Like a dictionary explaining
words / terms Concepts used
when processing

**Automatic
Data Processing
Handbook**

Other McGraw-Hill Handbooks of Interest

American Institute of Physics • American Institute of Physics Handbook
Baumeister and Marks • Standard Handbook for Mechanical Engineers
Beeman • Industrial Power Systems Handbook
Blatz • Radiation Hygiene Handbook
Brady • Materials Handbook
Buell · Handbook of Modern Marketing
Burington • Handbook of Mathematical Tables and Formulas
Burington and May • Handbook of Probability and Statistics with Tables
Condon and Odishaw • Handbook of Physics
Coombs • Basic Electronic Instrument Handbook
Coombs • Printed Circuits Handbook
Croft, Carr, and Watt • American Electricians' Handbook
Etherington • Nuclear Engineering Handbook
Fink • Electronics Engineers' Handbook
Fink and Carroll • Standard Handbook for Electrical Engineers
Gruenberg • Handbook of Telemetry and Remote Control
Hamsher • Communication System Engineering Handbook
Harper • Handbook of Components for Electronics
Harper • Handbook of Electronic Packaging
Harper • Handbook of Materials and Processes for Electronics
Harper • Handbook of Thick Film Hybrid Microelectronics
Harper • Handbook of Wiring, Cabling, and Interconnecting for Electronics
Henney • Radio Engineering Handbook
Heyel • The Foreman's Handbook
Heyel · Handbook of Modern Office Management and Administrative Services
Hicks • Standard Handbook of Engineering Calculations
Huskey and Korn • Computer Handbook
Ireson • Reliability Handbook
Jasik • Antenna Engineering Handbook
Jourdain • Condensed Computer Encyclopedia
Juran • Quality Control Handbook
Kaufman and Seidman • Handbook for Electronics Engineering Technicians
Klerer and Korn • Digital Computer User's Handbook
Koelle • Handbook of Astronautical Engineering
Korn and Korn • Mathematical Handbook for Scientists and Engineers
Kurtz • The Lineman's and Cableman's Handbook
Landee, Davis, and Albrecht • Electronic Designer's Handbook
Machol • System Engineering Handbook
Maissel and Glang • Handbook of Thin Film Technology
Markus • Electronics and Nucleonics Dictionary
Markus • Handbook of Electronic Control Circuits
Markus and Zeluff • Handbook of Industrial and Electronic Circuits
Maynard • Handbook of Business Administration
Perry • Engineering Manual
Skolnik • Radar Handbook
Smeaton • Motor Application and Maintenance Handbook
Stout and Kaufman • Handbook of Operational Amplifier Circuit Design
Terman • Radio Engineers' Handbook
Truxal • Control Engineers' Handbook
Tuma • Engineering Mathematics Handbook
Tuma • Handbook of Physical Calculations
Tuma • Technology Mathematics Handbook
Watt and Summers • NFPA Handbook of the National Electrical Code

Automatic
Data Processing
Handbook

Edited by
THE DIEBOLD GROUP, INC.

McGRAW-HILL BOOK COMPANY

New York   St. Louis   San Francisco   Auckland   Bogotá
Düsseldorf   Johannesburg   London   Madrid
Mexico   Montreal   New Delhi   Panama
Paris   São Paulo   Singapore
Sydney   Tokyo   Toronto

Library of Congress Cataloging in Publication Data
Main entry under title:

Automatic data processing handbook.

Includes index.
1. Electronic data processing. 2. Electronic digital computers. I. Diebold Group.
QA76.A888   001.6′4   76-28331
ISBN 0-07-016807-5

234567890   KPKP   78654321098

The editors for this book were Harold B. Crawford and Virginia Anne Fechtmann,
the designer was Naomi Auerbach, and the production supervisor
was Teresa Leaden. It was set in Caledonia
by The Kingsport Press.

It was printed and bound by The Kingsport Press.

CONTENTS

Section 7 SPECIAL INDUSTRY APPLICATIONS OF AUTOMATIC DATA PROCESSING

Section 8 THE COMPUTER AND SOCIETY

Index follows Section 8.

Contributors

DONALD K. ABE *Management Consultant; Lecturer, Graduate Business Program, Saint Mary's College, Morago, Calif.; formerly Division Manager and Senior Advisor, Mathematics, Computers, and Systems Department, Computer Sciences and Training, Exxon Corporation, Florham Park, N.J.* (SECTION 3, PART FIVE, CHAPTER 2).

WILLIAM M. ADAMS *Metropolitan Marketing Manager, Recognition Equipment, Inc., Indianapolis, Indiana; formerly Associate Director, Operations/Automation Division, The American Bankers Association, Washington, D.C.* (SECTION 7, CHAPTER 1).

IRA ADLER *Principal, John Diebold & Associates, New York, N.Y.* (SECTION 2, PART SIX, INTRODUCTION; SECTION 4, INTRODUCTION).

RONALD H. BALLOU *Associate Professor of Marketing and Logistics, Case Western Reserve University, Cleveland, Ohio* (SECTION 4, CHAPTER 4).

JAMES F. BARCUS, JR. *Plant Manager, Black & Decker Manufacturing Company, Hampstead, Md.* (SECTION 3, PART THREE, CHAPTER 1).

JOHN D. BEDNAR *Manager, Industry Marketing Development-Financial, Burroughs Corporation, Detroit, Mich.* (SECTION 7, CHAPTER 3).

TOBY S. BERK *Associate Professor of Computer Science, Mathematical Sciences Department, Florida International University, Miami, Fla.* (SECTION 3, PART THREE, CHAPTER 4).

HUGO BERLET *Vice President, The Diebold Group, Inc., New York, N.Y.* (SECTION 1, CHAPTER 2).

LEONARD A. BERNSTEIN *Manager, Teleprocessing Systems Department, Merrill Lynch, Pierce, Fenner & Smith, Inc., New York, N.Y.* (SECTION 3, PART ONE, CHAPTER 1).

DONALD L. BOYD *Assistant Professor, Department of Computer Sciences, University of Minnesota, Minneapolis* (SECTION 2, PART TWO, CHAPTER 2).

JOHN E. BUCKLEY *President, Telecommunications Management Corporation, Cornwells Height, Pa.* (SECTION 2, PART FIVE, CHAPTER 3).

ARTHUR J. BURKE *Manager, Corporate Systems Development, Westinghouse Electric Corporation, Pittsburgh, Pa.* (SECTION 3, PART FOUR, CHAPTER 4).

HOWARD H. CAMPAIGNE *Department of Mathematics, Slippery Rock State College, Slippery Rock, Pa.* (SECTION 8, CHAPTER 4).

ERIC H. CLAMONS *Director, Data Systems Standards, Honeywell Information Systems, Inc., Waltham, Mass.* (SECTION 2, PART SIX, CHAPTER 2).

WARREN A. COLE *Director, Markets Development, Business Systems Markets Division, Eastman Kodak Company, Rochester, N.Y.* (SECTION 2, PART ONE, CHAPTER 3).

JAMES F. COLLINS, JR. *Vice President, Management Information Services, Corporate Staff, Johnson & Johnson, New Brunswick, N.J.* (SECTION 1, CHAPTER 3).

JOHN E. COX *Vice President, International Telephone & Telegraph Corp., formerly Vice President, Engineering Division, Western Union, Upper Saddle River, N.J.* (SECTION 2, PART FIVE, CHAPTER 1).

IRVING M. CRUPAR *Technical Director, Wackenhut Electric Systems, Corp., Miami, Florida; formerly, Manager of Engineering, Holmes Protection, Inc., New York, N.Y.* (SECTION 5, CHAPTER 7).

R. L. DAUBENMIRE *Director, Information Systems Center, International Business Machines Corporation, Sterling Forest, Suffern, N.Y.* (SECTION 7, CHAPTER 5).

A. F. DERSHOWITZ *Corporate Strategy & Systems, General Electric Company, Fairfield, Conn.* (SECTION 3, PART ONE, CHAPTER 3).

P. J. DIXON *Director of Management Systems, Massey-Ferguson Limited, Toronto, Canada* (SECTION 5, CHAPTER 9).

J. K. DREYER *Executive Vice President, Association of Data Processing Service Organizations, Inc., Montvale, N.J.* (SECTION 6, CHAPTER 2).

J. C. DUFFENDACK *Vice President, ADP Network Services, Inc., Cyphernetics Division, Ann Arbor, Mich.* (SECTION 2, PART FIVE, CHAPTER 4).

JAMES C. EMERY *Vice President, EDUCOM, Inc., Princeton, N.J.* (SECTION 3, PART ONE, CHAPTER 2).

GEORGE J. FEENEY *Vice President and General Manager, Information Services Business Division, General Electric Company, Rockville, Md.* (SECTION 6, CHAPTER 5).

JOSEPH FERREIRA *Vice President, The Diebold Group, Inc., New York, N.Y.* (SECTION 2, PART ONE, INTRODUCTION; SECTION 2, PART FOUR, CHAPTER 2, APPENDIX; SECTION 3, PART FOUR, INTRODUCTION).

MICHAEL M. FLACK *Continental Telephone Laboratories, Hickory, N.C.; formerly Engineering Division, Western Union, Upper Saddle River, New Jersey* (SECTION 2, PART FIVE, CHAPTER 1).

JOHN FORD *Director, Management Systems and Controls Corporate, Rohr Industries, Inc., Chula Vista, Calif.* (SECTION 2, PART THREE, CHAPTER 5).

WILLIAM R. FRANTA *Assistant Professor, Department of Computer, Information, and Control Sciences, University of Minnesota, Minneapolis* (SECTION 2, PART TWO, CHAPTER 1).

DANIEL P. FREEDMAN *School of Advanced Technology, State University of New York, Binghamton, N.Y.* (SECTION 5, CHAPTER 3).

THEODORE J. FREISER *Senior Vice President, John Diebold & Associates, New York, N.Y.* (SECTION 2, PART THREE, INTRODUCTION; SECTION 5, INTRODUCTION; SECTION 6, INTRODUCTION).

S. E. FURTH *Industry Consultant, Information Systems Marketing, International Business Machines Corporation, White Plains, N.Y.* (SECTION 4, CHAPTER 3).

BRUCE GILCHRIST *Director of Computing Activities, Columbia University, New York, N.Y.* (SECTION 8, CHAPTER 5).

PETER J. GRAY *President, Symbiotics, Briarcliff, N.Y.* (SECTION 2, PART THREE, CHAPTER 2).

DAVID H. GREENBERG *Attorney at Law, Beverly Hills, Calif.* (SECTION 3, PART FOUR, CHAPTER 5).

ROBERT J. GREENE *Compensation Consultant, A. S. Hansen, Inc., Lake Bluff, Ill.* (SECTION 5, CHAPTER 4).

T. G. GRIEB *Universal Systems, Inc., Arlington, Va.* (SECTION 2, PART SIX, CHAPTER 3).

JOHN A. GUERRIERI, JR. *Consultant, Niles, Ill.* (SECTION 5, CHAPTER 8).

ROBERT A. GUIDA *Manager, Data Entry Division, Blue Cross of Massachusetts, Boston, Mass.* (SECTION 3, PART FOUR, CHAPTER 3).

G. J. HAHN *Research and Development Center, General Electric Company, Schenectady, N.Y.* (SECTION 3, PART ONE, CHAPTER 3).

WILLIAM J. HARRISON *Technical Consultant, Computer Services Department, Fireman's Fund American Insurance Companies, San Rafael, Calif.* (SECTION 2, PART FOUR, CHAPTERS 1 AND 2).

KEITH HARVEY *Operations Manager, Computer Communication Group, Bell Canada, Toronto, Canada* (SECTION 5, CHAPTER 5).

LEE F. HAYNES *Director, Management Information Services—Corporate, The B. F. Goodrich Company, Akron, Ohio* (SECTION 4, CHAPTER 2).

ALDEN HEINTZ *Vice President, Corporate Development, TYMSHARE, Inc., Cupertino, Calif.* (SECTION 6, CHAPTER 3).

F. M. HEINZMANN *Vice President, Computer Sciences, Eastern Airlines, Inc., Miami, Fla.* (SECTION 3, PART TWO, CHAPTER 4).

CARL HEYEL *Management Counsel, Manhasset, N.Y.* (COORDINATING EDITOR)

MARJORIE F. HILL *Manager, Marketing and Research, Control Data Institute for Advanced Technology, Control Data Corporation, Rockville, Md.; formerly Industry Standards Coordinator, Control Data Corporation, Minneapolis, Minn.* (SECTION 2, PART SIX, CHAPTER 1).

JOHN W. HOAG *Director, Strategic & Business Planning, Honeywell, Inc., Process Control Division, Phoenix, Ariz.* (SECTION 7, CHAPTER 4).

LANCE J. HOFFMAN *College of Engineering, Department of Electrical Engineering and Computer Sciences, University of California at Berkeley* (SECTION 8, CHAPTER 4).

E. G. HOLZMANN *Research and Development Center, General Electric Company, Schenectady, N.Y.* (SECTION 3, PART ONE, CHAPTER 3).

L. LEE HORSCHMAN *Director, Program Sales Development, Business Systems Markets Division, Eastman Kodak Company, Rochester, N.Y.* (SECTION 2, PART THREE, CHAPTER 4).

ELEANOR H. IRVINE *Director, New Concepts, Delhi, N.Y.* (SECTION 5, CHAPTER 2).

FRANKLIN M. JARMAN *Chairman, GENESCO, Inc., Nashville, Tenn.* (SECTION 1, CHAPTER 1).

EUGENE J. JONES *Management Consultant, Data Processing Systems, Huntington, N.Y.; formerly Vice President, Systems & Programming, Avis Rent-A-Car System, Inc., Garden City, N.Y.* (SECTION 7, CHAPTER 6).

EARL C. JOSEPH *Staff Scientist, Sperry Univac, St. Paul, Minn.* (SECTION 2, PART TWO, CHAPTER 5).

WALTER A. KLEINSCHROD *Editor,* Administrative Management, *New York, N.Y.* (SECTION 2, PART ONE, CHAPTER 1).

ANDREW KNOWLES *Vice President, Group Manager, Digital Equipment Corporation, Maynard, Mass.* (SECTION 2, PART TWO, CHAPTER 4).

EVELYN KONRAD *Evelyn Konrad Associates, New York, N.Y.* (SECTION 4, CHAPTER 6).

THOMAS E. KURTZ *Director, Office of Academic Computing, Dartmouth College, Hanover, N.H.* (SECTION 2, PART TWO, CHAPTER 3).

HAROLD LAZARUS *Dean, School of Business, Hofstra University, Hempstead, N.Y.* (SECTION 4, CHAPTER 5).

JOHN E. LETSON *Senior Vice President and Director, Computer and Communications Systems Group, Bache Halsey Stuart Inc., New York, N.Y.* (SECTION 3, PART FOUR, CHAPTER 1).

HUGH J. LYNCH *General Manager, Communications Systems Division, NCR Corporation, Columbia, S.C.* (SECTION 2, PART FOUR, CHAPTER 5).

NORMAN R. LYONS *Associate Professor of Management Information Systems, College of Business, University of Texas, Lubbock, Tex.* (SECTION 3, PART THREE, CHAPTER 3).

JAMES J. McSWEENY *President, Collieries Management Corporation, Philadelphia, Pa.; formerly, Vice President, Strategic Development, IU International Corporation, Philadelphia, Pa.* (SECTION 3, PART FIVE, CHAPTER 2).

DEAN E. McWILLIAMS *Products Manager—Automated Systems, Sperry Remington (Remington Rand Systems Div.), BlueBell, Pa.* (SECTION 2, PART ONE, CHAPTER 2).

WILLIAM MEYER *Fireman's Fund, American Insurance Companies, San Francisco, Calif.* (SECTION 3, PART FOUR, CHAPTER 2).

N. RICHARD MILLER   *Vice President, The Diebold Group, Inc., New York, N.Y.* (SECTION 2, PART TWO, INTRODUCTION).

CHARLES G. MOORE   *Cybernetics Division, ADP Network Services Inc., Ann Arbor, Mich.* (SECTION 3, PART THREE, CHAPTER 3).

J. P. O'BRIEN   *Manager, Personnel Administration Center, International Telephone and Telegraph Corporation, World Headquarters, New York, N.Y.* (SECTION 4, CHAPTER 5, APPENDIX).

JOHN W. OPLINGER   *Marketing Manager, The Diebold Group, Inc., New York, N.Y.* (SECTION 2, PART FOUR, INTRODUCTION; SECTION 3, PART ONE, INTRODUCTION; SECTION 8, INTRODUCTION).

DEREK O. ORAM   *Director of Engineering, Simplex Time Recorder Company, Gardner, Mass.* (SECTION 2, PART THREE, CHAPTER 1).

FRANK J. PERPIGLIA   *Programming Manager, Burroughs Corporation, Paoli, Pa.* (SECTION 2, PART FOUR, CHAPTER 4).

NORMAN C. PETERSON   *Executive Vice President, RAPIFAX Corporation, Fairfield, N.Y.* (SECTION 2, PART 5, CHAPTER 2).

WILLIAM R. POLLERT   *Manager, Soviet Commercial Development, International Paper Company, New York, N.Y.* (SECTION 5, CHAPTER 1).

ANTHONY B. RAGOZZINO   *Director of Peripherals, Honeywell Inc., Minneapolis, Minn.* (SECTION 2, PART THREE, CHAPTER 1 AND CHAPTER 3).

ROBERT REICH   *Corporate Planning Officer, The Cleveland Trust Co., Cleveland, Ohio; Instructor of Computer and Information Science, Cleveland State University, Cleveland, Ohio* (SECTION 4, CHAPTER 1).

WILLIAM F. REILLY   *Assistant, Office of the Chairman, The Diebold Group, Inc., New York, N.Y.* (SECTION 3, PART TWO, INTRODUCTION; SECTION 3, PART THREE, INTRODUCTION).

ARNOLD REISMAN   *Professor of Operations Research, Case Western Reserve University, Cleveland, Ohio; Vice President, University Associates, Inc., Cleveland, Ohio* (SECTION 4, CHAPTER 1).

PHILIP RICCO   *Principal, The Diebold Group, Inc., New York, N.Y.* (SECTION 2, PART FOUR, INTRODUCTION; SECTION 7, INTRODUCTION).

GEOFFREY A. RIGBY   *Manager of Marketing Services, Racal-Milgo Limited, Reading, Berkshire, England* (SECTION 2, PART FIVE, CHAPTER 5).

JEAN E. SAMMET   *IBM Corporation, Federal Systems Division, Cambridge, Mass.* (SECTION 2, PART FOUR, CHAPTER 3).

HUBERT J. SCHLAFLY   *Chairman and Vice President, Transcommunications Corporation, Greenwich, Conn.* (SECTION 8, CHAPTER 3).

ARNOLD SCHRON   *Manager, Data Administration, Merrill Lynch, Pierce, Fenner, & Smith, Inc., New York; Adjunct Assistant Professor, Computer Application Information Systems Department, The Graduate School of Business, New York University, New York* (SECTION 3, PART TWO, CHAPTER 2).

RICHARD F. SCHUBERT   *Director of Management Information Services—Technical Advancement, The B. F. Goodrich Company, Akron, Ohio* (SECTION 5, CHAPTER 6).

LEONARD C. SILVERN   *President, Education and Training Consultants Company, Los Angeles, Calif.* (SECTION 8, CHAPTER 1).

PRESTON SINKS   *Systems Officer, Morgan Guaranty Trust Company of New York, New York City* (SECTION 3, PART TWO, CHAPTER 1).

IRVING I. SOLOMON   *President, Aris Associates, Plainview, New York ; formerly, Vice President, Information Systems Division, National Retail Merchants Association, New York, N.Y.* (SECTION 7, CHAPTER 2).

GEORGE STEPHENSON   *Assistant Professor of Management, Fordham University, New York, N.Y.; and Consultant* (SECTION 1, CHAPTER 4).

MILTON M. STONE *President, Continental Information Services, Inc., Chicago, Ill.; formerly, Editor,* Infosystems Magazine, *Wheaton, Ill.* (SECTION 3, PART THREE, CHAPTER 2).

F. E. THOMAS *Partner, Thomas Friedman & Associates, Rosemont, Ill.* (SECTION 3, PART TWO, CHAPTER 3).

EDWARD A. TOMESKI *Professor of Management, Fordham University, New York, N.Y.; and Consultant* (SECTION 1, CHAPTER 4; SECTION 4, CHAPTER 5).

GERALD M. WEINBERG *President, Ethnotech, Inc., Lincoln, Nebr.* (SECTION 5, CHAPTER 3).

MICHAEL A. WEINER *Senior Associate, John Diebold & Associates, New York, N.Y.* (SECTION 2, PART FIVE, INTRODUCTION).

LEON WEISBURGH *President, Anstat, Inc., New York, N.Y.* (SECTION 6, CHAPTER 4).

L. A. WELKE *President, International Computer Programs, Inc., Indianapolis, Ind.; Past President, The ADAPSO Software Industry Association, Montvale, N.J.* (SECTION 6, CHAPTER 1).

HAROLD N. WELLS *Program Manager, Subsystems Product Marketing, Honeywell Information Systems, Inc., Wellesley, Mass.* (SECTION 2, PART THREE, CHAPTER 3).

LELAND H. WILLIAMS *President and Director, Triangle Universities Computation Center, Research Triangle Park, North Carolina; Adjunct Professor of Computer Sciences, Duke University, University of North Carolina at Chapel Hill, N.C. and North Carolina State University at Raleigh, N.C.* (SECTION 3, PART FIVE, CHAPTER 1).

Acknowledgments

Special acknowledgment is made of the work of Carl Heyel, who served as coordinating editor of this Handbook, in close collaboration with all contributors and the Diebold subject specialists. Mr. Heyel served for many years as editor of the Diebold ADP newsletter.

Acknowledgment is also made to Joseph Ferreira, of The Diebold Group, J. C. Duffendack, of Cyphernetics Division, ADP Network Services, Inc., and James F. Barcus, of Black & Decker Manufacturing Company, for advisory assistance in important areas of the work.

Introduction

by JOHN DIEBOLD

Chairman, The Diebold Group, Inc., New York

The Automatic Data Processing Handbook is offered as a comprehensive and readily accessible reference source on modern data and information processing, and on the management implications of present and foreseeable developments in computer and communications technology. The individual chapters have been written by recognized authorities in the fields covered, and the work thus represents the views of practitioners whose daily work keeps them abreast of advanced practice both here and abroad.

The Handbook is designed for several classes of readers:

1. Management generalists who seek a broad understanding of this fast-moving field to be sure that their organizations avail themselves of the applicable technology, and that they will make sound decisions and recommendations regarding the heavy investments called for by today's computer systems.

2. Professional data processing managers who seek to increase the internal efficiency of their departments as well as to enhance the department's effectiveness and status within the corporate structure, and who also wish to strengthen their grasp of the various technologies involved in their operations.

3. Specialists in one or more areas of automatic data processing who seek to advance themselves by broadening their horizons beyond the confines of their special discipline, and who, while not requiring this source as a reference with respect to their own field, need it to brush up on related areas where their present knowledge is marginal or non-existent.

4. Educators and graduate students in Business Administration who seek a comprehensive text on the broad field of automatic data

processing—a text that is organized in a way that clarifies broad principles first, and then follows with detailed treatments, permitting the reader to pursue any phase of the subject to the degree of detail desired.

5. Innovators and marketers who seek a broad view of "the computer industry" in order to gauge potentials for products and services to be sold to users of the technologies discussed, or for computer-based products and services where entrepreneurial opportunities are created by the computer and communications technologies currently developing.

SOME COMMENTARY IN POINT

A decade ago, that astute observer and articulate critic of the business scene, Peter F. Drucker, made the following points in speaking to a Senior Management Meeting of The Diebold Research Program. It is surprising and unfortunate that despite the tremendous technical strides in computer technology made in the intervening years, what he said then is still to so large an extent applicable today:

> This tool [the computer] can do five things. Today it is doing only one, in practically all business applications. It can do repetitive large-scale paperwork, production jobs. It can be used as a super clerk. . . . But that, surely, is not going to be its central use in the 1970s.
>
> We are now getting to the second use, one that exploits the computer's capabilities for information storage and retrieval. Unfortunately, in most places we do not yet know how to do that, partly because the wedding between the computer specialist who knows what the computer can do, and the manager, who knows or should know what he needs, has not yet taken place. We still largely believe that information consists of pouring out masses of data, which is the one absolutely certain way to *deprive* people of information.
>
> The third area, in which we have just made a beginning, is that of using the computer to control pre-established and present processes automatically, to maintain a pre-established norm, whether it is one of inventory or of machine speeds.
>
> The fourth one, which we are also now beginning to enter, is the use of the computer for the physical design execution. Here, again, the parameters and specifications have to be programmed. But it is the execution of essentially clerical or semi-clerical design work.
>
> Finally, there is the "tomorrowland" of the computer: *strategic decision making.* Of course, the computer itself will not be a *maker* of decisions, but a *tester* of decisions. We hear a great deal about this, but nobody really knows yet how to do it in business. We do know how to do this in laboratory exercises in universities, where we can state laws and hypotheses, and assume that what happened yesterday is going to happen tomorrow. In business strategy situations, however, we cannot as yet really do it effectively.

These are the five areas. How fast we are going to move into any of them no longer depends on equipment. The equipment is there, or it is in prospect. It depends on management, because from now on the ability of the computer to perform will increasingly depend on the willingness, ability, and understanding of management to think through its own needs, its own goals, its own specifications.

Who is to blame for the still slow penetration into Drucker's tomorrowland? It is not the man or woman who insists on talking about "how the watch works"—the technical professional. Actually, whether management wishes to face the fact or not, the blame must be laid on *its* doorstep—on top managers who have the power of choice in the first place, who are not "asking for the time" in the right way, who have not paid for the right kind of watch, and who have not employed the right kinds of "watch-man"—or trained the ones they have—to think of management's overall goals and needs . . . Eight years ago, I made the following comments in the *Harvard Business Review*,[1] and again, despite all that the business community has learned about computers since then, I submit them here for their relevancy today:

> Now that computers are becoming useful at a higher level of management and for more sophisticated tasks, top executives should use different yardsticks in evaluating and planning for them. But this is not being done; the old criteria are still in general use. By concentrating on savings and data processing costs, and on added efficiencies in routine operations, management exposes itself to serious errors of omission and commission . . .
>
> The problem is not lack of technical knowledge on the part of the experts. Rather, it is the failure on the part of top management to ask the right questions. It is the failure in particular to seek quantitative measurement of the very real benefits of automatic data processing to a business. I do not mean cost displacement, but rather increased management capacity to control and plan. Such benefits are not being considered in a serious and meaningful way; yet they are today the principal reason for computer use and for moving computers out of accounting and into operational use.
>
> The problem goes deeper still. Because top management has not asked the right questions, researchers have not yet addressed themselves sufficiently to producing useful methodologies for solutions. Technicians, too, have overemphasized system costs and given relatively little attention to system benefits to the company as a whole.

Obviously there is a communications gap that must be bridged between general corporate management and the professional technical managers in direct charge of the company's computer processing operations.

[1] John Diebold, "Bad Decisions on Computer Use," *Harvard Business Review*, January–February, 1969.

CLOSING THE GAP

The gap must be closed by greater involvement of top management in computer-system choices, by a greater familiarity with computer "state of the art" and developments ahead on the part of the general manager to whom the data processing manager reports, and by a more "management-eye-view" on the part of the professionals, namely the data processing manager and the computer personnel.

Greater involvement of top levels of management will come only if these decision makers can be made to see the exciting new dimensions of information technology.

Top management itself must take the trouble to understand what the new technologies make possible, and what is necessary to apply them effectively and imaginatively. Only if *its* imagination and enthusiasm are kindled will the climate be right for the proper basic computer choices to be made. Top management must be made to see the corporate implications of time-sharing systems and information networks and "corporate memories" and "real-time" computer query and response—and the whole new panoply and computer-powered armaments provided for decision making by the new management sciences.

How shall management achieve this? That is where the interpretive and liaison functions of an important management functionary come in—*the general corporate manager to whom the data processing manager reports*.

Hard-headed criteria for judging computer-operation efficiency can be established only when this general management executive has done sufficient "homework" to familiarize himself with the basics of how a computer works, and has undertaken to keep abreast of broad developments and directions of the technology.

Since its inception, automatic data processing has been one of the most casually managed activities in business. Awed by the mystique of computers, corporate executives tended to accept the data processing department's own judgments as to the efficiency of its operations, and, until the sharp business downturn of 1969–1970, meekly authorized purchases and paid the bills. Seldom was data processing measured against performance goals or other criteria related to profit-and-loss. Now that the field has matured, data processing is being subjected to closer scrutiny, although recent Diebold Research Program surveys show that most companies still have no clear criteria for measuring the performance of the function.

The advantage of the high-level corporate executive charged with overseeing the function—and, in a growing number of companies, the senior functional ADP executive—is that he was chosen because of his intimate knowledge of the business as a whole, *not* because of his knowledge of computers. This gives him the perspective needed in judging the practicality and applicability of plans of the computer specialists, and in applying the same kind of cost-benefit approach to computer operations as are applied elsewhere in the business.

A key responsibility of this executive must be to educate and orient operating executives in all divisions of the business regarding the computer system's capabilities in providing decision-making information, over and above the normal clerical, operational, and routine-report processing.

As for the data processing specialists, their goal must be to increase their broad awareness of management's needs, in addition to insisting that they impose internal controls on their own operations, governing equipment use, cost accounting, personnel selection, direction, and evaluation, and the like.

However, important though these aspects of their operations are, of even more significance is the new dimension to the specialists' thinking which must be provided. Over the years, a recurring problem confronting such personnel has been the hazard of a professional *cul-de-sac*. Their high degree of specialization, together with the often narrow technician-range of their thinking, has served to put a definite ceiling on their advancement. While in large corporations they have been able to achieve a certain degree of status and reward where they have attained the top classification in their specialty, few indeed have been able to break out of the confines of their professional enclave into the ranks of upper management.

For this they have by and large had only themselves to blame. Before they can aspire to management positions, they must *think* like management. Only if their thinking is broadened to encompass the goals and information needs of the corporation as a whole will they be able to come up with the imaginative information-system recommendations that will mark them for top-management responsibilities.

For all of the above levels of data processing management, this game is worth more than the candle . . . it is worth a whole bonfire!

Section 1
Basic Concepts

Chapter 1

Organizing For Effective Computer Utilization

FRANKLIN M. JARMAN

Chairman, GENESCO Inc., Nashville, Tennessee

This Chapter discusses the top-management approach that must be taken to assure effective utilization of computer resources, and the nature of top-management involvement in decisions on computer investment and choice. It does not go into the organization and operation of the computer department itself, discussion of which is reserved for Section 5. However, it discusses the place of the professional manager of the computer operation in the corporate organization, and especially the reporting of such a professional manager to a general corporate executive who must be the liaison with top management.

In the mid-1950s, business computers were an exciting innovation, and industry sages enthusiastically predicted that the total number of computers in use by 1970 would reach 100. The early installations were momentous events for their new owners, and ushered in a period of growth in the computer industry which has been unequaled in any other field. As an important symbol of corporate prestige, computer installations proliferated at a rapid rate during the 1960s. The prediction of 100 installations had to be revised upward repeatedly, and at this writing there are approximately 82,000 installations.

This almost incredible expansion was a result of continuous acceleration in both demand and technological development. However, the ability of business management to utilize the steady flow of innovations effectively was greatly outpaced by the advances in the technology. Accordingly, the contraction of the general economy at the end of the sixties brought with it not only a slower rate of expansion in the application of computer power and in budgets for computer systems, but, in many cases, an actual contraction. The period was clearly one in which management tended to "fall back and regroup," preparing for what promises to be another decade of growth.

Managing change always demands superb management talents. The new discipline of ADP, coupled with the confusion of continuing technological innovations, has not readily yielded to the application of traditional management procedures. With our present abilities to concentrate increasing data processing power into business applications, it is hoped the 1970s will be characterized in the future as a period when management began to manage ADP resources effectively, a period when traditional management practices and controls were applied to place ADP in an effective management harness.

MANAGEMENT'S ADP PHILOSOPHY

Top management bears the ultimate responsibility for establishing the policy and direction for every business activity. ADP is no exception. Setting the pace and creating a climate in which results can be both produced and measured will continue to be its key responsibilities. This does not mean that senior management needs to have day-to-day involvement with the ADP activity. However, by setting a direction and establishing a relatively small number of policies and control mechanisms, senior management can assure itself of an effective ADP activity.

General Management vs. Technicians In papers at professional societies and in articles in professional journals, ADP technical people have criticized corporate general management for an alleged lack of intelligent interest in ADP. For their part, general management people have severely criticized the technicians in ADP for not understanding the business, for not being profit-oriented, and for not being as interested in solving basic business problems as in solving technical problems.

However valid both of these criticisms may have been, there is evidence that the gap between the two groups is now narrowing. Developments in higher-level languages, widespread use of time-sharing terminals, improvements in displays and printouts, and other technological developments have greatly improved the interface between the computer and its users, permitting greater concentration on application aspects rather than on the technical aspects of computer operation. In addition, the mobility of ADP personnel and their steadily increasing numbers, together with educational efforts of manufacturers, business-education institutions, and business itself have created a large body of ADP personnel with a good exposure to business problems and business modes of thinking.

As to top management, the recent downturn in business, together with the large investments and operating budgets called for by widening computer applications, has brought home the realization that the ADP organization cannot simply be left to itself. Moreover, as systems development and implementation activity increase, ADP system personnel become more and more an integral part of the company. As this occurs, these employees grow in value to the organization and can make a contribution to creative managerial thinking. Their views, comments, and criticisms should be actively and continually solicited.

Systems development tends to cross traditional functional organizational boundaries; therefore the people engaged in such work tend to look at situations from a broad perspective. However, it should be recognized that this particular strength will at times threaten the security of the functional manager and can breed conflict. Careful selection of the ADP staff is vital to avoid such line-staff discord. Clear understanding of ADP responsibility by both line and staff, coupled with positive and constructive attitudes, will help create a climate in which teamwork can flourish.

Senior management should participate directly in the development of an expressed philosophy that includes, as a minimum, a statement of purpose for ADP, an explanation of organizational relationships within ADP operations and between ADP and line organizations, an indication of the process by which ADP is expected to align its objectives with those of the company, and basic guidelines for the day-to-day operation of ADP.

The establishment of a management philosophy for ADP will strengthen the relationships between ADP professionals and top management as they work out joint understandings of purposes and goals. Figure 1-1 is an example of a statement of doctrine on management information systems in use at one large company. A periodic rethinking of this philosophy will lead to later revisions as conditions within the company change.

The establishment of a management philosophy provides an excellent opportunity to recognize that ADP is composed of two major operational activities which are fundamentally dissimilar in terms of needed skills and the disciplines required for their effective management. The development of information systems is essentially a *project* activity that should be viewed as a continuing investment and measured by the return it produces. In contrast, computer operations—the "information factory"—is a

Doctrine on Management Information Systems

■ Because of its size and diversification within the apparel industry, GENESCO has the unique opportunity to develop a competitive advantage through properly planned and coordinated Management Information Systems. Implementation of such systems will result in improved service to our customers and more usable information for management decisions.

■ Adequate information systems may be manual or computerized. Where justified, the computer is a powerful tool for processing data for innovative management use.

■ For effective development and use of information systems, four important functions must be recognized. These are: Planning; Development; Electronic Data Processing; and Corporate Coordination of these activities.

■ PLANNING—Each operating company prepares an Information Systems Plan which will support their Strategic Plan. This Information Systems Plan serves as a guide in the justification and orderly development of manual and/or computer systems that support the needs of the business. Corporate Management Information Services (CMIS) provides consultive assistance to operating company management in preparing Information Systems Plans. Operating companies and CMIS should agree on Information Systems Plans before proceeding with development.

■ DEVELOPMENT—Individual operating companies have the responsibility for developing the systems needed to manage their business. This may be accomplished through the operating company staff or through CMIS, which maintains a staff to handle overflow work and special situations. In order to minimize duplication of effort and insure compatibility of systems, full use should be made of systems already developed centrally, by other GENESCO operating companies, and those available from outside sources. Decisions as to the use of systems development services from outside the corporation are made centrally. CMIS is responsible for developing systems required for central corporate needs.

■ ELECTRONIC DATA PROCESSING—EDP is a highly technical area subject to rapid technological changes. Opportunities exist for substantial savings through the pooling of processing demands. Therefore, all decisions on computing equipment matters and the use of service bureaus will be made centrally.

■ CORPORATE COORDINATION—CMIS is responsible for developing policies, guidelines, technical standards, and management training programs to support operating companies in the effective development and use of Management Information Systems.

GENESCO Doctrines are management guidelines based on past experience but the Responsible Executive, after careful analysis of various facts, may decide it desirable to follow a course of action that varies from the general doctrine.

Fig. 1-1 Doctrine on Management Information Systems, GENESCO.

process activity with the objective of producing its product at the highest levels of service and at the lowest possible cost.

Management Involvement "Management involvement" currently seems to receive the praise for most successes and the blame for most failures, while being misunderstood by almost everyone. Just what is the proper degree of management involvement at each level in the organization? To what degree is top management involved at each level in the organization? To what degree is top-management involvement necessary to ensure effective utilization of ADP resources?

Management involvement begins with the organization structure. ADP is properly viewed as a service activity, and as such it fits into the organization structure along with other service and staff activities. Under this concept it is felt that ADP must report to a high-level business executive, a generalist, a person with broad experience in areas of the business other than ADP. Such reporting will avoid problems that can arise where ADP operations report to highly competent specialists who may have limited experience in general business.

ADP must also function under the same conditions of responsibility and accountability as do other activities of comparable importance. Setting ADP apart and providing special treatment may have been necessary during its initial years of development. However, today it is no longer necessary or desirable to treat it as a sacred cow.

ORGANIZATION

In the most frequent pattern of successful organization, the ADP manager reports directly to a top-level general executive who has a title such as Chief Administrative Officer, or if not that title formally, has the responsibilities connoted by it, and thus typically deals in many areas that cross organizational lines.

Top management must make the overall policy decisions and determine the extent of computerization to be employed in achieving broad corporate goals. There is greater assurance that ADP activities will be supportive of the organization when directions and expectations are provided by top management. With such high-level participation in goal setting, ADP activities are less apt to be dominated by the technician's perspective.

Figure 1-2 shows a schematic of organization for ADP at GENESCO Inc. This is presented not as a blueprint for universal application, but simply as an organization of a specific company that embodies the philosophy here expressed. GENESCO is the largest manufacturer and distributor of apparel in the world. Operating from headquarters in Nashville, Tennessee, the organization comprises 80 individual companies that make and sell "everything to wear." Located throughout the United States, most companies are serviced by a large computing facility in Nashville. Growth through acquisition has generated a total of 16 separate computer facilities, most of

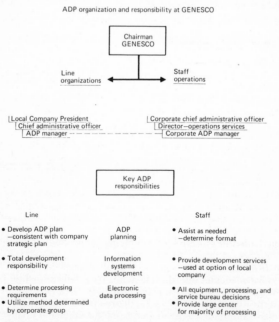

Fig. 1-2   ADP organization and responsibility at GENESCO.

which have now converted to the national facility for processing while retaining strong local control of information systems planning and development.

GOAL SETTING

In the company example here discussed, planning for the development of information systems parallels the approach used for weighing alternatives and establishing priorities in any investment activity. By concentrating emphasis on return-on-investment aspects, this conserves the time of key management personnel and ensures their involvement at the proper time: the basic planning stage.

ADP planning is a dynamic process. It begins with the identification of company objectives and goals. Working downward, the important opportunities for systems development are identified in every company activity. These opportunities are then ranked in terms of company objectives and goals by the key executives of the business.

Where the size of operations warrants, a number of the company's operating subsidiaries employ the "steering committee" or "policy planning committee" approach. Composed of the senior executives and key ADP personnel, this committee meets quarterly or seimiannually to set goals and evaluate progress for ADP. This technique thus calls for only a small number of high-level meetings, but these meetings are highly effective in determining broad priorities for systems development progress measurement. They also promote understanding of the overall ADP program and encourage support by line managements.

Broad planning of a conceptual nature which establishes the basic concerns and priorities can best be finalized by executives who do not have vested interests in lower functional areas. Under GENESCO's scheme of ADP organization, top local company managers working with their own ADP operating personnel can draw on the generally more experienced and less biased corporate ADP systems planners to assure objectivity. Plans are finalized with a time-phased action plan and a pro forma budget, usually looking ahead at least 24 months.

Systems planning is one of the most important responsibilities of ADP. Only the highest-skilled, most motivated and positive-thinking personnel should be entrusted with this responsibility. They must have sufficient contact with key executives to understand why changes in corporate thinking occur, and be perceptive enough to incorporate these changes into the planning process.

EFFECTIVE SYSTEMS DEVELOPMENT

The establishment of an information systems development plan approved by senior management is clearly the first step in assuring that ADP resources are directed toward areas of greatest opportunity and need. Past this point, much attention must be given to human-oriented factors if implementation is to be effective.

Human Factors All new systems development activities will have problems—and the greatest of these usually have to do with preparing an organization for change. Generally, the systems cover the activities of large numbers of operating people, and any changes in their jobs can be traumatic. Moreover, error lists and status reports issued for the first time on an activity tend to spotlight prior management problems (shortcomings). This will breed resentment unless handled tactfully. There are usually some inefficiencies beneath the surface of even apparently smoothly running companies, and these are often brought to light by technical ADP personnel who sometimes seem to enjoy gloating over their discoveries. Personnel of this type have to be weeded out of the organization or educated to recognize that their success will in the last analysis be dependent upon the relationships they establish with line managers. The latter often do not look at problems with the same motivation and willingness to change as do the ADP analysts. By the same token, line managers often see practical implications in proposed changes which may escape the eager designer of a new system.

Systems development opportunities receive more support by local management when local managers feel they were involved in the design effort. Key development and design activities must be conducted by ADP personnel who have taken the time to understand thoroughly the business needs in the particular system area. This may mean days, weeks, or months of "unproductive" effort spent in digging into the day-by-day operations. However, this "unproductive" effort will pay off immensely during the design and particularly during the implementation stages.

Opportunities and Accountability Systems developers have for years been telling management what they could not do because of technical limitations. Many of these limitations have now been overcome, and operating management today should be in full control in defining needs and expectations. The abundance and variety of available equipment and techniques will usually make possible a practical approach to fulfilling these needs and expectations. ADP personnel must be encouraged to apply these, and to be receptive to new methods, rejecting preconceived approaches.

Corporate systems planners should be held accountable for the degree of duplication in systems development efforts within complex organizations. All technicians enjoy developing a mousetrap with a slightly different twist. High development costs no longer allow organizations this luxury. Corporate systems planners must be aware of the system library available within the organization, and deal firmly with technicians who insist on redeveloping relatively common systems.

The ADP organization must become highly sensitive to shifts in management's desires and needs, and in the organization's ability to fund developmental work. Shifts and changes can represent an opportunity for resourceful ADP management.

Operating management should furnish the screen through which ADP technical innovations and creativity must be sifted to assure producing systems that are practical and economical to operate. Users should raise serious questions if systems justifications are confusing, and logical explanations are difficult to get from systems design personnel. Do the systems designers understand the business functions they are attempting to automate? Are user personnel receptive to and capable of implementing the changes required? Is the proposed improvement needed for continued success of the business, or is it merely something that challenges the designer's creative abilities? Line management must continue probing until revealing questions of this kind are satisfactorily answered.

PROBLEMS OF ORGANIZATION AND CONTROL

Centralization Many corporations attempt to design systems centrally or corporately to serve all their operating-unit needs. In select instances, the degree of central control may be sufficient, and the quality of the systems developed adequate, to accomplish this objective. In many instances, however, local operating managements tend to resist company-wide systems or those used by other operating units, feeling that the unique aspects of their particular operations are not properly recognized. While these reactions may be unfounded, they are valid concerns of the local management and, therefore, must be dealt with. Highly qualified systems planners from the central corporate group must establish credibility with local operating management in order to sell company-wide systems. This takes a tremendous amount of time and patience but assures support and use of the system when decisions are finally made.

From a purely managerial standpoint, centrally developed systems are cheaper. Additionally, the quality of the work from a large central staff is generally more professional and easier to manage when compared to fragmented systems groups scattered around an organization. However, in spite of the apparent economies of centrally developed systems, many fail for various reasons. Most common is the natural user-management resistance to the forced implementation of company-wide systems and concepts. Next in line would probably be lack of selling ability and persuasive management talents within the typical systems groups. It makes no difference how good the system actually is; it will not be used effectively until user-management is educated to its advantages and is convinced it will work for them. Gaining this level of support is essential.

Large user-departments should have systems-oriented individuals permanently assigned within their organization. These individuals can serve as a liaison with technicians and greatly reduce communication problems between the user-department and the corporate ADP organizations. Detailed system designers and programmers may be located either centrally or elsewhere in the organization with no significant communication problems if good systems personnel report directly to user-management.

Motivation Much has been said about the scarcity of talented ADP personnel. Companies go to great extremes to provide working environments that are conducive to productivity for ADP organizations. However, much attention is often devoted to working conditions, benefits, and other needs of employees that have long since been satisfied. Adequate working conditions are necessary for any progressive organization. Of much more importance than the conventional security needs of individuals is management's attention to morale and motivation through intellectual challenges. Those companies that make ADP personnel a part of the vital functioning of the organization and recognize their contributions fairly will attract talented people and will experience low turnover and high productivity.

Cost Allocation Allocation of the costs of information systems development is a key factor for effective management of ADP. The costs of all systems development should be charged directly to the individual activity for which the work is done. Rates established should include all fairly accessible overhead, such as training, administrative, and other indirect management costs. The objective of the ADP systems development group should be to break even.

When user-management begins paying for services on a basis they can understand, they, in turn, begin to control their costs. Arbitrary allocations of the total ADP overhead alienate users, who soon resign themselves to accept whatever charge is levied. This usually leads to unproductive competition for ADP assistance among operating groups. Direct charging, however, provides an excellent basis for the preparation of cost justifications for each systems development effort.

Charging for systems development, programming, and maintenance activities also greatly stimulates user-management involvement. If user-management is profit-oriented and is charged for these services, there is continuous interest in the progress of projects. Few projects should be allowed to get beyond the talking stage unless the head of the operating department is involved in the project, both financially and administratively.

Systems Performance Measures Long considered impractical or impossible, measuring the productivity of systems analysts and programmers can and must be accomplished.[1] Standards of output should be set for each person, taking into account general levels of experience, and factors such as vacations, sickness, holiday, etc., that reduce available time for productive work. By combining such a measurement with charging for systems development, the direct dollar contribution by each individual employee can be measured. Thus systems development group managers are provided with an excellent technique for managing each of their people individually, and managing their groups in a manner that will generate a break-even financial result. The real cost of hiring a new employee or transferring present personnel from project to project will reveal itself in terms of dollars under such a system and will influence the decision-making process.

EFFECTIVE COMPUTER OPERATIONS

Computer operations is the ADP activity responsible for converting input data into management information products. It essentially resembles any other production facility. Operating from a schedule, computer operations utilizes people and machine resources to produce finished products at the least possible cost. A strong "customer orientation" must be structured into its management process. Each individual user is concerned with his or her own product and resents continual lateness due to "other priorities." The computer operations activity must be structured to negotiate realistic data processing schedules and, having set them, must meet them on a consistent basis.

It may appear that the dual objectives of maximum service and minimum costs are inherently conflicting. This tension can, however, prove both creative and productive. The existence of a sound, detailed system for charging costs back to users can be a definite asset in resolving the differences between these two points of view.

Charge-backs As with systems development, it is essential that costs for data processing be charged to those who receive the direct benefits. Rates should be structured in a manner that will allow an extensive breakdown of each processing charge. Prices

[1] See Section 5, Chapter 8, "Evaluation of Computer Department Management and Personnel."

The
chief
manag
of cha
Top n
perioc
  Eac
Mana
minim
before
  Ope
shoulc
key m
manag
frustra
facts n
useful
for the
level
comp
  The
draw
volve
mana
can c
agers
on se
pany
will k

TOP

Few n
agem
  •
tion t
tions.
  •
ment
  •
align
devel
  •

th

  •
ADP a

mu
sy
pe
tha
tha

of
eit
dec
rec
me

qu
for
ope

ass
for
sid
son
wit

I
cos
ope
just
Onl
mal
plar

H
reac
dec
the
this

O
tabl
duce
posi
marl
thei
This
rent
fund
alter

Be
for e
The
and
As s
more
bette
a va
the r
their
for a

In
The
rializ
resul

² Se

Chapter 2

Integrated Data Processing and Management Information Systems: An Overview

HUGO BERLET

Vice President, The Diebold Group, New York, New York

Advances in information technology exert a primary influence on corporate planning. In line with its objective of identifying significant developments in this field for a decade ahead, the Diebold Research Program, beginning with its first conference in Brussels in January, 1965, has concerned itself with the evolving concept of the integrated management information system.

At that time, the concept was just emerging. One recalls the enthusiasm for it in America, where many envisioned a whole organization's data being digested and integrated by computers—managers would just push buttons to find out all they wanted to know about products, productivity, sales, financial results, and so forth. In other words, managers would make infallible decisions based on timely "total" information.

"With the present large-scale computers, management can now assemble in one master corporate memory all of its operations." This quotation, from an article on ADP in a large-circulation business magazine of 1965, is typical of the optimistic statements made at that time. Numerous articles prophesied a glorious tomorrow, in which management problems would be solved at the stroke of a light pen, or flash of a visual display unit, as executives availed themselves of the output of an integrated management information system (IMIS).

What was IMIS to be? Professionals in the field today are all aware that the realization has been less impressive than the advance publicity. Therefore it is fair to ask: Discounting some of the more ambitious visions of "total" systems to provide coverage of "all" operations, were and are the original basic ideas valid? Or was IMIS doomed to be, as Professor Dearden has called it, "a wild mirage, a wild goose chase, a will of the wisp by a fundamental flaw in the logic which gave it birth"?[1]

It is the purpose of this Chapter to attempt to answer the following three questions about IMIS:

1. What has been the experience in attempted implementations?
2. Are the original objectives still valid?

[1] John Dearden, "MIS Is a Mirage," *Harvard Business Review*, January–February, 1972.

3. In the light of experience, and with the benefit of hindsight, what conceptual changes should be made?

DEFINITION

The definition formulated by the Diebold Research Program, Europe, in 1965 still offers a valid objective: "IMIS is an information system making use of all available resources to provide managers at all levels and in all functions with the information from relevant sources necessary to enable them to make timely and effectively decisions for planning, directing, and controlling the activities for which they are responsible."

This definition is very similar to one advanced 5 years later by Walter J. Kennevan, in an attempt to clear up some of the semantic confusion that had by then surrounded the subject: "A management information system is an organized method of providing past, present, and projection information relating to internal operations and external intelligence. It supports the planning, control, and operational functions of an organization by furnishing uniform information in the proper time-frame to assist the decision-making process."[2]

The DRP-Europe conference in Bad Godesberg, in November, 1965, addressed the matter once more, and more thoroughly, because at that time many American companies were designing such systems *without* clear definitions and understandable guidelines. It was an attempt to draw attention to and to clarify semantic problems, and to alert DRP sponsors to the fallacy of the "all-things-to-all-men" approach.

DEVELOPMENT OF THE CONCEPT

While it is difficult to establish clear time boundaries, the following three phases in the development of and experience with the concept may be discerned:
- The first phase, from the early through the mid-sixties, characterized by great enthusiasm and optimism.
- The second phase, from late 1969 to 1972, marked by considerable disappointment.
- The third phase, in which we now find ourselves, characterized by a cautious reappraisal and implementation of the basic concepts.

The Bad Godesberg meeting in November, 1965, took place during the first phase. It considered "seven pillars" as the basic structure of such a system. Let us briefly review these here (see Figure 2-1):
- The first dealt with the necessity to set objectives — for example, with reference to "real time" management information needs: priorities, time, cost, etc.
- The second pillar dealt with the need for a methodology to embrace not only the concepts, but also the organizational and geographic elements, together with the hardware, software, and other technological tools.
- The third dealt with the common database. The principal characteristics of a common database which were identified then were:
  1. The possibility of file interaction.
  2. An organization to permit quick access.
  3. An organization to permit flexibility.
- The fourth pillar identified report stratification. Here, three questions posed to management still seem worth asking today:
  1. What per cent of the reports that you now receive do you read thoroughly?
  2. What per cent of the reports that you now receive do you read when they arrive?
  3. How long after you get the reports do you act upon them?

In essence, report stratification identified three levels of output to increase information effectiveness, but at the same time to reduce the number of reports. The first level called for *adaptive dissemination*, which, based on profiles of functions and their information needs, automatically generated certain reports necessary to the timely

---

[2] Walter J. Kennevan, "MIS Universe," presentation at the DPMA 1970 International Conference, Seattle, Washington, June 23–27, 1970; published in *Data Management*, September, 1970.

and effective exercise of each particular function. The intention was to put an end to the problems associated with obtaining information from another group in the organization (frequently more difficult than getting similar information from a competitor!). The second level called for the issuance of *performance reports*, highly condensed and summarized, with additional information for each particular line available on request through a key system. Finally, a third level of report was described, called the *demand report*, available only on request. For this, a catalogue system was used, which also indicated the cost of the report to each user.

● The fifth pillar dealt with the need to establish a communications-oriented data processing system with on-line/real-time capability. The factors determining the need for on-line/real-time usage were defined as response-time requirements, cost, and convenience.

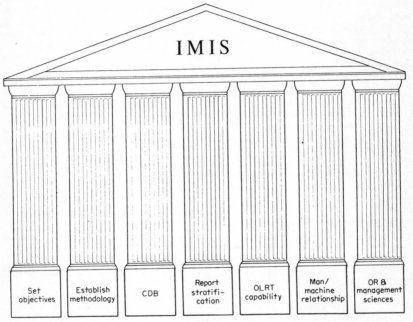

Fig. 2-1 Basic structure of an integrated management information system.

● The sixth pillar called for a better person–machine relationship—in today's terminology, the "user–system interface"—than was available in those days, particularly with reference to management.

● The seventh and last pillar dealt with the desirability of making use of operations research and other developments in the newer management sciences. Here the discussion was concerned with, for example, linear programming, network analysis planning, and simulation.

When the American delegates at the 1965 Bad Godesberg conference were asked by one of the participants from the floor to state their position regarding the above seven pillars, they responded for the most part positively. Their comments reflected the fact that at that time the concept was considered realistic, and, indeed, was being implemented in a number of American as well as European organizations.

PITFALLS

Some 2½ years later, in March, 1968, the XII DRP-European conference in Geneva again reviewed IMIS, which by that time was being referred to more frequently as MIS. Professor John Dearden of Harvard University had in the meantime written his much publicized article, "Myth of Real-Time Management Information," which added more fuel to the controversy that had grown up over the subject.[3] In this article, Professor Dearden stated that it would not be practicable to operate a real-time management control system, and that such a system would not help solve any of the critical problems even if it could be implemented, and delivered the following widely quoted indictment: "It is my personal opinion that, of all the ridiculous things that have been foisted on the long-suffering executive in the name of science and progress, the real-time management information system is the silliest."

While the experiences of successful implementors of MIS as related at this and later gatherings refuted this blanket charge, it was considered necessary at the Geneva meeting to call attention again to thirteen pitfalls which had been identified at the 1965 gathering:

1. Management does not cause all interested parties to become involved in the program at the outset. Frequently forgotten, for example, are external auditors and labor unions.

2. Management demands unreasonable objectives with reference to the time plan and the investment. You talk to management for months and years, urging that it do something about MIS, but when it finally agrees, it wants it all done at a fraction of the time and cost originally indicated as being required.

3. Management relies too heavily on the support of data processing manufacturers, all of whom make many promises.

4. Management accepts promises of delivery dates for hardware and software which are often unrealistic, and frequently not met.

5. Management overlooks the necessity for very early training of all persons who have to work with the system. A lack of training has a particularly undesirable effect on data input.

6. Management does not insist on appropriate standards and documentation.

7. Management does not concern itself enough about the system in the basic planning stage, as regards desired output.

8. Management does not recognize that highly qualified personnel, even though more costly per individual, are still less expensive in the long run than a larger number of less-qualified, lower-paid people.

9. Data processing management overlooks the need for appropriate measures designed for the possible failure of the automated system; unless it prepares for this eventuality, it will let itself in for a great deal of trouble.

10. Data processing management overlooks the need to build strong internal audit controls into the program at an early stage.

11. Data processing management overlooks the need for flexibility of hardware and software which would permit not only the increase, but also the decrease of the total system when changed requirements dictate.

12. Data processing management underestimates the time and costs involved in conversion and cutover.

13. Data processing management underestimates the increased problems of error generation, error transfer, and the compounding of these in an integrated system—the "rolling effect." In previous functional systems or subsystems or separate systems, an error in the system stayed there; but in an integrated system, one must be aware of and provide for the possibility that an error may generate compounding errors in other parts of the system.

Implementation Experience Four American and three European organizations have made presentations at DRP-Europe conferences concerning their implementation of management information systems during the 8 years from 1965 to 1973. With some generosity, one can say that two were successful, one was moderately successful, and four were total failures. In all of the last-named four one could discover only casual investigation or total lack of attention to one or (mostly) more of the thirteen pitfalls listed above.

Principal Causes of Failure Of five principal causes of failure, the first is found to be the attempt to design a system in one major effort, rather than to proceed with careful implementation of subsystems. Professor James C. Emery, director of computing

[3] John Dearden, "Myth of Real-Time Management Information," *Harvard Business Review*, May–June, 1966.

activities at the University of Pennsylvania, in a reply to Professor Dearden's criticism, has pointed out:[4] "Competent practitioners do not set out to design a totally integrated MIS. They rightly view the MIS — or whatever name one chooses to use — as composed of a collection of subsystems. In some cases a considerable degree of integration exists among these subsystems, but in most cases the subsystems are only loosely coupled or largely independent. The issue is one of degree."

Second, with reference to the setting of objectives, it became increasingly clear that the various levels of management found it very difficult to describe what they really needed by way of information.

Third, if they could indeed have done so, it was technically quite difficult and/or very costly to satisfy their information requirements with the tools available — until recently.

Fourth, although it was realized that in its details an MIS will, of course, differ from company to company, there was a belief that "the same overall description will apply to all." It appears now that the differences among companies were grossly underestimated. For example, with respect to their nature — if they were oriented to sales, manufacturing, or service; with reference to their type — if they were national, multinational, or conglomerate; and with reference to their structure or location, or whether they were profit- or nonprofit-oriented.

Fifth, it was not recognized that, with rare exceptions, top management would not accept as a solution to its problems the technical proposals of specialists whose language they could hardly understand.

A LESSON FROM SUCCESS

One of the two companies mentioned earlier as having installed a successful MIS is The Pillsbury Company in the United States. Details of the system are available in the literature.[5] Briefly, some salient points are recapitulated here:

As a decentralized firm, The Pillsbury Company operates through semiautonomous divisions and affiliates. The Executive Office in the company's chart of organization comprises the general executives who have a global responsibility for the affairs of the company, although each has his or her specific area of prime concern. The general managers are the executive heads of the operating divisions and affiliates. The corporate managers have charge of the functional departments of the firm: law, planning, information systems, personnel, finance. The general managers and the corporate managers report to the Executive Office. Referred to as middle management are the two or three echelons of managers immediately below the general managers, the corporate managers, and the principal executives.

To give an idea of the extent of Pillsbury's computer and related equipment in relation to its business, the Minneapolis computer installation will soon exceed in value the machinery and equipment investment in the company's largest manufacturing plant. In recent years, the purchases of electronic hardware have constituted more than 15 per cent of the company's capital expenditures in North America.

Parallel to Pillsbury's growth in facilities have been the growth in the status of the data processing and information systems function, and the rise in the skills and accomplishments of its staff. In 1956, the title of the data processing head was *Data Processing Coordinator,* and he then reported to the manager of the systems department. In 1959, the title became *Manager, Electronic Data Processing,* and the person reported to a divisional assistant controller. In 1962, the *Manager, Computer Department* reported to an assistant corporate controller. In 1965, the *Director of Information Systems and Services* reported to the corporate controller. Today the title is *Executive Director, Information Systems,* and this person reports directly to the Executive Office.

Pillsbury's communication system utilizes Teletype record communications and Data-Phone data transmission, either on a computer-controlled or personnel-con-

---

[4] In "Letters to the Editor," *Harvard Business Review,* May–June, 1972, p. 22.

[5] Terrance Hanold, Chap. 30, "Perspective on an Advanced Information System," in The Diebold Group, *Rethinking the Practice of Management.* Praeger, New York, 1973. A condensed and updated account appears as the entry "Management Information Systems: A Case Example," in Carl Heyel (ed.), *The Encyclopedia of Management,* 2d ed., Van Nostrand Reinhold, New York, 1973.

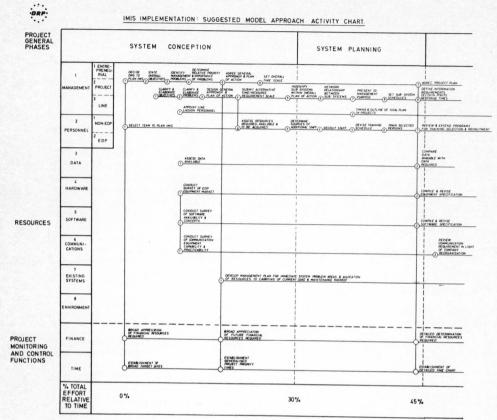

Fig. 2-2 Model approach activity chart for integrated management information system. (Diebold Research Program—Europe, Document No. E-46, Implementation of Integrated Management Information Systems.)

trolled basis, and transmits data originating at every point of importance to the company, to the central information system. While the data *assembly and processing points* are reducing themselves to one central system, the data *originating points* are as numerous and widespread as the needs of the business demand. While this concentration and computerization of information has achieved important savings, much more important is the fundamental shift that occurred in the time-place-quantum dimension of the information currents upon which the management of the business depends.

Data proceed immediately from points of origin in Production, Sales, Marketing, and Distribution to the computer. The computer accumulates, classifies, organizes, analyzes, and reports simultaneously and in the same context and the same detail, if it is desired, to every level of management and operations. As a result, the Executive Office has the ability, by inquiry to the computer, to examine data reflecting the present state of the business in whatever detail the inquiry specifies. It also has electronically at hand an immense amount of historical and environmental data to illuminate the present and suggest the future. But note that this system does *not* inundate the Executive Office with raw data and unneeded information. Coupled into it are mathematically based programs which analyze, simulate, forecast, and perform other operations important in the decision-making process.

Having created a system of great power, diversity, and capability, and having added

IMIS IMPLEMENTATION: SUGGESTED MODEL APPROACH ACTIVITY CHART

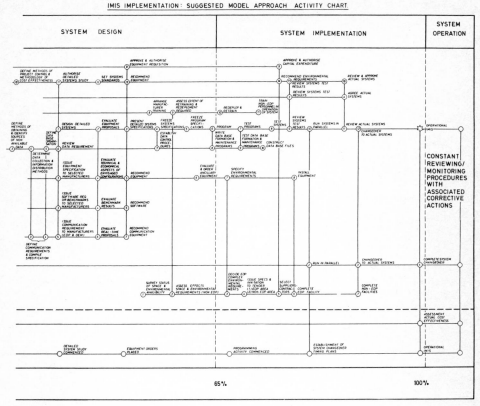

Fig. 2-2   (continued)

to it a group of highly trained people, the company found that the divisions and departments served had to add people of equal capability to work with the information system experts. As a result, there developed all around the information system a series of informal middle-management groups drawn partly from the information system and partly from the operating departments, which utilize information-based techniques to manage Pillsbury's operations.

Of the techniques used, optimization through linear programming is the primary one. This was used initially to formulate and cost products, select and blend materials, develop sales and distribution patterns, rank and allocate orders among plants and warehouses, schedule production, and so forth. The next step was to use simulation techniques based on mathematical principles: market simulation, sales forecasting, manufacturing models, and financial models to predict firm size, capital usage, and so on.

So long as the Executive Office was exposed only to historical data, 30 to 45 days behind the event, the executive officers were compelled to be involved in operations to maintain a feel of the status of the business. Now that current data are regularly available which properly reflect the existing state of affairs in broad outline, the executive officers are able to withdraw from operations to a point where they can better observe the workings of the entire enterprise *in true perspective*.

In an address discussing the workings of MIS at Pillsbury, with special reference to the criticism of the concept advanced by Professor Dearden, Terrance Hanold, Pillsbury president, had this to say:[6]

> Whether there can be a Management Information System was once a matter of great debate, and there were signs for a time that exhaustion had settled the issue. The debate had been prolonged, but hardly profound, so we were grateful for the respite. But the charge that MIS is a mirage has once more been raised in the *Harvard Business Review*. As the description of the system he proposes to disprove, Professor Dearden, in his article, "MIS Is a Mirage," quotes the Kenneron [sic] definition.[7]
>
> Whether or not acute analysis might modify it in part, this is a competent and sufficiently extensive description of a management information system. How does a scholar go about its destruction? His first effort at discreditation is to describe it as grandiose. Aside from the charge itself, he offers nothing but ridicule to support the description. Then, to give it a character it does not claim, he attributes to the definition the universal dimensions of a *total* management information system. Quite clearly, the author of the statement makes no such claim of universal content, and it is certainly not fairly subject to attack on that score. It includes only information capable of systematic collection and of organized processing and presentation in a business environment.

ASSESSMENT OF EXPERIENCE

Adverting to the questions posed in the opening of this Chapter, the first one asked: "What has been the experience in attempting implementations?" It would seem that there were more failures than successes. Some failures were inevitable because of the lack of management involvement and understanding. For example, a major European organization abandoned such an effort, and its action could be directly traced to this point. More specifically, it violated the second of the thirteen pitfalls by having approved a 250-person-year MIS project in 1969, and then insisting that the same result be achieved with half the money, personnel, and time resources.

Far different is the Japanese approach. Dramatic evidence of this is a relatively unnoticed 148-page report entitled, "The Plan for Information Society—a National Goal toward the Year 2000," published in May, 1972, by the Japanese Computer Usage Development Institute. Here we see a solid proposal for the establishment of a nationwide MIS program. It is almost incredible that only 120 years after Admiral Perry landed on the shores of Japan such gigantic steps in industrialization and technology have been made by the Japanese people that they are able to point out with understandable pride in this report that Japan will no longer "follow America," but in fact lead in the establishment of an "information society."

It may be somewhat disconcerting to note that one of the intermediate targets to be achieved within the next 10 years will be the establishment of what the Japanese call a "computer mind." In the words of the report, "Intelligent creativity, by fully using information output by computers, will become the general pattern of human behavior. Thus, daily habits and practices in the information society will be developed. This is the establishment of the computer mind."

Not only the amounts of money involved, but also the goals are staggering, proceeding from an operational management information system to a managerial MIS by 1980, a strategic MIS for top executives by 1985, and an international MIS for multinational enterprises by 1990. The Japanese quite correctly propose to leave the development of the MIS itself to each enterprise, with full assistance to expedite its development given by the government. This will include the establishment of an MIS education

---

[6] Terrance Hanold, "The Executive View of Management Information Systems," The Society for Management Information Systems *Special Report*, 1972.

[7] In the HBR article, through error, the author of the definition is referred to as Walter Kenneron, instead of Kennevan, cited correctly in fn. 2, this Chapter, and the error has carried over into literature taking up the Dearden criticism. After quoting the definition, Prof. Dearden wrote: "This is approximately what I perceive most people to mean by MIS. And if this definition seems grandiose, I can only remark that '*the* management information system' describes a grandiose idea. If the definition were less global in its scope, it would not measure up to the term. If, for example, one were to limit the definition to the context of a company's financial accounting programs, he would have to speak of the *financial* MIS of the company, rather than its general MIS. However, in practice, no such limitations are intended. Kenneron's [sic] inclusive definition of the MIS approach is quite consistent with the nearly universal benefits claimed for it."

center and the creation of data banks in 100 cities (classified by 50 industrial categories). In 10 cities, international trade data transmission centers will be opened, and these are expected to be operating within 3 years.

The second question raised in the beginning of this Chapter was: "Are the objectives still valid?" The strong evidence is that they are. Today the chances of successfully implementing management information systems are now much higher than they were in 1965. This is because more of the necessary tools and experience are now available. Newton appropriately said, "If I have seen further, it is because I have stood on the shoulders of Giants." The price of pioneering has been high, but those who study and heed the lessons of the past are now in a position to benefit greatly.

The third question posed in the beginning was: "In the light of experience and with the benefit of hindsight, what conceptual changes should be made?" DRP-Europe published a generalized MIS "Model Approach Activity Chart" in February, 1968 (see Figure 2-2). This suggested approach, broken down in terms of resources, project monitoring, and control functions, would still appear to be useful as a general guide. One constructive change that could be made today would be to assess cost effectiveness during systems conception, and to review it in the following phases of systems planning, design, and implementation. In general, the seven pillars as well as the thirteen pitfalls seem as valid today as they were in 1965.

Perhaps one of the most important things learned is that there is really no point in time at which one can say, "We have a management information system." It is a never-ending endeavor.

Chapter 3

ADP in Corporate Planning

JAMES F. COLLINS, JR.

**Vice President, Management Information Services,
Corporate Staff, Johnson & Johnson,
New Brunswick, New Jersey**

Planning ahead has always distinguished the successful manager from the ordinary, and especially from the unsuccessful. Throughout history leaders of any military, civil, social, or business enterprises have been judged on their ability to prepare in advance for future occurrences, and to influence those happenings over which they can effect some control and to be ready to adjust and cope effectively with those over which there is no control.

The outstanding person has been the most adept at using tools to extend his or her own abilities and those of associates to reach their goals. The stored-program electronic computer has been one of the most dramatic advances of all time in making a tool available to the competent manager for problem solving and information evaluation. But it is clearly a *tool* and in no way a replacement for the creative and judgmental responsibilities of the leader.

The remarkable rate of acceptance of computers in business management over the past few years has very rapidly caused them to replace repetitive record keeping and analysis by manual procedures, making well-organized information available quickly and to an extent that has truly revolutionized business operation and control. However, their use in decision making and for complex planning and forecasting has proceeded relatively slowly.

There are two reasons for this lag. First, certain developments in the technology were required, and second, an evolution had to take place in the confidence and desire of policy-level management to become involved in the use of computer technology for planning, predicting, and policy optimization.

With respect to the first, low-cost remote terminals with intelligent capabilities have only relatively recently become available, along with low-cost large-core capacities for the central processors. As regards the second, managers trained in the functional levels of business operations, where they gained experience in computer applications, have moved on up to general-management levels. They are familiar with the capabilities and limitations of computers, feel comfortable with systems and computer specialists, and are sponsoring the use of the technology for corporate planning and assistance in decision making. We are now about to see an explosion in the use of computer simulation and forecasting runs for these purposes that will be comparable to the fantastic growth of the past decade in the use of automated data processing for the transactions aspect of business operations.

However, the laws of economics have not been repealed for this phase of computer use, any more than they were for the previous one. A number of overenthusiastic managers came to grief when they allowed their computing costs to rise far beyond the value of the information in running the business. Designing systems, processing these on computer equipment, storing massive data files and keeping these up to date, extract a heavy toll. The resulting output must be substantially more valuable in aiding the managing of the business than all the costs.

APPLICATION BACKGROUND

Corporate planning, or forecasting, using available historical information fitted to predicted courses of events, has always been with us. Now there are cost-effective computer techniques to extend the effectiveness of forecasting by orders of magnitude. More information can be used, projected with far more variables applied, in an almost instantaneous time frame.

To achieve effective planning, the following components must be developed:
- Valid database information.
- Modular simulation and forecasting routines.
- Economical batch processing.
- Economical direct access of data files with analytical routines.

Database Information The database of information needed to project trends and forecast requirements is for the most part now readily available from an existing database of the company operations. This is a byproduct of the major operational systems, usually from the order service system that is the heart of the operations of the business. These data are current by the nature of the operations system, and pertinent to the scope of the business itself as well as being up to date. They are also error-edited and as clean as any information elements can be. They can provide the basis for forecasting in all the sales, marketing, financial, and production capacity areas. The file can be supplemented for special projections by special data files for demographic or new-product markets, obtained from specialized service agencies for a fraction of the cost of developing this information independently.

Simulation and Forecasting Simulation or forecasting routines need to be constructed as modularly as possible, with the capability of isolating those portions of the system pertinent to the evaluation at hand. In the recent past, generalized simulation systems, covering very large numbers of variables and often very complex in their programming, and using very specialized simulation programming languages, called for massive computer runs that not only were expensive, but produced fearfully complicated reports.

The currently more effective approach is to use retrieval routines to extract the data pertinent to the planning forecast from the available database, and then apply the desired variables to a forecasting routine used to process these selected data. If they are not already developed, serious consideration should be given to purchasing or even renting the appropriate software from service companies specializing in this.

One can develop the valid database pertaining to the company's operations in the normal course of running the business. This can then be used to select, extract, correlate, and then forecast, based on variables that can be applied and changed as required. Routines to accomplish this can be purchased from special service agencies, or in some cases rented or leased, usually reasonably economically. Or, if one does not mind having one's private database in someone else's hands, the analyses and forecasting runs can be made by the service agency for an agreed fee.

Batch Processing Batch processing is usually the most economical approach to relatively large corporate planning studies. This is especially true where the time element is not critical enough to justify instantaneous turnaround, and the matrix of the processing of the available data against the selected variables is large enough to make an interactive approach excessively costly as well as cumbersome. On the other hand, direct-access, interactive processing is feasible for many analytical routines.

Direct Access The advantages of direct-access interactive processing, where an experienced planning analyst can selectively modify his or her approach to the study as the forecasting develops, are very real—as long as the person–machine relationship is not misused. The required database cannot be too great, the simulation or analytical routines must not be too large, the simulation or analytical routines must not be too

001.64 c.1 Au82t

large, the number of variables must be reasonably small, and the operator must be clear as to what he or she is after. If these criteria are met, the analyst can truly effect improvements to the forecasting run by changing specifications based on relationships shown in the results. On the other hand, if it is a strategic planning run, or a "fishing expedition" in a large file of data to find relationships worth pursuing for forecasting, then the initial analysis must be carried out with a well-specified batch-processing approach.

Remote-terminal Access. It is worth noting that scientists and engineers have for many years been using remote terminals and directly accessing computers for solving equations and making correlations and evaluations of scientific data. They were some 5 years ahead of business-oriented analysts in the use of this form of computer-assisted decision making. This is not too surprising when we recall that electronic computers were first developed by and for scientific personnel to speed up calculations and to solve problems that were beyond the scope of existing mechanized computing technology. Business managers, on the other hand, have been oriented to the application of the greatly expanded electronic computing capabilities to tremendous volumes of operating transactions, rather than to using stored-program computers to analyze experimental data, compare them to hypotheses, and predict results. Now that computers and peripherals have become lower in cost and more flexible in their performance, business analysts should, like their scientific and engineering counterparts, welcome this increased capability to examine data, simulate problems, and forecast results—and to do this while sitting in front of their own inexpensive connecting terminal.

This is more and more the coming thing. Business managers and their staff associates will be catching up on computer-assisted planning and decision making, and the 5-year lag behind their scientific colleagues will rapidly vanish. Perhaps not every manager will have a computer terminal on his or her desk, as enthusiastic equipment manufacturers have hoped. But every manager can have one if he or she needs and wants one and will use it, or can have a specialized staff assistant to turn to who will use such equipment to make the inquiries, correlate the data, make the simulation runs, and furnish the selective decision-assisting information.

Approaches As indicated earlier, strategic planning models and all manner of long-range forecasting runs using large data files are best done in batch mode. This is by far the most economical approach, and where adequate capacity can be made available on in-house equipment, the processing can be scheduled for maximum convenience as well as minimum costs.

For analytical routines, selective data retrieval and comparison, and other relatively short problem-solving runs, the advantages of interactive computer processing for the flexibility and creativity this engenders have made individual terminal connections the most effective approach. Where there is plenty of available computer capability on in-house equipment for this person–machine interaction, this is an easy step. Where there is not, and this is certainly the more universally true situation, the use of outside time-sharing services, at least in the early stages of establishing computer-assisted planning, is the most cost-effective approach.

Outside Services. A fairly wide selection of specialized time-sharing services is available in almost all locations. These provide a pay-as-you-go, buy-as-much-as-you-need-or-can-afford approach to remote-terminal processing. As soon as the use of this interactive method of data analysis grows to a break-even point or beyond, the utilization of in-house facilities can be considered.

Even where large facilities are available within the organization, there may still be some occasions where consideration should be given to some specialized service facilities, or at least the rental of certain software available from them. An important factor here is to avoid tying up major portions of in-house facilities with massive simulation runs to the detriment of essential regular data processing.

The availability of specialized proprietary applications developed by some service bureaus is also a consideration. Many banks, for example, have excellent financial analyses and projection packages, and one would be ill advised to spend the redundant time and effort to reinvent them. Risk analysis, financial forecasting with multiple variables, the future value of present dollars or the discounted present value of future dollars, and many other highly useful packages are now available just for the selection.

IMPLEMENTATION

Three Categories of Planning   The use of computer processing for corporate planning may be categorized broadly into three groups. The first is *strategic planning*, usually thought of as long-range planning. The time frame is often 3 years, perhaps extended by means of projections of 5 or 10 years and more. Strategic planning models are best known in the areas of finance, with some fairly recent work in long-range marketing forecasting models. Strategic planning models are also being used in the evaluation of ventures and acquisitions.

The second general category is *short- to medium-range forecasting*. Here the models and analytical routines are most often used for financial projections, involving multivariable risk analyses, capital forecasting, cash-flow planning strategies, cash investment planning, and tax minimizing plans, and also for sales forecasting in summary and down to the product level. The periods most commonly used are a year's forecast, by month or other fiscal increment, although of course these can be carried forward if the forecaster feels comfortable in his or her assumptions.

Market conditions, historical seasonality, planned promotional activity, product changes, new-product marketing, all known and many more assumed variables can be fed in, and their effects individually and in concert can be observed. The value of the forecasting, of course, rests on the adequacy of the historical data selected as the basis for the projection, and on the judgment and experience of the modeler in designing the relationships and effects of the varied assumptions of changing conditions.

The third category may simply be termed *miscellaneous analyses*—a catchall for the many short-range evaluation and comparison runs or problem-solving processing. Typical of the large number of applications in this miscellaneous group are site-selection optimization routines, plant facility size as well as location optimization, project cost reporting and comparison, project status reporting, and project priority evaluation. The extent of computer evaluations for planning requirements in this category is boundless, limited only by the ingenuity of the planning analyst and the availability of resources.

The Implementation Process[1]   The successful use of a mathematical model to represent an operating environment rests upon effectively bringing together two different disciplines. The most important factor in model building is really good communications between the knowledgeable operations manager and the management-science specialist.

The operations manager must perceive a need for simulating portions of his or her operating environment to estimate results based on the selection of various conditions. Or, the manager may see the advantage of projecting past history and then observing the effects of varying elements of the environment. He or she will then call on the staff specialist who can translate this into a representational model that can be run on a computer to calculate the effects of the many assumptions and the variables involved.

The management-science specialist works with the operations manager to assist in defining the elements of the operations and the impact on these of changing conditions, or variables. The specialist will build a model to represent the environment, and using analytical techniques such as linear programming, and high-level computer languages such as FORTRAN, will prepare the model for computer processing. He or she will then arrange for the computer runs, and will assist the using manager in interpreting the results and work with the manager in varying the assumptions or changing variables for further analytical runs. Regular runs that are repeated at intervals, such as forecasting simulation runs, become routine, and a staff assistant to the manager can be readily trained to provide the new input, set the parameters of the conditions desired, and arrange for the computer processing.

Making the assumptions and weighting their relative importance are the most critical aspects in designing and building the representational model. Here is where communications and understanding between the manager and the technical specialist are crucial. The management-science specialist has a definite responsibility to learn and understand the operations being studied, so that he or she can agree with the relation-

---

[1] For in-depth development of the decision-making processes here discussed, see Section 3, Part One, Chapter 3, "Simulation and Models for Decision Making," and Section 4, Chapter 1, "New Tools for Decision Making."

ships being portrayed. The specialist must explain to the operations manager how the model functions, and advise the manager as to the meaningfulness of the results. The impact of small variations in each key parameter must be depicted clearly.

The operations manager is responsible for the assumptions and their relative weighting, for only the manager has the broad perspective as to the effects of changes on the operations. The operations manager must also be responsible for seeking external information that will improve the estimates. The technical specialist can quantify the assumptions, but only the experienced manager can make them in the first place, and ascribe the weighting for relative importance.

For example, how much influence do general economic conditions have on operations? The manager must look at past trends, and then test his or her assumptions. What is the impact of an increase in raw-material costs of 10 per cent? What is the impact on the selling price of a 10 per cent increase in wages? These and many other assumptions rely on the experience and judgment of the manager. Only the manager can make the best assumptions, although he or she has the right to expect good counsel from a technical assistant in establishing these.

The operations manager must exercise extreme caution, and not believe that after making several assumptions he or she will arrive at a completely valid projection of the future. Models fail when an assumption is considered an absolute fact just because it has been made a part of a simulation run. Only the interaction of an experienced manager and a competent management-science technician, who have learned to understand each other and to communicate effectively, will result in a valid and valuable model that will simulate variable conditions in a computer run and provide for better decision making.

EXAMPLES

The following examples of planning models currently in use in a number of operating companies show the characteristics of planning models:

Strategic Planning Model – 3-Year and 5-Year Horizons

Objectives. In conjunction with preparation of the 3- or 5-year financial forecast and planning, the model provides assistance in the reappraisal of present trends and the performance potential of the operations. The operating parameters of the planning model are to:

1. Optimize the total sales contribution, within the present manufacturing capacity, for the next 3 years, and also for 5 years. The production capacity of the various product lines versus sales plan can be varied to optimize profit. With a fixed total manufacturing capacity, profit returns can be optimized by concentrating on selected product lines.

2. Define the product mix and the pricing policy, and also which products to manufacture and at what price to market them, in each monthly planning period.

3. Determine optimum plant loading schedule – how many shifts, regular and overtime, for each machine.

4. Analyze machine utilization increases versus marginal increases in sales contribution. Does the increase in sales income justify the costs involved in the required increases in the number of shifts on a machine or production line?

Capabilities. After analyzing simulation runs:

1. Optional pricing policies related to capital investments in capacity may indicate revisions to current business operating policies.

2. Additional definition of marketing objectives, and conversion of plant operation to meet the optimal production sequences, will then be the primary concern to operations management.

3. Present equipment for one product line may possibly provide sufficient capacity to meet the forecast demand, if optimal product assignment or production sequences are followed.

4. Optimal investments for increasing the machine capacity for selected lines may be indicated. This would be based on a high return on these investments and their potential immediate effect on income contribution.

5. A substantial increase in income contribution may result from a concentrated program aimed at reducing waste levels.

6. Improvements in machine utilization, although desirable, may not justify priority attention until effort is invested in improving all other operations factors.

This planning model assists in the decision of how many of which products to manufacture on which machines. This consideration becomes quite complex with a number of products and their respective markets, and the building up of inventories to the optimal point for long production runs and reduced distribution costs. Anticipated future growth, additional capital investments in capacity required to meet that growth as well as the introduction of new products, combinations of machines to maximize output with minimum costs, market demand as influenced by pricing, competition, and changes in the economy, all combine to form a problem that cannot be solved piecemeal. The mathematical programming techniques of the model can provide combinations of actions to optimize results.

Sales Forecasting Model—Forecasting for 1 Year or Less

Objectives. The system is designed in program modules to meet the forecasting requirements of any company. It is usable by companies with different product types, business types, or systems structure. The specific objectives are to:
1. Increase forecasting accuracy by means of statistical techniques.
2. Improve customer service.
3. Reduce inventory level.
4. Reduce manual effort.
5. Communicate to production planning.
6. Offer flexibility and ease of operation.

General description. The forecasting system performs six basic functions:
1. Editing.
2. Seasonality testing.
3. Simulation testing.
4. Projection.
5. Adjusting.
6. Communicating to production planning.

Each of these functions is programmed separately so it can be run independently of the others. This permits independent use of any or all of these capabilities during the same run. This flexibility is advantageous because what might be an adjustment run for one user could be a start-up run for a second user, and a forecasting run for still another user.

Characteristics. The forecasting system is a person–machine system designed to support the sales and marketing forecasting operations. Forecasting consists of some extrapolation of past history plus a judgment of external influences, to arrive at an estimate of what to expect in the future. From historical data, the computer can pick up growth and seasonal patterns to project future demand. The forecaster adds expected significant influences such as a promotion, favorable or unfavorable publicity, a large contract, or the release of a new product. The forecaster also helps refine past history by making a one-time demand adjustment. Misleading data elements in a demand pattern will decrease the accuracy of seasonal indices, the selection of forecasting methods, and the forecast itself.

With this approach, the computer is used as a tool to create the historical basis for the forecast and to provide for easy flexible adjustments desired by the forecaster.

Capabilities. The sales forecasting system:
1. Performs strong data screening to identify questionable demand information. The edit-run program identifies questionable demand data by means of statistical comparisons. The questioned data items can then be further analyzed.
2. Calculates seasonal indices for each item.
3. Simulates to select the best forecasting method for each item, and makes projections of past demand patterns which are then compared with recent actual experience. The method showing the least cumulative error for each item is then selected for future forecasts.
4. Calculates statistical forecasts.
5. Accepts forecast adjustments, adjusts existing forecasts, records revised forecasts.
6. Provides confirmation of forecast adjustments.
7. Provides history of forecast revisions, on request.

8. Serves as a communication link between the forecasting function and production planning.

9. Provides measurement of forecast error for the calculation of safety stock.

10. Provides information base for creation of a production requirements planning report.

11. Performs internal checks on projection and adjustment accuracy. Projection formulas are self-correcting.

12. Provides the forecaster with the ability to override established forecast frequency and perform immediate reprojection whenever forecast error goes out of bounds for an item.

13. Allows easy addition of new statistical forecasting techniques, formulas.

14. Identifies items requiring manual forecasting and provides all capabilities, except projection, on such items.

15. Maintains complete information base for forecasting.

16. Establishes frequency of use independently by each user.

17. Makes any or all system capabilities available to all users during the same run.

18. Organizes data and forecasts to any of six levels: company, forecasting group, product group, product, distribution point, market area.

Benefits. Improved corporate planning is achieved through:

1. More accurate forecasting, ability to measure and react to shifts in forecast accuracy, ability to select hard-to-forecast situations and concentrate on them.

2. More economical safety stock levels, statistical foundation for item-by-item calculation of proper safety stock levels.

3. Improved communication of market requirements, from forecasting to production personnel.

4. Reduction in manual effort involved in forecasting production personnel.

5. Common research and development effort applied in the forecasting area. New ideas or improvements developed by one element of the company are made available to all parts of the company through use of the forecasting system.

Financial Consolidation System   Typical of the problem-solving or operational planning computer systems are the currently popular interactive consolidation routines for multicompany summary reporting and analyses.

Objectives. Provide a generalized, interactive computer system to:

1. Process and consolidate any data presented in the form of a financial schedule.

2. Provide for the retrieval of the information so presented in various report formats and comparisons.

Capabilities. The financial consolidation system:

1. Edits financial statements and schedules submitted periodically by all reporting units.

2. Makes all necessary reconciliations between statements and schedules.

3. Makes necessary calculations relative to revaluation and devaluation, and properly applies gain or loss.

4. Converts all statements received in foreign currency to U.S. dollars.

5. Provides consolidated U.S. dollar results at any level requested, e.g., country, continent, executive reporting arrangement, worldwide.

6. Processes journal entries entered at any level, through logical consolidation.

7. Accommodates swift retrieval of information in other than the format in which the data were originally presented: e.g., report of cash for all foreign affiliates.

8. Provides simple report-generator tools allowing Finance to format, and request from the information files, the many necessary internal reports.

CONCLUSION

Forecasting the course of the future based on the experience of the past has been attempted by all managers since time began. With today's available computer technology a whole new dimension has been added to corporate planning. Optimizing projections using more variables than ever before possible are not only technically available but economically possible now.

The company management that fails to make maximum use of this planning and decision-assisting tool is going to be at a severe competitive disadvantage. To use the automatic data processing approach to forecasting and planning is now not only a great assistance and convenience. Not to use it regularly and extensively could be disasterous. A little knowledge may be a dangerous thing, particularly if one's competitors have the advantage of a great deal of knowledge from computer-assisted planning.

Chapter 4

Understanding the Computer: Technical Background for the Generalist [1]

DR. EDWARD A. TOMESKI

Professor of Management, Fordham University, New York, New York; and Consultant

GEORGE STEPHENSON

Assistant Professor of Management, Fordham University, New York, New York; and Consultant

The most important feature that distinguishes the modern computer is its capability of holding an *internally stored program* (which prescribes a sequence of operations to be performed on data) that can be modified or replaced by another program. Indeed, this flexibility for almost limitless use has made the computer a truly general-purpose tool, which explains its important role in so many different organizations (manufacturing, processing, transportation, finance, education, government, technical fields, etc.).

The elements of a computer system can be separated into two major sections: equipment (or hardware) elements and analytical programming (or software) elements. An executive should have a basic understanding of these elements to obtain full satisfaction from the new technology. No one can use a computer, or manage it, without a reasonable comprehension of its capabilities and limitations. However, it must be realized that there are a vast number and variety of computers and related devices. Further, computer technology is quite complex. The treatment in this Chapter is necessarily generalized and summary in nature.

HARDWARE BASICS

Computer hardware consists of a central processing unit and auxiliary storage units, and of input and output devices. (See Figure 4-1.)

[1] This Chapter follows the treatment by the authors in their chapter, "Computer Basics," Carl Heyel (ed.), *Handbook of Modern Office Management and Administrative Services*, McGraw-Hill, New York, 1972, here updated.

Central Processing Unit (CPU) The central processing unit is the heart of the computer. It is the unit that includes the circuitry which controls the input and output units, and auxiliary attachments, and which interprets and executes the computer program. The unit contains fast memory (or storage) devices that can hold a computer program or programs and data. The memory devices have the ability to retain electrical pulses which represent, inside the computer, numeric, alphabetic, or special characters. Main fast memory, in the CPU, usually consists of magnetic cores. How-

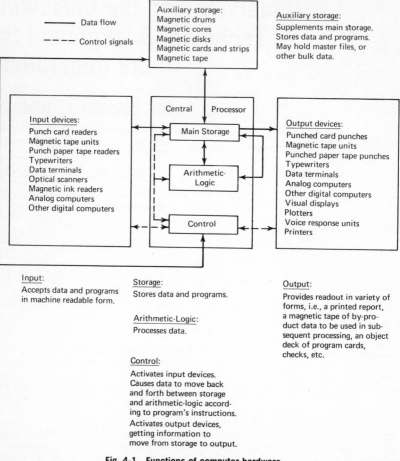

Fig. 4-1 Functions of computer hardware.

ever, thin film, semiconductors, and more exotic memory elements are beginning to be used. When additional memory is required, increments can usually be made to the CPU's storage (with an upper limit). Also, it is frequently possible to connect, via cable, auxiliary storage units to the CPU. Auxiliary storage may be magnetic cores, magnetic tapes, magnetic drums, magnetic disks, or other magnetic devices. The CPU frequently has other supplementary storage areas used for special purposes (index registers, counters, etc.). All these magnetic storage devices, under control of the computer program, can be magnetized or not magnetized in specific locations to represent a number, letter, or symbol in *binary form*, as explained below.

The memory of the computer is divided into a number of locations, each having a definite address, which permits orderly allocation and storage of data, and accessibility to these data as required. Figure 4-2 schematically illustrates the use of memory.

All data in the CPU are stored and processed in the form of *bits* (abbreviation of binary digits). In binary processing, only one of two possible states can exist—*on* or *off*. A bit is on when magnetized; it is off when unmagnetized. Thus, all data and programs are represented in binary form by combinations of 1 (on) and 0 (off). The computer is engineered to use binary digits because for its processing, it is much more efficient than our human language, which consists of 10 symbols (0 through 9) in the decimal system, 26 symbols in our alphabet, and numerous special symbols ($, %, etc.), and because there exist many bi-stable devices, devices with two stable distinguishable

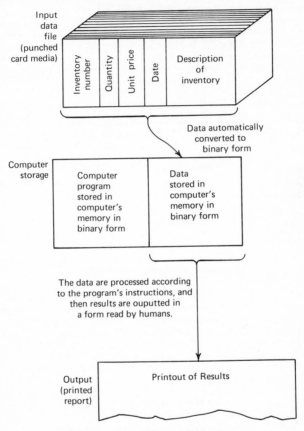

Fig. 4-2   The use of computer memory.

states, e.g., a transistor conducting or cut off, or a core magnetized in one direction or the other.

The binary system lends itself to a variety of coding. One version, shown in Figure 4-3, assumes that each location consists of eight bits. The bit at the extreme right has a value of 1, the second bit from the right has a value of 2, the third bit has a value of 4, and the next bit has a value of 8. Thus, any of our decimal digits can be represented with the four bits. Bits 5, 6, and 7 are used—in combination with the numeric bits—to represent an alphabetic character or a special symbol. The eighth, and leftmost, bit is a check bit used to provide an internal verification of the data; the check bit is added (automatically by the computer) to create odd parity check. That is, all data must be represented by an odd number of magnetized bits. (It should be mentioned that some computers use an even parity check.)

A series of memory locations are used to handle large numbers and other data. Such a grouping of locations, to handle a single related data element, is usually referred to as a *word*. The word is thus an ordered set of characters, made up of perhaps 32 bits, in the binary (or machine-language) form, and is treated by the computer circuitry as a unit. There are methods of coupling and uncoupling words to provide for both small and large data elements. Word lengths may be fixed or variable, depending upon the particular computer. Various methods are used to identify where a variable-length word begins and ends.

It is important to realize that the computer storage effectively keeps the data and/or program unchanged in storage until an instruction is given that deliberately replaces the contents of one or more storage locations with something else.

The CPU accepts programs and data from the input devices or from auxiliary storage, processes the data according to the program's instructions, and sends the results (information or byproduct data) to the output devices or to storage for updating or adding to information already stored there.

Engineered into the CPU are the circuits and controls that enable it to perform, at extremely high speeds, functions (operations) such as READ A RECORD, ADD, SUBTRACT, MULTIPLY, MOVE, COMPARE, BRANCH, WRITE, STOP, etc. Most of the functions entail arithmetic operations, logic, decision making, the movement

Decimal System	*Binary Digits System (Bits)*							
	B_8	B_7	B_6	B_5	B_4	B_3	B_2	B_1
	Check				*8*	*4*	*2*	*1*
Digit 1	0	0	0	0	0	0	0	1
Digit 2	0	0	0	0	0	0	1	0
Digit 3	1	0	0	0	0	0	1	1
etc.								
Alphabet								
Letter A	1	0	0	1	0	0	0	1
etc.								

Fig. 4-3   Example of binary coding.

of data, or the formatting of the data. A CPU may have the capability of performing a few dozen or several hundred different types of operations, depending upon its design. The CPU's control unit translates the program's operations and activates the affected components: input-output devices, storage, arithmetic units, etc. Time used in the translation of the program is known as *I time* (or instruction time), and time used in carrying out the operation is referred to as *E time* (or execution time).

Thus, computer storage is used for several purposes: storage of the computer program, storage of data, accepting (or reading in) data, and generating (or reading out) information. Careful planning is required to allocate storage appropriately among these several purposes. There is a technique (use of *compiler programs*, to be discussed later) which delegates to the computer the task of allocating storage.

Input and Output Devices   Input and output devices, interconnected by cable to the CPU, permit the computer to communicate with the outside environment—and allow people to communicate with the CPU. We say that such devices are "on-line" with the CPU.

The primary input devices are punched-card readers, typewriters, paper-tape readers, optical scanners, magnetic-ink readers, and data terminals (teletypewriters, data collection units, etc.). Magnetic-tape units, used in many large and medium-sized computer installations, are combined input-output and auxiliary storage devices.

Besides magnetic-tape units, the principal output devices are punched-card punches, punched-paper-tape punches, printers (which can produce hard-copy reports, etc., on continuous forms), data display tubes (similar to a television screen), plotters for graphic work, typewriters, voice response units, and data terminals.

Increasing use is being made of remote data terminals (which can be thousands of miles distant from the actual computer) which can communicate with the computer via telephone lines, Teletype lines, microwave transmission, or space satellites.

Some authorities put auxiliary storage, such as magnetic disks, in the input-output classification. Each computer is limited as to the number and kind of I/O (input and output) devices that can be connected to the CPU.

Machine-readable media are standard materials (paper, cards, etc.), conforming to predetermined uniform rules, on which are recorded data (in code or stylized print). Besides print, the recording may be in the form of magnetized spots or perforations. For the CPU to function, machine-readable media must be used for input. Examples of such media are punched cards (see Figure 4-4), punched paper tape, magnetic tape, and special preprinted forms. Usually, the input media are prepared from a manually created source document which reflects some activity (sales ticket, requisition, etc.). Such media are said to be generated off-line (by equipment not cable-connected to the CPU). For instance, punched cards can be prepared on special typewriterlike devices called *keypunches*. The keypunch operator, reading from a source document, depresses the appropriate keys on the keypunch machine, which perforates the automatically fed cards to be punched. Some standard data, such as dates, can be duplicated, thus eliminating the time-consuming depression of keys.

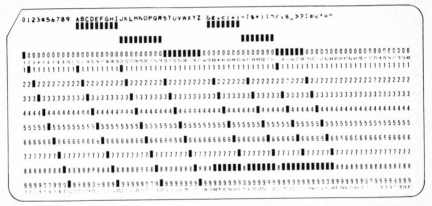

Fig. 4-4   The 80-column Hollerith card. About the size of a dollar bill, the punched card is the most prevalent medium used for recording both the data and the computer program for computer systems.

In other instances the input media are created as an automatic byproduct of another operation (e.g., as a purchase order is typed, a coupled keypunch machine automatically punches a card with all relevant data). This automatic creating of input media is sometimes referred to as *integrated data processing*. It is not infrequent that the computer itself, when processing one application, will generate output which will be input for subsequent processing.

The formats (or layouts) of input and output media must be carefully planned; for example, the maximum number of characters for each data element must be stipulated when designing the system. Forms design can be an important aspect of computer input and output, particularly when related to printed forms or the format of computer-generated reports.

The on-line input devices can read (or sense) the coded data on stylized media. They transmit the data, at high speeds, to the CPU. The CPU translates the media's coded data to binary form for manipulation as directed by the computer program. The computer program is also read into the CPU's memory via an input device; in fact, the program must be read into the CPU's memory prior to the data being read in. The computer program is recorded on media just like data.

The output unit takes information, as directed by the program, from the CPU's memory and records the information on some medium.

There is a wide range of input and output devices, and they have varying characteristics, speeds, and costs. Speeds can range from that of a typewriter (about 200 characters per minute) to transfer rates of millions of characters per minute when such devices as magnetic-tape units and magnetic-disk units are used. In general, the computer's speed of arithmetic and logical operations is so great in comparison with that of peripheral equipment that most computers are said to be "input-output-bound"; that is, the I/O devices cannot keep up with the greater speed of the CPU. This is particularly true of business as opposed to scientific computation.

COMPUTER SYSTEMS AND PROGRAMMING

Competent systems and programming work must be accomplished before a computer can be used. In some organizations the same individual performs both the systems and the programming work. In other organizations, these are considered separate jobs (although it should be recognized that there is an important interface). As a matter of convenience this chapter will treat systems work and computer programming as inter-related jobs performed by separate units.

Systems Phase   Systems design and analysis are the activities of analysis and synthesis that should precede programming. It is not altogether rare, however, to find organizations overlooking or even ("we can't afford it") deliberately bypassing these important phases.

Systems analysis involves an objective study of the existing system which is to be improved, and the detailed development of the new system. Systems design implies a higher-level overall planning of systems in sufficient detail for the systems analysis to proceed.

Systems analysis and design involve the following steps: (1) studying the problem, (2) developing a general scheme for solving the problem or improving the system under study, (3) justifying the new system, (4) obtaining approval for proceeding, and (5) developing details of the system. Analysts can employ a great variety of techniques in their work; some examples are flow charting, statistical analysis, work measurement, models, decision tables, organization analysis, cost-effectiveness analysis, and network analysis (critical path method [CPM] or program evaluation and review technique [PERT]).

The new system should be the best alternative. Of course, an adjective such as "best" will have different meanings and values to organizations and individuals. Therefore, some criterion should be set.

After the systems analyst has completed his or her work, computer programming can proceed. The systems analyst normally provides the programmer with the following kinds of guidelines: a flow chart (a diagram which indicates the structure of the system), specifications or examples of input forms and output reports, and related specifications about the new system (frequency of processing, size of files, length of records, exception cases, etc.). The systems analyst, obviously, will obtain many ideas, suggestions, and requirements from other people—particularly the executive(s) to be most affected by the new system. Conversely—the executives should show a lively interest in new systems that will be affecting them and their organization. It is during this stage that executives should let their preferences be known.

Programming Phase   With the guidelines provided by the systems analyst, the programmer develops a block diagram (a detailed chart of how the computer program will work), and prepares program coding sheets. Figures 4-5 and 4-6 illustrate a block diagram and a program using the FORTRAN language. The illustration demonstrates how decisions, program modification, and looping are built into a computer program.

Obviously, the programmer must be quite familiar with the system to be computerized as well as the computer and the available support from the computer manufacturer. The programmer must conform closely to relatively rigid programming and computer equipment specifications.

A keypunch machine, previously discussed, is then used to punch the program; the keypunch operator uses the programmer's program coding sheets as the source document. The deck of punched cards, punched by the keypunch operator, constitutes the source program.

Few computer programs are written in the actual machine language which the computer (CPU) uses. Most computer programs are written in somewhat more generalized languages (approaching normal English or algebraic statements) which then must be converted, automatically by the computer, to the computer's language. The conversion is accomplished by a *compiler* or *assembler* program provided by the computer manufacturer. The compiler or assembler is read into the CPU's memory, and then

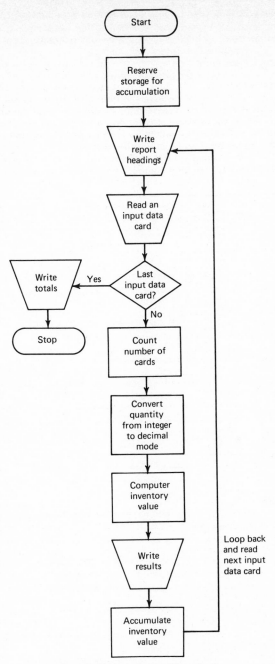

Fig. 4-5   A block diagram (flow chart).

the source program, which is to be processed by the compiler or assembler, is read, and the machine language is generated as output. The machine-language program is called the *object program*. A listing of both the source program and the object program can be made on the computer's printer.

The programmer tests the program against representative data to simulate, on the computer, how the new computer program would operate under real conditions. As a result of this, the program is "debugged" (errors are removed).

The person who will normally receive the output of the computer should review the test results. At that point the programmer should document the program. Documentation means a comprehensive and uniform record of the program. The documentation should be sufficiently complete for a systems analyst or another programmer, not familiar with the program, to be able fully to interpret it and if necessary modify it for required changes. At that point the program can be considered ready for routine operations in the computer center. Figure 4-6*b* shows a print-out of results from a

```
      CTHIS A SAMPLE FORTRAN PROGRAM NO 2
      CTHE APPLICATION IS COMPUTING THE VALUE OF INVENTORY
      CPROGRAM PREPARED BY E.TOMESKI AND L. CLARKE, JAN. 1970
0001        KOUNT=0
0002        TOTALV=0.0
      CSTMTS 1,2 RESERVE AREAS FOR ACCUMULATIONS
0003        WRITE(3,1)
0004      1 FORMAT(1H1,15X,'INVENTORY STATUS, XYZ CORP.,JAN. 1970')
0005        WRITE(3,2)
0006      2 FORMAT(1H0,1X,'INVENTORY   QUANTITY   PRICE      VALUE      DATE
            1DESCRIPTION')
0007      6 READ(1,3)INV,NQUAN,UPRICE,IDATE,D1,D2,D3
0008      3 FORMAT(I3,I2,F4.2,I6,3A4)
0009        IF(INV-999)4,99,4
0010      4 KOUNT=KOUNT+1
      CSTMT 10 WILL COUNT THE NUMBER OF INVENTORY ITEMS
0011        QUAN=NQUAN
      CSTMT 11 CONVERTS AN INTEGER TO A DECIMAL
0012        VALUE=QUAN*UPRICE
      CSTMT 12 COMPUTES THE VALUE OF EACH INVENTORY ITEM
0013        WRITE(3,5)INV,NQUAN,UPRICE,VALUE,IDATE,D1,D2,D3
0014      5 FORMAT(1H0,6X,I4,7X,I3,2X,F5.2,4X,F7.2,2X,I9,2X,3A4)
0015        TOTALV=TOTALV+VALUE
      CSTMT 15 ACCUMULATES THE TOTAL VALUE OF ALL INVENTORY ITEMS
0016        GO TO 6
0017     99 WRITE(3,7)TOTALV,KOUNT
0018      7 FORMAT(1H0,' TOTAL INVENTORY VALUE      ',F9.2,7X,'COUNT IS ',
            1I2)
      CSTMTS 17-18 WILL CAUSE THE TOTAL VALUE OF INVENTORY AND ITEM COUNT TO
      CBE PRINTED
0019        CALL EXIT
0020        END
```

(a)

```
                INVENTORY STATUS, XYZ CORP.,JAN. 1970

   INVENTORY   QUANTITY   PRICE      VALUE      DATE    DESCRIPTION

        1         20      5.00      100.00     13170   NYLON SHIRTS

        2         15      2.00       30.00     13170   SOCKS

       10          1      1.00        1.00     13170   RAYON TIES

       77         99      9.00      891.00     13170   SILK SHIRTS

      125          0      9.00        0.0      13170   SWEATERS

      370         33      7.00      231.00     13170   UMBRELLAS

      542         26      3.00       78.00     13170   SILK TIES A

      777         76      4.00      304.00     13170   SILK TIES B

      999         27      7.00      189.00     13170   GLOVES

   TOTAL INVENTORY VALUE            1824.00    COUNT IS  9
```

(b)

Fig. 4-6   (a) A computer program written in FORTRAN, one of the widely used generalized languages. The program corresponds to the block diagram in Figure 4-5. **(b) Computer output generated by the computer program.**

computer. Figure 4-7 summarizes the major steps in creating a computer program.

Software *Software* in the computer field means the collection of computer programs associated with the computer.

As previously mentioned, each computer has a set of operational functions engineered into its logical design. These operations are individually relatively simple. When used in combination, by the person programming the computer, the operation codes form a powerful set of instructions to process data and solve complex problems.

A computer program is a planned procedure for solving a problem or task through computerization. The computer program consists of a series of instructions to be performed on the data. Each computer instruction has two basic parts: (1) a statement (usually a verb such as READ, PUNCH, or CALCULATE) that specifies an operation to be performed, and (2) a statement (usually a noun) that identifies the location(s) of the data or thing which is to be referenced or manipulated (known as the *operand*). There may be more than one operand for an instruction depending on the computer involved. In sum, the format of a computer instruction is as follows:

Operation   Operand[2]
(OpCode)[2]
XX   XXXXX
(Tells computer   (Tells computer where to find data
what to do.)   to process, or device to use.)

As with a data word, the instruction word may be either fixed or variable in length— depending on the computer employed. Instructions, like data, are also stored in binary form in the computer's memory.

The computer is quite helpless until the instructions that the programmer has written are fed into the machine and the right computer buttons are pressed. While the programmer does not have to know all about the complicated electronic circuitry inside the computer, he or she must know the general organization of the machine, the kind of instruction statements that can be used in communicating with it, and how to write these statements sequentially to get the computer to perform as the programmer wishes.

An *application program* (used to process a particular job such as payroll, accounting, inventory, etc., or a phase of the job) may vary in size depending on the complexity of the job and capability of the programmer. A small program might consist of several dozen instructions, while a large program could contain hundreds of thousands of instructions.

Most computers are supplied with generalized programs by the computer manufacturers, or these are available from other computer service organizations. These generalized (or "packaged") programs are for wide use, and differ from the user's own application programs, which are developed for specialized use in a particular organization. The general programs facilitate certain routine and universal processing such as sorting and merging, or widely used computational routines related to such things as correlation analysis, multiple regression, linear programming, etc. Also, some organizations make available packaged (or generalized) application programs; however, not infrequently, the computer users must modify these programs if they wish to use them in their organizations. Few organizations wish to conform completely to someone else's systems.

Most computers are supplied with compiler and assembly programs. These programs, as indicated earlier, translate application programs written by the user (the programmer) into the actual machine language that the computer understands. Obviously, this simplifies the task of programming and delegates to the computer the tasks of converting to machine language and of allocating memory to the descriptive labels used for operands.

To give a grossly simple example, consider the symbolic instruction DISTANCE = RATE ∘ TIME. This instruction would be familiar to most readers if they knew that the symbol ∘ means "multiply" in Computer X's instruction set. Converted to machine language (or the digital equivalent), this single instruction might be several instructions (again depending on the computer used), as shown in Figure 4-8.

---

[2] The sizes of the operation code and operand(s) vary for different computers.

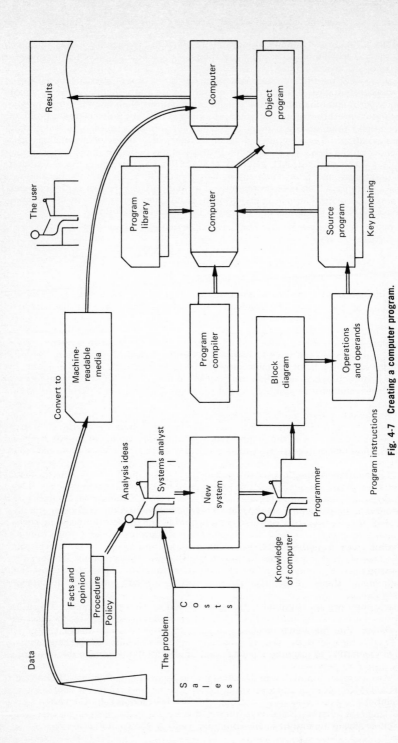

Fig. 4-7 Creating a computer program.

It should now be obvious why there is a trend toward using the higher-level programming languages, rather than the abstruse machine language; it simplifies the programming task. Assemblers are machine-oriented, i.e., different from computer to computer. Compilers are problem-oriented, i.e., more or less the same for different computers. Higher-level languages are said to be "problem-oriented" rather than "machine-oriented."

There is a plethora of programming languages. Generally, each computer manufacturer has created different programming languages and accompanying compilers and assemblers. This, when added to the extensive array of different computers and related equipment, compounds the complexity of the computer field and indicates why computer and programming standards have been difficult to achieve.

Programming languages are usually designated by acronyms. Among those in relatively wide use are FORTRAN (Formula Translator), ALGOL (Algorithmic Language), and COBOL (Common Business Oriented Language). COBOL has been strongly backed by the U.S. Government as a standard compiler for commercial-type computer applications, for its numerous computer installations. FORTRAN has at-

Operation	Operands Operand A	Operand B	Comments
10	0500	1222	10 means multiply. Rate is stored in 0500, and time is stored in 1222 of memory.
25	2001		The product will be developed in the arithmetic register. The content of the arithmetic register will be stored in location 2001 of memory; thus, 25 means store contents of arithmetic register. Location 2001 now contains the distance.

Fig. 4-8 A simple example of computer instructions.

tained very wide acceptance for more technical applications in such fields as statistics, research, and mathematics. Most computer manufacturers now supply COBOL and FORTRAN compilers with their computers. It has been said, however, that such high-level languages move the person further away from the computer and that a good programmer can write a more efficient (in the use of storage and speed) program using a machine-oriented computer language. There are thus arguments, as well as appropriate situations for use, for both higher-level programming languages and the machine-oriented languages.

Sophisticated Analytical Techniques Invariably, in addition to the already-mentioned techniques (problem definition, flow charting, forms design, block diagramming, programming, etc.), the systems analyst and programmer have other aids that permit them greater creative and problem-solving capability. Some of these techniques are associated with operations research (management-science) personnel, and in some cases industrial engineering staffs. But they also have a definite role in the field of systems design and analysis, as well as computer programming. Such techniques can range from well-known methods such as work measurement or statistical sampling to esoteric mathematical techniques such as simulation or linear programming. The more powerful of these techniques are frequently dependent on a computer to perform extensive iterations.

Mathematical techniques, combined with the great computational capability of the computer, provide powerful problem-solving capability in such areas as inventory, allocation, queuing, sequencing, routing, replacement, analyses of competition, search, scheduling, etc. It would be well, however, to caution that logical mathematical analysis cannot be accepted as the final answer to all the executive's problems. Successful use of the techniques requires a recognition that human behavior is difficult to quantify, good data must be available for manipulation, and the model must reflect a pragmatic situation. These mathematical techniques, as with the computer tools, are intended to be aids (not sources of final answers) for the executive. The more elaborate techniques usually require fairly large-scale computers since their memory and processing requirements are usually extensive and are beyond the capacities of small and medium-sized computers.

Operating Systems Many modern computers are operated under the overall control of a set of programs known as an *operating system* (monitor system, etc.). The operating system is usually provided with the computer by the manufacturer, and is intended to facilitate efficient and automatic processing of the computer and its input and output devices.

The operating system is quite complex and has increased the programming challenge to the programmer in interfacing with the computer.

SCOPE OF COMPUTER TECHNOLOGY

The entire computer field—equipment, software, applications—continues to undergo significant change. Concurrently there are changes, induced partially by computer technology, in traditional organizational and administrative concepts. Figure 4-9 traces some highlights of the evolution of computers.

Accomplishments	Pre-computer	Early computers	Common computers	Trend in computers
Correlation and consolidation of accounting and information by computer. Management has real-time, ready access to vital information for planning, decision-making, and control. All parts of the company are linked together to approach optimization. External information, as well as internal information, is available.				Compatible; mass storage; data transmission; operating systems; monolithic integrated circuitry; wide range of input and output devices
Forecasting, simulation, and management-by-exception reports prepared by computer. Large storage devices permit company files to be readily accessible for inquiry, retrieving, or manipulation. Integration of related applications.			Magnetic tape and disk; magnetic core; transistorized; higher-level languages	
Absorption of more clerical and computational tasks by the computer. Preparation of more complex reports by the computer.		Magnetic tape and punched card; vacuum tube; limited internal memory; symbolic programming		
Mechanization of routine and repetitive clerical tasks. Mechanization of many accounting-type jobs. Procedurization.	Mechanical punched card equipment; considerable manual handling			

Fig. 4-9 Evolution of computers.

SELECTiVE BIBLIOGRAPHY

Davis, Gordon B., *An Introduction to Electronic Computers*, McGraw-Hill, New York, 1966.

Heyel, Carl, *Computers, Office Machines, and the New Information Technology*, Macmillan, New York, 1969.

Tomeski, Edward A., *The Executive Use of Computers*, Colliers, New York, 1969.

——, *The Computer Revolution*, Macmillan, New York, 1970.

——, and Harold Lazarus, *People-Oriented Computer Systems*, Van Nostrand Reinhold, New York, 1975.

Acknowledgment: This Chapter and the more extensive treatment in the *Handbook of Modern Office Management and Administrative Services*, cited earlier, are derived partially from *The Executive Use of Computers*, listed above.

Section 2

The Underlying Technology

Part One

The Subcomputer Spectrum

Introduction

JOSEPH FERREIRA *Vice President, The Diebold Group, New York, New York*

Whenever "ADP" is mentioned today, the assumption usually is that the discussion concerns computer systems. However, computer systems cannot be looked upon in isolation. They must be seen in perspective as part of a complex and intertwined technology. Computer systems not only depend upon and tie into a host of equipment and subsystems and devices directly linked to their own installation, but also must compete with a broad array of mechanization, automation, and service configurations open to users, whatever their scale of operations may be.

In fact, today's office automation is not something that began in the midfifties when the computer first loomed upon the business horizon. It is part of an evolutionary process that has been going on for the past hundred years and more, paralleling mechanization in the factory. Thus the first practical typewriter appeared in 1867, and as long ago as 1963 the Dictaphone Corporation celebrated the 75th anniversary of the first commercial dictating machine. In 1884 the mimeograph machine was introduced, which for the first time enabled businesses to reproduce copies of paperwork rapidly and inexpensively. The addressograph principle of repetitive imprinting was developed in the 1890s, and the first model of a multigraph machine for form letters was built in 1902.

Presaging the age of high-speed punched-card equipment, Dr. Herman Hollerith adapted punched cards for sorting and tabulating in 1887, but the idea itself had been used to control the patterns of weaving textiles as early as 1801.

Thus today's most advanced computer systems are directly tied in or associated with a broad spectrum of peripheral and supporting office machines and appliances pioneered in the last century—and it is worth noting that of the prominent suppliers of complete electronic computer systems for business applications, four were long-established manufacturers of office typing, calculating, and tabulating equipment. And the general office equipment itself has profited from computer-stimulated technology, as witness the extent to which typewriters, calculating machines, and accounting machines have "gone electronic." Today small solid state hand calculators are being promoted commercially as "miniature computers," and the top-line electronic accounting machines are in fact small computers, with now only an indistinct line between what is to be classified as a computer, and what as a piece of sophisticated accounting equipment.

All of which means that a designer of a computer system must be fully cognizant of the "subcomputer spectrum" in order to achieve the best possible design of an overall system. The designer has to give as much thought to "word processing" and related activities that provide input to the computer, and to the multiplication and efficient dissemination of computer output, as to the computer-room operation itself.

Similarly, the administrative service manager or other functionary concerned with the selection of desk-top and related office machines of all types must be sure that the equipment whose purchase he or she authorizes not only will be suited to today's operations, but will be compatible with computer systems, even though for his or her company the latter may still be in the offing.

Chapter 1

Office Mechanization: Overview

WALTER A. KLEINSCHROD

Editor, Administrative Management, New York, New York

Office mechanization goes beyond the simple substitution of motors and linkages for operations that previously were handled manually. The mechanized office today embraces whole categories of equipment that have "gone electronic" to the point of behaving almost like computers. Indeed, they have the capability of fitting in with true computers either through an on-line connection, or by means of the specialized output the particular machine prepares. At the computer, that output becomes input as soon as anyone feeds it into the system.

True enough, office mechanization also includes its share of marvels that—to use a kitchen comparison—are in the "electric can opener" class. Electric paper-shredding wastebaskets, electric pencil sharpeners, even electric erasers are commonplace today. And in some cases, having survived the cost-justification wringer, their value would be hard to assail. After all, it was not too many years ago that the electric typewriter was treated as a luxury reserved for only the glossiest of secretaries; today the sight of a typing specialist plugging along at a nonpowered keyboard is by far the exception, not the rule.

What concerns us here, however, are not the stand-alone machines that whir away at some individual task, but the "subcomputer spectrum" of machines which, wholly or partly, operate in conjunction with computers themselves (Figure 1-1). They include such classes of equipment as bookkeeping-accounting machines, addressing machines, text-editing typewriters, keypunch units, and (while not strictly *office* machines, fully relevant just the same) point-of-sale equipment. Later in the Chapter, by way of rounding out the picture, several other important types of office equipment—calculators, copiers, dictating machines, and mechanized files—are discussed, even though they operate without direct hookup or output to a central computer.

MACHINES THAT TEAM UP WITH COMPUTERS

Accounting and Bookkeeping Systems One might think that machines specifically designed for functions as basic as accounting and bookkeeping would carve out a big share of the office equipment market. This used to be the case, but recently the advance of other equipment with greater general-purpose capabilities, such as the calculator and minicomputer, has curbed the importance of accounting and bookkeeping machines as such. Moreover, the distinction among these product categories is becoming increasingly vague.

Except for some nuances of internal logic, or some accessories around the keyboard, it is almost as hard to tell whether one is dealing with a high-end accounting system or a small-business minicomputer, as it is to distinguish the "mini" from a powerful programmable calculator. The differences have as much to do with semantics and marketing strategy as with any intrinsic differences in the equipment itself. Thus the manufacturer of a widely known line of programmable calculators states that his product is well within the minicomputer class, but the term "computer" has a way of

Fig. 1-1 Office machine or computer terminal? This input-output display device is actually both, a common occurrence today. (ITT)

scaring off potential customers. So he markets "calculators" and puts his customers at ease.

In truth, what the business shopper faces in the area of small-scale accounting and bookkeeping systems is an array of electronic equipment flowing imperceptibly from one price and performance level to the next—a continuum that, semantically at least, may eventually blur out those "separate" items that today still answer to the names of accounting and bookkeeping systems.

And, as is made evident in the next Chapter and through much of Part 2, the distinctions are not any clearer on the large-scale end of the spectrum either. It is more by arbitrary definition than anything else that minicomputers are separated from the "midis," and these from the "maxis." To say that a midi must have at least a 32K main memory may be one way of helping sort out the systems, but there is nothing "natural" about that figure, nor is there universal agreement that it is the best place to establish a cutoff.

Any fine-tuning within the accounting and bookkeeping zone is subject to similar quibbling. Even so, it is safe to divide the field into three general subcategories consisting of (1) posting/bookkeeping machines, (2) bookkeeping/billing machines, and (3) electronic machines ranging from minilike stand-alone systems to systems that can operate locally while also communicating remotely to a larger computer.

Posting/Bookkeeping Machines. These machines operate mechanically (that is, nonelectronically) for the most part. Used mainly for accounts payable and receivable— 90 per cent of all accounting and bookkeeping work—they are well suited to small businesses. Because of their speed and efficiency, they offer decided advantages to firms which still post by hand.

The machines improve the legibility of documents and speed collections. Statements which otherwise might be mailed between the fifth and fifteenth of the month are ready for mailing by the first. Because the machines do not require highly trained workers, they fit in well where staff is limited. A 10-key posting/bookkeeping machine is often no more complicated than a 10-key adding machine. At the end of the day it can tell the user how much money is coming in, how much is on the books, and how much is owed to suppliers. And the user is not likely to carry errors unwittingly, since the machine may be equipped with such proofing features as down-total and crossfooter registers. The latter add horizontally across a form as a check against sums arrived at vertically, or down each of the several columns. For all that, there is a limit to the kinds of tasks a posting/bookkeeper can perform. If needs also include payroll, general ledger, and statistical information, the next category should be considered.

Bookkeeping/Billing Machines. These, like their simpler cousins the posting/bookkeeping machine, operate mechanically for the most part. However, they have the ability truly to calculate, whereas with posting machines multiplication and division are achieved by repetitive addition or subtraction. Of course, the user pays more for these additional capabilities. Bookkeeping/billers are priced[1] in the low five figures, though some models are under $10,000. Posting/bookkeepers invariably carry four-figure price tags. Recently a number of electronic bookkeeping/billing machines have made their appearance. One versatile model dates, numbers, converts, spaces, totals, discounts, and computes taxes – all automatically. Another unit, suggested for systems producing a minimum of 50 invoices per day, employs a typewriter-printer dealing only in capital letters. It can process invoices at the rate of 80 characters per second.

Electronic Systems. The main things separating these machines from the electronic bookkeeping/billers just mentioned are the greater degrees of power and sophistication they possess. They are programmable, often with ready-made software packages for specific industries, banking, insurance, etc. They are expandable, accommodating various peripherals. Some can communicate in "real time" with central systems.

While unmistakably computerlike in operation, the electronic accounting systems look like nothing more formidable than a desk with keyboard and perhaps adjacent file-sized units – the memory and printer. Prices range widely from the low four figures into the low five. The NCR 399 unit shown in Figure 1-2, with its communications capabilities, serves as an "intelligent terminal" that can provide editing, formatting, validating, and batching of input data for transmission to another NCR 399, an NCR Century, or other computer, or to a data center. It can also format data received from a central computer, prepare reports, and handle on-site processing.

Beginning with the Burroughs F4200 Sensitronic, manufacturers have in recent years provided for storing data on magnetic stripes on the visible-record ledger cards, thus converting the ledger file into random-access memory. When the operator keys in a new entry, the machine will automatically update the balance from the last entry stored on the stripe. Magnetic stripes can store account balances, account numbers, marital-status codes, credit rating, control account designations, and other accounting and statistical data.

Addressing Machines The image of the mail room as a knockabout place under the hot-water pipes – forlorn equipment, forlorn people, piles of gray canvas bags – is as obsolete today as a 2-cent stamp on a first-class letter. In a growing number of modern offices, the mail room has become a colorful airy place, located centrally in the organization the way a communications hub ought to be. Its personnel are regarded as people with key skills and responsibilities; they themselves sense the importance of who they are and what they do. And the addressing equipment they operate possesses computerlike abilities to sort, select, and merge. The plates it imprints with may be readable as computer input.

While envelopes can be addressed by any number of machines from standard typewriters to card imprinters of the kind used by department stores for charge sales, two prevalent types of equipment are the addresser-printer and the labeler. The latter, as the name implies, prepares labels in sheets or strips by means of such common "repro" methods as xerography and spirit or stencil duplication; some also affix com-

[1] All prices mentioned in this chapter are as of 1974.

puter print-out labels. Addresser-printers on the other hand imprint directly onto envelopes from metal, foil, plastic, or mimeo address plates.

Labelers. Typical machines in this category include a spirit process unit capable of transferring 20,000 images per hour on labels from $2\frac{1}{4}$ to $4\frac{1}{2}$ inches wide; an electro-static unit producing 135,000 addresses per hour, or 38 five-line labels every second; an applicator which affixes up to 13,000 data processing print-out labels per hour onto envelopes and catalogues, and another machine which does the same thing with pressure-sensitive labels at the rate of 8,000 per hour.

Addresser-Printers. Key to mailing systems of greater computer involvement, these fast machines print addresses directly onto envelopes, brochures, or other mailing materials. While high-powered units capable of addressing hundreds of pieces in minutes are of most interest here, models range down to the simplest hand models (one envelope, one swipe of the printing arm at a time). Nevertheless, all models work from

Fig. 1-2 Electronic accounting machine or minicomputer? Again, the answer is both, the distinction being mainly semantic. (NCR)

data carriers—plates of credit-card size or slightly larger, capable of holding a surprising amount of information within their compact formats. A typical metal plate might hold 460 characters piled 10 lines high.

Mimeo plates are the least expensive, but have no value for direct reading as computer input. Plastic data carriers, the most expensive at around 5 cents each, can be embossed with a special OCR (optical character recognition) typeface for direct reading into the data processing system by means of a scanner. Somewhere in between, as far as price is concerned, are the metal and foil carriers. The former are lightweight and sturdy, making sharp impressions through several carbons. Their tabs allow individual plates to be selected, counted, or skipped during a print run. Foil plates, less expensive than the metal ones, are ideal for small lists or where information changes frequently. They can be quickly embossed on almost any electric typewriter. Two basic foil systems are available. With one, foil is separated from a perforated strip, inserted into a durable metal carrier, then tabbed or programmed for automatic selection. With the other, foil is supplied permanently mounted on $3\frac{1}{4}$- by $7\frac{5}{16}$-inch cards which hold up to 500 characters.

Text-Editing Typewriters and "Word Processing" Though the computer and the typewriter have coexisted for many years as a team of office workhorses, until recently they have had very little to do with one another. All that is changing, not only because some typewriter systems have also "gone electronic," but more importantly because this new technology is opening up a new profession for managing the secretarial environment as a high-production, cost-calibrated center for typewritten output. Paralleling data processing in more ways than one, this major development is known as *word processing*.

Heart of the modern word processing system is the mechanical text-editing typewriter, a machine capable of fast error correction as keystrokes are captured on magnetic media. The machine is also capable of extremely rapid playback of the errorless text. Present in most word processing systems, too, are centralized dictation systems — discussed more fully further on.

Although the majority of text-editing typewriters "stand alone," the state of the art is rapidly involving the memory and manipulative powers of the computer more fully and more imaginatively for large-scale word processing purposes. Using time-shared systems, or "dedicated" systems devoted solely to text processing applications in-house, word processing specialists are able to call paragraphs, pages, or entire reports from memory in a variety of formats. Very often the technologies of word and data processing are joined when a manager discovers that a computer brought into the company for other purposes has some memory space available — and some extraordinary capabilities not yet put to use — and the manager applies them by means of a productive tie-in to typewriter terminals capable of such communication.

Whether orchestrated in a system of this magnitude, or self-contained in a single unit with all the electronic gear tucked into one corner of the desk beneath the typewriter, word processing has the potential for such vast systems and social change within the office that an overview of these aspects is as important as the hardware itself.

For management, word processing can mean faster throughput rates, reduced costs, and an overall improvement in organization effectiveness. It can also mean some organizational upheaval.

For the typist, it means the "worry" is gone — that fear of making an error at the last minute and having to do the job over. Thanks to the electronic logic of editing typewriters, the typist can now type a fast draft and retype only the parts in need of change. Once recorded satisfactorily on magnetic tape, card, or disk, the whole text can be played back for one rapid final print-out, or for as many subsequent documents as necessary. Variables such as addresses may be typed manually, though in some systems this operation can be automated too.

The secretary who ostensibly types 60 words per minute on the normal office electric typewriter actually produces about 3 or 4 per minute when all the error whiteouts and page-length remakes are figured in. As a typing specialist with automated equipment and good supervision, he or she could achieve 15 to 30 words per minute, again taking into account all the practicalities of setup, referencing, and button pushing.

Of even greater significance to the typist can be the career paths that word processing is opening up. For workers restive in the dead-end "gal Friday" role, the prospect of rising to the position of word processing supervisor or manager offers encouragement and dignity, to say nothing of potentially higher salaries.

What word processing, in its full meaning, does is to make possible a *systematized approach* to secretarial work. The assortment of tasks which the traditional secretary has handled on a largely random basis — some typing, some filing, some "go-ferring" — are assigned now along definite work-flow lines to one of two new specialists: *Typing or Correspondence Specialists*, working with editing typewriters in a company's word processing center, transcribe dictation phoned to, or delivered to, the center. *Administrative Specialists*, outside the center, serving a number of executives or professionals in a work group, handle the files, phone calls, and other nontyping duties.

In general, all editing typewriters operate in a number of modes such as *record* and *play back;* they encode and automatically perform various positioning actions such as *margin return* and *tab;* at a button's push they move the recording medium forward to a desired point for a copy change, in increments of a *word, line,* or *sentence,* and often *paragraph*. Right-hand-margin control is another common feature; it can be set to prevent a too-ragged right margin by means of a "hot zone" control which stops the machine when it reaches a predetermined number of spaces from the desired end of a line. The "hot zone" can vary from 10 spaces down to zero. The operator can then manually complete the line, hyphenating if necessary. In large computerized systems, hyphenation can be accomplished automatically with a fair degree of accuracy.

In the hierarchy of automatic typewriters, the ones designed for repetitive letters are on the first rung of the ladder. Often called "automatic" typewriters, they do not afford the ease of change possible on, say, a magnetic-media editing typewriter—the next step up in sophistication. Machines here use the same principle for correcting simple errors as the tape recorder. The user backs up the medium and then records (types) new material over the old. Continuing up the ladder, the multiple-work-station, dedicated-computer type of system is next. Time-shared text processors represent another increment of sophistication. Occupying the top rung are video, or CRT (cathode-ray tube), editing machines. The operator can see and adjust the text on a screen before commanding the system to go ahead and produce it.

Some word processing professionals foresee an "ultimate" system involving no type-writers at all, though there will still be keyboards. The operator will key text noise-lessly onto a screen through a CRT device. He or she will edit, reformat, enlarge, or reduce the projected image. When all is to the operator's liking, he or she will press a button and in seconds have an electrostatic hard copy produced by a companion unit.

Compared to data processing, word processing is still in its infancy, but it is maturing rapidly.

Keypunches and Other Data Entry Devices   These units are described in detail in the first three Chapters of Part 3 of this Section. A somewhat special group of entry devices, the point-of-sale devices, are overviewed later in this Chapter.

Card Punching. This mechanical means of encoding tab cards is the oldest and still most widely used means of preparing data for computer entry. It is losing ground, however, to other more direct input methods using key-to-tape, key-to-cassette, and key-to-disk equipment; optical scanners; and, again, point-of-sale and other at-the-source terminals.

Not new but typical of high-end card processing equipment is a line available in punch/verify, punch/print, or punch/print/verify models. The machines can store six programs in their buffers, making changes in card format as simple as turning a dial. Buffered units represent the aristocracy of card-punch, or keypunch, equipment; not all models have buffers.

A popular attribute of many keypunches is portability. One simple "carry-around" unit electromechanically punches Hollerith-code holes into plastic as well as paper cards of varying size. Another portable unit, electronic, prints what is punched so that the operator can see what he or she keys and maintain high accuracy.

Key-to-Tape. These magnetic-tape units have in recent years garnered the lion's share of user interest. More sophisticated and versatile than the keypunch, usually more cost-effective than the higher-end magnetic entry devices, this category of equipment has many advantages and relatively few disadvantages. Briefly, key-to-tape devices access two kinds of tape: either computer magnetic tape, for direct use by tape drives feeding the central processor; or cassettes, processed by *key-to-cassette* devices which tend to be smaller, portable, and less costly. Whether to use tape-drive or cassette input depends on individual circumstances—both techniques can be worth-while.

Key-to-Disk Devices. Not as popular as key-to-tape units but with enormous po-tential for future data processing systems—that is a fair way of summarizing the current state of this category. Called *key-to-disk equipment* or *shared processing equipment*, multiple keystations input data to a central disk storage. The systems are complex but fast, providing good cost-performance ratios where data volumes are high. They are expensive, but advancements have made the price worthwhile for many companies staggering under massive input loads. Key-to-disk units can, for example, date, file, manipulate, and edit data off-line. A general rule of thumb for the high-volume user is that if real-time needs are not essential, key-to-disk may be the way to go; otherwise key-to-tape should be considered.

Optical Scanning.[2]   Seemingly a highly practical method of input because it "elimi-

---

[2] See Part 3, Chapter 2, "Optical Scanning, OCR, and MICR," in this Section.

nates the keypuncher," optical scanning has never quite fulfilled the boom its proponents predicted for it. The golden age of optical character recognition (OCR) seems always to be in some elusive "next year."

The beauty of scanners is that they read data directly from source documents into the computer. The problems, often enough, are the strict tolerances of forms design, and the shape and legibility of the alphanumerics which must be met for the system to work effectively. Cost is no minor matter either, though it has been said that a business with as few as 15 keypunches and 5 verifiers could justify OCR. For all that, more and more companies *are* dipping their toes into OCR waters—and making the plunge. Banks, for example, are using centralized OCR units to scan forms sent in daily from branches. In one, a job that formerly took 2 days now is done in 3 hours. The cost is one-tenth of keypunch, and the gross reject rate is 2 ten-thousandths of 1 per cent.

Fig. 1-3   Point-of-sale cash register is also a computer terminal. (Singer)

Point-of-Sale Terminals Call them "super cash registers" (they stand on store counters and they do hold cash). But call them also entry devices for they do access computers, inputting data on sales volumes, totally or by merchandise category, and outputting inventory levels or information on the customer's credit standing. The keyboards on most point-of-sale (POS) units look very different from those on traditional cash registers (Figure 1-3). Gone are the banks of buttons, replaced by a 10-key pad, function keys, and lights which guide the operator "teaching-machine fashion" through each sequential step to prevent keying errors.

In addition to handling a surprising number of administrative tasks, POS terminals are credited with saving substantial amounts which normally are written off as "cash register shortages." According to Peat, Marwick, Mitchell & Co., POS terminals reduce such shortages by $45,000 per each $100 million of sales, while saving an additional $10,000 a year by *not* making arithmetic errors in itemization and tax calculation.[3]

OTHER IMPORTANT OFFICE MACHINES

To discuss adequately, category by category, the many types of office machines available would require not a chapter but a book the size of this volume. A recent directory of products sold by office equipment dealers listed more than 130 kinds of machines. And that is only the "dealer segment" of the industry—which does not include all machines which *cannot* tie in directly with computers, let alone those that can. Here,

[3] See Section 7, Chapter 2, "ADP in Retailing: Point-of-Sale Automation."

selectively, among the "cannots," are overviews of those major machine categories which space allows:

Calculators The price of calculators has dropped in recent years, mainly because of breakthroughs in mass producing the electronic logic chips which most of these machines use. The consequent oversupply has flooded every stationer, electronics outlet, and discount house with big and little calculators to the point that they have become home, as well as office, items. Even so, for office use, price may not be the prime factor in calculator choice. Commercial-grade models are priced upward from about $400 or $500, but for that the user should get distinctly better quality, good local servicing, operator training, trial installation, and some analysis of systems requirements. Going lower, the user might end up without, say, 12-column display or print, direct-access memory, and decimal punctuation.

Although the trend in recent years has been to smaller equipment, down to the cigarette-pack-sized "hand-holdables," larger models are generally preferred for office use because of easier keyboard operation, better readability of display, and lesser chance of theft. Hand-holdables, of course, have won some acceptance in low-volume commercial applications. They run on batteries—sometimes rechargeable—whose life varies, and usually also on alternating current.

Important functional considerations to weigh when choosing a calculator include the number of registers and memories it has. The terms are often confused. A *working register* is the place where a number is held in transit. If you ask a calculator to solve the problem $2 \times 3 =$, it must have some means of holding the 2 and 3 while waiting for you to key in the = command. The average machine has two working registers, usually referred to as registers x and y. Some have three.

In a general way, working registers are an indication of the calculator's power, but *storage registers* and *addressable memories* are even more meaningful. Storage registers hold a number for continued use. If you want to multiply 10 different numbers by 3 (the 3 then being a constant), you can enter 3 into the storage register for this purpose. However you then must recall it through the keyboard for each of the multiplications. Memory, on the other hand, is a live accumulating feature. You can address a memory automatically and perform a series of additions or subtractions on it without recalling it each time. You can, for example, multiply 2×4, put the resulting 8 in memory, and subtract the number 3, and then another 3, from the 8 which you have stored. Other calculator features to consider include:

Type of Display. In some models, numerals "light up," illuminated by Nixie tubes, light-emitting diodes (LEDs), liquid crystal displays (LCDs), or similar means. Other models print their output, electronically or mechanically.

Number of Calculating Digits. They range from as few as 8 to 30 and more.

Number of Display Digits. Likewise.

Decimals. Floating or fixed?

Other Options. Overflow, underflow, true credit balance, constants, chain calculation, mixed calculation, programmability, rechargeable power source—to name a few.

Copiers, Duplicators, and Copier Duplicators There is no hard and fast rule, but if you make only a few reproductions of an original—less than 15, say—that is copying. If you make more, you are duplicating. Copiers and duplicators are designed to achieve these short or long runs cost-effectively. The hybrid copier/duplicators are price-scaled to permit any length of run with reasonable economy.

Duplicating tends to be a centralized function; one bank of machines handles all the work of this nature for the organization. Copying may be centralized or decentralized. The heavier-duty console-sized copiers and copier/duplicators generally operate in centralized "repro" areas, though it is possible that a company may place a few closer to high-use departments. Table-model copiers are more apt to be decentralized as "convenience" machines.

The particular physical or chemical process by which the machine operates is not as much of a factor as it used to be. Among copiers, the vast majority today are electrostatic. Among duplicators, offset has the strongest appeal, although mimeograph stencils and spirit masters will still give a good run for the money. Similarly, on the copier side, the magnetic, thermographic, and a few hybrid processes produce serviceable to excellent results, and capture a significant share of the market.

Even so, the big question asked of copiers is not what kind of process, but what kind of paper. Even the huge electrostatic segment goes two ways on this, because one version of this technology (known also as xerography) operates on *plain paper*, while the other version (Electrofax) uses *coated paper*. The convenience, the appeal, and the trend are all in favor of plain paper. The competition to develop good plain-paper machines is so furious that most authorities agree that *every* major copier manufacturer must soon have one in its line or lose considerable market standing and prestige. At this writing, only one nonelectrostatic plain-paper copier is on the market—a magnetic process machine. Even that process, however, is split; there are also coated-paper magnetic machines.

Spirit. Of the three main duplicating processes, spirit is generally considered the simplest, fastest way to produce runs up to 500 copies. Quality of reproduction, however, is usually well below that of the other two processes. But spirit has many important office uses, including forms production and internal memoranda. Spirit duplicators cannot reproduce photos, but can produce multicolored copies with one run through the machine. Such work is prepared by typing or drawing on the same master with differently colored carbons.

Stencil. This process, or *mimeograph* as it is often called, uses the familiar fibrous-tissue stencils which hold back ink except where cut by a typewriter key or stylus. Stencil machines can reproduce photos with fair fidelity. Runs of between 1,000 and 3,000 are common; special stencils can extend the total to around 5,000.

Offset Duplicators. Though often used for short runs, these machines are designed to accommodate volume work of high quality. They are an in-office adaptation of the offset lithography presses used by large commercial printers. Three types of masters are available: *paper*, for runs up to 2,000 copies; *plastic*, for runs to 5,000; and *metal*, to 25,000. Skilled operators can often manage to extend runs beyond the stated figures.

Many an offset master can be prepared on a copier. Some copiers can also make transparencies for projection. Other features to check out in selecting a copier include the cost of purchase, meter plans (if available), or leasing (if available); paper feed (flatbed or rotary); collator and automatic document feed attachments; reduction capabilities; maximum size of originals; speed; and the range of optimum use in terms of copy volume per month.

Dictation Equipment With their many models and features, dictating machines and the systems to which they connect can seem bewildering, but as with other office equipment, it is a matter of knowing one's needs and purchasing accordingly.

Dictating equipment falls into three broad categories, with each then subdivided:

1. Discrete media machines, both portable and desk-top.
2. Discrete media central recorder systems connected by private wire or PBX.
3. Endless loop systems, either individual or centralized.

Discrete Media Machines. These use a specific recording medium, one that can be stored, moved, mailed, or switched from dictation machine to transcription machine. Typical media include belts, cassettes, disks, and cartridges. As noted, discrete media machines come in portable, desk, and central recorder models.

Portables currently account for one-third to one-half of all dictating machine purchases. With productivity a watchword in business today—a $20,000 executive need save only 6 seconds a day to justify a $300 expenditure—executives are now carrying "electronic notebooks" which can be used almost anywhere under almost any conditions. They fill a long-standing need for a means of out-of-office dictation.

Desk-top models—the original design when dictating machines were introduced over a hundred years ago—typically incorporate such features as review, dictate, and start/stop capabilities; a conference capability to record multiple-person meetings for transcription; "quick erase" for error correction; indexing or digital counters to inform the transcriptionist of letter length or to give special instructions; automatic voice-level control; speed control to vary the rate for transcription; a telephone recording capability, and remote control microphones.

Central Recorders. These are expanded discrete media dictating systems. They play a major role in word processing systems (along with text-editing typewriters). Central systems are by no means the only way dictation can be accomplished in a word processing system, but because of their flexibility and centrality, they loom large. Instead of dictating into a portable or desk-top machine, the "word originator" (formerly called a "dictator," but that term is frowned upon now) picks up a phone and dictates to a recorder at some central location. The connection may be by way of a Bell System PBX or a non-Bell private wire system.

Private systems employ handsets with "push to talk" capabilities similar to those on desk and portable units. When a word originator pushes the record button, the centrally located medium starts recording. When he or she releases the button, the medium stops. Handsets are linked to the recorder in one of three ways: (1) *Non-selector stations* connect only one recorder. If it is busy, the word originator must wait until it is free before dictating. (2) *Manual selector stations* reach several recorders—the word originator selects the recorder which is free. (3) *Automatic selector stations* also link up with several recorders, but when the phone is lifted, the system automatically chooses the first one free. If all are busy—which should happen rarely unless too few recorders were purchased to meet existing needs—the word originator must wait until one of them is free.

Fig. 1-4   Supervisor in a word processing center monitors unit recording dictation phoned in from word originators throughout the firm.   (Lanier)

Except for the fact that they work through Bell System equipment, PBX central recorders are pretty much the same as private wire systems. The telephone company provides the following two types of interface between its gear and the central recording equipment:

1. *Trunk links* allow telephone equipment to interpret rotary signals from a dial phone, or Touch-Tone signals from a push-button phone, as instructions to the central system. Typical instructions: record, playback, back up, end of letter, correction, call the operator—all accomplished by entering one or another number according to instructions.

2. *Recorder couplers* perform all the functions of the trunk links except they cannot interpret tone or rotary signals as machine commands.

Endless Loop Systems. True to their name, these machines employ multihour loops of magnetic tape permanently fixed within a cabinet. The tape runs round and round across two tape heads placed a few seconds' distance apart. The first head records, spilling tape into a deep storage channel until the transcriptionist activates the second head, which draws the recorded tape from the channel and "reads" it through for eventual reuse by the same or a different word originator. (Figure 1-4.)

Endless systems do not need as much operator attention as do the discrete media types. Since the tape runs constantly, the machine is always properly loaded. The drawback comes in fast response to an urgent need to have some particular dictation transcribed. Its location must be searched out along the tape. Meanwhile the other messages on the tape, normally processed on a first-in, first-out basis, get shunted aside. With discrete systems, because of the very fact they are discrete, media containing rush work can be quickly picked out and assigned to a transcriptionist.

Mechanized Files While not a machine in the sense of a typewriter or copier, the mechanized file plays such an important role in records management that it must be mentioned in any discussion of the modern mechanized office.[4] Although vast numbers of administrative records are housed today in the invisible memory banks of computers, the need for "hard" documents is still very much with us. One should also not overlook the fact that microfiche, tab cards, and even cassettes, while of a far different order than original records, are eminently filable and retrievable, and mechanization can help speed these jobs just as it can for paper.

FURTHER OFFICE MACHINE INFORMATION

The reader is referred to the monthly magazine *Administrative Management* for further information on the office machines mentioned here, as well as information on many others. Subjects covered in this magazine fall in the general categories of information and records management, data processing, word processing, telecommunications, office environment, human resources, systems improvement, and the broad realm of "administrative overview." Other publications in the field are *Word Processing World* and *Office Procedures*. Publications such as these periodically present "factor-comparison" analyses of specific classes of machines, such as calculators, copiers, dictating equipment, and the like, giving machine specifications, price information, and application information.

SELECTIVE BIBLIOGRAPHY

Administrative Management, "EDP Input: The Six Choices," April, 1971.

Clark, Jesse, *Records Management by Clark*, Paperwork Systems, Newton, Mass., 1971.

Dickinson, A. Litchard, *The Right Way to File*, Geyer-McAllister, New York, 1971.

Hanson, Richard E., "Copiers '75: The Push Is On for Cost Control," *Administrative Management*, December, 1974.

Heyel, Carl, *Handbook of Modern Office Management and Administrative Services*, McGraw-Hill, New York, 1972.

Kleinschrod, Walter A., *The Dartnell Guide to Word Processing*, Dartnell, Chicago, 1975.

———, "Take a Postmaster to Lunch," *Administrative Management*, September, 1972.

Meisner, Dwayne, "The Ins and Outs of the Company Mail," *Administrative Management*, October, 1974.

Minicucci, Rick, "Automated Typing Systems," *Administrative Management*, May, 1974.

———, "Text Editors: Speed, Specialization," *Administrative Management*, November, 1974.

Word Processing Report newsletter (semimonthly), Geyer-McAllister, New York.

Word Processing World, "Dictation Equipment Going the Systems Route," March–April, 1975.

Zaffarano, Joan, "Tools of the Office: Accounting Systems," *Administrative Management*, March, 1973.

[4]See Chapter 2, "Information Storage and Retrieval (Noncomputer)," in this Part.

Chapter 2

Information Storage and Retrieval (Noncomputer)

DEAN E. McWILLIAMS

Products Manager — Automated Systems, Sperry Remington (Remington Rand Systems Div.), Blue Bell, Pennsylvania

The maintenance of records and documents has traditionally been considered a necessity, but nevertheless a matter of secondary importance. Until relatively recently, it was looked upon as drudgery which could be assigned to the lesser of the clerical staff, and it received little if any attention for improvement of storage and service. However, it is now generally realized that efficient storage and retrieval of information contained in transaction documents and reference documents are vital to any business, governmental, academic, and professional organization. Quite aside from the growing burden of paperwork in everyday business transactions, the ability to chart an organization's current position and desired direction is predicated on adequate documentation having been maintained for review and guidance. The ability to retrieve a particular record (or a copy or summary of its contents) for the user when required, quickly and efficiently, is today a prime criterion of good management. In far-flung organizations, and in organizations where the reference rate of specific classes of documents is high, with many people demanding the same information, problems of retrieval and delivery are compounded by the need to restore the documents promptly to their home locations, with minimum delay due to out-of-file conditions.

In all the foregoing, of course, the process of storage and retrieval, though highly important in terms of speed of access and return, is only one facet of records *control* that must be supported by proper systems and procedures as well as by the selection of the proper modes of storage.

With the continued growth of a business, and accentuated by increasing demands for records of all sorts by regulatory and taxing agencies and for fringe benefits and other personnel requirements, the sheer cubic volume of records to be maintained soon reaches cumbersome proportions, and storage in existing areas of office activity becomes increasingly difficult. In addition to the pre-empting of space disproportionate to that required by other administrative functions, the logistical problem is complicated by inefficiencies in accessibility, the need for growing numbers of support file personnel, untimely and inefficient retrieval, delivery, and restoring of records, and rising maintenance costs.

This Chapter addresses itself to advanced methods of filing and retrieval.[1] It assumes the necessary prior records analysis and establishment of procedures, to which we only allude here: Involved are the determination of the ratio of records volume to frequency of reference in established time frames, and consideration, for various alternatives of equipment and procedures, of the number of support personnel required to retrieve the document, complete the work function directly associated with the file operation, and delivery to the end user. The storage-retrieval-storage cycle is completed by maintaining proper file locator controls and returning the file to its home storage for later use.

File Mechanization In the approach to mechanized document storage and retrieval, a review of available equipment reveals variables in capacity and speed that must be related to the required file activity for proper cost justification. Specific filing media must be reviewed in terms of the function of the content and indexing needs before one decides upon a specific type of mechanized unit.

The final question is whether the documents involved will be converted to microsystem form or changed in form or subject to differing access because of planned computer processing. Many file items, because of their content and the way in which they are used by operating and file personnel, cannot be converted to other forms. Other documents, because of content such as signatures, seals of certification, or evidentiary characteristics, or because of other legal requirements, must be retained in their original form. Still others simply cannot economically be converted because of the sheer volume of data contained, or accompanying enclosures.

As part of a total systems approach, it is often best to convert to the chosen mechanized system those items of immediate use and high activity, together with all new incoming documents. This provides immediate partial and long-term progressive space savings, and makes possible a gradual phasing out of the older, less active items and the phasing in of new items, leading to a final result of maximum space and personnel savings through mechanization.

STORAGE AND RETRIEVAL CONCEPTS AND CHARACTERISTICS

Storage and retrieval of documents and records take many forms today, as dictated by the types of records, their volume, and the density of reference and activity. Following is an overview of the various forms of storage and retrieval. In discussing specific equipment types, the author may, to explain a point, refer to Sperry Remington equipment because of his familiarity with it; but it should be pointed out that all the types are available in varying form from others in the industry, and the illustrations accompanying the text are representative of the products of other well-known suppliers.

Table 2-1 provides a relative index ranking of each filing mode as to cost for application per unit filing inch for storage. The index is in point factor increments, ranging from a half point to five points, to indicate the cost relationship of each product class to the others.

File Cabinet The first concept of organized filing was an innovation of the founders of Sperry Remington (Remington Rand Systems). Prior to this time, records were stored in stacks or boxes, one on top of another. The use of the file cabinet as such was the first significant advance in records storage, and was the dominant form of storage for almost 70 years. As the demand for records increased, the use of the file cabinet also increased; however, at no point was the concept sufficient for exceptionally large and active files: Its domain was and is the files of moderate volume and activity.

Because of the open-drawer concept, files can be easily updated or added to chronologically without removal. If such files are used on a periodic basis, the normal open-and-close operation of drawers is no hindrance. However, productivity of files with high activity or involved file maintenance at the point of filing is greatly restricted with cabinets.

The Lateral File This is a present-day modernization of the file cabinet, and is a crossbreed of the storage cabinet and shelf filing. It is largely limited to the advantages of the cabinet, and because of its enclosed movable shelf drawer it loses the

---

[1] Microfilm in business applications is discussed in the following Chapter in this Section. Computer output microfilm (COM) is treated in Part Three, Chapter 4, in this Section. Computerized information storage and retrieval are covered in Section 4, Chapter 3.

advantage of mass storage and visible access found in shelf filing. Its height is limited to a low profile to provide visibility. However, because of its compact slim design, it does lend itself readily to small decentralized office applications. Its prime benefit is the versatility of housing file folder media that are either top-tabbed or side-tabbed. (See Figure 2-1.)

Shelf Filing The demands of a steadily increasing volume of records and greater records use and activity were met with the modern space-saving, divider-type shelving, a concept that utilized more air space, thereby housing more records in the same space taken up by the conventional file cabinets. In addition, this mode of filing provides

TABLE 2-1   Comparison of Filing Modes

Mode	Usage	Type of folder°	Cost-ratio points
File cabinet	Fixed module. Manual. Moderate activity. Medium-sized files	T	1.5
Lateral file	As above.	T	1.5–2.0
Shelf filing	Fixed module. Manual. Moderate to high activity. Moderate to very large files.	S	0.5
Motorized: shelving ranges	Fixed/expandable module. High capacity. Low activity.	S	1.5–2.0†
Automation	Automated rotary shelves. Unitization. High to extra-high activity files. Moderate to very large installations.	T & S	3.5
Automation	Fixed shelf. Automatic tray retrieval. Expandable unitization. High to extra-high activity files. Moderate to very large installations.		

° T = top tab; S = side tab.
† Range based on unit capacity.

the benefits of increased speed of record access and improved visibility in records location and refile. These benefits were achieved by the open-shelf concept with no drawers to open, close, push, or pull. The results are greater storage at a lesser cost and improved access to perform more record functions in less time.

Motorized Shelving Storage This more recent innovation meets the requirement for housing records that have passed the period of active use, must be retained in their original form for legal or technical reasons, have very low reference levels, and are large in volume. Records of this type require large amounts of storage in lesser amounts of floor space, but cannot justify the high cost of most conventional automated space-saving systems such as Sperry Remington's Lektriever and Supreme Equipment & Systems Corporation's Conserv-a-trieve discussed under "Mechanized and Automated Storage and Retrieval" below. However, they do call for greater efficiencies than conventional shelving.

Motorized shelving is a module or series of modules of movable track-mounted shelving accommodating letter, legal, X-ray, film, and computer-tape files. Heights vary according to the user's requirements, and can extend from the floor to the ceiling.

Modules have from 4 to 20 ranges of shelving, each with from 3 to 10 sections each. Size of the module and the floor plan are programmed to the individual user's needs. The shelving is compacted face to face on tracks, eliminating the need for any permanent aisle space and increasing the storage capacity of a given area by as much as 87 per cent as compared to conventional shelving. (See Figure 2-2.)

Access to a requested file segment is accomplished by moving the shelving manually, or automatically by electronic controls which on command will open an aisleway for access and retrieval. Principally, mobile shelving eliminates the aisleway and saves space. However, even in automatic systems, the operator still performs the time and motion functions of file search, retrieve, and restore by traveling to the

Fig. 2-1 Lateral file. (Sperry Remington.)

point of file of the records. Because of compacted aisles, access is restricted to a limited number of operators, and this limits file productivity.

MECHANIZED AND AUTOMATED STORAGE AND RETRIEVAL

Mechanized and automated storage and retrieval units are classified by record size and use. Classifications are determined by:

1. Total volume or lineal file inches of records.

2. Density of reference or number of references and refiles in a specific work time frame by a given number of personnel.

3. Descriptive work function performed with documents.

4. Consideration for present filing system, indexing, folders, etc.

Further physical delineation is made in terms of type of record housing module within the mechanized unit:

1. Letter-, legal-, or other large-size media such as films and magnetic tapes.

2. Card size: 3 by 5, 4 by 6, 5 by 8, tabulating, check sizes, and other variations of card-type documents.

3. Distinction as to unitized capacity, expandable in individual, independent, fixed-capacity modules.

4. Distinction as to large-capacity, singular modules available in variable sizes as required for the application.

5. Automated shelf.

The last two of the above factors have most impact in the application of the equipment to the document.

Automated Shelf The automated shelf or power-file product family is the mechanized form of open-faced shelving, typified by Lektriever and Conserv-a-trieve. For example, the Lektriever 100 is unitized, and provides filing capacity of up to 16 four-drawer files in less than 50 per cent of the space of conventional file cabinets. The shelving provides maximum visibility for quick reference access and fast refile, with no drawer operation. A prime feature is the ability to accommodate existing shelf file media without the time or expense for conversion of folders and indexing systems from existing shelf systems. Consideration must be given to the file function, because

Fig. 2-2 "Live aisle" mobile storage system. This installation (Nassau County Library System, New York) includes six mobile bases and two static racks, all 7 ft high. The bases, capable of supporting 8,960 pounds, ride along three 1-in. square steel tracks. In all, more than 12,000 linear shelf inches are created. (Dexion, Inc.)

file operation and maintenance require removal of the entire file. However, a convenient work-station surface that is adjustable to either a standing or seated position is provided for easy file processing. (See Figure 2-3.)

The automated shelf lends all the modern efficiencies of automation and space savings. Its solid state, electronically controlled ferris-wheel-type mechanism positions any one of up to 18 levels (each equivalent to over three file drawers) to the operator's work level in an average of 5 seconds. The unit delivers the file shelf to the operator rather than the operator traveling to the file. A push of a button on an indexed keyboard activates electronic logic that directs the delivery system always to take the shortest route to the operator, providing maximum productivity by the reduction of operator motion. In addition to solid state circuitry, electronic safety beams and pressure-sensitive touch bars stop the unit instantly should a file or an operator's hand enter the path of the moving shelf. Supplemental features include security locking doors, securing the files during periods of inactivity, and permitting controlled file access by authorized personnel for complete file integrity.

A product feature here is unitization: the housing of specific fixed capacities, with high-speed access to a select group of documents without the time delay of larger high-capacity units. This additionally provides specific operator responsibility and workload assignment. The rotary shelf concept makes possible fast sequential work operation for large-volume, high-activity files. Multiple units with individual operators provide maximum file productivity.

Automated Tray The automated tray concept is related to the oldest known form of filing, the file drawer. The efficiency of many file applications is improved by conversion to tray storage. Others, because materials are presently in drawer-type files, require no conversion. Because the individual tray is a small module and comes in variable sizes to accommodate records in numerous sizes, the application options are broad. Available are small unitized systems, and large mass-storage systems such as Conserv-a-trieve and Sperry Remington's Randtriever systems.

Product classifications are as follows:

1. Unitized capacity. Automated shelf with individual manual-extraction trays.
2. Unitized capacity. Automated shelf with automatic full-tray ejection.
3. Movable column. Individual tray location, retrieval, and delivery.
4. Card housing units. Unitized, low-volume. Unitized, high-volume.

Fig. 2-3 Lektriever 100 automated shelf filing unit. (Sperry Remington.)

Supplementing the power-file family, units of the type of the Lektriever 200 provide all the features of the automated shelf unit, but are equipped with individual trays. Each tray accommodates existing file drawer media and eliminates any conversion requirements. A salient point is that of front-to-back filing for accommodation of drop file procedures. This allows filing and chronological updates without file removal. All that is required is manually to eject the individual tray. As an added benefit, each tray can be removed for bulk file maintenance and other associated work functions. (See Figure 2-4.)

Improved enhancements, such as those of the Lektriever 300 systems, provide all the features of individual tray filing, but add the further sophistication of automated individual tray ejection upon positioning of the requested file level. Advantages here are for files that have a high degree of sequential filing retrieval and restore operations, with a minimal retrieval versus in-file activity ratio, although a higher cost factor is incurred than with manual systems. Another important factor in the use of the automatic ejection is that the operation generally reduces the work-counter surface to a minimum, making file maintenance at the equipment difficult. This restricts application of this concept to the retrieve or in-file functions only, with no provision for work-station operations or file maintenance at the unit.

Systems of the type described are unitized in fixed capacities, with the family of equipment ranging in capacity from the equivalent of 8 four-drawer files to 16 four-drawer files (letter, legal). This variation in fixed capacity makes the product suitable for all ranges of users who want the benefits of space and personnel savings in conjunction with modern efficiency. Thus this type of equipment meets the needs of the small file system, or, in multiple, the needs of the high-volume user.

Moving Column   The alternate form of automated tray ejection employs the method of moving a column equipped with a platform and extractor mechanism that locates, retrieves, and restores individual trays of filed media from the left or right of shelving modules. Figure 2-5 illustrates an advanced "off-the-shelf" compact automated record storage and retrieval system—the Conserv-a-file Minitrieve of Supreme Equipment & Systems Corp. The self-contained filing system is housed in a small rectangular enclosure, ranging from 7 to 10 feet high and occupying floor space from as little as 7 feet

Fig. 2-4   Lektriever 200 and 300 automated front-to-back filing system with individual trays for housing letter-, legal-, and card-size media.   (Sperry Remington.)

wide by 8 feet deep, expandable to accommodate increasing filing needs. Documents and other types of filed material are contained in letter- or legal-size file bins stored in facing banks of columns inside the enclosure. Control is by an adjoining desk-type keyboard console (work station). A touch of a push button orders a mechanism riding between the facing columns to couple itself to the file bin requested, and to transport it in seconds to the operator. The bin is presented at desk height in a top-access position ready to be worked on, and returned just as quickly by pressing a restore button. A center partition in each bin presents to the operator two facing rows of files, totaling 26 file inches, in one compact reachable location.

Enhancements of this type of system are activation and file access by tabulating-card input and computer control. Computer control can be a function of an off-line minicomputer control center or an interface with the user's mainframe computer. Byproducts are total file control and scheduled sequential access for maximum production.

For extremely large systems with a high ratio of activity, distribution conveyor systems for delivery of container storage trays to remote work stations can be implemented. Working applications where such large systems are justifiable are large medical record files, reference libraries, and insurance daily files or other voluminous archives.

The foregoing discussion has related the size and volume capabilities of the moving column concept. In addition to size and speed, consideration must be given to the matter of single-point access or multiple single-point access to very large volumes of files. Too few operators may have only limited access to large file volumes. As mentioned earlier, a detailed analysis as to densities of reference versus user need is most important.

Systems such as Conserv-a-trieve and Randtriever for moderately sized to large-sized files, if configured as a result of a detailed study and with sufficient care for heights and lengths of system as opposed to cycle time, productive capability as compared to file volumes housed, and work versus user needs, can be a most efficient

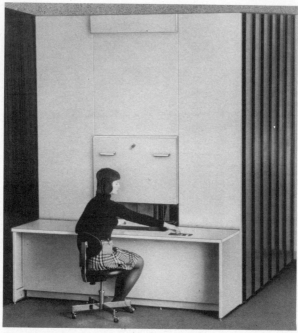

Fig. 2-5 Conserv-a-file Minitrieve record storage and retrieval system. A press of a push button locates file from within and delivers it to operator. (Supreme Equipment & Systems.)

means of storage. On large-capacity systems of low reference level, space savings because of height capability will surpass that of any other concept, and on singular large modules will progressively diminish in cost with size.

Card Housing Units Card housing is by nature of its physical dimensions confined to tray housing. Again, the type of mechanized housing must be related to its usage profile. Generally, cards are reference material and do not require removal from file. However, some applications do require removal from the file for temporary outside use. Such applications could be aperture cards or microfiche or film jackets containing documentation which is either reviewed or copied away from the storage module. Factors for consideration are:

1. Volume or lineal file inches.
2. Density of reference or activity in a specific time frame to a given number of items.

Automated Lektriever tray-type units provide storage capacities in ranges of 5,000 to 12,000 file inches. Because of the ease with which a voluminous quantity of card media can be stored in a singular unit, it is important to evaluate access requirements to volumes housed. This family of products is best suited for large files with minimal reference. Cycle times can approach 10 to 12 seconds on large units.

For files with high ratios of activity, smaller, compact, low-profile units are utilized. These units, referred to by Sperry Remington as Kardveyor, are capable of positioning a shelf or level of trays in less than 5 seconds, providing very high productivity levels. These products are frequently used in high-speed check-filing applications where sequential filing calls for in excess of 1,200 items filed per unit per hour. Speed is essential, and the smaller, low-capacity, higher-speed units improve access capability

Fig. 2-6   Kardveyor units position trays in less than 5 seconds. (Sperry Remington.)

Fig. 2-7   Simplafind system, for card-sized records, microforms, small parts, etc. Average time for positioning is about 3 seconds. (Wheeldex.)

and productivity. Kardveyor units range in capacity from 300 to 6,000 file inches.[2] (See Figure 2-6.)

Figure 2-7 shows the Simplafind system by Wheeldex, Inc., for card-sized records, microforms, small parts, etc. Upwards of 300,000 cards per unit may be handled, in

---

[2] In evaluating competing systems, care should be taken to be explicit about terms used. *File inches* may be *gross* or *usable*. For example, a tray accommodating 14 inches of cards cannot be loaded to that capacity. Some 2 inches must be allowed for comfortable working with the cards. Also, of course, size of card must be specified. Roughly, 100 cards per file inch are obtainable with standard 3- by 5-inch cards. Similarly, care must be exercised in discussing floor space used, allowing for operator comfort.

Fig. 2-8 Centrac rotary file, operating on the "Lazy Susan" principle. (Acme Visible Records.)

models ranging from 10 to 16 trays per cradle. When a cradle is selected by push button, it automatically positions itself by the shortest possible route. Thus the average time for positioning is about 3 seconds.

Not all large card systems need be automatic. Figure 2-8 shows the Centrac rotary file, operating on the "Lazy Susan" principle, marketed by Acme Visible Records, Inc. The slant-fin type illustrated accommodates computer print-outs for use in conjunction with the cards. Straight-finned units are used where print-outs are in hard-cover

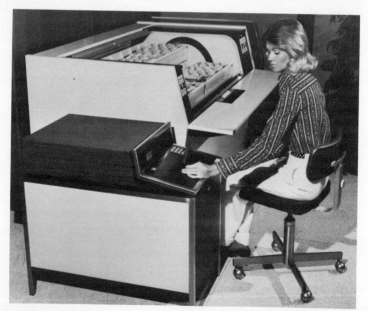

Fig. 2-9 In the Diebold D-550 system, closed-circuit television links desk-top monitors to a microform information bank at the transmitter unit illustrated. Monitor controls permit scanning of an entire microfiche. (Diebold.)

binders. Units such as these are used by utilities, banks, and savings and loan companies where there is need for immediate reference to balances and account statements to customers in telephone conversations.

Document Image Retrieval Systems are available which retrieve documents in ways previously described, and then incorporate closed-circuit television links to display the contents of the document at distant points, and, if desired, to many points simultaneously. This is useful, for example, in insurance company applications, where numerous individuals may wish to examine the same policy; and it has the added advantage of retaining important documents in the file location. Figure 2-9 is representative of the principle.[3]

COMPUTER INTERACTION WITH DOCUMENT STORAGE

The advent of electronic data processing has had significant effect on document storage and retrieval. The application of data processing can eliminate original-document form or diminish the volume of documents. Elimination is generally to banks of data that are basically reference-type files only. Access can now be gained through use of local print-out terminals and CRT display units. An additional form of reduction is the use of computer output microfilm for reduction of output mass and space savings, yet retention of original document format.[4]

Diminishing the volume of records is further accomplished by consolidation of portions of the database in computer memory banks and by improved information processing procedures for the balance. However, in many instances the information generating capability of the computer is such that vast amounts of management information are now available in a myriad of combinations and comparative displays. The result is more original-document generation and required storage than ever before with manual information processing methods.

With regard to original-document storage and retrieval, the prime computer benefit is in machine-processed documents. Examples are invoices, insurance daily files, order processing, and management reports. Now, as never before, the document is generated and automatically sorted into sequence for fast, efficient filing. For retrieval modes, many applications lend themselves to periodic computer-generated file retrieval listing, all in fast, efficient, chronological file-pulling order. Additionally, file locator controls can be implemented by the computer, providing data as to items scheduled for pull, their supposed work location while out of file, overdue listings for out-of-file conditions, and cyclical file maintenance operations. The computer is thus capable of providing highly automated forms of information processing, but it also can be an adjunct of efficient control for the original-document environment which does not lend itself to a computerized form.

[3] Reference is to Diebold, Incorporated, Canton, Ohio, which has no connection with The Diebold Group, editors of this Handbook.
[4] See Part Three, Chapter 4, "Computer Output Microfilm, (COM)," in this Section.

Microfilm in Business Applications

WARREN A. COLE

Director, Markets Development, Business Systems
Markets Division, Eastman Kodak Company,
Rochester, New York

During the second half of the twentieth century, society is relying on three principal media to record, assemble, file, manage, and distribute intelligence: paper, magnetic tape, and microfilm. Microfilm is used for both the old and the new. It helps to preserve the oldest organization records and to distribute the newest computer-generated data. Whereas microfilm's primary business use once was as a security medium, it is recognized today for its capability to solve many problems related to information storage and retrieval. Since paperwork is the largest single maintenance cost of a company of any size, there has been a strong incentive to find alternative information storage methods. Microfilm has become that method. Used alone or in conjunction with a computer, microfilm replaces paper mountains with a medium that greatly reduces the size of documents.

BACKGROUND

Microphotography got its start in 1839, just a few months after the introduction of the daguerreotype process, through some experiments performed by J. B. Dancer, an Englishman. But it was not until 1851, with the perfection of the wet-collodion process, that adequate definition could be achieved. Within a few years, Dancer and others were selling microphotographs as curiosities. Possibilities for this new medium soon came to mind; scholars of that era proposed the making and publishing of miniaturized reference books. It was suggested that secret dispatches could be filmed and concealed in tiny places.

Little use was made of these ideas until the introduction of modern microfilming by Kodak in 1928, with one notable exception. This exception—probably the first practical use of microphotography—was the Pigeon Post operated in 1870–1871 by Rene Dagron to send messages to Paris during the Franco-Prussian War. The Pigeon Post relied on carrier pigeons to carry microphotographs of official dispatches and civilian messages into the besieged city. It is interesting to note that the original specimens of Dagron's Pigeon Post messages that exist today are still in very good condition.

Microfilm's first business application made its debut in 1928. For 5 years, George L. McCarthy, vice president of a New York bank, searched for a means to establish proof that the checks written by a bank's customers had been paid. In those days, after the original checks were returned with a customer's statement, the bank had no legal proof of the transaction. To fill the need, McCarthy developed a microfilmer which was improved with Eastman Kodak Company's help. McCarthy became the vice president and general manager of a new Kodak subsidiary, Recordak Corporation, and in 1928 the first commercial microfilmer was installed in the Empire Trust Company, New York City. From that time on, banks have had positive proof of payments of checks, locked on film. (Many samples of microfilm that were made during the 1930s have been inspected and found to be in excellent condition.)

Records Preservation   As the popularity of microfilm grew, it became accepted as the medium for archival storage of records. Good examples of this acceptance are the time capsules buried at the sites of the 1939 and 1965 New York World's Fairs. These capsules contain a great mass of information on microfilm, the purpose of this information being to explain the civilization of our times to people 5,000 years from now. These time capsules are not the only examples of microfilm being used to archivally record documents for posterity. The New York Times began to microfilm its back files in 1939. The Genealogical Society of the Church of Jesus Christ of Latter Day Saints, Inc., has selected microfilm as the storage medium for more than 500 million genealogical statistics going back as far as the fourteenth century. The United Nations Education, Scientific and Cultural Organization (UNESCO) placed trained personnel and microfilming units at the disposal of countries around the world to microfilm documents these countries deem worthy of preservation. More than 2 million documents were recorded on microfilm in this program.

Stimulation   In 1937, about the same time the Federal Government was turning to microfilm to help handle the flood of data being created by the then-new Social Security Administration, the Kings County, New York, Clerk's office installed what may have been the first local government microfilm program. The reason was pure economics. Except for typing, photocopying was the only other means of duplicating a record; photocopies then cost about 12 cents each. Microfilm duplicates were a fraction of that.

At about the same time, the first state government microfilm application was initiated by the New York State Unemployment Compensation Board in conjunction with the Social Security program. Nine million checks were then issued to eligible recipients, each of whom had to sign a postcard affidavit that he or she did not earn more than $12 in the preceding week. Copies of 9 million checks and 11 million original affidavit cards had to be retained for record purposes. They would have taken up tremendous space, so all were microfilmed. Other states soon adopted similar unemployment compensation records procedures.

In 1941, the Pennsylvania Secretary of State became the first such office to install a microfilm program, converting to film all the recordings of corporation records. In the same year, the New York City Department of Vital Statistics embarked on the most ambitious retrospective microfilming job yet undertaken—involving all its records, back to Alexander Hamilton's 1801 death certificate. During World War II, microfilm was used by the Government for its V-Mail program. An estimated $1\frac{1}{2}$ billion letters were filmed, flown to and from combat zones, and reproduced as paper copy.

Also during the 1940s, a development occurred which opened industry's eyes to microfilm's potential in the engineering department. This was the introduction of the aperture card, a frame of 35-mm film mounted in a tab-size punch card. The aperture card enabled the reduction of large engineering drawings which could be readily blown back or enlarged, and the mounting in a tab card made them easily filed and readily retrieved.

However, it was not until about 1947 when the Social Security Administration converted a file of 90 million ledger sheets to film with provisions for quarterly updating that microfilm started to be accepted as an active office reference medium. The Social Security Administration's application proved so successful that large-scale conversions were made at many other Government agencies. Most of these were on 16-mm or 35-mm roll film, and the files created were largely manually retrieved.

True mechanization of microfilm began in 1949 when microfilms of engineering drawings were placed in electronic accounting machine aperture cards. One of the first to use this system for its engineering drawings was Hamilton Standard Division of United Aircraft Corporation. Others soon followed. In 1960, the Defense Department came out with specifications that required all military contractors to deliver copies of their engineering drawings on aperture cards. Thus the era of large-scale microfilm use in industry truly began.

Microfilm became increasingly visible on the local level after 1968. The spur was a trio of Federal acts which helped local agencies mechanize their record-keeping methods. (These were the National Defense Education Act, for educational institutions, then the Hill-Burton Act for hospitals, and third, the Safe Streets Act.)

Manufacturers of microfilm equipment have contributed to the growing use of microforms by introducing automated and increasingly sophisticated hardware. Typical are the use of magazines to eliminate the need to handle and thread roll film, and retrieval methods based on special codes recorded directly onto film during photography. The latter method enables specific information to be recalled on keyboard command.

Paralleling developments in roll film and aperture cards was the evolution of other microforms. One was microfiche, a sheet of film usually 4 by 6 inches on which 64 or more images can be recorded. Microfilm jackets, transparent jackets with channels that house individual or small sequences of images, have become a popular filing medium. New uses such as micropublishing and computer output microfilm emerged.[1]

Government action continues to help pace general acceptance of microfilm for information handling. In 1964, the Federal Government elected to distribute certain technical reports on microfiche; private publications on fiche began to proliferate shortly thereafter. More recently, in 1972, the Government Printing Office announced that within a few years it would probably distribute all Government documents on microfilm, some *only* on microfilm.

CURRENT STATE OF THE ART

The various *microforms*, as they are called, include roll film, microfilm jackets, microfiche, and aperture cards. Roll film on spools is used primarily for records not requiring frequent "look-ups" or reference. Roll film, loaded into magazines, is used for automated retrieval programs.

Microfilm jackets, usually about 4 by 6 inches in size, and aperture cards containing 16-mm film are often used to retain strips of film. Used as file folders, they can be added to and updated easily. It is quick and inexpensive to duplicate them.

Microfiches are "filmcards" which typically contain from 60 to more than 500 images. These are created by photographing pages in sequence and stripping groups of images together to form a printing master or by recording directly from a computer output microfilmer.

The aperture card, previously described, offers easy updating, usually by replacement.

Roll Film. In format, roll film closely corresponds to photography as it is known by the layperson. Roll film images are locked side by side as they are filmed, providing fixed file continuity. In the most basic approach, documents are filmed in some logical file control order (chronologic, alphabetic, numeric, etc.), and the user searches the film visually with a viewer to find the document needed. Traditionally, roll film on open reels, generally in 100-foot lengths and in widths of 16 mm and 35 mm, has been the most common microform. Sixteen millimeter is more often associated with in-house legal-size, letter-size, or smaller-size microfilming, while 35 mm is identified with engineer drawings, large bound books, and newspapers on film.

The roll takes on sophistication when it is transformed into a magazine, either by snapping the reel into a plastic "collar" or rewinding the film to a plastic container (usually 4 by 4 by 1 inches in size). The magazine acts as a labeled filing unit, protecting the film from foreign matter and most importantly providing faster access to its contents because it self-threads into the reader. Rolls and magazines display newest information first, since it is spliced to the leading edge of the film. Film that is coded for electronic retrieval is kept in a magazine.

[1] For computer applications, see Part Three, Chapter 4, "Computer Output Microfilm (COM)," in this Section.

Microfilm Jackets. As a microform, microfilm jackets lie midway between roll film and microfiche with some, but not all, of the advantages of each. Typically, jackets are made of polyester bonded together to form channels in which short strips of film (cut from larger rolls) can be inserted. Jackets come in various sizes and configurations, such as 4 by 6 or $3\frac{1}{4}$ by $7\frac{3}{8}$ inches.

The advantages are easy updating by removing and replacing individual filmstrips, and quick, inexpensive duplication in contact printers without removing the film from the jackets. Jackets are also easily filed and retrieved. The disadvantages: Jacketed film does not have the rigid file integrity of roll film; perfect alignment of film in jackets takes precise handling because of unitization of images; and it is somewhat more costly than roll film.

Microfiche. This is the fastest-growing microform. Though "fiche" comes in several sizes and reductions, one size has become accepted as standard—the 4- by 6-inch National Microfilm Association format with a maximum capacity of 98 images of $8\frac{1}{2}$- by 11-inch pages, each reduced 24:1. There is also 4- by 6-inch microfiche that contains fewer images (72 pages $8\frac{1}{2}$ by 11 inches reduced 20:1) or more images (as many as 208 pages reduced 42:1, generally computer output, printed directly onto microfilm). Within the fiche category are other reduction ratios referred to as *ultrafiche* and *superfiche*. Ultrafiche uses reductions of 150:1 going to 210:1. The superfiche reduction ratio of 48:1 is proving popular, and 50:1 is also used.

Microfiche has become a way of publishing a wide variety of information, in color as well as black and white. It enables readers to get material—technical reports, for example—at a fraction of the cost of a paper edition. Although microfiche is generally more expensive than roll film, it is easier to duplicate and handle. Microfiche viewers are simple to operate and require less investment than do roll film viewers.

Aperture Cards. As mentioned earlier, an aperture card is an electronic accounting machine card, $3\frac{1}{4}$ by $7\frac{3}{8}$ inches with a cutout surrounded by an adhesive material for holding a frame or frames of film. The film frame is usually 35 mm, although there are aperture cards that take 8-mm and 16-mm inserts, as well as others that take a combination of film widths. "Mil-D," a card which places the location of the aperture between card columns 53 and 76, and holds a 35-mm film chip, is the most common size. It is so called because this is the location standardized for military and Government use. One variation of the aperture card holds the film in a pocket(s) formed between two layers of optically clear, polyester material.

A drawback to the aperture card is that it is not a practical format for documents with an average of more than 16 pages, and is more expensive to create on a per-image basis than other microformats. It is, however, simple and fast to duplicate on a card-to-card duplicator and can be machine-sorted.

Retrieval Methods Selecting the desired microform from a group of microforms is simple. Merely choose the film cartridge or roll bearing identifying letters or numbers, the transparent jacket, or microfiche with a title on the header. Finding the one image needed out of thousands in the microform can pose a problem, but it can be avoided by the use of simple-film-coding techniques applied as documents are photographed.

The simplest code involves *flash cards* which bear large numbers or letters. These identify groups of document images on a roll and are photographed directly onto the microfilm. The card images are preceded and followed by clear film spaces. As the film is viewed, the operator sees what appear to be white flashes. Then, the operator stops and finds the letter or number signifying the sought-after group of images and looks for the exact image.

Documents can be filmed in chronological sequence, assigned a location number, then listed alphabetically or numerically in a log. Another method of coding is to expose automatically horizontal or vertical lines (*code lines*) on the film at escalating positions between document images. When seen on the reader screen, the lines change positions as the film advances or rewinds. The desired image or group of images is located when the code lines match sequential numbers or alphabetic characters on a scale adjacent to the viewing screen.

Automated Retrieval. For even faster image locations, there are *image control* retrieval approaches that place "blips" adjacent to each film image. These marks are exposed on the film during microfilming. In retrieving, the operator enters the desired image number on a keyboard coupled to a reader and presses the search button. The marks, or blips, are electronically counted at high speed until the precise image is located.

The most sophisticated coding of all uses *binary code* patterns. As each document or groups of documents is microfilmed, varied code patterns that correspond to subject matter in the documents are also exposed onto the film. When a magazine is inserted into the reader, the desired code numbers are entered on a keyboard. The code patterns on film are electronically scanned and the film stops at the images containing the desired subject matter. Searching thousands of images takes only seconds.

A BASIC MICROFILM SYSTEM

In a flow chart, the sequence of a basic microfilm system would consist of *input* (document organization and indexing), *microfilming* (camera work), *processing* (including duplicating), *filing*, and *retrieval* (including viewing and hard-copy print-outs where needed).

Input   Paper documents are the input in almost all microfilm systems. The major exception is computer output microfilm (COM) systems, which bypass paper and transfer data directly from magnetic tape using one of the four modes of microfilm in human-readable form described under "Current State of the Art," above.

Almost any type of document is applicable to some form of microfilming. This includes financial records, correspondence, drawings and diagrams, publications, and reports. The type of document and the way in which the information it contains will be used will determine the most suitable microform.

Microfilming   Two basic types of microfilmers are used for hard-copy (paper) recording: rotary (flow) and planetary.

Rotary microfilmers are designed for rapid, continuous, and automatic recording of documents. They can handle thousands of items per hour, from bank checks to legal-size papers. In a rotary microfilmer, a mechanical feed system, synchronized with the speed of film travel in the microfilmer, transports the documents. Because of the automatic nature of most rotary microfilmer operations, the reduction ratio is fixed (though it varies depending on the need and the lens used). Common reduction ratios are about 40:1, 32:1, 24:1, and 20:1. The typical rotary microfilmer uses 16-mm film. It records in any of three modes: simplex, duplex, or duo.

In the simplex mode, only one side of a document is filmed at a time. If information is contained on the reverse side of the document, it is turned over and the other side is photographed. On the film, the image of the front of the document appears immediately before the image of the back. In duplex mode, the microfilmer records both sides of a document simultaneously, through the use of a mirror system. The front and back images appear side by side on the film. The duo mode uses only half the width of the film at one time. After one complete side of the roll is filmed, the roll is turned over, loaded back into the camera, and used to film the other side.

Planetary microfilmers photograph one document at a time, and are handled manually, rather than automatically. The film and exposure unit are usually mounted on a vertical track above the document. The quality of the microfilm produced in planetary systems is considerably higher than rotary systems, because of the lack of document motion; thus these microfilmers are used to film engineering drawings and other large-size documents. Planetary microfilmers normally use 35-mm film; however, some can use 16-mm, 70-mm, or 105-mm film. Because they are manual, production speed rarely exceeds 300 to 400 images per hour.

A variation on the standard planetary microfilmer containing unexposed roll film is a microfilmer-processor which is loaded with aperture cards containing unexposed 35-mm film chips. This type of machine exposes the film, processes it automatically, and delivers a finished aperture card. There are also microfilmer-processor units which utilize 105-mm film and deliver finished 4- by 6-inch microfiche. Some microfilmers permit simultaneous exposure of two rolls at a time, for security purposes. Other security methods involve duplicating a processed roll, by a variety of means, and storing one roll in an off-premises vault.

Processing the Film   The one thing that processing units have in common is that they are designed to process roll microfilm. There the similarity stops. Some processors require darkroom facilities; some do not. Some require plumbing connections, while others use liquid or gaseous chemicals in cartridges, and still others operate on a heat-development principle. Some units occupy 6 square feet or more of floor space; others will fit on a tabletop. There are even processors so compact that they sit alongside the microfilmer, ready to accept and process exposed film from the same cartridge used in the microfilmer. Some processors will develop one roll at a time; others will handle several simultaneously. There are processing units that handle one or two film widths only, while others take a complete range of sizes from 16 mm to 105 mm.

After processing, roll film is left on the spool or put into cartridges or cassettes. Microfiche produced in roll form on 105-mm film must then be cut to size. A variety of hardware exists for these specialized functions, some manual, some automatic.

Duplicating Microfilm Because of its nature as a medium of information, a microform generally does not exist as only one original. It is duplicated for dissemination, often in thousands of units.

Most duplicating units are contact film printers, similar in principle to those with which photographers are familiar. Roll-to-roll duplication is the most common and is usually done by commercial services, except in those cases where a user has a continuous day-in, day-out need for a large number of duplicates. There are also duplicating units that print card-to-card, fiche-to-fiche, and jacket-to-jacket fiche, as well as other types of conversion units that will print roll-to-card and roll-to-roll fiche.

Aperture cards and microfiche can be reproduced at relatively low cost in a variety of units designed for low-volume, in-house operation. There are, for example, card-to-card duplicators that will duplicate one aperture card at a time for pennies. Similar units duplicate microfiche.

Recording original microfilm on silver halide film offers maximum sensitivity and resolution. Duplicates are often made on non-silver films, principally diazo (ammonia-developed) and vesicular (heat-developed) films. These films are less sensitive than silver halide film, but are well suited to most duplicating needs.

Filing Microforms are filed in a variety of retaining devices, from simple file boxes to computer-controlled electromechanical filing systems. As in all other areas relating to microfilm, the need determines the mode. Advanced filing and retrieval systems, whatever their technology (edge-notching of jackets, or aperture cards, optical film coding, etc.), are of two basic types. One type is tightly organized, such as catalogue files, directories, parts lists, maintenance manuals, inventories, name-to-account number files, and account files. The second type is a cumulative collection, assembled by the chronological addition of discrete units of information. Examples include libraries, technical and other management report files, and serial files of publication.

As a general rule, microforms should be stored under moderate temperature (50 to 80°F) and in 35 to 70 per cent relative humidity. Where temperatures or humidity may be expected to be outside these limits, it is recommended that temperature and humidity control be installed in the area where microforms are stored.

Retrieval, or "Look-ups" Information contained on microforms is ultimately retrieved by one of two basic devices: a reader, or a reader-printer. Readers range from simple hand viewers used for occasional reading of microfiche to units tied to keyboard-accessed logic systems. There are literally hundreds of models from which to choose, including portable readers, tabletop readers, and console models. Almost any magnification up to 150:1 is available, though 24:1, 40:1, and 50:1 are the most common. There are readers with vertical screen formats (for basic document reading), horizontal formats (for COM output), wide-screen formats (for newspapers and engineering drawings), and still others that allow two page-images to be viewed simultaneously.

Reader-printers allow an operator to view an image and, if desired, also make a paper copy. This is done by simply pressing a button. The entire copy-making process is self-contained in the unit; a print is delivered in seconds. Prints are made by one of five processes: photographic, electrolytic, electrostatic, thermal, or diazo.

Photographic-process reader-printers use silver-sensitized paper similar to that employed in the typical darkroom process, though automatically. The electrolytic process uses a paper laminated to a metallic foil which establishes the image through electroconductivity. Each of the other processes applies its own specific technology to produce a finished product automatically.

APPLICATIONS IN BUSINESS

A purchase order and the documents it generates — shipping invoices, bills of lading, statements, and the like — are ideal candidates for retention to active microfilm files. Other business records which are commonly on microfilm are address-change notices, corporate records, waybills, sales slips, personnel files, tax returns, requisitions, check vouchers, and canceled checks. Correspondence files increasingly are being converted to microfilm. An early problem of add-ons and deletions has been resolved with the use of microfilm jackets. Following are specific business gains available from microfilm:

Space. Records on microfilm need as little as 2 per cent of the space occupied by the same records on paper.

Convenience. Only seconds are involved in retrieving one of a million records filed within arm's reach of a seated operator.

Security. Duplicate microfilm files kept off premises protect against destruction and loss of vital information.

Lower Costs. Hours freed from sorting, filing, and refiling paper records are either recovered or channeled into more productive work.

Improved Service. Questions from customers and clients can be answered accurately and without the delays of searching paper files.

File Continuity. Records filed on microfilm are in fixed sequence, guarding against misfiling, mislaying, alteration, or loss.

Uniformity. Regardless of original-document size, images are reduced to fit standard microfilm dimensions for convenient handling.

Rapid Computer Print-out. Magnetic-tape data are made readable on microfilm in a fraction of the time required for printing out on paper.

Low-Cost Distribution. Economical film duplicates are quickly produced and inexpensively mailed.

Filing Equipment Saving. Far fewer filing cabinets are needed for microfilm records.

Easy Reversion to Paper. A paper copy of the original document is produced in seconds from the microfilm image.

Versatility. Microfilm can assume or supplement existing information handling methods with little change of current procedures or disruption of operations.

Legal Recognition. Federal and state legislation has provided for the admissibility of microfilm records as primary evidence in the courts.

The list of generalized applications is almost endless. Taking seven industries for the sake of illustration, following are some examples of specific microfilm systems.

Banking Banking was the first and continues to be a major application area for microfilm. Information on the faces and the backs of checks is recorded on microfilm. In the event of a loss, the checks can be reproduced in their entirety and sent on their way for collection.

Many banks now use a new microfilm application called *item address* for check processing. This combines computer processing's advantages with microfilm filing. Following proof encoding, the items are assembled into control groups, and each group is assigned a number. The microfilm operator enters the control information into a sequential imprinter on a microfilmer and begins filming. Each item is imprinted with the control and sequence information, and then receives its microfilm address. After the microfilm operation, the checks are forwarded to the data capture area, where under program control the computer in effect assigns the same control information as was physically stamped by the microfilmer.

Various listings then contain both the check data and the location of the item on film. Detail listings accompanying transit items ask correspondent banks to refer to the identification number that appears beside any item in question. Demand deposit transaction journals and customer statements also contain the film location of the items.

Retrieval of specific check images is a simple matter of referring to one of the records for the number assigned to the item, selecting the proper film magazine, inserting it in a reader, and rapidly locating the item.

The basic item address system — microfilming and sequentially numbering documents on receipt—is applied to a host of banking applications. Typical are transit and bookkeeping operations, account reconciliation, and audit trails on installment payments. Any random-input computerized billing system is facilitated by automatic sequential number indexing as items are filmed.

There also are many banking applications of microfilm in daily use other than item address systems. Single rather than multiple copies of customer statements are generated, then microfilmed, and mailed with checks and deposit slips. Microfilming statements eliminates extra forms, lowers costs, reduces storage space requirements, and shortens reference time. In another application, dividend checks are filmed immediately prior to mailing, and the film record takes the place of the check register.

Multiple copies of microfilmed signature card files are easy and inexpensive to keep and enable every bank branch office to have a copy of all customers' signatures for quick review on a reader. Aperture cards are used by some banks to retain a copy of a charge-card customer's basic application and a credit report.

Insurance Major insurance uses are for policy application files, premium payment systems, and policy status files.

Policy application forms are arranged in policy number order and photographed on a rotary microfilmer. The film is cut into strips which are inserted into microfilm jackets. As documents are added to the file—endorsements, correspondence, medical forms, etc.—they are microfilmed and added to the jacket in the same way. For easy retrieval, the policy number is typed in eye-readable type along the upper edge of the jacket, and the jackets are filed in standard card file cabinets, usually in policy number order.

In premium payment systems, a file control system similar in principle to banking's item address system is employed. As checks and vouchers are photographed, they are given a sequential number address. This same sequence number is used for computer entry and creation of an index to the items.

Policy status file systems utilize COM output which can be retained in microfilm jackets, or roll film in magazines. If jackets are used, the microforms are kept in policy number order with eye-readable titles. Updates are simple—additions of film chips to the jacket. If film magazines are used, the updated material is filmed, processed, and then spliced into proper sequence in the appropriate magazine.

Insurance companies use name-to-number microfilm filing to allow companies to deal with policyholders by name or policy number. Documents are keypunched and a listing is created via COM. At the same time, source documents are photographed in a sequential listing. The COM-produced listing—by name or number—is the index to the microfilmed documents.

Insurance companies have become involved in micropublishing. Microfiche is used to save about one-third of the printing costs of policy rate books and more in space, time, and convenience. In one company, each clerk has an up-to-date fiche file replacing piles of bulky and heavy books used to convert rate information for calculation of cash, loans, and death value of policies. Dividend books, technical publications, and cash value books are other examples where microfiche may prove very practical.

Transportation Airlines, motor carriers, and railroads are all major users of microfilm. Airlines use COM extensively to maintain records required by the Civil Aeronautics Board. They also apply microfilm to maintenance operations, pilot logs, credit billing, engineering drawings, air waybills, computerized reservation information, interline accounting records, personnel records, and lift tickets. To date, the greatest usage has been in the creation of microfilmed maintenance manuals, following general microfilm specifications published by the Air Transport Association of America. Most maintenance systems use film in cartridges and a visual code method such as code-line indexing.

The major microfilm application for motor carriers is a file system for freight bills. These bills, in 8 to 10 copies, come to a central accounting office from terminals and customers. There they have a microfilm address number added as they are filmed, and then they go to data processing where they are keypunched in the established manner with the simple addition of the microfilm address. Data processing creates a reference register which includes this address for future retrieval.

Railroads use basic automated information retrieval systems to handle waybills.

The documents are recorded at random, but with a binary code for each image. The code is logged, and when the document must be retrieved, the appropriate film code position is punched into a keyboard and the desired image is brought into view. The Interstate Commerce Commission is so satisfied with this method that it allows actual waybills to be disposed of within 3 months. Filmed data are readily accepted as a substitute for the originals.

Public Utilities   Telephone companies are also large users of microfilm. File control is widely used for retention of service order data. Toll libraries, where data are kept on all operator-assisted calls, use a variation of the system whereby the basic documents (mark-sensed tab cards) are filmed with a sequence number and also entered into the computer data bank with the same number. Computer output produces necessary statistical and operating data, while the original document is kept on film available for review if needed to answer customer inquiries. The document is easily accessed through its sequence number. In another application, classified directory sales contracts are microfilmed in random fashion and retrieved through their code numbers.

Possibly the greatest microfilm breakthrough in telephone company application will be directory assistance. Various experiments have been conducted to reduce bulky directories to easily accessed film files, and tests have shown that operator look-up time can be substantially reduced. Several microfilm directory assistance programs were in operation in 1975, and it is only a matter of time for more to be implemented.

In other utility applications, information that has been entered on meter orders, test records, service orders, and other field reports of electric, gas, and water utilities need no longer be transferred to meter record cards. Instead, the original papers are microfilmed, eliminating transcription errors. A record of each meter by district office and serial number is keypunched on an EAM card (electronic accounting machine card) and fed into the computer to create a master meter list. Subsequent meter transactions are also fed into the computer. Periodic print-outs provide a summary of all transactions on each meter. Each transaction provides a numerical address to the source document on film.

Retailing   To reduce internal operating costs and increase response capabilities, retail firms (as well as credit-card companies) have turned to extensive computer-supported information systems. COM complements computer processing to lower the cost and practicality of distributing data. Typically, updated credit information is fed into the computer once a month to create an updated master file tape. A special software package allows the tapes to be compatible with a COM system. The system's output—roll film or microfiche—is processed, duplicated, and sent to the central credit authorization point for telephone response to credit information inquiries. Roll film in magazines, microfiche, microfilm jackets, and aperture cards are all employed as the retrieval microform.

Image control techniques have been applied to retailing in such areas as accounts receivable. Even though charges and credits to customer accounts are handled by computers, many problems still exist which require recall and look-up of documents. By microfilming and sequentially numbering all input documents after proving, retrieval is fast and easy. Further, the microfilm address of the original-document image is carried on the customer statements created in data processing. The original sales slips are not mailed, saving postage charges. Instead, they are discarded, saving storage charges. They still exist on film, and can be reproduced in a hard-copy print-out if needed.

Manufacturing   All the universal document control systems for which microfilm is the ideal filing and retrieval medium apply in manufacturing. In addition, microfilm facilitates unitized engineering data control systems. In some cases, original drawings are microfilmed, along with supporting documents, on both 35-mm and 16-mm film sizes. The material being filmed determines the size; i.e., 35 mm for drawings, 16 mm for letter-size documents. The strips of 35-mm and 16-mm film are inserted mechanically into a microfilm jacket. At this point the drawing number is applied on the index strip along the top edge of each jacket. The jacket contains three times as much area for engineering drawings as a similar-size aperture card, plus all the support data. When updating is necessary, new or revised information is inserted into the master jacket and the obsolete film is discarded. Distribution duplicates are made on silver, diazo, or thermal film, and the duplicates are read on any standard microfiche reader.

Manufacturing, with so many diverse record-keeping needs, offers many other applications. For example:

Credit Files on Film. One large Midwest-headquartered company keeps current customer financial statements, credit investigations, trade clearances, collection transactions, and credit and collection correspondence for some 15,000 active accounts in one tabletop two-drawer cabinet. Use of microfilm virtually eliminates obsolete information, speeds the dispatching of collection letters, and reduces the space required for filing records by about 98 per cent. The average customer's credit file can be contained within one microfilm jacket. All aspects of creating the microfilm files are performed within the credit department, including filming and processing in a compact tabletop unit which requires no darkroom.

Paperless Purchasing Department. A Pennsylvania firm which controls an inventory of about 25,000 parts is virtually paperless. In addition to purchase orders, acknowledgements, receiving tickets, and correspondence, everything coming into the department that refers to a purchase order is filmed—between 3,500 and 4,000 documents of this nature a week. When an order is expedited with a vendor and the delivery date is obtained, the information is filmed. The film is encoded to allow automatic retrieval.

Microfilm is also used for a matching function. After a purchase order is on film, it is used to check against the vendor acknowledgement for verification of price and quantity. This enables the company to determine whether any price increases are authorized and whether it is obtaining the proper discounts.

Information on discounts is maintained in the computer. When a clerk places an order, the computer will indicate whether or not there is a price break for the particular company. If there is, the clerk need only pick the appropriate film magazine for that vendor, search for the particular part number, read what the price break is, and take action accordingly. With inflation affecting prices, the company can easily keep track of all changes through its computer and microfilm programs.

Customer Status Reports. Sometimes ready access to the status of customer equipment and component orders is vital when there is a considerable lag time between the placement of an order and its completion. In fields involving heavy industrial equipment the lag can be as much as a year on equipment, 28 weeks on some components. One Philadelphia manufacturer installed three microfilm programs, saving $175,000 in the process. Its customer order inquiry system has some 4,000 to 5,000 customer inquiries per week which are served through the use of microfilm. The number of characters of information previously needed to store customer data in the computer was becoming astronomical.

A customer accounting application involves COM: computer-generated documents are produced on COM and spliced into film magazines. A saving in print-out and computer time as well as referencing is the outcome. The company's engineering data are also filmed and encoded for microfilm retrieval.

Centralizing Microfilm. One major steel company established a central unit to plan and coordinate microfilm applications affecting all departments and plants. Uses included engineering drawings which are filmed, inserted into aperture cards, keypunched, and retained in a master file. Diazo film duplicates are distributed upon request. A computer-generated listing of all filed drawings is kept for cross-referencing. Keypunched aperture cards are machine-processed on a semiannual basis, and each of the company's many engineering departments is provided a copy of the drawing list generated by this operation.

The purchasing department closely integrates its functions with the accounts payable process. Interrelated records are generated every step of the way. Microfilm jackets are filed by district location code and then by order. Film in magazines contains images of invoices, checks, and correspondence.

In the salary and employee benefits accounting unit all records pertaining to each individual employee of the steel company are filed under the Social Security number. In addition, paper print-outs were replaced by microfilm in magazines in the market research department.

Order Processing. Manufacturers who sell their products directly to a large number of retailers find microfilm an ideal tool for information processing. Customer order, invoicing, packing tickets, notice of balance to follow, cancellation notice, and correspondence can all be filmed and retained in a magazine for prompt retrieval. Microfilm can provide an audit trail in considerable depth. Microfilming can be handled in a company's regional distribution center.

Warranty Records. One clothing manufacturer has an iron-clad guarantee pertaining to the life of the garment—provided the person requesting an adjustment is the one who originally ordered the merchandise. Since space did not allow the retention of records for more than 13 months, on premises, a problem used to be posed when the subject of a warranty came up. With all warranty records kept on microfilm, there is excellent file integrity. The paperless approach eases response to customer inquiries; virtually never does the company need to admit it cannot find a record. Encoded microfilm is used to retrieve customer records automatically, and responses can usually be given in about 10 seconds.

Publishing Micropublishing—the original publishing and distribution of information in some form of microfilm, in color as well as in black and white—is one of the fastest growing areas of microfilming. Companies and organizations publishing data in microfilm form are so numerous it would be impossible to compile a comprehensive listing of them. Parts catalogues, maintenance manuals, wiring diagrams, chemical and technical abstracts, newspapers, periodicals, student reference material, travel literature, medical studies, and financial publications are some of the areas to which micropublishing systems have been applied. In fact, just about every type of printed material is now available on one microform or another. These include commercial publications offered by subscription and proprietary publications prepared by or for an organization which recognizes microfilm as an ideal publishing means.

Microfiche is the most widely used microform because of its ability to accommodate multiple pages of information on a common subject, and its inexpensive nature. Printing costs are reduced at least to a third of those of standard publishing; mailing costs are reduced even more; and production turnaround time is far faster. A microfilmed publication can be duplicated and disseminated in days, compared to the weeks it would take for comparable hard copy. The recent introduction of good, low-cost readers also has been a major spur to micropublishing in the microfiche format.

GETTING INTO MICROFILM

How does a business go about creating a useful microfilm program?

The logical time to start is when an organization is investigating a systems change. At that point the company may engage the services of a reputable microfilm consultant. The consultant can assist in analyzing needs, developing systems, selecting and installing hardware, and training personnel.

In selecting a consultant, start by asking for whom he or she has worked in the past in a similar capacity or what experience and capability the consulting firm has in the problem area. Check through with other clients. The consultant will want the problem clearly outlined so he or she can determine what needs to be done—and not done. One way of forcing through such an outline is through a written statement of objectives. The actual work done, and how it is done, will vary from project to project, but the expertise and objectivity of an outside consultant can save a great deal of time and money.

Another source of help is systems specialists connected with major manufacturers. Their consultation is generally free and knowledgeable, and can be both extremely useful and valuable. Of course, they will have a bias toward their own equipment and methods, but by working with more than one supplier, the company can evaluate alternative proposals.

The education offered by manufacturers and vendors in the form of seminars and literature should not be ignored or overlooked. The latter, particularly, can be used to build up an excellent reference file. Also useful are a number of trade journals which cover developments in the microfilm field. In addition, seminars are offered by a number of organizations including the National Micrographics Association, American Management Association, Advanced Management Research International, and the Institute for Advanced Technology. These seminars are held on a regular basis in various cities and can serve as a useful introduction or update to microfilm.

Finally, and not to be overlooked, is membership in the National Microfilm Association and attendance at meetings of the group. The association has chapters across the country. It publishes a bimonthly journal and a series of publications on microforms subjects and holds a midyear meeting in the fall and an annual spring conference and concurrent equipment exhibition that offer the best opportunities to be brought up to date on developments in the micrographics industry.

THE FUTURE

During the period since World War II, microfilm has come a remarkably long way as a tool for the management of information. To date, most applications have been major in nature, involving large quantities of documentation. In the near future, such installations will increase in sophistication. Leading the way will be evolutionary developments wherein microfilm is married to the computer in a device to capture data and microfilm at the same time.

In the near future also is the extension of microfilm as an active tool into previously unexplored areas such as the small-office environment. This has already created yet another acronym, SOM (small-office microfilm). Inexpensive, desk-top readers, microfilmers, processors and duplicators, and filing systems are opening many new opportunities for the smaller businesses.

SOM programs and hardware may be roll film (8 mm or 16 mm) or microfiche. Recent low-priced desk-top readers and cameras, particularly for microfiche, jackets, and aperture cards, are pointing the way. Most small offices require only readers and perhaps a camera for a highly functional SOM program. Service bureaus can do the processing and can provide a wide range of services. Capital expenditures for SOM equipment easily fit into the budget of a small office, and, like most office equipment, it may be leased.

Undoubtedly the key element that makes SOM possible is the inexpensive portable reader, and particularly the microfiche reader. There are many manufacturers and commercial services companies which will provide microfiche for anyone at a reasonable price. They can take the original material, photograph it, and create a fiche master and duplicate it.

Facsimile microfilm is another area due for development. Facsimile transmission units exist that can scan a chip of microfilm and then transmit the data from the film, via telephone lines, in the same way that data from hard copy are transmitted. These units are in early stages of development and not yet in commercial application, but the possibilities are obvious—almost instant transfer of engineering drawings from one plant to another, immediate verification of documentation with carry-away available copies. In short, every potential benefit of facsimile transmission plus the advantages of microfilm data filing.

Finally, one of the largest potential areas for microfilm expansion is into the home. There are already a limited number of home study programs of material on microfilm. Many medical schools, for example, are now making color microfiche available to students rather than color slides; it is equally effective as a teaching tool and far less expensive. Some secondary school systems now have lending programs for microfilmed materials and readers, and experiments on the elementary and secondary school level have shown that children readily accept and use microfilm. There already have been some limited commercial microfilm efforts for home use outside of the micropublishing area. As the acceptance and use of microfilm grow, so will the business of getting microfilm into the home.

SELECTIVE BIBLIOGRAPHY

Avedon, Don M., *Computer Output Microfilm*, 2d ed., National Microfilm Association, Silver Spring, Md., 1971.
———, *User's Guide to Standard Microfiche Formats*, Microfilm Publishing, New York, 1971.
Badler, Mitchell M., *1972 Microfilm Source Book*, Microfilm Publishing, New York, 1972.
Ballou, Hubbard W., *Guide to Microreproduction Equipment*, 5th ed., National Microfilm Association, Silver Spring, Md., 1971.
Kish, Joseph L., and James Morris, *Microfilm in Business*, Ronald, New York, 1966.
Lee, Tom, *Microform Systems: A Handbook for Educators*, Ann Arbor, Mich., 1970.

The Management of Information, Eastman Kodak Company, Rochester, N.Y., 1971.

Nanney, Thomas G., *Using Microfilm Effectively,* Geyer-McAllister, New York, 1968.

Panorama, various issues, quarterly magazine published by Business Systems Markets Division, Eastman Kodak Company, Rochester, N.Y.

Wolf, David, and Charles Yerkes, *Microform Retrieval Equipment Guide,* General Services Administration, National Archives and Records Service, Washington, D.C., 1971.

Part Two

Computer Systems

Introduction

N. RICHARD MILLER *Vice President, The Diebold Group, New York, New York*

To a greater degree than one would hope for, application system design is reliant upon the hardware environment in which it will be run. Computer manufacturers, beginning with the third generation of computers appearing around 1965, have steadfastly pursued the doctrine of machine independence for data programs and applications (at least within their own product lines), but this kind of flexibility has been more apparent in the marketing effort than in the reality of implementation.

Many hardware vendors have conducted campaigns in which the theory has been propounded that the designers and programmers of application systems do not have to have substantial knowledge of the machine architecture to fulfill their missions effectively. While this theory is valid in a very limited sense, its realization is by no means typical. As anyone knows who has moved an application system from one machine to another (especially if they are of different manufacture), the transfer. whether made just prior to programming or after implementation, is anything but "transparent" to the user. It is obvious that the more nonuniversal features an application system takes advantage of, the more difficult it will be to reimplement on another machine. (See Part Six of this Section.) And the manufacturers generally provide some almost irresistible nonuniversal features, thus making difficult any vendor switching that a user may be tempted to undertake.

Substantial advantages of efficiency can be secured through the careful tailoring of application systems to specific hardware, and many computer users have chosen to do just that. However, this is done at the expense of maintaining flexibility in hardware selection and configuration in the future, since while these efficiency considerations are often moderately effective in the short term, their long-term impact is usually negative. But it would be unfair to place the entire onus for this upon the manufacturers, for while they may create and provide the attractive nuisances (i.e., unique hardware features), it is the managers of the installations that take advantage of those nuisances.

Many technicians on user staffs have an uncontrollable urge for efficiency —i.e., making the computer behave in the most technologically perfect manner possible—and become infected with the "tinkerer's syndrome," in which more often than not application effectiveness is sacrificed for "efficiency." Sometimes ultimate efficiency is sought with such fervor that the application system never gets into production, or has taken so long to perfect that the hardware has changed in the meantime. Computers in business must run application systems in support of the business activities if they are to be effective: efficiency per se must be a secondary consideration.

Considering the great variety of hardware and the nearly infinite number of combinations in which it can be configured, there is little wonder that many users are bewildered when they try to understand what amounts to a very complicated "Chinese menu." However, it is the trends in computer hardware and systems software technology and their associated costs that are of importance to the manager, not so much the technical details. The basic elements to be considered are the central processing unit (CPU), also known as the mainframe; secondary storage and associated control devices and channels; main memory; systems software such as operating systems; remote computing hardware (e.g., terminal devices), and services (e.g., time-sharing and computer utilities).

Discussions of mainframe computers generally place them into two classifications, scientific and general-purpose (business) computers. The distinction is essentially one of instruction repertoire and speed of solution of a particular type of problem: scientific computing is oriented toward elaborate and lengthy computation, whereas general-purpose computing is adapted to heavy data movement, minor calculation, and the associated substantial amount of data storage and retrieval to and from secondary storage devices. Associated with scientific computing is the analog computer as well as the digital computer, although the business computer is usually the latter. Analog computers are applied especially to simulations of physical phenomena (e.g, mass spectrometry) as well as to sensor-based manufacturing process measurement and control (e.g., an analog computer to control fuel mixtures in a boiler to maintain required temperatures and optimum fuel mix). It is also possible to feed analog data into a digital computer via a converter for analysis, and to send control signals through a converter from digital computers to analog control devices. While such engineering/scientific applications tend to be straightforward and definable, business applications on digital computers are not nearly as susceptible of rigorous specification. This makes hardware and systems (executive) software correspondingly more difficult to select properly.

Perhaps the most important trend to note is the increasing speed of computer mainframes and the substantial reduction in cost per unit of processing. This unit cost has decreased by whole orders of magnitude over the past decade, and it is expected that the trend will continue.

Cost factors for storage units (main memory and auxilliary or secondary storage) are also decreasing, and store/retrieve speeds are increasing. (See Chapter 3 of this Part.) This means that many a candidate for automation which was not cost-beneficial in the past can now be justified.

In addition to batch-oriented computers run in local mode, many remote computing services are available either as company internal services (such as the increasingly popular remote job entry) or as purchased services, e.g., from time-sharing vendors. The essential characteristics of such outside services are (1) the customer pays only for what storage and mainframe time he or she uses; (2) the customer always has access to the computer, although response times may be long during peak hours; (3) a wide variety of application software packages ("canned software") is available for use without each user having to develop his or her own; (4) reliability is continually improving; and (5) costs of various elements of the service are diminishing. (See Section 6.) It is anticipated that once costs have been sufficiently reduced, many households will subscribe to such services for a variety of uses as they now subscribe to telephone service. (See Section 8, Chapter 3.)

While the trend to centralized data processing was encouraged in the 1960s, it appears likely at this writing that decentralized processing will become increasingly the norm through the 1970s and 1980s, as technological advances bring about less and less expensive computers (in relative terms) and their associated peripherals. Satellite computers, ranging from minicomputers to large-scale units, will be located at the source of data (e.g., a branch of a department store to receive inputs concerning inventory and cash register receipts) and report successively through other computers finally to the corporate headquarters. There aggregate data will form the basis of the management information system discussed so much in the past but seldom successfully implemented. In such a network of computers, the variety of combinations staggers the imagination and introduces a markedly higher level of complexity even before we have truly mastered current application potentials.

Chapter 1

Computer Basics

WILLIAM R. FRANTA

**Assistant Professor, Department of Computer, Information,
and Control Sciences, University of Minnesota,
Minneapolis, Minnesota**

To every general statement on computers, an exception exists. In this Chapter on computer basics, by necessity, the objective is to describe the "general" case. It must be recognized, furthermore, that the composition of the "general" case is somewhat dependent upon the author's experience. It is hoped that readers aware of exceptions to statements made in the following paragraphs will also be mindful of the above constraints.

ANALOG AND DIGITAL

Two types of computers have been developed over the years. The generic labels associated with these types are *analog* and *digital*. As the name implies, in an analog computer, direct analogies are made between the variables of the problem to be solved and the variables within the computer. More specifically, the term *analog* is generally meant to imply continuously varying signals (voltages), the values of which correspond by analogy to the values of the variables in the problem being solved. In digital computers, on the other hand, variable values are maintained as sequences of digits rather than as the magnitudes of voltages. Consequently these values vary in discrete steps rather than continuously.

Although capable of slightly more general computations, the analog computer is usually used to solve differential equations. This capability is not as limiting as might first be imagined, for many problems can be cast into the mold of one or more such equations. As evidence of this fact, consider the models of urban and then world dynamics popularized by J. Forrester of M.I.T.[1] These models consist of sets of interrelated differential equations.

Since the analog computer has the potential to do many activities in parallel, the time required to solve a set of equations is usually the same as that to solve a single equation. The digital machine operates in a more sequential manner, so that a digital machine requires more time to solve a set of equations than is required to solve a single equa-

---

[1] J. Forrester. *Urban Dynamics*, M.I.T., Cambridge, Mass., 1969.

tion. These considerations appear to give the analog machine a net advantage over the digital, at least when solving sets of differential equations. Such is, however, usually not the case. This apparent anomaly is explained as follows. First, the capacity of analog equipment can be measured in basic units of varying types, known as *components*. The number and complexity of the differential equations being solved determines the number of components necessary to compute the solution. Many problems simply require more components than are available.

Second, because of the electrical nature of the analog components together with a need to produce digitized outputs, analog computations are limited to approximately four digits of accuracy. For many problems this is simply inadequate. Finally, analog components are subject to a phenomenon known as *drift*, which results in a component's deviation from its normal operating characteristics. Unless components are occasionally adjusted (aligned), the effects of drift can adversely affect solution accuracy.

Additional factors such as storage capacity and programming ease are also vital considerations in the assessment of analog and digital machines. The digital machine by its nature allows for the storage of far more information, in the form of digitized numeric values, than does the analog. This consideration alone makes activities such as customer billing nearly impossible for analog equipment. Programming ease qualitatively indicates the human effort necessary to place the problem, or more aptly the solution method, in a form suitable for presentation to the machine. In most cases the digital requires less effort. These considerations taken together show the digital computer to be the more viable and flexible machine.

For these reasons, although analog equipment is still used, digital machines predominate, and the remaining portions of this Chapter are devoted to them alone. We note in passing, however, that analog and digital machines can be connected (for intermachine passing of information), and made to operate in parallel toward the solution of a problem. This arrangement is generally referred to as a *hybrid* computer. If the work necessary to the solution process is appropriately assigned so as to take advantage of the unique capabilities of each machine type, and if the requirements on accuracy are not too stringent, the hybrid unit can simplify and speed the solution process for many problems.

GENERAL DESCRIPTION

A few pertinent notions relating to computers are presented at this point, and further elaborated upon in the following Chapter sections.

To begin, we may say that the elements of a computer system can be separated into two major sections, namely, equipment or *hardware elements,* and programmed or *software elements.* The hardware elements usually include a central processing unit (CPU), auxiliary storage, and input-output devices. (See Figure 1-1.) The central processing unit is the heart of the computer. It is the unit that contains the circuitry which controls the operation of input-output devices, and which obeys (executes) the computer program held in its associated storage unit. It must be realized that the central processing unit can manipulate only data that have been stored in its associated memory device. Similarly, programs must be placed in main memory to be eligible for execution. To mitigate this necessity, the CPU is capable of initiating and controlling the transfer of information from main memory to and from any of several input-output devices.

For most machines, information (i.e., data and/or programs) is stored and processed in the form of bits, the elements of a number system (binary) containing only the digits 0 and 1. Such a system is convenient as it is realizable in devices which are either *on* (0) or *off* (1). The binary system is quite adequate, furthermore, to represent not only numbers but symbols as well. The latter is accomplished by interpreting a series of bits as an encoded representation of the symbol. Figure 1-2 gives several examples.

Any given sequence of bits may represent an alphabetic character or characters or a numeric value. The distinction is one of context rather than form, and is determined and controlled by the program.

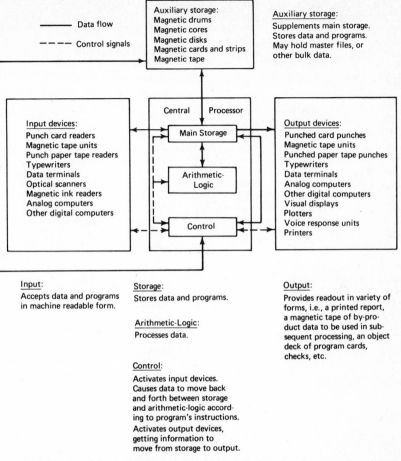

_____ Data flow

- - - - - Control signals

Fig. 1-1 **Functions of Computer Hardware.** (From Chapter 9-5, by Edward A. Tomeski and George Stephenson, in Carl Heyel (ed.), _Handbook of Modern Office Management and Administrative Services_, McGraw-Hill, New York, 1972.)

EARLY DEVELOPMENTS

The ancestry of both electronic analog and digital computers can be traced to mechanical devices, the first of which appeared in the seventeenth century. During the 1630s, W. Schickard developed a somewhat unreliable mechanical calculator in Tubingen, Germany. The first mechanical analog unit is perhaps the planimeter, a device developed by J. H. Herman about the year 1814, and used to evaluate the area bounded by a contour.

Continuing to outline the development of digital devices, we may cite as the next seminal development Blaise Pascal's adding machine built in 1641. Pascal's device exhibited the same

Decimal number	Binary equivalent
1	000001
5	000101
23	010111
(etc.)	
Alphabet	
A	010001
B	010010
(etc.)	

Fig. 1-2 **Example of binary coding.**

propensity for failure as Schickard's. Improvements by the mathematician G. W. Leibnitz resulted, in 1874, in the first desk calculator to be manufactured and marketed in quantity. Leibnitz made a further contribution by developing an arithmetic based only on the digits 0 and 1, i.e., binary arithmetic.

During the years 1823 to 1833, C. Babbage designed a mechanical computer based upon the arithmetic of Leibnitz. As pointed out below, Babbage's machine exhibited many of the main features of modern electronic computers. Unfortunately his ideas, although sound, were beyond the technical capabilities of his time, and he never realized an operational model of his design. Remarkably, his ideas lay unused until the 1930s, although technology was sufficiently sophisticated to have made possible a realization of his machine by the year 1910.

In 1934 Konrad Zuse, working in Berlin, Germany, began the construction of a mechanical digital computer. The machine became operational in 1937. He later perfected a revised version of the machine using electromechanical relays, which became operational in 1941.

In 1939 construction of an electromechanical computer, later known as the Harvard Mark I, was begun and directed by Howard Aiken. The design specified that the machine be controlled by orders encoded and punched on a paper tape, and further that it have the capacity to retain 72 numbers of 23 digits each. Data were to be supplied on punched cards. It was completed in 1944.

Aiken's machine, as well as those of Zuse and Babbage, exhibited many of the features of the modern-day computer. They all, for example, possessed some limited capability for retaining numbers and performing arithmetic. Furthermore, in each case, some provision was made for controlling and/or ordering the operations to be performed. In the case of the Mark I, control was provided by an encoded paper tape, while Babbage prescribed encoded punched cards. These provisions were most necessary, since all these machines were designed as general-purpose devices. That is, the designs did not restrict their applicability to the solution of any specific problem. It was intended, rather, that they could be used to solve a wide range of problems. Under these circumstances it is necessary to coordinate the arithmetic operations of the device with the computational recipe used to achieve the desired solution. The set of problems which could be solved was, quite obviously, limited by the availability of a computational recipe, computation speed, and the amount of numbers which the machine could retain. For many applications the ultimate constraints were those of speed and storage, limitations inherent in the mechanical nature of the machines.

The First Electronic Computer   The prospect of replacing mechanical and/or electromechanical components by electronic circuits promised to enhance significantly the speed and storage capacity of machines. A computing instrument designated the ENIAC (Electronic Numerical Integrator and Calculator) is generally regarded to be the first electronic computer. It was developed by J. P. Eckert, J. W. Mauchly, and coworkers at the University of Pennsylvania, and was completed in 1946. It contained nearly 18,000 vacuum tubes, the majority of which were obliged to operate if the machine was to function. Despite this demanding criterion, the machine was quite successful as evidenced by the fact that it was used at the Ballistic Research Laboratories in Aberdeen, Maryland, for scientific calculations from 1946 until late 1955.

The machine was somewhat awkward to use, in that the sequence which controlled the calculation, as well as numeric data, was specified by setting some portion of over 6,000 switches on a control panel. Further selections were made by appropriate plug wire patterns also established on the control panel. This specification convention, although flexible, meant that the changing of control sequences required considerable time, owing to the lengthy setup times which necessarily preceded the computations. It was fairly probable, furthermore, that altering a significant number of switches resulted in several that were inappropriately set. Such a contingency is especially likely if the switches are multiposition as was true on the ENIAC. Since inappropriately set switches could significantly, if not disastrously, affect the results of the computation sequence, much time-consuming checking was necessary to ensure correct settings. The situation could have been much improved if the specification of the computation could have been more easily manipulated by the programmer, and routinely placed in and removed from the machine as required. Machines following ENIAC, including all modern computers, possess features which provide this capability.

The difficulty described above is circumvented by the structure of the *stored-program computer* described in a report published in 1946.[2] As an indication of the stability of the basic notions outlined in that report, we can safely state that they apply quite well to all modern machines.

BASICS OF MODERN MACHINES

The modern stored-program computer is characterized by possessing four basic units responsible for the functions of *storage, control, arithmetic,* and *input-output.*

Storage   The storage unit consists schematically of a fixed number of "slots," each capable of retaining a fixed-length number. The slots can logically and physically be thought of as organized in a linear array within the device. The individual slots can then be labeled by an index number J, such that the value of J ranges from 0 to $N-1$ for a device containing n slots. Since the relationship between index number and slot is 1:1, any slot within the linear assemblage can be identified by stating its index number. In computer terminology the slots are known as *words,* and the index number associated with a given word is referred to as the *address* of the word.

Control   The control sequence is reduced to a numerical code and placed in the storage device along with the data associated with the computation. The set of operations allowed by the machine is known as the *order code,* while the sequence of orders selected to effect a computation is known as a *program.* It is the function of the control unit to locate the encoded instructions in the storage device, in the order necessary to effect the desired computation, and direct the arithmetic and/or input-output units to obey them.

To expedite the control function, most machines are constructed so that the control unit maintains, in a device known as the *program address register,* the address of the word containing the instruction being executed. The control unit normally assumes that the address of the word containing the next instruction is that word whose address is obtained by adding 1 to the current value of the program address register. The control unit can then ensure that the entire program is obeyed by cyclicly performing the following steps:[3]

1. Fetch from memory the instruction found in the word pointed to by the program address register.

2. Increment the program address register by 1. This is done without the aid of the arithmetic unit.

3. Cause the order just fetched to be obeyed.

To initiate the computation, the program must be placed in the storage unit, and the program address register set to the address of the first instruction. These tasks are usually performed under the direction of a supervisory program, to be discussed below.

It should be pointed out that since the program is stored in the machine as a sequence of numbers, it is self-modifiable. That is, the orders of the program can be thought of as data, eligible for use in arithmetic operations. Thus, programs can freely operate upon themselves, i.e., *alter their own composition.* The computational sequence can, therefore, be dynamically controlled by the program itself, alterations being made, for example, on the basis of intermediately computed values.

Input-Output   The input-output unit provides the tie between the storage unit, and thus the control unit, and the outside world. It is responsible for directing the transmission of numbers, hence information, from words in memory to and from the set of peripheral devices connected to the machine. The number and nature of the devices so connected depend upon many factors and are discussed in Chapter 2 of this Part. The input-output process is generally quite slow in relation to the computation speed of the control and arithmetic units, because of the physical nature of the peripheral devices. Often, on the other hand, data for a given program must be transferred periodically to and from peripheral devices. These conditions are mitigated by the possible parallelism now described.

---

[2] A. H. Taub (ed.), *Collected Works of John von Neuman,* Macmillan, New York, 1963, vol. 5.

[3] A provision to deviate from this sequence is also necessary. It is usually provided by the "jump" instructions contained in the order code set. See Part Four, Chapter 2, "Programming Techniques," in this Section, for further elaborations.

As stated earlier, the data transfers are initiated by the control unit in response to program orders. Once initiated, however, the input-output unit is usually able to effect the transfer independently of, and in parallel with, the activities of the control unit. Hardware components are usually included, furthermore, so that the control unit can be notified of the completion of a previously requested transfer. Thus the arithmetic and control units need not stand idle while input-output transfers are performed. The ability to overlap computational and input-output transfers for a program can in many instances be employed to minimize the control unit idle time sustained. This in turn increases computer utilization and shortens the time required to complete a computation. More will be said of this later. The concept of multiprogramming (see Part Four, Chapter 1, in this Section) was also conceived to reduce the potential idle time still further.

Arithmetic Unit The component not yet discussed, namely the arithmetic unit, is usually generalized in nature and can perform functions in addition to the standard operations of addition, subtraction, multiplication, and division. These additional functions generally include, for example, Boolean and cyclical permutation, or shifting operations. Most arithmetic units, and thus, computers, are designed and built to perform arithmetic on numbers expressed in binary notation, as previously indicated. Correspondingly, the words of the storage unit must be considered as consisting of a fixed number of binary digits.

Integer and "Floating-Point" Formats. Obviously, not all computations will produce integer numbers as results. Thus computer arithmetic must be capable of dealing with mixed numbers, i.e., numbers in the form of $xxx.xxx$, where the digits to the left of the period represent an integer, and the digits to the right represent the fractional part of the number. In daily life, where we are accustomed to dealing with the decimal system, the period is referred to as the decimal point. The digits to the right represent successive fractions formed by the powers of 10 in the denominator. Thus, $457.312 = 4 \times 10^2 + 5 \times 10^1 + 7 \times 10^0 + 3 \times \frac{1}{10} + 1 \times \frac{1}{100} + 2 \times \frac{1}{1000}$. In exponential notation, the portion to the right of the decimal is expressed as $3 \times 10^{-1} + 1 \times 10^{-2} + 2 \times 10^{-3}$.

Since computers usually do arithmetic in base 2 or 16, rather than 10, the period is referred to as the *base point*. Just as in the above example, digits to the right of the base point represent fractions of the powers of the base. Thus in binary representation, $101.110 = 1 \times 2^2 + 0 \times 2^1 + 1 \times 2^0 + 1 \times 2^{-1} + 1 \times 2^{-2} + 0 \times 2^{-3}$.

When formulating a scheme to handle mixed numbers, we must remember that since the word size is fixed, we wish to retain as many significant digits as possible, and we wish to represent very large as well as very small numbers. These goals are usually achieved in computers by consistently retaining a fixed number of digits, by assuming that the base point is located at one or the other end of the digits, and by specifying a second number, the exponent, which indicates how the given base point must be moved to represent the actual number.[4]

As might be expected, the two formats possess distinct virtues. The range of numbers which can be represented in the floating-point format generally far exceeds the capabilities of the integral format. On the other hand, integral representations are

---

[4] For an n-bit machine word, the largest binary integral number, i, which can be represented is, then, 2^{n-1}. In the "floating-point" format, the numbers are represented as $c \cdot b^m$, where (in binary) $b = 2$. For most machines, m is an integral quantity, while c is either a fractional or an integral quantity. Since the base number can be assumed by the arithmetic unit when manipulating floating-point quantities, only the values of m and c need be retained.

The usual procedure employed to retain both parts considers a word containing a floating-point number as divided into two segments, with both quantities packed into the word. A larger portion of the bit positions is usually reserved for the representation of c, the significant digits of the number. If the division specifies that k of n bits are used to specify the exponent m, and the remaining $n - k$ to represent c, then the largest binary number which can be represented is bounded above by 2^{2^k}, assuming c a fraction. Since provision is made for signed arithmetic, the corresponding lower bounds for negative integral and floating-point numbers would be -2^n and -2^{2^k}, while the smallest nonzero numbers, in magnitude, which can be represented would be 1 and 2^{-2^k}.

Actually, the above bounds must be considered approximations only (but sharp approximations) in that we have not deducted bit positions in either c, m, or i which must necessarily be used to represent the signs of the numbers. We add in passing that many machines manipulate numbers using a base 16 representation, known as *hexadecimal*. This is effected by manipulating and interpreting bit positions in groups of four.

exact, whereas floating-point representations are not. Adding two integral values together, for example, results in an exact integral value so long as the range restriction of the format, i.e., the number of bits that can be accommodated, is not exceeded. In other words, the magnitude of the sum is less than 2^n. · On the other hand, not every real number whose magnitude is between 2^{-2^k} and 2^{2^k} possesses a floating-point representation. Upon entry of a real number into the machine or following an arithmetic operation involving floating-point numbers, a rounding operation is usually necessary, which in essence forces the number to be represented by its nearest neighbor on the real number line which possesses a floating-point representation. This slight loss of accuracy is usually quite acceptable in computations in light of the possible extended range.

The inclusion of the two numeric formats does necessitate the inclusion of two sets of arithmetic commands within the order code of the machine. An arithmetic operation involving operands of unlike format is usually not allowed. Since the equivalents of the disallowed operations is desirable, provision either by short programs or order code is usually provided to transform numbers from one format to the other.

GENERATIONS OF MACHINES

Attempts to provide a broad classification of computer systems usually appeal to the notion of "generations" of machines. Labeling a machine as first-, second-, or third-generation equipment supposedly identifies, without explicit enumeration, the hardware-software features associated with it. The usual classification segments the period 1940 to date into three intervals, each corresponding to the basic development period of a generation of equipment.

Machines developed during the period 1940–1950 are referred to as first generation, those developed between 1950 and 1960 as second generation, and those developed during the period 1960 to present as third. Although some manufacturers may claim to have marketed "fourth-generation" systems, none to date seem to warrant that distinction.

In reality, the intervals of development are not as clear-cut as the segmentation would suggest. Nonetheless the classification is useful.

Associating a computer with any given generation characterizes both the hardware and software attributes of the machine. As the generation number increases, so generally does the machine computation speed and memory size, while the support software, that is, the executive and related programs, becomes more sophisticated.

A summary of certain salient features of the three generations is given in Table 1-1. A similar table has been prepared by Denning.[5] Not reflected in the table is the emphasis and technique, indicated below, that have affected computing.

First Generation First-generation machines were designed mainly for scientific and/or military computation. Each user of the machine could be considered an expert on computers. Each expected programming to be time-consuming and difficult. Since support software was usually nonexistent, each user generally entered his or her program into machine memory and controlled the computation by directly manipulating switches and/or buttons on the machine control panel (console).

Since the user was intimately familiar with the program, the user often detected coding errors by visually monitoring the executing program on the machine's console. Errors could then, oftentime, be patched immediately and the computation continued. The absence of support software implied, furthermore, that routines to calculate special mathematical functions (for example, square roots or trigonometric functions) would be coded and placed in memory by the user.

Scheduling of the machine was generally done by a log book, into which each user noted the hours during which he or she desired contact with the machine. Since programs were generally written directly as sequences of digits, finding and correcting errors in programs once entered into the machine (debugging) was often quite time-consuming. For lengthy computations, it was furthermore desirable periodically to produce and record on paper tape, cards, or drum a description of the state of the program. This ensured that the computation could be restarted from the last such record, rather than from the beginning, if a machine failure occurred before the computation had completed.

[5] Peter Denning, "Third Generation Computer Systems," *Computing Surveys*, December, 1971.

To complicate matters further, the small memory size, coupled with relatively slow speed, meant that many ingenious ad hoc coding schemes were used to reduce the size of programs and/or the amount of intermediate input-output required. This often reduced the readability of programs to nil. These factors narrowed the applicability of computers considerably.

Second Generation By the exploitation of core memory and circuits based upon transistors, second-generation machines realized significant increases in speed and reliability over first-generation equipment. The inclusion of hardware to support floating-point arithmetic and "interrupt" handling represented, as explained below, further significant improvements. These features were further augmented by much improved secondary storage devices.

TABLE 1-1   Salient Features of the Three Generations of Computers

Characteristics	Generation		
	First	Second	Third
Components	Vacuum tube	Transistors	Transistors or integrated circuits
Component operation time	0.1–1.0 ms	1–10 μs	0.1–1.0 μs
Processor memory technology	Electrostatic tubes or delay lines	Magnetic core	Magnetic core semiconductor registers (cache)
Memory–size in words (typical)	1–4K words	4–32K	32–300K
Memory–access time	1 ms	1–10 μs	0.1–1.0 μs
Machine–mean time to failure	Minutes–hours	Days	Early sixties, minutes–hours (failure usually due to software collapse); late sixties, many hours–days
Auxiliary memory types	Delay lines, paper tape, cards	Cards, magnetic tape, drums, disks	Same as second plus mass core, extended core

K$= 1024 = 2^{10}$; m$=$ milli $= 10^{-3}$; $\mu =$ micro $= 10^{-6}$.

During the first years of their existence, many second-generation machines were used in the manner outlined above for first-generation equipment. It soon became apparent, however, that such conditions did not foster the realization of such a machine's full potential. Increased utilization and productivity were achieved by a combination of developments, all contrived to reduce the time necessary to prepare and debug a program.[6]

Floating Points. The inclusion of floating-point arithmetic significantly reduced the time required to prepare programs, for it relieved the user of the necessity of carefully examining the computational algorithm and estimating the magnitude of all quantities formed, because the hardware associated with floating-point arithmetic ensures that the task is handled automatically and dynamically by the arithmetic unit. Quite obviously the time required to execute a program was also significantly reduced, since floating-point hardware obviated much coding otherwise necessary to bookkeeping operations associated with scaling numbers.

[6] We are thus equating potential with measures of machine utilization and throughput, i.e., the rate at which programs are processed.

Eliminating the need explicitly to scale numbers, however, removed the incentive to analyze rigorously the computation prior to executing the program.[7] Without such analysis, programs are more apt to attempt the formation of numbers, via the arithmetic process, that are too large for representation. Since the inability to represent the result of an arithmetic operation may invalidate the computation, it is generally desirable that a record of the violation be made and/or program execution aborted.

Interrupt. The interrupt mechanism greatly facilitates this checking. The interrupt hardware allows the control unit automatically to deviate from normal execution and execute a special program (designated the *interrupt handler*) upon receipt of a signal from the arithmetic unit that an attempt had been made to form an "illegal" operand. The interrupt handler can ignore the signal and instruct the control unit to continue executing the program which generated the error, or can "handle" the error condition in any number of ways. An immediate generalization provides similar "interrupt handling" on the other abnormal arithmetic conditions such as division by zero, etc.

An alternative approach to the detection of error conditions requires the inclusion within the order code of instructions which can be used to interrogate the arithmetic unit following each arithmetic operation. The use of interrupt to provide information on abnormal arithmetic processes is superior in terms of program length and preparation time.

Buffered Interrupt. A second hardware feature designed to decrease program execution time and included in second-generation hardware allows the computation and input-output processes associated with a given program to operate in parallel. Such a parallelism is generally referred to as a *buffered input-output capability*. To effect this parallelism, the input-output instructions of the order code must be of the initiate type only. That is, they are not handled to completion by the control unit before an attempt is made to obey the next sequential instruction. Rather, the associated input-output channel (in reality a rudimentary computer) is notified of the instruction, and it is then the responsibility of the control hardware associated with the channel to complete the data transfer.

Under these circumstances it becomes desirable to notify the program easily when the transfer is complete. This is necessary in order that memory areas involved in the data transfer are not used prior to completion of the transfer. Notification of completion is easily handled by expanding the interrupt mechanism capability. If so done, upon receipt of a signal from the input-output unit, the control deviates from obeying the executing program (that is, the program is interrupted), and begins executing a program especially written to process such signals. The processing may involve nothing more than setting a word, usually designated by the program which initiates the input-output transfer, to a value which by convention designates that the transfer is complete. The interrupt handler program can then instruct the control to continue executing the normal program from the point of interrupt.

If the concept of interrupt is generalized, immediate notification of anomalous or error conditions arising within the external or peripheral equipment can also be given the program. Quite obviously, the ability of a program to overlap computation and input-output is constrained by the logic of the computation, as represented by the program.

Support Programs. Certain support programs were also developed during the period associated with second-generation equipment. The utility of these programs was greatly facilitated by auxiliary storage devices which could be directed by program, rather than human, control. For example, a short "boot strap" program placed in machine memory by some means, could search for, find, transfer to main memory, and cause to be executed a program stored on an auxiliary storage device.

Obvious candidates for storage are programs which calculate commonly used functions. Such programs could then be developed, be placed upon the device, and be easily made available to all computations which required them. Such a collected store of programs is known as a *program library*. Since many programs so stored generally perform but a portion of a computation, they are known as *subprograms*, or *subroutines*.

---

[7] For a detailed account of scaling, see M. Stein and W. Munro, *Introduction to Machine Arithmetic*, Addison-Wesley, Reading, Mass., 1971, Chap. 7.

This procedure results in maximum flexibility while still relieving many machine users of complex programming tasks. For example, suppose that our computation demands that we calculate the square root of the return on an initial amount x invested for n periods at a compound rate of r per period. It is not inconceivable that the program library contains a routine for calculating $\sqrt{y}$, for arbitrary y, and a routine named, say, RET, for calculating the return mentioned. Our desired computation is then effected by simply writing $\sqrt{\text{RET}(x,r,n)}$ or, employing a more normal programming syntax, as SQRT(RET(x,r,n)). Be mindful that it is our *third* program which is referencing (i.e., causing to be executed) the other two. As is hopefully obvious, the reverse, RET(SQRT(X),r,n), and other combinations are also possible.

For this concept to be useful, the referencing program must be able to "link" with the desired routines stored on the device. For this reason, a program which locates and transfers the routines to main memory, and makes the referencing program aware of their placement, was developed and became known as a *loader program* or *linking loader*.

Two final remarks about these library programs are in order. First, as discussed in Part Four, Chapter 1, in this Section, the addresses used in conjunction with various instructions in a program are dependent upon the placement of the program in memory. Since the number and length of the subset of available subprograms referenced by any computation must, for flexibility, be completely arbitrary, the ultimate placement of any subprogram in memory cannot be known in advance of the "link" request. For this reason the library programs are sorted in a format in which the addresses can be adjusted, or specified, following the transfer of the subprogram to memory. This format is known as *relocatable binary*. Finally, if we allow subprograms to reference other subprograms, the generality is complete. A computation might then be specified as a collection of modules (programs and/or subprograms) from the library and a specification of which module should begin the computation.

Other support programs developed during this period include the assembly program and the FORTRAN compiler; the former around 1953, FORTRAN in 1957. Both were, of course, designed to reduce program preparation time. Both provide the means by which programs can be written in symbolic form with the reduction from symbols to integral numbers, that is, to machine code, being performed by the assembly program or the FORTRAN compiler. These reductions are known as the *assembly* and *complication* processes, respectively.

The assembly program statements mirror the machine order code, whereas FORTRAN statements are, in the main, machine-independent. For flexibility, and convenience, the processing (translation) programs associated with each of these languages are kept upon auxiliary storage along with the subroutine library. (See Part Four, Chapter 3, in this Section.)

Executive Program. The full potential of the machine with the complement of translation and subprograms found in the program library was realized as a result of the executive program. Development of executive programs began in the late 1950s. Such programs are assigned to eliminate the human operator in order better to utilize the equipment while still maintaining flexibility. These executive programs are also called *resident* routines, since in order to be useful they were required to be in memory at all times. The basic tasks handled by executive programs associated with second-generation equipment include: (1) limited scheduling of jobs, (2) collection and recording of accounting information, (3) handling of interrupt requests, and (4) handling of service requests. Since task 3 was discussed earlier and the meaning of task 2 is obvious, they do not receive treatment here. Tasks 1 and 4, however, require some elaboration.

Limited scheduling allowed decks of cards, representing a collection of independent computations (jobs), literally to be stacked on an input device, say the card reader. The executive program would monitor the device and "process" each job in turn. For this reason such executive programs became known as *batch monitors*. Batch processing was facilitated by the invention of command languages. Statements in these languages direct the executive program's processing of the job deck. They signal, for example, requests for the loading and/or execution of programs from the program library, including support programs such as the assembly program and FORTRAN compiler. Others might specify evocation of additional support programs designed to allocate equipment to jobs, to build, save, and alter program libraries, or to transfer blocks of data from device to device. By the early sixties the command language and executive programs found on most second-generation equipment were quite sophisticated indeed.

The availability of second-generation machines precipitated a rapid demise of first-generation equipment. The arrival of third-generation computers did not, however, have a similar effect upon those of the second generation. In fact, during the seventies many second-generation systems continue to operate quite effectively.

Third Generation In view of the coverage of later chapters, only highlights of this most significant generation are given here.

To begin with, in terms of basic hardware, the distinctions between second- and third-generation machines are not as clearly delineated as those between first and second. This is partially demonstrated by Table 1-1. The designation of a machine as third generation is partially dependent upon the machine's ability to support a subset of such features as multiprogramming, multiprocessing, time sharing, remote job entry, complete executive program scheduling of jobs, and a plethora of programming languages and program libraries.[8] Usually, moreover, they provide all the features discussed above for second-generation machines, only more so. In some cases, these features are facilitated by the support of hardware-software devices known as *paging* and *segmentation.*

Many third-generation machines were conceived as "giants," supposedly capable of handling all computing chores, including scientific computation, data processing, management information systems, information retrieval, etc., in many cases from time-sharing terminals. The initial performance of many of these systems was disappointing. This author, for example, ran several programs on one third-generation machine (in 1967) which required far more time to complete than they did on a much slower second-generation machine.

The reason for the unexpected failure lay in the complexity of the executive program. In attempting to support multiprogramming, internal scheduling, and the like, executive programs for third-generation machines became very extensive. Furthermore, the lack of adequate algorithms for automatically scheduling many resources among competing concurrent activities, that is, programs in the multiprogramming-multiprocessing environment, implied logically complex executive programs. This complexity coupled with their extensive size (in instructions) often caused the executive routines to be poorly designed, as well as poorly coded and debugged. The end result was often complete collapse of the system.

These early failures precipitated endless modeling and analysis efforts, mainly within university centers, which attempted to understand the reasons for and then correct the observed performance failure. This analysis activity was aided by performance data obtained from existing systems, collected by automatic data collection programs included within often hastily modified executive programs. (In more recent systems performance monitoring requirements are considered at the system design stage.)

The resulting analysis has provided many deep insights concerning system performance and has spawned many excellent allocation procedures. Only recently, however, have third-generation systems approached their original performance expectations. Most systems remain weak, however, in the critically important area of data security. That is, many systems process and retain "sensitive" data in auxiliary storage. In order to ensure that only authorized users gain access to the material, several levels of security are required. Some users may, for example, be authorized to use but not alter data, while others must be authorized to alter and/or extend the data set. At this writing, a considerable number of potentially useful procedures for security have been devised, but few have received extensive trial use. The importance of these security measures cannot be stressed too strongly in view of current observable trends in the use of large computer systems.[9]

[8] Complete executive program scheduling of jobs allows submitted jobs to be queued on secondary storage and executed at the discretion of the executive program in accordance with some scheduling policy or algorithm.

[9] See Section 8, Chapter 4, "The Computer and Privacy."

GENERAL CONSIDERATIONS

Costs   To give the prices of specific systems would be of limited value.   It would seem more useful to point out that the cost of computing equipment has been falling steadily since the fifties.   Some costs, such as those associated with logic circuitry and on-line storage, have been falling at an exponential rate.   Martin and Norman[10] state that circuit costs have been decreasing by a factor of 10 every 5 years.   This decrease in costs is, furthermore, in the face of decreased machine size and increased speed, both also changing at exponential rates.   Foster[11] believes that minicomputers occupying a single "chip" based on large-scale integration circuitry can soon be produced for around $3.

The costs and capacities of on-line storage have similarly changed.   Typical capacities have increased from 10^6 bits in 1955 to 10^{12} bits in the seventies, while costs have dropped significantly.   There are no indications these trends will not continue.

While the costs of equipment have been dropping, the costs for programming and related services have been increasing.   For many third-generation machines, the hardware development costs represent but a fraction of the costs associated with the development of executive and support programs (including language processors).   Relief from the exhorbitant programming costs is being sought in many ways, including improved programming techniques and program sharing.

Business Data Processing and Information Processing   Hardware designed to facilitate business data processing is usually provided by including instructions in the order code for manipulating characters and/or performing decimal arithmetic.   Character representation is effected by encoding schemes which usually require 6 to 8 bits per character, thus allowing for the representation of 64 to 256 unique characters. To conserve storage, text is usually stored in the form of several characters to a computer word.   On machines not in possession of character commands, manipulation of specific characters within a word can be time-consuming.   Character commands, on the other hand, usually allow specific character positions within a word to be referenced and/or altered.   Although such commands do not theoretically increase machine capability, they aid in reducing program length and preparation time.

"Information processing," as distinguished from "number manipulation," is usually characterized by a low ratio of arithmetic command to decision command, and a large data transfer requirement.   The reduction of data from a space probe or the manipulation of billing or accounting data are representative examples.   For efficient information processing, the system's auxiliary storage devices must be fast, and of large capacity and low cost.   These conditions are met by most third-generation systems.   Although scientific computation will always remain an important computing activity, it represents an ever-decreasing portion of the total computing spectrum.

Increased emphasis is now being placed on applications relating to education, computer-aided instruction, law enforcement, information retrieval, management information systems, real-time transaction systems, and the like.   Each area requires the development of specific methodologies.   All are related, however, in that they represent information processing activities.

Time Sharing   Considerable effort must yet be expended in the development of executive and support programs for time-sharing environments.   Work remains to be done, for example, in the development of resource allocation policies and algorithms, information storage and retrieval algorithms, data security and file management algorithms, etc.

It has become desirable, furthermore, not only for people to communicate with computers via telecommunications systems, but for computers to communicate with other computers by the same means.   This precipitates networks of computers and thus facilitates the sharing of data and programs among machines composing the network.[12]

Supercomputers   The development of supercomputers, mostly for scientific applications, continues.   The result of many of these efforts can aptly be labeled fourth-generation machines.   Two typical examples are the STAR-100 machine (developed

---

[10] James Martin and Adrian Norman, *The Computerized Society*, Prentice-Hall, Englewood Cliffs, N.J., 1970.

[11] Caxton C. Foster, "A View of Computer Architecture," *Communications of ACM*, July, 1972.

[12] See Section 6, Chapter 5, "Interactive Teleprocessing Network Services."

by Control Data Corporation) and the ILLIAC-IV (developed by the University of Illinois and the Burroughs Corporation). These machines achieve remarkable computation rates by operating on several sets of operands in a parallel (ILLIAC-IV) or pipeline (STAR-100) fashion.[13]

Minicomputers Increased emphasis is being placed on minicomputers, especially if they can be connected to form a supercomputer. A mini, in such a conceptualization, might be assigned to each major task performed, say, by the executive program of a third-generation system. The design would provide for flexible, easily expandable, hardware-software systems, each more easily tailored to a specific workload than existing third-generation systems.[14]

SELECTIVE BIBLIOGRAPHY

Communications of ACM, Anniversary Issue, Association for Computing Machinery, July, 1972.
  Denning, Peter J., "Third Generation Computer Systems," *Computing Surveys*, December, 1971.
Goldstine, Herman H., *The Computer from Pascal to Von Neumann*, Princeton University, Princeton, N.J., 1972.
Heyel, Carl, *Computers, Office Machines, and the New Information Technology*, Macmillan, New York, 1969.
——— (ed.), *Handbook of Modern Office Management and Administrative Services*, sec. 9, "Data Processing: Mechanization and Automation," McGraw-Hill, New York, 1972.
Martin, James, *Telecommunications and the Computer*, Prentice-Hall, Englewood Cliffs, N.J., 1969.
Pylyshyn, Zenon W. (ed.), *Perspectives on the Computer Revolution*, Prentice-Hall, Englewood Cliffs, N.J., 1970.
Rosen, Saul, "Electronic Computers: A Historical Survey," *Computing Surveys*, March, 1969.
Rosin, Robert F., "Supervisory and Monitor Systems," *Computing Surveys*, March, 1969.

[13] For a discussion of these concepts, see D. L. Slotnick, "The Fastest Computer," *Scientific American*, February, 1971; and William R. Graham, "The Parallel and the Pipeline Computers," *Datamation*, April, 1970.

[14] See Chapter 4, "Minicomputers," in this Part.

Chapter 2

Auxiliary Memories

DONALD L. BOYD

**Assistant Professor, Department of Computer Sciences,
University of Minnesota, Minneapolis, Minnesota**

One feature of computers which distinguishes them from other forms of calculating devices is their ability to store, to retrieve, and to modify information. A computer system can be defined as a collection of resources which maintain and manipulate information. Among these resources are information and hardware devices which maintain the information. Information consists of programs (the collection of instructions which, when applied to the computing system, implement an algorithm of manipulation) and data (the collection of information which defines an application of the program). The hardware devices for maintaining information are called *storage systems* or simply *memory*.

The Hierarchy of Memories The storage system of a computer forms a hierarchy of memories, beginning with devices which retain a small amount of information and allow very fast access, and continuing down to devices which retain massive amounts of information, but require more time for its access. This memory hierarchy is divided into two principal types, *main memory* and *auxiliary (or secondary) memory*. This division is defined primarily by the mechanism for accessing the stored information. In main memory, information is accessed directly by an instruction of the central processor and the same amount of time is required to access any stored unit of information. In most auxiliary memories, the accessing mechanism must move from its current position of access to the next position of access, thus requiring a varying amount time between accesses, depending on the distance between positions of access. Another distinguishing feature is that the instructions of a program may be accessed and executed directly from main memory, whereas information from most auxiliary memories must be transferred to main memory before direct access can take place. The transfer of information from auxiliary to main memory is known as *reading*, while the transfer of information from main to auxiliary memory is known as *writing*.

Auxiliary memories are further divided into two general classes, distinguished by their access and recording techniques. The *sequential* access devices require that information be recorded in an ordered fashion, and accessing a particular unit of information may require the accessing mechanism to pass over previously recorded information before arriving at the desired information. Examples of sequential devices are paper tapes and magnetic tapes. The other class of auxiliary memory devices allows accesses similar to that of main memory, and is referred to as *random-access* or *direct-access devices*. The accessing mechanism allows direct passage between units of information. Some random-access devices are disk, drum, and bulk storage devices such as the slow-access-time core storages of both IBM and Control Data Corporation (CDC). Information may be recorded and accessed sequentially on random-access devices as well as on sequential devices.

The medium used for storage of information is often referred to as the *storage medium* or *volume*. The recording and accessing mechanism is referred to as the *unit*. A different way of classifying auxiliary memories is by the length of time information' is to be stored. The *long-term* auxiliary memory devices allow the storage medium to be removed from the unit for permanent storage, whereas the *medium-term* auxiliary memory devices do not physically have this capability.

The medium-term storage devices are normally on-line to the computer system, and are generally used by the operating system or user programs for temporary storage of information. Information stored on these devices is often in a machine-readable form requiring little or no transformation when read into main memory. Examples of these devices are bulk magnetic core, drums, and some disks.

With the long-term storage devices, the storage medium may, as stated, be removed from the unit, allowing the recorded information to be retained indefinitely. This action may cause temporary delays in information accesses, since the storage medium may not be on-line, and it must be mounted on the unit. However, a convenience is achieved with these devices because they allow information to be transferred from one computer system to another by simply transferring the storage medium. To achieve this capability, information is often recorded on the device using standard codes which may be interpreted by different computer systems. This requires a transformation of information code when transmission occurs between auxiliary and main memory. Examples of long-term auxiliary memories are tapes and some disk units allowing pack removal.

Finally, the various memory devices may be classified by their storage capacities, access speeds, and costs. At the low end of this hierarchy are tape devices which allow the storage of large amounts of information, have relatively slow access times, and are relatively inexpensive. At the high end are bulk magnetic core and drums which have less storage capacity, have very fast access times, and are usually more expensive.

Under the next heading we discuss some characteristics of several common auxiliary memory devices, but first we define here some terms which relate to the organization of information stored in auxiliary memory. A *file* is any logical collection of data stored in auxiliary memory. Files are delimited by control information uniquely defined for the storage device. A file is not limited to one storage device, but may be spread across several devices. Conversely, several files may reside on one storage device. Individual items of information in a file are called *records*. The information transmitted between main memory and a file by a single read or write operation is called a *physical record*. The amount of information contained in a physical record is normally determined by the physical characteristics of the storage device on which it resides. A logical item of information in a file is called a *logical record*. (For example, the entire collection of information about an individual in a personnel file might constitute a logical record.) A single logical record may require several physical records, thus requiring multiple read or write operations for accessing or recording. Conversely, if a physical record is large enough to hold several logical records, the records are said to be *blocked*. The responsibility for blocking or deblocking records is a software function and lies with the operating system or the program making use of the file. When one deals with files recorded on sequential-access devices, accessing or recording a block of several logical records requires only a *single* read or write operation, representing a significant time savings.

SOME AUXILIARY MEMORY DEVICES

This discussion covers the physical characteristics and recording mechanisms of some typical auxiliary memory devices. Although the list of devices described here is not exhaustive when one considers all types of auxiliary memory, it contains the most commonly used devices. Each manufacturer produces variations of these devices, and only the most common characteristics are considered here.

Tapes   The simplest and least expensive form of auxiliary memory is tape. Two types of tape are commonly used, *magnetic tape* and *paper tape*. They are characterized by their shape as well as their recording and accessing techniques. They are long, thin, narrow, flexible strips wound about reels and they require that information be recorded and accessed sequentially.

Information is recorded on paper tape by punching holes in the tape, limiting the use of a single reel of paper tape to one set of information. Magnetic tapes are coated with an iron oxide which may be magnetized to record information. Magnetic tapes may be reused for new or modified information when the old information is no longer required. Because of the density at which information can be recorded, a single reel of magnetic tape will allow storage of more information than a reel of paper tape. Paper-tape units are less expensive than magnetic-tape units, and are often used as auxiliary storage devices on small computer systems or on terminals for time-shared systems as discussed in Chapter 3 of this Part. Since magnetic tapes are more often used as computer tapes, only magnetic tapes are discussed here.

A typical reel of magnetic tape is $\frac{1}{2}$ inch wide and 2,400 feet long. The width of the tape is partitioned into either seven or nine parallel *tracks*, with each track capable of holding a "0" or a "1" bit. Information on tapes is recorded one character at a time, vertically across the tracks of the tape. This requires that each character be coded into unique combinations of either six or eight 0 and 1 bits. The extra seventh or ninth bit is called a *check bit* (or *parity bit*), and is used to detect errors (the parity concept requiring that there be an even or odd number of bits in each vertical column).

To record or to access information on a magnetic tape, the tape reel is mounted on a tape drive (the "unit"). There is a take-up reel, and a capstan which pulls the tape past read and write heads. Information is written on the tape by sending current through the write heads to magnetize the tracks of the tape. Information is read from the tape by sensing the voltage induced in the read heads from the magnetized tracks.

Information is packed along a tape to allow fast access speeds and a large capacity of data. The standard *densities* are 200, 556, 800, and 1,600 bits per inch (bpi). A tape that is at rest must be accelerated to maximum speed before reading or writing can begin. It is not practical to write one character at a time, and so characters are grouped together into blocks (physical records) before being recorded on tape. Typical record and access rates are 30 to 320 kilocharacters (kc) per second.

The delay necessary to bring the tape to maximum speed is called the *start time,* and the time needed to decelerate the tape after an access is called the *stop time.* The gaps found on the magnetic tape due to start and stop times are called *interrecord gaps,* and are sometimes $\frac{3}{4}$ inch long. The last column of each physical record preceding the interrecord gap contains *longitudinal check bits* for each track on the tape.

There are two techniques for synchronizing the writing of characters on a tape. Either the tape has been preformatted with a special timing track containing a 1 bit to indicate each character position of the tape, or the synchronization is provided by an internal electronic clock during the write operation. The important difference between these two techniques is that when a timing track exists, it is possible to detect a character position on the tape and to rewrite the character. This capability allows the programmer to modify and to rewrite existing records without copying to a new tape. When clocking is used, it is nearly impossible to guarantee that the tape moves at exactly the same speed between two successive operations, and inserting a modified record between two existing records is normally not possible. This necessitates a strictly sequential use of the tape.

The advantage of variable-sized physical records is that the programmer may determine the number of logical records contained in one physical record. By allowing large physical records, the amount of information stored on a single reel of tape is increased, because of the decrease in the number of tape-consuming interrecord gaps.

At the beginning of each reel of magnetic tape there is a special sensing mark to denote the start of information; and at the end there is another mark denoted as the *end-of-tape* mark which prevents the driving mechanism from pulling a tape off its reel. Files written on a tape are separated by an *end-of-file* mark which may be written or sensed by programs. To make use of these special marks, a number of tape operations are available, in addition to the usual read or write of one physical record. In addition, many systems allow physical records to be read or written in either a forward or backward direction.

Many operating systems require that files be delimited by identifying records, called *header labels* and *trailer labels*. The labels are in addition to the end-of-file marks, and may in fact also be delimited by end-of-file marks. A typical header label would contain the name of the file and certain physical characteristics of the file. Any program which uses the file could then verify that the correct tape and correct file have been mounted on the tape unit for use. A trailer label may also contain information about the physical characteristics of the file. This may include information about additional reels of tape in the event that the file requires multiple reels.

Disks   Although tapes still remain a popular form of auxiliary memory, multiprogramming batch and time-sharing systems require auxiliary memory devices with much faster access times. Hence the disk has become a very popular device for auxiliary memory. Physically, disks resemble a stack of phonograph records on a playback mechanism.

Disks are found in two versions. One version allows the storage medium, called a *pack*, to be removed from the unit, called the *disk drive*. The other version has the recording medium permanently attached to the unit. Although disks are more expensive than tapes, they often have the same capacity for information. Disk units with removable packs, like tapes, may be used for long-term storage of information by allowing removal of the pack when the information is no longer needed on-line. Those that do not allow removal of the packs, as well as some that do, are more often used as medium-term storage devices for holding intermediate information, or information which must be on-line to the system at all times.

The recording medium of a disk usually consists of one or more stacked platters which are all rotating about a shaft at the same speed. The platters are coated with a magnetic material which, like magnetic tape, may be magnetized for recording purposes. The recording tracks are arranged in concentric circles on both the top and bottom surfaces of the platters. Many disk units with removable packs do not allow recording on the top surface of the top platter or the bottom surface of the bottom platter. The number of tracks per surface ranges from 100 to 1,000. The tracks are arranged in such a way that one could pass an imaginary *cylinder* through a given track on the stacked surfaces.

The accessing mechanism is a set of arms of equal length extending from an exterior shaft in a comblike fashion. At the end of each arm are read and write heads for each recording surface of the disk. During read or write operations, the heads are resting in a given cylinder of tracks. Upon command, the heads may be lifted off the current set of tracks and moved to any other cylinder of tracks.

Synchronizing the recording of bits is accomplished by timing tracks on one platter surface. This allows repeated recordings of information in the same relative positions on a track. Information is normally coded in a horizontal fashion rather than the vertical fashion of tapes. Furthermore, many disks require formatting information specifying the beginning of information on a track, as well as the physical record size. Formatting a disk is often accomplished by a maintenance program. Some disks require a fixed record size by dividing the tracks into equal-sized *segments* large enough to hold one physical record.

To access information recorded on a disk, the programmer must supply a disk address similar to a main memory address. The disk address must specify the desired cylinder of tracks, the specific track (surface or head number), and the relative record number from the beginning of a track (or the segment number). The operation required to move the head assembly between two cylinders is called a *seek*, and the delay in access time is called the *seek time*. This time is a function of the distance of head movement, and may range up to a maximum of $\frac{1}{4}$ second. The second delay in access time is the *rotational delay* necessary to locate a given record or segment on a track. Many current systems allow separate seek and locating operations to be performed before the actual read or write operation. This allows the connecting data channels to access information on other devices during these time-consuming operations. The actual rate of transfer of information to or from a given disk can be up to 800 kc per second.

Disk platters are shielded by protective covers, and are less prone to damage and errors than tapes. However, most disk systems require that a small number of tracks be set aside on each surface to be assigned as alternates in case of track errors. This assignment is accomplished by placing address pointers in the recorded formatting information.

Files on a disk are organized by cylinders. That is, the physical records of a file are stored sequentially, first through adjacent tracks of a cylinder and then through adjacent cylinders. This technique significantly reduces the number of seek operations required for sequential access of records in a file. The addressing form of access allows the programmer to locate records in a nonsequential fashion. If the disk address of any record is known, the location operators may be executed and the record may be accessed directly, eliminating the necessity of passing over all intervening records as required by tape accesses. This form of access justifies the name often given to disks, *random-access* or *direct-access* devices. Many operating systems allow the programmer to specify the relative record number of a given file, thus calculating the actual disk address. This is often accomplished by a mathematical function, and is referred to as *hashing*.

An "associativelike" address technique is allowed in many disk systems. Rather than requiring that a disk address or relative record number be specified, a specific record is located by its contents. Stored with each record is a piece of data called the *key*, e.g., part of a person's name. The accessing mechanism will locate the record by comparing the specified key to each recorded key. This technique eliminates the need of storing or remembering the locating information of each record.

A further advantage of the addressing form of access is efficient use of unused space on a disk. Rather than requiring that a file be stored on adjacent tracks and cylinders, stored address pointers may be used to locate the next collection of records in the sequence, and unused spaces on a disk may be used freely for recording files.

The same address pointer technique may also be used within a file for creating *hierarchial structured data files*. The programmer may organize a file in a treelike fashion by storing the branch information as disk address pointers with the records of the file. Different paths of linking information are followed to retrieve data in desired orders. The retrieval time of individual items of a large file will be greatly reduced when such a structure is placed on the file. The advantage of efficient retrieval in structured files must be weighed against the overhead cost in disk storage space required for the storage of linking addresses. It is not unusual to find up to 100 per cent overhead required for linkage information.

Drums Another form of direct-access auxiliary memory is the *drum*. Although historically the drum has been in use much longer than the disk, it is merely a variation of the disk. A drum is a rotating cylinder with parallel tracks around the circumference. There are fixed read and write heads for each track. By design, drums often rotate at a higher speed than disks. The tracks are divided into equal-sized segments providing fixed-length physical records. In addition, many drums allow several tracks to be accessed in parallel. Locating a record involves only rotational delay (on the average, a half-revolution), and information transfer rates are very high, up to 3,000 kc per second.

Although drums usually have faster access rates than disks, the design and the cost of a drum limit its capacity for information. Consequently, drums are almost always used for medium-term storage of intermediate information. On some very early computers, drums were the bulk of memory. Finally, it should be noted that because of the direct-access nature of drums, the same freedom in structuring data and using free space is obtained as with disks.

Variations Although drums and disks are the most popular direct-access auxiliary memory devices, there are several variations of these devices. Some devices combine the concept of fixed and movable heads on a drumlike device. The recording medium is partitioned into a section of small capacity for information with very fast access rates, and a section of large capacity for information of slower access time.

Other devices, such as the *data cell*, have direct-access potential while allowing the storage of large amounts of information. The data cell is composed of magnetic strips which are automatically inserted into a read and write mechanism. Although the access time for information on a data cell is slower than the conventional drum or disk, it maintains many of the direct-access features of these devices, and has a much larger capacity for data.

A recent development in auxiliary memory devices is the MSF (*Mass Storage Facility*). An MSF is composed of a very large number of high-volume cartridge tapes residing in an array of storage cells. There is a selector device which will automatically fetch a cartridge from its storage cell and move it to a read/write station where the tape is removed from the cartridge and made ready for information access. Although this mounting operation requires a few seconds, once mounted, data transfer speed is approximately the same as data transfer speed from a disk. When information access is completed, the tape is returned to the cartridge and the selector then returns the cartridge to its storage cell. Furthermore, the cartridges may be removed from the storage cells for archival storage. The volume of data on a single cartridge can be up to 50 million characters. The number of cartridges in an MSF system may be more than 4,000. The MSF is designed to provide a low cost per character, on-line, archival storage device. Under most applications, the MSF would reside at the lowest level of the hierarchy of auxiliary memory.

Bulk Memory   A final class of devices which may be used as auxiliary memory is that of the *bulk memories*. Bulk memory is usually made up of magnetic-core storage and uses circuitry similar to that of main memory for accessing information. Although the access time is slower than for main memory, bulk memories usually have a larger capacity for information. Like main memory, the time required to locate and access any unit of information is constant, making bulk memory the auxiliary memory with the fastest access time.

The size of a unit of information accessed in a single operation varies according to the design of the bulk memory. The IBM bulk memory, called Large Core Storage (LCS), allows information to be accessed and manipulated directly by the central processor. Although LCS is physically separated from main memory, the only distinction between them is the different access speeds. The CDC bulk memory, called Extended Core Storage (ECS), accesses 480 bits (eight main memory words) in a single operation. Thus, like other auxiliary memory, the primary operation is to move information between ECS and main memory.

APPLICATIONS OF AUXILIARY MEMORY

Although many applications have been implied in the above discussion, a few specific applications covering the wide spectrum of auxiliary memory functions are described briefly here. The use of auxiliary memory is often limited only by the imagination of the application designer, with some restrictions imposed by the characteristics of the storage devices.

Auxiliary memory is first viewed as an information store for its users, providing a long-term, temporary, or backup store of information. It is then viewed in terms of its position in the hierarchy of memories, that is, a logical extension of main memory. The goal of this application is to make the distinction between auxiliary memory and main memory transparent to most users.

Auxiliary Memory: An Information Store   Auxiliary memory is a collection of "warehouses" used by the computer system users for the storage of information. Here the term "user" means any entity, whether it is a human being or some other system component, which makes use of the computer system resources. Included in these resources is auxiliary memory. Users must have the capability of storing, retrieving, updating, and replacing information in these warehouses. The type of warehouse selected depends upon the requirements of the user. These requirements include a wide range of storage capacity, access speeds, storage costs, and information storage times. In order to make the selection, the general characteristics of auxiliary memory devices may be matched against these requirements.

The most obvious application, and historically the most common application of auxiliary memory, is the storage of large quantities of data. The user is either a programmer, the operating system, or an individual making use of existing programs. The data may be either the input to or the output resulting from a computer program. Examples of this type of application would be the storage of experimental data for statistical analysis, the storage of information files, such as employee data to be maintained by programs and used, for example, to calculate payroll, and finally storage of intermediate output from a scientific or engineering program requiring a large number of iterations in order to arrive at a solution.

A second application of auxiliary memory for these users is for the storage of program libraries. When a programmer has a collection of programs that are used repeatedly, auxiliary memory such as disks or tapes is used to store these programs in machine-readable format. This provides a safe, convenient, and fast method of retrieving these programs for execution.

Traditionally these applications have been performed on *batch-processing* computer systems. The user submits a job to a central input facility, the job is stacked along with other jobs into a batch, the batch is then executed sequentially by job, and finally, after the entire batch has completed execution, the results are printed and returned to the user. With the arrival of third-generation systems, two important variations of this scheme have come about. They are *multiprogramming batch-processing systems* and *multiprogramming time-sharing systems*, both with *multiaccessing* capabilities.

Multiprogramming is the concurrent use of main memory by several jobs that are competing for the use of the central processor and for the input-output processors. In most modern computer systems, these processors may be run concurrently; this is denoted as *parallel processing* or *multitasking*. The limited capacity of main memory often forces a program to use auxiliary memory for temporary storage of information. Two techniques are commonly used for accomplishing this. Either the programmer must organize his or her program and data in such a way that only the necessary information is maintained in main memory, or the operating system will automatically use auxiliary memory as a logical extension of main memory by exchanging information between the two types of memory, freeing the programmer from this responsibility. The latter technique is discussed in more detail in the second part of this section.

Multiaccessing capabilities imply that the users may submit jobs and receive the results at any one of a number of different locations. In batch-processing systems, this is referred to as a *remote-batch* facility.

Since relatively slow input readers and output printers are used to communicate with the user, auxiliary memory is used as an intermediate memory for user input-output. An operating system program places jobs from remote stations into a queue of requests for execution. At the appropriate time, jobs are selected from this queue and initiated for execution. During job execution the input is read from auxiliary memory, and the resulting output is stored in auxiliary memory to be sent back to the appropriate output station when execution is completed. This technique for batch input-output is sometimes referred to as *spooling* (*S*imultaneous *P*eripheral *O*perations *O*n-*L*ine). Note that multiprogramming and multiaccessing capabilities eliminate the need to run jobs sequentially as in the earlier batch systems. The typical batch job requires a large amount of execution time, may perform large numbers of input-output operations, and does not require immediate solutions. Examples of batch jobs are simulations, report generators, or long analysis programs.

For the user who wishes to have immediate results, does not require a large amount of execution time or input-output, and who wishes to converse directly with the computer, there exist time-sharing systems.

Time-sharing systems are often denoted as conversational or on-line interactive programming systems because they allow many programmers to converse concurrently and directly with the computer system through remote typewriter terminals or display terminals with keyboards. The characteristics of these systems are discussed in the following Chapter. As in the batch systems, auxiliary memory is used to store a job's input-output. Because of the large number of concurrent users and the direct interaction between the computer system and its users, it is imperative that fast-access auxiliary memory be used. The user's primary form of input is the terminal keyboard. He or she must rely on auxiliary memory for permanent storage of information between interactive sessions with the computer.

The final set of applications which make use of auxiliary memory as an information store is taken from the systems or subsystems that are dedicated to a particular use. Two examples are discussed here: the *database systems* and the *real-time systems*.

Database systems are designed around auxiliary memory. These systems are often transaction-oriented, and are referred to as information systems. The configuration consists of a computer system with a large capacity, fast-access auxiliary memory, and a set of remote terminals. Large files of information are stored in auxiliary memory, and transactions on these files may be directly effected by the users from the remote terminals. The transactions include interrogation of the files, updating of information in the files, addition of information to the files, or deletion of information from the files. Examples of database systems include airline reservation systems, employee record systems, financial systems, and inventory systems. Transaction response times, security and integrity of information, and user convenience are primary factors in designing database systems. Hierarchical data structures are often used to provide the access speeds necessary for good user response times.

Real-time systems are much like database systems but have deadlines imposed upon the response time — for example, an employee record system where the personnel file structure follows the corporate organization might allow immediate retrieval of data on all individuals in a given department. Fast response in a database system is a design goal, and often leads to the success or failure of the system. However, fixed response times are requirements in real-time systems. Real-time systems include process control systems such as assembly-line control, flight control systems, and certain medical application systems.

Auxiliary Memory: An Extension of Main Memory The cost of main memory and the multiprogramming capabilities of current systems require that auxiliary memory be used to supplement main memory for temporary storage of information. A goal of both computer hardware and software designers is to design computer systems that allow users to obtain as much memory as needed without making a distinction between main memory and auxiliary memory. Two techniques which have been used to achieve this goal are *swapping* and *virtual memory.*

The swapping systems allow each user to request as much memory as required to execute his or her program successfully within the bounds of main memory. A priority is placed on each job according to its response-time requirements or some other optimization criterion. If a high-priority job requires execution, the operating system copies the lowest-priority jobs from main memory to auxiliary memory until there is enough space for the high-priority job. The jobs that have been "swapped out" are then temporarily delayed until some future time when they may be "swapped in" to resume execution. The fast-access devices such as disk, drum, and bulk memory are used to allow fast swaps and to reduce operating system overhead. To maintain high utilization of computer resources, it is desirable to leave at least one job in main memory to make use of the central processor while swapping occurs.

Swapping has been used for a number of years, and is still a popular technique in many systems. However, swapping has several undesirable limitations. Among others, the programmer is forced to define his or her program within the limitation of main memory size. Second, in most swapping systems the entire collection of information belonging to a job is swapped to auxiliary memory. It is more desirable to transfer only the unused instructions and data to auxiliary memory. Consequently, with more jobs remaining in main memory, a higher degree of multiprogramming will occur.

Virtual memory is a more recent concept being used in some systems to eliminate some of these undesirable features of swapping. Here a memory much larger than main memory is made available to programmers for program definition. The entire memory is called a *virtual memory,* and that part used by an individual program is denoted as the program's *name space.* The computer hardware uses an *address map* to translate a program's name space address either to a main memory address if the information is located in main memory, or to an address fault if the information is located in auxiliary memory. The program's name space is segmented into blocks, and during program execution only the required blocks are maintained in main memory. When a reference is made to a block of virtual memory that is not currently resident in main memory, an address fault occurs and the operating system is notified. The requested block is then transferred from auxiliary memory to main memory, either by locating unused memory space or by replacing blocks which are not currently needed.

The block sizes vary from system to system and may be of fixed or variable length. Fixed-length blocks are called *pages,* and the corresponding memory blocks are called *page frames.* When a required page is not located in main memory, a *page fault* occurs and the transfer between main and auxiliary memory is called *paging.* If paging occurs only when page faults occur, the system is using a *demand paging* algorithm. A suitable *replacement algorithm* must locate a page frame for the required page. As in a swapping system, the auxiliary memory devices used for virtual memory must allow fast access of blocks; disks, drums, or bulk memory devices are normally used.

Virtual memory systems have become very useful in current multiprogramming systems. However, the system designer and the user must be aware of two important limitations of such systems: If name space is not properly segmented into blocks, address faults may become so frequent that the overhead of swapping blocks is very high. When this occurs, the system is said to be *thrashing*. Second, since swapping requires the use of the operating system, there may be a significant degradation in overall system performance. Virtual memory systems are highly effective in on-line interactive systems where central processor requirements are low, but they must be carefully studied in batch systems, particularly if the workload requires a large amount of central processor time.

SUMMARY AND CONCLUSIONS

We have defined auxiliary memory by its position in the hierarchy of computer system memories. We have looked at various ways of classifying auxiliary memory, and have looked at the characteristics of several commonly used auxiliary memory devices. Finally, we have looked at some of the applications of auxiliary memory, first as an information store for both batch-processing and time-sharing systems, then as a logical extension of main memory through swapping or virtual memory.

In conclusion, let us look briefly at the future development of auxiliary memory devices. The needs seem to dictate two directions: The most obvious need is for extremely large capacity devices that have access times comparable to those of main memory, but at a tolerable cost. Devices such as laser memories have been mentioned as a possible step in this direction. Also, accessing techniques must be designed to allow extremely fast retrieval of individual items from very large stores. This involves a combination of hardware development and development of new data structures for organizing information on these devices.

The second need is for medium-capacity, reliable, low-cost devices which may be used for field storage of information and may later be used on-line to a computer system. The development of the "floppy-disk" is a step in this direction. It is a small disk approximately the size of a 45-rpm phonograph record that weighs approximately 1 ounce, has a capacity of around 0.25 million characters, and is very inexpensive.

SELECTIVE BIBLIOGRAPHY

Chapin, Ned, *Computers: A Systems Approach,* Van Nostrand Reinhold, New York, 1971.
Denning, P. J., "Virtual Memory," *Computing Surveys,* September, 1970.
———, "Third Generation Computer Systems," *Computing Surveys,* December, 1971.
Gear, William C., *Computer Organization and Programming,* McGraw-Hill, New York, 1969.
Hellerman, Herbert, *Digital Computer System Principles,* 2d ed., McGraw-Hill, New York, 1973.
Maurer, W. D., *Programming: An Introduction to Computer Techniques,* Holden-Day, San Francisco, 1972.
Stone, Harold S., *Introduction to Computer Organization and Data Structures,* McGraw-Hill, New York, 1972.

Chapter 3

Time-Sharing Computers

THOMAS E. KURTZ

Director, Office of Academic Computing, Dartmouth College,
Hanover, New Hampshire

No term in computing has been more misunderstood or misused than *time sharing*. Since the early 1960s, when the term became common, it has been used to describe an extraordinarily wide variety of computers and computer services. About the only point of agreement was that two or more interactive terminals were involved. Thus, as manufacturers or service vendors attached personal terminals to their machines, they also attached the term time sharing to their marketing material. In order to distinguish between the wide variety of so-called time-sharing systems, and to discover the common elements, we shall carefully discuss both the physical and functional features of such systems.

HISTORICAL DEVELOPMENT

The very first computers had no software operating systems. All programming was done in machine language. As assemblers, and later compilers, were developed, their use placed great demands on the then-meager resources. Indeed, users discovered that some time could be saved if, after loading the assembler, all assemblies for the day could be performed in a *batch;* this process was, in fact, the source of the term *batch processing,* although as we shall see later, most contemporary batch-processing systems in fact do not batch.

It soon became clear that the throughput of one of these expensive computers could be greatly improved if certain software were made available to get user programs in and out of the machine quickly. For example, the last step of a user's program might read in a small program that could, in turn, read in the program of the next user, without directly involving the machine operator. Thus began the long development of operating systems.

In the late 1950s, these operating systems provided access to a variety of languages and services, but in most cases were restricted in two ways: first, they allowed only input by punched cards; second, since they provided each user with full access to all the resources of the given machine, they forced users to line up and wait, since only one could be computing at a given time. (The term *sequential processing* would thus seem to be a more accurate descriptive term than batch processing.) While such operating systems certainly improved machine efficiency, if a long production run were in progress, a programmer requiring a debugging run of 1 minute would have to stand around and wait. It was this dilemma that motivated the development of time sharing.

The first successful experiment with time sharing took place at M.I.T. and Bolt, Beranek and Newman, Inc. (BBN) in the early 1960s. A Digital Equipment Corporation PDP-1 was equipped with a drum auxiliary store and with a special multiplexer connected to several typewriter terminals. As programmers worked on these several terminals, their work would be rolled in from the drum, short debugging or editing calculations performed, and the entire result rolled out to make room for the next programmer. It was assumed that the users of such a system would be programmers working in the machine or assembly language of the PDP-1. If a production run were in progress, it would be interrupted (even though unfinished) and rolled out, to be rolled in and continued later.

One other early development deserves special mention. Jules Schwartz at the Rand Corporation devised a new programming language called JOSS,[1] and built an interactive interpretive system to deliver it to terminals. JOSS statements preceded with a line number became part of the program, while those without line numbers were executed immediately. Since each typed line had to be interpreted immediately in order to know what to do with it, such languages became commonly known as *interpreter languages*. JOSS thus served as the ancestor of a large number of similar languages, some of which are mentioned later in this Chapter.

About 1962, a group at M.I.T. under the direction of Dr. F. J. Corbato began modifying an IBM-7090 to allow the connection of several typewriterlike terminals. The goal was to provide to each terminal user all the services then available under the sequential or batch operating system—hence, the name Compatible Time Sharing System, or CTSS. The major importance of their work was to demonstrate the viability of the concept of time sharing, with particular reference to greatly improving the debugging process. So good was their work that CTSS served the M.I.T. community for more than a decade, and achieved a remarkably high level of reliability. Even so, the design was such that only one user's program could be in the core memory of the machine at a given time; therefore, considerable dependence was placed on swapping programs into and out of the core memory to auxiliary devices.

Another interesting development began in 1963 at Dartmouth College under the direction of John G. Kemeny and the author. While the machine configuration and general design of the Dartmouth system were different from that of CTSS and the earlier PDP-1, the main departure lay in designing "from scratch" a command language and a programming language especially suited for liberal arts undergraduates. Operational in May of 1964, it provided for between 20 and 40 users simultaneously, starting with the 1964–1965 school year. It was in this project that the computer language BASIC was designed. Built around GE-235 and Datanet-30 hardware, this system, slightly modified, became in 1965 the basis of the Mark I service offered by the time-sharing division of General Electric.

Still another important early development was the system developed at the University of California at Berkeley. Constructed around SDS-940 hardware, this small but sophisticated system included a JOSS-like language called CALTRAN, and later became the basis of the commercial time-sharing offerings of both Com-Share, Inc. and Tymshare, Inc.

Another project of note was the QUICKTRAN product of IBM and later of SBC (Service Bureau Corporation, now part of Control Data Corporation). It offered a FORTRAN service in which messages pointing out errors of form (typographical errors) were provided as soon as the typed line was entered. Although in the early days of time-sharing systems this immediate return of the error message was deemed to be of central importance, later developments tended to prove that a somewhat less immediate response was actually superior from the user's point of view, and in addition a whole lot cheaper in the use of machine resources.

Time sharing as a method for distributing computer resources and services to many users "simultaneously" becomes practical only for sufficiently large and fast machines. Generally speaking, such machines became available with the introduction of transistors. Besides the speed and capacity offered by third-generation hardware, there is

[1] For a discussion of programming languages, see Part Four, Chapter 3, in this section.

little inherent in their design not possessed by earlier machines that allows time sharing. The only necessary requirement is that each user's program be isolated from the operating system executive program; this may be accomplished by, for instance, a memory protection feature or by having the executive program reside in a separate but connected computer.

As is indicated elsewhere in this Chapter, time-sharing systems have been successfully constructed for almost every type of computer, including some very early models. But it soon became clear that certain special hardware features could greatly ease the construction of time-sharing operating systems, and allow their efficient operation. As a result, many special hardware designs were proposed and experimented with in the 1960s.

The first attempt to design a large-scale general-purpose time-sharing system from scratch without relying on existing hardware or software occurred at M.I.T.'s Project MAC. Started in 1964, and known as MULTICS, this system combined the special hardware features of paging and segmentation (see later herein) as provided by the GE-645 (now the HIS G645), a sophisticated software operating system programmed almost entirely in an enhanced version of PL/I, with advanced ideas in reliability and security. This project was sponsored by the Advanced Research Projects Agency of the Department of Defense.

The MULTICS system became a service offering at M.I.T. in October 1969. The system provides an environment for running very large programs, particularly those having a complex structure and perhaps requiring extensive human interaction. As of May 1973, the service MULTICS system could support 50 users simultaneously. While the cost of a MULTICS system is high, five such systems were operating in late 1973: two at M.I.T., two in Honeywell, and one in the Air Force.

Almost concurrently with the MULTICS development, IBM began a similar project, TSS, built around the 360/67, a highly modified version of the 360/65. Like MULTICS, TSS used the hardware features of paging and segmentation. A number of installations of the 360/67 were made, primarily in universities, but the acceptance of TSS was not as great. In mid-1973, there were only a few TSS systems still operating. The product TSS was not a market success, and has been essentially dropped by IBM.

An interesting variation on the time-sharing theme is provided by the CP/CMS system on the 360/67 hardware. Instead of providing the full range of time-sharing services, CP/CMS utilizes the paging features to establish a number of virtual machines within the same physical machine. Any existing software designed to operate in a standard 360 could operate in one of these virtual machines. Time-sharing services were successfully provided in a large number of installations using this approach.

BATCH VS. TIME SHARING

Batch systems developed along the lines that:
    1. The user should be able to reach all the physical resources of the machine hardware and its peripherals.
    2. The most important jobs were the long production runs, either compute-bound or input-output (I/O)-bound.
    3. The machine-room operator would be able to perform any duties that the operating system could not.
    Time-sharing operating systems, on the other hand, developed along the lines that:
    1. The user should be able to access a wide variety of services (such as languages and editors) interactively, but not necessarily be able to have access to all the available hardware.
    2. The most important jobs were the many small jobs and debugging runs, and the operating system must be able to allocate very small amounts of machine resource and time.
    3. The operating system must perform virtually all the functions such as resource allocation, scheduling, on-line file access, security, and isolation of users from each other, and complete accounting and performance statistics.
    These are highly simplified descriptions, and serve only to explain the different directions taken by the early batch systems versus the early time-sharing systems. Furthermore, operating systems of each variety were often so different as to defy

deriving general characteristics, or even intelligently discussing the question of "time sharing versus batch." In fact, it is the contention of the present writer that there is no fundamental difference between well-constructed batch operating systems and time-sharing operating systems, and that the actual differences between specific instances of each are gradually disappearing. The purpose of the remainder of this chapter is to compare and describe further examples of time-sharing systems, but always in the context of their being first and foremost simply operating systems.

Relation to Certain Hardware Developments   The early machines were designed for a single job at a time. Under this assumption, the user is merely provided with a collection of physical resources; what the user does with them is his or her business. If the program contains an error that destroys the files, it is not the fault of the computer vendor or operator.

The advent of time-sharing computers, with the eventual requirement that several jobs might occupy the computer's memory in order to share the processor, placed new demands on the hardware design:

1. The need for protection of the operating system from a runaway user program.

2. The need for user–user isolation, and to a lesser extent, isolation of data from program.

3. The need to provide exceedingly small, as well as exceedingly large, portions of machine resource, but without relinquishing control over these resources.

These needs are being met through some combination of hardware *segmentation* and hardware *paging*.

In order, first, to understand segmentation, we consider the problem of a program whose data occupy the middle regions of the computer's memory. As long as there is only this one job in the machine, there is no problem. But as soon as we require several jobs to occupy different portions of the memory simultaneously, we would like to be able to move both program and data to other portions of the memory. While index registers can often accomplish this moving or relocation, their use is subject to programming errors and, in some cases, places an added burden on the processor; further, their use is not transparent to the user-programmer.

Segmentation in its simplest form accomplishes the desired relocation. A *relocation* or *base address register* is provided for the user. This register maps the user's addresses to actual machine addresses by adding a certain constant number (the address of the base location) to each of the user program's addresses as they are being processed. The user then programs as if always starting addresses at location 0. If this program currently occupies locations 1000 and above, then a constant 1000 is added to each of the addresses as they are processed. Address 100 then becomes the actual address 1100, 101 becomes 1101, and so on.

One segmentation register is sufficient to allow easy relocation of a user's program and data. Additional segmentation registers allow the user to separate the program from the data, or allow several users to operate on their own data but from a common copy of a compiler, for example.

In addition to relocation, the segmentation register usually performs two other services. First, it can provide an upper limit on the amount of memory used; if the user attempts to access an address beyond the bounds provided, a fault will occur and some action will be taken by the operating system. Second, its use allows certain highly privileged instructions to be denied the user. These instructions include all direct I/O instructions, instructions that set or reset the timer, and instructions that provide the relocation address to the segmentation register. When the segmentation register is in use, the user is (1) limited to a certain region in actual memory, and (2) prevented from executing I/O and certain other highly privileged instructions. The operating system is carefully constructed so that it can operate without the limitation of the segmentation register, can access any memory location, and can issue I/O and other privileged instructions.

A survey of selected large machines shows that almost all have at least one relocation (segmentation) register. These include, for instance, Univac's 1108, Digital Equipment's PDP-10, Control Data's 6600, and Honeywell's 6000.[2]

---

[2] See, for example, C. G. Bell and A. Newell, *Computer Structures: Readings and Examples*, McGraw-Hill, New York, 1971.

Segmentation is under the partial control of the user or programmer, and he or she is certainly aware of its existence. For instance, the user will be painfully aware of any severe limitation on the amount of actual memory that can be occupied. On the other hand, paging is a technique for making much easier the allocation of memory but without the user's being aware of it at all.

Paging is associated with the concept of virtual memory, which can best be described in terms of how it is used. A programmer works with memory having consecutive addresses as usual. However, these addresses are not real addresses but are automatically converted to addresses in real memory by a *page table*, which usually resides in very high-speed associative memory. The programmer thus works not directly with real memory, but with an "image" of it called *virtual memory*.

Both real memory and virtual memory are divided into convenient-sized units called *pages*, perhaps 1,024 words. A given page of virtual memory can reside anywhere in real memory; all that is necessary is that its location in real memory be stored in the page table. It is thus possible that the pages belonging to a particular program will not be consecutively located in real memory, nor that all of them even be in real memory. If the desired page is in memory, processing takes place. If the desired page is found to reside currently on some auxiliary storage device such as a drum, disk, or bulk core storage, action is initiated to swap in that page into any available place in real memory to permit processing.

Because paging is accomplished through a page table in associative memory, it becomes easy to allow a very large number of segments, since they are accessed not through physical registers but merely as supplementary addresses in the page table. The programmer thus has the illusion that he or she has available a very large number of segmentation registers, each of which allows access to a very large amount of virtual memory. Machines employing this approach include the Honeywell G645 and 6180, and the IBM 360/67 and 370/168.

While paging has the highly desirable effect of allowing programs that are much longer than the actual memory of the machine, and gives the programmer the illusion of essentially infinite memory, this feature also has the severe drawback that excessive amounts of time may be spent in swapping, particularly if large programs are not organized properly. The term *page thrashing* is used to describe situations where more time is spent swapping in or out pages than is spent in actual processing.

Significant Considerations The main goals of both time-sharing and batch operating systems are the same: to provide access to the computational and information resources of the computer, and to do it efficiently. But there are several important subgoals which have tended to distinguish the instances of these systems in the past. We mention four considerations of special significance:

The first consideration is the choice between interaction and no interaction. The development of batch systems has tended to adopt the point of view that machine efficiency is compromised by the overhead of terminal services, and that conventional punched-card input is adequate for most needs. Time-sharing systems, on the other hand, have obviously assumed that programmer or user efficiency is as important as machine efficiency, and that some form of terminal or interactive service is needed to provide this efficiency. Consequently, time-sharing operating systems designed from scratch provide interactive terminal service reasonably efficiently, relatively speaking. Batch operating systems on which have been grafted terminal support subsystems usually place a heavy requirement on that subsystem, resulting in less efficient, and therefore more expensive, operation.

Another consideration of importance is that, while batch operating systems tend to allocate machine resources physically, such as with the allocation of disk storage, time-sharing systems usually provide a device-transparent interface between the user and the physical devices. One might say that batch systems provide for disk storage of user programs and data, while time-sharing systems provide a file system; the devices actually containing the user programs and data will probably not be known to the user, and may even allow for a single data set to be spread over several devices, possibly even of different types.

A third consideration is that in most time-sharing systems the task of program preparation and editing takes place on the system. Furthermore, the programs are usually stored on-line, thus eliminating or reducing the need for card files or tapes external to the machine. Batch systems, on the other hand, usually require that program preparation be done using keypunches and punched cards, or some similar arrangement, and further that editing and modifying of programs take place again at the keypunch, in between the debugging runs.

A fourth consideration is that since time-sharing systems automatically must be concerned with communications (in order to connect terminals to them), building them into networks becomes a much simpler task. The user identification, control, and billing needed for a larger network become a simple extension of these functions which are already included in the time-sharing system. Batch systems, on the other hand, have had to have these functions added later when the need for them was finally perceived, and the grafted-on services often require a much greater share of machine resource in order to be carried out.

Functional Characteristics We now review some of the functional characteristics that stress the distinction between time-sharing systems and batch systems. In all cases, the characteristic is desirable in a batch system, though perhaps not necessary, while it is mandatory in a time-sharing system.

Perhaps the first and foremost requirement is *reliability*. In the batch world, a delay of 1 hour because of hardware or software failure will be almost unnoticed by the users, who are prepared to wait awhile anyway. Even frequent "crashes" cause little trouble, except when the initial program load sequence requires a long period of time. But on a time-sharing system, not only must the system be up and available practically all the time (99.9 per cent, for instance), but when it does "crash," it must return to service within a few seconds or a minute at the most. This means that restart procedures must be built into the system and not depend in any way on manual intervention.

Another requirement made crucial by the advent of time-sharing systems is that of *security*. In a batch world, security is provided easily by having sensitive or proprietary data on individually owned tapes or disk packs. The machine-room operator, who can be assumed to be trustworthy, will mount these sensitive tapes or disks only when the corresponding programs are being run. Otherwise, they will be locked in cabinets. As a result, most batch systems have only a very crude method of providing logical security controls over and above those physical ones provided by the machine-room operator. With time-sharing systems, where many sensitive data belonging to a large number of users are stored in a common on-line file system, elaborate and nearly foolproof procedures are needed to ensure the needed security. Since this requirement is usually obvious at the time the system is designed, the security features are readily built in and can be carried out with a minimum drain on the system resources.

As stated earlier, one of the important functions of a time-sharing system is to provide logical access to the various resources of the machine. That is, rather than requiring the user to be familiar with the physical properties of the machine he or she is using, and rather than requiring the user to learn detailed and elaborate codes for obtaining access to these resources in any combination he or she wishes, a time-sharing system usually provides for reasonable user interfaces between the user and the resources. The time-sharing system "worries" about the sharing of resources so that different users do not conflict in their requests. But the users themselves may not even be aware that elaborate algorithms are being applied to match their needs with the available capabilities of the machine.

Perhaps the most noticeable distinction between systems that grew up as batch systems and those that began as time-sharing systems is that batch systems have traditionally assumed that all jobs are big. That is, they have been constructed to make available to a big job as much of the machine resource as it needs. Since big jobs occasionally require special services, all the overhead needed to provide these services is included in the job setup procedure. It has proved difficult to reduce this overhead when the job is small. Thus, large jobs have a large setup time, and small jobs also have a large setup time. In a time-sharing system, it is likely that most jobs are small. Therefore, the design of the system has allowed for very simple job setup procedures for extremely small jobs. While it has proved difficult to scale down batch systems to handle small jobs, it has proved simpler to scale up time-sharing systems so that they can handle large jobs.

A related consideration is the nature of the compilers provided. Since the assumption in batch systems is that all important jobs are large and long-running, extra emphasis is placed on compilers that produce efficient object code, even though the compilers themselves may be large and slow. In a time-sharing system, the emphasis is on many, many small jobs. Thus, the compilers tend to be small and fast, although they may not produce efficient object code.

One other distinction between batch and time-sharing systems lies in the richness of the services available on a time-sharing system. Various observers have commented on the "community of users" idea. As time goes on, the collection of library programs and special services, such as special editors or games, becomes richer as the users themselves add their own efforts to the mix already there. In a batch system, while it is likely that the users may be just as creative, it is not as easy to make the results of their efforts available to the other users of the batch system.

CURRENT STATE

A very large number of time-sharing systems are currently running on almost every brand and type of hardware equipment. Starting with the small computers, we may note that time-sharing systems have been prepared for and are being used on DEC PDP-8s and PDP-11s, Data General NOVAs, and Hewlett Packard 2000s, to name four of the most common hardware systems. Although limited to a certain extent in terms of the variety of services and languages offered, they have proved extremely successful in the educational and commercial world. Some of them operate with an extremely high degree of reliability, often much greater than that which can be obtained on larger systems.

Most of the commercial time-sharing vendors have prepared their own operating systems. The largest vendor, General Electric, uses a software system of its own construction with HIS G635 and HIS H6000 Series hardware. The company offers worldwide access to its network, in which a large number of systems are attached to a common communications network. A wide variety of language, editing, and data services are offered. Their system is patterned, from the user's point of view, from the earlier Mark I service, which was based on the original systems effort at Dartmouth College.[3]

IBM's early entry in commercial time sharing, QUICKTRAN, has been replaced by the CALL/360 system which offers both programming and editing services. This system operates on standard 360 or 370 hardware equipment.

There are a large number of commercial time-sharing firms in existence, too many to enumerate here with any accuracy. Suffice it to say that in most cases the hardware vendor's software is used only in part or not at all. Rather, the time-sharing service vendor or an independent software firm prepares the system from scratch, or adapts it from either the hardware vendor's software or a university-constructed system.

In almost all cases, the time-sharing software offered by a hardware vendor consists of additions to the standard batch operating system, or perhaps consists of a single batch job that provides time-sharing services to a number of users. The TSO option of the OS 360 operating system for the IBM 360 or 370 is such an example. Another example is the time-sharing component of the GCOS III operating system for the Honeywell G635 or H6000 Series. In almost all cases, the time-sharing service provided in this way tends to be inefficient, in relation to the hardware, in terms of the number of users that can be served simultaneously. Furthermore, the time-sharing component often does not allow the time-sharing user to have access to the file system of the principal operating system, or to its other services. One reason has been that the batch file system does not provide adequate protection from illegal incursions.

There are several examples of high-quality time-sharing systems provided by hardware manufacturers. Most notable is the APL system offered by IBM. Operating as a partition in OS 360, it can serve a large number of users efficiently, and it is very reliable. Other vendors have improved on the IBM APL system, but the fact remains that the original system was of high quality and has had wide popularity.

Another notable example is the operating system for DEC's PDP-10, which can serve 50 to 80 users on the larger hardware configurations. It is widely used in universities, and has been used with minor modifications by several commercial time-sharing firms such as Applied Logic Corporation and Cyphernetics.

[3] See Section 6, Chapter 5, "Interactive Teleprocessing Network Services."

Still another vendor-supplied system is KRONOS, which operates on CDC's 6000 Series. This system is used by several commercial time-sharing firms, including CDC's own SBC.

Much of the interesting development work in time-sharing operating systems has taken place in universities. Already mentioned was the early work such as the PDP-1 (M.I.T. and BBN), CTSS (M.I.T.), the GE-265 (Dartmouth), MULTICS (M.I.T.), and the SDS-940 (University of California at Berkeley). Some of these efforts have been commercial successes as well.

Despite the enormous difficulties, development of time-sharing operation systems in universities goes on. The reason is that the levels of sophistication and efficiency required by the universities cannot fully be met by the manufacturer's operating system. First of all, a much greater variety of language services is required. Further, since adding hardware in order to enhance performance is expensive, and therefore not often practical, universities often choose instead to tighten up the software, allowing more users to do more work on a given hardware configuration.

One of the best known of the university-developed operating systems not already mentioned is Dartmouth's DTSS. Built for HIS G635 or H6000 hardware, it was begun in 1967, and now serves several commercial and educational sites in addition to Dartmouth. It normally serves 180 or more users simultaneously, and offers the usual wide variety of languages, editing services, and file system services. As with most large time-sharing systems, file backup and restoring services are provided for within the system, thus relieving the user from this worry. Adequate user isolation and system protection features are built in, so that use by administrative offices is possible on the same system used by students. DTSS is an instance of a system developed entirely from scratch (as is MULTICS), but using standard hardware.

Another important university-developed system is Michigan's MTS. Using IBM 360/67 hardware, it operates at five university sites in addition to the University of Michigan itself. Other university-developed systems include ones that operate on the CDC-3600 at the University of Massachusetts, the CDC-3300 at Oregon State University, and on the CDC-6400 at the University of Texas.

CONCLUSIONS

The most important single conclusion that one can make about time-sharing computers is that the crucial ingredient is the software, not the hardware. Excellent time-sharing operating systems have been built for and operate well on hardware not particularly designed for them, and certainly not having all the features deemed desirable (such as paging.) On the other hand, less than excellent time-sharing operating systems have been constructed on hardware equipped with all the desirable features. Finally, it is almost true to say that every major brand and type of hardware has at least one good time-sharing system operating on it.

The second conclusion to be drawn is that the hardware vendors have not led the way in providing efficient and sophisticated time-sharing software. Their approach has almost always been to graft a time-sharing module onto their standard batch operating system. In part, the fact that there still is an argument about which is better, batch or time sharing, measures the extent to which the comparison is being made between the time-sharing service offered as a module on the batch system, and the batch service itself. Or perhaps the comparison is made between a full-scale batch system and the time-sharing service provided by a mini or small computer.

The final conclusion is that good operating systems will, in the future, offer a full range of services efficiently. These will include terminal services, services related to card input and printer output, language services available both through terminals and from cards, reliable operation, adequate user isolation protections, and so on. It is only an anachronism that there is currently such a visible distinction between time-sharing systems and batch systems.

Chapter 4

Minicomputers

ANDREW KNOWLES

Vice President, Group Manager, Digital Equipment
Corporation, Maynard, Massachusetts

From something unheard of at the beginning of the 1960s, the minicomputer has become an important factor in the whole computer industry. In the mid 1960s, the first minicomputer, the PDP-5, was introduced by Digital Equipment Corporation. Its development was brought about by the need for a unit to produce computer functions in a scientific and industrial environment, and provide those functions at low cost. Each of the PDP-5s was virtually handmade, and only 100 were assembled. But the reaction for the computer was so great that the first mass-produced minicomputer, the PDP-8, was introduced.

Since then, other minicomputers have been introduced, both from Digital Equipment Corporation and other manufacturers. By mid-1975, there were about 83,000 minicomputers throughout the world. Their uses had spread from simple calculation and control functions in limited types of applications to complex and sophisticated applications in nearly every major phase of human activity. And throughout this period, the power and speed of minicomputers has increased while the cost has diminished.

FUNDAMENTALS

Minicomputers are general-purpose electronic computers with many of the characteristics found on the larger computers, but there are differences. First of all, a minicomputer is physically smaller. Its word length is shorter—usually between 8 and 16 bits, as opposed to 32 to 36 bits in a large computer. It is considerably less expensive—a basic minicomputer system consisting of central processing unit, 4,096 words of memory, and a terminal, today costs as little as $2,200; this is orders of magnitude less expensive than the least expensive large computer system.[1]

Minicomputers are generally more rugged than large computers, and usually stand much higher extremes of ambient temperature and humidity. This characteristic makes minicomputers particularly useful for work in facilities that are not air-conditioned, in mobile installations such as trailers and ships, and in remote locations where environmental conditions may vary greatly.

Like all computers, minicomputers have elements such as a central processing unit (CPU), memory, and input-output interfaces. Some minicomputers have traditional or-

---

[1] Prices mentioned in this Chapter are as of early 1975.

ganization; others employ a newer bidirectional data path structure exemplified by the Digital Equipment Corporation UNIBUS®. In Figure 4-1, traditional minicomputer architecture employing two bus lines is shown. One bus connects the memory directly to the CPU and indirectly to the peripheral devices via a direct memory access (DMA) link. Thus, the processor must intervene in all normal (non-DMA) data transfers from and to memory. The DMA link is an option and is not found in all minicomputer systems. Without DMA, all data transfers require processor intervention between the peripherals and memory. This can restrict the rate of data transfer.

The bottom illustration in Figure 4-1 shows minicomputer organization on the UNIBUS principle. Here, both memory and peripherals are on the same bus, from which the CPU is also hung. The bus is asynchronous and bidirectional. Under this arrangement, any system element except memory (i.e., CPU or peripherals) can assume control over the bus and initiate functions such as data transfers. Data transfers

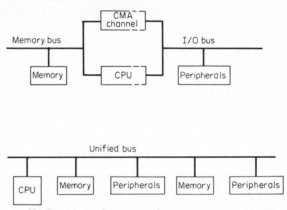

Fig. 4-1   Minicomputer architecture

can occur directly from memory to peripherals, between peripherals, or from peripherals to memory, without the need for a separate DMA link. Since processor intervention is not required for these operations, data transfer rates involved are considerably faster.

Although many minicomputers have raw computing speeds comparable or superior to those of larger computers, the amount of data handled at any period of time tends to be smaller, because minicomputers are physically smaller devices. Thus, for some applications, a basic minicomputer can be slower than a large computer in terms of throughput. However, for some types of calculation, the use of a second special-purpose processor in a minicomputer system can close this gap; but this requires specific system configurations.

The programs available for today's minicomputers are highly sophisticated and highly efficient. Early minicomputer programs were restricted to low-level machine or assembly languages; now most major minicomputers have at least one high-level language available. The most widespread of these is FORTRAN, followed closely by BASIC. Several manufacturers have developed versions of FORTRAN that are fully compatible with (and sometimes extensions of) the industry-standard FORTRAN IV. Some manufacturers have even developed their own high-level languages such as FOCAL®, which was developed for Digital Equipment Corporation computers.

A minicomputer is almost never used except in a system configuration beyond the central processor and the software. (Some purists insist on classifying a central processor, the software, and a terminal as a "system"; viewed in this light, even a tabletop minicomputer in its minimum configuration is a "system".) The third ingredient of a minicomputer system, as of any computer system, is its peripheral devices, which can roughly be subdivided into storage devices and input-output devices.

Minicomputer peripherals, like minicomputers themselves, generally are less expensive and more rugged than their large-computer counterparts. A wide range of computer peripherals are available for minicomputers, including line printers, CRT displays, plotters, magnetic-tape storage devices, card readers, paper-tape readers and punches, and magnetic-disk storage devices. Using these peripherals, powerful and versatile minicomputer systems can be created. The simplest system, to be sure, is a computer with one input-output device like a teletypewriter. Usually, though, a computer system has several peripheral devices. The most common is some form of mass storage device, although frequently printers are used.

Turn-key and General Systems   Minicomputer systems are often divided into *turn-key* and general categories. A turn-key system is one that is designed to do a specific job with no further effort on the part of the user. That is, all the user has to do is turn the power key on and the system is ready to perform its function. Such turn-key systems are sold as units with an integrated design of both system components and software. They are particularly useful to those users who have little or no programming experience and who see no need to learn programming. Such systems can be configured for most of the applications that computers are used for; and usually the manufacturer of the system will document, maintain, and service the system as a system.

A general system, on the other hand, is just what its name implies: a system capable of performing more than one function. Obviously, such a system cannot be turn-key, since it would require reprogramming in order to perform its different functions. Although many of the general systems are programmed in low-level languages, some systems employ high-level languages, which means that reprogramming general systems has become easier than was originally the case.

Multiple Computer Systems   In addition to being used in systems by themselves, minicomputers are sometimes used in systems employing more than one computer. Where this is the case, the minicomputer can be used in any of three ways: as an "assisting" device, to relieve another computer of some of its chores; as an element in a management chain, taking charge of certain operations with complete autonomy; and as a part of a network of minicomputers, where each minicomputer acts as an element of a total computer "team."

Minicomputers used as assisting devices are generally restricted in the type of actions they are programmed to perform. A minicomputer may be connected to a large computer, for instance, to take care of all the petty details so that more of the memory of the large computer can be dedicated to sheer computation. In such a case, the minicomputer's functions are usually communicative ones, acting as a link between the large computer and the user(s).

Systems in which minicomputers are used as part of a larger computing scheme may be organized to give the minicomputer a considerable degree of independence. In such systems, one or more minicomputers are connected via communication lines with a larger computer. Each minicomputer may in turn be connected either directly to a process or to more limited special-purpose computers or logic elements known as *controllers*. In either case, the minicomputer performs its functions largely as would an independent system; however, when it encounters a problem beyond its capacity, it contacts the large computer and "calls for help." It forwards such problems to the larger computer, which solves them and returns the answer to the small computer. Further, in some systems, the larger computer monitors the activity of the smaller computer and makes high-level decisions on the basis of the minicomputer's outputs. This arrangement of minicomputers and larger computers working in partnership is known as a *hierarchical arrangement*, and systems employing this principle are known as *hierarchical systems*, as further discussed under "*Applications*," below.

A computer hierarchy may parallel the management of a company. (See Figure 4-2.) Minicomputers are often used in a manufacturing environment to monitor the performance of special-purpose devices known as *programmable controllers*, which in turn control machine tools or equivalent manufacturing machinery. To this extent, the minicomputer is analogous to a supervisor overseeing a number of production workers. Like the supervisor, the minicomputer can act as a backup to those it monitors, augmenting the operations of a controller when the controller encounters a circumstance beyond its capacity. Just as a supervisor may report to a department manager, so a minicomputer in a hierarchy would report to a larger (medium-scale) computer. And just as each minicomputer would monitor the operations of a number of controllers, so a medium-scale computer would monitor the reports of a number of minicomputers.

While one minicomputer might be supervising the operation of a manufacturing process, another might be in charge of a materials handling and storage operation; thus, the medium-scale computer might alert a storage-application computer that it should ready a store of raw materials to be shipped to the manufacturing area because the manufacturing minicomputer informed the medium-scale computer that supplies were running low.

The medium-scale computer could also be hooked up to a large computer that would be the equivalent of the board of managers of a company. By correlating the inputs from a number of medium-scale hierarchies, the large computer could help develop the overall corporate strategies of the company's operations. With proper communication channels, the large computer could be connected to medium-scale computers at remote locations, thus permitting one centralized evaluation of a number of diverse operations to take place.

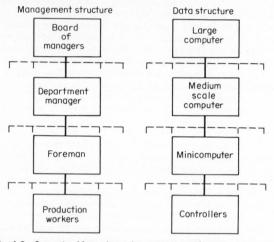

Fig. 4-2 Computer hierarchy and management hierarchy compared.

A third arrangement is one in which individual minicomputers are coupled together to produce the equivalent of a much more powerful computer. This may be done by organizing the computer's data paths and internal programming so that each can handle one aspect of a difficult problem. Also, other schemes can permit each minicomputer to work on a problem in parallel with other problems being analyzed by the other minis. Such multiple-computer arrangements could also be used as a section or level of a hierarchy.

APPLICATIONS

Dedicated Systems versus Multipurpose Within the parameters imposed by hardware considerations, minicomputers are limited when compared to large-scale computer systems. A typical minicomputer might have, say, 8K words of 16-bit length in its memory; a large-scale computer might have 8K words of 32 bits. In this situation, the minicomputer would already be limited by sheer memory capacity; in the hypothetical example, the large-scale computer has twice the memory. And since large-scale computers usually have more than 8K words of internal storage, it should be obvious that the larger machine has a greater degree of program flexibility because of the additional space to store instructions and data.

As a result of this situation, minicomputer systems tend to be "dedicated" to a single job. That is, they are programmed to concentrate all their resources in doing one thing. On that basis, minicomputer systems can be extremely effective.

A word about dedicated systems: A dedicated minicomputer system is not the same as a special-purpose system. Although it does only a single job at a time, it can be reprogrammed to do completely different jobs merely by reading a new program into the computer's memory. Through the use of a high-speed bulk storage device such as a disk, a minicomputer can be completely reprogrammed in a matter of seconds. Thus, the dedicated minicomputer system need not be a restriction to a computer user; the same computer system that is dedicated to a process control job in the morning could be used as a general calculating system in the early afternoon and as an inventory system toward the close of the business day.

A multipurpose computer system is one that can carry on several different operations during the same time period. Usually, minicomputers are not used in such applications, although some are used in time-sharing systems where one computer can service multiple terminals. Time sharing is usually considered a dedicated function in a minicomputer system, since the majority of minicomputer time-sharing systems employ the same database (e.g., a common language and stored constants), even though the different users may be requesting solutions to problems requiring widely differing calculations.

AREAS OF USE

In science, industry, communications, commerce, education, medicine, agriculture, and even entertainment, minicomputers are used for a variety of functions. And although the minicomputer's uses started in the scientific laboratory, its utilization has grown to the point where minicomputers are involved in every major phase of human activity.

Communications One application area in which minicomputers have been highly useful is data communications. Data communications is a large subset of the field of communications, but it is restricted to the transmission and reception of numbers, letters, and special "operator" characters such as punctuation, addition signs, etc. These characters are used as input data to computers, information for reservation and billing systems, and status information from remote stations. Minicomputers are used in data communications for message switching, data concentration, and front-end processing.

Message switching is the technique whereby a terminal sends information either to a computer or to another terminal. Previous to using minicomputers for this purpose, it was necessary for a large computer to control these functions and/or to employ a specialized form of hardware to do the job. Through use of minicomputers, the system can be adapted to the particular needs of a communications network through programming to achieve maximum efficiency. A hardware-based system would have a fixed number of channels, for instance, meaning that either some channels would go unused in an original configuration or that any additions might entail a rebuilding of the entire switching device. By contrast, reprogramming can make such alternatives trivial in a minicomputer system.

Beyond the area of message switching is the concept of data concentration. Here, the minicomputer takes data to be sent to a computer from more than one source and combines the inputs into a single stream in order to use the communication channel more efficiently. In some respects, it is like a form of remote-location time sharing. Such operations are possible because the operating speed of a minicomputer is considerably faster than that of a terminal. A standard teletypewriter terminal has an input or output speed of 10 characters per second. Since the normal operating speeds of computers are in millionths of a second, a lot of time is available between the input (or output) of one character and the next. If a computer is programmed and organized properly, it can spend this "spare time" interacting with another input device—in fact, with a number of them. The character data obtained from the individual terminals can be arranged in some fashion—either character by character or block of characters by block of characters—to permit the combined messages to be transmitted at the maximum data rate possible on the communication line. Similarly, the remote computer can send data back in an equivalent format for the minicomputer to distribute to the appropriate terminals that it is servicing.

Another communications-related application of minicomputers is that of front-end processing. When a large computer is used to service a number of terminals and/or other input-output devices, a portion of the computer's memory must be dedicated to programs required to switch messages between terminals, to interpret different input codes, and the like. This requirement diminishes the computer's processing capabilities, since it can devote less than its full resources to processing. However, if a minicomputer is used between the large computer and its terminals, the large machine can be relieved of most, if not all, of these nonprocessing functions. The small computer is pro grammed to do this detail work, freeing virtually all of the larger computer's resources from communication functions to analytical functions. Such an arrangement means that either the required analyses can be performed with a smaller large-scale computer than would otherwise be necessary, or an existing large-scale computer can be made substantially more effective at a relatively modest investment.

Business   Originally, business applications were the exclusive domain of the large-computer system. This situation has altered, and more and more minicomputers are being used for these functions. In part, this has been due to hardware and software developments that have made minicomputers considerably more effective than were the original models. Additionally, the price of minicomputers made it possible for smaller businesses to obtain computer power, whereas before they had to rent a terminal to an outside service, drop off forms to a service bureau, or do without any form of computer assistance.

For small to medium-sized businesses, minicomputer systems have been employed as total computing facilities. With the use of mass storage devices such as magnetic-tape drives and reels, data can be stored easily for use. Also, control programs on other reels of tape make reprogramming of such systems very rapid. Usually, the minicomputer-based business system employs a minimum of two tape drives and often uses more, sometimes with other high-speed input-output devices.

The normal procedure for operating a minicomputer-based business system is to run one business requirement at a time. That is, a control tape is fed into the computer's memory with the appropriate program. The data are accessed as required from another tape, with updates made by an input-output device similar to a teletypewriter terminal. Often the resulting data are transferred to another tape for record purposes, and concurrently, or immediately thereafter, the required printed information is output, usually on a high-speed line printer. Such systems can perform accounting, inventory control, billing (including discounting), sales analyses, and the like.

Business hierarchies.   Just as minicomputers can be used for manufacturing hierarchies, as previously discussed, so can they be used for business hierarchies. However, in these applications, we tend to depart more from the "classical" business uses—after-the-fact data processing—and concentrate, rather, on the "real-time situations," where business is being conducted immediately.

A typical application for a minicomputer in a hierarchy might be in a point-of-sale terminal arrangement. The minicomputer would be located in a store or department and would be connected to terminals at sales points. In the case of cash transactions, the information would be forwarded either to a mass storage area for temporary storage, or directly to the main computer located either at the central offices of the store or at the corporate headquarters of the chain. In the event of a credit sale, the minicomputer would access a mass storage device for credit information (if unavailable locally, the minicomputer could obtain the information from the appropriate storage device via communications through the main computer). If valid, the sale would be consummated; if not, an instant credit refusal could be made. Not only would the large computer be used for the appropriate data processing, billing, and—in advanced systems—even inventory checks, but in addition, it would be used for corporate-level sales analyses, top-level management strategies, and other executive analytical work.

Figure 4-3 is a schematic of a computerized point-of-sale business computer network. At each sales point, there would be two special terminals to communicate with the centralized departmental minicomputer. One would be connected to a cash register to record cash sales. This connection would be primarily for accounting purposes, though the register could indicate which "cash" sales were made by check, which were made by adjustments, credit slips, etc. The other terminal would be for credit-card sales.

The credit terminal would permit credit cards and checks to be verified before purchases were made. In the case of a check, the terminal would be used for verification only; the sales clerk could enter the customer's name and both the account bank numbers of the check along with the check's amount. An indicator light would verify whether the check was approvable or not on the basis of checking the system's files to determine whether any bad checks had been passed under those numbers. In the case of the credit-card sale, the operator would enter the customer's name and the designation of the credit card (i.e., whether it was a store card, a bank card, or other card recognized by the·establishment) as well as the charges. The information would be checked against the store's files by first searching against the local storage for "bad card" information, or upper purchase limitations. For very large orders, if the card cleared this first stage, the data could be sent to the store's central computer for further verification.

The store's central computer would be located in the accounting area. For a single store, such a system could be a medium-scale computer; for a store chain, a large computer. In a chain, the departmental minicomputers could be connected remotely to a large computer in another location via communication lines. The large computer, which would be at the top of such a hierarchy, not only would correlate sales informa-

Departmental minicomputer

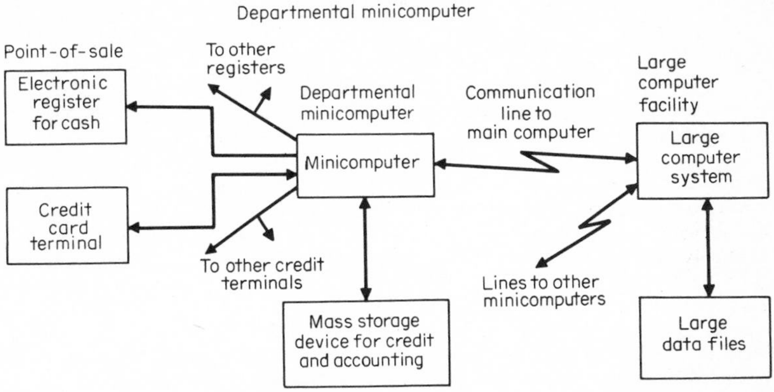

Fig. 4-3 Schematic of a computerized point-of-sale business computer network.

tion from the different store locations, and verify credit when queried, but could "alert" the local computers about bad checks, stolen or invalid credit cards, and the like.

Industry Minicomputers have been used for a large number of industrial applications, from stand-alone "supercalculators" all the way to elements in plant-wide hierarchies. Automation via minicomputer has been demonstrated to be a highly efficient means of running a process or activity. In industry, minicomputers are used for monitoring a process, controlling a process, or acting as a communication link between more than one related activity.

The simplest form of minicomputer application is that of monitoring processes. In the crudest form, the minicomputer is connected to instrumentation that in turn is connected to the process or activity under scrutiny. The data from the item being monitored are transmitted to the minicomputer, which in turn translates and "preprocesses" the data, outputting the results onto magnetic tape or punched paper tapes. The tapes are periodically forwarded to a larger computer for detailed analysis.

In more sophisticated systems, the minicomputer has sufficient power to perform the analyses itself. Usually, such a system makes use of some form of temporary data storage or uses extended memory, or both. Minicomputer systems used for this purpose can monitor a variety of operations simultaneously. Some minicomputers are used in this fashion to determine the performance of one or more entire processes in a manufacturing environment; others are used to monitor similar parameters in a number of equivalent operations (e.g., fuel and materials consumption in a catalytic process in a petrochemical plant).

In some cases, such monitoring and data acquisition systems are part of a computer's hierarchy. In such an arrangement, the processed results of the minicomputer system's activities would be transmitted to a larger computer for correlation. Such inputs from a number of monitoring stations could permit the logistical and maintenance requirements of the manufacturing operations to be performed with utmost efficiency.

The step beyond monitoring in industrial systems is control. Here, the minicomputer is required to perform some task. It might be the control of the precision machining of automotive parts or of the blending of ingredients to achieve the proper octane level in gasoline production, or even of mixing solids, such as baked goods dough or concrete. In systems used for control, the minicomputer is programmed to keep the process within certain limits, which may include such parameters as materials flow, temperature, pressure, and container volume. Sensors in the equipment performing the process transmit data to the computer, which in turn analyzes the data and, when required, transmits commands to return the process to an optimum performance from any deviation. The minicomputer is highly useful for certain manufacturing functions where the work is dull, repetitive, or requires very fast reactions, since the minicomputer does not get bored and can react to a situation in millionths of a second.

Scientific and Engineering Research In scientific and engineering research, minicomputers have made what is perhaps their strongest impact. The use of minicomputers to analyze and control scientific experiments was the first major application to which minicomputers were put. As in other areas, a minicomputer can be used for analysis, control, or both.

The simplest form of use for a minicomputer in analysis is as a data processing or calculating device. The majority of minicomputers currently available are capable of running programs in a high-level programming language such as FORTRAN IV or BASIC—languages that were once the exclusive province of large-scale computers. A minicomputer that is capable of running a high-level language like FORTRAN permits the scientist or engineer to have the computing power normally expected only on a terminal connected to a remote computer through a communication line, but without requiring the large computer. Experience has shown that the average rental costs for a time-sharing terminal are sufficient to purchase a minicomputer in 6 months to a year.

Having a minicomputer as a data processing calculator is also useful in other ways. For instance, if a facility is renting time from an external computer bureau, often the time-sharing channels are obtainable on a "first-come" basis. This means that on busy days, a considerable amount of time may be wasted just establishing connection to the computer from the terminal. Then, there is also the matter of possible malfunctions. If there are problems in the communication lines, the terminal may be disconnected from the remote computer halfway through a job, and contact may be difficult to re-establish. Also, there is the possibility that the large computer might fail. If some malfunction should happen to a large remote computer, all those who have terminals connected to the machine will be put out of action; with an equivalent number of minicomputers used for the same sort of analyses, the malfunction of one will not affect the operations of others.

This is not to say that a minicomputer will do all the analyses that a large-scale computer will do. A large-scale computer is invaluable for in-depth analyses such as mathematical simulations, or for other operations that require broad-scale operations and databases; but most of the time-sharing requirements do not necessitate any operations of that magnitude. Where more complex problems appear, a minicomputer can often be connected to another mini or in a hierarchical arrangement to a larger machine to solve the problem.

Indeed, often the situation is that the mini is sufficiently powerful so that it can form the basis of a time-sharing activity in its own right. There are several commercial minicomputer time-sharing systems, most of which can service over a dozen users simultaneously.

Beyond calculations, minicomputers are used for analysis and control in experiments. Coupled to instruments, minicomputers can decrease markedly the time required to perform the analysis or experiment. As a consequence, more experiments can be performed in a given period of time, with the computer doing the slow, boring work that previously had to be done manually by the researchers. In addition, any interesting or significant effects show up immediately in the course of an experimental run, permitting unusual effects to be investigated in detail without waiting for rescheduling or setting up the experiment again.

Biomedicine and Health Minicomputers have found many applications both in biomedical research and in medical care. Vital functions can be monitored by minicomputers through the use of special electronic interfaces. As in other fields, the inputs to the minis can be monitored.

In addition to pure research in biological laboratories, these monitoring functions can be particularly important in hospitals. Minicomputer systems can be programmed to monitor instrumented patients in intensive-care wards. Should any monitored vital function (breathing rate, pulse, etc.) fall or rise beyond previously established limits, the computer will alert the medical staff so that the patient can receive treatment with a minimum of delay. Such patient-monitoring systems are usually employed in a time-shared environment; thus, one minicomputer generally monitors six or more patients simultaneously.

In addition to monitoring, minicomputers are also used for normal analytical work. Interfaced to blood-serum analyzers, the minicomputer can perform the necessary calculations to determine the proper blood fractions that a doctor needs to know—and it can print out the results in a standardized form. Other instrumentation, when computerized, is equally useful in medical analyses.

Finally, minicomputers are even used to perform patient interviews before the doctor examines the patients. In such an arrangement, the computer flashes questions on the screen, and the response of the patient determines the next question that the computer asks. The results are presented to the doctor as a report before the patient is examined, giving the doctor time to become familiar with the patient's medical history.

Other Applications With literally tens of thousands of minicomputers in the world, the number and variety of applications grows each day. Minicomputers are used for virtually every major phase of human activity. They have gone exploring with teams in the field—for example, a minicomputer was aboard the *USS Manhattan* when it sailed the Northwest Passage. They are used in entertainment, from selling tickets at reservation agencies to controlling scoreboards at baseball stadiums to producing animated films. They are used to handle baggage at airports, to sort tea in English warehouses, to monitor pollution, and to raise poultry. And the list keeps growing. With newspapers being typeset by minicomputers, packages being sorted by minicomputers, food being processed by minicomputers, the chances are that almost everybody in the United States has been in contact with at least one minicomputer-processed or minicomputer-influenced item each day.

CONCLUSION

From something that was thought of as an upstart device when first introduced, the minicomputer has grown into an important segment of the computer industry. Because of its ruggedness, durability, and low cost, it will continue to play an important role, both in individual systems and in partnership with other computers.

Chapter **5**

Design Trends

EARL C. JOSEPH
Staff Scientist, Sperry Univac, St. Paul, Minnesota

Management's attitude toward computers has matured to the point where most users are far less interested in the "geewhiz" equipment components and far more concerned about what ADP systems can do for their organizations. The emphasis today is on effective and practical application of computer systems. Current management interests when upgrading to newer systems are thus in the key areas of:

- Application cost-effectiveness — more throughput per dollar invested.
- Direct program compatibility. (Current investments in programs now far exceed hardware cost over life of system.)
- Total systems availability and reliability of hardware and software.

Since the digital computer was first used to assist in the management of business some 2½ decades ago, it has significantly reshaped the management task. In fact, the very foundation of management — the acquisition, interpretation, and use of business information — has been altered. Over this period, computer alternatives and options have proliferated with explosive acceleration, and it may be expected that this trend will continue. Industry forecasters have estimated that by 1980 millions of remote terminals will be communicating with computers,[1] and certainly many of these will be used directly by managers. Thus an even greater impact of computers on management can be anticipated in this decade, with the capability of extending (or, in computerese, "remoting") the computer's power to where managers manage — at their desks and throughout the organization.

However, while innovative technological leaps will continue to characterize developments in the computer industry, it should be pointed out that today's computer technology already suffices for a major portion of business ADP needs. That is, the main developments in the application of computers will not lie in hardware technology per se, but rather in the software areas of programming, systems, applications software, and management. At the same time, management cannot ignore orders-of-magnitude changes in hardware technology which reduce costs, increase efficiency, increase capability and capacity, increase reliability, and make computers easier to use. Users must expect radical departures in computer architecture to continue, and such advances will further expand the use of computers.

Time sharing, low-cost hardware, minicomputers, availability of a multitude of pro-

---

[1] The author is of the opinion that this may well be an understatement, considering forecasts for computer usage in community information systems, schools, medicine, customer contact in banking and retailing, and others.

grams, and computer networks are changing the heretofore universal economy-of-scale rule of thumb—"the bigger the cheaper." For a large number of business applications, the economic route is via distributed smaller systems rather than a larger central computer system. This opening of the door for management to alternative choices, for centralized versus noncentralized and specialized versus general-purpose systems, calls for considerable knowledge about these systems—in terms of comparative advantages, not necessarily in terms of detailed technology. The wrong choice could be costly—millions of dollars could be wasted, not necessarily in terms of not providing the needed capability, but in terms of how much less costly the choice could have been. The right decision could bring many added values and offer easier evolution (upgrading) into the future.

COMPUTER TRENDS

Computer System Architecture It appears that the demand for computers in any specific application area will not significantly affect the development of general-purpose computer technology. Computer system architecture design innovations are emerging to allow computer systems to be tailored (pieced together) to meet specific application requirements. While many special-application computers are again beginning to appear, in many cases the special systems are attachable to and/or require general-purpose computer systems.

The major factor in the movement into fourth-generation computer systems design is the evolution of third-generation systems. Thus far this transition is largely characterized as the "3½ generation." The evolved changes include the addition of some new features, new technology, and new additions to the families of processors and peripherals. In most, if not all, cases, the key enhancement achieved is more cost-effective computing while maintaining direct program compatibility with the past generation. In the process, many new architectural features are in a sense presently being "batched," waiting to be incorporated into the true fourth-generation systems.

As of this writing, a considerable ferment is brewing in semiconductor technology. This ferment will bring about revolutionary changes as the industry moves further into fourth-generation computers. The resulting new computer architectures, now just emerging, offer a varied spectrum of choices to the user. The visible growing trend is the movement toward what may be characterized as *polysystems*.

Polysystems use low-cost, standardized-function *macromodules* (both hardware and software). These "off-the-shelf" modules can be pieced together to form a wide variety of computer systems. In general, the newer architectures are application-tailorable, specialized, dedicatable, and dispersible. They also allow high-speed emulation of past programs, and the continuation of the trend toward common system software. Many are essentially networks of computerlike functions. These networks are organizable to adapt to a wide range of architectural environments for effectively increasing throughput (performance) and greatly reduce programming and hardware costs. Thus, the result of moving toward higher levels of integration of hardware is now drastically impacting the design of future computer system architectures.

Additionally, these same hardware modules are being used to (1) replace costly and high-usage software—"hard software"; (2) make things more "intelligent" (such as memory, peripherals, processors, machines, tools, instruments); and (3) automate computers—programming, debugging, maintenance, simulation, and a host of applications.

Polysystems can be configured and dynamically reconfigured to form a wide variety of architectures to fit application requirements. In this proliferation of variety, the winner is obviously the user. The newer architectures allow computers to be molded and system-integrated to fit within management and application environment needs. Even though the trend is toward specially tailored systems, the emerging polysystem architectures are general-purpose.

Computer Generations In the past, it was relatively easy to spot the demarcation points between computer generations. Historically, the introduction of new computers has occurred after revolutionary advances in hardware technology: vacuum tubes for the first generation, transistors for the second, and integrated transistor circuits for the third. Lately, however, the introduction of many other new features—in the repertoire, memory, peripherals, communications, programs, remote terminals, operating systems, architectures, and the like—have made the distinction between generations increasingly fuzzy. Therefore, it is far from adequate to characterize such a complex structure as a modern computer system by a simple generation breakdown along hardware lines. Further, with the advent of the third generation, the switch was made from manufacturers providing *computers* (the central part of an ADP system) to the era of supplying computer *systems*—processors, memories, software, and peripheral systems for doing total tasks. In the main, each generation characteristic falls within a different time scale. Thus to give a date for the introduction of fourth-, fifth-, and sixth-generation systems will depend on the feature, or features, which each user or designer sees as the major distinguishing mark.

The average lifetime of a computer generation is approaching one decade and soon may approach two decades (through piecemeal updating). Yet each next generation comes along after an interval of about 6 years. The lifetime of a computer generation therefore considerably overlaps previous and future generations. The rapid evolution into the fourth computer generation—spurred on primarily by the immense proliferations of low-cost hardware and minicomputers—is as of this writing now under way. Fourth-generation computer systems are characterized by trends such as the moves toward medium- and large-scale integrated (MSI/LSI) circuits, extended families of computers, semiconductor memories, programmable repertoires, microprogramming, processors for special functions, greater reliability and availability, subprograms in hardware, automated debugging of programs, a multitude of different computer peripherals, remotes, and terminals, and computer networks.

Further, fourth-generation computer systems will be tied even more to the telecommunications systems, allowing the computer to "remote" its power to where it is needed. Indeed, the telephone will probably become the most widely used "terminal" of the late 1970s or early 1980s—incorporating voice input and output. Such an availability of computer power is bound to have an immense impact on management, far greater than the computer has had to date. Figure 5-1 summarizes trends in past, present, and expected future generations of computers.

ADP Feature Trends   In the past, considerable insight into the near future could be gained by looking at the best features which each individual computer, peripheral, memory, or semiconductor manufacturer was capable of, without considering possible new breakthroughs. Even today, if we assume that sometime in the future the best features of each individual manufacturer will be synergistically combined, the computer industry would be capable of producing systems with a thousandfold reduction in cost! (In the past, only a factor of 10 or so was available from such combinations.) When will this happen? In the recent past, up until the late 1960s, such a combination could have occurred and did occur within a time span of a few years (2 to 5 years).

Today, there are many reasons why it will take much longer. First, because of the economic conditions of the early 1970s there is less mobility of people in our industry—and thus, less mobility of proprietary ideas. Second, there is considerably less Government-supported computer R&D—and thus, computer innovations now supported by industry take longer to emerge into the public domain. Third, and perhaps most important, the initial expense of launching a new generation is far greater than making evolutionary changes to the current generation to increase cost effectiveness.

The result of the foregoing developments has been the spawning of a considerable variety in systems, in which one or more advances are incorporated. Such fragmentation causes waves of new products from which it is difficult for users to make a choice. It also leads to the use of multiple manufacturers' products in typical systems, with corresponding multiplication of product mixes.

The second-generation computer's capability was somewhat measurable from knowledge about the execution time of its instructions—the number of instructions executable per second. Early in the era of the third-generation computers it was common to compare computer capabilities in terms of MIPS (millions of instructions per second). However, it soon became apparent that such a measure was inadequate for determining or comparing how well a computer would perform on a specific application. One major reason why this simplistic measure was inadequate was the diversity in features and instructions incorporated in different computer systems. That is, to do a certain task, some computers would need to execute as few as 100 instructions, while others would require as many as 1,000—i.e., as much as a 10 to 1

Generation and date introduced	Character-izing computing	Architecture	Primary logic/hardware	Modularity	Software characteristics
Pre-1940s First	Calculation	Stored Program	Relays	–	–
1 1951–52	Business and Scientific – Automatic Computation	Special-Purpose Computers	Vacuum Tubes	Electrical Components	Machine Language, Subroutines, Utility Routines, Libraries, Symbolic Assemblers
2 1958–60	Data Processing	General-Purpose Computers	Transistors	Logic Gates	Higher-Level Languages (COBOL, FORTRAN), Monitors, Macroassemblers, Supervisors and Executives
3 1963–65	Information Processing	Systems · Centralized · Multiple · Families	Integrated Circuits (IC/SSI)	Multiple Circuits	Operating Systems, Many Languages, Multiprogramming, Packaged Programs, Simulation Languages, Modular Programs
4/3½ 1970–72	On-line Information Processing	Networks of Systems · Dispersible · Application or function dedicated	SSI/MSI/LSI	Subfunctions	Extendible Languages, Metacompilers, Interacting Conversational Systems
5 1976–78	Man's (Intelligent) Assistant – Mind Amplifiers	Polysystems and "Intelligent" Adjuncts	MSI/LSI/GSI	Macrofunctions	"What" (in place of "How") Type Programming, "Hard Programs," Natural Languages

Fig. 5-1 Computer generation characteristics.

difference. Thus, a slower MIPS computer, in some instances (those with a "richer" instruction repertoire in terms of the specific application), could actually have a considerably higher throughput than a "faster" computer (one with a higher MIPS, but with a repertoire not as well suited to the application). Thus, users turned to "benchmarking" their applications before deciding which computer to purchase (i.e., running a typical or simulated problem on each computer under consideration).

As the industry moves further into the fourth generation of computers, the trend toward expanding repertoires – programmable (usually) microcoded repertoires, higher-level instructions, and application-tailored repertoires – it becomes increasingly more difficult to compare computer systems.

Logic (Hardware) Design Trends Dynamically variable computer system architectures are now emerging. They allow their hardware and software to be modularly tailored and reconfigured for each application. It is expected that such tailored systems will remain program-compatible with one another. Yet the many hardware and software complement choices of application-tailored systems could mean that each computer system may be architecturally different from all others. This rebirth of special-purpose systems can evolve without the past evils of incompatibilities.

A major element that is causing drastic potential changes in computer design comes from the tremendous strides now being made in the semiconductor industry. From a consideration of semiconductor technology it now appears that semiconductor prices for the 1970 decade are accelerating downward at a rate of a factor of 10 less (i.e., to one-tenth) each 5 years. In the 1960s the curve was a factor of 10 less each 10 years. Even though we are in an era of evolutionary computer change, such a rapid evolution must be considered revolutionary.

The projected low cost of hardware logic is causing an upheaval in design considerations for future computers. The small computer on a chip has emerged; some microcomputers on a chip are already being designed today, and the calculator on the chip is a reality. Before 1980, very capable (as capable as first-generation computers and many of today's minicomputers) data processing functions may cost less than $100 each in high-volume production. Thus, since the hardware of computers is approaching "zero cost," we will lose interest in keeping such resources busy. As a result, operating systems will require considerably less storage; and they, as well as the total ADP system, will become more efficient.

The growing ferment in the semiconductor field is leading to a large number of contending technologies: bipolar (BIP), metal oxide semiconductors (MOS), ion implantation, field effect, small-, medium-, large-, and grand-scale integration (SSI, MSI, LSI, GSI), charged coupled devices, hybrid, flat packs, thermocompressing bonding, beam leads, isoplanar, chip, monolithic, micromosaic, and others. To describe in detail the design trends in even a few of these areas is beyond the scope of the present discussion. However, general design trends in some of these computer logic areas will be highlighted.

There is a definite trend toward higher levels of integration of circuitry from small-scale through medium-scale to large-scale toward "grand-scale" integration. This trend offers lower cost, physically smaller size, and greater reliability for computer hardware, and there is thus a trend toward incorporating considerably more hardware in computer systems. With lower-cost logic comes the ability to incorporate many more functions and features in computers to enhance their performance and make them more cost-effective—that is, hardware logic for programs, for increasing system availability, and for making equipment "smart." As a result, each scale of ADP system, from the small to large, is becoming considerably more capable and easier to use.

In the larger- and super-scale computer systems, and in some medium-scale computers, the trend is to use the faster technologies offered by BIP and small-scale integration. For the small-scale, mini, and microcomputer systems, the trend is toward the lower-cost technologies gained from MOS—MSI, LSI, and GSI. Soon the era of the "computer on the chip" will become a common building block. However, the performance range of microcomputers is rapidly growing, and is invading the realm of small- and medium-scale computers.[2] Many computer designers are also turning their attention toward the design of multimicrocomputer systems (polysystem networks), which could also foretell the demise of large-scale "dinosaur" systems. Thus, soon only super-scale and microcomputers will be left as the types (range) of general-purpose computers and micro special-purpose computers (computerlike ADP devices).

With the availability of "zero cost" hardware logic and local small memories, considerable design attention is being given to building major segments of the software into the hardware—"hard software." Such considerations point to a trend toward dedicating processors and memory to functions and applications. The major result is an expected two-thirds reduction in the executive portion of the operating system software, again bringing considerably more efficient and cost-effective use of computers, as well as 10:1 and 100:1 cost savings in application programs.

The gross expected rate of change resulting from these semiconductor advances for the 1970 and 1980 decades are:

● System speed (throughput) and reliability enhancement advances—more than a factor of 10 improvement per generation.

● System storage capacity advances—more than a factor of 100 increase per generation.

● System hardware cost reductions—to a factor of 10 less per generation.

● System size, weight, and power reductions—about a factor of 10 less per generation.

Since the design parameters of computer circuits (through the use of higher levels of integration), are revolutionally different, it follows that new system design techniques and architectures will evolve. Some architectural considerations are:

● Application-tailorable systems—systems tailored to applications to achieve cost-effective performance.

---

[2] See Chapter 4, "Minicomputers," in this Part.

- Piecemeal updatable systems.
- Fault-tolerant architectures—self-repairable systems.
- Macromodular systems.
- Multimicrocomputer systems—networks.
- "Hard software" (software in logic or ROMs—read-only memories).
- Dedicated ADP functions—distributed systems.
- "Intelligent" functions.
- Extendible repertoires.
- Dispersed decentralized and federated architectures.
- Bus-oriented systems.
- Maxi (large and super) computers pieced together from multiminicomputers.

Since logic has become an extremely low-cost item, the connections and cables (to the logic) now loom as a high-cost hardware item. It follows, then, that the designers' new problem is to minimize the number of connections rather than the amount of logic used. Further, contemporary large computers require massive amounts of wire and cable. To reduce costs as well as weight and power consumed, more and more systems designers are turning to serial high-speed (single) bus systems.

Distributed ADP System Design Trends A major trend in ADP design is toward distributed function systems and networks. The fact that in the past most general-purpose computers could be used for any application did not mean that they performed each application equally well. They performed some applications more effectively than others, because of the mismatch of general-purpose computer resources to the requirements of the specific application area—and thus variety in computers proliferated.

In recognition of this problem inherent in general-purpose computers, future architectures will tend to be modularly tailorable to application needs. But this new modularity will offer much more. It will also allow the computer to be removed from the confines of centralization. It will permit the dispersion of ADP functions throughout systems, internally and externally to the computer, to wherever data are handled or wherever control functions are performed—allowing further automation of these functions to occur. Because thousands and tens of thousands of logic gates and bits of memory will soon be available as single components, "intelligent" data processing functions (adjuncts) will be attached to such devices as:

- Instruments: autopilot, meters, oscilloscopes, etc.
- Source-data automation devices: collection and dissemination.
- Communication devices: switches, terminals, telephones, concentrators, multiplexers, etc.
- Automobiles and home appliances.
- Sensors and controllers.
- Computer subfunctions: processor, memory, I/O, peripherals, and "old" computers.

This dispersion of computer functions, distributed where data are handled—processed, collected, or disseminated—has now become practical. Lower hardware logic costs allow ADP systems to become more useful and "intelligent." Each such use will spawn a variety of new stand-alone computerlike architectures and new applications of computers. In addition, dispersed ADP systems are more and more being netted together.

This trend of netted computer system architectures will grow. Each unit will be dedicated with its own "hard program" to the function it supports. Most will probably be made from universal functional micromodules that are applications tailored for the dedicated function they perform. They will allow rapid technological advances to be incorporated as they occur; that is, many third-, fourth-, and fifth-generation computers will be *piecemeal updated* into future-generation systems. Thus, no longer will we convert to a new system by bringing in a total new computer; rather we will add new modules, without self-obsoleting the system. Further, this trend foretells the end of computer generations.

Polysystem Design Trends There are four basic types of polysystem computer networks:

- Communication-system netted computer systems.
- Maxis from micros—e.g., multiple microcomputer configurations.
- Arrays (e.g., ILLIAC-IV).

● Central processors with multiple remote terminals.

With the advent of distributing the computer's power, three distinctive types of central processors (CPUs) are also beginning to emerge: (1) The classical "number cruncher" (high-speed arithmetics) CPU-type system, where the data processing and dispersed file processing functions are performed in remote systems. (2) The file processor CPU operating on central files, with remote access and processing of local data. (3) Polysystems – microcoded ADP functional modules netted into computers and ADP systems.

The features and repertoires of polysystems will be extended and enhanced through:

● Microprogram and hardwired controlled modules.

● Microprogrammed control over repertoire as well as hardwired high-order languages.

● Addition of "application engines" which incorporate the processing functions, local memory, and the dedicated application program in the computer hardware.

By allowing microprogram control over the I/O and memory as well as the repertoire, a computer system can truly emulate another computer for both the instruction and data differences, as well as the I/O variations. Users will gain by being able to use past programs directly on next-generation computer systems. Since such ADP adjuncts are modular, by virtue of small units of processing capability and local memory capacity, future systems can be uniquely tailored to achieve application optimum cost- and performance-effective systems. Dispersed- and federation-oriented data processing hierarchies could thus become the common system architectures for future computers.

Recent architecture studies show that it is practicable to build universal microhardware and microsoftware system modules that can be cost-effectively used in a wide variety of computer systems. A high degree of replication can be achieved across and within computer types rather than only from within a single system family. That is, computers would be "pieced" together from an inventory of "off-the-shelf" universal polyunit micromodules. Thus computer system users will reap large cost savings through the replicated use of universal micromodules.

Through the use of universal micromodules, polysystems allow the structuring of all past computer structures. Polysystem architectures, using dedicated hardware and software micromodules, have four basic (optimal) forms:

● Federated/dispersed/distributed polysystem architectures (Figure 5-2) – networks tailored to management functioning and organization.

● Centralized polysystem architectures (Figure 5-3) – networks tailored to emulate current ADP architectures.

● Application federated polysystem architectures – networks tailored to application hierarchy and functioning (Figure 5-3).

● Program/programming federated polysystem architectures – networks tailored to "natural" programming dichotomizations.

Micromodular polysystems are typically pieced together from hard programs (application engines) which are universally applicable microcomputerlike modules. Typically, each microcomputer module is dedicated to a specific function for relatively long terms; dynamic rededication normally occurs only when drastic changes in system application occur. Thus, future polysystems will have dedicated microcomputers that are:

● Tailored to programming dichotomization:

CPU ADP section – multiple micropolymodules for: application executive tasks, individual applications and/or tasks (many), processor intelligent adjuncts.

ADP memory section for: memory executive, data, and storage management, intelligent adjuncts for stores.

ADP I/O section for: channel intelligence, I/O executive, I/O processing (multiple) tasks, communications, remotes and peripherals – adding intelligence.

● Tailored to application functioning:

Dedicated multiple micros for: individual/independent tasks, cooperative dependent tasks.

● Tailored to management organization:

Dedicated multiple micros for: individual managers (and others), terminal intelligence, instruments/machines intelligent adjuncts.

In addition, these same micromodules can be incorporated into subsystems and added as intelligent adjuncts to *existing* ("old") systems and subsystems for updating them to be program-compatible with new systems, and for greatly extending their capabilities.

Since the micromodules find application in such a wide variety of systems and subsystems, considerable economies are achievable in design, development, manufacturing, testing, number of parts, documentation, training, and programming. Through the use of polymodules, usually 100 per cent of a specific system is implementable from universal micromodules. Few if any modules of a new system need be uniquely designed. With such standard hard-programmed modules, general-purpose computer systems which are tailored to end-use requirements can be constructed. Thus, new

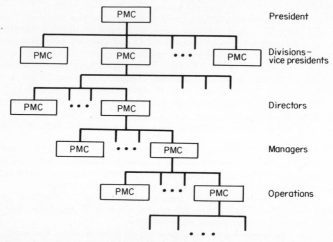

Fig. 5-2 Federated (dispersed) polysystem architecture. Each processing node in this type of network is a collection of polymodules (micro or miniprocessors, local memory, buffers, etc.) distributed throughout the organization via a communications net. Such a federated ADP architecture emulates the natural decentralization of typical management organizations. Each polymodular computer (PMC) assists the individual staff in the typical hierarchical structure by providing computer-assisted processing, storage, retrieval, and communication of information. Generally each PMC is tailored differently in capability and capacity to the individual staff needs, and has varying numbers of remote terminals connected.

computer design becomes a system integration procedure—eliminating much in the design process:

- Time—weeks or months are required instead of years.
- Testing—becomes a simple system functional verification procedure.
- System design and manufacture—module level only, a one-time task not for each system, system integration procedure thereafter.
- Prototyping and simulation—accomplished using the actual micromodules (if result is not what is desired, micromodules can be easily added, subtracted, or recycled).

The common availability of these universal polymodules allows very low cost and short schedules for new computer developments—down from years to months and even days. Conceivably some users will design (piece together) their own system rather than obtain a system from some computer manufacturer. Further, this procedure gives the user a new dimension and freedom for evaluating and obtaining optimum systems for the application. That is, it allows dynamic or short-term design and reconfiguration of computer systems.

Already languages are being developed to allow noncomputer designers to "program the design of their new computer system" as well as to allow the recycling of computer modules from such systems design and to upgrade into "newer" systems. Additionally, in the design or simulation of special systems (for example, in control systems, factory automated systems, military systems, etc.), polymodules can be pieced together much faster and for less cost than writing a program for system simulation or benchmarking. Programs, both application and operating types, are also implemented as compatible software micromodules, and vastly reduce programming costs.

Memory Design Trends A number of trends are observable in memory design. There is an increasing number of levels of memory, from fast, small-capacity, and costly, to

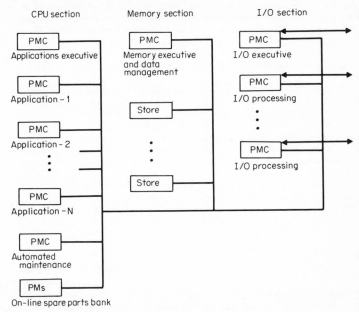

Fig. 5-3 Centralized polysystem architecture. In this polysystem the architecture is organized (tailored) to "natural" programming functions, separating control (executive program), individual applications, memory operations, and I/O processing. Such an architecture emulates a maxicomputer using a network of polymodular microcomputers (PMCs). This organization can be either centralized or decentralized. Note the inherent parallelism in program execution gained through dedicating polymodules (PMs) to such natural program functions, thus greatly increasing ADP system throughput. In this network, each PMC contains a local high-speed buffer for dedication of the high-usage portion of the program associated with the PMC function. This allows the architecture effectively to use a serial high-speed bus for inter-PMC-node connections. (For some applications, multiple serial busses are required in portions of the network to avoid excessive queueing up of waits.)

slow, high-capacity, and low-cost. Many new hardware aids are being added to make the various levels "smart" and "transparent" to the programmer. For each hierarchy level there is now available a diversity of technologies, with considerable diversity between levels—technologies such as magnetic, semiconductor, optical, and holographic, in both the rotating and nonrotating types. Each technology is carving out its own niche in the spectrum of systems, depending upon requirements for speed, capacity, versatility, reliability, and environment.

Typical computer systems use multiple technologies in the memory hierarchy. This increase in storage options offers the user a wide and growing range of cost, capacity, and performance choices. Even so, the predominant memory technology still remains magnetic—specifically magnetic core. However, use of semiconductor memories is rapidly growing. The major application of LSI is for high-speed memory, and this semiconductor technology is rapidly moving down the hierarchy, supplanting some magnetic-core memory areas. MOS memory technology is spurring this trend along. There is a discernible trend toward the use of optical memories for very large capacity memories.

A second major trend, from the viewpoint of ADP use, is that on-line storage capacity is growing much more rapidly than processor performance. Application programs are getting bigger, system software is doing more (thus getting bigger), and more data are being stored for computer manipulation and retrieval. Additionally, the management of storage is being automated more and more through hardware features and system software, thus relieving the application's programmer of this difficult task.

Virtual Memory. Virtual memory is a technique for assisting memory management, and incorporates hardware to automate the process. Its prime purpose is to make the distinction between mass memory (disk or drum storage) relative to main memory largely transparent to the programmer. It manages the limited amount of high-speed, high-cost main memory and a much larger amount of lower-speed, low-cost mass memory in such a way that the programmer, together with system software, does not directly provide the transfers and storage control operations between these two memory hierarchies.

The technique usually entails a means of swapping segments of programs and data from the mass memory into the main memory as required for execution. Virtual memory is the hardware facility for managing (controlling) such segments. To the programmer and user it means that larger jobs can be run, those requiring considerably larger amounts of main memory than is in the system, without requiring the programmer to write unique user code. For those tasks which are not time-sensitive, it allows the requirement for main memory to be reduced by 10 to 100 times. Virtual memory is another of the growing list of operating system features that are being cast into hardware on the pathway toward a future in which the programmer or user will need only be concerned with application algorithms instead of having also to be concerned with system overhead tasks.[3] Successes with virtual memory systems are turning designers toward making the total system virtual (e.g., to errors, I/O, etc.).

RELATED PROGRAM DESIGN TRENDS

In consequence of the foregoing, program costs will tumble by much more than an order of magnitude in this decade, also primarily because of on-line computer interactive program development. Even so, program costs will remain the dominant cost in the use of computers. The dominant hardware cost in most ADP systems is for peripherals, because of the large number used. Memory is the next most high-cost hardware area, again largely because of the large amount used and the growing requirements for more, even though the cost per bit is tumbling rapidly. The CPU hardware, when considered as part of a total system, represents in most cases less than 5 per cent of the total investment. Today, the overwhelming cost to the user over the life of a computer system is the cost of the programs—now approaching 80 per cent of the total cost. Actually this is a desirable trend: We are spending more to use the computer than the cost of the tool.

Computer software design continues on its dynamic march, with frequent changes and enhancements causing the user constantly to be faced with decisions for updating. Usually the decision must be to implement the next revision, or watch the old version quickly be obsoleted and unsupported. Fortunately for the user, designers and manufacturers are aware of this problem and are implementing the new products so that they are generally, if not completely, compatible with past versions in the evolution cycle. Therefore, the major event of the transition between the third- and fourth-generation ADP systems is the stabilizing of software. Operating systems stabilization is being provided even with the simultaneous accelerated proliferation of variety in system families, processors, memories, peripherals, and programs.

A typical task of most programmers soon will be piecing together the desired collection of polysoftware modules. Thus, programming will become characterized as the "what" type rather than the costly "how" type performed today. That is, the typical programmer will describe "what" modules rather than describe to the computer "how" to execute, as is the common programming method today. New languages and new program architectures are already being developed for this micromodular type of programming. As memory becomes less costly, more and more programs will be dedicated

---

[3] For further discussion of virtual memory, see Chapter 2, "Auxiliary Memories," in this Part.

for the long term to specific hardware memory modules. Further, the art and science of programming (methodology) is reaching the point (in the near future) of giving the capability to write correct programs and to prove them correct.

Software Enhancements Computer software enhancements offer probably the greatest opportunity for improvement. But because of high software costs and the user commitments involved, operating systems have an attendant high-risk factor in any design consideration for radical departures. Therefore, most design is directed at evolutionary-type enhancement changes. To this end a variety of hardware features are being added to the architecture of ADP systems to facilitate updating and make operating systems more efficient. Some hardware-related programming design trends are:

- "Hard software" and application program parts incorporated in hardware.
- Microcoding.
- Modular or block-structured programming.
- New system software compatibility with old/past systems.
- Emulation.
- Program products — sold programs.
- Proliferation of application problems.
- Structured/constrained programming.
- Quality control of programs — software reliability.
- Program transferability and transportability features.
- Proliferation of variety in languages: application oriented, enhanced and extensible.
- Standardization of common-use languages (compilers).
- Extensive (almost 100 per cent) use of higher-level languages.
- "What"-type programming.
- "Language-directed" processor design.
- Proving-program-correctness approaches.
- Benchmarking of systems.
- Performance monitoring for optimizing programs and systems.
- Interactive (on-line remote terminal) program development.

Through the use of hard application programs, drastic cost reductions can be expected by the typical user through the elimination of much, if not all, of the programming task now performed on site at user installations.

INSTRUCTION REPERTOIRE DESIGN TRENDS

The instruction repertoire of contemporary computers was somewhat generically crystallized in and based on second-generation logic speeds and memory speeds and their gap ratios. In the intervening years memory technology advances have closed the speed gap. Logic still is considerably faster however: The gap is now about 10:1, whereas it formerly was more nearly 100:1. With the advent of new approaches to microcoding, designers are finding it increasingly difficult to obtain similar system speed (throughput) enhancements offered by the higher-speed logic and memory devices.

Recent experiments vividly show that if computers move away from instruction repertoires toward the incorporation within the hardware of a higher-level language (fed directly to microcode bypassing instructions), a factor of 10 or more speed gain is possible, using present hardware. As yet, no label has been attached to this language level — some candidates are "primitives," "macros," "operators," and the like. In any event, whatever they will be called, they will certainly soon be incorporated into new computers, especially since they additionally offer a similar factor of 10 or more gain (reduction) in amount of storage required for programs. That is, they considerably reduce the number of operations to be written by programmers and stored for execution. They also greatly ease the programming problem by reducing the amount to be coded, debugged, maintained, documented, etc.

The "hard software" in future computer systems will be both wired in logic and microprogrammed in ROMs. High-level language macros being considered as candidates for casting in the logic are:

- Software-type hardware subroutines: compiler macros, language macros; executive macros, operating system macros; data management operators/macros; error detection and correction operations; interface matching operations; repertoire extensions; debugging macros, allowing the semiautomation of debugging.

- Application-type hardware subroutines: high-usage special application subroutines; application processing adjuncts.
- I/O-type hardware subroutines: conversion, coding, etc.; interface matching and switching, multiplexing, etc.; high-usage I/O processing subroutines.

Some additional architectural repertoire feature trends are:
- Stack operations: "addressless coding."
- Descriptor base referencing: data "naming" instead of addressing memory.
- Virtual systems: hierarchical transparency.
- Backward-compatibility mechanisms: microcodes, emulation.
- Local microprogram controlled high-speed memory buffers: in processor, main memory, and I/O sections; peripherals enhancement; remoted and dispersed file operations; data capture and dissemination operations.
- Data management features: operation (type of arithmetic, etc.) attached data; in remotes and peripherals, search, edit, sort, etc.; data naming rather than addressing; associative operations; paging/segmentation operations; variable word operations; automated store and retrieval operations.
- Programmable repertoires.
- Dynamically restructurable and reconfigurable systems.
- Common/standard/universal microprogram controlled functional macromodules.
- Performance monitoring and measurement features.

COMPUTER PERIPHERAL DESIGN TRENDS

The proliferation in variety of computer peripherals includes:
- More flexibility.
- Greater efficiency.
- Lower cost.
- More reliability.
- "Smart"/"intelligent" peripherals: remote devices, microcomputer and memory, terminal systems; tapes, disks, drums, etc.; instruments, tools, sensors, controllers, etc.
- Interactive.
- Tailorable (to application requirements).
- Graphics and CRT.
- Voice output (voice input later in the 1970s or early 1980s): telephone-connected.
- Optical: character and page readers.
- Higher speed.
- "Paperless" types: electronic, microfilm, etc.
- Enhanced standard peripherals.
- Computer communications: digital; serial bus systems; ADP integration via communication networks.

COMPUTER SYSTEM RELIABILITY DESIGN TRENDS

With low-cost modules, maintenance becomes simple and inexpensive through the use of "throwaways." By on-line "wiring" the spares in, self-repair of computers becomes economically practical. This is accomplished by including diagnostic (error-detection, location, and some correction) logic coupled with redundancy techniques and programs the self-repair (programmed switching of macromodules). Such a self-healing computer system need be maintained manually only when the spare parts bank becomes exhausted. Thus applications requiring both remote and long-term unmanned operations will become practical.

Computer system reliability design trends encompass:
- Greater systems availability.
- Expanded error-detection, control, and recovery features.
- Error-correction features.
- Self-repairable system: on-line spare parts bank.

- Off-site semiautomated remote maintenance.
- Fail-safe, fail-soft systems.
- Fault-tolerant computer systems.
- Redundant systems.
- Locks and keys: program, file access, terminal access, and data security features.
- System integrity features.

SUMMARY

The new features and terminology of computers encompass: modular hardware and software, polysystems networks (of micros), "piecemeal updatable" systems, "application-tailored" systems, federated systems, "hard software" and application "hard programs," dedicated ADP resources, and microprogrammed systems. Taken in total, they offer users of next-generation ADP systems many economies and ease of use, and widen the application areas wherein computer-automated systems can greatly assist industry, government, and our total society. Many current computer system design trends highlighted in this Chapter are now occurring which will make ADP extremely cost-effective, even for very small businesses and individuals in their homes. Cost-effective ADP will cause the further proliferation of computers into society (distributed-function networks), spawning the introduction of many new computerized services to assist business (and people in general) through the telephone and a variety of remote terminals.

SELECTIVE BIBLIOGRAPHY

Gruenberger, Fred (ed.), *Fourth Generation Computers: User Requirements and Transition,* Prentice-Hall, Englewood Cliffs, N.J., 1970.

Joseph, Earl C., "Evolving Digital Computer System Architectures," *IEEE Computer Group News,* vol. 2, no. 8, pp. 2–8, March, 1969.

———, chap. 51, "The Coming Age of Management Information Systems," in Peter P. Schoderbek, *Management Systems,* 2d ed., Wiley, New York, 1971.

———, chap. 4, "Computer System Architecture," in Alfonso F. Cardenas, Leon Presser, and Miguel A. Marin (eds.), *Computer Science,* Wiley-Interscience, New York, 1972.

Pylyshyn, Zenon W. (ed.), *Perspectives on the Computer Revolution,* Prentice-Hall, Englewood Cliffs, N.J., 1970.

Part Three
Computer Peripherals

Introduction

THEODORE J. FREISER   *Senior Vice President, John Diebold & Associates, New York, New York*

Hardware peripherals to the mainframe (central processing unit) present the fundamental limiting factor of throughput in the computer system. They must therefore receive substantial attention from those involved with evaluation, selection, and operation of computer equipment, as well as from those engaged in designing and implementing application systems. Because the peripheral devices invariably rely upon mechanical movement, there are inherent limitations in speed and capacity which apparently, like absolute zero, cannot be surpassed. In many instances these mechanical limitations have already essentially been reached, and only a new approach which minimizes or eliminates reliance upon mechanical movement will renew vigorous advance in peripheral technology. At least one exploratory probe has been made toward a storage device having no moving parts: Large-core storage (LCS) serves as a lower-speed adjunct to main memory and is, of course, available at lower cost than main memory. When monolithic memory has been further substantially reduced in cost, it may well offer a faster replacement for LCS, although core memories are less expensive at this writing.

As Part Two of this Section demonstrates, computer hardware poses complex problems in evaluation, selection, and operation. Nowhere is this complexity more severely aggravated than in peripheral devices. Significantly more option features are offered by many more manufacturers than is the case with the mainframe computer. The ability to mix and match vendors offers many potential cost savings, but at the same time poses some truly high-risk situations. It is also important to recognize that while the computer mainframe seldom "goes down" (becomes inoperable as a result of electronic failure or mechanical failure), the same observation can hardly be made about peripheral devices. This, of course, is almost exclusively because peripherals have so many more moving parts and are electronically attached to the mainframe by external cables which are not always the most reliable. The peripheral devices are also in significantly more physical contact with human beings than are the mainframes that control them.

The standard kinds of peripheral devices, many of which have been available for years, are for bulk storage of data and use a moving magnetic medium. Magnetic tape, disk (fixed and movable head), drum, and data cell are the most familiar of these devices, and each medium has undergone substantial improvement during the years since its inception. Faster mechanical speeds combined with higher recording densities have greatly improved their cost performance. Better electronic circuitry has improved reliability, as have improved encoding techniques that allow more perceptive hardware error detection and recovery features.

Paper media are still widely used and are still undergoing minor technological improvements. The most frequently used paper media include the ubiquitous 80-column punched card, the 96-column card, and punched paper tape. Punched mylar tape is also used for such things as numerically controlled machinery.

As a direct result of extraordinary advances in input-output computer peripheral device technology, new media have been developed (though not yet perfected) and are both commercially feasible and in current operation. Among these are: (1) optical scanning devices, offspring of magnetic-ink character recognition (MICR)—used, for example, on checks; optical character recognition (OCR); and mark-sense devices which read hand- or machine-produced paper documents; (2) laser-encoded photographic plates; (3) computer output microfilm (COM) which has become increasingly popular as costs of paper and special forms soar and as bottlenecks become more aggravated when more and more printed computer output is generated. Concomitantly, the cost of microfilming has constantly been going down.

Several other media are receiving increasing attention for input, among them voice recognition and magnetic-stripe cards (such as many credit cards now in circulation). Voice recognition shows great promise because no special equipment is needed by the initiator of the input data. Significant advantages of key entry over voice recognition at this time are its considerably lower cost and higher reliability.

Audio response (the output counterpart of voice recognition) has enjoyed a significant degree of popularity in such diverse applications as credit authorization and telephone number information. Again, the primary advantage in having audio response is that the receiver of data need not have any special equipment.

A fundamental breakthrough in remote peripheral input devices was the advent of the "Touch-Tone" facility for telephones, which allows subscribers to send data to a computer over any voice-grade dial-up line by a series of distinct tones, e.g., produced on a 12-key portable pad acoustically coupled to any telephone. Many such devices are in use today, often in conjunction with an audio-response unit.

One paper medium that has long been available is the printer output. Drum printers, typewriters, and impact, electrostatic, and ink-jet printers are among the different means of producing computer print-outs. Advances in this technology (speed, reliability, and quality) have continually been made. A limiting factor to speed, however, came to the fore when 2,000- and 3,000-line-per-minute printers were introduced, and problems were encountered with paper transport. Forms, especially multipart, and heavy or thin stock tended to come apart. While the printed reports will never completely disappear, they will decrease in number and volume as on-line systems and COM replace them. Exception reporting, which has not gained nearly as widespread acceptance as it merits, is established at least as a trend which also reduces volume and frequency of printed output.

The most significant advances in peripheral computer devices have recently been and will continue to be in source-data automation (SDA). These include scanning and voice recognition already mentioned, as well as continuing improvements in point-of-sale (POS) types of devices and extended application for them.

Because of the ever-reducing cost of core memory and electronic circuitry, minicomputers are becoming cheaper. And because the demands and needs of each remote user of a computer differ, even though they may use a common data bank, more and more terminals are joining stand-alone minicomputers to be linked as polyprocessors. There is an increasing trend toward the "intelligent" or "smart" terminal with integrated processing capabilities. In a very real sense, then, these terminals are the peripherals of polyprocessor systems.

Linked into the technology of the polyprocessor will be the terminal— either one per processor or else buffered and with more terminals per processor. There are several ways in which terminals are developing.

The keyboard is the most common form of data input used today, whether in conjunction with punched cards, punched tape, or the modern key-to-tape or key-to-disk systems. On terminals, the keyboard is commonly connected with a typewriter or cathode-ray tube (CRT). It is not thought likely that much gain in speed will be achieved through the traditional keyboard, since there is a limit to typing speeds. There are some developments in the field of pressure-sensitive devices which may well be cheaper. Other systems using 5 or 10 keys and codes are much less expensive, but require more operator training. There are also interesting developments in analog devices, such as graphic interactive systems using light pens or track balls.

As far as display or output devices are concerned, the greatest breakthroughs will be in CRTs. The teletype is no longer the most popular output method, at least not as a stand-alone terminal, and it will more and more be used simply to provide hard-copy confirmation of CRT display when requested. Technical developments will move away from the slow, cumbersome typing method, and even away from very fast, electrostatic printing processes, toward facsimile reproduction of complete pages using techniques such as fiber optics or half-silvered mirrors. Hard-copy speed will then be similar to the CRT itself. The CRT will increase in usage, since it is invaluable for providing information where no hard copy is required, particularly in query systems. Present technology is moving toward cheaper substitutes for the CRT, such as raster scanning as used in commercial television. One computer could be shared between 64-plus terminals and would need one rotational disk to store and refresh display images. However, the "bi-stable storage" tube (an alternative CRT technology) requires no expensive controller or direct memory access to a computer. Now mainly used in expensive oscilloscopes, technical developments and the demands of interactive terminals are producing significant price reductions.

Much promising work is also being done in the field of lasers as an alternative to the CRT. These are particularly useful for large screens and where little interactive transmission is required. Laser-photochromic displays will become competitive with the CRT, and three-dimensional output by holographic displays will become available, though only to engineering and design outlets until costs come down.

Much research is also being carried out in other fields, including plasma (ionized gas) and liquid crystal display, and by 1985 costs will be so low that a complete all-purpose terminal for visual display, perhaps with microfilm backup, will be available even to households.

The major trends in peripheral computer devices can be summarized as follows: (1) for bulk storage, faster, denser, and cheaper (per unit of data); (2) for input, source-data automation and collection of data close to or at their source; (3) for stored data, to keep them physically as close as possible to the major users but available to low-frequency users over communications lines; (4) to minimize, in general, special interface equipment required of the user of ADP. In short, the eyes, ears, and tongue of the computer will become even closer analogies to their human counterparts.

Chapter 1

Input Devices

DEREK O. ORAM, M.S.E.E.

Director of Engineering, Simplex Time Recorder Company,
Gardner, Massachusetts

ANTHONY B. RAGOZZINO, B.S.M.E., M.S.

Director of Peripherals, Honeywell Information Systems, Honeywell, Inc.,
Minneapolis, Minnesota

The program and data for a computer system are entered into the computer by input devices such as card readers, tape or disk drives, and optical and magnetic character recognition devices, and by paper-tape media or by direct on-line entry via a keyboard. The program and data are recorded and stored on media such as punched cards, marked or imprinted documents, magnetic tape, or disk.

OVERVIEW

Historically, the first significant method of entering data into a computer was via the punched card. The punched card was first developed by Dr. Herman Hollerith to summarize and tabulate the results of the 1890 U.S. Census, since the 1880 Census still had not been completed by 1887 using the old hand methods. Census data were recorded for each person by means of punching holes in a card. The cards were then run through tabulating machines to add and compile the census data. The punched cards were produced on a machine that we now know as the keypunch. Despite new developments, the keypunch is still far and away the dominant method of data entry into a computer. The tabulating machines and their successors were the bases for IBM's initial success in the data processing field.

The punched card invented by Hollerith reigned supreme until IBM introduced a new type of punched card for the System 3 computer system in 1969. This is a punched card that is smaller, packs more data onto the card, and is mechanically easier to handle. To produce the System 3 punched cards also requires a machine similar in function to the Hollerith card keypunch, called a *data recorder*.

An alternative method of data entry is the key-to-magnetic-tape devices first seriously introduced by Mohawk Data Sciences in 1965. In this system the data are recorded on magnetic tape rather than punched cards, the advantage being that the format of the data is not restricted to the size of the card (80 characters of information for the Hollerith card), but can be variable. Since the data are keyed into a buffer memory first, operator-detected errors can be corrected on the same machine before the data are permanently recorded on the magnetic tape. In the unbuffered keypunch system the data have to be verified on a separate machine called a *verifier*.

The next development which has in certain respects superseded key-to-tape is key-to-disk. It differs from key-to-tape in that as many as 64 key input stations are controlled by a computer, which transfers the data from each station onto disk storage, and at the same time can perform more editing and validation of the data while they are being entered. Data can also be generated for input into each record. Despite the fact that on a per-station basis key-to-disk is more expensive, it is more economical because of the increased operator efficiency. As a result, key-to-tape is being relegated to the low-volume data entry user who cannot afford the fixed costs of a minimum key-to-disk configuration. Another variation on the key-to-disk system is the key-to-cassette, which is based on a microcomputing capability in the system, but in which the data are recorded on magnetic cassette tapes. Key-to-cassette is used for the smaller-volume data entry requirements, or where the data entry input points are decentralized into small subunits.

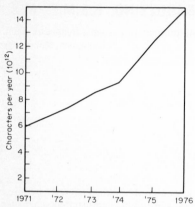

Fig. 1-1 Volume of source data handled by data entry equipment (excluding verification).

Most of the devices introduced have been centered in the computer room, but recently data are increasingly being entered directly into the computer system via communication lines such as voice-grade telephone lines, e.g., from point-of-sale terminals in department stores and data collection terminals in factories. This technique eliminates many second keying operations, and enables data to be entered on a real-time basis for such things as inventory control and ordering.

A sophisticated technique for data entry already being tried experimentally employs voice recognition machines that convert the spoken word (numerals at present) into machine language. The problem of course is the many different accents and dialects that can cause errors; however, with adaptive recognition systems that are trainable to each person using the machine, even this problem is on the way to being overcome. Voice recognition might typically be used for credit checks over the phone.

The objective of most data entry methods is to reduce the number of human keystrokes to a minimum, since input costs are directly related to keystroke volume. One approach to reducing or eliminating keystrokes that has been developing since the 1950s is the use of optical and magnetic character recognition for the entry of data. In this technique, data printed on documents (such as bills, premium notices, checks) are read directly from the original or source document because the characters have been printed in machine-readable form (i.e., use a standard font). This technique thus eliminates the keystrokes necessary to translate the document into machine language. For handling of exception information (e.g., when the check does not equal the bill), this information may be keystroked in, or a technique called *mark sense* may be used, in which data are hand-encoded by pencil on the original document, and then read by the same machine that read the preprinted characters.[1]

The need for the newer, more efficient types of data entry machines is illustrated by Figure 1-1, which shows the volume of source data estimated to be handled by data entry equipment (excluding verification) for the years 1971 through 1976.

MAJOR DATA ENTRY TECHNIQUES

Keypunch The keypunch machine converts data into machine-readable form on punched cards, so that they can be physically entered into the computer via a card

[1] See the following Chapter, "Optical Scanning, OCR, and MICR."

reader. The data are stored in the punched card in the form of punched holes that are a binary representation of each character.

Figure 1-2 shows the standard punched card encoded with the basic characters available on an alphanumeric keypunch. Each card can store up to 80 characters, each character being represented by one to three punched holes in a column. Numeric characters are represented by one hole in one of the rows zero through nine. Alpha characters are represented by two holes in a column, and symbols such as % and $ are represented by three holes in a column.

Keypunch machines are of two basic types, numeric or alphanumeric. Each of these types can be equipped with an interpreting feature that prints the character above the punched column (as shown in Figure 1-2), for easy human readability.

Since the bulk of data recorded is numeric, and since the human keystroking of numeric data is more prone to error because of its monotony, several additional features are available on keypunch machines to reduce errors significantly. For example, when money amounts are being keypunched, the input documents are often batched into groups of, say, 100 documents, and the total money amount is added on an adding machine. The input documents are then keyed on a keypunch equipped with an adding machine (operated from the keypunch keyboard numeric keys), which again adds the money amount. The totals of each tape are then compared for accuracy.

Another feature available on keypunch machines is check digit capability, which is commonly used when account numbers (e.g., credit card and employee numbers) are being keypunched. In a typical so-called Mod 10 check digit system, the account number is divided into odd and even columns, the additional check digit being an even column. The odd-column numbers in the account number are doubled. If this number exceeds 10, 9 is subtracted. Odd and even columns are then added, and for the check digit to check, the sum must be a multiple of 10. (Figure 1-3.)

As the operator is keystroking the account number, if an error is keyed, e.g., a wrong number keyed, or digits are transposed, as the check digit is keyed the keyboard will lock up, and no further processing will be possible until the card is removed for rekeying, and the release button is pressed. Thus positive action has to be taken to correct the error.

For alphanumeric keypunching, the most common method of checking the recorded data is to use a verifier machine. This machine is identical in appearance to a keypunch, the difference being that it does not have the punching capability. The operator in this case inserts the already punched card into the machine and rekeys the input data. The verifier reads the punched holes on the card and compares the data read with the keyed data. If the characters do not match, the error column is marked by a notch on the top edge of the card, and the process is then continued through the whole card. Error cards must then be rekeyed.

Data are usually organized into groups in designated columns on the punched card. This is called *formatting*. In order to speed the movement of the card between groups, the card is skipped at high speed to the next column. The high-speed skipping and control of the card through the punch are directed by the program card that is specially punched and mounted on the program drum of the keypunch machine.

Buffered Keypunch. Obviously, keying the data twice is time-consuming and costly, and with the availability of low-cost memories, the buffered keypunch evolved. In the more expensive type, the data are first keyed into the buffer memory. If the operator senses that an error was keyed, and in a very high percentage of cases this is true, he or she backspaces to eliminate that character from the memory and then rekeys the correct character. When the buffer is loaded, the punch key is depressed, and the data in the buffer are punched into the card. While this is taking place, the operator can be keying the next record, thus avoiding delays in card transporting that occur in conventional keypunches. Also the speed of the operator is not limited by the mechanical speed of the keypunch, which is often slower.

For full verification, the buffered keypunch has a read capability, so that the data punched on the card can be read and loaded into the buffer. By rekeying the data and comparing them with the data in the buffer, the operator can verify the card. Verification is usually done by another operator for more integrity. If an error is detected, the card has to be replaced by a new repunched card.

Another means of hand-entering data into a computer is via mark-sensed punched

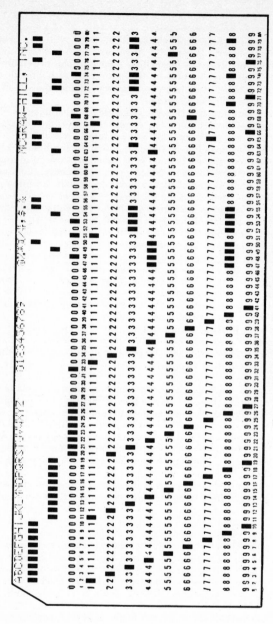

Fig. 1-2 Punched card with Hollerith-code characters.

cards. Data are marked in specific locations on the card by means of pencil strokes. The card is then placed in a special machine that converts the pencil mark into the character, and punches the appropriate holes.

System 3 Card. A significant keypunch development is the introduction of the System 3 punched card. It is different in that it can store 96 characters instead of 80 on the standard 80-column card. The card is approximately one-third the conventional size, and therefore is lower in cost and easier to handle both by the operator and the machine. The data are recorded by means of small round holes instead of the rectangular holes in the standard cards. (Figure 1-4.)

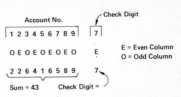

Fig. 1-3   Mod 10 check digit system.

The functions of the System 3 data recorder are very similar to those of the buffered 80-column keypunch. One machine, manufactured by Decision Data, has an additional significant feature: two input hoppers and two output stackers. This is very useful when cards are prepunched and in sequence for additional data to be entered on them. When an error is detected in the verification mode, the error card can be routed automatically to the second stacker, and a new card from a blank deck in the second input hopper can be reinserted and totally repunched

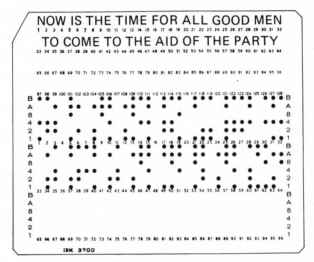

Fig. 1-4   Ninety-six-column punched card.

with the correct information and put back into the deck in correct sequence. System 3 data recorders are typically faster in operation than 80-column, particularly when they have the high-speed skip capability (useful when keying money amounts), and because the mechanisms are simpler and can physically punch faster.

Key-to-Magnetic-Tape   Here magnetic tape is the data storage medium instead of punched cards. Key-to-magnetic-tape has the following advantages:

- Storage is significantly more efficient volumetrically.
- Data are entered more rapidly into the computer because tape-drive data transfer rates are significantly faster.
- Tape equipment is mechanically much simpler and more reliable than punched-card equipment.
- Tape media are reusable.
- Use of operator for greater throughput is more efficient.

Data to be transcribed are keyed on a standard keyboard into a buffer memory. When the buffer memory is filled up, the data may then be automatically transferred onto magnetic tape at a density of from 200 up to 1,600 bits per inch, depending on the system requirements. Since the buffer memory can be many hundreds of characters long, the record size is consequently much greater than is possible with a keypunch machine limited to 80 or 96 characters per record. This feature considerably eases format requirements and increases the efficiency of the operation. Also, the operator can type at his or her maximum capabilities, whereas in most unbuffered keypunches, there is a mechanical limit to speed, and operators frequently overtake the keyboard.

Another significant advantage of key-to-tape is that the characters keyed are displayed on the keyboard, so that if the operator senses an error, he or she can instantly verify it and, if an error was made, backspace and rekey correctly. Most keyboards also have so-called audible feedback. Since the machine is very quiet, every time a key is depressed, a click relay gives audible feedback to the operator.

Formatting control of data is a very powerful tool for error control and for orderly storage of data. The format of each type of record may be entered into the key-to-tape control memory via the keyboard. For convenience, where many different formats are frequently used, a punched card or mark-sensed document is typically used for storage and encoding of formats, and the latter are entered into the device via an appropriate reader. Key-to-tape machines typically have options for check digit verification for numeric fields, plus the ability to add numbers for zero balancing. Full verification is again done on a separate key-to-tape, in a fashion similar to that of the buffered keypunch. In this case the records are read from the tape into the buffer, and the data are rekeyed for a character-by-character comparison and corrected as necessary.

In installations requiring many key-to-tape machines, it is inefficient to load tape reels from each machine into the main computer tape drive; therefore, most key-to-tape machines have the ability to pool or consolidate data from several key-to-tape machine tapes onto one tape.

Many optional configurations are possible. One popular use of key-to-tape is as a communication device, by having the equipment connected through a modem to a communication line such as a voice-grade telephone line. Data may then be transmitted from a remote source, loaded into the buffer memory for format control if necessary, and then transferred to the tape if the record is valid. If the record is not valid, the key-to-tape system can tell the system to transmit the data again. Data can similarly be transmitted to a remote site. High-speed line printers can be attached to a key-to-tape to enable off-line printing from a tape, thereby freeing the main computer system from this time-consuming chore.

Key-to-Disk   Key-to-disk systems differ from those previously mentioned in that one or two disk memories are used as the intermediate memory for input keyboards. The latter may number up to 64, as compared to key-to-tape, where one tape drive per keyboard is required.

The keyboards are typically controlled by a minicomputer that not only provides the format control, check digit verification, or editing features for each keyboard (each keyboard is completely independent of another and can be keying different types of records or formats), but also loads each record onto the disk pack for intermediate storage, and then typically sequences the records into logical order by job and batch for entry into a magnetic tape which is the output medium.

Key-to-disk systems are typically provided with a supervisory station to enable the supervisor of operators to monitor and control the total operation of all keyboard units. For example, this station can be used for monitoring operator performance as regards error and speed. Additionally, the supervisor controls the loading of data from the disk memory onto magnetic tape.

The key-to-disk system, because of its high fixed cost due to the minicomputer and disk drive, requires a higher volume of input data to cost-justify it. However, once this threshold has been exceeded, the cost per key station, including labor costs, becomes significantly less, as shown in Figure 1-5.

The savings in key-to-disk stem primarily from reduced labor costs. These result from improved operator efficiencies due to such items as reduction in verification required, range checking of money amounts, character validation, and check digit and zero balancing capability.

Key-to-Cassette   Key-to-cassette is used in smaller installations where the volumes are not great, and where more flexibility is required. Operation and use are similar to those of key-to-disk. Key-to-cassette devices typically consist of keyboard, micro-processor, and two cassette tape recorders. One cassette tape is used for storing of the microprocessor control program, plus the format and verification data; the other is used for storing of the keyed data. Most key-to-cassette devices are also equipped with a CRT display that can display the format, so that all the operator has to do is fill in the missing information. Key-to-cassette devices can also be equipped with communica-tion adapters or connected to the telephone via acoustic couplers for communication to a centralized computer system. The program and memory capabilities of these devices

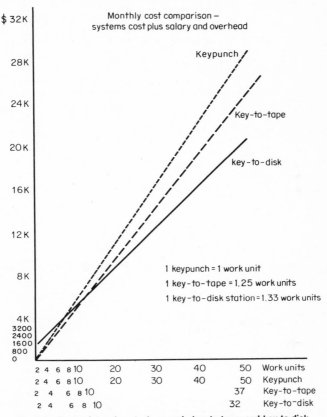

Fig. 1-5 Comparison of costs: keypunch, key-to-tape, and key-to-disk.

are growing to the point where many standard peripheral devices can be attached—so that the key-to-cassette actually becomes a miniprocessor.

Point-of-Sale Devices and Source-Data Collection Point-of-sale devices have bur-geoned in recent years, with more than a dozen different types available to retail stores. They are typically on-line to a central computer operation, and have the capability to communicate information keyed by the sales clerk, such as money amount, commodity, code, and quantity, to the computer.[2]

Some point-of-sale devices have the capability to read special credit cards, the data from which are transmitted to the central computer for instant adjustment of a cus-tomer's account, or for validation of credit. Some have the additional capability to read punched garment tags attached to the item sold.

[2] For additional details, see Part One, Chapter 1, "Office Mechanization: Overview," in this Section, and Section 7, Chapter 2, "ADP in Retailing: Point-of-Sale Automation."

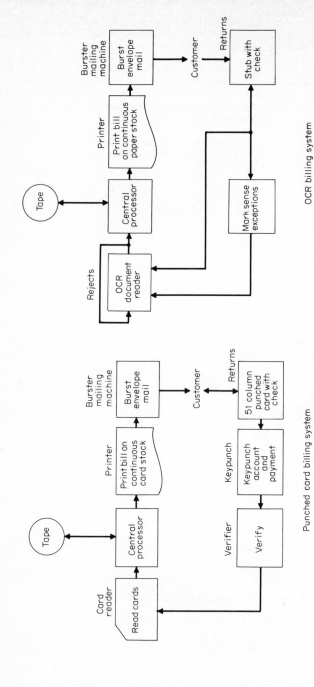

Fig. 1-6 Punched-card and OCR return-media systems.

OCR billing system

Punched card billing system

Factory-data collection is growing in utility. Typical machines have the capability to read an employee card, and are equipped with a time clock and means of reading, say, a punched card that contains information relative to the job (for example, make 10 of a part on drawing No. 157653).[3]

All these systems have the basic advantage that the data are being recorded at the source point, and will not require rekeying by a centralized data entry operation.

OCR and MICR Optical character recognition (OCR) and magnetic-ink character recognition (MICR) were first introduced in the 1950s as a replacement for punch-card keypunching. MICR is universally used for the processing of checks in banks—without it banks would have been buried in paperwork in view of the explosive growth in the use of checks over the past 20 years. OCR has not yet completely fulfilled its

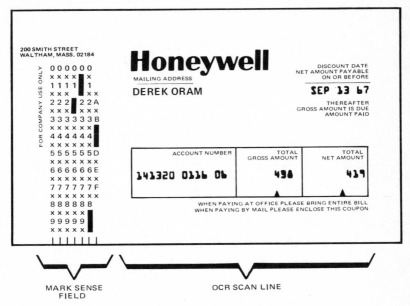

NOTE: The mark sense characters shown correspond to 2.19c

Fig. 1-7 Sample turnaround document.

promise, because initially the machines introduced were complex, unreliable, and expensive to use. By the time these problems were reduced, other techniques were available such as key-to-tape and key-to-disk which were in many cases more general in application. However, in many cases, OCR can provide a lower-cost means of data entry than any other techniques.

A typical OCR example is the return-media billing application used for bank mortgage payments, utility company payments, subscription notices, and insurance premiums. A block diagram of typical return systems using punched cards and OCR respectively is shown in Figure 1-6.

In the OCR system, the bills are printed on paper forms by a high-speed printer (less expensive than punched-card stock, and more amenable to decorative printing), with an additional line of machine-readable characters for OCR scanning, containing the account number and the amount billed. The paper forms are burst into individual documents and mailed to the customer, who returns a portion (stub) of the paper bill with his or her payment. If the bill is only partially paid, the amount submitted is recorded on the bill (by the office) by means of mark-sense pencil marks written into the appropriate mark indicators as shown in Figure 1-7.

[3] See Chapter 5, "Source-Data Automation," in this Part.

All the documents are then fed into the document reader to transfer the data on the OCR scan line and mark-sense field into the computer, to update the customer account. An additional benefit may be gained from the use of an optical character reader in this application; utility meter readings may be inputted to the computer by mark-sensing this information on paper documents.

Another factor in the OCR system is the problem of handling reject documents. Since the OCR device is reading printed information rather than binary punched holes, the document reject rate is a function of the quality of the printing. This reject rate can vary from 0.001 per cent when reading lithographed printing, to 1 to 5 per cent when reading high-speed printer printing, to 25 per cent when reading gas company credit-card invoices. The reject documents may be re-entered into the computer by retyping the documents, mark-sensing the reject documents, or ultimately using key-to-tape devices. The cost of handling rejects has to be considered when calculating the total cost of an OCR system.

The advantage of OCR systems over other systems of handling the return-media problem is that human operations have been reduced to handling the exception and reject documents because the "source" documents are being read automatically, and the number of machine operations to complete the billing cycle have been reduced.[4]

SUMMARY

The basic methods of data input have been discussed in historical sequence. However, the relative importance of each method is changing; as data input volumes have increased, the shift from punched-card techniques to magnetic techniques is becoming more significant. OCR is at last showing signs of burgeoning, as lower-cost techniques become available. Point-of-sale and factory-data collection devices are growing in use. Each of these developments is in response to the increased volume of data input, and the significant increase in the cost of labor. The trend in data input is to capture data at the source, and to reduce the number of rekeyings required. The reduction of human keystrokes by machine reading of data from bills, credit cards, and checks also reduces the labor cost, and significantly reduces the error rate.

SELECTIVE BIBLIOGRAPHY

Keypunch Replacement Equipment, Modern Data, Framingham, Mass., 1969.

Oram, Derek O., "Optical Character Recognition," *Honeywell Computer Journal*, vol.2, no.3, Fall, 1968.

Samson Report, *Data Entry*, Quantum Science Corporation, New York, 1972.

[4] For further details, see the following Chapter, "Optical Scanning, OCR, and MICR."

Chapter 2

Optical Scanning, OCR, and MICR

PETER J. GRAY

President, SYMBIOTICS, Briarcliff, New York

With the introduction of each new generation of computers, faster, more powerful processors provide the ADP user with more computer capability per dollar. High-speed printers and other output devices generate more information at a greater rate than ever before, and new applications are constantly being developed for the computer. The stress on internal processing and output speeds has aggravated the data input problem of increasing volumes of data to be entered or re-entered into ADP systems. Tight schedules, queuing delays, the shortage of keypunch operators, high personnel turnover rates, inaccurate data transcription, and generally increasing costs of data entry have created unsatisfactory operating conditions for many data processing users. It has been estimated that 30 per cent or more of systems costs are spent on computer input of information.

In addition to such data entry devices as keypunches, verifiers, key-to-tape and key-to-disk systems, and remote on-line terminals, alternative devices such as optical scanners, and particularly optical character recognition (OCR) systems, promise to be the most practical means of direct source-data entry to modern data processing systems.

One of the most important differences between OCR and the other input methods is the degree of labor intensiveness required to operate each system. The use of optical readers dramatically reduces the clerical task of transcribing data into punched cards or paper tape, and obviates the need to enter information manually through a keyboard. Optical readers provide the fastest means of data conversion, with the least potential to introduce errors, and at a lower cost per record or form than either the traditional keypunches or the newer key entry devices.

There are a number of reasons why optical readers are being increasingly accepted by ADP users, and why OCR may become the dominant computer input method in the future. The productivity of manual key entry methods is limited by human skill levels, despite the introduction of improved keyboard devices. Meanwhile, labor costs of keyboard operators are rising rapidly, and such work is becoming less attractive with time. Improvements in capabilities, reliability, speed, and cost-performance ratio are helping to make OCR a more widely acceptable method of data entry. The development of improved software, technological advances in character recognition, and the trend toward fewer restrictions on forms-preparation requirements also contribute to OCR's increasing acceptance by computer users. In addition, users now have a choice from among a wide variety of OCR systems designed to satisfy their needs at a cost they can afford.

DEFINITIONS

Optical scanning is a generic term which includes optical mark, code or bar, and character reading. However, optical scanning is only one of the functions of an optical reader. Scanning involves searching a form for marks, bars, or characters, and conversion of the reflected optical impulses to electrical signals. *Recognition* is the process of comparing these signals with matching sets of stored signals in order to determine their identity. Optical mark and code readers correlate the position and location of marks, bars, or lines with predefined characters, while optical character readers identify each character by comparing its features or characteristics with those features or characteristics stored in memory.

In *magnetic-ink character recognition* (MICR), signals transmitted via magnetized characters are picked up by a read head, identified, recognized, and compared with predefined positions on an electronic grid. MICR is primarily used in check mechanization procedures. Some reader-sorters can read MICR-encoded characters both magnetically and optically. This capability is particularly useful for reading and sorting check rejects.

Check Standardization and MICR   In July 1956, after many years of effort by the American Bankers Association, magnetic-ink characters were approved as the most suitable for check mechanization. However, it was not until December 1968 that the E-13B font for MICR was unanimously accepted as the Common Machine Language Standard by manufacturers of check printers and other interested groups. E-13B consists of ten stylized numeric digits and four symbols for the transit number, amount, "on-us," and dash. (It is illustrated in Figure 2-1, later in this Chapter.)

The need for a check standard was clear. Over 90 per cent of business transactions are handled by check, and nearly $10 billion changes hands in the United States by check every day. Furthermore, despite some preliminary steps toward a "less-check society," check volumes continue to grow from 14 billion in 1960 to 22 billion in 1970 and a forecasted 32 billion in 1976. In the late 1970s we shall begin to notice some substitution of electronic transactions for paper checks, but significant impacts will not be seen until the late 1980s.

Today, nearly 98 per cent of all checks cleared through Federal Reserve Bank offices are MICR preprinted. These checks are processed by MICR reader-sorters at speeds of between 600 and 1,600 documents a minute. Although MICR is a generally reliable and accurate method of processing checks, an average of 2 to 3 per cent of checks handled by any bank are rejected by MICR reader-sorters. These rejects may be keypunched, processed via CRT terminals and other key entry devices, or optically read by OCR equipment. In addition to checks, loan coupons, utility bills, credit-card slips, and deposit slips are MICR encoded and read.

HISTORY OF OPTICAL CHARACTER RECOGNITION

Optical character readers have a relatively long history, dating back to the early 1800s, when devices were patented as reading aids for the blind. In 1870, C. R. Carey patented an image transmission system using photocells, and in 1890 P. G. Nipkow invented sequential scanning, whereby an image was analyzed line by line.

However, no practical OCR devices were developed until the early 1950s. D. H. Shepard founded Intelligent Machines Research Corporation (IMR) in 1951, and developed the first commercial optical reader for typewritten data. Two years later, Shepard and the Stanford Research Institute built a machine to read serial numbers from travelers checks and create a punched-card record. In 1954, Shepard developed a machine for the petroleum industry designed to read imprinted customer account numbers from tab card charge slips and create a punched card. The Farrington Manufacturing Company entered into a marketing agreement with IMR to provide optical readers to the petroleum industry. In 1955, the first Scandex "self-punch machine" was installed for test purposes at the Standard Oil Company of California in Salt Lake City, Utah.

In 1956, Reader's Digest installed the first paying OCR machine developed by IMR to convert typewritten documents into punched cards for a subscription application. In the following year, IBM licensed from IMR, Shepard's inventions relating to OCR. IMR was acquired by Farrington in 1959. Also during this year, the first page reader was put to use by the U.S. Air Force in Rome, New York, and the first document reader was delivered to an electric utility, Arizona Public Service Company, Phoenix.

It was only slightly over 10 years ago when OCR began to make a noticeable impact on commercial and Government data processing installations. IBM entered the field of commercial OCR in 1960 by announcing the 1418 document reader, an on-line machine to the 1401 computer. The next year, Farrington delivered its first page reader using 12F font (Figure 2-1) and National Cash Register installed the first production model of a journal tape reader. The Control Data Corporation acquired Rabinow Engineering Company in 1964, and in the same year, the first Recognition Equipment Corporation multifont reader was installed. In 1965, the first CDC 915 page reader was installed at Crocker-Citizens National Bank, San Francisco, California.

Impeding the growth of commercial OCR devices was a lack of flexibility and versatility in fonts and character sets. In 1966, a Business Equipment Manufacturing Association (BEMA)[1] committee proposed a set of stylized characters for OCR which was adopted as a United States standard by the American National Standards Institute. This standard is known as the United States of America Standard Character Set for Optical Character Recognition (USASCSOCR), or in short, OCR-A. In addition, the European Computer Manufacturers Association adopted a different standard known as OCR-B.

During 1967, IBM delivered the 1287 document reader, and in 1968, it added the capability of reading handprinted numeric characters and five alphabetic symbols. This opened up a whole new range of applications permitting direct source-data entry. However, the 1287 was restricted to reading documents, and could not handle standard size $8\frac{1}{2}$ by 11 inch or larger pages. Also, like the earlier IBM scanners, the 1287 could only operate on-line to a System 360 computer. Cognitronics offered the first remote OCR terminal service in 1969, while both Compuscan and Information International provided the first microfilm readers.

In 1970 there emerged the first high-speed OCR systems capable of reading a wide variety of forms sizes, from small documents to large pages, and during the following two years these systems were further enhanced to incorporate journal tape reading. This permitted data processing users to handle the bulk of their applications on a single multipurpose, off-line system, without requiring the purchase or rent of two or three special-purpose machines. In 1972 and 1973 a number of manufacturers introduced "multimedia" systems combining OCR and key-to-disk stations. Scanning wands and stations at retail stores and in business operations were becoming increasingly popular in the mid-1970s.

Growth of OCR   Although only 5 per cent or so of United States commercial and Government computer sites have OCR equipment installed today, this direct computer input method is finding ever-widening acceptance, and OCR is predicted to account for 15 to 20 per cent of these computer sites within the next 5 years. In 1966, the market for OCR in terms of annual value of shipments was less than $20 million. In 1970, the estimated level of shipments was $150 million, and as of 1975 estimates put the market at between $400 million and $500 million a year.

The acceleration in the growth of OCR has been caused by a number of factors. Optical readers have become less expensive, more versatile, faster, and more reliable. Today, systems are available that require few forms restrictions, and are supported by general-purpose, user-oriented software packages. More and more data processing users find it easy to cost-justify a sophisticated OCR system if they have 10 to 12 keypunch operators. In addition, other key entry devices are often considered intermediate steps between keypunching and OCR, because major improvements in accuracy of data input and significant cost savings can be achieved only by minimizing the amount of direct and indirect labor associated with keyboard terminals or key stations. There is a trend toward decentralization of optical scanning from back office batch processing to direct data capture at the source of entry. This means that many more optical readers will be installed to perform specialized data entry tasks.

OCR READERS

OCR systems can be classified by type of input form processed. Thus there are *document readers, page readers, journal tape readers,* and *multipurpose readers* capable of

[1] Now Computer and Business Equipment Manufacturers Association (CBEMA).

handling a variety of input media. A document reader is generally capable of scanning one to five lines of data in fixed locations on a document at a single pass. Page readers are capable of scanning many lines of data during a single pass of the form. Journal tape readers can process rolls of paper tape generated by adding machines and cash registers.

If the data processing user has a simple, numeric data collection application such as inventory, or a limited order entry requirement, he or she might consider using an optical mark reader. Such readers are cheaper than OCR systems, but they restrict the user to a few well-defined applications. Similar restrictions apply to OCR document readers and special-purpose journal tape readers. For data processing users having a variety of input applications, including pages, documents, and sometimes journal tapes, the logical choice should be a multipurpose OCR reader capable of processing a wide range of forms sizes and types.

A multipurpose OCR reader should be capable of reading alphanumeric characters from turnaround documents, such as invoices, that are usually computer-generated and returned to the issuer for computer re-entry via OCR equipment. In addition, such equipment should be able to read and process handprinted information, marks, encoded, typed, or printed page-sized forms, and journal tape rolls without major modifications to the equipment. For example, such applications as sales orders and inventory reports ideally lend themselves to the recognition of handprinted characters. No typing or retranscription is required, with a consequent improvement in the speed and accuracy of data entry.

Many readers are available to satisfy specialized user requirements. For example, in the publishing industry, scanners are increasingly being used for text input and conversion. Newspapers and printers of all kinds can perform editorial and ad copy error correction, editing, formatting, hyphenation, and justification functions for typesetting. Microfilm readers can convert character or graphic images from analog to digital form, and record them on magnetic tape. However, such systems are currently extremely expensive and do not have a wide market.

Scanning Techniques   Among the scanning techniques used in optical readers are mechanical disk, flying spot, photocell or photoarray, Vidicon, image dissector, and laser. Mechanical disk scanners use a light source which is reflected from the form being scanned, through a series of lenses, and onto a rotating disk containing multiple apertures which slice each character into segments. Light reflected through these rotating apertures and a fixed aperture plate permits a full character to be scanned for each disk revolution. The fixed aperture plate controls the light and directs it to a photomultiplier for conversion into electrical signals. This method is relatively slow — e.g., 400 to 500 cps (characters per second) — and subject to mechanical problems.

Flying-spot scanners use a CRT-generated spot of light which moves across a form to locate characters and trace their shapes. The intensity of the reflected light is measured and converted by photomultipliers and amplifiers. These scanners are of medium speed (e.g., 1,000 to 2,000 cps), and have the ability to do curve tracing and line finding. However, flying-spot scanners do not have the resolution capabilities of some other techniques, and they require strict control to prevent entry of ambient light.

In the photocell scanner, a light source is used to reflect a character image onto a series of photocells that are used to sample a number of points adding up to a character slice, or to sample a complete character at a time. The photocells generate signals which are quantized into shades of gray, black, or white. This scanning technique is quite expensive, but scanning speeds of 2,400 to 3,600 cps can be attained.

The Vidicon or TV camera approach involves scanning characters projected onto the surface of the tube, rather than scanning the form directly. The quantized video signals indicate the degree of blackness or whiteness that exists. This technique is limited by the low number of characters that can be stored on the tube surface. The image dissector method also involves scanning the face of the tube. A high-intensity light source illuminates the read area, reflecting and converging information through a lens and onto the face of the tube. The image dissector tube is a high-resolution, medium-speed (e.g., 2,000 cps) means of scanning. Some readers use a laser light source for scanning. A beam from a continuous laser is expanded and controlled to ensure uniform intensity. Then, a spinning mirror directs the light beam onto the document, scanning the characters column by column.

Hand-held optical scanning wands are increasingly being used in supermarkets, retail stores, and warehouses. Fiber optic bundles carry light beams through a flexible cord. Variations in the reflected light from a bar-coded item tag are converted into electronic impulses that are deciphered by the data terminal. Such systems are generally limited to reading prices, quantities, part numbers, or other bar-coded numeric data.

Recognition Methods The most commonly used recognition methods are matrix matching, curve tracing, and stroke or feature analysis. In matrix matching, the electronic signals representing the scanned character are stored in a series of shift registers connected to register matrices. Each matrix represents a single character, and is connected to another register containing a voltage representation of the referenced character. The voltage representations in the two registers are compared, and recognition is accomplished. This technique permits the recognition of full alphanumeric fonts and facilitates font changes.

Curve tracing in conjunction with flying-spot scanning involves following the outlines of a character and recognizing features to identify the character. However, problems are encountered with broken lines and other character imperfections.

Stroke or feature analysis uses selected sizes and positions of strokes to identify a character. The form of the character is matched against a "truth table" representing each reference character. Some scanners incorporate an image enhancement technique prior to recognition, which permits poor-quality characters to be read and reduces the number of rejects and substitutions.

Fonts The user of optical readers has a wide choice of fonts (shapes of characters and symbols) in either numeric or alphanumeric character sets. Multifont readers are available, with most manufacturers offering a basic system and additional fonts as options.

In an attempt to standardize, the United States of America Standards Institute, now known as the American National Standards Institute (ANSI), adopted OCR-A, a stylized font which consists of alphanumeric characters and a set of special symbols. The use of this standard by optical readers generally provides higher accuracy than nonstylized fonts because each character has been designed to differentiate it absolutely from another character. The use of nonstylized fonts may result in increased reject and error rates. Although there are a number of ways to prevent rejects from occurring, the substitution of one character or symbol for another is a more serious problem that occurs more frequently with nonstylized fonts. The objection to such stylized fonts as OCR-A is that they are not esthetic, but in reality, the characters are as easily read by the human eye as by scanners. (See Figure 2-1.) Most users require little or no adjustment to OCR-A, and this font is now used more extensively than any other. OCR-A is usually created by typewriters or line printers, but it is also available in larger sizes for cash registers, adding machines, and credit cards.

A variety of special fonts are still in use that were developed prior to the acceptance of OCR-A. Some fonts, such as 407 and 1428, are generated by IBM accounting machines, line printers, and typewriters. As stated earlier, the font recognized by most MICR and some OCR readers is E-13B, which is limited to ten numeric characters and four special symbols. A font known as CMC-7 (not shown in Figure 2-1) is also used by MICR systems, particularly in Europe. Most embossed credit cards, including American Express, Diners Club, and Master Charge, use the larger characters in the 7B font, although 1428E and 407E-1 are also employed by certain airlines and retail chains.

OCR-B font is widely used in Europe and Japan and is being proposed for adoption as an international standard. However, changes are still in progress, and some problems remain to be resolved between ANSI and the European Computer Manufacturers Association before a standard becomes acceptable to all.

There is a trend toward the development of systems capable of reading an even wider range of characters through the use of a combination of both hardware and software recognition. Some systems are now capable of "learning" fonts directly from pre-scanned material using software, but this method of recognition is slower and less reliable than the hardware method.

Paper Transport A key factor to be considered in evaluating optical readers is the paper handling capability of the transport. The paper transport moves forms from an input feeder, through a read area, to output stackers. Most paper transports use a friction or vacuum feeder with rollers and belts. However, in a rotating vacuum drum system, one drum is used to pick up a document and the other moves it past a read head and to the stackers. In the case of journal tape or microfilm, spools are used to feed and take up the materials.

The speed and efficiency of the transport, together with the speed and capability of scanning and recognition, determine the throughput rate of the optical reader. The throughput rate of a particular form will depend on the size of the form, the number, type, and quality of the characters, and the number of lines to be read. Rescanning characters many times, and manual character insertion after display, reduce the number of forms rejects, but these methods slow down the throughput rate of the system.

	Font I.D.	Category	No. of char.	Character set
All machines			4	space, reject character, | (word separator), — (line delete)
Standard	OCR-A	Numeric	18	0123456789 Y$+-⊓⌐⏴■
	OCR-A	Alpha-numeric	58	0123456789 ABCDEFGHIJKLMNOPQRST UVWXYZ "Y$%&'{}*+,-./:;⊓=⌐⏴■?
Other	OCR-A	Special symbols	8	▵°‡⁄⋈↓↑⊓
	1428	Numeric	18	0123456789 -=⋈+$,,/
	407-1	Numeric	18	0123456789 -+,./⌐⊇⌐.
	E13B	Numeric	14	⑂123456789⓪ ⑊: "' ⑊' ,.'
	7B	Numeric	10	1234567890
	12F	Numeric	18	0123456789 -+$,./⊢⌐
	OCR-B	Numeric	17	0123456789 +-./FHL
	Handprint	Numeric	17	1234567890 CSTXZ +−
	Gothic	Numeric	10	1234567890

Fig. 2-1 Typical fonts.

Although most users initially install a scanner to process one or two applications, such as one-line documents of a similar type, they will want to utilize their systems more effectively by adding other types of forms to be read, such as multiline documents and pages. Today, multifunction transports are available, capable of handling a wide variety of forms sizes, weights, thicknesses, and textures. Forms design specifications and restrictions are becoming less and less severe. For example, some readers can process forms without reference marks, with formatted or unformatted data, with variable data locations, and with no aspect ratio (length to width) constraints.

ECONOMIC JUSTIFICATION

Two popular methods of measuring the relative capability of optical readers are the price-performance ratio, and the cost per character or cost per thousand characters processed during a given period of time. Potential scanner users can best determine throughput rates, price-performance ratios, and cost per character processed by testing their forms on various scanners and comparing results.

Optical scanning is typically compared to keypunching and verifying, or other keyboard data entry methods. Tangible dollar savings can be established by calculating the costs of manual keying, including equipment, labor, cards, overhead, benefits, and other factors relative to the performance of the equipment in terms of accurate quantities of data produced.

An average keypunch operator can generate 120 to 130 keystrokes per minute, but the effective throughput rate is reduced to 70 or 80 characters per minute because verification is generally required. In contrast, an average typist can produce data at a rate of 100 to 140 characters per minute, with error correction. Even if we assumed the total costs of keypunching and typing were equivalent at $5 per hour, the productivity-cost ratio of typists is more than twice that of keypunch operators. For example, the breakeven point between keypunching and a $4,000 per month OCR system reading typed pages is about 15 keypunches and verifiers. When reading computer-generated turnaround documents, the breakeven point is about 10 keypunches and verifiers.

Such an OCR system is also justified versus alternative key devices when the volume of forms input exceeds 5,000 per day. However, these comparisons are not fully indicative of the costs involved. Manual key entry devices of all kinds are labor-intensive. The costs of hiring, training, turnover, salary increases, benefits, overtime, and other factors must be accounted for. Most optical readers require one operator, or with high-speed readers, only a part-time operator. There are also a number of intangible savings involved in speeding up the data processing billing cycle, and thereby improving the cash flow. Reduced order processing time means faster revenues and reduced inventories, and improved accuracy of data entry means better operating decisions. Pre-editing and formatting of data also helps save CPU time.

A major benefit of using high-speed data entry devices such as optical readers is the improvement in utilization of installed computer systems. An EDP system costing the user $100 per hour or more, waiting to process key-generated data, is typical of many installations today, and computer utilization is likely to become even less efficient as users upgrade to larger, more powerful systems. Priority should be given to improving input methods that will in turn improve the utilization of mainframe systems.

In evaluating optical scanners, the subject of off-line versus on-line readers must be considered. The on-line CPU costs of a system should be added to the price of the scanner, because some portion of computer time is dedicated to the operation of the reader, rather than to performing other processing tasks. Unused time on a computer costs the same as full utilization. Less flexibility in scheduling input jobs, and dependency on the main computer, are also restricting features of on-line systems. Remote-terminal readers should be priced including communications line costs, modems, and other devices. Another important consideration is the software, systems, and training support provided with the readers. Some vendors offer complete support within the price of the system, while others are partially or fully unbundled.

APPLICATIONS

A wide range of applications is being processed by the 3,000 or so scanners installed as of this writing. Such business applications as billing, order entry, file maintenance, and inventory control are common to all types of business and Government organizations. In addition, scanners are reading specific forms pertaining to individual companies and industries.

For example, publishers are using equipment to read subscription and book club notices, address lists, invoices, premium forms, and coupons. Manufacturers are reading inventory forms, job tickets and time cards, work orders, production and test reports, and payroll lists. Utilities use scanners to process meter cards, repair reports, and change notices. The retail industry uses optical readers for sales order entry, inventory control, and price changes. Banks are processing loan records, payments, stock transfers, trust accounts, dividends, and service bureau applications. Insurance companies read premium notices, claims forms, medical records, and accident reports. In the area of education, scanning is used extensively for student tests and records. State and Federal governments use scanners for tax statements, motor vehicle registrations and licenses, payment reports, allotment forms, and many others. The airlines read tickets, and the oil companies and credit card issuers read credit card stubs by means of scanners.

Data collection, preparation, and recording for optical scanning may be accomplished in a variety of ways. For example, computer-generated turnaround documents such as bills are prepared by chain or drum printers. The returned stubs of these documents are read back into the OCR system, which initiates a file update and new billing cycle. Credit-card imprinters are used to generate OCR-readable documents for oil companies, retailers, restaurants, and other businesses. Cash registers and adding machines create journal tapes to be optically read by special OCR equipment or multifunction OCR systems with journal tape features.

The office typewriter is commonly used to generate lists or prepare forms for subsequent entry to computers via an optical character reader. Forms may also be generated by handprinting characters or by marking. For example, sales order slips are filled out at the data source with a date, quantity, description, and prices. These sales orders can be read directly into the system without retranscription. There are a number of other methods of recording data, such as garment tag perforators and notching devices. Another retail application involves point-of-sale scanning devices that automatically read the price or a code from each item purchased, and transmit this information to a computer which calculates taxes and total amounts, and maintains inventory status records.

TRENDS

Until recently, OCR systems could be justified only for high-volume applications such as credit-card stubs and airline tickets. However, rapid technological improvements in hardware will continue to bring about lower costs for improved systems, so that many more lower-volume users of data processing equipment will be able to afford OCR equipment.

The versatility of modern optical character readers is constantly being increased. For example, many more OCR systems will be communications-oriented, with either remote or centralized recognition capabilities. Remote OCR terminals are typically slow-speed, low-cost, source-data collection devices that permit data communications over voice-grade telephone lines through a modem, or that may be on-line to a central processor. Remote recognition is technologically feasible, but the overall systems costs of hardware, I/O channels, communications lines, modems, etc. are still expensive, although these costs are likely to experience a relative decrease during the next few years.

Although there has been a tendency for users to prefer off-line systems, the distinction between on-line and off-line is disappearing as software improves, and as minicomputer systems become more powerful and capable of performing many of the same processing functions as major CPUs. Combination systems of OCR and key-to-disk equipment sharing a common processor will become more popular. Applications that naturally lend themselves to scanning, such as computer-generated turnaround documents, can be directly scanned and processed, and rejects may be entered via keyboard stations. Other applications with lower volumes or special requirements may also be entered via keyboard entry systems that include CRT displays and disk files. By adding a high-speed line printer to the system, OCR turnaround documents may be created for subsequent scanning, and in addition, the system may be used as an off-line print station for other data output applications. Combination systems, such as that described above, permit the user to handle a full range of data input-output applications.

Future OCR systems will put fewer constraints on the customer by permitting the use of simpler forms, and by providing virtually unlimited font recognition. The technology is available today for reading the full range of alphanumeric handprinted characters, but the cost of such systems is still prohibitive, and the constraints on the user are still too severe. Many characters are similar in shape so that they may be confused and substituted for each other. For example, to avoid substituting a "D" with an "O," "B" with an "8," "U" with a "V," etc., the user would have to write each character in a predefined, unnatural style to distinguish it and avoid confusion. (See Figure

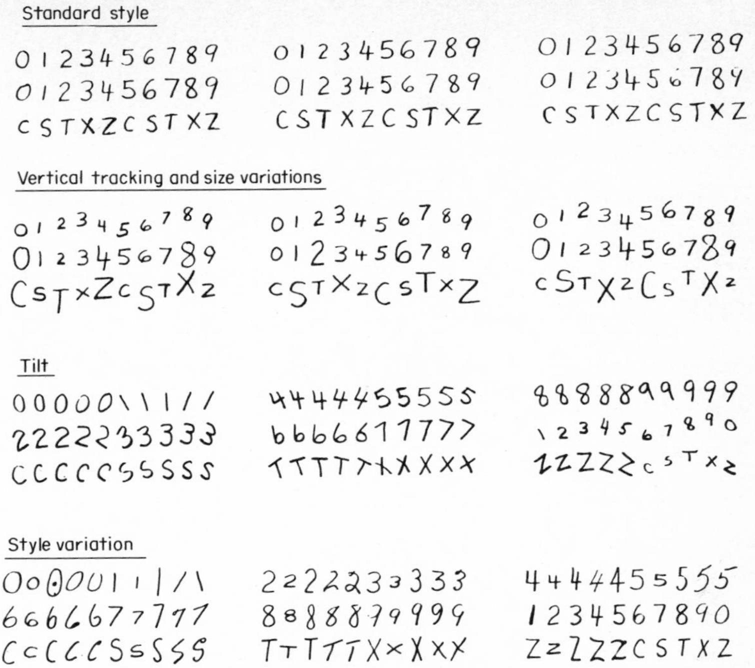

Standard style

0 1 2 3 4 5 6 7 8 9   0 1 2 3 4 5 6 7 8 9   0 1 2 3 4 5 6 7 8 9
0 1 2 3 4 5 6 7 8 9   0 1 2 3 4 5 6 7 8 9   0 1 2 3 4 5 6 7 8 9
C S T X Z C S T X Z   C S T X Z C S T X Z   C S T X Z C S T X Z

Vertical tracking and size variations

0 1 2 3 4 5 6 7 8 9   0 1 2 3 4 5 6 7 8 9   0 1 2 3 4 5 6 7 8 9
0 1 2 3 4 5 6 7 8 9   0 1 2 3 4 5 6 7 8 9   0 1 2 3 4 5 6 7 8 9
C S T X Z C S T X Z   C S T X Z C S T X Z   C S T X Z C S T X Z

Tilt

0 0 0 0 0 \ \ 1 / /   4 4 4 4 4 5 5 5 5 5   8 8 8 8 8 9 9 9 9 9
2 2 2 2 2 3 3 3 3 3   6 6 6 6 6 1 7 7 7 7   1 2 3 4 5 6 7 8 9 0
C C C C C 5 5 S S S   T T T T T X X X X X   2 2 2 2 2 C S T X 2

Style variation

0 0 0 0 0 1 1 1 / \   2 2 2 2 2 3 3 3 3 3   4 4 4 4 4 5 5 5 5 5
6 6 6 6 6 7 7 7 7 7   8 8 8 8 8 9 9 9 9 9   1 2 3 4 5 6 7 8 9 0
C C C C C S S S S S   T T T T T X X X X X   Z Z Z Z Z C S T X Z

Fig. 2-2   Variations in handprinting.

2-2.) Nevertheless, systems capable of recognizing the full alphanumeric handprinted character set will be in limited use for specialized applications within the next 2–3 years, and their use will gradually increase as improved systems become available and costs are reduced.

CONCLUSION

The major limitations to broad acceptability of OCR have been the high cost and inflexibility of the equipment, and inadequate software capability. However, prices are going down, and in addition, modern OCR systems are becoming faster and more versatile, handling a wide variety of applications on all types and sizes of forms, containing data generated by hand, line printers, keyboards, imprinters, or other devices. General-purpose, powerful software packages are available for easy addition of applications, and for greater processing capabilities. Improved reliability means that data of poor quality can be recognized with increased accuracy of input. Whether the user requires a sophisticated multimedia OCR system, or a limited-purpose decentralized scanning device, he should be able to satisfy his need for improved direct data entry with currently available equipment.

Chapter 3

Remote Terminals

HAROLD N. WELLS, B.S., M.B.A.

**Program Manager, Subsystems Product Marketing,
Honeywell Information Systems, Inc., Wellesley,
Massachusetts**

ANTHONY B. RAGOZZINO, B.S.M.E., M.S.

**Director of Peripherals, Honeywell Information Systems, Honeywell, Inc.,
Minneapolis, Minnesota**

Remote terminals have been evolving over many years. Their application in large numbers, however, is a relatively recent phenomenon. For many of us, the initial contact with some form of remote terminal may well have been the remote coin box and music selector for the jukebox at the diner on a Saturday night. It contained the functions of the remote terminal – communications, a remote database, input of coins, a "tutorial" to step the customer through the music selection process, a keyboard, and of course output of the music played back through a speaker. This is a very simplistic example of the terminal – the extension of a desired function to a remote point through communication lines.

For purposes of definition in the data communications and computer environment, we can consider the *terminal* to be a logical extension of a subset of the computer facility to some remote place, either through a direct cable, private wire, or the common carrier networks. Examples of the use of remote terminals today are found in retailing, banking, airline and hotel reservation systems, car rentals, stock brokerages, off-track betting parlors, and in engineering and manufacturing locations.

Data processing terminals can be traced back to the telegraphic typewriter, which replaced the hand-driven key of the telegraph operator. It provided a keyboard, a serial printer, and communications capability through telegraph lines and over radio networks. It was this teletypewriter, originally designed for message communications, which became one of the key elements in the early era of time-sharing networks. It was adopted because it was available and because of its low cost, reliability, and existing interfaces to communications networks. The teleprinter obviously was not designed with time sharing or computer communications in mind, and has many drawbacks when applied interactively. As yet, however, the various evolving technologies have not entirely displaced the old reliable teletypewriter as a means of supplying low-cost hard copy.

The next logical extension of the remote terminal from the computer room was the communications-oriented remote batch terminal. The remote batch terminal allowed the essential functions of the computer room (card input, card output, and printing) to be extended to more convenient, distant locations by means of controllers, communications interfaces, and telephone lines. The continuing extension of computer power from the computer room to the remote sites was stimulated by a variety of motivations, the most basic being remote duplication of a basic computer capability at a low cost. Further, remote job entry results in a considerable convenience to a number of intermediate-sized users affiliated with a larger central facility, and allows a centralized computer system to maintain procedural control.

The teleprinter and remote batch terminals were followed by the alphanumeric display terminal. It was applied in those cases where interaction with databases, the retrieval of customer files and records, and the provision for editing and reinsertion of data to the file were essential, and where hard copy was not. Examples are airlines and other reservation systems. The next proliferation of remote-terminal applications was in banking, point-of-sale credit authorization, time sharing, and on-line data entry systems which combined interactive requirements with special functions such as ticket printers, cash drawers, and passbook printers.

In recent years the role of remote terminals has grown significantly, and now all major systems manufacturers and a number of specialty suppliers offer hundreds of models. An increasing number of computer installations have added communications facilities, random-access memories, and communications-oriented operating systems, anticipating the accelerating use of data communication terminals through the seventies.

Computer data entry has traditionally involved key-to-media capture for later batch processing, with the data stored on cards, tape, or disk. Conceptually, the task, *source-data entry*, is really a key-to-database capturing system. The dividing line between source-data entry/capture systems and general interactive terminal applications is indefinite. The trend in computer systems is to update databases directly through interaction with terminals or other input methods such as OCR or MICR readers, so that intermediate batching and processing of data are unnecessary.

SYSTEMS ASPECTS

The use of a terminal as a systems element is heavily dependent upon the technological advances in the related areas of communications, database management, and systems software. All these have progressed to the point where the use of a terminal as an integrated and conceptually balanced portion of the overall communication system is possible. Figure 3-1 shows typical relationships between terminals and the tasks which they are designed to perform. Terminal characteristics are determined by the mode of operation, application orientation, human or media orientation, required speeds for data transmission, and the degree of functional capability which must be incorporated within the terminal.

Some applications depend on operator speeds and throughputs because the task at hand is to a high degree operator- or job-oriented. Others, such as the remote batch application, are media-oriented, with speeds and processing designed to service the higher-speed peripheral devices. The data rates designed for computer terminals are also dependent upon the expected duty-cycle requirement for either continual low-speed interaction with a central computer, or shorter periods of high-speed data transfers.

Communication A large on-line dedicated network including the communication links, the modem and data sets, and the associated terminals can easily cost as much as the entire central system that is supporting the network. The ability to have reliable, accurate, instantaneous connection to communication networks is basic to the success of the remote terminal.

Common carriers such as the traditional telephone and telegraph companies are being joined by new data communications–oriented common carriers such as Datran (Data Transmission Company) and MCI (Microwave Communications, Inc.), which are operating dedicated microwave links for the transmission of computer data. The Bell System is offering new modems and services. The connection of outside vendor

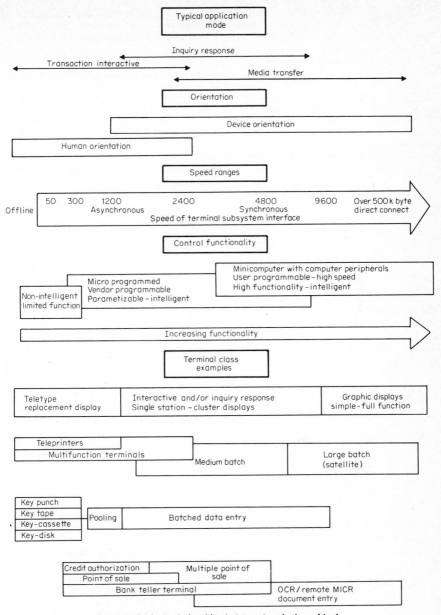

Fig. 3-1   Typical relationships between terminals and tasks.

modems and services to the common carriers has been allowed as a result of the Carter-fone decision in 1968, opening the way for interconnection of a variety of equipment not previously allowed on the common carrier systems.

Some sophisticated large users—for example, ARPA (Advanced Research Projects Agency)—have created a network of communications and high-speed data links nation-wide, connecting a variety of defense and university research computer establishments. Minicomputers are used at the nodes of this network to provide standardized data interfaces and computer disciplines. Continuing efforts are being made in the industry to standardize interfaces, line disciplines, procedures, and code sets. Occasionally the terminal must be capable of operating in a stand-alone mode in case of failure of the communications facility.

The typical systems environment (Figure 3-2) encompasses the host computer-room processor, the communications front end, and the database. To reach the variety of remote terminals connected, both switched and dedicated networks are used. The example of the switched network in Figure 3-2 shows an automatic dial unit and its associated modem automatically switched through the telephone company network to the individual modems and terminals desired. These connections may be initiated or terminated by either the host processor or the terminal, depending on the system's organization.

The dedicated network frequently has several remote modems located along one leased line in several cities. The terminals alternately use the communications

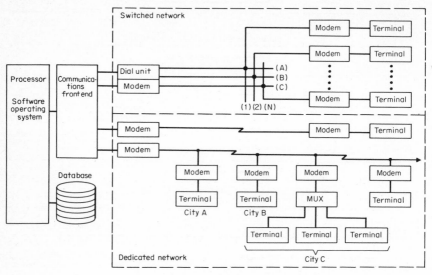

Fig. 3-2   Typical systems environment.

facility on a polled basis. An inquiry to the line status is made by either the processor or the terminal, and when the line is free the messages are transmitted from individual units. This is typically called *part-line operation*. Cost-saving techniques employed in the data communications networks involve the use of multiplexers where a number of low-speed data rates are interleaved and transmitted at a higher speed on one circuit, resulting in lower operating costs.

Database   Another requisite of major on-line terminal systems is an adequate database to contain the files required for the variety of real-time and on-line applications. Database trends are toward decentralization to localized files as required by the application. These are typified by the magnetic-tape cassette, the small, floppy disk or diskette with removable cartridge memory, small removable disk pacs, and some solid state memories. Larger central files are also available, using the combined software, central system hardware, and advanced mass storage techniques. Techniques of the future will include holography, electron beam, bubble domains,[1] and other developments which will allow the remote terminal access to a vastly expanded central database, as well as its own smaller local database.

Distributed Intelligence   Circuit components, ROM/RAM LSI memories, modems on a chip, microprocessors on a printed circuit board, and increasing applications

---

[1] Holography and bubble domains are coming technologies related to very high density memory techniques.

sophistication on the part of terminal designers have tended to distribute intelligence outward from the central computer. The terminal impact of this capability is discussed herein under "Intelligent Terminals."

Software Systems software allows the integration of terminals, communications, database, and sophisticated application packages into complex real-time systems. Typically the software should have the capability to manage the database, establish communication link control, deal with multiple terminal types on common communication lines, and handle the administrative overhead of network security, password recognition, error recovery, on-line diagnosis of network faults, and the proper queuing of jobs. The foregoing is a large task, and one not always accomplished in today's systems. Further, real-time terminal-oriented applications must now make a distinction between those software functions which are to be resident in the host computer and those which are to be resident in the intelligent terminals at the nodes of the network.

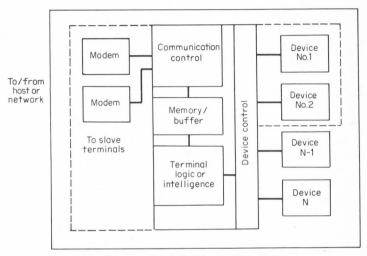

Fig. 3-3 Terminal device/element interaction.

Human Factors Terminals are located in computer rooms, factories, banks, retail stores, service stations, police cars, and ordinary offices. Environmental factors are important considerations in the design of the applicable systems and hardware. Equally important is the attention that must be placed on the human-factors aspects of the hardware design.

Typically involved are attention span, fatigue, decision time, and the execution and waiting times for the tasks as they relate to the operator. Also important are styling, color, general size and compactness, location of switches and controls, acoustic noise levels, and the quality of audio-visual sensory outputs. Other person–machine interface considerations are: ease of correction, the maximum number of characters that may be presented simultaneously, editing capability, and the need for standardized format.

PRESENT TERMINALS

For convenience of discussion, terminals can be classified as (1) *displays*, (2) *keyboard printers*, (3) *intelligent terminals*, (4) *remote batch terminals*, (5) *industry-specific, applications-peculiar terminals*, and (6) *personal terminals*. Not all of these classes are mutually exclusive, since many of the differences are found in the rearrangement and packaging of basic elements, or in the emphasis on the functional capability gained with particular elements added for varying applications. To illustrate the basic organization of devices or elements of a current terminal, Figure 3-3 and Table 3-1 cover respectively the logical interaction of the devices and the primary and secondary applications generally associated with each terminal class.

All or none of the depicted functions may be housed logically and physically within the main control. The main control may reside within an element. Small tabletop or portable terminal devices are examples of a completely integrated unit. A satellite remote batch terminal, or a point-of-sale terminal with optional cash-dispensing or credit-card readers may have some elements or device modules packaged separately.

The interface from the device to the control elements may be unique to the device, such as a keyboard, or be an industry-standard interface, as illustrated by an ordinary

TABLE 3-1   Examples of Application by Terminal Class

Primary application	Secondary application
DISPLAY	
Teletype replacement	
Interactive time-shared computer access	Minicomputer console
Interactive display	
File access/interrogation	Airline reservation
Data edit, entry, storage and retrieval (IRS example)	Computer-assisted instruction
	Plotting—limited graphics
	Stock quotation
Graphics	
Engineering design	Production of movies—cartoons
Manufacturing simulation	Computer-assisted instruction—
Medical simulation	pattern recognition
Air traffic control	
Data reduction	
KEYBOARD PRINTER	
Teleprinter	
Record communications and messages	File inquiry
Interactive time-shared computer access	Minicomputer console
	Order entry
	Invoicing
	Data logging
	Computer-assisted instruction
REMOTE BATCH	
Remote media entry	Satellite mode (free-standing operation)
Remote media output	
Remote computing with centralized system control	Limited inquiry—response
INTELLIGENT	
Decentralization of work functions from CPU to terminal	Accommodation to host central processor communication disciplines
Control of local database	
Localized error correction and input data editing	Emulation of hardwired terminals
Localized processing of data in event of communications failure	Manufacturer's flexibility in changing functionability
INDUSTRY-ORIENTED	
Normal terminal features plus specific functionality to a market segment and application such as:	Some specific functions not allied with data transfer or control such as:
Automobile rentals	Incorporation of cash drawers
Commercial and savings Bank teller stations	Merchandise dispensers (i.e., tickets, vouchers, cash, stamps
Credit authorization	Passbook printers
Factory data collection	
Medical services	
Point of sale	

teletypewriter connected to a display subsystem to provide hard copies. Some terminals also have available a variety of interface speeds, with direct memory access, to allow operation of higher-speed peripherals and communications lines with minimum absorption of control logic capability. The logic and memory for control of devices usually resides in the terminal controller, but may also be decentralized within an attached device.

The organization of the devices and control is related to a number of factors such as cost, usage expected, orientation to the operator or to media, ease of maintenance, and the need to provide enhanced function by addition or substitution of devices and options without basic terminal redesign.

Displays Displays may be classed in three basic ways: (1) *Teletype replacement*, (2) the *interactive display* in single and multiple stations, and (3) the sophisticated, highly functional *graphics terminal*.

Teletype Replacement. The Teletype replacement display is primarily the result of needs of the time-sharing market. The development of a teletypewriter or other printer-based terminal mechanism normally traces several years of major efforts in tooling, mechanical design, testing, and reliability improvement. In contrast, the technology of the cathode-ray display tube, solid state keyboard, microcircuits, solid state memories, and the basically electronic content of a Teletype replacement display has allowed entry by many independent firms in a short time and without appreciable investment. The goal of Teletype replacement or Teletype compatible display terminals is to provide the functional capability of a Teletype Model 33 or 35 at approximately the same price. Other goals are to avoid noise, provide editing flexibility, and allow easy revision of keyboard entries without overstrikes or full-line re-entry.

Key features of the Teletype replacement display are low-speed communications over acoustic couplers or Bell 103 modems, a 72- to 80-column line width, an uppercase character set, occasionally a lowercase option, 6 to 24 lines of data on the screen, at an 80-column width, and roll-up of data to simulate teletypewriter paper motion. Unlike a hard-copy teletypewriter, the data rolling off the top of the CRT screen are lost to the user. In time-sharing environments, the users require program access, data access, and insertion and deletion of data into the file. Should a time-sharing user of a Teletype compatible display require a hard copy, an optional receiver-only printer can be used.

The Teletype replacement or compatible display has further characteristics in its communication mode which may or may not be available in a particular model, depending on its pricing and targeted market functionality. The strict Teletype replacement display operates in a character serial mode, transmitting each keystroke to the computer just as a teletypewriter does. Some models offer block transmission, allowing the complete message to be buffered on the screen, edited, and corrected to the satisfaction of the user. The message may then be transmitted in a teletypewriter compatible message format, but in an entire block sequence. The latter mode requires additional electronics, and is not always available in the basic Teletype replacement displays. Teletype replacement or compatible displays sometimes offer communication baud rates up to 9,600 baud (asynchronously; see Figure 3-1). Since 9,600-baud rates are normally synchronous in nature, asynchronous transmission at 9,600 bauds is not always practical for use in normal communication systems, because the possibility of data errors exists in high-speed asynchronous transmission.[2] The need for specially conditioned lines to utilize higher baud rates makes this an impractical sales feature. The typical user operates asynchronously over the dial network at speeds of 300 to 1,200 bps (bits per second), and only in short-duty cycles.

Interactive Display. The interactive display is by far the largest and most popular display terminal in today's markets. It is normally applied in a dedicated network for applications such as airline reservations systems, bank teller inquiries, stock quotations, computer-assisted instruction, text editing, information storage and retrieval, and data capture. Depending on the application, a computer communications port may communicate with one or more interactive displays on the same communication line in a dedicated network application.

The terminals are much like the Teletype replacement in physical appearance and size, but have other functions to a significant degree. Like the Teletype compatible

---

[2] For communications concepts, see Part Five of this Section, Chapter 1: "Communication Basics."

display, they have a display screen, keyboard, communications control, refresh memory, and options such as hard-copy printer cassettes. In addition, they normally have a full-page communication buffer which allows block transmission of the data at speeds ranging from 1,200 baud at the low end of the spectrum to direct-connect speeds of several hundred thousand characters per second in local environment. High speed is particularly useful for computer console applications where pages of information must be displayed instantaneously to an operator without any appreciable delay. At 1,200 baud, a 2,000-character display takes almost 20 seconds to fill from a phone link.

The interactive display in cluster environments utilizes a poll-and-select mode. A block message is transferred to a terminal when it has requested access to the computer program, has been polled, and has been selected by the communication system. One of the additional features an interactive display may possess is the capability to "protect" data fields, normally called a *forms mode*. Fixed data are put on the screen to assist the operator with data entry. Variable data are entered in the areas left unprotected, and transmitted back to the central system in preselected formats. This allows an economy in transmission line utilization, since constants are not shuttled back and forth.

Some typical editing facilities provided in this class of display are erasure of a full page, erasure of any selected line, cursor movement to any selected character position, and deletion or insertion of additional characters. Other available features are forward and reverse, horizontal tabulation, selective transmission of data, and split-screening two or more areas on the screen so that separate fields of information may be treated uniquely. In some split-screen models, the display area is effectively two, three, or more separate display areas, each of which may be separately manipulated.

Graphic Displays. The graphic display terminal is normally a highly sophisticated, finely adjusted, and highly precise electronic device. It offers high-resolution data display, very flexible and powerful editing, and special image manipulation capabilities such as display enlargement or miniaturization, rotation, circle generation, vector generation, and very dense packing of displayed information on the screen. Typical applications are engineering design, medical simulation such as the depiction of the human heart in cross section through the various phases of a heartbeat, air traffic control, and general data reduction.

The graphics display normally has localized intelligence in the form of a minicomputer for its control, and its operating software allows many of the terminal's functions to be exercised locally. Extremely heavy computation workloads are shared with a larger central computer facility. The software burden imposed upon the overall system for its image generation and constant refresh is very large.

Special features and functions of graphic terminals also include the capability to isolate data with a "light pen" pointed to specific locations on the screen, and have the coordinates of that point recognized by the system for reference to the corresponding data in the program. Other methods of doing similar functions are available in the form of a "joy stick"—a small control like the joy stick of an airplane which moves the cursor in the direction of pressure.

Graphic terminals normally utilize a cathode-ray display, but some lower-cost models also use a visual display storage tube to retain the data, which does not require a refresh memory. The disadvantage of the storage tube graphics display is that dynamic depiction of motion is not possible; any change of displayed data requires an erasure of the entire image.

Keyboard Printers Keyboard printers form the largest population of an individual terminal class in today's markets. The Teletype Corporation's Models 33 and 35 and the IBM 2740 and 2741 constitute a major portion of that population. Generally, teleprinters are classified in terms of low speed (10 characters per second), medium speed (15 to 50 cps), and high speed (above 50 cps). Keyboard printers normally communicate in the same manner as the printing is accomplished, that is, character by character in a serial mode. Most print mechanisms are serial printers, that is, each character is formed and printed before the carriage moves to the next print position. This is in contrast to a line printer where the entire line of print is deposited on the paper by a series of print mechanisms and hammers operating as soon as all of the specific characters of the line are available to the print position.

Keyboard printers have the following general characteristics regardless of speed:

• They are relatively "nonintelligent."

• They run at asynchronous communication line baud rates ranging from 110 to 1,200 bps.

• They are available in keyboard send/receive, receive only, and automatic send/ receive versions. Some means for capturing data other than the printed page, such as a punched paper tape or a magnetic-tape cassette, is usually offered.

The first application of the keyboard printer was record communications and message transmission. The primary computer terminal application is in the interactive time-shared computer access environment. Secondary applications include minicomputer consoles, general file inquiry, order entry, invoicing, data logging, and computer-assisted instruction. Recent evolutions in keyboard printers have included nonimpact technologies as well as higher-speed impact technologies.

The demands made by customers of computer time-sharing networks have led to the development of readily portable nonimpact keyboard printers operating at 30 cps. These incorporate in a single carrying case an acoustic coupler, a keyboard, a printer, and associated control electronics. They are considerably more portable than the Model 33 or terminals using similar impact technologies, and seem to give satisfactory operation. Keyboard printers are also incorporated into larger, more sophisticated terminal devices such as the low end of the remote batch family, and are sometimes attached to displays to provide hard copy.

Another trend in teleprinter features is the increasing sophistication in the degree of paper handling capability available from various manufacturers. These include extended forms handling, horizontal tabulation, forward and reverse line feed, vertical form feed, automatic positioning to the head of the next form, multiple forms handling with tractors, single ledger card insertion, and other paper handling features.

The buffered teleprinter is advantageously applied where a large number of dedicated keyboard printers are required on a single line, since the associated communication line costs for a number of individual communications lines would otherwise be excessive. The technique utilized is that of operating a keyboard printer in a local mode, buffering a full message, verifying its accuracy, and then requesting selection on a polled network, thus allowing several keyboard printers to operate from one higher-speed communications line. Normally, buffered teleprinters operate at 1,200 to 2,400 bps line speeds rather than the lower speed of the serial printer mechanism. Operating on a poll-and-select network, a buffered teleprinter can access the line for only the time that its own transmission is required. Other buffered teleprinters are allowed access to the line while its next message is being formatted.

Intelligent Terminals[3] "Intelligent" terminal systems are one of the more recent trends in data communications and terminals. For years, manufacturers have been offering terminal systems with fixed functional capability. In the past, displays, small remote batch, keyboard printer, and application-specific terminals, all of which can be intelligent today, were offered in nonintelligent versions with the manufacturer's best estimate of the required functional capability hardwired in fixed logic. Today's intelligent terminal is the result of advances in technology which allow more distributed intelligence to be placed at the terminal location. Because of the lower costs and less critical speed requirements, logic and memories made of MOS/LSI circuits (metal oxide semiconductors and large-scale integrated circuits) are incorporated into the terminal. (The fact that the speeds of terminal operation are generally governed by a human interface makes unnecessary the nanosecond speeds and expensive circuitry associated with central processing units.)

Terminal intelligence can take many forms, ranging from the simple ability to change operating parameters of the terminal to the power of a full-register microprocessor capable of executing user programs. Terminals can include a completely functional central processing unit with an instruction set, registers, memory, and local terminal resident software including compilers and assemblers. Intelligent terminals are able to emulate many different communication line procedures and disciplines. Thus a small, independent equipment manufacturer may provide terminals that connect successfully to various central systems merely by emulating a terminal class supported by that system.

[3] Intelligent terminals applications are discussed in Section 6, Chapter 4, "The Computer Business Utility."

Intelligent terminals in some clustered display and remote batch families utilize the intelligence of a minicomputer to control connected components, such as keyboard displays, card readers, punches, or line printers. One of the advantages of terminal intelligence to an equipment manufacturer is that it enables the manufacturer to offer a wide variety of terminal functional capability with one basic model of terminal. For various functions, the terminal is tailored to suit the need of the particular customer or industry segment by means of specific software. The software is generated by the user, using compilers or software generators located within the terminal itself. An operating system and a compiler which are resident on a magnetic-tape cassette or a small disk memory are furnished by the terminal manufacturer. Other alternatives include the use of a remote time-sharing system or a host central processor for generation of the specific programs to be loaded in the terminal. This offers the advantage of computer power not inherent to the microprocessor or minicomputer of the intelligent terminal system itself.

From the foregoing, it is obvious that an advantage of the intelligent terminal concept is that a retailoring of the basic system installed in a customer's site may be accomplished by reloading software when additional functional capability or peripheral capabilities are desired, rather than having to replace an entire system with each change in requirements.

In general, the power of a particular intelligent terminal subsystem can best be measured by a user in terms of an analysis of present and anticipated needs. Some of the terminal considerations are the communications system and its general range of speeds, the variety of peripherals which can be added, the speed of the basic processor or microprocessor inherent in the terminal, the overall structure of the terminal system, the software which supports it in terms of utility routines, emulators, and languages, and the basic memory options available.

A basic systems question which should be addressed is: Will this terminal subsystem allow a distributed database to be used, thus off-loading the host computer system and lowering the communication access requirements? Another basic consideration is the degree of flexibility inherent in an intelligent terminal system, enabling it to do different kinds of tasks in different periods of time, or even concurrently, which are necessary for the application environment. For example, a number of data entry and editing tests that previously had to be made by the central processing system can be made by the terminal subsystem. Examples are account number transposition check digit calculations, accumulations of local control totals, or field checking for error control in data entry environments. Housekeeping tasks such as cyclic redundancy checks, forward-error detection, and code translation are easily implemented and changed via the intelligent terminal logic capability. However, an intelligent terminal is not necessarily the universal solution to all terminal-oriented problems, since applications may be such that high-volume simple-function terminals using a hardwired simple-logic approach may be indicated because of their lower costs.

Remote Batch Terminals Remote batch terminals can be generally classed as (1) *multifunction*, (2) *remote job entry*, and (3) *satellite*. They are mentioned here in the order of increasing speed, functional capability, and cost.

Multifunction. The multifunction terminal is a general-purpose, operator-oriented, low-cost terminal that can be configured for a wide range of applications. It is an example of the intelligent terminal class in that it usually has local programmability or accepts parameter tables specifying functions from either a local or remote program load. It is able to communicate in batch- or transaction-oriented mode, and in an inquiry-response mode, to satisfy application needs. The typical multifunction remote batch terminal includes one or more operator keyboard stations, either a display or a serial printer for a record of the data entered, communications, and a local database (a cassette or series of cassette drives, a floppy disk, or a drum memory).

The terminal is user-programmable to allow tailoring of the terminal to a number of specific user applications. It is generally operator-oriented, rather than media-oriented (refer to Figure 3-1). A multifunction terminal may include higher-performance peripherals as options, including 7- or 9-channel tape, disk, and a low-speed line printer.

Remote Job Entry. The remote job entry batch terminal is essentially an extension of the peripheral capability of the computer system to which it is attached. At a remote location it extends, with control, the functions of card reading, card punching, and line printing, but not necessarily intelligence. The principal function of a remote job entry terminal is to allow the data to be transmitted to a central computing facility in such a way that remote entry and centralized processing are accomplished with a centralized system control. Some remote job entry terminals are hardwired, and some have local programming facilities, particularly for control of formats and communications.

Satellite. The satellite remote batch terminal includes all the functions of the remote job entry terminal with the added ability to conduct free-standing operations as a computer system in its own right, as well as having the communications capability to deal with a remote site as a master or as a slave. In some cases it may have the capability of limited inquiry response to the central database. A satellite batch terminal more typically includes disk and tape capability, and processing power for manipulation of its own localized database.

Some specialized satellite processors include not only the basic functions mentioned, but also keyboard displays, magnetic data cards, magnetic-ink character recognition, paper-tape capability, and higher-speed serial printers.

Industry-Specific Applications-Peculiar Terminals Not all terminal applications can be satisfied by general-purpose terminals and their associated elements. In some cases, special functions and features are needed to satisfy a particular market need or application peculiarity. Examples are found in brokerage houses, banks, factories, stores, and hospitals. Savings banks have specialized terminals accepting passbooks; automobile rental agencies have terminals uniquely oriented to reserving cars and writing contracts; stores have terminals which offer combined credit authorization and cash register functions, including sales slip generation; factories have terminals which allow the feedback of factory data from the manufacturing floor to the data processing centers for control of production, monitoring of inventory status, and related functions. With respect to these applications, the terminals will also include components not allied with data transfer or control, e.g., cash drawers, change dispensers, merchandise dispensers (in terms of tickets, vouchers, cash, stamps), and (in the case of banks) specialized passbook and journal and validation printers.

Industry-oriented terminals are to a large degree normally used by noncomputer, non-terminal-oriented personnel. Banks, for example, have a large turnover of personnel and wish to minimize retraining costs. Therefore, in many of the industry-specific terminals there are some special functions which are helpful in training new operators. These are called *tutorial functions*, and they normally take the form of sequence lights or instructions indicating the current operation and the next operation, and indicating error conditions as well. In a banking example, the sequence of light presentations to the operator may be "enter transaction type," "enter account number," "insert passbook," "enter old balance," "enter dollar amount," "check journal for correct entry," "transmit," and "print." Similar sequence indications are available for point-of-sale terminal operators in stores, or for personnel on the factory floor who have only occasional need to access the terminal.

Figure 3-4 shows the Honeywell 7340 Bank Teller Terminal, an application-specific terminal created for the mutual savings banks and savings and loan industry. It offers the functions of a normal remote terminal plus those required by the savings and loan associations, which use a unique medium, the customer passbook. This bank teller terminal allows different function sequences to be performed at the customer's option. In initiating the terminal operation on a communication line, a set of parameters is loaded into it which gives it its specific "personality" with respect to the bank's need. The general functions of the terminal include a keyboard with numeric and function keys standard, optional alphabetic keyboard, a journal and receipt validation printer, a passbook printer, a tutorial display for procedure instruction to operators, security key locks, and the ability to capture data off-line on cassettes.

Personal Terminals The personal terminal may be defined as a remote data communications facility of low cost and low power consumption, occupying small space, and requiring no special power or air-conditioning provisions. Familiar examples are the stock brokerage quote terminal, the executive keyboard display terminal used for inquiring into the status of sales activity, inventory, and other management information data, and the keyboard terminals used in connection with the time-sharing services discussed in Chapter 3 of Section 6. The personal terminal is thus not actually a special class of terminal, but rather a form of the keyboard and display terminals previously discussed.

Personal terminals are available that offer features of easy portability and easy acoustic coupling to the telephone system. For the traveler or person working at home, the personal terminal offers convenient access to remote computation and databases.

Special Types. Ingenious special types of personal terminals are available today. An example is a portable model which includes a keyboard, an acoustic coupler, and logic—when combined with an ordinary home television set it becomes a time-sharing display terminal. It can function in a motel room where a television set and a telephone are available. Another example introduced in recent years is a portable low-cost, acoustically coupled, battery-driven keyboard data inquiry system, working on audio response from a remote database. This terminal can be used for applications such as

Fig. 3-4   Honeywell 7340 Bank Teller Terminal.

inventory status inquiry, sales order entry, or other uses where timely access to a remote database is important.

FUTURE TERMINALS

System Trends The system trend is toward larger host processor systems which incorporate a large database with complete random access and a powerful front-end processor capable of dealing with the communications needs of a dedicated on-line system. Routine tasks such as editing, format control, simple check digit calculations, some arithmetic functions, and other tasks which are capable of completion without reference to the centralized database are being distributed to the remote-terminal site. In addition, with the advent of appropriate hardware, the distribution of the database or a subset of the database to the remote terminal is also occurring. There are several systems reasons for this, prime among which is the fail-safe capability that is provided. In an on-line customer-related environment, loss of the link between the main computer and the subsystem must be compensated by the utilization of local intelligence and a local database as an interim measure. The transaction data accumulated during periods of outage are stored and transmitted to the central processing system when communications have been resumed.

Another major trend is a complex and somewhat user-invisible software system allowing cooperation between the software resident in the host processor and the software resident in the remote intelligent terminals. The technique, particularly for intelligent terminal applications, is for a user-available compiler or assembly language to be resident within the terminal. Thus the user has a small-business computer available to assume some of the tasks which have been delegated by a larger host processor.

The trend to distributed databases, hierarchical file structures, and distributed intelligence does not totally imply that today's nonintelligent terminal is obsolete. The true significance of the intelligent terminal is twofold: first, for the equipment manufacturer, it allows an increased ability to tailor the terminal elements and modules into an applications-specific configuration. And second, for the terminal user, the availability of local intelligence allows increased system connection and application flexibility with fine tailoring of terminal functional capability to specific user needs, not necessarily requiring full application support from manufacturers.

Hardware Trends Cost and technology trends go hand in hand. Terminal costs are decreasing, particularly for electronic components. Very low-cost Teletype compatible modems are available on a chip. Similar cost reductions are true of solid state memories, MOS/LSI circuits, and low-cost microprocessing units which give terminals the intelligence function. The development of mechanical components has also experienced cost reductions and technology improvements, but at a slower pace. Mechanical improvement in card readers, printers, and specialized devices for specific applications involves relatively more design and development effort.

Further cost reduction is also achievable through combinations of functional capabilities. Key entry of source data applied directly to a local database is now made possible by accurate and low-cost electronic keyboards, improved local processing, and disk technology. Another example of combining functions is the use of a remote batch or remote job entry terminal which also incorporates a communication line concentrator.

Application Trends The span of application innovations has increased. The basic tasks to be served by data processing systems now penetrate further into application-oriented areas. Application terminals which have become very prevalent include point-of-sale credit authorization terminals; commercial and savings bank teller terminals; brokerage, airline, and automobile reservation systems; order entry terminals; and hospital admissions, medical history record keeping, and remote diagnosis terminals. The concept of the less-check and less-cash is merely an extension of the philosophy that database update will be accomplished by rapidly capturing source data.[4]

Communications The trend in modem cost and communication line cost is increasingly in the direction of higher speed at equivalent costs, which implies synchronous transmission. A further trend is the integration of modems and other communication functions into terminals. It is very likely that the Bell System and other common carriers will continue to lower data tariffs, enabling most users to have dedicated private line systems where needed. This is particularly true because of the increasing general competition in the data network area.

Cable television is in its infancy and certainly represents a major opportunity. The communication bandwidth and information content represented by CATV, particularly if communication both to and from the studio is implemented, should have a drastic effect on computer communication networks.[5] Flat-screen display technologies, inexpensive keyboards, microprocessors with local intelligence, a personal database, and instant communication feedback over a CATV reverse channel, all at a subscriber price equivalent to today's telephone prices, are very exciting developments.

In introducing the topic of terminals the authors have drawn on an analogy of the jukebox in the corner diner. The blue sky extension of the analogy may very well be

[4] See Section 7, Chapter 1, "The 'Less-Cash, Less-Check' Society."
[5] See Section 8, Chapter 3, "The Computer in the Living Room."

the CATV terminal and personal database just described, performing the function of home entertainment, personal financial database management, and the initiation of personal and professional conferences from one's own home. The implication is future access to business files, public library records, university courses, and the complete library, say, of all Buster Keaton films from a home CATV terminal!

SELECTIVE BIBLIOGRAPHY

Lapious, Gerald, "MOS/LSI Launches the Low Cost Processor," *IEEE Spectrum*, November, 1972.
Machover, Carl, "The Future of Information Displays," *SID Journal*, May–June, 1972.
Martin, James, *Future Developments in Telecommunications*, Prentice-Hall, Englewood Cliffs, N.J., 1971.
Salzman, Ray M., "An Outlook for the Terminal Industry in the United States," *Computer*, November–December, 1971.
Sprague, Richard E., "Personalized Data Systems," *Business Automation*, October, 1969.

Chapter 4

Computer Output Microfilm (COM)

L. LEE HORSCHMAN

**Director, Program Sales Development, Business Systems
Markets Division, Eastman Kodak Company
Rochester, New York**

Although techniques and equipment for producing computer data directly onto micro-film have existed for almost 20 years, it is only recently that computer output microfilm, or COM as it is called, has been recognized as a more useful and economical way of re-cording computer information. The usual method of producing information from the computer has been impact printing (paper print-out, or "hard copy"). The increasing complexity and cost of working with and storing paper print-out are primary reasons for the growing popularity of COM.

In simple terms, COM enables human-readable information to be recorded onto film at speeds far in excess of those possible with an impact printer. Data can be viewed on microfilm readers and, when necessary, a copy can be made directly from the film through the use of a printer. Film complements computers in many ways. It provides an excellent medium for storage; it provides security, integrity, and economical trans-mission because it is difficult to change or destroy. It easily records graphic informa-tion.

It has been demonstrated that by using microfilm to reduce the physical size and complexity of a computerized database, personnel costs for software maintenance can be reduced. In addition to being a good storage medium, microfilm also demonstrates its cost effectiveness in recording large amounts of computer input.

For these reasons and for cost advantages cited herein, COM is rapidly becoming integrated as a major link in many companies' processing chain.

COM ADVANTAGES

COM does more than merely write human-readable data on microfilm quickly. It makes possible substantial economies through:

- A saving in computer time no longer dedicated to conventional impact printing.
- Greatly reduced duplication and distribution costs. A 100-ft reel of 16-mm film containing 2,500 pages of information can be duplicated and put in a magazine for approximately one-twentieth the cost of standard continuous-form paper. This ex-cludes costs for decollating, bursting, and binding. The cost of producing micro-fiche duplicates is even less. More impressive is the saving in mailing costs realized from lighter weights. A 100-ft film magazine weighs less than 6 ounces. A set of 12

microfiche containing roughly the same number of images is even lighter: less than 2 ounces. By contrast, a hard-copy set of 2,500 continuous-form pages weighs 20 pounds. The savings in handling time and costs are proportionate.

● Compressing the time required to generate and distribute a finished report.

● An enormous speedup in retrieval time. Locating information on microfilm usually takes far less time than equivalent searches with hard copy.

Of course, COM is not the only alternative to paper as an information storage and retrieval medium. Computer core memories, disks, data cells, magnetic tape, and punch cards all store data and support access to it. But where daily or weekly updates are satisfactory, COM has proved to be the most economical alternative.

COM RECORDERS

There are three basic types of COM: alphanumeric, scientific, and graphic arts. COM recorders used in business generate high-speed alphanumeric output onto 16-mm nonperforated film or onto 105-mm film. The 105-mm film is subsequently cut into 4- by 6-in. sheets called *microfiche*.

Scientific COM units are designed to record graphic information. These machines have a slower throughput time than alphanumeric recorders, but are much faster than a mechanical hard-copy plotter. The normal output medium is 35-mm or 105-mm film.

As their name indicates, graphic arts recorders are designed to generate both graphic and alphanumeric output of the very high quality required for offset reproduction.

Three basic techniques are usually employed in COM recording: a cathode-ray tube (CRT), an electron beam, or fiber optics. A fourth and newer technique uses a laser beam as the energy source. CRTs are the most widely used method. With CRT, information is written by exciting the face of the tube and forming characters on it. This happens at extremely high speeds—up to 120,000 cps. The image is photographed directly onto unexposed film. In an alternate CRT technique, an electron beam passes through the image of each character in a miniaturized matrix within the tube and then onto the face of the tube.

The second technique involves characters "written" by an electron beam directly onto unexposed film, which in this case is a dry-silver film (silver film that uses heat rather than chemical development).

The third method has the selective illumination of a matrix of luminous fibers which form the characters in a single line of data; recording is done a line at a time.

In all three techniques, forms overlays for heading-column designations, company logotypes, etc., can be superimposed on the image as it is recorded. This is done either through the use of slides, or less commonly, through programmed merging of film images. Thus, preprinted information that would normally appear on paper stock can be generated automatically onto COM-produced output.

After exposure, the film (except for the dry-silver film) is processed in a fashion similar to that used for any other microfilm and can then be duplicated as many times as is necessary without significant loss of quality.

On-Line and Off-Line   COM recorders may be used on-line (recorder attached directly to the computer) or off-line (using a magnetic tape or disk as input at a different location). Both have advantages.

The on-line technique requires no special programming, providing the user desires only uncoded microfilm, since the computer treats the COM as it does any other peripheral device. The job goes through in one operation at extremely high speeds when compared to a line printer.

With an off-line operation, tapes coming from mainframe computers are sent to the off-line COM recorder. If a job has to be rerun for any reason, no computer time is involved. The COM recorder can be located physically away from the computer room. (Since most recorders require chemicals for film processing, this is an important consideration to many companies.) Generally, off-line recorders offer a wider selection of options in font size, image rotation and indexing capabilities, and microforms, than do on-line recorders.

COM recorders range in price from approximately $30,000 for the simplest on-line unit, to well in excess of $200,000 for complex scientific and graphic arts recorders.

Most alphanumeric business recorders fall in the $90,000 to $150,000 range (1975 prices).

As with most things, the buyer gets what he or she pays for—with added capabilities increasing the price. For example, COM recorders with graphic capabilities are the most expensive, particularly those producing output that is suitable for offset reproduction. Similarly, a recorder with a universal camera will cost more than a recorder with a camera capable of producing only roll film.

The number and size of character sets (fonts) as well as forms merging capabilities, all bear on the price of the recorder, as does the availability of retrieval codes (put on during filming). Still other cost considerations are the number and type of software packages available for and with a given recorder.

WHEN TO USE COM

Typically a business executive considering COM examines it as an alternative to paper print-out. Answers to questions such as the following may show whether COM is justified:

- Does the time required to get data on hard-copy print-out consume computer time that could be used for other data processing work?
- Must the same program be run twice or more to produce the required number of copies; or must the same program be run on more than one impact printer?
- Is the need for information so urgent that it is impractical to wait for computer print-out, yet to have the same data available on-line would be uneconomical?
- Are multiple copies needed for distribution to a widespread network of offices and end users?
- How is retrieval of information handled now? How long does it take to get information to the people who need it, and how much does it cost in terms of paper, storage, and personnel?

Whether an in-house COM recorder is the best solution depends on the amount of work to be run on it. A rough rule of thumb is that between 100,000 and 200,000 computer-printed pages a month must be produced to warrant an in-house COM unit. If fewer pages than that are involved, it is more economical to deal with a reliable service bureau, most of which provide 24-hour service with pickup and delivery of tapes.

Once the decision to use COM is made, the most efficient way is to treat it as an information system, not just an economy measure. The needs of the end user should determine the nature of the specific COM system chosen. To that end, another series of questions should be asked:

- What does the end user need and in what form is it needed?
- Is roll film or microfiche the best output for the application?
- How often will the specific data be referenced?
- What indexing techniques are required?
- In what final format will the information be most useful? What software and programming are available to do the job—and, again, what equipment is compatible?

Hard answers to these questions and others like them are a must before a successful COM application can be created. In effect, the hardware is one of the last considerations—though a vital one.

Growing Interest As mentioned in the first sentence of this Chapter, although the term COM is still new to many, its capability is proved. Eastman Kodak Company developed its own version of a COM device called a Dacom microfilmer in the late 1950s. Stromberg-Carlson Division of General Dynamics Corporation developed a recorder combining graphic and alphanumeric capabilities which it introduced in 1960. Priced at more than $200,000, the unit was widely used for the next 5 years. In the second half of the 1960s lower-price recorders with only alphanumeric capabilities were introduced by an increasing number of manufacturers.

The growth of COM in many ways paralleled the growth and acceptance of electronic data processing a decade earlier. Acceptance was slow for the first commercial computers, which made their debut in the 1950s, but quickly grew in the later half of the decade, as EDP equipment improved and became more sophisticated and less costly.

The advent of second- and third-generation computer hardware, and increased application of computers to business data processing, have caused many companies to examine COM more closely.   Many EDP applications involve the printing of large masses of data but only relatively minor computer processing.   In such instances it becomes too costly to lose high computer processing speed and capability through relatively slow electromechanical printing time.   And then, too, the former criticism of COM has passed.   The chief objection used to be that despite film's obvious benefits, people were more comfortable with paper.   This waned as handling paper became more and more difficult because of sheer volume, and as office workers became accustomed to working with microfilm.

Studies have shown that success in overcoming employee resistance depends on how the users are educated in using film.   Often people are dubious when first exposed to microfilm.   But when they are shown how easy it is to use, and how improved optics in today's readers make viewing comfortable rather than eye-straining, they soon become microfilm advocates.   This is not to say that the paper habit is broken; it just does not have quite the stranglehold it once did.   And that hold becomes weaker as new applications come to the forefront.

Where COM Is Growing Fastest   Generally speaking, any activity which requires frequent information searches of a large data file and/or large distribution of reports is a prime candidate for COM.   In terms of industries that are extensive COM users, banking, insurance, and utilities stand out.   Most banks in the United States use COM, either through an in-house COM recorder or through the COM facilities of an outside service bureau.   Typical applications include general accounting reports, credit files, demand deposit reports, personal finance histories, travelers check listings, and stock transfer journals.

Insurance applications include recapitulations of claims and claims histories, group history files, group activity analyses, sales reports, credit files, personal histories, and group annuity and accounting reports.

In addition to common applications such as payroll and general accounting records, utilities also use COM for customer registers and history files.

Large retail organizations are a growing area of COM potential.   Above and beyond the essential accounts payable and accounts receivable records applications, these retailers find COM invaluable for account credit status reports, customer directories, customer name and address files for account look-ups, invoice histories, and transaction indices.

Probably the largest potential for COM use is in manufacturing, an area that presently is largely untapped.   Obvious applications include standard office records such as accounts payable and receivable, payroll records, bill of materials listing, product cost breakdowns, parts lists, and project analyses, as well as inventories.

The Federal Government is probably the largest single user of COM, and state and local governments are increasing their uses by justifying COM in a variety of daily activities.

TYPICAL INSTALLATIONS

The range and value of COM can be seen in these typical installations.

Electric and Gas Utilities   One major Midwestern utility prints customer records, its transaction and open balance registers, the refund check register and deposit control report, on a computer output microfilmer.   Microfilm serves as a backup to a real-time system providing traceable information after the latter has been purged from the real-time system.   On-line data are available only for the most recent 12 months.   Without the microfilm records there would be no way, for example, to answer a customer's question about a current charge as compared with a similar one a year or more earlier.   A reduction of 48:1 was selected because it allows the placing of 777 customer data records on a single microfiche, and is easily readable.

A large Northeastern utility found that whereas it takes 16 to 17 hours at 1,600 lines per minute to print a 27,000-page report on paper, the report can be COM-generated at 22,000 lines per minute in less than $1\frac{1}{2}$ hours.   This same power company uses microfiche to replace all paper records.   One example is the company's stockholder records, now managed internally with changes being prepared on a daily basis, and information printed out by a COM onto fiche. Just as accounting clerks have their latest fiche in three-ring binders near a reader in order to answer customer inquiries, so do clerks in the stockholder records department.

Insurance One insurance company found that its COM enables 29 clerks to do the work of 60 persons in less than half the time. COM is involved in helping to control the company's outstanding check file. Nearly 2 million sheets of computer print-out paper were previously used each year. The saving in paper costs alone paid for the COM equipment. By using image control retrieval keyboard techniques, rather than going through an entire roll of microfilm, it is estimated that the time required to find a check is cut almost in half.

The future will see an even closer relationship between microfilm, computers, and the insurance industry. Microfilm fits in nicely in that it can maintain information flow by capturing documents. As records are altered, an audit trail record can be kept on film by use of COM. Film can be referenced by various departments which might wish to learn what a picture looked like 6 months or even 1 month ago. This kind of information is not feasible to keep on cathode-ray tubes because of the cost of maintenance in the computer file. For current information, companies can reference a computer. To get past information status, they can go to film.

Banking Prior to the use of COM, one Southern bank's statewide operation center received daily computer-generated paper reports on various banking transactions. With retention time for reports varying from 3 months to 7 years, paper storage became a great problem. Also, it was not economical to print out reports for all those smaller city branches. Consequently, when customers came to local branches with questions about their accounts, it was necessary to call the main office to obtain information.

This was changed by having paper stop at the regional level as these reports were put onto magnetic tape and microfilmed. The COM-generated roll microfilm is programmed with a code-line indexing to ease retrieval of information. Branch offices are equipped with a microfilm reader for viewing COM-generated fiche. COM is used to keep track of charge accounts for 125,000 customers. Volumes of print-out gave way to more easily retrievable microfiche files for answering customer inquiries. Two clerks handle inquiries which formerly required six clerks. The yearly saving in computer time in this operation alone has more than paid for the investment in COM equipment.

COM is an integral part of the data processing operation at another large Southern bank. Telephone transmission of daily reports going to the regional centers was becoming very time-consuming and costly. The faster processing speed of COM allowed the bank to eliminate Saturday work and one shift at three centers. More than 2.5 million frames per month, or more than 50 per cent of the total computer output of information, is produced on the COM in lieu of paper print-out.

A Midwestern bank developed several methods for use of computer and microfilm technology that eliminated large amounts of cost from various banking operations. In 6 months alone its COM operation saved more than $70,000 in paper cost and almost 1,000 hours of computer print-out time. It eliminated the need for extra personnel to handle a growing workload, and minimized equipment investment. The daily deposit trial balance is on COM. Whereas previously it took between 2 and $2\frac{1}{2}$ hours of print-out time, it is now produced within 20 to 25 minutes. One of COM's interesting applications is a trust company accounting method wherein personnel within the trust company can feed information via a cathode-ray tube into a computer. From there it goes to a computer output microfilmer and becomes encoded microfilm. The encoded film is back in the department the next day for retrieval. It takes about 10 seconds to look up a report on the microfilm retrieval terminal.

Hospital A Baltimore hospital used to operate its computer continuously, 24 hours a day, 7 days a week, to print out reports which range from a 1,500-page patient listing to a 12,500-page accounts receivable report. The use of COM has speeded up production of records and made the computer more readily available. The hospital's COM equipment generates the equivalent of 0.5 million pages of information per month. The paper cost saving in $4\frac{1}{2}$ months of operation offset the cost of the new equipment.

Automobile Club Conversion from paper filing systems to COM-generated microfilm helped a Midwestern automobile club save more than $200,000 a year in paper handling procedures, while also streamlining record-keeping methods. Each day approximately 11,000 policies or renewals are printed out. These documents are formatted onto disks for COM. Subsequent computer programs are used to produce an index to the microfilm information. Each 4- by 7⅜-inch microfiche contains 260 images of computer-size pages. The daily total of 11,000 documents is contained on 16 fiche.

Diazo film duplicates are distributed to various clerical units. To obtain data relating to a policy, the policy number is keyed into the console of an on-line teleprocessing terminal. Dates, fiche numbers, and document types of all the documents in the fiche file for that policy number are accessed from the microfilm index file and displayed on the terminal screen. The appropriate fiche is removed from the tray and viewed. COM-generated 16-mm roll film is also used in the collections department for open and closed account registers.

Industry As implied earlier in this chapter, COM applications are rapidly coming into play and are subject to constant improvement. Although one large rubber company's early application has been substantially updated, even the initial benefits are worth reporting. Six distinct advantages were realized.

• By using computer output microfilm in place of paper in billing, sales reporting, accounts payable, order entry, and personnel records, the company was able to eliminate 132 preprinted paper forms from its inventory.

• Because microfilm takes about 5 per cent of the space devoted to paper storage, the company was able to convert 4,000 square feet of stock-room space into offices. And, of course, considerable paper handling costs were eliminated.

• File integrity proved to be a third benefit of COM. The ability to print large and small reports on microfilm gave impetus to improved file organization.

• A fourth advantage is considerably faster report turnaround. Generating COM reports 100 hours a month produces more than 2 million frames of data. This is comparable to 2,000 hours on an impact printer. Three copies of a 20,000-page report are produced in 2 hours. Printed on a 3-part form and decollated, the same report would require 40 hours, and might be available a week later than the microfilm.

• The fifth advantage is a reduction in mailing costs. Where it used to cost $875 to mail 36,000 pages to 44 locations, by film the cost was reduced to $35.

• Finally, the sixth benefit is reduction in the on-line disk storage space required to support various real-time information retrieval systems. The marriage of microfilm and on-line direct access can be extremely beneficial when one considers the possibility of storing a large expensive database on inexpensive microfilm, and using direct access to the disk file only for dynamic occurrences that have transpired since microfilm was created. An example of this might be distribution in an inventory control system. It would be very expensive to store on-line a complete history of all transactions for all shipments and sales, so the company prints it on microfilm. Transactions occurring since the microfilm was created are stored on disks. Portions of the database which represent active items are stored on disks, and a complete history of all transactions is stored on microfilm. The company has real-time direct access to current data in the disks or the historical data on film. The combination of two information sources provides all valuable data including the most current updates of the film. Microfilm duplicates serve as a backup for security. This one company has more than 200 computer output microfilm applications. Reportedly, the saving from its first application – involving invoices produced each day – was enough to justify the entire COM installation.

GETTING STARTED

One way to start in COM is to use one of the many independent service bureaus to initiate a program. Work with a bureau to determine the turnaround time that you need, the programming that may be required, the film type, etc. Then turn over the tapes to the bureau, and it will return the film to you. Working with a service bureau will enable your company to get valuable experience in the use of COM technology without having to make any capital expenditure.

Later, increase the number of applications at an orderly rate. Justify each one economically. At a certain point – which can be predetermined by a cost analysis – the output volume at the service bureau will justify consideration of an in-house system. Even when you reach this point, you should still move slowly.

Take over the in-house system yourself when the equipment costs, supply costs, and labor costs equal the price being paid to the bureau for its services. At this point, an in-house operation can be justified. If you have facilities to preplan your installation and train your personnel in the effective use of COM, as well as sufficient volume to justify this approach, an initial installation of your own will probably be most satisfactory. With either course you will be in the COM business, and realize benefits impossible with "traditional" output methods.

CONCLUSION

Computer output microfilm is becoming far more than just an alternative to paper or a backup records file. It brings a new dimension to the use of the computer—a saving of time. COM facilitates faster distribution of data than does printing, allowing computer time to be used more effectively. It can improve information flow and allow historical information to be viewed quickly for reference. The future will show many examples of outstanding information systems based on the interrelationship of computers and microfilm.

SELECTIVE BIBLIOGRAPHY

Avedon, Don M., *Computer Output Microfilm*, 2d ed., National Microfilm Association, Silver Spring, Md., 1971.
Ballou, Hubard W., *Guide to Microreproduction Equipment*, 5th ed., National Microfilm Association, Silver Spring, Md., 1971.
Bird, Michael G., "Indexing is the Key to Retrieving COM-Stored Data," *Computer Decisions*, May, 1971.
Information and Records Management, monthly (includes a monthly COM section).
An Introduction to COM, Dataflow Systems, Bethesda, Md., 1971.
Microfilm Source Book, Microfilm Publishing, New York, annual.
Panorama, quarterly magazine published by Business Systems Markets Division, Eastman Kodak Company, Rochester, N.Y.

Chapter **5**

Source-Data Automation

JOHN FORD

**Director, Management Systems and Controls Corporate
Rohr Industries, Inc., Chula Vista, California**

Source-data automation refers to the creating or preparing of input data for the computer automatically, at the point of origin of the data, as a byproduct of some other necessary procedure or by some minor added procedure such as inserting a card in a slot. Where production data entry is being automated, methods include in-machine sensors and in-plant data entry terminals. The sensors or the terminals may be on-line to the host computer, or an off-line system may collect and batch the data for the computer.

The intent is to replace a manual data preparation procedure, such as card keypunch or other keystroke data entry, in whole or in part. The gains from successful source-data automation are threefold: data are more timely, since preparation times are eliminated; data preparation costs are reduced or eliminated; and error rates are reduced.

Other chapters in this Section describe techniques for reducing or eliminating manual data capture procedures (such as magnetic-ink and magnetic-stripe encoding of cards and documents) in commerical and financial applications. This Chapter focuses on applications in the industrial environment: capturing inventory and inventory-movement data, tracking work in progress and production machinery operations, monitoring and controlling tool utilization and inventory, automatic monitoring of materials and production in refining and primary metals processing, and monitoring railroad and utility operations—in general, the creation of an automatic or semiautomatic data link between the physical operations of an organization and its management information system.

In the 1960s, the concept was developed of a hierarchy of computers in the large-scale production environment; in-machine sensors connected to minicomputers—one minicomputer to each group of machines or production area—which accumulated and interpreted the signals (e.g., converted sequences of in-machine switch actuations into parts counts and machine-speed calculations). In turn the minicomputers were to forward their formatted data to plant-level computers which track inventory, schedule production, track work in progress, and respond to inventory and order status inquiries. Finally, the plant-level computers were to report to corporate management information systems which would abstract and interpret the production, inventory, and backlog position of the company.

While this concept has not developed in reality as quickly as its most optimistic proponents expected, major elements of it are a reality in various industries. The automobile industry and allied piece-part manufacturing industries, in particular, have implemented quite ambitious systems, in which elaborate automatic material handling systems—stacker cranes and conveyor systems—automate the routing of materials through the production process. Signals from the material handling system and from in-machine sensors in the production equipment are interpreted by computers to develop and present complete current pictures of plant status.

In addition, the in-machine sensors permit another computer function—timing analysis of production machinery (e.g., transfer machines)—permitting the computer to pinpoint the cause of slowdown in large multistation machines.

The philosophy of in-machine sensing is usually to piggyback on a signal required for the operation of the machine itself where possible, rather than add a sensor, since this increases the reliability of the data. Typically such a signal would be derived from a *limit switch*—a switch actuated by a machine movement (at the end or "limit" of part travel), used as a control signal in sequencing the machine through its cycle. To sense the presence of parts or machine movements not detected by limit switches, a variety of sensor devices using different technologies are available: magnetic sensors, electrostatic proximity sensors, pneumatic sensors, pressure sensors, level sensors for liquids and bulk solids, etc.

The outputs of all such sensors are passed to interfacing boxes which transform the signals electrically to computer-compatible forms, performing any digitizing or time sequencing required for computer input.

Complementing the data automatically acquired from machinery are the data which must be entered manually—worker identity, production lot number, manual work-in-progress movements, etc. These consist of data of a somewhat fixed or repetitive nature—worker identities, part numbers, work-order numbers, etc.—and variable data such as quantities, hours, reject rates, etc.

In-plant terminals have been developed for entry of this type of data. After some early failures showed the special characteristics required for such terminals—rugged enclosures, dirt- and contamination-resistant working parts, large push buttons and manual controls not requiring delicacy of touch, positive confirmation of input, etc.—special terminals were developed for this function. Long-term fixed data such as employee identity are encoded on durable media such as machine-readable plastic cards, and shorter-term fixed data are encoded on punched paper cards which accompany work in progress, and which are manually inserted in slots in the in-plant terminals.

Another expedient, still widely used for many applications, was the development of *mark-sensing* cards, introduced early by IBM. Here the person capturing the original data uses a special graphite pencil to make marks in specified locations on a card, which is later fed into a card-punch machine that senses the marks and produces punched cards as output—a technique applicable in low- to moderate-volume applications like meter reading and questionnaire surveys.

Where accurate tracking with minimum time lag is essential, data acquisition terminals on line to a computer which processes each input as a separate transaction to disk-resident files is indicated. Where a lag of several hours in updating of files can be tolerated, it is more economical to accumulate and store data in an off-line system, with periodic batch input to the computer system.

One method, pioneered in the early 1960s by three manufacturers in the aircraft industry, involved the use of the IBM Automatic Production Recorder System. This system utilized a variety of physical sensors imbedded in production and handling machinery—strain gauges, weighing devices, counters, pressure and temperature sensors—to detect and quantify production and material handling activity, and accumulate and format the data for computer input.

The system was set up to handle fixed and variable data. Variable data were entered by pressing keys on a 12-key keyboard on manual entry stations in the fabrication area. The system used consoles at which fixed data were entered by manually inserting punched cards. The console then produced output punched cards that were the medium of data transfer to the host computer.

About 75 per cent of the data to be entered were fixed, leaving only about 10 characters to be manually keyed in per transaction, minimizing manual data entry errors. The system produced a computer-readable transaction card immediately upon data entry. In subsequent expansions, the users began collecting labor and attendance information, in addition to data on shop-order movement.

Although these early efforts to automate data collection were not without successes, management recognized certain limitations: device costs limited expansion, the output was still a punched card, equipment maintenance was costly, and relocation of terminals was not simple.

Touch-Tone Data Entry An innovation in source-data automation was the use of Touch-Tone[1] telephones in 1966. Initially, these phones were used as input to IBM 026 keypunches. In mid-1967 Touch-Tone input was coupled to a host computer and an audio-response unit (Figure 5-1). A small vocabulary of words was recorded on a

Source Data Automation   A NEW PRACTICAL WAY USING AUDIO RESPONSE

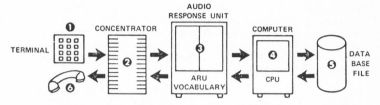

1. DATA IS ENTERED VIA THIS TERMINAL,
2. THROUGH THE CONCENTRATOR WHICH ACTS AS AN AUTOMATIC SWITCHBOARD,
3. THROUGH THE ARU,
4. TO THE CPU WHERE THE COMPUTER PERFORMS THE NECESSARY LOGIC AND ACCESSES ANY DATA FILES REQUIRED.
5. THE RESPONSE IS ROUTED BACK THROUGH THE ARU WHERE IT IS CONVERTED TO VOICE SIGNALS
6. AND TO THE SENDER AT THE TERMINAL.
   (CYCLE IS REPEATED AS MANY TIMES AS NEEDED TO COMPLETE THE TRANSACTION.)

A Typical Audio Response Labor Transaction

EMPLOYEE	VOICE RESPONSE MABEL	
13	Man Number?	*NOTE: Mabel checked to see if the man number was a current employee and if the work order was active. She assigned the work location automatically, because she knew what telephone was talking to her, and assigned the time reported to the work order. If the employee makes an error, Mabel points it out and in some cases automatically activates a teletype in timekeeping to get the problem solved.*
Man Number	Work Order?	
Work Order	Operation Code?	
Operation Code	O. K.	

Fig. 5-1   Source-data automation using audio response.

drum, and under computer control phrases were formed to guide the employee through input transactions.

More applications followed, and the CRT terminal soon joined the Touch-Tone telephone as a computer input device. One user was able to reduce punched card usage from 80 million cards per year to 10 million. While this cut in card volume was being achieved, system accuracy in parts tracking increased from 55 per cent to 96.5 per cent.

KEY QUESTIONS

In analyzing a functional area of a business to determine if source-data automation is feasible, the following specific questions must be answered:

[1] Touch-Tone — ®American Telephone and Telegraph Co.

1. Do large data processing input volumes exist?
2. Are response-time requirements short?
3. Are data handling errors too large?
4. Are the same data elements being transcribed repeatedly?
5. Are the personnel requirements for data handling too costly?
6. Are the computers devoting too much time to input processing (reading cards, balancing, error listing, and correcting bad data)?
7. What will future trends be with respect to the foregoing points?

Collateral Problems   Another key question is: Can source-data automation be accomplished without seriously disrupting current systems?   By planning implementation of a system in a series of manageable steps, one can minimize the disruption of operations.

Finally, it must be remembered that source-data automation usually affects many people in a plant—e.g., in production and parts tracking.   Therefore heavy participation from the affected organization units must be solicited.   Success or failure of the project will depend in large measure upon the degree of commitment obtained from the people who will use the system.   If the groups who will be most affected by the change are invited to join in analyzing the conditions that call for a new system, their instinctive opposition can usually be converted to cooperation.   And, of course, *management involvement* at all levels is necessary.

JUSTIFICATION

While tangible, direct-cost justification is definitely important, there is a tendency to overemphasize it, instead of looking for *total* P&L impact.   All collateral costs and savings that will reflect on the balance sheet should be developed.   Generally, a system implementation should not be undertaken unless the annual savings exceed the annual costs by a sufficient margin to amortize rapidly the one-time start-up costs.   Important areas to consider for savings are:

Personnel—both in user areas and in data processing (keypunchers, machine operators, clerks).   Obtain specific commitments of these forecast personnel savings in writing, and follow up on them after implementation.

Forms and supplies.

Storage and file space.

Equipment—typically, keypunches and unit record equipment.

Major items of cost which must be taken into account are:

Systems and programming.   The nature of the collection systems (usually on-line and often real-time) demands specialists of high caliber.

Equipment—purchase versus lease trade-offs.

Communications—includes the cost of all hardware necessary to interface with the computer (typically data modems, transmission controllers, and special multiplexers).

Hardware maintenance costs.

Training.

Lost Production—disruption caused by installation and start-up.

DESIGN AND IMPLEMENTATION

Error Checks   A careful network of error checks and safeguards must be designed into the system.   It is inevitable that some errors will occur in every procedure involving human operators and mechanical equipment.   As a matter of fact, even when the data are entered via devices such as optical scanners, a certain amount of error will occur due to smudges, torn documents, and other input media defects.   Software validity checks should be programmed to detect and, where possible, correct such input errors.

One of the most common is the self-checking number routine (check digit).   Check digit verification simply requires that a formula be used to calculate a single digit based on the combination of digits found within a field.   A typical example is an employee number.   Each employee can be provided a check digit to enter along with his or her employee identification when entering data.   Then when the employee number is entered, the same calculation that originally provided the check digit is performed upon the basic employee number. If the calculation yields a result different from the check digit inputted by the employee, an error will be noted. Check digits are also used to catch digit transposition mistakes. This technique can be used to validate employee numbers, tool numbers, shop-order numbers, and similar identifiers.

Many other validating techniques exist. Typical are field length tests, tests of the type of data within a field (all numeric or all alphabetic, for example), range tests, and reasonableness tests.

A range test can be included when the programmer knows in advance the highest or lowest magnitude an input variable can be expected to reach. The system can be programmed to reject, or flag for attention, any input outside these limits. A good example of a reasonableness test would be in the area of retail credit sales within a store. If a particular credit account had shown a pattern of an average of five transactions per month over a period of time and suddenly in one day six transactions were made, it might be reasonable to verify that nothing was amiss. In a manufacturing situation, the number of parts leaving one work station can be a test of the reasonableness of the number arriving at the next station.

Master data tables and files can be used to validate portions of incoming data transactions. An example is a labor and attendance collection system. One such system collects attendance arrivals and departures on 95 per cent of hourly employees in a company, handling about 18,000 transactions per day. An employee making use of this system must input his or her employee identification number. In addition to performing a check digit calculation on this number, validation is made against an on-line master employee file. When the employee reports labor data for a particular shop order, this number is validated against another on-line file. If an employee makes an error, he or she is told to "redial." If the employee fails to enter valid data on the second try, then the data are accepted but reported as being in error. Specific steps taken at the time an error is made can contribute to both a timely correction of the error and prompt education of the using employee. Typical labor data mistakes cause an immediate print-out on a teletypewriter located in the timekeeping office. A call to the supervisor of the employee serves two purposes: The correct data are relayed to timekeeping where they are promptly re-entered on-line, and the supervisor instructs the employee in correct procedures.

Safeguards Specific safeguards for the data collected can be employed. Depending upon the device on which the data were entered, the employee can be given feedback as to the way the computer received that data. Moreover, the employee can be prompted, particularly on a CRT, teletype, or audio-response unit, leading him or her through the transaction and minimizing errors or omissions in the transaction procedure. Additional safeguards include: (1) Require only a minimum of data to be entered. (2) Keep all transactions simple. (3) Indicate positively to the terminal user that all data have been accepted. (4) Update files only when a transaction is complete. (5) Design transaction procedures to give multiple opportunities to enter valid data. (6) Provide adequate error indications. (7) Terminate the transaction if no data are entered within a predetermined interval. (8) Attempt to signal user when the system is inoperative. (9) Maintain tape or disk backup of all data transactions entered.

Backup A typical system design error is to provide inadequate backup provisions. Most systems will be inoperative or "down" at least occasionally. Typically, heavy periods of downtime will occur whenever new systems are implemented, new hardware is first used, or extensive changes have been made to a system. A backup (usually card-oriented) means of entering data should be provided.

Equipment backup can be as simple or as elaborate as the reliability of system requires. It is good practice to arrange the placement of terminals so that if one terminal fails, the user has access to a nearby alternate. When telecommunications are employed, backup transmission lines may be leased in case the primary line(s) fails. This type of precaution may be extended to power sources, air conditioning, and the computer mainframe itself. The degree of backup is determined by how critical downtime is and how much downtime is tolerable.

Data Security It may be necessary to consider the security aspect of the actual data. Although security may not be so critical as to mandate lead-shielded transmission lines, protocols should include identifying the terminal user and the terminal. User identification can be via password. Usually, the system can be designed to allow an individual user to select his or her own password. And the system can be programmed to restrict specific types of transaction to selected terminals and/or persons.[2]

Planning Larger projects are best planned in relatively short increments, each resulting in added system capability. This will mean that: (1) Cost estimates are more realistic. (2) Management begins to see results soon after the funds are committed. (3) Implementation usually occurs before any major corporate policy changes.

Diagnostic Routines and Tracing If a system uses a type of terminal that is unsupported in software by the host computer, it will be necessary to write diagnostic routines to assist support personnel to isolate hardware failures. A selective tracing function to provide a print-out of computer memory at key points during program execution is also a useful aid. This should be controlled through a master console, and will prove of particular value during program test and troubleshooting. The key here is to be highly selective, so that meaningful output data are generated. The on-line program should be segmented into smaller subtasks by function, so that program or hardware malfunctions in one area do not disable the entire system. A task monitor can be created at the highest level that governs the start and restart of independent subtasks. One purpose of such subtasking is to separate older and more stable functions from newer ones which are more subject to problems.

TRAINING

Good training will diminish the natural distrust of an employee toward this type of innovation. This includes a continuing follow-up program. Keeping records or entering data is an annoyance or distraction to a factory employee whose attention is focused on his or her primary production task. If employees are provided with a clear understanding of how the new data collection system will benefit them, their confidence and cooperation can be obtained.

Such benefits can include simpler, less bothersome procedures (e.g., using a Touch-Tone telephone instead of finding and using a pencil in a gritty work environment), the worker's own confidence that data relating to his or her work are accurately entered, and the pleasure of using a sophisticated automatic system and having it respond (e.g., by recorded voice in a voice-response system).

Training includes indoctrination sessions, the provision of instruction manuals, and follow-up sessions to ensure that workers are using the system properly. Training must also include supervisors and management people, as well as production workers. People involved at every level must understand the system.

EQUIPMENT

For collection of large volumes of largely numeric data in an environment where great numbers of terminals are needed, there is no more flexible and economical medium than the Touch-Tone telephone. Alphanumeric data are usually best collected via CRT terminal, teletype, or one of the various key-to-tape or key-to-disk systems.

It will be necessary to establish a central point for reporting equipment malfunction. This part of the system must operate the same hours as the equipment, and this may be 24 hours per day, all week long. Prompt attention must be given to malfunction problems, or user dissatisfaction will soon set in. This implies that trained equipment specialists must be available at all times. It is advisable to handle minor problems in-house, but major problems require vendor-trained specialists.

A reliable, financially stable vendor with a proved product is a necessity. There are usually new companies with attractive products about; they should be treated carefully. Before entering any agreement, it is best to arrange face-to-face contacts with satisfied users, if possible. Demand proof of performance not only along equipment lines, but also service. Many firms have found that prolonged downtime of equipment negates the benefits of the data collection system.

[2] See Section 8, Chapter 4, "The Computer and Privacy."

Minicomputers   In some systems, minicomputers can economically off-load data accumulation, formatting, and validation procedures from the host computer, working either in a stand-alone mode or as a front-end processor to the host computer.   When the minicomputer acts as a stand-alone processor, the accumulated data can be transferred as a batch to the host computer on tape or a removable disk.[3]

[3] See Part Two, Chapter 4, "Minicomputers," in this Section.

Part Four

Computer Programming and Languages

Introduction

PHILIP A. RICCO, *Principal, The Diebold Group, Inc., New York, New York*

The technology of creating programs (software) to make computers do useful work has lagged behind the hardware technology almost from the beginning of computer science. Many computer users have spent much more money to develop software than to acquire the computer systems to execute it. More significant than the direct dollar outlays, however, are such factors as the unreliability of software—especially new software—and the inability to predict or control the amount of time required to provide it.

As many managers have learned, the number of lines of code written is a poor indicator of the amount of work related to a computer program. This is because *debugging*—finding and correcting logical and functional errors in the code—often is more difficult than writing the original code. And, once written and placed into production use, a program may still be unreliable: it may contain hidden bugs which do not become apparent until a specific combination of input conditions occurs.

There have been successive generations of programming tools, comparable to the generations of hardware. These started with the painstaking process of writing in machine language—the long strings of ones and zeroes the computer itself recognizes—and proceeded during the 1950s and early 1960s to assemblers, macroassemblers, compilers, and interpreters—each a type of computer program which converts a notation convenient to humans into the machine language of the computer.

The first of these, the assemblers, permitted programmers to use mnemonic instruction codes, symbolic labels for data and addresses, and decimal numbers for constants and locations. When macros were added, making macroassemblers, they saved programming time by permitting frequently used sequences of instructions—such as a decimal-to-binary conversion—to be specified in a single line of code. When the idea of the subroutine—a small program that can be "called" (invoked) by other programs—was developed, it made possible major savings of both programmer and machine time, and of machine memory space.

Assemblers, like machine language, keep the programmer close to the mechanics of the machine, since—in both languages—the programmer specifies each movement and manipulation of data into and out of registers and memory locations. The late 1950s saw the emergence of compilers, which permitted the programmer to express the program in a *higher-level* language, specifying what the computer must calculate, but not the individual machine steps of the calculation, which now would automatically be selected by the compiler. These languages, such as FORTRAN for scientific and engineering work and COBOL for commercial applications, are called "higher-level" because of their one-for-many relationship: one line of FORTRAN code generates, through the compiler, many lines of machine language.

Interpreters, which began appearing in the mid-1960s, are also high-level, but differ from compilers in that programs are executed by interpreters a few lines at a time, as they are entered into the machine. Interpreters were originally designed as simple languages for nonprogrammers to use interactively, at terminals, but they are now expanding from this role to become programmers' languages for certain types of problem.

Another powerful boost to programmer productivity came with the development—also in the 1950s and 1960s—of *operating systems:* resident software which includes *monitors* or *executives* to handle all the input and output activities of the system and to control the complex flow of data traffic to and from and within the hierarchy of storage media in the modern computer. This simplified programming greatly, since these procedures—among the most tedious to code—could now be invoked by simple CALL statements.

But these improvements in programming technology were constantly overmatched by the more rapidly increasing complexity of the computing environment and of the applications themselves. Tasks became larger in scale, progressing (in the commercial realm) from simple ledger accounting to such applications as complex financial simulations, or production and inventory control systems with complete product-line bill-of-material explosions. As *batch* processing was mastered, there emerged *on-line* and interactive processing, in which the program path is dynamically determined by input from terminals. On-line or transaction-oriented processing opened vast new dimensions of programming complexity, with such requirements as error recovery, transaction-conflict resolution, procedure re-entrancy, and data protection and security.

This outpacing of programming capabilities by hardware resources and by the increasing complexity of new applications has meant that the sorest spot for many data processing managements has been the project area—the activity of specifying, designing, and implementing new applications and getting them into routine production. It is here that time and money estimates most frequently break down, and performance commitments are broken.

Up to now, the technical innovations which have been offered as solutions to these problems have not proved to be panaceas, though compilers—and the newer, labor-saving *precompilers*—have eased many specific burdens, and such software as terminal managers, database languages, and ever more sophisticated operating systems have all made important contributions. But there is reason to hope that some emerging technologies—some not really new, but newly revived and developed—may at least bring controlled confusion, if not order, out of the chaos of traditional software development.

Programming has traditionally been regarded as an art: Efficient, economical utilization of machine resources has been thought of as a matter of talent and insight, not readily taught, explained, or transferred to others. One effect of this "art" psychology has been the tangled and forbidding characteristic of much computer code—a web of cross-references between and within routines, difficult to read or follow, and especially difficult to analyze backward to an understanding of the application. This unreadability, of course, has been a major factor in the time and cost overruns of projects, since communication among programmers on a project has been inhibited and it has been especially difficult for a new programmer to pick up the thread of a departing programmer's work.

Compounding the problem has been a correspondingly poor quality of program documentation: the written record of a program's underlying procedural sequence—its algorithm—and the other details required to use, understand, modify, or enhance it. Documentation has often been created as a hasty afterthought, with attention during most of the project time focused on "getting the program up and running." Then too, programmer "artists" have often not been disposed to document their oeuvres too completely.

Now, however, there is a movement in the software community to convert programming from an art to a science, or an engineeringlike discipline. Widely regarded as the father of this movement is Edsger Dijkstra, a Hollander also credited with advancing the fundamental ideas of Structured Programming. Dijkstra counseled the avoidance of GO-TOs—the jumps which often make programs such tangles of internal references—and described a limited set of structures, or flow progressions, into which, he argued, all program looping and other conditional execution forms can be fit. Further, he argued, these forms can be imposed in hierarchical levels, so that a simple block at one level can be decomposed into structures of one of the basic forms at the next lower level. This organization of the work permits programmers to start at the highest block-diagram level, writing "nucleus" code which links the major procedural blocks, and writing executable "stubs" which substitute for as-yet-unwritten modules of code. This Top-Down Programming reverses the traditional "bottom-up" approach, in which detailed procedures are written first and must later be integrated into a larger program. In Top-Down Programming, integration proceeds continuously, and executable code exists from the very beginning of the project.

Structured Programming is often used in conjunction with a Chief Programmer Team, which enforces the discipline, and organizes both the programming and the documentation, and sets up continuing communication among the programmers on the project. Methods called Egoless Programming and Structured Walk-Throughs further this communication by making all code "public": All code is read by all team members, and no segment of the program is considered the preserve of one author. Structured Programming is also usually accompanied by a new notation, using an identation scheme and a *pseudocode language* to represent the structure at each level. This notation has made Structured Programming largely self-documenting, as a byproduct of the application design and programming process.

Early trials of these techniques have been very promising, with far fewer bugs appearing in the test phase, and significant employee-hour savings, as measured against estimates based on conventional project methods. Equally important, maintenance—the process of repairing and enhancing production programs—has been greatly facilitated, as has communication between project and maintenance programmers.

Another trend which promises a measure of relief for application development problems is the emergence of very small business computers not intended to be programmed by the user. The vendors are providing complete, ready-to-run programs for specific applications for these computers. Generally, these are designed to meet the needs of small companies, or for limited, remote-site ("distributed processing") applications within bigger companies with larger machines in headquarters locations. Typical of these remote-site applications are customer order entry, inventory transaction processing, and production monitoring.

More remote as a significant alternative to general computer programming, but still an interesting development, are the microprocessors presently undergoing rapid development—particularly by a number of semiconductor firms. Many of these units are controlled by programs in read-only memory, and this type of "firmware" may well eventually supersede certain categories of conventional programming.

Chapter 1

Programming Basics

WILLIAM J. HARRISON

Technical Consultant, Computer Services Department, Fireman's Fund American Insurance Companies, San Rafael, California

Computers, as we have seen in earlier chapters, are complex machines which must be instructed in detail if they are to perform useful work. The art and science of programming concerns the way in which computers are told what to do.

ELEMENTARY OPERATIONS

The vast majority of business computers are medium to large general-purpose machines which are directed by a long series of binary zeros and ones. The latter constitute *instructions* consisting of *operators* which define the type of operation intended by that instruction, and one or more *operands* which tell the machine where the data to be operated upon by that instruction are located. A group of these instructions, taken together in some specified order of execution, is called a *program*.

Each of the machine instructions is in reality a fairly complex operation in itself, as far as the machine is concerned. For example, one of these machine-level instructions may cause the machine to perform a series of steps internally and externally. (See Figure 1-1.)[1]

If a person had to consider each of these steps while writing a program to direct the execution of a complex external problem, such as preparing a payroll, the workload

---

[1] Figure 1-1 is offered as an example of the complexity involved in writing machine-level instructions. For the reader interested in knowing what the notations mean, an explanation of the steps called for is as follows: The first step is to express the binary string in line 1 into an equivalent but more convenient notation known as *hexidecimal* or *hex* (line 2). If this hex string appears at a location in memory where it would be encountered by the machine's flow of control, it would be interpreted as an Operation (58), a First Operand (4), and a Second Operand (OD7F8). The First Operand is a General-Purpose Register number, in this case GPR 4. The Second Operand is interpreted as an Index GPR 0 (zero), a Base GPR D (hex for 13), and a Displacement 7F8 (hex for the decimal number 2040). The total operation instructs the machine to add whatever number is in the Base GPR 13 to the Displacement 7F8 in hex, plus any index value (none in this case since the index position is zero), and use the sum as an address in the computer's main memory. From this calculated address exactly 4 bytes (32 bits) of data are moved into GPR 4. The exact interpretation of each Operator code is dependent upon that code, and the machine hardware (wired or solid state circuits), not the programmer, handles this interpretation. (The reader is referred to the Appendix at the end of Chapter 2 of this Part for a detailed discussion of binary and hexadecimal representation.)

would be unbearable. The presence of the machine's repertoire of instructions, known as a *machine language*, makes the solving of external problems possible, but even machine language constitutes a very difficult and unwieldy mechanism for programming.

EVOLUTION OF HIGHER-LEVEL LANGUAGES

In the early days of computers, when attempts were made to work directly with machine language, it was noticed that certain aspects of the work proceeded more easily if the location of instructions and of data in the machine's memory could be referred to by name rather than by numerical location. Especially, whenever it was necessary to move programs in memory, or to add new requirements, or to correct errors, the

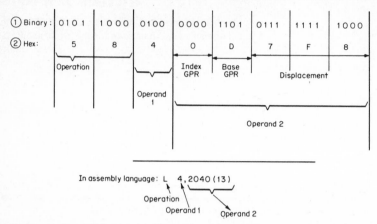

Fig. 1-1   How a string of binary 0 and 1 characters might be used to represent a computer instruction.

address numbers used to express the location of data or of other instructions might change, but the names did not.

New programs were written that took other programs and changed the names to the absolute numbers required by machine languages. Thus was born the earliest of the symbolic programming languages: the *assembly* languages. The programmer now wrote the program—for example, a series of instructions for the solution of an accounts aging procedure—without concern for the actual location of the program in memory. The result was a great increase in programmer productivity and, because there could be greater concentration on the external problem, improved accuracy and greater quality all around.

The next big step came quickly when it was noticed that certain similar sequences of operations were being written again and again, with only minor changes from one to the other. This led to the *macroassemblers*, which allowed single-programmer-written instructions called *macros* to be generated into large groups of machine-language instructions, with those parts which differed being provided as *parameters*.

In the 1950s the *high-level* languages came into being. These tended to be concerned with ways of stating a solution procedure, and attempted to make a program independent of particular machines. Complete with syntax (a definition of the order of words in statements expressed using the language) and semantics (the meanings of particular words), languages such as FORTRAN (Formula Translator) and COMTRAN (Commercial Translator) were invented to express external problems in terms meaningful to the specialist in the external problems. (Figure 1-2.)

THE PROGRAMMER TODAY

The introduction of the high-level, problem-oriented languages in the 1950s was widely believed to spell the demise of the programming profession as such. Businesses were supposed to express business problems in the newly developed Common Business Oriented Language (COBOL), and let the computer do the rest. The engineer was to do the same with FORTRAN or any of the host of other engineering-scientific-mathematical languages invented.[2]

However, the machine knows only machine language. The high-level languages must be converted into it before the computer can run the program. And since the machine is an expensive resource, its effective utilization requires detailed knowledge of programming theory as well as knowledge of the problem area. For this reason, the profession of programming continues, with several major specializations.

Application Programmers The application programmer needs to have some idea of system organization and the nature of logic in such systems. He or she also must be familiar with the external problem, or "problem area," which is to be dealt with. The first of these, system organization and logic (or simply *programming theory*) is learned directly in a special computing science curriculum, or indirectly in the more common mathematics, physical science, engineering, or liberal arts programs. Modern business systems are learned in the business school or in actual practice or work experience.

Machine Language:	58 40 D7F8 41404001 50 40 D7F8
Assembly Language:	L 4,ECOUNT LA 4,1(4) ST 4,ECOUNT
FORTRAN:	ECOUNT = ECOUNT + 1
COBOL:	ADD 1 TO EMPLOYEE-COUNT

Fig. 1-2 To illustrate the evolution of languages, a simple case of adding 1 to a counter is shown in machine, assembly, and two higher-level languages, FORTRAN and COBOL. Note the increase in human readability.

One major area of external problems or applications area with which the business manager and the programmer must be concerned is that of managing the work of the computer itself. The programmers concerned with this highly technical area are known as *systems programmers*.

Systems Programmers The typical business computer operation forms an increasingly major support to the corporate organism as a whole, and requires an equally increasing portion of its budget. The speed with which a computer works makes personal human supervision impossible, so the machine must perforce be made to supervise itself. This is done by means of a highly sophisticated set of programs known as the *operating system*. Although the machine's vendor provides the operating system, there is always a great deal that the individual machine installation management can do, and indeed *must* do, to ensure that the computer operates well and as inexpensively as possible in its environment. Since the operating system is itself a massive program, specialized programmers known as *systems programmers* are used to install, tune, and modify the operating system to an individual user's needs.

Support Staffs: Technical Staff and Operations Staff The systems programmers are usually organized at a business installation into a unit known as the *technical staff*. This staff considers not only the major problems of using the operating system effectively, but also all major program matters that are common to all the applications programmers.

The actual running of the machine is handled by a different staff, the *operations staff*. There is an obvious interaction between the operating system and the men and women who operate the system. The technical staff controls this interaction and is cognizant of the problems of both the users of the computers and its operators. Any large business organization will have other support functions as well, such as testing, documentation, standards, etc. (Figure 1-3.)

[2] See Chapter 3, "Programming Languages," in this Part.

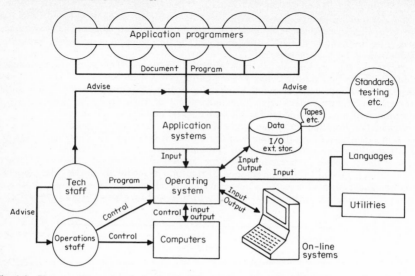

Fig. 1-3 The operating system is the heart of the modern data processing shop. The application programming groups are supported by the various support groups shown.

OPERATING SYSTEMS

Although Chapter 3 of this Part investigates this topic in detail, the three major types of operating systems in use are mentioned here:

Multiprogramming. (Often called MVT or MFT.) The machine's memory is divided into many different regions, each of which is capable of acting like a separate computer for one program. Many programs are running at once, and the computer will move from one to another, overlapping some activities—e.g., waiting for relatively slow externally attached devices such as disk or tape memories to work—with faster activities such as calculation.

Mutiprocessing. Here the operating system runs two or more computers at once. Each computer may in turn be multiprogrammed, and the highly sophisticated multi-processing system divides work between the two, keeping both (or many) machines running at maximum efficiency. Typical are IBM's MP or ASP systems.

Virtual Systems. In virtual systems, many machines are considered to exist at the same time, but only one physical machine is actually used. Any of the machines that the system considers to "exist" may in fact be far larger than the actual machine present. All these nonexistent, or virtual, machines are run simultaneously within the one "real" machine by the operating system. This involves the use of *paging* principles in which each virtual machine is divided into many "pages," only a few of which are actually in the real machine's memory at any one time. Virtual systems may also look like MVT systems far larger than the actual machine memory, or like single (typically 16-million-position) regions overlaying one another in a far smaller physical memory.

SUPPORT PROGRAMS: UTILITIES

Problem programs, those programs which the programming staff will write to service business problems, will often share certain functions. These very common functions may be handled directly by either the operating system or a class of programs known as *utilities.* Input and output of information between the internal memory of the computer and any externally attached devices such as disks, tapes, drums, or card reading-punching equipment are usually handled by portions of the operating system known as *access methods.* Aside from data transfer of this type, one of the most common major functions is changing the sequence of data. This is handled by a separate program, generally not part of the operating system but usually supplied by the vendor, known as a *generalized sort and merge system*. Many other functions needed by many users are also provided as utility systems.

SYSTEM DEVELOPMENT CYCLE

Writing the application (or "problem") system involves these steps:

1. System analysis, to determine just what is to be done, and how the results are to be evaluated.

2. System design, or deciding how the problem is to be handled. A number of separate programs (called *modules*) may be defined in order to solve the problem efficiently.

3. Writing the modules, or the actual writing of the programs.

4. Modular testing, to ensure that each module (part of the system) performs to specification.

5. System testing, to ensure that the entire system developed does the job that it was meant to do.

6. Placing the application program into production.

System Analysis and Design. System analysis, the first step, is covered in Section 3 of this Handbook. System design is a specialized task, often combined with system analysis, of dividing the system into parts. This division may be based upon workload considerations, schedules, machine limitations, program functions, or just plain convenience.

Through the *application system* resulting from this system design, the following two flows must be considered. (Note that both of these flows also apply to individual program modules and are discussed in that light in Chapter 2 of this Part):

1. Flow of control viewed as a step-by-step operation. The sequence of steps known as the *flow of control* may pass from module to module, or "loop" through the system or perform *subroutines*. The techniques of electrical circuit diagraming are used to state flow of control as *flow charts*, or they may be stated as sets of logical directions called *decision tables*.

2. Flow of data. Data enter the system at specified points, and are manipulated by the system, transformed into other forms, used in calculations, etc., until they finally emerge in the form of reports or files, or in other ways. The flow of data through a system is highly complex at times and difficult to express, but the same means are used to express it as for the flow of control. (Figure 1-4.)

Programming Discipline. In recent years, working programmers have begun to look at their methods, and to study those which have worked best for them. This study has led to statements of various disciplines which are known collectively as *Structured Programming*, or SP for short. But only a small part of this work has originated in commercial applications programming. Rather than providing an overview of these disciplines and techniques here, those which are useful in commercial programming are discussed as the need arises in this Chapter and the next one. The Bibliography at the conclusion of this Chapter includes several of the major works on SP for those interested in detailed coverage.

Writing the Modules. The system design step serves to divide the system into a number of individual *modules*. The programming team then takes over actually to write the program for those individual modules, which means to code, using a programming language such as COBOL. Programmers have a great many techniques at their command in performing the writing and testing stages of the development of the application program. These are discussed in some detail in Chapter 5 of this Part. Generally, the design of the module is a smaller version of the system design task:

1. Identifying the data into and data out of the module.

2. Determining a way of getting from the data put in, to the data put out.

3. Designing the flow of control within the module.

4. Identifying common functions which can be done by subroutines.

In this design stage, it is common to use the Structured Programming approach known as *Top-Down* design. The system is first designed so that the total system can be represented as major functions within a space easily grasped by a human reader, typically on one sheet of paper. Each of these major functions is further represented on single sheets in terms of lower-order functions, and so on until the "programmable" function level is reached.

The foregoing is a very rough description of Top-Down, but it encompasses the general idea. Related topics include HIPO (Hierarchies plus Input-Process-Output), Composite Design, and Structured Flow Charts. The Bibliography contains several excellent references on these topics.

Writing the Program. When a definitive level of description has been reached in the design stage, the design should conist of many individual logically related blocks.

The next step is to group these blocks, or modules, into physical groupings, or pro-

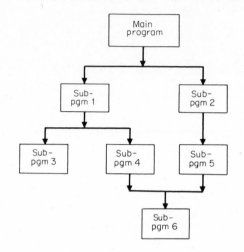

Flow of control

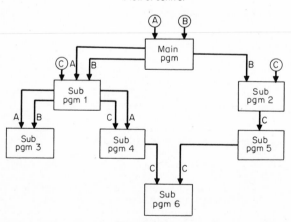

Flow of data

Fig. 1-4   The charting of both the flows of control and the flows of data through the same hypothetical program. In the bottom illustration, Records A and B are introduced in the Main Program. A is used in Subprograms SP1, SP3, and SP4, while B is used in SP1, SP2, and SP3 only. C, on the other hand, may be introduced in either SP1 or SP2, and is used in SP4, SP5, and SP6, as shown. Data flow is usually more complex to chart than control flow, but its value in system testing and debugging is great.

grams. If the design has been well done, this grouping might be on a one-to-one basis. Efficiency and machine environment considerations also come into the picture during this grouping. The exact nature of the communications between the programs which will make up the system must now be considered, and this is sometimes referred to as *interfacing* the programs.

Environmental matters such as use on on-line systems, invocation techniques, access methods, database interfacing, and memory usage are just some of the major technical decisions to be made prior to the start of the actual programming project. Test procedures, programming group organizations, and scheduling are management problems to be solved prior to this stage. Perhaps a much earlier decision, timewise, is the choice of programming language and programmer's techniques (i.e., shop standards) to be used. The actual writing and testing of the programs themselves are the subject of the next Chapter and will not be covered here in detail.

Modular Testing. Here the programmer is concerned with the following functions:

1. Determining which parts of the system are missing during the programmer's test (for a module is only a part of the total application system), and providing for simulation of the rest by means of "dummy" modules, or preferably by utilities known as *linkage monitors*, or by suppressing those parts of the module which depend upon the missing parts.

2. Selecting the test data with which the programmer will test the module. Two major sources of test data are available:

 a. Artificial test data. These data are contrived to test those functions of the module in an orderly and predetermined pattern. Artificial data may be hand-coded, or parametrically generated by test data generation programs.

 Worst-case data are also widely used. "Worst-case testing" is a term borrowed from engineering to describe the testing of a system at the extreme values which it is expected to encounter in practice. The theory is that if a system works when presented with the most extreme sets of inputs, it will work in between. All extremes should be covered. For example, in a payroll program, one employee at the lowest possible salary level, with the maximum conceivable number of dependents and with the maximum number of deductions, would be used, as well as one with the highest allowable salary, no dependents, and no deductions. Use of extreme values of all variables may result in a very large test, but the average case should also be included, lest the test does not detect that the average case does not work at all.

 b. Live Data. Actual data taken from real situations or existing files ("stripped off") may be used.

3. Systematic testing of the module.

The flow of control and the flow of data through the program may be studied, and all unique "paths" (or at least the major ones) through it may be identified. Then, data may be designed or selected to exercise each of these paths in turn.

System Testing. After all modules have been tested, a system test must be made. The final system must be thoroughly checked out, using both artifical and live data. Random, or "Monte Carlo," data are often used, on the theory that combinations will be checked which may not be thought of in direct testing. System testing culminates in clearing the new system for actual use. This is known as "putting the system into production."

An application system should handle all situations which it is designed to encounter within a given business environment. Two problems are typically encountered here: First, no testing (except in the simplest cases) will allow complete check-out of all situations to be encountered. Second, business situations have a way of not standing still, but rather change and introduce new situations from time to time. These circumstances are the basis of the very important topic of system maintenance.

SYSTEM MAINTENANCE

Often, changes are desired in a production system. The changes must be made and the system retested, and put back into production, without upsetting the production itself. The change to be made may be fairly minor, such as a minor error ("bug," in programmer's jargon) in the system which showed up only after the system had been in production for some time, or it may be a change of specifications due to a changing business environment, or a change in the computer environment itself.

Normal Maintenance Detection of bugs in the system, or changes in the business need being serviced by the system, look very much like initial development situations discussed earlier. Conformance to legal requirements such as new laws affecting a business are known as *statutory maintenance*. After making the change in the module, a complete testing procedure must be performed before the new system replaces the old system in production. In business environments, years may pass between initial development and maintenance operations, in which time the original programmers may have left the organization, or may have forgotten the details of the system. This illustrates the major need for standards, for thorough documentation, for annotation of systems as they are initially developed, and for keeping these up to date as maintenance takes place. Systems must also be initially developed with the idea of ease of maintenance in mind. (Figure 1-5.)

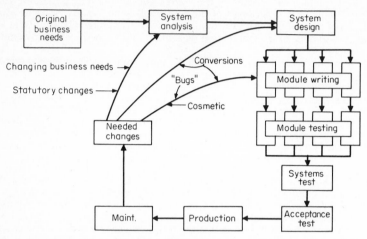

Fig. 1-5 System development cycle, with addition of the all-important function of maintenance. The latter may go on for years after the system is "up and working."

Conversions If the computer environment changes, changes to all systems may be needed. If a new computer is purchased which is incompatible with the old one, or a new language is adopted as the shop standard, those systems affected will have to undergo a process of "conversion" to continue to operate in the same business environment. Three means of converting a system are used:

1. Conversion at the language level. Programs may be converted from one language to another, or from one "dialect" of a language into a newer dialect of the same language. Language conversion aids are usually available in the form of special-purpose programs, but a conversion on the source-language level needs careful planning.

2. Simulation, in which the new environment "simulates" the old environment. Usually this means that the new environment treats the old programs as data, and operates entirely in the new environment but performs the same useful work as the old program did in the old environment.

3. Emulation. The new environment can be made, usually through electronic circuitry, to look just like the old environment. This is done either by means of a switch on the main computer, or preferably, by region control within the computer in multiprogramming operating systems. This latter case, in the virtual operating systems mentioned earlier, results from the fact that virtual systems act as if they are running many computers instead of only one, but there is only one real computer present. One or more of these virtual systems happens to be the old environment, while the others are the new environment.

Other Considerations One important class of languages deserves mention here. These are the *nonprocedural* languages. The procedural languages, such as COBOL, FORTRAN, BASIC, PL/I, and ALGOL, permit the programmer to define, step by step, the procedure to be used in transforming the input data into output. Nonprocedural languages do not. Instead, they permit a description of the input and output data desired, together with some sort of description of how these are related, and the language translation does the rest. Many of these nonprocedural languages are tailored to report writing (e.g., RPG—Report Program Generator) or to other specialized applications. High-level procedural languages, in some of their more generalized features, approach nonprocedural language in form.

Standards The establishment, codifying, and enforcement of standards are every bit as important in a programming shop as in a tool and die shop. This often-neglected area of the computer software field is now beginning to receive the major attention it needs, largely as the result of bitter experience of the lack of it rather than for any idealistic appreciation of its value. The major national and international standards (in the United States, the ANSI standards) for COBOL and FORTRAN are the most important examples.[3] But every shop should establish its own standards (or buy and tailor standards developed for general-purpose) to ensure that it will be able to continue its effectiveness through the years without depending on any one individual or group of programmers remaining available during that time.

SELECTIVE BIBLIOGRAPHY

Dahl, O. J., E. W. Dijkstra, and C. A. R. Hoare, *Structured Programming*, Academic Press, New York, 1972. Dijkstra's portion presents many insights into the decision process of program design. Hoare covers data structures and Dahl covers hierarchical program structures. The classic book on the subject (but perhaps difficult reading).

Gruenberger, Fred (ed.), *Effective v. Efficient Computing*, Prentice-Hall, Englewood Cliffs, N.J., 1973. A collection of papers on management aspects of the modern commercial programming shop.

HIPO, *IBM Manual GC20-1851*, International Business Machines Corporation, Armonk, N.Y. 10540.

Kernighan, B. W., and P. J. Plauger, *The Elements of Programming Style*, McGraw-Hill, New York, 1974. Analyzes a number of programs, pointing out lessons in style, good and bad.

McGowan, Clement L., and John Kelly, *Top-Down Structured Programming Techniques*, Mason and Lipscomb, New York, 1974. Covers a major design technique widely used but only now being formalized.

Myers, Glenford, *Reliable Software through Composite Design*, Mason and Lipscomb, New York, 1974. Covers a technique widely used by PL/I programmers.

Weinberg, Gerald M., *An Introduction to General Systems Thinking*, Wiley-Interscience, New York, 1975. On how to think the way a computer programmer should. A nontechnical presentation of systems thinking for managers and teachers.

———, *The Psychology of Computer Programming*, Van Nostrand Reinhold, New York, 1971. Looks at programming as a human rather than a machine activity. Includes topics such as team programming and "egoless" programming, along with such factors as the effects of personality and work environment on performance. Written for data processing management.

[3] See Part 6, "Standardization," in this Section.

Chapter **2**

Programming Techniques

WILLIAM J. HARRISON

Technical Consultant, Computer Services Department,
Fireman's Fund American Insurance Companies, San
Rafael, California

Volumes could be written on the subject of programming techniques. In this Chapter's necessarily short treatment, an overview is presented on the following major aspects of the subject: computation; logic; input and output; algorithms; special major applications such as reporting and sorting; debugging; and the program development cycle. The discussion of each of these aspects provides insight into the problems met by working programmers, and how they handle them.

COMPUTATION

Computation is the "crunching of numbers." Adding, subtracting, multiplying, dividing, and rounding are the more obvious examples of number crunching. But there is more to it than just arithmetic. To be sure, scientific and engineering data processing shops do computation in far greater volume than do commercial shops, but the basic problems met with are the same. The concepts developed below are drawn from *numerical analysis.*

Numbers in computers are expressed as strings of zeros and ones, called *binary bits,* as explained in Chapter 4 of Section 1. The interpretation of these bits varies from one type of computer to another, and even within one computer from instruction to instruction. Usually, however, there are a limited number of interpretations in all, and a few of the more common such interpretations, or encoding, will be covered here.

Arithmetic and numeric operations are of three basic encoding types: binary, packed, and binary coded decimal (BCD). A fourth type, floating point, is not widely used in commercial work and will not be covered.

In binary encoding, a value is assigned to each bit. A number is represented by the sum of the values of those bits which contain a one (or are "turned on"). The usual values are the "powers of 2" series, 1, 2, 4, 8, 16 . . . , and the values are assigned from right (low-order) to left (high-order). The high-order, or leftmost, bit is often reserved for the sign of the number (zero for plus, one for minus). Since binary strings of numbers are awkward to read by a human, they are often read in groups of three bits each (*octal*) or four at a time (*hexadecimal*). Eight bits constitute a *byte* and 32 bits a *word.*

Packed coding takes advantage of the fact that the numbers 0 through 9 can be represented by four bits. Numbers written in normal Arabic form are encoded into four bits per digit. BCD uses six bits for the same purpose, allowing the letters of the alphabet to be encoded, as well as the numbers. Extended BCD (EBCDIC) is a standard eight-bit encoding which allows special characters for a total of 256 characters to be represented.

Since binary encoding is based upon the "powers of 2" number system, it is known as *base 2*, or *Mod 2* arithmetic. Packed and BCD-type encodings are based upon 10, and use *Mod 10* arithmetic. The choice of type of arithmetic is handled automatically in high-level programming languages such as COBOL, but the effects of the different Modulo numbering systems are different in terms of precision, rounding, truncation rules, and propagations. These effects are of concern to programmers. The subject of encoding is broad and detailed, and is best studied in the context of the particular equipment available to the user.

With the higher-level languages discussed in Chapter 3 of this Part and elsewhere in this Handbook, the programmer need not be concerned about the details of translating

FIND one-third of $27.95		
Multiplier	Answer	Answer rounded
.3	$8.385	$8.39
.33	$9.2235	$9.22
.333	$9.30735	$9.31
.3333	$9.315735	$9.32
.33333	$9.3165735	$9.32
.333333 . . .	. . .	$9.32
Ideal:	$9.3166666 . . .	$9.32

Fig. 2-1   The decimal value of the fraction $\frac{1}{3}$ can only be expressed as an infinitely long string of 3s after the decimal point. In practice, only some finite number of 3s may be used, representing a loss of precision due to the low-order truncation of the excess 3s. This makes the result less than ideal. But the rounding process causes another loss of precision in this already less than ideal number. However, accuracy might be taken in this example as a measure of how closely the result approximates the "ideal" result after rounding. Four 3s at the end provide this level of accuracy, and increasing the number of 3s does nothing to improve the "accurate" answer. Indeed, using more than four 3s might be considered a waste of computing power. The programmer must consider the trade-off between accuracy and the cost of obtaining that accuracy.

between the various forms of numbers, but he or she must be concerned with the effect that a *change of base* has in the program. These effects usually are confined to the decimal places and their precision.

Precision   When applied to data, the term *precision* refers to the number of decimal places which an individual piece of data contains. To illustrate, 0.333 is an imperfect representation of the fraction $\frac{1}{3}$. A better representation is 0.33333, while 0.333333333333 is better yet but still not perfect. These three examples illustrate increasing precision. Just how much precision can be kept in computer storage is a function of the space available (usually one computer word in the case of binary items, or two computer words which is commonly called *double precision*), the number base used to store the number, how much precision is really needed of the number, and efficiency considerations. Generally, any loss of precision is called *low-order truncation*. The dropping of bits off of the front of a number is called *high-order truncation*. A distinction is also made between *significant* and *nonsignificant* digits. Truncation of the latter (usually zeros) is quite acceptable, but truncation of the former is a serious matter. For instance if an amount of $0,152,435.17 has its nonsignificant leading zero truncated, no harm is done. But if the next digit, a significant 1, is truncated, a full tenth of a million dollars is lost—a serious matter. Digit significance is not determined by individual cases, but by analytical procedures.

One factor should be pointed out in connection with this discussion of precision and related topics. All the subjects thus far discussed are objective—they can be handled by analytical means and the mathematics are generally understood by programmers.

But there is also a factor known as *accuracy*. This one is subjective. Since exact precision is not always practically or even theoretically possible, then how much do we need? How much rounding error is acceptable? These questions require business judgment and common sense. (See Figure 2-1.).

Scaling Adding a two-decimal-place number to a four-decimal-place number producing an integer result (i.e., no decimal place) requires that the numbers be internally "lined up," or scaled. Although this is automatic in most programming languages, the programmer is very concerned with the many ramifications of scaling. (See Figure 2-2 concerning multiplication.) Related topics in computation are signs, overflow (when precision is greater than the storage assigned number), justification (actual location of the number within the storage assigned), and synchronization (actual location of the storage assigned within the larger area of storage).

Discrete and Nonnumeric Discrete numbers are those which represent values not continuously related. For instance, in answers to a questionnaire, five selections of multiple-choice answer 1, and five selections of multiple-choice answer 3, certainly cannot be averaged out to indicate that multiple-choice 2 was selected. Answers 1, 2, and 3 in this case could be rearranged in any order with no loss of informational value. They might even be called A, B, and C instead.

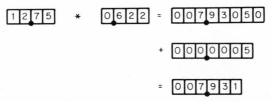

Fig. 2-2 **A two-decimal-place number is multiplied by a three-decimal-place number to produce a three-decimal-place result, rounded.** The allowance for enough storage positions follows normal rules of algebra. Note the selection of the number of decimal places in the "half adjust" or "round-off" quantity of 0.0005, which propagates the carry digit into the final result (bottom line). When rounding, it is important that the actual position rounded (the fourth decimal place in this example) be dropped, or a danger exists of "propagating a round-off error."

Another common example of discrete numbers is found in counting money. The denominations of coins and currency are related in terms of absolute value (a quarter is worth more than a dime) but not in continuous values. There is no coin for 7 cents, for instance, so one may not use exactly four coins to make a dime, while it is perfectly possible to find four numbers (e.g., 7, 1, 1, 1) to add to 10. Discrete numbers often affect more problems than change making by implying a rounding off in money figures to the smallest denomination unit. In United States money, a dozen widgets may cost 1 dollar, but how much does one cost? It must be some multiple of 1 cent, so a round-off error is introduced which, as discussed above, causes a loss of precision.

The topic of discrete mathematics is a broad and fascinating one, and one which is highly pertinent to commercial programming. Nonnumeric data, on the other hand, are not used directly in computations, but are widely used in comparisons for control of both continuous (common) and discrete arithmetic. The key point to keep in mind is that nonnumeric data, like numeric data, are stored simply as a long string of zeros and ones. Programmers take advantage of this situation, which tends to appear quite obscure to the uninitiated.

Figure 2-3 shows that 16 bits (each of which may take the value of either zero or one) can be used to store a variety of data. Since the long string of zeros and ones is difficult to read easily, a shorthand notation is often used, called *hexidecimal* (or *hex*). This shorthand shows the values of four consecutive bits—0000 is hex Arabic 0; 0001 is hex Arabic 1; and so on. At the tenth pattern, 1010, the hex character A is used, on through the ultimate pattern of four bits, 1111, which is shown by the hex character F.

Hexidecimal shorthand can be used regardless of the coding scheme used. EBCDIC coding used Arabic 8 bits to represent an actual letter or number or special character. The character "blank," for instance, is represented by the binary bits 01000000, or in hex notation, Arabic 4 Arabic 0. (Note: ƀ in Figure 2-3 is used by programmers to designate "blank.") The letter A, on the other hand, is represented by the binary bits 11000001, or in hex notation, letter C Arabic 1. Thus the text string ƀA is represented by the EBCDIC coded binary bits (in hex shorthand) Arabic 4 Arabic 0 letter C Arabic 1. In binary coding, binary bits 11000001 are identical for the number Arabic 16,577. All EBCDIC coded character strings may also be interpreted as binary numbers.

	Hex	Binary
"ƀA" in EBCDIC code:	4 0 C 1	0 1 0 0 0 0 0 0 1 1 0 0 0 0 0 1
16,577 in binary code:	4 0 C 1	0 1 0 0 0 0 0 0 1 1 0 0 0 0 0 1

Fig. 2-3. The letter A, preceded by a blank, when encoded in the common EBCDIC coding scheme of the IBM 360/370 line of equipment, is identical to the Arabic number 16,577 expressed in binary code.

LOGIC

Logic in a program concerns the making of decisions and the flow of control through the program. Generally more significant in commercial than in engineering processing, a great many of the programmer's tools are related to logic and control. The workhorses are PERFORM in COBOL, and the GO TO and IF statements in any computer language.

IF Statement This powerful statement is the prime method of making decisions in programs. Numbers can be compared to see which is larger, names can be checked against a master file, drafts returned from the bank can be checked against drafts written, and so on. In any individual check, only one situation is of interest: Is the comparison being made true or false? If it is true, then one action is taken; otherwise another action is taken. In fact, the last sentence is almost a model of the IF statement. Generally, the format is: IF condition, THEN true−action; ELSE false−action. (Figure 2-4.)

This is a *binary* (or two-way) decision. The *condition* is defined as a single binary variable. However, it may actually be quite complex, so long as in the end, after an evaluation procedure, it comes out to a simple yes/no answer. The principal ways of writing conditions include:

Simple condition, a single comparison giving a yes/no answer.

Negation, using the word NOT to reverse a yes/no answer.

OR, to relate two conditions into a single new condition which is yes if *either* of the two related ones is yes.

AND, to relate two conditions into a single new condition which is yes if *both* of the two related ones are yes.

Parenthetical grouping, use of parentheses to group conditions so that they are considered as a group. Also known as levels.

Compounding, use of several or all of the above techniques.

Nesting, writing a second IF as part of the true or false action following an IF statement.

Abbreviations, language rules which permit leaving out operators or operands in some cases (a specific technical meaning).

All the above IF capabilities provide tremendous logical power to the programmer, but some have also proved error-prone, and thus are quite often restricted or considered bad technique in some data processing centers.

The type of action taken depends upon the programming language used, and in COBOL it may be any of a wide variety. But the most common is the GO TO. (In fact, this is always taken, regardless of whether the programmer states it explicitly.)

GO TO Statement A computer is essentially a serial machine. It does one thing after another, literally. To solve a problem, the programmer may wish to execute different parts of the program, depending on decisions made, or to combine common pieces of processing for different purposes. However, the best way of solving a problem may not always involve a straight-line approach.

To illustrate, in a payroll procedure there is no reason to go through New York State tax processing for an employee who lives and works in California. One would wish to make a decision on the applicability of each processing section for each particular case, and direct the flow of control accordingly. Those programmers who attempt to visualize the application problem using the popular "top-down" approach will attempt to avoid the use of the GO TO statement[1] as much as possible, and when it is used they will restrict it to exception cases and error handling, thus confining its use to downward directions only. This particular approach emphasizes the use of the PERFORM statement.

PERFORM Statement Quite often, when a decision is made it is desired to do something about it and then continue. Rather than put that "something," which might

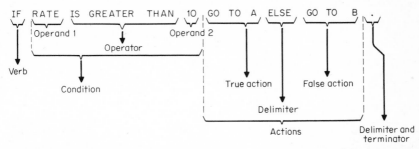

Fig. 2-4 Typical COBOL language IF statement. If, at the time it is executed and for the particular information available at that time, a data item RATE is larger than 10, it can direct the flow of control to procedure names A (specific places in the program in which the IF statement occurs); if not, to procedure B. The three major parts of any conditional statement—verb, condition(s), and action(s)—are further broken down into their components. The word THEN, optional in the COBOL rules, is not used here. The ELSE could be replaced by OTHERWISE if desired. The word ELSE and the final period serve to end the major parts in which they appear; thus they are called *delimiters*. In practice, a literal number would usually not be used as the comparahend (operand 2), but rather a data item containing that number would be used.

consist of a considerable amount of code, right in the true section of the conditional, it is better to place it elsewhere in the program. The mechanism by which the distant code, often called an *out-of-line subroutine*, is executed is the PERFORM statement. The PERFORM has numerous options in COBOL which permit control over its execution and especially over how to determine when it should finish its work. Closely related to the PERFORM in COBOL is the DO of FORTRAN and other languages, and the DO-WHILE and DO-UNTIL of Structured Programming texts[2] (Figure 2-5).

Decision Tables Often a body of data is presented which must be considered as a group, in order to determine the proper action to be taken. For example, hours worked, class (salary, hourly, piece), and pay rate must all be considered in arriving at gross pay in a (simplified) payroll system. The method by which gross pay is calculated depends upon these factors. It is the "method of calculation" which is the "action" to be determined by the logic. The actual value of gross pay is then determined by executing the calculation chosen.

The point is that the procedure to be used is dependent upon the particular combination of data presented to the program. The major considerations here are that the selection of procedures covers all possible cases, and that any one case will lead through the logic to just one of the procedures, and do so efficiently. These attributes are known as *completeness* and *noncontradiction*, respectively. The decision table (depending on support available) permits the simple and automatic handling of sets

[1] GO TO is also known as JUMP or BRANCH in some languages. One form, the GO TO . . . DEPENDING ON is used in major control and in editing areas, and is sometimes called the *transfer vector.*

[2] The PERFORM facility is related to the ALTER facility. The ALTER dynamically changes the operation of its target GO TO, but this facility has proved highly error-prone in practice and has given way to the safer and more easily maintained PERFORM statement.

of parallel and interrelated complex logical situations with attention to these two attributes. (Figure 2-6.)

Decision tables are usually preprocessed (processed by a computer program which translates them into a traditional programming language such as COBOL), but studies are under way in several quarters to combine decision tables directly into COBOL.

```
MAIN-STREAM SECTION.
M-S-1. PERFORM INIT-PGM.
       PERFORM PROCESS-TIME-CARDS
           UNTIL EOF-SW IS EQUAL TO EOF-TRUE.
       PERFORM TERM-PGM.
       STOP RUN.
PROCESS-TIME-CARDS SECTION.
P-T-C-1.
       PERFORM READ-TIME-CARD.
       IF EOF-SW IS EQUAL TO EOF-TRUE
           GO TO P-T-C-EXIT.
       PERFORM PAY-CALC.
       PERFORM WRITE-CHECK.
       PERFORM WRITE-REGISTER.
P-T-C-EXIT. EXIT.
READ-TIME-CARD SECTION.
       . . .
PAY-CALC. SECTION.
       . . .
       . . .
INIT-PGM SECTION.
       . . .
TERM-PGM SECTION.
       . . .
```

Fig. 2-5 Procedure coding of a simple COBOL language program to read input records, calculate pay amounts, write checks, and prepare the check register report. It consists of a MAIN-STREAM section which contains the overall logic of the program, and four specific function sections (detailed coding not shown here) to handle the actual operations indicated by their names.

Conditions	1	2	3	4	5	6	7	8	9	10	11	12	13	14	15	16
Is item stocked?	N	N	N	N	N	N	N	N	Y	Y	Y	Y	Y	Y	Y	Y
Quant. ordered > Quant. on hand?	N	N	N	N	Y	Y	Y	Y	N	N	N	N	Y	Y	Y	Y
Item already on backorder?	N	N	Y	Y	N	N	Y	Y	N	N	Y	Y	N	N	Y	Y
Item in-house produced?	N	Y	N	Y	N	Y	N	Y	N	Y	N	Y	N	Y	N	Y
Actions																
Ship full order.									X	X	X	X				
Ship partial order.													X	X	X	X
Backorder partial order.													X			
Prepare in-house work order.														X		X
Modify existing backorder.															X	
Reject order.	X	X	X	X	X	X	X	X								

Fig. 2-6 Decision table to look at an incoming transaction, ship from inventory, and prepare a work order, or back order, for that item. Four things are known about the inventory (the conditions), and thus there are in theory 16 possible combinations, known as rules. Given a combination of yes (Y) or no (N) answers to the various conditions, those actions which are appropriate are shown as X. Decision tables in COBOL or other language programs vary widely in format and implementation; therefore a general text format rather than an actual programming format is shown here.

INPUT-OUTPUT

Data may be stored internally in the computer's memory, but this storage space is a scarce resource, and is expensive. Moreover, data originate from outside of the computer, and results must be presented outside of the computer to do any good. This means that input from the external world, including externally stored data, must be a major concern of the programmers. In fact, emphasis on the organization of data storage and on inputting and outputting of data is the prime characteristic of the commercial data processing program. The principal types of I/O are *sequential, indexed, random,* and *database.*

Sequential These files can be read, one record after another, or written upon in the same way. Straightforward and simple, they are the most commonly used file type. They may be disk, tape, or cards, but the medium is of far less interest from the program point of view than is the sequential nature of the file. Recent innovations include extendability (adding onto the end of the file), reading in reverse (last record first, down to the first record), update-in-place (actually changing the contents of a record on the medium itself), and others.

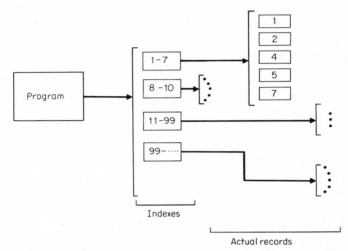

Fig. 2-7 Indexed data. To obtain a specific record from a large file, the program looks it up in the index. It is easier to look through the index than through the main file if records are to be accessed only occasionally, e.g., matching transactions for a single day against a very large master file which does not have activity on every item every day.

Sequential files, and many others as well, provide for the "blocking" of records. That is, actual data records, called *logical records,* may be collected. These collections of logical records may be stored within a single area of magnetically recorded data known as the *physical record,* or *block.* Logical records may also span two or more physical blocks, be fixed or variable, or be undefined in length. (All these aspects of records are more or less transparent to the programmer, except for a major case of variable-length records known as *occurs depending on* records. The ODO will not be covered here.)

Indexed Like books in a library, data may be stored away and the program may search only through the *indexes* set up for them, rather than through the files themselves. When the desired index is found, the actual data can be retrieved from the file. Indexed files come in various types. (Figure 2-7.)

Random Here, data records are stored with no particular regard to how they may be related to one another. When records are retrieved, each record is as accessible as any one of the others. One can read Record 20 and then read Record 526 next, as easily as one can read Record 21 next. In a sequential file, Records 21, 22, 23 . . . 524, and 525 would have to be read before Record 526 is read.

Keys are often used for searching for specific records. These keys are specific portions (*fields*) of the logical record which contain indicative information, and which may be searched easily and directly by any one of a number of mechanisms. Sometimes these keys are separated from the actual file itself, providing something like the indexed files discussed above. (Figure 2-8.)

A point to be emphasized is the difference in the organization of a file and the way a program accesses it. The organization is how the file is placed onto its storage medium. It may be stored in a sequential fashion or in an indexed or a random fashion. Access, however, is how the program chooses to read the file. A file may have been created as indexed, but the program may choose to read it as sequential rather than as indexed. There are some obvious, and some much less than obvious, complications in mixing organization and access methods of which programmers must be aware.

Database In the types of I/O thus far discussed, the programmer must be concerned with the individual files upon which the data are stored. The concept of database relieves the program, and hence the programmer, of this concern. The program merely describes the data needed, and the *database handler* (usually a separate utility-type computer program) locates and obtains the data. It is not all quite this simple, of course, but that is the general idea. Database also implies that all corporate data are collected, organized, and controlled by a central authority, usually called the *database*

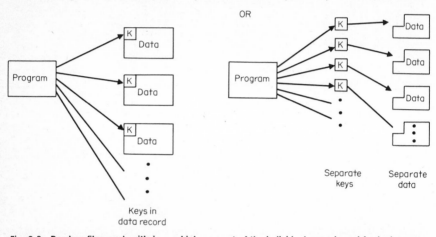

Fig. 2-8 Random files work with *keys* **which are part of the individual record used for look-up purposes—employee numbers, stock numbers, etc.** The keys may be specially located in the record so that they may be searched quickly, or they may be separated into a new file.

administrator. This may be a computer program or a person, or a combination of both.

To corporate management, the database concept is a means of maintaining control over the massive mountain of information needed to operate a modern organization, and the data themselves are sometimes carried on corporate books as an asset. To the programmer, it means relief from the tedious and frequently changing chore of needing to know how and where data are stored, in addition to what they mean. Now the programmer can concentrate on proper use of the data and forget the problems of where they are coming from and where they are going (externally to the machine, that is). Database administration is the new challenge. If properly and wisely applied, database concepts will succeed, but if not well controlled and administered, database concepts could be serious problem areas to everyone concerned.[3]

Interactive I/O Today, computers are often talking to people, and people are talking back. Consoles, or remote terminals where people sit to communicate with the machine, require some special programming consideration. The program cannot ask a tape reel what it meant by that last data record it sent, but it can ask human console operators about their last transmission. Video terminals also introduce the esthetics of screen layout in the person-to-machine environment.

Tact and a little applied psychology are required of the programmer who is writing the interactive program. This need arises when framing the prompting questions which the "computer" will ask the human subjects, and the "forgiveness" the computer will have when the human, as humans sometimes do, goofs a reply.

[3] See Section 3, Part Two, Chapter 3, "Planning-Level and Operational-Level Files and Databases."

Even system design requires consideration of the human with whom the "computer" (actually the program, i.e., the programmer) interfaces. How much problem solution work should be done before prompting the human for more information? Should all information be stored until completely entered and then evaluated, or should it be evaluated immediately? Should potentially long waiting-time activities be undertaken while out there somewhere a real person is logging idle time waiting for a reply? And if that person is a customer or a potential customer, should the programmer use the same tactics in the interactive program which he or she would use with an employee? Such questions, and many more, are facets of programming which the interactive-program programmer often unexpectedly finds to be part of the job.

Printing Files to be printed have special requirements. Since they are to be read by people, layout and appearance are important. Volume is often large, with much wasted storage capacity inherent in the files. They are technically just sequential files, but the volume and unavoidable waste make it imperative that these files be produced, stored, and printed with the greatest haste. The concept of "spooling" print-out, or placing it on a low-cost storage medium such as magnetic tape until it can be printed, is used to reduce storage expense. Also increasingly popular is the use of microfilm (COM).[4]

ALGORITHMS

This "elegant" word simply means a procedure by which a problem is solved. It contains all steps: manual activities, computer logic, arithmetic, formulas, and so on. Several features, as indicated below, occur quite often in algorithms.

Loops It is often necessary to do some work over and over again, with perhaps some minor difference, and to use separate items of data each time. Here so-called loops are employed.

There are two types of loops. Refinement loops are those in which some sort of approximation is made and the looping process serves to make the approximation better each time through. This type of loop, sometimes known as *iterative loops*, or *iteration*, is far more common in engineering and scientific work than in commercial. The second type of loop simply repeats a set (or logically variable) amount of work each time through, but on different data each time. One common example is the main processing loop in many programs. (See Figure 2-5.) Here, each pass through the loop causes the action to take place on a separate entry of a table (see "Table Handling," later in this Chapter).

Loops, in COBOL, may also be handled by PERFORMs or by the equivalent combinations of IF and GO TO.

Increasingly, higher-level language techniques are being enhanced to eliminate the explicitly programmed loop. The COBOL tape handling statement SEARCH is a good example of the basic table look-up being expressed as a single nonloop statement.

Formulas A formula is simply an equation with operands related by operators. Formulas may also be used in IF statements. Of particular interest are leveled or grouped formulas.

Levels and Parenthetical Grouping In both formulas and logical IF statements, parenthetical groupings are used. These represent levels in which the expression so grouped is evaluated. Related to this concept is that of *binding power*. Some operations bind more tightly than others. Without going into all the rules which the programmer must know, we discuss the following example: $X = (A + B \circ C \circ (E - F))$. The lowest level of parenthetical grouping (most tightly binding) is $(E - F)$. Next, since the $\circ$ (multiply) binds tighter than does the $+$ (add), the product $B \circ C \circ E \circ (E - F)$ is computed. Lastly, the sum of A and this product is calculated and stored in X. (Figure 2-9).

Data Manipulation Data can be moved about and changed in programs. Whenever this movement or change is for other than arithmetic or logical purposes, it is called *data manipulation*. This technique is also useful in producing report formats and in preparing data for external storage purposes.

[4] See Part 3, Chapter 4, "Computer Output Microfilm (COM)," in this Section.

MAJOR APPLICATIONS

Certain applications occur frequently in commercial programming. Some of these are discussed here, partly because of their importance and partly to illustrate topics thus far discussed.

Master Transaction Updating   In this common application, a sequential transaction file, such as payments or address changes, is read while a master file is also being read. The transactions are posted to the appropriate master record, and the master is written out again. The master may be sequential, in which case the procedure consists of a match-merging step. The incoming transactions are matched against the incoming masters, and those matching are "merged" (cause updating or posting) into the master. If both files are sequential, both will have been presorted to be in the proper sequence. The transaction "drives" the master file in this case, since the activity on the master is entirely determined by incoming transactions. (Figure 2-10.)

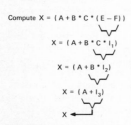

Compute $X = (A + B * C * (E - F))$

$X = (A + B * C * I_1)$

$X = (A + B * I_2)$

$X = (A + I_3)$

$X \leftarrow$

Fig. 2-9 In a calculation involving more than two operands, binding rules determine the order of execution. In this example, one may think of an intermediate result being calculated each time another operand is used. The order is always from the most tightly grouped parenthetical sets outward toward the more encompassing parenthetical sets. Within a parenthetical set the particular operation involved determines the order of execution. Here, $E - F$ is calculated first, and that intermediate result is treated as though it were a single operand in the equation, replacing that parenthetical set. Since more than two operands are in the new equation thus formed, the stronger operation, multiply (*), is done next, followed by the other multiply and finally by the add. At the end, the equal sign (=) binds the least, and in the last step the final result is placed into X, rather than into an intermediate result.

Report Preparation   The report is the final output of the data processing job in human-readable terms. The reader must be able to obtain useful information from it easily and quickly. Thus considerable programming attention is paid to report layout and generation. Special report-writer language elements are available in COBOL which handle a great deal of the detail of data manipulation involved with reports. A few report terms may be of interest here.

Headings and Footings. These identify the report, provide page numbers, identify field in the reports, etc. Headings come at the tops of reports or report groups, footings at the bottom. Footings include total lines.

Detail and Total Lines. Reports summarize information for presentation. If the information being summarized is shown, it is called *detail* information. The summaries themselves are called *total footings*. A body of information which is summarized is called a *report group.* When only summary information is to be printed, *group indications* are shown to identify the group.

Control Levels. Totals are often presented in levels. Although the actual levels are arbitrary and dependent upon the report design, the traditional levels are *minor, intermediate, major,* and *final.* It is perhaps more common now to identify totals by the *control field* which creates that particular level of *control break,* or total. Thus levels might now be city, state, country, and final. Totals can be developed in any of several manners, but *rolling* of totals from one level to the next is common, and has definite efficiency aspects to recommend it. The report programmer must also be very aware of round-off errors, and the effect of cumulative errors on the accuracy of information presented.

Sorting   Almost all sorting is now done via manufacturer-supplied major utility *sort/merge* programs. Thus the details of resequencing one sequential file of no particular order into a specified order are not of serious concern to most programmers. However, understanding how to specify that new order is of concern.

Keys. A record is traditionally sorted on *keys.* Specific fields within that record are specified as keys. These keys are then used to instruct the sort/merge utility to resequence the file in the desired order. Any individual key may be specified as either ascending or descending, and the keys are specified as to importance. Thus, specifying in a particular file the fields EMP-NUMBER and GROSS-PAY as keys, then requesting the utility sort/merge to sort on GROSS-PAY DESCENDING, EMP-NUMBER ASCENDING, will result in listing the highest-paid employee(s) first and the lowest-paid employee(s) last. Where several employees have equal GROSS-PAY amounts, these will be in order by EMP-NUMBER.

Other Sort Features. As the name implies, sort/merge utilities allow several files already sequenced on some field to be merged together into a new file. Sort/merge utilities also provide many "exits," two of which are particularly important. To use COBOL terminology, these are INPUT and OUTPUT PROCEDUREs. The first of these allows a COBOL language program to process the records to be sorted as they are actually coming into the sort/merge utility. The second allows similar processing as they leave the utility. A related technique is sequence checking, in which each record encountered is saved to be compared to the following record.

Table Handling and Look-up Tables, arrays, vectors, or OCCURs groups all represent data collections in which one data item or an organization of data is repeated a number

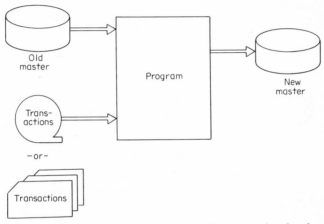

Fig. 2-10   Master transaction updating. The master may be sequential, indexed, random, or a database. The old and new files may share the same space, or the new file may be an entirely new, recreated file, depending on the application.

of times. They differ from sequential files, which might be described the same way, in that tables, etc., reside within a single overall or group data item defined within the program, since files are external to main memory and tables reside in memory. There are two major ways of getting at any single occurrence of these repeated data items: *subscripting,* and *indexing.* Subscripts permit the address of the specific item to be calculated automatically every time a reference is made to an occurrence of a repeated item. Indexes (not to be confused with indexed files discussed previously) permit a simplified calculation of the address and more flexibility in addressing these repeated data items. Arrays may be multidimensioned, with three dimensions being the usual maximum.

Modularity Breaking a program down into various parts for ease of programming, debugging, and maintenance is a common technique. Often this means the development of subroutines consisting of a commonly useful code. Techniques of modularity include, briefly, *overlay* (letting modules use the same space when executing), *dynamic invocation* (loading a new module into core based upon decisions made by the program on an as-needed basis), *phasing* (a series of programs following one another under the control of a monitor program), and use of libraries of programs or even of pieces of coding which are used in several or more programs. As the cost of program maintenance increases, concepts such as modularity take on ever greater importance in commercial shops. (Figure 2-11.)

Modularity is not really a programming problem. Rather, it is a systems design problem, and as such subject to many tools of the system designer. Unfortunately, however, it is rare for the job to be done completely at the design level, and thus programmers have traditionally handled the matter of modularity.

DEBUGGING

Debugging is the time-honored name for the process of testing out a new program to see how well programmed it is. Although the entire test procedure may be considered

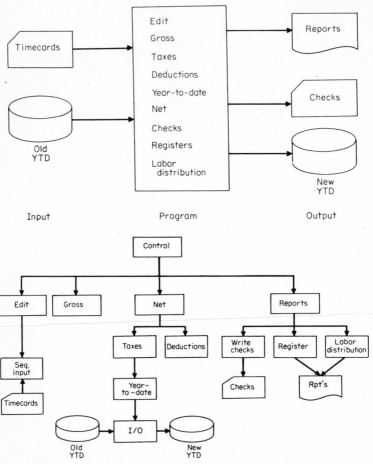

Fig. 2-11 Modularity. At the top, a large payroll program contains all its functions in a single module (monolithic source program). While feasible, the size of the single module presents problems of allocation of work within the programming team, of difficulty in changing the program when situations change, and of finding errors. At bottom, this one large module is redesigned as 12 smaller modules which do the same work. The added module CONTROL may or may not be needed, depending on the situation.

as debugging, the term usually is used only for that testing which the actual programming team performs. A separate validation or acceptance test by the end user is not usually thought of as debugging, for the emphasis here is on how well the program meets the original specifications, which is sometimes a different viewpoint.

Debugging is a complex procedure, and one which is not entirely a science. Much of it is still practiced mainly on an everyone-has-his-own-way basis. Following are a few points that can be made on the subject:

Testing Plan   A testing plan is usually developed for larger systems. Even for smaller development plans, some sort of testing plan is evolved, although it often is done very informally. The usual test plan is tied in with the concept of modularity, discussed above. Each individual module is tested by itself, then subsystems of modules are tested together, and then the entire system is tested. This is followed by placing it into "parallel" production with the old system which it is intended to replace until confidence increases to the point that will allow the new system to "take over" from the old.

Test Data   Two primary sources of data are available for test situations: dummy and real. *Real data* are "stripped off" of "live" files, if such files are available. *Dummy data* are made up specifically for the test, and not related to any real-life situation. In this area, automatic test data generation systems are very useful in providing vast quantities of highly varied data with minimal human effort. The greatest problem with dummy or generated data is verifying the results.

Other Test Data.   A technique widely used is *worst-case data* in which the limits of the system are heavily tested.[5] *Mainstream testing* attempts to identify flows of control through programs and, starting with the most common ones, branches out until all paths are tested. *Linkage monitors* allow testing of in-core passed data in modular situations where the modules are incomplete. Many other test data concepts are used by working programmers.

Other Tools   *Dumps* are actual print-outs of the machine's core in machine language. These are very useful in locating and solving very technical problems and program errors. *Traces*, on the other hand, document the actual flow of control in the same language in which the program is written. Especially useful in locating errors in logic, traces can usually be dynamically turned on or off by the program based on counts, conditions, etc. *Monitoring techniques* in higher-level languages stand in the program, and record when the specified data are referenced (flow of data), as opposed to the trace technique of following along with the flow of control.

Exhibiting data is useful in validating data manipulation and calculation results. *Packets* are convenient ways of inserting debugging tools into programs without upsetting the program itself, and certainly simplify their removal. Generally all debugging tools should be removed or disabled before a program is placed into "production."

Interactive Debugging   This style of debugging was at one time the only available means of checking out a program in detail. It meant stopping the computer at predefined points and investigating the status of the machine directly. As machine costs increased and as other methods discussed above were developed, interactive debugging fell from favor. However, the recent introduction of the time-sharing concept in multiprogrammed machines has once again made it possible to give the programmer a "machine" of his or her very own, which the programmer may stop, start, and even "crash" at his or her pleasure without adverse effects on the many other users of the physical machine in which the testing is being done. Many techniques of interactive debugging exist, but they are all based upon the idea that the programmer does have his or her own personal (virtual) machine and can stop and inspect it any time he or she wishes.

THE PROGRAM DEVELOPMENT CYCLE

The source program, once written, must be compiled, tested, corrected, recompiled, retested, recorrected, etc., until the program is acceptable. Then it is combined with other programs (modules), and the entire system of which it is a part is tested. Once passing an acceptance test, a system is usually put into "production" doing whatever job it was intended to do. A period of parallel operation with the system which was previously used to do that job (if any) is simply good business sense. Any changes required while the system is in production are called *maintenance*—a major activity in most large shops after a few years' operation.

Editing   The procedure of correcting the source program is known as *editing*. Editing is quite similar to the master transaction updating procedures discussed earlier.

[5] See Chapter 1, "Programming Basics," in this Part.

The principal actions which might take place are addition of records, deletion of records, or changing of records.

Security Adequate records of changes must be kept (known as the *audit trail*), and programs are usually saved at major levels in their development in the event that a new direction in development might later be deemed unwise. Interactive editing is becoming extremely popular in shops with some interactive facilities. Security in this process is aimed at recreatability of the edited program at some trade off in security versus likely costs of repeated work.

CONCLUSION

In this Chapter we have tried to give the reader some insight into the nitty-gritty of the programming task. While in this limited space it is impossible to introduce great depth of coverage of techniques, a good idea of what is involved in a large-scale commercial programming shop can be gained. In smaller shops, matters are still about the same, but less formal. Standards for the programmer can vary widely from shop to shop, regardless of size. Some shops combine noncommercial work with the more business-oriented, such as a common computer shared by the front office and the engineering staff. In such shops each group affects the other's use of the equipment in various ways. But in the final analysis, the problems of the programmer are essentially the same regardless of the nature of the programming installation or of the hardware installed.

SELECTIVE BIBLIOGRAPHY

Chapin, Ned, *360/370 Programming in Assembly Language*, McGraw-Hill, New York, 1973.
McCracken, Daniel D., *A Guide to COBOL Programming.* Wiley-Interscience, New York, 1970.
Maynard, J., *Modular Programming*, Auerbach, Philadelphia, 1972.
Naftaly, Stanley M., *COBOL Support Packages*, Wiley-Interscience, New York, 1972.
Pollock, Solomon L., H. Hicks, and W. J. Harrison, *Decision Tables: Theory and Practice*, Wiley-Interscience, New York, 1971.
Saxon, J., *System 360 Programming*, Prentice-Hall, Englewood Cliffs, N.J., 1968.

APPENDIX

Some Newer Programming Methods

JOSEPH FERREIRA   *The Diebold Group, New York, New York*

In the last 4 or 5 years, a new set of implementation disciplines has emerged—involving some wholly fresh concepts and some older ones extended and formalized—under the names Top-Down Programming; Structured or GO TO-Less Programming; Chief Programmer Team; and Egoless Programming and Structured Walk-Throughs. (See box, Figure 2-A-1.)

Some of these terms date back to 1968, and most have been widely discussed since IBM published its account of implementing the now-famous New York Times Information Bank System in 1972. (It has been reported that this large interactive system—over 83,000 lines of code—was completed, including system integration and testing, within 132 employee-months, including management, professional, and clerical effort. Integration testing also went very rapidly, with few and minor programming errors.)

Then, in December, 1973, *Datamation* developed the concepts thoroughly in five articles of a special issue.

Taken together, the new techniques seem to "front load" a project, adding much more detailed system design work before coding begins. Users have stated emphatically that they have realized direct savings in system integration, testing, and debugging. The methodologies, they say, enforce consistent data definitions and adequate definitions of module interfaces, and eliminate many of the causes of logical and functional errors.

THE NEW PROGRAMMING METHODS

1. Top-Down Programming. Job Control Language and a nucleus of control code establishing relations of major system modules are written first. Unwritten modules are simulated by executable "stubs" of dummy code, resulting in an executable program before any modules are written.

Modules are created by a downward iteration of this process: at each level, a module is first a control nucleus with stubs representing the (as yet unwritten) modules at the next lower level. At each level, there is executable code, with successively more operational features. At the lowest level, the last stubs become code.

2. Structured or GO TO-Less Programming. Structured Programming embodies the proposition that any program can be implemented using only three flow progressions, each with just one entrance and one exit:

A. Sequence

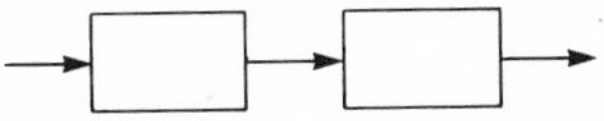

B. IF-THEN-ELSE

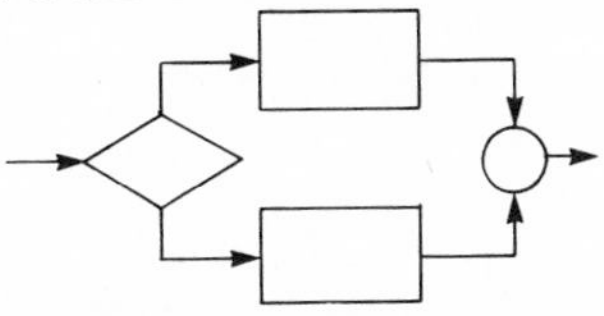

C. DOWHILE

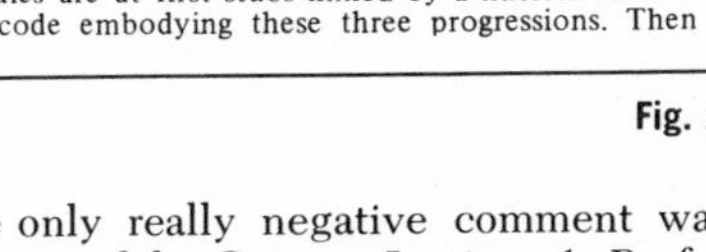

Since all branching is controlled by the IF or DO-WHILE syntax, GO TO is never used.

Structured Programming is generally used in combination with Top-Down Programming. The major modules are at first stubs linked by a nucleus of control code embodying these three progressions. Then each module is decomposed into next-level modules similarly linked.

When used with certain coding conventions (e.g., indicating interior or "nested" progressions by indentation), Structured Programming makes for code strikingly easy for programmers other than the author to read – to the point that structured code is sometimes called self-documenting.

In some languages, including Cobol and Fortran, these principles are more easily implemented if certain (presently non-standard) verbs are added to the language.

3. Chief Programmer Team. The nucleus of the Chief Programmer Team consists of the Chief Programmer, a Backup Programmer, and a Programming Secretary or Programmer-Librarian. The Chief Programmer designs the overall system architecture, either working with or acting as a system analyst, and writes the nucleus of JCL and control code. He will probably write other difficult or key code in the course of the project. He assigns modules to other programmers, and oversees their work.

The Backup Programmer closely assists the Chief Programmer, reads all his code, and stands ready to assume his role if he leaves the program.

The Secretary maintains all coding sheets and program decks, project notebooks and status records. He is the interface to the machine for the rest of the team, initiating and monitoring all machine runs. He has a complete picture of the status of the program at all times and makes any required program segment available to any team member.

The Chief Programmer Team can procedurally follow the Structured Program progression, spinning off programmers as Chief Programmers for new teams as modules are carried to lower levels.

4. Egoless Programming and Structured Walk-Throughs. Under these concepts, all code is "public." Team members all read code written by each, and no segment of the program is considered the preserve of one author. The walk-throughs are actually "talk-throughs" -- group sessions in which program segments are followed by verbally "playing computer." The purpose is to discover errors, not to evaluate programmer performance, and supervisors are generally not present.

Fig. 2-A-1

The only really negative comment was made in an ACM paper by Prof. Paul Abrahams of the Courant Institute.[1] Professor Abrahams voices concern that the new methods will "[create] the illusion that difficult problems are easy. If Structured Programming is treated as a collection of good programming practices, it is immensely helpful; but it will not decrease our programming efforts by an order of magnitude. If it is treated as a collection of inflexible rules which can replace good judgment, it will ultimately increase rather than decrease our efforts, while concealing from us the fact that this increase has occurred." He insists that the inherent difficulty of certain computer applications will make it difficult to enforce the top-down approach

[1] "'Structured Programming' Considered Harmful," by Paul Abrahams, Courant Institute of Mathematical Sciences, New York University, *SIGPLAN NOTICES*, April, 1975.

rigidly. He also points out that the New York Times project involved innovations in both programming and managerial methods, and suggests that the managerial changes (the Chief Programmer Team organization) may have been the more important.

Professor Abrahams also raises an issue of widespread concern and debate among the developers and users of Structured Programming: the memory-space and execution-time efficiency of the resulting code. Both COBOL and FORTRAN lack the syntactical forms required to implement the IF-THEN-ELSE and DO-WHILE progressions directly. In standard COBOL, for example, IF can conditionally invoke a string of statements only by the use of the forbidden GO TO or the use of PERFORM. And, it is pointed out, some COBOL compilers handle PERFORMs inefficiently.

One response has been the introduction of new, nonstandard verbs to COBOL and FORTRAN. In COBOL, for example, a new END-IF is used, permitting nested IFs in a block structure. DO-WHILE . . . END-DO is a similar construct. Precompilers are now marketed (Applied Data Research's MetaCOBOL, for example) which translate COBOL programs including these forms into compilable COBOL.

Interestingly, however, several COBOL users reported to The Diebold Group's publication, *ADP Newsletter*, that the deficiencies of the language were not a signifi-

Type of Program	Program Complexity	Lines of COBOL Code	Lines Written Per Day	No. of Tests		Costs		Percent Actual to Budget	Percent Complete
				Budget	Actual	Budget	Actual		
Load	Average	1,287	121	6	4	$ 1,280	$1,184	92%	100%
Edit	Very High	6,186	76	20	10	16,880	7,496	44	80
Update	Average	2,319	64	12	4	4,800	290	6	80
Conversion	High Average	831	50	16	14	3,000	1,620	54	100

Fig. 2-A-2   Results of a large accounting area project using Structured Programming and Structured Walk-Throughs.

cant problem. Some used the COBOL PERFORM; one installation used a COBOL object-code optimizer after compiling to reduce the inefficiencies. But as one user pointed out, design and implementation costs are becoming more visible as other costs go down, and it has become attractive to tolerate some machine inefficiencies to obtain project cost savings.

In FORTRAN, there are said to be 30 to 40 precompilers at various universities, and Dr. Selden Stewart, at the National Bureau of Standards, is at this writing completing development of a new FORTRAN-like language, STAPLE, with a block structure oriented to Structured Programming.

Several users provided *ADP Newsletter* with details of projects they clearly regarded as striking successes. One large East Coast user provided quantified results of a large accounting area project using Structured Programming and Structured Walk-Throughs (Figure 2-A-2). This user cited as advantages increased programmer productivity and ability to respond to users; forced additional forethought and planning, increased program reliability; more standardized and readable programs; and backup of key people. This user also cited some difficulties, described as transitional: the need to develop new programming standards, the need for large-scale programmer training or retraining, personnel resistance to change, prolonged maintenance on two types of programs (structured and unstructured), and a need to revise estimating and budgeting methods.

A project manager for a Department of Defense agency reported that a test group of 32 people writing a "very large subsystem" entirely under Top-Down Structured Programming concepts was "very successful," with completion well under initial estimates based on complexity and scope.

Users varied in their priorities among the new techniques, with some emphasizing top-down design and team walk-throughs over coding in pure structured form. Top-down coding, as noted, provides executable code very quickly, permitting testing to start early in the project, and thus, several users report, tending to produce more reliable code. Similarly, these users indicate, the team reviews, such as the walk-through, succeed in catching errors and producing reliable code.

One user specializing in remote-access business services cautioned against taking too big an initial bite in converting to the new techniques. To the four techniques cited in the box in Figure 2-A-1, he adds a fifth which he actually regards as the most important: A System Design Language. His organization uses a "pseudocode" which resembles a structured COBOL but is freer, more like English, and more legible to non-programmers, in which to express the program in a rigorous form in which errors can be detected and corrected. He urges newcomers to get command of Structured Programming and Top-Down design before trying to institute Chief Programmer Teams. (His in-house Structured Programming training program runs 10 days.)

The IEEE Computer Society sponsored a workshop on Structured Programming at Lake Arrowhead, California, in September, 1974, and the society's magazine published a brief report on the meeting. The author, Dr. R. R. Brown of Hughes Aircraft Co., noted a consensus of the meeting on the following significant points:

● Benefits apply to a wide spectrum of application areas: business systems, avionics, system software.

● Some users have realized savings of over 50 per cent through the use of the techniques. An "extensive" IBM database on software experience indicates an average saving of 40 per cent.

● Bright, motivated project leaders are important, but inexperienced or run-of-the-mill programmers can be used successfully.

● Productivity savings are realized primarily in the test and integration phase.

Chapter 3

Programming Languages

JEAN E. SAMMET

IBM Corporation, Federal Systems Division,
Cambridge, Massachusetts

Programming languages are widely used tools for writing programs, yet they remain one of the most controversial subjects in the entire computing field. Even the definition is disputed among experts, and the views in this article are solely those of the author. The ANSI (American National Standards Institute) glossary states that a programming language is "a language used to prepare computer programs," but this is not very illuminating. Furthermore, it does not include the frequently used term *higher-level language*.

BASIC CONCEPTS

Terminology In order to make the entire Chapter understandable, it is necessary to establish what is meant herein by the term *programming language*. It is important to note that from the viewpoint of *this* author the terms *programming language* and *higher-level language* are interchangeable. However some other knowledgeable people make a distinction which allows a symbolic assembly language to be included in the former definition but not necessarily in the latter. (An assembly language generally has instructions which are identical to machine instructions.) Other points of controversy surround whether RPG (Report Program Generator) and similar tabular shortcuts to programming should be considered as programming languages.

This author excludes both symbolic assembly language and RPG; the reasons for these decisions are based on the following definitional concepts:

A programming language is considered a set of characters with rules for combining them (= syntax) which have the following four major characteristics:

1. *No necessity for machine-code knowledge*. This is a shorthand way of saying that the user does not have to know the actual instruction code of the machine on which he or she expects to run the program. This does not mean that one can ignore idiosyncrasies of a particular machine and still obtain maximum efficiency. The basic concept merely means that it is not logically necessary to know any actual machine code in order to write a program in a higher-level language.

2. *Strong conversion potential*. Originally this concept was stated by many people as saying that programming languages were "machine-independent"; this objective still remains, but we do *not* have true machine independence in any of the higher-level

languages in use in the mid-1970s. The state of the art has not progressed to the point of knowing how to develop completely machine-independent practical languages and simultaneously retain a reasonable amount of efficiency. Thus efficiency of the programs written in the higher-level language is the constraint; without it we could indeed obtain true machine independence. A good illustration of machine dependence which is of concern to business data processing people is the collating sequence on a machine, i.e., the rules for sorting the character set into a high-low sequence. Thus, if a program segregates various classes of input data and has tests which depend in any sense on the actual internal value of the characters involved, then the program may give different results on another machine.

3. *Expansion of instructions.* For every "instruction" written in a higher-level language in the original program, more than one machine-code instruction is generally produced. This is normally done by another program called a *translator*, of which the two major kinds are *compilers* and *interpreters*. Of the two, only the compiler actually produces machine code, i.e., the compiler translates the original program (called the *source program*) into a form known as the *object program* which can actually run on the computer. An interpreter produces answers directly from the source program.

A discussion of translators is beyond the scope of this Chapter. It is essential to realize that a language and its translator are *not* the same thing; in loose or inaccurate terminology they are frequently used interchangeably but this is quite wrong and tends to mislead. The fundamental difference is as follows: A translator is a program which converts sequences of statements into some other form, e.g., machine code. A language is a set of rules for writing the sequence of statements. For any language there can be (and usually are) many translators. It is important to note that the code-expansion characteristic of programming languages rules out basic assembly language. It even excludes macroassemblers because the latter must involve machine language.

4. *Problem-oriented notation.* This concept certainly involves a value judgment on the part of the user, but is meant to convey the spirit that a higher-level language should be more natural to the user than is machine code or assembly language. Thus the way in which the user is able to state the problem in the higher-level language should be as natural and close to the actual notation used within the problem area as possible. A subsidiary feature of this characteristic is to eliminate systems in which the user fills out forms. This effectively rules out, or eliminates, the concepts of decision tables and report program generators from being classified as programming languages. *This in no way implies any failing or lack of importance of such systems, but it merely excludes them from the class of languages being considered here.*

Ways of Classifying Languages There are many ways of classifying programming languages; in this author's opinion the most important by far is by the application for which the language is actually designed. Thus, languages might be classified as being useful for numerical scientific computations, general business data processing, insurance, banking, civil engineering, check-out of equipment, simulation, etc. Not only is the application area of prime importance, but one's depth of knowledge affects the view of an application and the languages designed for use in it.

An individual with relatively little knowledge is more inclined to feel that a single language can cover a wide scope. For those who are very familiar with a subject area, it is clear that individual aspects of the subject might require specialized languages. For example, while there do not appear to be any languages developed specifically and uniquely for processing insurance, one might envision some. One could also envision not only a single language for dealing with all insurance problems, but different types of languages for writing programs in life insurance, automobile insurance, homeowners' policies, etc.

Another major way of classifying languages is in terms of the detail with which the procedure must be specified. At one extreme, one can envision saying CALCULATE THE PAYROLL, while at the other extreme one writes the detailed sets of instructions required in a higher-level language such as COBOL. The term *nonprocedural* is frequently used to indicate some absolute classification of language; in reality it is a relative term which changes as the state of the art changes. For example, in the mid-1970s, CALCULATE THE PAYROLL was considered nonprocedural, whereas in the early 1950s the statement CALCULATE NET PAY = GROSS PAY − DEDUCTIONS was considered nonprocedural.

Among other concepts related to "nonproceduralness" are such terms as problem-statement language, problem-defining language, requirement-defining language, automatic programming, etc. There is generally *not* agreement within the field as to explicit definitions of each of these, although they are frequently used interchangeably.

Related topics which are not discussed here include (1) database management systems which generally tend to include some language capability for querying the database and (2) data description languages which are discussed in Chapter 6 of Section 5.

One distinction that is frequently difficult to discern is the difference between an application package and a programming language. The former is a carefully designed collection of programs for a well-defined application (e.g. inventory control for wholesale warehouses). In general, a programming language allows the user more flexibility while application packages usually have only a fixed set of routines whose sequence of execution is often fixed. Application packages generally operate on the basis of a set of control cards to supply input parameters for the various routines. Sometimes the control cards also allow choice and sequencing of the routines available within the application package; more often they only tailor the package to the user's volume and report preparation requirements.

HISTORICAL DEVELOPMENT

Just as the early usage of computers was primarily scientific (excluding of course the first commercial computer sold, which was to the United States Census Bureau), so the initial developments in programming languages were aimed at simplifying the coding process for scientific problems. As early as 1954 there were preliminary specifications for FORTRAN. That system was released in 1957 by IBM, and has become one of the best-known and widely used programming languages. It was preceded and paralleled by other languages with similar objectives. In 1955, Remington Rand UNIVAC began the development of a language known as FLOW-MATIC. This was designed to be used primarily for business data processing applications.

FORTRAN concentrated on fixed- and floating-point numbers and various types of arithmetic computations; it assumed a need for only a short data name. The ideas in FLOW-MATIC were heavily concentrated on such features as alphanumeric data, meaningful data names (e.g., SOC-SEC-TAX) and the recognition that the data description should be separated from the instructions (i.e., procedures) which were to operate on the data. Not long after FLOW-MATIC was made available to UNIVAC users, development started on two other languages, namely FACT (Honeywell) and Commercial Translator (IBM). FLOW-MATIC and Commercial Translator were the major inputs to the development of COBOL, which was started in 1959 by a committee involving manufacturers, users, and Government representatives. Although COBOL was originally meant to be only a "short-range" language, it rapidly became widely established when the U.S. Government required that computer manufacturers supply COBOL compilers for virtually all Federal Government computer orders. Since 1959 there has been a steady and continuing development of COBOL to handle new equipment and new concepts, from such well-known ideas and needs as sorting and merging, to the random-access equipment, to more recent consideration of databases. Virtually every computer manufacturer has one or more COBOL compilers.

It is worth noting that by the mid-1970s only FORTRAN, COBOL, and two other languages—APT and ALGOL—had actually been processed and accepted as standards by ANSI (American National Standards Institute) and ISO (International Standards Organization). Both FORTRAN and COBOL started on their second round of standardization (i.e., the mandatory revision and reconsideration process) not very long after their approval as standards in 1966 and 1968 respectively. A revised COBOL standard was issued in 1974. Further development work in COBOL continues under the CODASYL Programming Languages Committee.

A portion of a COBOL program is shown as Figure 3-1. It illustrates the separation of the machine description, the definition of the data, and the executable procedures.

The development of interactive systems in the 1960s made it desirable to have languages which were more suitable for use by a user at some type of terminal. Of the many languages created for this purpose, BASIC (which was developed at Dartmouth in 1965 as a tool for students) is the most widely used. Although originally designed as a very simple language to be used for numerical computations, some of the later versions had included data and file handling facilities.

Another significant facet of language development is the large number of simulation languages, exemplified by SIMSCRIPT and GPSS which are used for modeling the behavior of processes (e.g., assembly lines, traffic flows, and even computer programs).

In 1964 the first preliminary specifications of PL/I were produced by a joint IBM-

```
IDENTIFICATION DIVISION.
PROGRAM-ID.  UPDATING.
REMARKS.  THIS IS A SIMPLIFIED UPDATE PROGRAM, USED AS AN EXAMPLE OF
    BASIC COBOL TECHNIQUES.  THE PROGRAM IS EXPLAINED IN DETAIL IN THE
    INTRODUCTION TO THIS MANUAL.
ENVIRONMENT DIVISION.
CONFIGURATION SECTION.
SOURCE-COMPUTER.  IBM-360-H50.
OBJECT-COMPUTER.  IBM-360-H50.
INPUT-OUTPUT SECTION.
FILE-CONTROL.
    SELECT MASTER-FILE ASSIGN TO DA-2311-D-MASTER
        ACCESS MODE IS RANDOM
        ACTUAL KEY IS FILEKEY.
    SELECT DETAIL-FILE ASSIGN TO UT-2400-S-INFILE
        ACCESS IS SEQUENTIAL.
    SELECT ACTION-FILE ASSIGN TO UT-2400-S-OUTFILE.
DATA DIVISION.
FILE SECTION.
FD   MASTER-FILE LABEL RECORDS ARE STANDARD
        DATA RECORD IS MASTER-RECORD.
  01   MASTER-RECORD.
        05   ITEM-CODE          PICTURE X(3).
        05   ITEM-NAME          PICTURE X(29).
        05   STOCK-ON-HAND      PICTURE S9(6).      USAGE COMP SYNC.
        05   UNIT-PRICE         PICTURE S999V99     USAGE COMP SYNC.
        05   STOCK-VALUE        PICTURE S9(9)V99    USAGE COMP SYNC.
        05   ORDER-POINT        PICTURE S9(3)       USAGE COMP SYNC.
FD   DETAIL-FILE LABEL RECORDS ARE OMITTED
        DATA RECORD IS DETAIL-RECORD.
  01   DETAIL-RECORD.
        05   ITEM-CODE          PICTURE X(3).
        05   ITEM-NAME          PICTURE X(29).
        05   RECEIPTS           PICTURE S9(3)       USAGE COMP SYNC.
        05   SHIPMENTS          PICTURE S9(3)       USAGE COMP SYNC.
FD   ACTION-FILE LABEL RECORDS ARE OMITTED
        DATA RECORD IS ACTION-RECORD.
  01   ACTION-RECORD.
        05   ITEM-CODE          PICTURE X(3).
        05   ITEM-NAME          PICTURE X(29).
        05   STOCK-ON-HAND      PICTURE S9(6)       USAGE COMP SYNC.
        05   UNIT-PRICE         PICTURE S999V99     USAGE COMP SYNC.
        05   ORDER-POINT        PICTURE S9(3)       USAGE COMP SYNC.
WORKING-STORAGE SECTION.
  77   SAVE                     PICTURE S9(10)      USAGE COMP SYNC.
  77   QUOTIENT                 PICTURE S9999       USAGE COMP SYNC.
  01   FILEKEY.
        05   TRACK-ID           PICTURE S9(5)       USAGE COMP SYNC.
        05   RECORD-ID          PICTURE X(29)
  01   ERROR-MESSAGE.
        05   ERROR-MESSAGE-1    PICTURE X(20).
        05   ERROR-MESSAGE-2    PICTURE X(36).
        05   ERROR-MESSAGE-3    PICTURE X(46).
```

Fig. 3-1 **Complete UPDATING Program (Part 1 of 2).** (SOURCE: *IBM OS Full American National Standard COBOL Compiler and Library*, Version 4, *Programmer's Guide*, p. 32. Reprinted with permission. © International Business Machines Corporation, 1972.)

```
PROCEDURE DIVISION.
OPEN-FILES-ROUTINE.
  OPEN INPUT DETAIL-FILE.
  OPEN I-O MASTER-FILE.
NEXT-DETAIL-RECORD-ROUTINE.
  READ DETAIL-FILE AT END GO TO END-ROUTINE-1.
NEXT-MASTER-RECORD-ROUTINE.
  MOVE ITEM-CODE IN DETAIL-RECORD TO SAVE.
  DIVIDE 19 INTO SAVE GIVING QUOTIENT
    REMAINDER TRACK-ID.
  MOVE ITEM-NAME IN DETAIL-RECORD TO RECORD-ID.
  READ MASTER-FILE INVALID KEY
    PERFORM INPUT-ERROR GO TO ERROR-WRITE.
COMPUTATION-ROUTINE.
  COMPUTE STOCK-ON-HAND IN MASTER-RECORD = STOCK-ON-HAND
    IN MASTER-RECORD + RECEIPTS – SHIPMENTS.
  IF STOCK-ON-HAND IN MASTER-RECORD IS LESS THAN ZERO
    PERFORM DATA-ERROR GO TO ERROR-WRITE.
  MULTIPLY STOCK-ON-HAND IN MASTER-RECORD BY UNIT-PRICE
    IN MASTER-RECORD GIVING STOCK-VALUE
    IN MASTER-RECORD.
  IF STOCK-ON-HAND IN MASTER-RECORD IS NOT GREATER THAN
    ORDER-POINT IN MASTER-RECORD PERFORM REORDER-1
    THRU REORDER-2.
WRITE-MASTER-ROUTINE.
  WRITE MASTER-RECORD INVALID KEY
    PERFORM OUTPUT-ERROR GO TO ERROR-WRITE.
  GO TO NEXT-DETAIL-RECORD-ROUTINE.
REORDER-1.  GO TO SWITCH-ROUTINE.
SWITCH-ROUTINE.
  ALTER REORDER-1 TO REORDER-2
    END-ROUTINE-1 TO END-ROUTINE-3.
  DISPLAY "ACTION FILE UTILIZED."
  OPEN OUTPUT ACTION-FILE.
REORDER-2.
  MOVE CORRESPONDING MASTER-RECORD TO ACTION-RECORD.
  WRITE ACTION-RECORD.
ERROR-WRITE.
  MOVE DETAIL-RECORD TO ERROR-MESSAGE-2.
  DISPLAY ERROR-MESSAGE.
  GO TO NEXT-DETAIL-RECORD-ROUTINE.
INPUT-ERROR.
  MOVE "KEY ERROR ON INPUT" TO ERROR-MESSAGE-1.
  MOVE SPACES TO ERROR-MESSAGE-3.
DATA-ERROR.
  MOVE "DATA ERROR ON INPUT" TO ERROR-MESSAGE-1.
  MOVE MASTER-RECORD TO ERROR-MESSAGE-3.
OUTPUT-ERROR.
  MOVE "KEY ERROR ON OUTPUT" TO ERROR-MESSAGE-1.
  MOVE SPACES TO ERROR-MESSAGE-3.
END-ROUTINE-1.
  GO TO END-ROUTINE-2.
END-ROUTINE-3.
  CLOSE ACTION-FILE.
END-ROUTINE-2.
  CLOSE DETAIL-FILE.
  CLOSE MASTER-FILE.
  STOP RUN.
```

FIG. 3-1 Complete UPDATING Program (Part 2 of 2). (SOURCE: *IBM OS Full American National Standard COBOL Compiler and Library*, Version 4, *Programmer's Guide*, p. 33. Reprinted with permission. © International Business Machines Corporation, 1972.)

SHARE committee. (SHARE is one of the IBM user groups.) In its later stages PL/I had many objectives, including the effective use of third-generation computers and operating systems, while simultaneously providing the features needed for both scientific computations and business data processing.

Finally, the trend in the late 1960s through the mid-1970s was toward languages for very specialized application areas (e.g., civil engineering, social sciences, graphics), and languages with narrow application relevance represented about half of all the languages used in the United States. (While this statistic is certainly true, it is nevertheless somewhat misleading, since many of these languages were used by only a very small group.)

MAJOR TECHNICAL AND NONTECHNICAL ISSUES

Technical Issues When one considers the technical issues pertaining to a programming language, one generally tends to include the actual elements of the language. Thus one naturally considers the form of the language, including the character set, methods of defining variable and statement names, and the physical input format. Another major technical characteristic of the programming language is the actual structure of the program (including its subroutines) built up from the smallest subunits; the latter include both the nonexecutable declarations and the smallest executable units (frequently called *statements*).

A major feature of any programming language is the types of data which are allowed and the computations that can be performed with them. Not all languages allow all the major types of data; the latter include arithmetic (e.g., fixed mode, floating mode, mixed mode, rational mode, and double precision), logical variables (i.e., truth values), character variables (for alphanumeric information), strings (i.e., sequences of characters), and others.

There are various ways of grouping data items. The two most common are *arrays* and *hierarchies*. (Arrays are essentially tables which can have many dimensions, e.g., a three-dimensional array is a three-dimensional table. All elements in an array are the same type. This contrasts with a hierarchy which is a way of representing subunits where all elements are not necessarily alike. Thus, an address is composed of a street number, street address, city, state, and Zip Code. These individual elements can be grouped and used together when the need arises.)

The heart of the executable portion of a program is the set of executable statements such as assignment statements, alphanumeric data handling, control-transfer statements, conditional statements, loop control statements, and various types of error-condition handling statements. The last major remaining category of statements are those which involve interaction with either the operating system and/or the equipment, e.g., input-output statements, debugging statements, and storage allocation statements.

Finally, all programming languages tend to have declarations which are not directly executable but which provide information about the data. It is a major characteristic of languages designed primarily for use in the business data processing environment that the descriptions of files and individual data items are a major portion of the program, albeit generally kept independent from the executable statements. This permits the user to change a data file without having to rewrite the entire program.

Functional Issues While the technical elements of a programming language are obviously crucial, they are frequently less important than the nontechnical or functional characteristics of programming languages. The latter include such concepts as the purpose of the language, which would in turn include the application area for which the language was designed, the type of user (e.g., professional programmer, novice, systems analyst), and the planned physical environment and equipment (e.g., typewriter, keypunch, display device, etc.).

Conversion and Compatibility. One of the major nontechnical characteristics of programming languages pertains to conversion and compatibility. Machine independence of the programming languages was discussed in our introductory remarks, and it should be clear that there are certain difficulties in moving from one machine to another. While the collating sequence is one of the most striking examples, differences in word length, machine idiosyncracies pertaining to how the value zero is handled, and other examples all lead to difficulties in taking a program from one machine to another. Each of those items could be avoided theoretically, but only at the cost of intolerable inefficiency.

In other words, if the user wishes to obtain maximum efficiency on a particular computer, he or she must know (and use) some of the hardware characteristics, e.g., size of machine word and its subunits, types of storage devices available. However, in planning a program to be efficient in a particular hardware situation, the direct transferability of the program to a different machine is made much more difficult. As a trivial example, suppose a particular computer can read a tape backward and suppose the high-level language contained a command to allow this. If the user included such a command in a program because his or her machine had that capability, then the program would not run (or would be intolerably inefficient) on a machine without such a command.

While machine independence (or lack thereof) is well known, the issue of compiler independence (or lack thereof) is not as well known but is equally important. Because of the state of the art of language definition and compiler writing in the mid-1970s, it is extremely difficult to find two compilers which handle a given language exactly the same way. Compiler writers differ in their philosophies of handling errors in the source program; their concern for efficiency sometimes has subtle repercussions. Even such mundane subroutines as those converting decimal to binary numbers can occasionally play havoc when one changes compilers.

Although the previously mentioned problems are caused by the state of the art, there are also many instances in which users bring additional incompatibility grief upon themselves by using special additional features of a language which are provided to them by a particular vendor; when they try to switch to another compiler or another machine they find these features are no longer available. Thus their desire to have something more than the standard language in which to write their programs will cause them difficulty when trying to run their programs with a different compiler or on a significantly different computer.

The final point on conversion is that converting of the *program* may in fact be only the tip of the iceberg in the difficulty of actually switching machines; the difficulty of getting the database transferred may far surpass the difficulty of moving the program itself.

One of the major attempts to minimize the trauma of conversion is by way of standardization, which is done in the United States as a voluntary activity under ANSI. The procedures are extremely lengthy and time-consuming but have the major objective of making sure that all views are carefully heard and appropriately represented. Thus when a standard is finally promulgated, most organizations have had a chance to have their say and there is a general consensus on the merits of the standard itself. (See Part 6 of this Section.)

It might be thought on the basis of the above comments that there is no validity to the concept of being able to transfer a program in a higher language from one computer (or compiler) to another. On the contrary, this is probably the greatest advantage of a higher-level language, and will be discussed under the next heading. The difficulties in transferral are not negligible, but are minimal when compared with moving a program written in assembly language. The latter must be rewritten *entirely*. The main reason for citing the difficulties is to attempt to redress the imbalance of claims that all programs written in a higher-level language can immediately be run on another computer without any effort.

LANGUAGE SELECTION AND EVALUATION

Any user is faced with the primary problem of whether to use a higher-level language or an assembly language, and, if he or she chooses in principle to do the former, how actually to go about selecting a specific one. In order to consider this matter, let us examine some of the advantages and disadvantages of using higher-level languages.

Advantages The primary advantage to a higher-level language is that it reduces the actual amount of time to get a particular task done. This time reduction occurs because the higher-level languages are generally easier to learn, to code, to debug, to maintain, to document, and to convert. This "ease" factor applies basically when comparing against an assembly language of equivalent complexity.

The reasons for these advantages stem from the basic characteristics of a higher-level language as discussed in the first section of this Chapter. The problem-oriented notation means that users are able to understand what they are looking at more readily. Thus writing

IF A IS GREATER THAN 0

is clearly easier to understand than

CLA A
TRZ

This notational advantage carries over into the documentation, since higher-level languages are inherently self-documenting because of their understandability. The programs are easier to code and debug because the user needs to write less; this is a direct result of the characteristic of instruction expansion discussed earlier in this Chapter. Generally the number of errors made in a program are directly proportional to the size of the program and hence anything which reduces the amount of writing will reduce the number of errors.

One of the major advantages of a higher-level language is the ability to move the program from one computer to another. This concept is often referred to as *transportability*. This facility derives from the basic characteristic that a higher-level language has good potential for conversion to another computer, since this is one of the defining characteristics discussed in the first section of this Chapter. The realistic problems in doing this which were discussed under "Conversion and Compatibility" above do not remove this inherent major advantage.

Disadvantages There are some disadvantages which are often cited as reasons for not using higher-level languages. These tend to be (1) the time required for compilation, (2) potentially inefficient object code, and (3) the inability of the language to express all the needed operations.

This author wishes to make clear the opinion that these disadvantages do not exist in most realistic cases. First, little extra time is required for compilation with compiler techniques that are known at the time of this writing. With regard to inefficient object code, it may be true that the very best programmers can produce better code than the very best compilers. However, what normally tends to happen is that mediocre or novice programmers use fairly good compilers; in such a situation the compiler will generally produce better object code. Furthermore, there are relatively few really expert coders, and many of them are the developers of the compilers! Thus the most realistic situation seems to be that when a "mediocre" programmer uses a "good" compiler, the resulting code probably will be "good" and so the other advantages apply.

As far as the language being unable to express all the needed operations (e.g., lack of character handling or adequate input-output), this is indeed frequently a legitimate complaint but often comes about because the incorrect language was chosen in the first place. There are several instances of complaints about the inadequacy of FORTRAN for writing payroll programs. This is similar to complaining that an automobile will not cross a river. FORTRAN was designed for use in numerical scientific computations, not for business data processing.

Selecting a Language There is no simple procedure for choosing a language and evaluating it. However, various types of numerical techniques can and have been used (e.g., weighted factor analysis).

The first factor that one should consider in the choice of a language is the actual suitability in terms of having the available features that are needed for the particular set of problems and the class of users. Furthermore, one must make sure that the language is available on the desired computer, and that training costs for the potential users (if needed) are within tolerable bounds. It is important to distinguish between the efficient implementation of a particular compiler which is a meaningful concept and the efficiency of the language. The latter concept is generally not very meaningful because most interpretations of it relate to the applicability of the language to a particular problem. Finally, in selecting a language one must give due attention to the compatibility with the present environment and the growth potential. In other words, a simple language which is suitable today might be outgrown by the installation within a year, and it might have been better to choose a more powerful language in the first place.

MAJOR LANGUAGES

In trying to assess what is meant by the term *major language*, a significant amount of value judgment is required. There are many ways in which one can measure the usage of languages. For example, one can consider the number of people who have been trained in the language, the number of people who are actually writing programs, the number of programs that have been written, the amount of machine time spent in compiling, the amount of machine time spent in running production jobs, etc. Since it is extremely difficult to obtain statistics of this kind, it is necessary to make essentially intuitive value judgments.

It would appear that probably the most widely used language (by many of the above criteria) is actually COBOL. This is reflective of the very large number of smaller computers which are being used for business data processing. Other major languages in use in the mid-1970s are FORTRAN and BASIC. Both of these tend to be used more for numerical and scientific computations, although each in turn has actually been used for data processing applications. Another language significant for business data processing is PL/I, which has within it the broad capability of dealing effectively with both numeric and nonnumeric (i.e., business data processing) applications. PL/I is a very large language, but does not have the English language features that many users tend to like in COBOL.

Many installations are heavily concerned with applications involving very large databases. A discussion of the database management systems which are frequently used in this context is beyond the scope of this Chapter.[1] However, attempts are being made to provide much of this facility in COBOL.

LANGUAGES FOR SPECIALIZED APPLICATION AREAS

As indicated in the beginning of this Chapter, all languages are application-oriented, but some applications are more specialized than others. For example, business data processing is a broad application, whereas civil engineering, economics, graphics, simulation, equipment check-out, etc. are much more specialized. Note that some application areas (e.g., simulation, graphics) really span many user applications, whereas others (e.g., civil engineering, equipment check-out) are highly specialized to a particular discipline.

As far as this author can determine, approximately half the languages actually implemented and used within the United States are for these very specialized application areas. It is not surprising that most of these tend to be more scientific- and engineering-oriented because of the wide variety of discipline-oriented jargon. The enormous usage of COBOL, and the apparent lack of necessity of developing languages for sub-specialties in the business data processing areas, have prevented the significant growth of specialized languages in business data processing. There are some languages used for social science, and an example from one of these, namely DATA-TEXT, is shown as Figure 3-2.

SUMMARY

Of the several hundred different programming languages in use in the United States, less than a dozen are really widely used. Included are FORTRAN, COBOL, BASIC, and some of the languages for specialized application areas. Most programming is done in higher-level languages, and most of the business data processing programming seems to be done in COBOL. In addition to the technical features of a particular language, one should always consider such nontechnical issues as the amount of compatibility associated with it, and the status of the official standardization. There are

[1] See Section 5, Chapter 6, "The Technology of Database Management."

```
Col. 1                                                                      Col. 8
   ° DECK COLLEGE STUDENT STUDY
   ° READ CARDS
   ° CARD(1-2)FORMAT/UNIT = COL(1-4),CARD = COL(5)
   ° AGE =            COL( 5- 6/1)   = AGE OF STUDENT
   ° SEX =            COL( 7/1)      = STUDENT'S SEX(0 = MALE/1 = FEMALE)
   ° RACE =           ACOL( 8/1)     = RACIAL BACKGROUND(B = BLACK/
                                                        W = WHITE/
                                                        O = OTHER)
   ° INCOME =         COL(10-14/1)   = FAMILY INCOME
   ° CLASS =          COL(15/1)      = COLLEGE CLASS(1 = FRESH/2 = SOPH/
                                                     3 = JUNIOR/4 = SENIOR)
   ° ABILITY =        COL(27-28/1)   = SCHOLASTIC APTITUDE TEST
   ° ITEM(1-4) =      COL(31-34(4)/1) = WILLING TO BE DRAFTED(1 = YES/
                                                        2 = NO)/              °
   °                                 APPROVE OF SDS POLICIES()/               °
   °                                 LIKE NIXON()/                            °
   °                                 LIKE AGNEW()
   ° ACTIVITY(1-50) = COL(6-55(50)/2) = SCHOOL ACTIVITIES(0 = NO/1 = YES)
   ° VAR (1) =        COL( 9/1)      = FATHER'S EDUCATION(1 = SOME HS/        °
                                                        2 = HS/
                                                        3 = SOME COLL/
                                                        4 = BA/
                                                        5 = BEYOND BA)
   ° VAR (2) =        COL(21/1)      = FUTURE PLANS(0 = GRAD SCHOOL/          °
                                                    1 = PROF SCHOOL/
                                                    2 = BUSINESS/
                                                    3 = TEACHING/
                                                    4 = OTHER/
   °                                                5 = DON'T KNOW)           °
   ° VAR(3) =         MEAN ITEM(1,3-4) = PRO-ESTABLISHMENT SCALE
   ° INDEX =          SUM ACTIVITY(1-50) = ACTIVITIES INDEX
   ° VAR(4) =         1 IF VAR(1) = 4,5 AND INCOME GREATER THAN 20000 =       °
                                     SOCIAL CLASS INDEX
   °                                (1 = UPPER/2 = MIDDLE/3 = LOWER)
   ° OR =             3 IF VAR(1) = 1,2 AND INCOME LESS THAN 10000
   ° OR =             2
   ° VAR(5) =         RECODE(A) VAR(2) = FUTURE PLANS II(1 = SCHOOL/
                                                         2 = WORK)
   ° CODE(A) =        (0,1 = 1/2-4 = 2/5 = BLANK)
   ° VAR(6) =         (ABILITY/AGE)° 100 = AGE-GRADED ABILITY
   ° CHANGE(1-10) = POSTEST(1-10) − PRETEST(1-10)
   ° WRITE DATATEXT DISC 4
   ° COMPUTE STATISTICS(AGE, INCOME, ITEM, VAR(6)), SKEW
   ° COMPUTE T-TESTS(ABILITY, VAR(3)), GROUP BY SEX
   ° COMPUTE FREQUENCIES
   ° COMPUTE CORRELATIONS(ACTIVITY),TEST
   ° COMPUTE CROSSTABS(VAR(2), ITEM BY SEX, RACE, CLASS), CHI SQUARE
   ° COMPUTE REGRESSION(ABILITY ON AGE, SEX, VAR(1), INCOME), GROUP
     BY CLASS
   ° COMPUTE ANOVA(SEX BY RACE BY VAR(4)), ABILITY
   ° START
```

Fig. 3-2   A Sample DATA-TEXT Program. (Source: D. J. Armor, "The Data-Text System: An Application Language for the Social Sciences," *Proceedings of Spring Joint Computer Conference*, AFIPS Press, Montvale, N.J., vol. 40, p. 336, 1972.)

many languages for very specialized application areas and in some ways users might be well off to develop their own specialized languages, providing they have the in-house talent or wish to pay another group to do it for them.

SELECTIVE BIBLIOGRAPHY

American National Standard, *Programming Language COBOL*, ANSI X3.23–1974, American National Standards Institute, New York, 1974.

Armor, D. J., "The Data-Text System: An Application Language for the Social Sciences," *Proceedings of Spring Joint Computer Conference,* vol. 40, AFIPS Press, Montvale, N.J., 1972.

CODASYL COBOL Journal of Development, 1973. Available from Technical Services Branch, Department of Supply and Services, 5th floor, 88 Metcalfe St., Ottawa, Ont., Canada, K1A OS5.

Naftaly, S. M., B. G. Johnson, and M. C. Cohen, *COBOL Support Packages . . . Programming and Productivity Aids,* Wiley, New York, 1972.

Sammet, Jean E., *Programming Languages: History and Fundamentals,* Prentice-Hall, Englewood Cliffs, N.J., 1969.

Chapter 4

Operating Systems

FRANK J. PERPIGLIA

Programming Manager, Burroughs Corporation, Paoli, Pennsylvania

A computer is valuable only to the extent that problems can be solved more economically by it than by other means. Realization of this has caused the evolution of operating systems from a haphazard collection of programs and subprograms to a vital and integral part of computer systems. The evolutionary aspects of operating systems are necessary to understand, for where the hardware has changed through technology from tubes to transistors to integrated circuits, software has primarily evolved through management and control. The plethora of programming languages existing today notwithstanding, the significant strides in software's ability to make computers more available and easier to use have been made with very little change in the software technology and with no change in the stored-program concept.

What has changed is the recognition that a program, that funny set of instructions written by funny kinds of people, is a product that consumes enormous time, energy, and costs. A program may be invisible — one can see only its printed form — but it is valuable: it is expensive to produce, expensive to change, and expensive to repair. With this realization has come the attempts at standardization and modularity, and the exploitation of programs already in existence. Operating systems embody the recognition that programs required by everyone need not, should not, and cannot be written by everyone. Functions and programs that have previously been done by users are finding their way to the basic system, simply because they are becoming better defined, their generality and frequency of occurrence have been verified, and finally because there are performance benefits to be gained by implementing certain functions closer to the hardware.

Let us examine the functions that must take place in a computer system in order to execute a program. First, the program must be written; second, it must be keypunched or otherwise presented in a form that is recognizable by the system. Once in this form, it must be loaded into the executable portion of the system. Once loaded, it must be given control of the system or at least those components that it requires. During its execution it must have access to the resources of the system that it requires. Finally, on completion the processor must transfer control away from the program, or the program must have a way of terminating the execution of the system resources it controls.

On small systems any one program has a high probability of using all the resources available, and loading, starting, and stopping features might well be built into the hardware. For example, a small system with a paper-tape input might have a load button to introduce programs. Pressing this load button would cause the paper tape to

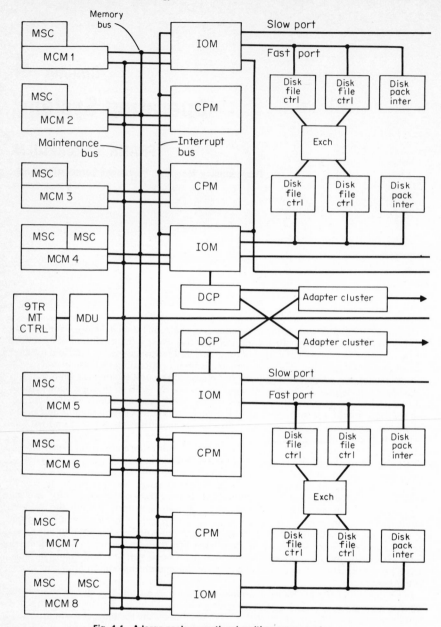

Fig. 4-1   A large-scale operational multiprocessor system.

be read and transformed into a format that could be executed by the processor of that system. A start button might exist which would cause the execution of the processor. In this kind of system, operating systems may be very trivial, and sometimes they are nonexistent.

The other end of the spectrum is somewhat different. Consider a large-scale general-purpose computer system which is constructed with multiple central processors, multiple input-output processors, and multiple memory modules which are shared by both the I/O processors and central processors. If we add a peripheral complement of

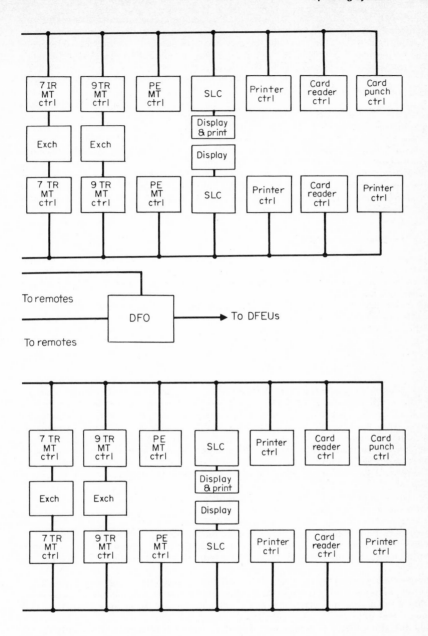

30 million bytes of secondary storage disk, disk packs, a half dozen magnetic tapes, two card readers, two line printers, and two operator consoles with CRTs for operator and system communication, we have a very flexible and powerful computer system which may rent for $60,000 per month. Many systems of this size or larger are in use today.

An example of a large and modular system of this type is depicted in Figure 4-1, representing the Burroughs B7700 multiprocessor system. If we attempt to apply the rules of executing a program on a system of this size, it should be obvious that inefficiencies will be encountered, for without an operating system it will be necessary for a programmer to take his or her program, load it into the machine, begin its execution, and await its results. This was the standard mode of operation in the early fifties, and is the mode today for some smaller systems. The problem, of course, is that the setup time required for each program is usually greater than the time to execute the program itself. If problems occur during the execution of the program, much time is spent in debugging the program or isolating the failure in the hardware. Therefore most of the resources are not used most of the time. Thus, operating computer systems can be a great source of inefficiency. Users and manufacturers recognized this problem and began to look for ways to reduce these operational inefficiencies. The decision was to delegate the operations of the system to the system itself. This was achieved through the development of monitors or control programs, and was the beginning of the development of operating systems as we know them today.

Thus an operating system may be defined as the master program that controls the execution and flow of all other programs and attempts to maximize the utilization of central processors, input-output channels, memory, and peripheral devices in an effort to achieve greater work per unit time.

NEED FOR OPERATING SYSTEMS

If we view computer systems as a set of "function boxes" communicating with one another to achieve a desired result, then hardware may be viewed as the collection of the physical function boxes, and operating system software may be viewed as the function box coordinator.

An operating system is defined, then, as a program or set of programs that:

1. Controls the physical devices that comprise the system, i.e., the hardware.

2. Aids user programs or application programs in their execution.

3. Acts as an extension to the machine hardware to ease the interface between a user and the hardware.

4. Manages the utilization of the hardware by providing efficient execution of application programs.

Operating systems, therefore, help bridge the gap in the complexity of systems, help effectively utilize the resources of systems, and help toward achieving the machine independence that users rightly demand. Through operating systems, users are freed from concern with the physical components that help solve their particular problems. Operating systems provide the interface between users of the system and the system itself, and they are needed to provide effective utilization of all the resources that make the computer installation work.

There are, however, many users of systems—e.g., the software programmer, the application programmer, the computer operator, the data processing manager, the bank teller, and the airline reservationist. Each of these users has a different view of the system, and each view imposes different requirements on the operating system. Thus, the adaptation of a general-purpose computer system toward the support of each of these users falls within the jurisdiction of the operating system. Effective, well-designed operating systems can increase not only the productivity and throughput of people's usage of computer systems, but the productivity and throughput of the people as well.

There should be no doubt that there is great need and demanding requirements for operating systems. It is precisely these great and diverse requirements that cause most of the problems for manufacturers and eventually for the users themselves. Let us examine four different views of operating systems.

The Operator's View The computer operator's view has changed significantly as the operating system has taken over functions previously in his or her domain. Where once the operator directed the operation of the system, today's operators are directed by the system itself. Indeed, some installations exist where the nature of the operations is completely defined, and operators are necessary only in emergency situations. Process control monitoring by computer systems is an example. For most data processing installations, however, an operator is still a necessity in running the computer system. Status information, resource utilization, and hardware reliability information are required from the operating system when overt action is to be taken by the operator. Operators expect ease of interaction with the operating system, and expect that the responses they are required to make to the operating system be as direct and as simple as possible.

The Data Processing Manager's View   The data processing manager views the operating system through the eyes of a resource manager. The operating system is considered a "master" program whose combined functions include allocating resources as required by user application programs, and the apportionment of time in an accounting fashion to each of these programs. The data processing manager views the installation as a "factory" where programs introduced into the system occupy and utilize certain resources. When the programs have accomplished their task they leave the system, but their existence and resource utilization are logged by the operating system for auditing purposes. The operating system monitors the flow of programs into and out of the system and regulates the state of the system during the execution of the various programs.

From this viewpoint, the data processing manager expects to see detailed reports on a daily basis, reports perhaps ordered by time, indicating the arrival time of a particular job, the exit time, the amount of processor time expended on a particular job, the amount of I/O time, and even the amount of memory used. In short, a log should contain the percentage of total resources used on any one job. This information is required to measure the utility of the system. Programs or jobs which take large amounts of resources can be identified, and perhaps optimized. The needs dictated by this view demand that operating systems provide effective utilization of resources, allow scheduling of work to be predefined to the system, and provide for logging facilities by which an accounting of resource utilization can be made.

The Programming View of Operating Systems   The programmer in trying to use the system to solve a particular problem has a totally different view of the operating system. In many respects he or she is more intimately involved. The programmer must first ascertain from the operating system what tools are available to help solve the problem. This view includes not only control programs or monitors, but also compilers, data communication facilities, data management systems, job control managers, and various utility functions. Thus, in many respects, the programmer views the operating system as *the system*, since the operating system represents the programmer's only means of communication with the system. The programmer is no longer concerned with processor modules, memory modules, or channel activity. After all, what do they have to do with the solution of an equation or with the posting of a transaction? The programmer's only concern is the best way to express the algorithmic solution to the problem and the solution itself. The needs dictated by this view demand that operating systems be simple to use and to interface with, and that they mask from the programmer all functions not related to the logical solution of the problem.

The User's View   A bank user has an altogether different view of the operating system. Take the bank teller as an example. For the teller the system is dedicated to serving his or her request and responding to commands. The requests and commands are usually in the form of specific buttons that exist on specific teller-type terminals. These buttons or commands are the only means of communication, and whether the commands are interpreted and handled by the terminal, by an application program, by the operating system, or by a special-purpose processor is of no concern whatever to the teller. Nor should it be. The needs dictated by this view cannot easily be ascribed to one part of the system or the other. System design and implementation will specify functional assignments within the hardware, software, operating system, and application program hierarchy. Performance and cost objectives will indicate where within the hierarchy the specific functions are implemented.

From each of the views described above, it can be seen that an operating system means different things to different people. The further removed one is from the computer system, the less concerned one is with the placement of functions within the system. Only as one moves closer to the system and within the system is one concerned with the placement of functions. "How" a system works is important only to the designer.

THE MANUFACTURER'S ROLE

The development of operating systems offers significant problems to the manufacturers of computing equipment. One problem is the seemingly simple decision regarding the content of the operating system. The mere establishment of priority for the development of the various functions is a nontrivial task. Further, the operating system designer and developer is not always in control of these priorities. On the contrary, most times he or she has least control. It is easy to recognize that almost all customers and potential customers have requirements that are unique to their own installations. Further, they would like to see these unique requirements reflected in the system they buy. From the customer point of view, each request is certainly reasonable. If it can be a part of the operating system, then "obviously" that is the best place for it. Many times this can be self-defeating. When the number of users is large and the number of demands, therefore, is equally large, an individual user may have requirements which work to the detriment of other users by imposing performance or stability degradation on customers who will never use that particular function. The manufacturer's ability to solve this dilemma is a function of the basic operating system structure and the programming tools used to implement this structure.

Implementation Problems Manufacturers must be responsive. However, they are faced with the difficult role of determining the essential from the seemingly essential, of having to respond to realistic demands but objecting to demands that would disturb the structure and content already established in the system. Since the operating system is an open-ended one, one that is never complete, one that is never put to rest, one that is always in a constant state of change, achieving stability while accommodating change is the manufacturer's paradoxical situation.

That is not to say that the problems faced by the manufacturer are not controllable, for certainly they are. In many respects operating systems development is quite similar to other large-scale programming projects. There are at least two techniques employed in the development of the large-scale programming projects and they have been applied to the development of operating systems. One technique is to build large operating systems with large groups of people. This is the divide-and-conquer approach, which assumes that a 9 employee-month effort can be achieved by nine employees in one month. In such cases it is not unusual for manufacturers to employ literally hundreds of people on any given operating system. Such an approach is very rarely successful. It has been shown that a limit exists such that the more people on a project, the less is actually accomplished.

Use of Compilers Another technique that has been used successfully has been to analyze the tools needed to develop operating systems, to provide a proper design and structuring of these tools, and to assign small groups to work with these tools in the implementation. One tool that has significantly increased the productivity of user programming development is higher-level languages.

While higher-level languages have been successfully employed for many years in the development of user programs, their use for system software development has not been accepted as standard throughout the industry. Two notable exceptions are the MULTICS systems at M.I.T., with their use of PL/I, and the Burroughs Corporation, where use of higher-level language is the rule, without exception, throughout its EDP product line. Burroughs has successfully employed compilers in the development of all system software since the early sixties.

While there are significant economic advantages in the use of higher-level languages, the important motivation behind their use is control. With higher-level languages fewer programmers are required, communications problems are minimized, the documentation levels of each program are increased, and maintenance aspects are simplified. Use of higher-level languages allows the manufacturer to be more responsive to change. In every way imaginable, the use of higher-level languages makes software development more manageable. The use of assembly languages for system software development is open admission that the architecture of the system does not efficiently support the higher-level languages that are available to the user.

Operating System Reliability High-level languages also help to increase the reliability of operating systems, and reliability is probably the most significant problem for user and manufacturer alike. This is a manifestation of a more global problem in the computer system, i.e., the lack of proof of correctness of a computer program. The approach to program verification has always been, and is today, to try various data patterns or to run specialized test routines. One cannot deny that these techniques are better than doing nothing, but in a formal sense, all that is verified is the program's ability to execute properly in that particular environment. These techniques verify the existence of errors — not their absence. By invocation of Murphy's law ("Whatever can go wrong, will"), it can be guaranteed that some other environment will uncover a logic problem at some later time.

Release levels of operating systems are further proof of the lack of reliability. Each new release attests to the inefficiencies of prior releases. Unfortunately, new release levels contain not only corrections to previous release levels, but also additional functional levels. Since these additions have not been completely verified, they are the source of even more errors. It is well known that each new release level is treated with much suspicion by the user community in general, and so it should.

All other problems with operating systems are dwarfed by the reliability question, since any operating system deficiency means system degradation. Manufacturers are coping with this problem by converting operating systems developed for earlier machines to the new machines. That is, hardware is being built to support and exploit existing software. Again, the use of higher-level languages provides additional leverage in controlling such conversion, and is a further step in the development of machine-independent operating systems.

THE USER'S ROLE

The user groups have played and continue to play an extremely vital role in the development of operating systems. User groups provide the feedback to manufacturers that is vital to understanding the market requirements. Most user groups have established procedures for specifying and requesting additions or modifications to manufacturers' operating systems. Such requests usually have associated with them an indication of the importance of priority of the proposed feature or modification. These priorities are valuable in helping the manufacturer assess the need and provide the scheduling required to satisfy customers. Further, many users develop additional operating system functions on their own, or modify existing features to the overall benefit of the use or performance of the system. Such user-generated modifications sometimes receive wide distribution, and if generally applicable, may well be incorporated and supported by the manufacturer.

As indicated earlier, this question of operating system content is a difficult one to solve. While users recognize the need and potential offered them through the operating system, nonetheless operating systems tend to be a constant irritant between the two groups. One cause of this controversy is the "overhead" of operating systems. The very word itself is controversial, and a meaningful definition is lacking. One view holds that the entire operating system is overhead, while the other view states that the operating system is a consolidation of functions that would have to be distributed to user programs anyway — ergo, no overhead exists. As with most such disagreements, the truth lies somewhere between.

Operating systems do consume substantial amounts of hardware resources, particularly processor time and storage space. Well-structured systems, however, adapt to the hardware, so that functions not being used consume only backup store. Users should consider this consumption factor when evaluating systems — it does represent a cost item.

OPERATING SYSTEM FUNCTIONS

The functions of operating systems are many and varied, but the following adequately characterize most of the operating systems in existence today. There are functions to provide for:
1. Interrupt processing.
2. Input-output processing.
3. Command/control language.
4. Initiation/termination.
5. Job control and scheduling.
6. Memory management.
7. Data management.
8. Logging and accounting.
9. Recovery.

Interrupt Processing Interrupt processing is the interpretation of hardware-generated signals by the operating system. The interrupt handler is invoked by the hardware processor upon the occurrence of a well-defined set of conditions. Hardware faults, illegal operations, and data transfer parity errors are examples of conditions which may be detected by the hardware and reported, usually at the time of occurrence, to the interrupt handler.

Most hardware systems are interrupt-driven. That is, the hardware exists in one state and remains in that state until an interrupt occurs to alter that state. An interrupt represents a transfer of control from one system state to another. This is the primary source of control exercised by the operating system in the utilization of the hardware.

Input-Output Processing Input-output processing is the initiation, termination, error handling, and control of data transfers between central processing elements and the peripheral devices. The mapping of data to and from their storage media is removed from the concern of the user.

Command/Control Language The command/control language represents the communication medium between the users and the operating systems. Examples are commands to execute a job and terminate a job, and interrogations as to device status. It is through the command/control language that operators communicate their desires to the system, primarily in communicating with the scheduling functions of the operating system. This language is used to define the work flow through the system.

Initiation/Termination Job initiation provides for the retrieval and setup of the structures and data required to begin processing a job. Termination is responsible for the cleanup and file storage, the logging, and accounting of the job.

Job Control and Scheduling This function is responsible for the allocation of processors to programs (jobs), for determining priorities of jobs in the schedule, and for altering the number of jobs and the priority as a function of the status of the resources. The scheduling functions determine the order of execution of jobs awaiting service, and have the objective of maximizing the utilization of all system resources.

Memory Management (Virtual Memory) Memory management is responsible for allocation and deallocation of main memory, for administering the transfer between main memory and extended memory, and for allowing a program's execution to be independent of the size of main memory.

Program structures must be resident in main memory for execution to begin. Since main memory is expensive relative to backup storage (disks, drums, disk packs, etc.), the memory management algorithms are responsible for maximizing the usage of main memory and minimizing traffic between main memory and backup store. Some manufacturers have recognized the importance of this requirement and have designed hardware functions to support this important operating system function. Burroughs first introduced the concept of virtual memory in 1962.

Data Management Data management and file management are responsible for the collection, organization, storage, and retrieval of data and for establishment of protective accessing methods. The objectives are to provide the user with a standard representation of information in a form which, through simple commands, permits easy storage, retrieval, and updating of information.

Logging and Accounting The logging and accounting functions are required to provide a history of arrival times, initiation times, termination times, and utilization of processor and storage. The logging and accounting functions are service functions performed under the auspices of the operating system, but the actual recording of the data is well distributed throughout the functions of the operating system. For example, the time that a job arrives into the operating system's schedule is first determined by the scheduler. Such time would have been logged by the scheduler but would have been available to a logging routine for recording.

This collection and statistic-producing function is helpful in determining system and individual program performance, as well as distributing costs relative to usage.

Recovery Recovery from errors is the responsibility of every part of the system. That includes the hardware and the operating system, as well as the user application program. Further, error recovery implies not only recovering *from* the error but also recovering from the *effects* of the error. That is, it is possible to recover in the face of a failing memory, but to recover the data that existed in the memory is another matter altogether.

The need for error recovery is a manifestation of the requirement for system availability. An unavailable system is no system at all, but what needs to be understood is that achieving a continuous processing capability is a function of the entire systems design. Continuous processing is a very important aspect of the computer industry today, particularly where computers are an essential and integral part of the operations of a business. Certainly space probes would have been impossible without computers, and an unavailable system at launching time means either no launch or catastrophe. On-line banking, process control of oil refineries, and other commercial installations have similar stringent needs. Because of this ever-increasing reliance on computer availability, it is worthwhile here to describe a set of necessary conditions to achieve continuous processing:

1. The hardware must be modular—both logically and physically—where modularity implies complete independence, including power supplies.

2. The software or operating system must recognize the hardware modularity and be able to commit and decommit these modules without impacting the rest of the system.

3. The operating system itself must be modular, must have extensive error checking, and must be capable of recovering from its own failures.

4. The hardware must have total duplication, i.e., no single modular failure should be capable of rendering the entire system inoperable.

5. The operating system must be designed to accommodate component failures. This can be achieved only by recognizing that failures will occur, and providing a system design to detect and recover from such failures.

6. The operating system must accommodate the changing system configuration with minimum impact to operating programs. That is, the operating system, when recognizing a failure, must attempt to minimize the impact of that failure and to localize that failure relative to the set of jobs that may be in execution at the time of failure.

7. The operating system must provide functions for user application programs, to allow the user program to be structured to accommodate failures. Features such as the ability to duplicate files, provide dual recording, and provide checkpoint and restart upon user invocation must exist.

8. The user programs themselves must be structured to accommodate failures. The user program must recognize that, despite the efforts of hardware reliability, despite the efforts of operating systems software, there will be times when failure occurs. User programs must be aware of this possibility. It is unreasonable, for example, for a program that processes sequentially 500 reels of tape to be capable only of beginning with the first reel. The program must recognize that a failure could occur during its execution, and prudence dictates that recovery points be taken, for example, after every reel. Thus, instead of an error requiring the reprocessing of all previous tapes, only the tape in process at the time of failure need be reprocessed.

MULTIPROGRAMMING

Perhaps no other feature has caused so much change or required so much energy within the development of operating systems as multiprogramming. Multiprogramming is defined as the interleaved execution of two or more programs. Perhaps a way to understand that is to view a system schematically. Figure 4-2a depicts a memory and a processor. The memory has Programs A and B resident within it. The arrow between the processor and the program represents execution, that is, the processor is pictured as executing Program A. When Program A cannot proceed, the processor is switched to Program B. Figure 4-2b shows processor switching as a function of time. Thus the processor works on only one program in any one instance, but on both programs for a given interval of time. The rationale behind multiprogramming is to attempt to economize a system or to match the speeds of processors with input-output devices.

Most programs have a cycle consisting of getting the data, operation on the data, and storage of the data. Usually the time frame for the processor to operate on data is significantly shorter than the times either to get or store the data from or to a peripheral device (cards, tape, etc.). When one considers that processor speeds are measured in microseconds, disk pack speeds are measured in milliseconds, and card reader speeds are measured in seconds, then perhaps one can understand that a typical program might cause a central processor to be idle for significant periods of time while the data are transferred from or to the device.

There are two ways in which one might eliminate this inefficiency. One is to increase significantly the speed of the peripheral devices. This is a nontrivial task. The second is to multiprogram—that is, to have another program resident and capable of executing. Then when a processor goes idle, the idle state can be recognized and the operating system can switch it to the waiting program.

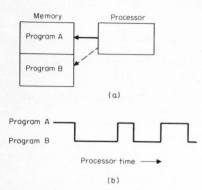

(a)

(b)

Fig. 4-2 Multiprogramming schematic: (a) memory and processor; (b) processor switching as a function of time.

Burroughs Corporation, for example, has recognized that this disparity of speeds will continue to exist for at least a long period of time and perhaps forever, and so has constructed architecture to support naturally the multiprogramming aspects required to keep systems running efficiently. This concept has allowed the creation of time-sharing utility systems and has tremendously increased the productivity of computer systems as we know them today.

MULTIPROCESSING

Multiprocessing is the ability to control the execution of more than one processor, and is a natural byproduct of a proper systems design for multiprogramming. The following benefits ensue from multiprocessing:

1. Ease of increasing throughput. Processing power is increased without reprogramming or recompilation. Growth is accommodated easily.

2. Fault tolerance. Multiprocessor systems allow all processors to do useful work, but allow graceful degradation, since the failure of any one processor does not cause the entire system to be inoperable. Failures are accommodated naturally.

Thus, although multiprogramming/multiprocessing concepts and implementations have existed since the early sixties, these concepts are only now gaining wide acceptance and understanding.

SUMMARY

The tremendous cost and complexity of computers demand that they be run effectively and efficiently, and since the early days of data processing, much effort has been expended toward achieving this goal.

Operating systems today are the result of the evolution of the industry as a whole, and represent the means of identification of a system—that is, a computer system is only as good as the operating system controlling it.

It is reasonable to expect that operating systems will continue to mature and evolve in the future as they have in the past. Operating systems have become well-defined structures and have been, in some instances, well integrated into the hardware; and many hardware supporting features exist solely to aid operating system implementation. It is expected that this trend will continue, and operating system functions will continue to find their way into the more basic hardware structures.

Eventually, we shall begin building machines that will be self-adapting for specific applications, and we shall see the implementation of all operating system functions integrated within the hardware itself.

SELECTIVE BIBLIOGRAPHY

Burroughs B6700 Master Control Program, Burroughs Corporation, Detroit, 1970.

Dijkstra, Edsger W., "The Structure of 'THE' Multiprogramming System," *Communications of ACM*, vol. 11, no. 5, pp. 341–346, May, 1968.

Lampson, B. W., "A Scheduling Philosophy for Multi-Processing Systems," *Symposium on Operating System Principles*, Association for Computing Machinery, October 1–4, 1967.

Randall, B., and C. J. Keuhner, "Dynamic Storage Allocation Systems," *Communications of ACM*, vol. 11, no. 5, pp. 297–305, May, 1968.

Sayres, Anthony P., *Operating Systems Survey*, Auerbach Computer Science Series, Auerbach, Philadelphia, 1971.

Chapter 5

Application Programs

HUGH J. LYNCH

General Manager, Communications Systems Division, NCR
Corporation, Columbia, South Carolina

Application packages began to receive attention in the early 1960s. Up until that time, hardware and software technologies were the central concerns of the user community. While hardware and software technology has continued as an area of major interest, a growing part of the user community has become actively concerned with the availability of application packages. This is a natural development following the achievement of a minimum standard of capability in hardware and operating software. The next obvious priority to basic technical capability is to achieve greater utilization by placing more work on the computers through the vehicle of application packages.

A major problem characterizing the efforts of the 1963–1965 application development efforts was that of scale. From the beginning, it was possible to identify applications within industries in which years of accounting practices, mobility of personnel, legal requirements, and competitive customer service requirements had resulted in a great deal of standardization. The most difficult variable remaining was the size of companies in the same line of business. The size of the equipment to be utilized and the amount of on-line storage and throughput requirements are differences that must be dealt with. There are also substantial differences in the degree of integration of application systems with other management information systems, depending on the size of the business.

In 1965–1967, third-generation hardware and software began to appear, providing major relief for these problems. It became relatively inexpensive to reconfigure an application system, in terms of size of both software and hardware. (It should be noted that the term used here is "relatively inexpensive," not "automatic.") The increased facilities and flexibility of compilers and I/O systems have also made it easier to redefine file interfaces so that system interfaces are more flexible. This is particularly true when the initial design anticipates flexible interfacing. As a result, application packaging provides greatly expanded opportunity insofar as the software and hardware technology base is concerned. Today, the majority of ADP users have had some involvement with application packages. Thousands of sites are running multiple packages and, in fact, have a majority of their processing workload based upon application packages.

Two major conditions govern the continuing growth of application package availability. One is the quality of application software products in terms of content, reliability, economy, and flexibility. The second is the attitude and willingness of the ADP users to take advantage of application packages.

Many applications are available. In addition to a wide selection of generalized accounting packages such as Payroll, Accounts Payable, Accounts Receivable, and General Ledger, there are many industry-specific processes. Bills of Material, Order Entry, Inventory, Central Information File Banking, Medical Audit, Fashion Reporting, Credit Authorization, Trust Accounting, Vehicle Scheduling, and Route Accounting are but a few examples of industry-specific packages. Any industry that has achieved a number of computer users within it can be expected to have some useful application software already available.

Such programs range from an individual ADP user system made available as a spin-off of the user's effort, to sophisticated systems designed for the express purpose of establishing a wider user base. The latter are designed with multiple users in mind originally, and with many tools and service options to facilitate use as a package. Unfortunately, individual investigation is required to qualify these products and to relate them to the user's need. In many cases, the single-user-developed program will perform excellent service, and in others it will not. In still other instances, the relatively expensive package program with extensive options and installation aids will provide the most economic and satisfactory installation. The main purpose of this Chapter is to provide some guidelines to help the potential user of packages find and evaluate these offerings.

Continued growth of application package selections and quality is of course directly related to investment capital available. The business recession of 1970–1971 saw numerous failures of application projects. Future expansion will be slower, but should provide a higher percentage of sound, well-conceived application packages.

The user attitude is the most essential single ingredient to evaluate and use packages successfully. To install a package, the user has to *want* to do it. Specifically, all the user's personnel must want to make reasonable trade-offs. Since a computer application must reflect the finite operating details and individual processing of the information upon which a given segment of the business is operated, it directly and indirectly affects operating policies.

A degree of flexibility is usually available in a well-conceived package, but some reasonable compromises usually must be made. It is unfortunate, but true, that in most businesses individual clerks have sole possession of the mechanical details of the information processing for which they are responsible. These personnel are not usually in a position to make the necessary compromises. Management's involvement and ability to exercise balanced judgments to make operating policy compromises is the key to finding a package to fit the user's needs. The economic potential of application packages provides strong motivation to management.

WHAT IS AN APPLICATION PACKAGE?

The term *application package* like many coined phrases obscures more than it tells. Commonly covered by this name are entire systems, including conversion and all management reporting and input systems, as well as necessary education, documentation, and supporting services to bring about an installation. However, application package is also used to describe individual programming techniques or modules that must be augmented to provide a single application program which represents only a portion of a system. Further, some application packages provide only an overall design architecture with selected support programs for that architecture, but leave the burden for many of the key programs containing the essential application logic on the individual user. Others provide no input system or require that the user provide all reporting systems. In common usage application package is applied to almost any preprogrammed tool that allows a data processing user to achieve an installation of a specific application and avoid some of the software development that would otherwise be required on the user's part.

Many application packages need to be specific to a particular industry, while others can move readily between industries. This is a matter for caution. Payroll in a department store and payroll in a construction firm or a manufacturing concern have different requirements. Therefore, in examining many packages, the user should immediately establish the user base being discussed. Later in this Chapter, some guidelines are provided for evaluating packages. Competitive offerings must be qualified to determine if a basis of comparison exists. Points for comparison are:

- How many users are there?
- Is the application industry-specific?
- Does it provide a conversion system?
- Does it provide for all input requirements?
- Are all file processing systems provided?
- Does it provide all reporting systems?
- Are file maintenance systems provided?
- Is the package designed modularly?
- Are the above fully programmed, or are they building blocks to be operated on first by the user?
- Does the design include the ability to integrate with other packages — existing or planned?
- Is there complete documentation?
- Are training services available?
- Are support and installation services available?

To proceed with selection, users must survey the functions they are trying to implement. They must compare the available packages. They must evaluate the best return. These steps require allocation of resources prior to purchase.

INVESTMENT CHARACTERISTICS

The obvious investment benefit of an application package is to purchase it for less dollar investment than would otherwise be required for in-house development. Based

TABLE 5-1   Return-on-Investment Computation

	Application package	In-house development
Benefit	$1,000 per month	$1,000 per month
Benefits start	9th month	18th month
Life	48 months	48 months
Cost Period Yr. 1	$19,000	$20,000
Period Yr. 2	3,000	10,000
Period Yr. 3	3,000	3,000
Simple ROI	192%	145%
Internal Rate of Return	48%	16%

on the source of the package in question and the breadth of the market for the package, this benefit normally can be expected. However, there are other tangible investment benefits that are less obvious than the one mentioned above. For example, an application package typically can be purchased one month and installed the next. Normally, invoicing takes place at the time the system is certified as operating. (Note: This is usually based on test data sets rather than waiting for the user to complete conversion.) However, even better start-up terms are negotiable. The dollar benefits of computerized applications may be considered as a return on investment. (Note: As with any process improvement, cost savings will not automatically yield expense savings.)

To secure an application package with immediate dollar benefits realizable in the same time frame as the cost, as compared with in-house development expenses accrued perhaps 18 to 24 months prior to receiving any benefits, is a significant business opportunity. Table 5-1 is an example of ROI computation.

The internal rate of return shown in Table 5-1 is obtained utilizing present worth of dollar computations. The effect of small cost increase with delays in benefits can change a program from attractive (48 per cent) to marginal (16 per cent). This example is conservative in comparing both cost and time frames.

Cost of money difference alone can in many cases determine the favorability of the entire undertaking. Further benefits may be achieved if the application package provides a rental plan. In the example discussed above, as shown in Figure 5-1, the application package 48-month return is realized by the end of the 57th month. The in-house 48-month return is not realized until the end of the 66th month. The risk of achieving a 48-month life should be better for the package.

Comparison of finished application packages versus in-house development should not ignore the opportunity to place the expense in a desirable accounting period. The lead times and continuing nature of in-house expense do not give this flexibility to the financial manager.

A significant issue that should be considered is the opportunity to achieve greater productivity of existing computer facilities. Application packages can achieve in a shorter period of time more rapid buildup of utilization of rental or purchased equipment. Typically, if a company uses all possible application packages, the in-house staff still has a full development agenda.

Greatly significant is the investment risk. The prudent evaluator will place heavy weight on this factor. The investment risk in an application package can be reduced to almost nothing. As a finished product it has greater visibility if management will invest the necessary effort to investigate. In-house system development carries a high number of risks. Management control in any development area over cost overrun, serious schedule slippage, systems deficiencies, and processing speed is hard to achieve. These risks of internal development must be assigned high value based on the history of the industry today. A further aspect of this management problem is the continuing maintenance costs which one must expect with a new software development. This might conservatively be expected to be as much as 50 per cent of the original development cost (10 per cent in each of five subsequent years). A well-seasoned application package would minimize the maintenance expense.

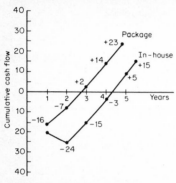

Fig. 5-1   Cash-flow comparisons.

In the experience of the author, few companies weigh all the above factors in considering application packages. Typically, a comparison of in-house development versus application packaging greatly understates the cost of in-house development. Most users do not have internal accounting systems to produce factual costs of in-house development. Therefore, in-house costs are usually higher than anticipated.

There will continue to be many instances where in-house development is the best answer. However, the point to be gained by careful analysis of the investment characteristics of a package is that the management concerned should have a very carefully constructed idea of what the unique requirements that disqualify an application package are actually costing the company. If the above factors are known, or at least recognized and guessed at, in-house development decisions will come under much greater scrutiny in the future.

PART OF AN INFORMATION SYSTEM

To evaluate an application package in its proper perspective, it is necessary to have more than just the computer room in mind. The relationship of the computer processing to the total information system is critical to understanding and evaluation of application software. This perspective applies to in-house development as well as to applications obtained from an outside source. The essential requirement of any system is that the processing volumes, deadlines, and departmental reporting and feedback systems are adequately met. This is the logistic and human-factors requirements of the system. The more complex the system, the more critical this requirement becomes. The direct operation of a computer system may affect 10 to 20 employees. However, preparation of the input, setup of new file records, handling of the reports, and in turn the preparation of feedback to the system can and probably will involve the majority of clerical and supervisory employees as well as customers in many systems.

For this reason, evaluation of an application package should begin with establishing a documented, graphic overview of the information system involved. Figure 5-2 shows a simplified MAP (**M**ake **A P**lan) diagram of an order billing and inventory. The

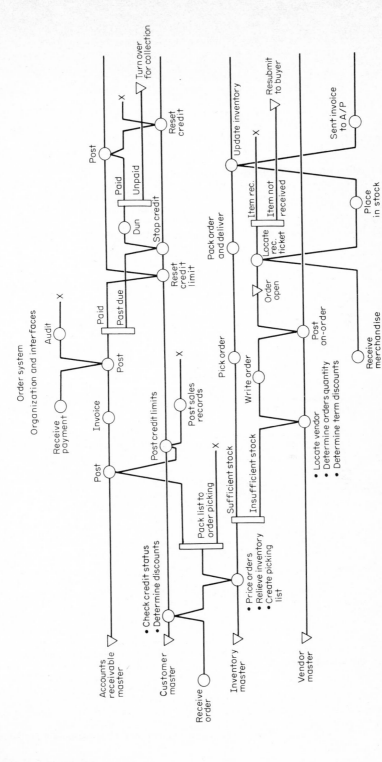

Order system
Organization and interfaces

Fig. 5-2   Diagram of organization and interfaces, order billing and inventory system.

MAP System Charting Technique[1] manual published by NCR provides an excellent method for achieving overall visibility of information flow in an organization.

As can be seen, this system integrates all the major functions of the business: order department, credit, receivables, inventory, order packing and delivery, purchasing and receiving. Each function forms a subsystem of the information system.

A broad-scope concept of *system* made up of operating control information, management information, subsystems, and interlocking organizational interfaces is essential to understand what the information system is. All these elements must be evaluated, planned, and synchronized in making and realizing the benefits of an investment in information systems. Studies of application packages can be conducted only within a clear understanding of these fundamentals. This application must be in keeping with the long-range organization and systems plan.

How Flexible Are the Information Requirements? In considering the opportunities for application packages, it is useful to classify information systems as they relate to their potential impact on the business. Obviously, classification along these lines can be utilized to establish priorities and to yield insight into the required flexibility. Management can change some business methods more readily than others.

A simple classification of information within each application is to view it as operating control information versus management information. Operating control information is defined as data having to do with the physical and financial disposition of assets

Fig. 5-3   Schematic of information relationships.

of the business. Management information has to do with comparative data on performance or status for use by management in making decisions on the future of the business. It can be observed that what has been considered management information may in the future perhaps be considered operating information. Thus the first aged-accounts receivable was part of an "advanced management information system," whereas today it is standard operating practice. However, management must be wary of the current fashion to extract management information that results in no action. A simple illustration of information relationships is shown in Figure 5-3.

Typically, the basic *operating* information requirements can most readily be satisfied by application packages. It is in the area of *management* information that variances will be found. This naturally reflects the philosophy and criteria of the individuals making up the company. The author anticipates that growing use of computerized applications will result in more direct flow of pertinent management information, eliminating some of the lower-level interpretation of critical information.

An additional view of application packages is to see them in their perspective relative to the key operating controls and central policy questions of the business. Figure 5-4 relates outside controls versus internal options, depending upon application. There are many ways to approach this area. The point of Figures 5-3 and 5-4 is that the user should consciously approach the issue, and achieve an understanding of options available.

Computer-Room Requirements Shopping for an application package is an educational process. As major features of competing application packages are presented, they will stimulate further questions about the nature of the users' business processes. Users should first establish a complete understanding of their own computer requirements and document them so that they may conduct their evaluations of application package offerings with a minimum of confusion and delay.

There are three areas for which users should have documented detailed statements of their requirements:

1. *The operating environment.* Obviously, the equipment configuration available

[1] Copyright 1961.

needs to be understood. All equipment and features should be listed in detail. If new equipment is to be purchased, then the requirements of the application will govern the equipment. In such a case, nonstandard configurations should be avoided.

A critical additional consideration is the operating software environment and language. These must be compatible with existing operations, or serious operational and software maintenance problems may be introduced that will surface in future years.

2. A further consideration is to document operating schedules and deadlines. It is most important that the user have a very clear understanding of cutoff times for all input sources and operating hours and reporting deadlines. This must be matched with not only the amount, but time of day of computer availability within the data processing facility. Few facilities are able to schedule effectively around the clock. The critical turnaround time period is the key to scheduling computer equipment, not gross hours.

All operating files, exceptions, input volumes, and output volumes should be established and documented. Typical and peak levels need to be established. The timing of peaks must also be determined. In many cases estimates are used for certain exception items and other low-percentage circumstances. In any case, it is important that these be documented, and that a common basis of comparison be established for evaluating purposes. An amazing amount of systems evaluation time is wasted today on wrong or contradicting or changing volume data. It is also important that this information be maintained, so that subsequent evaluation of performances during installation will be related to original assumptions. Frequently, this will eliminate much wasted effort spent addressing the wrong problem.

3. A final area, the most difficult one, is to identify in one list the major operating policies, departments, and organizational responsibilities that this application will directly affect. This can be initiated with the technique mentioned earlier, called MAP. After a MAP is prepared, each

Fig. 5-4 **Outside controls vs. internal options.**

major database can be reviewed to make a list of major operating features that are sought. The actions shown against each database provide the basic guide to the information necessary. It can be anticipated that such a list will continue to grow as additional applications are investigated. It is most important, however, that priorities be established in such a list of features, so that cost and benefits are maintained in perspective.

SOURCES OF APPLICATION PACKAGES

Application packages are available from a number of sources, of which the following are representative.

Equipment Manufacturers Computer equipment manufacturers provide a wide range of application packages. Some are available for purchase or rental; others are available "bundled" in the hardware price without separate software pricing. Frequently such packages are part of a larger marketing plan that includes education and installation support plans. Manufacturers have a growing commitment to this area of offering.

The most rapidly expanding application software offering from equipment manufacturers today is associated with minicomputers and/or terminals. For the most part, these products are sold as a "total system" dedicated to a single application or closely associated applications. The application software in the minicomputer is the essential element integrating all the hardware into a system. At present, this newest type of application package is found almost exclusively with equipment manufacturers.

Consulting Firms Business consulting firms have been providing increasing offering of application packages for general-purpose computers. These have frequently been developed with a specific client and then modified for more general use. Normally, they include or are a part of a broader consulting package.

Software Houses Packages from this source differ from those of the consulting firms only in that generally the offering is exclusive to software and computer services, and would not include the business services one would anticipate from a consultant. A vast array of software packages is available from this source. Some have been developed and documented as proprietary package offering; others are a result of a single installation which is now being modified to achieve a broader offer.

ADP Users Many ADP users have made their application software available to other users. This is a growing trend with larger ADP users.

User Groups and Software Exchanges ADP and trade user groups maintain software exchange activities as a major benefit of membership. In addition, there are industry publications dedicated to cataloguing and listing software applications and resources.

DESIGN CHARACTERISTICS

Standards do not exist for systems design and architecture within any given application, let alone standards inclusive of all applications. However, there are commonly needed provisions that can be examined with a checklist. The concern is not the specific answer provided, but whether the requirement has been anticipated. The checklist of design characteristics given below will provide a rapid means of organizing information and comparing application systems to evaluate their completeness and serviceability in a working environment:

Systems Content Considerations

- Was the system written from a complete market survey?
- Is the application defined to encompass the entire market or aimed at a specific segment—e.g., accounts receivable (general, retail, or industrial)?
- What type of businesses apply within the market—e.g., grocery, plumbing, electrical distributors, etc.?
- What is the size of the business served within the industry?
    Volume of dollar business?
    Transaction volumes?
    Size of the required files?
    Are the estimated volumes stated accompanied by equipment configuration?
- Are conversion aids provided?
- Is upward compatibility a consideration?
- Have reports been efficiently consolidated?
- Are many preprinted forms required?
- Is there a sound approach to solving a business problem?
    Is input control and audit satisfactory?
    Are the reports efficiently designed to consolidate information for ultimate use (clerk, buyer, etc.)?
    Are file maintenance transactions provided and practical on all master files?
- Reports
    Are report fields defined in documentation?
    Are report headers and editing complete?
    Are report controls and totaling clearly defined?
    Are report options clearly explained?
    Are unusual report requirements identified?
- Input definition
    Are all input fields clearly explained?
    Are all validation rules specified?
    Is each punched format described?
    Is there room to add transaction codes?
    Do input field sizes correspond to field sizes in the history definition?
- Computation definition
    Are all major computations clearly identified?
    Are computations calculated according to existing user practice?
    Do narratives supplement the computation; do they sufficiently explain the computation?

- History definition
    - Are all fields properly identified?
    - Is the size of the field realistic?
    - Is file maintenance indicated for each field?
    - Are unused fields available for expansion?
- Logic definition (tables and branching conditions)
    - Does the definition communicate each condition?
    - Are all major and branch conditions covered?

In addition to systems content, the performance of the process within its hardware and software environment is a key measure of its suitability for a user's needs. The following questions on technical considerations are aimed at this area.

Technical Considerations

- System design approach
    - What are the objectives of the system?
        - Processing time of the system?
        - Minimum number of programs?
        - Use of consolidated files?
        - Ease of integrating into other systems?
        - Ease of programming?
    - Is the design problem- or hardware-oriented?
    - Can the applied programs be run on multiple systems configurations?
    - What type of file processing technique was chosen and why?
        - Random?
        - Index sequential?
        - Serial sequential?
        - Serial selective?
        - Nonstandard technique?
    - What are the maintenance advantages or disadvantages of the approach?
        - Programming?
        - Testing?
        - Implementation and training?
    - Are the following operating requirements considered in the system design?
        - Number of disk pack changes to operate the system?
            - Daily?
            - Periodic?
        - Number of paper changes?
        - Number of disk packs required for running the entire system including backup?
    - What conversion problems are unique to the system?
        - What is the data format?
        - Are production controls different from conversion controls?
        - Are special conversion programs required, and why?
    - Is the system compatible with the available equipment configuration?
        - Memory size?
        - Peripheral requirements?
        - Running time?
    - Are there deviations from computer department standards, and why?
    - Are general software tools included? List all available. (Many packages are based upon and include report generators, generalized input systems, and data editing utilities.)
- Hardware
    - What is the minimum configuration for the system?
    - What is the effect of hardware changes?
        - To the system flow?
        - To the performance of the system?
        - To implementation and training?
    - Has auxiliary input or output equipment been considered—e.g., types and manufacturers of input equipment?
- File construction
    - How many files are there?

Have files been consolidated when possible?
What are file sizes?
What are the file types?
    Standard file structure ("father-son")?
    Chained file structure?
    Destructive update file structure?
    Combinations of file structures?
Are records fixed or variable length?
Are there special file maintenance characteristics, and if so, what are they?
Which files are involved in cyclic processing?
How much backup is required on each file?

- Systems controls
What are the internal controls?
    What are the rescue and restart procedures for each file?
    What files use trailer records?
    Are hash and/or actual totals used in the trailer records?
    Which files are controlled by record counts?
What are the external controls?
    Type of preaudit system used?
    Type of postaudit system used?

- System timing
Were any significant timing problems encountered, and if so, what were they?
    What timing method was used?
    Do the timings represent average and peak volumes?
    Is the timing critical to running the system?
Have samples of live situations been produced?
Has setup time been considered in the timings?

- System test plans
Have test plans been provided?
    Is testing of one program contingent upon a file produced by another program?
    Is it possible to create test files to avoid this contingency?
    Are test data being provided?
    Are live data provided with special test cases?
Are guidelines documented to show all phases of system conversion and start-up?
Are fallback plans provided to protect current operations during trial periods?

USER RESPONSIBILITY FOR INSTALLATION AND MAINTENANCE

Application software is frequently marketed with installation services and ongoing software maintenance provided. This may be available as a part of the initial purchase, or as an additional service at extra cost. These two areas are both critical to successfully using an application package. The amount of vendor service ranges widely. The provisions for such services from the vendor should be carefully considered. Frequently, offerings represent a minimum level of service and should not be confused as the total required service. Even in circumstances where the vendor service is liberal, major responsibility remains with the user. All using departments must be properly staffed and trained in the utilization of the new system. All file record conversions must be undertaken and errors reconciled, and the past system must be accurately maintained to avoid losses of information during conversion.

The modifications required to achieve the initial installation will vary with the application and the user. Application software that is in wide use and that must meet legal or accepted accounting practices such as payroll will generally be most flexible and readily installable. Specific industry processes mentioned earlier will be likely to require more initial modification. User motivation to keep software cost to a minimum is a key to flexibility in considering system features. A minimum of from 70 to 80 per cent of the original package coding must be preserved and utilized to achieve economy. Many application installations are 98 to 100 per cent package software.

Typically, a business system will require a third of its total software investment for maintenance. This is spread over the life of the system. In other words, an initial $100,000 software development may require an additional $50,000 of maintenance over a 5-year life of the system. Typically, the cost of maintenance is greatest in the initial year. An additional point to observe is that installation cost may exceed software cost. These observations apply to in-house developments and to some extent are avoided in an application package, depending on the maturity and maintenance service accompanying the package. Obviously, the maintenance requirements vary widely, depending upon the nature of the system and the quality of the original product, its vulnerability to changing business climate, etc.

A substantial amount of management dissatisfaction experienced with systems results from inadequate planning for systems maintenance. Recognition of this need and adequate planning for it will permit several major benefits to be realized. First, the initial requirements can be more realistically limited if additional follow-on maintenance is known to be planned. Second, a maintained system is responsive to new requirements and to the demands of the people utilizing the system. System acceptance, effectiveness, and the morale of the organization are improved by a properly maintained system. Third, the life of a systems investment is a direct function of the maintenance it receives. Properly controlled maintenance is essential to the extended useful lifetime of an application system. Once a user has decided to buy a package, the user's attitude should be the same as if it were owned from that point on.

There is no standard prescription for a user installation and user responsibility. There are many workable solutions. Any evaluations of application packages or in-house developments must include specific plans and cost estimates for installation and ongoing maintenance. Outside maintenance will serve in some circumstances. However most situations favor users doing their own maintenance.

OTHER BENEFITS OF APPLICATION PACKAGES

There are several useful benefits that application packages provide that do not require installation of the software on a production basis.

One of these is the opportunity to do equipment evaluation in terms of specific results the user is interested in. Application packages exercise the machinery in a process similar if not identical to that required for any user of that application. Application packages allow equipment evaluations to avoid unnecessary entanglement in technology and concentration on final results.

There are several ways to utilize an application package in this activity. One, of course, is to ask that it be set up on test data sets and run on the equipment. Then it is possible to make a direct evaluation of the result. This, of course, is ideal but may not be possible because of limits on time and cost. A second method would be to use the specific process as designed in the package, and perform desk analysis to evaluate the various pieces of equipment under consideration. A third method found highly reliable is to establish a simulation based upon a running application package. The simulation can be verified against a running, production installation of the package. Once this is done, equipment substitutions can be made into the simulation model with a fairly high degree of confidence. This permits the evaluation of technological improvements in terms of results in a specific process.

A further use of application packages is to facilitate the design and implementation of in-house systems development for which a package can be found. By using a package as a starting point, the final design can be achieved more rapidly with a higher degree of reliability. It is a much more predictable process to review and revise a running systems approach as implemented, than to start at the beginning with a survey of the management requirements of the area in question. As a result, application packages are very frequently used only as "design road maps," replaced with the user's or unique coding.

Table 5-2 helps show the cost areas that "road-map use" of a package does not relieve. It might also be observed that even full use of a package does not eliminate all inside cost. The point at which sufficient system change is required to justify complete reprogramming is difficult to specify, and is obviously a decision that must be carefully made. Even in cases where such a decision is taken, a very substantial amount of time can be saved in the design phase by modifying the design of an existing package.

An additional point recommending this approach is that all strong features of a package would naturally be preserved, whereas an original design might not.

An important point to consider in package selection is hardware configuration. Multiple sources will result in a wide variety of hardware and software technique, whereas a single source of packages comprising a complete system will tend to be standard on hardware and ease selection and evaluation chores.

TABLE 5-2 Typical Division of Application Program Development Cost

	% Cost	% Lapse time
Feasibility	15	15
Functional requirements	15	25
Design	10	15
Develop	35	30
Install	10	15
Maintain	20	Ongoing not included in %

FUTURE TRENDS IN APPLICATION SOFTWARE

Application generators or constructors are an extension of the application package. As application packaging has matured, a wide selection of options has become available for election by the individual user. When a range of options is available, it becomes possible to assemble the options automatically. For example, seven or eight interest calculation methods might be included in an application, or a dozen types of withholdings within payroll. With generators, the user assembles these options, usually by completing a questionnaire. A program is provided using the questionnaire response as input to the application program library, and the appropriate options are included in the end program. Obviously, such an approach is limited by the options that are in the basic library. However, this type of construction makes it extremely convenient to set up an individual program, and for the developers to continue to add optional modules to application. It also facilitates users' supplying their own codes when necessary.

This type of packaging will increase as more application software specifically designed for multiple users is made available. This will be particularly prevalent in terminal systems, where the number of applications is reasonably narrow and the computer support programs are designed to concentrate on offering the user a wide variety of options that are likely to be required.

A second major trend is in the integration of applications. First-generation application packages ignored other processes, and were treated as straightforward, narrow problems. Limitations of software and compilers along with the newness of the concept of application packages resulted in that limited outlook. When second-generation application systems began making their appearance, systems information interfaces provided common input systems and common file maintenance systems.

Most application systems designed to date are of the second-generation variety. There are, of course, wide ranges of sophistication in the integration of such systems. However, integration is achieved in the second generation through a program or process which passes data from one system to the next.

Third-generation systems, in their infancy today, will provide for systems integration through the use of common files. The interface process will disappear as data sets become common between systems. This approach holds a great deal of promise, but also introduces problems. Maintaining application modularity and dependence for software maintenance and fast implementation is a totally different problem in a second-generation system, from one with a common database. Initial design must be more farsighted. Initial cost and time will be greater. For the immediate future, most application package users will find second-generation systems least risky. However, after problems on third-generation designs are solved in use, the organization and information benefits of third-generation systems will have a dramatic impact on hardware and software approach throughout the industry.

Part Five
Communications Technology

Introduction

M. WEINER   *Senior Associate, John Diebold & Associates, New York, New York*

From a layman's perspective, data communications is any process of transmitting information. The processes range from the audio communications used in speech, to the visual communications used with semaphores, to the electronic communications used in high-speed transmission of data between computers. In the field of automatic data processing, however, data communications has a rather esoteric definition. It is usually defined as the movement of information encoded in machine-processable form between two or more machines, by means of electrical transmission systems. Transmission systems usually include input-output devices, the electrical transmission links proper, and related communication switching systems.

From a management perspective, data communications is usually considered to be the physical movement of information between remote locations of a company's operations by means of machine-to-machine communications technology. In a typical corporate data communications system, geographically dispersed factories, field offices, distribution points, and regional, divisional, or corporate headquarters locations are linked together for the purposes of information flow, accessing of centralized data files, or the accessing of raw computer capability at a centralized or regionalized data center. Effective utilization of data communications can result in reduced costs, increased speed in the flow of information to all levels of management, and increased managerial control of the corporation.

During the past 5 years, data communications has been characterized by a rapid if not frantic pace of change in technology, economic relationships, government regulation, and user demand for services. The rapid growth in data communications is expected to accelerate during the next decade. Primary impetuses for the growth in the use of data communications are cost reductions due to technological changes and improvements; the introduction of an old but now-revitalized concept known as competition to make the regulated communications carriers (primarily telephone companies) more responsive to user demands for new and improved services; and the basic need for faster, cheaper, and more efficient ways to move expanding quantities of information. From a management perspective, the forecast of continued rapid technological and regulatory change argues well for the growth in opportunities to exploit data communications in a cost-effective manner. In particular, management will have a wider spectrum of cost-effective alternatives to consider, as the cost premium for more rapid transmission of data declines.

In evaluating the need for a data communications system, management must consider two basic factors: (1) the success of a corporation or other large organization is to a considerable extent dependent upon information and the movement of this information, and (2) a data communications system can be used to increase the speed of information flow almost to the point of "instantaneous" transmission over considerable distances. A perspicacious management will not be befuddled by esoteric jargon and complex technology, but will focus on the primary investment decision. Conceptually, evaluating a data communications system is no different from evaluating any other investment. The countervening costs and benefits are measured and the impact on the corporation's bottom line is determined. For a data communications system, in particular, the investment decision for management should be based on whether the benefit from a faster and perhaps more error-free delivery system is sufficient to justify the high cost premium inherent in the use of data communications. The trend toward less costly data communications in itself does not negate the need to cost-justify any data communications system.

Before embarking on the installation of a data communications system, alternative means for information flow should be examined. Mail, airmail, messenger services, and voice telephone are examples of alternatives that can be equally effective at a much reduced cost. Do the incremental benefits from the use of data communications compensate for the incremental costs? Will the success of the corporation be sufficiently enhanced by faster information flow to offset the cost of using data communications?

Often the need for a data communications system is based on the requirement to respond to a very rapidly changing environment. An airline reservation system that relies completely on a single inventory of seats exemplifies a rapidly changing environment requiring a fast response. In other cases, the need for data communications is based upon the desire of senior management to exercise closer control over the company's operations. In either case, estimates of the dollar value of improvements, though intangible, in faster information must be developed not only to justify a data communications system itself but also to evaluate the incremental benefits of the wide spectrum of alternative systems and associated costs.

The use of cost-benefits analysis techniques is not the only prerequisite for effective evaluation of a proposed data communications system. As a general rule, data communications systems are characterized by the highest levels of complexity, sophistication, and cost in hardware, software, ADP personnel skills, and ADP management skills. Therefore, management must ensure that the basic parameters of the proposed data communications system are properly defined. From client experience, John Diebold & Associates has found five major parameters that must be thoroughly investigated in the evaluations of a proposed data communications system. These are:

1. *What is the function of the data communications system?* A clearly defined and detailed set of functional objectives is prerequisite for a success-

ful management evaluation. The objectives provide the basis for identifying and quantifying the potential benefits to be derived from the proposed systems. The objectives also serve as a uniform standard or benchmark for evaluating alternative systems. Moreover, clearly defined functional objectives will preclude the situation where the technical experts propose state-of-the-art solutions and then hunt for problems to solve.

2. *What are the volumes and distribution of data to be transmitted?* The costs of a communications system are directly related to the transmission volumes. The consequences of inaccurately estimating the transmission volume can be sizable. Moreover, the estimates of peak transmission volumes are most important, since the system must have adequate capacity to handle peak transmission. On the other hand, a system can be designed with less peak capacity, if the consequences of occasional delays are not significant. In either case, peak transmission volumes are prerequisite for effective evaluation of alternative designs.

3. *What is the reliability of the system?* Any proposed data communications system will be susceptible to hardware and software failures. The consequences of a failure itself and the consequences of alternative recovery times must be evaluated, so that the costs to maintain backup systems and recovery procedures will be compatible with the economic consequences of a system failure.

4. *What is the capability for growth?* A corporation is a dynamic entity. New additions to product line, new markets, growth in markets, changes in market penetration, etc., all impact the company's information network. Corporate growth itself usually dictates higher data transmission volumes in the future. Moreover, as corporate users become more knowledgeable about a company's data communications system, demand for data communications service will grow. Therefore, the proposed communications system must have adequate flexibility to absorb larger transmission volumes with minor changes to the system. Moreover, the data communications system should be designed based upon planned or anticipated changes in the structure or needs of the corporation it will serve.

5. *What is the total cost of the system?* A total cost-benefits analysis of all alternative data communications system is prerequisite for effective evaluation.

In summary, as in any financial decision, the evaluation of corporate investments in data communications systems requires clearly defined functional objectives, well-thought-out alternatives, and carefully calculated cost-benefit analyses.

Chapter 1

Communication Basics

JOHN E. COX

Vice President, International Telephone & Telegraph Corp.,
Stamford, Connecticut; formerly Vice President,
Engineering, Western Union, Upper Saddle River, New Jersey

MICHAEL M. FLACK

Continental Telephone Laboratories, Hickory, North Carolina;
formerly Engineering Division, Western Union, Upper Saddle
River, New Jersey

One of the earliest forms of electrical communication was the telegraph. The message to be transmitted was coded into a form that could be described by the presence or absence of an electrical current. This permitted transmission between remote locations over an electrical conductor, usually a single copper wire, with the ground providing a return path. While this unsophisticated arrangement bears little resemblance to a modern data communication system, it does provide the basic requirement of the latter, the transmission of information in a symbolic language by an "on-off" signal.

In more recent years the means of transmitting information between locations has been determined by the predominant requirement for voice communication. A circuit used for the transmission of speech is not designed to convey the "on-off" signal which is characteristic of telegraphic or digital communication. As a result, it is necessary to translate the digital signal (dc pulse) to an *analog form* (a sinusoidal frequency signal) for transmission over these facilities.

With the increasing demand, in recent years, for data communications, the pendulum has started to swing the other way. Emphasis is being placed on the transmission of digital information without the traditional conversion to analog form. Plans are well under way for the construction of communications networks dedicated to this form of transmission. The first leg of one such system is at this writing operational between Atlanta and Cincinnati, and will soon be extended to serve all major Eastern United States cities and eventually the entire nation.

One might question the wisdom of segregating the network used for transmitting digital information from that presently employed for analog transmission. The answer is twofold. Performance impairments, such as noise, once introduced into an analog system cannot be readily removed. On the other hand, a digital signal may be easily regenerated at intermediate locations to its original form, with most of the impairments contributed by the transmission system erased. The result: less errors. The other advantage is increased efficiency in the utilization of the facility. Thus, the transmission system designed primarily for digital communication promises improved performance at lower cost.

In practice, the two networks may not be completely separated, but may share some portion of a common transmission system when there is a requirement for both analog and digital traffiic. This technique is discussed later in this Chapter.

The User's Stake The majority of communications users will prefer to leave the many intricate decisions and trade-offs required to establish a viable digital transmission system to the common carrier from whom they lease services. However, a basic understanding of the transmission equipment employed, together with their limitations, will be invaluable, to many, in selecting the most suitable and economical services and offerings for their particular requirements, and in planning for expansion of their data processing systems.

CIRCUIT PERFORMANCE

The performance of a data circuit can be most easily measured by one criterion: the number of errors received that were not transmitted. An error may thus be defined as the reception of an information bit that was not transmitted, the absence at the receiver of a bit that was transmitted, or the change of state of an information bit.

Transmission errors may result from various disturbances to which the transmission medium may be subjected. While any one of these perturbations may, if of sufficient magnitude, cause an unacceptable performance, it is more usual to find that this condition results from a combination of several causes, of which the following are typical:

Noise Electrical "noise," i.e., unwanted signals, is inherent in all forms of electrical communication. The very flow of electricity through a conductor produces noise due to the collision of electrons within molecules. The amount of noise produced in this manner is proportional to the temperature of the conductor. At normally encountered temperatures and with proper design techniques, this source of noise is not usually serious. A similar source of noise, which is also proportional to temperature, is caused by radiation from a mass. This form of noise becomes an important consideration when extremely sensitive receivers are employed to detect weak signals, such as those in a microwave system. Noise from these sources is usually termed *thermal noise*.

Many elements of a communication system are nonlinear by nature and, as a result, cause unwanted modulation products which appear as another form of noise. The resulting interference is often referred to as *intermodulation distortion* or *intermodulation noise*.

Because noise generated by the means described above is usually randomly distributed, its energy may be considered to be uniformly spread over the entire bandwidth of a communication channel. The absolute quantity of noise energy present is of little importance. It is the amount of noise power relative to the power of the desired signal that controls the degree of communication impairment, called the *signal-to-noise ratio* (S/N).

For error-free digital transmission, it is necessary to detect accurately which of two possible states exists, and when a transition between them occurs. By the selection of an appropriate threshold, this detection process can be accomplished in the presence of noise levels which would make an analog circuit unusable. For this reason, uniformly distributed noise (so-called white noise) is seldom encountered at such excessively high levels that it will cause a digital circuit to be unusable. However, this form of noise does reduce the tolerance of the circuit to withstand other impairments. (See Figure 1-1.)

Impulse Noise. This form of noise can be a serious cause of errors in data transmission, particularly at the higher speeds. Unlike the types of noise previously discussed, impulse noise does not have a uniform distribution of energy. As the name implies, the energy is concentrated in short-duration impulses which may have a very great amplitude.

Impulse noise may be generated in a number of ways. The most troublesome sources are lightning, power line transients, switching and relay operation, and rotating machinery in communications rooms. Unlike white noise, impulse noise often exhibits amplitudes exceeding that of the desired signal. If an impulse occurs at the instant that the receiving equipment is expecting to receive a change of digital state, it may be interpreted as a signal when none is actually present. The result will be an error.

Delay Distortion The absolute time taken by an electrical signal to travel from the transmitter to the receiver will not affect the data signal if this delay is constant across the frequency spectrum of the communication channel. However, communications systems contain electrical filters and capacitive and inductive elements which cause the delay to be greater at some frequencies than it is at others. This "relative delay characteristic" will typically be as shown in Figure 1-2, with the lower and higher frequencies taking longer to traverse the system. The shortest delay will usually be

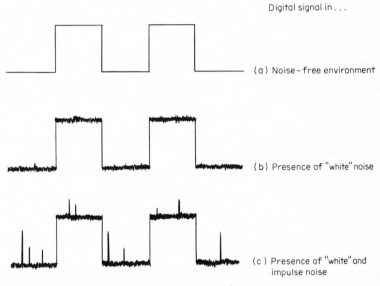

Digital signal in . . .

(a) Noise-free environment

(b) Presence of "white" noise

(c) Presence of "white" and impulse noise

Fig. 1-1   Types of noise.

experienced near the center of the band at about 1,800 Hertz. (Hertz = cycles per second, commonly designated Hz.)

Since the data signal in analog form will utilize different frequencies, some components will be delayed longer than others.

Fortunately, corrective measures can be taken to reduce the relative delay. Since the absolute delay is of little consequence, within reasonable bounds, it is possible to add delay to the circuit selectively by the use of an external network. This network, or "equalizer," is arranged to introduce greater delay in the center of the band and lesser amounts toward the edges. Because the equalizer contains several tuned circuits to provide the desired characteristic, the resulting equalized channel characteristic will not be perfectly flat, but will contain a slight ripple as is shown in Figure 1-2.

Amplitude Distortion This characteristic refers to the amplitude of the waves transmitted by the communications channel relative to their frequency. The ideal channel would provide a uniform signal amplitude across the bandwidth required for transmission. Outside of the desired band it should exhibit very high attenuation to eliminate interference from out-of-band-signals and noise. (Attenuation is the loss of amplitude of the signal.)

In practice, the idealized situation cannot be attained. The filters employed in communications systems cannot suddenly change from low to very high attenuation at a particular frequency. Instead, they will gradually increase the attenuation over a range of frequencies. The attenuation of cable, an integral part of all communication systems, will increase with frequency. Transformers, capacitors, and inductors will also add to this form of distortion.

Amplitude distortion can be reduced by equalization in a similar manner to that employed for delay distortion. If amplitude distortion were allowed to accumulate without correction, some frequencies, particularly at the high-frequency end of the channel (i.e., of the band of frequencies used) would be attenuated more than others. This would cause distortion of the data signal and, if severe enough, cause errors or reduce the margin against other impairments. As the speed of the data to be transmitted is increased, the frequency response of the channel must be flatter.

Phase Jitter Although this form of distortion has always been present in communications channels, it has been of little significance in voice or low-speed data transmission.

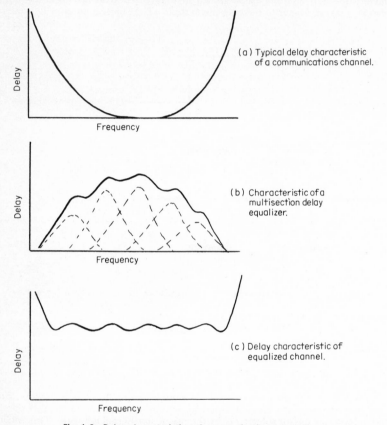

(a) Typical delay characteristic of a communications channel.

(b) Characteristic of a multisection delay equalizer.

(c) Delay characteristic of equalized channel.

Fig. 1-2 Delay characteristics of communications channels.

At speeds above 1,800 bps (bits per second), phase jitter becomes a critical consideration in the design of a circuit.

Phase jitter is the unwanted phase or incidental frequency modulation of the wanted signal as it traverses the transmission path. The major source of phase jitter originates in the carrier frequencies used to translate the channels in a frequency division multiplexing (FDM) system as discussed later herein. (Multiplexing is the combining of discrete units of information, each of which is carried within its own frequency band, into a larger bandwidth for a single transmission.)

Every effort is made in the equipment design to produce pure, noise-free carrier sources. However, because of ground currents and ripple on the power supplies, there is always a small amount of phase modulation present on the carrier supplies, which is transferred to the channel. The modulation is usually directly related to the power line frequency or its harmonics and, as a result, modulation products above 300 Hz are rare.

Impairment and Data Speed Trade-off All the impairments described above are present in every communication channel in varying degrees. The error performance of a data channel will be determined by the combined contributions of all impairments. It is, therefore, possible to make trade-offs of one type of distortion against another. If, for instance, a channel is found to have a very low noise contribution, then a greater amount of, say, amplitude or delay distortion could be tolerated for a given error performance.

As the data speed is increased, the tolerance to withstand the shortcomings of the channel is reduced. Thus, for a given speed of transmission, the channel may be considered to require a minimum figure of merit for satisfactory performance. This hypothetical figure of merit would be determined by the combined weighted effect of the impairments. If the data speed is increased, then a higher figure of merit will be required. This may be achieved by reducing only one or two of the impairments. Usually, the necessary improvement is obtained by more careful equalization of delay and amplitude distortion, which is much easier to achieve than reduction of the other impairments. This process is termed *circuit conditioning*, and may be ordered from a common carrier in several grades to meet most data requirements. It accounts for the higher price attached to higher grades of circuits, independent of distance.

THE ANALOG TRANSMISSION MEDIUM

The Elements of a Network There are several methods of transmitting information between two locations. Each has advantages and disadvantages, both technical and economical, which makes it more attractive for a particular application. The typical circuit will utilize several of these transmission methods, each selected to provide optimum performance and cost for a particular portion of the network.

A circuit between two subscribers may be considered as consisting of three elements: the *local loop*, the *intracity trunk*, and the *intercity trunk*. The number of each required will be dependent on the geographic location of the two subscribers and the overall length of the circuit. The local loop provides the connection between the subscriber and the local central office or equipment room of the carrier. The intracity trunk extends this local central office to another in the same city, which may be co-located with the long-haul transmission equipment. The intercity trunks, as the name implies, provide the long-haul portion of the network between cities.

Fig. 1-3 Typical multipair plastic insulated cable. (*Courtesy Northern Electric Co., Ltd.*)

Transmission by Paired Cables Where the distance to be traversed is short, a cable consisting of a number of pairs of copper conductors enclosed within an outer moisture- and abrasion-proof sheath is an economical solution (Figure 1-3).

The characteristics of paired cables are such that the attenuation increases with frequency, typically doubling from 1,000 Hz to 3,000 Hz. In addition, the attenuation is relatively high, of the order of 2 decibels per mile, depending on the size of the copper conductors. These characteristics can be reduced by adding external inductive components to the cable at regular intervals, usually every 6,000 ft.

These characteristics limit the use of paired cable to only short distances when digital transmission is employed. When the digital signal is converted to analog form for transmission, the length of the cable can be extended, but equalization becomes more difficult. As a result, it becomes economical to use time or frequency division multiplexing techniques on the cable when the distance exceeds a few miles. Thus, transmission directly over cable pairs is used almost exclusively for local loops and short intracity trunks, where the impairments can be tolerated.

Carrier Transmission Cable pairs can be arranged to accommodate more than one circuit by taking advantage of the wideband characteristic of unloaded cable which is not utilized for voice or low-speed data transmission. Voice transmission requires only a small portion of the available frequency spectrum, from about 200 Hz to a little over

3 kilohertz (kHz). Paired cable is capable of transmitting information in excess of 1 megahertz (MHz), although with greatly increased attenuation.

Multiplexing With carrier transmission, a number of voice channels are multiplexed by modulation techniques to permit their simultaneous transmission over a single facility. When these channels are stacked one above the other so that each occupies a discrete but separate portion of a wider frequency spectrum, they are said to be "frequency division multiplexed" (FDM). At the receiving end they are "unscrambled" into the original voice channels.

This concept can probably best be understood by analogy with a number of radio broadcast stations. Several radio stations can each carry different programs by transmission on different frequencies via the same transmission medium (electromagnetic waves). At the receiving location, a receiver can be tuned to any one of the transmitting stations, or a number of receivers can be employed so that all the programs can be received separately. In the case of carrier transmission by cable pairs, the transmitters are of much lower power, the transmission medium is a pair of copper wires, and the receivers are not tunable. However the basic concept is the same.

The multiplexing process may be accomplished by either frequency or amplitude modulation. That is to say, variations of the amplitude of the signal to be transmitted change either the frequency of a carrier frequency, or the amplitude of a carrier frequency.

For example, suppose one is "stacking" 12 voice channels of 4 kHz each.[1] A total bandwidth of 48 kHz would be required. Carrier waves of much higher frequency than 48 kHz would be used, but the total frequency spectrum taken up would be 48 kHz. With frequency modulation, the top 4 kHz of the spectrum would be used for the top channel. Transmission would be at constant amplitude, but the frequency would be made to vary within the 4-kHz range — say from 104 to 108 kHz. At the receiving end, the signal would be demodulated to reproduce the variations in amplitude of the original signal. The second channel would be frequency-modulated within the 100- to 104-kHz range, and so on. With amplitude modulation, the top channel would be transmitted at a constant frequency of 106 kHz, but the signal would be amplitude-modulated to correspond to the amplitude of the original signal. The next channel would be transmitted at 102 kHz, and so on.

These modulation processes are illustrated in Figure 1-4. Again, it should be stated that the carrier frequency is very much higher than the highest modulating frequency. Although frequency modulation does offer some potential improvement in noise performance, it requires a greater bandwidth for near distortion-free transmission than does amplitude modulation. In addition, the cost of equipment for frequency modulation and demodulation is generally slightly greater. For these reasons, amplitude modulation is the almost universal choice for frequency division multiplexing.

When a carrier is amplitude-modulated by a signal, a complex waveform is produced which contains components comprising the original two frequencies (i.e., the carrier frequency and the modulating signal frequency), the sum and difference of these two frequencies, and their harmonics. The original modulating frequency, which is much lower than that of the modulated signal, and the harmonically related products are readily removed by simple filters. This leaves a spectrum of bandwidth occupied by the carrier frequency in the center and with sidebands above and below this frequency. These sidebands will extend to the highest modulating frequency above and below the carrier. If the information is transmitted in this form, it is referred to as *double sideband, transmitted carrier transmission* (DSB-TC).

DSB-TC is a low-cost form of transmission, since the signal filtering requirements are minimal. For this reason, it is occasionally employed for carrier systems with only a few channels operating over short distances, for instance local loops. However, the theoretical minimum frequency spacing between channels is twice the highest modulating frequency, and in practice, additional separation must be provided to permit filtering between channels. This limits the number of channels that can be transmitted.

The resultant transmission will concentrate the power at the carrier frequency, rather

---

[1] Although useful bandwidth of a voice channel is 3 kHz (in multiplex systems), we speak of a 4-kHz-wide channel in order to comprehend the separation between channels when stacking them. This separation is called *guard band*.

than in the information-carrying sidebands. A number of techniques are available to avoid handling this high carrier power, which would add to cost. It is not practical, because of the proximity of the wanted sidebands, to remove the carrier by filtering. The same effect can, however, be achieved readily in the modulator itself. The amount by which the level of the carrier can be suppressed is determined by the degree of balance obtained between the diodes or transistors used in the modulator. This technique is called *double sideband, suppressed carrier transmission* (DSB-SC) and is often employed for multichannel systems used over short distances such as intra-city trunks and local loops.

Each of the two sidebands completely describes the information being transmitted,

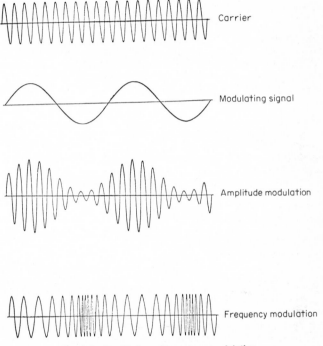

Fig. 1-4 Amplitude and frequency modulation.

so that only one is essential. The other contains redundant information and occupies valuable bandwidth. Frequencies below about 200 Hz contribute little to the fidelity of speech. Since this unnecessary band of 0–200 Hz is adjacent to the carrier after modulation, it provides a region of about 400 Hz between the two sidebands. This is sufficient spectrum to permit removal of one of the sidebands with conventional filtering techniques. This *single sideband, suppressed carrier* (SSB-SC) method of modulation is more costly to achieve because of the stringent filtering requirements, but permits channels to be spaced very closely, usually only 4 kHz apart. For these reasons, SSB-SC carrier systems are most commonly employed on intercity trunk routes where the added equipment cost at the terminals is offset by the larger traffic-carrying capacity. If these routes are of relatively short length, the carrier system may be applied to paired cables. Longer and heavier density routes will employ coaxial cable or microwave radio as the transmission medium.

Frequency Division Multiplexing Carrier systems designed for use on paired cables will usually employ only one or two stages of modulation, and will provide up to 24 circuits. Microwave systems and coaxial cables can accommodate many more channels, often thousands, so the multiplexing scheme must provide a logical building-block arrangement to permit economical growth and circuit routing. This is achieved by consecutive steps of modulation.

Although minor differences are encountered between the various common carriers and equipment manufacturers, one universal modulation plan is representative. This plan follows the recommendations of CCITT (The International Telephone and Telegraph Consultative Committee). Twelve individual channels are modulated to form a *group* occupying the spectrum from 60 to 108 kHz. Five of these groups are then modulated to provide a 60-channel *supergroup* occupying the spectrum from 312 to 552 kHz. If the system is to have a capacity of less than 900 channels, the requisite number of supergroups are each modulated with an appropriate carrier frequency to stack them one above the other for application to the coaxial cable or radio system.

Larger-density systems employ another step called a *mastergroup*. The CCITT recommends a 300-channel mastergroup comprising five supergroups in the band from 812 to 2,044 kHz. AT&T and some national administrations employ a 10-supergroup, 600-channel mastergroup. A final modulation step places the required number of mastergroups in their specific line assignments for transmission. Provision is made for very large coaxial cable systems to have an added level of three 300-channel mastergroups, called a *super mastergroup*. This degree of standardization permits end-to-end compatibility of equipment made by different manufacturers, and is invaluable on international systems where equipment built and designed in different countries must be interconnected.

When paired or coaxial cables are employed as the means of transmission, the signal is attenuated by the cable facility, with the greatest attenuation at the higher carrier frequencies. This attenuation must be overcome by amplifiers and equalizers, called *repeaters*, spaced at intervals along the cable. These repeaters will reinforce the signal strength well before it is indistinguishable from the noise present in the cable.

Since the attenuation of the cable varies significantly with temperature, means must be provided to adjust automatically the amount of amplification provided within the system. *Regulation*, as this process is called, is accomplished by constantly monitoring the received signal for changes in level. The change in level is then used to control the gain of amplifiers in sympathy with variations in the attenuation of the cable. In large-capacity systems, each group, supergroup, or mastergroup may be individually regulated at the terminals and variations in the frequency-attenuation characteristics may also require compensation.

The heart of a frequency division multiplex system is the supply used to generate the various carrier frequencies. Not only must they be stable, but they must also be very accurately tuned to avoid a displacement of the signal frequencies between terminals. When the carrier is transmitted this is not a problem, because the carrier itself provides an accurate means of demodulation. When this is not the case, the carrier must be regenerated at the receive terminal at exactly the frequency used at the transmit terminal. For this reason, it is common practice to transmit a reference frequency between the two ends of a system. This frequency is used to synchronize the receive oscillator to the oscillator employed at the transmit end of the system.

Time Division Multiplexing With frequency division multiplex, the bandwidth is subdivided into a number of channels on a full-time basis. Another multiplexing approach, called *time division multiplexing* (TDM) makes available the full bandwidth of the system for all channels but allocates only a portion of the time to each. This process requires that the information to be transmitted be sampled repetitively to ascertain the signal level. Provided that this sampling is carried out at a rate of not less than twice the highest modulating frequency to be transmitted, there is little impairment to the intelligibility of the channel. In the case of a nominal 4-kHz voice channel, the sampling rate must be at least 8,000 times each second, or alternatively stated, each channel must be sampled once every 1/8,000 sec (125 ms). The time between these consecutive samples of a channel can be used for sampling other channels. It is, of course, necessary that the transmitter and receiver be kept in synchronization, so that the received samples can be associated with the correct channel. This is achieved by the transmission of a synchronizing pulse during each frame.

When analog information is to be transmitted by time division techniques, the pulses representing each sample must be modulated in some manner. This can be achieved by varying the amplitude, width, or position of the pulse in sympathy with the amplitude of the modulating signal. However, because of the degradation of the pulses by the transmission medium, these modulation methods have not gained wide acceptance. Another modulation method which overcomes these disadvantages is *pulse code modulation* (PCM). This technique eliminates analog transmission completely and, instead, codes the sampled analog amplitude information into a binary format. As a result, it is necessary only to determine the presence or absence of information bits to reconstruct the intelligence.

T Carrier Systems   Pulse code modulation carrier systems have become a major transmission method in the past decade, and are widely used for intracity and short intercity trunks on paired cables. New systems are under development which will permit the application of PCM to long-haul trunks using microwave radio or coaxial cables. These systems have come to be called generically *T carrier systems*, although this is a misnomer, since that designation actually describes the conditioned line over which the systems operate. In Bell Laboratories/Western Electric Company terminology (the first United States company to exploit this type of transmission), the terminals are designated as D-1, D-2, or D-3 channel banks. Although there are substantial

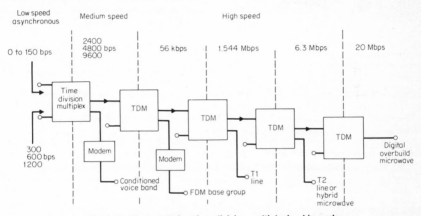

Fig. 1-5   Western Union time division multiplexing hierarchy.

differences in the configuration and application of these terminals, they all operate in a basically similar manner and provide a line bit rate of 1.544 Mb per sec. The D-1 and D-3 channel banks are designed for relatively short-haul applications, whereas the D-2 bank is designed for medium-haul applications over 1.544-Mb-per-sec T-1 lines or, with further multiplexing, over 6.3-Mb-per-sec T-2 lines.

The multiplexing scheme adopted by Western Union is shown in Figure 1-5. This hierarchy is typical of that which will be employed by other carriers. It should be noted that the 56-kb-per-sec, 1.544-Mb-per-sec, and 6.3-Mb-per-sec levels are established by the characteristics of the T carrier systems. In some instances, the total digital capacity shown at the higher level of multiplexing may not be available to the user because of the need for overhead bits in transmission to ensure frame and system synchronization.[2]

[2] A sampling rate of 8 kHz is employed for each of the 24 channels in the system. Since the sampled analog signal level is to be converted to binary form, the amplitude must be approximated to one of a number of quantum levels. The number of quantizing levels that can be employed is restricted by the practical consideration of the number of bits that can readily be transmitted.

Most systems employ an 8-bit "word" with one of the bits used to transmit signaling information either exclusively or in every sixth frame. A 7-bit word will provide 128 levels; however, a code of 7 zeros may be troublesome to the transmission line where timing information is recovered from the digital signal. As a result, 127 quantizing levels are available to describe the sample amplitude. This amplitude may be either positive or negative, so 64 levels are employed for positive values and 64 for negative values, with one level representing zero level. Since the number of quantizing

The analog information is transmitted as a digital signal and is completely described by the presence or absence of pulses. While this signal will suffer the same impairments as are experienced by analog signals during transmission, such as noise, attenuation, or pulse distortion, it would require a very major impairment to make the pulse unrecognizable. As with FDM systems, PCM systems employ repeaters (or more correctly, regenerators) at intervals along the cable, typically 6,000 ft apart. The purpose of the regenerator is to recognize the presence or absence of the distorted received pulse and regenerate a clean new one at the appropriate time for retransmission. It should be noted that this eliminates the cumulative effects of circuit impairments and, apart from quantization noise, transmission can be free of most forms of distortion. It is this feature which makes pure digital transmission so attractive for both analog and data circuits.

Fig. 1-6 Six-tube coaxial cable. Note the complement of paired conductors in the centers of the coaxial tubes.

Since systems of this type can make use of modern low-cost integrated circuit components, they offer potential cost savings over FDM systems which employ costly filters.

Coaxial Cables Coaxial tubes consist of a center conductor surrounded by a circular outer conductor. The center conductor is kept at the exact center of the outer conductor by means of special insulating disks. A cable of this type will be made up of several coaxial tubes surrounded by an outer moisture- and abrasion-proof sheath. It is also common practice to include a number of paired conductors in the cable for voice frequency and control applications. (See Figure 1-6.)

Great care must be exercised in the installation of this type of cable to ensure that no irregularities are introduced. The installed cost of coaxial cables is high, but they are capable of carrying several thousand channels using FDM or PCM techniques. To minimize temperature variations and physical distortion, they are usually buried or placed in ducts and, consequently, provide highly reliable communication over long distances.

MICROWAVE RADIO

Microwave frequencies extend upwards from about 1 gigahertz (1 GHz = 1,000 MHz). Below these frequencies, noise from both human-made and natural sources requires

---

levels is limited, and the signal amplitude must be transmitted as the nearest of these levels, the received decoded information will have a slightly different level from that of the original. This level difference is termed *quantization distortion* or noise.

The greatest quantization distortion that can occur is one-half of the difference between levels. If the levels were each of equal value, the amount of quantization distortion would be relatively much greater at low-amplitude levels than it would be at high values. To illustrate this point, assume that each of the 64 quantizing levels represents a step of one unit of amplitude. The maximum quantization distortion that can occur will be one-half of a unit. A low-amplitude signal of one-half a unit will be coded as level 1, an error of 100 per cent, while an amplitude of $63\frac{1}{2}$ units will be coded as level 64, an error of less than 0.8 per cent. To reduce this problem, the quantizing steps are compressed at low-amplitude levels. In earlier systems this was achieved by compressing the analog signal prior to encoding at the transmitting terminal followed by a corresponding expansion at the receiving end after decoding. More recent equipment achieves the same result by using nonlinear coding steps.

Since 8 bits are required to describe each amplitude sample for 24 channels, the frame length is 8×24 or 192 bits, to which an additional synchronization or framing bit is added, making a total of 193 bits. Each frame is repeated 8,000 times every second so that the line rate is $193 \times 8,000$ or 1.544 kb per sec. If the digital information were transmitted in this form, with unipolar pulses, there would be a significant amount of meaningful energy at frequencies from direct current all the way up to twice the bit rate. This wide frequency spectrum is difficult for the transmission facility to accommodate. To overcome this problem, each alternate mark or binary "1" bit in the code is reversed in polarity. This process changes the transmitted energy in such a way that the maximum energy is concentrated at one-half the bit rate, and there is no dc component.

the use of high transmitter powers to provide an acceptable signal-to-noise ratio at the receiver. As the frequency increases, noise from these sources reduces, and noise generated within the equipment becomes a more significant factor and provides an upper-frequency limitation.

The Federal Communications Commission (FCC) has the mandate to control the use of radio frequencies in the United States, and it has established several microwave bands for communications use. Separate bands are assigned for use by common carriers, government, right-of-way companies (railroads, pipelines, etc.), general business, and other categories. In each of these bands, the FCC rigorously controls the type of emission and the amount of bandwidth that is utilized. The allocations shown in Table 1-1 are presently employed by common carriers. Each of these bands is subdivided to permit a number of microwave radio channels to be operated in parallel, each occupying a discrete portion of the total bandwidth. Each of the bands has characteristics which make it more suitable for some applications than for others.

TABLE 1-1   Spectrum Allocations Employed by Common Carriers

Band	Spectrum	Total bandwidth
2 GHz	2,110–2,130 MHz	20 MHz
	& 2,160–2,180 MHz	20 MHz
4 GHz	3,700–4,200 MHz	500 MHz
6 GHz	5,925–6,425 MHz	500 MHz
11 GHz	10,700–11,700 MHz	1,000 MHz

The 2-GHz band has a very limited bandwidth, and the radio equipment to operate at this frequency can be produced at relatively low cost. Consequently, its use is appropriate for light-density routes where only a small number of channels will ever be required. The 4-GHz and 6-GHz bands are usually employed for long, heavily loaded routes, since they can provide a wide bandwidth and good propagation conditions. Transmission at 11 GHz and higher is severely affected by attenuation due to heavy rainfall. As a result, this band is more suitable for transmission over short distances even though it can accommodate a large number of channels. It is particularly useful as an entrance link to large cities where congestion of the lower-frequency bands may be severe.

With the burgeoning demand for communication in recent years, the valuable commodity of microwave bandwidth is rapidly becoming depleted. Each year it becomes more difficult to plan new microwave paths without causing interference to existing systems or employing circuitous routes. To alleviate this situation, serious consideration is being given to exploiting presently unused bands at higher frequencies. While these bands will be suitable only for very short distances, they will provide relief where the congestion is most critical: in and around large metropolitan areas. They will also provide another means of furnishing intracity trunks and, for some large bandwidth users, local loops.

Characteristics of Microwave Radiation   Radiation of microwave energy has many properties in common with light. It can be concentrated into a narrow beam. It will be attenuated according to the inverse square law; that is, if the length of the path is doubled, the attenuation will be increased fourfold. It can also be reflected and refracted by changes in density of the transmission medium.

The microwave transmitter provides a relatively small amount of power to the antenna, typically 1 to 10 watts. If this energy were to be dispersed omnidirectionally by the antenna, only a very small portion would be radiated in a particular direction. Since our concern is with transmission between two fixed locations, most of the radiated energy would be wasted. To overcome this, highly directional antennas are employed which concentrate the radiation in a specific direction toward the receiver. Virtually all microwave communications systems employ a metallic parabolic reflector in one form or another to achieve this. The microwave energy is radiated toward the reflector at its focal point and concentrated in a narrow beam. The larger the reflector, the narrower the beam. Reflectors for this purpose are available with diameters ranging from 2 to 15 ft and larger, with 6 and 8 ft being the most commonly used.

Microwaves are radiated in an essentially straight-line path between the transmitter and the receiver. It is, therefore, important that there be no obstruction between them, such as hills, mountains, or large buildings. To provide an optical path over such obstructions, it is often necessary to mount the antennas on tall towers or buildings. In practice, the microwave horizon can be further distant than the optical horizon, because the microwave beam is bent slightly downwards by variations in atmospheric density. This permits the antenna to be pointed slightly upwards, so that the microwave path can be extended beyond the optical line of sight.

The length of a microwave path is limited by the amount of signal provided to the receiver. In addition to receiving a signal strength much greater than the noise, a margin must be provided to guard against abnormal propagation conditions. The factors which control the received signal strength are the transmitted power, the diameter of the antennas, the attenuation of the path and, of course, the microwave horizon and path obstructions. These considerations will yield paths of typically 25 miles in length, although under some circumstances they may be very much shorter

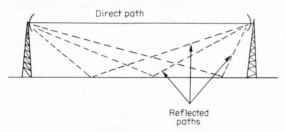

Fig. 1-7 Multipath microwave reflections.

or longer. Microwave systems may be made up of many microwave paths connected in tandem; in fact, several systems span the entire continent.

Fading The microwave beam radiated by the parabolic reflector is not completely parallel. Some of the signal energy will be transmitted at an angle to the straight-line path and may be reflected by an intervening surface before reaching the receive antenna. The reflected path will be longer than the direct path and there will be a difference in the phase of the two received signals. Depending on the phase relationship of the two receive signals, they may tend to reinforce or cancel one another. When cancellation occurs, the signal provided to the receiver will be smaller and the performance will be degraded. This condition is called *multipath fading*. The microwave path is engineered so that the normally received signal is greater than that required for satisfactory operation to provide a margin against fades (see Figure 1-7).

Because the atmospheric and surface conditions are continually varying, the points of reflection and the amount of energy reflected will also vary continuously. The resulting fade conditions can be predicted accurately in terms of what percentage of time the received signal will be above certain levels. It would be very uneconomical, if not impossible, to engineer the path so that the received signal is always in excess of the required strength.

For systems where a high degree of reliability is required, additional steps must be taken beyond providing a large fade margin. The increased reliability is obtained by employing two receivers to detect signals which have arrived by separate paths, and then selecting the best one. This process is called *diversity operation*. When two antennas are employed with adequate vertical separation between them, there will be only a small probability of fading occurring on both paths simultaneously. In this space diversity arrangement, it is necessary to provide only one transmitter, although a second one will usually be provided to yield a further improvement in reliability from equipment failures.

Different frequencies, even in the same band, will experience unrelated fading conditions. This fact leads to the use of another diversity arrangement, called *frequency diversity*, which employs two transmitters and two receivers each tuned to a different frequency, but connected to a single antenna. Since this arrangement is wasteful of microwave spectrum, it is more commonly used with one diversity channel serving several working channels as protection. When one of the working channels fails or fades, the information is automatically switched over to the protection channel for transmission.

Modulation   In communication systems, the microwave carrier frequency is almost universally frequency-modulated. This method offers two important advantages over amplitude modulation. At relatively high signal levels, it provides an effective improvement in the signal-to-noise ratio, and the amplitude of the demodulated signal can be substantially constant, even in the presence of large variations of the received microwave signal.

Each modulation and demodulation process adds to the system noise, which is accumulative. On long multihop systems this can result in a serious performance degradation. To reduce this noise contribution on trunk route systems, the signal is not demodulated and remodulated at intermediate stations. Instead, the microwave signal is shifted down in frequency to an intermediate frequency (IF), usually 70 MHz, where it can be readily amplified. After amplification, the intermediate frequency is shifted back to microwave and retransmitted. This type of repeater is referred to as an IF Heterodyne type.

Although the cost of establishing a microwave station is fairly high, once construction is completed, expansion to provide large numbers of channels can be achieved at a low cost. For this reason, microwave systems provide the majority of long, heavy-density communication routes throughout the world.

SATELLITE COMMUNICATION

No discussion of modern communication methods would be complete without at least briefly mentioning this important new medium. Until recently, satellites have been reserved for international communications; however, the FCC has now cleared the way for their use by domestic carriers. The first domestic satellite was launched by the Western Union Telegraph Company in 1974.

Satellite systems are a special application of microwave communications. They are effectively a two-hop system with an intermediate repeater orbiting the earth at an elevation of some 22,300 miles. This particular height was selected so that the satellite orbits the earth in the same time that the earth makes one revolution. This is called *synchronous operation*. Since weight, power, and space limitations restrict the design of the orbiting transmitters and receivers, their shortcomings must be offset by the ground-based equipment. This demands the use of high-power transmitters, very sensitive noise-free receivers, and large parabolic antennas. To minimize interference and provide a large communication bandwidth, different frequencies are used for transmission from the ground to the satellite (the *uplink*, usually 6 GHz) and from the satellite back to earth (the *downlink*, usually 4 GHz).

Because of the distance that the signal must travel, the time taken to reach the receiver is considerable, about 0.3 sec. This requires that special precautions be taken to reduce the echo on voice channels, and may reduce the throughput of data circuits using conventional error-detection and error-correction schemes. These disadvantages are more than offset by the potentially low cost of transmission for longer circuits, particularly coast to coast.

DATA TRANSMISSION OVER ANALOG FACILITIES

An analog circuit is not capable of transmitting digital data in an "on-off" form. It is, therefore, necessary to convert the signal to a form that can be transmitted over an analog transmission channel. The digital-to-analog, analog-to-digital signal converters are commonly called *modems*, a contraction of "modulator-demodulator." The simplest modem will transmit and receive a single frequency tone within the passband of the analog channel. This tone may then be switched on and off to represent mark (binary "1") and space (binary "0") conditions. Although easy to achieve, this method is not commonly used because it is uneconomical in the utilization of bandwidth, and is extremely sensitive to transmission impairments, particularly impulse and "white noise."

When used for medium-speed data transmission, the nominal 3,000-Hz analog voice bandwidth channel has an effective bandwidth of 1,800 Hz. The effective bandwidth is that portion in the center of the channel that is relatively free from amplitude and delay distortion. The effective bandwidth of a channel may be extended from 1,800 Hz to about 2,400 Hz by the addition of amplitude and delay equalizers to condition the channel.

Digital data information is usually transferred over an analog channel at the rate of one bit of information for every hertz of effective bandwidth. Sophisticated modem designs permit the transfer of data information over a channel at rates up to four information bits for every hertz of effective bandwidth.

Data are transmitted over analog voice channels at rates from 45 bps up to 9,600 bps. Modems that transmit data at rates up to 300 bps are classed as low-speed, and modems that transmit data at rates between 300 and 10,000 bps are classed as medium-speed. High-speed modems transmit data at rates in excess of 10,000 bps over wide-band channels whose effective bandwidth is greater than 4,000 Hz.

Asynchronous Transmission Asynchronous data transmission is the transfer of information character by character. Each character is framed by a start and stop bit, consists of from five to eight information bits, and is independent of the character it precedes or follows. Asynchronous data are originated by keyboard teleprinters, tape transmitters, and simple buffered terminal equipment operating at rates between 45 and 1,800 bps. Frequency shift keying (FSK) modems employing two adjacent frequencies provide a practical approach to asynchronous transmission. One frequency represents a mark or binary "1," the other a space or binary "0." The tone transmitted to the analog channel is shifted between these two frequencies in sympathy with the digital data signal. The minimum frequency separation between the two frequencies is determined by the maximum data rate to be transmitted. For low-speed transmission, it is possible to combine a number of frequency pairs over one voice channel using FDM techniques. Typically, up to twenty 100-bps signals may be multiplexed in this manner.

Synchronous Transmission Synchronous data transmission is the transfer of information serially, block by block. Each block of data is framed by framing characters, with block lengths typically ranging from 25 six-bit characters to 1,000 eight-bit characters. The bit integrity of the data channel is preserved by the data receiver remaining in bit synchronization with the data transmitter. Synchronous data are originated by computer, magnetic-tape terminals, and buffered data terminal equipment operating at 2,400, 4,800 or 9,600 bps over analog voice channels.

Synchronous modems employ digital coding techniques to convert the serial data information into multilevel signals that are phase-shift-keyed (PSK) or PSK and amplitude-modulated to provide analog signals that are within the effective bandwidth of the voice channel.

Typically, a PSK synchronous modem using "two-to-one coding" will examine the incoming serial data two bits at a time: Each of the four possible combinations of data (mark-mark, space-mark, mark-space, or space-space) is then represented by a unique phase position of a single-frequency line signal. This arrangement permits a data transfer rate of two times the effective bandwidth of the channel. The receiver derives timing information from the incoming data signal, and modulates the line signal and reassembles the serial data information that is synchronized to the data input of the distant transmitter.

Synchronous modems that use ratios of data rate to effective bandwidth in excess of three to one normally include automatically trained adaptive amplitude and delay distortion equalizers. These equalizers, once trained to the characteristics of an analog channel, will compensate for minor changes experienced in these impairments. All 9,600-bps modems include these automatic adaptive equalizers.

DIGITAL TRANSMISSION OF DATA

If data are transmitted in a digital form, many of the impairments associated with analog transmission become inconsequential, since periodic regeneration is feasible.

The error rate of a digital channel is determined primarily by the signal-to-noise ratio of the channel, impulse noise, and interruptions or "hits." Information can be transmitted digitally by wire lines or microwave radio. The ubiquitous T carrier system discussed earlier in this Chapter is a means of digitally transmitting analog information using time division multiplexing techniques.

TDM is even more attractive for the transmission of data, since no analog-to-digital conversion is required. When the data are synchronous or at a constant asynchronous rate, each digital channel can be assigned a sequential time slot, and the binary condition can be detected and interleaved with other channels. Some TDM systems sample each bit and interleave the individual channel bits sequentially. Alternatively, for asynchronous transmission, each channel may accumulate a complete character and transmit this in its entirety between characters from other channels.

Each asynchronous character contains start and stop information which may be longer than an information bit. When character interleaving is employed, each character is transmitted as a complete entity. The start and stop bits, being redundant, are removed at the transmitter and reinserted at the receiver. This results in efficient transmission. However, because a complete character must be accumulated before it is sent to the line, there can be a two-character transit delay. Bit-interleaved systems transmit each bit of a character independently. It is, therefore, necessary to transmit every bit provided to the input, including the start and stop information. Although slightly less efficient than character interleaving because of the transmission of these additional bits, transmission delay is limited to only two bits.

When the data signal is not of constant speed and code, it is necessary to detect and transmit each transition from one digital state to another. A code of three or four bits is used to describe fully the occurrence of a transition. As a result, this technique is considerably less efficient than other TDM techniques.

The high-speed output of TDM equipment may be subjected to further multiplexing, as with FDM systems or may be connected to a digital transmission facility. Alternatively, the digital signal may be transmitted over an analog network by the addition of modems.

The hierarchy of TDM multiplexing which will be employed by common carriers is controlled to a considerable extent by the wide acceptance of T carriers in their existing plant. (Refer back to the discussion of Figure 1-5.)

Microwave   An entire microwave system may be dedicated to digital transmission using phase, frequency, or multilevel amplitude modulation of the microwave carrier frequency. Very few systems have, until recently, been implemented for purely digital transmission, and most of these have used conventional microwave equipments with the same FM modulators and demodulators that are employed for analog transmission. With several transmission companies planning large digital networks, increased emphasis is being placed on the development of microwave equipment specifically designed for digital communication. Most of these systems are expected to employ phase shift modulation using four or eight phase conditions.

Where analog microwave systems are pre-existing, the digital capability can be achieved by the addition of a further channel of microwave radio equipment. The buildings, towers, antennas, feeder, power equipment, etc., would be shared between the analog and the digital system.

When the total analog and digital traffic is not sufficient to justify separate microwave facilities for each, both services can be combined and transmitted over the same microwave channel. The low-frequency end of the microwave baseband is assigned to digital traffic, while the analog traffic is placed above it on the baseband. Western Union installed the first system of this type, which it calls *hybrid* microwave, between Atlanta and Cincinnati. This system provides 6.3 Mb per sec of digital capacity. The Bell System plans to use a similar technique, which it terms Data Under Voice (DUV) to provide 1.544 Mb per sec of digital traffic below the normal analog baseband.

TARIFFS

The user has a wide choice in selecting services furnished by common carriers. These services and their associated tariffs are in a continual state of flux as improved offerings become feasible and as costs change. Traditionally, there has been no differential in the price of service between major cities over high-density routes or small villages over lightly loaded routes, even though there can be a wide variation in the cost of providing these two services. As the new specialized common carriers begin to offer service between large business centers, without the burden of high-cost, lightly loaded routes, there are indications that the existing carriers may modify their policy of nationwide average pricing.

Switched Services The present switched-service offerings of the carriers are in the main aimed at providing services other than data transmission. There are three major switched networks: the direct distance dial telephone network (DDD), the Telex network, and the TWX network. Each permits a subscriber to contact any other subscriber on the same network and, in addition, subscribers on the Telex and TWX network can interchange traffic by means of computer-controlled store-and-forward switches. The record communication networks provide a reliable and economical means of transmitting low-speed data. The DDD network can provide a reasonable grade of service for medium-speed data, although the user will experience a wide variation in the quality of communication channels selected by the switches due to the numerous routes available.

Private Services As higher-speed transmission is required, or as traffic requirements demand high usage between a limited number of locations, private wire services will become economically attractive. These services provide dedicated service between two or more locations, and can be tailored to meet virtually any requirement. Private wire services are classified by series which describe the type of service:

1000 Series. This series covers unconditioned channels for transmitting dc mark-space or binary signals at rates up to 150 bps. These channels are not suitable for the transmission of ac tones.

2000 Series. This series covers channels with a bandwidth not exceeding 4,000 Hz, suitable for voice transmission.

3000 Series. This series covers channels with a bandwidth not exceeding 4,000 Hz, suitable for data transmission and for remote telemetering, supervisory control, and miscellaneous signaling purposes. These channels are not suitable for the transmission of dc pulses and a modem must be provided by either the user or the carrier.

4000 Series. This series covers conditioned channels with a bandwidth not exceeding 4,000 Hz for facsimile transmission and for remote metering, supervisory control, and miscellaneous signaling purposes. These channels are not suitable for transmission of dc pulses.

5000 Series (TELPAK). Series 5000 channels are designed for large-capacity facility requirements between specified points. Base capacity is provided for transmitting voice, teletypewriter, data, and other services. Two arrangements are available, providing 60 or 240 maximum equivalent voice-grade channels.

8000 Series. This service provides transmission paths of approximately 48 kHz for use as wideband channels suitable for high-speed data or facsimile transmission or for use as individual voice-grade channels up to a maximum of 12 for voice, facsimile, data, and remote metering.

Datacom. This service, offered only by Western Union, is an economical arrangement for the high-volume, low- and medium-speed data user. Various arrangements are available to provide a wide variety of speeds and channels. For example, a user could select twenty-four 75-baud circuits or four 600-baud and ten 150-baud channels.

Conditioning. Circuits provided under series 2000, 3000, 5000, and 8000 tariffs may be conditioned to provide a specified maximum delay and amplitude distortion. The most commonly encountered grades of conditioning, in increasing order of channel quality, are C-1, C-2, and C-4.

Equipment. In addition to the transmission facilities, a wide range of equipment to terminate circuits is available. This includes such devices as modems, teleprinters, tape perforators, switchboards, and in fact, everything required for a complete communications system.

SELECTIVE BIBLIOGRAPHY

Boxall, Frank, "Pulse Code Modulation in Telephony," *Telephone Engineer and Management,* Reprint, September, 1968–January, 1969.

Carl, Helmut, *Radio Relay Systems*, MacDonald, London,

Davenport, William P., *Modern Data Communication*, Hayden, New York, 1971.

Schwartz, Mischa, William R. Bennett, and Seymour Stein, *Communications Systems and Techniques*, McGraw Hill, New York, 1966.

Whittaker, A., and Michael M. Flack, "Microwave Communications," *Telephone Engineer and Management*, Reprint, 1968.

Bell Telephone Laboratories, *Transmission Systems for Communications*.

Chapter 2

Facsimile Communications

NORMAN C. PETERSON

**Executive Vice President, RAPIFAX Corporation,
Fairfield, New Jersey**

Facsimile is the transmission and reproduction of an image over a distance by electronic means. Facsimile machines accept input originals (which may be documents, photographs, microimages, or other forms of graphic information) at a scanner or other appropriate transmitting terminal, and translate the image into electronic signals. These signals are sent over communications facilities to a receiving terminal or printer where a facsimile reproduction of the input original (possibly at a different linear scale) is created. The basic idea of facsimile was conceived in Scotland and demonstrated in primitive form over 125 years ago, but for many years it attracted no commercial interest. Facsimile had to await the growth of long-distance telephone communication networks in order to become a practical possibility and begin to attract users.

The first routine application of facsimile began some 50 years ago, for news wirephoto. Pictures accompanying news stories could be transmitted by wire or radio in parallel with the stories. The news services found a broad and eager acceptance of the novel service by newspapers across the country and abroad. A second early application was found in the transmission of weather maps which are needed by meteorologists in preparing weather forecasts. This application also found and retains wide acceptance. A third application was found in military operations, where maps displaying reconnaissance information could be sent instantly to command posts for use in making troop movement decisions and in the direction of artillery and aerial bombardment.

Each of these applications had several common denominators. The information was graphic and could not be sent by the use of printed or spoken words or symbols. Also, the information was "time-vital," since in the delivery time offered by such alternatives as mail or messenger, the information would become essentially useless. Weather maps that are 3 days old are of no use to forecasters. Three-day-old news photos are of no interest after the story has left the pages of the newspaper.

Beyond these few applications mentioned, where there was no viable alternative, facsimile found very little use in the early years. The available equipment was bulky, inconvenient to use, slow, and unreliable. Transmission times were long and communication costs correspondingly high. High image quality could be obtained only by the photographic processes of wirephoto, for which the cost and processing inconvenience were unacceptable for general business use. Thus, as the nation's businesses moved into the technologically explosive 1950s, facsimile had still found no appreciable use in business communication.

The need, however, for improved graphic communications was growing rapidly. Large multiple-site organizations perceived a need that was not being met by the communications means available. The mails were (and are) slow and to a degree undependable; telephone is fast and convenient for the spoken word, but does not provide a written record that can be copied, filed, distributed, and consulted after the fact; Teletype record communication provides the written record, but requires that documents be retyped from the original onto the teletypewriter keyboard, with the attendant operator costs and propensity for error. The means available could not provide adequate communications capability to the multiple-location organizations of business and government that needed rapid, accurate, and economically practical record communication to function efficiently.

By 1960, businesses had begun to experiment with facsimile to solve some of their record communications problems, even though the equipment then available was primitive and but little improved over what had been available for many years. During the 1960s, the need became relentlessly more urgent: Computers began to become important and required accurate and timely input information; the postal system began to show symptoms of a growing inability to handle efficiently the enormous volume of mail generated by modern society. Fortunately, the fields of data communications and of integrated circuits yielded technologies that would enable increased speed and flexibility for facsimile communications. By the end of the decade major advances in technology, plus favorable government regulatory changes, had created the bases that would permit facsimile to become a convenient and economical communications tool.

FACSIMILE TECHNOLOGY

A facsimile transmission involves the following seven basic steps:

1. *Input paper handling.* This function brings the document, from which the image is to be transmitted, into the proper position to be scanned and then to be removed from the machine after scanning. Input can be manual or automatic.

2. *Scanning.* This step is the process of translating the light and dark areas along successive scan lines into an electrical signal that represents the image. The resulting signal, called the *video baseband signal,* is then turned over to the next system component for further processing.

3. *Encoding.* The baseband signal may be encoded in a variety of ways intended to make the subsequent transmission fit into the available bandwidth of the communication channel or (in a digital system) to eliminate redundant information, thus minimizing the number of bits to be transmitted, or to make the transmitted signal less susceptible to errors, noise, and interference, or for crypto purposes. Not all facsimile machines employ encoding.

4. *Modulation, line coupling, and transmission.* The encoded or unencoded baseband signal (as the case may be) is passed through a modem (i.e., modulator-demodulator) which puts it into a signaling format appropriate to the transmission channel employed (digital or analog, two-wire or four-wire, or wireless). The signal thus reaches the receiving terminal. An important step in the transmission process is that of establishing the link to the receiving terminal and instructing that terminal to prepare for reception.

5. *Reception, demodulation, and decoding.* The transmitted signal is detected on the communications channel, demodulated into a format suitable for decoding, decoded, and passed to the printer in a form equivalent to the original video baseband signal. These processes can occur either *open loop* (no communication from receiver to transmitter about the quality of the transmission and reception) or *closed loop* (i.e., with such communication).

6. *Printing.* This step recreates a facsimile of the original input image on paper, film, or a display.

7. *Output paper handling.* This step is the bringing of the recording medium into position for printing and removing the medium after the image is implanted. Usually processing of some sort is required after printing to develop and fix the image. This step may occur either before or after removal of the medium from the receiver, and may be manual or fully automatic.

Input Paper Handling The input document must be put in position to be scanned. All facsimile systems use a raster (i.e., television) scan. The image is scanned along closely spaced parallel lines with the scan head reading the image density along one, two, three, or even more than three, contiguous scan lines simultaneously. The scan proceeds across successive sets of scan lines in the same direction. The same raster pattern must be created in both the scanning and the printing processes. Synchronism between scanner and printer must be maintained so that each starts a new line (or set of lines) at the same time.

There is no limit to the number of ways a raster can be created. Several of the more widely used means are noted below. Each has its advantages and disadvantages to be considered by the equipment designer and the user.

Rotating Drum. Perhaps the simplest and least expensive method for implementing a raster scan is to mount the input image or document on a drum which rotates at constant speed. Scanning optics are focused at the drum surface and either the drum or the optics is moved in a line parallel to the drum axis by a lead screw. If the scanner is reading one scan line at a time, the lead screw advances the assembly by the space between scan lines for each complete revolution of the drum. The document length is limited to the length of the drum in this method; no practical method for the continuous feeding of documents has been found. Between sheets, the drum rotation must be stopped to permit replacement of the completed sheet by the next sheet.

Ingenious mechanisms have been developed for automating the input paper handling on drum-type machines. The drum, at rest, presents a slot to the input document. When the document is inserted, it is clamped along a narrow margin (usually less than $\frac{1}{8}$ inch) and the drum rotation starts, thus wrapping the width of the document about the drum.

Interestingly, the most sophisticated high-resolution facsimile machines, those used to transmit full-page newspaper plates between editorial offices and printing plants, employ completely manual rotating-drum input paper handling. The page plate is accurately positioned and stretched tightly about the drum, and held in place by pressure-sensitive tapes.

In all rotating-drum systems in general use, the image side of the document faces outward. Obviously a drum with a transparent surface could be devised, where the document faces inward and the scanning optics are inside the drum. This configuration has not found favor.

Rotating Turret. This method reverses the roles of the scan optics and the drum. The document is wrapped around the surface of a nonrotating transparent cylinder, and the scan optics rotates at high speed inside the cylinder. As before, relative motion of the two elements is provided by a lead screw, and either element may be the one that moves in translation. Efficient mechanisms for handling continuous lengths of input document have been developed for rotating-turret systems. These devices have found use in the transmission of seismic records, drilling logs, and continuous roll-feed meter records of arbitrary length.

Flat Bed. A flat-bed system does not bend the input document, but holds it flat on a scanning platen. A very large number of practical mechanizations are known, some moving the document in relation to the scan station, either by a lead screw (which translates the entire scan platen assembly) or by rollers driven by stepper motors which slide the input document past the scan station. Other assemblies hold the input document stationary and translate the scanner. Also, a rocker-type flat-bed input has appeared where the line of sight of the scan optics is swept down the page by a rotating mirror while the flat-bed rocker tilts to keep the optical path length constant.

Flat-bed input paper handling is the method least affected in performance by variations of document thickness, stiffness, fold lines, and size.

Scanning The heart of the scanner is a photosensitive element which outputs either a voltage or a current proportional to the intensity of the incident illumination. The scanner measures the surface optical density at the location of the resolution element (picture element, or *pixel*) being scanned. Either the document is floodlighted and the scanner optics are sharply focused on the pixel, or the scanner optics may be defocused and only the pixel illuminated by a sharp spot of light. This latter method is termed *flying-spot scanning.* Both methods can yield excellent results and both are widely employed.

Drum-type Input Stations. In general, these employ floodlighting with focused optics serving the photodetector.

Turret-type Input Stations. These are found in both the floodlighting and flying-spot mechanizations. Usually the lighting beam is fed down the hollow rotating shaft on the end of which the turret is fitted. A 45-degree-angle mirror at the turret site directs the light to the inner surface of the cylinder where the document is illuminated. This structure eliminates the need for sliding power contacts by keeping the light source stationary. In all instances the photosensitive element is kept close to the pixel to minimize the light loss due to the inverse square law of light intensity variation with distance from the source.

Flat-bed Scanners. Flat-bed scanners are used in a wide range of implementations:

CRT (Cathode-Ray Tube) Scanners. CRT scanners are of two kinds. In one, a sharply focused electron beam creates a tiny bright spot which constantly sweeps out the same or almost the same line on the tube face. The spot is imaged on the input document by a double convex lens, and thus constitutes a flying-spot illuminator. The light reflected from the input copy is sensed by a linear photodetector whose optics are defocused to maximize the capture of light. Either the CRT or the input copy may be the moving element. For this implementation, the CRT used is broad and thin, shaped rather like a paddle.

In the other CRT implementation, the electron beam is enabled to sweep in rapid succession a number of lines of the scan raster. This mechanization is employed in line-skipping systems where the scanner moves with extreme speed over blank regions of the copy. The scanner must have the ability to scan a number of successive lines to allow time for the physical movement of the CRT with respect to the input document to be accelerated to catch up to the raster line being scanned. This multiple-line CRT system is also employed in some implementations of *data compression algorithm* facsimile systems, described in later paragraphs.

Spinning Mirror. A focused light beam can be swept in angle by reflection from a rocking or rotating mirror. Using this fact, both flying-spot and floodlight scanners have been implemented.

Rotating Spiral. The intersection of a rotating spiral slit with a stationary radial slit creates a moving aperture. Light passing through the aperture can be used for a flying-spot illuminator. This scheme was widely used in early weather-map facsimile systems. Rotating-spiral mechanisms are used in send-only systems; no satisfactory means for using the spiral idea in a printer has been found.

Line-to-Circle Converters. Optical means that can enable a straight line—the scan line—to be imaged on a segment of a circle permit the line to be scanned by a simple rotating element. One implementation of this idea is in the fiber optic scanner. A sheet of fine parallel optical fibers, laid in parallel, and in the width desired, is held linear at one end while the other end is curled into a circle. The circular end is scanned by a rotating element. Such scanners can achieve rather high resolutions and scanning speeds and, when used in the floodlight structure, require only modest levels of light intensity because the end of the optical fiber is held in physical contact with the pixel. Hence, light losses are minimized.

Other line-to-circle converters using both transmissive and reflective optical trains are in use. These structures overcome the fragility of fiber optics and are finding use in operational facsimile systems subjected to sustained heavy usage.

When light-sensitive recording paper is used for the copy output, the line-to-circle converter systems, CRT, and spinning-mirror systems can be used both to read and to write.

Scan Arrays. Several electronics components manufacturers are now marketing strips of discrete photosensitive elements upon which a raster scan line can be imaged by a lens. Such strips require the same number of discrete sensitive elements as there are pixels along the scan line. The array is scanned electronically and can operate at very high speeds. The potential advantage of such solid state photosensitive linear arrays is low first cost, once production quantities reach a sufficient level. The prime disadvantage until quite recently has been the difficulty of obtaining uniformity of response from element to element along the strip. As the cost and uniformity problems are overcome, it is probable that solid state scan arrays will find substantial use in flat-bed input facsimile transmitters.

Encoding To discuss encoding it is first necessary to distinguish between synchronous and asynchronous systems. For a synchronous system, one may visualize the raster scan line to be marked off by a fine ruler into individual fixed-position resolution elements. As the scanner examines each resolution element, it must decide if that element is a white or a black. That decision is easy if the element is all white or all black, but is equivocal if a transition from white to black (or vice versa) takes place toward the center of the element.

Decision rules are built into the scan logic which attempt to make the decision on a consistent basis. However, such rules are imperfect, and in the scanning of curved characters or inclined lines, the scanning yields image signals equivalent to ragged or stepladder edges in the received copy. This result is called *quantizing noise*. To overcome it, the resolution of synchronous systems is increased to the point that the edge imperfections are too small for the unaided eye to detect. It is a thumbrule in the graphics trade that a synchronous scan requires about 30 per cent higher resolution than an asynchronous scan to yield output copy of equal apparent sharpness to the eye.

An asynchronous system does not have fixed-position resolution elements along the scan line. Instead, the scanner merely outputs a signal proportional to the average image density it sees in the resolution spot. This signal then may or may not be *thresholded*, or interpreted in binary digital form. If it is not, the printer is commanded to make a mark on the output copy of the same density seen at the corresponding spot by the scanner. If the signal is thresholded or digitized, the printer prints white until the threshold is exceeded, then makes a mark. An asynchronous digitized system is thus also afflicted with quantizing noise, but to a lesser degree than a synchronous system.

The great advantage of synchronous systems is that the data output of the scanner is in synchronous binary form and can thus be processed by data handling circuits of arbitrary sophistication to accomplish a variety of goals.

Consider now an asynchronous analog scanner feeding an analog modem. Very little can be done with the signal stream. It is comparable to a voice signal. Its exploitation of the total information carrying capacity of the channel is low and, unless the channel itself is very broad, the transmission time for such a system will be long. (Concerning bandwidth compression of such signals, see "Modulation, Line Coupling, and Transmission," below.)

The bit stream from a synchronous scan is susceptible of substantial beneficial processing. The dominant effort in the trade is to develop and implement means for the efficient encoding of *run lengths* of white or black resolution elements. The scanner output may be in the form: white, white, white, white, black, black, black, for example. A first-level encoding of such a stream would be "four white, three black." Thus, seven "words" have been compressed to four. In recent years, a great deal of effort has been invested in the search for efficient procedures, called *data compression algorithms*, for transmitting all the information in a bit stream while using the minimum number of bits for doing so and yet avoiding ambiguity.

One next notes that the "words" (or symbols for) white and black are unnecessary. The polarity alternates, and hence it is only necessary to know the first polarity, each following one then being the opposite. Thus the four "words" above can be cut unambiguously to three by the equivalent statement "four white three" meaning "four white, three black." A compression factor of $7/3$, or $2\frac{1}{3}$, has been achieved.

The efficient encoding algorithms focus on the lengths of the runs of bits between transitions from white to black, or black to white. But a problem now arises. The signaling between the facsimile machines is in terms of the binary digits "0" and "1." Those are the only symbols. There are no commas, decimal points, signs, or spaces. One must find a way for the decoder to know where the binary number for one run length ends, and the number for the next one begins. The simplest way to do that is to rule that all the run-length numbers are of fixed length, say four bits, and to rule that one four-bit number, say 0000, means a transition to opposite polarity. If a given run length is too long to be encoded by one four-bit symbol, two, three, or more symbols are used as needed, preceding the transition symbol. Such encoding means have been built and used, but are somewhat inefficient on "busy" copy where the information is dense and the transitions are numerous.

The next level of improvement involves the use of variable-length binary numbers to encode run lengths, while avoiding the wasteful practice of inserting transition symbols between binary numbers. Various means of achieving that end are known, but in general are regarded as trade secrets by the owners and are not revealed. Such *adaptive run-length encoding* results in quite efficient encoding. All these schemes rely on the observation that there is a great deal of correlation, along a scan line, among the alternate run lengths. That is to say, roughly, that all the letters in a given type font are about the same size. The amount of white is about the same from letter to letter, and the amount of black is about the same from letter to letter.

Yet further improvements in data compression efficiency are attained when use is made of the fact that the correlation of run lengths is very high from one scan line to the next. A letter of typescript, for example, may be 12 scan lines tall. In its center portions all the scans will be approximately the same. Using this fact, algorithms which encode two or even three lines in parallel have been demonstrated. One may also reserve special symbols to designate a scan line that is entirely white or black. Such a line is then not encoded as a run length per se, but as an instruction to the printer to skip a line (or print a line all black). Such line-skipping routines can be quite efficient on copy free of vertical margin lines or other long vertical markings.

Modulation, Line Coupling, and Transmission   Techniques for modulation and transmission of facsimile signals are available in endless variety. Only the more widely used ones are mentioned in this summary.

Modulation. The public telephone network is engineered and maintained for voice communication even though a substantial portion of the traffic is made up of data or facsimile signals. Such signals must then be put in a form that the telephone plant can handle. This function is accomplished by a modem. The most widely used form of modem operates by frequency modulation; that is, the modem emits to the line a continuous tone signal whose frequency changes up and down in step with the input to the modem from the facsimile encoder. The simplest such modems use two tone levels, for example, 1,800 Hz may be "0" and 2,100 Hz may be "1."

Nonencoding facsimile machines designed to transmit not just black and white, but also shades of gray, are served by a modem whose emitted tone signal can assume any frequency between the mentioned 1,800 Hz and 2,100 Hz. (These example frequencies are arbitrarily chosen. There exists no obligatory standard.) The receiving modem recognizes each frequency and enables the printer to reproduce approximately the same shade seen by the scanner. Such *binary FM* modems are limited by nature to a maximum of about 2,400 picture elements per second.

A more advanced form of FM modulation is called *duobinary FM*. In this technique, there are three tone levels. For example, the center frequency may represent "0," and the upper and lower frequencies each represent "1." Alternate "1"'s are above and below the center frequency. This method almost doubles the information capacity of the channel, and is the method employed in some intermediate-speed facsimile machines entering current use.

High-speed facsimile machines (1 minute per page and less) employ one or more of the following: extensive encoding, and either high-capacity (analog or digital) channels, or very efficient modems that can make the most use of the bandwidth offered by a channel. The fastest machines (30-seconds-per-page range) exploit both encoding and efficient modems. These more efficient modems do not employ FM, but rather employ a library of (usually) 8 or 16 different waveforms, each of which represents three successive data bits, or four such bits, respectively. Such modems routinely transmit 4,800 bps over direct-dialed long-distance connections. Their ability to talk through noise and interference is remarkable, in that such modems will accept and use almost 95 per cent of long-distance connections.

Line Coupling. The modem can be coupled to the telephone network either acoustically or electrically, the latter requiring the use of an isolation circuit called a *data access arrangement* (DAA).

Acoustic coupling has been important to the acceptance of facsimile. Today, it means the placing of the standard telephone handset into a cradle with the earpiece and the mouthpiece adjacent to opposing microphone and speaker elements. Isolation from ambient noises is provided by sponge rubber seals. Prior to 1966, all facsimile devices had to be connected electrically to the communications lines through cumbersome isolation devices specified by the common carrier companies. In some instances the cost of the connection, particularly to the voice-grade public switched network, approached the cost of the facsimile device. The introduction of acoustic coupling permitted much simplification. Most of the low-speed facsimile devices now in use are acoustically coupled. That means is both flexible and, on a first-cost basis, inexpensive. It enables portable machines to be offered which can receive or transmit from any telephone in the office, home, or elsewhere. Acoustic coupling is limited to the lower rates of data transfer, for when high rates (above about 3,000 bps) are attempted, acoustic standing waves develop in the coupler and destroy the data stream.

An electrical connection is necessary for high data rates. The signal passes through the DAA, an element that has been vastly improved since 1966. Its purpose is to protect the facsimile machine and the telephone plant from each other, whatever may happen (e.g., lightning on the phone lines, or a short circuit or other malfunction in the machine). The telephone companies are now coming under substantial public and regulatory pressure to publish required isolation specifications so that the needed safeguards can be built into data and facsimile equipment, as they are built into telephones, so that the expense and installation delays of the DAA can be avoided. The issue today stands unresolved in the United States. In Japan and much of Europe the needed regulations exist and the external DAA is not required for facsimile machines.

An advantage of the electrical connection in addition to its high data capacity is the feature of unattended answering of incoming calls, and hanging up after transmission. Most acoustic coupling systems require operator participation at both the transmitting and receiving ends.

Transmission. Analog modems operating above about 2,400 bps make such thorough use of information capacity of a channel that the electrical distortions inherent in long telephone circuits must be considered. These distortions are overcome by an *equalizer* in the receiving modem which applies a counteracting or inverse distortion to the incoming signal so that it can then be accurately decoded. Such equalization can be set once for all, or be *fixed* for data speeds up to about 3,600 bps. Above that rate, modems employ *adaptive equalization,* which is implemented by active circuits in the receiver that automatically and constantly retune the receiver circuits to balance out the distortions of the line.

Analog modulation has dominated the discussion to this point. But, it is also possible to use digital lines (offered now by a number of common carrier companies), which are lines explicitly engineered and maintained for the transmission of data signals. Coupling to a digital line does not require a modem. Instead, the Electronic Industries Association has standardized (for the United States) a set of interface connection arrangements which permit a data machine (including digital facsimile) to be coupled directly, by hard wire, to the channel network. The standard most employed is termed RS232C.

If the traffic load is more than roughly 5 million bits per day (15 to 20 pages of high-speed facsimile), then digital channels, where available, should be considered and in many instances are less costly than analog (voice-grade) channels. Digital channels are substantially free of noise and errors, and can be ordered in almost any speed capacity desired. To exploit them, new superspeed facsimile machines are being developed and will be offered to commercial users.

Reception, Demodulation, and Decoding These processes are simply the inverses of encoding, modulation, and transmission, and their end result is the video baseband signal, fully provided again with all its redundant data bits, which is fed to the printer.

In the less sophisticated facsimile machines, the reception is *open loop,* which means that the receiver does not communicate automatically with the transmitter to report on the quality of the reception. With such systems, the success or failure of the transmission can be established only by voice discussion after the fact between operators at both ends of the connection.

Closed-loop systems are provided at several levels of refinement. At the high end, the transmitted data are formatted into *blocks,* or groups of 500 to 1,000 bits. These blocks are verified as to freedom of error one by one between transmitter and receiver. Unacceptable blocks are retransmitted until correctly received, and the receiver can cause the transmitting scanner to pause in place while any transmission problems are waited out. If the receiver logic is unsatisfied with the quality of reception, it can interrupt the transmission and demand a new connection. Such systems ensure that the sending operator knows precisely the disposition of each transmission without requiring an operator at the receiver. Other systems do not correct incorrectly transmitted blocks, but keep a record of their number and distribution. Blocks in error do not disturb output copy quality unless they occur in a lengthy sequence. A copy quality rule is built into the receiver which, if violated, causes the receiver automatically to reject the connection and demand a retransmission.

Printing Alongside the overall cost of usage (i.e., fixed cost plus variable charges), the companion feature of facsimile systems most important to the end user is the apparent printing quality on the output document. Here psychological factors come into play, for it has been found that the eye attaches roughly equal weight to the contrast between the whites and blacks of an image and to the actual resolution of the process, in forming its subjective assessment of copy quality. Resolution is defined as lines per inch: a resolution of 100 lines per inch means (in facsimile) that if the input copy presents two parallel black lines 1/100 inch wide, spaced by 1/100 inch, then both of the lines and the gap will be discernible on the output copy. If the same image is printed twice with exactly the same resolution, but once with low contrast (gray on white or black on gray) and once with high contrast (black on white), the eye will believe that the high-contrast copy is much more crisp and sharp. Hence, facsimile manufacturers work hard to achieve high printing contrast. Systems have been offered in the trade which, from a speed, reliability, cost, and resolution viewpoint were excellent, but which had low-contrast output copy, and which were commercial disappointments to their sponsors.

Another interesting psychological fact is that the eye attaches greater importance to horizontal than to vertical resolution. (The raster scan lines of a television picture are scarcely noticeable in the normal viewing attitude, but try looking at a TV picture with the head slanted 90 degrees to one side!) Hence, almost all facsimile machines use greater horizontal than vertical resolution, usually by about 20 to 25 per cent.

Commonly used facsimile printing processes are:

Electroresistive. This process is simple and produces a good image at some cost for the special paper, and a minor production of odor. The process passes a current through a three-layer paper composed of a base stock, a carbon layer, and an opaque white layer atop the carbon. As the current is increased, more of the white layer burns off, giving a darker image. Thus the process can produce continuous-tone pictures on analog machines. The cost of the paper makes the process somewhat uneconomical for high-volume users, and the stiff "feel" of the paper is found to be undesirable by some users.

Impact. This method uses a hammer to strike a special paper with a blow proportional in strength to the desired image density. The paper may be either a carbon or carbonless formulation that darkens upon impact. The process is simple and inexpensive, and can produce multiple copies if desired. The disadvantages are that the process is slow and noisy.

Electrolytic. In this process a thin paper moistened by an electrolytic solution changes color when a current is passed through the paper between opposed electrodes. The process has been widely used by the weather services. It is simple and inexpensive, but the resolution and the contrast are both low. Also, the paper supply roll for the printer must be kept moist.

Xerographic. This process, also employed in many office copiers, is applicable to facsimile. A photoconductive medium has the image written upon it by a modulated light beam performing a writing raster. This image transfers a dry toner powder to the print paper to which it is quickly fused by heat. The process offers high contrast, high speed, and low print paper cost. The equipment is expensive, however, and not practical for low-volume applications.

CRT/Electrostatic. An image can be placed on photoconductive copier paper by imaging the facsimile raster on the paper from the faceplate of a CRT. The process is capable of very high speed, but is plagued by low printing contrast. CRT printing is favored by machines using line-skipping encoding because the electron beam of the CRT has zero inertia and can be skipped over blank areas at great speed.

Dielectric. In this process the image is written on a charge-retentive paper by an array of fixed styli. The image is developed by contact with a liquid toner and fixed by evaporation of the toner solvent, a process completed in seconds before the copy reaches the output tray. The process offers high contrast, resolution, and speed at intermediate print paper cost. The printing system cost is comparable to the xerographic system previously mentioned and is not practical for low-volume use.

Output Paper Handling Substantially all business facsimile machines in use today discharge the output copy into a tray or pop open a door so that the output copy can be removed easily. The output of most of the high-resolution machines in use for wirephoto or newspaper page plates is manually removed from the receiver for processing. Automation of the chemical photographic processing is coming into use on recently manufactured machines.

SYSTEM DESIGN

Today there is a considerable array of facsimile equipment. The user must understand his or her requirements, develop selection criteria, and acquire a system that complies with them. The most important considerations are the overall usage cost of the system (i.e., equipment costs and communication costs, both of which have fixed and variable elements), output copy quality, the convenience of use of the equipment, and the assurance that a transmission sent is in fact received and printed at the destination.

The user must decide what operating speed is needed, or whether several speeds are required—that is, whether top-of-the-line equipment is needed at certain offices, but less sophisticated can be used at other offices. Selection must be made among transmitters, receivers, and transceivers, or some mixture. A decision must be made on communication facilities, and terminals must be selected with the proper degree of automation for demonstrated needs. The user must select the communication network interfaces that best fulfill the company's needs, and consider which optional attachments should be ordered with the equipment. Thus the user is the final designer of his or her own system.

Understanding the Requirement The burden is upon users to understand their communications needs and to develop a clear understanding of what a graphic system is worth to them, in dollars. The marketing personnel of the equipment vendors are well experienced in these analyses and are of course anxious to help and should be consulted. However, users are wise always to bear in mind that the salesperson is out to sell; such counsel must be evaluated objectively.

Only a very small fraction of potential or actual facsimile users have a good grasp of what fast graphic communication can do for them in improving the efficiency of business and government administration. In many organizations, facsimile is "saved" either for use of the top executives exclusively, or for only super-urgent communications, while the great bulk of traffic is committed to other and slower means. But companies should evaluate the cost of having receivables documents and order entries tied up in the mails for two days or more. The 1975 average delivery time for first class air mail, coast to coast, office to office, was over 4 days. In litigations, what is the value of access to distant documents in minutes as compared to days? In management and control, what is the value of having the weekly operating reports, with total accuracy, in the hands of the supervision in minutes instead of days? As to accuracy: a facsimile machine, in contrast to all other means of electronic record transmission (all requiring an operator at a keyboard at some point in the process) cannot transpose a number.

Usage Cost The usage cost of a facsimile system is made up of the fixed charges for the machines and the communication channel terminations (both in general are monthly rentals), plus machine variable charges and consummable supplies, plus the cost of the use time on the transmission channels. Some organizations have dedicated and private communication networks, or have "unlimited-use" long-distance call contracts with the communication companies. In such instances, a serious error is sometimes made by the analyst who assumes that the variable cost of the transmission channel is free, because the channel is in being and paid for regardless of the facsimile decision. Of course, all channel users should absorb a duration-of-use proration of the transmission costs to ensure that each contending user makes an economic use decision.

The trade-off between speed (or throughput) and cost must be evaluated. Equipment is available in various speed configurations. In general, higher transmission speed ability means higher monthly rental charges, coupled with lower transmission line costs. The break-even monthly volume between two different units (subscripts a and b) can be calculated as shown in the accompanying boxed calculation.

$$V = \frac{R_b - R_a}{(L_a + S_a + M_a) - (L_b + S_b + M_b)}$$

Where V = break-even transmission volume (in pages) per average unit time
R = rental per unit
L = line charges per page
S = supplies cost per page
M = meter cost per page

As an example, suppose a comparison is desired between a 2-minute metered unit and a 4-minute unit with lower monthly cost. Assume the following:

R_2 = \$200/month
L_2 = 2 minute $\times$ 38¢/minute = 76¢/page
S_2 = 2¢/page
M_2 = 10¢/page

R_4 = \$50/month
L_4 = 4 minute $\times$ 38¢/minute = \$1.52/page
S_4 = 5¢/page
M_4 = 0

The break-even volume is calculated as

$$V = \frac{200 - 50}{(1.52 + 0.05 + 0.00) - (0.76 + 0.02 + 0.10)}$$
$$= 217 \text{ pages/month or } 10 \text{ pages/day}$$

This formula finds the intersection of two lines, each representing the usage cost of a machine as a function of the volume. These curves have the familiar appearance of Figure 2-1.

The numbers employed in our example are purely illustrative. For an actual business decision, it is imperative to consult the pertinent vendors and common carriers to ensure that the input figures employed are current and inclusive.

The following figures are representative for 1975 equipment and transmission costs for an even mix of transcontinental and midcontinental calls. The 4- to 6-minute units are least costly (all-inclusive) at a daily page volume per unit of 7. The 1-minute units (for which the rental is higher but the channel costs are less) are most cost-effective at daily page volumes of 14 or more. The mid-speed (2- or 3-minute) units are best suited to the range between those shown in Figure 2-2.[1]

One more comparison: For reasonable traffic levels, teletype is about five times as costly, word for word, as high-speed facsimile.

Output Copy It is worth the cost to employ facsimile equipment with high-quality output copy (high resolution and high contrast) if any of the following are true:

1. Copies of the received copy are likely to be made for further distribution.

2. The received copy is to be marked up, corrected, signed off, or otherwise reprocessed and then transmitted again.

3. Received copy is to be of archival quality, be filed, and be kept for any lengthy period of time.

[1] The calculations are for fax (facsimile) transmission only (not comparing fax direct cost with mail, for example) and are for an even mix of mid-range (1,000-mile) and long-range (3,000-mile) calls. An average of 14 transmissions per day is not much for an office of any appreciable size, and hence such offices, if they treat with other offices in other cities, should logically use high-speed fax. With any alternative, that office is wasting money and time. Not many firms as yet appreciate this. Rapifax's largest customer, with more than 60 facsimile machines, does. Each of its machines averages about 1,000 transmissions per month, or about 45 per day. The average customer makes about 400 transmissions per month, or 18 per day. Experience shows that usage of equipment always rises from month to month, for each installation, as users become accustomed to the speed and confident of delivery on the other end.

4. Received copy is to be scanned by character reader devices, either of the optical or mark-sense variety.

5. Received copy is to be used (if only occasionally) as input to a duplicator.

Operator Convenience   In general the internal operating logic of facsimile machines is not interesting to office personnel, and they should not be called upon to be sympathetic with the machine's problems.   Therefore, success in routine operations demands that the machines be highly automated so that the operator has only to instruct the machine on the intended address, the page size, and the desired speed.   Experience has shown that if the operators have to do more, they tend to fear the machine, and fear begets error.

The 3-hour time shift between the coasts of the United States means that East and West Coast offices are out of step for part of each day.   It is thus desirable for some users to have the feature of completely *unattended receive* in their facsimile equip-

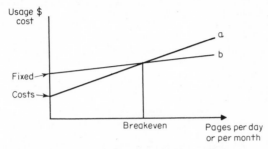

Fig. 2-1   Facsimile usage break-even chart.

ment.   With that feature, the East Coast offices can make routine transmissions west while the address offices are still not opened up in the morning.   And similarly, after 2 P.M. in the West, transmissions east remain practical, and will be on the addressees' desks the following morning while the senders are still in bed.

Assured Delivery   An important requirement for a true unattended receive function is that the transmission be *closed loop*, so that the receiver automatically informs the sender whether the copy was properly received or not.   If not, the copy can be sent again.   Without assured delivery, the transmission may be a failure and neither the sender nor the intended receiver would know.   Days (and valuable business!) could be lost.   Unattended receive equipment without the feature of assured delivery should not be considered.

Transmit-Only and Receive-Only Units versus Transceivers   With separate consoles, electronics, power supplies, and channel interfaces, it is clear that the cost of a transmit-only unit plus a receive-only unit will be greater than the cost of a transceiver.   Hence, if a given facsimile transaction point is to have both transmit and receive functions, it is usually true that transceivers are the preferred equipment.   There are, however, two circumstances where this simple conclusion does not hold:

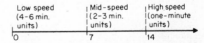

Fig. 2-2   Comparison of facsimile units for maximum cost effectiveness over a range of usage.

1. In the circumstance of very heavy operational use (many hours per day of either transmission or reception at one point) a transceiver could be so busy sending that an outside sender could rarely get "in"—the sender would almost always get a busy signal; similarly, if a transceiver is almost always busy receiving, the local personnel would have to get into a queue to get "out."   The solution to such problems is to have multiple communication lines and multiple machines, some for transmit only and some for receive only.   Thus, the cost of a transmitter plus the cost of a receiver can be less than the cost of two transceivers.

2. In the circumstance of highly skewed usage, with almost all transactions being transmit, transmit-only units are frequently preferred.   The reason here is that, in general, a transmitter is less costly than a receiver with the same quality of performance.

Thus, from points with high outbound traffic and little inbound traffic, several transmit-only units plus one transceiver should perhaps be considered.

Communication Facilities and Communication Interfaces   In addition to the public switched telephone network (PSN), most large firms and almost all branches of government employ one or more networks of privately owned or leased and dedicated communications facilities.   Until the early 1970s these networks were usually analog voice circuits set up for economy or privacy or both.   More recently such networks have shown a trend to be digital, and to be intended primarily for data links among computers or between computers and terminals.   Facsimile equipment can be set up to operate very well on these lines.   (The configuration and protocols of digital channels are discussed in Chapter 1 of this Part.)

For organizations contemplating the routine operational use of facsimile communication, it is usual to set up the equipment for primary operation on the private network, with access to the PSN available as a backup should the private network be out of commission or overloaded.   For this purpose, both the public and private lines are brought to an interface switch on the machine, enabling the operator to select the channel to be used for transmission.   Normally, this interface is set up to receive an incoming call on either line, if not busy, without operator intervention, and without regard to the switch setting for outbound calls.

Standard interfaces are available which enable a facsimile transmitter to make a *broadcast* or simultaneous transmission to all or any subset of the facsimile machines on a network.   These arrangements prevent an unauthorized point from eavesdropping, but do not prevent a station on the network not involved in a broadcast from calling any other station not on the broadcast, to transact its own business without any interference to or from the broadcast.

Also, standard interfaces are available for facsimile *hot lines*.   These are dedicated lines among two or more points, and available for use without operator dialing.   The operator merely hands the documents to the machine, which automatically "wakes up" and immediately begins transmission to the other point or points.

Hot-line installations find use within large plant sites, among main offices of corporations, and notably in the financial institutions of New York City between midtown and Wall Street.

Optional Attachments   The line interfaces already mentioned (digital line, broadcast, and hot line), and the unattended receive/assured delivery feature may be regarded as optional attachments to a basic facsimile equipment.   They do not alter the basic performance of a unit, but rather enhance the convenience of its use.   Further optional features available which the system buyer should consider are:

Unattended Send.   This feature enables a machine to make a transmission at an arbitrary interval of time after it has been instructed to do so.   Suppose, for example, that the field sales offices are to send in, daily, by facsimile, the sales results for main-office study.   Each office is assigned its time slot during the night for transmission.   The document feeder (discussed below) is loaded with the day's sales report, a clock timer on the unit is set, the *unattended send* button on the facsimile machine is asserted, and the address (phone number) of the main-office machine is dialed in.   That number goes into a temporary memory.   At the appointed hour, the clock starts the transmission and it proceeds to completion.

Store and Forward.   The idea of unattended send is carried to its logical end point by the *store and forward* attachment.   This unit enables a number of transmissions to a number of different addressees to be stored on magnetic tape during the course of a business day.   Then, at a preselected hour, the unit initiates transmission activity to the various addressees.   The unit pauses at prearranged intervals so that the parent facsimile machine can make receptions if someone (e.g., another store and forward) is attempting to call in.   The unit is set up to retry calls that do not get through, and to keep a complete record of its work so that the following morning the operator is fully informed about what was and was not achieved.

Multiple-Page.   This important feature enables a facsimile transmitter to hold a connection so that many sheets can be transmitted on the same call.   This capability is inherent in all voice-coordinated-type machines (i.e., those requiring an operator at both ends). It is not inherent in all unattended receive machines. Machines without this feature should not be considered for any but the most occasional use.

Document Feeder. Once the benefits of graphic communication are appreciated by an organization, the process is organized for efficiency. Transmissions are grouped by addressee, and multiple pages are sent on each call. It is costly to have an operator do manual feeding, a page at a time (e.g., one per minute, or one per 2 minutes, which is just sufficiently frequent that the operator could not do something else in the meantime), and hence an automatic document feeder is usually an attractive investment. Most mid-speed and high-speed facsimile equipment offer this option.

Shorthand Dialer. Experience shows that most facsimile transmissions are made to a very few addressees. Any one machine will make 85 to 90 per cent of its calls to one of nine frequently called numbers. It is time-consuming, boring, and hence conducive to operator dialing errors for an operator to dial the same two or four numbers several times a day, day after day. The facsimile industry is now offering a *shorthand dialer* attachment which will enable the most frequently called numbers to be stored in memory in the machine. These numbers (including the area code and intermediate pauses for dial tones) can be called forth by the operator by dialing only two digits. The actual network control signals (dial pulses or tone signals) that go to the telephone plant are generated electronically by the shorthand dialer circuitry.

Compatibility. There are many facsimile units, from many vendors, in use throughout the world. Some of these machines will work across family lines with machines of another family, and some will not. There is growing appreciation of the proposition that compatibility between families of machines is desirable for several reasons:

1. It would permit high-speed machines to be used between high-traffic locations, and yet allow low-traffic points to communicate with high-traffic points without requiring the duplication of equipment at the latter.

2. It would facilitate lateral facsimile communication between companies using equipment from different sources.

It is, however, clearly unwise to attempt to fix and finalize the signaling format of facsimile machines, since that act would foreclose progress to more efficient encoding means, higher speeds, or other innovations. The solution lies in the compatibility options offered by several equipment manufacturers. These attachments will allow the host machine to send to and receive from machines in one or more other families of machines, in at least one of the speed modes of the other machines.

The facsimile equipment buyer should consider compatibility requirements and ensure that the compatibilities he or she requires can be obtained.

Computer Compatibility. Facsimile equipment can be used in the role of a computer printer. For this purpose there must be a character-generation function either as part of the computer program, or as part of the internal writing control logic of the facsimile printer. This function receives the character codes from the computer, and from a look-up table stored in memory, outputs the raster scan equivalents to the printer mechanism, line by line.

APPLICATIONS SUMMARY

Facsimile today is finding broad, general-purpose use in a variety of industrial, service, governmental, and professional applications.

In a message communication system, facsimile is used to communicate time-vital information of all kinds from the source point directly to the end user. In this application, facsimile offers the flexibility of maintaining the original format of the message with no possibility for a transposition or omission error by an intermediate operator, while providing the most rapid system possible at a surprisingly low cost. The features of the contemporary equipment such as quiet, simple, and odorless operation that permit its placement in the office instead of in the communication center make a facsimile system practical and desirable.

In data collection, facsimile permits the capture of operating data at the source and their transmission to the central point for study or entry to data processing. Facsimile data entry can be used in the small sales office as easily and effectively as in a major facility.

Acceptance of facsimile as a major means of communication in business and government has been progressing on a large scale since about 1970. But today, both the technology, and the full benefits of its use, are still being discovered and developed. The applications are limited only by the imaginations of the users. Equipment improvements and extensions are coming forth rapidly, and facsimile promises to provide the same widespread, convenient, instantaneous, and readily available communication for graphics as we have all come to take for granted for voice, via the telephone.

Chapter 3

The Communications Subsystem

JOHN E. BUCKLEY

President, Telecommunications Management Corporation,
Cornwells Heights, Pennsylvania

All communications data processing systems exhibit a very similar architecture with respect to their associated communications subsystems. The communications subsystem of an automatic data processing system is that series of functional devices that permits the reliable exchange of data between remote locations and a central processor or computer. While each specific system has a unique configuration of these functional building blocks, their existence is common to all such information systems.

The components of a generalized communications subsystem are as follows:
1. Data communications terminals.
2. Modulating-demodulating units.
3. Transmission channels.
4. Network multiplexers.
5. Computer communications controllers.

Of these five major component classifications only the network multiplexers may be optionally applied, depending upon the relative economics of the particular system. The other four classifications are mandatory for a computer communications system. This Chapter introduces and discusses the role of each of these components in today's information system applications. In this manner the reader can obtain an accurate overview of the interrelationships of these components, as well as being able to assess the system economic factor with respect to each component's presented scope of performance.

COMMUNICATIONS TERMINAL SYSTEMS

Terminal devices are used in all data communications systems. Even when two computers exchange data through a communications channel, one computer is considered a terminal to the other computer. And even the normal I/O peripheral devices associated with a computer can be properly considered a level of terminal devices. Following is a classification of the various terminal devices which can be used to satisfy a variety of applications:

LEVEL 5: Applications-Sensitive Terminals
LEVEL 4: Conversational and Interactive Terminals
LEVEL 3: Batch Transmission Terminals
LEVEL 2: Satellite Processor Terminals
LEVEL 1: Central Computer I/O Peripherals (Central computer and files)

Any application may be satisfied by terminals at any of the specified levels. The single factor that is normally influenced by a replacement of specific terminal level by another terminal level is the responsiveness or timeliness of the system's resulting data. The relative factors illustrated in Figure 3-1 compare some of the other more pertinent aspects of each terminal-level classification in a generalized application.

Other schemes of classifying data terminal devices relate to the inherent transmission speed of the terminal. Figure 3-2 presents a terminal speed spectrum with illustrative candidates.

A push-button telephone instrument can be used as a terminal device. The push-buttons on the instrument each generate discrete tones. These tones can be decoded into binary-encoded signals at the computer end. Response, however, must be oral. Several voice-response devices are available which can be programmed to generate a number of spoken words over the return path to the Touch-Tone telephone terminal user.

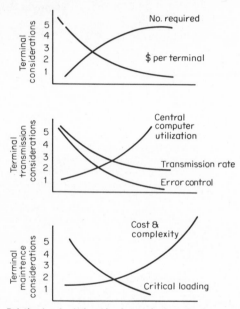

Fig. 3-1   Relative-level relationships in terminal application classifications.

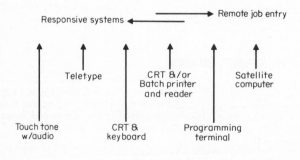

Fig. 3-2   Terminal speed spectrum.

Probably the most common terminal in use today is the typewriterlike teletypewriter. These devices are characterized by a hard-copy printing mechanism and a keyboard. In some configurations the keyboard can be left off for receive-only applications. The operating rate of these devices is on the order of 10 to 15 characters per second (cps).

Other typewriterlike devices on the market are being operated at 30 to 40 cps. These are more correctly referred to as *conversational terminals*. Such typewriterlike terminals have also led to the development of much faster terminal devices which still have the same basic characteristics. Several manufacturers now offer printing devices (with or without keyboards) which will print 120 cps or even up to 250 cps. These are usually called *serial* or *character printers*. The basic printing mechanism is like a typewriter in that each character is printed individually, and an entire line is constructed in a character-by-character manner from the left margin. This mode of operation is chosen to eliminate the need for some local storage at the printer site, since a character may be printed before the next character is received.

Higher-speed printing mechanisms, identical to those used as computer peripherals, are also used as terminal devices. The entire line is printed in a single operation. Since characters are received through the communications medium in serial order, some local storage is necessary to assemble a print line. These printers are called *line printers*.

Where the need for hard-copy output is not desirable, CRT terminal devices are used. The CRTs used in terminals have the same basic characteristics as those used in commercial television sets, and the associated electronics convert the digital bit sequences into the proper signals acceptable to the display. These devices usually include a keyboard for data transmission.

Display devices may be of two kinds: limited and vector. Limited display systems include the ability to exhibit a limited set of symbols, in specific locations on the face of the screen. This type is most often used in information-query types of commercial applications. A vector display permits arbitrarily drawn straight lines. By drawing short lines at various points, figures such as circles, alpha letters, numeric digits, and other symbols can also be constructed.

The use of a high-speed line printer in a terminal provides for batch data output. If the terminal also includes a card reader, the terminal may be used to submit jobs to a central computer through the card reader, and receive output on the printer. In many applications, a keyboard is desirable. The keyboard is often associated with a display, so that the user can request certain limited information directly from the system. Such a terminal, with four components (printer, reader, CRT, and keyboard) can be used for communicating with both batch-oriented and responsive systems.

Some terminals include a programmable minicomputer which can perform a limited amount of processing at the user's site. These satellite processor terminals are available to permit local data acquisition with local data editing performed by the minicomputer to edit and store the information.[1] At the same time, the minicomputer is also used as a terminal to some larger system. The advantage of a programmable terminal is that its characteristics may be programmatically changed to emulate different terminal devices. If the terminal is used to communicate with more than one computer system, the programmable computer can be used to create the data transmission characteristics required by each individual computer system.

Output Media The choice of the output media of the terminal is an important factor in system design. The media selection must be made on the basis of the intended applications of the system, not just the availability of terminal devices. Some of the most common media are:

- Printed page.
- Punched card.
- Punched paper tape.
- Magnetic tape.
- Visual display.

Printed pages may be typed by one of the various hard-copy mechanisms and are probably the most common output form of a terminal communications system. The volume and variety can dictate the use of either a low-speed typewriterlike character printer or a high-speed line printer.

[1] See Part 2, Chapter 4, "Minicomputers," in this Section.

Punched cards represent a very common data medium for high-volume applications. These can be prepared off-line, and provide a physical, tangible document from which to work. Punched cards are also used as an output medium in data communications, depending on the specific application. Their major use, however, is to input data.

Punched paper tape is a very common data communications medium. Many terminals are designed to handle only paper tape. Paper tape is often produced as a byproduct from accounting machines, and can be used as a direct data entry medium. Paper-tape speeds are also compatible with punched cards, with many of the same physical problems. Paper tape demands that some transcribing equipment be available if output is provided only on tape.

Punched cards and paper tape are now being replaced by magnetic tape as a local terminal storage medium. There are many terminal devices which use small audio cassettes, with relatively low recording densities. Magnetic tape offers the possibility that higher transmission speeds can be used than with the limits imposed by mechanical printing devices. The speeds of contemporary magnetic-tape facilities at a terminal are normally designed to be compatible with the other media of the terminal.

Visual display devices exhibit a need to refresh the display several times a second. The refresh function is most often done by requiring the terminal to have some local storage which is cycled for refreshing the local display.

Hard-Wired vs. Stored-Program Terminals   When considering the application characteristics of the terminal, one may be faced with the question of selecting either a hard-wired or a stored-program device. Hard-wired terminals are generally satisfactory with low-speed, keyboard, or hard-copy applications. Magnetic-tape, punched-card, and punched-paper-tape terminals, however, are most often used where the output media will be direct input to a central processor. Because of normal program maintenance, it often becomes more desirable to make any required changes in the terminal program, rather than in the main processor program. Under these circumstances, a stored-program data terminal becomes more useful and more economical than a hard-wired terminal. It is also possible to utilize a stored-program terminal for off-line listing compilations, sorting, etc., by adding low-cost peripherals, if the traffic flow for communications permits this kind of scheduling.

Hard-wired terminals have traditionally had the advantage of lower cost per capacity, and in most cases, required less maintenance. These factors are rapidly changing, however, with current technological advances, resulting in more reliable and lower-cost circuitry, particularly in the MOS/LSI semiconductor areas.

Error Control   The kind and type of error-control technique required will influence the selection of the data terminal. If the data traffic contains sufficient redundancy, relatively simple error detection with operator-initiated correction provisions may be acceptable. This function is carried out by either the processor or the human brain. If no redundancy or very little redundancy is present in the data traffic flow, or if the data are to be directly interpreted by a computer, it is important to keep the residual error rate at a very low value, and an elaborate error-control scheme will be required.

It can be deduced that the choice of the terminal will be influenced by the complexity of the error control required. The more sophisticated codes generally require a stored-program terminal for execution. Character and block parity check schemes can be readily handled by hard-wired machines.

Hidden Costs   Some hidden costs which may be overlooked but should be examined when choosing data terminals for a system are personnel costs related to data preparation, data distribution, training and staffing, etc. The costs for parallel operations while switching over to a new data communications system must be calculated. Other charges, such as the supplies for magnetic tapes, punched cards, documentation, etc., are sometimes significant.

MODULATING-DEMODULATING UNITS

The communication network used for voice and data transmission is an analog system.[2] Voice generates an analog signal made up of a number of frequencies capable of having a number of levels. Data generated by or required by a digital computer are binary in nature, and the information signal within such a computer has only two

[2] See Chapter 1, "Communication Basics," in this Part.

states or levels: "1" or "0" value. In addition, the computer communicates between its internal components using direct current (dc) signals rather than frequencies. In order for a standard dc binary signal from a digital computer to function with a frequency multilevel signal communication network, a converter must be utilized. This converter is called the *modem*.

From the dc binary signals, the modem creates a signal compatible with the communication network. Conversely, the modem transforms a frequency signal from the communication network into a dc signal compatible to the computer.

The term *modem* is a contraction of the two functions to be performed, i.e., modulating and demodulating. Modulating is converting the dc signal into a compatible frequency signal. Demodulating is converting the frequency signal into a dc signal.

The term *data set* is also used to identify a modem.

Modulation   There are three basic types of modem designs, classified with respect to their associated methods of modulating (and demodulating):

- Amplitude modulation (AM)
- Frequency modulation (FM)
- Phase modulation (PM)

An AM modem transmits a constant frequency. Amplitude, however, varies depending upon the value of the dc binary information. For example, a dc "1" level will be full amplitude, while a dc "0" level will be a lower amplitude.

Amplitude modulation is generally used for low-speed data transmission (up to 300 bps). While an AM modem is the least complex to design and manufacture, this technique tends to be susceptible to burst noise which varies the amplitude or energy level of the transmission signal. Burst noise coincident with a "0" level can raise the amplitude so that the demodulator interprets the received signal as a "1" level.

An FM modem transmits a constant level or amplitude while frequency changes depend upon the value of the dc binary information. For example, a dc "1" level will be frequency 1, while a dc "0" level will be frequency 2.

Frequency modulation is generally used for medium-speed data transmission (300 to 1,800 bps). While more complex to manufacture than an AM modem, the FM modem has a higher immunity to burst noise than the AM modem.

PM modems transmit a constant amplitude and frequency, but the changes in phase depend upon the value of the dc binary information. For example, a dc "1" level will be phase 0 degree, while a dc "0" level will be phase 180 degrees.

Phase modulation is generally used for high-speed data transmission (2,000 bps and higher). The design and manufacture of PM modems is quite complex. However, since it uses constant amplitude and frequency, the PM modem has excellent noise-immunity characteristics. Phase modulation coupled with other data manipulation techniques can provide reliable data transmission at speeds of 9,600 bps using a typical voice circuit.

Some modems in operation today use AM for high-speed transmission (AM "vestigal sideband"); and some low-speed modems (under 300 bps) use FM rather than the AM techniques.

At the higher transmission speeds, circuit conditioning is mandatory. In addition to the circuit conditioning provided by the common carrier (C-1, C-2, C-4), some high-speed modems also contain equalizers (conditioners) as part of their design. The equalizers contained in these modems are intended to complement, not replace, conditioning provided by common carriers. These modem equalizers essentially accomplish the "fine tuning" required for the high transmission speeds.

Recent high-speed modems have automatic equalizers, an advancement which permits more practical application. With automatic equalization, the receiving modem can sample the delay variations present in a received signal and automatically introduce delay at the appropriate frequencies to ensure that all frequencies are received at the same time as the slowest frequency.

Timing   Modems can also be classified with respect to method of timing: asynchronous and synchronous.

An asynchronous modem reacts to any change occurring at its dc interface regardless of the rate of change. Realistically, if the rate of change exceeds the internal limitations of the modem, such as the bandpass of the output line filters, the modem will not operate properly.

An asynchronous modem designated as having a maximum 300-bps transmission rate will operate very reliably at only 100 bps or at any other speed within its stated limits. A synchronous modem, however, operates only at specified speeds. These modems also require a clock or timing signal, either generated internally by the modem or provided by the data processing equipment. This clock is used to sample the dc signal and activate the modulator. For received data, the clock identifies to the data processing equipment when a new bit has been demodulated. Asynchronous modems are generally used at up to 1,800 bps, while synchronous modems are generally associated with the higher transmission speeds.

In a low-speed data transmission application, the digital bit-per-second and transmitted baud[3] rates may have the same value. For each unit of information on the digital side of the modem, there is a corresponding unit on the analog side. Such a system might utilize a modem device which is essentially passive, and generates a unit of analog information for each unit of digital information presented to the digital interface.

Multilevel Modulation With higher-speed systems, modems perform functions other than simple modulation and demodulation. Because of the limitations of available communications channel bandwidths or passbands, the digital data must be compressed so as to reduce the number of actual units of information transmitted. This is accomplished by transmitting to the communications channel a single unit of information representative of a number of digital bits of information generated at the interface between the data processing equipment and the modem. Such data transmission systems are referred to as *multilevel modulation systems* and are most common at the higher transmission rates.

If a transmitted unit of information can be used to recover more than one digital bit, the number of digital bits which can be transmitted in a given period of time may be greater than the transmission rate (baud) of the communications channel. For example, a system using amplitude modulation may employ two discrete signal levels to represent the different binary values. The maximum number of bits which can be transmitted in one second is equal to the baud rate of the communications channel. Assume that an amplitude modulation system actually had four discrete amplitude levels that could be transmitted and detected. Two digital bits would be represented for each signal unit transmitted. In such a system the baud rate would be half the bit rate:

Transmitted signal level	Digital bit values
A	11
B	10
C	01
D	00

Other modulation schemes can also use this technique. By using four different frequencies in a frequency modulation system or four distinct phases (045, 135, 225, and 315 degrees) in a phase modulation system, the same type of bit rate compression can be achieved. This concept has been carried further with eight discrete steps where three consecutive bits are transmitted in a single unit of transmitted information. With these techniques, commercially available modems are able to transmit 4,800, 7,200, and 9,600 bps on a communications channel with less than 3 kHz effective bandwidth.

TRANSMISSION CHANNELS

Precise uniformity of transmission facilities is not a characteristic of today's communication network. Transmission facilities can be classified into three levels. These levels are based on the transmission capacity of the service as expressed in bandwidth. The wider or larger the bandwidth, the greater the potential capacity for data transmission. Table 3-1 presents these service levels and their associated characteristics. While all services may be used for data transmission, the voiceband is the most widely utilized. The transmission parameters of the voiceband are also applicable to the other two

---

[3] One baud = 1 pulse per second.

service categories.   However, in view of the predominant use of voicebands, this discussion is limited to the voiceband characteristics.

As shown in Table 3-1 a typical voiceband has a nominal 4-kHz bandwidth.   This means that when voicebands are frequency-multiplexed for long-distance carrier transmission, the centers of two adjacent voicebands are spaced 4,000 Hz apart.   The actual bandwidth available for data transmission is significantly less.   The actual bandwidth is identified as the circuit's effective bandwidth.   Such transmission equipment as bandpass filters, inductive loads, amplifiers, etc. cause the difference between the nominal bandwidth and the effective bandwidth.

TABLE 3-1   Transmission Facility Classification

Designation	Bandwidth	Transmission rate	Remarks
Narrowband	Variable – generally up to 300 Hz	150–300 bps	Generally private line except for Telex and TWX services
Voiceband	Nominal 4 kHz	2,000–2,400 bps and higher with COAM modems	Private and dial lines
Wideband	48 kHz and up	40.8 kb per sec and higher	Generally private line except Data-Phone 50 service from Bell System

TABLE 3-2   Conditioning

Voiceband	Conditioning	Delay distortion	Band
3002	None	1,750 μs	800–2,600 Hz
3002	C-1	1,000 μs	1,000–2,400 Hz
		1,750 μs	800–2,600 Hz
3002	C-2	500 μs	1,000–2,600 Hz
		1,500 μs	600–2,600 Hz
		3,000 μs	500–2,800 Hz
3002	C-4	300 μs	1,000–2,600 Hz
		500 μs	800–2,800 Hz
		1,500 μs	600–3,000 Hz

When a modem transmits data, a series of frequencies are simultaneously generated. Generally, these frequencies can be considered the carrier frequency and the associated sidebands.   In order for the receiving modem to detect the transmitted frequencies for either a "1" or "0" bit, the carrier frequency and a number of the sideband frequencies must be received within the duration of the bit.   Electrical signals have different propagation times depending on their frequencies within a typical communication circuit.   If the transmission rate is low (up to 1,800 bps) the bit duration is usually long enough to allow all necessary frequencies to appear at the receiving modem, permitting recovery of the bit.   As the transmission rate increases (2,400 to 4,800 bps and higher) the transmission circuit must be "treated" to ensure all frequencies are received at the required time.   This is accomplished by "slowing down" the propagation of the faster frequencies to match the slower frequencies.   This "treatment" is called *circuit equalization* or *circuit conditioning*.   Table 3-2 presents typical conditioning available for a 3002-type voiceband data channel.

Transmission facilities are available on both a private line or dial line basis.   A private line is a full-time circuit between two specified locations.   The circuit charge is based on the airline mileage equivalent between the two locations.   A dial line is established when needed and dissolved when not needed.   The charge is based on the airline mileage equivalent and the time the connection was established.

Both of these services may be used for data.   Since the dial line is established in a random manner, there is no way to predict the resulting connection quality.   A dial connection may exhibit excellent transmission characteristics at one time, and totally inoperative data characteristics the next time the same location is dialed. Because of this variability of characteristics, a dial line normally has a lower transmission rate capability than a private line. Conditioning, for example, is available only with a private line, since it is a permanent connection.

Voiceband circuits are generally available on a half-duplex or full-duplex basis. Half-duplex circuits (2-wire) permit two-way, nonsimultaneous data transmission. Full-duplex circuits (4-wire) permit two-way, simultaneous data transmission. All the circuits between the telephone companies' switching offices are full-duplex (4-wire) lines. These interoffice circuits are called *trunk facilities*. The circuit between the telephone company end office and the customer is a pair of wires normally capable of transmitting one voiceband. These circuits are called *local loops*. In order to conserve on physical wire, and in view of the original voice transmission requirements, the local loops are half-duplex (2-wire).

When a private line is installed as full-duplex (4-wire), an additional local loop is assigned between the customer's location and the trunk facility. The switching centers, originally designed for voice, can accept only 2-wire local loops. A dial connection is, therefore, only half-duplex.

Since a dial connection is randomly established, a mismatch of trunk circuit characteristics normally occurs. This mismatch can cause the resulting connection to oscillate or "echo," because of the reflection of the transmitted signal. In order to prevent this echo, which could destroy the quality of voice transmission, echo suppressors are installed in the telephone trunk circuits. These echo suppressors will amplify in the direction aiding the higher-level signal, and attenuate the lower-level reflected signals from the opposite direction.

When the other end of a connection begins to transmit, the higher-level signal will be coming from the opposite direction. The echo suppressor will then reverse its direction of amplification, the reversal being called the *turnaround* of the connection. This function takes a certain amount of time (turnaround time). Voice transmission can usually continue during this time without loss of intelligibility. For data transmission, however, this turnaround time is dead time. Information cannot be transmitted until the turnaround is complete. While turnaround time is normally stated as 150 ms, this time can significantly reduce the effective throughput of a data transmission.

NETWORK MULTIPLEXES

The nature and design of telephone carrier systems allows a number of independent transmissions to be simultaneously achieved over the same physical trunk circuit. The same technique is utilized in digital multiplexer equipment.

The requirement that a separate physical circuit is needed to transmit an information signal can easily become an economical liability. Digital multiplexers allow a number of independently generated digital signals to be combined and transmitted on a single physical circuit. The system network economies that are possible through the use of multiplexing are the primary consideration for the use of this technique; that is, the basic justification for the use of digital multiplexing equipment is a reduction in system communication cost. Fundamentally, there are two types of digital multiplexers: frequency division multiplexers (FDM) and time division multiplexers (TDM). Each has applications in today's telecommunication systems networks.[4]

A typical FDM configuration consists of a number of small bandwidth circuits which are combined and transmitted simultaneously over a wider bandwidth circuit. The wider bandwidth circuit, also known as the *trunk circuit*, is frequency divided into a number of smaller bandwidth channels.

The primary disadvantage of frequency division multiplexing is the limited number of low-speed circuits that can be combined into a high-speed trunk. If the low-bandwidth circuits are to be used at a lower transmission rate, i.e., 75 bps, additional low-speed channels could possibly be realized, since each low-speed channel could be filtered into channels narrower than 300 Hz. The electronic circuitry is extremely simple: to a large extent, the majority of the electronics are passive analog circuits with the only active element being primarily associated with amplification circuits.

[4] For detailed discussion, see Chapter 1, "Communication Basics," in this Part.

The cost per low-speed channel for an FDM is generally lower than for a comparable TDM. This cost advantage is primarily evident when only a small number of low-speed channels are to be multiplexed. Once the number of low-speed channels to be multiplexed increases, time division multiplexing becomes more attractive economically. This particular economic crossover varies with each manufacturer's equipment, because of variances in pricing and system modularity. Whenever a number of low-speed circuits are multiplexed using frequency division, they must be demultiplexed before the low-speed data signals can be introduced to a digital computer. In evaluating computer communications system cost, operational duplication of FDMs must be considered.

Another advantage of frequency division multiplexing is the lack of required synchronization. Each low-speed channel before and after the multiplexing function operates as an independent transmission circuit. As such, the timing technique (asynchronous or synchronous) is indicated solely by the termination equipment or each low-speed channel. Between the FDMs there is no timing or synchronizing activity required. The multiplexers are passive and transparent transmission elements with respect to the information and data transmission activity.

A time division multiplexer, unlike an FDM, utilizes the full spectrum of the trunk circuit. A typical configuration for a TDM system also consists of a number of low-speed circuits being combined for transmission over a high-speed trunk. The combining, however, is achieved by an allocation of time rather than an allocation of space or frequency spectrum.

If a bit of information requires X ms to be transmitted on a low-speed channel, and the high-speed channel can transmit this same bit of information in one-twentieth of the time ($X/20$ ms), the capacity of the TDM is theoretically 20 low-speed channels. For example, assume 75-bps low-speed circuits to be multiplexed using time division and a trunk circuit transmission rate of 2,400 bps. The theoretical capacity is 32 such low-speed circuits.

The determination of theoretical multiplexer capacity using frequency division was achieved by dividing the bandwidth of the low-speed channels into the bandwidth of the trunk circuit. With time division, the theoretical capacity of the multiplexer system can be calculated by dividing the band rate of a low-speed channel into the band rate to be used on the high-speed trunk circuit.

The most important consideration, however, in the design of a TDM is the synchronization necessary over the trunk circuit. The TDM operates on a cyclical basis, such that a cycle must be completed within the transmission time of a unit of information on the low-speed circuits. A complete cycle or scan of all low-speed circuits is called a *frame*. Each frame transmitted over the trunk circuit is divided into a number of *bytes*, where a byte is a unit of information that can consist of a data bit or a data character depending on the multiplexing equipment.

If the TDM is designed to multiplex data bits of information, one bit from each low-speed circuit would be scanned and transmitted in the sequence. More commonly, a complete data character is multiplexed and would, therefore, be transmitted over the trunk circuit in sequential bytes. In both cases, each frame must contain unique synchronizing information which is used to synchronize the demultiplexing equipment with the multiplexing equipment. A unit of information obtained from low-speed Circuit No. 1 by the multiplexer must be properly delivered to low-speed Circuit No. 1 by the demultiplexer. This order is assured by designating one or more bytes of the frame as synchronizing bytes, containing unique characters which cannot be duplicated by data. The byte following the synchronizing bytes is always assigned to the first low-speed circuit followed by the byte from the second low-speed circuit, etc.

The application of digital multiplexers is primarily of value when a system uses a number of low-speed circuits (less than 300 bps) and voice-grade trunk circuits. The other requirement for the use of multiplexing equipment is that each low-speed circuit, and hence each device, requires continuous access to a central point. If the access to the central point can be scheduled, the use of the switched or dial communications generally offers a more economical system solution to the communication network requirement.

The major advantage of a TDM is the high multiplexing capacity. While a significant amount of common electronics is used by all the low-speed circuits, present TDMs generally represent a level of reliability comparable to FDMs. It is also interesting to note that if the data to be time-division-multiplexed are destined for a digital computer, it is not mandatory that the high-speed trunk be demultiplexed before interfacing with the digital computer. It is possible to interface the high-speed trunk directly to the digital computer and allow the computer to perform the synchronizing functions.

COMPUTER COMMUNICATIONS CONTROLLERS

The communications controller is a peripheral to the central computer, and generally interfaces with the modems or data sets through a separate *data set adapter* (also called

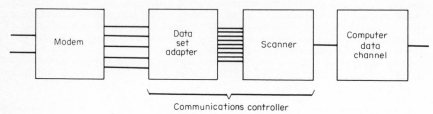

Fig. 3-3   Communications controller configuration.

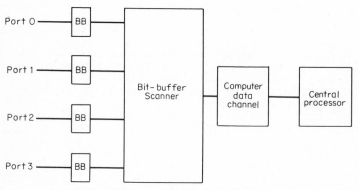

Fig. 3-4   Major components of a bit-buffer scheme.

a *line termination unit*) for each modem. For each modem there is a data set adapter (DSA) which performs the interface function of matching the computer's internal conventions to those of the data set supplied by a communications vendor. Most data transmission is performed serial by bit, while digital computers deal with bit clusters called *bytes* or *characters*.

The data set adapter must contain the logic necessary to commutate the character's bits one by one for transmission, and aggregate bits into characters on input for parallel presentation to the computer. It is important to note that the data set adapter just described is exemplary, and not all DSAs do character-bit manipulation. Most data set adapters do, however, carry certain control lines from the data set into the computer. The sensing of conditions is also performed by the data set adapter, as well as the conditions that cause interruption of processes inside the computer to invoke unique actions. (See Figure 3-3.)

The simplest kind of I/O communication scanning transfers bits, as received, into the computer on demand. The bits are not normally deposited directly into central memory, but are deposited into a special register in the central processor which is accessible to a program in memory. This memory implies that the data set adapter must have a one-bit memory, and for that reason is called a *bit buffer*. Figure 3-4 shows the major components of a bit-buffer scheme. Each individual modem and associated transmission channel is referred to as a *port* when viewed from within the computer.

Since bits arrive through different ports of the scanner asynchronously, some control outside the scanner itself must be responsible for timing in this kind of system. Each port is equipped with a bit buffer which senses and holds the current logical state of the communications channel. During one bit interval the multiplexer scans each active port and presents the current logical state to the central processor.

The scanner which controls the bit buffers typically works as follows for data reception. Assume that only port number 2 is active, and the maximum bit rate is 150 per second. Each $6\frac{2}{3}$ ms, an incoming bit obliterates the last bit. Each $6\frac{2}{3}$ ms the computer is interrupted by the scanner with the address of port 2. The current state of the bit buffer for that port is presented to the central processor, and is available to the programs designed to do communications servicing.

Each time the scanner senses the state of port 2, a logical 1 is detected, since no data are being sent from the terminal and the communications channel is in the quiescent

Time since start bit (ms)	Bit received	Car	Bit counter
			8
$6\frac{2}{3}$	1	00000001	
			7
$13\frac{1}{3}$	0	00000010	
			6
20	0	00000100	
			5
$26\frac{2}{3}$	1	00001001	
			4
$33\frac{1}{3}$	0	00010010	
			3
40	1	00100101	
			2
$46\frac{2}{3}$	1	01001011	
			1
$53\frac{1}{3}$	0	10010110	
			0
60	Stop bit	10010110	
			0

Fig. 3-5   Scanner operation.

state. When a key on the terminal is depressed, the next port sample will yield a logial 0—the start bit. The next eight bits are then collected and transferred as data.

Each port of the system has two unique words in central memory. Once the start bit is detected, the *character accumulation register* (CAR) is cleared to zero, and the *bit counter* is set to eight as shown in Figure 3-5. After one bit interval has elapsed since the start bit ($6\frac{2}{3}$ ms in our example), the received bit is shifted into the character accumulation register, and the bit counter is decremented by one. Bits are placed into the character accumulation register by shifting the previous contents left by one bit position, and placing the newly received bit in the low-order (vacated) position of the register. This corresponds to the standard convention of transmitting the most significant bit first.

After all bits have been collected, the bit counter will eventually reach zero. Then, the software which accumulates the bits into characters will recognize that subsequent one-bits represent the quiescent state of the communications link, and a zero in the bit counter means a new start-bit is to be expected. This may happen as soon as one bit interval ($6\frac{2}{3}$ ms) has elapsed after the CAR has been filled. Therefore, the communications software must unload the character accumulation register as soon as possible. This is accomplished, in the software, by passing the contents of the accumulation register to a buffer elsewhere in central memory reserved for this port. The buffer is a consecutive group of memory locations which will hold the successively received characters.

Assuming a 30-port system, with all ports active, all terminals will be simultaneously transmitting or receiving. The scanner which controls bit buffers will generate heavy demands on the software system. The bit-sensing operation of the scanner must be performed 150 times each second for each of 30 ports, or 4,500 times each second, whether data are being received or not. To be able to continue to transfer logical bits of data, a computer interrupt must be performed 4,500 times each second. If each interrupt requires an average of 50 μs (which represents only a few executed instructions), 450 ms per second are used up, or 45 per cent of the processor's capacity for computing is usurped by the communications servicing of bits.

Under the worst conditions, each terminal could supply 15 characters each second, and 450 characters must be placed into buffers each second. Normally, output and input are not performed concurrently in half-duplex operation. If the software requires 100 μs to install one received character or select one character to be transmitted, another 45 ms are required.

Finally, the buffer-switching operation will occur about every 30 characters, which is the approximate length of the average record received from and transmitted to a terminal. Then, the buffer switching must take place 15 times each second. This operation might take an average of 250 μs each, requiring a total of about 4 ms out of each second.

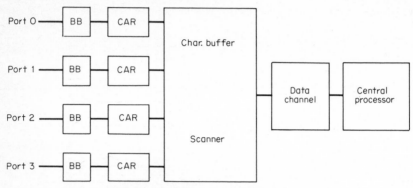

Fig. 3-6   Character-buffer data set adapter.

The bit-buffer controlling technique, in this example, has used about half the time available in the central processor at full system load. The number of bits per character, the operating bit rate of the channel, and the synchronous/asynchronous network controls are all under the control of the communications software. These parameters can be varied as required by modifying the software. As terminals on ports change dynamically (by dialing or by mixing varieties of terminal types on a multidrop polled line), the appropriate software changes can be made automatically.

A character-buffering scanning system configuration permits establishing fixed parameters for the three attributes of:
- Maximum number of bits per character.
- Bit rate.
- Synchronous or asynchronous timing.

Efficiency can be gained by providing a more sophisticated data set adapter. Such a data set adapter includes the necessary logic to collect bits into characters.

The character-buffer data set adapter (see Figure 3-6) includes the bit buffer, as well as a character accumulation register and counting logic. The hardware in the DSA is responsible for detecting the start bit, accumulating characters, and notifying the central processor when a character is done. Many data set adapters of this type include a pair of character accumulation registers; one contains the last complete character received (or next full character ready for transmission), and the other is empty (in the quiescent state) or partly used. If only a single character accumulation register is available, then when a character is received, the central processor must clear the CAR between characters. With two accumulation registers, the processor has a full-character interval time in which to clear the holding CAR. This time permits a load leveling which can be used to enhance system efficiency through scheduling in the software.

Once a character being received is detected as complete by the data set adapter, the active character accumulation register's contents are transferred to the holding register and the processor is notified of the character's completion. Once the software answers the interrupt, the character may be read from the data set adapter through the scanner into the central processor memory.

Characters received must be placed into the memory buffers, and characters to be transmitted must be selected from these buffers, with the associated software actions. The efficiency of a character-buffering system is higher than that of the bit-buffering system, since software is not involved in collecting bits into characters. If the character-servicing software still requires 100 μs per character, then the worst conditions of system activity will still yield a consumption of 45 ms per second (or 4.5 per cent) of the processor's capacity.

Since buffer servicing is also identical with the bit-buffering case, this kind of data set adapter will require the associated software to occupy a total of about 5 per cent of

TABLE 3-3

	Bit interrupt	Character interrupt	Buffer interrupt
Bit program time	45.0%	—	—
Character program time	4.5%	4.5%	—
Buffer program time	0.4%	0.4%	0.4%
Total program time	49.9%	4.9%	0.4%

the processor's time. The next obvious step is an interface which not only collects characters, but deposits them in buffers in the central memory, interrupting only when buffers are full. Such scanners are called *buffer controllers*. The buffer controlling scanner services data set adapters, which include individual bit buffers and character accumulation logic for each port.

When a character is received, the data set adapter collects the bits into a character. Once the entire character has been recognized, the scanner deposits it into central memory. The data set adapter contains the logic required to determine the number of bits which constitute a character, and the time interval between bits. Generally, this fixes the characteristics of the terminal devices which may be serviced on a particular port. However, different ports may be characterized by different data sets and adapters to support the specific mix required by the installation.

The buffer control word pointer table is known to the multiplexer. The servicing of a particular buffer is determined by adding the port number to the base address of this table to arrive at the location containing a pointer. Assume that a character has been sensed and collected for Port 3. The base address is added to 3, and the pointer in this computed address is read from memory. This content points to a set of *buffer control words*. To distinguish between different buffer control words for a particular port, this will be called BCW3.

The buffer control word basically contains two addresses. As with the software-controlled buffering schemes of previous techniques, these pointers refer to the next and end character positions. When the character arrives, and the buffer control word is accessed via the pointer, the character may be deposited in the location addressed by the *next character* pointer. The pointer is then incremented by 1, and checked against the end-of-buffer pointer. If the end has not yet been passed, the multiplexer recognizes that servicing is finished for this character for this port. If, on the other hand, the buffer has been filled, an interrupt is generated.

In summary, the impact of the multiplexing method on the central processor is shown in Table 3-3. For the purposes of an example, this case has been chosen to be consistent for all three communication controller transfer techniques, in order to be able to show this comparison.

Chapter 4

Regulatory Considerations in Data Communications

J. C. DUFFENDACK

Vice President, ADP Network Services, Inc.,
Cyphernetics Division, Ann Arbor, Michigan

Over the years, common carrier regulation and communication tariffs have become quite complex, requiring much interpretation by those who would begin to understand them. This is certainly the impression one often has after discussing some special need, innovative idea, or critical communication requirement with a communications common carrier. The presentation here is intended to shed some light on common carrier regulation and several related tariffs in order to give communications managers and system designers additional insight into the alternatives open to them in the design and operation of a data communications system.

A thorough understanding of the regulatory and legal aspects of communication is equally as important to the operation of a large telecommunication network as is a thorough understanding of communication technology, engineering, operations, administration, and maintenance. In this Chapter, we look primarily at the underlying regulatory structure of common carrier tariffs and their provisions in an effort to gain understanding of the services offered to the data communications customer and the techniques available to the customer for minimizing his or her costs.

CARRIER REGULATION

Regulation of the supply of communication services, as we know it today, was instituted by the Communications Act of 1934 creating the Federal Communication Commission and defining its authority for the regulation of interstate communication. The supply of common carrier communication services serving locations within a given state (intrastate) is regulated by each state's public utility or public services commission. Under the 1934 act, communications common carriers within a given area are granted monopolistic power and are required to file before the appropriate regulatory bodies Certificates of Necessity and Convenience as well as tariffs for services. The purpose of these tariff documents is to record the products and policies of the communications vendor (e.g., the telephone company). In effect, any standard service that a communications vendor offers is described and priced in its tariff.

Federal vs. State Regulation   As a general rule, the state regulatory commissions follow the precepts of their Federal counterparts (or, perhaps more exactly, the Bell operating companies within each state follow the lead of AT&T). There are, however, several fine distinctions worth noting in this relationship.

1. As a general rule, changes in intrastate services or the introduction of new services wi'hin a state follows the interstate service filing, but lags from several months to several years behind it.

2. Prices (rates) are generally higher for intrastate than for similar interstate services.

3. As a matter of philosophy, a common carrier service is generally considered intrastate (subject to state regulation) if it can be used for communications wholly within the state. For example, the telephone handset and attached line at your home or office are considered intrastate services even though you may call locations in other states. It is only the rates for interstate calls which are subject to Federal regulation. This fact has interesting ramifications when one studies the interconnection of various devices to the telephone network.

The distinction between intrastate and interstate communication regulation may seem inconsequential. However, consider for a moment its effect upon a specific communication requirement (voice-grade, lease-line, and series 3000) between San Francisco, Los Angeles, and ˚Phoenix. The situation can be demonstrated graphically as shown in Figure 4-1.

The surprising point here is that in this case, the intrastate leg of the network is over 3.7 times as expensive as the interstate leg of approximately the same length. In fact, for the price of the intrastate line from San Francisco to Los Angeles you can get an interstate line from Los Angeles to New York. Even more interesting is the fact that, if you request the carrier to install a switch linking the lines in Los Angeles, the San Francisco to Los Angeles link becomes interstate under the tariff, and its cost drops to

Fig. 4-1 Intrastate and interstate legs of a network compared.

$589 per month, with an overall system savings of $1,627 per month or over 73 per cent. In order to install this switch, you must have a legitimate requirement for through service between San Francisco and Phoenix.

TARIFFS

General Several common interstate tariffs filed with the FCC which specify communication services are:

Federal tariff	Subject
254	Western Union Private Line Services
255	AT&T Administrative Rate Centers and Central Offices
259	Wide Area Telecommunication Service (WATS)
260	AT&T Interstate Private Line Services
263	Long-Distance Message Telecommunications Service

Because these tariffs are representative of many common principles of communications regulation, and since state tariffs tend to follow Federal tariffs, it is instructive for our purpose here to study specific clauses of a single tariff. Therefore, let us look at AT&T's Interstate Private Line Tariff, FCC 260.

FCC Tariff 260

Usage Provision. One of the most significant provisions in this tariff specifies the allowable uses of a leased, point-to-point, voice-grade telephone line.[1] Basically, this provision says that as a telephone service customer, you are permitted to use this service for transmission of communications to or from yourself, where such communication is directly related to your business. The provision also allows transmission relating directly to the business of a wholly-owned or controlled subsidiary, or simultaneous transmission relating directly to matters of common-interest parties who are in the same general line of business and who are connected to the communications facility. In addition, the facility must be terminated (at least on one end) on your property.

The important point to note here is that the tariff states that you may use your communications facilities for yourself and may not provide a communication service to others. The only exceptions to the above rules are for joint use (discussed later), for governmental use, for use by members of a commodity or stock exchange or members

TABLE 4-1   Prorated Credits for Service Interruptions

Interruption	Credit
Less than 30 minutes	None
30 minutes to 3 hours	1/10th day
3 hours to 6 hours	1/5th day
6 hours to 9 hours	2/5th day
9 hours to 12 hours	3/5th day
12 hours to 15 hours	4/5th day
15 hours to 24 hours	One day

of an electrical power pool, and for certain use by a licensed aeronautical communications company.

Reliability and Responsibility. For damages arising out of mistakes, omissions, interruptions, delays, or errors associated with the purchase of communications service, the tariff specifies that the common carrier assumes no liability greater than the proportionate charge for the service period in which the defect occurred. The courts, of course, have held that these tariff provisions do not protect the common carrier in the event of its negligence.

It is interesting to note that tariffs say nothing about the quality of service the carrier must offer its users. There are no minimum provisions for reliability, error rates, noise levels, etc. Tariff 260 does specify the bandwidth and delay distortion characteristics for the various levels of conditioning of a voice-grade line. However, this is a far cry from actual specification of the communications channel characteristics which determine the reliability of transmission.

Service from a common carrier is generally provided on a 1-month-minimum-period basis, with pro rata charges for fractional portions of a month. Generally, credits for service interruptions are given on the pro rata basis shown in Table 4-1, assuming a 30-day month.

It is the customer's responsibility under the tariff to provide space and power for common carrier facilities installed on his or her premises, as well as to provide access to common carrier employees for the installation and maintenance of such equipment. In addition, of course, the customer is responsible for all payments and, in some instances, the common carrier is allowed to require a 2-month advance deposit as a guarantee for payments. The common carrier, however, must pay approximately 6 per cent interest on the deposit.

The common carrier, by written notice to a customer, may immediately discontinue providing communications service for nonpayment or for violation of various conditions governing the furnishing of service. Disputes leading to service termination over the past few years have centered around violations of interconnection provisions or usage provisions of the tariff.

[1] Generally used for dedicated data transmission up to 9,600 bps.

Joint Use. The "Joint Use" provision of the tariff allows a communications customer to share his or her common facilities with other "shared users" where each such user has a legitimate communications requirement as defined under the Usage provision discussed above. The important criteria here are (1) the primary user must have a legitimate requirement for the facilities (i.e., communications to or from this user and directly relating to his business), as must each joint user, and (2) the joint user must have a station or service terminal on his premises and a "through" connection to all portions of the network being shared. Each joint user is billed by the common carrier a pro rata charge for his share of the common carrier facilities, as specified by the primary user. In general, there is also a charge for each individual joint user connected to a "shared user network."

The general intent of the Joint Use tariff provision is to allow increased utilization of the telecommunication resources of the country while precluding the resale for profit of communication services by entities other than common carriers. In effect, the primary user is allowed to defray communication costs by letting joint users share unused facilities without allowing the primary user to profit by the supply of a communication service. There are some services where joint use is precluded. For example, joint use is specifically not allowed on WATS, foreign exchange lines, and certain wideband facilities. In considering any specific joint-use arrangement, it is recommended that approval from both the common carrier and the appropriate regulatory bodies be procured.

SUPPLY OF COMPUTER/COMMUNICATIONS SERVICE

In March, 1972, the FCC released its Final Decision and Order with respect to regulations that control the independent relationship between computer and communication service. This action was reviewed by the Second Circuit Court of the U.S. Court of Appeals which, by its decision of February 1, 1973, affirmed the Commission's ruling with certain minor modifications.

As a direct result of the Final Decision, the Commission concluded that no public interest would be served by the regulation of data processing services, whether or not the sale of those services involves the use of communication facilities to provide access by the customer to the computer of the data processing supplier. On the contrary, the Commission decided that the existing market for the sale of data processing services was inherently competitive and that this market would develop and flourish best in a competitive environment. With respect to communications common carriers, the Commission found no reason to require the carriers to withdraw from the data processing market. In fact, the Commission felt that the competitive environment might well benefit from carrier participation under appropriate conditions.

Thus, the Commission invoked the doctrine of "maximum separation" to ensure that the regulated activities of the carrier are in no way commingled with any of its non-regulated activities, including data processing. The rules adopted by the Commission and affirmed by the court provide that a common carrier must set up a separate corporate entity to furnish data processing to others. That separate entity must maintain its own books of account, have separate officers, and utilize separate operating personnel and separate equipment and facilities. Further, the Commission's regulations bar a carrier from selling, leasing, or otherwise making available to any other entity any capacity of a computer used by the carrier in any way for the provision of its common carrier communications services.

Essentially, the degree of separation required by the Commission was based on the following regulatory premises:

1. That the sale of data processing services by carriers should not adversely affect the provision of efficient and economic common carrier services.

2. That the costs related to the furnishing of such data processing services should not be passed on directly or indirectly to the users of the common carrier services.

3. That revenues derived from common carrier services should not be used to subsidize any data processing services.

4. That the furnishing of such data processing services by carriers should not

inhibit free and fair competition between communication common carriers and data processing companies, or otherwise involve practices contrary to the policies and prohibitions of the antitrust laws.

To maximize separation, the Commission also ruled that no carrier may engage in the sale or promotion of data processing activities on behalf of its data processing affiliate.

As is pointed out in other Chapters of this Handbook, the versatility of computers readily enables their use both for data processing and for switching of messages among terminals connected by communication channels to the computer. Message switching, including the storage and forwarding of correspondence, is regarded by the Commission as inherently a communication operation. When performed as a service for hire, the services are therefore subject to regulation as common carrier service. Thus, the intriguing issue confronting the Commission is whether or not to regulate a specific computer entity offering a mix of data processing and message switching services.

In effect, the Commission's decision ruled that hybrid services, namely those combining into a single integrated service both data processing and message switching procedures, would be subject to regulation if their primary purpose was communication. On the other hand, to the extent that message switching is merely incidental to the sale of data processing, the hybrid service would not be subject to regulation. Clearly the regulatory treatment of hybrid services does not lend itself to generalized formulas. The possible combinations and permutations of different services capable of being amalgamated in a common service offering by a computer entity are too many and too diversified for categorical definitions. It is for this reason that, subject to the very generalized guidelines mentioned above, determination by the Commission concerning hybrid services will be made on the basis of review and evaluation of particular factual situations as they develop.

SUMMARY: A CHOICE OF ALTERNATIVES

In this Chapter we have looked briefly into several specific current tariff provisions, as well as some considerations of the overall regulatory environment which currently prevails. The keyword of this environment is one of competition and an increase in the alternatives open to the computer communications system designer and manager.

As a result of the FCC's interconnect decision in the Carterfone case, users have a much wider range of equipment options. This has created a new interconnect industry which, in the best tradition of a market economy, has introduced new equipment and lower prices. The new interconnect policy has also galvanized Bell and other common carriers into competitive marketing efforts. Bell has revised its prices on existing modems and has introduced a new series of modems. It has marketed a new family of PBX equipment, key telephone systems, and CRT terminals. It has also responded with a re-evaluation and revision of its tariffs dealing with leased private lines, PBX hardware, and station equipment.

In the specialized common carrier field, new carriers are mainly engaged in the construction of their systems and the initial offering of services. Here again, Bell has responded on a broad front by restructuring the existing tariffs and announcing plans for a new end-to-end all-digital service. With the introduction of these competitive carriers has come the dissolution of the age-old concept of "nationwide rate averaging." Further, the FCC has approved open entry for domestic satellite systems which will undoubtedly result in the establishment of several competitive long-haul satellite transmission facilities by 1976 or 1977.

The provision for competition in what has traditionally been a regulated monopolistic industry has mobilized great concern for assuring a fair competitive environment, where cross-subsidy from a carrier's noncompetitive products to its competitive products is closely monitored. Both the carriers and the FCC are taking broad steps in order to prepare for this increasingly competitive marketplace. For example, common carriers are showing significant new interest in cost-related pricing, and all carriers must have greater knowledge of their costs in order to meet the outside competition. This is promoting greater operating efficiency within the carriers and an increase in the concomitant benefits to the user.

SELECTIVE BIBLIOGRAPHY

Greenberger, Martin, *Computers, Communications, and the Public Interest*, Johns Hopkins, Baltimore, 1971.

Jones, Malcolm M., Chap. 26, "The FCC Inquiry and the Data Communications User," in The Diebold Group, *Rethinking the Practice of Management*, Praeger, New York, 1973.

Trebing, Harry M., *Essays on Public Utility Pricing and Regulation*, Michigan State University Press, East Lansing, 1971.

Chapter **5**

Communications: International Regulations in Western Europe

GEOFFREY A. RIGBY

Manager of Marketing Services, Racal-Milgo Limited,
Reading, Berkshire, England

A user in Western Europe wishing to have a data communication link joining two locations on separate sites has a multiple choice as to how this will be achieved, but basically there are two choices. The user can either install a private link (subject to any regulations that apply) which could be a line or a radio link, or hire the facilities from the established communication authority—usually the telephone company. The former choice is usually not possible on the grounds of expense, except short-line links such as exist on one site (a university campus, for example). The latter choice is therefore almost the universal one. Technically, it may not be the best choice, but financially it is usually the only choice. Thus, with few exceptions, data communication links and networks are based on channels which were originally designed and intended for use as voice channels, i.e., telephone channels, and consequently the regulations which have evolved are specifically related to their use as such. Regulations are designed to prevent interference with the satisfactory operation of the voice channel and are discussed in some detail later.[1]

Types of Line A line is dedicated or leased when it is permanently connected between two or more locations, or the link may be provided by the public switched network (PSN) on dial-up operation. In general, different regulations apply, those for dial-up operation being more stringent than those for leased-line operation. Interference from a leased line can be caused only by cross-talk, whereas on the PSN there is direct connection to the telephone system.

[1] *Author's note:* In this Chapter, basic concepts and philosophies of communications regulations are discussed, and specific detail is given only by way of illustration and example. There are two reasons for this: First, the number of individual regulatory authorities concerned is large, generally one per country; and second, the situation is by no means static. It could be misleading to make statements purporting to be factual which may well be outdated by the time the Chapter is published. All comments made are believed to be true at the time of writing. Intending users should check either with their equipment supplier or the local regulatory authority before making connections to a nonprivate line.

REGULATORY AUTHORITIES: PTT

Throughout Western Europe, telephone networks are owned and administered by a government department responsible for Posts, Telegraphs, and Telephones. Although the actual title of the department varies from country to country, they are known collectively as the PTTs, and reference to "the PTT" in any country is understood to mean the department concerned. In general, one PTT covers a complete country, but in Finland and Yugoslavia, for example, where there are a number of regional authorities, this is not so.

Each PTT is completely autonomous and has absolute right to determine what equipment it shall permit to be connected to its telephone system. In practice, PTTs do not exercise their rights in an autocratic manner. Each publishes its requirements, and, provided that these requirements are met, permission to connect is not withheld.

PTT Approval or Homologation Before any equipment is connected to equipment owned by the PTT, it must be approved by the PTT. Stiff penalties may be applied to unauthorized connection. Note that it is equipment *directly connected* to the telephone line which is primarily subject to approval. In data communications, it is the modem (or data set) which *must* be approved. Other equipment making connection to the line only through the modem may or may not require approval, depending upon its nature and upon the PTT concerned.

Each PTT publishes regulations and requirements which must be followed. The technical requirements are concerned with three aspects:

1. Safety of plant and personnel.
2. Interference with other equipment.
3. Correct performance.

The safety aspect is concerned with preventing dangerous voltage levels being applied to PTT equipment. In particular, it must not be possible for the power supply voltage, which in Europe is generally in the range of from 210 to 250 volts at 50 Hz, to be applied to the telephone line either under normal operating conditions, or under fault conditions. The PTT inspects the specifications and construction of the power transformer and of the line transformer to satisfy itself that they are suitable for the purpose.

To prevent interference with other equipment, the PTT specifies the frequency bands and maximum level of the signal transmitted to line. This ensures that common equipment is not overloaded and that a continuous tone could not be confused with a control tone used by the PTT and cause spurious operation.

Procedure for Obtaining Approval It is usual for approval to be requested by the manufacturer or supplier rather than by the intending user. The PTT normally requires this, as the user may not be in possession of sufficiently detailed technical information relating to the equipment, and would therefore require a statement of compliance from the manufacturer. Thus responsibility for ensuring that equipment complies with the technical requirements is more easily placed on the manufacturer or the manufacturer's appointed representative. From the manufacturer's point of view, it is much more satisfactory to deal directly with the PTT. This also has the advantage that the PTT has a smaller number of people to deal with, and offers the manufacturer the opportunity of reaching a close understanding of the requirements of the PTT and of establishing a beneficial relationship with the PTT based on mutual trust.

While business users of data communications are not likely to find themselves in the situation of having to make their own PTT approval application, they should understand the fundamentals and place their reliance upon the manufacturers. In most cases the manufacturer will already have obtained approval, as a necessary preliminary to marketing operations.

The first action is for the manufacturer to prepare a detailed technical document which describes the equipment for which approval is required. Manufacturers with previous experience are best fitted to do this, as they know the type of information and form of presentation preferred. The document must give sufficient detail of the equipment's operation, function, and performance, to enable the PTT to assess its effect when connected to line. Thus the technical description includes block schematic diagrams, operating instructions, power output levels and frequencies, specifications of transformers, and so on. Such a document does not normally form part of a manufacturer's publications, as it is neither a sales data sheet, nor a technical manual for operation and maintenance. Nor is it yet a design manual. Nevertheless, it is a very important document, and a well-prepared one can be of great assistance in obtaining approval. The same information can, of course, be used for all PTTs, so that the investment made in it can be recouped.

Some PTTs, particularly those of the more nationalistic nations, require the approval document to be presented in the language of the country concerned.

The approval document is formally presented to the PTT with a request that the equipment to which it refers be considered for approval. Having inspected the specifications and found them to be satisfactory, the PTT then requests the loan of equipment for evaluation. Such a loan enables the PTT to inspect the construction of the equipment and to carry out any tests it wishes as a check that its performance complies with the previously submitted specification. If all is well, the PTT then issues a letter or other document to the applicant, which formally states that the equipment is approved and sets forth the conditions which apply to its use. Usually the approval is given a reference number. The PTT makes a charge for the evaluation which is payable by the applicant—who, as a manufacturer engaged in commercial operation, would not normally charge a customer.

If, during the initial study of the approval document, the PTT finds the equipment has a feature or characteristic which is not acceptable to it, the applicant is then informed and allowed the opportunity of modifying the equipment accordingly and resubmitting the application. If, during the evaluation loan, the PTT decides that the equipment is not acceptable, it may either reject it or grant an approval subject to certain changes being made in the equipment. For example, the equipment may permit adjusting the transmitted output level, and thus the maximum output level may exceed that permitted by the PTT. Although it is possible for the level to be adjusted to be less than the maximum permitted level, the PTT may insist on the equipment's being modified so that the output level is fixed at less than the permitted level, or so that when adjusted to give its maximum output, the latter is less than the permitted level. Normally, approval would not be withheld for such a reason, but the applicant would not be allowed to connect equipment which had not been modified as required. Some PTTs require a label to be fixed to the equipment, stating that it has been so modified.

The time taken to process an approval application varies with the type of equipment, the PTT concerned, difficulties encountered, and the workload at the time. An average time is 2 to 3 months. In the planning stages of a new network it is essential that sufficient time be allowed for approvals to be obtained for equipments requiring them.

Permission to Connect. It is not permissible to connect approved equipments without authority of the PTT. Normally this is a formality, a courtesy even, but it is the means PTTs adopt for keeping themselves informed of equipments connected to line. It is sufficient to give approval reference numbers where they exist, and to give details of the line to which connection is to be made.

Permissible Operations In the above discussion it has been assumed that approval has been required for a specific modem, but we must now return to the general situation and examine that more fully. At the start of this Chapter it was stated that user's have a choice of either installing their own lines or renting from the PTT. This is generally true, but the situation is somewhat more complex than that simple statement implies. It must first be established whether the intended mode of operation is one that is permitted by the PTT. If it is, the next point is whether or not the PTT operates a monopoly, and if not, whether the equipment is approved by the PTT. Interwoven with the above is the question of whether the line is to be leased, or whether operation will be by the PSN.

Most PTTs are monopolistic on PSN operations—that is, modems for connection to the PSN must be obtained from the PTT and modems from other sources are not permitted. Certain PTTs do not permit access to a multiplexer over the PSN. Thus it is important to establish at an early stage, preferably directly with the PTT or PTTs concerned, whether the intended mode of operation is permitted in principle.

For operation over leased lines, there is less tendency to operate monopolies, but the trend is for PTTs to extend their monopolies, presumably for commercial reasons. For example, at the time of this writing, in Belgium there is a monopoly up to and including 2,400 bps, but it is expected that this will be extended to 4,800 bps in due course. In Italy there is a complete monopoly at all speeds, whereas in the Netherlands there is no monopoly. However, even where there is no monopoly, the PTT always requires a modem to be approved before it is connected to line.

A time division multiplexer falls into an interesting category. Because it is not connected directly to line, but via a modem, some PTTs take the view that approval is not required (although it must be checked that multiplexing is a permitted mode of operation). A few PTTs require the multiplexer to be approved.

International Links The above discussion has been in reference to links wholly contained within a specific country. There are many European links which connect locations in two or more countries, some of which connect to locations in the United States. Of particular concern are those links which have a location within a country where the PTT exercises a monopoly at the intended operating speed. This implies that the modem must be obtained from the PTT, but this modem may not be on-line compatible with the modem it is desired to use in the other countries. In certain countries (Sweden is an example), the PTT permits the use of an approved modem for international links, even though it operates a monopoly for internal links.

SUMMING UP

The intending users of data communication within Europe should first check with the PTT or PTTs concerned regarding the intended mode of operation to ensure that it is permitted. They must also check whether the PTT exercises a monopoly at the intended speed of operation and, if not, they will then check with the modem supplier of their choice as to whether the modems are approved or if approval can be obtained. It is the responsibility of suppliers to obtain approval; it is the responsibility of users to notify the PTT of the intended connections.

The regulations governing the connection of modems to telephone lines are numerous and complex. Fortunately users do not need to be familiar with them in detail, for they will rely upon the PTTs in monopoly situations or upon suppliers otherwise.

ADDRESSES

The addresses given below are those to which initial enquiries should be made by intending users.

Austria

Bundesministerium für Verkehr
  und Verstaalichte Unternehmungen
Generaldirektion für die Post und
  Telegraphenverwaltung
1011 Wien
Postgasse 8

Belgium

Regie van Telegrafie en Telefonie
1030 Brussel
Paleizenstraat 42

Denmark

Ministeriet for Offentlige Arbejder
Generaldirektoratet for Post og
  Telegrafvaesenet
Favergade 17
1007 Kobenhavn K

Eire

Department of Posts and Telegraphs
Marlborough Street
Dublin 1

France

Ministere des Postes et Telecommunications
Direction Generale des Telecommunications
20, Avenue de Segur
Paris 7

Germany

Deutsche Bundespost
Fernmeldetechnisches Zentralamt
61 Darmstadt
Postfach 800

Italy

Ministero delle Poste e delle
  Telecomunicazioni
Ispettorato Generale delle Telecomunicazioni
Direzione Centrale Telegrafi
00100 Roma

Luxembourg

Administration des Postes et
  Telecommunications
Division Technique
17 rue de Hollerich
Case Postale 2061
Luxembourg

Netherlands

Staatsbedrijf der Posterijen
Telegrafie en Telefonie
Centrale Directie
Kortenaerkade 12
'S—Gravenhage
Postgirorekening 45100

Norway

Teledirektoratet
Universitetsgata 2
Oslo 1

Spain

Compania Telefonica Nacional de Espana
Avda de Jose Antonio 28
Madrid 13

Sweden

Televerkets Centralforvaltning
Projekteringsavdelningen
Marbackagatan 11
123 86 FARSTA
Stockholm

Switzerland

Schweizerische Post, Telephon und
  Telegraphenbetriebe
Generaldirektion
Viktoria strasse 21
3000 Bern 33

U.K.

Post Office Telecommunications Headquarters
Tenter House
45 Moorfields
London EC2Y 9TH

PART SIX

Standardization

Introduction

IRA ADLER *Principal, John Diebold & Associates, New York, New York*

Throughout history, the development of standards, especially in conjunction with high technology, has been of fundamental importance in determining how far a particular technique can advance in practical application. Standards have certainly played a key role in commerce among people, companies, states, and nations, because they have provided a common understanding with a minimum of explanation. A volt of electrical energy is the same unit of potential difference regardless of what country it is measured in. An erg is a unit of physical work—universal regardless of where it is measured. No translation or equivalency tables are needed by people dealing in such standard measures in order to understand exactly what is being expressed.

Notwithstanding the general agreement that standards are inherently valuable and cost-beneficial, we are all familiar with elements of our daily lives where the standardization effort, if it existed at all, failed miserably, or where failure to standardize early in the development of a particular area proved extremely costly to institute later on. Unusual currency units (such as the old English currency) eventually had to be changed to decimal, at great cost; those not now using metric weights and measures will eventually have to submit to the costly (in terms of education and money) conversion to that system; and Japan, Britain, and some other countries will eventually change to driving on the right as Sweden did several years ago at substantial expense (although at least most of their vehicles were left-hand drive to begin with).

It is rather easy to cite myriad examples to prove the economic desirability of standards without even mentioning the aesthetic appeal they have to the orderly, logical mind. While the quantifiable worth of standards manifests itself in economic benefit, less precise value can be attributed to them for practical and procedural reasons. It is helpful to understand why standards should be developed, implemented, and enforced in the business world in general and ADP specifically. Exact communications is of course the paramount reason for standards. This means that ideas and facts can be transferred from one entity to another with a maximum degree of terseness and precision and a minimum of ambiguity and confusion. In ADP there are person-to-person, person-to-machine, machine-to-person, and machine-to-machine communications, each of which is susceptible of standardization.

While there may be peculiar circumstances in which one wishes to compare apples and oranges, most often the desired comparison is between like items measured in the same units: When apparently dissimilar items are compared, it is essential to define explicitly the terms and measures used as the basis for the comparison. The expression of comparison using standard terms obviates such definition. Things equal to the same thing or equal things are equal to each other.

At the same time that effectively defined, implemented, and enforced standards seek to restrict the number and different kinds of ways a job can be performed, they also provide an almost limitless flexibility. If the hardware (and its concomitant control systems software) of one manufacturer conformed to the same standards as that of another, an ADP installation would have the ultimate freedom to modify configurations by intermingling manufacturers' equipment or by completely switching manufacturers essentially at will. If the systems development/project management procedures for ADP systems were standard from one company to the next, personnel transferability would be greatly enhanced, and training in redundant development concepts embodied in different procedures would be obviated. In short, standardization is the essential foundation upon which to build flexible resource acquisition and allocation.

It is only in the best of all possible worlds that effective global standards will be found. In the meantime it is appropriate to seek an inclusive set of international standards and to define a compatible subset of those standards which is practical for a particular ADP installation. Organizations not choosing the path of standardization do so at the risk of higher operating costs and very likely the inability to take advantage of future technological development without undergoing the painful and expensive conversion to standards which may be a practical necessity regardless of any technological advance. If the organization does choose to ignore standards, it had better identify the risk costs incurred.

An almost endless number of groups have been organized to develop or sanction standards, many of which are discussed in the Chapters of this Part of Section 2. These organizations range in scope from international to national to industry to company, and are of greatest long-term value in the order mentioned. It is appropriate to consider a standard as having increasing value in direct relation to its acceptance. Because standards in the ADP industry have not yet been generally legislated, people involved in data processing have an opportunity to organize intelligently and contribute to the inevitable standardization effort by participating in one or more of the national and international committees, as well as working toward a set of compatible standards for their own installations.

A number of specific topical areas must be addressed in the standardization effort. Certainly one of the first that has met with moderate success is the area of programming languages, though much work remains to be done. Other areas which have not yet enjoyed substantial standardization treatment include documentation, systems development methodology, terminology at every level, storage media encoding procedures, data representation (e.g., EBCDIC or ASCII), data communications interfaces, and the like. Standards for data center operations hold the key to effective and controlled machine-room and ancillary-services operations for both the testing and production environments. Certain key interfaces are also appropriate candidates for standardization. Hardware-to-hardware, hardware-to-systems-software, systems-software-to-systems-software, and systems-software-to-people interfaces are among those that must be addressed. Data entry is part of the people-to-system interface which may be susceptible to a degree of standardization. Again, standards in the interface area will improve transferability of applications systems and people, thus reducing (or eliminating in the perfect system) conversion and retraining costs.

A substantial difference exists between a *guideline* and a *standard:* The first is a suggested procedure, and the second a rule established and enforced by authority. The implication is that if a specific procedure or rule cannot be enforced, it is not a standard. There are several criteria that determine a successful standard. Among them are: *understandability* of the content of and necessity for the standard (i.e., it must not be ambiguous or irrational, and it must be published and understood by those whom it affects); *enforceability* (i.e., ability to measure the degree of adherence and the ability, as a matter of course, to detect violations); *durability* (frequent changes of existing standards imply that they are not standards at all to any significant extent); *maintainability* (i.e., a formal mechanism must be available to add new, delete obsolete, and amend existing standards as the environment governed by the standards changes); *economic justifiability* (i.e., there must be conclusive evidence of economic justification, considering costs to develop and administer, and benefits which will accrue over time); and *timeliness* (ex post facto standards tend to be very costly to implement on a retroactive basis).

Meaningful standards to govern the ADP environment are essential to help maximize the long-term benefit and growth of the technology. The more formal and the more generally accepted the standards, the more valuable they will be to the industry. Both national and international ADP standards organizations will continue to contribute to this vital effort, and one can hope that their positive efforts will become even more significant in the coming years.

Chapter 1

The Standards Development Environment

MARJORIE F. HILL

Manager, Marketing and Research, Institute for Advanced Technology, Control Data Corporation, Rockville, Maryland

The development of standards is a vast worldwide activity which could almost be classified as an industry in itself. Thousands of individuals are involved in standardization for ADP. In ANSC X3 alone (American National Standards Committee for Computers and Information Processing), there are about 500 individuals engaged in some phase of developing standards. It is reported that, on the average, five meetings of the International Organization for Standardization (ISO) take place somewhere in the world every working day of the year.

Standards for ADP have been under development for over 10 years, yet very little is known about how standards are developed, how consensus is achieved, or the organizations that are a part of the process. This Chapter explains how a standard developed in Midtown, U.S.A., can move through the approved procedures to become a standard recognized by the United Nations.

BACKGROUND

Recognition of the value of standards has existed for centuries. The Magna Carta contained a chapter on standards, and our own Constitution authorized Congress to "fix the standards of weights and measures." The early growth of the railroads in America was aided by standards for track width that made it possible for all railroads to share tracks and expand routes and services.

When the first suggestions were made that standards should be established in the field of computers and information processing, there were well-established, mature organizations for standards development to accept the responsibility. At an ISO meeting in early 1960, Sweden recommended that a new ISO technical committee be formed to develop standards for information processing. The United States was asked to accept the role of secretariat.

Upon the return of this country's participants in the ISO meeting, the heads of manufacturing companies in the United States and officials of the Office Equipment Manufacturers Institute (OEMI),[1] were invited to a meeting to discuss the steps that should be taken. At this meeting it was recommended that an organization be formed to develop standards in the computing field. As a result, the X3, X4, and X6 sectional committees of the American Standards Association (now the American National Standards Institute, ANSI) were formed. In 1965, the X6 Committee was disbanded and its work was taken over by a group within the Electronic Industries Association (EIA).

USEFUL ACRONYMS

ANSC	American National Standards Committee
ANSC X3	American National Standards Committee for Computers and Information Processing
ANSC X4	American National Standards Committee for Office Machines and Supplies
ANSI	American National Standards Institute
CCITT	International Telegraph and Telephone Consultative Committee (a division of ITU)
ECMA	European Computer Manufacturers Association
FIPS	Federal Information Processing Standard
IAC	International Advisory Committee of ANSC X3
ISO	International Organization for Standardization
SAB	Standards Advisory Board of ANSI
SPARC	Standards Planning and Requirements Committee of ANSC X3
SSC	Standards Steering Committee of ANSC X3
TC	Technical Committee
X3	Short form of ANSC X3

Two years earlier, CODASYL had been formed, and soon COBOL existed as a language. When the announcement of the formation of X3 was made in September, 1960, COBOL and codes were emphasized as the standards to be developed.[2]

At the first organizational meeting of X3, which was held in February, 1961, seven major topics were identified: Optical Character Recognition (OCR); Magnetic Ink Character Recognition (MICR); Data Transmission; Programming Languages; Terminology; Problem Definition and Analysis; and Codes. The activities on keyboards and other office machine standards became a separate committee known as X4. The Computer and Business Equipment Manufacturers Association (CBEMA) accepted the secretariat of both committees.

At a Round Table Conference organized by ISO and the International Electrotechnical Commission in May, 1961, two ISO technical committees and one IEC technical committee were formed. ISO TC97 and TC95 were modeled along the lines of X3 and X4 respectively.

The European Computer Manufacturers Association had just been founded, and at the 1961 meeting of ISO, ECMA was invited to become a liaison member of TC97. The American National Standards Institute officially accepted the secretariat for TC95 and TC97.

Figure 1-1 shows an exploded view of the founding dates of organizations involved solely in the development of standards for the computing industry. It is interesting to note that once the need for standards was recognized, the organizations were quickly formed.

---

[1] OEMI later became known as Business Equipment Manufacturers Association (BEMA), and, since January 1, 1973, as Computer and Business Equipment Manufacturers Association (CBEMA).

[2] CODASYL: Conference on Data Systems Languages; COBOL: Common Business Oriented Language; see Part 4, Chapter 3, "Programming Languages," in this Section.

STANDARDS ORGANIZATIONS

The objectives of all the international and national standards bodies are so similar that they can be thought of as carbon copies of one another. Basically their objectives are:

Promulgation of standards.

Coordination of standards development.

Establishment of standards.

Exchange of information.

It is well to note at this point that the standards organizations act as the vehicles for the approval of standards, but that the initiation of a standards project is voluntary.

1959	J F M A M J J A S O N D	CODASYL organizational meeting. First International Conference on Data Processing. COBOL existed as a language.
1960	J F M A M J	IFIP founded. Proposal to ISO that a TC for information processing be formed. ECMA formed. COBOL-60 published. CEN formed. ASA called meeting as proposed secretariat for new ISO/TC.
1960	J A S O N D	X3/X4 organization announced with CBEMA as sponsor (now secretariat).
1961	J F M A M J J A S O N D	First ANSC X3 meeting held. ISO meeting, TC 95 and TC 97 officially formed. ECMA officially registered. Round Table Conference organized by ISO and IEC. IEC TC 53 approved.

Fig. 1-1 Chronological chart showing the founding of standards organizations associated with computers and information processing.

The development of technical standards is not planned and directed in the way that an industrial organization plans and develops a product.

Membership The membership of standards-making bodies varies, but at the international level, the members are nations. The nations are then represented by the leading standards organizations interested in the subject matter. At the national level, members represent individual interests such as consumers, producers, or general interest groups. Each organization has its own membership rules and voting requirements.

Organization All organizations are structured to accommodate a high-level board for policy direction, a board for approval of standards, one or more technical advisory boards, an administrative board, and the standards development committees. Figure 1-2 shows four types of organizations and their corresponding functional bodies.

All technical development work is accomplished in the technical committees, whether a national or an international standard is involved. The hierarchical structure of boards is maintained to ascertain that a consensus has been reached and that the primary interests concerned have been involved in the process.

Relationship of Standards Organizations A complicating factor in the development of standards is the interwoven relationships at the international level and the increasing complexity of these relationships at the local or national technical committee level.

At the international level, member bodies of one council may also be member bodies of another; members of working groups of an international body are often members of a technical committee of yet another. American technical committees may meet in joint sessions with European technical committees to develop an international standard.

Both the Japanese Standards Association and the American National Standards Institute have offices in Geneva, so as to be close to ISO headquarters. The European Free Trade Association and European Economic Community maintain close liaison with ISO, the International Electrotechnical Commission (IEC), and the International Telecommunications Union (ITU).

Complex as are the relations and the interaction between and among the standards-

Type of Organization	International	National	Standards Committee	European
Example	ISO	ANSI	ANSC X3	ECMA
Membership	Country represented by leading standards organization	Trade and professional associations, companies, government agencies	Equal number of consumers, producers, and general interests	Companies which manufacture DP equipment in Europe
Type of Membership	Participating (P) Observer (O) Correspondent	Company member Government member Organizational Individual Sustaining Honorary	Principal and alternate Liaison Observer	Ordinary member Associate member
Approved By	ISO Council	Board of Directors	Secretariat	Two-thirds vote of the membership
Officers	President, Vice President, Treasurer, Secretary-General	President, three Vice Presidents, Managing Director	Chairman, Vice Chairman, Secretary	President, Vice President, Secretary
Executive Officer	Secretary-General	Managing Director	X3 Secretary	Secretary-General
Governing Body	Council	Board of Directors	None	General Assembly
Technical Advisory Body	Advisory Committees as required	Standards Management Boards	SPARC	Coordinating Committee
Administrative Body (Standards)	Council	Executive Standards Board	X3/SSC	Coordinating Committee
Highest Level of Standard	International Standard	American National Standard	Proposed American National Standard	ECMA Standard
Adjudicating Body	Council	Board of Standards Review	Secretariat	General Assembly
Vote Required to Approve	75% of Member Bodies	$\frac{2}{3}$ of Board of Standards Review	80% of the X3 Members	$\frac{2}{3}$ of the Ordinary Members

Fig. 1-2 Comparison of standards organizations functions.

making bodies, all activity comes to focus at ISO, IEC, and ITU. These organizations are recognized by the United Nations as the responsible bodies for standards development for both the developed and underdeveloped countries of the world.

The ANSI/ISO relationship is that of a country standards organization (ANSI) serving as a member of an international standards organization (ISO). When ANSI is asked to serve as the secretariat for an ISO technical subcommittee, ANSI is merely fulfilling its responsibility as a member of ISO in much the same way as a member of a task group or technical committee serves as the secretary. The work is more complicated because of its scope and the international protocol involved, but the function is much the same.

It is becoming increasingly important to hold joint technical meetings with the European Computer Manufacturers Association (ECMA), so that European and United States standards can be developed in parallel. In this way, technical issues can be resolved prior to an international meeting. The beneficial effects of this coordination can be seen in the ANSI COBOL standard, where the ANSI, ECMA, and ISO standards are identical.

Finance Although many international and national organizations derive their operating revenue from membership dues and the sale of standards, others are wholly or partially supported by their governments.

Several national standards organizations have extended their activities to include a certification program which contributes to their income.

Most of the standards organizations are portrayed as self-sustaining nonprofit organizations.

Technical Committees Most technical committees have an organizational structure similar to that of the parent organization, with the appropriate quota of administrative and advisory groups to supervise the progress of the technical work.

Each technical committee is chartered to develop standards within its range of interest. Since this charter or scope generally covers a broad range, each technical subject may be subdivided into its component parts. Some topics may be interlocking, and some may be totally independent of any other topic within the technical committee. Still other technical committees may establish liaison with technical committees or other standards organizations.

Technical Work Since standards organizations are partially dependent upon the revenue from standards, the technical development work is of prime importance.

Most of the developed countries of the world take an active part in the development of the contents of standards. However, some elect merely to monitor the international development work which is then evaluated in terms of that nation's requirements. Australia and Canada are examples of this type of participation.

It is also common practice for some international organizations to adopt the international standards developed by the ISO technical committees.

DEVELOPMENT AND PROCESSING OF A STANDARD

The development of standards is voluntary and based upon the premise that the project must be cooperative in nature and the technical content must represent a consensus of the parties involved. The theory of consensus applies to Federal standards as well as to national and international standards. Federal standards are subjected to review within the Federal Government, and when a consensus has been reached the proposed standard is published in the Federal Register. Following this cycle, the subject becomes a Federal Information Processing Standard (FIPS). Standards developed by the Electronic Industries Association and other organizations are treated in much the same manner. Standards developed by these bodies may be proposed as American National Standards.

The philosophy of consensus imposes a responsibility upon the organizations that form the framework within which standards can be initiated, developed, and approved. It naturally follows then that the organizations must develop methods, a process, and operating procedures to guarantee that this consensus has been reached.

In the United States, the three accepted methods that may be used to show evidence of consensus are the canvass method, the accredited organization method, and the standards committee method. A proponent may elect to use any one of the methods.

Canvass Method The canvass method may be used when a standards-making organization or any other responsible organization has developed draft standards it wants to have considered as American National Standards, but does not have procedures to show broad-based consensus. In this event a canvass or mail poll is taken of all organizations which are known to have concern and competence in the subject.

The organization that proposed the standard becomes the proponent, and is responsible for preparing the canvass list, which is approved by ANSI. Generally 6 months is allowed for responses to the poll.

A standard submitted under this method is processed within the standards-approving organization in the same manner as one submitted under the standards committee method. In other words, at the close of the canvass period, the proposed standard is submitted to ANSI in the same way as a standard developed by one of the technical committees of X3 is submitted.

Accredited Organization Method Where an organization has its own procedures for demonstrating evidence of consensus, it may apply to ANSI for accreditation. The organization must be able to show the same broad-based participation in the standards development as provided by the standards committee method. A standard developed by such an organization is submitted to ANSI in the same way as one developed by ANSC X3. No further canvass or approvals are required of the proponent.

Standards Committee Method This is the method best known to the computing industry. It is used when one or more organizations have developed or are developing standards on the same or related subjects.

The method described here is based upon the ANSI version. However, the fundamental principles, the decision base, and the decision points are identical to those at the international and local levels. As an example, the factors applied to the decision to form a standards committee are the same in ANSI as in ISO, and as in ANSC X3.

The ANSI responsibilities in establishing a standards committee, watching its progress, and acting upon its output are identical to those of the comparable ISO councils. The duties and responsibilities of an ANSI secretariat are identical to those of an ISO or IEC secretariat.

The standards committee method, as used by ANSI, consists of a secretariat and a standards committee embodying a balanced representation of consumers, producers, and general interests. Such a committee assures in advance that a consensus will be self-evident when the members complete their assignment.

Secretariat. One of the most important functions in the standardization process is that of the secretariat. It is also probably the least understood. The terms *secretariat* and *sponsor* are often used synonymously, but each has a distinct place in the standardization process.

A sponsor, as defined by ANSI, is "an organization or group which assumes responsibility for development and publication of its own standards where no standards committee exists." As an example, the American Society for Testing and Materials acts as a sponsor of ASTM standards when proposed as American National Standards.

A secretariat is "an organization or group authorized to assume the responsibility for a standards committee." A secretariat is always associated with a standards committee, a sponsor is not. As an example, the Computer and Business Equipment Manufacturers Association was authorized by ANSI to act as the secretariat for American National Standards Committees X3 and X4.

The secretariat plays an important role in the efficient functioning of the standards committee activity. A national secretariat must interact with the international secretariat and with all organizations that have an interest in its work.

Standards Committee. Standards committees are organized with a chairman, vice-chairman, and secretary as officers. The chairman and vice-chairman are appointed by the parent body for a specified period of time; the chairman appoints a recording secretary.

Standardization Process The objective of a process which leads to approval of a standard is to confirm that consensus has been reached. Such a process (see Figure 1-3) must be carefully designed so as to provide:

- Several review cycles of adequate length to permit response.
- Balanced representation of those interested in the subject.
- Approval bodies at each level of development.

- A document flow which guarantees that all interested parties are informed.
- Announcement to the public at the completion of selected milestones.

The process which is almost universally employed consists of three phases:

1. *Planning.* A topic is proposed as a candidate, and a judgment is made as to its value to the industry. A committee is authorized to accomplish the work, and a public announcement is issued to that effect.

2. *Development.* A committee is formed to develop the standard or standards. When work is completed, the proposed standard is transmitted to the approving body.

3. *Approval.* Approval through the hierarchical structure and then final publication.

To satisfy the commitment to consensus, each phase includes requirements for balanced representation, distribution of information, and approvals. Entwined

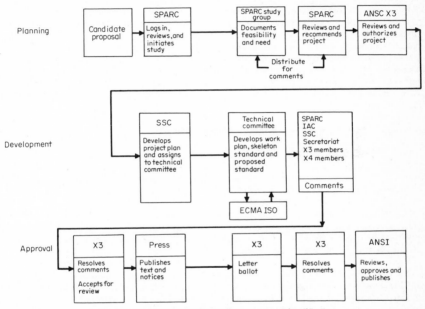

Fig. 1-3 ANSC X3 standardization process (simplified).

throughout are the international liaison and joint participation for the purpose of developing an international standard.

Planning Phase. The planning phase is heavily oriented to planning for the successful completion of the project. In this phase, all aspects of the need for the standard, organizations interested, and feasibility of successful completion are considered. When the decision has been made to form a standards committee, appropriate notices are issued to the press and interested parties are encouraged to participate.

The completion of this phase results in the formation of a standards committee of the ISO TC97 class, the ANSC X3 class, or the X3 project class.

Development Phase. The administrative procedures during this phase are relatively uncomplicated, starting with the formation of the committee.

The first task of the new committee is to prepare a scope and program of work for the project. Following the acceptance of the scope and program of work, the committee sets up liaison with ISO and related organizations. During the life cycle of the standards development committee, the efficient and timely flow of information and the interactions with relevant technical committees are vital to the successful completion of the task.

Many informal papers may pass between and among the organizations involved, but the formal papers such as country positions on issues, formal ballots, etc., are always transmitted by the national ISO member body. For example, ANSI, as the United

States member body, transmits all papers on codes to the secretariat of that committee, which is the French member body.

The work of the standards committee culminates in the transmittal of a proposed standard to the cognizant authority. This is preceded by a ballot to verify that consensus has been reached. If only one topic was assigned to the standards committee, the committee ceases to hold meetings, but holds itself in readiness to process the comments generated during the approval phase.

Approval Phase. The approval phase begins with the receipt of the proposed standard at the secretariat with the request that it be processed as a national or international standard. The secretariat first determines that all the required documentation has been submitted and then distributes the document for review prior to taking a formal ballot. Either the proposed standard is published in its entirety or a notice is published indicating that the document is available.

If comments are received, these are forwarded to the development committee for resolution, and the proposed standard may then be returned to the secretariat for review. The nature of the comments (substantive or editorial) determine future changes or transmittal to the next higher level of authority.

The proposed standard now enters the stage where processing will be completed to make it a national or international standard. From this point on, no decisions are made on the technical content; the total emphasis is on the evidence of consensus. When consensus has been validated, the life cycle of the development of a standard is complete.

WORKING STRUCTURE OF STANDARDS ORGANIZATIONS

International Organizations In order for the development of standards to proceed in an orderly manner, there must be organizations to act as the vehicles for the process.

In the international arena, the International Organization for Standardization is concerned with the broadest range of topics. Other organizations such as the International Telecommunications Union confine their interests to one topic.

Membership in ITU is composed of two classes of organizations: (1) the telecommunications administrative bodies of each country and (2) the recognized private enterprises of each country. The interests of the United States are held by the U.S. Department of State, which has delegated responsibility to the International Division of the Federal Communications Commission. The data processing community's main contact is with the International Telegraph and Telephone Consultative Committee (CCITT), a division of the ITU. The CCITT contributed heavily to the development of the International Code for Information Interchange. Our national version of the code is known as the American Standard Code for Information Interchange, or ASCII.

Many of today's electronics engineers are surprised to learn that the organization that serves as the electrical division of ISO was formed in 1906. The International Electrotechnical Commission (IEC) became affiliated with ISO in 1947, but continues to retain its technical and financial autonomy.

ISO membership is composed of member countries and liaison members. A member country is represented by a member body, which is the national body most representative of standardization in that country. The American National Standards Institute, with headquarters in New York City, serves as the United States member body.

ISO has been granted consultative status with the United Nations and many of its agencies. In addition, individual technical committees of ISO maintain special liaisons with more than 200 international and regional bodies interested in particular aspects of ISO work.

Over the past 10 years, the work of ISO has expanded to include more and more projects related to information processing. For example, the banking industry originally was concerned with magnetic ink character recognition for use on checks. Recently the work of TC68, Banking Procedures, was expanded to include several other projects, and a new American National Standards Committee was formed.

To understand the scope of the topics being undertaken by one of the technical committees of ISO, the subcommittees of ISO TC97, Computers and Information Processing, are shown in Figure 1-4a. The liaison relationships required to develop the standards from this group are shown in Figure 1-4b.

European Organizations   In Europe, the European Computer Manufacturers Association is the organization most familiar to those concerned with data processing standards. ECMA is composed of manufacturers only, as is the Computer and Business Equipment Manufacturers Association in the United States.   However, its relationship to standards development is quite different: ECMA develops ECMA standards; CBEMA does not develop CBEMA standards.   ECMA enjoys a liaison relationship with a technical

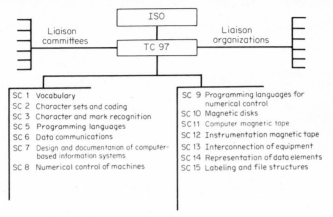

Fig. 1-4a   Subcommittees of ISO/TC97.

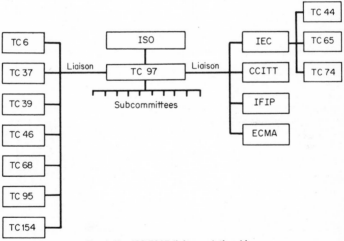

Fig. 1-4b   ISO TC97 liaison relationships.

committee of ISO (ISO TC97); CBEMA acts only as the secretariat of an American National Standards Committee, i.e., ANSC X3.   ANSC X3 is composed of an equal balance of producers, consumers, and general interests; ECMA is composed of producers only.

ECMA members are drawn from all Europe, therefore ECMA members may join their individual country delegations at an ISO meeting.   For example, an ECMA committee on COBOL may include members from organizations located in France, Germany, United Kingdom, etc.   At an ISO meeting, each representative joins his or her nation's delegation, thus providing the delegation the benefit of his or her expertise.

Another organization of interest is the European Standards Coordinating Committee (CEN).   CEN was born out of the European Economic Community (EEC) and the European Free Trade Association (EFTA).   The purpose of the organization is to secure full and identical implementation of international recommendations developed by ISO, IEC, and ITU.

National Organizations   The American National Standards Institute is the member body of ISO, and represents the interests of the United States in international standardization organizations of a nongovernmental nature.

ANSI is a federation of trade and professional associations, companies, and Government departments and agencies.   The scope of the work addressed is as broad and inclusive as that of ISO.   It has standards management boards to act in an administrative capacity, a review board to determine that consensus has been reached, and an approval board.

The groups developing standards for the data processing field are the responsibility of the Information Systems Standards Management Board, which is responsible for coordinating standardization projects and harmonizing conflicts.

Organizations such as the Electronic Industries Association (EIA), or the American Society for Testing and Materials (ASTM), or the Underwriters' Laboratories may seek accreditation and submit standards developed within their organizations for approval as American National Standards.

The technical committees of ANSC X3 are responsible for the development of standards such as those for programming languages, data transmission, media, magnetic

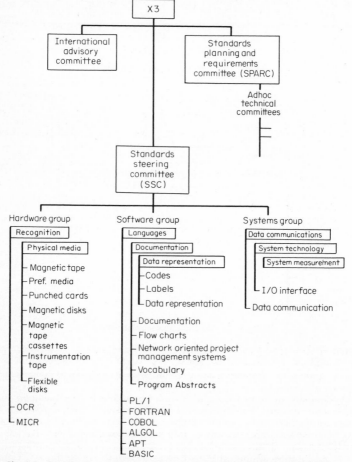

Fig. 1-5   Organization of American National Standards Committee X3 (ANSC X3).

recording, etc. The standards developed by the technical committees of X3 are approved by the membership of X3 before being transmitted to ANSI for final approval. X3, aided by its technical committees, also develops technical responses to ISO ballot issues for its national standards body.

The work of ANSC X3 is probably best known to the ADP community through the standards for programming languages. However, X3 is responsible for a myriad of projects, as shown in Figure 1-5.

An organization which holds a unique position in the standards development field is the Conference on Data Systems Languages (CODASYL), which is dedicated to the development of COBOL. Standardization of the language is the responsibility of a technical committee of ANSC X3.

The Underwriters' Laboratories, which is familiar to us through its work on electrical safety standards, is influential in the development of standards that provide specifications and requirements for safety standards for computing installations. Many of the standards developed by ULI have become American National Standards.

FEDERAL STANDARDS PROGRAM

In 1964, the Secretary of Commerce designated the National Bureau of Standards to serve as the focal point within the Federal Government for the advancement of technology in industry and commerce.

Under the Brooks bill, passed in 1965, NBS was charged with providing recommendations for uniform Federal ADP standards through the Secretary of Commerce and the Bureau of the Budget (now the Office of Management and Budget) to the President of the United States.

In response to the new responsibilities given it under the Brooks bill, NBS brought together several units in 1966 to form the nucleus of an organization known as the Center for Computer Sciences and Technology (CCST). This organization functioned for some time under the Institute of Applied Technology but recently was made an independent organization.

An important part of the Federal program of standardization is the Federal Information Processing Standards (FIPS) Register, established in 1968. This register serves as the official source of information throughout the Federal Government. It is divided into four technical sections: Hardware, Software, Applications, and Data Standards. Each section is subclassified as to standards which may be required, and each standard is appropriately numbered for retrieval purposes.

In 1969, NBS stated the objectives of the program as:

1. The ability to provide maximum compatibility among Federal information processing systems in the acquisition, use, and interchange of equipment, information, programs and personnel, by providing independence from a particular manufacturer or make of hardware, software, and supporting components.

2. The ability to acquire systems or components from all reliable sources at competitive prices and still retain maximum compatibility.

3. The ability to interchange information among systems without the need for conversion or translation.

4. The ability to eliminate duplication of effort in the development and application of information processing systems.

5. The establishment of standard application packages for Federal use.

6. The ability to interface, where necessary, information processing and communications systems.

7. The establishment of compatible standards applicable to both information processing and telecommunications systems.

To develop Federal standards, a procedure similar to that used in the development of national and international standards is employed. A coordinating and advisory group serves as a vehicle for coordinating the work assignments of the FIPS task groups and also acts as a general advisory group on information processing standards.

The FIPS program is more than just the development of Federal standards and the acceptance of national and international standards for Federal use. FIPS task groups may be organized for such purposes as providing advice to NBS on specific draft standard proposals, making recommendations on specific problems, and developing draft proposals in specific standards problems areas as assigned in work-scope statements.

The Federal program is important to every user as well as to manufacturers, since it defines the basic benchmarks that are used by the Government in defining basic standards.

FOR ADDITIONAL INFORMATION

Below is a roster of organizations which can furnish lists of existing standards and information on work in progress.

American Bankers Association (ABA), 1120 Connecticut Avenue, N.W., Washington, D.C. 20036. Attention: Director of Standards.

American National Standards Institute (ANSI), 1430 Broadway, New York, N.Y. 10018. Attention: Information Processing Systems Engineer.

Canadian Government Specifications Board, Department of Supply and Services, 88 Metcalfe Street, Ottawa, Canada (for *CODASYL Journal of Development*).

Computer and Business Equipment Manufacturers Association (CBEMA), 1828 L Street, N.W., Washington, D.C. 20036. Attention: Director of Standards.

European Computer Manufacturers Association (ECMA), Rue du Rhone 114, 1204 Geneva, Switzerland. Attention: Secretary General.

Institute of Electrical and Electronics Engineers, Inc. (IEEE), 345 East 47th St., New York, N.Y. 10017. Attention: Professional Group on Electronic Computers.

International Electrotechnical Commission (IEC), 1, Rue de Varembe, 1211 Geneva 20, Switzerland. Attention: Secretary General.

International Organization for Standardization (ISO), 1, Rue de Varembe, 1211 Geneva 20, Switzerland. Attention: Secretary General.

Japanese Standards Association, (publishes *JISC Yearbook*).

Society of Certified Data Processors, 38 Main Street, Hudson, Maine 01749.

Underwriters' Laboratories, Inc., 207 East Ohio Street, Chicago, Ill. 60611.

United States Government Printing Office, Public Documents Department, Washington, D.C. 20402. (FIPS publications may be ordered from the GPO individually, or on a subscription basis.)

SELECTIVE BIBLIOGRAPHY

ANSI Materials: *ANSI Catalog of Standards,* published yearly; *ANSI Reporter,* monthly; *ANSI Standards Action,* published biweekly, lists all standards in the ANSI approval process.

Hill, Marjorie F., *The World of EDP Standards, 1972,* Control Data Corporation, Minneapolis, 1972 (now published by NBS as a GPO document).

ISO Materials: *Status Report on ISO Draft International Standards,* issued quarterly; *ISO Memento; ISO Participation,* published yearly, lists the ISO technical committees and membership by country; *ISO Catalog,* published yearly with supplements distributed periodically; *ISO Bulletin,* monthly; *ISO Directives,* published as required.

Chapter 2

ADP Standards

ERIC H. CLAMONS

Director, Data Systems Standards, Honeywell Information
Systems, Inc., Waltham, Massachusetts

". . . the progress of a profession is usually marked by the
cumulation of an increasing number of generally accepted
practices."

WILSON AND TAUBER, *The University Library*

The impact of computers on our society since World War II is difficult to imagine
unless one was privileged to witness it. Desk calculators, punched-card machines,
and a few electromechanical calculators so expanded the mental productivity of human
beings that when the first electronic computers became available there were waiting
lists of users, all of whom needed the results that now could be attained at lightning
speeds. However, little thought was given to the problems that would be generated
as developers took any available input-output device and attached it to a computer.

EVENTS LEADING TO ADP STANDARDIZATION

The first input-output media used with computers were punched cards and paper tape.
Hollerith had no idea that Baudot's punched paper tape would some day have to work
with his punched cards, and designers of computers were too busy to worry about
common interfaces. In the excitement that the first "giant" computers worked at all,
only the glitter of the trickle of results previously not attainable by any other means
was of importance. It was not until the early 1950s when avalanche after avalanche
of new computers flooded the market that users suddenly realized the lack of transferability of the fruits of their labor.

By the mid 1950s, intellectual efforts were started to reduce the manual labor of
coding. It was hoped that the design of better, simpler coding systems would so
reduce the labor of recoding as to reduce the problems of transferability to insignifi-
cance. The burden of bookkeeping was transferred to the computer and, thus, assemblers (closely related to machine code) and interpreters (simulation of one machine
on another) were born. With these developments, the productivity of coders increased
significantly, but not enough to put a dent into the need for transferability of programs.
Assemblers produced good machine codes at a high cost of labor, and interpretive
programs took about ten times as long to be executed as those coded in machine
language—a luxury one could ill afford not only because of the cost, but also because
machines were still scarce.

By the late 1950s, a number of compilers were in use, notably FORTRAN and FLOW-
MATIC (the forerunner of COBOL). Compilers were to be the answer to transferability

of programs. Their execution times were nearly as good as those of hand coding, their language as simple as that of the interpreter. However, the time required to compile a program and the number of times one had to compile it to obtain a correct result were still unreasonable. Over the years, compilers improved, and today they are the backbone of the industry.

During the late sixties, productivity of compiler coding took yet another turn for the better by the use of time sharing. The fast turnaround time, improved diagnostics, and high reliability all combined to increase the speed of coding by a factor of five over older batch methods of producing machine-encoded programs.

Time-sharing reintroduced interpretive programs, but by now the early restraints of cost and availability had all but disappeared, bringing with them better diagnostics and debugging aids.

As all these advances took place, and as better-trained personnel became available, the storehouse of programs essential to the conduct of science and business became so large that it contradicted the original premise that it would not take much effort to redo a program once coding were simplified. From this realization grew ·the early efforts to standardize the major languages. Early in 1960, efforts were started to develop standard FORTRAN, COBOL, ALGOL, and APT languages.

Programming is only one facet of standardization to conserve the user's investment; data are another. Almost 1 million data entry and capture devices attest to the importance of data to the user. Much of these data are discarded. Those data which are retained are assets to the continuance of the activity for which they were created. Some of the data which are captured in machine-readable form are proprietary to the conduct of one's business. However, an ever-increasing share of the captured data represents a commodity which can be traded commercially: market data, scientific data, library references and indexes, etc. Like programs, data must be recorded so as to be transferable. Ultimately, the ability to exchange and manipulate data freely will open up new uses for computers which will further expand the power of the human mind.

Early Approaches   The computer industry is unique in its approach to standardization. Instead of waiting for practices and techniques to settle to a steady state to be standardized later, a number of forward-looking projects were undertaken. No other industry has dared anticipate its needs to the point of standardizing practices which have not yet been proved. But the need for conventions was so great that it induced much selfless cooperation among the individuals who pioneered data processing standards.

The Office Equipment and Machines Institute (OEMI) started a standards program for optical character recognition during the early 1960s. Later the OEMI was reorganized into the Business Equipment Manufacturers Association (BEMA), which was recently renamed the Computer and Business Equipment Manufacturers Association (CBEMA). Seven major projects were started by 1962:

>   Optical Character Recognition.
>   Codes and Input-Output Media.
>   Data Communications.
>   Programming Languages.
>   Vocabulary.
>   Documentation.
>   Magnetic Character Recognition.

From these early beginnings there grew to be about 50 committees working on well over 100 active projects, all of which are well planned and controlled by a knowledgeable group of individuals representing producers, users, and interested professional associations.

NEEDS AND OBJECTIVES

Needs   Almost any attempt at utilizing computers represents a considerable expenditure of time and money. It is in the interest of both the user and the supplier to reduce the overhead of rewriting programs and re-entering data. Standards release the user from the cost and the drudgery of redoing his or her work. They also encourage more use of computers and therefore increase the usefulness and hence the market base of data processing devices. Standards are also needed to take care of overloads, to share the use of computers with others, and to communicate with other computers.

The preservation of the user's assets in programs and data is essential for the user's continued existence in case of disaster. ADP standards are an indispensable ingredient for all such contingency planning. Standards are also essential for the user's continued existence in a competitive environment. Without standards the cost of converting an installation to a completely new data processor may be so high as to discourage the updating of a system; yet, the longer it is postponed, the harder conversion becomes. Finally, faced with an obsolete machine, competitive pressure, and an insurmountable budget problem, a company could have to fight for its continued existence.

An accumulation of personally owned data and programs (as contrasted with an employer's proprietary material) represents an individual's intellectual property. The employee could be deprived of it if he or she changed employment to an organization in which this accumulation of know-how would be destroyed by inability to transfer it to the new job. Data and programs are marketable entities. Lack of standards limit their marketability.

Objectives The basic objective of data processing standards is *transferability*:

• Transferability to enable a meaningful interchange of information between systems, subsystems, and peripherals – local and remote.

• Transferability to enable data once entered into the processing stream to be captured and stored in central store, auxiliary store, and input-output media.

• Transferability to enable data stored for use in one system to be entered meaningfully into another.

• Transferability to enable programs written for one system to be executable by another.

• Transferability to enable information streams, data, and programs to be relayed meaningfully to remote sites.

• Transferability to enable people to communicate meaningful data processing information to each other.

AREAS OF STANDARDIZATION

Common Intelligibility The first requirement for machine-sensible information is to come up to the level of common intelligibility which visibly legible, written, typed, or printed information has achieved. To accomplish this one must establish:

• Dimensional and physical transferability of media from one system to another.

• Electromechanical transferability of recorded matter on media.

• A convention for relating machine-sensible patterns (codes) to the characters used in visibly legible records.

Telecommunications needs for standards are similar to those of the media. They require additionally:

• Physical interconnection standards for communications devices.

• Electrical interface standards.

• Conventions for actuating and conversing with other devices (control codes, control procedures).

One notes that telecommunications and media require standards not needed in communications between people. People can determine when to start, stop, or continue, etc., machines must be told. The signals which tell machines what function to perform are called *control codes* and the methods of using these control codes are called *control procedures*. Standards are needed for them.

Person–Machine Communication A second requirement is that of person–machine communication standards. Just as human beings have a language in which to converse, so must there be programming languages for people to talk to computers. Some of the more commonly used ones are FORTRAN, COBOL, PL/I, ALGOL, and BASIC. These languages must be standardized in order to permit the meaning of a program written in a given language to be executable on machines other than the one for which it was written originally.

A standard language alone does not ensure transferability of programs any more than common knowledge of, say, the English language ensures communication among people. The transfer of semantics (meaning) is the responsibility of the writer of a program and probably not subject to generalized standardization. Specific applications permit standardization of semantics, e.g., the APT (Automatic Part Tooling) language permits tools to produce identical parts.

The standards above are written for the intellectual level of communication. There are other person–machine standards intended for the physical intercommunication. Only one area has been tackled by standardizers: keyboards. Future standards will probably unify general-purpose communications terminals to eliminate the current needless proliferation of differences between them.

Person-to-Person Communication A third area of standardization is person-to-person communication. Here the most important work is the generation of a common set of words. This is a never-ending task which results in periodic revisions of a dictionary published by CBEMA.

Documentation standards are needed primarily for programs and data. They are applications-oriented. As a first step various data elements are being standardized. Program documentation has not reached the national level of standardization; it is being practiced within organizations.

Documentation of systems and systems software is also standardized by each manufacturer. However, standardization of such documentation on a national or international level is not likely to be undertaken.

The three areas of standardization enumerated above are functional in scope. The National Bureau of Standards (NBS) has embarked on a study of computer performance. As the industry matures, standards of performance will be established. In the strictest sense these are not standards; they are purchase specifications.

STANDARDS FOR MEDIA

Early attempts at unifying the recording of data fell short of today's needs. From the proud moments of the early 1950s when it became apparent that we could store data externally (mostly on magnetic tape) to the realization in the early 1960s that recorded media are a valued property of a user, manufacturers prided themselves in offering an ever-increasing variety of recorded media. A frenzied activity of code standardization was sparked by the early successes of the machine-tool industry when it standardized a code on paper tape. By the end of 1962, a committee of the American Standards Association (now the American National Standards Institute, ANSI) had erected a framework for the transferability of data. It developed a correspondence between binary numbers and graphic characters (called a *binary representation of graphics*), and was busy defining the recording of this "code," which by now had been dubbed ASCII (American Standard Code for Information Interchange—pronounced "as-key") on media. This same committee also sponsored the work which created the physical and recording standards for the media: punched cards, punched paper tape, magnetic tape, magnetic disks, etc.

Figure 2-1 shows the interrelation of several standards. The binary representation is derived from the column/row coordinates of a graphic symbol. For example, the letter A is in column 4 row 1, the binary representation of 4 is 0100, and of 1 is 0001; hence the binary representation of A is 0100 0001. Also shown for each entry is the punched-card code, e.g., the letter A is represented by holes in rows 12 and 1 of a given column. ·Columns 0 and 1 show equivalent graphic symbols for the control characters of ASCII. The letters and symbols of columns 2 to 7 have the shapes (font design) prescribed for optical character recognition by the OCR-B standard. The Japanese characters (Katakana) shown in columns 10 to 13 also have OCR shapes rather than the traditional brush stroke design. Finally, columns 12 to 15 show the U.S.S.R. standard Cyrillic characters in relation to the Roman characters. An interesting design feature of the Russian standard is that if one overlays the right half of the code on the left, and omits the lowercase characters of both the Roman and Cyrillic alphabets, one obtains a dual Roman-Cyrillic set ideally suited for telegraphic equipment.

These standards activities represent a "first" in the history of standardization. The representation of data on media was the first attempt ever to break completely with the past and to adopt a logically correct standard. The work took place during an era when it was accepted that (1) the present computer would be replaced sooner or later, and (2) the process of replacement of equipment would entail a changeover of files and programs. Unfortunately, foot-dragging and competitive pressures held up the final approval of these standards until the late 1960s. Consequently, the very chaos these standards were supposed to avoid exists today. However, not all was lost. Users and producers alike are slowly converging toward the use of only two codes: ASCII and EBCDIC (Extended Binary Coded Decimal Interchange Code), the latter being the de facto code introduced in the IBM 360 product line and since copied by a large segment of industry.

Paper-Tape and Magnetic-Tape Cassettes Paper tape is truly the only medium which can be said to be fully standardized. It is 1 inch wide and has eight information tracks and a sprocket track. Seven of the information tracks are used to record ASCII characters; the eighth is optionally used either for parity or as an additional information bit. Standards for magnetic-tape cassettes followed closely on the heels of paper tape because they would eventually replace paper tape. These two media are deemed functionally equivalent.

Punched Cards Punched cards are also standardized internationally; the punched holes are those defined by EBCDIC (see above). Interestingly, the significance of the standard punched-card code lies more in the tie which it forms between ASCII and EBCDIC, than with the fact that it ties punched holes to ASCII. Nonetheless, over a period of time, we may find as uniform a representation on punched cards as we find on punched paper tape.

Magnetic Tapes The progress of standardization in magnetic tapes is phenomenal. From a plethora of products varying in every conceivable physical or electrical factor—materials, dimension, recording method, density, etc.—we have settled to one standard for all unrecorded tapes and three recording densities: 200, 800, and 1,600 pulses (bits, characters) per inch. A fourth density of 6,250 ppi will be standardized shortly. There are eight data channels and the recording method is self-sprocketing. Simply put, one can take a tape from one machine to another and use it. But beware: only the electromechanical factors are compatible. The recording conventions imposed by a program can still prevent carefree exchange of recorded tapes.

Disks Disks are another medium for exchange of recorded data. Most of the effort in standardization has been directed toward the physical exchange of unrecorded disks. The recording of data and its organization on disks are more complex than, say, on magnetic tape because of the close relation between it and the processor system design, and therefore do not lend themselves to standardization. Luckily, in this sense, magnetic disks have not proved a successful medium for data exchange because of their bulk and weight.

Machine-Readable Fonts Magnetic ink characters (MICR) are the stylized characters now found on personal checks. The American Bankers Association developed these in the early 1960s and they are the salvation of the banking community. They have proved to be reliable means of encoding billions of documents generated by banking transactions. The characters are not pleasant to the human eye and not easy to read; however, they are easier to proofread than uninterpreted codes on paper tape or punched cards.[1]

Optically recognized characters (OCR) have been standardized for some time. Without a specific industry's backing, OCR has not been as successful as MICR. An early method of recognizing characters was a stylized bar code, CMC-7, used in European banking circles. In the United States the OCR-A character font was originally designed as a stylized numeric set which was to rival MICR in other than banking applications. Since then it has been expanded to include the capital letters of the alphabet and most of the symbols used in business correspondence. OCR-B rivals OCR-A; it is more pleasant to look at and by today's technology no more difficult to read than OCR-A. This font was originally proposed by ECMA and was vigorously opposed by manufacturers who had only OCR-A to offer. All three methods offer the opportunity to use an office typewriter to generate machine-sensible documents. MICR does not, a fact which makes it desirable for checks but not for data entry.

[1] See Part 3, Chapter 2, "Optical Scanning, OCR, and MICR," in this Section for discussion and examples.

The Hollerith card code for 256 characters is constructed from

1 or 2 or 3 ... or 7 or blank (no punch)
+ any combination of 12, 11, 0, 8, and 9 → X 32 (2^5)
(from none to all) = 256

For historical reasons, the assignments present little in the way of a regular pattern, but they are the key to translate to and from IBM EBCDIC.

REFERENCE CHART ISO CODE (ASCII IN THE USA) AND ASSOCIATED RELATIONSHIPS

Note: this is not a standard in itself.
Refer to the appropriate documents.

Note 1
These 12 positions are variable — 2 for currency, 7 primary national usage, and 3 secondary usage which are diacritical marks used for alphabetical extension when preceded by BS. Positions 2/7 and 2/12 are invariant but also serve as diacritical marks. The presently-known assignments are given in the table

JISCII (Japanese Industrial Standard Code for Information interchange) is an 8-bit code consisting of the ISO characters plus the Kata Kana characters shown in the upper row positions of columns 10-13 (columns 8 and 9 are reserved for additional controls, 14 and 15 for additional graphics).

GOST 13n52-67 defines the USSR set, shown in the lower row entry positions of columns 12-15. Actually, the standard defines these characters for columns 4-7 of a 7-bit set (SO= Russian register, SI= Latin register). Columns 8-11 are identical to 0-3.

	currency	1st 7 national	dia	1st 7 national	dia	dia	1st 7 national	dia
	2/3 2/4	4/0	5/11 5/12 5/13	5/14	6/0	7/11 7/12 7/13	7/14
Netherlands—A								
Australia								
Belgium—A								
W. Germany—A								
US								
Japan								
UK								
Italy—A								
Switzerland—A								
France—A								
USSR								
Netherlands—B								
Belgium—B								
France—B								
Switzerland—B								
Italy—B								
Switzerland—C								
Hungary								
W. Germany—B								
Switzerland—D								
Sweden								
Finland								
Denmark								
Norway								
Spain								

even parity — feed hole — odd parity

track of 8-track paper tape

(b_1 is the first bit sent in serial transmission, then b_2, etc. to b_7 (b_8), then parity)

channel of 9-track magnetic tape

Fig. 2-1 ISO Code (ASCII) relationships.

Direct Data Entry   Direct data entry, with or without visible records, vies for a share of the market for encoding data for machine use.   As a first step a general purpose keyboard standard was developed which unfortunately offers two options; one typewriter-like and the other teletypewriter-like.   In addition, for commercial data input the IBM keypunch keyboard appears to be the de facto standard.   Future standards for terminals may bring uniformity to this area.   There will be two types of standards, one for general-purpose terminals, the other for applications-oriented terminals.

STANDARDS FOR LANGUAGES

There are six standards currently active in software standardization.   One of those is an applications language, APT (Automatic Part Tooling), which is used primarily by users of numerically controlled machine tools.   This language was originally invented at M.I.T. and is currently maintained by the Illinois Institute of Technology Research Institute.   The standard for APT was approved in 1973, nearly 17 years after the language was first invented.   APT is basically machine-independent, i.e., independent of the machine tool for which it is intended; therefore it needs a postprocessor which transforms the results of the APT program into an input for a machine tool.   A project to standardize a postprocessor is under way.

The other five projects deal with systems languages.[2]   The oldest of the languages, FORTRAN, was originally introduced by IBM about 1954.   It is used primarily in engineering.   A FORTRAN standard was written in 1966 and is about to be updated (1975). A subset of FORTRAN, Basic FORTRAN, was also standardized in 1966; it is used by smaller machines.

COBOL, a business programmer's tool, is a more recent entry into the family of systems programs.   It was originally started by Dr. Grace Hopper as FLOWMATIC. A first version of FLOWMATIC was in existence in 1959.   Two years later, largely through the efforts of Charles A. Phillips, then with the Department of Defense, CODASYL, the Conference on Data Systems Languages, was formed to develop COBOL (Common Business Oriented Language).   CODASYL has remained the recognized development authority for COBOL.   The CODASYL Committee keeps COBOL dynamic, and a number of revisions to COBOL have been made by it.   An independent COBOL Standardization Committee acts as a filter for stabilizing implemented versions of COBOL.   The first standard COBOL was issued in 1968 and its first revision was published in 1974.   The CODASYL Committee is currently very active in the development of a standard data management system and a standard data descriptive language.

Although a better language than FORTRAN, ALGOL has been the stepchild in computer implemented languages.   A number of ALGOL versions are implemented but are used primarily in academic institutions.   An international version of ALGOL is about to be published, but a standard ALGOL will not be adopted by the United States.

PL/I is one of the more recent additions to the family of programming language standards.   The language PL/I was developed jointly by IBM and by SHARE and GUIDE, the IBM user organizations.   PL/I is an effort to combine the best features of FORTRAN, ALGOL, and COBOL into one language while, at the same time, enriching it for uses not possible with the other three languages.   PL/I represents a novel approach to language standardization because the development, as well as the standardization of the language, rests in the same organization.   It is also remarkable because it is an outstanding effort of cooperation between the United States and Europe.   PL/I was first introduced in 1963 and a number of implementations exist in the field.   First publication of a PL/I standard was scheduled for late 1975.

The most recent effort at standardizing a computer language is the standardization of BASIC.   BASIC was first implemented at Dartmouth College around 1964.   It has since been adopted by every time-sharing service in the world.   Current efforts are aimed first at defining the minimum level of implementation and, second, at defining a common set of language extensions.   The work is progressing well.   A draft "Minimal Basic" was scheduled for availability late in 1975.   The advanced modules will take between 3 and 5 years to complete.

---

[2] For a further discussion of programming languages, see Part 4, Chapter 3, in this Section.

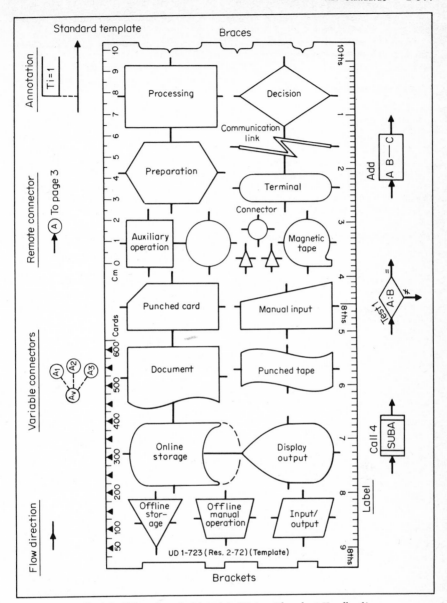

Fig. 2-2 Univac flow chart template (*Univac Flowchart Handbook*).

DOCUMENTATION STANDARDS

Two documentation standards have been issued so far: One is a standard for flow chart symbols and their use in information processing (Figure 2-2)[3]; the other is a dictionary for information processing.[4] A draft "Guidelines for Technical Documentation of

---

[3] ANSI X3.5-1970, *American National Standard Flowchart Symbols and Their Usage in Information Processing.* A useful manual is the *Univac Flowchart Manual,* Sperry Rand Corporation, 1972, which conforms to the ANSI standards.

[4] ANSI X3.12-1970, *American National Standard Vocabulary for Information Processing.*

Computer Projects" was issued in 1974. Work in network-oriented information systems is unpredictable at this time.

Two separate additional efforts at coming up with a vocabulary for information processing are taking place. In the United States the effort is directed primarily toward the accumulation of a dictionary which enumerates all the terms that are currently in use. The international effort is on a more intellectual level. The ISO (International Organization for Standards) bases its work on the work of IFIPS (International Federation of Information Processing Societies) and the ICC (International Computer Center).

The IFIPS/ICC vocabulary was first published in 1965 through the Holland Publishing Co. and has been updated since. The international effort is to analyze the work of the IFIPS/ICC critically, to add terms, revise definitions, etc. The ISO vocabulary differs from the work in the United States in that it defines each term in context and therefore provides a more rigid framework for an understanding of the language of computers. This kind of preciseness is necessary in an international environment, where language barriers could prevent a dictionary such as that developed in the United States from ever being properly translated.

DATA REPRESENTATION STANDARDS

Three areas of data representation are being standardized. The first is on the elementary level of the code itself. In this area, a number of standards have been published for the basic set of ASCII. The most important work still going on at this time is the work in code extension. As now envisioned, code extension will make it possible to represent almost any character regardless of its origin or language on a computer.

TABLE 2-1   Types of Labels, Names, Identifiers, and Numbers

Type	Name			Identifier and number
Beginning of volume	Operating system	Volume header label	Required	VOL1
			Optional	Prohibited
	User	User volume header label	Optional	UVL1 to UVL9
End of volume	Operating system	End of volume label	Required	EOV1
			Optional	EOV2 to EOV9
	User	User end of volume label	Optional	UTLa
Beginning of file	Operating system	File header label	Required	HDR1
			Optional	HDR2 to HDR9
	User	User file header label	Optional	UHLa
End of file	Operating system	End of file label	Required	EOF1
			Optional	EOF2 to EOF9
	User	User end of file label	Optional	UTLa

There are over 10,000 different symbols used in connection with the Latin alphabet of 26 characters. Accommodations are being made to permit each one to be encoded uniquely. The Japanese, too, have worked on standards to encode their pictograms (about 20,000) by the method of code extension. This work represents a giant step toward the further encoding of business and scientific information.

A number of standards are being developed which define in a descriptive label what the data which follow are. This work applies primarily to tapes and disks. A standard label was developed for magnetic tapes. Table 2-1 shows what a magnetic-tape label may contain. In this table the word "volume" is taken to be synonymous with "tape reel." Standards for magnetic disks and for tape cassettes are being developed.

One of the biggest projects is the effort to standardize data elements. To enumerate just a few, there are the representation of dates, time elements, individuals, organizations, accounts, states, counties, cities, towns, places, point locations, mailing and shipping addresses, countries, subdivisions of countries, continents, and water areas. These should all be extremely important in future communications between users of ADP systems.

TELECOMMUNICATIONS STANDARDS

Early attempts at communicating data were based on the existing telephone and telegraph networks. The 5-bit Baudot code in use then was better suited to communication between typewriters than to communication between typewriters and computers. ASCII was developed in its place. It took the cooperation of many domestic and international organizations to accomplish today's advanced communications technology standards. In the United States, ANSI combined efforts with the Electronic Industries Association (EIA). They divided the work between logical and electromechanical interfaces. Internationally the work was divided among and coordinated between the European Computer Manufacturers Association (ECMA), the International Organization for Standards (ISO), the International Electrotechnical Commission (IEC), and the Consultative Committee International, for Telegraph and Telephone (CCITT). The relationships between the committees are too complex to discuss here but the interests covered are those of the users, manufacturers, and the representatives of the Departments of State of all countries having an interest in communicating across borders.

The first giant effort was the standardization of start-stop data communications based on ASCII. Ten control codes in ASCII have been set aside for use in data communications. These codes are used in the "hand shaking" between computers. The procedures for the use of ASCII in communications links were first published in 1971 and will be revised soon. They are in daily use today. In addition to these standards there are a number of mechanical and electrical standards which permit the interconnection of systems with a data network, etc.

At present, the work is concentrating on standardizing a code-independent method for communicating data. Originally introduced by IBM as the Synchronous Data Link Control (SDLC), an Advanced Data Communications Control Procedure (ADCCP) was developed by ANSI for standardization in the United States. A subset of ADCCP was developed in Europe by ECMA and is being introduced as the High-Level Data Link Procedure (HDLC) in ISO and CCITT. These standards permit the transmission of any digital data regardless of its content. In these procedures the "envelope" of bits which surround the message is completely separated from the message itself, thus eliminating the possibility that a user-generated message might interfere with data transmission. This eliminates a weakness of today's ASCII-oriented communications links.

Network control procedures are also being standardized in recognition of the need for the many private and public data communications networks to work together someday.

REFERENCES

No attempt has been made in the foregoing few pages to be all-inclusive as regards standardization activities. The reader is referred to the listing and addresses given at the conclusion of the first Chapter in this Part. The Computer and Business Equipment Manufacturers Association (CBEMA) and the European Computer Manufacturers Association (ECMA) act as the focal points respectively in the United States and in Europe for the gathering and dissemination of information on ADP standards.

A significant contribution to understanding the worldwide standards making process was made by Marjorie F. Hill, Control Data Corporation, TECH MEMO TM 4 *The World of EDP Standards*. The book, now out of print, has been updated by the author and is now published by the National Bureau of Standards, Washington D.C., 20234.

Chapter 3

Software Standardization: Management Perspectives

T. G. GRIEB

Universal Systems, Inc., Arlington, Virginia

The scope of this Chapter includes the standardization of all areas of software and interfaces with software systems. The responsibility for standards falls into one of three categories according to the scope of application, importance, and projected life. These categories are:

1. *National (and international)*. These are standards that the user may have or want to adopt; one has no control over these unless one participates in their development (e.g., American National Standard COBOL). All national standards may be submitted, as is or modified, as candidates for international standards.

There are two subcategories here:

    a. Standards which are required by law, e.g., Federal information processing standards or military standards which one must follow when dealing with or for the Federal Government or the Department of Defense.

    b. Standards created, used, and sometimes promoted by professional societies (e.g., IEEE), trade groups (e.g., ABA), interchange committees, mutual help groups (e.g., NASIS), and some commercial groups. Such standards may have broad application and be candidates for national standards, or have limited application for specialized groups only.

2. *Installation*. These are standards candidates that are only beginning to be addressed by national standards bodies, local organizations, and companies. In this class, the problems are not yet well enough known to classify them specifically.

3. *To be determined.* This is a catch-all category that includes systems documentation and otherwise unclassified candidate.

SOFTWARE STANDARDS: WHAT, WHY, AND HOW

There is very little published information on the *theory* of standardization. The concepts of how and when to develop or adopt standards and how and when to establish their use are still unclear in the minds of those who manage the data processing industry and profession.

But just what are standards? Standards are methods, procedures, and techniques which have been proved or are believed to be the best and most workable for the overall desired results. The answer to "Why standards?" now becomes easy: Workable software standards allow *order* in the process of developing, producing, and maintaining software systems. Order increases understandability and manageability. Are software standards too expensive? Software standards are often neglected because the costs of the lack of these standards are ambiguous, hidden, and once discovered, difficult to quantify. It is possible that the shortage of software standards costs computer users as much as (or more than) their hardware.

What is the effective level for software standardization? It has to take place at an elementary level. The more complex and sophisticated the component being standardized, the less useful it is to standardize.

The scope of software standardization is still limited by the status of hardware standardization. At this time, for example, it is impossible to make a clear separation between (1) standards for data representation and data handling, and (2) hardware and media capabilities and standards. Available equipment has to be able to handle easily the standardized methods produced in the software area, or else they are too expensive to implement and are perhaps even useless. For example, if there were a national standard print character set (data representation) that was too large to be implemented on current printers (hardware), the standard would be useless, at least for the time being until the printer technology caught up.

What role do software standards play? The full extent to which software standards affect the data processing industry is still to be determined. We have learned, however, that some of the benefits of extensive and valid software standards are:[1]

- Systems of higher quality.
- Better utilization of valuable personnel.
- Better communication between data processing personnel and other sectors of the company, especially management.
- Better communication among data processing personnel.
- Better protection of valuable programs and data, and documentation of the entire systems.
- Fewer errors in design, programming, testing, and operations.
- Simpler, less costly maintenance process.
- Less time and energy spent on "reinventing the wheel."
- More efficient process of teaching established methods to personnel.

An effective standards approach aims for a balance among at least the following:

1. Costs.
2. Control.
3. Development efficiency.
4. Production efficiency and ease.
5. Preservation of continuity throughout a software system in documentation and naming, etc.
6. Thorough and readily accessible historical operations documentation.
7. Ease of maintenance.
8. Ease of conversions.

The amount of emphasis to be placed on each of these areas is a management decision. That is, management of the data processing department decides on the definition of balance according to what it thinks will best support the purposes and goals of the company, and makes necessary budgetary and policy recommendations to higher management for implementation.

What about the timely implementation of software standards? Is there a secret for success? In order for software standards implementation to be successful, one or more of the following conditions have to exist:

1. The recognition by management that firm economic or business goals cannot be reached without certain standards.
2. The enforcement of standards by government.
3. Sufficient pressure placed on the producers of software by the consumers of software, so that standards are needed to satisfy their demands for efficiency, uniformity, performance, predictability, understandability of the product, etc.

[1] See also J. O. Harrison, Jr., "Role of Standards," *Proceedings of the Society for Information Display*, vol. 13, 3d quarter, 1972.

The tendency is to do things "my way" unless a critical need to standardize is recognized by management and clearly communicated to the producers of the software. On the other hand, the mere existence of one of the above conditions does not guarantee success of implementation. The pitfalls of the management of any implementation process are forever present.

HISTORY, NEEDS, AND PROBLEMS

The first national standards in the software area were created about 15 years ago. The data processing profession was then just an infant, and thus things were done in any way which produced something somewhere near the desired results. The capabilities of hardware increased at a fantastic rate and the complexity of applications followed the trend. Interchange of information and programs among manufacturers and among users became important.

About 1960 it became obvious to perceptive decision makers that the process of software development had to be disciplined on a national scale, just as had been done by architects and engineers in their respective fields. They went to work and produced many good standards. Some of the people who launched this work for data processing are now authorities and even "giants" in this industry.

Without the knowledge of the standards which have been developed and are being developed nationally, those in charge of an installation can waste an unbelievable amount of money, time, and energy trying to do without standards or to develop all their own. Obtaining all applicable published EDP standards from the American National Standards Institute (ANSI) is, of course, important. The American National Standards Committee on Computers and Information Processing (ANSC X3) is responsible for national standards, and relates to international standards projects having to do with hardware and software interfaces. (Chapter 1 of this Part describes the environment, process, and organization for the development and publication of standards.) A knowledge of standards under development by the applicable American National Standards committees, especially ANSC X3, and by other organizations, would also be of value to every company using a computer. The Computer and Business Equipment Manufacturers Association (CBEMA) in Washington, D.C., acts as the secretariat of the ANSC X3 and has copies of all proposed standards and information about all current projects.

There are hundreds of methods, tools, techniques, etc. within the software arena which still need to be considered for standardization at a national level.

The most neglected areas of software standards are those controlled totally within an installation. First, there is a lack of recognition of the value of adopting or modifying standards developed for and by another installation. There is a reluctance in user companies to give up the notion of "almost total uniqueness." There seem to be infinitely more common problems among user companies than unique problems. Second, because of the overhead expense of developing standards, their development and application are usually assigned a low priority unless and until there has been a serious crisis due to a lack of applied standards in a particular area. For instance, in one computer installation which employs about 500 people, inadequate naming standards were a serious problem. That is, the names for all the components of software systems (programs, modules, fields, jobs, data sets, etc.) were not standardized adequately. The documented costs in terms of employee-hours and machine-time due to errors caused by inadequate names amounted to $41,000 in one year. The head of this large installation stated that the actual costs would be between 10 to 100 times the documented amount. That means a reasonable estimate would be 0.25 million dollars a year for inadequate naming standards alone!

The following pages contain some general information about areas in which standardization is much more valuable than is normally expected. Each type of standard is identified as to category: national, installation, or to-be-determined.

Programming
Design (Installation Standards). The first attempts to standardize the design of programs were made with the introduction of the *performed subroutine* concept. That is, the main logic could be written in a continuous flow without the interruption of

I/O functions or detailed data manipulation. The I/O and manipulative instructions could be separate (perhaps at the end of the program) and could simply be referenced and performed; then control would be returned to the main logic where execution had left off. In a sense, this was modularity. However, in order to make a change in any part of the program, one had to check for uniformity throughout the program and had to recompile the entire program every time there were changes.

To solve this problem, the true modular programming concept was developed.[2] That is, the modules of the program are self-contained, separately compiled, and testable. The modules are combined into one program only when it is time to execute. The complete program can also be stored in the final or "load" form. For each type of module, (control, I/O, manipulative), standards were also developed by some installations to encourage a common approach to the logic flow through these modules. Such standards allow one programmer to understand the work of another programmer in the same installation with much less difficulty. Such relative independence of the program from its author can be achieved only with standardization, *even at the installation level*.[3] The standardization of modular program design imposed by some manufacturers upon their users also allows the complete separation of the definition of data from the program. This, then, is the capability which serves as the stepping stone to database systems. This step could be achieved only through the implementation of this standard, although standards still vary with different manufacturers. This standarized approach has cost the industry millions of dollars, but may save billions.

Languages (National Standards). Programming languages were the first area of the software development process for which national standards were created. One simply could not write a program and have a compiler available to translate it without a standardized and agreed-on programming language. However, each manufacturer had a unique version of each programming language to use with its particular hardware and control or operating systems.

In 1966 and 1968 technical committees of ANSI produced the first national standards for FORTRAN and COBOL respectively. The international standards are based upon the ANSI standards. The value of the universality of these, the first standard languages, cannot even be measured. The 1974 revised COBOL contains many extensions and improvements.

A proposed revision to the present standard FORTRAN is at this writing being prepared by an X3 technical committee. The APT language was approved in 1974, and PL/I is in progress. There is an international standard, but not a United States standard, for ALGOL. When a standardized language is given extensions for a particular computer, the extensions make the use of the language nonstandard and once again dependent. Such extensions are studied for possible inclusion in the standard when it is revised.

There has been an active effort to publish and administer a standardized set of audit routines (also called *validation routines*) for various language compilers. Many administrative, technical, and legal problems have detained their publication and distribution. Studies to obtain answers to all the anticipated problems for COBOL, for instance, are being directed by the National Bureau of Standards. (For further discussion of standards for languages, see Chapter 2 of this Part.)

Testing (Installation Standards). As recently as 10 years ago, the process of testing programs was completely unstandardized, i.e., unpredictable. The evolution of today's standardized approaches was a slow one. However, now there are testing "software packages" that were developed by specialists, which give the capability to adopt or modify rather than develop a standardized approach from scratch. We also have software which allows us easily to generate comprehensive test data, thereby giving us the possibility of having standard test data installation-wide. Some installations and some service organizations have developed standardized testing procedures for both the testing of individual programs and modules as well as the testing of entire systems by separate groups. In other words, when the testing process is standardized, it is a

[2] *Improved Programming Technologies: Management Overview*, IBM Corporation, Data Processing Division, White Plains, New York, August, 1973.

[3] See G. I. Myers, "Characteristics of Composite Design," *Datamation*, September, 1973, pp. 100–102.

workable part of the overall flow of systems development. There are many valid approaches to testing and each is usable with different equipment and different operating systems. However, there are many good products on the market which are valuable in standardizing the testing process in-house.

Problems which should be addressed as possible standards candidates in the programming area include:

1. Currently it is not possible to do in one program what is possible in a multimodule program. A standardized block-structured language would have this capability.

2. There are many different operation codes and variables in the different instruction sets of the different languages. It may be desirable to have some degree of standardization in this area.

Documentation Documentation standards play an especially significant role in the definition, design, programming, implementation, and maintenance of systems and their component parts.[4] Good documentation standards can serve as a guideline, a checklist, and an aid to organization and formatting, as well as promote a comprehensive, easy-to-understand record of the entire system. The more clearly defined and the more detailed the documentation standards are, the less difficult and less costly is the system development/production/maintenance process.

Management (Installation Standards). Managing a data processing project is an aspect of software standardization, because workable standards in this area can ensure that the project is predictable, communicable, controllable, and measurable.

Project estimating, when standardized properly, gives us the capability to segment the entire system into defineable "project modules." These modules, with the use of some equations, can be translated into exact units of employee-hours and machine-hours. Standardized forms, which call for all the necessary information, serve as a vehicle for the translation process and are a permanent record of how the estimate was derived.

Effective project control and measurement has been difficult to implement.[5] One of the reasons is that, in an attempt to make it meaningful, we tend to create too much detail and people balk at complexity and discipline. However, again, with a valid and standardized approach and supporting forms, software, and reports, project control (including machine utilization control) does work.[6] When the project manager combines workable, standardized estimating techniques with an effective project control standard, projects can be finished on time and within budget. This is true for all sizes of projects. In large ones we simply have more segments or "modules," and increased interrelationships.

Possibly the most important part of project control is project accounting. Computers cost money. Programmers and analysts cost money. Damaged customer relations and failure of a business system to do its job cost money. The details of how this money is charged is not in the area of standards, but standards (standardized methods and documentation) must be concerned with seeing that adequate information is available to support the charging procedure used by an installation. Accounting information in job cards and on-line user identification are examples of this type of documentation.

Systems Documentation (To-be-determined Standards).[7] There are database systems and application-oriented systems. Additionally, each of these types can be designed to be batch– or on-line–oriented, or a combination of the two. No matter which type of system or which method of processing is involved, the development process must be predictable, therefore standardized. A lack of good standards in the systems development and documentation process is more costly than in any other area.

When all aspects of the systems process are clearly defined and standardized, the forms which document that process are designed accordingly. When all the information called for on the forms is provided in proper sequence, the tasks of the systems process will tend to be performed properly and in proper sequence. Thus, proper

[4] See Max Gray and Keith R. London, *Documentation Standards*, Brandon/Systems Press, New York, 1970.

[5] Dick H. Brandon and Max Gray, *Project Control Standards*, Brandon/Systems Press, New York, 1970.

[6] Robert S. Kuehne, Herbert W. Lindberg, and William F. Baron, *Manual of Computer Documentation Standards*, Prentice-Hall, Englewood Cliffs, N.J., 1972.

[7] See also the discussion in Chapter 2 of this Part.

standardized forms can assure adherance to workable systems standards, and can take all the unnecessary guesswork out of the systems process.

Documentation standards play an important role, starting with the statement of *general design.* The conclusions of the general design process must be recorded in a systematized way. Preprinted forms are usually used. Such forms make it easy to record-as-you-go, and they serve as a handy checklist for completeness. All the general design considerations should be recorded in such a way that independent persons or groups can study and evaluate the document and the design. At this point, the systems designer has to be careful to be detailed enough so that he is forced to consider in his mind what the final detailed solution will be like. However, it is also easy to work out and document too much detail, so that specific design considerations are solidified too early. Later, when it becomes apparent that it would be best to modify the design, it often is too costly and time-consuming to make the necessary changes in all the documentation.

In the general design phase, all operational, programming, and data components should be referred to by general, descriptive, but independent names. Any dependence, interrelationships, or sequence implied in names at this time will certainly prove to be restrictive and awkward during the programming and implementation phase. In other words, the *independent design* approach could be and commonly is hampered by the practice of dependent names.

At the end of the *detailed design* phase, all standardized documentation required for programming except for the exact programming solution should be complete. Again, as in all good documentation standards, preprinted forms should be used. Specific programming names which show relationships or sequence are still premature.

The documentation at this level should include:

1. Design goals.
2. Design trade-offs.
3. Constraints.
4. Systems flow charts.
5. Processing descriptions.
6. File definitions.
7. Record definitions.
8. Field definitions.
9. Security requirements.
10. File protection and retention requirements.
11. Hardware requirements.
12. Data communication requirements.
13. Personnel requirements.
14. Needs and justification for outside contractors.
15. Languages to be used.
16. Software support requirements and restrictions.
17. Costs and schedules.
18. Glossary of all terms used.

This subject of *systems documentation* is temporarily placed in the "to-be-determined" category because feasibility studies are currently being conducted in this area at the national level. The *Automated Data Systems Documentation Standards Manual,* published by the Office of the Assistant Secretary of Defense (Comptroller), has been introduced into X3 as a candidate for a national standard.

Program Documentation (Mixed Categories of Standards).[8] The design, coding, polishing, testing, and maintenance of individual computer programs are time-consuming and expensive processes. Each of these processes as well as the resulting documentation must be standardized in order to work. Generally speaking, the more standardized these processes are, the more accurate is the final solution as intended by the user and by management. While it is possible, in theory, to overstandardize, that does not appear to have happened yet and is not too likely to happen.

The documentation for each finished program should include:

1. Record source list.
2. Program source list (with proper internal documentation).

---

[8] See also the discussion in Chapter 2 of this Part.

3. A map of the linkage of all program modules.
4. Narrative descriptions of the program and all modules.
5. Data name cross-reference listings.
6. Listings of all test data.
7. Listings of test outputs.
8. Reference to test data files.
9. Listing of control statements or catalogued job procedures used for testing.

The documentation for all programs of the system, collectively, should include:

1. Documented results of systems tests and related user sign-offs.
2. Documented package to include description of system test files, data set names, and related job control language.
3. Complete set of operations documentation for the execution of the system.

The life of the system during the operational phase is much longer than during the development phase. Therefore it is very important to keep the needs of the maintenance teams in mind. No part of the information of the system, especially the programs, should be taken for granted. Everything must be recorded somewhere, in a standardized way.

These documentation standards for programs are usually installation standards; however, a standard "program abstract" is currently being considered by a technical committee of ANSC X3.

Manual Procedures (Installation Standards). All manual procedures that are a necessary part of the (new) data processing system must also be documented. Here, too, having standardized methods and forms is essential to the effectiveness of these procedures, and therefore of the system.

Procedures are needed for:

1. The preparation and validity of input data.
2. The transformation of input data into machine-readable representation.
3. The control of all work and schedules for the computer room.
4. The preparation for the processing of data through the computer.
5. The quality control and distribution of all work leaving the computer room.
6. The teaching of any part of the systems process, wherever needed.

Techniques, Methods, and Tools (Mixed Categories of Standards). In order to accomplish any defined activity in the area of software development, we must have standardized techniques, methods, and tools to work with. This is particularly true in the areas of programming and documentation. To reiterate, documentation is the tangible result of the entire process of creating solutions. As such, a standardized documentation approach has a very powerful influence on the process and on the result of the creating process. Therefore, the influence should be as supportive and as complete as possible. Following are some of the main techniques, methods, and tools that should be made available to the data processing technician:

1. *Standard vocabulary.* The American National Standards Institute has published a standard vocabulary.[9] All the major manufacturers and many major users in the country took part in the development of this standard. The final result is a workable and valuable document and tool. The industry now has a generally agreed-upon, manufacturer-independent, easily available set of definitions of technical terms.

2. *Flow charting techniques.* ANSI has produced a good, manufacturer-independent standard for flow charting. The meanings of the symbols and of identifiers and explanations have often been confusing because one never knew which method of flow charting was used. The adoption of this national standard is wise for any company.[10]

3. *Naming standards.* Standardizing names for all system components within an installation is a tricky business. There are many needs within an installation that have to be answered by the naming standards. Often the needs of the development groups, the maintenance groups, and the operations personnel are in conflict with each other. Thus, priorities in terms of costs and workability have to be established. Then, unless each component and all possible effects of the names are thoroughly studied, inadequate standards are the result. Nothing can be taken for granted.

---

[9] ANSI X3.12-1970, *American National Standard Vocabulary for Information Processing.*
[10] See Figure 2-2 in Chapter 2 of this Part.

Needed information is often not supplied in the names, and this causes confusion and loss of time in operations. On the other hand, information is sometimes included in the names which causes arbitrary restrictions, and unnecessary work and frustration in both development and operations functions.

A company either chooses to adopt a standard which has been published, or must take the following steps to develop effective naming standards:

   a. Generally list and define all system components, present and anticipated.

   b. Categorize these components into at least the following: organizational, operating, processing, and data components.

   c. Obtain agreement on the specific definitions of these components.

   d. Determine all the elements of information which the names should contain.

   e. Define the exact interrelationships and nonrelationships among the components.

4. *Decision tables.* These have not yet been standardized on a national level, but have been defined very clearly by authorities on the subject. Several approaches are widely accepted and form a basis for common understanding, and could become input for a national standardization project. A major problem is that this, possibly the most powerful documentation tool we have, is not understood and not used by the majority of data processing personnel. A national effort to standardize decision tables would help to correct the situation. The book by Pollock and Harrison on the subject is clear and comprehensive.[11]

Other current national standards projects under way in the documentation area include: (1) a standardized graphical representation of networks, (2) a network glossary, (3) a network-oriented computer systems guide, (4) network-oriented project management systems, and (5) a national standards guideline manual for the entire systems documentation process.

Representation, Recording, and Transmission of Data   The major objective of standardization in the area of data is to achieve understanding and agreement about: (1) a common character code set for a particular scope of uses and the bit configurations which define (equate to) the characters of the agreed-upon set, and (2) common information units (data elements) and their representation and handling in data systems.[12]

Representation, recording, and transmission are the elementary levels at which standardization within this subject area can be most effective and workable. The higher the component level of a standard in this area, the more restricted is its scope and usefulness, and the more difficult is its implementation and the measurement of its effectiveness. It is useful here to keep in mind that programs are data also.

The most popular standard for code representation was and still is the Hollerith punched-card code (X3.26). The BCD (binary coded decimal) and the EBCDIC (extended binary coded decimal interchange code) are also widely used.

At the national level, the American Standard Code for Information Interchange (ASCII) has been established (X3.4). ASCII is currently used by some companies (1) for government requirements of data, (2) for interchange with other companies when code compatibility is required, and (3) when they need to provide information to some central organization within their particular industry. The general effort at the time of this writing seems to be for the adoption of ASCII as the basis for data created, processed, stored, or transmitted electronically.[13]

Subject areas covered within current development projects include flexible disks; recorded magnetic tape and tape cassettes; special-purpose cards; graphics; magnetic disks; tape labels and file structures; and data elements such as identification of places and organizations. In the data transmission area alone the following are under development: transmission signaling rates; heading formats; code-independent control procedures; network control procedures; data interfaces; and systems performance. Other

---

[11] S. L. Pollock and W. C. Harrison, *Decision Tables: Theory and Practice*, Wiley, New York, 1972.

[12] The ANSI X3L8 subcommittee of X3 is processing a "proposed American National Standard technical report" entitled "Guide for the Development, Implementation and Maintenance of Standards for the Representation of Data Elements." The main topics covered are: (1) background and concept of data standardization, (2) codes and coding, and (3) the current organizations and activities of data standardization.

[13] J. L. Little, "ASCII Code Applications," *Proceedings of the Society for Information Display*, vol. 13, 3d quarter, 1972. See also the discussion in Chapter 2 of this Part.

subject areas under study include interchangeable data files; collating sequence; and display parameters.

CONCLUSION

Awareness of the need for software standards has increased considerably in the past 5 years and continues to increase, especially with database systems.

Standards in electronic data processing are a necessity just as standard units of measure are in the field of medicine and standardized symbols and signs are in regulating traffic.

Those standards which have broad applicability and benefit in the industry can be submitted for possible standardization by ANSI and ISO as they have in the past. Installation standards, which have a smaller scope of users, will probably be developed by individual companies and perhaps shared with others.

Company personnel who have an intimate knowledge of and take part in the local, national, and international standards program have an advantage. They are informed about the current problems of the industry and are in an excellent position to enhance the standards awareness and programs in their own companies.

The ratio between dollars spent on software and dollars spent on hardware is constantly increasing. Therefore the value of software standards will become more and more evident. And, since there is a strong trend toward generalized software and the possibility of entire software-generated systems, software standards will no longer be looked upon as a luxury, but as the necessity and asset they really are.

SELECTIVE BIBLIOGRAPHY

Brandon, Dick H., and Max Gray, *Project Control Standards*, Brandon/Systems Press, New York, 1970.
Clamons, E. H., "Character Codes: Who Needs Them?" *Honeywell Computer Journal*, vol. 5, no. 3, 1971.
Gray, Max, and Keith R. London, *Documentation Standards*, Brandon/Systems Press, New York, 1970.
Harrison, J. O., Jr., "Role of Standards," *Proceedings of the Society for Information Display*, vol. 13, 3d quarter, 1972.
Kuehne, Robert S., Herbert W. Lindberg, and William F. Baron, *Manual of Computer Documentation Standards*, Prentice-Hall, Englewood Cliffs, N.J., 1972.
Little, J. L., "ASCII Code Applications," *Proceedings of the Society for Information Display*, vol. 13, 3d quarter, 1972.
National Aeronautics and Space Administration, *Computer Program Documentation Guideline*, Superintendent of Documents, U.S. Government Printing Office, Washington, D.C. 20402
Pollock, S. L., and W. G. Harrison, *Decision Tables: Theory and Practice*, Wiley, New York, 1972.

Section 3

Computer Systems Design and Installation

Part One

Computer Systems in Perspective

Introduction

JOHN W. OPLINGER, *Marketing Manager, The Diebold Group, Inc., New York, New York*

Those who have been involved in ADP since the 1950s can appreciate the tremendous change that has taken place in computer technology in the last 20 years. We can remember programming an IBM 650 in actual, that is, using binary code — not octal. We can remember wiring output panels and sitting at the console long into the night debugging programs. We then discovered SOAP, an early assembler, and said goodbye to endless visions of dancing "I's" and "O's."

We were introduced to the IBM-1401, a machine which by today's standards is little more than a minicomputer, but one which, because of its tremendous acceptance, must be considered the forerunner of commercial data processing. Many of us went to IBM schools to learn AUTOCODER. No one had ever heard of programmed instruction courses in those days. Somehow around that time, we also learned FORTRAN and discovered that a computer could understand such simple English words as "do," "if," and "format."

In the early 1960s, technology moved quite rapidly. Commercial programs for some of the larger machines were being written more and more in COBOL, and we were introduced to the first primitive operating systems, on such machines as the IBM-7094 or the CDC-3600. One still mounted one's own tape and could play with the console to debug a program, but a vague feeling began to creep in that it would never again be possible to understand fully what was going on inside the machine. Macros from nowhere were found in core dumps, and who knew what the compilers did to COBOL READ statements. But, by 1964, IBM introduced, with great fanfare, the System/360. We were told that at last we had one machine that could combine the needs of both the commercial and scientific user; that tape and sequential processing were now obsolete; and that what we called a RAMAC was now a direct-access storage device, or a DASD. We had to learn a whole new vocabulary, including such words and terms as *multiplexer* and *selector channel, index sequential access method* (ISAM), *job control language* (JCL), *tasks,* and many more. We were told that multiprogramming was just around the corner, and that a new language called PL/I was the answer to all a programmer's prayers. After going through a score of operating system releases and half a decade, many of these promises have been fulfilled.

Since the mid-1960s, change has continued, but has tended to be much more gradual. In 1975, we found ourselves in a world of multiprogramming, databases, minicomputers, and massive memory; we find people today trying to cope with virtual storage, much as they were trying to cope with operating systems 10 years ago; and we find ourselves waiting impatiently for the latest in laser memories, trillion-bit storage, distributed networks, and parallel processors.

ADP EFFICIENCY AND EFFECTIVENESS

In spite of these dramatic advancements in ADP technology, those of us in consulting practice must conclude that for many reasons only a small number of organizations have learned to utilize data processing equipment with the efficiency and effectiveness of other capital equipment. (One finds numerous examples of machine utilization of less than 10 per cent.) Worse, organizations are getting even lower utilization out of ADP personnel. One finds many cases in which such personnel make contributions to their organization which are worth less than their actual salaries, as opposed to being respectable multiples as they should. Further, far too many ADP projects, when given a stringent cost-benefit analysis, are found to have a negative return on investment.

One of the main causes of this situation has been an overconcentration on the technological rather than the business aspects of ADP. Companies launched huge computer system projects that held more technical interest than promise of return to the company. Large development projects ran virtually unmonitored and uncontrolled; costs and time schedules ran wildly over projections, and technical problems persisted chronically — sometimes they were never cleared up and the projects failed.

In any other corporate function — engineering, manufacturing, R&D, physical distribution, marketing — fundamental management principles apply: Spending projects are submitted to management with budgetary projections, a set of economic benefits are cited and quantified, and a payback period and return on investment are stipulated. Managers of such projects are held closely to these projections and are disciplined if they are missed. (Missed in *either* direction: A project too far *under* budget is viewed as a sign of inability to budget well, and hence a sign of a poor manager.) However, for a long time, company managements felt unable to exert management control over the ADP function: to apply conventional return-on-investment standards and budgetary discipline to spending for ADP, pass judgment on the recommendations of the technical people, or distinguish between normal operating problems and a department in serious trouble — much less react effectively to cure severe problems as they emerged.

It is a sign of a new maturity of the ADP function, however, that top ADP managers are increasingly just that — managers — and decreasingly technical personnel. Departments are increasingly cost centers, controlled by users who are charged, in internal accounting, for the data processing services they use. This puts a premium on efficiency and effectiveness, so that departments are increasingly focusing away from ambitious new projects and toward improvement of operations and productivity, budgetary monitoring and control, and close supervision to ensure responsiveness to users' real needs. *Effectiveness*, cited above, is a distinctly different value from *efficiency*. Efficiency measures the cost of accomplishing a function; effectiveness measures the extent to which the ADP function meets a valid corporate need. Efficiency has been a concern of data processing management for some time; effectiveness is now getting the management attention it deserves.

The new maturity is measured, too, by new relationships with the end users of ADP services. Each function — data processing and the user — talks the other's language to a greater degree. Users, in addition to paying for application development and operations, participate in choosing the application, designing it in detail, setting priorities, participating in implementation, and evaluating performance.

Now, too, there are moves to exchange personnel, placing ADP specialists in user-departments, to make the technical people more user-minded and make the user-departments more technically competent — and to place user-personnel in the data processing department, to train them and to bring a user perspective into the technical group. In the meantime, rapid advancement on the purely technical side of data processing has continued.

LOOKING AHEAD

At any point during the last decade one could say, "The next 10 years will bring significant new developments in the computer field." This is still a reasonable assumption at the time of this writing. But we must proceed with great humility. Rereading articles only 5 or 6 years old, one finds carefully reasoned forecasts concluding that by the early 1970s we would see the end of the programmers, with systems that could easily be programmed by untrained managers; the end of tape systems; the death of the keypunch; the explosive use of OCR (optical character recognition) and COM (computer output microfilm); and the certainty that every organization would have an MIS (management information system). Recently, The Diebold Group, Inc., undertook a research project to forecast the direction of data processing hardware and software through 1985. Some of this work is drawn upon in summary fashion as follows:

Developments are emerging from laboratories throughout the world which have a chance of impacting future technology. It is expected that, through improved MOS (metal oxide silicon) and LSI (large-scale integration) technologies, semiconductors will become smaller, be produced at lower costs, and increase in reliability by at least two orders of magnitude. These will impact terminal, memory, and processor design. Fiber optics, film optics, and laser technology will have a major impact on information acquisition, optical character recognition, and facsimile and information display. It is also expected that optoelectronic developments will find their way into the design of large-scale memory systems. In the area of magnetics, it is expected that bubble memories of some form will be in major use by the late 1970s.

Computer architecture will be dramatically impacted by these developments, especially LSI. Major impact will come at both ends of the computer size spectrum. Minicomputers will continue to become smaller and cheaper. Eventually, microcomputers will allow the inclusion of whole functions (such as inventory control) on a single chip. Experience gained with giant processors such as the ILLIAC-IV and the STAR, and the use of parallel processing, will merge into minicomputer technology and together with a more sophisticated telecommunications environment and software systems will produce what will be called *distributed networks* or *polyprocessors.*

Telecommunications is at last coming into its own. This is the result of a number of simultaneous developments, including (1) the introduction of sophisticated specialized terminals for a number of applications, such as POS (point-of-sale) terminals for retailers and supermarkets, and financially oriented devices for banks; (2) the approval by the FCC of services to be offered by specialized common carriers, and the resultant competitive offerings in data transmission service forthcoming from AT&T and Western Union; (3) the launching of communication satellites; (4) the introduction of low-cost intelligent terminals, permitting editing and data reduction at the site of origin of data with a cost reduction due to lower transmission volumes; (5) the availability and acceptance of communication-oriented database software; (6) the wide acceptance of large service-bureau-type time-sharing networks of both a generalized and a specialized completion; and (7) the success of a number of large and well-publicized systems including airline reservations, stock market quotations, automobile rental, ticket-dispensing, and off-track betting. Naturally, along with these successes the reader is cautioned to expect failures caused by the application of teleprocessing technology to areas where its particular advantages are not warranted.

Coupled with these changes in software, because of the huge current investment, reasonably standardized COBOL and FORTRAN are expected to remain the preeminent computer languages for the foreseeable future, with some trend toward making computers less dependent on programmers. These will be supplemented, where justified, by comprehensive database manipulation software. A trend for installations to use purchased software packages is now accelerating as the full impact of unbundling becomes known. This trend should accelerate even more in the coming years.

A concentration on increasing programmer efficiency is also expected. This would come from such developments as (1) structured programming, which has had significant impact in reducing program maintenance costs; (2) the wider use of virtual storage concepts to relieve programmers of the chore of storage allocation; and (3) the use of chief programmer teams and "egoless programming" concepts. Finally, we expect to see significant breakthroughs in the use of software for both multi- and polyprocessor systems.

This speculation into future developments in computer technology would not be complete if we did not at least mention certain new developments whose immediate applications remain cloudy, but which have a good probability of affecting the field at some future date. These include research into the molecular nature of the human brain, artificial intelligence, the general theory of automata and self-organizing systems, theories of natural language, and pattern recognition studies. If the increasing management professionalism continues, the corporate world should be well positioned to extract the real potential of these developments as they emerge.

Chapter 1

Characteristics of Modern ADP Systems: Management Options

LEONARD A. BERNSTEIN

Manager, Teleprocessing Systems Department, Merrill Lynch, Pierce, Fenner & Smith, Inc., New York, New York

To balance the internal forces represented on the one hand by the inertia of the managers and users of the older manual or data processing systems, and the often freewheeling propensities of the professionals in charge of the extension of modern computer applications, the criterion of cost justification must constantly be applied. Top management must continually emphasize this rule. Thus, one of the chief characteristics of modern automated data processing systems is the need for visibility at the higher levels of management. Under these circumstances, (1) new projects or hardware acquisitions cannot be started before their need is demonstrable and their timing is sound, (2) company funds are not wasted on unnecessary expenditures for hardware, software, and personnel, (3) management's desires and expectations are reasonably stated, and (4) management is apprised regularly and in ample time on the status of all major projects.

ENVIRONMENT

The various hardware, software, and personnel elements do not occur in a vacuum. There exists a general tone which in a variety of ways affects the data processing effort. In some installations, there is an air of obvious professionalism. One can sense that decisions will be reasonable, that schedules will be met, and that projects are cost-justified. In other installations, "fire fighting" a series of crises is an everyday occurrence. Decisions are rarely final. Existing systems are barely adequate. Improvision and stopgap measures are the hallmark of their systems.

It is obvious that the decision-making processes and the results are entirely different in these two types of installations. Naturally, a wide range in the quality of installations exists. In many ways, it is unfair to criticize harshly any particular installation without knowing how it came to be that way. The classic reason for failure is the lack of top-management support, interest, or imagination, and this manifests itself in hundreds of different ways. But as data processing costs grow—either proportionately or absolutely or both—upper management will be forced to take a more active role.

This increase in participation is important for several reasons. First, the necessary decisions to get a project started affect other areas of the organization. It is almost axiomatic that the greater the project, the more widespread will be the areas concerned. In most cases, there will exist other units of the firm capable of directly or indirectly vetoing the project unless upper management takes an active hand. Second, the time horizon for results is becoming longer and longer. And lastly, the cost of systems is growing, overall, so that cost justification becomes more necessary. Even when all proposed or active projects are cost-justified, it is necessary for management to set the priorities among them.

The ideal source of project requests is upper management itself. But since this initiation procedure is rare, the second choice is a receptive management ear. After listening to the yeas and nays from below, management must be capable of deciding which projects should be implemented and whose objections must be overridden. There are practical mechanisms for achieving these results, but they are meaningless without the active support of upper management.

One alternative to management participation is to "let nature take its course": management hears about data processing problems when the crisis is here or imminent. Then the only recourse for the company is to buy its way out, or rush half-thought-out systems to early completion, with the likely result of purchasing continual operational problems. A second way out of participation is to write a blank check hoping that money alone can solve all problems. This "overkill" approach may be valid militarily, but it is a disaster in a data processing installation. In short, there does not seem to be a valid alternative to the intelligent participation of management.

Assuming that a proper managerial posture exists, the next important environmental characteristic of modern ADP systems is the mechanism for initiation, definition, staffing, scheduling, management, and implementation of a given project. Though they are only listed here, each of these functions is a major topic in itself. It is specifically in these basically nontechnical areas that the managerial attitude will be reflected. In any company, there are many possible uses for data processing resources and talent. How are the important projects identified? How are priorities set? How are resources obtained? How are resources committed?

Also flowing from the managerial attitude will be the nature of the various suborganizations of the firm. Will non–data processing managers participate and innovate or be passive? Cooperate or resist? Will the data processing arm be business-oriented, cost-conscious, professional, and imaginative? The answers to this group of questions depend heavily upon the demands made by management. Management cannot be presumed to have the technical excellence required to make specific decisions, except, perhaps, through staff personnel. Therefore, decisions will either be made by "political" considerations or personnel whims, or by the professional yardstick of cost justification—either savings or income

One major aspect of automated data processing not touched upon here is the content and purpose of the jobs themselves. It is assumed that the information flow to and from the system meets the needs of the organization with regard to accounting, management reporting, research and development, and required reports to regulatory agencies.

In many ways, the most crucial environmental factor is the competence of the personnel within the data processing group, especially its departmental management. Foremost among that management's responsibilities is the integrity of the operation. That is, all currently operational systems must be run on schedule. Next, efforts must be directed toward improving the efficiency of the firm—more dollars spent on ADP services should result in an even greater dollar saving or net increment elsewhere.

The tendency always is to talk about dollar *savings*, when it is just as appropriate to discuss increased income. The possibility of greater revenues, however, is generally harder to prove. It is in these areas that an astute top management can play an effective role.

Programmers, analysts, operating personnel, and intermediate management should be the best available in that geographic area given the aims of the company. Skills improvement should be encouraged by in-house classes, attendance at conferences and seminars, classes given by vendors or trade groups, support library facilities, and/or by whatever other means are available. It goes without saying that the company should also supply adequate working quarters, and that salaries must be competitive, or, better yet, attractive.

In summary, the single most important characteristic of modern data processing is the posture of management.

HARDWARE

Hardware is a general term which includes anything physical. As indicated in previous Chapters, the basic component is the central processing unit (CPU) and its memory, where programs act upon information. The next elements are the tape and disk drives, which house the tape and disks upon which the information resides. Channels and buses provide a path between the CPU and the various drives. Information into the above system flows from punched-card readers, optical scanners, keyboards (local or remote), sensing devices, and other computers. Output from the computer ultimately goes to printers of all kinds, visual televisionlike displays, servomechanisms, and other computers.

Tapes, disks, punched cards or paper, extra memory, and other computers are intermediate storage devices where information is temporarily stored for future use or for backup purposes. The term *disks* is meant to include all rotating-type devices. The difference between the terms *local* and *remote* used above implies the use of Teletype or telephone lines in the case of remote.

Characteristics   The chief characteristics of the *CPU and its memory* are memory size, memory speed, number of bytes fetched, instructions set, and execution speed. Translated into application terms, these characteristics involve the following: How much information or how many programs can memory hold (memory size)? How fast can program instructions or data be delivered to the CPU (memory speed and number of bytes fetched)? How many different types of operations can the CPU perform (instruction set), and how fast does it do them (execution speed)?

The important physical characteristics of data processing *peripherals* are:

Disks and Tapes Drives
  1. The quantity of information that is contained on one disk or tape.
  2. The number of units (disk drive or tapes) that can be accessed during computer operations.
  3. The time it takes to start transferring information over a channel.
  4. The speed at which information is transferred.

Channels
  1. The operation speed of the channel. Usually much greater than any device can provide.
  2. The operating characteristics of the channel.
  3. The number of channels that a CPU can support.
  4. The type of devices that a channel can support.

Other Peripherals
  1. The type of channel required for operation.
  2. The speed of data transfer.

The above lists are an oversimplification. Not only are there a variety of combinations for any one manufacturer, but different manufacturers employ entirely different techniques. And in many larger firms, equipment is obtained from more than one vendor.

In almost every computer running today, there is a special type of software called variously a *control program, operating system, monitor, driver,* etc. Most control programs are supplied by the manufacturer. To the extent that hardware does not operate without a control or operating program, this software will be lumped together with hardware.[1]

Cost Performance and Trade-offs   We now have in the list of options mentioned above one of the three major elements in deciding what kind and how much equipment to obtain. The other major elements are (2) the job to be done (which is here considered to be a "given" and is not discussed), and (3) the software to do the job (discussed later). No implication is intended that these major elements can ever be truly separated, but it is done here for discussion's sake.

[1] See Section 2, Part 4, Chapter 4, "Operating Systems."

Given the job (or job mix) and the software, how does one select hardware? The answer is *cost performance*. Is it better to finish a job in 1 hour for $10,000 than in 2 hours for $5,000? The answer is not obvious. If finishing sooner gains $8,000 somewhere else in the organization, then, of course, it is worth spending the extra $5,000. The problem of hardware selection is further complicated by the method of payment. In other words, the $10,000 mentioned above could be straight rental. A lease rate for the very same equipment might be $8,000, and $6,000 for outright purchase. An offset of $4,000 elsewhere in the firm would not justify the faster operation under straight rental, but would under lease or purchase. The biggest danger in not having a cost-justification procedure in the selection of hardware is that many computer people want the "newest toy" or recommend new equipment as a way of solving problems that are amenable to other, less costly techniques.

Nothing in the world of computers comes free. The way of life is *trade-offs:* To get cost performance down to a minimum requires a "feeling" for the various sacrifices that have to be made. In computers, as in chess, you sacrifice, if you can get more in return. The following "trade-offs" are most relevant to our time and the immediate future.

Trade-off No. 1: Used vs. New Equipment A relatively few years ago, the used-computer equipment market was not a major factor in the acquisition of computers and peripherals. That situation has now changed for a variety of reasons. The so-called third generation of computing equipment is solid state electronic, giving rise to the easiest of maintenance conditions. Much of the equipment is like a camera lens. That is, light passing through the lens does not wear it out. Second, a tremendous market in subsystems has grown up during the third-generation years. There are independent manufacturers of memories, disk subsystems, tape units, printers, etc. This growth of competing sources of computer system components means that managers of data processing can show dramatic performance improvements without buying new systems.

For example, suppose throughput is limited by the speed of tape drives. Then faster tape drives could be supplied by independents, if these drives were not available from the central processing unit manufacturer. All too frequently, a faster CPU is provided by a new system with only limited improvement in overall performance. Thus, the time to read and process two tape records might be 22 ms based upon 10 ms per tape read, and 1 ms to process. The faster computer can save only something less than 2 ms. But faster tape drives can save 10 ms if their speed is double that of the drives displaced.

In this case, it is obvious that throughput gains by virtue of the faster tape, and not by the faster-performing new CPU. What is of major importance is that faster tape drives are much less expensive than a new CPU. One does not have to buy new equipment while current equipment is still cost-effective.

Another reason for the growth of the used-computer market is the tremendous investment in third-generation software. These accumulated programs are owned not only by the manufacturer, but also by its customers. It is obvious that a new line will have very, very slow acceptance if a given user could not use his or her existing programs. Therefore, for many practical purposes, new and old equipment can be interchangeable. Any movement away from this goal causes difficulties for both manufacturer and customer.

If the cost of new, better performing equipment were the same as that of old equipment, then for the same money, one might as well acquire the new. But used equipment is roughly half the price of new equipment and, very often, real bargains can be obtained. Thus when acquiring equipment, one should survey the resale market before purchasing new equipment. If expanded capability is needed, one should see what steps could be taken to improve the current installation. All that might be required is bigger and faster memories, greater capacity and faster disk drives, etc.

Trade-off No. 2: One Vendor vs. More than One Vendor Implicit in the discussion above is that the most cost-effective shop may be the one with equipment from various vendors. That is fine when the system is functioning, but when the system is not performing, which component is the culprit? There is no question that a mixed shop poses some difficulties and some added cost to the running of the installation. If the shop is small, the added cost may well offset the dollar savings elsewhere.

The managers of larger installations have more options open to them than do their fellow professionals running smaller ones. They can employ an independent organization to do all maintenance. They deal with one outfit in much the same manner as if they were a one-vendor shop. The added costs in a mixed-vendor shop are the hidden costs resulting from delays while determining whose equipment is causing system failure.

A second alternative for the manager of a mixed-vendor installation is to establish a department of engineering services. This group could pinpoint the problem and call in the right vendor. In cases where two or more vendors have to cooperate, this department would coordinate their activities. In addition, much immediate action could be taken to eliminate the need to call any vendor. Lastly, such a department could relieve data processing management of the apprehension that exists in a mixed-vendor installation when that management does not have an engineering background or the time to be involved in engineering problems. The costs of this department are offset by the direct saving in equipment costs as well as the indirect benefits of improved service to the rest of the firm.

Trade-off No. 3: Rent vs. Purchase vs. Lease[2]   In one sense, the most costly way to use data processing equipment is to rent it. In general, the shorter the rental period, the greater the cost. The major argument for renting equipment is the flexibility provided in replacing it when the need arises. At the beginning of the 1970s, approximately half the larger computers were rented from the manufacturer, while the other half were either purchased outright, or leased from third parties for varying time periods. In the case of the smaller companies using medium-sized computers, rentals predominated as the method of payment.

Since third-party lease rates and amortized purchase costs can run as much as 50 per cent less than rental, the burden should always be on cost-justifying rentals. Obviously, more planning for future needs is required when considering purchase or lease, since the commitment is longer. The degree of planning depends upon needs of the individual organization. If the current data processing situation is under control and no major systems are unaccounted for in the present installation, then planning for the future is relatively easy. If the current operation is loaded with first- and second-generation maintenance problems, and the demand for new systems is widespread but ill-defined, then planning will be a monumental task.

The flexibility inherent in straight rentals has some additional costs built into the situation. There is usually a great deal of disruption to the smooth performance of an installation when equipment is moved in, out, and around. Second, there is the danger that clever use of existing equipment will be ignored in favor of bigger, faster equipment. Frequently, additional equipment is cost-justified, but the cost could be further minimized.

The potential danger in longer-term commitments is freezing oneself out of benefits resulting from technological advances. Since the original lease or purchase was cost-justified, the possibility of even greater profits must be viewed with only mild regret. Another weakness is the possibility of having underestimated or overestimated future requirements. Underestimation is only a calamity when it is impossible to improve the capability of the current equipment. In many cases, more and faster peripherals can be acquired or extra memory can be added. Furthermore, inflexibility is not total, since purchased equipment can be sold or leased equipment swapped. It all depends on the situation at that time. Overestimation, of course, will result in idle or under-utilized equipment.

Another offset to purchase or lease savings is the amount of time and effort that must be spent or delegated by management in arranging lease or purchase terms, researching legal questions, and comparing equipment options. These activities are not for amateurs or fainthearted professionals. The above costs, however, are usually small relative to savings.

Trade-off No. 4: Tapes vs. Disks   The dictates of the job mix at a given installation will determine the equipment configuration. These mixes are so varied that it is difficult to talk in general terms. At one extreme is the installation with tremendous data files that have to be accessed relatively infrequently. In some cases, these files (usually on magnetic tape) can be organized in cycles. That is, only part of the total is used at any

---

[2] See Section 3, Part 4, Chapter 4, "Lease vs. Purchase or Rental of Computers."

one time, e.g., files organized by billing date. In other cases, the total file has to be available. An example would be the case of claims against insurance policies. The latter situation would require a great many more tape drives. One trade-off would be to have fewer drives, but more operator intervention.

In the example of billing date files, every record is read and processed. In the case of claims, only a small percentage of the records are processed. Nonetheless, all the tapes have to be spun, since the required records are scattered throughout the total file. If possible, operation would be faster if each record could be randomly accessed. Disks are ideal for this type of retrieval, but disk drives and disks are expensive compared with tapes and tape drives. In addition, the physical tape size is small relative to disks. Therefore, off-line storage of many tapes takes far less physical room than would the storage of disks. Another trade-off then involves the use of tapes versus disks. There is no pat answer.

Trade-off No. 5: How Many Tape or Disk Units? When a production shop has a variety of jobs, as such shops usually do, the worst case will almost always determine the minimum equipment requirement. In our example, the insurance company has both a billing data program and a settle claims program. Therefore, the more demanding requirement for tape drives will be the constraint. When less demanding jobs are run, there will be excess tape-drive activity. Ideally the schedule for completion times is sufficiently flexible and other resources sufficiently available that another job will be able to use the tape drives at the same time as the less demanding job.

The production schedule is also important. It could well be that both jobs are required to be finished at the same time, and their ability to run separately in time is not feasible. That is, during some period of the day, both jobs are active, We now require more tape drives or more operator intervention than when each job was tackled individually.

Fortunately for the users, there is a tremendous competition in the area of tape drives. Tapes themselves are being spun faster, and each tape is packing more bits per inch. Tape drives offered for sale today now pack 6,250 bytes per inch and spin tape at 200 inches per second. These figures translate to a transfer rate of 1,250,000 bytes per second. Therefore, fewer tapes and tape drives can do the job. A similar situation holds true for disk drives. They are becoming faster, and have increasing storage capacity.

At this writing, there are at least two manufacturers offering mass storage devices that promise to revolutionize the field. A single system holds on-line over 450 billion bytes. Few, if any, tape libraries store that much information. These devices are so cost-effective that it is easy to imagine their ultimate success. In the smaller installations, tapes and disks will likely remain more cost-effective than these mass storage devices.

Trade-off No. 6: The Computer Itself The significant components of the CPU are memory width and speed, execution speed, memory size, channel interference, and control program overhead. All but the last element are hardware characteristics. If the job mix and scheduling algorithm find that CPU resources are inadequate, then a series of options must be considered. First, a less costly control program can be used. Control programs waste both memory and cycles. All too often, the most complex control program is used when a more effective one for that particular installation is available.

Second, if there are physical limitations beyond control program requirements, it is possible that extra memory can offer a solution. Each CPU has some limitation on the size of memory. One-way memory is limited because of the addressing schemes of the program instructions. Another limitation stems from electronic or physical constraints. Nowadays, the manufacturer of the CPU will offer memories up to a certain maximum, but independent memory manufacturers frequently can supply greater capacity. In smaller and specialized computers, there is the possibility that faster memories and/or faster execution speeds can be installed. This third option is open to few installations, because most equipment is not of this type.

The fourth choice offered to an installation where the CPU is the limiting factor is whether to acquire a bigger, faster computer or to live with a degraded system. For example, the CPU may be using excessive memory for data transfer buffers. These buffers increase the efficiency of channel utilization at the expense of memory. Reducing buffers may increase the running time of the program because of delays in transferring information across the channel from the peripherals. If the overall operation can tolerate the delay, then the acquisition of a new computer could be postponed.

A final choice is to examine the programs to determine if any are unduly wasting CPU resources. In a well-run organization, it is presumed that programs are efficient at run time. That is not always true. There are special program analyzers that reveal where any program is spending much of its time. (These analyzers are special programs written by systems programmers or software companies.) It is possible that a reasonable examination of these areas will reveal inefficiencies. Improved coding could reduce the demand for CPU cycles and return added capacity to a marginal computer.

TRENDS IN DATA PROCESSING EQUIPMENT[3]

Computers themselves are becoming more cost-effective, as shown by recent trends in performance. Memories are becoming larger, faster, and less expensive. Execution speeds are becoming faster. Electronic advances include associative memories, master buses, direct paths into memory eliminating CPU interference, a single more intelligent controller for various types of peripherals, etc. These advances are dramatic. There are other advances which are less dramatic but probably just as useful from a business point of view. Among these must be considered the following:

1. The replacement of keypunch units by data entry systems. The use of programs to aid data preparation has markedly reduced errors and delays normally associated with keypunch operations.

2. The rapid development of equipment for data entry at the point of origin. Chief among these are the terminals associated with retail sales, bank teller operations, on-line credit verification, and sale of reserved tickets.

3. Rapid improvement in the handling of data over telephone lines. These communication gains have made many operations economically feasible. For example, fast printers were long available, but their remote operation was retarded by the inability to transfer data rapidly over long-distance telephone lines. The transfer speeds have gained dramatically in the last few years. Reports and information can now be cost-effectively transferred via telephone lines between branches and the home office.

4. The development of intelligent terminals further enhances the possibilities of remote operations. The term *intelligent* means that the terminal is capable of performing a relatively complex series of operations independent of the CPU. For example, data can be checked for validity before transmission. That is, only numbers can appear where numbers are required, and the same is done for letters. Terminals can present a format for the operator to complete.

Other items are gaining in importance. Microfilm units are well established, as are magnetic ink and optical scanning equipment. Gaining ground are audio-response devices and all sorts of analog inputs.

SOFTWARE

Software is a general term covering programs (sets of instructions) that drive and control the computer and its associated peripherals. One group of programs is supplied by the manufacturer and is rarely tampered with by the individual customers. This group includes the control program, utilities, compilers, assemblers, and special-purpose programs. The rest of the programs are either written by the installation's programming staff or outside software personnel, or purchased as packages.

In this connection, there are two nonsoftware items that will gain in importance. The first is called *firmware*. The second has no specific name, but it is the development of "intelligent" channels and peripheral equipment.

Firmware   Firmware, or microprogramming, is the ability to create special machine instructions which are then used following regular programming methods. Most computers come with an existing structure of electronic components capable of performing

[3] See also Section 2, Part 2, Chapter 5, "Design Trends."

fixed operations. The program provides the sequence in which these instructions are used. Occasionally, it takes several instructions to do what one instruction would. For one reason or another the manufacturer has not provided that particular instruction. Manufacturers have to think in general terms, but the customer sometimes is faced with unique situations. The ability to create one's own instruction or modify an existing one is now available in some minicomputers. There does not seem to be a great future in this capability unless it finds some application in the larger computers. This turn of events does not appear to be a reasonable expectation at this time.

Intelligent Peripherals   A more likely expectation is the continued growth of intelligent peripherals and control units. For one thing, computer applications are dependent upon input from some source. The more work done outside the CPU, the more effective the total system could be. In many cases, the outside intelligence derives from exporting CPU functions to another, smaller CPU with specialized instructions. For example, as of now, programs in the CPU have to keep track of all devices and contain special programs to "talk" to each different type of unit. It will not be surprising to find by the end of the present decade that these programs have been converted to electronic circuitry and exported to one generalized control unit for all peripherals. If so, this step will eliminate many software headaches that currently plague control programs.

Control Programs[4]   The control program is generally that set of software programs supplied by the manufacturer to enable the customer to execute programs written in assembler or higher level languages.[5]   Modern large-scale computers could not be sold without these programs – the vast majority of computer users are completely dependent upon them. This dependence has led manufacturers to write control programs in a very general manner. They are forced to consider the needs (or whims) of many customers with widely diverse requirements. As a result, control programs have been either notoriously late, woefully inefficient, or riddled with problems. Probably more money has been wasted by customers because of control program problems than for any other single reason. Nor do customers, generally, help themselves. They have collectively permitted manufacturers to alter these programs, thereby forcing customers to absorb the cost of change. The manufacturers have dropped support for various control programs, forcing customers to more costly systems.

The change from one control program to another upon securing larger computers is a traumatic experience, despite manufacturer statements about "compatibility." And customers generally tend to harm themselves by poor use of these systems. Occasionally, there are installations where the expertise exists to make changes to the control programs. These alterations are designed to serve specific purposes or to overcome control program inefficiencies.

As long as users are unorganized and manufacturers not penalized, there does not seem to be an end to the troublesome situation, although fortunately for the customers, the trend indicated above has been accompanied by more than offsetting improvements in hardware effectiveness. The net result has been improved throughput, despite the dilemma of the ever-changing control program.

The best course for any given company is to hire programming personnel and data processing managers who have experienced the disparity between marketing claims and actual performance. They can utilize this experience to keep the manufacturers in line, and if they cannot succeed in this, they should be capable of doing what must be done.

Software Houses and Proprietary Packages   The customer has one other resource that should be exploited to the fullest. There are many competent independent software houses.[6]   While these firms do not generally supply control programs in direct competition to the manufacturer, they do supply more efficient subsystems. These subsystems refer to such items as sort routines, compilers, report writers, application program control monitors, input-output routines, etc. It would seem that the very existence and profitability of these software firms attest to the difference in efficiency between the two sources of software mentioned. It is rare that an individual customer can afford to develop these routines in-house. Therefore, the only real alternative to

[4] See Section 2, Part 4, Chapter 4, "Operating Systems."
[5] See Section 2, Part 4, Chapter 3, "Programming Languages."
[6] See Section 6, Chapter 1, "Software Houses."

manufacturer-dependence is an open mind with respect to proprietary software packages.

Proprietary software packages available from manufacturers, consultants, and software houses are also of interest. For example, there are program packages for payroll, inventory control, billing, and many others. There is definite merit in reviewing what is available rather than "reinventing the wheel." The major obstacles to the extended use of proprietary packages are, first, the real or imagined uniqueness of the customer's application and, second, the variety of computers on which these programs are run. Computer manufacturers have shifted in recent years from providing free programs to charging a fee. This change of policy has aided the independent software developer.

In the case of proprietary software, the outsiders generally offer a proven product. But where an outside firm is developing a program for a client, there are elements of risk. First, with time and material contracts, there is the danger of cost overrun. The later the schedule, the more costly. Losses tend to compound. The customer's protection arises from the reputation of the software house plus the willingness of ADP management to keep a tight rein on project control. A second element of risk is the financial stability of software houses themselves. It could be embarrassing or a disaster if part way through a project the software concern collapses.

Fixed-fee contracts with reputable consultants are becoming increasingly popular. The use of software consultants is growing, if one judges by the proliferation of these firms, and their increasing size. ADP management, however, must become increasingly willing to enter into complicated negotiations, share or delegate project control, and abide by commitments.

Future Software   The bulk of software in the future will still be developed by internal programming and systems staffs, despite the gains in the use of proprietary products. The major programming languages seem to be entrenched. It is difficult to imagine one language attaining any kind of supremacy, without some kind of enforced industry standard.

All languages are being extended to include special database commands, communications interfaces, and other "goodies." These gains enhance the language, but do nothing for such characteristics as program design, testing, maintenance, and programmer productivity. It is in these last three elements that the future is likely to see some significant strides.

There is a growing use of techniques which strive to convert programming from an art to a technology. These techniques are largely language-independent. The most promising is called *structured programming*, or *segmented level programming*. The object is to create a hierarchial arrangement of small modules. The characteristics of each module are that the module is small, has only one entry point, and is passed and returns a few fixed number of parameters; its internal code permits no branches; and each module can be individually tested. System complexity may expand the number of modules, but never complicates a single module. A special testing program is an essential part of the process.

Eventually a library of these modules will be available at each installation. Each module is specified before it is coded, and serves as the documentation. There are a variety of ways in which modules are specified—in English, by decision tables, or by structured diagrams. In any case, the use of complicated flow charts and rigid documentation practices is ruled out. Maintenance or changes to existing programs should become easier under these techniques. Thus, while each major programming language grows in power and versatility, it seems that its use will become more structured and more technological.

Chapter 2

Concepts of Management Information Systems

JAMES C. EMERY

Vice President,
EDUCOM, Inc., Princeton, New Jersey

Although the term *management information system* — or MIS — has been used widely for a number of years, there exists no general consensus as to its meaning. Some authorities in the field feel that the term has become a mere collection of buzz words without real meaning. Others find the term useful enough, but restrict its meaning to include only those parts of the overall information system that are closely connected with management decision making. Some authorities further restrict the meaning to include only the on-line, interactive decision components.

The viewpoint taken in this Chapter is a fairly broad one. The MIS is defined to be the overall formal information system that serves the organization. Thus, the MIS includes both routine transaction processing as well as the information processing associated with decision making.

This does not imply that the MIS is a single, monolithic thing that closely integrates all information processing activities; on the contrary, in practice decision-making subsystems are likely to be largely decoupled from transaction processing subsystems (for reasons that are discussed below). Nevertheless, it is often useful to view the collection of subsystems in their entirety, and therefore it is desirable to have a name to attach to this collection.

CHARACTERISTICS OF AN MIS

An MIS is closely linked to day-to-day operational matters, such as the handling of customer orders and generating paychecks. It also provides varying degrees of aid to decision makers concerned with such things as production scheduling, market analyses, and long-range financial planning. Even though we are still in the relatively early stages of information technology, the clear trend is toward more and more comprehensive systems that pervade virtually all aspects of the organization's activities. This is true whether the organization is a profit-making firm, an agency of government, or a nonprofit unit.

Person–Machine System A well-designed MIS draws on the capabilities of both people and machines. The computer, of course, typically handles well-defined data processing tasks; to an increasing extent it also aids human decision makers in various ways. The assignment of tasks between person and machine depends on a variety of factors, including the size of the organization, the volume of routine processing tasks, the complexity of the management processes, and management style and sophistication.

Collection of Subsystems An MIS is far too complex to be implemented and managed as a single entity. Instead, it is broken down into a collection of parts as a means of simplifying the overall system. The various subsystems may be tied together very closely; more often they are only loosely coupled.

The MIS is often structured to correspond to organizational boundaries. For example, a manufacturing firm may be organized by major product groupings, and each group may have its own information system. Within each product group the organization and the MIS may be broken down by functional department (e.g., marketing, manufacturing, etc.).

Activities often may cross organizational boundaries, and consequently a strict adherence to organizational boundaries may unnecessarily restrict the usefulness or efficiency of the MIS. In these cases the MIS may be structured along the functions performed. For example, an order entry subsystem, which handles sales orders from customers, may include functions falling within the responsibilities of marketing, manufacturing, engineering, and accounting.

Hierarchical Structure The subsystems composing an MIS constitute a hierarchy of activities. The lowest level deals with *operational* matters, such as order entry, payroll, invoicing, and the like. In many systems these functions may be highly automated. Intermediate-level subsystems deal with relatively short-term *tactical* decisions, such as the ordering of inventory items and scheduling production. These decisions can often be at least partially automated through the use of a decision model, but human decision makers still play the dominant role at the tactical level. This is even more true of the *strategic* level of the MIS, which deals with the broad, long-term decisions facing the organization. At this level, decisions tend to involve many factors that are ill-defined and difficult to quantify; accordingly, relatively little progress has been made in automating strategic decision making.

Heavily Database-Oriented One of the dominant technical characteristics of an MIS is its heavy reliance on stored data. The system must have access to data dealing with such matters as customers, suppliers, employees, production facilities, inventories, costs, current plans, and past performance. The collection of stored data is termed the *database* of the organization.

The database provides a formal analog of the organization and its environment. It is kept more or less current through periodic *updating* that adjusts the stored information to reflect new events that have occurred in the real world.

Decisions based on the formal information system rely on the description of the real world contained in the database; they are not based on the real world itself. The intent, of course, is to have the database give a faithful enough representation of the real world so that good decisions can be made. Inevitably, however, the representation introduces distortions due to errors in data collection, delays in updating, gaps due to significant omissions, and all the filtering and condensation that takes place within an information system. These distortions generally carry some penalty, but reducing them (through faster updating, more accurate data collection, etc.) increases the cost of information processing. The objective should be to strike the best compromise between the quality of the database and the cost of providing it.

PROCESSING FUNCTIONS PERFORMED WITHIN THE MIS

Data Collection[1] The data collection function serves as the sensory organ of the MIS. It is the source of new information about events that go on in the real world that require formal information processing. A huge volume of data may enter the system — describing new sales orders, receipts from suppliers, activities within the production process, hours worked by each employee, and similar events. The cost of data collec-

---

[1] See Section 2, Part 3, "Computer Peripherals"; specifically Chapter 1, "Input Devices," Chapter 2, "Optical Scanning, OCR and MICR," and Chapter 5, "Source-Data Automation."

tion can easily constitute over 25 per cent of the total cost of operating the MIS. Furthermore, errors in data collection are persistent sources of inaccuracy in the system.

The common keypunch is gradually giving way to newer forms of data collection technology. Optical scanning has a useful, if somewhat limited, range of application. A wide variety of keyboard devices have been developed for recording data directly in magnetic form (typically on magnetic disk). This approach is particularly attractive when the keyboard is on-line to a computer (very often a specialized minicomputer), thereby allowing the computer to perform certain logical functions at the point of data entry. Included in such functions are the selective display of required input data (on the face of a CRT, for example) and the performance of editing checks for completeness, correct format and mode, numeric values within prescribed ranges, and logical consistency across fields. The more powerful the on-line processor available at the data entry point, the wider the range of aids that can be provided to the data entry clerk.

Data Storage[2] The database of an MIS may consist of billions of characters. The data have widely varying economic values, access frequencies, and response-time requirements. In order to store such data, a physical storage hierarchy is used that consists of devices with diverse performance and cost characteristics. High-performance, high-cost storage (such as primary storage or a fixed-head auxiliary storage device) is reserved for data accessed very frequently and with short response-time requirements. Data having a very low probability of being accessed, and with little urgency if they are needed (such as archival data retained for legal purposes), are relegated to a low-cost medium such as magnetic tape or perhaps microfilm.

One of the more difficult aspects of designing the database is to choose its logical and physical structure. The structure defines the way in which data elements are partitioned into records and allocated among physical storage media. It also establishes the logical links among records. For example, the structure governs the ability of the system to relate an inventory record to other inventory records and to the records of the suppliers of the item. Logical relationships of this kind can be established by storing the data contiguously — all inventory records stored on the same sequential file, for example — or through the use of pointer addresses that link one record with another. The rapid progress being made in direct-access storage and database management software makes it technically and economically feasible to employ a much richer interlinking of records than was previously feasible. This development can significantly enhance the ability of the MIS to be more responsive to user needs.

Data Retrieval[3] Retrieving specified data from a massive database can present a formidable task. If information needs can be anticipated in advance, they can be satisfied in the form of periodic reports. Often such a report can be generated from a single file — such as a monthly inventory analysis report based on input from a sequential inventory file. Under these circumstances, the retrieval function is quite straightforward and relatively inexpensive. Problems arise when dealing with requests that could not be anticipated in advance or that require access to records in separate files. For example, many existing systems would find it difficult and time-consuming to cope with an ad hoc inquiry asking for a list of the suppliers of all inventory items of a given product grouping that have a back-order balance greater than $100.

It is impossible to anticipate all the information needs of decision makers. This is particularly true of higher-level managers who often deal with ill-structured, one-of-a-kind problems. However, if the MIS is to be truly responsive it must provide a means of handling ad hoc inquiries. The conventional approach of preparing tailor-made reports by programming them in a standard programming language (such as COBOL) does not offer a satisfactory solution to this problem — it is too time-consuming and too expensive. Managers soon learn that they cannot get a suitable response to ad hoc requests for information.

An approach that is gaining increasing use is the implementation of a database management system that permits the processing of ad hoc inquiries. The manager requesting information — or, more likely, a technical staff person supporting the man-

[2] See Section 2, Part 2, Chapter 2, "Auxiliary Memories," and Section 5, Chapter 6, "The Technology of Database Management."

[3] See Section 4, Chapter 3, "Computerized Information Storage and Retrieval."

ager—expresses the information requirements in the form of an English-like statement (or perhaps on a standard retrieval form that permits the user to specify the inquiry in a more structured way). For example, a request might be expressed in the following way:

FOR ALL INVENTORY_ITEMS WITH PRODUCT_GROUP= 'HARDWARE' AND BACK_ORDER > 100,
PRINT LIST: ITEM_NUMBER, BACK_ORDER, ON_ORDER, SUPPLIER;
ORDERED BY BACK_ORDER

The retrieval software then translates the inquiry into the necessary program to cause the actual processing of the inquiry. The retrieval may be processed in batch fashion, permitting, say, an overnight response time. If information needs so dictate, the system can be designed to provide very rapid response from an on-line database. The cost of handling ad hoc inquiries can be quite low, especially if batch processing provides a suitable response time (as it very often does).

Display The display function provides the interface between the MIS and its users. Most conventional reports are presented in tabular format. This has the virtue of being inexpensive, familiar to users, and precise. In many cases, however, it is difficult for a user to perceive underlying relationships among variables. For example, a report showing the relationships among actual versus planned orders received, orders shipped, and inventories would be very difficult to comprehend when displayed in tabular form. The same information displayed in graphical form would much more effectively show the essential facts.

Graphical display has not been widely used in most MIS because of the cost and time to prepare graphical reports, and perhaps because of their unfamiliarity to some users. Considerable progress has been made, however, in display hardware and software. It has now become relatively inexpensive automatically to prepare graphical outputs in hard-copy form or on a transient CRT display device. The next few years will undoubtedly witness the widespread use of this technology in management applications.

DECISION MAKING AND THE MIS

Hierarchical Decision Levels Decisions take place throughout an organization. Their nature, of course, varies greatly, depending on the type of organization, style of management (e.g., centralized or decentralized), and level in the organization of the decision maker.

At the lowest level, decisions deal with such routine matters as the choice of job to assign to a machine, the payment of an insurance claim, or the ordering of food for the hospital food service. Intermediate-level decisions tend to deal with less routine matters and have longer-range consequences; the determination of a quarterly production schedule, the selection of a new regional sales manager, or the preparation of an annual operating budget typify such decisions. High-level decisions have broad implications and long-term consequences—such as the determination of the organization's basic goals, structure, principal activities, and sources and uses of its major resources. It is convenient to attach the labels *strategic*, *tactical*, and *operational*, corresponding to the highest, intermediate, and lowest decision levels respectively, although the boundaries between them may be indistinct and ill defined.

Strategic decisions are typically unstructured, encompass multiple organizational units, and have a long planning horizon (several years or more). They are made infrequently, and are often nonrepetitive. The information needed for strategic decisions is difficult to predict in detail; it tends to be highly aggregated and low in volume, often comes from informal external sources, and does not impose particularly severe requirements for timeliness and accuracy.

In contrast, operational decisions are typically highly structured and well defined. The scope of a given decision is usually quite narrow. The planning horizon can be a matter of a few days or even a few minutes. A given type of decision may be made repetitively and at frequent intervals. The information required is usually quite predictable, comes from formal internal sources, tends to be detailed, and often has stringent requirements for timeliness and accuracy. Tactical decisions tend to have characteristics and information requirements intermediate between the two extremes.

Flow of Information among Decision Levels   Most formal information processing takes place at the operational level. Data enter in the form of transactions, which are coded descriptions of events of significance to the system. The transactions are then processed by one or more subsystems, and various working documents are produced as output. A sales order, for example, enters as a transaction. It is processed by the order entry subsystem. Shipping papers and an invoice are printed as a result of the processing. If the order brings an inventory item below its reorder point, a requisition is prepared. In addition, various database records are updated as a result of the transaction (such as inventory balances and the customer's accounts receivable balance).

Data entering an operational subsystem can often be supplied as input data for tactical decision making as a byproduct of transaction processing. For example, sales data from the order entry subsystem might feed into a forecasting subsystem, which in turn feeds into an inventory decision model (for determining order points and order quantities, say). Such byproduct information is somewhat limited, however, because information significant for purposes of predicting the future may often not be available as a byproduct of transaction processing.

This is true, for example, in sales forecasting. Future sales are influenced by anticipated changes in marketing strategy, new product developments, actions of competitors, actions of customers, and general economic conditions. Information of this sort is typically not included as part of the routine transaction data.

Information about significant external matters is collected in the form of *environmental* data. Some systems formally provide for the routine collection of such data. For example, salespersons may submit periodic reports on their customer's future plans or the actions of competitors. Economic data (such as time series data on gross national product and other important economic variables) may be obtained from information utilities that provide such services. Thus, tactical decision makers obtain data from both internal and external sources.

Strategic decision making obtains input data from similar sources. However, environmental data become increasingly important the higher the level in the decision hierarchy. Since strategic decisions are concerned with long-term issues, current events of the sort that get processed at the operational level are not especially relevant. Furthermore, very often the needs for environmental data cannot be anticipated and provided for as part of the formal information system. If these needs are satisfied at all, it is through such informal sources as casual conversations with colleagues and reading newspapers or business publications.

We have seen that data flow upward from the operational level to provide input data for tactical and (to some extent) strategic decision making. A similar flow occurs in the downward direction. Decisions, the output of decision processes, must be fed to lower-level subsystems in order to be implemented. Thus, strategic decisions impose constraints on tactical decisions, which in turn constrain operational subsystems.

Consider, for example, inventory decisions. For some businesses (such as a supermarket firm) the decision as to the total amount of money that can be invested in inventory is a relatively high-level decision, accounting for a significant proportion of total assets. This aggregate decision should then constrain individual inventory decisions in such a way that the resulting aggregate inventory conforms to the amount specified at the strategic level. These individual decisions in turn should be fed into the order entry subsystem at the operational level so that inventory replenishment orders are generated for the specified quantity when the actual balance reaches the order point.

Degree of Aid Provided to Decision Makers   The formal information system provides varying degrees of aid to the decision maker. The appropriate degree depends on such factors as how well defined the decision process is, the number of variables and relationships involved, the frequency with which a given type of decision is made, and the potential payoff from improved decisions.

Decisions Receiving No Significant Aid.   Some decisions receive no significant aid from the MIS. An ill-defined, one-of-a-kind decision may not be susceptible to much formalization. Politically sensitive decisions and the setting of basic organizational philosophy may, for example, not be aided by the MIS. This is true even though such decisions may be exceedingly important ones.

Unselected Display of Decision Information. For many decisions, the system may at best provide relatively unselected information in the form of periodic reports. Accounting, market analysis, and inventory reports may be prepared on a monthly basis, for example. Each report is then available to decision makers during the interval until the next report is prepared.

Although such reports can be useful, their lack of selectivity limits their value. In an attempt to meet a broad range of information needs and avoid the risk of not displaying useful information, the designers of such reports often include information that has a low probability of being needed during any given reporting interval. Because precise information requirements cannot be predicted in advance (certainly not over an interval as long as a month), a considerable amount of unused information inevitably gets published in such reports. (A common example of this is the conventional telephone book, which contains a very low density of useful information for any one subscriber.)

Selective Display of Decision Information. The density of useful information can sometimes be substantially increased by use of tailored exception reports. This requires the decision maker to specify in advance the conditions under which information will be displayed. In principle, the intent should be to report only the information that will improve the decision process. In practice, we generally have to settle for a much less stringent screening criterion, because it is rarely possible to define in advance precisely what information is relevant to a given decision.

Greater selectivity can often be achieved through the use of ad hoc inquiries. Rather than predicting information requirements in advance, an ad hoc retrieval system responds to specific requests for information. The retrieval request can be as specific as the user can define within the capabilities of the retrieval language and the comprehensiveness of the database. Because only specified information is reported, the density of useful information is likely to be much higher than with a periodic report.

Decision Models. Simple aggregation of extracted data, or the calculation of standard statistics such as the mean or range of a set of data, is usually the limit of the calculations that can be expressed in a conventional retrieval language. The MIS begins to play a more active role in a decision process when it allows the decision maker to perform more complex transformations of extracted data. The ability of the MIS to respond to "What if . . ." questions provides a very powerful tool for exploring alternative plans. The calculations involved in such a system are based on an analytical or simulation model.[4]

Consider, for example, the question: "What will happen to indirect labor costs if sales increase by 10 per cent?" The determination of the correct answer may require (depending on the accuracy desired) considerable computation based on analytical relationships between the volume of output of each product group and the various components of indirect labor. If some of the relationships are too complex to be conveniently expressed in analytical form (e.g., the relation between work-center capacities and the volume of output in a job shop), conceivably they could be estimated by means of a simulation model (in this case, one that "runs" the job shop to see how output responds to changes in capacities).

A computer-based decision model must, of course, be expressed in a computer language. Most models are written in a general-purpose procedural language such as FORTRAN. This provides great generality, and thus permits the model builder to tackle a wide variety of decision problems.

A well-designed model is normally highly parameterized in order to handle a range of problems within the context for which the model was implemented. For example, a budgetary model should allow the decision maker to alter any of its basic inputs (volume, cost relationships, etc.) in order to test the effects of such changes. Similarly, it is desirable to permit the user to request different forms of output (choice of variables, degree of aggregation, etc.).

---

[4] See Section 1, Chapter 3, "ADP in Corporate Planning," Chapter 3 of this Section, "Simulation and Models for Decision Making," and Section 4, Chapter 1, "New Tools for Decision Making."

The notion of generalized models can be extended. Many of the functions performed in building and operating a model are common to a wide variety of problems. The definition of functional relationships, the generation of random variables, the retrieval of stored data, and the preparation of specified output reports are examples of these common functions. A set of such generalized functions can be viewed as a special-purpose modeling language. A number of these languages have been developed, and some are available commercially. The experience gained from their use suggests that they, like other special-purpose languages, can greatly increase the efficiency with which a given problem can be expressed (as long as the problem fits within the range of models expressable in the language).

Person–Machine Decision Systems. A model combined with a human decision maker constitutes a *person–machine* system. The computer can be assigned the chores of manipulating vast quantities of data and performing elaborate transformations both quickly and accurately. The human is free to exercise his or her special strengths: flexibility, adaptability, and the ability to recognize subtle relationships and to generalize from past experience. The great virtue of such a combination is that it can exploit the best features of both people and machines.

The typical person–machine decision process works as follows: The person proposes an alternative plan. The computer then evaluates the alternative based on some sort of model. The human then decides whether to accept the alternative. If he or she does, the decision process is complete; if not, the human proposes another alternative (typically adjusting the previous alternative in a way that he or she feels will correct or improve upon it). The trial-and-error process continues until the decision maker is satisfied that further search will not produce a significant improvement over the best current plan (at least not enough improvement to justify the cost of further search).

Automatic Decision Models. A person–machine decision system includes the human decision maker as an integral component. In certain cases it may be possible to assign to the computer all direct responsibility for the decision process; the human in such a process is left only the responsibility to monitor results and make appropriate modifications in the automatic process.

The requirements for an automatic decision process are quite severe, however. First, the problem must be expressable in the form of a model – i.e., analytical relationships among variables or an explicit procedural definition of the process (as in a simulation program). Second, there must exist an objective function that can be used to compute the relative values of alternatives being evaluated. Third, there must exist an automatic process for generating alternatives and terminating the search.

An *optimizing* model is a special case of automatic decision model. In such a process, the generation of alternatives and the termination of the search guarantees that the best possible alternative will be found among all alternatives permitted by the model. (Note, however, that the model is only an approximation of reality, and that therefore certain alternatives possible in the real world may be ruled out by the constraints or procedures defined by the model. It is always possible that one of the excluded possibilities is the true optimum.)

Linear programming is probably the most common form of automatic decision making. The model (consisting of a series of constraints) and the objective function are expressed in the form of linear equations or inequalities. The algorithm used to compute the optimum assures that each new alternative evaluated will improve upon the last one evaluated (or at least not worsen it). The optimum alternative will be found after a finite number of iterations, and the algorithm identifies when this point has been reached.

An optimizing model of this sort offers the obvious advantage of finding the best of all possible alternatives. Often, however, there exists no known algorithm for computing the optimum (or at least not one that is computationally feasible). In this case, if automatic decision making is to be employed, one must settle for a nonoptimizing search strategy. Various heuristic or "hill climbing" techniques have been developed for this purpose. Included in the search technique must be a means for automatic termination of the process.

Although the human does not play a direct part in such a process, he or she nevertheless fills the vital role of monitoring the system. In some cases the human might modify a decision in order to take into account intangible factors not included in the model.

The person's more fundamental role is to serve as the adaptive mechanism by which the system is modified to correct for imperfections in the model or to respond to changes in the environment. A well-designed system allows the human to examine the operation of the model in order that he or she can better perform the adaptation function.

Automatic decision making is almost always confined to lower-level decision processes. Higher-level processes generally have multidimensional, incommensurable goals; consequently, it is usually not possible to find suitable trade-offs among goals in order to determine a single (composite) objective function. Furthermore, a high-level decision process is usually too complex for the application of automatic search or optimization techniques.

Future Decision-Aiding Systems   The trend is clearly toward the implementation of information systems that provide a greater aid to decision makers. Any such aid should, of course, recognize the costs as well as the benefits of developing the system.

Often a selective retrieval system offers the best balance between costs and benefits. The real payoff appears to lie, however, in the more widespread development of person–machine decision aids. Such systems are powerful enough to deal successfully with a wide range of decision processes, including many that occur at the strategic level. Despite their power, they are well within the state of the art of computer science and management science.

INTEGRATED DECISION SYSTEMS

Any (human-made) system must be broken down into a collection of subsystems. The degree of interaction among the subsystems depends in part on the way the system is designed and operated. Interactions can be substantially reduced by a suitable choice of structure that combines closely interacting activities within the same subsystem boundaries. The impact of interactions that cross boundaries can also be mitigated through various forms of decoupling. For example, buffer inventories decouple subassembly departments from the assembly department, and message buffers decouple remote terminals from a central processor. Duplication of resources within each using subsystem (such as an independent minicomputer dedicated to separate processing tasks) avoids interactions that would otherwise arise in sharing a common resource.

An integrated system is one in which a high degree of coordination takes place among subsystems. Activities of one subsystem that interact with activities in other subsystems are explicitly coordinated in order to mesh them together and achieve the best overall result. A great deal of resource sharing takes place in an integrated system in order to reduce duplication and gain economies of scale.

The trade-off between independence and integration is one of the more fundamental issues facing the system designer. Independence provides simplicity, but it does so at the cost of duplication, suboptimization, increased buffers, lower resource utilization, and foregone economies of scale. Integration can increase efficiencies, but at the cost of greater complexity, sophistication, and risk. Conceptually, the designer should strive to achieve the best balance between these opposing effects.

An integrated MIS, like any integrated system, achieves a relatively high degree of coordination and sharing. There are two aspects to such integration: the information system itself, and the organization it serves.

Integrated Information Processing   Integration of information processing is aimed at greater efficiency. It is manifested in a number of ways:

- *Data entry.* A fragmented system usually collects a considerable amount of duplicate data, whereas an integrated system tends to eliminate such duplication. For example, in an integrated MIS, sales data might be collected by the order entry system; all other subsystems (forecasting, inventory control, accounting, etc.) would then obtain sales data from this source.

- *Database organization.* An integrated information system tends toward consolidated records, rather than duplicating data elements in fragmented records. For example, a single employee record may be used instead of maintaining separate records for payroll and personnel administration.

- *Program organization.* Programs tend to be consolidated as integration proceeds. For example, a consolidated inventory control program might combine routine file maintenance, retrieval and report generation, physical and financial control functions, etc.

• *Resource sharing.* An integrated MIS achieves a high degree of sharing of processing resources, communication lines, personnel, and programs.

It is by no means true that the ideal MIS is the one that achieves the highest degree of integration. Integration of the MIS, like all integration, is a matter of trade-offs between efficiency versus complexity. However, as advances take place in the technology of information processing, the balance between independence and integration tips in favor of greater integration. For example, advances in multiprogramming operating systems and communications favor greater computer sharing. Advances in database management software and auxiliary storage hardware favor the sharing of data as a means of reducing duplicate collection and storage. The completely integrated, monolithic MIS—the so-called total management information system—remains a figment of the imagination of unrealistic dreamers, but current technology certainly supports a much higher degree of integration than existed a few years ago.

Integration of Organizational Activities   The second major aspect of an integrated MIS is the integration of organizational activities. The purpose of such integration is to coordinate the activities more closely and to achieve more global planning and control. In a multiplant manufacturing firm, for example, an integrated planning and control system might schedule the production and distribution of each plant's outputs in a way that results in the lowest cost for the company as a whole, rather than suboptimizing by scheduling on a plant-by-plant basis.

Integration of this sort requires a centralized database that spans the organizational units included in the coordinated plan. For example, a multiplant logistics system would require data about manufacturing, transportation, and warehousing costs; available capacities; forecasts for each item; and current inventory levels.

Coordinated planning also requires a model of each unit included in the plan. Without the ability to examine the detailed implications of an alternative plan, decision makers would have no basis for choosing the plan that achieves the best overall result. As a practical matter, a high degree of integration generally requires the use of formal models, for in no other way is it possible to manipulate the complex relationships and large number of variables involved in multiunit centralized planning.

The degree of integration in the planning process can vary greatly. It may take the form of relatively infrequent, aggregate planning, such as monthly scheduling of aggregate output of each major product group. At the other extreme, it could involve real-time scheduling of detailed production and distribution at multiple manufacturing and distribution facilities. The tighter the integration, the greater the efficiencies in shared utilization of resources, reduced buffer stocks, reduced suboptimization, and so forth. This is gained, however, at the cost of increased information processing and greater complexity.

Integration of information processing and integration of organizational activities are related but separable issues. It is possible to have highly integrated information processing without also integrating organizational activities. Each decentralized activity might, for example, draw upon the processing resources of a centralized computer system by means of remote terminals linked through communication lines. The centralized resource in this case could merely provide efficient processing services; how each decentralized unit uses the services could be handled on a strictly local basis.

Integration of organizational activities, however, calls for at least some degree of integration of information processing. The minimum requirement is a centralized database that spans the units being coordinated, combined with centralized decision aids that permit coordinated planning. In short, integrated information processing is a necessary, but not sufficient, condition for integrated planning.

INTEGRATION OF DECISION MODELS WITH TRANSACTION PROCESSING

An important issue in the design of a comprehensive MIS is the nature of the link between decision models and transaction processing. If a model is completely integrated into the MIS, it obtains inputs and disposes of outputs automatically. In a less thoroughly integrated system, at least some human intervention must take place.

Consider first the case of a completely independent, or nonintegrated, decision model. All input data for such a model are obtained manually. The original source of the data may be accounting or other types of reports coming from the transaction processing system, but the transformation of these data into the form required by the model is handled by a human. A transformation is necessary to convert historical transaction data into planning data. For example, the actual unit cost of various replenishment orders of a raw material must be converted into a projected unit cost suitable for planning purposes (budgeting, say). Typically, the projection involves an averaging process and perhaps adjustments for unusual conditions in the past or for expected changes in the future. It is also necessary to transform the data into the format and coding required by the model.

Outputs from a nonintegrated model are handled in a manner similar to the inputs. The outputs are first displayed for use by a human. If a decision from a model (an inventory order quantity, for example) is to be fed into the operational part of the system (which in general must be done for the decision to be implemented), a human must intervene to convert the decision into input data having the required form.

Many of the applications of linear programming models are of the nonintegrated type. Suppose, for example, such a model is used to determine the optimum blend of grains in a flour milling operation. All the inputs—giving the current price of different grains, capacity constraints, production requirements, and the like—are typically collected manually and keypunched into the proper input format. The decisions from the model are executed through human intervention, such as placing orders for the specified quantity of each grain (modified, perhaps, to take account of intangibles not included in the model). If a decision is required as an input to the transaction processing system—to prepare a purchase order, for example—it is manually entered into the system.

Nonintegrated versus Integrated Models   A nonintegrated model offers the great advantage of simplicity. Humans supply all the intelligence required to extract data, transform them into input data having the correct format and coding, and handle output decisions. Expressing such intelligence in the form of a completely explicit program can be enormously difficult and expensive. If the volume of input or output data is fairly limited, the nonintegrated approach is usually best. As the volume grows, however, a nonintegrated model may eventually collapse from the burden of the required manual support. The preparation of inputs becomes increasingly expensive, time-consuming, and error-prone. The number of output decisions may become too large to permit careful review and implementation.

These difficulties can be partially relieved by implementation of a system with a *static* database. In such a system, the input data are originally collected in the same fashion as in the nonintegrated model. Once the data are stored in the static database, however, they then can be manipulated automatically or by a person–machine process. For example, the input data for a linear programming model can be stored on magnetic disks. Any modifications or reformating of the data can be performed by the computer. Data elements can be updated selectively, without having to feed in the entire set of inputs. Outputs from the model can similarly be stored in detailed form, permitting specified reports to be prepared by means of a retrieval program.

The complete integration of the model comes with the introduction of a *dynamic* database. In this case the model is automatically linked to a database that is updated as a byproduct of routine transaction processing. Input data are extracted automatically and transformed into the required form. Outputs feed back to the database where they are then made available automatically to the operational part of the system. (The transformations of the inputs or outputs may be performed by means of a person–machine process, rather than by a completely automatic process, but the routine clerical functions of collecting, coding, and rearranging the data are eliminated.)

Inventory models offer perhaps the best examples of highly integrated models. The principal inputs are the sales forecasts for each of the items being controlled. The forecasts might come directly from a forecasting program, which in turn obtains its inputs from the order entry subsystem. Reorder points and order quantities may in some cases be fed back automatically to the order entry system, in which a purchase requisition is generated for an item when its stock level falls below its order point.

However, complete integration rarely, if ever, exists. Even a highly integrated model obtains some of its inputs through human intervention. For example, it is unlikely that an inventory model would be provided cost data (e.g., ordering cost, stockout cost) automatically from the accounting subsystem. These data are low in volume, are subject to relatively infrequent changes, and require subtle transformations to convert transaction data into planning data. For these data, the trade-offs strongly favor nonintegrated links between the model and the transaction processing system (although the high-volume input data, such as sales forecasts, may still be obtained through integrated links).

CONCLUSION

A well-designed MIS should reflect the trade-offs that exist between independence and integration. A suitable balance will certainly not result in a "total" monolithic system that at one time captured the imagination of the more fanciful members of the ADP profession.

A successful MIS is carefully structured so that each subsystem exhibits considerable independence. It is implemented step by step, so that worthwhile interim benefits are generated while moving toward the long-term MIS plan. It avoids unnecessary technical sophistication that yields potential benefits too low to justify its substantial added costs and risk. In short, its designers recognize the enormous complexity of organizational activities and the limitations of information technology.

As information technology advances, the design of an MIS should shift toward greater—but by no means total—integration. This has been the clear trend over the past decade. It has been manifested in the greater sharing of common data, sharing of processing and communication resources, consolidation of programs, and more powerful decision aids. A cautious, realistic, deliberate, and carefully planned movement toward increased integration is a sure sign that an organization is properly exploiting information technology, and thereby increasing the efficiency of its component parts.

SELECTIVE BIBLIOGRAPHY

Blumenthal, Sherman C., *Management Information Systems*, Macmillan, New York, 1969.

Davis, Gordon B., *Management Information Systems*, McGraw-Hill, New York, 1974.

Emery, James C., *Organizational Planning and Control Systems*, Macmillan, New York, 1969.

Emery, James C., "Decision Models," *Datamation*, Sept. 1 and Sept. 15, 1970 (reprinted in William C. House (ed.), *Operations Research: An Introduction to Modern Applications*, Auerbach, Philadelphia, 1972).

Mader, C., and R. Hagin, *Information Systems: Technology, Economics, Architecture*, Systems Research Associates, Palo Alto, Calif., 1974.

McFarlan, W., R. Nolan, and D. Norton, *Information Systems Administration*, Holt, Rinehart and Winston, New York, 1973.

Morton, Michael S., *Management Decision Systems: Computer Based Support for Decision Making*, Graduate School of Business, Harvard University, Cambridge, 1971.

Simon, Herbert A., *The New Science of Management Decisions*, Harper & Row, New York, 1960.

Chapter **3**

Simulation and Models for Decision Making

A. F. DERSHOWITZ

**Corporate Strategy & Systems,
General Electric Company, Fairfield, Connecticut**

G. J. HAHN

**Corporate Research and Development Center,
General Electric Company, Schenectady, New York**

E. G. HOLZMANN

**Corporate Research and Development Center,
General Electric Company, Schenectady, New York**

Modeling and computer simulation provide powerful tools for evaluating business decisions. Just as ordinary hand tools improve the ability of the mechanic to attack physical problems, computer simulation allows the manager to extend his or her ability to *understand, plan,* and *control* complex operations. The procedure involves representing the effect of various decision and environmental variables on business performance by a series of logical and algebraic relationships, known as the *simulation model.* These relationships are then programmed into a computer.

Evaluation of a particular business strategy generally involves a series of computer runs of the simulation model to allow for unpredictable variations in the environmental variables and for uncertainties in the decision maker's knowledge. The output of the runs gives a statistical distribution of the possible values of the business performance variables. These can be examined by the decision maker to evaluate the consequences of the given strategy. Alternative strategies may be compared by running different series of simulation runs and comparing the outputs.

The main point of the simulation procedure is that it permits the decision maker to evaluate the consequences of different business strategies *before* implementing one of these strategies. It becomes economically possible to compress many years of potential business experience into a few minutes of time on a high-speed computer. A further advantage of the simulation is that it forces the decision maker to define formally the variables which affect business performance to determine how they relate to each other. Thus, the discipline required in developing the simulation model, and the resulting improved insight, are important fringe benefits.

The purpose of this Chapter is to provide the reader with insight into the construction and use of simulation models for business decision making. Some typical simulations are discussed first. Next, six specific steps in conducting a simulation analysis are outlined, and each of these steps is illustrated by an example. Generalized computer programs for simulation analysis are then described, and some alternative tools to simulation for decision making are given. Information on further reading material concerning simulation is also provided. This includes references to the well-known *Industrial Dynamics* developed by Forrester.

SOME TYPICAL SIMULATION PROBLEMS

Sizing a Waste Water Treatment Plant[1]

A producer of chemicals was required to develop a waste treatment plant into which liquid residues would be fed, thus preventing their discharge into a nearby river. The problem was to determine the required

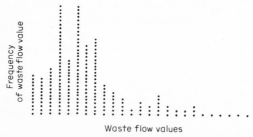

Fig. 3-1   Histogram of waste flow from simulations. Each asterisk represents an occurrence of a simulated waste flow within a given range. Thus, the first column of asterisks represents the count of simulated flows of 0–4,999 lb/day; the second column, flows of 5,000–9,999 lb/day, etc.

size of the plant in order to accommodate the waste output a very high proportion of the time. The problem was complicated by the fact that in processing over 1,000 process grades, the manufacturer used roughly 50 different major operating stations which generate waste.

The process streams can be likened to a river system with flows from numerous branches, each representing a station operating on an individual schedule and feeding the central mainstream. Whether or not a particular branch is feeding waste into the system at any instant of time is a matter of chance, depending on whether the process representing that branch is active at that instant.

Reliable information was not available on how much and what waste could be expected to be fed from each process into the waste treatment plant, or on what schedule the wastes would be generated. Therefore, each process area was reviewed, operation by operation, product by product. Where possible, current waste was measured or calculated to serve as a base for future projection. From all this, data on flow rates, duration, frequency, and characteristic flow cycles were compiled for each independently operating station. Some typical resulting information is shown in Figure 3-1. This provided the input to the computer simulation which would generate a distribution of total waste.

The simulation model essentially involved shooting "computer dice" for each station to determine whether or not it was creating waste, and, if so, for how long. For example, Station A (see Table 3-1) was estimated to create waste 42 days per year, with a probability of $42/365 = .11$ on any given day. A random number generator would then choose a number x between 0 and 1. If $x \leq 0.11$, the computer logic considered Station A to be

---

[1] Taken in part from M. Kopp, H. Lapidot, G. Hahn. (See Selective Bibliography at end of the Chapter; all subsequent references in this Chapter are documented in full therein.)

creating waste that day. By generating random numbers, the computer would determine the starting times of the first waste creation for each station for each day. The waste flow rate was assumed to be constant over the period during which the waste was generated—for example, the rate for Station A was assumed to be 4 pounds per hour—but it could easily have been made variable.

TABLE 3-1   Typical Waste Generation by Station
(Input data for simulation)

Station	Waste pounds per hour of operation	Days run in a year	Hours of waste per run	Length of run hours
A	4	42	24	24
B	62	210	5	12
C	780	12	2	24
D	−24°	125	1	24
E	−110°	125	1	24
F	23	310	24	24
G	1,250	10	1	24
H	1,960	25	1	6
I	2,280	18	1	8
J	2,600	45	1	8
K	200	17	1.5	6
L	555	24	1	12
M	1,720	99	5	12
N	3,300	25	3	8
·	·	·	·	·
·	·	·	·	·
·	·	·	·	·

° Negative amounts indicate process is using up waste material.

The computer examines each station in this manner and "generates" the appropriate waste amounts. A total waste profile for each period of the day is obtained by summing the waste values for the individual stations. The whole procedure is repeated many times, providing simulated waste values for randomly selected days. The resulting information is summarized by the computer by means of a histogram, as shown in Figure 3-1. This histogram provides a picture of the waste flowing into the system each day and gives the necessary information for sizing the plant.

In this example, consideration was also given to adding a smoothing lagoon to the system through which all waste would be fed. The effectiveness of such a smoothing lagoon was also evaluated by an extension of the simulation analysis.

The steps involved in this simulation are summarized as follows:

- At each station determine from random numbers:
- Whether waste is generated by that station that day.
- If so, determine if waste is flowing at the *start* of the day. If it is, determine how long and when else it will flow that day. If not, determine when it will start flow for the rest of the day.
- Sum wastes over all stations to obtain total waste generated each hour of the day.
- Calculate hourly outputs from different-sized lagoons and/or provide input of total hourly waste generation to the surge reservoir simulation.
- Repeat preceding procedure for total of N days.
- Calculate summary statistics and plot histograms for results over N days.

Estimating Product Liability   A manufacturer of equipment that is required to operate under field conditions subject to performance warranties wanted to estimate the magnitude of the dollar risks incurred because of product problems or malfunctions over a specified time period. This information was required to set aside appropriate reserves to cover such warranties. The information was also needed to evaluate the effect of design changes on product liability and to establish warranty policies.

As input, the business forecast included fixed numbers of units of different types in the field, in different stages of installation or operation at each particular time during the projected interval. The units were subject to various problem modes, depending upon their predicted operational status. Whether or not any problem actually occurred on one unit or on more than one unit, and the costs required for fixing the problem during the projected time period, were matters of chance. Thus, the liability to be incurred was also probabilistic in nature. The purpose of the computer simulation was to obtain a histogram (similar to that of Figure 3-1 for the waste flow problem) to describe the statistical distribution of product liability in dollars.

The specific input information required for this problem included:

• A description of each possible problem mode, and information on whether the problem mode was one which would occur independently on individual units, or one which would occur simultaneously on groups of units, such as on all units manufactured during a particular month.

• Estimates of the probability of occurrence for each problem mode.

• The estimated probability distribution of the resulting dollar liability if the problem mode occurred.

The simulation model consisted of a series of equations involving the above variables. These equations express the dollar liability as a function of the probability of occurrence of the individual problem modes and the costs associated with each of these modes. A run of the resulting simulation program then involved selecting random values from each of the appropriate probability models, entering the resulting values into the programmed equations, and using these equations to calculate a value of total dollar liability. This procedure was repeated many times. The histogram of the resulting total dollar liabilities from these simulation runs provided an estimate of the statistical distribution of the product liability costs.

The manufacturer thus was able not only to estimate the magnitude of dollar risks incurred, but to provide for flexibility in bank credit arrangements to cover likely alternative patterns of liability.

Planning a Material Handling System   The problem in this example arose in the planning of a new major appliance factory. The engineers responsible for the layout of the manufacturing and storage system had decided to employ the concept of *point-of-use storage:* purchased and manufactured parts and subassemblies were to be stored in high-rise racks directly adjacent to the assembly areas. Compared with traditional warehouse storage, this new concept promised to shorten the cycle time and the total amount of material being held in inventory.

Additional savings were sought by using stacker cranes in place of forklift trucks to store and retrieve parts containers for the assembly lines. Stacker cranes require an aisle width of 4 feet contrasted with about 20 feet for forklift trucks. Also, forklift trucks are slower than stacker cranes and more limited in their vertical reach. Finally, it was expected that the stacker crane operation would be under the partial control of minicomputers, backed up by the larger memory of a full-size host computer. The fringe benefits of this system included instant availability of inventory data for management decision making and control.

Manufacturing engineers, working with advance-planning engineers and a consulting service, had calculated the design parameters for the high-rise storage racks and the associated container handling system. The calculations were based on an average expected product mix, and yielded average container cycle times, crane travel and usage times, etc. But neither these calculations nor any existing statistical theory was able to predict peak load conditions, the dependence of stockouts on numbers of containers in storage, on crane lift velocity, and on other important design variables.

The engineering calculations clearly showed that four stacker cranes could easily handle the average production load under normal conditions. However, they were unable to give a conclusive answer to the question of whether a fifth crane would be needed to ensure continuity of production in case of a crane malfunction and to cope with peaking conditions. Stacker crane outage or overload could result in stockouts or complete shutdown of a production line. To counter this, the installation of an extra crane as insurance had to be considered. The installed cost of each crane was roughly $100,000.

In this situation, simulation helped to evaluate the risks under several design assumptions and many operating conditions. In essence, the computer described a day in the life of a stacker crane system, operating with three or four cranes at different speeds, with different production rates and initial conditions. It turned out that even as few as three cranes could support the assembly operation for about half a shift. Furthermore, the expected return on the cost of a fifth crane was found to be quite small, and the added investment was not deemed necessary (Holzmann).

A simulation program like the one required for this example, once developed, can be readily adapted to help in the evaluation of other planned manufacturing facilities. In fact, this type of simulation problem is so common that special high-level computer languages are now available to help with the task of writing the computer code. (See "Generalized Computer Programs for Simulation Analysis," later in this Chapter.)

STEPS IN CONDUCTING A SIMULATION ANALYSIS

The specific problems which can profitably be subjected to a simulation analysis differ widely. However, the general approach for attacking each problem is reasonably consistent. The following steps are generally involved:
1. Problem definition and statement of objectives and criteria.
2. Development of an appropriate model.
3. Obtaining valid input data for the simulation model.
4. Translation of the simulation model into a computer program.
5. Validation of the computer program and its use to obtain the desired information.
6. Summary and analysis of results.

Step 1: Problem Definition and Statement of Objectives and Criteria The reasons for conducting the simulation analysis need to be clearly stated. Also, the criteria for evaluating the results, that is, the output variables from the simulation analysis, must be defined precisely. Some examples are:
1. To compare the effect of specified alternative bidding strategies on net income.
2. To evaluate the effect of a policy of aggressively building market share on cash-flow distribution, income distribution, and the distribution of rate of return on investment.
3. To determine the minimum number of stations required by a test and repair facility so as to assure waiting times of 1 hour or less on 99 per cent of all units going through the station.

Step 2: Development of an Appropriate Model The development of an appropriate model is the most challenging step in the decision analysis. It requires the development of a set of relationships between the input variables and the output, or performance, variables, that realistically represents both the mathematics and the logic of the problem.

There are two basic types of simulation models—those which are *time-dependent* and those which are not. Time-dependent models generally are required in servicing or manufacturing problems, such as the stacker crane problem already briefly described. Such models are characterized by the fact that the values of the variables in the model change with time. Frequently business decision problems, such as the problem discussed below, under "Example of Simulation Analysis," can be reasonably formulated so as not to be time-dependent, and in this Chapter the main emphasis is on such time-invariant models. However, generalized simulation languages for time-dependent processes are discussed briefly under "Generalized Computer Programs for Simulation Analysis," later in this Chapter.

Another important way of categorizing models is according to whether they are probabilistic or deterministic. Deterministic models are ones which include only input variables whose outcomes are known exactly at the outset of the simulation analysis. The stacker crane problem discussed earlier is an example of a situation which can be handled by a deterministic model. Probabilistic models are ones which include one or more variables whose outcomes are a matter of chance. The waste water treatment and product liability examples are illustrations of problems which require probabilistic models. Most business decision problems involve probabilistic models; a deterministic model is sufficient for some simulations of physical and manufacturing situations.

The input variables for the simulation model may be further classified into two categories: variables under the control of the decision maker, and environmental variables. Variables under control might include such factors as the size of the advertising budget, the product sales price, etc., and would usually include the variables whose effect on business performance is being studied in the simulation analysis. Environmental variables are generally beyond the control of the decision maker, and might include such factors as gross national product, competitors' advertising budgets, and weather conditions (for example, the effect of a cold summer on the manufacture of air conditioners). The exact values of such environmental variables are often unknown, and estimates of their values are subject to random fluctuations. Thus, they must be entered into a probabilistic model as random variables with specified probability distributions. Each run of the computer simulation then involves the selection of a random number from the distribution of each of the random variables in the model.

Since the output of the simulation depends on assumptions concerning the input variables, it is necessary for the model builder to work closely with the decision maker to obtain agreement on the assumptions. A workable simulation will ordinarily provide output describing the simulated input variables, as well as the desired output variables, so that their reasonableness can be checked.

An important design consideration in building the model is cost of the simulation versus level of detail desired from the simulation. An effective simulation will provide for the most important results to be obtained economically, and will provide for additional results to be included as their cost is justified.

Some of the decisions that need to be made in developing the model are:

1. Is a deterministic simulation sufficient or is the element of randomness essential?

2. If the model is time-dependent, will changes in the state of model variables be keyed to equal time increments (*time pacing*) or to occurrence or completion of specific events (*event pacing*)?

3. How can the model be made sufficiently simple, so as to be easy to use, but still be precise enough to be realistic? Will the theoretical framework of the model give adequate answers, and in any case, what are the limits to the answers and the assumptions of the model?

Step 3: Obtaining Valid Input Data for the Simulation Model Each term in the model for which data must be provided is now examined. Where a detailed study of a business is required, projects must be set in motion to gather and validate the required information. Examples of some of the data to be obtained are:

• What is a "typical" mix of orders?

• How often does each type of machine break down? For how long?

• How do the actions of competitors depend upon economic and marketing factors and how might these actions affect our business?

• What is the chance that Company X will begin to buy our product? If so, how much? When?

Frequently, this step involves obtaining subjective probability estimates and distributions for many of the input variables. (See "Example of Simulation Analysis," below, for a specific example; some of the techniques involved in this step are discussed by Dalkey et al. and some of the pitfalls are indicated by Hahn, and both articles provide further references.) The specific input data used for such analyses generally have a very profound effect on the resulting output. However, the effect of the assumptions concerning input constants and random variables can be evaluated by conducting *sensitivity analyses* using the simulation model. Such sensitivity analyses involve rerunning the simulation model with perturbations on some of the input data and observing the effect on the simulation output.

Obtaining input data for the simulation model can proceed in parallel with programming the simulation model (Step 4). In fact, it often turns out that some of the required information is obtained only after the simulation is first run and the sensitivity of the results to the input variables is evaluated.

Step 4: Translating the Simulation Model into a Computer Program Programming a simulation model usually involves more complex decisions than those involved in computerizing a payroll or a market analysis. The key decisions include:

1. Can an existing special-purpose or generalized simulation program be used, requiring only data, but essentially no new computer code? Or does the problem call for the coding of a specialized program? In the latter case, what is the most suitable language?

2. Is the simulation small enough to be programmed on a time-sharing computer? The interactive capability of time-sharing is such that it often pays to conduct part or all of the simulation analysis in this manner.

3. How will the input data be provided? Do bridges to data banks have to be programmed?

4. What output displays should be provided?

A probabilistic simulation model will require generation of random numbers. This feature is generally available in computer library programs for a variety of statistical distributions. If a new computer program is to be developed, the procedures for obtaining random values from a variety of distributions given by Hahn and Shapiro and also by various books on simulation methodology will be found useful. (See Selective Bibliography.) These books also provide information concerning certain *variance reduction* techniques which may be programmed into a simulation routine to make it more economical to run for various purposes. Such techniques can be of critical importance in some technical applications of simulation.

Step 5: Validation of the Computer Program and its Use to Obtain the Desired Information

Program Validation. This involves not only the routine checkout of the computer program, but also the evaluation of the reasonableness of the generated distributions of the input random variables and of the output calculations for "known" situations.

Planning of the Simulation Runs. The combinations of values of strategic variables to be considered by the simulations, including the combination of values for the sensitivity analyses, should be organized so that a meaningful evaluation of their effect on the output can be made. Often the help of a professional statistician will improve the resulting experimental design. Such organization is especially necessary for batch computer simulations. However, even with an interactive simulation using a time-sharing computer, one must decide on priorities and the necessary number of runs. The required number of simulations depends upon the degree of statistical precision desired in the results. (This subject is discussed by Hahn.) In any case, the specification of the required degree of precision in the output, and the resulting sample size, must be tempered by one's confidence in the input data from which the output is obtained. High statistical precision in the output when the given input is coarse would be unrealistic and could be misleading, besides being a waste of money.

Operational Use of the Simulation Program. Operational use of the simulation program to obtain the desired answers is straightforward. With large simulations, recovery routines should be provided to protect against the risk of program interruption, and the computer operators should be instructed in the use of such routines.

Step 6: Summary and Analysis of Results The most effective display of the results of a simulation analysis is often a graphical one, as suggested by the examples herein. In some cases, the results of the simulation are summarized by one or more summary statistics, such as the estimated mean and standard deviation of some performance value, calculated from the results of the simulation runs. On occasion, statistical models, such as a normal distribution or a beta distribution, are fitted from these summary values. This might be the case, for example, if the results of the simulation are to be used as the input to some subsequent computer analysis. In most cases, however, this approach is not as informative as a direct display of the results. Thus, for the waste treatment plant sizing problem, the output distribution is decidedly nonsymmetric, and it is more informative to draw conclusions from Figure 3-1 directly, rather than to deal with calculated summary values.

EXAMPLE OF SIMULATION ANALYSIS

Given below are the steps and some of the details involved in conducting a simulation analysis. To provide the full "flavor" of the simulation, the discussion is necessarily more technical than much of the rest of this Chapter.

Step 1: Problem Definition and Statement of Objectives and Criteria A manufacturer of a large subsystem which is part of some heavy industrial equipment desires to compare the effect of three alternative operating strategies on total sales for next year. (A comparison of the costs associated with each of the strategies will be part of a subsequent simulation analysis.) Sales stem both from new units and from replacement units on each of 10 product lines. Replacement sales may come either for units originally sold by the company or for units sold by its competitors.

The first strategy continues the present pricing, delivery, and distribution strategies, and is consistent with the trend of the business.

The second strategy seeks to gain a larger market share by building up field service forces, and by providing an outstanding improvement in warranties and a decrease in installation time. The established product quality levels justify the improved warranties if customer personnel can be adequately trained and helped in maintaining the equipment.

The third strategy extends the second strategy by expanding the market to installations currently being serviced by lower-rated competitive equipment. This strategy requires selective price reductions and could backfire by resulting in reduced sales income if the reductions spread through all elements of the line.

Step 2: Development of an Appropriate Model The model may be regarded as time-invariant; however, it is decidedly probabilistic in nature. The formulation of the model, as described here, remains the same for each of the three operating strategies.

Let S = total sales for next year, in dollars

$\quad S_i$ = sales in dollars for next year for product line i, $i = 1, \ldots, 10$

$\quad N_i$ = new business sales in dollars for next year for product line i, $i = 1, \ldots, 10$

$\quad R_i$ = replacement business sales for next year in dollars for product line i, $i = 1, \ldots, 10$

The total sales are obtained by adding the new sales and the replacement sales for the 10 product lines, i.e.,

$$S = \sum_{i=1}^{10} S_i = \sum_{i=1}^{10} N_i + \sum_{i=1}^{10} R_i \tag{1}$$

The models for new business sales and replacement sales for product line i will be developed separately.

In determining the new business on product line i for next year (N_i),

$\quad G$ = general economic condition indicator for next year, relative to average economic conditions

$\quad V_i$ = dollar values of all current units for product line i

$\quad Z_i$ = proportion of the dollar value of current units that new industry sales for product line i represent under average economic conditions

$\quad C_i$ = company share of market for product line i (fraction)

Then the total new product sales for the next year are seen to be

$$\sum_{i=1}^{10} N_i = G \sum_{i=1}^{10} V_i Z_i C_i \tag{2}$$

The total dollar value of all current units (V_i) is known for each of the product lines. However, all the other terms in this part of the model are random quantities whose actual values are determined by chance (see Step 4 for more detailed specification). Note that different values of V_i, Z_i, and C_i are specified for each of the product lines, but that the value of the economic indicator G is the same for each product line.

In indicating the replacement sales (R_i) for product line i for next year, the subscript i, denoting product line i, will generally be omitted for convenience in this discussion. Also, all terms will continue to refer to next year. In particular, let

$\quad J$ and J' = number of company and noncompany units, respectively, in the field

$\quad B_j$ and $B_{j'}$ = probability of need for replacement of company field unit j and noncompany field unit j' respectively

$\quad L_j$ and $L_{j'}$ = probability company gets replacement order, given need for replacement of company field unit j and noncompany field unit j' respectively

$\quad W_1(B_j) = \begin{cases} 1 \text{ if unit } j \text{ actually needs replacement} \\ 0 \text{ otherwise} \end{cases}$

and $W_1'(B_{j'})$ is defined similarly for unit j'. Thus, $W_1(B_j)$ and $W_1'(B_{j'})$ take on the value 1 with probabilities B_j and $B_{j'}$ respectively.

$\quad W_2(L_j) = \begin{cases} 1 \text{ if company gets replacement order on unit } j \text{ given need for replacement} \\ 0 \text{ otherwise} \end{cases}$

and $W_2'(L_{j'})$ is defined similarly for unit j'. Thus, $W_2(L_j)$ and $W_2'(L_{j'})$ take on the value 1 with probabilities L_j and $L_{j'}$ respectively.

M_j and $M_{j'}$ = magnitude of replacement order size for company field unit j and non-company field unit j' respectively

Then the replacement sales for product line i can be determined:

$$R_i = \sum_{j=1}^{J} [W_1(B_j)] \ [W_2(L_j)] \ M_j + \sum_{j'=1}^{J'} [W_1'(B_{j'})] \ [W_2'(L_{j'})] \ M_{j'} \tag{3}$$

Equations (1), (2), and (3) are the relationships which define the simulation model for a particular strategy. These equations involve a number of simplifying assumptions, whose validity must be evaluated. For example, the model implies that the variables are independent of one another. Thus the probability that the company gets a replacement order for a particular order is assumed to be independent of the probability of obtaining such an order for any other unit. This might in actuality not be the case, since both units might be in the hands of the same customer and this customer might have a preference for or against the company or a policy of splitting sales among vendors. The model could, of course, be generalized to include various interdependencies at the cost of additional complexity.

Step 3: Obtaining Valid Input Data for the Simulation Model This step involves obtaining valid deterministic or probabilistic estimates for the terms in the simulation model defined in Step 2. This must be done for each of the 10 product lines under each of the three strategies.

The model requires subjective estimates for many of its terms, such as the probabilistics B_j, $B_{j'}$, L_j, and $L_{j'}$. Such estimates are subject to management judgment, but ordinarily are derived initially from historical frequency records (such as a histogram of past equipment life for units made by the company and by its competitors) and the judgment of the company's field representatives (such as their estimates of the change in the number of replacement orders for next year compared to this year due to company policy changes). The resulting input will be illustrated only for product line 1 (again dropping the subscript $i = 1$) under Strategy 1. For this case, the following data are obtained:

G = general economic condition indicator for next year. This is a random variable which is assumed to take on the values 1.0, 1.1, 1.2, or 1.3 with probabilities of .1, .3, .4, and .2 respectively. Thus, over a series of many simulation runs, the computer will select the value 1.0 in 10 per cent of the runs, the value 1.1 in 30 per cent of the runs, etc.

V = dollar value of current units. This value is known to be $122 million.

Z = proportion that new industry sales represent of dollar value of all current units. This is a random variable which is assumed to take on any value between .1 and .2 with equal probability. For a particular simulation run, this value is generated by the computer as a uniformly distributed random variable with values from .1 to .2.

C = company share of market. This is a random variable which is assumed to be between .1 and .2 with a probability of .4; between .2 and .3 with a probability of .3; between .3 and .4 with a probability of .2, and between .4 and .5 with a probability of .1. Thus, over a series of many simulation runs, the computer will select a uniformly distributed random variable between .1 and .2 in 40 per cent of the runs, a uniformly distributed random variable between .2 and .3 in 30 per cent of the runs, etc.

J and J' = number of company and noncompany units in field: 15 and 35.

B_1 and B_1' = probability of need for replacement for the first (i.e., $j = 1$) of the 15 company field units and for the first of the 35 noncompany field units: .1 and .2, respectively.

L_1 and L_1' = probability that the company gets order, given replacement need for the first company field unit and the first noncompany field unit: .6 and .3, respectively.

M_1 = magnitude of replacement order size for company field unit 1. This is assumed to be a normally distributed random variable with a best estimate of \$10 million and an optimistic estimate of \$12 million. Best estimate is assumed to be the median, or 50 per cent point, of the normal distribution, and the optimistic estimate is assumed to be the 90 per cent distribution point, i.e., that value which one would expect to be exceeded with a probability of only 10 per cent. Then the mean, μ, and the standard deviation, σ, of the normal distribution from which the computer will generate a random number in each simulation run are obtained from the relationships $\mu = 10$ million and $\mu + 1.28\sigma = 12$ million.

M'_1 = magnitude of replacement order size for noncompany unit 1. This is assumed to be a normally distributed random variable with a best estimate (median) of \$15 million and a pessimistic estimate (10 per cent point) of \$12.5 million.

Similar information is provided for each of the other product lines and for each of the strategies. In so doing, one must also indicate for each of the probabilistic terms in the model whether the random values to be generated remain the same from one strategy to the next, or vary independently, or are correlated in some specified manner.

Step 4: Translating the Simulation Model into a Computer Program A specialized computer program—either batch or time-sharing—could be developed for this problem. Alternatively, a generalized program could be used (see "Generalized Computer Programs for Simulation Analysis," below, for further discussion concerning such programs). In either case, the computer program translates the information specified in the previous steps into a form that will permit rapid repetitive calculation of total sales from the given input data.

Step 5: Validation of the Computer Program and its Use to Obtain the Desired Information The validation run of the computer program is conducted by setting each of the probabilistic variables at their median conditions and observing whether the resulting output value appears to match up with expectations. Some validation runs are also performed at "extreme" conditions.

It was determined that, in light of the coarseness of the input estimates, 100 simulation runs for each of the three strategies would provide sufficient precision. Each of the resulting runs calls for selecting a series of independently generated random values from the various statistical distributions of the probabilistic variables specified in Step 3 and then using these in the equations given in Step 2 to arrive at a total sales figure for that simulation run. The 100 simulation runs for each strategy yield 100 values for total sales for each of the three strategies. Additional runs are conducted to evaluate the sensitivity of the results to variations in the input values. For example, the effect on the distribution of total sales of changing Z_1 (the proportion that new industry sales represent of the dollar value of all current units for product line 1) from varying between 0.1 and 0.2 to varying between 0.1 and 0.3 might be examined.

Step 6: Summary and Analysis of Results The output of the computer simulation, in addition to providing a tabulation of the estimated distribution of total sales in dollars for each of the three strategies, also provides:

1. The distribution of the randomly generated values of each of the input values (as an additional check).

2. The distribution of the components which make up the total dollar sales—in particular, new product sales and replacement sales, for each product line.

Comparison of the outputs for the simulation runs for each of the three strategies reveals that:

- The chances are one in ten that total dollar sales will be:
  \$325 million or more under Strategy 1
  \$355 million or more under Strategy 2
  \$375 million or more under Strategy 3
- The chances are even that total sales will be:
  \$275 million or more under Strategy 1
  \$320 million or more under Strategy 2
  \$300 million or more under Strategy 3

- The chances are nine in ten that total sales will be:
$200 million or more under Strategy 1
$210 million or more under Strategy 2
$225 million or more under Strategy 3

The preceding results are shown graphically in Figure 3-2. From these curves, one can conclude that:

- Strategy 1 appears inferior to Strategies 2 and 3.
- Strategy 3 is riskier than Strategy 2. (It provides better chances of high sales, but has a higher probability of resulting in low sales.)

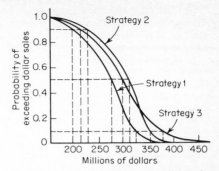

Fig. 3-2 Comparison of dollar sales distribution for three alternative marketing strategies.

Costs will of course also differ for the three strategies. Now that the effects on sales of each of the strategies is known, the simulation model can be extended to permit consideration of the viable alternatives.

GENERALIZED COMPUTER PROGRAMS FOR SIMULATION ANALYSIS

Generalized Programs vs. Specialized Computer Languages Simulation analysts have to choose one of three possible alternatives:

1. Use an existing generalized program (such as GPSS or ADA, discussed below).

2. Write their own simulation programs in one of the special higher-level simulation languages (such as SIMSCRIPT or CSMP, discussed below).

3. Develop their own computer programs or simulation "languages" based on a general-purpose computer language such as FORTRAN, COBOL, ALGOL, or PL/I.[2]

Regardless of the chosen approach, a certain amount of specialized learning and experience is required. Generally speaking, the first approach is the easiest to master and the least time-consuming, because the instruction set is strongly application-oriented and involves a minimum of "computerese." The price paid for this convenience is a higher computer running cost, because of the additional overhead burden that must be assumed by the computer. Also, in some cases, the memory requirements of a generalized program somewhat restrict the size of the problems that can be handled.

The development of special simulation languages has progressed to a level where coding and debugging of a program using such a language often costs less than the definition of the problem and the collection of the input data. However, the effort required to master one of these higher-level simulation languages can be a substantial stumbling block. One may prefer to engage the skills of an experienced analyst to help in planning and executing simulation projects that are too large to handle by an existing generalized program.

The third approach, developing one's own program from scratch, is recommended for very small or very specialized problems, where existing programs may be too inefficient or too restricting. Otherwise, it is difficult to justify duplicating the efforts already invested by others with resources that generally dwarf those available for a single undertaking.

Two kinds of generalized programs will be discussed. These apply principally to time-invariant and time-dependent processes, respectively.

Generalized Computer Programs for Time-invariant Processes The example in the preceding discussion involved a time-invariant process with two basic elements, the specifics of which differ from one application to the next, namely:

- Functional relationships describing the simulation model.
- The generation of random values from specified statistical distributions.

[2] See Section 2, Part 4, Chapter 3, "Programming Languages."

The remaining steps in many computer simulation analyses are essentially the same from one simulation analysis to the next. Generalized programs for time-invariant simulation analysis have capitalized on this similarity by providing a general structure to which the user need add only the following:

1. Specify by means of a FORTRAN (or BASIC) type statement the relationship between the input variables and the output variables for the specific simulation.

2. Select random values from a series of already programmed statistical distributions for generating such values by specifying the appropriate distribution type and the parameters of the distribution (or, more usually, by specifying percentage points of the distribution from which these parameters are calculated).

3. Specify certain options with regard to desired output, etc., and indicate the desired number of simulation runs.

Such generalized programs are highly attractive to the decision maker with limited background or training in simulation analysis, statistics, or computer programming. Such an individual would, for example, find it relatively easy to perform the analysis described in the previous section of this Chapter by using one of the available generalized programs for this purpose. In contrast, it might be a very burdensome job for such a person to write the required program from scratch and he or she would undoubtedly be hesitant to do so.

Many of the generalized computer programs for time-invariant simulation analysis have been developed on time-sharing computers for maximum simplicity and interactive use. Brief descriptions of available batch and time-sharing programs are provided by Berger (see Selective Bibliography).

Computer Languages for Time-dependent Processes Common to all time-dependent processes is a cause-effect relationship that involves time delay. For example, the temperature at one point of a pipeline is causally related to the temperature upstream of that point, with a delay that depends on the flow rate. Likewise, the number of available tables in a restaurant is a delayed function of the arriving guests and the service rendered by the waitresses. Stock market indicators are believed to be precursors of market action. Thus, all these cases are time-dependent processes.

The flow rate and temperature in an oil pipeline are examples of continuous types of time-dependent processes. The arrival of guests in a restaurant and the assignment of tables are discrete time-dependent processes. Stock market fluctuations may be considered continuous or discrete, depending on the time scale of interest.

Continuous-Process Simulation Languages. Algorithms descriptive of continuous processes always involve accumulation. The mathematical model takes the form of a set of differential equations. An analog computer solves the differential equations by the use of electrical integrators, combined with adders, multipliers, and nonlinear elements. (See Soroka, Korn and Korn, and Warfield.) A digital computer can solve the same differential equations by substituting a method of numerical integration. The key to economical digital integration is the ability to control the increment of time for integration, according to the problem requirements.

The following digital programming systems (or *languages*) are commonly used for continuous-process simulation (references are cited in full at the end of this Chapter):

1. CSMP – IBM's Continuous System Simulation Program. (See Brennan and Silberberg.)

2. ADA – General Electric's Automation Dynamic Analyzer. (See Watson and Moore.)

3. DYNAMO – A versatile language usable for a broad range of continuous closed-loop systems (see Pugh). It has been associated with the modeling activities using the Industrial Dynamics approach. (See Forrester and the other references under "Industrial Dynamics.")

4. ISL – an interactive continuous simulation "language" (really an assembly-language program), designed for high-speed operation on minicomputers. It is especially suited for hybrid analog-digital simulation, where the speed of the dedicated digital computer can often be a limiting factor. (See Benham and Taylor.)

These systems accept user-oriented input statements for constructing the simulation models and controlling the simulation runs. Current development efforts aim at improving the use of remote consoles operating within a time-sharing environment, to give the simulation user a computer tool that provides the desired on-line interaction in handling complex problems.

Discrete-Process Simulation Languages. A digital computer simulating a discrete process usually works differently. Logical rather than mathematical relationships advance the computation from one discrete event to the next. The key concept here is the method of ordering the events in time.

The simulation "looks ahead" to each occurrence of a significant event and then evaluates the new state of the system, characterized by a set of variables. The changes of state in the interval between such occasions are not of direct interest and therefore require no explicit computation.

In discrete-event simulation of large-scale complex systems, the major concern is with:

1. Queues waiting for service, subject to capacity constraints and priority logic rules.

2. The chaining of related activities.

3. The effects of random events specified to occur with given probabilities.

In addition to the traditional "custom" programming approach, using FORTRAN or BASIC, the following generalized programming systems for discrete-event simulation are in wide use:

1. GPSS—General Purpose Simulation System. (See Gould.) This block-oriented program features a simple flow-chart language for describing the problem or system to be simulated. When this description is fed into a computer, the program automatically carries out the simulation. (See Reitman.) One of the prime objectives of the GPSS language development is to make it relatively easy to change logic and data, and to select results. Graphic presentation of the results is part of the language. Batch versions of GPSS are available on computers of various manufacturers (e.g., IBM, Honeywell, Univac); time-sharing versions are also available (e.g., GE).

2. SIMSCRIPT (Markowitz, Karr, and Hausner). This is an activity-oriented simulation language designed for use with larger and more sophisticated models than GPSS. The designer requires more programming competence, since both the model structure and the data organization are largely left to the programmer. SIMSCRIPT has special features for added convenience, such as initialization and definition tables and a powerful report generator. Graphic relationships can be used to structure input data. Computers of many manufacturers have SIMSCRIPT compilers.

3. SIMULA (see Dahl and Nygaard) is a simulation language for discrete-event models frequently used in Europe. It is based on the ALGOL general-purpose computer language which is widely used there.

4. GASP IV—a FORTRAN-based "general application simulation program," especially designed for combined continuous and discrete simulation problems, and suited for use on minicomputers having main memory of 32K words or more. (See Pritsker.)

5. MODSIM (See DRI), SIMPLAN (see SSI), and XSIM (see Dynamic Associates) are among languages oriented toward deterministic projection of combined business and econometric time series models. Such models often involve recursive solutions of simultaneous equations, and interactive rather than probabilistic exploration of variables.

The purpose of higher-order programming languages is to simplify the user's task by shifting to the computer some of the routine problems of programming. While FORTRAN and ALGOL were developed for the solution of equations, and basically are not suited for discrete-event simulation, skilled programmers have adapted them successfully to such uses—at great effort and expense. (See Clementson, Pritsker and Kiviat, and Dahl and Nygaard.)

SOME ALTERNATIVES TO SIMULATION FOR DECISION MAKING

The basic technical problem in many simulation analyses is to determine the distribution of some output (or performance) variable given the relationship between the input variables and the output variable and given information on the statistical variation of the input variables. There are general approaches other than computer simulation which allow one to attack this problem, either exactly or approximately. These include *probability theory* and *error analysis*.

Technical descriptions of these methods are provided elsewhere. Therefore, rather than giving a detailed account here, we limit ourselves to a brief description of these two methods. The advantages and disadvantages of these alternative approaches relative to simulation are summarized in Table 3-2. Some further methods are also reviewed and compared with simulation.

Probability Theory Finding the distribution of some output variable as a function of input variables is a standard problem in probability theory, and is generally discussed in books on probability, mathematical statistics, and related topics under the heading "Transformation of Variables," and related techniques. (See Hahn and Shapiro, Chapter 5, which also provides further references.) In particular, this method allows one to obtain the distribution of an output variable which is a known function of some input random variables, the distribution of each of which is completely specified. Unfortunately, the procedure is a complicated one and is intractable for many situations. Thus, its usefulness is limited to some special simple cases, such as finding the distribution of the sum of a small number of random variables.

Error Analysis The error analysis method, also known as the *propagation of error* method or the *delta* method, is a procedure for approximating the mean and standard deviation of the distribution of an output variable. The procedure uses the means and standard deviations of the statistical distributions of each of the input variables

TABLE 3-2 Comparison of Features of Alternative Technical Methods for Decision Analysis

	Technical Method		
Feature	Probability theory	Error analysis	Simulation
General applicability	Very limited	Moderate	Extensive
Intuitive appeal to management	Low	Low	High
Statistical exactness (assuming correct model)	Exact method	Requires approximation to input and output distributions	Only limited by number of simulations
Computation costs	Generally low	Low	Could be high for many simulation runs and sensitivity analyses

which affect the output variable. Thus, in the marketing strategy example previously given, error analysis might be used to obtain approximate values for the mean and standard deviation of the distribution of total sales, given the means and standard deviations of the distributions of the specified variables which affect total sales. The details of the method, and some extensions, are described by Hahn and Shapiro, Chapter 7, which also gives additional references.

An advantage of error analysis is that for sufficiently small problems the method can be used without a computer. Even when the problem size dictates the use of a computer, error analysis is generally more economical with regard to required computer time than is simulation. This is especially so if the sensitivity of the output variable to perturbations in the input variables is to be evaluated. However, the disadvantages of error analysis are:

1. The basic method provides only the mean and standard deviation of the distribution of the output variable, rather than the complete distribution. Thus, to obtain percentiles of the output distribution or a distribution histogram, an approximation, such as assuming a normal distribution, is required. (However, an extension of the basic error analysis method does permit some added information about the distribution of the output variable to be found, other than its mean and standard deviation. See Hahn and Shapiro.)

2. The method becomes complicated when one is dealing with a highly complex relationship, especially one which involves correlated variables.

Error analysis is thus a convenient and economical approach for certain relatively small problems. It is less useful for large, complex problems.

Other Techniques   Various other analytical techniques are sometimes applicable in place of simulation analysis. These are specialized methods which, if applicable, are often preferable to simulation. Analytical techniques provide exact results, but only under highly restrictive conditions. Thus, such methods sometimes provide elegant solutions to an unrealistically oversimplified version of the real problem. In fact, in some cases, the literature on these techniques gives examples of simulations to avoid the restrictiveness of the methods.

Markov Processes. These are probabilistic models which deal with the probability of transition from one state to another. It is assumed that the state of the system today depends only on the state of the system yesterday (although some extensions have been developed). Such models have been used, for example, in studies on how to distribute a company's advertising budget so as to capitalize on the public's brand-switching habits.

Queueing Theory. This theory deals with the analysis of waiting lines and service facilities and is used, for example, to make decisions concerning the required number of facilities for various customer servicing problems. Queueing models have been used in such diverse areas as the design of tool cribs, the layout of major freight terminals, and the specification of rules for traffic lights.

Theory of Games and Business Gaming. Game theory is an elegant mathematical technique to study the behavior under uncertainty of competing individuals, companies, or nations. It has had limited practical application to date. Game theory should not be confused with business gaming. The latter is a simulation game in which teams of decision makers compete to test their skills in attacking a business decision problem. Business gaming can be used to provide a better understanding of the competitive environment, and to provide training in decision making and simulation analysis.

Mathematical Optimization and Linear Programming. Many problems involve finding the optimum of some mathematical function, or model. If the model is deterministic, various mathematical techniques may be applied to find the optimum. These techniques range from the use of elementary calculus for very simple situations to the use of such methods as mathematical search and "hill-climbing" techniques for more complex problems. If the function is subject to one or more constraints, mathematical programming techniques become applicable. (See Springer, Herlihy, and Beggs.) The simplest mathematical programming method is linear programming. This requires both the function to be optimized and each of the constraints to be linear. There are also more advanced mathematical programming techniques, such as integer programming, quadratic programming, etc., and methods which take random variability into consideration.

Simulation Flow Analysis   This form of analysis, which is common in electrical engineering, models a system by assuming that a flow of service passes through processing stations which delay, combine, and divide the flow. The resulting analysis of the system can be evaluated mathematically or numerically at low cost, compared to a full simulation of the same system.

Simulation vs. the Other Techniques   The main advantage of simulation versus most other techniques is its applicability to a wide variety of problems, including some that are too complex to analyze any other way. Essentially all that is needed for the simulation is a statement of the model, a description of the random input variables, and a means of generating random values from these input distributions. The results may be obtained with as high statistical precision as desired by conducting a sufficient number of simulation runs. (In practice, the loss in statistical precision due to the variability introduced by the generation of random numbers is generally much less important than inaccuracies in the model and in the input data.) Also, simulation has the important advantage of high intuitive appeal—that is, it can be readily explained to, and understood by, those with limited mathematical interest and/or background. If need be, a computer program for simulation analysis can generally be developed somewhat more easily by individuals with limited mathematical training than can a program using a more sophisticated statistical approach.

The disadvantage of simulation is that it may sometimes be more expensive than certain other methods. For example, a simulation analysis generally involves higher computation costs than an error analysis for the same problem. However, in many analyses, the computer costs are small relative to the cost of the analyst's time.

Analytical and simulation methods can often be fruitfully applied to complement each other in attacking a particular problem. For instance, analytical methods may yield a check on the results of the simulation for special conditions. Also, analysis may provide additional insights into the behavior pattern to be expected from the system under varying conditions. Conversely, simulation is often used to test proposed analytical models that can serve more economically to represent complex situations.

In summary, then, simulation is used extensively as a technique for decision analysis because of its great generality and high intuitive appeal. For some problems where alternative tools can be used, simulation may be a less economical approach than the alternatives.

SELECTIVE BIBLIOGRAPHY

Simulation has been applied widely, so there is a splendid opportunity to obtain specialized additional insights as follows:

Introductory Material

Hillier, F. S., and G. J. Lieberman, *Introduction to Operations Research*, 2nd. ed. Holden-Day, San Francisco, 1974.

Wagner, H. M., *Principles of Operations Research*, Prentice-Hall, Englewood Cliffs, N.J., 1969.

Primers on Simulation

Barton, R. A., *A Primer on Simulation and Gaming*, Prentice-Hall, Englewood Cliffs, N.J., 1970.

Meier, R. C., W. T. Newell, and H. L. Pazer, *Simulation in Business Economics*, Prentice-Hall, Englewood Cliffs, N.J., 1969.

Smith, J., *Computer Simulation Models*, Hafner, New York, 1968.

Technique

Hammersley, J. M., and D. C. Handscomb, *Monte Carlo Methods*, Methuen, London, 1964.

IBM Corporation, *Analysis of Some Queueing Models in Real-Time Systems*, 2d ed., Armonk, N.Y., 1969.

Mize, J., and J. G. Cox, *Essentials of Simulation*, Prentice-Hall, Englewood Cliffs, N.J., 1968.

Reitman, J., *Computer Simulation Applications*, Wiley, New York, 1971.

Tocher, K. D., *The Art of Simulation*, Van Nostrand, New York, 1963.

Applications

Naylor, T. H., J. L. Balintfy, D. S. Burdick, and K. Chu, *Computer Simulation Techniques*, Wiley, New York, 1969.

Schrieber, A. N. (ed.), *Corporate Simulation Models*, Graduate School of Business Administration, University of Washington, Seattle, 1970.

Industrial Dynamics

The Industrial Dynamics continuous-process simulation model has received wide publicity, and its application to worldwide problems has provoked an extensive literature of enthusiasm and criticism. It is usually implemented via the DYNAMO language (see Pugh, 1963), although many variants and extensions exist. Some variants include stochastic considerations. Forrester's emphasis is on information feedback systems where "the environment leads to a decision that results in action which affects the environment and thereby influences future decisions." A few of many possible citations are:

Forrester, J. W., *Industrial Dynamics*, M.I.T. Press, Cambridge, Mass., 1962.

———, *Urban Dynamics*, M.I.T. Press, Cambridge, Mass., 1969.

———, "Counterintuitive Behavior of Social Systems," *Simulation*, 1971, pp. 61–76.

———, *World Dynamics*, Wright-Allen, Cambridge, Mass., 1971.

Hueckel, G., "A Historical Approach to Future Economic Growth," *Science*, March 14, 1975, pp. 925–931.

Meadows, D. H., et al., *The Limits to Growth*, Potomac Associates – Universe Books, Washington, D.C., 1972.

Pugh, A. L., *DYNAMO User's Manual*, 2d ed., M.I.T. Press, Cambridge, Mass., 1963.

For a more extensive bibliography, see E. R. Johnson, *Simulation and Gaming in Business and Economics in the 1960s: A Bibliography*, College of Business Administration, University of Iowa, Iowa City, 1969.

CITATIONS IN TEXT

Benham, R. D. and G. R. Taylor, *Interactive Simulation Language for Hybrid Computers*, Interactive Mini Systems, Inc., Kennewick, Washington, 1975.

Berger, R. W., "Implementing Decision Analysis on Digital Computers," *The Engineering Economist*, vol. 17, no. 4, p. 241, 1972.

Brennan, R. D., and M. Y. Silberberg, "Two Continuous System Modeling Programs," *IBM Systems Journal*, vol. 6, no. 4, pp. 242–265, 1967.

Clementson, A. T., "Extended Control and Simulation Language," *Computer Journal*, vol. 9, no. 3, pp. 215–220, 1966.

Dahl, O. J., and K. Nygaard, "SIMULA: An ALGOL-Based Simulation Language," *Communications of the ACM*, vol. 9, pp. 671–678, 1968.

Dalkey, N. C., et al., *Studies in the Quality of Life*, Lexington Books, Heath & Co., Indianapolis, Ind., 1972.

DRI, *The MODSIM Reference Manual*, Data Resources, Inc., Lexington, Mass., April 18, 1972.

Duersch, R. R., *Bibliography and Discussion of Business Modeling and Simulation*, Report 73CRD-303, Corporate Research and Development Distribution, General Electric Company, P.O. Box 43, Building 5, Schenectady, N.Y. 12301.

Dutton, J. M., and W. H. Starbuch, *Computer Simulation of Human Behavior* (especially chapter on "The History of Simulation Models"), Wiley, New York, 1971.

Dynamics Associates, *XSIM Reference Manual*, Cambridge, Mass., 1974.

Forrester, J. W., "Industrial Dynamics: A Major Breakthrough for Decision Makers," *Harvard Business Review*, vol. 36, no. 4, pp. 37–66, 1958.

Gould, R. L., "GPSS/360: An Improved General Purpose Simulator," *IBM Systems Journal*, vol. 8, no. 1, pp. 16–27, 1969.

Hahn, G. J., "Sample Sizes for Monte Carlo Simulation," *IEEE Transactions on Systems, Man, and Cybernetics*, vol. SMC-2, no. 5, p. 678, 1972.

———, and S. S. Shapiro, *Statistical Models in Engineering*, Wiley, New York, 1967.

Holzmann, E. G., "Stacker Crane System Simulation," *Proceedings of 1970 Summer Computer Simulation Conference*, Denver, Colo., pp. 400–405.

Kopp, M., H. Lapidot, and G. J. Hahn, "Estimating Plant Wastage Using Simulation and Other Techniques," A.I.Ch.E. 74th National Meeting, 1973.

Korn, G. A., and T. M. Korn, *Electronic Analog Computers*, Prentice-Hall, Englewood Cliffs, N.J., 1956.

Markowitz, H. M., H. W. Karr, and B. Hausner, *SIMSCRIPT: A Simulation Programming Language*, Prentice-Hall, Englewood Cliffs, N.J., 1963.

Pritsker, A. A. B., *The GASP Simulation Language*, Wiley, New York, 1974.

Pritsker, A. A. B., and P. J. Kiviat, *Simulation with GASP II: A FORTRAN-Based Simulation Language*, Prentice-Hall, Englewood Cliffs, N.J., 1969.

Pugh, A. L. (see under "Industrial Dynamics," above).

Reitman, J. (see under "Technique," above).

S.S.I, *Simulation Users Manual*, Social Systems, Inc., Chapel Hill, N.C., 1975.

Soroka, W. W., *Analog Methods in Computation and Simulation*, McGraw-Hill, New York, 1964.

Springer, C. H., R. E. Herlihy, and R. I. Beggs, *Advanced Methods and Models*, vol. 2, *Mathematics for Management Series*, Irwin, Homewood, Ill., 1965.

Warfield, J. N., *Introduction to Electronic Analog Computers*, Prentice-Hall, Englewood Cliffs, N.J., 1959.

Watson, J. M., and H. W. Moore, *ADA70 Users' Manual: Automated Digital Analyzer 1970*, General Electric Technical Information Series No. 70C263.

Part Two

Developing the Overall Systems Configuration

Introduction

WILLIAM F. REILLY, *Assistant, Office of the Chairman, The Diebold Group, Inc., New York, New York*

The development and yearly maintenance of a general system design (GSD) is essential to the operation of a well-run ADP organization. It specifies which computer systems will be developed and implemented to assist management during a particular time period, preferably 3 to 5 years. The GSD provides both a description of *what* functions will be performed by computer systems, and a definition of *how* the functions will be performed. The former are the functional specifications; the latter, the technical system design. The GSD consists of a description of management information requirements, the design of the computer systems which fulfill those requirements, estimates of the costs and benefits of implementation, hardware and personnel requirements, database designs, communications requirements (including telecommunications networks), estimates of the costs and benefits of implementation, and an installation plan. Each of these elements is necessary in order to have a complete GSD.

The GSD has an important position in the overall framework of functions performed by an ADP department. It should result in the development and approval (by management) of a long-range data processing plan. The plan calls for the development and installation of a variety of computer systems designed to meet user needs. Following the approval of the GSD, detailed system design is begun for those systems scheduled for earliest implementation. After the detailed design is reviewed and approved by management, programming, testing, parallel runs, user training, conversion, and installation are performed for each of the systems in the GSD. In summary, the GSD provides the blueprint for all the new system development activity in a data processing organization.

The Diebold research and client experiences have shown that those companies that do not have a GSD have common characteristics. First, their computer systems tend to be developed in isolation from each other. Therefore, they do not have integrated systems which pass important data automatically from one system (and user functional area) to another. This results in a situation where the ADP department has great difficulty in filling user requests for new reports, especially when the new report is intended to contain information collected by more than one system. Second, the ADP department tends to spend most of its time and resources working on minor enhancements to existing systems. (For example, constantly changing basic systems such as payroll, billing, accounts receivable, etc.) This firefighting activity becomes so time-consuming that new system development work drops to a minute fraction of total work performed. As this continues for a number of years, a company falls farther and farther behind its competitors in the development of systems designed to help operating management make better decisions, plan marketing strategies, schedule production, and prepare financial plans. Finally, the company recognizes its ADP deficiencies and goes into a "crash" effort to plan and develop new systems. This is the best approach if there has been a lack of planning but obviously, the longer the company proceeds without a plan, the more expensive and disruptive is the crash effort.

The major problems which ADP organizations will encounter when commencing the development of a GSD are (1) definition of the scope and duration of the effort; (2) training staff members in performing generally unfamiliar activities; and (3) achieving sufficient user-management involvement in the process. Since the project has the goal of providing a long-term plan for computer system development and installation for an entire organization (division, company, etc.), its scope should be as broad as possible. Generally, the entire organization should be included in the fact-finding portions of the project.

Because development of a GSD from scratch is a difficult and expensive task, it will not be done frequently in any organization. Therefore, its scheduled duration should be long enough to perform a thorough fact-finding and analysis job. The duration of the project depends on the size and complexity of the company and its information processing procedures. The Diebold firm has found durations of from 4 to 8 months to be appropriate for a large number of organizations ranging in size from $100 million to $2,000 million in revenue.

Proper selection and training of ADP personnel to participate in the GSD project are essential. Generally, the most experienced systems analysts and project leaders will be required for successful completion of a GSD. The staff members should receive special training, preferably from those already experienced in using the necessary tools and techniques.

Besides receiving training from experienced personnel, the participants in the GSD project should be provided with a set of good data processing principles which they are expected to follow. This assures consistency and increases the quality of the work performed.

The third major problem in developing a long-range data processing plan is getting sufficient user involvement in the process. The results of not getting enough involvement are visible in many companies. An example of one of the worst of the problems which can arise occurred in a large, multi-divisional manufacturing company. This organization has both corporate and divisional ADP organizations. The corporate department prepared a detailed plan for the implementation of new computer-based systems with little or no consultation with divisional management or divisional ADP departments. The plan was approved, and considerable new and sophisticated hardware was purchased. As detailed design and programming proceeded, the corporate department discovered that the volume of transactions which it was required to process could not be handled by the new equipment with its existing software. The ADP personnel proceeded to develop new software packages to try to overcome the problems, but were unable to do so. The basic failure to discuss the plan with the actual users—the divisions—resulted in the design of systems which did not and could not meet the needs of the organization. The plan was neither understood nor approved by the users. It was designed with insufficient knowledge of business plans and implementation problems. Attitudes of corporate ADP and user-management became a problem. The former felt the users did not understand data processing (or their business), and the users believed the corporate department was in an "ivory tower." Finally, the entire project was scrapped. The company spent many millions of dollars with no useful result, and the corporate ADP manager was fired. Later, the corporate department was dissolved.

In summary, lack of user involvement leads to systems being designed in isolation from management. This sometimes results in spectacular disasters such as the example described above. More frequently, it results in systems being designed to reduce clerical work or to accelerate the billing process rather than to help management make decisions; or in ADP resources being spent in aiding functional areas which have little impact on the profit-and-loss statement, rather than those which are critical to a company's success. All these deficiencies can best be avoided by attaining and keeping close cooperation with user-management throughout the system design, development, and installation process—especially when preparing a long-range plan.

The preparation of a cost-benefit analysis is one of the most important phases in the preparation of a long-range data processing plan. It is of major importance among the many criteria used in preparing an implementation schedule for systems included in the GSD. The net savings shown by the analysis, if any, constitute the economic justification, in terms of return on investment, for the direction, growth, level of sophistication, and service capability the ADP department plans to provide to users. If an organization does not prepare a cost-benefit analysis of its proposed implementation plan, it is left without a rational means of determining the best level of resources which should be spent on ADP. The inability to make rational decisions, of course, does not mean that decisions will not be made (or even that they will be made incorrectly). It does mean that ADP resources will be allocated to those users who make the loudest outcry ("squeaky wheel") or to those whom the decision maker chooses to favor. (The decision maker can be the highest ADP executive or a member of operating or corporate management.) Neither of these alternatives is likely to result in the highest return on ADP investment. Management should recognize that the process of allocating ADP resources is analogous to that of preparing capital budgets, and should be subject to the same careful analytical procedures.

In summary, the preparation of a general system design with associated cost-benefit analysis is a key element of every data processing organization's activities. The successful completion of this long-range plan will provide substantial assurance that the users will receive a good return on their ADP investment.

Chapter 1

Organizing and Conducting the Systems-Needs Survey

PRESTON SINKS

Systems Officer, Morgan Guaranty Trust Company
of New York, New York City

The systems-needs survey can vary in scope depending upon the nature of the company and the complexity of the problems being investigated. However, there are certain basic common denominators that hold true for all surveys, and this Chapter is directed to a discussion of these common denominators. For illustrative purposes, the reader should assume that the survey being done is a fairly substantial one in a large commercial business, and that the survey team is composed of one project leader and three or four team members.

STEPS OF A SYSTEMS-NEEDS SURVEY

The following steps of a typical systems-needs survey are discussed in the order in which they should be performed.

1. Establishing the Scope First, someone will initiate the survey. It may be higher management. It may be the head of the Systems Department. It may even be a large computer vendor who has sold the corporate president on a new technology. Be that as it may, the first points that the director of the Systems Department must determine are management's goals and the reason for wanting the survey.

Why does management believe that it wants or needs better systems? Have competitors developed systems that are truly giving them an edge in the marketplace? Is management simply enamored with computers? Have some members of management just attended one of those 1-day pie-in-the-sky seminars on the "everything database" to answer the "everything" inquiry, and now believe that they too must have the latest database management information system? If their reasons are irrational and their goals are impractical, the director of the Systems Department must explain why.

Often the current state of the art simply will not permit the attainment of the lofty heights of systems utopia. On the other hand, management may know that it wants to expand the business and that the existing localized, decentralized, essentially manual systems just will not do. Or it may want to standardize the accounting practices throughout the whole corporate structure, which has expanded rather suddenly in the past few years by the acquisition of many small independent subsidiaries. Or there may be layers and layers of white-collar staffs in various offices throughout the country, and management wants to assess the possibilities of regionalizing or centralizing these staff functions.

Second, the director of the Systems Department must work out agreements on the time duration of the survey, the personnel who will be allocated, and the budget that will be allowed. The agreements may be rough yardsticks, but some guides must be established.

Third, the scope of the survey must be determined. Should it be company-wide? Should it be restricted initially to one division and then, depending upon the findings, broadened later on? Should it be restricted to particular staff functions? Are there any particularly sensitive areas that definitely should not be surveyed?

Fourth, the director of the Systems Department should discuss how much management would be willing to commit to the development of new systems. If the top price for implementing new computer systems is $500,000, then it makes little sense to spend $100,000 on a systems-needs survey. But if management is willing to spend up to $10,000,000 on new systems, then $100,000 for a survey would be reasonable.

Fifth, the director of the Systems Department should mention that the survey team will probably have to have access to salary figures in order to cost out new systems versus existing systems, and that the team will have to have clearance from top management to obtain this information. Salary information can be dynamite, and it pays to lay the groundwork early to pry this information out of the accounting departments.

Sixth, the format of the final report should be discussed. Large companies often have standard operating procedures that will determine this, but smaller companies seldom have such standards. Should the final report be written? Will a flip chart presentation with summary handouts suffice? Also, are interim status reports expected; and if so, what should their frequency be?

Last, all parties should agree on the urgency of the survey vis-à-vis other projects already going on in the Systems Departments, and specifically when the survey should begin.

2. Selecting Members of the Survey Team   Though this step might appear routine and trivial, it is probably the most important step in the entire survey. People determine the end result, and their particular experiences and views will, of course, influence their final recommendations. Obviously, the budget allocated to the project and the availability of uncommitted analysts will also have a bearing on the composition of the team. But if the project is fairly significant, then perhaps some knowledgeable and experienced people should be released from their present projects to work on the survey.

Consultants may be used if the budgets permits. Charges of $30 to $40 per hour are not uncommon in the consulting field. While care must be exercised to keep the scope of consultants' assignments within immediate needs, advantage can be taken of their expertise to point the way to the systems sophistication to which the company may eventually progress. Additionally, they provide competition and challenge to the in-house staff, and thus often serve as catalysts, so that the entire project may end up being done sooner and better because of their presence.

In-house personnel must be selected judiciously. The young, enthusiastic analyst can bring great energy to the project, but often has much to gain and little to lose, career-wise, from the eventual implementation of an involved computer system. Thus such an analyst is likely to favor the most sophisticated on-line, real-time database data management system and the latest version of the most complex operating system just to enhance his or her own personal experience and open-market value. The older analyst, on the other hand, may be so gun-shy from past conversion nightmares and systems failures that he or she no longer has the spark and the imagination to run the survey. Such a person could, however, contribute a wealth of detailed knowledge on how the company functions today.

There is no set of rules for selecting the project leader. Obviously it is wise to choose a person who has demonstrated an ability to handle people and to delegate work. Ideally the leader should have 8 to 10 years of experience in systems and in data processing—preferably in the same industry as the one being surveyed. He or she should be knowledgeable in the state of the art, though not necessarily a super computer technician. The project leader should have a sense of what applications have been installed successfully and which ones have failed and why. Further, he or she should be aware of the systems ramifications and the cost implications of major systems changes. Naturally this person should be capable of writing a final report and presenting the various cost figures in an acceptable accounting manner. Most important, the leader should be able to plan, execute, and control.

Reporting to the leader can be a combination of young, not-too-experienced analysts to do the leg work, and some experienced, seasoned analysts. Generally it is wise to have no one on the team who is older than the project leader, because the older members will be difficult for the project leader to control. The project leader may also have some proven colleagues that he or she will wish to requisition for the project team.

3. Planning the Survey Once the project leader has been designated and the team has been selected, the project leader should develop a work plan for controlling the progress of the survey. As a prelude to writing the work plan, the project leader should become familiar with the organization of the company, or department, or district, or whatever it is that the team is to review. The leader should obtain organization charts from the Personnel Department, together with the names of all the key managers and supervisors, and be briefed on the functions and responsibilities of the various departments. Furthermore, he or she should attempt to sense the "politics" involved, and be forewarned of any characteristically unpleasant managers who may attempt to scuttle the project. The leader should also become familiar with the background of any recent mergers and acquisitions. Bitterness engendered by mergers can smolder for years and cause obstructions to efficiency.

After obtaining this background information, the project leader should make brief tours of representative departments. During these tours he or she should meet the key personnel and observe operations sufficiently to obtain a "feel" for the scope and complexity of the survey. The leader should converse with the key managers and let them brief him or her on their functions. Top management should, of course, alert the various departments that this survey will be occurring and request that all managers and personnel cooperate with the survey team.

After the tours, the project leader should write the initial draft of the work plan. A work plan is really nothing more than a giant "to do" list. The project leader lists the broad categories of work down the page and then fills in the specific tasks under the category titles. A *task* is loosely defined as a logical unit of work of no less than 5 and no more than 40 employee-days. For example, "Review the Accounting Department" might be a category of work, but "Document the Work Flow in the Invoicing Section" could be a task. Across the top of the page, the project leader writes captions for "Estimated Employee-Days," "Scheduled Start Date," "Scheduled End Date," "Actual Start Date," "Actual End Date," "Persons Assigned," "Actual Employee-Days Expended to Date," and "Status." These captions will be written over separate columns; and because many columns will be required, it is wise to use 14-column accounting spread sheets for the work plan. The estimated employee-days and the scheduled start and end dates can also be filled in at this time, but the remaining data will have to be filled in during progress reporting sessions as the survey takes place.

Though the exact contents of a work plan can vary endlessly, a typical systems-needs survey would have to accomplish these broad categories of work:

1. Conduct the departmental overview.
2. Document the existing functions and work flow.
3. Interview higher management for their suggestions.
4. Assess the effectiveness of existing systems and procedures.
5. Compile a list of the most promising systems improvements.
6. Screen the systems improvements with higher management.
7. Set the priorities of the systems alternatives.
8. Compile cost figures of operating the existing systems.
9. Do conceptual systems design of the improved systems.
10. Calculate the development costs of the improved systems.
11. Calculate the operating costs of the improved systems.
12. Calculate the paybacks and rates of return.
13. Develop a plausible implementation schedule.
14. Write a final report for management.

The remainder of this Chapter will deal primarily with the first seven topics on this list, since other topics are covered in other Chapters of this Section.

4. Conducting the Departmental Overview The departmental overview can be accomplished by the project team worker in much the same manner as the project overview was accomplished by the project leader. First the project leader should brief the project worker on the functions, the approximate size, the organization, and the politics (if known) of the department the worker is to review. The project worker should also be told what tasks to perform in the department (e.g., survey all, survey parts, manage a small team, etc.). Then the project worker should be introduced to the departmental managers and supervisors.

During the initial conversations with the departmental managers, the project worker should ask them for a briefing on their operation as well as for an organization chart, a personnel chart, and a list of any special machines (e.g., super bookkeeping machines, computers, calculators, etc.). He or she should let the managers talk freely and at length. They will be better disposed to helping if the survey member is courteous and a good listener.

The managers should be asked to notify their subordinates that the surveyor will be around to see them and to request that the subordinates cooperate. The goals of the project (if not highly secret), the tasks assigned to the project worker, and the target dates should also be discussed. If this is done, the managers can advise the project worker as to what areas are most difficult and where he or she might want to start to use the time to the best advantage. The managers should also be asked if they have personnel available who could aid in the data collection portion of the survey. For example, departmental personnel could be helpful in collecting samples of all the reports used by or produced by the department. The extent of their participation can vary, but should be clearly understood and agreed upon at the outset. Arrangements should also be made for desk space for the project team members and for conference-room space for meetings.

After the initial meetings with the managers, the project worker should be taken on a tour of the department to learn where the various sections are located. If the department is large enough, he or she should be given a floor plan layout. Also, during the tour the managers can introduce the project worker to some of the chief supervisors with whom he or she will be dealing later on.

5. Documenting the Existing Functions and Work Flow There are a number of ways of documenting the existing functions and work flow. Three proven ways are (1) interviewing the key supervisors, (2) sitting with the clerical personnel and actually following the logical work flow, and (3) reviewing any existing procedures manuals and flow charts.

Usually, the project worker will start by conducting individual interviews with key supervisors. Each supervisor should be told why the project leader is there, how long he or she will be around, and what the survey is intended to accomplish. Presumably the supervisors will have been notified ahead of time by the managers that the survey will be occurring. Then the project team worker should ask the supervisor what the section does, when, why, where, how, and how often. Naturally, the project worker should take extensive notes and should collect samples of any forms and reports that are discussed. Each supervisor should be asked for any suggestions for improvements to systems, organization, floor plans, etc. Copies should be requested of any existing procedures manuals, flow charts, volume figures, production reports, organization charts, and staffing schedules. Arrangements should then be made with the supervisor for the project worker to watch the clerks as they perform their daily work.

Following the flow of the daily work and documenting it are, of course, the best ways to learn the existing systems. However, this approach is time-consuming, and the project worker must ration time carefully in order to meet deadlines. The project worker simply starts at the logical beginning and observes the work flow step by step. He or she should make careful notes of what is being done and should collect samples of all forms and reports. The project worker should record the names and the telephone extensions of the various clerks in case it becomes necessary to call them for clarification of points later on.

The usual commonsense questions should be asked, namely: Who does it, when, why, where, how, where does the source data come from, where do the results go, and how often is it done? Questions that the clerks cannot answer should be noted for subsequent resolution with the supervisor. The project worker should also be constantly asking himself or herself whether the current system is sufficient, whether the controls are sufficient, and whether the information is timely. There is absolutely no substitute for thoroughness when doing this type of fieldwork.

In addition to following the work, the team member should collect any work standards and frequency figures that are available. The supervisors may be able to help with this because they may maintain production figures and volume reports for management. Frequency distribution reports showing the number of transactions processed in half-hour intervals can also be helpful. These reports can indicate when the peaks tend to occur and when the slack periods occur. If the area is critical and no norms or frequency distribution figures exist, the project member should request of the project leader that work measurement people be sent into the area to develop some standards. For example, if the area being studied is a typing pool that may be converted to a keypunch group, it would be essential to know the average keystrokes per minute or per hour that the typists are attaining.

If there are existing computer systems, these too must be documented, and some of the departmental programmers or analysts may be pressed into service for this. Typical documentation of a computer system would include:

"Balloons and boxes" flow charts of the runs.

Short narratives of each run.

Record layouts.

Input formats.

Output formats.

Computer configuration and monthly rental costs.

Number of keypunch and verification clerks.

Number of computer operators and shifts.

Number of personnel in input-output control groups.

Computer usage time.

Transaction volume figures.

Report volume figures.

If the department has any existing current procedures manuals and flow charts that are reasonably accurate, the team member should obtain copies of these and digest their contents. Unfortunately, in more companies than not, procedures manuals and flow charts of clerical work steps are nonexistent.

After surveying a particular area, the project team member should return to his or her desk to put the notes into sensible order. The interviews should be written up and notes on the work flow should be drafted into logical, readable procedures. The project worker may wish to augment written procedures with flow charts; however, there are so many different ways to draw flow charts that a flow chart that is clear to one person may be incomprehensible to anyone else. If flow charts are used, the techniques should be standardized throughout the entire project team. These written interviews procedures and flow charts should then be filed in one part of the team member's work papers.

In a second part of the work papers should be filed all documentation relating to existing computer systems.

In a third part, samples of all the reports and forms should be mounted into a scrapbook. Next to each form should be written a short narrative describing who prepares each, who uses it, how often is it produced, and in how many copies.

Fourth should be a section in which are filed all papers relating to production statistics, frequency reports, work standards, etc.

The fifth section should show the departmental organization, the staffing, the floor layout, and any special machines used.

The sixth section should contain all reasonable suggestions for improvement—whether they be the project worker's own ideas or someone else's.

Usually, the project leader will want to review periodically the progress of the project team member to determine where the review stands versus the schedule and to ascertain what the project worker has learned. Typically, the project worker will first report progress and justify accomplishments. The worker should also request more help if he or she is falling behind schedule or if the area of study is proving to be more difficult than was initially visualized. Afterwards, the project worker can give the project leader an oral run-down of what the department does as well as a run-down on the staffing levels, production volumes, schedules, etc. The project leader may wish to review the work papers that the team member has compiled; and it is at this point that well-written procedures will prove their merit. Generally, during these question-and-answer sessions, fuzzy points will be uncovered, and the team member may have to return to the department for more investigation.

The project leader should be quite busy during the early phases of the survey reviewing the work of the three or four assistants, talking to various departmental managers, keeping political fences mended, taking key managers to lunch, etc. He or she should also, rather early in the survey, prod higher management to supply wage, salary, and benefit figures for the areas being surveyed. Preferably the leader should also be given figures showing the growth of the number of employees as well as the average annual increases in compensation over the past few years. These figures will be essential in the later parts of the survey for comparing the costs of continuing the current operations with the projected costs of operating any new proposed systems.

6. Interviewing Higher Management for Suggestions Members of higher management should also be interviewed for their opinions on the systems needs of the company. They will obviously have a broad grasp of the company as well as a historical perspective of how it has grown and where it is headed. (Additionally, some of them who are not interviewed may make trouble later on when the final report is rendered by saying, "I was never consulted.")

For protocol's sake, meetings for this purpose should be arranged by the top operating officer in the area that controls the Systems Department—typically by the financial vice president. The managers should be briefed ahead of time concerning the purpose of the meeting and given a short list of discussion points so they may better prepare their suggestions. The interviews should be kept fairly short—say an hour or two with each top manager and a half day or so with the slightly lower echelon managers. Naturally the project members attending should take careful notes for inclusion in their work papers. A few typical questions that might be discussed include:

- What do you think are the most important systems improvements that should be made in this company?
- What systems improvements might open up new areas for marketing?
- What do you think are the most important systems improvements that could be made in your area of responsibility in this company?
- Are communications between districts and territories sufficient and timely? Can they be improved by better telecommunications networks, or tie lines, or phone systems, or even on-line computer systems?
- Are the information retrieval systems and management reporting systems sufficient?
- Are our customers expressing satisfaction or dissatisfaction with our services?
- Are we planning to open up any new divisions or branches or markets which might cause problems for our existing systems, or which might require the development of new systems?
- Are there any political developments occurring in Washington that may require us to report new and different data that we have never had to report before?

7. Assessing the Effectiveness of Existing Systems and Procedures Now will occur the step where the backgrounds and experiences of the members of the survey team will have a major bearing on subsequent events—namely, the assessment of the effectiveness of existing systems and procedures. As each team member was doing the field work, he or she should have noted areas of deficiency; these plus any suggestions for improvement should have been recorded in the member's work papers. Armed with these points, the team members and the project leader should conduct a series of lengthy brainstorming sessions to discuss the possibilities of improvement. A number of questions could be pursued, varying widely with the type of company and the situation being studied; but for the normal commercial business the following might be typical:

- Is each day's work completed on time without excessive overtime and weekend time?

● Does the work flow from one section to another reasonably on schedule? Are there bottlenecks? How can these be eliminated?

● Has the labor force increased faster than the growth of the business in the past few years? Have labor costs increased faster than productivity per employee-hour?

● Can the work in certain areas be level-loaded? For example, if the bulk of the work arrives at the end of the day, can part of it be held over to the next morning?

● Can labor task forces be set up to be dispatched to departments that are working at peak volumes or that have a high absentee rate on a given day?

● What is the average number of days required to fill an order from the time the salesperson submits the order until the goods are shipped? Has the average time grown worse in the past few months or years?

● Is the inventory under control? Can the warehouse people tell what is on hand? What goods are on order? How much is work-in-process and when will it become finished goods? Are the records accurate?

● Is the company experiencing an ever-increasing quantity of stock outages and back orders? Are there mysterious inventory shrinkages?

● Has the number of customer complaints increased lately?

● Are all items that are shipped billed?

● Are all bills collected? Is there a sound system for following up on open accounts receivable and rebilling periodically?

● Do the open accounts receivable agree with what the customers say they owe us? (The internal and external auditors may have statistics on this.)

● What about order and accounts receivable controls? Are all orders initially logged and monitored and tracked from the time of receipt through shipping and through to the final collection of the bill?

● What is the average number of days required to collect a bill after mailing? Has it grown worse?

● Does the company have a sound, comprehensive sales analysis system which accurately measures the various products being sold, by whom, to whom, and in what territories? If not, why not? If so, do the various sales managers believe that the reports are accurate and useful? What improvements do they want?

● What about the warehouse situation? Are the warehouses optimally located? Are there duplicate facilities in the same cities that could be merged? Are the systems the same in the various warehouses? Can they be standardized with benefit to the parent company?

● Is there a standard cost system in the company? Would such a system give better controls in this type of company?

● Are reports from the existing systems flowing to management on time? Have deadlines been missed more frequently lately?

● Have the users expressed satisfaction or dismay with the existing reports and systems? Have the users repeatedly asked for small changes which never seem to be made to the reports? What improvements have the users suggested?

● Are all purchase orders controlled and monitored until the goods arrive?

● Are competitive bids used for purchases? Who checks up on this procedure?

● Does the company have a system for reporting cash-in-bank balances accurately at day's end in all accounts all over the country? Does financial management know what the company's cash commitments are in the next few days, weeks, and months? Does it know what is left over to invest?

● What systems improvements can be accomplished easily and quickly by conventional approaches such as time and motion studies, forms redesigns, and new floor plans? For example, in a city government agency, four different departments needed the same information, and each department typed its own form. A methods analyst simply designed one 4-part form to be typed once with copies to each of the four departments. The labor and paper savings was calculated at $50,000 per year as a result of this simple forms change. In another case moving the desks around to different locations in the floor space cut down on excessive walking between work stations, and more work was accomplished in the same length of time by the same staff. Obviously these types of changes should be considered as primary candidates for immediate implementation.

● What types of improvements can be made by semiautomation? Can super bookkeeping machines and super calculators be installed? Can semiautomated type-writers driven by paper tapes be utilized to grind out the standard descriptions on forms while the clerks key in the variables? Can power-driven rotary files be used?

• What types of improvements can be made only by full computer automation? Can the company somehow still do the job in a less sophisticated way? Or is the computer at this time, with existing volumes, the best answer?

These brainstorming sessions among the project team can and probably should continue for many days and perhaps even weeks. Many of the questions asked will require statistical answers, and the team members may have to return to the field for more research.

8. Listing the Most Promising Systems Improvements   After many days of brainstorming sessions spent assessing the effectiveness of existing systems, the project team will have to compile a list of the most promising systems improvements.

Initially, they should also identify those defects which are most urgent and can be rectified most quickly with a minimal investment of analyst time. While cost and payback analyses can be useful in making these selections, the project team will be dealing at a less quantified, more intuitive level at this point in time. More fundamental systems questions are at stake. For example, in the 1967 heyday of the stock brokerage business, one profitable brokerage house simply could not balance the cash in the receive and deliver cage. The number of trades had risen too fast and the company system, which was essentially a clerical one with numerous old-fashioned adding machines, simply could not cope with the volume. The urgency of the situation was such that, like it or not, the company had to install a simplistic computer system just to add up and pair off all the cash debit and credit tickets. The system literally saved the company.

Another corporation in a totally different industry had difficulty with sales statistics. This company sold typewriters. Because of all the combinations of colors, type fonts, carriage lengths, keyboard layouts, etc., the clerical force could not compile accurate sales statistics of what was being sold, let alone by whom and where. Furthermore, because of "cannibalizing" of existing typewriters in the warehouses to make up the particular configurations ordered by the customers, management no longer knew exactly what was in stock. Eventually, the company installed a small minicomputer system to keep track of inventory and to produce sales reports.

These two examples are extreme cases where the most pressing needs were fairly obvious. More typically, different departments in the corporation will be vying for the services of the Systems Department to develop their own pet projects. For example, the personnel director will want a personnel information system which, along with the usual administrative information such as employee name and address, department number, employee number, and Social Security number, will have a data bank of employee skills and experiences—all instantly accessible when openings occur that must be filled from within on a crash basis; also, he or she will want it to tell the department head when each employee is due for a salary review.

The production manager perhaps will want a sophisticated production control system with model production scheduling, model explosion, machine loading, inventory control, automatic reordering, open order control, and accounts payable. Again all data should be instantly available by poking a few buttons.

The sales manager will want an accurate and timely sales reporting system that will tell what products are being sold, by whom, when, and where. Furthermore, it should be capable of making comparisons to prior years' equivalent records, and it should report salespersons who are over and under quota. Case example: One very profitable small company had no sales reporting system for many years, but the company made so much money that when the owners divided up the profits at year-end, they went home quite happy and quite rich. Then the company started to grow, and the owners hired salespeople with no stock in the corporation. After a while certain salespersons claimed that they were doing a "land-office" business and were not receiving their just rewards. The owners could not dispute these salespersons because the owners could not measure who their good employees were. Eventually, they installed a sales reporting system so that they could be equitable instead of arbitrary in the distribution of commissions.

Finally, there will be the financial vice presidents and the controllers who will want "the whole world" in management information reports, with all the financial facts and statistics stored on-line in a giant computer instantly accessible by a magic general inquiry language.

How to weigh these demands and settle on the most important ones will require great experience, skill, and diplomacy on the part of the members of the project team, particularly later on when they are defending their final report. But at this point they should apply a few fundamental objective criteria to enable them to list the most promising improvements in some reasonable order. Suggested criteria in priority order are:

1. What existing systems need immediate attention because they are threatening to go out of control? These systems should be attacked first, particularly if the problems can be rectified quickly by conventional systems. The money-proof system mentioned above that was installed in the brokerage house is an example of this type of situation.

2. What is the main business of the corporation? Making widgets? Selling stocks? Warehousing goods? What systems can be installed that will have a positive impact on the main thrust of the business? These systems should be implemented second. A centralized order entry system with warehouse control, invoicing, and accounts receivable would be an example of this type of system for a company that is primarily in the mail-order business. An automated deposit, withdrawal, and balance updating system would be the best candidate for a savings bank.

3. What systems—though neither critical nor essential to the main thrust of the business—could be installed that would result in major labor savings? These should be implemented on the third-priority basis. Payroll systems fall into this classification. Customer billing and accounts receivable systems in the utility industry are additional examples.

4. What potential systems fall into the category of nice-to-have-but-not-essential? These systems should be done last, if at all. Personnel database systems usually fall into this category and often lose out to higher-priority projects. Similarly the "everything" inquiry systems with the "everything databases" for the financial departments are also usually classified in this category.

The project team should weigh every worthwhile systems improvement identified against these four criteria, and they should end up with a list in priority order. Next they should prepare for a screening session with higher management. Generally, two types of visual displays should be prepared: (1) a flip chart listing the tentative improvements in priority order, and (2) a typed handout which describes each systems improvement in a short paragraph or two and which also cites reasons for the priority level assigned by the team. Then the project team should simulate conducting the screening session by bombarding each other with management-oriented questions. Finally, the project leader should schedule the screening session with higher management.

9. Screening the Systems Improvements with Higher Management The list of potential systems improvements, arrayed in tentative priority order, should now be reviewed with higher management. The purpose of the review is to ascertain which of the projects management thinks are most important, roughly how much management is willing to pay for these improvements, and how long it is willing to wait for their completion. When the managers review the long list of alternatives and hear what each of these can do, relative to another, for the business, their perspectives may be quite different from what they indicated in their individual interviews.

Although the project team will not yet have done detailed cost estimates of the development costs of each improvement, based upon their experience they should be able to give rough guides on the time and costs of the different alternatives. Some of these estimates may truly shock management, and the project team should discern this before wasting more time on a particular course of action. The managers may not be able to tell the project team what systems the company needs, but they may very well be able to tell them what the company does not need or "isn't going to have for that price!"

For example, in one survey conducted in an investment firm, all the members of the project team agreed that money management, run on an on-line computer, would be a desirable technique for controlling cash balances of the firm. The concept was that each time a trade was made or a settlement occurred or a cash movement transpired, it would be recorded on an on-line terminal. A central computer would keep track of committed cash by commitment date as well as free cash balances. At any moment throughout the day, the computer could spew forth the total money position of the firm, and this magic ability would give the firm an edge in the money markets.

This concept was suggested to the key partners in the firm; and much to everyone's surprise, the partners said that the system would be of no help to them. They said that, as human beings, they would be unable to react on a second by second basis to their constantly fluctuating cash position and that the deals did not occur that way anyhow. They said that when an attractive financial deal was presented to them, they would recognize that it was attractive; and if they did not then have the money, they could always raise it. True, there might be some supervisors in the cage who could benefit from this current information, but not the investment decision makers of the firm. Hence, the project team scratched that idea off the list.

In another case, a commercial business indicated to an electronics firm that it felt it needed a more comprehensive and accurate quote system for maintaining the prices of the company's products. Preliminary engineering studies were conducted, and finally the electronics firm made its presentation. The presentation seemed to be going well, and the commercial business managers seemed enthused about the exotic features being offered. Then the question of money arose, and the electronics firm cited the costs—$20 million to develop the system. The business managers swallowed hard and replied that $20 million was more than all the combined rentals that the company had paid to computer vendors in the past 10 years. Management firmly declined the proposal, and the whole idea quietly died.

Another benefit of the screening session will be derived from gauging management's reactions to the urgency of implementing the projects that it does want. It may say that it considers all projects to be so important that they should be developed in parallel. The project leader should point out the pitfalls of this approach, which will obviously dictate the formation of a very large systems programming department that, like a building construction labor force, will have to be collapsed after the projects are completed. Alternatively, much of the programming could be subcontracted to software houses, but at higher prices per hour than would be expended if the work were done in-house. On the other hand, management might be willing to wait for many years as the projects are implemented serially. Then the systems programming staff could be relatively small and permanent, and the implementation dollars would probably be lower. The major disadvantage would be the extensive elapsed time until the last project was completed.

As was mentioned before, the purpose of this screening session is to gauge the relative reactions of the managers to the various systems improvements. Some sales ability will undoubtedly be required on the part of the project team; and this will be particularly true in cases where management wants a final management information reporting system, but does not understand why it has to wait for many years until the basic accounting system, which provides and maintains the database, is developed first.

The screening session may be quite lengthy, and more than one may have to be scheduled. After the sessions have been completed and some measure of compromise has been achieved, the project team should retire to fix the priorities of the various alternatives.

10. Setting the Priorities of the Systems Alternatives   After the screening sessions with management, arraying the systems alternatives in priority order will be a relatively straightforward process. The team will simply list them in descending order of priority, using their own judgment in cases where management has expressed no preference.

Once the list has been compiled, the project team will proceed with the subsequent steps in the work plan, which are concerned with doing the conceptual design of new systems, costing the existing and the proposed systems, and writing the final report. These steps are listed as numbers 8 through 14 in the hypothetical work plan outlined earlier in this Chapter. Because these topics are the subject matter of subsequent Chapters in this Section, they will not be discussed at this point. Suffice it to say that the most difficult costs to estimate for the new systems will not be hardware costs or the development costs. The most difficult costs will be the people costs of the clerks that will be required to run the new systems performing jobs for which no counterparts exist today.

SUMMARY

This Chapter has attempted to describe the conduct of a systems-needs survey not just from the "how to do it" point of view, but also from the management point of view. An underlying unwritten theme has been that the company can survive only if it continues to make a profit. Systems analysts and programmers can make a contribution to the corporate well-being as long as they make practical decisions to install practical systems. The fact that a system *can* be computerized does not mean it *should* be computerized. Frequently basic systems needs can be fulfilled better by simple conventional systems changes and not necessarily by installing a sophisticated computer system. The most difficult judgment is to determine when the fine line has been crossed where the simple solution must and should give way to the more costly computer solution.

Chapter 2

Survey and Analysis Techniques

ARNOLD SCHRON, M.S. (O.R.)

Manager, Data Administration, Merrill Lynch, Pierce, Fenner & Smith, Inc., New York, New York; Adjunct Assistant Professor, Computer Application Information Systems Department, The Graduate School of Business, New York University, New York, New York

Survey and analysis techniques deal with three different aspects of facts: (1) fact finding, (2) fact recording, and (3) fact analysis.

FACT FINDING

The identification and collection of facts requires that one get the complete story (accurately and in detail) from the people who know it best, namely, the people who do the work. Those who supervise and direct the work are the best source for information on company policies, organizational statistics, and planning. All facts should be verified as they are recorded. The fact finder should determine in advance which facts are wanted and how they are to be used. This avoids the problem of too many or too few facts in the analysis phase.

Research into background material will yield data on objectives, functions, methods cost, etc. It will also describe how the work and responsibilities are distributed according to official plans. Research will also identify segments the survey is concerned with, and their relationships to other areas in the organization. Report statistics will measure the effectiveness of various operations within the organization and the performance of the total organization (versus stated goals). These data can usually be found in the Budget and/or Accounting Departments.

Personal Observation Personal observation is the only dependable method for measuring the validity of data collected from administrative reports, through interviews, questionnaires, etc. In addition, management is usually more receptive to recommendations based on personal observation. The dangers inherent in personal observations are the following:

If the current volume of work on current operating conditions are not normal, an incorrect diagnosis will result.

The presence of observers may be a disturbing influence on operations, and cause an abnormal work performance.

Personal observations can include the following:

1. *Desk audits.* This activity combines the features of the interview with observation of work in process. It is a valuable technique for determining work-flow details, individual responsibilities, personal knowledge, and accuracy of stated organizational relationships. Be certain that desks being audited are representative. Determine *where* the work comes from, *where* it goes, and *why.*

2. *Following transactions.* Transactions should be followed through each position. Determine frequency for each transaction type, and the procedure for handling exceptions.

3. *Work volume.* Study of work volume should cover a time period large enough to be representative of the normal working environment. The analyst must provide definite instructions of *what* is to be counted, *where* it is to be counted, and detailed *definitions of work units.* A method for checking the accuracy of the count must also be provided. The count must be properly timed in the survey, so the data will be available when needed.

Interviewing   Interviewing is an important method in the fact-finding phase of surveys. It is the only way to secure facts not recorded anywhere except in the mind of the person being interviewed. It gives the analyst an opportunity to judge a person's attitude, way of thinking, and knowledge of the job. The major drawback to the interview technique is that the interviewee may answer the analyst's questions the way he or she believes the interviewer wants them answered, rather than stating true beliefs.

The analyst's preparation for the interview should include careful determination of the kinds of data the analyst wants to elicit. The interviewee should be given advance notice of the subject matter to be discussed so that he or she can prepare adequately. The interview should be limited to fact gathering and recording. Doubtful facts should be checked by asking questions, or repeating information back to the interviewee. The analyst should also check and digest facts from one interview before starting another interview.

Questionnaires   Questionnaires have a special but limited use in the fact-gathering activity. They are used under the following survey conditions:

1. There is insufficient time to interview all the people from whom information is needed.

2. It is the only means of reaching people far removed from the scene of the survey.

3. Time is needed to reference records for detailed answers to questions.

Many weaknesses are inherent in the questionnaire approach to fact gathering. The single major weakness is the respondent's interpretation of the questions. If you have 10 respondents you may receive 10 different interpretations for the same question. In addition, those who have the time and disposition to answer questionnaires are often the least qualified to answer them. Thus a study group which is unbiased statistically may yield a respondent group which is biased (depending on who answers the questionnaires). In general, this technique can be used with some measure of safety to collect quantitative data, i.e., volume statistics on work load, number of forms or other articles used, etc. This method is not practical as a fact-finding medium where narrative work descriptions, opinions, etc., are required.

FACT RECORDING

Fact recording is a corollary to fact finding. The recording of facts can be divided into four distinct methods:

1. Note taking.

2. Completion of special-purpose forms.

3. Collection and notation on related forms, records, charts, etc., as to data, source, and use.

4. Collection of original or copy (duplication) of tables, graphs, charts, etc., containing desired data without regard to format.

Note Taking   Note taking is usually done during interviews and observations. The format of the notes is unimportant, and where possible the notes should be expanded and rewritten as soon as possible after the interview.

Special-Purpose Forms   The captions on special-purpose forms classify collected data. Typical forms are:

- Procedure analysis work sheets.
- Preprinted process charts with symbols for operation, delay, transportation, storage, etc.
- Work distribution charts.
- Work flow notes: task lists.
- Interview with supervisor, section head, etc.

The analyst should record facts in the simplest manner possible consistent with completeness. In addition, the recorded facts must be comprehensible to someone *not* a member of the procedures staff. The information should be classified in such a way that it can be found easily, and related information can be brought together and coordinated.

The arrangement of data in proper relationships, collated and organized for summarization, is simultaneously part of the fact-recording activity and part of the fact-analysis process. The two categories for organizing factual data are:

1. Narrative: Limited to reports and other types of descriptive material.
2. Graphic portrayal: This method tells a story quickly, and can illustrate a procedural story in broader perspective. Many types are available, e.g.:

TITLE		NAME
Collection Control Clerk	TASK DATA SHEET	K. White
DATE 4/20/71		DEPT. Customer Collect

To gather data for preparation of your Task List, you may wish to keep track of things you do, in the columns below. Write the description of your first Task in the morning under item #1. Then mark #1 opposite ALL times you work on item #1. Do the same for #2, #3 etc. as you go through the day. Interruptions: mark A, B, etc. in that column, and describe under "Description". Phone interruptions, show tally marks for each one, opposite the time they occur. In this way you can summarize the DATA at the end of each day, and use as a guide for your TASK LIST.

ITEM NO.	DESCRIPTION	TOTAL TIME	ITEM NO.	DESCRIPTION	TOTAL TIME
1	Process Mail	60	11	Maintain Postage Supply	15
2	Maintain Ind. Accts.	45	12		
3	Maintain Mdse Accts.	75	13		
4	Post Bad Debts Pmts.	—	14		
5	Process Agency Accts.	—	15		
6	Prep. N.Y. Coll. Rte.	75		TOTAL TASK TIMES (1 TO 15) EXCLUDING LUNCH ETC.	
				INTERRUPTIONS	Quant
7	Process Field Colls.	—	A	Phone Calls Re. Collect	2
8	Investigates	30	B	Phone Calls Re. Credit	2
9	Process Applic E B D	150	C	Questions from Employees	2
10	Typing Route Sheets	—	D		

TIME	ITEM NO.	INTERRUPTIONS A	B	C	D	MISC	TIME	ITEM NO.	INTERRUPTIONS A	B	C	D	MISC	TIME	ITEM NO.	INTERRUPTIONS A	B	C	D	MISC
8:00	6						11:00	6				1		2:00	9					
:15	6						:15	6						:15	|					
:30	2		1				:30	6				1		:30	|					
:45	1		1				:45	3						:45	↓					
9:00	1						12:00	3						3:00	Break					
:15	1						:15	3						:15	9					
:30	2						:30	Lunch						:30	1					
:45	8						:45	|						:45	11				1	
10:00	8						1:00	|						4:00	9					
:15	3						:15	↓						:15	|					
:30		Break					:30	2						:30	|					
:45	3						:45	9			1			:45	↓					

Fig. 2-1 Task Data Sheet.

- Procedure charts.
- Process charts.
- Work distribution charts.
- Bar graphs.
- Pie charts.
- Schematic outlines, etc.

FACT ANALYSIS

If the fact-finding and fact-recording phases have been executed properly, the existing organization and its methods can now be analyzed.

The analyst should arrange facts in *proper relationships*, collated and organized for interpretation. Discrepancies or omissions in the facts will be verified at this point. Conclusions and tentative recommendations will be put together by the analyst. This is also the proper time to test or experiment with any doubtful recommendations, before they are submitted to management.

The analyst should consider every technique and worthwhile method he or she knows to identify (in the organized data) clues for needed improvement in the organization being surveyed. The analyst should then develop ideas to implement these improvements, recommend these ideas to management, and promote the solutions to the point of acceptance and adoption. He or she should also discuss with management the necessary controls for the improvements program.

ORGANIZATIONAL UNIT CHARTED Credit and Collection			
EXISTING ORGANIZATION x	DATE 4/26/6[illegible]	NAME J Brown	NAME L Black
RECOMMENDED ORGANIZATION		POSITION Supervisor	POSITION Clerk
CHARTED BY J Brown	APPROVED BY G King	GRADE Section	GRADE Senior

ACTIVITY NUMBER	ACTIVITY (FUNCTION)	HOURS PER WEEK	TASKS	HOURS PER WEEK	TASKS	HOURS PER WEEK
1.	Collection, Current Accounts	63	Investigate Pymt	1	Current Acct Rev.	5
2.	Collection, Closed Accounts	60½	Rev. Incom Mail	1¾	Cl. Accts Rev.	12½
			Investigate Pymt	3	Dictate Letters	5
3.	Bill Distribution	51½				
4.	Credit	29¾	Appliance Svcs	1½	Rev. Non Rev.	5
			Dictate Cr. Letters	5		
			App Cred Non Rev	1¾		
5.	Administration & Training	31¼	Daily Att: Rpts	¼	Lead Clerk	5
			Supervision	15		
			Meetings	1¾		
			work Simplification	3	Job Training	5
			Quality Control	1		
6.	Miscellaneous	27¼	Files & Miscell.	2½		
	INSERT SUB-TOTALS OR TOTALS (MANHOURS)	262½		31½		37½

Fig. 2-2 Work Distribution Chart.

This is the final stage of the survey and analysis activities, and several pitfalls exist which can negate much of the good work done in the previous two steps.

The analyst must discuss facts with personnel in the organization being studied to determine whether or not the facts mean what they seem to mean. A second danger point is the failure to check the facts learned from one source with those learned from a second source, to be certain that they are properly integrated. The final and major pitfall is the analyst's tendency to come to a conclusion too quickly, especially if a pattern solution is applicable.

THE STEP-BY-STEP PROCEDURE

The foregoing has discussed survey and analysis techniques in terms of basic principles. This general description may leave the reader without a specific step-by-step procedure that can be used in survey and analysis work. Accordingly, presented below is one version of the survey and analysis method with suggested forms for data collection.

1. Use a Task List Form Begin your system survey with a *Task Data Sheet* form (Figure 2-1). This form has the following features:

a. It introduces the systems analyst.
b. It is completed by the staff in the areas being surveyed.
c. It gives the staff a chance to assess their own work.

NAME R. Green		NAME R. White		NAME M. Blue		NAME J. Jones		NAME M. Schwartz	
POSITION Coll Acct Clerk		POSITION Coll Acct Clerk		POSITION Coll Acct Clerk		POSITION Coll Chkg Clerk		POSITION Mail Clerk	
GRADE Utility		GRADE Utility		GRADE General		GRADE General		GRADE Service	
TASKS	HOURS PER WEEK	TASKS	HOURS PER WEEK	TASKS	HOURS PER WEEK	TASKS	HOURS PER WEEK	TASKS	HOURS PER WEEK
Process Notices	7	Maint. [illegible] Accts	4	Prep. Field List	1¼				
Process MVA's	3½	" Mts"	3	Filing + Check'g	2				
Arrange MVA's	6½	Prep. Field Wk	5	Check'g Pymts	4				
Review Field Work	6	Rev. Field Wk.	1¼						
Checks Activity	1	Investigate Pyml	12½						
Phone Inquiries	5½	P.O. Pymts	1¾	Closing Bill Notices	8¼				
		Trans. Agency Accts	¾	Final Bill List	1				
		Transfer EBO's	3¼	Bad Debt List	2				
				Collection Agency	6¼				
				Checking Accts	1½				
				Transfer Proposal	2				
				Returned Mail	¾	Returned Mail	¾	Bill Processing	37½
						Operate Postal Eqpt	12½		
						Chkg Deposit T.C.	10		
						Review Deposit	¼		
Stationery Inventory	2	Process Mail Pymt	2½	Return Contingency Memos	¾	Door Box Payments	6½		
		Miscel Typing	2¼	Miscel	2	Miscel	7½		
		Miscel Interrup	1¼						
	37½		37½		37½		37½		37½

    d. It provides the analyst with a quick appraisal of what his or her course of action may be.

    e. It provides information for the development of a *Work Distribution Chart*.

The Task Data Sheet (task list) is a tool for job analysis. It is also very helpful for people who find it difficult to keep track of how the day is spent. People are interrupted frequently by incoming phone calls, or by visitors. Some may change tasks several times during the day. They will find it difficult to keep track of how the day is spent. The form has a timetable in 15-minute intervals. The task is listed under "Description" and given a number. This number is then posted in the timetable part of the form. Interruptions are tallied as they occur. In totaling for the day, the interruptions can be given some nominal value, such as 5 minutes each. Figure 2-1 has a Task Data Sheet form and is completed for the collection control clerk's position.

2. Complete the Work Distribution Chart   Completion of the *Work Distribution Chart* (Figure 2-2) achieves the following:

    a. It summarizes tasks.

    b. It permits immediate review of work distribution and work relationships.

    c. It establishes basic functions:

    • Activities required per function.

    • Systems required per activity.

    • Procedures per system.

    d. It isolates problems for detailed *flow process charting*.

The Work Distribution Chart provides the analyst with a three-dimensional view:

View 1. The Activity column (as a whole), i.e., the *organizational* view. This dimension examines the activities of a department, which can then be compared with the official purpose of that department. Perhaps changing times, decentralization, or the centralizing effect of electronic data processing have made many departmental functions obsolete. Total hours for each activity can be compared with the activity's relative importance to the departmental mission.

View 2. Each Activity, *independently*. Look across the chart, at one activity, independently. Ask of each task: What is the purpose? If it does not fulfill the purpose of the activity, then eliminate the task. If it does seem to fulfill the purpose, ask in what alternative ways it can be done. Compare the cost and reliability of each.

View 3. Each Person, *independently*. Check to see if people are working at tasks below their skills. We want to upgrade skills continually while we downgrade tasks. This will give everyone a maximum chance for regular promotions. A skill inventory might prove useful, particularly for new people in the department. Look for unfair workloading which leads to poor human relations. Try to distribute work evenly within the skill grade and across all deadline work. Be sure that people do not jump from one task to another all day. This results in very little job satisfaction and in deteriorating work morale.

Figure 2-2 shows a Work Distribution Chart completed for a credit and collection department.

3. Complete the Flow Process Chart   The *Flow Process Chart* (Figure 2-3) is designed to achieve the following objectives:

    1. It provides a step-by-step appraisal of work flow, systems, procedures, and volumes. It develops the *why, when, what, where, who,* and *how* of a task.

    2. It gives a primary analysis of a job: Makeready, Do, Put-away.

    3. It identifies and emphasizes undue disparity in the relationships of Makeready, Do, Put-away.

    4. It gives a secondary analysis which shows the *what* of each step through the use of the symbols shown in Figure 2-4. Use of these symbols graphically confirms work flow and problems. It also indicates shortcuts and delays, and gives the analyst a *precise* view of the problem.

The chart can follow either one person or one material. In general the *person* type chart will be useful where the same person carries the action from place to place. This is the case of a maintenance worker, a bank teller, or a messenger. The *material* type chart is recommended where one material carries action from place to place. This would happen in most factory operations on a product, or clerical operations, or some work paper in a procedure. For more than one person or one material, make additional charts.

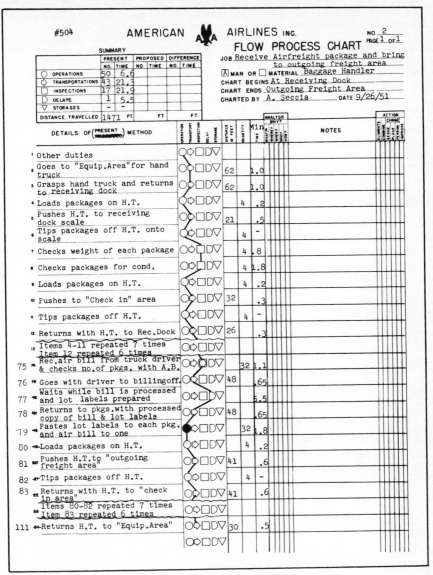

#504 AMERICAN ✈ AIRLINES INC.

FLOW PROCESS CHART   NO. 2 PAGE 1 OF 1

SUMMARY	PRESENT		PROPOSED		DIFFERENCE	
	NO.	TIME	NO.	TIME	NO.	TIME
○ OPERATIONS	50	6.6				
⇨ TRANSPORTATIONS	43	21.3				
□ INSPECTIONS	17	21.9				
D DELAYS	1	5.5				
▽ STORAGES	–	–				
DISTANCE TRAVELLED	1471 FT.		FT.		FT.	

JOB Receive Airfreight package and bring to outgoing freight area
[X] MAN OR [ ] MATERIAL Baggage Handler
CHART BEGINS At Receiving Dock
CHART ENDS Outgoing Freight Area
CHARTED BY A. Seccia   DATE 9/26/51

DETAILS OF (PRESENT) METHOD		DIST. IN FEET	QUANTITY	Min. TIME	NOTES
1	Other duties	○⇨□D▽			
2	Goes to "Equip.Area" for hand truck	○⇨□D▽	62	1.0	
3	Grasps hand truck and returns to receiving dock	○⇨□D▽	62	1.0	
4	Loads packages on H.T.	○⇨□D▽	4	.2	
5	Pushes H.T. to receiving dock scale	○⇨□D▽	21	.5	
6	Tips packages off H.T. onto scale	○⇨□D▽	4	–	
7	Checks weight of each package	○⇨□D▽	4	.8	
8	Checks packages for cond.	○⇨□D▽	4	1.8	
9	Loads packages on H.T.	○⇨□D▽	4	.2	
10	Pushes to "Check in" area	○⇨□D▽	32	.3	
11	Tips packages off H.T.	○⇨□D▽	4	–	
12	Returns with H.T. to Rec.Dock	○⇨□D▽	26	.3	
13	Items 4-11 repeated 7 times Item 12 repeated 6 times	○⇨□D▽			
75	Rec.air bill from truck driver & checks no.of pkgs. with A.B.	○⇨□D▽	32	1.1	
76	Goes with driver to billingoff.	○⇨□D▽	48	.65	
77	Waits while bill is processed and lot labels prepared	○⇨□D▽		5.5	
78	Returns to pkgs.with processed copy of bill & lot labels	○⇨□D▽	48	.65	
79	Pastes lot labels to each pkg. and air bill to one	●⇨□D▽	32	1.8	
80	Loads packages on H.T.	○⇨□D▽	4	.2	
81	Pushes H.T. to "outgoing freight area"	○⇨□D▽	41	.6	
82	Tips packages off H.T.	○⇨□D▽	4	–	
83	Returns with H.T. to "check in area"	○⇨□D▽	41	.6	
	Items 80-82 repeated 7 times Item 83 repeated 6 times	○⇨□D▽			
111	Returns H.T. to "Equip.Area"	○⇨□D▽	30	.5	
		○⇨□D▽			

Fig. 2-3 Sample Flow Process Chart.

Pick a starting point, where the action begins in your department and ends in your own department, unless you work as a member of a team. The chart can then cover the departments within the team.

Fill in the headings at top of the chart. Walk from station to station where each step is performed. Discuss each step with the person on the job. Avoid any criticism, but note any suggestions made by the operator or clerk. If the activity is important, try to estimate an average time for each work station. Count the steps to the next operation and convert into feet traveled.

To visualize the flow, or change of action, from step to step and as an aid to analysis, a *flow line* is traced on the chart. A line is drawn from the bottom of one symbol to the top of the next as shown.

Operations are classified as Makeready or Do or Put-away.   The *Do* operations are those that alter the product, or carry out the function of the process or procedure.   The preparatory steps are called *Makeready*, and the clean up or disposal steps are called *Put-away*.   On the chart, blacken in the symbols for the Do operations so that they can be analyzed first.   If a DO operation is eliminated, we automatically eliminate both the Makeready and the Put-away.

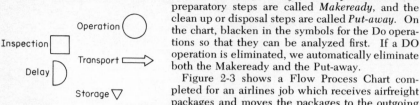

Fig. 2-4   Flow-process symbols.

Figure 2-3 shows a Flow Process Chart completed for an airlines job which receives airfreight packages and moves the packages to the outgoing freight area.

4. Confirm the Work Flows   At this point, the analyst may want to confirm the work flows that have been developed.   Standard confirmation techniques include the following:

a. Actual work count:
   • Provides confirmation of information received.
   • Frequently points up problems which were ignored earlier.
b. Random sampling:
   • Provides a faster method for obtaining trends than does the actual work count.
   • Can be used when data that would provide an actual work count are unavailable.
c. Delay ratio:
   • Simultaneous spot checks at different stages of the work flow to determine ratio of idle to productive time provide useful data.

5. Develop Analysis and Problem Definition   Develop alternative solutions through questioning the data collected in terms of *why*, *when*, *what*, *where*, *who*, and *how*. Test these solutions in terms of:

a. Better systems.
b. Proper work relationship in the distribution of work.
c. Elimination of duplication of effort.
d. Proper time proportions devoted to the true objectives of the area being studied.
e. Improved work flow.
f. Better layout and working conditions.
g. Equipment and facilities.
h. Cost and savings.

This leads to the development stage, where alternatives to the current systems are tested for their effectiveness.   If the tests are successful, the stage is set for the final implementation of the proposed alternatives.

Chapter 3

Planning-Level and Operational-Level Files and Databases

F. E. THOMAS

Partner, Thomas, Friedman & Associates, Rosemont, Illinois

The terms *data* and *base* are highly relevant to the computer system professional when charged with the responsibility of developing an integrated information system. The objective is to take various pieces of data (on-hand, on-order, unit price) and organize them for meaningful and efficient storage, update, and retrieval activity. This means that the data fields need to be classified, associated and related to a file key (part number, policy number, employee number, etc.), to form a record.

Record was consistently used as the term to describe the lowest key unit of associated data that was usually processed "whole" by sorting or indexing through data processing systems of the 1950s and 1960s. However, with the advent of cheaper, randomly accessed disk storage devices, it became apparent that more and more data would be stored in this medium, and that the fields of data would be associated with many more relationships (keys). It then became considerably more complicated and much less obvious which major file should contain which fields of data. To many managements' chagrin, systems personnel under heavy workloads and short deadlines would often take an easy way out. They would simply create another file, thus duplicating some of these data fields in order to complete the program and not have to get into another programmer's jurisdiction. As a result, data-field relationships (records and files) tended to grow without control, and were influenced by factors other than good integrated systems design.

This, then, has become the systems manager's new responsibility—to design records to be put together as an integrated information system. The term *integrated* really means to break the data fields down to the lowest practical common denominator of relationships (a segment of related fields), and then to interrelate these segments. This interrelation function was previously performed by batch sorting the records to a different sequence (key) and then processing them in separate computer programs.

In an integrated database these different sequences (e.g., factory labor tickets related by employee number for payroll calculation, and then by part number for production control and cost reporting) of stored data are developed when the data are updated, and thereupon available to the program at that same time to process either sequence. This capability is necessary for the new-generation systems design that heavily utilizes CRT inquiry, high levels of exception reporting, and on-line updating.

The term *base* then describes these arrangements of other relationships, ranging from a single sequence (payroll master records by employee number) to many (three to six) additional sequential relationships.

The foregoing has only introduced the technical definitions of database terminology. The fact is, however, that these considerations are relatively "pat" compared to the major efforts or expenditures in developing operational- and planning-level systems. The most important considerations, to be further discussed, are:

1. Company organizational lines.
2. Functional application boundaries.
3. Systems organization.
4. Technical complexities.

COMPANY ORGANIZATIONAL LINES

Any information system worth its salt will have as one of its objectives to "cross all organizational lines necessary" in order to interrelate data germane to supporting management decisions. This is much easier said than done! Whenever organization lines are crossed, the size of the educational effort increases disapportionately. Not only do the operational personnel need to understand the effects of the system and their contribution to its success, but the management group needs an even larger dose of education. This is usually necessary to allay fears of a manager about encroachment and lack of control of his or her destiny. Without adequate education, the result is, at best, tacit argument, but unless the incentive of early payoffs is apparent, implementation may be severely affected. To put it another way: For all organization lines the system crosses, the pre-selling/educating/measuring effort pyramids. *The most obvious reason for integrated system failures is the systems technician who designs a degree of integration from the database standpoint that cannot be pulled apart when it finally becomes apparent that the organizational problems cannot be overcome.*

For this reason, if possible, the systems design should be implemented one organizational unit at a time, and each manager's responsibilities and contributions should be clearly measurable. Each industry has its own implementation pattern and modules that become more apparent as a company visits others in its own related field. The review of successful packaged programs can also be of help, since they are normally designed to be implemented in stages.

Many companies are recognizing the need for a new function—database manager. However, the job definition of this function still varies widely. Most large companies have an operating systems software function that has been in existence for some time. The temptation is normally to take one of the technicians out of this group and assign this person the additional function of coordinating all database designs. This can be a serious mistake if the individual does not have the sales ability or political capability to sense organizational conflicts. This person must be able to resolve a plan for the database that is several steps ahead of the ideas of the organizational line managers as well as the systems programmers, in order to reduce the necessity of "downstream" changes. Since database design is not only a function of computer file interrelationship needs, but also very sensitive to traffic volumes through these paths, it is probably much more important for this database manager to have a heavy application background rather than purely technical software experience.

The next 5 years will be the testing ground for the importance of this function, and companies should be aware of leadership experience in their industry. The experienced companies, noted for their leadership up front, can generally be easily recognized by all the "arrows in their backs" and experiences that have not always worked out successfully. But, once on a successful path, they generally manage to stay far ahead of the rest in their industry because of this newly developed experience and maturity.

FUNCTIONAL APPLICATION BOUNDARIES

Almost in spite of the above concern over organizational boundaries, an effort to keep integration and implementation consistent within function should be attempted. Systems design is no different from many other tough decision areas: it is merely a matter of balancing opposing forces. When one application is designed, the follow-on use of the data developed should be expedited as much as possible. A manufacturing example would be an application sequence of a stock status on-hand, open-purchase-order file maintenance, receiving and inspection reporting, and finally accounts payable. Following the previous recommendation, this series would be implemented in steps involving the organizational departments of Inventory Control, Purchasing, and Accounting.

Highly important is the recognition of the human factors involved. For example, the precise habits and influences of accounting personnel are really needed to enforce the accuracy of the on-hand balances in the initial application subsystem. If this initial application is promptly followed by the succeeding control-oriented applications, success of the whole string is likely to be enhanced. On the other hand, if the database design and implementation does not follow through, not only will the first application be in danger, but a database redesign will probably be necessary in order to carry on and "get out of the hole."

At this point, the "art" of database design becomes highly visible. The assurance of on-going flexibility is highly important, but not to the point that the future possibilities are "ground so fine" and the only accomplishment is "planning."

Another application example of staying within functional boundaries when implementing is the order entry, billing, accounts receivable, and sales analysis string of events. This series would likely force the detailed implementation of several inter-related database files: Customer Master, Product Master, Open-Order Detail, Accounts Receivable Detail, and Sales Analysis History. It would also limit the general organizational line involvement to sales and financial, with the manufacturing function utilizing the open-order detail results. The problem, of course, is that this series still involves several departments. If the total series presents a large enough problem, then it should be broken up into steps, but with the following considerations in mind:

Data Processing Expertise Can the systems design work where all files will be tied together initially, or can only a couple be initiated at the beginning? What degree of mechanization is already being performed, and will parallel runs be useful? Will the new application provide more detail than prior to augmentation of this parallel, such as a new open-item accounts receivable vs. the old balance forward method? If so, then certain control summary levels can be used to evaluate the parallel check-out period. If the application is handled in an entirely different way, then in all probability smaller steps and more testing will be required prior to cutover. Some new applications provide different answers because they accomplish results in a completely new and different way. This generally necessitates additional user personnel for educational purposes, and sometimes calls for entirely additional job descriptions and resources.

Does the application require significant new data processing skills, such as the first use of CRT displays or the first on-line update experience? In all cases, this data processing learning curve should not be "taken out on the users," since the user will never understand the complexities of the effort. Very simple, "user-shielded" application uses of these new techniques should be implemented first, wherever practical. If not justifiable, however, then applications with the smallest number of exposed users and those where the highest level of comprehension exists should be selected initially.

User Learning Curve If part of the new application was performed under the old method, then it would be an early candidate for conversion. Also, dry runs without live update can be utilized, such as writing orders for a portion of the day's work without storing the results. The amount of parallel personnel available will dictate how long this can go on until the live cutover is accomplished. Dry runs can be successful in exposing the operators to all the tough exception routines, a few at a time, until volume and speed can pick up. In our example, the downstream departments of Marketing, Accounts Receivable, and Manufacturing can take an implementation "back seat" until the work done on the open-order detail file is completed. However, it does not let them off the hook to participate in the initial overall design effort.

One more important human factor is the need for recognition of one's own environment. Generally, operational users do not easily perceive how an application will actually work until they see their own live data. They do not have the background or generally the interest to comprehend flow charts, printer layouts, or CRT screen layouts; hence a lot of learning will not be accomplished until they actually start to work with the live system. For this reason, systems design should always take place with at least two major steps in mind—initial "bare-bones" essentials, and then user-initiated embellishments. This means database records should be constructed with sufficient space for additional information that invariably will be required. That is why the ability to add additional data to database records easily is so important a consideration in database design. (The requirement will appear anyway, no matter how well the job is done initially.)

The users just do not comprehend the concept that a computer program is a series of instructions that must have a solution for *all* possible events given to it; hence they will want to "roll with the punches." They have normally operated in an environment where they try to cover most of the important situations and will "play it by ear" on those lesser items remaining. Users therefore get impatient with preciseness, and will inevitably fail to think through all aspects completely.

As a result, a lot of time can be wasted by having the systems designer continue to grind out routines for all possible error conditions, and then dump these volumes back on the users. A "sense of significance" has to be developed between the users and their systems counterpart, whereby the exceptions are delineated by an "ABC" strategy or the 80/20 rule (80 per cent of the problems are caused by 20 per cent of the error conditions and should have primary attention). Again, this type of implementation strategy dictates a *growing/learning* approach to application development, and has to be supported by database facilities that operate in the same mode.

In looking at the selected application series again, the maturing, and therefore the believability of the file status of the open-order detail records should be proved in the first steps. The Billing and Accounts Receivable departments then should have the confidence that the input to them from the order entry system has matured. Then, when they begin their own parallels, any errors are generally within their own control. If this procedure is not followed, it is extremely difficult to pinpoint where errors are coming from in a long string of integrated programs. Organizational lines crossed by the series generally erect barriers, making error analysis even more difficult.

In summary, after the general application series is designed and the database is laid out, the most important work has yet to be done—that of carving it up into modules and steps for implementation. Generally, a good rule to follow is that after you have decided on each step, plan one more "back-off step" within each step as a fail-safe point in case you run into trouble. A good database manager will understand the importance of these steps and will have these alternatives thought through sufficiently in order to keep implementation efforts on target.

An obvious result of this near-term and far-term trade-off database design is a continuous process of re-evaluating plans against volume changes and application learning curves. The best, most professional, and most experienced database manager will be able to take the user's learning rates into consideration (on an application basis) and anticipate the major changes necessary. This will enable the manager to absorb near-term deviations within the original implementation design and provide bridging or an easy conversion to a higher functional capability.

The most obvious frustrations foreseen will be in keeping up with the computer vendor's strategy, in that the utilization of the latter's database software will place any company in a highly dependent mode on its vendor. Even so, the old days of "writing one's own" operating systems and sort utility programs ended with the 1960s. Database software is now so complicated that most companies will not write their own any more. Any indication of a significant investment in tailoring or rewriting the vendors' database software should be an immediate warning to the company's management that its Data Processing staff is working on questionable priorities. The more aware managements should be able to sense this, and give the warning signal that Data Processing's efforts are not being placed on good business-type payoff applications for which the data processing investment was initially planned. In other words, they should determine to "make the best of it" within major database/operating systems software offerings available from the vendor.

What Others Are Doing Whenever a significant integrated systems project is embarked upon, there is generally an industry model of the results similar to what the company is attempting to achieve. In some cases, there is an actual successfully installed system in a company often acknowledged as one of the industry leaders. More often, however, there is an ideal or "dream" of an ideal system promoted by computer vendors as an industry-oriented marketing effort. These are almost always designed for "some time in the future" in order to stimulate another round of computer hardware buying. But, when you come right down to the basics, these ideals will eventually have to stand the test of the marketplace, so therefore should be seriously reviewed for developing industry direction. The important thing, however, is that there *is* an ideal objective providing something for all systems and user personnel to study in detail.

This situation has tended to be a boon for the individual systems planner in that most of his or her designs are targeted toward the industry ideal. The problem, though, is that most mature systems designs and objectives tend eventually to look quite similar. The Data Processing staff then tends to look at the techniques and results as if the whole thing were already accomplished. To wit, they tend to overlook the most obvious problem — that everyone is trying to get to the same point, but all are coming from a different position of present implementation. As a result, each company should have an accurate assessment of where it is, how good it is in each area, and where the greatest return is by balancing the learning curve lead time of each step.

This is extremely important when visiting other companies in the same industry. Too often, when visitors who do not completely understand their own systems view someone else's accomplishment, they tend to be impressed by the end results and think that the method of accomplishment is universal. The background and level of expertise of present systems in each company range so widely that these differences become the real "meat" to be gained from visitation. It is through these very valuable comparisons that blind alleys can be avoided and stimulation developed, in order to ensure that "the thing might really work after all."

As more companies develop integrated systems, the one single thing that will tend to become more and more similar will be the basic database design. The arrangement of information, traffic through the files, and levels of summarization will tend to look similar within an industry. User-managers will eventually see that the differences in report formats are minor, and that the structuring of the basic records is the real key to the desired levels of sophistication. Therefore, cross-talk within an industry by systems people should be strongly fostered for the next several formative years. As a result of these efforts, a master database plan can become the common denominator of, first, systems, and then user communication. This will result in a greater understanding and determination of actual implementation steps practical for each company's unique situation.

SYSTEMS ORGANIZATION

Just as there are many requirements and ways to organize a company's management, there are similar variations in the Data Processing Department's requirements. This Chapter does not discuss the organizational structure of the Data Processing Department, but it covers a very important new function beginning to show up in medium and large firms — the Database Manager.

Only over the last year or two has this function become important enough to give it the recognition and genuine title, but we may expect it to expand much more rapidly in the next 5 years. It is important to note that the function is not yet widely established, but is growing in importance, i.e., firms are just sensing the need. Even when the need becomes apparent, the beginning responsibility is generally limited, and not earth-shaking in scope. As a result, the function is often handled like a fish out of water, i.e., "Where should it be reporting as it grows in stature?" This attitude is not inappropriate, because until any new function or title earns its keep and departmental respect, it should report only as high as it can be successfully managed. Therefore, with a limited, more technically oriented charter initially, the database manager should report to a technically oriented management level. As the responsibilities broaden and take on a more policy-oriented nature, the level of reporting should heighten, maybe even to the extent of moving outside the Data Processing Department, and taking up the company's entire function of "Organization of Data."

In any case, the steps that might be taken in sequence by this function in terms of formal reporting (see numbers on the possible Data Processing Department Functional Organization Chart, Figure 3-1), are as follows:

Computer Operations (1)   Most medium and large companies have (it is hoped) grown out of a tape-oriented into a random-access disk storage environment as the price-performance ratio has improved.   The customary database management function used to be accomplished rather straightforwardly by the tape librarian.   The programmer would label and call out tape files as required, per processing run.   The operations manager would normally schedule these runs, and thus was in the best position to know where all the files were used and on what schedule they were required.   As these tape

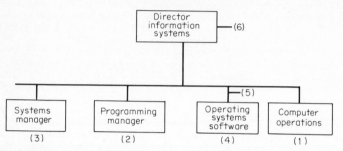

Fig. 3-1   Sequence of possible formal reporting arrangements for the database manager.

files were gradually converted to disk and integrated through rather simple linkages, the operations manager still had the basic run-control problem of which files to use per program job stream.

The operations manager is probably still the most logical person to whom the newly created database manager should first report.   This would not shake up the whole organization and threaten other functions within the department, and the new function might not even be called by its ultimate title.   There is one great danger, however, in that the database manager is likely to come from a purely technical background and not be up to the total job later, in its full development of responsibility and corporate stature.

Program Manager (2)   The second level of involvement begins when the programmers see the need for education and guidance on the programming interfaces to the new database software packages.   Since these vendor-furnished program products are quite complex, a big load of database self-education and further programmer education is necessary.   At this time the programming manager is most likely to relate closest to the management responsibility required, because the database manager now looks like a superspecialist programmer inside the Programming Department.   Again, the title Database Manager might not be officially used, and the person would function more as a lead programmer with special database responsibilities.

Systems Manager (3)   As the full significance of the database manager's position finally becomes recognized—requiring (*a*) a good grasp of where the company is heading from a computer applications standpoint, and (*b*) a sensitivity to current and potential traffic volume through the database—there comes a full realization of the expertise requirements.   Here is where an improper, technically oriented personnel selection previously made would show up.   It now becomes apparent that the database manager has to be able to comprehend all the major applications to be integrated, and most importantly, must evaluate initial learning curve volumes through their eventual maturity.   He or she will have to develop a plan to change database formats, linkages, and access techniques as the applications grow in complexity and volume.   In larger companies, this level may be the initial entry point for this function, but with an upward look toward the potential corporate "political" problems to be encountered.

Operating Systems Software (4)   In large companies with an established operating systems software staff that normally works with O/S, RJE, CRT, switching, etc., the database package program from the vendor may be so technically complicated that the database manager function might initially fit with the software group.   This helps integrate the database software into the learning process with all the other systems software, and give the Data Processing Department personnel a "leg up" on the learning expertise prior to exposing themselves to a user's implementation schedule. In large, on-line terminal update shops, this degree of coordination with Systems Software is highly desirable if not downright mandatory.

Head of Operating Systems Software (5) The next step, however, comes when the individual selected for the database manager function on the merits of potential application and corporate political expertise constantly sees the broader picture and can therefore evaluate the trade-offs in a businesslike way. When this happens, the individual is the likely candidate to manage the Operating Systems Software Department, except that this person may now have higher nontechnical visions of his or her true responsibility to the company's development.

Ultimate Level (6) At this point, it becomes apparent that the database manager is in the best position to dictate who (what organizational department) is responsible for creation, update, and maintenance of each data element in the entire system. He or she then has to negotiate run-time schedules and cutoff, as some files have to be updated prior to other file cutoffs (back to his or her beginning in the Operations Department); determine the application use of on-line CRT interference with batch updating; and decide whether the files should be decentralized as a distributive database, etc. In other words, the database manager really becomes a technical/application/organizational aide (or challenge) to the director of information systems.

The point of this whole discussion is that this function will most likely grow faster than any individual can, and that several expertises at different times and budget levels may actually be required. It promises to be one of the most interesting and challenging job descriptions yet to hit the data processing industry, and will require the entire latter half of the 1970s to mature.

TECHNICAL COMPLEXITIES

As stated initially, the technical considerations of a database structure are rather "pat." It may be stated (even though most data processing professionals at this time will not be in complete agreement, on the point) that most companies during the remainder of the 1970s will be constrained to utilizing a relatively limited selection of vendor-furnished software programs. The obvious reason for this is that computer manufacturers are now in the process of integrating their hardware, operating systems software/firmware, and database software into a single-package strategy. This means that the average customer company will not be able, let alone inclined for resource reasons, to write its own variations. Therefore, when a company's hardware vendor is selected, the vendor's database software offerings will likely constitute most of the reasonable alternatives. To be sure, independent software houses will always be a factor, but as hardware and operating systems change, the customer will be even more vulnerable to "marketing strategy obsolescence."

The basic architecture of database software is very closely dependent on the computer systems hardware and operating system; therefore the resources and lead-time advantage to coordinate changes falls highly in favor of the manufacturer over outside software houses. Bridging techniques to aid these conversions are very important to the customer company that has heavily invested in its own application programming. For this reason, companies will realize more and more how heavily they are becoming "locked in" to their vendors—a condition that will be due not to hardware or operating system compatability, but more likely to the database features. This will come as a rude awakening for most data processing personnel, who are accustomed to the present freedom of picking and choosing database software for specific applications. They will now have to consider a much broader horizon, and consider including more esoteric features in their earlier learning curve time frames.

This will include the immediate involvement with backup and recovery systems overhead, on-line terminal support, remote job entry, concurrent updating of the same data from more than one program or CPU, CPU downtime recover capability, and "failsoft" considerations. The downtime and recovery problems will precipitate the most important decisions required of data processing personnel in a long time. As more data are updated in an on-line mode, and therefore, more and more of the company's operating records are required for hour-to-hour decisions, the vulnerability to down-time (of any type) increases.

Decentralized Databases For a long time to come, the reliability of a single huge system as the sole source of processing will be risky. There will, therefore, be a significant trend to "distribute" databases to other CPUs and operating systems whenever practical. This trend will probably be the most important to multiplant, multiapplication users over the next 5 to 7 years. The cost of telephone transmission of all detailed transactions will also foster this cycle, in that it is still relatively too expensive to transmit all the transaction detail. At present, with slow telephone transmission rates, telephone transmission is still an underpowered way of feeding the large centralized CPU. It is generally more reasonable to update a smaller database at the remote location and then batch transmit the summarized information periodically to the central CPU.

This decentralized "distributive" database presents a whole new set of challenges and opportunities. In most cases, for each industry, it is relatively obvious where the databases should be split, i.e., decentralized. The number of print lines of output, detail transaction of input, database capacity residual in the local CPU to edit detail input transactions, and expense and reliability of telephone transmission are all key items that determine the split. Here is where the vendor's support strategy is so important—the degree and level of supported interface software available. Since vendors are just developing this area, it is now imperative that the customer closely monitor the progress and commitments made.

The type of distributive support presently available, even if it is only the commonality of languages supported, may well be the key to how database jobs are carved up into implementable steps. Often the remote database that is initially determined as practical may be designed to coincide with the steps of implementation. This also reduces interference with testing, and reduces the esoterics of the application to the main "skin-and-bones" of the user's needs. It also may reduce the programming language sophistication requirement—e.g., COBOL vs. RPG (report program generator)—reduce the telecommunication expertise required, and provide for more effective decentralized corporate management, since the remote manager can exercise control over his or her own destiny.

This last point is the one most often overlooked when plans are made to centralize and standardize corporate data processing support. In most cases, the remote manager feels a lack of control over his or her own system's operation, and if "those guys at corporate" promise to do it all, the remote manager will be likely to give up too much involvement. This initially leads to misunderstandings, and planning may fall down, defeating the purpose of decentralization in the first place.

When dealing in a decentralized mode, the role of the database manager becomes much more critical and political. He or she can easily be held responsible for standardization and conformity at the level of interface while dealing with batched summarized records. The tricky part, however, is keeping in touch with the detail-level records on the basis of expectation of recentralizing them at some time in the future. Here the database manager is much more likely to run into resource problems due to the lack of vendor's software support compatible at the remote level. This situation will improve as the state of the art develops and the esoterics of the large system support filters down to the smaller remote-type hardware and software support.

Another major design consideration of a centralized/decentralized database is the hierarchical levels of summarized information. Of course, the higher the level of summarization, the less record volume produced. This provides a database usable for higher-management-level analysis and reporting, and therefore, possibly one that is less rigorously formatted. Instead of repetative-type reporting cycles, a host of query-type program languages will probably be developed. These make it easier to set up one-time programs to process this high-level summarized data. (Sometimes the executive can personally handle the report generating programming.)

The significant advantage, however, of a well-designed database system would be to provide the capability to go down to lower depths of detail whenever required. If this can all be accomplished within the same database system, then the top-level cut-and-try cycles with the summarized data can be processed through many, many iterations until a close relative fit of the results is apparent. Then the final assumptive result can be further processed against the full level of detail, also tied efficiently into the same database system. This will have a resounding effect when it can also be easily accomplished through a physically decentralized set of files and CPUs.

Bridging Techniques   Various *bridging* techniques are now becoming available whereby old-style languages and databases are made compatible with newer systems, but most importantly, in the new system's format. This means that old programs can still be processed (without significant degradation, it is hoped) against their old database records which are actually formatted and controlled by the new database software. All new programs, however, can be written in native mode under the new software control. This protects the major investment that the customer has in the original system, but gives the customer the full advantage of all the newly supported features. For this reason, any company that goes too far on its own without fully assessing these new bridge conversions is likely to forfeit the advantages of newer support, as well as suffer a continuing burden of converting its own code later anyway. These bridges will probably be furnished for cross-vendor conversion as well, but most vendors will invest heavily within their own line first, before going after competitive markets.

Security   As this vendor database software matures, undoubtedly outside software firms will offer modular enhancements, especially query-retrieval-type high-level languages. This will then open up a new problem — that of security of the information in the files. Since many databases will be on-line, terminal-oriented, on a dial-up basis, this could mean that a clever outsider could call up your system and inquire into your database if this outsider knew your operation.

Because many query software systems could be in use on top of the database program, the security of the total systems will have to reside in either the operating systems or the database software. Since this function is more closely tied into the structuring of the database calls and instructions, it will probably become an increasingly important feature of database software. This function not only is required for outside control, but is just as important inside the company. The classic issue of everyone getting into confidential payroll records is only one aspect. The most important aspect is the various file protection techniques that can prevent testing being done on one file from accidentally wiping out another file. As these features become available, more and more companies will take advantage of them and eventually consider them as a minimal requirement of any database support.

CONCLUSION

As can be seen from this Chapter's emphasis, the subject of planning-level and operational-level databases involves problems similar to that of shooting at a moving target. There will be a severe challenge to data processing professionals to provide continuing support to their users without committing their companies to inordinate and unnecessary conversion efforts later. This will be a highly dynamic subject for the remainder of the 1970s.

Chapter 4

Criteria for Basic Systems Decisions

F. M. HEINZMANN

Vice President, Computer Sciences, Eastern Airlines, Inc.,
Miami, Florida

The analytical description and affinitive understanding of the potential area of automation are fundamental foundations to a viable system. The systems designer must be sure the system solution embraces the problem—rather than a problem adjusted to a preconceived system solution.

Once the overall problem definition has been developed, the systems planners must embark upon a program of balancing the user's needs and desires against the economics of change. The objective of such a program is to produce a refined description of a system which will provide the greatest benefit to the business enterprise as a whole. A corollary objective is to develop quantitative tools that will enable management to predict with an acceptable level of confidence the effect of implementing the system and to measure its actual effects after implementation.

Since the evaluation and refinement process is, of itself, an expensive undertaking, a truly *optimum* systems design, even if achievable, is seldom justifiable. Instead, the systems planners must execute a finite and sometimes quite limited number of iterative approximations to the optimum design. In the course of those iterations, numerous basic systems decisions must be made. Frequently, the decision must be made in the face of considerable uncertainty.

The intent of this Chapter is to identify the common basic systems decisions and to recommend criteria for decision making. While references are made to numerous analytical tools, and a few are defined for purposes of illustration, this work is not offered as a "cookbook" approach to decision making. Rather, it is hoped that the reader will upon completion be better equipped to develop sound decision criteria of his or her own.

PRELIMINARY JUSTIFICATION

The process of preliminary justification often begins with an educated guess on the part of management that the benefits of an automated system outweigh its cost. Although the system's users may know generally what they want, their wants are predicated on the assumption that the system will prove to be cost-effective. The responsibility of the systems planners is to apprise management as early as possible of cost effectiveness and to identify changes which can increase cost effectiveness. This can be accomplished through proper use of preliminary costing.

No system can properly be costed until an overall systems description has been developed. Certain cost judgments must be made at a very early stage. The nature of the dilemma facing the systems planners at this point can best be summed up by the rhetorical question: "Does the probability of this system's becoming a cost-effective system in operation justify the development and evaluation effort necessary to determine this system's probability of becoming a cost-effective system?"

The question obviously leads in a circle. If the wrong answer is given to the question, then a beneficial system is scrapped before it gets off of the drawing board, or resources are wasted on an unprofitable system. Obtaining the answer to this question is the purpose of a feasibility study.

After the overall systems description has been developed, costing can take place with minimal reliance on intuition, best estimates, or judgments. This is not to say that the system should be costed out to the last penny. To do so would probably be a wasted effort since the costs will be used to determine if the overall systems description should be redefined. All the major costs, however, should be identified and examined in some detail.

Identifying Major Costs The following paragraphs identify some of the areas where major costs may be found. The list is not complete, as each system will have its own unique costs; however, all systems should be analyzed for at least these major cost items.

Hardware acquisition costs are usually one of the major cost items in automated systems. Although the subject of hardware planning is beyond the scope of this Chapter, it should be mentioned that cost estimates should reflect the provision for sufficient hardware to support testing, training, and maintenance activities in addition to the normal system operation.

Use of existing hardware presents special problems to those attempting to price a system. If the capacity of the existing and planned hardware is great enough to accommodate the new system without displacing or degrading any existing or planned systems, a fully allocated cost of hardware resources should be employed. Remember that preliminary justification is not developed for cost-accounting purposes, but is intended solely to predict the profit effect of the proposed system.

Associated with hardware acquisition costs are *hardware maintenance costs*. These maintenance costs usually represent a significant portion of the total hardware costs when extended over the life of a system.

The overall systems description will imply a number of costs relating to *personnel.* Under the heading of one-time personnel costs are: systems design and evaluation, management and supervision (of the development team), program development, database creation, acceptance testing, training, and facilities modification.

It should never be assumed that there will be no *software development costs* when software is being purchased from an outside vendor or is being supplied by the hardware vendor. Even the most versatile and comprehensive software packages may require some modification to meet a unique set of circumstances. This is especially so if the new software must interface with existing software.

Under the heading of *continuing personnel costs* are: management and supervision, operating personnel, program maintenance, and database maintenance. Operating personnel includes computer operators, keypunch operators, clerical support, and any additional personnel *including those in the user-department* required to support the day-to-day operation of the system.

Some of the other areas where major costs might be found are: communications lines, real estate, physical plant facilities, forms, and supplies.

Allocation of Costs The well-known "Pareto's Law," that 20 per cent of the effort produces 80 per cent of the benefits while it takes 80 per cent of the effort to achieve the final 20 per cent of benefit, is valid to a great degree for most automated systems. Therefore, it will often be helpful to allocate systems costs into several distinct implementation phases, with each phase representing a successively higher level of sophistication. Even when there is no intent actually to implement the system in phases, viewing it in this manner helps the planners make value judgments on its various components. Since this method of costing is merely being used as a guideline to re-evaluate the systems description, it is not to say that two or more phases may not actually be implemented on the same date.

When applicable, costs should also be allocated by geographic areas. This is because the location showing the greatest benefit might also have a prohibitive cost due to length of communications lines or other factors.

Systems costs may also be allocated by function, since most systems consist of several major functions. In order to determine the strong points and weak points of the system, an attempt should be made to determine the cost of each major function.

Before allocating the cost of the system by any of the methods mentioned above, it should be established that the expected *benefits* can be allocated on the same basis as costs. Otherwise, it will be difficult to re-evaluate the overall systems description on a cost-benefit basis.

After the several sets of cost figures have been developed (by implementation phase, geographic area, and function), some preliminary tests may be made to determine economic feasibility of the total system and of each of its components. Techniques for determining economic feasibility by return-on-investment analysis and identification of intangible benefits are discussed elsewhere in this Chapter. It frequently happens in these preliminary stages that not all costs can be estimated with satisfactory precision. A "worst case–best case" approach can be used in this situation. Caution should be used with this approach, since the result may be almost meaningless if too many of the component costs are expressed in terms of worst-best case.

Refining the Systems Description After costs and benefits have been allocated, the overall systems description can be refined with an eye toward increasing cost effectiveness. The obvious course of action is to attempt to eliminate those components of the system not having a favorable cost-to-benefit relationship. This, however, is only one-half of the re-evaluation phase. The cost figures should also be used to determine if the scope of the system can be expanded to provide greater benefits. Components of the system having a highly favorable cost-to-benefit relationship should be analyzed to determine what factors make them have a high yield. Patterns may emerge which point the only way for justifiable expansion of the system.

For example, consider a real-time system that is to serve a number of nationwide branch offices from one central computer. The overall systems description may have specified that only the larger branch offices were to be automated, since they represent the greatest apparent potential for cost reduction. An examination of the geographically allocated costs of the proposed system may reveal that the size of a branch office is not as important as proximity to the central computer.

Identifying components of the system that should be eliminated because of an unfavorable cost-to-benefit relationship can be a fairly straightforward process. There are, however, a number of other factors to be considered before reducing the scope of the overall systems description.

The systems planners must be alert for the existence of synergistic relationships between the various cost components—i.e., whether the whole is greater than the sum of its parts. Any given component may not prove to be economically justified on its own merits; however, it may be critical to the successful operation of the system. If a particular function or geographic area is to be eliminated, assurance must exist that the database still can be maintained with integrity and that the system can perform as intended. The elimination of one or more components of a system may require exception coding and exceptions to procedures. Such provision for exceptions can prove to be so expensive that it is sometimes better to accept certain "unjustified" system components in order to maximize the cost effectiveness of the entire system.

If it is decided to eliminate a component of a system because of an unsatisfactory cost-to-benefit relationship, then the costs of other elements may undergo a change. This will be the case when central-site costs have been allocated to geographical or functional areas. These costs must be reallocated and the affected components re-evaluated. If elements in a communications network are eliminated, then, of course, the network must be reconfigured and the affected system components re-evaluated.

The overall cost effectiveness of a system may be improved in some cases by expanding the user's functional description to include additional related applications.

For instance, the user may have defined an air cargo information system without requesting automated printing of waybills (possibly because the user *assumed* this function to be economically unjustifiable). The systems planner, in the course of analyzing the system components, may discover that another justifiable component will create a database from which waybills can be generated for little or no incremental cost. If the addition of this unrequested function will improve the cost-to-benefit ratio of the total system, it certainly should be recommended.

Sometimes a tendency on the part of systems planners under user pressure is to slip some of the economically unfeasible elements in on the coattails of the more profitable elements of the system. The purported logic behind doing this is that no harm is done as long as the total system is economically feasible. This is faulty logic. No component of a system should be accepted unless the benefits (real or intangible) justify its cost. The purpose of preliminary justification is not only to determine if a system is economically feasible, but also to ensure that the ultimate scope of the system is no more and no less than the most cost-effective system attainable.

EVALUATION OF INTANGIBLES

Having satisfactorily identified and quantified new costs to be incurred for equipment, personnel, and facilities, and having done the same for existing costs to be displaced if the proposed system is implemented, there remain to be examined other areas of potential gain or loss.

A term frequently used in reference to areas of potential gain is *intangible benefits*. This term is somewhat deficient in that it not only ignores potential loss, but also connotes a lack of reality or measurability.

Most so-called intangible factors are classified as such for one or more of the following reasons:

1. A demonstrable cause-and-effect relationship to the proposed system has not been established.

2. There is no known *direct* measure of the factor which can be expressed in dollars.

3. Estimates of the future behavior of the factor are believed to have very poor precision.

The quantity of resources to be devoted to examination of these areas will be influenced by a variety of factors. The initial tendency will be to provide for only cursory examination when the ratio of new cost to old cost appears highly favorable. If this tendency prevails, the user will, at best, run substantial risk of failing to realize achievable benefits or, at worst, implement a system having a real cost substantially greater than the value realized.

Identification of Items for Evaluation   The list of questions in Table 4-1 is intended to stimulate thought leading to identification of areas a system user might decide to investigate for intangibles. The list should be viewed as suggestive rather than comprehensive. The key point is to establish recognition of the fact that any system of appreciable size is likely to create many corollary benefits, and possibly some adverse effects.

Decision whether to evaluate will be assisted by obtaining judgmental rough estimates of value. Following ranking of values, initial appraisal of resources required for refining estimates may be used to adjust the rankings, to select items to be evaluated, and to allocate resources for evaluation effort.

The iterative nature of the processes employed in developing a basic system design is evident in the inference readily drawn from the foregoing. The information fed back to systems designers from the evaluation processes will obviously affect design decisions, normally to the degree suggested by the relative net values.

A valuable benefit derived from the evaluation process is the educational effect on all participants. Previously obscure relationships come into sharper focus. Communication and understanding (team consciousness) are provided stimuli for growth.

In developing methods for portrayal of the so-called intangibles, it is highly desirable that the principal yardsticks employed to forecast system results have the following characteristics:

1. Durable business health index.

2. Endorsed by executives of user-departments.
3. Endorsed by postimplementation evaluation authority.

Each industry, each company, and each department within a company are likely to have a set of performance indexes developed over many years, and viewed as reliable measures of the health of the business. Such performance indicators are most useful for a variety of reasons, directly related to the *authority, responsibility*, and *accountability* vested in the various executives.

The first listed characteristic—*durable business health index*—implies an ability to apply an acceptable standard of measurement over a time period beginning not later than initiation of system development, and continuing well beyond stabilization of operation of the system implemented. A vehicle is thus afforded for measuring the quality of the forecast of results to be achieved.

The second characteristic—*endorsed by executives of user-departments*—provides a basis for commitment. An automated data processing system does not operate in a vacuum. Its contribution to the health of the business is dependent upon many extraneous factors in the operating environment. Many of these factors are subject to control by the departmental executives. Thus, an executive commitment to the achievement of specific goals through system implementation can exert a beneficial influence on system design decisions and on the results achieved during system operation.

TABLE 4-1   Suggested Areas of Search for Intangibles

PERSONNEL

User-employees:
  Will the system improve or hinder important lines of interpersonal communication?
  Will employees using the system identify it as a help or a hindrance in performance of their daily job?
  Will the new job environment increase or decrease the potential for labor relations problems?
  Will the system increase or decrease the employee's sense of involvement in and contribution to the success of the company? To his or her personal success?
Nonuser-employees:
  Will employees in related jobs be affected and, if so, will their reaction be favorable or unfavorable?
  Will the quantity of employees and their locations and work procedures be affected? If so, what adjustments will be necessary and what costs or benefits will be entailed?

CUSTOMER SERVICE

Will customers be affected favorably or unfavorably at time of sales or service contact? Will there be favorable or unfavorable effect on delivery of product or service?
What will be the effect on quality of product or service?

MARKETING

Will the new system provide advertising advantage?
Will the system enhance ability to deploy sales forces more effectively?
What is the marketability of the system itself?
Will the sales and service advantages increase our share of the market?
What is likely to be the effect on marketability of our product if the system is *not* implemented?

FINANCE

Will financial controls be improved?
What is the expected effect on capital requirements, cash flow, insurance, taxes, etc.?

COMPUTER SYSTEMS

What is the effect on other computer systems requiring exchange of data with the new system?
Will the new system provide a base for expanding into other applications?

PLANNING

Will the new system provide data not previously available or affordable for research and planning?
What is the relationship between the plans for this system and other plans currently contemplated or being developed?
Are the units of measure and definition of terms employed in the new system compatible with those employed in analytic processes?
Do the assumptions made in the system prospectus agree with your view of the future?

The third characteristic—*endorsed by postimplementation evaluation authority*—is intended to operate much as an acceptance by a referee, before the game, of the rules of play. Failure to develop specific plans for postimplementation evaluation renders highly questionable the expenditure of the substantial resources required for identification and quantification of decision criteria. The prophet whose predictions are not subsequently tested against actual events has reduced incentive to remain honest. The principal objective is the definition and acceptance of measures adaptable to conversion to units of monetary value—the best available common denominator.

Evaluation Techniques   There is no mystique surrounding evaluation of results to be achieved through implementation of an automated data processing system that does not also surround evaluation of results to be achieved through other endeavors.

When the anticipated result lies, for example, in the area of changes in morale, one should look to the personnel specialist's bag. However arcane they may appear to the data processing specialist, the evaluation techniques employed by the professional trained in the specific area are likely to be those generally acknowledged as the best available. The most significant contribution the data processing specialist is likely to make is the proffer of computerized aids to computation, simulation, and analysis.

The rule best held inviolable is explicitly to identify qualitative evaluation as such and to identify the evaluating authority. When appropriate, range of values should be given along with the rationale used in establishing the limits of the range. Many different techniques for the ranking and weighted scoring of attributes have been published. Sharpe describes a typical matrix manipulation technique, but hastens to add that "weighting schemes must be used with considerable care."[1]

In the final analysis, a "worst case–best case" evaluation, coupled with a positive, measurable commitment by the appropriate managers, is probably the most reliable method. Effective managers, unlike the poor workers, seldom blame their tools. Instead, having committed to a goal, they will make every effort to achieve it, frequently offering constructive recommendations for the improvement of their tools.

THE INCREMENTS OF CHANGE

When the automatic data processing function was initiated, there must have been an economic justification process. This justification, in all probability, was based on the total benefit to be derived from the automation of certain application systems. The benefit or payback is the difference between the cost of operating the previous systems (maybe manual), and the cost of the new systems (automated). When all the applications included in the original plan have been implemented and the expected benefits have been achieved, the ADP function can be regarded as a unit that contributes to the profitability of the corporation.

How then do we proceed when a new application is to be added to the existing ADP function? How do we justify it? How do we proceed when, during the development of a system, opportunities are presented to add new procedures to the already existing overall system plan? In either case, the principles of differential or incremental profit analysis should be used.

Incremental Costs and Benefits   In costing a system, each application must bear its share of expense according to its usage of the various human, machine, or material resources.

Cost estimating has already been described as an iterative process during the development of the system. As design criteria change or external influences modify the environment, the cost-estimating process is repeated until the system description is finalized.

Justification, on the other hand, deals with an entirely different situation. Since existing costs have already been accounted for, we are now asking what are the additional (incremental) costs that must be incurred to implement a new system. Justification cannot be entirely separated from the area of priorities. Once part of the corporate information system is automated, the decision is not merely what to automate next, but which one of many opportunities should come first.

For example, an airline, having developed a passenger reservation system as part

[1] William F. Sharpe, *The Economics of Computers*, Columbia University Press, New York, 1969.

of an overall plan to automate the passenger processing function, sees an opportunity to enhance its service to the passenger by incorporating the facility to handle hotel reservations for passengers in their destination cities. The costs that must be considered are only those associated with the addition of this capability. In the case of the example cited, it would be necessary to obtain answers to such questions as:

- Are additional ADP or user-personnel needed?
- What is the cost of programming to incorporate additional segments in the existing reservations software structure?
- Will it be necessary to make any hardware additions or changes?
- Will there be additional communications needs?
- Will there be additional building requirements?

For purpose of justification, only such incremental costs must be borne by the new function. If the expected profit increment exceeds the total incremental cost, the new function is economically justified.

In a broader sense, whenever change occurs, the cost and benefits associated with that change are incremental. Dean identifies incremental costs as "the additional costs of a change in the level or nature of activity."[2] Incremental costs include costs that are usually classified as fixed or semifixed, and differ from marginal costs which relate to a single kind of increment and ignore fixed costs. For example, increasing the number of seats in an aircraft would incur marginal costs, while adding a new flight to a schedule would result in incremental costs.

A new application to be developed and implemented will create a need for a large number of questions to be answered. The answers, and the decisions which result from those answers, will determine the incremental impact of the new application on the entire organization. For example, an existing computer installation processing data for a variety of users bears certain fixed costs, such as building and equipment rental, utilities, etc. To add a new application will increase the machine processing load, but unless the system performance is unacceptably degraded, the new application will not add to the fixed costs.

If the computing system is nearing an overload condition, the new application should be analyzed to determine how it will add to the computing system load. As a result of the analysis, it should be apparent where the critical load will be. If the overload is on the input side, then consideration must be given to the addition of a card reader, front end computer, multiplexers, or channels to provide relief. If the problem is in throughput, adding core or increasing the number of regions might solve it. If the load is on the CPU, going to a more powerful computing system may provide the additional capability that is needed to run the application when it is developed. Whatever decision is made to provide the expanded capability, the incremental cost should be borne by the new application. Where such hardware increments are already planned to keep pace with normal business growth, however, the new application need only justify the cost of acquiring the additional hardware earlier and, perhaps, amortizing it over a shorter useful life.

Large incremental changes in hardware will frequently have the dual effect of improving the processing performance of existing systems and providing additional capacity for future ones. On the other hand, the incremental loading of new systems on an already heavily loaded hardware configuration may impair the justification of systems that follow.

The usual method for justifying the cost of developing a new application, addition to hardware/software, or a new report in a system compares the cost to the benefits to be expected. In the machine-accounting and early computer era, these benefits were usually displaced persons. Each new application was expected to stand alone, and its value was measured by its ability to reduce headcount in the user area or absorb increasing volumes of input without adding more people.

As more and more functional areas of the company are supported by ADP systems, there is a need to develop higher-level integrated systems, and the benefits to be derived from these are less visible. Tangible benefits like reduction in personnel, reducing inventory costs, or faster order processing will usually justify the costs of design, construction, and implementation of a system, but the creation, for example,

---

[2] Joel Dean, *Managerial Economics*, Prentice-Hall, Englewood Cliffs, N.J., 1951.

of a database which is the single authoritative source for data concerning aircraft movement and passenger and cargo loads may be justified only by the intangible benefits of better control, standardization of reporting, or quality of editing and auditing. Yet, it is in this direction that ADP is moving because of the need to provide increasingly relevant data to management.

Schwartz points out that an automated accounts receivable system not only provides reduced costs of operation and improved speeds in the billing process, but "perhaps more importantly, it can be the first step towards automating information flow that will help improve corporate cash management." He further argues that although it is difficult to quantify in advance the payoff of such projects that enhance the financial manager's capability, it is clear that an improved cash management information system can become a very profitable possibility after implementation of other financial transactions processing.[3] In other words, the size of the incremental change needed to design, construct, and implement a management information system may be considerably reduced if the results of already automated systems can be integrated into a database.

System Increments: The Phased Plan There are several very good reasons for developing a system in phases or increments. Perhaps the most important is that the impact of change on the user is spread over a longer time span while some of the benefits can be realized early.

The initial phase of an application might be undertaken to provide "hands-on" experience for the user, so that user-personnel are better prepared to work with the complete system when finally installed. This is particularly true in those applications where the data entry point is transferred to the user area, as in on-line and real-time systems.

Another important consideration is the length of the development cycle. The size of each phase should be tailored to the specific needs of the user, but the user should begin to see some useful results within 12 to 18 months, or there may be a loss of interest on the user's part.

A lack of available resources may also cause a system to be developed in several phases. Unforeseen changes in priority can cause diversion of some of the systems development team, with a result that the development cycle is extended. Again, the problem of how long a user will wait to receive useful output must be measured against higher-priority tasks, and the overall systems development plan should show a consistent commitment from both the user and the ADP group.

It should be quite evident that a detailed ADP master plan for application development is an extremely valuable asset which permits evaluation of the full impact of change, not only in terms of the system being scheduled next for implementation, but also on future systems. In some instances, large incremental changes could be justified by several systems planned for consecutive development. It is clearly unwise to consider such changes without having an ADP master plan against which to measure the full impact.

COST TRADE-OFFS

Identifying Potential Cost Overruns In the later stages of the development of the overall systems description, the level of detail with which the analysts are working should enable them to uncover potential problem areas which could lead to cost overruns.

Cost overruns result from many different causes, but the most common are (1) permitting significant changes to be made to the systems specifications during systems construction, and (2) poor estimating because of a lack of experience on the part of the estimator. Other causes of cost overruns include:

- Systems implementation taking place during months when there is a high incidence of absenteeism or other unusually heavy demands on involved personnel.
- Changes in personnel, particularly the project manager, during the systems construction stage, causing a loss of momentum and continuity.

[3] M. H. Schwartz, "Computer Project Selection in the Business Enterprise," *Journal of Accounting*, April, 1969.

• Using the systems construction stage to provide on-the-job training for less experienced programmers.

• Poor project management.

• Conflicting corporate priorities which may cause valuable personnel to be switched to a higher-priority task.

• Lack of complete and mutual understanding between the user and the ADP group of what the system must do.

Analyzing Trade-offs   Once the potential for cost overrun is discovered, it is necessary to take corrective action by planning to avoid the overrun or at least to minimize its impact. To do this requires analysis of the choices or trade-offs.

The three choices that are available involve time, cost, and quality. It is generally safe to expect that any change to one of these three elements will have a corresponding effect on the other two.

The Make-or-Buy Decision. More frequently corporations are buying software, both application and systems software, rather than developing their own in-house. This is a good example of balancing the time and cost to develop against the benefit of earlier implementation. Of course, the quality of the software, in terms of how easily it can be installed in a specific environment, may suffer.

This make-or-buy decision may be made at any time during the systems construction stage, but should never be made before the overall systems description has been completed. Only then can it be determined how well the vendor's software will fit the needs and how much modification to the purchased software will be required. Also to be considered is who will make those modifications. If it is the vendor, there will usually be an additional charge, and if it is to be done by the buyer's own ADP group, the time and the cost of the programming resources to make the modifications may erode the benefits that justified the decision to buy.

The ideal time to decide whether to make or buy is, of course, before systems construction begins. However, changes in corporate needs resulting from increased volumes, acquisition, or mergers may make it necessary to consider the value of having the capability now, versus the cost involved in jettisoning a systems construction activity in which millions of dollars may have been invested. In such a trade-off, sunk costs should not be considered. The trade-off is strictly between the cost of acquisiton and the incremental cost to complete the in-house system.

For general-purpose software, such as database management, information retrieval, and report writers, the trade-off decision is easier to make because few companies have the programming resources to dedicate to the development of such software. The salability of such products after development should be considered, however, since it is usually possible to recover some, if not all, of the development costs over a period of time.

Trading Quality for Time. Many constraints on the systems design, construction, or implementation will have been identified during the systems-needs survey. All those constraints force decisions to be made which usually involve trade-offs.

In order to satisfy a user demand for a particularly stringent implementation date, for example, it may be necessary to sacrifice the quality of the system initially installed. This may reduce the cost of the initially implemented product, but subsequent modification to produce the desired quality may be more costly. Alternatively, if the required date can be met by adding more people to the systems development team, then a cost increase would occur. Analysis of the incremental cost required to meet the due date versus the cost of missing it would determine whether a cost overrun would be justified.

Prototype Systems. If the time and the application permit a prototype system to be developed on a small scale, it is very much easier to detect possible cost overruns, but again the trade-off in cost and time has to be measured against the value of being able to control the possible cost overrun. Such an approach has merit in that it may well provide a rapid, if not completely satisfactory response to the user's need.

An additional benefit which can be derived from the use of a pilot or prototype system is that it provides the user with a working model, permitting some experimentation with the system. This proves to be very helpful if the user has not had previous experience with ADP, for it provides training for the user's people and gives greater assurance that the system ultimately installed will satisfy clearly understood and defined needs.

This type of system can be developed by the use of commercially available file management systems or by the use of time-sharing.

Trading Cost for Quality. A frequent cause of cost overruns is the desire to create a "quality" system. This overrun may be caused by the programmer who is allowed to indulge in "cosmetic" programming, or by the user who insists on adding unjustified frills during the systems construction effort. The primary measure of the quality of a system is its acceptability to the user. This should never be sacrificed without a complete analysis of all other possible trade-offs and full concurrence of the user. Other measures of quality which may have trade-off potential are *resilience, operability, performance,* and *salability.*

The resilience of a system, that is, its ability to continue to support the information needs of the user for which it was developed, despite changes in volumes, other systems, or user-management, is a major determinant of the system life. It is often worth a cost overrun to achieve this kind of quality in a system. This is particularly true when the ADP group is faced with the enormous costs associated with conversion to new hardware. The vendor will usually provide the software to emulate the hardware that is being replaced; however, an inefficient system running on current equipment will be more inefficient in a new computer. The longer a system can be run, even under emulation, the greater the payback from the original investment. Of course, the costs associated with maintaining the integrity of the system may become excessive, in which case a rewrite or redesign may be justified, but the quality of systems design is a major factor.

Quality in design is also reflected by the way the system runs. During systems testing, the operations team has an opportunity actually to work with the job procedures, and can often suggest ways of improving them. Excessive tape handling and mounting of "private" disks add to the time it takes to process the data in the system. While the systems designer is usually conscious of the need to minimize the possibility of overruns of the nonrecurring developmental costs, the recurring costs to operate the system can be overlooked. Without proper awareness and concern, the cost overrun can exist for the life of the system.

Systems performance is particularly concerned with recurring costs. The increasing use of higher-level languages has reduced the complexity of programming and made it easier to implement new systems. The continuing reduction in the cost of memory has lessened concern for application program efficiency, and these are valid trade-offs. However, inefficient programs will continue to be inefficient and add to the run time unless reworked. The reworking may take place much later in a system's life, but careful supervision of the techniques in use by programmers can eliminate the need for these additional costs to be incurred.

In most industries, there are certain major applications for which each member company shares a need. Reservations systems in the airline industry, refinery processing optimization and tanker scheduling in the petroleum industry, and demand deposit and mortgage loan accounting in banking are some examples. A generalized, but high-quality system for providing this application support can often have a high market value. In fact, many companies have recovered significant amounts of their original development cost by outright sale, leasing, or selling service to other member companies of their industry. The majority of business-oriented applications, when developed to satisfy the needs of a specific company, are not easily adapted to satisfy the needs of another, but subsystems can often be marketed. The salability usually depends on the quality of the product and its ease of adaptability to another corporate environment. If there appears to be a market for the system after it is developed, then it may be a worthwhile trade-off to build in more generalized procedures, better performance, and operability, even at the cost of overruns in dollars.

ANALYTICAL METHODS

The various cost considerations identified in the preceding pages can be analyzed by a variety of methods. The tools and techniques available to the systems planning and design team include the traditional ones associated with cost accounting, and some newer techniques.

Traditional Techniques   The traditional financial tools include marginal analysis, return-on-investment analysis, using either average rate of return or net present value methods, differential profit analysis, and break-even analysis. *The Accountants' Cost Handbook*, edited by Prof. Robert I. Dickey of the University of Illinois, describes these methods in great detail.[4]

Return-on-Investment Analysis.   ROI is a very widely used tool, one which has been used successfully to justify the expenditure of corporate funds. It specifically identifies the profitability of a corporate venture, and provides a standard against which performance can be measured. For these reasons, it is an appropriate tool to use in justifying the expenditure of ADP and user effort to design and implement large applications. Steiner states that "used with caution, and used wisely, there are few more useful tools for planning and judging results." He further points out, however, that it is not without shortcomings. Technical progress, morale, stability, and growth are among factors which may be more governing, on occasion, than ROI.[5]

Differential Profit Analysis.   This technique is used to assist decision making when there are alternative choices. *The Accountant's Cost Handbook* describes this method as being the most useful since it shows the fundamental causes of profit and of loss under actual or hypothetical circumstances. The concept of differential profit analysis includes marginal analysis, which considers only the variable costs associated with a change.

Break-even Analysis.   This is a simple but effective method for identifying the point in time when the payback will exceed the cost of development. It is an extremely useful tool when faced with the "emulate-or-convert" decision.

Cost-Benefit or Cost-Effectiveness Analysis.   This is a frequently used technique for measuring the cost of an alternative course of action against the benefit to be derived from taking that course of action.[6] Although similar in concepts to differential profit Analysis, the cost-benefit approach makes it easier to deal with relationships where the full extent of the decision cannot be measured in dollars alone. When faced with alternative choices, such as frequently happens in the early stages of developing the overall systems plan, this technique is particularly suitable for use.

Cost-benefit analysis is usually applied to evaluate hardware or software. The most common form is benchmark testing in which one or more computing systems manufacturers run the same problem or problems, as specified by the buyer, on the vendor's recommended configuration.

Similar benchmark testing can be conducted with software vendors, but as Sharpe states in *The Economics of Computers*, "the imposition of any sort of rigid measure of performance and/or requirement for performance is almost certain to lead to less-than-optimal result." He further states that given the "time, resources and interest," a subjective selection procedure is preferable provided "the selection is in the hands of unbiased and thoroughly knowledgeable individuals."[7]

Weighted Scoring.   In this technique, nonquantifiable factors, such as vendor reliability and support, general programming support, and data management, are subjectively rated with respect to each significant attribute. In weighted scoring, cost is used as a weighting factor, but normally is not allowed to dominate to the exclusion of other significant considerations. Weighted scoring is particularly useful in the reiterative processes of design and evaluation, because it allows so-called intangible considerations to be included in the development of overall systems justification.

Planning for Postimplementation Evaluation   A very important decision criterion too often overlooked in the early stages of systems design is the establishment of a post-implementation evaluation procedure. Such a procedure, agreed to in advance by the user, the ADP department, and top management, can play two vital roles in the development and operation of the system. Obviously, it provides management with a yardstick and a unit of measure for after-the-fact monitoring of the system's effectiveness. Not so obvious, however, is the role this criterion can play during the design, evaluation, and development phases.

[4] Robert I. Dickey (ed.), *The Accountants' Cost Handbook*, Ronald, New York, 1960.
[5] George A. Steiner, *Top Management Planning*, Macmillan, New York, 1969.
[6] Steiner, op. cit., p. 412.
[7] Sharpe, *op. cit.*

A simple, unambiguous standard for evaluation can serve as a constant beacon, reminding the systems planners of the tangible objectives of the system. Certainly, the ultimate objective of any system is to improve corporate profitability. During the re-iterative design phases, however, planners and programmers can more easily identify with this complex objective if it is stated in terms of *how* the system is expected to improve profitability.

For example, SYSTEM ONE, Eastern Airlines' automated reservations and passenger service system, was originally justified on the basis of reducing the total reservations cost per passenger. Since personnel represented the greatest variable (and displaceable) cost component, the system's objective was translated into a management

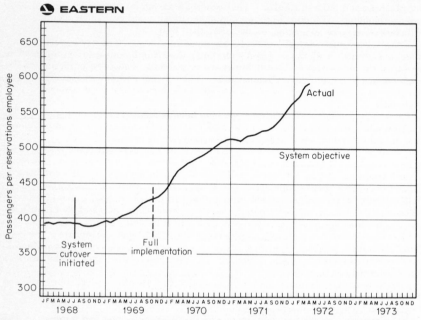

Fig. 4-1   **Performance of Eastern Airlines' reservation agents before, during, and following implementation of SYSTEM ONE* automated reservation and passenger service system.** An objective was to raise the ratio of passengers boarding per reservations employee to 500. Prior to the system implementation, the actual ratio was relatively constant at 390. The ratio improved steadily during and after implementation, surpassing the objective one year after full implementation. (*°Service mark of Eastern Airlines.*)

commitment to increase the ratio of passengers boarded to reservations employees. Throughout the long, complex development process, many routine trade-off decisions were made easier by applying this simple criterion. Figure 4-1 depicts this technique in graphic form, as it is used today by Eastern management as a measure of the system's continued effectiveness.

There is no doubt about the need to have both a costing system from the very inception of an ADP operation as well as a justification system to complement it. The costing system will indicate the distribution of ADP operating expenses by the various applications, and the justification system will indicate the payback from each one of them. Together they will produce a sort of profit and loss statement for ADP. At some point in the life of an ADP installation, usually in periods of economic recession, senior management may question the profitability of computers. By that time, original justifications are often forgotten, and this tool would be very useful to present a convincing case for ADP. Certainly, it might be easier for management to measure the performance of the ADP group more effectively.

Management too often seizes on per cent computer utilization as an easy and immediate way to measure the effectiveness of the ADP installation. However, as Rau points out, this line of reasoning, followed to its logical conclusion, could place a premium on inefficiency.[8]

Rau recommends measuring system performance by applying the simple equation:

$$\frac{R_1}{R_2} = M$$

where M = a measure of performance

R_1 = the ratio of total benefits to total costs for the system as it exists today.

R_2 = the ratio of the sum of current benefits and potential benefits to the sum of current costs and additional costs required to provide the potential benefits.

A "perfect" system would earn a value of unity for M. A value of 0.5 would indicate the system is operating at only half its potential effectiveness.

Another way of measuring cost effectiveness of ADP is to develop a series of cost ratios for each system or group of systems, such as: cost per company employee for payroll, cost of reservations per passenger boarded, cost of handling inventory per 1,000 aircraft flying hours, etc. Obviously, these costs must include not only ADP costs, but also equivalent user costs. If these ratios are historically constant or on the decrease, then there is an incontrovertible proof that the ADP function continues being profitable.

Estimating System Life One of the decisions that must be made during the cost-estimating process is, "How long will the system operate?" This estimate must be made in order to determine the ultimate payback. The true life of a system cannot be predicted easily, because a system is composed of many subsystems, each with its own probable true life and each affected by different influences. The *hardware subsystem*, for instance, is subject to the forces of physical and technical obsolescence, but may have a real life in the range of 6 years. The *software subsystem* often has a somewhat shorter life when viewed as a relatively temporary set of procedures subject to continuous refinement and amplification. The *information subsystem* described by a carefully developed system definition may have the longest life of all, since it defines the functional objectives and can transcend several generations of hardware and software. Brandon points out that "in general, a system should be designed and built to allow recovery of the planning costs (design, programming, conversion, parallel operation, testing and the like). Since the planning costs for all applications appear to exceed, in most organizations, the purchase cost of the equipment, the planning amortization period usually exceeds the breakeven period on equipment acquisition."[9]

It is probably safe to assume that the life of an average system, when all factors are considered, is in the range of 3 to 5 years; however, there are other influences which may extend its life significantly.

For justification purposes, management frequently requires a payback period considerably shorter than the probable true life of a system. Such a policy assists in the ordering or prioritizing of opportunities for automation by establishing a threshhold for acceptability.

The pilot or prototype system approach could have an important bearing on the ultimate life of a system, since the user has the opportunity to change the system specifications in a "live" environment. There is an advantage also if the prototype can be run in a decentralized mode during its shakedown period, allowing the user even more freedom to play with the system specifications in a "what if" mode. The finalized system that results from this approach should be very efficient and should satisfy the user's needs for many years.

The resilience and flexibility of a system have a direct relationship to its effective life, but other factors may cause the life of a system to be shortened unexpectedly. Two of the many possible causes for a system to be discontinued or replaced are *improper systems definition* and *changes in user-management*. Improper definition usually results from the lack of clearly understood system functional requirements or performance criteria. Unionization of user-personnel, disagreements developing with unions subsequent to implementation, major changes in corporate management or

---

[8] Paul Rau, "Evaluating the EDP Function," *Datamation*, September, 1972.

[9] Dick H. Brandon, "Computer Acquisition Method Analysis," *Datamation*, September, 1972.

policies, and shifts in emphasis on major products all may have a direct impact on the estimated life of a system and, therefore, on the expected payback. Changes in functional responsibilities in the user area can result in the loss of the system's sponsor.

Bear in mind that while corporate organization and the assignment of functional responsibilities may change from time to time, the basic functional responsibilities themselves rarely change. The best automated systems are designed to perform a *function* rather than merely to automate the current procedures of a particular organizational entity.

A final caution: Beware of the "personality cult" whose propensity to hip-shooting —an art practiced by some users, data processors, and EDP salespeople—involves drawing quickly, firing into a blank wall, painting a circle around the hole, and proclaiming "bull's-eye."

A simple summary of six words to ask and to answer are: *why, what, where, who, when, how?*

SELECTIVE BIBLIOGRAPHY

Blumenthal, Sherman C., *Management Information Systems: A Framework for Planning and Development*, Prentice-Hall, Englewood Cliffs, N.J., 1969.

Hare, Van Court, Jr., *Systems Analysis: A Diagnostic Approach*, Harcourt, Brace & World, New York, 1967.

Martin, James, *Design of Real-Time Computer Systems*, Prentice-Hall, Englewood Cliffs, N.J., 1967.

Rau, Paul, "Evaluating the EDP Function," *Datamation*, September, 1972.

Schwartz, M. H., "Computer Project Selection in the Business Enterprise," *Journal of Accounting*, April, 1969.

Sharpe, William F., *The Economics of Computers*, Columbia University Press, New York, 1969.

Steiner, George A., *Top Management Planning*, Macmillan, New York, 1969.

Yourdon, Edward, *Design of On-Line Computer Systems*, Prentice-Hall, Englewood Cliffs, N.J., 1972.

Part Three

Detailed Systems Design

Introduction

WILLIAM F. REILLY,   *Assistant, Office of the Chairman, The Diebold Group, Inc., New York, New York*

In a modern large-scale ADP operation, the detailed systems designer may be supported in his or her work by a variety of staff functions. The programming languages may have been standardized, documentation policies formalized, database content defined, and the hardware configurations stabilized. It is hoped the systems designer will have the guidance of a general systems design that is part of a long-range plan of development for the ADP function.

If this state of affairs exists, the designer of a major system will find the task somewhat easier, or at least beset by fewer pitfalls. However, regardless of such supports, it is the responsibility of the systems designer to come up with a system that will satisfy the needs of the user and will operate effectively, accurately, and dependably under the conditions that exist in the user's particular environment.

The systems designer is, in truth, the pivot between the user, the programmer, and the ADP staff services. It is this person's function to translate the features of the general systems design into terms of the user's detailed operating needs, and to do this in such specific terms that the computer programs can be effectively written and tested. To accomplish this, the systems designer, in one way or another, will have to perform the following functions:

Starting with the features of the general systems design, the systems designer will (or should) work closely with the user to firm up the functional characteristics of the system. What will it do? How will it do it? When? How often?

From this point, still working with the user, the systems designer defines the external inputs, the desired outputs, and the system logic. Such basics as the content and frequency of action documents, print-out of management information reports, need for human interaction with the computer, audit trails, controls, and validity checks are thrashed out. Decision rules and equations for any mathematical decision aids are also developed at this time.

More or less concurrently, the systems designer is developing the file content definition and file organization data. If working in an environment with an established, well-organized database, the systems designer need only confirm the presence of the necessary data and their location in the overall file structure. As is more often the case, the system will involve the establishment of new files as part of a projected integrated database. Under these circumstances, the systems designer will coordinate his or her plans with the data management specialist or other central authority to assure uniform treatment. At this time, any questions of confidentiality of data or of file security are worked out.

Up to this point, the systems designer has not had enough information to confirm the viability of the detailed system as it has evolved from the general systems design. File content and data volumes can now be accurately estimated and related to known capacities of files and processing equipment. Decisions can then be made as to hardware availability or needs. In-house processing, remote job entry, commercial time-sharing, or other alternatives can be evaluated. If uncertainty regarding hardware capability or system performance exists, pilot operations or simulations can be planned. Although programming specifications have not yet been developed, it is possible to make decisions as to the most appropriate programming language to be used, special considerations involving the operating system of the computer, and the practicality of using available standard program packages. Finally, a more precise estimate of system development and operating costs can be obtained.

Once the viability of the system has been confirmed, there remains the exacting task of translating the details of the system into formal programming specifications. In addition to providing precise information regarding inputs, outputs, files, and logic of the system, the designer will also specify the program modules into which the functional elements of the program will be grouped and will identify the linkages by which the respective modules are connected. In this way the designer maintains control over the precise nature of each program module. He or she then prepares specific test data to prove out the reliability of each individual module. As a result, testing on a module-by-module basis is greatly expedited, and overall system testing is considerably simplified.

At this point, detail system design is complete, and the designer can go on to other tasks. It might be well, however, to explore some of the characteristics that identify a "good" system design from a "bad" one.

Perhaps the most important single characteristic is summed up by the phrase "user satisfaction." Does the system, in fact, satisfy the needs of the user? In many cases, user satisfaction is nearly synonymous with user participation, particularly in the early stages of detailed design. If user participation can be achieved at that time, it is usually possible to find out what the user really needs to run the operation. If, for any reason, a compromise between need and fulfillment is necessary, the user will generally recognize the realities of the situation.

In the course of a recent ADP performance audit, it became obvious that an entire user-department was enraged because of the utter uselessness of a complete configuration of management information reports that had been designed within the past year. Upon further inquiry, it was learned that the systems designer (no longer with the company) had developed the report configuration without any contact with the user-department whatsoever. Strangely enough, it was later ascertained that most of the information actually needed was available in the system files and was easily retrievable in acceptable format.

Another case of user dissatisfaction came to light during a general system design study for a large financial organization. In that situation, however, user participation and understanding were excellent. However, because of a basic defect of system design, it was economically impractical to retrieve additional management information from the database on a selective basis. Consequently, although both the designers and the users understood the problem, there was little that could be done to satisfy changing management information needs short of the complete restructuring of the database, which has since taken place.

Another case of user dissatisfaction involved an extremely long delay at program testing. In this situation, a decision had been made to subcontract the programming of the system to a presumably qualified software house on a fixed-fee basis. The systems designer responsible for the project prepared precise and detailed system performance specifications, together with comprehensive system performance test data. Neither party recognized the necessity for logical modularization of the program, and for development of carefully planned test data for each module. The system was installed 6 months late, the systems designer is still bleeding, and the contract programmer is still blotting red ink.

How do you recognize a good system design? Very simple. Nobody ever complains about it. They just take it for granted.

Chapter 1

Operational-Level Subsystems Design

JAMES F. BARCUS, JR.

Plant Manager, Black & Decker Manufacturing Company, Hampstead, Maryland

Usually systems design occurs in two different stages. The first deals with conducting the systems-needs survey and feasibility studies, etc., already discussed in the four preceding Chapters. In that stage, the system normally exists merely as a general approach with only the essential key beams of its architecture defined. A comprehensive statement of purpose has already been prepared, which should give a rather finite definition of what the system *will* or *will not* do. Organizational relationships and responsibilities have been defined, including external regulations or requirements. Last but not least, an economic evaluation has been prepared which documents the statement of benefits, cost of the current system (if one exists), cost of the proposed system (initial and operational), and finally a return-on-investment analysis which should also consider the systems maintenance required after installation.

In stage one, it is necessary to carry the design only to the level of detail needed to generate and support the management proposal. Additional design effort at that time is not justifiable unless management accepts the design concept and authorizes the project. Just where to draw the line between stage one and the subsequent detailed systems design is not easily defined. However, the reader should remember that the design in stage one must be complete enough to evaluate the need, concept, and solution or, in short, generate sufficient information to make and defend the management proposal.

After management's approval, the next step or second stage of systems design is to convert the proposed system's general architecture into detailed design. The development of the detailed system design that defines the data (input) required, the logic to be performed (processing), in order to generate better information (output) to help people perform better on their jobs has to be the most critical task of the entire ADP systems job. This is where the real quality is built into the system. The success of the whole computer venture will be most heavily influenced by the quality of the system being computerized and not from automation of existing or some new procedures. This is the place to spend the time to do it right.

The central thrust of this Chapter deals with this conversion of general design into detailed design and computer specifications ready for programming.

Currently most data processing organizations are pretty good at determining technical feasibility, and are getting better at measuring economic feasibility. But what about *operational feasibility?* The data processing organization has to keep reminding itself that the company is in business not to "manufacture systems," but to manufacture products and sell them at a profit. Therefore the intent should be to provide systems which support the various operations of a company by supplying integrated, timely, and accurate information.

Management and User-Department Involvement   The first and most important step is to gain top-management focus. Actually, this has to be accomplished during stage one of the systems design. Without this element, the task is almost impossible and at best will be long and drawn out with end results considerably less than expected.

Management focus starts with communication of computer plans. This forces the data processing staff to lay out *specific* plans, both short-range (to keep the business running) and long-range (to make sure you get where you want to be at the time you want to be there). These plans should consist of objectives, criteria, and priorities presented in a form that management will understand and will pass judgment on. Once these plans are generally tuned in, probably adjusted many times and then approved by top management, they must be integrated as a part of operating objectives and budget preparation. Continual performance reviews and considerable special training throughout the line organizations will also be needed. User-management as well as top management must be involved and fully committed to the development and successful installation of the automatic data processing system.

User-department participation is also crucial to the development of detailed subsystems design. The user still has the responsibility for the function, and the system has to end up being *the user's system*, since the user will be the one who must live with it. When the systems project is at stage two and the detailed design is undertaken, make certain that appropriate user-management personnel are assigned to the project on a full-time basis. As the system design evolves from the combined design team, it should be reviewed constantly, with additional key user-personnel from the operations that will be affected. This constant review, sometimes on a weekly basis, brings about a growing awareness of the system within the user-department, and gives the data processing people the opportunity to discover special problems and needs in ample time to do something about them.

Once the detailed design has been approved and the detailed specifications have been generated, the continuity of user participation can be preserved by having the design team split its function. While the data processing people program, code, and debug, the user members of the team design the training and communication package. It is highly important for user-personnel to perform the training at the *doer* level, which means they are talking to their own people about *their* system. Finally, the actual implementation is a joint effort. Test and parallel results are checked jointly. The user has the final say so—is the system ready to turn on?

User participation is an absolute ingredient for successful development of computerized systems. Getting a system installed without user participation is at best a horrendous task. Gaining the desired results from an installed system without user participation is practically impossible. Therefore, any further comment in the remainder of this Chapter in regards to steps to be taken in developing design of operational-level subsystems assumes complete user participation—*it is a must!*

THE SYSTEM PLAN

A successful business or operations support system calls for a master systems plan—a master plan which is one level of planning lower than the overall data processing plan. Without a master blueprint of the system, it is difficult to determine in what sequence the systems development work should occur in order to achieve a logical and orderly systems buildup. The chances then are that the user will end up with a patchwork structure of unrelated and perhaps incompatible subsystems.

Figure 1-1 shows the eight operational-level subsystems of the logistics system installed at The Black & Decker Manufacturing Company. The logistics system at B&D was conceived late in 1966 as an integrated information system supporting the basic operational functions of the manufacturing cycle. It was quite apparent that not *all* the problems could be defined and solved, and not all new systems could be created and implemented at the same time—business had to go on as usual. Therefore this huge undertaking was broken down into chewable bites and installed a block at a time. Some of the subsystems were further broken down into stand-alone logic modules, such as the creation and maintenance of bills of material and other basic manufacturing files from the product parts planning subsystem. These were implemented before the inventory update module was installed. In this way, a computerized product structure was available to the sales forecast and manufacturing planning subsystems before the total product parts planning subsystem was installed, without the need to create duplicate files.

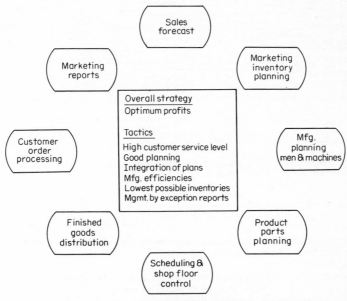

Fig. 1-1   The logistics system.

The systems plan must be detailed enough to define the major elements of the job, how much work must be done, who will do it, and when it will be completed. All interrelations between elements must be recognized and included in the schedules so that completion dates flag any instance where a dependent element must wait for its interface. Figure 1-2 shows the schedule portion only of the system plan followed to improved communications in the customer order processing subsystem several years after the original installation.

A comprehensive systems blueprint requires an early investment in time and effort, but this expense is paid back manyfold during the programming, debugging, and implementation of stages of the systems project. However, there is one problem. Many computer-oriented people put a great deal of stock in the importance of the overall, integrated system design in an attempt to avoid pure data processing inefficiency down the line later. Data processing inefficiency should not be ignored, but one should always be aware of the objectives of the system that is being developed. If too much time is spent attempting to design the absolutely optimum way to run the system on the contemplated data processing hardware, it is very probable that the payback potential of the system itself will never actually be realized. The payback money is with the overall system, and not with how well the specific data processing equipment operates. However, it is important to strike a balance between the two extremes. It has been said that "when the systems effort becomes totally subordinated to an overall program and high payoff applications are postponed for the sake of integrating them more efficiently

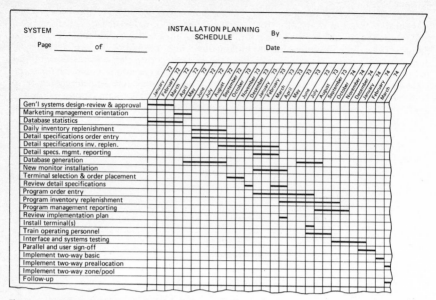

Fig. 1-2   Schedule portion of the system plan to improve the customer order processing subsystem at Black & Decker Manufacturing Company.

into an imagined future total system, the company is being run for computer efficiency and not for operating efficiency."[1]

To summarize the prescription here advocated: Develop an overall system design and implementation plan. Know where you want to be, where you are going, and how you are going to get there. Detailed development of how you are going to get there will bring about changes and adjustments to the plan, but the original intent should remain intact. Good systems development must be a well-managed, evolutionary process, reinforcing the best features of previous methods, discarding less effective techniques, and eventually achieving the much touted goal of an *effective* computerized information system.

Reducing the System into Modules   The magnitude of details to be addressed during the development of a large system is almost beyond comprehension. When all elements or functions of a system are developed simultaneously, the job becomes extremely unwieldly and practically unmanageable. Indeed, it would be unique for a systems development team to be staffed with enough people to develop all functions on a concurrent basis. Trying to develop the total system with relatively few people usually results in very long delays. Also, the completed design (if it ever happens) would likely be a "rambling system" that would probably require very complex programming and be almost impossible to debug and extremely difficult to change or expand.

Another good case for subdividing systems is that in this way it is often possible to realize some of the objectives more quickly. Some subsystems certainly can be implemented as stand-alone modules at a much earlier date. Producing some early tangible results is always desirable in order to improve the system's credibility with using departments as well as with top management. Furthermore, some degree of success is always an uplift to the systems team, since not seeing any results from long hours of labor for months on end is demoralizing to even the most experienced systems designer. Providing an earlier opportunity for user-department exposure and a more gradual acclimation to the expected final operating environment is another positive reason for subdividing a large system.

[1] Oliver Wight, *The Executive's New Computer*, Reston Publishing, Reston, Va., 1972.

Dividing the system into subsystems should be done with great care, because these will be the units of work to be dealt with throughout the remainder of the detailed design, programming, testing, and implementation of the system. The design objectives of the total system should never be lost sight of. Sometimes glossing over the importance of the various interdependencies of the subdivided parts results in subsystems which fit together poorly, both logically and functionally. (For example, has coding within a transaction already been validated? Have certain quantitative fields in master files been previously updated? Are all the data needed for the logic to be performed in the transaction actually available?)

Another pitfall to avoid is inadequate communication and reviews between the groups working on the various subsystems. This usually results in a complete breakdown of the integrated system when the modules are brought together for the first time.

Some of the more critical items that should be considered during this subdivision are:

1. Do not attempt to subdivide the system strictly along organizational lines. Try to group together the common or like business functions where common logic can be performed within a system. Take this thought process all the way down to the actual examining of the like types of transactions that will flow through the system, also keeping in mind those peculiar transactions that always seem to be within a system.

2. It is usually wrong to attempt to tailor the subdivided parts to match the talents of the design group working on a particular subsystem. An unanticipated change in project personnel will later completely wipe out the logic applied when using this as one of the concepts for subdivision.

3. Attempting to subdivide based on planned processing schedules (daily, weekly, monthly, and so forth) is usually a mistake. Actually, the design should include flexibility which will allow this function to be user-defined and subject to changeable schedules. Normally the pressures of work to be performed will have some influence at a later date within the data center as to the timing of actual computer runs. This is another reason not to build timing into module definition.

4. The number of the various inputs and outputs required between the subsystems (actual interfaces) must also influence the division. Obviously, if the number of inputs and outputs exceeds the physical hardware capabilities of the computer system (the number of tape and/or disk files or memory capacity, etc.), there is no way subsystems can be structured for that configuration.

5. Careful attention should be paid to common master and historical files. Critical are the number of passes that must be made against large files in order to keep processing time to a minimum. There should also be concern that all inputs and data elements have been updated at the particular time the logic is to be performed. It is also a good practice to separate *file maintenance* (addition of qualitative and descriptive information) from *updating* (posting of new quantitative data) and from logical conclusions.

6. Another good practice is to keep the basic system logic functions separate from data collection, input, validation, and reporting modules.

7. Refer to the systems plan and be aware of the desired implementation sequence, i.e., which parts must run first.

8. Make certain the approach to subdivision is consistent with the planned hardware acquisition. Address such questions as: When must data capture devices be available? Are all the data storage media necessary for the subsystem installed? Be alert to the completeness of the processing capabilities or configuration of the mainframe, such as level of memory capacity. Is availability in the same time frames required by the defined modules?

9. The techniques necessary and the amount of computer time required to test a stand-alone module should be given consideration, as well as whether you can really recover from an error, and what file backup or regeneration is necessary for testing the module. These same module considerations for the actual production environment must be addressed.

10. Last but not least, the actual number of project people available to be assigned to the subsystem will have some impact on the division of work in the light of target dates.

DEVELOPMENT OF THE DETAILED SUBSYSTEM DESIGN

There are many definitions of the word *system*. Most seem to reflect a combination of people, documents, and procedures working together with equipment and material in harmony to accomplish specified purposes. This general thought, coupled very closely with a clear understanding that successful computer applications will be most heavily influenced by the *quality* of the systems being computerized, should be the governing principle behind all elements of the detailed subsystem design. In other words, systems by themselves do not achieve results; but people with a good working knowledge of their jobs and their function, using accurate, complete, and timely information, can achieve results.

Unfortunately, the prevailing tendency during detailed design of subsystems is to perform a "what copy goes where" study and to speed up, add to, or combine reports. This type of approach usually ends up as a computerization or further automation of *present procedures*. Frequently present procedures were designed under constraints set by the low information processing capabilities of punched cards or even an older manual system. Also, it is not uncommon to find that a company's objectives, organization, marketing strategies, product complexities, or in general, "what makes the company tick" have changed since the functional system in its present form or degree of automation was installed. Now is the time to find out how the system works, and to look closely at the function the system is to support, and its purpose. The point is, do not automate existing procedures, but design for improvement in information availability that will assist those responsible better to perform the function being computerized.

Criteria for System Success Computerizing existing procedures is not really a very tough job, but the development of a good system to support an operating function is quite difficult. Far too many people direct the preponderance of their attention to the electronic mystique of computer-aided automation instead of to the system being automated. In the end, the real judge of success of the system should be by the usual business standards, such as: Are there more sales? Have inventories been reduced? Has productivity increased? Have services offered been improved? Is the product being produced at a lower cost with better quality? Have key financial ratios improved? . . . And so forth. Prescription: Use your computer resources where the dollars are. Do not develop an electronic superclerk. Develop operating systems that support applications controlling the cost of the product or service while maximizing your ability to seize marketing opportunities with minimum financial investment.

Once the intent and objectives of the system and its supporting subsystems have been defined and clearly understood, the next most important design element is to make sure that these requirements are met by the outputs of the various subsystems.

It is during the detailed design of the system at the subsystem level that the design team must ensure that output will really support the user, and that it will help the user solve day-to-day operating problems. The information should be looked at as needed by the decision maker only as a basis for a decision. If information is not furnished where it is needed, and timely enough to take the action indicated, its value is strictly historical. In the dynamic marketplaces of today, historical information alone is of little value in day-to-day decision making. The man or woman on the firing line is the one who has to take action immediately. Such persons need to know their current status, and should have some feel for the problems they will be facing, particularly in the immediate future. Certainly, some historical information has to be retained as required by law and as desired by higher authority in the company, and as needed for comparison purposes. However, the decision making of the people who are taking action has to be assisted by information accurately describing *current* situations.

Analysis for Decision Making An accurate determination of the decisions needed to execute the function being computerized must be made early in the analysis. Next, who makes these decisions, and when, should be ascertained. It is usually fairly difficult to establish what information is needed, and in what form, to help in decision making. Here the joint efforts of the user and systems people as a team definitely pays off, for sometimes the decision maker may not really know his or her true requirements. Also, a careful examination of how the information is used is in order, since misuse of information or a misunderstanding of data content is usually more dangerous than leaving operations status quo.

The next step is to determine if all inputs necessary to provide this output (information) is available, either in this subsystem or within other subsystems of the total system. Note that under the procedure described, the files are not designed first. The needed output must first be determined; then files that support the true information requirements can be developed. It is usually pointed out that files have to be set up first during implementation of the system. However, that is not to say that they must be designed before the content and relationships between data elements are determined.

It is usually a mistake to attempt to design a database that will support all future information needs. If you do attempt that, you may spend all your resources developing a so-called total database that turns out to have limited practical value in furnishing users critical operational information because of improper output format, poor timing, or incompleteness.

Proper Level of Automation The principal strengths of a computer are its ability to scan masses of information and perform arithmetic calculations and simple yes/no logic steps at phenomenal speeds—all with consistent accuracy. Humans, on the other hand, do far better than the computer in dealing with unstructured, unanticipated changing conditions. A successful automatic data processing subsystem should combine the best of these capabilities.

Close attention should be given to establishing the proper level of automation. Programming or designing for all possible events soon reaches a point of diminishing return. One should not fall into the trap of automating what people can do better. Programming and designing for the last 15 to 20 per cent of possibilities (and you will never think of them all anyway!) usually adds a tremendous amount of cost to the project, and most certainly will lengthen greatly the time span before actual results will be realized.

Actually, most effective systems allow for exception reports, and then provide for human override. Almost every subsystem needs a feedback mechanism which allows for timely human intervention before data are stored in final form or passed on for further processing. Care should be used in designing intervention so that the provision for override, correcting, or re-entering information is kept simple. For the intervention to be effective, the user must understand the basic logic performed by the computer subsystem, and the content, timing, and other data relationships of the information being supplied to the user. Oliver Wight calls this the "rule of system transparency."[2] He underscores the need to have that user who has the responsibility for the system results understand the logic of the system. This is a must in order to have effective human override capability.

Referring back to Figure 1-1 as an example, the sales forecasting subsystem performs an evaluation of actual sales in a current month as compared to forecast sales, and generates exception reports that allow marketing managers readily to investigate any problem products. Where the computer is not doing a good job of projecting actual results, human judgment is exercised to override the computer for fine-tuning of the forecast. The adjusted forecast then becomes one of the inputs to the marketing inventory planning subsystem.

Integrated vs. Fragmented Subsystems At this point the advantages of an integrated subsystem, one that transcends organizational lines, should be stressed; but at the same time a caution flag to avoid unnecessary complexity should be raised. Complexity is always undesirable, and certainly drives costs ever upward and upward. A "sophisticated" or very complex system may never be finished!

The objective in an integrated subsystem is to capture the data as close to the source as possible, and then to handle the entire data processing requirements of a specific function as a single entity, regardless of organizational lines. The integrated subsystem processes both the original data and additional data available in the total system, using the principle of once in, many times out, to supply the total information requirements.

On the other hand, in a fragmented subsystem each application exists as a separate entity, and files are normally maintained separately for each application. Considerable

[2] Ibid.

duplication usually exists when common data are maintained by different functions in separate files. Probably the most severe problem of fragmented systems is the possibility of generating different answers about some function or element of the business from common data introduced and maintained separately in systems developed along strict organizational lines. As an example, payroll data used in standard cost calculations in support of product parts planning (make-buy decisions) may not include latest wage increases, since the Production Planning Department is not the department that pays the employee.

There are many advantages in an integrated system. Usually the data are more accurate, complete, and timely, and this provides potentially better information for improved savings or profits generated by use of the system. Duplicate records with their duplicated supporting efforts and random uneconomical practice are eliminated. Also, the need for interfunction controls is reduced. Based on how well the original design work is done, the need for change due to inadequate systems design is reduced. As pointed out previously, it is practical to implement subsystems individually, thus realizing partial benefits earlier. As the total system or a subsystem's requirements expand, the need of costly reprogramming is generally reduced.

The disadvantages all center around complexity. An integrated system is more difficult and costly to design and install, and thus takes considerable more time. The degree of planning required and special training of personnel increase manyfold, and in addition, many organizational changes must be anticipated. Probably some meaningful early savings will tend to slip away while one is awaiting the design of the totally integrated system.

Actually, it is very difficult to visualize the complete system in detail. As was pointed out previously in discussing reducing systems to modules, very few systems departments are blessed with the number of people required to design and implement a totally integrated system in one huge bite. It may be doubted whether developing a total integrated MIS as one system is even possible.

So-called sophistication, which always leads to complexity, should be absolutely avoided. Reducing the system into chewable bites to be built as operational subsystems and installed a block at a time is by far the most desirable approach. Subdividing a large system and developing programs fashioned out of linked modules reduces the problems of complexity considerably. Business functions can be effectively integrated, but the technique should be that of building meaningful blocks or logic modules centered around mutual input-output requirements.

Controls   We have previously discussed the desirability of making the logic transparent to the user. The controls within the system—to be sure that it operates in the manner intended—should be equally apparent. The integrity of the system, that is, of the information generated from the system, must be clearly obvious to the user. Controls can be both internal and external. A high degree of credability must be established not only with the user but also with other and higher levels of authority, including the public accounting firm that certifies the company's financial records. Also, each higher level of management should have some assurance that all this invisible manipulation of pulses that represent information within the computer hardware is indeed functioning properly.

Inexperienced systems designers sometimes get carried away with the computer's ability to generate control information, and ignore the ability of the user department to digest or react to the control information. It should be remembered that control data normally play no part in the decision-making information being provided, and should be considered as an overhead burden to the system. The main thrust of data control should be aimed at validating the nonrecurring data that are inputs to the system. Many different methods are used to validate incoming records, including the use of check digits to assure that critical codes or identification numbers are valid. Hash totals of identification numbers, accumulated dollars, total pieces, or document numbers are examples of input controls used to assure that all documents sent were actually received and introduced into the system. Quantitative fields within data or master files can be electronically cross-footed, to check that all additions or deletions to values or transactions have been included in an updated computer file. These are just a few of the many types of checks that can be programmed.

Deciding whether or not to install a control is usually based on a comparison of the cost of the control versus the probable loss if the control is not installed. This is tempered somewhat by the principle of generating the necessary "comfort feeling" within the user department and various functional levels of responsibility.

Another necessary element of control is the ability of the system to generate periodic or upon-demand audit trails of lower levels of supporting details. The user sometimes may believe that supplied information when compared to past history does not seem logical, or may question changes in values or volumes that are being reported. The person using the information has to have the ability to get in and examine the detail when he or she feels that to be necessary, rather than being covered up every day with page after page of detailed transactions that are almost never looked at.

Operational Awareness　Early in the subsystem design, ground rules or specifications are established that define the logic steps and calculations to be applied to data within the system in order to generate the information or output to be used within a department. *Operational awareness* means that there are provisions within subsystems so that certain maximum or minimum conditions or other early warning signals are brought to the attention of user-departments through special or exception reporting when defined limits have been exceeded. It is up to the users to determine for themselves if actions are to be taken, but they should be given as much assistance as possible in flagging the conditions where they should use their human intelligence to take a look and see if things are as they should be.

Always try to provide some form of diagnostic outputs which tell users in advance what appears to be wrong, or about to be wrong within their function. One sure way to "turn a user off" is to report nothing but history that points out problems only after the time to control or effect change has passed—historical information that documents problems of last month or last accounting period. It is also well, when practical and justifiable, to provide some degree of simple simulation. In other words, give the manager some limited ability to play "what if" without committing his or her resources or changing the actual live information within files. The manager can then test ideas before taking action. For example, one could develop what the effect in finished goods inventory month by month might be, based on next year's sales forecast, if the customer service level were raised from its present actual by 5 per cent.[3]

System Obsolescence　To the extent possible, the subsystem should be designed with system obsolescence in mind. Internal operations of the subsystems should be independent of policy change or existing organizational structures. Do not tailor internal operations to the labor that prevails in an area the system covers. Anticipate the system's effect on its environment. For example, a remote data capture subsystem's communication capability should expect increases in traffic and be capable of handling it. Consider systems availability as it affects the way the business is run. As an example, where finished products are currently distributed through decentralized distribution centers on a weekly basis, the system should be designed to accommodate daily movement of product if that physical requirement seems practical to expect if the business continues to grow.

Providing for systems growth is a must. Unanticipated systems growth will render the original design inadequate and is the most common cause of obsolescence. Absolutely avoid embodying nonlogical considerations in program procedures or code specifications. As an example, the absolute value of the alpha factor used in an exponential smoothing formula in forecasting sales should not be a program constant. Instead, the entire values of the formula might be maintained as a data element in a master file which can be changed by the user without requiring program modification. Another common pitfall to avoid is fixing the number of variables in a file design—for example, provision for the address of a customer that permits only three lines, or allowing for only two "quantity buy" prices for a product.

Purchased Software　The final major element that should be considered during detail design is to consider the use of purchased software to perform part of a subsystem's function. In some extreme cases the entire subsystem may be purchased.

Software packages vary widely from modules or routines such as functional square root routines to complete packages for an application such as accounts payable or general ledger packages. Some software may not offer problem solution, but are more

---

[3] See Part 1, Chapter 3, "Simulation and Models for Decision Making," in this Section.

like compilers offering sets of means for converting files generated on one manufacturer's computer to be accessible by programs running on another manufacturer's computer.

In considering purchased software, one should make sure to evaluate the documentation provided, who will maintain the software and how this will be done, the hardware and operating environment requirements, and finally whether the package will solve one's problem. Make sure the predescribed inputs and outputs or generalities of logic or calculations do not place constraints on the design objectives. If all this fits within your parameters, it then is an economic decision versus in-house development.[4]

COMPUTER PROGRAM SPECIFICATIONS

Having broken the system into subsystems made up of logic modules centered around mutual input-output requirements, it is now time to convert the detailed design into computer specifications for programming. The cardinal principle to observe at this step is to generate very explicit program specifications that reduce the programmer's design responsibility or interpretation of design to as close to zero as possible. Every possible transaction the system will encounter, its appropriate processing (logic and calculations to be performed), and its influence on output, either internal files or printed reports, must be resolved and recorded within the program specifications. This will add time to the detailed design phase, but will shorten considerably programming and testing time and should add an additional degree of quality to the design, since the original intent will be preserved and generated into computer code.

This Chapter has already stated that the computer is best at dealing with highly structured, recurring kinds of data manipulations. This is a strong indication that it is possible to define specifically what processing the subsystem is to perform and how it is to do it, and in what format results are to be reported or recorded. Actually, if the design cannot be reduced to precise statements, it is doubtful the design is complete enough to be valid. There are many forms which detailed subsystem design specifications can take, but it is not the format that is important—what is important is the discipline of putting it precisely on paper. The remainder of this Chapter refers to the standards used at The Black & Decker Manufacturing Company to indicate how one firm has approached this difficult and tedious aspect of developing automatic data processing systems.

There is really no absolute sequence of exact steps to be taken. Actually some of the steps go on concurrently. Following are the major events in moving from subsystem detail design to program specifications:

1. Development of a very precise and detailed narrative of the subsystem which tells what the system will do and how it will be accomplished.

2. Definition of outputs required, content, timing, and format.

3. Definition of inputs needed to generate above outputs.

4. Analysis of database considerations, then actual record layouts for all inputs and outputs.

5. The logic steps and calculations to be performed to get the right answer.

6. Functional information flow of the subsystem which blocks out the various programs and defines their limits.

7. The detailed decision tables which put all the above into very finite steps that the programmer will follow in developing computer codes for each program.

Using Black & Decker's two-way communication, order processing, and inventory replenishment module as an example, the above major steps are highlighted below in translating general design documentation into detailed design, and then into programming specifications. It should be pointed out that this new module replaces the order entry module of the customer order processing subsystem within the larger integrated logistics system already described in Figure 1-1. In this case the updated subsystem replaces an already computerized subsystem in an installed operating integrated system.

Step 1 The general design was documented in very good detail. (See Figure 1-3 for the content of this documentation.) First note the purpose and objectives (Figure

[4] See Section 6, Chapter 1, "Software Houses," and the extended discussion of software in Chapter 4 of this Part, and in the first three Chapters of Section 2, Part Four.

CONTENTS

Fig. 1-3 Black & Decker two-way communication, order processing, and inventory replenishment module: Table of Contents for documentation.

INTRODUCTION AND PURPOSE OF THE TWO-WAY SYSTEM

This general systems design has been undertaken by the Marketing Distribution Management and Management Information Systems under the direction of a steering committee.

Our existing Distribution Operating and Information System is over six years old and has served us well. However, our management has recognized the growth and changes we have experienced during this time. When we look forward and anticipate future objectives and problems it seems appropriate that now is the time to update and improve this vital area of our operations.

Our purpose is to provide an advanced order processing system utilizing two-way data communication to minimize distribution operating and inventory cost, while maximizing customer service and management control.

Two-way Systems Objectives

Provide flexibility in the methods of shipping to customer to offset the rising costs of transportation.

Minimize inventory carrying expense while maintaining management's desired customer service levels.

Monitor the effects of the system on inventory levels and customer service.

Simulate the effects of changes in inventory and service levels through the total system.

Route orders to alternate shipping points as required.

Provide alternative methods of stocking and replenishing various classes of inventory.

Maximize the efficiency of distribution personnel by minimizing and simplifying paperwork and maximizing the timeliness of information.

Project future warehousing requirements for budgeting purposes.

Fig. 1-4 Statement of purpose, in documentation referred to in Figure 1-3.

SYSTEM ELEMENTS—*Order Entry Will:*

1. Process customer orders and intracompany orders for finished goods tools and accessories through the current physical distribution system.
2. Require an order entry data capture and a billing data capture.
3. Acknowledge and record customer orders on the day received thus reflecting demand on DC inventory one to three days earlier than the current system.
4. Process customer returns and billing adjustments.
5. Process receipt of intransit and outside vendor material.
6. Provide for telecommunication and printing of shipping documents to the DCs and base warehouses.
7. Provide for message switching between terminals on a dial-up basis.
8. Provide for dial-up inquiry capability from the DCs and base warehouses to Towson for customer order and inventory status information.
9. Maintain balance on hand, intransit, available, committed, reserved, etc. for product by the various locations.
10. Provide the necessary correct count and exception procedures required to maintain accurate inventory statuses.
11. Use standard pack, weight, items per skid, and cube information to provide for increased shipment of economic handling volumes.

Continued for 21 items.

Order Entry Will Not:

1. Prebill shipments.
2. Provide pricing and billing for customer orders.
3. Be a real-time system.
4. Control items other than finished goods inventory.
5. Maintain stock locations in the base warehouses or distribution centers.
6. Maintain customer and product databases.
7. Support centralized order entry.

Fig. 1-5 "Will" and "will not" statements for module of Figure 1-3.

1-4) and portions of the "will" and "will not" statements for *just* the order processing element (Figure 1-5). This should produce a feeling for the level of detail contained in the narrative of the general design. Now examine Figure 1-6. This is the Table of Contents of the narrative portion *only* of the detailed design documentation. From Figure 1-7 one can see the explosion of detail, since this example is only a part of specifying the parameters for only the customer and product code validation routine — actually a very small piece of the order entry portion of the order processing element.

All this looks like a tremendous amount of detail (and it is) to get down on paper, but it is necessary in order to generate complete decision tables as the last step of de-

---

TABLE OF CONTENTS

I. *Introduction*

II. *Inputs*

This section contains a description and example of each type of input transaction.

III. *Customer and Product Validation*

This section describes the types of customer and product validation which will be done to each transaction and the possible errors that may occur. It also describes how a shipping location is assigned to an order line for alternate shipment.

IV. *Contract Order Processing*

This section describes the two-way processing of orders applied to contracts. It describes how to set up the different kinds of contracts and how orders are processed.

V. *Order Valuation and Policy Selection*

This section describes the extent to which the system will place a value on orders and the technique used to select the policies which must be applied to the order.

VI. *Policy Application*

This section will describe in detail the technique used to apply the selected policies to orders. It will also describe the method of establishing policies in the two-way system.

VII. *Order or Transaction Acceptance and First Inventory Update*

This section describes how orders are examined for errors and disposed of accordingly. It also describes how inventory records are updated with receipts or shipments.

VIII. *Correct Count Process* ·

This section describes the procedure to be followed and the system processing support provided for correct counting. Both the annual count and intermediate counts are discussed.

IX. *Protected Deferred Item Processing*

This section describes what a Protected Deferred Item really is and how it works. It describes in very detailed specifications how the system allocates inventory dynamically to Protected Deferred Items.

X. *Inventory Allocation*

This section describes how inventory is allocated to Back Orders and New Orders other than PDI Items. It also describes how the Inventory and Order Files are updated.

XI. *Program Item and New Product Processing*

This section describes a new philosophy in distributing items on sales programs and new products from base warehouses to distribution centers using the Sales Forecast rather than historical sales data. It describes the interface with the Sales Forecasting System.

XII. *Replenishment Calculations*

This section describes the calculations involved in deriving replenishment quantities for distribution centers. It also describes the allocation routines for items in short supply as well as "near order point" quantities for rounding out trailers.

XIII. *Create Trailer Shipments from Base to Distribution Centers*

This section describes the analyzation of the imaginary trailers and the creation of real trailer shipments. It also describes the technique for rounding shipment quantities into economic handling quantities as well as the technique for rounding out partial trailers.

XIV. *Create Shipping Paper and Distribution Center Control Reports*

This section describes the process involved in generating the required shipping paper as well as the zone and pool accumulation reports and related shipping summaries.

Fig. 1-6   Table of Contents of the narrative portion of the documentation.

CUSTOMER AND PRODUCT VALIDATION

The two-way system if fully utilized will require many different types of input coming from many different sources. This will require that all transactions entered be passed through a very stringent edit procedure. It is the purpose of this module of the system to perform this particular function. The editing breaks into three basic areas:

- Customer Information
- Product Information
- Order Information and Content

Customer Information—All transaction types which require customer data will be edited as follows:

1. The Customer File will be checked to insure that the customer is a valid, active customer.
2. The Customer File will be checked to see if there are any particular process override codes that are peculiar to this customer. These codes will be inserted in the order header only if there was no override captured as part of the order.
3. Information such as customer type, national accounts number, and any permanent special notes will be inserted into the order.
4. Any errors detected during this process will be flagged but editing will continue.

Product Information—All transaction types which require product data will be edited as follows:

1. The Product File will be checked to insure that the product is valid and is active.
2. If the product is discontinued the appropriate rules will be applied as to whether a substitution should be made. If a substitution is made the original catalog number will be noted on the shipper and the new catalog number inserted in the order.
3. If the item is a structured item (Explosion, etc.) the component items will be inserted in the order for picking and shipping along with the top number.
4. The product file will be checked to insure that the location concerned is eligible to *accept orders* for this product. If not the appropriate notes will be inserted in the order.

Continued for two more full pages.

Fig. 1-7   Detail explosion of item III, Figure 1-6.

GENERAL SYSTEM—*Control and Management Reporting*

At the completion of any batch run for one or several locations for either the partial job stream midday run or the complete evening run, system control, management reports, and location reports will be processed.

System control will be maintained and balanced internally using the two-way control file. Processing control errors will cause termination of the system and messages to operations indicating that problems exist on the database. The integrity of the database must be maintained for the security of all systems.

All processing errors which have been detected by the two-way programs will be placed on the report file. Depending on the type of transaction and severity of the error, items will be suspensed and/or reported back to the locations responsible for error correction.

Each location will receive a register of items entered, items rejected, items suspensed, and items processed for their internal control. We intend that the detail to support this control will be as simple as possible. This will be defined in the detail design.

Each location will receive control registers, shipping documents, prioritized messages, other location volume reports, etc. depending on transactions entered and run of the day (either midday or evening). This communication will be initiated from the data center to the appropriate location using existing WATS lines.

Management reports, center maintenance, audits, etc. will be printed at the data center depending on need as defined in the detail design by the steering committee.

Periodically (weekly, monthly, etc.) analysis reports will be run to monitor the performance of the system, distribution centers, warehouses, and the center. These are to be defined in the detail design.

Fig. 1-8   General systems definition for control and management reports.

fining for the programmer exactly what the computer should do. The narrative portion of the detailed design of this real-life module of a subsystem required over 400 pages to record the necessary level of detail.

Step 2 The general systems definition for control and management reports is shown in Figure 1-8. Figure 1-9 illustrates the data functional flow. During detail design the contents of output and actual report formats are designed as already described. Figure 1-10 is an example of just *one* of the 26 outputs developed to supply the in-

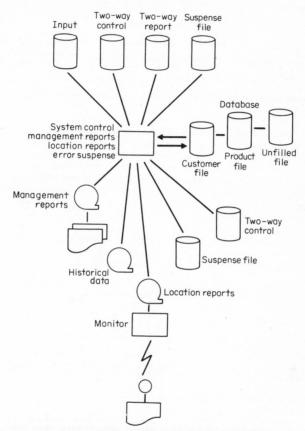

Fig. 1-9 Control and management data functional flow.

formation indicated by the general design in Figure 1-9. The reader by this time can begin to see the huge amount of additional definition that must be developed from the parameters set forth by the general design before the detail design is complete enough to program.

Steps 3, 4, and 5 The next three sets of tasks are performed concurrently. The inputs necessary to generate all the outputs are developed in detail. As the input requirements and formats take shape, the detail logic steps and calculations needed to produce the outputs must be examined. Usually these steps cannot be accomplished separately, since defining logic and calculations to be performed will cause further examination of input, and usually changes in content or format become necessary.

Figure 1-11 is an example of input information flow as it is documented in the general design. See Figure 1-12 for an overview of information flow at a decentralized distribution center. Working backwards the many, many input, logic, and calculation

THE **Black & Decker**• MANUFACTURING COMPANY
POWER TOOLS SHIPPING ORDER

MID. ATLANTIC DISTRIBUTION CENTER
P.O. BOX F
HAMPSTEAD, MD. 21074

BD

SHIPPER NO. | CUSTOMER NO. | REGISTER NO. | CUSTOMER ORDER NO. | ORDER ENTRY DATE | SHIPMENT DATE

Sold to:

Ship to:

WAREHOUSE INSTRUCTION:

Routing:

Ship Via:

Transportation Charge:

F/A
x

LINE NO.	DISTRIBUTION INFORMATION	QTY ORD.	QTY BACKORD	QTY SHIPPED	NUMBER	DESCRIPTION	WHSE. LOC.	SHIP. CTNS	WGHT (LBS)	CUBE	FRT. CLASS

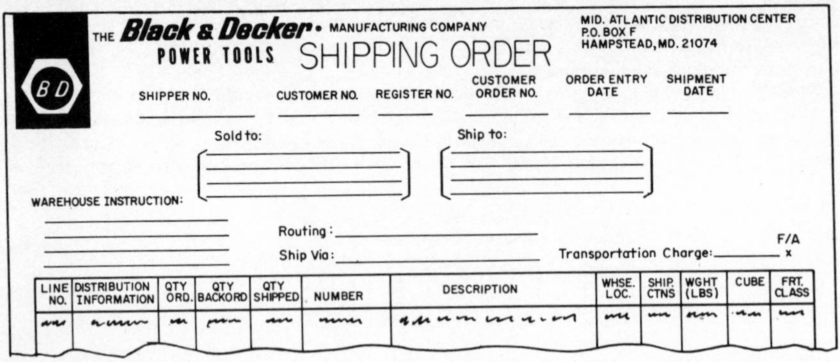

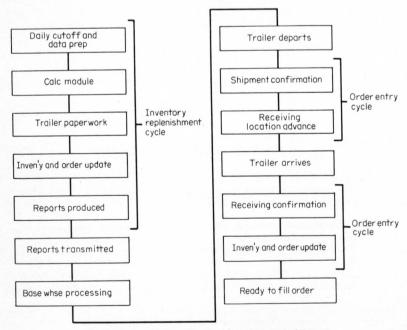

Fig. 1-10 Example of one of the 26 outputs developed to supply the information indicated in Figure 1-9.

considerations are analyzed and documented one at a time until every input, output, and process step is down on paper.

Step 6 The work done in Steps 3, 4, and 5 starts to spill over into Step 6. Database considerations, and determinations as to whether the information will be introduced by the subsystem or retrieved from existing files, begin to formulate a functional flow. The functional flow becomes the basis for establishing the scope of programs, which files each will process, create, or update, and which outputs will be generated by each program. In other words, the detailed functional flow establishes the logic sequence of program functions, details the functional content of each program, and spells out the various files used or generated. The reader can best recognize the magnitude of the job by realizing from the simple functional flow shown in Figure 1-13, that the detail design is expanded into 19 elements. See Figure 1-14 for the complexity of just one of these elements. The example element contains four programs,

Fig. 1-11 Input information flow, inventory replenishment.

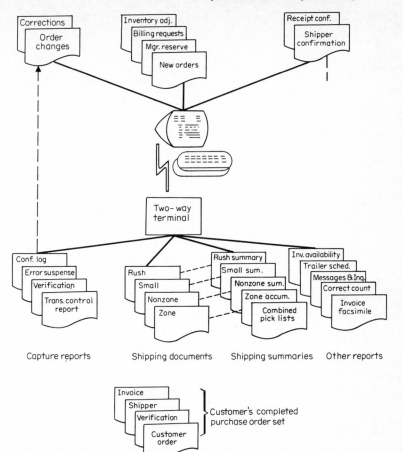

Fig. 1-12 Overview of information flow at a decentralized distribution center.

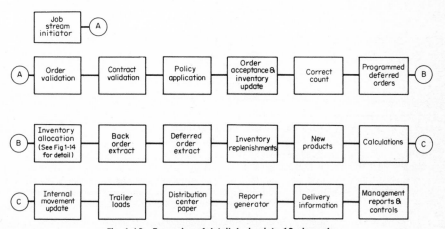

Fig. 1-13 Expansion of detail design into 19 elements.

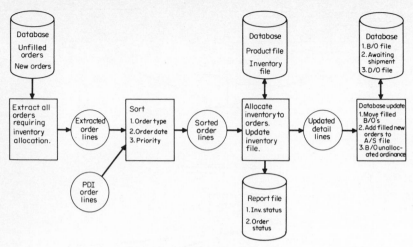

Fig. 1-14   Inventory allocation module.

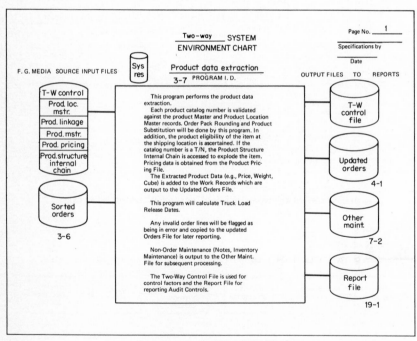

Fig. 1-15   Sample program environment chart.

and the total module (19 elements) of this subsystem requires 76 different programs.[5]

Step 7   All the above is then further backed up in detail by program environment charts, record layouts, and decision tables.   The environment chart (Figure 1-15) tells the programmer what files are used or generated by a program and what functions the program is to perform.   The record layout (Figure 1-16) defines exactly the content

---

[5] Part Two, Chapter 3, in this Section, describes in detail the considerations in developing computer files and databases.

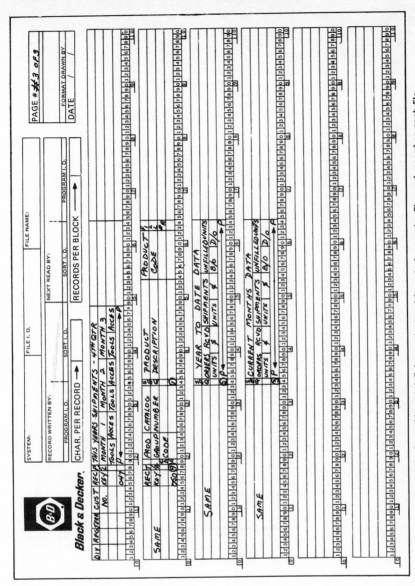

Fig. 1-16 Record layout defining content and format of computer files and record on each file.

CONDITION/ACTION — **DECISION TABLE**

CONDITION STUB — RULE NUMBERS	1	2	3	4	5	6	7	8	9	10	11	12	13	14	15	16	17	18	19	20
IS CONT. FILES FROM SUFFIX VALIDITY CHECK = LOC	Y	N	N	N	N	N	N	N	N	N	N	N								
" " " " = DCS		Y	N	N	N	N	N	N	N	N	N	N								
" " " " = BMS			Y	N	N	N	N	N	N	N	N	N								
" " " " = SVC				Y	N	N	N	N	N	N	N	N								
" " " " = DRP					Y	N	N	N	N	N	N	N								
" " " " = 900						Y	N	N	N	N	N	N								
" " " " = 901							Y	N	N	N	N	N								
" " " " = 902								Y	N	N	Y	N								
" " " " = 903									Y	Y	Y	N								
IS 'OP' FROM-ACCOUNT SUFFIX 2 = 155									Y	N										
" " " " 1 = 158									Y	N										

ACTION STUB

ACTION STUB	1	2	3	4	5	6	7	8	9	10	11	12
MOVE 'OP' FROM-ACCOUNT SUFFIX 1 → VAL-LOC	*	*										
" " " " → VAL-SVC				*	*							*
SUFFIX 2 → VAL-LOC			*			*						
MOVE 'OP' DIST CTR → "VAL-LOC"										*		
MOVE 'OB' → "ERROR-C.O"							*	*				
PERFORM DT#14A (ALL LOCATIONS EXCLUDING CANADA ARE VALID)	*						*					
DT#14B (ALL DIST CTRS VALID)		*										
DT#14C (ALL BASE WHSES VALID)			*									
DT#14D (ALL LOCATIONS VALID)					*						*	
DT#14E (ALL SVC CTRS VALID)				*					*	*		
DT#14F (VALIDATE DRT & PAYROLL #)						*						
GO TO DT #15	*	*	*	*	*	*	*	*	*	*	*	*

PURPOSE:
VALIDATE THE FROM-
ACCOUNT SUFFIX
USING THE CONTROL FILE

ENTRANCE CONDITIONS:

DECISION TABLE # 14

Sheet 1 of 1

DATE: 8/14/69

NAME: J. MORE

SYSTEM: FINISHED GOODS

PROGRAM: MKG 10611

Form No. 2025

Printed in U.S.A.

Fig. 1-17 Decision table.

and format of each computer file and each different record on each file. Finally the decision tables (Figure 1-17) define to the programmer the exact logic steps and calculations the program must perform. From this documentation the programmer will develop computer code or write in some computer language (COBOL, FORTRAN, etc.) a program to execute on the computer hardware the function as defined.

DOCUMENTATION

The key to ease of maintenance in an automatic data processing system is standard, accurate, and complete documentation. In any data processing organization, changes will occur after a system or program is in operation. The efficiency of updates to and possible conversion of systems and programs will depend considerably upon the adequacy and maintenance of the system documentation. Also, the historical record provided by standard documentation can serve as a valuable pool of experience in the development of future systems. It can be used as a reference in estimating necessary personnel, scheduling, project control and progress checking, and user orientation.

The subsystem narrative is the initial step in documenting the detail design. It becomes the base from which the remaining documentation is developed. Care should be taken that it is a concisely written description of the system and covers completely each type of input transaction and data validation. Also, every policy application, calculation, logic step, and output requirement must be spelled out in detail.

The functional information flow of the system is a graphical representation of the overall logic of the system. The main areas for standardization are overall layout chart, paging and identification, symbols, program identification and description, connector symbols, and system recovery and control. The chart should be as clear and simple as possible, reflecting clearly understood symbols.

There are many very adequate forms for defining input-output layouts, printer formats, keypunch documents, and program environment charts. The principle is standardization, so that every programmer and every systems designer are documenting in the same way. The ease in later maintenance, transfer, or loss of project personnel more than makes up for the effort of enforcing standardization. Do not let systems designers or programmers attempt to build in job security by not documenting or recording their efforts in a unique manner. Make certain that documentation is complete during the various phases of design and programming, because after-the-fact documentation almost never gets done.[6]

The final step of detail design definition, decision tables, is the most important part of the documentation. This is what tells the programmer exactly what the program is supposed to do and how it must function. The purpose of a decision table is to exhibit in a clear and concise manner the way in which each relevant factor relates to the problem structure, and how every possible combination of these factors leads to which actions or solutions. This technique shows the logical relationship between conditions and actions in such a way that the related data manipulations are clarified. (Refer again to Figure 1-17.) The Black & Decker experience has been that decision tables are far more effective in defining program logic than program flow charts, and are much more compact and much easier to keep up to date. Gildersleeve makes the point that decision tables are immediately comprehensible and more amenable to standardization than flow charts, and their structure tends to force the organization of the procedure into sets of relatively independent modules.[7]

SUMMARY

1. The success of the whole computer venture will be most heavily influenced by the quality of the system being computerized, not by automation of existing or new procedures.

[6] See Section 2, Part Six, Chapter 2, "ADP Standards," and in this Section Part Four, Chapter 3, "Documentation, Standards, and Controls."

[7] T. R. Gildersleeve, *Decision Tables and Their Practical Application in Data Processing*, Prentice-Hall, Englewood Cliffs, N.J., 1970.

2. User-department participation is most crucial to the development of detailed subsystems design. This is the way to assure that the system is being designed for the user. Keep user interest always in mind and make certain the objectives of the system are fulfilled.

3. Develop an overall systems design and implementation plan. Know where you want to be, where you are going, and how you are going to get there.

4. Subdivide large systems into operational-level subsystems, but integrate the business functions. Business functions can be effectively integrated, but the technique should be that of building meaningful blocks of logic modules centered around mutual input-output requirements. Complexity should absolutely be avoided.

5. Design to use computer resources where the dollars are. Do not develop an electronic superclerk. Develop operating subsystems supporting applications that are used to control the cost of the product or service while maximizing the ability to seize marketing opportunities and minimizing financial investment.

6. The cardinal principle to observe in converting the detailed design into computer specifications for programming is to generate very explicit program specifications that reduce the programmer's design responsibility or interpretation of the design to as close to zero as possible. Put it all down on paper.

7. The key to ease of maintenance of an automatic data processing system is standard, accurate, and complete documentation. The efficiency of updates to and possible conversion of systems and programs will be heavily influenced by the adequacy and maintenance of the system documentation.

SELECTIVE BIBLIOGRAPHY

Brandon, Dick H., *Data Processing Organization and Manpower Planning*, Petrocelli Books, New York, 1974.

Gildersleeve, Thomas R., *Decision Tables and Their Practical Application in Data Processing*, Prentice-Hall, Englewood Cliffs, N.J., 1970.

Hartman, W., H. Matthes, and A. Poeme, *Management Information Systems Handbook*, McGraw-Hill, New York, 1968.

Lindgren, L. H., "Auditing Management Information Systems," *Journal of Systems Management*, June, 1969.

Orlicky, Joseph, *The Successful Computer System*, McGraw-Hill, New York, 1969.

Rullo, T. A., "Understanding the Software Packages Market," *Data Processing Magazine*, July, 1970.

Wight, Oliver, *The Executive's New Computer*, Reston Publishing, Reston, Va., 1972.

Wofsey, Marvin, *Management of Automatic Data Processing*, Thompson, Washington, D.C., 1968.

Chapter 2

Planning-Level MIS Design

MILTON M. STONE

President, Continental Information Services, Inc., Chicago,
Illinois; formerly Editor, Infosystems Magazine, Wheaton,
Illinois

Information for management is useless unless it is closely and explicitly related to the activities being managed and to the actions that management can take. Therefore, in conceptualizing an information system for management, we must be concerned with business activity—but our examination of the activity must be from a specific viewpoint.

Doing and Managing Consider the subject of information for *doing*. Doing is the process of taking care of the day-to-day transaction of business—in accordance with the policies and procedures currently in force—on a routine basis. The process can be accomplished with little or no managerial intervention. Information for doing helps to answer such questions as: (1) What products must we deliver? (2) Which salesperson is responsible for the order? (3) Where must the products be delivered? (4) How will we get paid? (5) What finally happened?

Now consider the subject of information for *managing*. Managing is the process of adjusting the levels of allocation of resources, evaluating performance, deciding what to do next, and issuing the necessary managerial orders. Information for managing—much of it derived from the information required for doing—helps to answer such questions as: (1) What will sales be like? (2) What should be our pricing action? (3) What production rates should we maintain? (4) What is the best pattern of distribution, taking into account the level of sales, transportation, and inventories? (5) How do we determine where to make capital expenditures and in what amount?

How can we identify and catalogue this kind of *planning information* or *management information?* Our aim should be to identify information that will:
- Report what of significance is happening.
- Help to explain why it is happening.
- Help to forecast what will happen.

In addition, we want the method of organizing the information to be simple, logical, and direct—and flexible enough to remain useful when ideas or circumstances change.

MANAGEMENT INFORMATION: CONCEPTUAL APPROACH

In general, companies have used one of three conventional methods of identifying management information requirements:

• *Interrogation*, or the process of interviewing key executives to determine what reports each executive feels he or she needs.

• *Attrition*, or the process of experimental elimination of reports to determine whether or not a real demand exists for the information no longer being produced.

• *Recombination*, or the process of analyzing existing reports for duplication and overlap in order to synthesize a new and streamlined set of reports.

In general, the information supplied to management as a result of the above methods fails to focus attention on the relevant problems of management, fails to explain or provide insight, and is too rigidly tailored to the tastes of a specific organizational format and a specific personnel lineup.

To overcome these deficiencies, the focus of pertinent management information must be on: (1) results, (2) the influence of competition and environment on results, and (3) the influence of the actions of management (of management strategy) on results.

One of the difficulties of identifying this "pertinent" information is the complexity of the typical business function. For example, consider the extent of the marketing system of a major oil company. The system starts with the assumption of control of products at the refinery gate (or at their point of entry into marketing, if the source of supply is outside the company) and ends with the transfer of title, physical possession, and positive control of the products to their ultimate consumers.

Missions   Regarded as a complete entity, a system such as the one mentioned is extremely difficult to study. But we can help ourselves by dividing the function of marketing into a limited number of missions. Each of these is a fundamental task that must be performed continuously as long as the company is in the oil business.

It would be possible to subdivide these missions into smaller, less inclusive missions with more limited purposes, or to group them into larger, more inclusive missions with broader purposes. Hence, subdivision of the business of marketing (for example) into these specific missions is a somewhat arbitrary choice of what we feel is the most useful way of concentrating managerial attention on the basics of the business. This concentration helps to cut through the mass of information that *could* be developed. Attention is focused on a limited number of information requirements that are urgent because they relate to the fundamental missions of marketing, and to the important, nontrivial management actions that can be taken to accomplish those missions.

In defining missions and the management actions that have an influence on the accomplishment of each mission, we should be governed by the following principles:

1. A mission attacks a problem area — it must be accomplished.

2. A mission can be accomplished in more than one way — a choice of fundamental methods is involved.

3. A mission is under the control and the close scrutiny of management.

4. The accomplishment of a mission is a positive reason for spending money — not a justification for an unavoidable expense.

5. In each instance, a mission accepts an existing set of circumstances and produces a resultant set of circumstances.

6. A mission is arbitrarily defined in each instance so as to accept significant inputs and produce significant outputs and, hence, be worth significant managerial attention.

7. In general, except for terminal situations, outputs from one mission are inputs to a subsequent mission.

8. There is a fundamental difference between the influencing actions of management (as we define them here) and the skills of management (which have to do with intangible and subjective abilities). The management actions used in our analysis should either:

a. Select a resource or resources to use, or

b. Adjust the rate or level of utilization of these resources.

9. For each mission, general statements can be made for the influencing management actions. A specific and limiting version of the general statement of the action can then be developed for a particular level of manager.

Input-Output Model   The process of defining and examining missions is, in essence, a technique for organizing our thinking about information requirements. It is the basic tool to use in specifying those information systems designed to support *planning* or *managing* as opposed to *operating* or *doing*.

Briefly, the technique first scrutinizes the content of company operations, managerial functions, and those elements of performance that are influenced by managerial actions. The product of this scrutiny is an input-output model of the activities of the company. The input-output model is then used as a basis for describing the significant actions that management can take. Finally, study of the management actions leads to an identification of the cause-effect relationships between actions and events (or results). Measures of these results and their relationship to actions taken are indicators of the various elements of successful operation—indicators that management should monitor.

What do mission descriptions look like? In the case of the oil company, the marketing function might be described in terms of missions as follows:

MARKETING FUNCTION MISSIONS

1. *Maintain and improve the product line.* Concerned with evaluating the present and future contribution to profitability of each product marketed by the company—and with determining whether the company will continue to market the product.

2. *Create retail demand for products.* Concerned with the use of advertising, promotion, credit—or any other means—to create a preference for company products among potential retail consumers.

3. *Maintain and improve channels of distribution to retail markets.* Concerned, in general, with the buildup of a network of service stations to sell products to the retail consumer—but, where appropriate, could be concerned with other types of channels of distribution to the retail consumer.

4. *Help individual dealers to maintain and improve the effectiveness of service-station operations.* Concerned with aiding the individual service-station operator—through pricing action, training, company services, etc.—to increase the volume and profitability of the business.

5. *Create commercial and industrial demand for products.* Concerned with the use of advertising, promotion, credit, technical services—or any other means—to create a preference for company products among the potentially large commercial users or the industrial users of the products.

6. *Maintain and improve channels of distribution to commercial and industrial markets.* Concerned with the selection of potential commercial and industrial markets and the maintenance of a sales force—or the use of any other channel of distribution—to sell to the selected markets.

7. *Contract for the sale of products to commercial and industrial accounts.* Concerned with the negotiation (including pricing action, extension of credit, commitment to provide service, delivery commitment) of the terms of sale of products to commercial and industrial accounts.

8. *Maintain and improve channels of distribution to outside marketers and to cargo buyers.* Concerned with the development of high-volume, low-cost-of-marketing sales of products to accounts who may, in effect, market on a retail or commercial and industrial level in competition with the company.

9. *Contract for the sale of products to outside marketers and to cargo buyers.* Concerned with the selection of accounts and the negotiation (including pricing action, extension of credit, delivery commitment) of the terms of sale of products to outside marketers and to cargo buyers.

10. *Move products to storage and processing locations.* Concerned with the transportation of products from the points at which they enter the company marketing system to appropriate terminals and depots.

11. *Store and process products at terminals and depots.* Concerned with the storage of products at appropriate terminals and depots—and the required blending, chemical treatment, canning, packaging, etc.

12. *Move products from storage locations to customers.* Concerned with the delivery of products ordered.

13. *Maintain and improve channels of product supply (from both company refineries and outside suppliers).* Concerned with the development of offers to sell or to transfer products to company marketing.

14. *Supply products to company marketing.* Concerned with the determination of requirements for products and the negotiation of purchases, exchanges, or transfers of products to company marketing to supply the requirements.

15. *Accumulate money.* Concerned with making appropriate collections and payments.

Or, missions can be described more succinctly and they can be more inclusive. For example, the functioning of an entire company could be described in terms of the missions, inputs, and outputs, as shown below for a food canning company.

COMPANY MISSIONS

Planning

    A. *Develop the Product Line*

Procurement and Manufacturing

    K. Supply Raw Materials—Tomato-based Products.
    L. Supply Raw Materials—Oil-based Products.

  M. Supply Raw Materials—Fruit-based Products.
  N. Supply Raw Materials—Other Products.
  O. Manufacture Tomato-based Products.
  P. Manufacture Oil-based Products.
  Q. Manufacture Fruit-based Products.
  R. Manufacture Other Products.

Marketing

  B. Create Institutional Demand for Products.
  C. Create Grocery Demand for Products.
  D. Create Consumer Demand for Products.
  E. Create Government Demand for Products.
  F. Create Export Demand for Products.
  V. Create Industrial Demand for Products.
  G. Sell to Institutional Accounts.
  H. Sell to Grocery Accounts.
  I. Sell to Government Accounts.
  J. Sell to Export Accounts.
  W. Sell to Industrial Accounts.

Physical Distribution

  S. Position Inventory.
  T. Fill Orders.

Paying/Collecting Money

  U. Collect/Pay Money

INPUT-OUTPUT TO COMPANY MISSIONS

  1. Cash.
  2. Specification of Company Product Line.
  3. Present Markets.
  4. Suggested Markets.
  5. Specification of Suggested Products.
  6. Respecification of Company Product Line.
  7. Anticipated Markets.
  8. Anticipated Sales to Accounts.
  9. Consumers with a Preference for Company Products.
  10. Accounts with a Preference for Company Products.
  11. Positioned Inventories of Raw Materials.
  12. Inventories of Products.
  13. Anticipated Requirements for Positioned Inventories.
  14. Positioned Inventories of Products.
  15. Orders.
  16. Anticipated Collections.
  17. Potential Payments.
  18. Products Delivered to Customers.
  19. Payments.

When we put these inputs, missions, and outputs together we have a graphic representation of the food canner—a model of the company (Figure 2-1.) We see clearly that

---

Figure 2-1 shows a conceptual model of the food canner—an input-output diagram of the company's operation. The starting input (1) is Cash, and this is also the final output.

The lettered symbols between first input and final output identify the missions that must continually be accomplished if the company is to stay in business. The numbered symbols between first input and final output identify the intermediate conditions created by the use of Cash. They are inputs and/or outputs along the way.

Obviously, Cash is required to accomplish each mission. Thus, a vertical arrow (labeled to indicate that it comes from (1) or Cash) points to the top of each mission symbol. But more importantly, a set of starting conditions (input) is accepted by each mission which has been defined (and is necessary) to produce a set of changed conditions (output).

Thus, for example, on the right side of the diagram: Starting with the conditions of Inventories of Products (Input 12) and Anticipated Sales to Accounts (Input 8), Mission S (Position Inventory) is necessary to produce the conditions of correct Positioned Inventories of Products (Output 14) and updated statements of Anticipated Requirements for Positioned Inventories (Output 13).

The input-output diagram is almost a closed-loop representation of the company's operation. Nearly all inputs are outputs of a previous mission. All missions accept inputs (existing conditions) and create outputs (changed conditions). Nearly all outputs become inputs to a different mission.

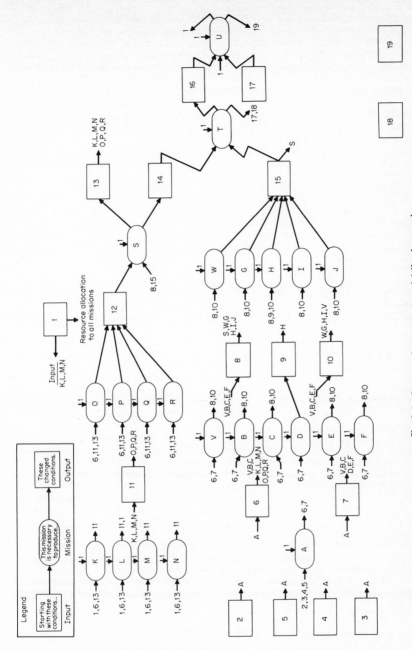

Fig. 2-1 Company input-output model (food canner).

the company's business goals are stated in terms of products, services, markets, and money. Accordingly, the inputs to and outputs from missions are business results; they describe the various stages in the development of products, services, and markets, and the exchange (between the company and its customers) of products and services for money. The total company mission is "to create customers" by providing better and more economic goods and services and by marketing these goods and services. The output from the total company system would be delivered orders and money which would flow back to the company.

Mission Analysis A major reason for identifying and analyzing missions is to break the total company system into logical elements which can be studied successfully. Mission analysis serves to focus management attention on:

1. The various stages in the development of business results.
2. The corresponding influence of competition and environment on these developing results.
3. The corresponding influence of the actions of company management on the various stages of developing results.

Mission analysis does not replace profit planning by organizational unit, or product profitability analysis. However, the performance of individual organizations and/or individual products is of less concern to management than an understanding of the working of the total company system as it moves a complete range of products and services closer and closer to its customers.

Definition of company missions serves to focus attention on relevant matters. Examination of the nature of management action leads to the identification of information requirements for decision making. We have said that there is a fundamental difference between the *actions* of management and the *skills* of management. The general statement of the management actions identified in mission analysis is action to:

1. Select a resource or resources to use, or
2. Adjust the rate or level of utilization of these resources.

To illustrate, a manager selects a resource when he or she decides to use a particular channel of distribution, or decides to acquire a particular piece of production machinery. In general, these are discrete choices; the manager must select one or more out of a number of alternatives. The manager may also "select" by changing the criteria established to make a selection. A manager adjusts a rate of expenditure (or level of effort) when he or she adjusts prices, level of personnel, or dollars expended for advertising.

The first and most basic adjustment of level of effort made by the food canner management was indicated on its total company mission diagram. In principle, there are 23 lines connecting Cash to the 23 company missions. Given a fixed amount of cash, company management either actively or by implication determines how much of this cash will be allocated to each of these 23 missions. In identifying the other management actions which apply to each of the missions, however, money is excluded from consideration. The choice of resources and the adjustment of the rate of utilization of resources is in terms of those things that money can buy. If this is not done, the analysis becomes so general that it is completely superficial.

What must be done is to develop an expanded statement of the content of each mission (so that there is no uncertainty on this score). Then, for each mission, we should develop a statement of the management actions that influence success or failure in the accomplishment of the mission and a statement of the results of (or factors influenced by) these management actions. Using the food canner as an example, the exercise is as follows:

Mission Content

The mission (A. Develop the Product Line) contains the following elements:
A. Collect and interpret intelligence. This activity involves a determination and review of the current and anticipated state of:
1. The environment in which the company moves.
2. The technologies we do or could use.
3. Our capabilities and skills (manufacturing, marketing, technical).
4. Our present products, markets, and strategies.
5. Our competitors' products, markets, and strategies.

. . . in order to suggest the need for (and the nature of) product changes, new products, new skills and capabilities, new facilities, new strategies—and/or the elimination of any existing products, facilities, or technologies.

B. Search for applicable ideas. This activity includes:

1. Collecting or requesting ideas from various sources such as customers, suppliers, agencies, inventors, and employees (including, but not limited to, marketing research, R&D, marketing, sales, and new products).
2. Generating new ideas or products by systematically combining various elements of environmental and technological information.
3. Reviewing submitted acquisition proposals as well as initiating searches for acquisitions which will fit company policies and plans.
4. Screening or applying ideas received against specific company and product criteria to determine whether to continue researching the product or idea.

C. Prepare selected products for inclusion in the product line. This activity includes:

1. *Business analysis:* Predicting the business potential of an idea utilizing internal and external sources of information. This involves collecting specific data on size of market, expected share, and gross margin, as well as cost of entry including investments in R&D, capital equipment, promotion and advertising, marketing research, packaging, etc. Additionally, at this stage, the required contributions of other departments are defined.
2. *Development proposal:* Preparing plan for developing, testing, and preliminary marketing of a product. This involves a plan for financial commitment, including time and cost for each developmental level for a subsequent period. Additionally, specific inputs are collected from all participating departments.
3. *Consumer tests:* Testing consumer reaction to products, concepts, advertising, and packaging. Additionally, other tests related to processing techniques and capabilities.
4. *Marketing strategy:* Planning the strategy for full distribution of a new product. The sales force is oriented and introductory promotional materials are created.
5. *Preliminary production:* Working through the problems of production of a new product and the manufacture of the product for test marketing.
6. *Test marketing.*

D. Establish and maintain specifications for finished products, ingredients, packaging, and raw materials.

Note: It is worth emphasizing that in this mission, *continuing* attention is paid to a refining of estimates of anticipated markets (Output 7) and to the respecification of existing products—perhaps improved—as well as the original specification of new products (Output 6).

MANAGEMENT ACTIONS

The success of the mission (A. Develop the Product Line) is determined by the way the following management actions are taken:

A. Select specific criteria, or measuring devices, for stating company goals, including such factors as sales, margins, earnings before taxes, and return on investment.
B. Select the parameters within which products will be developed in terms of markets served, needs satisfied, etc.
  1. Select vital ongoing or expected environmental trends to be exploited.
  2. Select specific company resources which will be strengthened or exploited.
C. Adjust the quantitative levels which are applied to achievements of goals.
D. Adjust the ratio of internal versus external growth sources.
E. Adjust the resources applied against the planning activity.
F. Select the sources to be used in collecting ideas for new products.
G. Select the organizational structure, administration, and processes for optimizing ideas.
H. Adjust the effort (time, talent and money) applied to searching for new ideas.
I. Select the criteria against which ideas will be screened, or new products will be evaluated.
J. Adjust the acceptance level of these criteria.
K. Select the techniques (strategies) for filling consumer and customer needs for new products.
L. Adjust the expenditures against individual marketing elements.
M. Select the types of measurements for determining acceptance of new or existing products, concepts, or strategies.
N. Adjust the time and effort applied to measuring this acceptance.
O. Select the source of production for initial development of new products.
P. Select the methods for measuring product quality acceptance levels.
Q. Adjust the levels of criteria for product quality acceptance levels.

FACTORS INFLUENCED (*Selected Example*)

The management action (C. Adjust the quantitative levels which are applied to achievements of goals) affects or has an influence on all departments' planning activities, size of organization, and extent of progress.

1. Buildings—number, location, type, size.

2. People — recruiting, compensation, personnel development.
3. Equipment — number and type.
4. Programs — how to utilize your resources.
5. Policies.
6. Operating effectiveness of all departments.
7. Timing of product development sequence.
8. Marketing strategies for ongoing products.

Allocation of Resources   When we identified missions, we said that they are basic, fundamental tasks that have to be accomplished as long as the organization lives. An urgent problem facing management is the allocation of its available resources to accomplish these missions as successfully as possible. Management must (1) plan to allocate its resources among the various missions, (2) measure what the allocation ac-

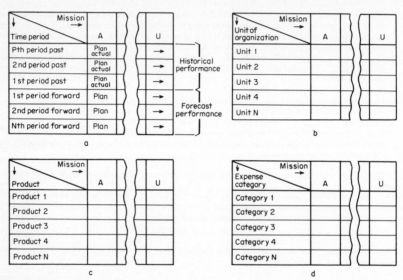

Fig. 2-2   Information matrices.   (a) For total company or for specific organizational unit. (b) For any specific period of time. (c) For any specific period of time. (d) For any specific period of time.

tually is, (3) measure the effect of the allocation, and (4) adjust its allocation plan as required.

The information matrices (sets of reports) suggested in Figure 2-2 are powerful aids to the execution of these four steps. These report sets help in differentiating between real allocations and apparent allocations. They help in determining what should be the division of resources among organizational units. And, they can be useful in measuring the "contribution to each mission versus cost incurred" — the performance — of each individual organizational unit.

The *column labels* for all the suggested report sets are identical. They associate data with specific individual missions. Thus, every entry in column A has to do with "Mission A: Develop Product Line." Every entry in column U pertains to "Mission U: Collect/Pay Money."

The *row labels* for each of the four suggested report sets are different. In Figure 2-2a, the row labels identify time periods, past and future. This is a *mission cost* analysis. In the historical section of the report, the intent is to show the relative importance of the various missions (in terms of planned expenditures) and to compare the actual expenditures with the plan. The forecast section indicates the updated plan. When correlated with a report on, say, product performance, Figure 2-2a becomes an indicator of the effectiveness of a particular pattern of resource allocation.

The row labels in Figure 2-2b identify organizational units; in Figure 2-2c they identify product lines; in Figure 2-2d they identify accounting expense categories. Each of these report sets is prepared to describe what happened over a specific period of time. Each report set permits a comparison of mission cost (related to an organizational unit, a product, a type of expense) with the benefits derived from the execution of the mission at that level of effort.

These information matrices do not record the history of any activity in an exhaustive fashion. They are merely a starting point, a concise way of beginning to list information requirements. They start the process of developing reports designed to alert management to the (1) effect of allocation decisions on results, (2) status of the business and possibilities of a change in status, (3) emergence of a need for additional investigation, and (4) specific matters that should be investigated.

A SUMMING UP

The best way to describe a true *planning* or *management* information system might be to list its distinguishing characteristics. These characteristics, one group having to do with the *mechanism* of the system and the other group having to do with the information *content* of the system, can be used to reveal the significant differences between an information system and a reporting system.

First, however, one characteristic distinguishes both the mechanism element and the content element. An advanced management information system is open-ended. Both mechanism and content are flexible, expandable, capable of modification to take advantage of new opportunities (new data, new techniques, new hardware) or to satisfy new requirements (imposed by management, competition, the economy).

Mechanism This element of a management information system has three identifying characteristics. The first of these results from the fact that every organization has in its possession a body of facts or data about the organization and about the environment in which the organization operates. Thus, a first, definitive characteristic of the mechanism of the advanced management information system is the availability of an organized, comprehensive, and (probably) automated file of data—data conveniently amenable to subsequent manipulation.

A major factor in the effective development and use of a management information system is the ability of the organization to assemble this body of facts in such a way that the facts can be interrelated. This is not always as easy to do as it sounds. For example, accounting and financial people who are in possession of what they call "clean" data are not anxious to have these data fed into a system that also stores the relatively "unpurified" data of production operations. Another example: Line sales management can make it difficult to insert its "dynamic" data, gathered from the field sales force, into a system which also stores the relatively "static" data generated by an invoicing operation. A third example: Data describing the progress of a product development project may be segregated from environmental data used to estimate the anticipated timing of the market requirement for the product being developed (and the relationship between these two categories of data should certainly be examined).

The second characteristic of the mechanism of the advanced management information system is its ability to interrogate its comprehensive file of data at irregular times, and in nonregimented ways. If we call this file of data, this body of data, a "bucket of facts," then we are talking about an ability to dip into the bucket of facts, with irregularly shaped dippers, at various locations in the bucket, to various depths, at odd times.

The business community has greatly improved its ability to use data processing gear effectively for this sort of random, curious poking and prying in search of answers to management problems. At first, management and technicians alike shackled their most flexible potential tool—the infinite variability of general-purpose computer programming. They organized their information development operations into stately, unvarying, hard-to-interrupt, do-it-the-cheapest-way patterns. But today's advanced management information system makes readily available, upon demand, varying patterns of information—patterns that reflect variation in the methods of interrelating raw data.

The third characteristic of the information system mechanism is its ability to turn out—smoothly, effectively, and accurately—management-oriented reports produced on a periodic basis for use in decision making and performance measurement.

Content The identifying characteristics of the content of a management information system are four in number. First, a management information system is set up to produce *information*, not raw data. Raw data, probably in large amounts, are fed into the system. What is produced by the system is information (derived from the manipulation, analysis, and interpretation of raw data).

This emphasis on the production of information, as opposed to data, calls attention to the next two characteristics of the content element of a management information system. One of these is the use of *discrimination*, or *filtering*, to hold down the output of the system. A desirable filter allows the passage of all valid and valuable information, automatically rejecting invalid and valueless information (probably, raw data).

Further, emphasis on the production of information stresses the close relationship between information content, the functions of each managerial job, and the controllable

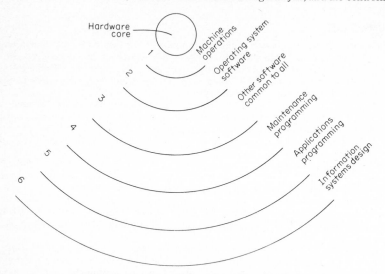

Hardware core

Machine operations

Operating system software

Other software common to all

Maintenance programming

Applications programming

Information systems design

Fig. 2-3   The scope of information systems service.

elements of these functions. Hence, a third characteristic of the content element of an information system is that the content results from the use of a *rigorous, analytical method to specify information requirements.*

Finally, a fourth characteristic of the content element of a true management information system is that it is designed to *benefit the company first,* and then its subordinate parts. The implications of this rather simple-sounding view are considerable, for it contradicts two very widely and tenaciously held notions: (1) that the whole is nothing more than the sum of its parts, and (2) that what is good for a division or a department must inevitably be good for the company as a whole. Neither of these notions is valid for today's complex business enterprise.

The Computer System The computer hierarchy upon which information systems are based can be represented by a series of concentric circles (see Figure 2-3). At the center is a core of hardware—computer and supporting equipment. Ring 1 includes the personnel who operate the equipment. Third-generation computers are run automatically by software (for the most part). The operator is primarily responsible for mounting information and media on input and output devices—and for reacting to instructions and observations generated by the software. Ring 2 includes the software which sequences the work, and Ring 3 includes such things as commonly used methods for sorting or for maintaining a tape library.

Ring 4 includes responsibility for keeping existing programs up to date. In an unpublished study made in 1968–69, IBM learned that two out of every three programmers (in the companies studied) were working on existing programs—and that 75 per cent of the time of these maintenance programmers was spent in making parameter changes. Maintenance is a heavy load, and maintenance responsibility requires detailed knowledge of the existing programs. As computer-based systems become more pervasive in a company, the newly developed programs are more closely related to the existing programs.

Finally, more recent computer-based information systems design has emphasized the development of the user's database (files) as the foundation for most of the user's transaction processing. Systems design—the design of networks of interrelated series of computer programs and human activities which feed the database and use the database—becomes much more closely tied to programming (the development of individual programs) than before. In addition, the quality of the systems design work heavily impacts the quality and cost of the programming work, and of the required processing work.

But, in spite of this impacting, the effectiveness of the information system as a tool in operating the business is primary—and the efficiency of the data processing required is secondary. No system design should ever be compromised in the name of efficient computer utilization when the compromise means ineffective company operation. The job is to use *computer-based systems* as effectively as possible in support of the company—and that is different from the mission of using *computers* as efficiently as possible.

Chapter 3

Hardware Requirements

NORMAN R. LYONS

Associate Professor of Management Information Systems,
College of Business, University of Texas, Lubbock, Texas

CHARLES G. MOORE

Cybernetics Division, ADP Network Services, Inc.,
Ann Arbor, Michigan

Like many practical problems one encounters, the problem of selecting a hardware configuration for an information processing system is difficult to consider in isolation. If asked to state exactly what the problem is that we are trying to solve, we might propose the following:

Problem: Given the demand that will be placed on the system, find the hardware configuration which gives the best performance at the minimum price.

The way in which this problem is attacked in practice is generally as follows. First, estimate in some way the demand to be placed on the system. Second, for each of the possible hardware configurations estimate the performance of the system, under the demand estimates previously formulated. Given the cost of each hardware configuration, some decision is then reached.

Assuming that the first step has been accomplished by techniques discussed in previous Chapters, this Chapter discusses the approaches and techniques for estimating and evaluating the performance of the hardware configuration, given the use to which it will be put. The methods vary widely in a number of ways. They vary in complexity and completeness, and therefore in cost. They vary greatly in what they produce as performance estimates. Some produce meaningful quantities, such as predicted turnaround time. Others simply produce a relative score for each configuration in which higher scores (or sometimes lower scores) indicate better performance. The methods also vary considerably in the way they require the demand on the system to be characterized. At one extreme is benchmarking, which uses the actual programs to be run to allow observation of system performance. At the other extreme are the queueing theory models. These require the user to estimate program running time on the configuration before using the model. The model then predicts the congestion and delays which will result from this demand on the system.

Selecting the best-performing hardware for the given demand is of course not the entire problem. A number of less quantifiable factors must enter into the decision. System reliability must be adequate, and depends on the quality of the maintenance.

Questions of compatibility with past and future computer systems are often of overriding importance. Another criterion in the selection process is flexibility of the configuration. It is often overlooked, but can be of significant value. If the demand increases by 15 per cent a year, can the hardware configuration be expanded in approximately the same increments? Additionally, how long can this incremental expansion go on? A 15 per cent increase per year doubles the demand in less than 5 years. In a situation where equipment has been purchased, there are compelling reasons to expand rather than replace already acquired equipment. Additionally, with shared databases and interactive use of a system, the alternative of simply buying a duplicate of the first system to double the capacity is an unattractive one.

NONMATHEMATICAL EVALUATION METHODS

A number of techniques have been proposed for estimating the effectiveness of a proposed or given computer system configuration. Most of these measures of system performance are fairly simple and do not by themselves provide a fully adequate measure of the power of any given computer system. What they do contribute is some readily understood measure of certain aspects of system performance, and they offer a first approach to the comparison of one computer system with another.

Effectiveness Formulas and Scoring Systems A number of effectiveness formulas have been proposed, purporting to provide a measure of the "power" of a given computer. One example is the effectiveness formula offered by Gruenberger[1]:

$$G = \frac{B(N_a + N_m)}{L}$$

where G = measure of effectiveness
B = core memory capacity (in bits)
N_a = the number of additions per second
N_m = the number of multiplications per second
L = instruction length

The measure above is directly related to the speed of arithmetic operations and the size of the memory. The inclusion of the instruction length is justified on the grounds

TABLE 3-1 Weights for a Scientific Mix and a Commercial Mix

Instruction class	Scientific weight	Commercial weight
1. Fixed-point additions and compare instructions	0.10	0.25
2. Floating-point addition	0.10	0
3. Multiplication instructions	0.06	0.01
4. Divide instructions	0.02	0
5. Other instructions	0.72	0.74

that it provides a correction for inefficiencies "due, for example, to decimal capability." This measure has a number of obvious problems. First, there is the difficulty of specifying L on machines with variable instruction lengths. But beyond that, there is the simplicity of the measure itself. The use of number of additions and multiplications per second prejudices the measure in favor of scientific-type applications, while for many types of applications, character manipulation and nonnumeric instructions may be more important. Finally, there is the problem that Gruenberger's measure of effectiveness is only a measure of computing power in some absolute sense. It does not attempt to relate the power of the machine to the applications for which the computer is to be used.

One way around this problem has been to use weighting schemes for classes of instructions. These weights are derived from "typical" scientific or commercial jobs and represent the importance of that category of instruction for a given class of job. One proposed weighting scheme is given in Table 3-1.

[1] Fred Gruenberger, "Are Small, Free-standing Computers Here to Stay?" *Datamation, April,* 1966, pp. 67–68.

These weights were given by Kenneth Knight in his doctoral thesis, and were derived from a dynamic trace of instructions executed on an IBM 7090 for a set of scientific and commercial jobs. These weights are then multiplied by the costs of execution for the various classes of instructions, and these are summed to give the measure of effectiveness for a given machine for a given application. This formula is

$$E = \sum_{i=1}^{N} C_i W_i$$

where E = effectiveness
       C_i = cost of execution of instruction class i
       W_i = relative frequency of instruction class i

One problem with this kind of effectiveness measure is that it is difficult to break jobs up into the "scientific" and "commercial" classes envisioned by the weighting system used. For new computers, the relative frequency of the instruction classes may depend on the compilers supplied with the machine, and it may be very difficult to get information on what to expect from them.

This kind of weighted score approach has been extended beyond a simple evaluation of the CPU of the machine. Sharpe[2] gives an example of one computer systems study that used a weighted score where all aspects of the computer system were considered and then subjective scores were assigned for each computer system considered. The weight table used in this study is given in Table 3-2.

TABLE 3-2   RAND Weighting System

Divisions	Items evaluated	Weight
1. Hardware	38	0.27
2. Supervisor	18	0.27
3. Data management	8	0.08
4. Language processors	31	0.16
5. General programming support	4	0.02
6. Conversion considerations	8	0.12
7. Vendor reliability and support	16	0.08

The weights given in Table 3-2 are then combined into an overall score in the same way by multiplying the individual weights by the scores below:

$$S = \sum_{i=1}^{n} W_i S_i$$

One possible problem with this type of scoring system is the linearity assumption that it implicitly makes. It assumes that the score on one factor is independent of all other factors. Economically, this means that for two factors in the evaluation, there is a marginal rate of substitution W_i/W_j between them. In fact, this may not be the case with a real-world computer system. Suppose that one system rates high for hardware speed, but the vendor support is very poor. The superior hardware speed may never be used because of the poor support, and the two factors are really not substitutable.

This problem could be handled by modifying the objective function to one of the form

$$S = \prod_{i=1}^{n} S_i^{W_i}$$

or

$$\log_{10} S = \sum W_i \log_{10} S_i$$

The scoring system above has the mathematical disadvantage that a zero score on any one factor, no matter how unimportant, gives a zero score for the overall evaluation.

[2] William F. Sharpe, *The Economics of Computers*, Columbia University Press, New York, p. 285.

(In the first expression above, the Greek pi means "take the product of all the terms," in the same sense that sigma means "take the sum of all the terms.")

The primary advantage of weighting systems like that presented in Table 3-2 is not that they provide absolute answers to computer system comparison and evaluation questions, but rather that they force the persons selecting the system to sit down and state their needs explicitly, and give the criteria for meeting these needs. This is an important first step in system selection, but the use of these means by themselves is not sufficient.

Kernel Evaluation   Moving beyond these scoring systems, another approach that has been suggested is the development of *kernels*. A kernel is the central processing required on a given machine to execute a specific task, such as matrix multiplication, calculating a Social Security tax, or evaluating a polynomial. The problem is assumed to have been coded by assembly language programmers of similar levels of sophistication for the machine involved. This particular approach to hardware evaluation is seldom used. The design of a representative set of tasks to qualify as kernels is difficult, as is the requirement that the programs be done by programmers of comparable levels of skills for the machines being tested. In any event, the use of kernels concentrates solely on the evaluation of CPU performance, and does not consider the total performance of the system.

Benchmarks   The problem of evaluation of the total system can be handled to some extent through the use of benchmark programs. Benchmark programs are test programs coded in a higher-level language that can be run on the different machine configurations being compared. Benchmark programs may be actual production programs from the organization doing the evaluation, or they may be specially designed test programs. In either case, an attempt should be made to ensure that the programs represent an adequate sample of the type of work the computer will be used for.

The Auerbach Corporation, which publishes *Standard EDP Reports*, proposes a series of six major benchmark problem classes for purposes of comparison of the different machines they evaluate:

Updating sequential files
Updating random-access files
Sorting
Matrix inversion
Evaluation of complex equations
Statistical computations

These tests are for a general-purpose evaluation of computers, and any organization considering a computer acquisition would have to design a set of specific tests to meet its needs. If the computer were to be used primarily for scientific and engineering computations, then benchmark tests designed to test the I/0 features of the machine would not have to be especially sophisticated. A company planning to use the machine for data processing only could do without the benchmark tests for mathematical manipulations.

In the preparation of benchmark programs, care should be taken to avoid such things as nonstandard coding or dependence on special routines such as random-number generators that may change the path of execution from one test to another. An attempt should be made to stay close to defined standard languages such as FORTRAN or COBOL, so that fair tests can be run across machine lines.

One problem in the use of benchmark programs comes when the programs are being run on a multiprogramming machine. In this case, it may be difficult to obtain meaningful figures on elapsed time or resource usage for a given program. Such figures may not really be relevant anyway, since what one is interested in is the throughput or number of jobs that can be put through the machine in a given period of time. In this kind of situation, one approach might be to duplicate groups of the benchmark programs and see how many such programs could be run on different configurations. Again, some thought should go into the programs selected for the tests.

Multiprogramming systems can achieve some of their economies by having I/0-bound jobs in one partition, and compute-bound jobs in another, so that the two jobs are not competing for the same resources. A sample of benchmark programs selected for testing a multiprogramming system should include jobs of both types.

MATHEMATICAL MODELS: QUEUEING THEORY

Mathematical models from queueing theory are at the same time the simplest and most difficult tools to use. When an appropriate model exists, it may be a simple matter of plugging the parameters into the model. When an appropriate model does not exist, or to be more precise, has not been solved, considerable mathematical expertise will be needed to solve the problem, if it can be solved at all.

Our approach here will be to outline briefly some of the queueing theory models for which solutions exist, and which have been used in investigating computer system performance. Those wishing to use these models should refer to one of the texts mentioned in the Selective Bibliography for more detailed information.

Nonmultiprogramming Models The simplest queueing theory models are still useful for estimating throughput and waiting time in a nonmultiprogrammed batch system.

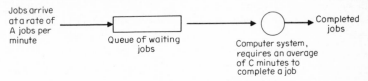

Jobs arrive at a rate of A jobs per minute — Queue of waiting jobs — Computer system, requires an average of C minutes to complete a job — Completed jobs

Fig. 3-1   Model of a batch system.

It is assumed that the general characteristics of the jobs to be run are known. In particular, the time required to execute the average job must be known. The model assumes that the jobs to be run arrive at random, but at some average rate of A jobs per minute. They are placed in a first-come, first-served queue, and each job is run to completion when it reaches the head of the queue.

Let us assume the average execution time for a job is C minutes. Schematically then, we have the model of Figure 3-1. The solution of the model then provides the following results for the average number of jobs which will be found in the queue, and the average time a job will wait from the time it is submitted until it has been completed:

Average queue length: $AC/(1 - AC)$

Average waiting time: $C/(1 - AC)$

For example, if the arrival rate is one job every 5 minutes on the average $(A = 0.20)$, and the average time required to complete a job is 4 minutes $(C = 4)$, then the average number of jobs waiting will be four and the average waiting time will be 20 minutes.

Though the average arrival rate of jobs is known, as is their average running time, the actual moments of arrival and execution times for individual jobs will vary from this average. The average running time for 10 jobs is 1 minute if each job requires 1 minute or if 5 jobs take 30 seconds and 5 jobs take 1 minute and 30 seconds. The degree to which the running times (and arrival intervals) differ from the average is characterized by a mathematical curve called the *probability distribution*.[3] Certain such distributions appear so commonly that they have been given names. One of these is called the *exponential distribution*. It is the simplest and often most reasonable distribution to use in modeling computer arrival and service processes.

The preceding results are not exact unless the service time distribution is exponential. Certain other assumptions made in solving this model must also be verified before the predictions of the model can be considered reliable. When the service time distribution is not exponential, or when more detailed predictions, such as the waiting time distribution, are wanted, other models are available. If A and C are known only approximately, the additional accuracy gained by using a model which more precisely reflects the structure of the system being modeled may be minimal.

Multiprogramming Models A multiprogrammed computer system is structurely quite different from a nonmultiprogrammed one. Jobs are processed in a pseudoparallel fashion. They do not usually finish execution in the same order they started execution, or in the same order they were submitted. A different kind of model is needed to reflect

[3] See E. G. Coffman and P. J. Denning, "Operating System Theory," McGraw-Hill, New York, 1973.

this structure. The central idea of a multiprogramming system is to switch the central processor from job to job at a rapid rate, giving the appearance of sharing the processor among the jobs. The rule governing the assignment of the processor to jobs is called the *processor scheduling algorithm.* The scheduling algorithm is implemented as part of the operating system or supervisory program of the computer. Much of the motivation for the development of multiprogramming models was to study such scheduling algorithms. Consequently models predicting system performance under a variety of scheduling algorithms are available.[4]

The use of a multiprogramming system does not affect the jobs to be run, so the characterization of the demand requires the same parameters as in the nonmultiprogramming model. Jobs are assumed to arrive at a rate of A jobs per minute, and require C minutes of processor time to complete. The schematic of the model, however, looks slightly different (Figure 3-2).

Since the processor is switched from job to job, the queue may contain new jobs, which have yet to be run, and also partially completed jobs, which have received some

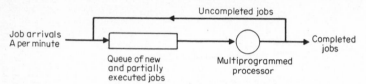

Fig. 3-2   Model of a multiprogramming system.

processor time, but not enough to complete execution. Jobs are selected from the queue according to the scheduling algorithm. It is no longer necessarily a first-come, first-served procedure. In fact there are usually a number of separate queues. There may be one queue of new jobs, one of jobs which have executed for a short time, and a third for longer-running jobs.

We note in passing two limitations to the multiprogramming models for which solutions exist. The first is that they ignore all aspects of the jobs other than their use of the central processor. Input-output activity in particular is not reflected in the model. Second, there is an implicit assumption that the multiprogramming level is unlimited. Any job which arrives is submitted and is immediately eligible to be run. The job scheduler, a component of many operating systems, is not reflected in the model. Of course, if sufficient memory is available and the number of waiting jobs is not too great, the assumption that the multiprogramming level is equal to the number of jobs submitted but not completed may be valid.

Predictions available from multiprogramming models are similar to those available from the nonmultiprogramming class. Average queue length and waiting time are usually available. Another measure of interest is the average waiting time for jobs which require a given amount of processor time. Since scheduling algorithms are designed to favor short jobs, the average waiting time for a job requiring one minute of processor time may be considerably less than the waiting time of a job requiring two minutes of processor time.

Time-Sharing Models Both the preceding models assume that jobs continue to arrive at a rate A, independent of the number of jobs already in the queue. This is obviously an incorrect assumption. The longer the queue gets, the less likely it is that new jobs will be added to it, since more and more of the potential job submitters are waiting for their jobs to be completed. This independent arrival stream assumption is reasonable in many cases, especially when the user population is large. In an interactive system, however, requests for service come from terminals, whose number is relatively small and well known. Each of these terminal users acts more or less independently. He or she presents a request for service to the computer and awaits a response (the completion of the request). The servicing of requests made from the terminals can be treated in the same way as it was in the multiprogramming or nonmultiprogramming models presented above. The difference is in the way in which jobs arrive. In an interactive

[4] Ibid.

system *job* has a different meaning. It is the service required to respond to a user's input. Instead of turnaround time, the usual performance measure of an interactive system is response time, the time to complete a terminal request. With our changed interpretation of a job, however, it is the same measure, in terms of the model.

As an example of time-sharing models, we present a modified version of the non-multiprogrammed model discussed above (Figure 3-3). In this case the system is assumed to have a fixed number of "users," each of whom independently makes requests for service. When the user makes this request, he or she joins a queue of other requests made from other terminals, and makes no more requests until receiving a response from the system. The computer time required to make this response is again some random amount of time whose characteristics must be determined from knowl-

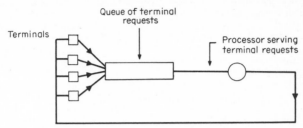

Fig. 3-3   Model of a time-sharing system.

edge about system demand and performance, as in the original nonmultiprogramming model.

In this case, the results to be derived are primarily the average response time, which corresponds to waiting time in a batch model. For example, where the mean time to *make* a request, for a given user, is A seconds, a system with N users will have an average response time of

$$\frac{NC}{(1 - P_0)} - \frac{1}{A}$$

P_0 is the probability the computer is idle, and can also be calculated from the model.

This type of model, called a *finite source* model, can be extended to the multiprogramming case as well, to examine the effects of different scheduling algorithms.

Limitations We list here a few cautionary notes which apply to the use of queueing theory models to estimate system performance. The models generally oversimplify the system structure. They require system demand to be characterized by at most a few numbers—for example, arrival rate of jobs and average computing time for a job. Thus they can be extremely sensitive to the parameters supplied. An error of a few per cent in estimating average job execution time can in certain cases cause the model to overestimate or underestimate turnaround time by a factor of 2. (True, the cases when this may happen are unusual, and they are easily recognizable to someone familiar with the techniques. It is mentioned here to warn the uninitiated not to plunge ahead blindly believing his or her results are the gospel truth.)

As has already been mentioned, queueing theory models place considerable emphasis on the central processor as the cause of delays in the computing system. Contention for other resources, such as memory, I/0 channels, and peripheral devices, is ignored. Where this is important, the models outlined are not likely to be accurate, though they may still be useful. In these cases, it may be possible to use a fairly recent development in queueing theory models for computer systems. These models are called *network models* and allow each resource in the computer system to be represented independently.[5]

SIMULATION TECHNIQUES

In all the approaches to computer system evaluation discussed so far, the measures provided are along only one or two dimensions. One approach that can be used to

[5] Ibid.

provide more detailed evaluations is computer simulation. In this approach, the characteristics of the job mix being fed into the computer are specified, and a simulated model of a given configuration is developed and tested against the job mix. Performance figures are given along a variety of dimensions for the machine being simulated. Computer simulation models can be implemented using any of the standard simulation languages such as GPSS or SIMSCRIPT, or a special-purpose language for the simulation of computer systems can be used. Examples of such languages are IBM's CSS (Computer System Simulator), Lockheed's LOMUSS II (Lockheed Multipurpose Simulation System), or Comress's SCERT (Systems and Computer Evaluation and Review Technique).

Of the systems for computer simulation, SCERT is probably the most widely known and used. It was developed by Comress Inc. and is rented to companies considering a computer acquisition. SCERT is not exactly a simulation system in the sense that a GPSS or SIMSCRIPT model of a computer system is. It does not simulate detailed job arrival and processing events. It utilizes a heuristic approach of estimating the performance of a given configuration based on empirically derived equations that propose to predict performance under a given job mix.

A SCERT run is divided into five phases. In the first phase, the job mix and system environment are input. In the second phase, the configurations of the different computer systems selected for evaluation are built up. In the third phase, the simulation preprocessing is run, and in the fourth phase the simulations themselves are run. Finally, a series of reports are produced for the user, giving the results of running the job mix on the simulated systems.

Simulation can be a valuable planning tool, but like the other methods discussed earlier, it must be used carefully. Sometimes, relatively small changes in the initial assumptions can cause large changes in the final results. It is difficult initially to gauge the sensitivity of a simulated system to these changes. It is always important in using a simulation model to set up some validation runs with the model. For these runs, test data are used where the results in the real-world system are already known. These real-world results are then compared with those generated by the model to assess the ability of the model to make predictions.

SELECTING EVALUATION METHODS

One test of the effectiveness of these various methods of computer selection is a look at the practices used in actual computer selection decisions. A survey was made in 1967 of the selection practices of 69 computer users in business, government, and universities to determine their computer selection criteria. One perhaps expectable result that emerged from this study was that the methods used in making such decisions depended heavily on the amount of money involved and the sophistication of the organization making the decision. (See Table 3-3.)

In all classes of organizations, benchmark programs and test programs were heavily used. Their use was lowest in the lowest rental categories, probably because this category included companies that were first-time computer users and did not have a backlog of usable programs or experienced programmers. In this category, there was a larger reliance on published reports as a means of evaluation. In the intermediate

TABLE 3-3   Computer Selection Practices as Related to System Billings*

	Method				
Monthly rental	Benchmark programs	Published evaluations	Test programs	Simulation	Models
$0–$14,000	50.0	80.8	53.8	7.7	0
$15,000–$49,000	81.8	77.3	54.5	13.6	4.5
$50,000 and up	76.9	53.8	61.5	46.2	30.8

* *Note:* The totals across rows exceed 100 per cent because some organizations used more than one method.

SOURCE: Norman Schnirdewind, "The Practice of Computer Selection," *Datamation*, February, 1967, pp. 22–25.

price ranges, the use of benchmark programs increased by 60 per cent over the lower rental category. This no doubt occurs because users in the intermediate category are upgrading their equipment and have a good idea of the types of performance standards required.

Only in the very large rental category were simulation and mathematical modeling techniques used to any great extent. There are a variety of reasons for this. First of all, users who can spend that kind of money on computer systems are also likely to be technically very sophisticated and quite capable of designing and using advanced modeling methods. Second, computer systems in this rental category are much more likely to be large systems embodying the latest technological advances, and conventional methods of system evaluation may not apply. For these systems, it may be necessary to use simulation or complex mathematical models to obtain an idea of the factors that will affect system performance.

The applicability of any of the methods of estimating system performance discussed herein will depend to a large degree on the size and use of the computer equipment being considered. The mathematical approaches such as queueing theory and the various power formulas apply primarily to relatively simple systems. Such an approach may prove useful for comparing one minicomputer to another for a fairly standard application. However, such techniques break down when complicated systems with a nonstandard mix of jobs are being considered.

For more complicated systems, the scoring approaches may be a useful beginning to system selection. The answers this method provides tell the decision makers more about the goals of the organization than they do about the particular computer system, but the determination of organizational goals is an important first step in deciding upon a specific computer system. If the organization has the capability available, mathematical modeling and simulation may prove helpful also. The only relevant question is which system can most effectively process the computing work of the organization, and in the end, this is usually a matter of selecting from among several serviceable computing systems and then fine-tuning the system over a period of months or years to meet the changing needs of the organization.

VENDOR SELECTION

In addition to hardware performance and feasibility, two important issues to be considered in the selection of a specific vendor are the time before the system will be operational, and the specific type of support the supplier will provide along with the hardware.

Of these two considerations, the timing of system availability is probably the most critical. A computer system is usually used to augment or replace existing systems, and successful computer systems installations require a great deal of advanced planning. There is usually a period where the old and new systems are run in parallel to work out the problems and ease the introduction. In some cases, increasing workloads make it imperative that a new computer system be operational by the date for which it was promised. Failure to meet the due dates can be financially disastrous.

The second consideration, system support, has always been a potential source of misunderstanding between the supplier and the customer. Originally, the customer paid for the hardware and the software support was provided "free" if at all. The responsibility for maintenance of the system hardware was usually provided for by advance agreement, and could be handled either by the customer or by the supplier for a standard rate. Since the unbundling decision of IBM in 1969, the range of system options has become a good deal more complex.

CASH-FLOW ANALYSIS

Hardware selection cannot be considered apart from the impact of a new computer installation on the entire organization. Since one of the primary concerns of any new system installation is obtaining the system needed to handle the data processing needs of the organization in a reasonable time frame, a cash-flow analysis of the project is necessary. This type of analysis naturally assumes that the time commitments implied in the analysis can be met, and that the system being considered is a technically feasible system for the organization.

As an example of cash-flow analysis, consider an organization that is replacing a traditional card-oriented system. The system installation is to take place over a 2-year period with delivery on the computer system taking place at the beginning of the first year. The first 6 months of the first year will be spent in planning for the new system. During the last 6 months of the first year, computer time will be rented on a similar machine at a local service bureau, so that program development can take place in advance of the delivery of the new machine. During the first quarter of the second year, both the old and new systems will be run in parallel to iron out any problems. During the second quarter, part of the old equipment will be phased out, and during the third quarter, all the old equipment will be removed. The project staff will continue to operate at a reduced level during the third quarter of the second year, and by the fourth quarter, the system should be fully operational.

To facilitate control of the project, a series of three charts were developed outlining the expenditures and the timing of the project development. The figures are hypothetical, but they represent the type of calculations that should be made. The first chart, Table 3-4, gives the development costs of the systems project itself. For the first year, training costs are $1,000 a quarter. They jump to $3,000 a quarter in the first half of the second year as training for the operational staff of the system is done. There is a staff of systems analysts and programmers associated with project control and the implementation of the new features associated with the systems installation. This staff is gradually decreased as the project becomes fully operational. In addition, there is also a group of analysts charged with the responsibility for conversion of applications on the old system to the new system. Finally, during the last half of the first year, outside computer time is rented so that development work can begin in advance of the delivery of the new computer. The column labeled "Total Development" gives the total cash flows in each period associated with the development aspects of the project.

Table 3-5 gives the operating expenses of the new system. The equipment rentals

TABLE 3-4   Project Development Costs

Year	Qtr	Training costs	Equipment and supplies	Project staff	Old-system conversion	Computer rentals	Total development
1	1	$ 1,000	$ 500	$ 15,000	$ 0	$ 0	$ 16,500
1	2	1,000	500	15,000	0	0	16,500
1	3	1,000	1,500	25,000	10,000	2,000	39,500
1	4	1,000	1,500	25,000	10,000	0	39,500
2	1	3,000	500	25,000	10,000	0	38,500
2	2	3,000	500	15,000	10,000	0	28,500
2	3	0	500	10,000	10,000	0	20,500
2	4	0	0	0	0	0	0
Totals		$10,000	$5,500	$130,000	$50,000	$2,000	$199,500

TABLE 3-5   Operating Expenses

Year	Qtr	Communications equipment	Computer rentals	Software rentals	Staff	Supplies	Total operating expense
1	1	$ 0	$ 0	$ 0	$ 0	$ 0	$ 0
1	2	0	0	0	0	0	0
1	3	0	0	0	10,000	500	10,500
1	4	0	0	800	10,000	500	11,300
2	1	20,000	25,000	800	15,000	2,000	62,800
2	2	20,000	25,000	800	15,000	2,000	62,800
2	3	20,000	25,000	800	20,000	3,000	68,800
2	4	20,000	25,000	800	20,000	3,000	68,800
Totals		$80,000	$100,000	$4,000	$90,000	$11,000	$285,000

for both the computer and the communications begin in the second year and are $25,-000 and $20,000 per quarter respectively. In addition to the hardware rentals, some special software packages are rented, and their cost comes to $800 per quarter. These rentals begin in the last quarter of the first year as the software packages are first tested on the rented computer equipment. The costs for the operational staff and supplies for the new system begin in the last half of the first year and reach their permanent levels by the second half of the second year. The final column, "Total Operating Expense," gives the totals of the quarterly figures.

TABLE 3-6   Savings and Cash Flow.

Year	Qtr	Personnel savings	Equipment savings	Total savings	Yearly cash flow
1	1	$ 0	$ 0	$ 0	$−16,500
1	2	0	0	0	−16,500
1	3	0	0	0	−50,000
1	4	0	0	0	−50,800
2	1	5,000	1,500	6,500	−94,800
2	2	20,000	13,000	33,000	−58,300
2	3	40,000	30,000	70,000	−19,300
2	4	40,000	30,000	70,000	+ 1,200
Totals		$105,000	$74,500	$179,500	

The last chart, Table 3-6, gives the savings generated by the introduction of the new equipment. These savings begin in the second year and are generated as the old equipment is phased out and the old operating personnel are retrained, transferred, or released. The column labeled "Total Savings" gives the total amount saved in each quarter as the old system is dismantled, and the column labeled "Yearly Cash Flow" represents the total investment in the project (project development and costs plus operating expenses) subtracted from the total savings. The total investment in the project comes to $306,200 over a period of 21 months, and this investment generates savings of $1,200 per quarter for the life of the system.

This investment can be analyzed by conventional capital budgeting techniques[6] to determine whether or not the investment is worthwhile. A straight cash-flow analysis should be used cautiously, however. In this example, the cash flows turned out to be positive, and this may not always be the case. The investment in the example assumed that the new machine would be able to pay for itself by displacing old personnel and equipment. The clerical displacement cost justification will not necessarily hold when new applications are being considered. New applications may have to be justified on the basis of such things as better service, timeliness of information, and so on, and these factors are not readily computed in a standard cash-flow analysis.

What the cash-flow analysis does give is an explicit determination of the costs associated with the project. Even if the flows are negative through the life of the system, this shows management what price it is paying for the improved service. The cash-flow analysis also provides a means of comparing one computer system with another on the basis of the cash flows each generates.

CONCLUSIONS

It is not possible in a treatment such as this to cover in detail all the pitfalls and problems of selecting a hardware configuration and a vendor for that configuration. The problem can generally be simplified if approached in an orderly fashion. The structure and organization of the system should be well defined before the question of hardware requirements is considered in detail. What kinds of demands are to be placed on the system must be fairly well known before hardware can be evaluated. These initial phases of system design may often severely restrict the possible hardware configura-

[6] See, for example, Harold Bierman, Jr., and S. Smidt, *The Capital Budgeting Decision*, Macmillan, New York, 1971.

tions. Adoption of a particular programming language or software system may require the acquisition of a particular vendor's hardware.

A good rule is to attempt to consider separately quantitative and qualitative questions. The decision to develop an on-line, real-time information system instead of using more traditional batch techniques cannot be made without some estimate of system cost and feasibility. As far as possible, however, one should consider this question without regard to a particular vendor's equipment. This will avoid the mistake of rejecting a system design because it is uneconomical when in fact that is not the case. This can easily happen if the hardware configuration is selected simultaneously with system design. The system design may be entirely reasonable, but not suited to the particular hardware chosen. If the system design is reasonably well fixed before hardware is evaluated, the most economical system can be chosen, or the nonexistence of a feasible system can be determined. It is to the solution of these questions that the tools of this Chapter are directed.

SELECTIVE BIBLIOGRAPHY

Bierman, Harold, Jr., and S. Smidt, *The Capital Budgeting Decision*, Macmillan, New York, 1971.
Coffman, E. G., Jr., and P. J. Denning, *Operating System Theory*, McGraw-Hill, New York, 1973.
Dearden, John, F., Warren McFarlan, and William Zani, *Managing Computer Based Information Systems*, Irwin, Homewood, Ill., 1971.
Herman, Donald, "SCERT: A Computer Evaluation Tool," *Datamation*, February, 1967, pp. 26–28.
Sharpe, William, *The Economics of Computers*, Columbia University Press, New York, 1969.

Chapter **4**

Software Requirements

TOBY S. BERK, Ph.D.

Associate Professor of Computer Science, Mathematical Sciences Department, Florida International University, Miami, Florida

A number of crucial decisions concerning software must be made while creating the detailed design of an ADP system. These include the overall software organization of the various components of the system, the choice of the computer language or languages to be used, the choice of operating system features which are needed for the system, and the decision whether to use a commercially available system or subsystem rather than producing the needed software in-house.

The individual or group responsible for the detailed system design must have expertise which overlaps that of the systems analyst on one end and that of the programmer on the other. He or she must have a good overview of the role of the system as part of the total ADP environment of the firm, and also have considerable technical knowledge concerning the details of programming, file storage and handling, etc.

It is of great importance, especially at this stage, that the initial system design remain flexible. Often during the detailed system design it will become apparent that minor changes in the specifications can greatly simplify the implementation. Of course, the overall information needs of the organization should not lightly be compromised in the name of efficiency. Nevertheless, channels of communication must remain open between the designer (and later, the programmers) and the analyst.

One of the most important decisions to be made is that of programming language or languages to be used. As we shall see, this choice can have great effects upon the overall structure of the system, its file handling techniques, etc. Another software consideration is that of the operating system. The operating system in a modern computer installation performs a major part of the total work done in an ADP system.[1] Furthermore, operating systems are very difficult to modify, and the nature of successive new releases provided by the manufacturer makes the maintenance of modifications a continual task. Thus, operating system considerations often lie at the very heart of the system.

Computer programming and the implementation of computer systems are very expensive operations, and it is often difficult to guarantee the final cost or performance of the system. A significant question, therefore, is whether or not to produce the

---

[1] See Section 2, Part 4, Chapter 4, "Operating Systems."

needed software in-house, or to make use of an increasing number of commercially available systems.[2]

SOFTWARE ORGANIZATION

Flexibility One aspect of data processing systems all too often overlooked is that any system will probably be changed several times during its useful life. In fact, the length of the useful life of a program is dependent on how easily it can be changed. Figure 4-1 shows the cost of a typical system over a period of years under two assumptions.

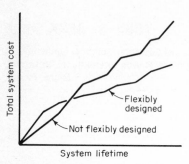

Fig. 4-1 **Cost advantage of flexible design.**

The system can be designed from the start to be flexible, with some increase in initial cost (although such an increase is by no means inevitable in a flexible design), or considerations of flexibility can be ignored. One should be extremely cautious of statements to the effect that a system will not be modified in the future (although sometimes such statements can be made safely, especially for systems which have a short intended life). The best way to minimize the long-run costs of a system is through careful planning at its inception. One of the best techniques for constructing a flexible, easily modified program is that of *modular* system design.

Modular System Design A modular system (or program) has a structure like that shown in Figure 4-2. Each subtask to be performed has a corresponding program module (represented by a circle in the fig-

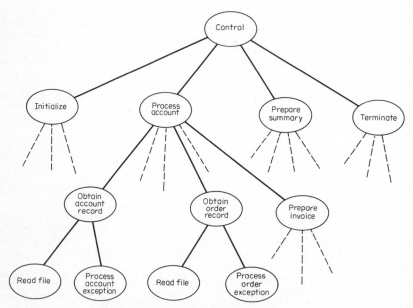

Fig. 4-2 **Modular system (or program) structure.**

ure). Each module should be of moderate size (100 to 300 statements) and should be *self-contained*. By making each module self-contained (i.e., its results depend only on the data passed to it), it becomes much easier to debug and modify modules individually.

[2] See Section 6, "Outside Services for Data Processing."

If the logical subtasks of the system are properly assigned to modules, modifications become an almost routine procedure. For example, a system might consist of one primary module which merely calls on the other modules in the proper sequence. This module would appear at the top of a diagram such as shown in Figure 4-2. Below the top module, and called by it, are modules which are responsible for performing the basic subtasks of the system (such as "process customer account," "prepare summary report," etc.). These perform their tasks by using modules at a still lower level ("obtain next order record," "prepare invoice").

All input and output, all report generation, and all reference to particular file structure will occur in low-level modules and will be isolated in them. Thus, a change in file elements (perhaps the addition of more information) will affect only the module that performs the actual file reading. Furthermore, if it becomes desirable to have other programs and systems utilize the same file at a later time, the same module can be used.

In addition, changes in logic can be made at the level of the control module without having to consider the detailed file structure. Changes in equipment can be made without having to consider the control structure. Changes in report format can be easily made because there is one module which is responsible for that format.

One of the main benefits of modular design is that each module can be tested separately. The entire system can be tested by replacing the "read file" modules with modules which generate test data, and all other modules can be tested by examining only the output which they produce for proper input. Also, a change in the system can be debugged separately and then later added to the system with the expectation that the system will run correctly.

CHOICE OF LANGUAGE

The choice of the programming language (or languages) to be used for the implementation of the system may be more important than it first appears. The language used in writing a program has a significant effect on the way that the program is organized, on the way that the data files are structured, etc. Unfortunately, many factors are involved in the choice of language, and therefore there is no one choice which is best for all applications.

General Considerations The following are some of the factors which should be considered when choosing a programming language.

1. *Ease of programming.* If early completion is very important, efficiency of the final product may be sacrificed for a reduction in the total programming and debugging effort. This will also be true if the phase of the system will have only limited life, such as a program or set of programs to convert an existing data file into a different format for use with a new system.

2. *Efficiency of result.* If the system is going to be run often, and will use a large amount of time and/or memory, then the size and speed of the resulting machine language program will be important. The efficiency of the available compilers and translators must be examined. In very extreme cases it might even be necessary to code certain key modules in assembly language. (This should be avoided if at all possible.)

3. *Ease of documentation.* Because programs are inevitably maintained and modified by programmers who did not write them, the ease with which they can be understood will have a significant influence on their long-run cost. Some high-level languages such as COBOL and PL/I are more easily understood, read, and therefore documented. Assembly language, as an example, is extremely difficult to document properly, and therefore very expensive to maintain and modify.

4. *Ease of debugging and maintenance.* It is axiomatic that no large system is ever completely debugged. It is also true that correcting one bug often creates another in some obscure manner. The choice of programming language used for a system can have a major influence on the ease of tracking down and removing errors which may surface long after the system is in production. Some languages (such as PL/I) contain powerful facilities for finding and correcting errors. Other languages, without such facilities, may require laborious pouring over core dumps. Often, the availability of such features is not actually a characteristic of the language chosen, but rather a characteristic of the compiler supplied by the manufacturer.

5. *Ease of conversion.* A crucial time in the life of any system comes when the

equipment upon which it runs is upgraded or replaced. At current rates, such a change can be expected at least every 4 years or so from technological advances, and more often as a result of the growth of the data processing sector of the organization. In order to make such conversions tolerable and still retain a degree of flexibility in the choice of equipment (avoiding the necessity to stay with the same line of equipment merely in order to run the old system), the system should be written in a *machine-independent* and *standardized* language. The use of special features added to a standard language by the manufacturer should be avoided, even though this may mean that the programmers must be instructed to use only a subset of the language chosen. Beware of a language that is not in wide use by a number of manufacturers.

6. *Effect on file and program organization.* The choice of programming language can have an effect on the overall organization of the programs and the files it references. Some languages facilitate the division of programs into modules, while others make it difficult or inefficient. Also, some languages do not provide efficient means of accessing certain file structures. Furthermore, the files produced by a program written in one language may not be accessible to other programs written in other languages.

7. *Programmer hiring and training.* If the firm has an adequate programming staff for the implementation of the system, the choice of a language that does not match the staff's experience will incur training costs and will also raise the cost of producing the final system. On the other hand, avoidance of change will cause the organization to be locked into obsolescent technology. If the system being developed will cause additional new staff to be hired, other considerations apply. Some languages (notably COBOL) are easier to staff than others because of the number of programmers available with proper experience. On the other hand, the need to hire new staff may provide an opportunity to use a more modern and flexible language (such as PL/I).

Common Choices   Most systems used in industry are now written in a high-level procedural language. In fact, the vast majority are written in either COBOL, FORTRAN, or PL/I. FORTRAN is used primarily where large files are not handled by the system, and the main thrust is computational. COBOL is the standard choice for applications which are oriented toward the handling of large files. PL/I combines both file handling and computational power in a structure which makes modularization very easy. In addition, PL/I contains good debugging facilities.[3]

Special-Purpose Languages   For certain pieces of a system, special-purpose languages may be used to advantage. Languages such as APL (for interactive systems), SNOBOL4 (for performing one-time conversion and special modification of file items), and various simulation languages[4] can greatly simplify certain tasks. The special-purpose languages are especially attractive for systems which will not have long life (thus eliminating considerations of conversion, maintenance, etc.). Such applications might include one-time simulation studies and one-time database conversions. Other special-purpose languages have application in special areas, such as computer graphics and computer-aided design.

Database Languages   In an environment which supports a large database, certain file processing operations are performed over and over again. These operations include the following: file creation (initial creation of a file from other files or new input data); file validation (checking the entries in a file to ensure that they do not contain, for example, alphabetic characters in numeric fields); file maintenance (insertion, deletion, replacement of file items without any arithmetic operations involved); sorting of the items in a file according to some key; data retrieval (obtaining a particular item of information, or set of items, from a file); and report generation. Special database languages have been developed and are widely used to facilitate these operations.[5]

The use of a suitable database management language, or system, allows all programs to access data files without any need to consider their storage and organization. This is in contrast to the usual situation where each program specifies and describes its own data files. If files are handled separately, they are frequently designed to optimize processing for only a few programs. In addition, they may reflect the file structure used by one particular language, and thus be inaccessible to other programs.

---

[3] See Section 2, Part 4, Chapter 3, "Programming Languages."
[4] See Section 3, Part 1, Chapter 3, "Simulation and Models for Decision Making."
[5] See Section 5, Chapter 6, "The Technology of Database Management."

One of the major attractions of a database language is the ease with which management can obtain specific information from the database via terminals. Requests can be formulated fairly clearly, and can make use of combinations of keys in the retrieval process. For example, one may request the TOTAL SALES in REGION SIX for DECEMBER EXCLUDING ACCESSORIES.

Considerations in the evaluation of a database package include the following:

1. *Security.* Does the package include effective controls on both interrogation and alteration of key data? The use of frequently changed passwords, automatic recording of all accesses to certain files, and the limitation of certain operations to specified terminals are common techniques applied to this problem.

2. *File organization.* The system should not excessively limit the structure of the files which it references.[6]

3. *Size.* If the database package is to be used by various other programs, it must share memory with them. Therefore the amount of main memory required to run the package should not be any larger than necessary.

4. *On-line operations.* Does the package allow on-line inquiries? Does the system allow on-line updating of files? What is the response time of on-line operations?

5. *Audit trail.* Will the package automatically record all inquiries and changes made to confidential or critical files?

6. *Report generation.* Does the package allow data items to be combined with arithmetic operations while generating reports? The ability to form totals, differences, and percentages is an important part of any report generating system.

In-House Language Creation In very special applications within very large organizations with big, capable staffs, it may be justifiable to design and implement a special language. However, such undertakings are best left to organizations the size of Boeing Corp. or General Motors. There are, of course, exceptions, but suggestions to design special languages which originate from the programming staff should be treated skeptically.

Installation Standard Language Many organizations adopt the policy of using a single language for all their programming. Such a policy can have several advantages. For one, the use of a standard language makes it easy to specify and enforce installation-wide documentation standards. This can make maintenance and conversion much easier. The use of a standard language also makes the staffing of the data processing section easier. In addition, if all programs are written in a single language, both files and program modules can be freely used in more than one place.

There are also, however, drawbacks to a single-language policy. No single language is best suited to all the programming tasks in a modern installation. Thus, by choosing a single language one causes certain inefficiencies. Also, the choice of language can influence the choice of techniques used in programming. Once a policy has been established which sets up a single language for the entire installation, it may be very difficult subsequently to introduce new techniques and different languages. The use of a single language may also have negative effects on the upgrading of skills by the programming staff and tends to encourage a degree of stagnation.

OPERATING SYSTEM REQUIREMENTS

With the introduction of the third generation of computer systems, it has become almost impossible to consider the performance of a computer without considering the associated operating system. Modern computers are designed from the start to use a complicated operating system as an integral part of any program or system that is run. The performance of the operating system is probably the major factor besides basic memory speed influencing the total performance of a system.

Basic Operating Services The services provided by the operating system which have an influence on system design include the following:

1. *Job scheduling.* Some operating systems run jobs on a strict first-in, first-out basis. For many systems this is adequate. There are other systems which provide the ability to schedule jobs on the basis of some calculated priority system. In some, it is possible automatically to delay the execution of one program until another has com-

[6] See Section 5, Chapter 6, "The Technology of Database Management."

pleted its execution. This may be of advantage in systems where, for example, one program prepares a file that will be referenced by another. Some systems give the ability to attach a deadline to a job. The operating system can then schedule to utilize computer resources most efficiently and also guarantee that the deadline be met.

2. *Multiprogramming.* Computer systems that run one program at a time are inefficient in their utilization of the available resources of the system. For example, most programs do not use all the memory in the system. A program which does a great amount of input-output may use the central processor only a small part of the time, since most of the time it will be waiting for the completion of a (relatively) slow input-output operation. In a multiprogrammed system more than one program is "active" at a given time. Thus a small report generating program can share memory with several other programs at the same time.

When one program has to wait for some input or output, the operating system will assign the central processor to another program. The result of this multiprogramming can be increased production from the total computer system. In a multiprogramming system it is often possible to "roll out" a program temporarily (when a required device or other resource is not available, for example) and then roll it back in later for completion. When this feature is coupled with a priority scheduler, it is possible for one job to interrupt a currently executing job of lower priority and run immediately. Such a feature can, of course, make the operation of scheduling the computer shop much easier.

3. *Resource allocation.* In a multiprogrammed environment conflicts can arise between two or more programs that are running at the same time. For example, if the system has three tape drives, two programs can be executing, each of which is using one tape drive and requesting two additional tape drives in order to continue. Such a deadlock can occur in other ways as well. A good operating system will schedule jobs in such a way as to prevent such a conflict from "hanging" the system and requiring operator intervention. Also, a good operating system will have the facility to check and determine that the necessary resources are available before they are needed. This would include automatic verification that the proper disk pack, for example, is mounted *before* making an attempt to read from or write on it.

4. *Remote communication.* The operating system is responsible for handling all communication with remote terminals and remote computers. This includes automatic error checking, resending any message which is not properly received, and freeing the programmer from any need to have specific knowledge of the devices which are serving the remote function. In fact, the system should be completely "transparent" to the type of terminal being used without having to change the program itself.[7]

5. *Communications with operator.* In modern computer systems, most communication between the running program and the operator is done via the operating system. This includes instructions to mount and dismount data files as well as error messages. The messages given to the operator should be clear, and not require reference to a large book of translations. In addition, the operating system should allow the operations staff some degree of flexibility.

One recent system would issue a message to dismount a tape when processing of that tape was complete. It would then check that the dismount was proper. If the operator had anticipated the message, and already dismounted the tape, the system required that he or she remount it, so that the operating system could give the message to dismount it. Such practice can obviously reduce efficiency of the computer operation. At the same time, the operating system should check everything that the operator does before accepting it and continuing.

6. *Accounting.* Depending upon the nature of the organization, it may be very important to obtain a detailed accounting of the cost of each job run on the computer. This is particularly true when funds from an outside source, such as the Government, are being used to pay for some of the computing being done at an installation. In a multiprogramming system, it might be difficult to calculate the total cost of running a program. This is true because the program may sit idle in memory while other programs are running, or it may tie up the very expensive central processor for long periods of time. There may also be costs associated with the use of tape and disk

---

[7] See Section 2, Part Three, Chapter 3, "Remote Terminals."

drives, with mounting and dismounting of data files, and with the printing of output. The operating system may make it easy to write and install an accounting system by providing the needed information. The accounting system supplied by the manufacturer with the operating system may, in itself, be adequate.

7. *Input-output control.* The operating system handles all communication between programs and input-output devices. As such, it is responsible for handling input-output operations with a minimum of delay and with a maximum of reliability. The programmer should be able to leave details of access to the operating system, and should not have to worry about the detailed characteristics of the particular devices being used. Furthermore, errors should be handled in a flexible manner. One bad record should not necessarily cause an entire job to be terminated without the alternative of continuing with the rest of the run. Because all input-output operations are handled by the operating system, the availability of certain data-access facilities in the operating system limits the possible file organizations which can be used. Alternatively, the desired form of file organization will often be a significant factor in the choice of operating system and operating system components.

8. *Program organization.* Many programs are too large to reside in the memory of the computer at one time. Other programs contain modules which are executed only at the beginning of the run, or only at the end, or only in response to certain rare error conditions. It is wasteful of computer memory to have those modules resident at all times while the program is running. In order to handle both of these situations, operating systems have facilities which allow programs to be *segmented* into small pieces, which are then loaded into memory only when needed. Other operating systems support *virtual memory,* in which a programmer can treat the machine as practically infinite in size and the operating system takes care of the task of seeing that the necessary parts are actually present in memory when needed.

The nature of the program segmentation facilities provided by the operating system can have an effect on the modularization of a system. Some systems require that if a module is in memory, all modules above it (see Figure 4-2) must also be in memory. Other operating systems (including virtual systems) do not make this requirement.

9. *Error handling.* The operating system provides the mechanism which handles errors in the system. Bad information on external storage devices, errors in the behavior of input-output controllers, errors in memory storage and reading, as well as errors in programs which make them attempt to read from devices which do not exist, etc., result in control being given to the operating system. In addition, operating systems themselves always contain "bugs." Their very size and complexity make it impossible ever to remove all errors from them. Therefore, from time to time any system will "crash."

The process which must be undergone to restart the system is an important factor in the choice of the system. Similarly, a good operating system will protect data files from being destroyed or lost in the event of a system crash. In hardware, program, and operating system error handling, the operator must be notified (if possible) by the system and as much diagnostic information as possible must be supplied.

Operating System Options   Many manufacturers provide the user with numerous options in the choice of operating system. One or more basic systems can be embellished with numerous refinements, each at a cost in dollars and computer memory space. The choice of operating system and system options greatly influences the design and performance of any system as well as its cost. Let us now examine some of the alternatives.

Mode of Operation   Most small installations operate in a *batch* mode, where each program is run in the machine alone and programs are run strictly in the order submitted. Such operation gives the most memory to the programs running, since the operating system can be relatively small. The disadvantage to batch operation is that the computer resources may be completely tied up by a small program. Memory must be adequate for the largest program to run, and when programs smaller than the largest are run, much of the machine may be unused.

One of the most common extensions to a batch system is a multiprogramming system with two jobs running at once. If a system generates large amounts of printed output, it is extremely wasteful to tie up the entire machine while waiting for the printing to be completed. One approach is to run a *spooling* program in a small part of memory along with other programs. The running programs send their output to some storage device such as a disk. Then, as time becomes available, the spooling program will copy output from the storage device to the printer. In the meantime, other programs might also be running in memory. In such a two-partition system, the two jobs are often referred to as *foreground* and *background*.

When a system supports remote terminals and remote inquiries to a database, one of the jobs in the machine must be available to respond to remote input. When several requests are being processed at once from remote terminals, the system is referred to as a *time-sharing system*. In a time-sharing system, several jobs take turns running in the machine, each for some fixed *time slice*. This system guarantees that no one job will hold the others up. A standard arrangement for large installations is to have time sharing going on in the foreground and batch production going on in the background.

Some operating systems which allow multiprogramming, or the running of several programs at once, require that memory be divided into fixed areas when the system is initiated. Each job is then run in one of these fixed areas. Other systems allow the memory to be shared among the jobs as the needs change, with the size of each of the areas changing from job to job. The latter mode of operation allows more efficient use of memory, but may carry a greater cost in terms of the size and efficiency of the operating system itself.

Data Access Facilities   Various forms of file organization and various types of storage devices require different *access routines* in the operating system. These routines should have the property that they are referenced in the same manner no matter what type of storage device is actually being used. Thus, devices can be changed to keep up with technology and the expanding needs of the organization without having to reprogram.

Data access facilities are expensive, both in terms of cost and memory usage, so unneeded facilities should not be used. The simplest file organization that can be used for the system being designed is probably the best. If data can be processed in a strictly sequential manner, there is no need to bear the overhead of a random-access organization.[8] Real-time and teleprocessing systems carry with them associated requirements for the proper data access facilities in the operating system.

Utilities   Operating systems include various *utility routines* that perform such operations as copying files. The availability of a good set of utility routines will often save the effort required from time to time to write special routines, for example, to convert a file or perform some simple editing function.

As an example, the ability to compare two files for identical contents with a utility routine makes it easy to check the output of a modified program with the results of the previous (correct) version without having to examine all output by hand.

Performance Monitoring   Some operating systems contain facilities which can give a profile of the places in a program where the time is being spent and of the machine operations (such as waiting for a particular input-output facility) that account for the elapsed time as used by the machine. Such a facility, which is often overlooked even when available, can be invaluable. One way in which such a facility is useful is in locating the bottlenecks of a system. Information about the number of conflicts encountered while trying to read information from external storage devices might indicate that the addition of, for example, another data channel will improve overall computer system performance.

The ability to monitor program operation and locate those modules which account for the majority of the running time can usefully direct attention to those areas where careful program optimization will pay off. It will also avoid the expenditure of much effort trying to optimize areas which account for only a small part of the total system operating cost.

File Handling   If the information system contains files of sensitive information, the operating system must provide adequate guarantees of security of information. If the system provides for the simultaneous use of files by, for example, an update program and an on-line interrogation system from a terminal, the operating system should have facilities to permit such simultaneous access at certain times and at other times prevent it. If the system includes a large number of data files, the operating system may need a

---

[8] See Section 5, Chapter 6, "The Technology of Database Management."

comprehensive facility for grouping the files into a hierarchical structure of libraries and sublibraries with suitably restricted access to each level. Provision to save one or more previous versions of each file can automatically provide backup in case of failure.

Many of these facilities can, of course, be provided in the programs written to implement the system, but most of them can and should be provided in the operating system itself.

Operating System Performance The major requirement for any operating system component is that it be *reliable*. If a new feature is being offered by the manufacturer, it is wise to contact other users and run careful benchmarks to determine its reliability. There are few things which can ruin the performance of a system as well as a renegade operating system component which periodically goes berserk and writes random data over large portions of critical files.

After reliability, the most important qualities of operating system components are probably size and efficiency. Operating systems which perform most or all of the operations described above are large and very time-consuming. When the third generation of computer systems was first introduced, many users were most disenchanted with their overall performance because of the inefficiency of the operating systems, although the concept is now universally accepted. Again, careful benchmark tests in *your own environment* are the only way really to know how the total system will perform.

Modifying the Operating System Although it is always possible to modify the manufacturer-supplied operating system to provide some needed facility, such an undertaking should be reserved to the large installation with a competent staff of systems programmers. One of the main difficulties with such modification is that as successive versions of the operating system are released by the manufacturer, the same modifications must be made over and over again. Also, since operating systems are so complex, a local modification may give rise to other bugs in the system which may not be corrected by the manufacturer.

COMMERCIALLY AVAILABLE SOFTWARE

There is a large and growing industry which produces applications software packages for sale or lease.[9] The option, therefore, often exists of choosing an available system (or system component) rather than creating it in-house. The logic behind the software industry is very appealing. The primary factor is that there is no need continually to "reinvent the wheel." By bearing the overhead cost of developing a package only once, the software firm should be able to spread that cost and provide the system to a number of users for less than it would cost the users to develop it themselves.

Development Time It is notoriously difficult to estimate correctly the total amount of time needed to develop a software system. Furthermore, the estimates obtained are almost always too low, rather than too high. As a result, as the deadline date approaches or is passed, proper design techniques and documentation are often overlooked in the rush to complete the system. This causes increased maintenance costs later. A commercially available package is often immediately available.

Performance One major advantage of a commercially available package is that it can be tested. Even if the system cannot be tested directly (because, for example, needed hardware is not yet installed), other users of the system can be contacted. When obtaining performance data from other users, the prospective user should try to get quantitative data such as, "For 2,000 employees the payroll takes us X hours per week," rather than general statements such as, "We like it just fine." Such general evaluations may be an attempt to cover up a bad decision.

Staff Effects If the organization's own technical staff is overloaded, or if there are more productive things which it can be doing, the commercially available system may be more attractive. In addition, obtaining software from an outside source avoids the situation of being dependent on the individual who is working on the project.

Total Costs When comparing the cost estimate for in-house development with the cost of using commercially available systems, it is important to include the *indirect* costs associated with the system. These costs include overhead for secretarial staff, office space, and benefits for the programming staff. Also included are the costs of

[9] See Section 6, Chapter 1, "Software Houses."

system installation, staff training, the establishment of clerical and control procedures associated with the system, etc. With an in-house system, initial maintenance and installation costs will probably be less because the program authors are available. This advantage will decline as time passes and the staff is transferred or replaced.

Upgrading   The costs of upgrading the system to new versions of the operating system as they are released by the manufacturer should be included in any cost comparison. Will such upgrading be included with the package or must it be performed by your own staff?

Language   The commercially available system will eventually have to be maintained by the in-house staff. Therefore, it must be in a language which they can handle. If the installation uses an all-installation standard language, caution should be exercised about incorporating any system which is in another language. In any case, the system should be written in a standard *dialect* of its language and not be dependent upon particular features available only in one particular compiler.

Organization   The same criteria of flexibility and modularity of design which apply to an in-house programming effort should also apply to any software purchased from an outside source. If the system is leased, and if maintenance is provided by the vendor, these criteria may be somewhat less important.

Documentation   Any purchased or leased system should come with a full set of documentation. This documentation should include system operation documentation, program documentation, user's manuals, flow charts, and anything else appropriate to the system.

Vendor's Reliability   It is extremely important to have a vendor who will be in business to make needed changes and corrections to the system. The financial position of the software firm should be carefully examined, as well as the length of time it has been in business. It is also good practice to determine how readily the vendor responds to requests for maintenance and other services. This can be done by contacting the vendor's other users.

Generality   Any system, be it created in-house or purchased, should allow logical extensions. The system being offered should be examined carefully to see whether, for example, it is possible to add new fields to the data format and how the system will behave if the quantity of data to be handled grows significantly. A program which just fits in memory may not have room for certain key tables to be expanded.

Pricing and Maintenance Options   There are several common pricing options for software. In an outright *sale*, the buyer contracts for the purchase of a package, with some guarantee that it will actually run on the buyer's system. Usually all bugs which appear during some specified initial period are corrected by the vendor. Software may also be *leased* for a set monthly or annual fee. The lease may include periodic updating to new operating system releases, and it may also contain debugging service for the entire life of the lease. Sometimes software is available for a *lease plus installation* fee, which includes a set fee at installation plus a set amount per month or year. Another form is the *lease plus usage* fee, where the set fee is incremented by an amount depending on the amount of use given the package. In any system obtained from a vendor it is very important to have a clear understanding of what the system does and how it works. Disputes can easily arise between a vendor and a buyer over whether a particular operating characteristic is a bug or is included in the system design.

SELECTIVE BIBLIOGRAPHY

Auerbach Task Force, "Understanding the Software Package Market," *Latest Developments in Electronic Data Processing*, Auerbach, Princeton, 1971.

Canning, Richard G., and Roger L. Sisson, *The Management of Data Processing*, Wiley, New York, 1967.

Head, Robert V., *Manager's Guide to Management Information Systems*, Prentice-Hall, Englewood Cliffs, N.J., 1972.

Ogdin, Jerry, "Designing Reliable Software," *Datamation*, July, 1972.

Scharf, Tom, "Management and the New Software," *Datamation*, April, 1968.

Weinberg, Gerald M., *The Psychology of Computer Programming*, Van Nostrand Reinhold, New York, 1971.

Part Four

Systems Implementation

Introduction

JOSEPH FERREIRA *Vice President, The Diebold Group, Inc., New York, New York*

Within any given company, the methods of the various operating departments tend to be relatively stable. In the accounting function, the emphasis is on stability and continuity; the legal department is conditioned to the respect for tradition and precedent; the manufacturing department is concerned with change primarily when a direct benefit is perceived as possible. The ADP function, on the other hand, is still in the grip of the technical revolution that began with the invention of the Hollerith machine, expanded with the introduction of electronic computers, and exploded with the arrival of the third generation. Moreover, since ADP is essentially a service function, it is affected by changes in the operations of other elements of the organization.

Because of these and other factors, introduction of change has been and continues to be the normal way of life in the ADP environment. New applications are regularly introduced, existing applications extended, and old applications upgraded as new opportunities are recognized or new technology is developed. The implementation of new, enlarged, or improved systems throughout the company is therefore a major part of the ADP function.

A recent study by the Diebold Research Program showed that approximately 25 per cent of ADP personnel costs are for systems design and programming staff. These resources are therefore major controllable items in the ADP budget. More importantly, the effectiveness with which improved systems can be implemented directly affects the potential contribution to profit of the operating departments that rely on these systems.

The implementation of a system can be as large or as small an activity as circumstances dictate. It can be a conclusive one-time effort or a continuing way of life. Regardless of the circumstances, however, the implementation of an ADP system normally includes all the following elements, to a greater or a lesser degree:

- A feasibility study is made.
- Management authorizes the action.
- The user departments approve the feasibility study.

- A time schedule is developed.
- A budget is prepared.
- Someone designs the system.
- Someone programs it.
- Equipment is made available.
- The system is tested.
- It is documented.
- There is some form of conversion activity.
- The system is turned over to the operating personnel.

The following illustrates, in capsule form, how these elements apply to implementation of even the simplest and least formal of systems: The director of Personnel of a large oil company needed a special, one-time analysis. He called in his resident programmer-analyst (who was actually a member of the central ADP department). "George," said the director, "do you think you can write us a program to pull some information off the file and correlate it with this new data we have come up with? We need the job by Friday." "Sure," said George, "I can write the program today, and test it tomorrow, but I have to have the data to keypunch by Wednesday if we are to get the job onto Thursday's computer schedule. It's a fairly long run and they will bill you about $250. OK?" "OK," said the director, "go ahead." "Don't forget," said George over his shoulder, "I have to have that data to keypunch by Wednesday—early!"

Note that most of the elements of a classic systems implementation procedure came up in the conversation.

A more typical situation involved a medium-sized company with an aggressive systems modernization program under way. The overall feasibility study had been completed, and an average of three or four individual project teams were functioning at any one time. Typically, a senior analyst was designated project manager, supported by a junior, a programmer-analyst, and one or two programmers. Representatives of user-departments were involved part time during design and programming and full time during conversion.

Hardware requirements, documentation procedures, and programming standards had been previously developed on a corporate basis. Consequently, a project manager was primarily concerned with the scheduling and coordination of design, programming, and conversion operations, leaving considerable time for concentrating on the technical aspects of the assignment. This approach to systems implementation worked well and developed a high degree of technical competence and project flexibility. Again, all elements of the typical implementation program were provided for, although many were basics of the total company effort.

A somewhat more complex situation is illustrated by the experience of a multiplant manufacturing company that developed a real-time database system to process customer orders and schedule production. The plan called for a leased private wire network with a dedicated central computer. All hardware was superimposed as a new function in addition to the existing ADP operation. To implement the system, an ad hoc project team was organized, consisting of representatives from sales, engineering, and production departments, in addition to systems designers and programming personnel. The regular project team was supplemented from time to time by software consultants and technical personnel from the hardware supplier and the communications company. Project feasibility was verified, budgets were approved, schedules were developed, documentation procedures were recorded, and programming standards were established. Altogether, about 50 employee-years of effort were committed. In spite of the comparative size of the project and the relative sophistication of its technology, it is interesting to note that the functions performed by the project team involved essentially the same elements of systems implementation as were demonstrated by our friend George in the first illustration.

Regardless of the nature of an application, one characteristic is common to all systems implementation efforts. Each one is a self-contained project, with a beginning and an ending, and each has someone who functions, either formally or informally, as project manager. The techniques of management of systems implementation include many that are common to project management everywhere, whether in construction of a rocket to the moon, a high-rise office building, or the latest version of a luxury yacht. In each case, the technology, the jargon, and, of course, the end product may differ widely, and competence in the particular field of effort is essential. You do not normally take a shipbuilder from the Banks of the Clyde and make him a project manager for a real-time computer system. You use a computer professional, with the appropriate experience and personality traits.

Depending on the size and nature of the system, the project manager may devote a greater or lesser part of his or her time to the technical aspects of the effort. However, in essence, the function is "the art and science of making things happen." Typically, the project manager begins an assignment with an objective, a budget, and a target date. In addition to technical contribution to the effort, he or she must schedule the activities that must take place, and expedite the phase-by-phase completion of the project. Generally, the project manager has strong support from high management, but limited policy guidance and direction.

The material presented in the Chapters of this Section discuss the factors that must be dealt with by the project manager during the course of a major systems implementation.

Chapter 1

Organization for Systems Implementation: Timetables and Follow-through

JOHN E. LETSON

Senior Vice President and Director, Computer and Communications Systems Group, Bache Halsey Stuart Inc., New York, New York

The management of computer systems development activity is not well organized in many companies today. This is probably due to the fast expansion of the systems development function since the advent of large-scale general-purpose computers of the mid-sixties. The expanded demand for implementation and maintenance of sophisticated business systems has outgrown the supply of good systems development managers. The education institutions are just beginning to recognize the need for applying standard management techniques to the data processing functions and to develop adequate training programs and seminars to fill the need for these managers.

The lack of professionalism in data processing management is most notably indicated by the growth of the facility management companies—an entirely new industry whose major service is to manage the data processing/telecommunications facilities of corporations, government agencies, etc. These facility managers apply their services both to the production function of data processing and to systems development activities.

In addition, many users of data processing have gone to consultants for assistance in the development of complex computer systems. Another route is for a company to close down its data processing activities entirely and utilize a computer service bureau operation. While the decision to use facility managers, consultants, service bureaus, etc. is a complex one with many financial, technical, and business facets, one of the most pressing reasons is to obtain *professional managers* for the data processing/telecommunications production and development activities.[1]

THE PROJECT MANAGEMENT ENVIRONMENT

Three primary functional areas must be recognized, and certain underlying assumptions and techniques must be understood in order effectively to manage a major systems development project:

[1] See Section 6, "Outside Services for Data Processing."

Senior Management Senior management is primarily non-computer-oriented, and therefore should not be confronted with "supertechnical" presentations that have no meaning to general managers. There are few general managers who are not "turned off" by a computer technician who uses extensive data processing "buzz words" in oral or written communications with them. The approach with senior managers should concentrate on the *business benefits* to be gained with computer systems, the *development costs, personnel scheduling,* and *computer operating costs.* These analyses may be refined further to capital expenditure requirements, depreciation schedules, application cost-benefit analyses, and budget cash-flow schedules. In short, the project manager must be able to communicate systems development and implementation activity in "noncomputerized" language that reduces technical details to business terms utilizing well-developed accounting and corporation finance concepts.

Users User-personnel vary in number and level of professionalism. For example, if a project manager is involved in an order entry system using remote input terminals, his or her user group may be spread geographically over many states or even worldwide, and probably is largely composed of semiskilled order clerks. The project manager could also be working on a sales analysis and reporting system whose users are three or four senior managers from the home office who are directly concerned with sales promotion and management. These two types of users must obviously be handled differently. The philosophy a good project manager must adopt is that the success of the development effect depends on a *joint* working relationship of the application user group and the development staff. The manager should not undertake any project development and implementation effort without the full understanding and cooperation of the primary user group.

Some projects require an extensive analysis and review of the details of a specific application, e.g., inventory control. Under these circumstances, the user is instrumental in the development of the detailed systems design. Here the project manager must gain the confidence and cooperation of the users, but at the same time recognize that after the system has been implemented, the user-personnel instrumental in the design may not be required—i.e., the function has now been automated. Therefore, in cooperation with the management of the user area, the project manager should face up to this problem at the start, and consider and discuss how experienced user-personnel can be useful to the company after system implementation. There are many constructive ways to accomplish this through transfers and retraining of user-personnel.

Computer Technicians Systems analysts, programmers, console operators, data entry clerks, and others in the organization must all be combined and controlled effectively to obtain the final product—*successful project implementation.* The project manager must get across to the various levels of technical computer personnel that this is "the name of the game." This may be difficult because of the different level of knowledge and motivation at each level of technical expertise. Many programmers have an idea that their performance is directly related to the number of lines of software code they can write per day. Of course, what really counts is *to obtain a working program within the budgeted time and cost that functions properly upon application.*

The attitude the project manager must drill into each worker is that a successful project depends upon each team member's obtaining useful results from his or her effort, and that a useful result is related to bringing that application in within budget, and having it work properly in a business sense. Useful business results are more important than technically operating systems. The technical activity involved in getting the project implemented is the means, not the end.

PROJECT ASSUMPTIONS AND TECHNIQUES

Certain necessary conditions must exist if a project is to have a good chance of success. If they are not present, the project development and implementation activity should not be undertaken.

Analysis and Review The most important aspect of any computer systems project is that there exist sound *business reasons* for undertaking the expensive activity of systems development and implementation. To this end there should be an extensive analysis and recommendation by the project manager or some other analysis group.

This should include the tangible and intangible costs savings to be derived, and/or the improvement in customer service, and/or the compliance to new governmental regulatory requirements. Any business benefits must, of course, be related to the cost of systems development and implementation as well as the continuing operational costs.

The project plan, including the business benefit-cost analysis, must be formally presented to and approved by senior management. The level of review required will vary from company to company, but generally the greater the impact the system has on the operation of the company and the greater the funds required, the higher the approval level needed. It is important that senior management take part in the review and approval of all major system projects. Often the data processing management is left with the job of project review and approval, but this can be dangerous because of the special interests the data processing managers have in expanding their areas of responsibility and control. The problem becomes especially acute as companies grow larger and their data processing budgets rise to the order of millions of dollars annually, with perhaps millions of dollars needed, in addition, to fund further systems development and implementation projects.

Project Funding A formal method of project funding must be part of the project review and approval procedure. The project manager must know how the funding flow will affect his or her budget, and in turn the time span of project development and implementation. The formal funding must of course also consider the equipment expenditures for computer mainframes, communications circuits, terminals, and additional peripherals that may be required for implementation of the new system. The project manager should take an active part in the accounting mechanics of funding, i.e., systems development budget adjustment and capital expenditure budget adjustment.

User Approval Another assumption involves user review and approval of the general design of the application under consideration. The project manager must obtain prior user approval of the general design package included in the management presentation referred to above. This approval controls the scope of the development and implementation effort, and provides a high level of confidence that the system designed by the computer technicians is in fact a reasonable business system, with projected personnel and equipment needs and funding estimates based on a computer application whose scope has been preapproved by the primary user-organization.

Project Management Techniques The project management techniques to be employed (developed in detail later herein) should include at least the following:

• There should be a complete layout of all tasks in sufficient detail to permit effective project control and review.

• Tasks should be quantified in terms of employee-days, -weeks, etc., and be related to specific individuals assigned and referred to explicitly by name. Phantom or unavailable personnel cannot complete projects, and should not be included in any personnel assignment schedules.

• A standardized graphic procedure should be used to report the project status to all levels within the company. This will simplify the preparation and reporting of project status reports.

• The various management levels of reporting should be defined at the outset. Levels of reporting require preparation and presentation of project status at various frequencies, and concern different levels of project development and implementation detail. These must be considered in advance, so that the project manager can include the staffing requirements and corresponding costs related to project report preparation and presentation.

• An attempt must be made to control the allotted time spent in project management activities. This time should be contained within a 5 to 10 per cent level, so that the project personnel can have sufficient time to spend on project execution activity. The specific percentage of total time spent on project management is related to the complexity of the systems, the total number of concurrent activities being performed, and the professional level of the primary user-group.

• The project manager must ever be conscious of the amount of time the project personnel spend on project status review, and attempt to limit this effort so that they can get on with their assigned tasks.

STAFFING CONSIDERATIONS

Knowledge and Experience   The project manager should review each of the individuals to be assigned to project tasks to ascertain that each is capable of performing adequately. Three specific areas of knowledge and experience are required: (1) managerial ability, (2) application know-how, and (3) technical competence in computer hardware and software.

Managerial ability is difficult to define. However, it is primarily concerned with effective motivation, coordination, and leadership of people. The person assigned to task leadership should be a good manager who can communicate effectively with people and coordinate the many activities of a project. To be an effective project manager, one should be a doer, i.e., oriented toward getting the job done within the cost and time budgets. The coordination responsibility involves the work of the professional computer development staff and the primary user-personnel, as well as project review and reporting to senior management of the company.

The second area of competance is a good working knowledge of the application area. Such knowledge helps to build confidence in the business reasonableness of any system development and implementation effort. Data processing professionals with good application background can contribute ideas on an application level, and they can also pass judgment on the various pieces of information put forward by the user-group.

The third competance required is technical knowledge about the computer hardware and systems software that the application software will utilize. This ability is probably the easiest to obtain because of the good training materials and schools that are available. Generally if a systems analyst or programmer has a proven experienced record, he or she will have qualified for technical computer assignments. A good project manager should be able to determine quickly the adequacy of proposed additions to the project staff as regards technical ability.

Levels of Personnel   Three distinct levels of personnel assignments are needed to carry out project development and implementation effectively: (1) project leader, (2) systems analysts, and (3) programmers. On the larger-scale projects, the project leader will assist the project manager in carrying out the project management function. On smaller projects, project leaders may not be required. A project leader usually controls a portion of a large project development and implementation effort, i.e., a subsystem. If, for example, there are four subsystems, each may be headed by a different project leader. The functions performed are those of motivation, coordination, and leadership of the computer staff and the assigned user-personnel.

The job of the systems analyst is to survey the user operation functions in detail, and, working closely with user-personnel, to prepare preprogramming specifications of the system. These specifications consist of a series of written reports defining how the system should function on the computer. The analyst must be a good communicator and have a working knowledge of the application area under design. He or she must be able to formulate and outline the business specifications in a systematic form that can be readily used by the programming staff.

Finally, the programmers are required to convert the programming specifications to machine code, and to test, debug, and document these programs. This is a task fairly well defined and primarily dependent on the programming staff alone. The project manager usually has fewer problems in this area than in project management or systems analysis because it is the best-defined area.

External versus Internal Personnel   One of the major decisions to be made by firms developing a major system is how to staff for those peak periods of 12 to 24 months. For obvious reasons, it is not good practice to hire, train, and assign personnel, and then dismiss them after the project has been implemented. In these situations a company can profitably make use of external service personnel, i.e., professional staff not on the company payroll, but contracted for on either a fixed-fee or a time-and-material basis.

Generally three types of external personnel are available, and the project manager should make sure that he or she understands each type and when to use them: (1) general consultants, (2) vendor systems engineers, and (3) software-house personnel.

General data processing consultants should be used primarily for specific applications know-how and/or project management responsibility. This class of personnel is generally experienced and well educated, and consequently the costs are quite high—about three or four times that of the same level of employee on the company payroll.

It is important for good cost control of project development that general consultants are employed only when definitely required for the specific functions outlined above.

Vendor systems engineers are best utilized when the project manager needs assistance in specific systems software development and/or knowledge of source application software. More often than not, the vendor systems engineers are used strictly for training or semitraining activities. Their costs are generally too high to employ on a continuing basis. Usually they are used to assist the in-house professional staff in such areas as operating systems generation and setup of job control procedures from a training standpoint.

Because of the close ties of vendor systems engineers to the manufactured computer systems, level of competency varies. Bundled companies may supply trainees and unbundled companies more experienced systems engineers. However, it is not unheard of that in a small unsophisticated company the unbundled vendor may supply trainees at normal per diem rates. The project manager must be aware of this possibility and attempt to ensure that performance of vendor systems engineers matches the costs billed. He or she should also consider employing the vendor systems engineers on a fixed-fee basis or performance-related contract arrangement. Obviously nonperformance of vendor systems engineers will delay systems implementation and negatively reflect upon the project management functions.

The third source of external personnel for hire are the software companies that usually supply systems analysts or programmers or both. Their functions are primarily technical, and the project manager must be sure that these professionals have been adequately trained for the business application–hardware/software environment in which they are to be employed.

It is dangerous to employ software company personnel under loose contractual arrangements. The payments for service rendered must be related to quality performance—the extremely rapid growth and decline of some software companies has put experienced project managers on guard. There are many frustrated project managers or former project managers who were brought down by poor software company performance related to quality, timeliness, costs, or all three.[2]

Misuse of External Personnel   The very nature of consultants, vendor systems engineers, and software staffs creates a management problem for the project manager, and can negatively impact the project progress. The project manager must exercise administrative control over all personnel, but can he or she really control the compensation, holiday schedule, termination, or promotion of external personnel? That is obviously impossible in its entirety. However, the project will not be implemented on schedule if the project manager allows the external personnel freedoms different from those of the in-company professional staff. This not only is unproductive as far as the external staff is concerned, but also negatively impacts internal personnel morale and could increase personnel turnover within the company.

A good example of unfair treatment concerns off-hour assignments. Quite often during the fast pace of systems test and check-out or system conversion, the professional development staff is called on to work nights or weekends. It is important that the project manager insist that the external and internal personnel continue to work in cooperative teams regardless of the time schedule. The same work standard must be used for all if the job is to be done within budget with a consistent team approach.

Selection of User-Personnel   User-personnel are extremely important because they provide two important keys necessary for effective project implementation. The first key is the daily working knowledge of the particular application area to be automated. The second key is the fact that these same user-personnel are the ones who must operate the system after implementation. By operate we mean prepare the proper input, control the master files, and employ the many outputs of the system. The automated system will not be successful unless the project manager selects superior user-staff who have the ability to train the personnel who in turn will operate the system.

This aspect of project staffing is the most important because, classically, user-management will attempt to assign "expendable" personnel as project support. The type of user-personnel required are exactly the superior workers the user-management requires for managing the daily production. Therefore, some compromise must be

---

[2] See Section 6, Chapter 1, "Software Houses."

worked out. It is important that the user-management does not rotate many different personnel into and out of the project assignments during systems development and implementation. If a few superior user-personnel are selected at the outset, and allowed to remain on the project, they will contribute more effectively than rotating user-staff. When the project has been implemented, these personnel will have a good knowledge of the automated system and they can train other user-personnel in the daily operation of the system.

User-personnel will, of course, have to be exposed to the fundamentals of data processing and telecommunications in order to develop good communications with the computer technicians. This training can be accomplished by informal in-company seminars usually given by the management of the computer systems development group. This user training can be enhanced by inviting all user-personnel to the weekly project review meetings. Effective organization of the project development team, and good written procedures, will greatly assist the user-personnel. They will undoubtedly have a difficult time in coping with the special jargon or "computerese" the systems analysts and programmers will use in their communication, but training can help them deal with this technical language barrier.

In summary, the quality and attitude of the assigned user-personnel are probably the most important project personnel ingredients, and the project manager should give special attention to this area.

PROJECT MANAGEMENT REPORTING

Review and reporting procedure is at the heart of effective managerial control of the project. To make the present discussion more meaningful, we shall describe a modified three-level Gantt technique currently in use at Bache Halsey Stuart Inc.

The three important characteristics of any project reporting system are:
- Graphic presentation.
- Ease of updating.
- At least three levels of reporting detail.

It is extremely difficult to review the many tasks within a project quickly and effectively in narrative form. Since the essence of project review is to concentrate on *variance from budget*, one must first be able to locate the variances quickly at a glance. A diagram of the various parts of a project makes efficient project review possible. The actual method of preparing the charts, i.e., manual or automatic, depends upon the number of project activities monitored and the frequency of review.

The second important characteristic is ease of updating. Most of the business system development and implementation projects have less than 50 personnel assigned concurrently. This could be subdivided into 30 computer technicians, 5 external personnel (i.e., consultants, vendor systems engineers, and software company personnel), 12 user-personnel, and 3 project management staff persons. A project of this size can usually be controlled manually.

Updating project charts involves:
- Maintenance of project integrity by always referring back to original budgeted activities and resources.
- Using a cumulative update schedule which separates activities for the last report period from activities of prior reporting periods.
- A quick, low-cost method of reproducing updated charts to be used for progress meetings and for general distribution.

In conformity with the third characteristic mentioned, the charts used to represent activity status should be developed at three levels of detail. If all these charts are interrelated, i.e., Level 1 is combined for Level 2, which in turn is summarized for Level 3, then the only review with project personnel is for the basic Level 1. The other two levels are simply a higher level of reporting and are used primarily for management review and discussion.

By relating the levels of reporting, the project manager can conserve time and ensure that all reporting levels are based upon the same staff review and therefore are compatible. The levels that are of interest start at individual assignment level, then expand to the functional group, and finally can be summarized as overall project summary data.

AN EXAMPLE OF THE PROJECT MANAGEMENT REPORTING

The example discussed here has all the three attributes mentioned above. The charts used are illustrated in Figures 1-1a and 1-1b.

First, let us get the conventions of the charting technique out of the way: What is important to realize is that the progress of each time phase of the project is shown by writing over the prior graphic form. This technique lends itself to easy updating. One is always adding to the prior status, without ever redoing a prior chart.

Updating and Distribution   The distribution method is composed of three operations:

1. Using the master schedules that contain the original estimates plus progress to the prior updating period, an updating procedure for the current date of review should be completed. This adjusts the master schedule for work accomplished during the last period.

2. The master schedule charts are now copied for additional updating. What is important here is that special notations are placed on the *copy* of the updated master schedule, i.e., dates, new estimated completion dates, status evaluators, etc. In essence, this operation customizes the schedules for each particular reporting period.

3. Finally, the customized copy of the master schedule is mass-reproduced for distribution. Because the charting technique represents project status at three levels, it may not be necessary to distribute all levels to everyone. Senior management is interested only in the top-level charts, while a project leader may require only the most detailed level.

Chart Format   Three charts all using the same scheme of simple presentation—two are illustrated in Figures 1-1a and 1-1b—are used for three levels of activity: (1) the phase level (a), every 4 weeks; (2) the task level (b), every 2 weeks; and (3) the step level (not shown here), every week. The charted data for each level form the basis for the next higher chart.

These are essentially Gantt charts that pinpoint status at a glance. A big advantage is ease of updating. A master drawing of a chart is made at the start, showing original bar projections and completion dates, which are never changed. This master chart, upon which budgets are based, is thus always the benchmark for comparisons. At reporting time, a copy is run of the original, the copy is updated with bar shadings and explanatory entries, and copies of this are then run off for distribution.

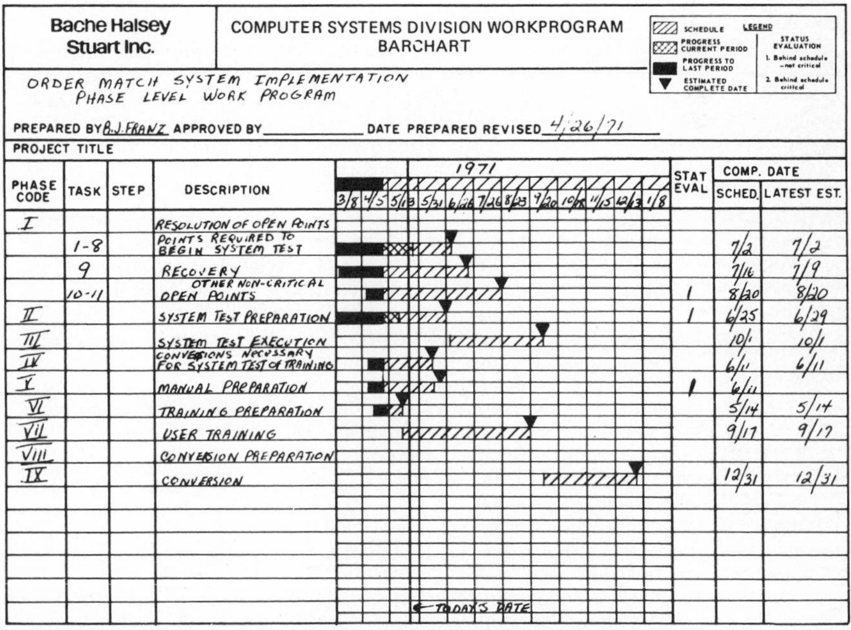

Fig. 1-1a   Chart for project management reporting.

Bache Halsey Stuart Inc.	COMPUTER SYSTEMS DIVISION WORKPROGRAM BARCHART	LEGEND — SCHEDULE, PROGRESS CURRENT PERIOD, PROGRESS TO LAST PERIOD, ESTIMATED COMPLETE DATE / STATUS EVALUATION 1. Behind schedule —not critical 2. Behind schedule critical

ORDER MATCH SYSTEM IMPLEMENTATION
RESOLUTION OF OPEN POINTS TASK LEVEL WORK PROGRAM

PREPARED BY _R.J. FRANZ_ APPROVED BY _____ DATE PREPARED REVISED _4/26/71_

PROJECT TITLE

PHASE CODE	TASK	STEP	DESCRIPTION	1971 (6/3 6/3 7/2 7/8 9/8 9/1 5/3 5/1 5/31 6/14 6/2 7/7 7/21 7/2 8/9)	STAT EVAL	MAN DAYS	PERSONNEL ASSIGNMENTS
I	1		PROJECT TEAM TRAINING			45	PROJECT TEAM
	2		PBC CHANGES			70	JENNIE SEGAL
	3		CANCEL AN EXECUTION			70	LAMONICA/MANDELL
	4		TPS SWITCHOVER & BOOTH CHANGES	COMPLETE		25	MARK IRGANG
	5		SHD INQUIRIES TO 100+	COMPLETE		20	AL PEARSON
	6		ADDITIONAL TESTING			20	AL PEARSON
	7		ASE ODD LOT INPUT			15	AL PEARSON
	8		7080 INTERFACE		2	110	CARTY IRGANG
	9		RECOVERY			90	CHUCK DONAGHY
	10		SYSTEM CONTROL			90	OMAR HOLQUIN
	11		6 MONTH RENEWALS	← TODAYS DATE	1	65	NOT YET ASSIGNED

Fig. 1-1b Chart for project management reporting.

Total length of each bar is in terms of estimated employee-days for completion. Solid shading shows portion completed at time of reporting; ruled portion shows remaining days scheduled. Cross-hatching shows portion completed in current reporting period. Column widths represent 4 weeks (Figure 1-1a) and 2 weeks (b). Dates shown are for end of period (right edge of column). Arrowheads indicate latest estimated completion dates. (The arrowheads are changed on the copies if necessary when charts are issued, but never, as stated, on the original.)

Note the long bar at the top of each chart. In a this represents the cumulative employee-days for all the separately barred phases indicated by the Roman numerals. Similarly, in b, this represents the cumulative employee-days for all the separate tasks numbered below. And in a, the bar for I, Steps 1–8, represents the cumulative employee-days for Steps 1–8 in Figure 1-1b. The chart not shown here, for the step level, follows the same logic, showing the steps making up a given task.

Status Review The importance of a particular level of charting depends upon the level of personnel reviewing the project status, and what type of project information is required. For example, if the phase level charts show a negative variance, it probably would be necessary to reference the task level and step level to determine exactly what is the root of the problem. This additional detail is of paramount importance in determining the type of corrective action to be taken. Under certain circumstances, it may not be necessary to review the task or step level work programs because the phase level review is adequate for good project management.

It should be noted that the special graphic notations are placed on each updated master copy to customize the charts for a given review period. This customizing will not be discussed in detail. However, a list of primary considerations follows:

• Updating the "current" estimate to completion enables one to ascertain if the activity will be completed prior to, on, or after the original estimate-to-complete date.

• Use of status evaluators for each activity lets one focus on negative variance situations. By using a further breakdown for critical-noncritical negative variances, one may concentrate upon those individual activities that will cause the project implementation to be delayed.

• If the estimated employee-days of effort for a particular activity are increased, this can be noted by a footnote to the employee-day column. It is important that major expansion of work effort from original estimate be explicitly noted, so that objective project review is possible.

- It is also important to footnote any personnel reassignments due to employment status change, or need for additional staff due to project scope expansion, etc.

An additional tool available to the project manager to control the performance of individuals is shown in Figure 1-2. The purpose of this work program is to standardize the manner in which a programmer and/or systems analyst goes about completing a specific assignment. The chart subdivides the program activity for each program into

Bache Halsey Stuart Inc.	PROGRAM CONTROL	RUN DESCRIPTION AND PROGRAMMER	EDIT	M. DIBENEDETTO UPDATE	G. RODBEN	R. HIPKISS FIGURATION	RPT FILE GEN	F. CARTY		
System **P4S PROJECT**										
Project Manager **B COOK**										
Date **7/20/73** Schedule **7/15/73**										
WEEK OF ASSIGNMENT		NO.	403	408	410	412				
12 13 14 15 16 17 18 19 20 21 22										
1 Programmer Analyst Assigned			6/10	6/10	6/16	6/10				
2 I/O Layouts Complete			6/11	6/12	6/12	6/12				
3 I/O Layouts Approved			6/11	6/12	6/12	6/12				
4 Specs Completed			6/11	6/15	6/16	6/15				
5 Specs Approved			6/30	6/30	6/19	6/20				
6 Programmer(s) Assigned			6/24	6/30	6/18	6/24				
7 Detail Flowchart Completed			6/24	6/24	6/23	6/24				
8 Detail Flowchart Approved			6/27	6/25	6/26	6/27				
9 Program 50% Coded			7/5	7/10	7/5	7/5				
10 Program Coding Completed			7/10	7/25	7/10	7/10				
11 Program Keypunched			7/12	7/28	7/12	7/12				
12 Test Data Available			7/15	8/5	7/15	7/15				
13 Quickdraw Completed			7/17	8/7	7/17	7/17				
14 Desk Checked—Quickdraw Precompile			7/18	8/10	7/17	7/18				
15 First Assembly/Compile			7/20	8/12	7/19	7/20				
16 Clean Assembly/Compile			8/1	8/20	7/25	8/1				
17 25% Testing Completed			8/5	8/27	7/29	8/5				
18 50% Testing Completed			8/9	9/7	8/3	8/9				
19 75% Testing Completed			8/15	9/12	8/10	8/15				
20 Operating Instruction Completed			8/21	9/12	8/12	8/21				
21 Ready for Systems Test			8/30	9/22	8/30	8/30				
22 Systems Test Completed			9/5	9/30	9/5	9/5				
23 Documentation Completed			9/15	9/30	9/15	9/5				
24 Documentation Approved			9/20	10/2	9/20	9/20				
25 Program Operational			9/22	10/7	10/7	10/7				
TESTING TOTALS										
COMPILATIONS / CLEAN										
COMPILATIONS / TEST										

Bill Cook
Signature

Fig. 1-2 Chart for program control.

25 discrete steps, each of which has a completion date. These schedules are especially effective for controlling trainees and external personnel. A trainee may not be aware of precisely what is expected of him or her, and a chart of this detail spells out all the activities with expected completion dates. The external programmer, e.g., from a software company, may also not be familiar with the mode of operation of the company. This chart thus becomes a tool to get everyone on the same standard programming procedure. It also allows each programmer to give an opinion on his or her written schedule, and therefore builds confidence since everyone knows at the outset what performance is expected.

Again, the updating procedure is simple. A master is reproduced with a copy made for each week of the program schedule, and predated as to reporting period. The analyst or programmer simply shades in those activities completed as of the reporting date, and submits a copy of the schedule to the project manager. The original activities and dates *never* change, and therefore, there is no requirement to reestimate any dates or prepare new schedules. An inspection of Figure 1-2 indicates those activities completed, those activities not completed, and the original completion estimate and the reporting date for the period. An analysis of the dates of the uncompleted activities when compared with the reporting date automatically indicates the status of each program step.

SYSTEMS TESTING

The biggest effort in any project development and implementation activity is the systems test activity. This is the first time that a set of machine-coded programs is grouped into a system for processing simulated business. The systems test phase of any project requires an interaction of the computer/communications operation staff, the systems development staff, and user-personnel.

While the importance of systems testing may be obvious, it is usually the one activity that is not adequately planned and executed. Consequently, systems test activities are usually very costly because of the many false starts, stops, and subsequent restarts. The project manager must truly approach systems testing from a user orientation, i.e., be concerned completely with the business aspects of the system.

The primary objective of the systems test is to prove that the system correctly performs all intended business functions and is operating efficiently. If this objective is not met, any possible conversion would be a disaster, and would probably result in a systems audit being performed of the entire development effort. Needless to say, the project manager of any ill-fated systems test would come under severe criticism and could possibly even be replaced.

We shall discuss here a comprehensive systems test procedure that includes: (1) prerequisites; (2) preparation; (3) timing; and (4) organization groups by function—(a) input preparation; (b) data check-out; and (c) discrepancy resolution.

The systems test procedure to be used depends, of course, upon the complexity of the system. It is not necessary to develop an elaborate systems test procedure for "shaking out" a small system or an operationally proven package. The procedures, regardless of complexity, must recognize the difference between systems testing, and unit or program testing. The data must be prepared from actual business conditions and be manually selected to reflect a real environment.

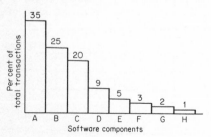

Fig. 1-3 Program logic modules arranged by frequency distribution.

One of the most common pitfalls in data selection is to select certain actual business transactions simply because they are the test data most easily obtainable. They may take the form of a day's business, a week's business, or the like.

While this approach is still used in systems test procedures, it is not the proper one to take. As an illustration, let us just select one program from a system that is to be tested. Assume that this program is composed of eight discrete logic modules or software components, as shown in Figure 1-3. Each of these software components is executed according to the transaction types that enter the system, i.e., Transaction Type A requires servicing by Software Component A, Transaction Type B requires servicing by Software Component B, etc.

Assume that the probability that a transaction is a specific type is as shown in Table 1-1. Such a distribution is due to two primary factors: (1) there are definite variations in business transactions, with a statistical tendency for a few types to be very popular while the others occur infrequently, and (2) business systems are run in cycles that usually include daily, weekly, monthly, quarterly, and annual cycles. The business cycle distribution is usually related to transaction type, i.e., Transaction Type H may be related to the annual business processing cycle.

TABLE 1-1 Probability of Transaction Input Streams

Transaction type	Probability
A	.35
B	.25
C	.20
D	.09
E	.05
F	.03
G	.02
H	.01
	1.00

From these relationships we can conclude that the probability is quite high that by selecting a day's business transaction we will not select *all* possible transactions. This means that we are *not* exercising all software components, and therefore not adequately performing the systems test. It is not uncommon that even if we select a week's or month's transactions, we still have not properly selected the test data to reflect those transaction types that occur only quarterly or annually. Obviously there is need for user-prepared test conditions that reflect all possible situations. This can be best carried out by good systems test planning and execution.

Systems Testing Prerequisites Prior to starting the systems test procedures, the following preliminary checks must be made:

- All programs must be on the systems library file.
- Test data should be organized by cycle.
- Each cycle should be defined from a business viewpoint.
- Master cycle schedule should be prepared.
- Check-out procedures must be developed.
- A systems test activities chart must be prepared to define the interaction of user, development, and operating personnel responsibilities.
- There must be detailed definition of all functions to be performed during the test, including personnel assignments.
- Space must be made available, including furniture and proper working materials.
- Adequate computer time must be available on a timely basis.

We shall expand on some of the more important prerequisites, but let us first look at the adequacy of the program test function. During the development of the programs, each is being tested as a unit to "shake out" program bugs. It is imperative that all these program faults be isolated and corrected during unit testing.

Occasionally the development team may be eager to progress to systems testing without completing the unit test. The project manager must ensure that expensive systems test activities are not wasted in resolving program faults that should be isolated by unit testing. The systems test is designed to catch systems bugs that are usually related to program interface problems, e.g., the result of linking many programs together.

The organization of test data by cycles is most important, so that the overall systems test can be subdivided into several discrete cycles that can be separately controlled. This allows the project manager to step into the systems test in ever-increasing cycles of business complexity. The increasing levels of complexity actually represent the systematic addition of a new aspect of the business, as shown in Table 1-2.

By separating each of these functions into cycles, the project manager can readily segregate the software components that have possibly caused the fault. Once a lower-cycle fault is corrected, one may progress to the next level in confidence, and thereby build credibility into the system from a business viewpoint. The final cycle should be exactly the same as a typical daily business cycle, so that the operation of the system is no different from the real thing. The cycle approach also allows for overlapping cycle activities, i.e., the preparation of input for Cycle 8 can be accomplished concurrently with the systems check-out of Cycle 7. This allows the project manager more efficiently to schedule fewer personnel for the systems test activities.

A systems test activity chart, referred to earlier, lays out all discrete functions in time sequence, and relates these assignments to three responsibility areas: users, development staff, and operating staff. The primary function of this chart is to illustrate the necessary steps required by each systems test cycle and the urgency of completing such tasks on time. The cost of running a systems test is extensive, and every project management effort should be directed toward controlling these costs by completing the activity on time and effectively.

TABLE 1-2 Typical Test Cycle Schedule

Test cycle	Test objective
1	ESTABLISH FILES
2	INPUT VALIDATION
3	UPDATE FILES
4	RECYCLE UPDATED FILES
5	ACTIVATE DAILY PROCESSING
6	ACTIVATE WEEKLY PROCESSING
7	ACTIVATE MONTHLY PROCESSING
8	ACTIVATE ANNUAL PROCESSING
9	UPDATE FILES, VALIDATE INPUT, ACTIVATE DAILY, WEEKLY, MONTHLY, AND ANNUAL PROCESSING
10	VOLUME TEST OF ACTUAL DAY'S BUSINESS

Systems Test Preparation The thoroughness of preparation contributes to a *controlled test*. Some of the major considerations are as follows:

Test Conditions Catalogue. A test conditions catalogue must be prepared, so that the numerous business transactions can be documented in a systematic manner and the documentation made available for reference by the systems check-out team. By formalizing all business conditions to be tested, a common standard is developed which will allow the team to ascertain the reasonableness and accuracy of the system under test. The catalogue is used in the user area in researching how the system should have performed as related to actual results.

The catalogue of conditions is also used in the preparation of the physical input media, i.e., punched cards, paper tape, etc. Further, it is used to resolve differences between the user area and development personnel as concerns specific test results. In summary, the conditions catalogue is "The Book" that defines all business conditions that must be met for a successful system.

Data Preparation. The data preparation function involves the generation of the physical information media to be used during test execution. This includes the establishment of files, databases, input data elements, message streams, etc. Of particular importance in the preparation of input data is the concept of cross-referencing of the physical media to the condition catalogue. This allows the systems check-out team to ensure completeness of data preparation, and contributes to ease in referencing all test data. For example, during systems test check-out it may be determined that a given condition was not properly functioning in Test Cycle 4. The condition catalogue /data input cross-reference would indicate what combination of input data should be reselected and placed into the next cycle (Cycle 5), to retest this business condition. Of course, this assumes that the software fault causing the improper processing has been isolated and fixed prior to running Cycle 5.

The test data must be grouped into cycles so that the system can be subjected to ever-increasing business complexity within a controlled environment. The typical systems test might result in 10 cycles, as shown in Table 1-2.

Note that the first four cycles are related to the development of the environment in discrete steps. If problems considered critical exist here, the systems test cycle progression should not continue. The test environment must be in proper operation in order to obtain useful results from business transaction streams.

The next four cycles (Cycles 5, 6, 7, and 8) test the prepared business transactions according to the design specifications. By segregating these transactions into four cycles, we are able to isolate possible software faults by transaction type. This improves the efficiency of resolving discrepancies encountered. Cycle 9 contains all prior test conditions, and represents, from a business condition viewpoint, a live processing environment.

The only other condition to test is a *volume condition.* This can be accommodated by selecting a typical day's peak business and running it through the system in Cycle 10. The primary purpose of a volume test is to check out various upper limits of systems, such as message or transaction input rates, volume overflows for a file or database overflow procedures, output print time, etc. The volume test is *not* used to check out various business conditions; it is used only to force the technical extremes of the system to be exercised.

Systems Activity Chart. The systems activity chart is a time-sequencing of systems test check-out activities. A list of the items that should be included in such a chart is shown in Table 1-3.

TABLE 1-3   Systems Activity Chart

Cycle	Activity	Day	Time
1	a. Select and prepare test data	1	1000–1600
	b. Execute Test Cycle 1	1	1600–2400
	c. Prepare output for check-out	2	800– 900
	d. Check out results of test	2	900–1100
	e. Resolve and correct discrepancies	2	1100–2400
	f. Reselect conditions to be Retested in next cycle	3	800–1000
2	a. Select and prepare test data	3	1000–1600
	b. Execute Test Cycle 2	3	1600–2400
	Etc.	Etc.	Etc.

As can be seen, all tasks are spelled out by cycle, and specific times are alloted for their completion. The cycles are time-sequenced to each other, with provisions made for reselecting test conditions and including these in the following cycle to retest a prior faulty condition. This technique expedites the systems check-out because the project manager does not have to repeat a complete cycle to retest corrected software faults, but can selectively add these conditions to the following cycle.

The systems test cycle schedule should be completed with the cooperation of user-personnel and formally published. The data should be selected and grouped by cycles, and a checklist should be prepared on what to look for and how to complete the execution of the check-out activity. The systems test functions should be formally scheduled and assigned to specific individuals in the user, computer development, and computer operations areas. Finally, adequate computer time, work space, and check-out materials must be made available.

It is the responsibility of the project manager to set up an effective professional environment for checking out the system. This can be accomplished only by segregating user-personnel from their normal operating environment. A separate area should be established for the systems check-out team which includes office furniture, telephones, calculators, etc. This will allow the test check-out to be executed with minimum interruption due to regular operating responsibilities, and make it easier for the project manager to control the timeliness and quality of the test check-out activity.

Systems Test Organization   Figure 1-4 illustrates one possible approach to organization of the systems test function. The systems test manager is the overall coordinator, and is usually selected jointly by the user and development heads. This person is usually a project leader from the development staff. Although technically oriented, the systems test manager must have extensive knowledge of the application area under test and be able effectively to work with people. Other duties are:

• Responsible for progress and quality in all areas of the systems test.

• Keep user-departments and data processing management apprised of systems test status.

• Monitor progress on a minute-by-minute basis.

• Determine when the next cycle will be run by close monitoring of all outstanding discrepancies.

The input preparation group is responsible for the systematic preparation and control of all input data. It should be supervised by a lead person from the primary user-department. The primary purpose is to prepare data that effectively reflect true business conditions, and to maintain effective control on the system as it concerns check-out status. These duties may be summarized as follows:

- Perform all functions necessary to use the system, and execute the systems test cycle in accordance with previously developed user reference and procedure manuals.
- Maintain and control all systems test data and report files.

User-department personnel also make up the data check-out group, whose primary duty is to assure the quality of output of the systems test. This is done by using the conditions catalogue as a standard of measure. The main duties of this group are:

- Check all systems test data against system output to be certain that (1) the intended test condition was adequately tested; (2) the system processed the condition correctly; and (3) all discrepancies are recorded and given to the discrepancy controller.
- Select and prepare all systems test cycle output for check-out.

To repeat our basic theme of user involvement, we note that control by the user area of the data check-out group gives us the essential check and balance over the system. This function should not be performed by the development group.

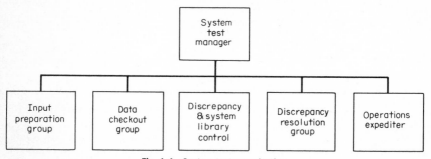

Fig. 1-4 System test organization.

The discrepancy and systems library control must be assigned to a single person. Usually this is a senior systems analyst who has superior leadership capabilities. Let us review the procedure for processing systems discrepancies by referring to Figure 1-5. This is a four-part form that is used to report, maintain, and control the status of all systems discrepancies. It is used as follows:

1. The data check-out group has an inventory of these forms prenumbered, i.e., each discrepancy is referred to by number and its status related thereto for accounting purposes.

2. When a discrepancy is found, a description is prepared by a member of the data check-out group that includes details of the cycle data used, as well as the error indications.

3. The report is received by the discrepancy controller, logged into the discrepancy file, and assigned to the discrepancy resolution group for research and correction.

4. The resolution group completes a description of the cause of the fault and the action taken, with notations to specific program patches and source updates.

5. The discrepancy controller discusses with the input preparation group a reselection of test conditions to be added to the next cycle for retest processing.

6. The discrepancy retest description is completed, and the discrepancy form (controller's copy) is filed into the completed file.

By tracing the completion of the activities required by this form, the project manager is able to review in detail the responsibility of the discrepancy controller. The duties of the controller are:

- Receive discrepancies on prenumbered forms from the data check-out group.
- Assign each to the discrepancy resolution group for research and correction.
- Maintain a discrepancy log that identifies the resolution analyst assigned and the status of assignment.

• Monitor progress on all outstanding discrepancies and report it to the systems test manager.
• Receive corrected discrepancy sheets and program corrections.
• Maintain a systems patch deck.
• Schedule and control all permanent changes to the systems library.
• Control and maintain security of the systems library.

The discrepancy resolution group is usually a subset of the original systems development team. It is headed by a senior systems analyst who is also a working member of the resolution group. It is the duty of this group to research and correct discrepancies as reported to them by the discrepancy controller. Following is an outline of these steps:

1. Research all discrepancies on a superpriority basis.
2. Correct and test the appropriate programs.
3. Give corrections and annotated discrepancy sheets and program corrections to the discrepancy controller on a timely basis.
4. Keep discrepancy controller current as to status of all uncorrected discrepancies.

Bache Halsey Stuart Inc.

Members: All Leading Exchanges · Founded 1879

Discrepancy #__________

COMMODITY SYSTEM TEST
DISCREPANCY FORM

SECTION A DISCREPANCY IDENTIFICATION

Cycle Number__________ Run Date__________ Initials__________

Checkout Date__________

Erroneous Document(s) Input ID and Type

Description:

SECTION B DISCREPANCY RESOLUTION

Assigned Programmers	Programs	Date Assigned	Controller Initials	Date Completed	Programmer Initials

Description of Modifications:

Date System Program Tape Update: __________

System Program Tape Number: __________

SECTION C RECYCLE INFORMATION

Cycle Number__________ Run Date__________ Initials__________

Input ID__________

Fig. 1-5a Test discrepancy form.

```
                          Bache Halsey Stuart Inc.
                            P&S SYSTEM TEST
                            DISCREPANCY FORM              DISCREPANCY #_____

 (A)   DISCREPANCY IDENTIFICATION:

       Cycle #_____ Condition #_____ Name_____ Date_____

       Erroneous Document(s)_____

       Description:_____

       _____

       _____

       _____

       _____

       _____

       _____

       _____

       _____

       _____

       _____

       _____

       _____

 (B)   DISCREPANCY RESOLUTION:

       Classification:  SA_____  ND   DK   DQ   A   B   C   D   E

       Assigned Programmers   Programs   Date Assigned   Date Completed   System Tape#   Date Updated

       _____       _____   _____   _____   _____   _____

       Resolution:_____

       _____

       _____

       _____

       _____

 (C)   RECYCLE INFORMATION:                                        DISCREPANCY #

       Cycle#_____   Paper Tape#_____      _____
```

Fig. 1-5b   Test discrepancy form.

The final area of responsibility is that of the operations expediter. This job can be performed by a member of the data processing operations staff. However, it would be preferable to use a systems analyst here also. The duties of the operations expediter are:

- Write systems operating procedures.
- Serve as liaison with computer operations, and schedule the analysts to be on site for the running of each cycle.
- Coordinate computer time requirements with data processing operations.
- Ensure that all operational inefficiencies or discrepancies are noted on discrepancy forms, and turned over to the discrepancy controller.
- Collect all systems output and turn it over to the data check-out group.
- Prepare critique for each completed systems test cycle.

This completes the organization of the systems test activities. Again, we should recognize that this organization is required so that the systems test can be effectively completed within both time and cost budgets.

MOST COMMON DANGERS

In summary, let us examine some of the most common dangers that could contribute to a system not being implemented. These may be grouped under three headings:

User-Related The most common contributors under this heading are:

- Insufficient personnel involvement.
- Low-level personnel assigned.
- Systems specifications not reviewed and approved by user.
- User reluctant to implement system.
- Changes in user-personnel during implementation.

The user is a primary ingredient in all systems development, but usually causes the *most* number of abortive implementations. This is not always the user's fault, but generally the fault of the systems development staff and in particular the project manager, who must insist upon detailed user involvement. The nature of new systems is such that the user usually comes out with a completely changed business environment that may include reduced administrative responsibility. Because of these facts, the user involvement must be controlled by the development staff to ensure that the common dangers listed above do not occur.

Data-Processing-Related Here the common contributors are:

- Lack of a detailed conversion plan.
- Underestimated personnel requirements.
- Loss of key personnel during development.
- Inadequate computer test time.
- Systems discrepancies not controlled.
- Detailed test procedure not prepared.
- Conversion and cutover not adequately planned and controlled.
- Systems development personnel not trained with application knowledge.
- Project manager not concerned with business aspects of the system.

The data processing development staff is generally guilty of poor consideration of the application or business side of any systems development activity. Although this is changing, most project managers are primarily "technical animals" and do not have an adequate appreciation for the responsibility of developing an operationally effective business system.

Other Dangers Listed here are:

- Management shifts development priorities because of unforeseen events, e.g., merger activity.
- Business volume surges, creating operating problems which have the effect of removing the primary user.
- Business volume collapses, resulting in budget changes that negatively impact existing development budget.

These general business dangers are usually unforeseen and result in short-term interruptions in a given development effort. They are, however, very costly for the company, because any stop/restart situation creates additional activities that are expensive. Also, a time delay in the original system implementation schedule is experienced, and that postpones the expected benefits to the corporation. These general dangers also negatively affect the morale of the systems development staff and the primary user-departments.

Chapter 2

Installation and Testing Techniques

WILLIAM MEYER

Fireman's Fund, American Insurance Companies,
San Francisco, California

The rapid growth of computer systems in the past 10 to 15 years has been accompanied by significant testing problems, but these problems are more a result of design weaknesses than of size. Computer installation testing methods are not always successful, as the cost overruns of computer systems amply demonstrate. In order to eliminate or at least control cost overruns, a rigorous *structured testing* plan should be developed in conjunction with the system.

Introduction of a structured testing system is a complex effort which requires time and cooperation. A system cannot be implemented overnight. Time and effort are required to train and orient all those affected by it. Since planning and control capabilities must be developed before implementation of a new system, a full-blown testing procedure cannot be imposed upon an organization. However, a structured testing procedure can be developed in much the same way as a computer *software system* is developed.

Feasibility A system may not be feasible for a variety of reasons — e.g., a necessary piece of hardware may not be available, or the current operating system may not be capable of handling the demand that would be placed on it — or if it is feasible, it may not be practical because of costs or because it would demand an unsupportable drain of resources. Assuming that the system is feasible and practical, a major part of the developmental funds is expended in analysis of the functions the system is to perform, and another large part is spent on the programming of those functions. Usually very little is *allocated* directly to testing, although a great deal is actually *spent* on it. Also, the costs that are incurred when a system continuously malfunctions are nearly impossible to calculate, but they are no doubt considerable.

SYSTEM ASSURANCE TESTING

In general, there are two testing activities, *developmental* and *acceptance*, which make up the activity called *assurance testing*. System assurance testing is the procedure which ensures that a computer software system performs as it is meant to.

System Assurance Group The system assurance group oversees and evaluates the effectiveness of the assurance testing. It should be made up of people who are highly competent and who possess wide knowledge. All parts of the system involve the system assurance group—from the methods used for data collection to the procedure designed to place the final product in the hands of the user, from the initial design to the postevaluation.

The system assurance group's working tool is the *system documentation*. From the documentation the testing plan is developed, and it then also becomes part of the system documentation.

A *test plan* is a technique used by the system assurance group to anticipate problem areas and to see that they are corrected before a system goes into production. The test plan will lay out the strategy to follow, so that the most efficient use is made of available resources. There is difference of opinion as to the value of a too rigorous test plan, on the grounds that it adds unnecessarily to the cost of the project, but thoroughness at this point will appreciably cut down unexpected cost overruns at a later time. There is no easy road to assurance testing, and no single path that will lead to complete assurance. The assurance group must take into account a number of fundamental considerations, such as availability of test data, file security, accessability of computer resources, control of program changes, and the like.

Purpose of Testing Assurance testing is designed to uncover bugs. A *bug* is an error in a program. A debugged program is one which, on testing, has not been presented data which will cause it to fail. However, while testing may uncover bugs, there is no assurance that *all* the bugs have been found. All that can be claimed for debugged programs is if the data they process stays within certain bounds, their reliability may remain high. It is the assurance group's responsibility to see that the reliability is and will remain high.

A bug in a system, on the other hand, is not always caused by a bug in a program. All the programs in a system may function perfectly, but if the wrong version of the master file is processed, the output will be useless—or worse yet, critical files may be irreparably damaged. A design weakness may allow perfectly valid, but nevertheless nonsense transactions, such as issuing blank invoices or writing checks or bills for zero or negative amounts. Or perhaps there is no method to prevent the same transaction from being processed a number of times, or no procedure to back out such activity. It is the system assurance group's responsibility to locate and remedy these types of bugs before they cause problems.

System Assurance Group Management A system is only as reliable as its least reliable component. While it is the job of the assurance group to identify and then strengthen this component, the full cooperation of the users, analysts, operations staff, programmers, and data entry personnel is also required—in short, everyone who interacts with the system. To gain this cooperation requires tactful and thoughtful management.

Management should be aware that the creation of a system assurance group will require some functional and administrative changes. During the developmental and installation phases of a project, the system assurance group becomes a superstructure that oversees and evaluates all the interfaces the system will have with all sections of the company. Obviously, the manager chosen to head such a group must be extremely talented.

The nucleus of the system assurance group should be a personable and intelligent analyst who is knowledgeable about the way the organization really works, a senior programmer who knows the operating system and the languages in which the system is written, and a technical writer who can write clear sentences. Personnel should be selected from each department, division, and section affected by the system. The commitment of each member of the assurance team will vary, depending on the impact the system has on each member's department, but each should be scheduled to attend periodic assurance review meetings.

Communication The review meetings are designed to open and maintain lines of communication (Figure 2-1). Each member brings from his or her department knowledge of activities or changes in procedures which will affect the system, and takes back to his or her department an intimacy with the system. For example, the member from the equipment planning section may have knowledge that certain remote terminals will not be delivered when they were scheduled. The data may now have to be entered via cards. However, there may not be a keypunch available at the remote site, and the manager of that department may be reluctant to release the original source

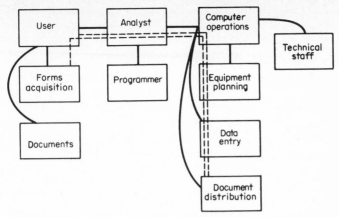

Fig. 2-1   Lines of communication for assurance testing. Typically, lines of communication between various affected sections are not well defined, as indicated by broken lines.

documents. Or the member from the technical staff may know of a planned operating system change that will affect the assurance schedule. Any number of things can and probably will happen that affect the assurance testing of a system, so it is absolutely vital that all possible lines of communication be kept open. Not all these lines of communication need be formally defined.

TEST DESIGN

Planning Tests One part of the system assurance test plan is directly concerned with the manual and clerical operations required by the system. A means to account for the human factor during system development rather than at conversion or implementation time simplifies system assurance. All important human operations, including training and orientation, are covered in this part of the plan, as well as personnel requirements and a schedule for predicting and measuring progress.

A broad outline of the plan can be developed directly from the system flow chart (Figure 2-2). First, a list of all areas to be covered by written instructions is extracted from the flow chart. The level of detail of this list will be determined by the needs of the application as defined by the assurance group. Included in the list may be, for example, design of input forms, balancing controls, document distribution, data entry, who is to be notified of changes to the system, and how they are notified.

Every subject on which a significant amount of time will be required to produce instructions should be included in this list. After the outline is developed, the details should be filled in: Who is to design the forms? How are they to be ordered? What about training? Will the users need special training? Will computer operations need special training? Are special one-time installation instructions necessary? Etc.

Testing Strategy The testing strategy must take into account the function and purpose of every module in the system (see Check-off List, Figure 2-3). Agreement has to be reached as to what constitutes a successful test. An edit module requires different testing than does a calculation module, and range edits have to be tested differently than do relational edits. Here is a good place to question the program design. Have all the programs been sufficiently modularized by function so as to make their testing an almost trivial operation? If not, they should be redesigned. (See Figure 2-4).

The name of the items to be tested within each module, along with a description of the data and the test cases required to ensure that each function within the module is correct, should be described at this point. The techniques used to develop test data and the test validation method should also be described. It would be useful to develop a PERT network[1] showing the critical path at this time. The PERT network chart will

[1] See, for example, the entry "PERT (Program Evaluation and Review Technique)," in Carl Heyel (ed.), *The Encyclopedia of Management,* Van Nostrand Reinhold, New York, 1973.

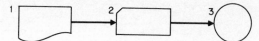

Source document gets transformed to cards then to tape.

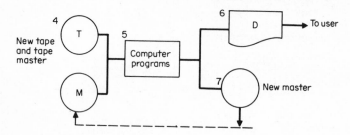

QUESTIONS FOR SYSTEMS ASSURANCE ACTIVITIES

1. a. How are source documents collected? Purchased? Distributed? etc.
   b. How are source documents coded? Is special training needed?

2. a. How are documents converted to cards?
   b. Training? Special cards? Are keypunches available?

3. a. How does data on cards get to tape? Optimum block size?
   b. Is special program needed? Training?

4. a. How are tapes identified?
   b. How long should they be retained?
   c. How many tapes in a file?

5. a. Identify record types.
   b. Identify field types.
   c. What do programs do?
   d. What happens to each field? How is it tested? What should be tested first?
   e. What is successful test?

6. a. Are forms designed? Ordered? Available? (When?)
   b. Special instructions for printing?
   c. What about distribution?

7. a. Name of new master different than old?
   b. What happens if it is damaged?

Fig. 2-2   Questions for system assurance activities developed from system flow chart.

A.   What does system do?

   1. What are input documents and files?
   2. What tasks and transactions are performed?
   3. What outputs are created?
   4. What becomes of output?

B. How does system do it?

   1. What are names and descriptions of data?
   2. What are edits on fields? Balancing?
   3. What happens when invalid data encountered?
   4. What are output fields?
   5. How are output fields related to input?
   6. What about equipment?
   7. Computer language?

C. Who uses the system?

   1. User manuals needed? Who writes them?
   2. Balancing/control operations? How? Who?
   3. How do source documents become usable data?
   4. Delivery of output to user.
   5. Training needed?

D. When does sytem run?

   1. How many programs?
   2. What are machine requirements?
   3. What if system doesn't run when scheduled? Who's notified? How?
   4. What if the system does not run successfully? Recovery? Restart?

Fig. 2-3   Check-off list.

enable the assurance group to direct its efforts where they will be most effective. In addition, it aids in the development of logical checkpoints. During the reviews, the assurance group will find the network charts a great aid in showing how well the testing is proceeding, how much is yet to be done, where the problems have been, and where they are likely to be. Also, the charts should prove useful in the development of future systems.

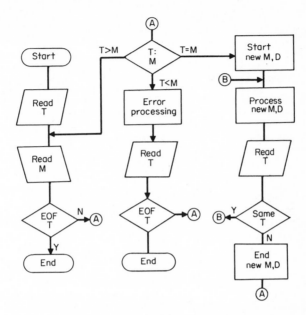

1. What does program do? What is successful test?

2. What are valid values? Explicit values? Range?

3. What happens when invalid values are encountered?

4. Is program designed well? What happens in START NEW M, D, PROCESS NEW M, D?

5. Can later changes be incorporated easily?

Fig. 2-4 From the program flow chart, the system assurance group develops test strategy and test cases.

Test Data To enumerate all test cases for a particular module may be impossible. For example, if a module contains tests for 50 fields, to ensure that every possible case is tested might require 2^{50} tests. However, if the functions can be separated into 10 groups of 5 tests, the number of tests required becomes 10×2^5 or 320, still a large number, but manageable.

Test cases for numeric fields should include positive and negative values, large numbers, and zero. If the module contains edits on numeric fields, a test case should be developed for alphabetic blanks and other invalid characters in the fields. Test cases should also be made for overflow, rounding, truncation, zero divide, and alignment.

Rather than expend all the effort required to develop these test cases, it may seem reasonable to strip off data from an existing master file and use it directly. The problem with using this approach is that no matter how large is the master file used, there is no certainty that all the possible logic paths within a program will be tested. Also, the larger the master input file, the more difficult will be the task of validating the output. However, data can be stripped from an existing file and then modified according to the rules developed for the test cases.

Test data can also be generated by using any of the *data generators* now on the market. Most of these generators can create data fields that will satisfy all test cases. Using the test data generator, it is possible to create wide ranges of valid and invalid data. The difficulty once again is in predicting the output. For every possible input value, the output must be predictable, else there is no certainty as to what the program is doing.

Testing Routines When testing a particular routine, it should be kept in mind that the test is being performed to check out the logic of the routine and not the machine's circuitry. While the possibility certainly exists that the computer itself can malfunction and cause errors, the probability of this happening is extremely low. What a test is designed to ensure is the correctness of the logic in the *program*.

For example, if there is an instruction that causes Field A to be added to Field B and the results placed in Field C, there is a high degree of certainty that the machine will execute the operations called for. The questions a test has to answer are: Do Fields A and B contain the correct values? Will they *always* contain the correct values? In order to answer these questions, all the ways values can be placed into Fields A and B must be tested. Whether or not all the logic paths that cause values to be placed in Fields A and B can be tested depends primarily on the program design. Since most programs are generally not designed, but rather grow wild like untended shrubbery, it may not be practical or possible to test all the paths.

Referring to the example above, suppose each of the 50 tests resulted in a different value being placed in Field A and/or Field B. Clearly, this would be a difficult routine to test. Suppose, on the other hand, that a detailed analysis of the routine showed that each field test is associated with a particular function and that if the program was designed by function, the testing problem would practically disappear.

FUNCTIONAL APPROACH TO TESTING

Program Design There are many advantages to designing programs by *function*. First, a function is always a closed routine; that is, it has only one entry point and one exit point. Second, a function always accomplishes a particular task, whether it be creating a detail line on a report, matrix multiplication, or adding Field A to Field B and giving Field C. Third, a function always posts back to the routine that invoked it a completion code indicating its success or failure. Fourth, when a function is tested, as with the add example above, it never has to be tested again.

Program switches and GO-TOs make a module difficult to test. A switch is usually set in a program when a condition is encountered at a point where the program cannot take the proper action to resolve the condition. The switch is tested somewhere else in the program to see if the condition has been encountered. A general rule is, the more switches there are in a program, the worse the program is. A switch may be set on any number of places in a program and set with any number of values, all of which must be tested. Maintenance and modifications to a program which has a number of switches are extraordinarily expensive. The maintenance programmer usually has no idea of the purpose of the switches and does not know all the values of the switch or all the places that a switch is set. Rather than take a chance in upsetting some hidden logic in the program that he or she does not understand, the maintenance programmer will normally add another switch to satisfy his or her needs, and on and on it goes.

GO-TOs compound the difficulty. They are often used in conjunction with testing of a switch. A GO TO says, "Stop what is being done here, go somewhere else, and do not come back." Testing of a program with a great many GO-TOs is especially difficult because following such a program's logic is difficult. Another general rule for evaluating a program is: If the GO-TOs branch to a reference point which is more than 50 instructions away, the program was not designed, it merely grew. The more GO-TOs there are and the further they branch, the more difficult is the job of testing.

Function Testing In any well-designed system, function testing should be possible as soon as the source coding has been successfully converted into machine code. When the higher-level languages (COBOL, FORTRAN, etc.) are used, a function would probably not consist of more than 20 source statements (excluding data definitions). This function would be tested by the development group according to the system assurance specifications. The test results would be evaluated, and if they check out, the function would be marked successfully tested.

When a function, module, or program has been successfully tested, it should be placed immediately on a *protected library*. Any accesses to this library by other than the *change control subgroup* of the system assurance group will be *read only*. The module becomes the property of the system assurance group. The developmental group can read and copy the module, but cannot update it.

Changing Tested Functions When changes are required in a tested module, they should be applied in a well-defined manner. The module should be copied from the protected library to a *test library*. The necessary changes should be applied to the test library version and the module used by the developers until they are satisfied with their changes. It is then turned over to the systems assurance group.

The changed module is in effect a new module, and as such its function and the testing techniques used to ensure that the function is performed have to be analyzed once again. A minor change may result in little more than retesting, while a major change may alter the whole system and may mean that everything done previously must be changed.

Whatever the case, the changed module is compared to the original. All changes are fully documented. What was changed? Who made the change? Why was the change made? When was it made? This document becomes a permanent part of the system documentation maintained by the system assurance group. The old module is then replaced by the new one and is protected from any more changes.

These documenting activities would be nearly impossible to do manually, but fortunately they are not difficult to automate. A program to compare the two source programs and produce a change listing is a relatively simple one. The name of the program, the name of the requester of the change, the date of the change, and the reason for the change are printed at the top of the listing, with the changes following. A description of the change is printed preceding the printing of the change. For example, there is a deletion message, "The following card was deleted," followed by the printing of the line of code that exists in the original module, but not in the new one. Similarly, there is an addition message, "The following card was added," preceding the print of the source record that is found on new module, but not on the old. This type of documenting program will be a valuable tool for the system assurance group, and its output has been of great assistance to the developmental teams in typical cases.

Test Drivers In spite of the best efforts of the designers to create modular programs, some routines may require some type of *driver* in order to be tested. A test driver is a program that simulates the activities of some other program that may not yet exist. It controls the execution of the module being tested by supplying data under controlled conditions and (usually) monitoring the output of the module. It allows testing of modules without delay, i.e., the modules can be tested before the main module being simulated is written.

If at all possible, the technique of using drivers should be avoided. A driver is, after all, another program, and as such requires analyses, specifications, programming, and testing. A driver adds more complications to an already complicated activity. But if a driver is necessary, it should be developed entirely by the system assurance group. The developmental group has enough to do without requiring more, and a driver may prove useful to the assurance group at a later stage, especially if it is generalized.

Acceptance Testing As the functions are developed and tested, they are combined into modules. The modules are tested and then combined into programs. The programs are tested and then combined into job streams. Finally, the job streams are combined into the fully developed system. Each step is checked off the PERT network and documented when it is completed according to the test plan specifications. When all the programs have been developed and their functions tested, the developmental testing phase is finished and the *acceptance test* phase can officially begin.

By this time most, if not all, of the documentation should be in existence. The users, operations staff, data entry personnel, and others concerned will be familiar with most of the systems characteristics. Whatever documentation is missing should now be completed, reviewed, and published.

The acceptance testing should simulate the actual production environment as closely as possible. This testing is meant to minimize and eliminate production malfunctions due to errors, omissions, or inadequacies within the system which are not discovered during the developmental phase. Acceptance testing may require a number of complete simulated test runs. Processing for different cycles may activate different sections of the system and each should be tested.

The user should now be fully trained and prepared to receive and operate the system. The user should be prepared to change his or her mode of operation to fit the new system and be satisfied that the new system operates as specified.

POSTIMPLEMENTATION CONSIDERATIONS

System Reviews   After the system has been in operation for a reasonable length of time, a *postevaluation* should be initiated. A review of the entire system and of the effectiveness of the assurance testing will provide reliable information which will prove useful for future projects. The review will indicate if the system is functioning effectively and if the anticipated benefits are being achieved. The possibilities for additional benefits may come to light at this point. Recommendations for improvements and solutions to problems should be included in the review.

Cost of Testing   Testing is a horrendous task. The costs incurred by a company in testing of computer systems make up a considerable investment. Unfortunately, much of this investment is spent haphazardly with little means of evaluating the payoff. The value of the testing methods used is a difficult figure to determine. A company's decision as to how much to invest in a particular testing method can be made less difficult if the true costs can be determined, that is: How much will it cost to train and orient all the people concerned? What will the machine costs be, using a structured testing approach? When these costs are estimated, they can be compared to the actual costs incurred on previous projects when testing was less than thorough.

A company's decision as to how much to invest in a particular implementation plan should be based on objective facts, and made when the decision to develop a system is made. Without a detailed testing plan, the decision is taken out of management's hands. By the time system testing begins, so much has been spent on development that management has little choice but to pay whatever it costs to do the testing. The purpose of a structured test plan is to put this decision back in the hands of management. The purpose of the system assurance group is to see that the plan is developed and implemented.

Some sort of a test plan usually evolves when implementing a system, even if it is done more or less informally. The software part of a system undergoes some degree of testing, though it may be haphazard, before it goes on the air. Clerical and manual operations, on the other hand, are generally not tested at all until the system goes into operation. (This placing of manual operations in a kind of limbo is probably a blessing to the system's analysts and programmers, for a breakdown in the manual functions takes some of the heat off of them that is generated when the software develops bugs.)

Monitors   Every system has errors or bugs built into it. The more errors there are in a program, the shorter the period it will run. For example, if there are a given number of errors in every 1,000 lines of code, and each has an equal probability of happening, then the longer a program runs, the higher is the probability that it will encounter a bug and terminate unsuccessfully. The longer a program runs before encountering a bug, the higher are the costs—which is a good reason to have monitors and restart capabilities.

The bugs in the manual part of a system are not normally critical, because people can always somehow muddle through. Software can be created that will muddle through also. Routines can be incorporated into the software that monitor number fields for improbable values (whether large or small), or monitor for unlikely relationships on edited fields. When the monitors find an illogical condition, error handling routines can be performed and processing can continue. Whether to use a monitor is a design decision, but it needs to be tested as does any other software routine.

Communication   A great many bugs are a direct result of inadequate communication between the user and the programmers. The programmer incorrectly implements the design and the user misunderstands the output. The user must know what he or she wants, and the systems people must understand the user's problem *before* the design is implemented. Many systems people believe they can solve problems better than the user can, when in fact they often do not understand the problem or the practical considerations of the solution. The user may be continuously changing the system requirements, and the initial design of the system, in all probability, does not lend itself to change.

Feedback is an absolute prerequisite to successful data processing. Responsibility for seeing that the right kind of information is given to the right people must be defined. A successful implementation requires a clear, concise, objective description of what the system is to do and how it is to do it, and a schedule of what is to be done, when it is to be done, and how it is to be done. All involved must be kept informed as to how the project is progressing, where the real problems are, and where the potential ones may be.

SUMMARY

A structured test plan is a technique for assurance testing a system. It is a technique to ensure that most of a system's problems are solved before they cause complications. But there must be a balance between techniques and end results.

Detailed test plans should themselves be tested for realism. A plan, especially in its early stages, must undergo constant change and tailoring to make it more effective. Changes and refinements in the original test plan should be made as soon as their need becomes apparent.

To oversee and evaluate the implementation of a system needs several pairs of eyes. The efforts of the user, analysts, programmers, operations staff, data entry people, etc. must be coordinated. This coordination can best be achieved through the system assurance group.

The successful installation and testing of programming systems requires periodic reviews by the assurance group during the target period. The reviews measure performance, check the validity of the testing, and suggest remedial action.

The costs of implementing a structured test plan may be very high. The creation of a system assurance group that in effect oversees the activities of the developmental team will not be looked upon with favor. The test plan itself will be expensive to develop and implement. However, balanced against this is the fact that these costs are already being incurred because of the low effectiveness of the developmental team operating without a test plan. Even if the costs do increase, the increase in check-out speed and decrease in undetected errors, the complete documentation, and the greater confidence in the system will make the investment a wise one.

Chapter 3

Documentation, Standards, and Controls

ROBERT A. GUIDA

**Manager, Data Entry Division, Blue Cross
of Massachusetts, Boston, Massachusetts**

Many individuals in the computer industry mistakenly believe it should be possible to develop data processing systems without difficulties or problems. They refer to similar engineering disciplines and point out that bridge building, for example, is partitioned into manageable phases. What they forget, however, is that such engineering disciplines are founded on proven theory, law, and practice, while the disciplines involved in developing data processing systems may be described as still rather loose or unproven.

The disciplines used by engineers follow proven approaches to the fabrication process from concept to completion. The methods used in developing each specification and drawing are governed by a myriad of standards of precision and accuracy to ensure that each part will fit together properly. To make sure that proper cross-checks and controls are built into the structure, facts such as weight, strength, and stress, as well as durability and adaptability to surroundings and environment, are given full consideration.

Similar disciplines are needed in designing, developing, and implementing data processing systems. It is important to structure the development process and base it on a series of phases, as evidenced by the preparation of written specifications. The whole approach and the individual tasks undertaken must be guided by a precise methodology so that the system produced is capable of withstanding tests of performance throughout its life cycle.

This Chapter deals with the nature and scope of the disciplines that must be applied in developing data processing systems. Too often, the disciplines that govern this function are considered mere appendages to the total development process, rather than essential and integral parts. The successful management of such projects will depend largely on adhering to, applying, and practicing the disciplines used in a professionalized approach.

DOCUMENTATION

Documentation is not always completely understood, even by those who use it. Documentation serves many purposes, including its use in the implementation process.

While some of its aspects are discussed in other Sections of this Handbook, this Chapter considers the significance of documentation as it applies to the design and development of data processing systems as well as to their implementation.

What Is Documentation?   Documentation of ADP systems is a coordinated effort to communicate information about them in written form. Usually it consists of descriptions, specifications, and instructions, and includes narratives, charts, graphs, diagrams, etc. Its purpose is to make sure that the details of the data processing systems are understood by all concerned in their development. Documentation explains what each system is; why it was created; how it operates; how it relates to other systems; and how it should be installed. It also provides information for continued maintenance, as well as a base line for reconstructing a system.

Need for Documentation   Whether a system is manual, uses office machines and tabular equipment, or uses computers, it needs written instructions to ensure proper processing of data. Today the need is much greater than before. As business grows more complex, equipment for the processing of data grows more sophisticated, and the need for integrating formerly isolated applications has become vital. In the broad sense, documentation is a matter of sound economics and management practice. For example:

- It closes the communication gaps among top management, users of systems, and the designers of data processing systems.
- It forces a standard approach to the design, development, and installation of data processing systems.
- It provides the necessary information to develop the education and training programs that are necessary for installing and operating the system.

Objectives   While detailed objectives vary with the system being developed, some fundamental objectives are common to the documentation of most data processing systems. They include:

- Creating a medium of communication for all management levels.
- Standardizing presentation in order to make it easier to prepare documentation and, later on, to locate specific information within the documentation.
- Creating a vehicle to provide evidence of progress in the development process and to monitor its progress.
- Creating a means for testing a system in order to verify its performance against pre-established, written criteria.
- Providing a means to determine in advance what will occur and when.
- Establishing a control on modifications to the design and implementation process.
- Creating a means for making the most efficient use of all resources and facilities applied in the development process.

Characteristics of Good Documentation   To be effective, documentation must have the following characteristics:

- *Availability.* After it is prepared, it must be accessible to those for whom it is intended.
- *Objectivity.* It must be clearly stated in language that is readily understood.
- *Completeness.* It should contain everything needed so that those reading it can fully understand the system being discussed.
- *Appropriateness.* It must use no more and no less detail than is needed, in a form that can be used by those for whom it is intended.
- *Standardization.* It should conform throughout to the same basic pattern in order to obtain maximum effectiveness.

The Control Process and Documentation   As in other corporate projects, the development of data processing systems has a beginning or point of initiation followed by other distinct phases which may be related to a step in the system development and control process. (See Figure 3-1.)

To initiate a project, the usual approach is to submit a request for services. This is made directly to the data processing services area or to a committee of top user corporate officers whose function is to guide and coordinate the data processing area services in accordance with corporate objectives and goals.

Regardless of the mechanism used, initial review and selection of a data processing project usually begins with the preparation and submission of a *User Request*, often referred to as a *Work Request*.

Essentially, the User Request delineates a need recognized by the user. Often a number of such needs are identified and considered simultaneously, each vying for the resources of the data processing area. The committee's function is to select, evaluate, and establish priorities. To assist the committee in the selection process, preliminary or feasibility studies are often conducted.

Once the need is recognized as valid by the committee, its preliminary approval to proceed is granted. The user then prepares a Functional Specification, which identifies the background, scope, and reasons for the request. It provides a problem-oriented

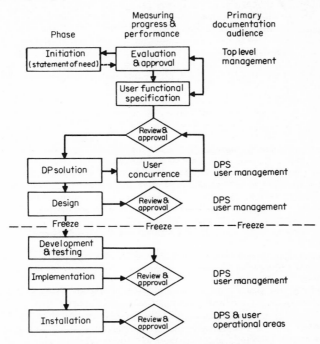

Fig. 3-1   System development control process.

definition of what is needed, with emphasis on user-visible features and short- and long-range requirements. It also provides specifications for the operational requirements of the system being requested, as well as the measures of performance the user intends to employ in evaluating the finished product's effectiveness.

The completed Functional Specification is usually submitted to the governing body for final approval and concurrence. In this way, top-level representatives of the company act as a group on behalf of all the interests of the company in authorizing the development of a data processing system.

The steps of initiating, approving, and authorizing the project thus become the first phase in the system development control process.

Once it is authorized, the actual process of developing a data processing system includes a number of distinctive phases, each of which incorporates several steps. Each phase is earmarked by the preparation of a document or documents which contain information appropriate and vital to the particular phase involved. Each document produced, if properly handled within established minimum requirements, becomes evidence of the completion of the particular phase. Thus, the documentation process may be viewed as a series of logical checkpoints, serving as tangible, objective control of progress.

Figure 3-1 graphically displays the structure of a set of development phases and how each phase relates first to the control process and then to the audience for whom the documentation is intended. As each phase is entered and concluded, a method of measuring progress and evaluating performance is provided by means of a formal *review and approval* session. More important, the requirements of the system are under constant review. (An excellent treatment of the control process is contained in Lecht's book listed in the Selective Bibliography at the end of this Chapter.)

Audiences for Documentation The total effectiveness of documentation can best be measured by its ability to keep those involved in the development process fully informed. System documentation is intended not for one audience, but for several that may be grouped into three general categories: management, users of the system, and data processing services personnel.

An effective documentation program will serve these three audiences in different ways. Management will be kept aware and thus be in control at all times. The various users of the system will be in tune. They will know what the system can provide and, equally important, what it cannot provide. Data processing service personnel will be able to proceed in logical sequence in developing the system.

Documentation for Management Relying on the approved Functional Specification prepared by the user, management should be able to authorize the data processing services area to develop a solution to the user needs.

The document written by data processing services in answer to the user request is called a *Product Specification*, often referred to as a *System Proposal*. Thus, via the Functional Specification, the user has asked that a certain product (system) be built. The Product Specification, therefore, represents the data processing solution to the problem presented by the user. It should cover five points:

- *Concepts.* The architectural design intended to meet the system's requirements.
- *Functional design.* The new system's functional requirements.
- *Resources required.* The proposed type and kinds of resources required to develop the system.
- *Development schedule.* A preliminary development schedule for the entire system, identifying the major phases.
- *Cost-benefits analysis.* A detailed cost-benefits analysis that covers present costs, costs to develop the system, estimated costs to operate it, as well as tangible and intangible benefits the company will derive.

Documentation for Users A system obviously cannot operate smoothly unless its users understand it and are fully aware of what is expected of them to make it work successfully. Therefore, user-oriented documentation should describe the system in such a way that the users understand that they are an integral part of it. It should also make them realize that they can easily work and communicate with it in simple, direct terms. Even more important, users should understand that it is *their* system, designed to solve *their* problems and meet *their* stated needs.

For purposes of clarification, a distinction must be made here between documentation addressed to user-management and documentation addressed to user-personnel who perform the detailed operating functions involved.

System Description for User-Management. User-management needs to understand the system in its broadest concepts. Therefore, a document sometimes referred to as a *System Description* is generated. A typical System Description should explain, in nontechnical terms, all aspects of the system from the user-management's point of view. It should explain how the system will operate when installed (operational characteristics), with reference to user functions in support of its continuing operation. It should also include a sample and explanation of each input document and transaction unique to the system, as well as descriptions of files or databases to be maintained by the system, and reports or other outputs of the system.

It should explain briefly the system's purpose and how it affects other systems and divisions in the company. It should explain fully any reassignment of responsibilities, possible reorganization requirements, and decision-making authorities affected by the system.

To promote better understanding at all levels of user-management, the description might explain the deficiencies of the existing system and the evolution of the new one. It should define responsibilities to make sure the user and data processing services agree on the functions needed to support the system. If subsystems are involved, the purpose of each and how each interrelates as part of a total system should be explained.

The System Description should also include such items as:

• *A work plan.* This would be a chart with supporting narrative that itemizes the tasks to be completed by data processing services and the user before the system can be completed. It should include such items as user testing, required file conversion, necessary training, etc.

• *A testing plan.* This section should define the tests to be conducted, their specifications, and what criteria are to be used for system acceptance.

• *Controls.* This section should provide a description of the internal and external controls to be built into the system. It should itemize procedures and responsibilities for the user and for data processing services in administering the operational process and controls provided. The size of this document will vary according to the size and complexity of the system being developed. However, the work required to produce a complete and comprehensive document is well worth the effort, since it will set the stage for the remainder of the development process and will provide user-management with a valuable reference for guidance in implementation and planning.

User's Guides. In addition to the System Description intended for user-management, user-personnel also need to know what roles they play in running the system. Therefore, documents sometimes referred to as *User's Guides* are generated. Typical User's Guides instruct user-personnel in the "what, who, when, and how" of the system. Thus they are intended to improve the operational interface between users and data processing services. Several types of guides are usually developed. However, each guide should have a standard introductory format which indicates the name of the guide, its purpose and aims, its intended readers, and how it should be used and updated. Among the several types of User's Guides that can be produced are:

• *Conversion instructions.* This particular guide provides a step-by-step instruction on how a manual system should be converted to a computer-oriented data processing system. Specifications are provided so that data currently maintained manually can be converted into machine-readable media in order that supporting informational files may be structured to eliminate data redundancy. Procedures for putting a new system "on the air" should include the development of charts, reports, and other techniques to keep on top of the conversion effort.[1]

• *Training manuals.* These are the guides that introduce user-personnel to the system. Training guides explain the overall system and the responsibilities of the user. The guide brings together typical examples of procedures to be followed, processes to be controlled, and work-flow guidelines to be maintained.

• *User operating instructions.* This guide specifies procedures for such operations as completing source documents, schedules for submission of data, and brief descriptions of the content of output reports.

The complexity of a system may require other types of User's Guides. For example, if the user has access to remote terminals and/or off-line data transmission facilities, specific instructions should be provided for their operation and use. Special instructions should be provided for transmission times, call-up and closing messages, etc.

To sum up, documentation for users of a system should comprise documentation which presents information to the user, regardless of level, and enables the user to recognize and understand his or her part in the operation of the system.

Documentation for Data Processing Personnel Documentation for personnel involved in the design, development, implementation, and operation of data processing systems should be divided into three separate categories: documentation first for systems designers, second for analysts and programmers, and third for operational personnel.

Documentation for System Designers. Once top management approves the system's architectural concepts and functional design as presented in the Product Specification, work can begin on its detailed analysis and design.[2] The analysis and design effort expended in the development of a data processing system is the most important building block in its fabrication process. To crystalize this effort, it is necessary to put in

---

[1] See Chapters 1 and 2 of this Part, "Organization for Systems Implementation: Timetables and Follow-through" and "Installation and Testing Techniques."

[2] See Part Three of this Section, "Detailed Systems Design."

writing the technical and design specifications that constitute the system. This document should be a detailed description in computer terminology of the system and its component parts. Frequently, it is referred to as the *System Specification*. A typical System Specification includes the following:

- *Purpose.* The objectives to be attained.
- *Scope.* The extent of the system. Enough information should be provided to place the system in proper perspective and to indicate its impact on other existing systems.
- *System flow chart.* The structure of the system, showing the logical flow of data through the system and the relationship between information processed and the operations performed.
- *Input-output summary.* The relationship of the input-output to the system's information needs, processing functions, and reporting requirements.
- *Interface.* This information is particularly needed in highly integrated systems. It should clearly define the various system devices through which input data or transactions are received and processed. Typical devices include driver programs, control programs, queueing programs, etc.
- *Master files.* A detailed description of the files, data sets, or specific databases used by the system.
- *Hardware-software.* Environmental requirements of the system.
- *Test plan.* Test objectives, the source of test input, the testing sequence, the means of measuring effectiveness, and the level of accuracy that is acceptable for the entire system.
- *Audit and control.* Specifications required to ensure the accuracy, maintenance, and control of the data processed by the system.

Documentation for Analysts and Programmers. The tasks of analyst and programmer are frequently performed by the same individual. However, the tasks themselves are distinct and separate, and are so treated in this Chapter. The specific document relative to each task is identified and described below.

The first document is a *Program Specification*. It is a functional description of each program, and defines what each program is, what it does and why, its relationship to the system, and its special features, if any. The Program Specification is essentially a statement of the design and logic requirements of a program and should include the following:

- *Purpose.* An abstract of the program, stating the major functions to be performed.
- *Background.* Additional information that would be helpful to the programmer in understanding the intent and scope of the program.
- *Program flow charts.* The first of these two charts is the macrochart, which shows the processing steps of the system and how each program relates to the others. The second is the microchart, which shows the logic of the program itself.
- *Input data.* Fields, data elements or records to be processed by the program, including definition of media type (card, tape, disk), sequence of elements, access method, record length, blocking factor, etc.
- *Output data.* A description, by record or data element, of the output generated. This could be a print routine, CRT screen display, etc. A sample should be included if the output is a formatted display or report. Details should include output media (card, tape, disk, CRT screen, report), sequence of elements, header/trailer label, record length, blocking factor, etc.
- *Database elements affected.* A list of file or database elements required by the program, showing how each element will be affected by the program.
- *Processing logic.* A descriptive narrative of processing steps to be carried out by the program with descriptions of special coding structures, table structures, algorithms, access, search and randomizing formulas, and other special techniques to be used.
- *Controls.* A description of the methods to be employed by the program to ensure that all data have been properly processed.
- *Test plan.* Procedures and requirements to be met before the program can be considered operational.
- *Subroutines.* Library and nonlibrary routines available to the programmer.
- *Glossary.* Alphabetical list of definitions of the terms peculiar to the system.

The second document is the *Program Manual*. It is prepared by the programmer to describe the finished product—the program. The contents specified for this manual have come, for the most part, to be accepted as the industry standard over the past few years. However, the particular installation environment in which the programming is done may require a particular structure and level of program documentation. Among the factors that influence the method to be used are: use of general-purpose software; impact of application packages; and impact of high-level languages. When these influences are encountered, a review of the approach described below is recommended before adhering to its requirements. A typical Program Manual should include the following:

- *Identification.* Identifies the program, that is, system name, author's name and title, preparation date, etc.
- *Program description.* This includes the functions to be accomplished by the program if they differ from those prepared by the analyst. Otherwise, there should be a statement that the program has been written in complete compliance with the program specifications.
- *Data specifications.* A finalized layout of the input, output, or file, if different from the specifications.
- *Programmer's guide.* This section of the document should explain how the program was written. It should also include a complete explanation of peculiar aspects of the program's development to make it easily understandable to another programmer or analyst.

The programmer may wish to reorganize flow charts, decision tables, search techniques, randomizing formulas, and special access formulas not called for or included in the original specifications. In coding, the programmer may make use of a "micro flow chart" or other techniques to simplify his or her own work. Program default, ABEND (ABnormal END of task) routines, etc., should be clearly described. It is precisely these extra notations that will be invaluable in facilitating reader understanding at a future date. If the program is modularized (segmented), the role of each segment should be described.

- *Listings.* The appropriate source and job control listings should be included.
- *Stand-alone test plan.* This should show steps to be followed by the programmer in testing the program independently. Results obtained should be clearly outlined.

Documentation for Data Processing Operational Personnel. This type of documentation is usually supplied by the analyst and/or programmer or a group of specialists with whom this function is placed. Ordinarily it falls into three distinct categories related to the data processing function involved: documentation for machine operations, for data preparation, and for data control.

In many installations these three functions are sometimes combined or interleaved. Although the organizational structures which support them may differ from one installation to another, the functions can usually be clearly identified.

The documentation that supports these functions should include general information, such as a brief narrative of the application system, a flow chart, background information, and other details that will assist the operational areas to recognize and understand their roles in the total system. This information can be considered universally needed by the operations people regardless of their specific functional responsibilities.

In most installations, the other operational information and documentation required are usually adequately provided by the system development group. (Space limitations in this Chapter prevent a detailed treatment of this type of documentation. For further guidance, see the Selective Bibliography at the end of this Chapter.)

STANDARDS[3]

Documentation is only one element of standardization. The following discussion defines standards and relates the use of standards to functions other than documentation within the data processing field.

What Is a Standard? Probably no definition could improve on the one offered by Dr. Astin, former director of the United States Bureau of Standards: "A standard is an arbitrary solution of a recurring problem." However, a dictionary definition might be

---

[3] See also Section 2, Part Six, "Standardization."

more in keeping with the philosophy of standardization in the development of data processing systems. According to *Webster's Dictionary*, "a standard applies to any definite rule, principle, or measure established by authority which constitutes or affords a means for comparison or judgment." It is within this framework, as it applies to the data processing services function, that standards are discussed here. Within that context, standards may be defined as rules and procedures to be followed by data processing managers, analysts, programmers, and operators in their everyday work activities.

Standards represent a yardstick for measuring the performance, integrity, and quality of the product built by the data processing professional. They are usually present in some minimum form in most data processing installations. Formalizing standards would undoubtedly be of benefit to all those internal to the data processing function. More importantly, the guidance offered by written standards bolsters the user's confidence, since it indicates that the product is being built within a fabrication process that is well defined and structured.

Data processing standards are concerned with such matters as processing integrity, data validity, and adequacy of control. Intangibles such as these are not readily recognized and, therefore, need to be carefully spelled out so that all concerned are in agreement as to what they mean and how they are to be employed.

The more standards are used in developing a computer system, the less difficult the process becomes. Standards not only simplify—they help establish and solidify the development process by promoting consistency. At the same time, they serve another function—probably their most important one—in providing a means of measuring actual performance against specified goals, thus making it easier to review current practices, estimate future requirements, and implement necessary changes. They also offer protection against turnover of personnel and provide a means to train new employees.

Another valid reason for standards is the desire on the part of many data processing practitioners to be recognized as professionals. If those engaged in data processing system design and management activities are seriously striving for acceptance of their services as truly professional, they must be willing to establish a minimum core of knowledge, discipline, and practice that will stabilize the quality of their product.

When Should Standardization Begin? The installation of a data processing function should be the signal to establish a set of installation standards. The standards need not be perfect at first. The important fact is that they exist and can be improved and changed as necessary. In this way, right from the start, everyone in the installation will be familiar with the practices and procedures to be followed.

Particular attention should be given to the development of documentation standards. Such standards are inherently present in most installations because of the tremendous amount of written communication involved: user to designer, designer to programmer, programmer to operational staff, etc. Since much of this communication is written, it would seem logical to establish standards that are based on an acceptable level of documentation dictated by a sound process of development and control. This point was strongly emphasized earlier in this Chapter.

For installations which lack standards, a basic set of documentation standards should immediately be established, and every effort should be made to bring past system development documentation to a minimum level. Its value will quickly be recognized when efforts are made to maintain or redevelop old systems.

What Should Be Standardized? Standards are treated in this Chapter as they apply to the data processing services function within an installation. If appropriate, any existing practices or standards that have been previously accepted should automatically become part of an installation's formal standards.

Standardization for the installation should begin with its development methodology —that is, how to go about performing the functions of analysis, design, programming, and implementation of a system. In other words, a method should immediately be adopted for the development and subsequent operation of a system to be produced. However, such methodology must not be looked upon as static and unchanging. On the contrary, as methodology itself continues to improve, there is bound to be an inevitable upgrading of standards.

The tools used in the fabrication process, that is, the specifications themselves, should be standardized, particularly the format for presenting the specifications.

Preparing specification documentation will be easier when all who prepare it do so in the same general way.

Actually, there are two sets of standards to be taken into account—industry-wide standards that are commonly accepted throughout the industry and should be adhered to, and local standards established by the company or organization. In large installations, the company or organization is usually able to develop its own in-house standards. But when the installation is small, the company frequently has to piece them together by adapting standards which have been previously developed elsewhere and are available in published manuals.

Obviously, an installation's standards should not conflict with the company's basic policy or procedures. Therefore, management should approve standards before they are formally accepted. In addition, it should support all standardization efforts.

The Standards Manual One way to speed up the acceptance and use of standards within the data processing environment is by developing and publishing a Standards Manual. Policy and Procedures Manuals have long been used to simplify and standardize other business activities, minimizing the necessity for involving upper management levels in routine matters. Similar results can be obtained if the same principle is used in publishing data processing standards.

The development and publication of a Standards Manual should be treated like other projects undertaken by the data processing function. A development team should be established with authority and responsibility to develop and publish a manual, and the manual's contents should be agreed upon early in the development process.

The system development control process, with the accompanying documents and checkpoints described earlier in this Chapter, is a valid, basic theme around which the manual should be built. The manual should trace the development process from the initiation of the project to its installation and subsequent postaudit. The development of specific documents should be the backbone of the development process and, as stated earlier, would provide for progress and performance review.

Enforcement of Standards. Since standards are useless unless adhered to, the best set of standards is one with which it is easy to comply. At every stage in the development of a system there should be checkpoints. For maximum effect, the standards should be built around the planning, design, development, and control process. (See Figure 3-1.) The standards thus become a set of guidelines and procedures well integrated into the structure of the actual development process. This is done so that the process becomes objective and acts as a check not only of progress but also of quality of performance. A well-defined set of standards makes the development process easier to administer and provides a clear path for development review. Thus adherence becomes not a forced issue but an accepted method of procedure.

There should be a designation of responsibilities for each phase defined in the development process and for which methods and procedures, documents, and guidelines have been specified. Since performance and progress cannot be measured unless they are traceable to an individual, the practice of adhering to standards becomes part of any acknowledged procedure and an understood role of each task assignment.

The assignment of responsibilities has the added advantage of preventing duplication of effort. Confusion is avoided. Certain elements in the development process are normally completed by the project supervisor or designer, while others are completed by the analyst or programmer. Thus, the development process flows in an understandable pattern, with guidance and direction inherent in the standards provided.

Need to Review Standards Requirements for the development of data processing systems are constantly subject to revision because of the dynamic and prolific nature of improvements in the field, and constant changes in hardware and software capabilities. The spiraling effect of these new methods and techniques implies anything but a static condition. Therefore, standards should be made to reflect methods as they exist and as they continue to enter each state of change. The establishment of a viable set of standards is not a one-time venture. Obviously, there must be a well-structured, management-controlled program for the constant reviewing, maintaining, and upgrading of the established standards.

Such a program is essential if the standards are to fulfill their function and continue to serve the organization. To make sure they do, two vital steps must be taken. First, responsibility for the maintenance of standards must be clearly assigned. Second, a standards officer should be carefully chosen. A prerequisite for this job, of course, should be a thorough knowledge of data processing and of the installation itself.

CONTROLS

In the past several years systems of control have been increasingly emphasized by the business community. The control process is as apropos to the data processing function as it is to the broader business environment. Quality assurance, too, has the same functional relationship and responsibilities to data processing as it has to the business itself. Since data processing methodology is simply a tool used by business to conduct its day-to-day activities, it is easy to appreciate the need for controls internal to the data processing function and the systems it develops.

What Is a Control? A suitable dictionary definition for *control* would be "to check, test, or verify by evidence or experiment." What definition then would suffice for *internal control*, the devices, procedures, and methods a company invokes to maintain integrity in its daily business transactions? To quote the American Institute of Certified Public Accountants, it is "the plan of organization and all the coordinate methods and measures adopted within a business to safeguard its assets, check the accuracy and reliability of its accounting data, promote operational efficiency, and encourage adherence to prescribed managerial policies."

Need for Controls In many companies today, electronic data processing systems have become the main source of data gathering and processing. Since the information used by management is generated from the manipulation of these data, it is necessary to maintain a system of controls of the data processing function to assure the quality of the data.

Types of Controls in Data Processing In the data processing function, controls can be divided into three categories: management, organizational, and procedural.

Management Controls. This type of control is concerned with the administrative and supportive management of the data processing installation. It involves not only the daily administrative supervision common to the management role, but also the establishment of a supportive staff group that is responsible for a variety of necessary control functions. One such control activity is the development and maintenance of installation standards, as discussed above. Standards, properly developed and adhered to, are essential in order to perform these two major management control functions:

1. Provide a means to measure the performance of data processing staff members and the systems they develop.

2. Enable corrective action to be taken as soon as problems arise.

In addition to maintaining standards, the four additional responsibilities frequently assigned to the supportive staff group are:

1. Administering a project control and reporting mechanism to handle details regarding the initial receipt and approval, budgeting and estimating, charge-back and reporting of projects undertaken by data processing.

2. Conducting the various approval and review sessions inherent in a well-defined system development and control process, as discussed earlier in this Chapter.

3. Providing a centralized writing function for software documentation. Although documentation writers need not possess a degree or extensive data processing background, college training and some data processing experience are helpful. Additionally, they must demonstrate a capacity to write logically and functionally.

4. Organizing and managing a library facility which will review and register, store, distribute, and maintain development documentation.

The centralization of these functions provides the management of the data processing installation with a strong support and control force. It also removes many time-consuming but necessary chores from the designer, analyst, programmer, and supervisor.

Organization Control. One of the basic principles of internal control is the need to distinguish the personnel who authorize a transaction from those who have custody of the asset required and those who record the accountability of the asset. In a manual system, internal control is concentrated in the review and cross-checking by the individuals involved in processing a transaction. However, in electronic data processing systems, internal control is very often concentrated in the system. Thus the authorization, recording, and processing functions can be an inherent part of the system itself. A typical example is an inventory management system which automatically generates a purchase order when the inventory for an item falls below a specified minimum.

To maintain the integrity of the internal control process in such a data processing environment, the systems development, operational process, and data control functions should be separated. The separation of each of these functions is itself another aspect of organization control. Essentially, then, each function serves as a cross-check for the others and, in essence, replaces the individual checks associated with the manual system. In turn, an audit function, usually the responsibility of a company's internal or fiscal auditor, provides another check.

Procedural Controls. In addition to proper management and organization control, a third control function is necessary to establish proper recording, processing, and output control procedures. It should concentrate on three areas: data source input; internal processing, and output.

1. *Data source input controls.* Basically, these have two objectives: First, to ensure that all transactions are properly recorded at the point of origin; second, to ensure that all transactions are transmitted from the point of processing.

The characteristics of currently available hardware and software provide a wide range of edit, validation, and control capabilities. Thus, systems which use conventional data source documents are as capable of performing such checks as are those systems where the source document is either eliminated or cannot be subjected to human review. In the latter situation, two basic methods are used to assure the validity and integrity of the source data.

The first method builds the controls and checks into the system itself, while the second places them at the point of source-data origin. Thus, remote recording and transmitting equipment uses built-in programmed controls and checks to assure authorized use and quality of input. Chapter 5 of Part 3, Section 2 of this Handbook provides coverage on the subject of source-data automation.

2. *Internal processing controls.* Internal processing controls become necessary once the source data have passed the input edit and validation checks and are residing within the computer's data storage devices. The various calculations, manipulations, and processes that are performed on the data must be subject to control and verification as well. All data processing equipment has built-in hardware controls to ensure that the data are correctly used, processed, and transferred within the system and are properly recorded for future processing. In addition to hardware checks, properly designed and comprehensive program checks assure the accurate processing of data within the system. The article by E. B. Dickey listed in the Selective Bibliography outlines a quite complete treatment of validation, processing, and control techniques that can be used in a data processing system. Further information is contained in the book by Gordon B. Davis, also listed in the Bibliography. Space restrictions prevent a detailed review of these techniques.

3. *Output controls.* The most basic output control is the comparison of control totals of data processed with totals independently obtained either from original source-data input or from prior processing.

In addition, the output control function should be geared to determine four points: (1) that the data processed do not include unauthorized alterations; (2) that all errors detected in the processing cycle have been corrected; (3) that output data are substantially reasonable; and (4) that a review of reports produced does not uncover any unusual or abnormal conditions. Here again, the techniques referred to in Davis's book are appropriate.

Control Groups within the Data Processing Environment Because the three types of control in the data processing environment are not automatic and self-perpetuating, it is necessary to have functional organization groups which will be responsible for continued administration and maintenance of the controls. These groups should be established within the data processing area, to provide direction and substance to the control effort.

Essentially, there are two types of control groups. One deals with the operational aspects of the data processing function. The other devotes its attention to management control, as discussed earlier.

The operational control group should confine its activities to functions that relate directly to the procedural controls: receipt of source data; processing of the data; and distribution of output reports which result from the processing cycle.

Audit Program The management of a company's internal audit function plays an important role in determining the integrity of data processing systems. It does so by continued surveillance and by determining the existence and effectiveness of the various controls described. Usually the internal auditor or the company's financial auditor has an established audit program.

The auditor should use the data processing installation's standards and procedures as a base line for assessing the installation's effectiveness. Whenever the auditor does not find installation standards, he or she should be severely critical, because this deficiency increases the difficulties involved in measuring the performance of the installation. The auditor's function, therefore, is to review and appraise the existing controls, not only within the data processing function, but also in each data processing system within the company. The auditor's responsibility is coexistent with the management function, and his or her report and recommendations should be responsive to the goals, objectives and plans of the company.

CONCLUDING REMARKS

Current trends point to an increasing concern for data processing systems which management can use with complete confidence to support its business ventures and to assist it in its administrative and decision-making functions. If a data processing system is to be reliable, efficient, and effective, as well as reasonably priced, it must be designed, developed, and implemented with great care. This means that the actual process used in developing the system must also be well structured.

It is not surprising then to note a change in the attitude of more and more company managers regarding the data processing function and the systems developed by it. Where they were somewhat passive and uninvolved in the past, they are now becoming more vigorous and direct in their participation, not merely in activities of the data processing installation itself, but also in the actual process of system development. This is a trend which some data processing managers may find hard to accept, particularly if the areas discussed in this Chapter are not given full attention. Ultimately, the measurement of the professional competence of a data processing practitioner, as well as the excellence of the data processing systems he or she develops, will depend on just how faithfully the principles discussed in this Chapter have been followed.

SELECTIVE BIBLIOGRAPHY

Books

Davis, Gordon B., *Auditing and EDP*, American Institute of Certified Public Accountants, New York, 1970.
Gray, Max, and Keith R. Landin, *Documentation Standards*, Brandon/Systems Press, New York, 1969.
Krause, Leonard I., *Administering and Controlling the Company Data Processing Function*, Prentice-Hall, Englewood Cliffs, N.J., 1969.
Lecht, Charles Philip, *The Management of Computer Programming Projects*, American Management Association, New York, 1967.

Articles

Bemer, R. W., "Information Processing Standards," *Data Management*, September, 1970.
Brandon, Dick H., "Data Processing Needs Management Standards," *Systems and Procedure Journal*, November–December, 1966.
Harper, William L., "Documentation for Application Programming," *Modern Data*, September, 1969.
Henderson, Reid, "Internal Control Safeguards for EDP," *Data Management*, September, 1970.

Chapter 4

Lease versus Purchase or Rental of Computers

ARTHUR J. BURKE

Manager, Corporate Systems Development, Westinghouse
Electric Corporation, Pittsburgh, Pennsylvania

The approaches to the lease vs. buy decision for electronic data processing equipment are basically no different from those for other types of capital equipment. Both quantitative and nonquantitative factors are analyzed and weighed. If the projected costs and benefits extend over a number of years, then present-value techniques of financial analysis should be used to reflect the fact that future dollars are not so valuable as cash on hand today. Where a capital investment requiring significant short-term cash outlay is involved, the return on investment should be calculated and compared against appropriate ROI standards. Such standards should be based on the organization's cost of capital and other investment opportunities. Where applicable, the effects of the decision on book profit should also be evaluated.

Our purpose is to discuss the financial elements of the lease vs. buy decision as they relate particularly to data processing equipment. The data processing industry is characterized by a high degree of technological change, an interrelationship of individual decisions, and a need for ongoing support, all of which make these decisions difficult even when a clear financial analysis is made. Nevertheless, a systematic approach to the financial factors permits evaluation of the associated risks, and should result in better decisions.

METHODS OF ACQUISITION

The financial methods generally used for procuring computer systems may be classified as follows: (1) rental directly from the manufacturer; (2) operating lease from a third party; (3) financial lease from a third party; and (4) outright purchase. Variations of these approaches are also used, such as time purchases and lease arrangements with options to modify or substitute equipment. The ingenuity of the financial community produces many such variations, but most can be analyzed in terms of the four common methods mentioned.

Rent, as the term is used here, is a form of lease distinguished by the fact that it is provided directly by the manufacturer. Periodic payments, usually monthly, are paid for use of the equipment. This form of acquisition is more widely used for data processing equipment than for most other capital equipment. Rent is usually available on short-term agreements of 1 year or less; and in recent years, commitments of up to 5 or 6 years at reduced rates have become available. Most rental agreements include maintenance in the charges. Title to the equipment, of course, remains with the manufacturer. A percentage of the payments is often available as credit toward subsequent purchase.

The operating or non-full-payout lease from a third party has been used as a logical alternative to rental. A leasing company purchases the equipment from the manufacturer or supplies the equipment from its own inventory of used equipment. The user makes a commitment to a series of periodic payments; but the lessor does not recover its full costs during the initial term and, therefore, assumes some risk of obsolescence. Longer commitments produce decreased charges. Maintenance is usually obtained by the lessee directly from the manufacturer. If the equipment is returned when the term expires, the lessor must find another user to recover full costs and achieve its projected return on investment.

The financial or full-payout lease with a third party is an agreement in which the user agrees to make a series of payments to a lessor, which in total exceed the purchase price of the equipment and return the cost of money, expenses, and a profit. Maintenance is contracted separately. Payments are typically spread over a period of time approximating the expected useful life of the equipment, which in the case of new computing equipment is usually 5 years or more. Title remains with the lessor at the end of the term, or may be available to the lessee to purchase at fair market value.

Outright purchase, generally the most common way of obtaining capital equipment, involves the immediate passing of title to the user in exchange for full payment. Until the past few years, purchase of data processing equipment by the user had been common in financially oriented organizations, such as banks and insurance companies, but had been used sparingly by most industrial firms. This pattern in industry has changed somewhat as a result of judgments that the rate of technological obsolescence of computers is slowing, coupled with the limited availability of attractive third-party operating leases during the past several years.

Use of the Methods   Short-term rental from the manufacturer is normally the most expensive method of obtaining equipment. It should be used only where no other alternative exists or where maximum flexibility for change is necessary. Longer-term rental commitments or third-party operating leases provide discounts from short-term rental for those in a position to commit for an intermediate term of 2 to 5 years. These agreements will, of course, limit flexibility for equipment changes, although some changes can be anticipated and contractually provided during the period.

Purchase should be considered when longer-term usage (over 5 years) is projected, or if the salvage or residual value is expected to be high after a shorter usage period. The financial justification for purchase is made by comparing the investment with the best viable alternative, including longer-term rentals or operating leases. A purchase which is justified by comparing it with short-term rental figures is meaningful only if this is the only alternative method of obtaining the equipment.

The use of financial leases can be viewed primarily as an approach dictated by organizational financial strategies. Such leases involve a full commitment of funds required for ownership of the equipment by the buyer, as in an outright purchase. Simultaneously, they provide a source of the funds. Other sources and their costs, as well as judgments of the effect of these leases on the total funds available to the enterprise, enter into the decision to use financial leases.

QUANTIFIABLE FACTORS IN EVALUATION

A number of costs will vary under rent, lease, and purchase. In comparing alternatives, many cost items will be unaffected. For those items which are affected, the actual differences in cost should be determined. In general, when estimating differential costs, prorated or allocated costs produced in the accounting system must be treated with caution, since such figures may not reflect actual differences in costs arising from the alternatives.

The discussions that follow are designed to point out items to investigate and evaluate for cost effects, but are not intended as definitive guides to governmental regulations or accounting practices. Taxes, insurance, and accounting procedures should be reviewed with those qualified to provide information on current practices and regulations. The view of a profit-making organization has been adopted, and modifications may be necessary when considered by other types of institutions.

Rental, Lease, and Depreciation Charges   The primary costs under rental or lease arrangements are, of course, the required periodic payments. Rental is often expressed in terms of prime shift usage, and additional charges for overtime are frequently required. Rental charges are subject to change, and anticipated changes should be estimated.

The outright purchase of equipment involves an immediate capital outlay, and the full amount is a direct deduction from available funds. The investment is expensed over a number of years, with a certain portion of the original investment charged to each year. This periodic expense, called *depreciation*, affects the cash flow through the years by its impact on income taxes, both Federal and state. Since it is an expense, it provides a deduction to reduce the income taxes and thereby increases cash flow. Of course, items which affect cash flow through income tax deductions assume profits that make the deductions possible.

The depreciation time period and method permitted an organization by the Federal Internal Revenue Service and respective state revenue departments for the determination of income taxes should be utilized in the cash-flow analysis. These may or may not correspond to the depreciation used for book profitability. Several methods of depreciation are used. The straight-line method gives an expense for each period merely by dividing the investment by the number of periods. Other methods permit acceleration of the depreciation expenses in the early years and thereby defer income taxes and improve cash flow.

Maintenance   Manufacturers' rental charges usually include maintenance, but maintenance is contracted separately by the user under third-party lease and purchase. Overtime, as well as prime shift maintenance costs, should be estimated. If a choice is available, a comparison between fixed-price and "on-call" overtime maintenance costs should be made, based on projected needs. Provision should also be made, where appropriate, for anticipated changes in maintenance charges. Since maintenance costs are largely determined by personnel salaries, they can be expected to increase over a number of years. Some suppliers provide contractual protection limiting yearly increases.

Taxes   Data processing industry practice, for the most part, has the manufacturer absorbing equipment personal property taxes under rental agreements. Third-party lease agreements are made with either lessor or lessee being responsible for these taxes. If applicable, they are a cost to the user of purchased equipment. Personal property taxes vary extensively depending upon the state or locality and do not apply in some areas.

Sales or use taxes are widespread, and must be added to periodic lease and rental charges. Normally, the full sales tax amount will be due on the outright purchase by the user at the time the purchase is made. It can be expensed immediately, and can thus provide an income tax deduction and not be treated as part of the capital investment and depreciated. If a third party buys the equipment for the purpose of leasing, then the tax usually is not due at the time of purchase but will be covered by the periodic payments.

Insurance   Insurance on the equipment is another item that is normally covered in manufacturers' rental agreements and may or may not be covered under third-party leases. When equipment is purchased, the insurance responsibility, of course, is with the buyer along with the corresponding cost or risk.

Salvage or Scrap Value   When purchased equipment has reached its economic life within an organization, it must be disposed of. The net proceeds from the disposal (the salvage or scrap value) will add to the cash flow for that year. Normally, the proceeds differ from the depreciated tax-based value of the equipment carried on the organization's books. If the disposal price varies from net depreciated value, the effect of the gain or loss on income taxes, and thus on cash flow, must also be considered.

Investment Tax Credit or Job Development Investment Credit   Credits for new investments applied against Federal income taxes, which have existed in several forms in recent years, can be a crucial factor in capital decisions. The existing rules for job development investment tax credit (JDTC) in the 1972 tax law permit 7 per cent of the investment to be taken as an immediate after-tax deduction for newly purchased capital items to be depreciated over a period of 7 years or more. The credit may also be deferred. If the depreciation schedule for the item is between 5 and 7 years, two-thirds of the 7 per cent is allowed. If the depreciation schedule is between 3 and 5 years, one-third is allowed. The depreciation is based upon the investor's schedules for the type of equipment.

For purchased equipment, this tax credit accrues to the buyer. Rental or lease agreements may or may not provide JDTCs to the user, depending upon the policies of the renter or lessor. Some manufacturers optionally give the credit to the user. When passed on in this way, the credit will be based upon the manufacturers' depreciation schedules, which typically are less than 7 years, and so less than the full 7 per cent maximum credit is available to the user. With third-party lessors, the credit is often a negotiable item with differing periodic charges available, depending upon whether the credit is given to the lessee.

Support Services Services associated with a computer system include personnel assistance for installing and maintaining systems software and applications, systems and applications program products, training, installation planning, preinstallation testing, and documentation, including manuals. With some manufacturers, all, or nearly all, of these services are included in the rental contract. With others, substantial fees may be involved for some of the services, particularly personnel assistance, training, and program products.

Manufacturers generally offer support for purchased systems similar to the support provided for those which are rented. However, differences may be possible even if they are not obvious from marketing policies. Once equipment has been purchased, the user's leverage with the supplier from ongoing rental payments is eliminated, and support services, especially those not charged for, can deteriorate over time. This is especially likely to occur when the supplier offers new competitive models and the user continues to use the older purchased system.

When a new or installed system is purchased by a third party for lease, the manufacturer's services should be equivalent to that furnished for direct purchase by the user. However, if the equipment is supplied from a lessor's inventory, the manufacturer normally will charge fully for any support provided, except for items that may be included within the scope of its maintenance contract. Some of these support services may be furnished by the leasing company.

APPROACH TO FINANCIAL COMPARISON

Data processing equipment is typically justified initially on the basis of the usual method of procurement used by an organization, whether this be rental, lease, or purchase. The quantifiable factors reviewed above, which vary under the different financial approaches, together with other quantifiable costs and benefits related to the systems development and applications, are the financial basis of the justification. Once the equipment selection and justification by the usual method are completed, alternative financing methods may be evaluated. Such a sequential approach to justification and financing separates the justification from the rent, lease, or purchase decision.

While separation of the decisions is desirable from an analytical viewpoint, it should be recognized that in many cases the decisions are interrelated. A favorable cost picture under a financial alternative not initially considered may cause a re-evaluation of the equipment selection. Therefore, it is desirable to examine the financial alternatives for competitive items of equipment before the selection is finalized.

For a selected item of equipment, the financial evaluation of rental, lease, or purchase is based upon the quantifiable costs which vary under these alternatives and does not involve costs related to systems development and applications. Quantifiable costs which differ should be projected for the planned equipment life. One of the alternatives is established as the cost base and the others are then related to it. If the projected equipment life is relatively short (less than 2 years), then a comparison of net after-tax cash flows for the feasible alternatives constitutes the key financial data for decision making.

If longer periods are involved, then the cash flows should be compared by means of the present-value method. One dollar at the end of one year is worth somewhat less than one dollar today. The expectation of receiving one dollar at the end of the year, therefore, has a present value of less than one dollar. Tables in financial handbooks permit the determination of the present value of a stream of earnings based on various required earnings rates or, as they are termed, *discount rates*. The required earnings rate to establish the present value of alternatives should be greater than an organization's capital costs and related to its return-on-investment standards.

DEMONSTRATION OF COMPARISON

Table 4-1 lists the parameters of an example which illustrates the use of the present-value technique in comparing rental, lease, and purchase for a piece of data processing equipment. The parameters are chosen to be representative of typical relationships among manufacturer's purchase, rental, and maintenance costs for new equipment. The indicated monthly lease rate would typically require a firm commitment from the user of 3 years or more on an operating lease. Miscellaneous expenses are incremental expenses assumed under a purchase or lease, such as maintenance beyond the prime shift, personal property taxes, and insurance, which are included in the manufacturer's rental charges.

Tables 4-2, 4-3, and 4-4 show the net after-tax cash flows for rental, lease, and purchase respectively for an 8-year period. A half-year convention is used to list the costs with Year 0 representing the initial 6 months and Year 8 the final 6 months. The cash flows for each year have been discounted to present value at a rate of 10 per cent. The cumulative value of these cash flows can be compared for different

TABLE 4-1 Data Processing Equipment (Example)

Purchase price	$88,000
Monthly rent	2,000
Monthly overtime (rent)	400
Monthly maintenance	200°
Monthly miscellaneous expense (purchase and lease)	33
Monthly depreciation—straight-line, 8 years	917
Monthly lease	$ 1,600
Income tax rate	50%
Sales tax	None
Investment tax credit (rent)	4⅔%
Investment tax credit (lease)	None

° First-year maintenance covered by manufacturer's warranty on purchase and lease.

TABLE 4-2 Rent—Cash Flow (In Thousands of dollars)

Year	Rent includ. maint.	Tax credit	Net cash flow	Discounted net cash flow @ 10%	Cumulative discounted net cash flow
0	$14.4	$4.1	−$ 3.1	−$ 3.1	−$ 3.1
1	28.8		− 14.4	− 13.0	− 16.1
2	28.8		− 14.4	− 11.9	− 28.0
3	28.8		− 14.4	− 10.9	− 38.9
4	28.8		− 14.4	− 9.8	− 48.7
5	28.8		− 14.4	− 8.9	− 57.6
6	28.8		− 14.4	− 8.1	− 65.7
7	28.8		− 14.4	− 7.4	− 73.1
8	14.4		− 7.1	− 3.4	− 76.5

TABLE 4-3 Lease—Cash Flow (In Thousands of dollars)

Year	Lease	Maint.	Misc. expense	Net cash flow	Discounted net cash flow	Cumulative discounted net cash flow
0	$ 9.6	—	$0.2	−$ 4.9	−$4.9	−$ 4.9
1	19.2	$1.2	0.4	− 10.4	− 9.5	− 14.4
2	19.2	2.4	0.4	− 11.0	− 9.1	− 23.5
3	19.2	2.4	0.4	− 11.0	− 8.3	− 31.8
4	19.2	2.4	0.4	− 11.0	− 7.5	− 39.3
5	19.2	2.4	0.4	− 11.0	− 6.8	− 46.1
6	19.2	2.4	0.4	− 11.0	− 6.2	− 52.3
7	19.2	2.4	0.4	− 11.0	− 5.6	− 57.9
8	9.6	1.2	0.2	− 5.5	− 2.6	− 60.5

TABLE 4-4   Purchase—Cash Flow (In thousands of dollars)

Year	Purchase payment	Maint.	Depr.	Misc. expense	Tax credit	Net cash flow	Discounted net cash flow @ 10%	Cumulative discount net cash flow
0	$88.0	$ —	$ 5.5	$0.2	$6.2	−$79.1	−$79.1	−$79.1
1		1.2	11.0	0.4		+ 4.7	+ 4.3	− 74.8
2		2.4	11.0	0.4		+ 4.1	+ 3.4	− 71.4
3		2.4	11.0	0.4		+ 4.1	+ 3.1	− 68.3
4		2.4	11.0	0.4		+ 4.1	+ 2.8	− 65.5
5		2.4	11.0	0.4		+ 4.1	+ 2.5	− 63.0
6		2.4	11.0	0.4		+ 4.1	+ 2.3	− 60.7
7		2.4	11.0	0.4		+ 4.1	+ 2.1	− 58.6
8		1.2	5.5	0.2		+ 2.1	+ 1.0	− 57.6

estimated lives. Rental shows the most attractive net cash flow for Year 0, since the effect of investment tax credit more than offsets the lower monthly charges of a lease. However, these cash flows are not meaningful if it is assumed that the equipment is to be removed after such a short period of time. The lease charges imply a longer commitment by the user, and return of the rented equipment would mean a cancellation of the investment tax credit. Beyond Year 0, lease produces a more attractive cash flow than rental.

The yearly cash flow from purchase in Table 4-4 assumes an ongoing use of the system, and does not provide for resale of the equipment if its use is ended with a remaining residual value. The purchased cash-flow present value breaks even with lease between the seventh and eighth year. In the seventh year, the cumulative discounted cash flow is −$57,900 for lease and −$58,600 for purchase. In Year 8, the cash flow for lease is −$60,500, and for purchase it is −$57,600. Put another way, the expected life for the equipment should be over 7 years if a purchase is to return 10 per cent on the investment relative to lease.

If it is assumed that the purchased equipment can be sold at a given point in time at book value, then improved cumulative discounted cash flows result. Table 4-5 summarizes the flows based on this assumption. The cumulative discounted cash from purchase breaks even with lease between the sixth and seventh year. In Year 6, the cash flow from lease is −$52,300 while that from purchase is −$52,600. In Year 7, the cash flow from lease is −$57,900 while from purchase it is −$55,800.

If an outright purchase is one of the alternatives being evaluated, then a capital investment is involved, and the return on investment should be a major criterion in the decision. The return-on-investment calculation compares two alternatives, i.e., the projected investment and either the status quo or another method of financing the investment without the use of capital funds.

The return on investment should be based upon present-value methods. Using this approach, the return on investments is defined as the discount rate which, when ap-

TABLE 4-5   Purchase—Cash Flow (In Thousands of dollars)

Year	Cumulative discounted net cash flow without salvage	Cash flow if sold at salvage-book value	Discounted cash flow in selling year	Cumulative discounted cash flow including salvage
0	−$79.1	−$ 2.8	−$ 2.8	−$ 2.8
1	− 74.8	+ 70.0	+ 63.6	− 15.5
2	− 71.4	+ 58.4	+ 48.2	− 26.6
3	− 68.3	+ 49.5	+ 37.4	− 34.0
4	− 65.5	+ 38.5	+ 26.3	− 42.0
5	− 63.0	+ 29.5	+ 18.3	− 47.2
6	− 60.7	+ 18.5	+ 10.4	− 52.6
7	− 58.6	+ 9.6	+ 4.9	− 55.8
8	− 57.6	+ 2.1	+ 1.0	− 57.6

plied to future net cash flows, makes the present value of future cash inflows equal to the investment.   The discount rate is determined by a reiteration of the discounting calculation at several different rates until the present value of the net cash flows is equal to zero.

Table 4-6 illustrates the development of the return on investment for the example with an estimated life of 6 years and a residual value equal to the book value at that time. Purchase is compared to lease, since lease is a more favorable alternative than rent, as indicated by the present-value calculations.   If a purchase is made, then the lease will not be executed, and the cash outflow from lease will be avoided.   Thus, the net-cash-flow effect of purchase as compared to lease is the algebraic difference of the purchase and lease cash flows.

If the resulting differential cash flow is discounted at 10 per cent, the total over 6 years is −$600, which indicates that the return on the investment is less than 10 per cent.   At a 9 per cent rate, the resulting total cash flow is +$2,100.   At 9.8 per cent, the total cash flow is zero, and this is the return on investment over 6 years.

The present-value and return-on-investment calculations did not take into account

TABLE 4-6   Return on Investment (In Thousands of dollars)

Year	Purchase net cash flow	Lease net cash flow	Difference net cash flow	Discounted cash flow @ 10%	Discounted cash flow @ 9%	Discounted cash flow @ 9.8%
0	−$79.1	−$ 4.9	−$74.2	−$74.2	−$74.2	−$74.2
1	+ 4.7	− 10.4	+ 15.1	+ 13.7	+ 13.8	+ 13.6
2	+ 4.1	− 11.0	+ 15.1	+ 12.5	+ 12.7	+ 12.5
3	+ 4.1	− 11.0	+ 15.1	+ 11.4	+ 11.7	+ 11.4
4	+ 4.1	− 11.0	+ 15.1	+ 10.3	+ 10.7	+ 10.4
5	+ 4.1	− 11.0	+ 15.1	+ 9.3	+ 9.8	+ 9.5
6	+ 18.5	− 11.0	+ 29.5	+ 16.6	+ 17.6	+ 16.8
Total				− 0.6	+ 2.1	0.0

interest or cost of money for the funds invested in the purchase.   An investment should logically be charged with the cost of such funds, and this cost cannot be ignored in evaluating the return.   However, if the cost of money is eliminated from the ROI calculation, then multiple ROIs may be compared directly and alternative uses of funds evaluated.   The cost of money, as well as available investment opportunities, is used in establishing the required ROI standards for investments and in this way affects the decision-making process.   Allowance should also be made for costs of funds when determining net profitability of investments.

CONCLUSION

While the parameters of the example are typical, many significant variations can exist in the purchase, rental, and maintenance relationships, depreciation methods, tax rates, and differential costs.   Each item of equipment in a system should be individually evaluated if different relationships among these parameters exist.

Often, the most difficult task in comparing alternatives is the estimation of the expected life of the equipment and the residual value.   These estimations are dependent upon future hardware and software changes resulting from technological developments and marketing strategies of suppliers.   Expected improvements should be related to the planned usage to determine when new equipment might be desirable or necessary.

If considerable uncertainty exists in the estimates of critical items, then several calculations are appropriate, covering a range of estimates so that comparative risks may be analyzed.   A matrix showing present values and ROIs under differing assumptions can be a valuable tool in focusing on sound financial decisions.

The increased attention given by users to the financial aspects of the procurement process is further evidence of the maturing of the data processing industry.   The cost savings made possible through purchase or long-term rental or lease can be significant. However, the planning required to use these tools effectively is difficult because of the many uncertainties in future hardware, software, and applications development.   The professional manager must examine these issues objectively with long-run price-performance as a primary goal. The lease, rental, or purchase decision is an appropriate focus for data processing management today.

SELECTIVE BIBLIOGRAPHY

Burke, A. J., "Third Party Leasing from a User's Viewpoint," *Datamation*, November, 1969.
Griesinger, Frank J., "Leasing of Industrial Equipment," in Carl Heyel (ed.), *The Encyclopedia of Management*, 2d ed., Van Nostrand Reinhold, New York, 1973.
Gushee, C. H. (ed.), *Financial Compound Interest and Annuity Tables,* Financial Publishing Company, Boston, 1966.
Vancel, J. R., "Leasing of Industrial Equipment," McGraw-Hill, New York, 1963.

Chapter 5

Legal Aspects of Computer Contracts

DAVID H. GREENBERG

Attorney at Law,
Beverly Hills, California

The field of automatic data processing presents a high degree of exposure to risk because (1) contractual arrangements are often authorized by members of management who are not sufficiently conversant with the technical aspects of the subject to be aware of the full implications of commitments they are making; and (2) technically oriented personnel often subject their companies to unexpected liability because, while they are knowledgeable of the subject, they are unaware of the full legal implications of commitments they enter into.

UNDERSTANDING TERMS

For a contract to be enforceable, the parties must have agreed to the same thing. This is referred to in law as *mutuality of understanding*. Therefore, words used in a contract must have the same meaning to both parties. The courts use the following methods to determine mutuality of understanding:

1. Words used ordinarily in the everyday world are interpreted by the courts to have their usual and customary meaning.

2. Words used as words of art, that is, words applicable to a certain industry, are interpreted by the courts to have their usual and customary meaning within that particular industry.

3. Words used with special meanings should be defined within the contract itself.

The biggest problem area is No. 2, words of art. Many of the words used as words of art in the ADP field have not had universally accepted definitions. A few examples will quickly illustrate this point:

Downtime. Are we talking about clock time or meter time, or are we talking about time the system is not being used or cannot be used?

Software. Are we talking about all programs, or the operating system?

Senior programmer. Are we talking about a person with a Ph.D. or a person with 10 years of experience? There are no formal qualifications for any job titles in ADP. Unlike law, public accounting, architecture, etc., anyone can call him or herself a programmer, and any programmer can call him or herself a senior programmer.

Hardware. Again, are the operating system programs an integral part of the hardware? What about microprogramming—is it hardware or software?

If people in the industry do not agree on the definitions of their terms, how can the courts find the necessary mutuality of understanding?

Defining Terms While there is no recognized "official" glossary of ADP terms, there are a number of published sources—e.g., the Department of the Navy's *ADP Glossary* (S/N 0840–0051) available from the U.S. Government Printing Office, and the American National Standard *Vocabulary for Information Processing* (X3.12–1970). When applicable, a contract should indicate that words used in the agreement are defined as indicated in a given authoritative source, and should be used accordingly. If this is not feasible, the words of art should be defined in the contract itself.

Another problem in understanding and defining terms is understanding the general definition without describing the specifics. An example would be a payroll program. We all know what it means. However, how much core does a particular program require? Does it handle state withholding tax if applicable, is it easily modifiable, what language is it written in—ad infinitum.

An example of failing to reach a mutual understanding would be in asking a supplier if your old programs will run on the new central processing unit the supplier is trying to sell, and the answer is yes. Does the supplier mean in emulation, or at the new speed and with taking advantage of the maximum capability of the new CPU?

When you ask the programmer how long it will take to write the program, do you mean just write it, or write it, test, debug, and complete the documentation?

Make sure that you and the supplier understand the same thing when you are negotiating. Do not assume the supplier knows what you mean.

Effective Negotiations Developing mutuality of understanding comes about through effective negotiations. Most companies allow their data processing personnel to determine their own needs and to negotiate for and order the products or services to fill those needs. If your company does not provide competent legal assistance in drafting and negotiating a technical contract, the following are a few basics to remember:

Makes notes and keep them regarding each contact you have with the supplier. After each meeting you have with a supplier where you come to some form of oral understanding, immediately reduce it to writing in the form of a letter confirming the understanding. If you are not an expert in the technical area you are discussing and you rely on the supplier's expertise, let the supplier know it in writing. If you are not sure you have all the answers, do some comparison shopping. Suppliers will not let you know of their shortcomings, but their competitors will. Remember, the salesperson is not there to do your job for you, but to sell his or her product or service regardless of whether or not there may be a better product or service on the market to fill your needs, or whether there would be a better way of accomplishing the same thing.

Consider the price of the product or service you are negotiating for. Chances are you will be spending more money on behalf of your company than you have ever spent in your life at one time. If you know what you want, but have difficulty expressing it in writing, ask your company for legal or other appropriate professional assistance. Again, do your homework before you meet with the supplier. Do not rely on the supplier for your education; it may be an expensive lesson. If you do not know all the answers, know all the questions. If you do not know all the questions, do not buy until you do.

THE CONTRACT

Chances are you will be required to sign a contract with the supplier. More than likely this contract will be a preprinted form prepared by the supplier and therefore favor the supplier in its terms. The first thing to remember is that a preprinted form is not the "Holy Graille." It can be amended, deleted, changed, and replaced. If the supplier is in a position of absolute dominance and you must sign the supplier's contract as presented, it may not be enforceable as a contract of adhesion.

In signing the supplier's contract, beware of waiving your legal rights. These would include your right to sue for loss of profits and consequential damages. Also, you may be giving up your legal protections, such as warranty of merchantability and fitness for a particular use. Are you agreeing to the supplier's right to injunctive relief, where the supplier might not otherwise be entitled to this special remedy? Remember that you are buying a complex and expensive product. Do not try to simplify the contract or discount its potential importance in order to save a few dollars.

A usual type of waiver taken from a standard contract reads as follows: "It is expressly understood and agreed that the liability, if any, of Supplier for errors and omissions shall be limited to the total charge for services as provided herein. Supplier shall not be liable for any special, consequential or exemplary damages."

Negotiated Contracts Most people are accustomed to buying on an "as is" basis. When we buy a car, we do not have the dealer or manufacturer custom-design the product to our particular need. However, in the purchase or lease of ADP products or services, there must many times be negotiated terms and conditions in order to have the product or service fit your particular needs. When your company is negotiating for a custom-usage product or service, a trained negotiator should work hand in hand with the data processing people. Be sure that the terms that you have negotiated orally are put in the contract.

Following is an example of not getting in writing what you think you have been promised:

You want to lease some hardware for 5 years. The salesperson shows you that the cost of this hardware for 5 years plus the projected cost of maintenance for 5 years is less than that of a competitor. The figures check out, so you take this lease and maintenance agreement instead of a competitor's. The lease is for 5 years, but the maintenance agreement is for 1 year. After the 1 year, the maintenance price can be increased, so that the total 5-year cost of lease and maintenance exceeds that of the other product you were considering.

It would now be too late to get out of the lease. The salesperson had projected the cost of the maintenance for 5 years, with no guarantee that the figure would in fact remain constant, and you have no escape clause when the maintenance fee is raised. This is only one example of how unsuspecting ADP people who are not trained in negotiating can be "taken."

The following is a true case that turned into a law suit:

The client, to whom we here refer as "User," is a company in the trucking business. The User went from a manual system to an automatic bookkeeping machine, and now felt it was ready for a computer. The treasurer started to read about computers, and believed a tape system would best suit his company's purpose. He called in a consultant to help advise him.

The major suppliers were contacted, and salespeople came out to see the User. Each supplier indicated some expertise in the User's business. Each supplier laid out a preliminary outline on the type of equipment it would recommend.

One supplier professed a special expertise in the User's business, and indicated that even though it would recommend a tape system which could be installed almost immediately, it would program for a transition to disk and that its small disk system would be ready in 6 months. The supplier further claimed an ability to write the applications programs, test, and debug, and stated that it would have a fully operational installation within 3 months.

A contract was signed (the supplier's preprinted form), and the User started to build a computer room. As the 3-month installation deadline approached, the supplier advised that the application programs would not be ready. No programming schedule had been prepared prior to the programming effort. The User had already built its installation, and had sent its key employees to school to prepare for the arrival of the system.

From this point forward things went from bad to worse. When the supplier indicated to the User that the programs would be written in one more week, the User thought that this meant "ready to use," not "ready to test," and therefore prepared for the changeover in processing.

The User's paperwork costs started to skyrocket because of the testing. The User had not realized that one can go through a carton of paper to get to the end of the program before realizing that there has been an error.

The preliminary preparation for the programs had been poor, and now the programs did not do everything that the User wanted. There was a high turnover of programmers, and as a result the programs were poorly documented, and not easily modified.

After the tape system was installed, the User made a cost study, and realized that its per-unit cost of processing had increased. Many of the things promised orally by the supplier had not come to pass. The tape system was makeshift, but the supplier's promises regarding the new disk system were more fancy than fact. The supplier had software problems with the disk system, and could not deliver as promised.

The User was not a large company with many levels of top executives. The time and expense of computerization thus cost the company dearly in misdirected executive time.

The problems of putting the tape system on line without dual processing caused numerous mistakes in billing and deliveries, and this led to lost customers.

Disputes arose as to whether the substantial downtime that occurred was the fault of the supplier's software and programs or the User's newly trained personnel.

The supplier never installed the disk system. The User finally had the tape system removed and went back to its more reliable and less expensive manual system.

The User received a bill from the supplier. This infuriated the User to the point of calling its attorney (for the first time). The attorney saw the problem, but was unable to decipher the facts, being unfamiliar with ADP terminology, custom, and usage. The attorney called in another attorney who was better prepared to litigate an ADP case. The User ultimately recovered in excess of $200,000 from the supplier, after four years of litigation.

Moral: During negotiation, try to be aware of the contractual pitfalls.

Contractual Pitfalls   Almost every Chapter of this Handbook calls for a different product or service, each with its own pecularities regarding the nature of the contract to be used.

Obviously, you cannot use the same contract to purchase time-sharing services as you would to hire a service bureau or to lease a CPU. Therefore, a cure-all contract cannot be drafted to serve all your needs and to protect you from all the potential pitfalls in all areas of ADP.

It is impossible to list all the potential pitfalls you may encounter in negotiating and drafting a contract. Listed below are samples of potential problem areas.

1. Waiving your right to punitive damages.
2. Waiving your right to ordinary damages.
3. Obligating your company to add on services.
4. Failure to provide for maintenance.
5. Failure to define or clarify terms.
6. Purchasing incompatible products or services.
7. Purchasing unmodifiable programs or services.
8. Obligating your company for products or services beyond a useful time period.
9. Failure to provide for a change of circumstances.
10. Failure to provide for specific supplier performances, rather than a "best efforts" basis.
11. Failure to provide for supplier penalties for nonperformance.
12. Failure to provide for suspension of payments upon an interruption of service.
13. Failure to provide for payments to commence on the system or program being fully operational rather than on installation.
14. Failure to provide for the supplier's warranty of title.
15. Failure to investigate the supplier's financial strength to ensure continued service.
16. Failure to provide for rights to product mix regarding CPU, peripherals, software.
17. Finding that prices can be raised after the system is installed.
18. Failure to understand and provide for personal property tax consequences.
19. Failure to clarify when title vests in the purchaser.
20. Allowing the seller to repossess without notice and without judgment.
21. Coordinating date of delivery of hardware to programming schedule, facility construction, and changeover.
22. Failure clearly to define and coordinate requirements and responsibility of installation.
23. Failure clearly to define responsiblity for training user-personnel.

24. Failure to protect against your legal liabilities. In this regard, insurance becomes an important factor.

PROTECTION

Insurance Coverage Your company may be large enough to have its own insurance department. If so, you may very well say to yourself, "It is nice to have the above list, but our insurance department handles that." Do not assume that even in a large company an insurance specialist is an ADP specialist also. You should have your insurance specialist, whether in-house counsel or an outside consultant, meet with your data processing manager, security manager, administrative manager, and your attorney. Together they can uncover the potential risks involved and determine if these risks are insurable and whether you have in fact insured against these risks. Following are some of the potential liabilities involved:

1. Confidential information. If you are a service bureau, or if you handle or come in contact with someone's confidential data, you can be liable for the theft, destruction, or unauthorized dissemination of the information.

2. Fire. Whether you lease or purchase equipment, that equipment can be worth millions of dollars, and your present fire insurance may not be adequate.

3. Business interruption. After having your records reduced to tape or disk, and that tape or disk is destroyed, how would that affect the operation of your business?

4. Theft. You may have leased a program for which you are responsible, and that program can be stolen. In addition, records and equipment should be protected.

5. Patent or copyright infringement. You may purchase or lease equipment and software only to find out that another party has claimed a patent or copyright interest in that equipment and software, and you can be joined as a defendant with your supplier.

Generally, does your insurance coincide with your contractual liability? As an example, your insurance may cover only property you own, rather than property under your control. You may have agreed by contract to be responsible for all damage to leased or rented hardware or software. What happens if the property is destroyed by an act of God, or by radiation or vandalism, which are not covered by your insurance?

One of the numerous areas in which the ADP department can expose its company to substantial risks is that of leased equipment and software. Even if your lease agreement indicates that the lessor will carry insurance on the leased equipment, this does not relieve your company from damage to the equipment caused by your company's negligence. You could find yourself being sued by the lessor's insurance company under their subrogation rights. Also, you may have signed a contract to be responsible for leased equipment or software without notifying your insurance company.

Clearly, a thorough review of your insurance coverage periodically is a must.

Employee Agreements One of your best protections against theft is a pre-employment agreement with your ADP personnel. Companies that are already involved in a high-technology product or service usually have their employees sign a pre-employment agreement. If your company is not in that category, or your company does not require a pre-employment agreement, you should consider such an agreement for your ADP personnel.

Trade Secrets and Confidential Data. The very nature of your ADP installation implies an intent to put all your data into a computer system, and then to allow the system users to extract data in numerous forms. This allows ADP personnel access to every piece of confidential data a company possesses, and further allows them to copy these data in seconds and at will. Having the employee sign an agreement that he or she will not divulge or disseminate this information will not stop the hardened thief, but it will give the impulsive potential thief second thoughts. It may also be wise to see if your ADP personnel are bondable.

Ownership of Developed Software or Programs. ADP personnel should also sign an agreement clarifying ownership of software developed by the employee while in the company's employ. A programmer employed by the company may develop an idea for software to make your installation more efficient. He mentions the idea to you, and you tell him to develop the program using the company installation, but not to let it interfere with the performance of his other work. The program turns out to be a highly marketable product, so the employee leaves with the software before it is fully documented. Does the company have the right to ownership or to receive any of the proceeds from the sale thereof?

Another point to cover is modifying existing company-owned programs. Most programs can be rewritten and accomplish similar results. At what point has a modified proprietary program become a new program? If an employee modifies your program, has he or she changed the ownership? The best answer is to clarify in writing the employee's rights and duties.

Patentability of Software Now that the Supreme Court has held that software cannot be protected under the patent laws, is there any way legally to protect proprietary software? Your only practical recourse is to protect yourself by contract. You can have each outsider who comes in contact with your proprietary software sign an agreement providing you with the same or greater protection you would have been entitled to under patent or copyright law.

UNBUNDLING AND ITS LEGAL CONSEQUENCES

Bundling In the early days of the computer industry, a user purchased all hardware, software, and maintenance from one supplier under one agreement, and was billed one price. If something went wrong, there was one company to go back to, one company to blame. This practice of one price for a *package* of hardware and software and specified services came to be known as *bundling*.

Unbundling Many suppliers and some users objected to bundling. This objection was primarily directed at IBM, the company that had a major portion of the ADP hardware market. With bundling, IBM also had a major share of the software, peripheral, and maintenance market. Through court actions and competitive pressures, other suppliers in the early 1970s brought about a move on the part of computer manufacturers toward *unbundling*, and thus improved the smaller supplier's chances of selling software, peripherals, and maintenance.

With the advent of unbundling, a greater sophistication on the part of the user in contracting and negotiating is required. Today you find yourself dealing with many different suppliers, and this obviously complicates the task of pinpointing responsibility when something goes wrong. Thus you may purchase equipment and peripherals from several manufacturers, maintenance from another source, and communications services from still another. In contracting with these various suppliers, you should read each contract carefully to avoid overlapping services and conflicting responsibilities.

If you find yourself in a position of having to buy one product or one service in order to obtain another product or service from the same company, you should discuss the situation with your attorney. The practice could be illegal and subject the offender to substantial damages under certain circumstances.

Some of the areas of future legal changes in the ADP industry might be as follows:

GOVERNMENT REGULATIONS

There are myriads of Government regulations that may affect a company because of its ADP involvement. Again, you should check with your attorney to see which rules apply to you specifically and to the contract you sign. Some of the more common regulating agencies you might come in contact with are the Federal Trade Commission, Federal Communications Commission, National Labor Relations Board, and the Securities and Exchange Commission.

Government regulations, if applicable, may very well affect the legality of your agreements, and may subject your company to civil or criminal sanctions.

RECOMMENDATIONS FOR NEW DEVELOPMENTS

Arbitration Board An arbitration board should be established to arbitrate disputes and set standards within the ADP industry. Computer-related contracts are highly complex, both technically and legally. Each such contract should contain a clause requiring submission of disputes to mandatory arbitration rather than resorting to the courts.

The board would be made up of members who have training and experience in both ADP and the law. The board would be established broadly upon the format of the American Arbitration Association. This would allow judgments to be rendered by people who can grasp the technical concepts involved, and therefore more justly decide each case on its merits. Also, each case would be adjudicated more quickly, thereby avoiding the 2- to 4-year wait to go to trial as is now required in many state courts. The cost of justice, which in a more complex case can be astronomical, would be greatly reduced, thereby diminishing the larger company's financial ability to defeat the smaller company before the case can be tried on its merits.

The idea of mandatory arbitration within an industry is now new. Within the entertainment industry, the standard guild contracts call for arbitration of disputes between contracting parties. In the insurance industry, it is common to see uninsured motorist provisions of automobile policies include mandatory arbitration of disputes.

Standards and Practices Committee As an adjunct to the arbitration board, there should be a committee to set standards and practices within the industry. This committee would have the task of defining job titles and requirements for job categories. There would then be some meaning in the terms *Junior Programmer* or *Senior Programmer* or *Senior COBOL Programmer*. Standards would be set for proprietary software packages, so that if the supplier's package has had the board's approval, the buyer would know that there is proper documentation behind the software and the program would be fully tested before marketing.

Industry-Wide Software Development The cost of software and programming now exceeds the cost of hardware in the average installation. This trend will continue.

To a great degree, the reason for this tremendous cost is duplication of programming effort within an industry. Within each major user-industry, a nonprofit software and programming group should be established. Joint programming efforts should be discussed and determined. Programs should then be written that would fit the needs and hardware of the majority of the users. The programming effort should be funded as a joint effort.

Again, this joint industry-wide effort is not unknown in other areas. The insurance industry has established a similar effort regarding insurance claims.

GENERAL CONSIDERATIONS

The following are a few helpful suggestions to avoid a lawsuit.

1. Do not stop processing work under your old system until your ADP installation is on line and fully operational. It is cheaper in the long run and good insurance to duplicate process for awhile.

2. Understand the differences between fixed-price, time-and-material, and cost-plus contracts. If you have been given an estimate on a time-and-material contract, put a cost ceiling on the contract.

3. Understand the total cost of ADP. Prepare a budget and list all items of cost, such as hardware, software, programming, paper costs, retraining personnel, tapes, disks, racks, consulting fees, installation, facility construction, security, maintenance, etc.

4. Take advantage of your in-house counsel. If your company does not have in-house counsel, it may have an attorney on retainer with whom you may consult.

Tell your attorney what you plan to do *before* you do it. Ask the attorney what the legal consequences will be. Advise the attorney of the known pitfalls and give him or her your checklist of potential problem areas. If your attorney deems it necessary to consult with a specialist before giving an opinion, allow him or her to do so and consider yourself fortunate to have wise counsel. Attorneys, like management, cannot be expected to know all the answers. It is the intelligent person who knows when to seek expert advice.

5. Finally, if you think your company has been wronged, discuss the situation with the company's attorney. Most attorneys will try to settle a dispute without litigation. As a last resort, your attorney may recommend litigation.

If you feel you have been wronged and your attorney does not recommend litigation as a last resort, consider asking another attorney for advice. Some attorneys who are unfamiliar with this industry might be afraid to handle a lawsuit involving complex, technical matters.

If you think your company could not afford legal action based on an hourly fee, ask your attorney if he or she will take your case on a contingency basis. Do not think that because your adversary is a giant company, you have no rights. Finding an attorney who will represent you against a giant company on a contingency basis can be a big equalizer.

Part Five

Case Examples

Introduction

What follows is a small sample of specific case examples of successful computer system implementations. Specific examples of this type are useful for conveying an insight into the practical possibilities — and very real practical problems — of application-oriented computer systems. However, the reader should keep in mind the inherent limitation of the case study approach: no two applications, situations, or sets of needs are ever exactly alike. Like the lessons of history in general, case studies should be applied with due recognition of changed circumstance.

Chapter 1

Case Example:

Triangle Universities Computation Center — Shared Computing for Higher Education in North Carolina

LELAND H. WILLIAMS

President and Director, Triangle Universities Computation Center, Research Triangle Park, North Carolina; Adjunct Associate Professor of Computer Science, Duke University, University of North Carolina at Chapel Hill, and North Carolina State University at Raleigh

Successful extensively shared computing is demonstrated by the Triangle Universities Computation Center (TUCC) and its participating educational institutions in North Carolina. Included in the network at this writing are three major universities and many other institutions. This Chapter gives some insight into the economic, technological, and political factors involved in the success, as well as some measures of the size of the operation. Also addressed is the organizational structure, which is interpreted in terms of a "wholesale-retail" analogy. The importance of this structure and the division by means of software of the central machine into essentially separate submachines for each retailer is emphasized.

Adopting terminology from Peterson and Veit,[1] TUCC is essentially a centralized, homogeneous network comprising a central service node (IBM 370/165), three primary job source nodes (IBM 360/75, IBM 370/135, IBM 370/135), 36 secondary job source nodes (leased-line Data 100, Cope 1200, IBM 1130, IBM 2780, IBM 3780, Nova 1220, IBM System 7, and leased- and dial-line IBM 2770), and about 375 tertiary job source nodes (136 dial or leased lines for Teletype 33 ASR, IBM 1050, IBM 2741, Cope 1035, NCR 260, Perry PE 8000, Hazleton 2000, Tektronics 4000, etc.). (See Figures 1-1 and 1-2.) All job source node computers in the network are homogeneous with the central

---

[1] Jack J. Peterson and Sandra A. Veit, "Survey of Computer Networks," *Mitre Corporation Report*, September, 1971.

service node, and although they provide local computational service in addition to teleprocessing service, none currently provides (nonlocal) network computational service.   However, the technology for providing network computational service at the primary source nodes is immediately available.   This is mentioned later in the Chapter under "Prospects for TUCC."

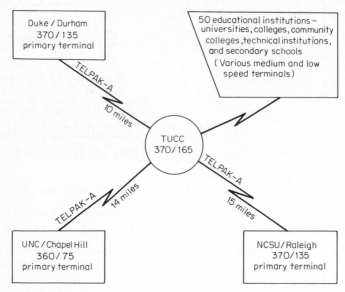

Note: In addition to the primary terminal installation at Duke Univ. at Durham, Univ. of North Carolina at Chapel Hill, and North Carolina State Univ. at Raleigh, each campus has an array of medium/and low-speed terminals directly connected to TUCC.

Fig. 1-1   The TUCC network.

BACKGROUND

The Triangle Universities Computation Center was established in 1965 as a nonprofit corporation by three major universities in North Carolina—Duke University at Durham, The University of North Carolina at Chapel Hill, and North Carolina State University at Raleigh.   Duke is a privately endowed institution; the other two are state supported. Among them are two medical schools, two engineering schools, 30,000 undergraduate students, 10,000 graduate students, and 3,300 teaching faculty members.

The primary motivation was economic—to give each of the institutions access to more computing power at a lower cost than they could provide individually.   Initial grants were received from the National Science Foundation and from the North Carolina Board of Science and Technology, in whose Research Triangle Park building TUCC is located.   This location represents an important decision, both because of its geographic and political neutrality with respect to all three campuses, and because of the value of the Research Triangle Park environment.   See Figure 1-3 for an impression of the pleasant environment.

The Research Triangle Park is one of the nation's most successful research parks. Located in a wooded tract of 5,400 acres in the small geographic triangle formed by the three universities, the Park has 11,000 employees, a payroll of $160 million, and an investment in buildings of $160 million plus $140 million committed.   The Park contains the research and development facilities of 48 separate national and international corporations, government agencies, and other institutions.

TUCC was a pioneer of extensively shared computing; hence there were many technological, political, and protocol problems to overcome.   Successive stages toward

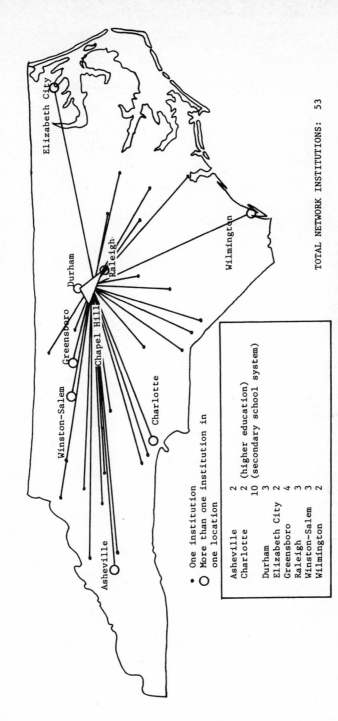

TOTAL NETWORK INSTITUTIONS: 53

- One institution
○ More than one institution in
  one location

Asheville	2	(higher education)
Charlotte	2	(higher education)
	10	(secondary school system)
Durham	3	
Elizabeth City	2	
Greensboro	4	
Raleigh	3	
Winston-Salem	3	
Wilmington	2	

Fig. 1-2 Network of institutions served by TUCC/NCECS.

Fig. 1-3   TUCC's pleasant setting.

solution of these problems have been reported by Brooks, Ferrell, and Gallie,[2] by Freeman and Pearson,[3] by Davis,[4] and by Williams.[5] This Chapter will focus on the present success.

PRESENT STATUS

TUCC supports educational and research computing requirements at the three universities, at 50 smaller institutions in the state, and also at several research laboratories, by means of multispeed communications and computer terminal facilities. In addition, TUCC supports the registrar and library computing requirements at Duke University and administrative computing at several of the smaller institutions.

TUCC operates a 4-megabyte, telecommunications-oriented IBM 370/165 using OS/360-MVT/HASP and supporting a wide variety of terminals (see Figure 1-4). For high-speed communications, there is a 360/75 at Chaptel Hill, a 370/135 at North Carolina State, and a 370/135 at Duke. The three campus computer centers are truly and completely autonomous. They view TUCC simply as a pipeline through which they get extensive additional computing power to service their users.

TUCC's version of the 370/165 has processed a peak of 8,620 jobs per day without saturation. In October, 1975, 181,500 jobs were run using 1,036 hours of computer time calculated by the formula given in the Appendix at the end of this Chapter. This total includes 91,200 batch jobs, 65,300 autobatch jobs (WATFIV, PL/C, WATBOL, etc.), and 25,000 interactive sessions. Of the 91,200 batch jobs, 58,100 were run at normal priority ($f_i(P) = 0$, cf. Appendix) and 73 per cent of these were processed with less than 30 minutes delay, 97 per cent with less than 4 hours delay. Of the 65,300 autobatch jobs, 64,500 were run at normal priority, and 97 per cent of these were processed with less than 30 minutes delay.

    [2] Fredrick P. Brooks, Jr., James K. Ferrell, and Thomas M. Gallie, "Organizational, Financial, and Political Aspects of a Three-University Computing Center," *Proceedings of the International Federation of Information Processing Societies Congress 68*, August, 1968.
    [2] David N. Freeman and Robert R. Pearson, "Efficiency vs. Responsiveness in a Multiple-Service Computer Facility," *Proceedings of the 1968 Association of Computing Machinery Conference and Exposition (ACM)*, August, 1968.
    [4] M. S. Davis, "Economics — Point of View of Designer and Operator," *Proceedings of "Interdisciplinary Conference on Multiple Access Computer Networks,"* sponsored by the University of Texas and the Mitre Corporation, April, 1970.
    [5] L. H. Williams, "A Functioning Computer Network for Higher Education in North Carolina," *AFIPS Conference Proceedings*, vol. 41, 1972, 1972 FJCC, pp. 899–904.

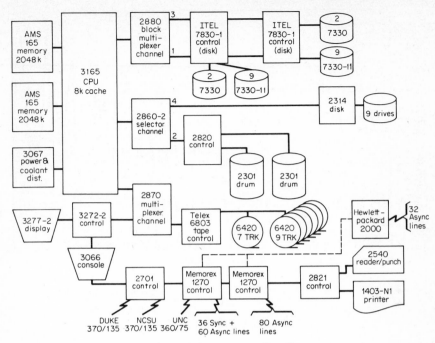

Fig. 1-4 TUCC hardware configuration.

At the present time, about 8,000 different individual users are being served directly. The graph of jobs processed per month as illustrated in Figure 1-5 is one indicator of growth in user needs.

Services to the TUCC user community include both remote job entry (RJE) and interactive processing. Included in the interactive services are programming systems employing the BASIC, PL/1, and APL languages as well as TSO. There is also a Hewlett-Packard 2000 for low-cost BASIC interactive computing. Available through RJE is a large array of compilers including FORTRAN IV, PL/I, COBOL, ALGOL, PL/C, WATFIV, and WATBOL. These language facilities, coupled with an extensive library of application programs, provide the TUCC user community with a dynamic information processing system supporting a wide variety of academic computing activities.

Advantages The financial advantage deserves further comment. As a part of the planning process leading to installation of the Model 165, one of the universities concluded that it would cost about $19,000 per month more in hardware and personnel costs to provide all computing services on campus than it would cost to continue participation in TUCC. This represented a 40 per cent increase over their expense for terminal machine, communications, and their share of TUCC expense.

There are other significant advantages. First, there is the sharing of a wide variety of application programs. Once a program is developed at one institution, it can be used anywhere in the network with no difficulty. For proprietary programs, usually only one fee need be paid. A sophisticated TUCC documentation system sustains this activity. Second, there has been a significant impact on the ability of the universities to attract faculty members who need large-scale computing for their research and teaching, and several TUCC staff members have adjunct appointments with the university computer science departments.

A third advantage has been the ability to provide very highly competent systems programmers for the center. In general, these personnel could not have been attracted to work in the environment of the individual institutions because of salary requirements and because of system sophistication considerations.

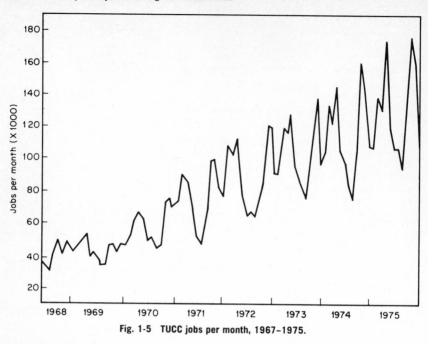

Fig. 1-5   TUCC jobs per month, 1967–1975.

Documentation   With the large community of users associated with the Triangle Universities Computation Center, it is essential that a formal system of communications be maintained to ensure that all necessary information is provided to all concerned.   A series of numbered documents is used to achieve this purpose.   All users and others associated with TUCC are urged to make use of this system.   The Information Services office at TUCC has overall responsibility for TUCC documentation, and maintains the numbering system.   Authors are drawn from the TUCC staff and the entire user community.   In some instances, Information Services initiates a document and seeks an author for it; it is also appropriate for an author to propose a document to Information Services.   Documentation updates are issued by TUCC in the form of addition, replacement, or insertion pages or in the form of a complete revision of the document.

There are basically two series of TUCC documents for users, the LS and GI series. Each of these series designations may be suffixed by the letter "R" (LSR or GIR), which indicates that one or more TUCC campuses may restrict distribution of the document according to some locally defined plan, generally because of document cost or the specialized nature of the information.   Procedures for acquiring "R" documents are announced separately by each campus to its users.   LS publications include documentation describing programs, subprograms, programming systems, and programming languages.   GI publications contain information to assist users in using the programming facilities described in LS publications.   Included are programming guidelines, announcements, terminal operation instructions, and software comparisons.

To ensure that LS/LSR and GI/GIR documents are maximally useful to all user communities, prepublication review of these documents includes a 14 day first-draft review opportunity for each Triangle campus/NCECS (North Carolina Educational Computing Service, described below).   This review and any other reviews deemed necessary are managed by TUCC Information Services, which has overall responsibility.   Periodically, TUCC issues various indexes to documentation and catalogues of documented programs.

Another memorandum series, IM (Installation Management), is used to facilitate documentation and communications between TUCC and the Triangle campus centers and NCECS.   The IM series is intended primarily to be of interest to, and for the use of, the Triangle campus centers and NCECS staffs. The content of this series includes scheduling priorities, partition and core allocations, accounting procedures and related policies, disk/tape handling procedures required by TUCC, services available, and other matters concerning TUCC management and operational policies which affect the campus computation centers and NCECS. A separate index for the IM series is prepared periodically.

NORTH CAROLINA EDUCATIONAL COMPUTING SERVICE

The University of North Carolina, which comprises 16 separate campuses, also maintains a Program Division known as the North Carolina Educational Computing Service (NCECS).[6] This is the successor organization to the North Carolina Computer Orientation Project,[7] which began in 1966. NCECS participates in TUCC and provides computer services to public and private educational institutions in North Carolina other than the three founding universities. Presently about 50 public and private universities, colleges, community colleges, and technical institutes plus one high school system are served in this way. NCECS is located with TUCC in the North Carolina Board of Science and Technology building in the Research Triangle Park. This, of course, facilitates communication between TUCC and NCECS, whose statewide users depend upon the TUCC telecommunication system.

NCECS serves as a statewide campus computation center for its users, providing technical assistance, information services, etc. In addition, grant support from the National Science Foundation has made possible a number of curriculum development activities. NCECS publishes a catalogue of available instructional materials, provides curriculum development services, offers workshops to promote effective computer use, and visits campuses, stimulating faculty to introduce computing into courses in a variety of disciplines. Many of these programs have stimulated interest in computing from institutions and departments where there was no interest at all. One major university chemistry department, for example, ordered its first terminal in order to use an NCECS infrared spectral information program in its courses.

The software for NCECS systems is derived from a number of sources in addition to sharing in the community-wide program development described above. Some software is developed by NCECS staff to meet specific and known needs, some is developed by individual institutions and contributed to the common cause, and some is found elsewhere and adapted to the system. NCECS is interested in sharing curriculum-oriented software in as broad a way as possible.

Serving smaller institutions in this way is both a proper service for TUCC to perform and is also to its own political advantage. The state-supported founding universities, University of North Carolina at Chapel Hill and North Carolina State University at Raleigh, can show the legislature how they are serving much broader educational goals with their computing dollars.

ORGANIZATION OF TUCC

TUCC is successful not only because of its technical capabilities, but also because of the careful attention given to administrative protection of the interests of the three founding universities and of the NCECS schools. The mechanism for this protection can, perhaps, best be seen in terms of the wholesaler-retailer concept.[8] TUCC is a wholesaler of computing service; this service consists essentially of computer cycles, an effective operating system, programming languages, some application packages, a documentation service, and management. The TUCC wholesale service specifically does *not* include typical user services—debugging, contract programming, etc. Nor

[6] L. T. Parker and J. R. Denk, "A Network Model for Delivering Computer Power and Curriculum Enhancement for Higher Education," *Sprint, EDUCOM Bulletin,* vol. 9, no. 1, 1974, pp. 24–30.

[7] Louis T. Parker, Jr., Thomas M. Gallie, Frederick P. Brooks, Jr., and James K. Ferrell, "Introducing Computing to Smaller Colleges and Universities—A Progress Report," *Communications of the Association of Computing Machinery (ACM),* June, 1969.

[8] David L. Grobstein and Ronald P. Uhlig, "A Wholesale Retail Concept for Computer Network Management," *American Federation of Information Processing Societies Conference Proceedings* (Fall Joint Computer Conference), December, 1972.

does it include user-level billing nor curriculum development. Rather, these services are provided for their constituents by the Campus Computation Centers and NCECS, which are the retailers for the TUCC network. (See Figure 1-6.)

The wholesaler-retailer concept can also be seen in the financial and service relationships. On an annual basis, the founding universities and TUCC negotiate to establish the TUCC machine configuration, each university's computing resource share, and the cost to each university. This negotiation, of course, includes adoption of an operating budget. Computing resource shares are stated as percentages of the total resource

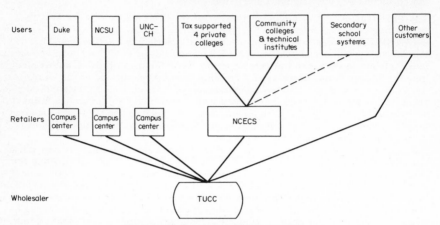

Fig. 1-6 **TUCC wholesaler-retailer structure.**

Fig. 1-7 **The scheduling algorithm and the organizational structure effectively partition the M-165 into four separate machines.**

used daily. These have always been equal for the three founding universities, but this is not necessary. Presently each founding university is allocated 25 per cent, the remaining 25 per cent being available for NCECS, TUCC systems development, and other users. This resource allocation is administered by a scheduling algorithm which ensures that each group of users has access to its daily share of TUCC's computing resources. (See Appendix at end of Chapter.) The algorithm provides an effective trade-off for each group between computing time and turnaround time; that is, at any given time the group with the least use that day will have job selection preference.

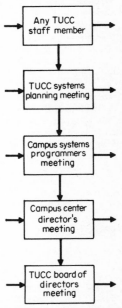

Fig. 1-8 TUCC decision flow chart.

The scheduling algorithm also allows each founding university and NCECS to define and administer quite flexible, independent priority schemes. Thus, the algorithm effectively defines independent submachines for the retailers, providing them with the same kind of assurance that they can take care of their users' needs as would be the case with totally independent facilities. This is illustrated graphically in Figure 1-7. In addition, the founding university retailers have a bonus because the algorithm defaults unused resources from other categories, including themselves, to one or more of them according to demand. This is particularly advantageous when their peak demands do not coincide. This flexibility of resource use is a major advantage which accrues to the retailers in a network like TUCC.

There are several organizational devices which serve to protect the interests of both the wholesaler and the retailers. (See Figure 1-8.) At the policy-making level, this protection is afforded by a board of directors appointed by the chancellors of the three founding universities. Typically each university allocates its representatives to include (1) its business interests, (2) its computer science instructional interests, and (3) its other computer user interests. The University Computation Center directors sit with the board whether or not they are members, as do the director of NCECS and the president of TUCC. A good example of the policy-level function of this board is its determination, based on TUCC management recommendations, of computing service rates for NCECS and other TUCC users.

At the operational level there are two important groups, both normally meeting each month. The Campus Computation Center directors' meeting includes the indicated people plus the director of NCECS and the president, the systems development manager, and the systems services manager of TUCC. The systems programmers meeting includes representatives of the three universities, NCECS, and TUCC. In addition, of course, each of the universities has the usual campus computing committees.

ADMINISTRATIVE DATA PROCESSING

TUCC has for some time been handling the full range of administrative data processing for three NCECS universities, and is beginning to do so for other NCECS schools. The primary reason that this application lags behind instructional applications in the NCECS schools is simply that grant support, which stimulated development of the instructional applications, has been absent for administrative applications. However, the success of the three pioneers has already begun to spread among the others.

The three larger universities have shown greater reluctance to shift their administrative data processing to TUCC, although Duke has already accomplished this for its student record and library processing. One problem which must be overcome to allow these universities to spend more administrative computing dollars on the more economic TUCC machine is the administrator's reluctance to give up a machine on which he can exercise direct priority pressure. This problem has been addressed for Duke by extending the submachine concept (job scheduling algorithm) described above, so that Duke University has both a research-instructional submachine and an administrative submachine. This extension is illustrated in Figure 7 by means of a dashed line separating the Duke submachine into an administrative submachine (A) and a research-instructional submachine (I&R).

PROSPECTS FOR TUCC

TUCC continues to provide cost-effective general computing service for its users. Some improvements which can be foreseen include:

1. An increased service both for instructional and administrative computing for the other institutions of higher education in North Carolina.

2. Support of more administrative data processing requirements.

3. Development of the network into a multiple-service node network by means of the symmetric HASP-to-HASP software developed at TUCC.[9]

4. Development of the HP 2000 to enable it to serve either at TUCC or at a remote site, not only as a BASIC language computer, but also as a 370/165 interface providing a HASP multileaving work station and HP 2000–IBM/370 file transfer, and access to 370 interactive services for low-speed terminals, thus minimizing communications costs and allowing low-cost program editorial work on the HP 2000 to be efficiently followed by cost-effective 370/165 computing which can be monitored via an HP 2000 terminal using TSO.

5. Additional use of line multiplexors to reduce communication costs.

6. Complementation of the (paper) documentation system with a computerized information retrieval system.

7. Participation in a resource-sharing large-scale distributed network.

SUMMARY

Successful extensively shared computing has been demonstrated by the Triangle Universities Computation Center and its participating educational institutions in North Carolina. Some insight has been given into the economic, technological, and political factors involved in the success, as well as some measures of the size of the operation. The TUCC organizational structure has been interpreted in terms of a wholesale-retail analogy. The importance of this structure and the division of the central machine by software into essentially separate submachines for each retailer cannot be overemphasized.

APPENDIX

TUCC Job Scheduling Algorithm

The TUCC job scheduling algorithm operates under two basic assumptions:

1. TUCC must distribute its resources equitably among its major users.

2. The major users will determine for themselves, within certain limits, the order in which their jobs will be run.

The selection formula is

$$S = f_i(P) - T - g_i(E,P,P_{min},P_{max}) - L_i \circ U_i$$

where the dimension of S is minutes. The job with the highest value of S is selected, unless one of several special conditions prevails. Generally, these conditions are designed to enhance throughput.

[9] James F. Walker and William F. Decker, "TUCC/Iowa Remote HASP-to-HASP System," *Triangle Universities Computation Center Report*, December, 1971.

$f_i(P)$ is an installation-dependent function of job card priority. A value may be specified for each acceptable job card priority. This value represents the number of minutes bonus to be awarded.

T is the age term and is the number of minutes from midnight January 1 to job submission. Since the T term is subtracted, the later a job is submitted, the lower its S value will be.

The $g_i(E,P,P_{min}P_{max})$ term is an installation-dependent function of estimated time, priority, minimum priority, and maximum priority. Each installation may specify P_{min} and P_{max} at and between which g_i will be nonzero. For priorities within the specified range, g_i is a piecewise linear function with slope changes at 5 minutes, 10 minutes, and 20 minutes. The function can be expressed:

$$g_i(E,P,P_{min},P_{max}) = 0, \text{ for } P < P_{min}$$
$$= 0, \text{ for } P > P_{max}$$

For $P_{min} \leq P, \leq P_{max}$, the function is

$$g_i(E,P,P_{min},P_{max}) = M_{1i}E, \text{ for } 0 < E \leq 5$$
$$= 5M_{1i} + M_{2i}(E - 5), \text{ for } 5 < E \leq 10$$
$$= 5M_{1i} + 5M_{2i} + M_{3i}(E - 10), \text{ for } 10 < E \leq 20$$
$$= 5M_{1i} + 5M_{2i} + 10M_{3i} + M_{4i}(E - 20), \text{ for } 20 < E$$

L_i is a multiplier which ensures the ith installation's access to its authorized share of TUCC facilities. These parameters are in proportion to the authorized shares and are sufficiently large to effectively isolate each user group from the others. Therefore, the values of the installation-dependent parameters of one installation have no effect on the selection of any other installation's jobs.

U_i is the cumulative computer use of the ith installation; it is reset to zero each morning when production time begins (approximately 0900).

For each installation, U_i is calculated by the following formula:

$$U_i = (\Sigma U_{ij})/60$$

where U_{ij} is the computer use, in seconds, of the jth job from the ith installation, and it is given by

$$U_{ij} = \Sigma \text{ CPU time} + \Sigma \text{ EXCP time}$$
$$+ 0.00085 \Sigma \text{ memory time}$$
$$+ 0.0083 \Sigma \text{ interactive connect time}$$
$$+ 0.67 \Sigma \text{ I/O wait time}$$
$$+ \text{ interactive memory add-on}$$

where Σ EXCP time $= 0.0076$ UREXCP $+ 0.011$ DEXCP $+ 0.019$ TEXCP and interactive memory add-on $= M(\Sigma \text{ CPU} + \Sigma \text{ EXCP} + \Sigma \text{ I/O wait})$, where $M = 1.57$ for APL and 0.215 for TSO.

Memory time is measured in kilobyte-seconds, I/O wait time is TSO swap time induced by terminal input-output, UREXCP means channel program execution for a unit record, TEXCP means channel program execution for a tape record, DEXCP means channel program execution for a disk record, and TSO means time-sharing option.

Examples Assume the following installation values in the priority-selection formula:

PRIORITY, P	$f_i(P)$	
0	−1,440 (one day in minutes)	$M_{1i} = 30$
1	0	$M_{2i} = 20$
2	300	$M_{3i} = 10$
3	1,740	$M_{4i} = 0$
4	1,920	$P_{min} = 0$
		$P_{max} = 2$

and assume that all example jobs come from the same installation.

Example 1:

JOB A	TIME = 1	PRTY = 0
JOB B	TIME = 2	PRTY = 1

If JOB B is submitted 23 hours and 31 minutes after JOB A and JOB A has not already been run, then JOB A will run before JOB B. The value of g_i is 30 (1 minute times factor of 30) for JOB A and 60 (2 minutes times 30) for JOB B. JOB B has a 24-hour bonus over JOB A because of the priority difference. TUCC normally catches up overnight, so a difference of 1,440 between priorities would usually ensure that a higher-priority job would run before a lower-priority job, but as can be seen from the above example, there could be exceptions.

Example 2:

$$\text{JOB C} \quad \text{TIME} = 11 \quad \text{PRTY} = 1$$
$$\text{JOB D} \quad \text{TIME} = 7 \quad \text{PRTY} = 1$$

The value of g_i for JOB C is 260 $[(5 \times 30) + (5 \times 20) + (1 \times 10)]$ and for JOB D it is 190 $[(5 \times 30) + (2 \times 20)]$. The difference is 70, or 70 minutes. Therefore if JOB C is submitted 71 minutes or more prior to the submission of JOB D it will be selected in preference to JOB D.

Example 3:

$$\text{JOB E} \quad \text{PRTY} = 4$$
$$\text{JOB F} \quad \text{PRTY} = 3$$

The value of g_i is zero for both jobs in this example because the priorities of both jobs are outside the range specified. JOB E would be given a 3-hour bonus over JOB F $(1,920 - 1,740)$. If JOB F were submitted 3 hours and 1 minute before JOB E and had not run within that period, it would be selected before JOB E. Unless great numbers of PRTY 3 jobs are being submitted, however, no PRTY 3 job should stay in the system for 3 hours and the situation would not normally occur.

Chapter 2

Case Example: A Strategic Management System[1]

JAMES J. McSWEENY

President, Collieries Management Corporation, Philadelphia,
Pennsylvania; formerly Vice President, Strategic
Development, IU International Corporation, Philadelphia,
Pennsylvania

Systems are feasible today that can meet the demanding requirements of business management by permitting managers and their staff personnel to interface and interact directly with the systems. Managers can thus bring subjective information acquired through experience together with more rigorously determined information.

The system described here was developed by International Utilities (IU) for making many of the company's strategic decisions. It contains no new management-science tools. Familiar models, algorithms, theories, and programs have been applied in what is sometimes a new application or form. The original aspects are the system engineering and the organization of management roles and methods that provide a variety of powerful tools for decision making.

IU was founded in 1924 and grew in its first 35 years around a nucleus of electric, gas, and water utilities. In the last decade and a half, a series of selective acquisitions and internal growth combined to shape it into a diversified operating company. Today IU is a billion-dollar company providing products and services to worldwide energy, transportation, distribution, and environmental markets.

Although many business management systems, models, and management-science tools have been applied to business firms, most of them have been tactical or functional. The strategic management system described here has a different scope. It has been designed to be interactive with management people performing the nonroutine functions of general or corporate management through the broad use of computer graphic interfaces.

---

[1] This chapter follows the treatment by the author in a paper originally presented before the Society for Management Information Systems. The basic paper appeared in the *Proceedings of the Fourth Annual SMIS Conference*, 1973, pp. 87–111.

THE NATURE OF STRATEGIC MANAGEMENT

Strategic management processes are comprehensive networks of data, information flow, estimation, evaluation, and decision making that continuously provide for optimization of total operation by directing action in a highly dynamic state. Figure 2-1 illustrates the general system flow in such a business economy. The four significant hallmarks of this microeconomy are:

1. *It is multivariate.* There are usually five or ten simultaneous goals and a larger number of constraints. A large number of controllable variables interact to influence the achievement of goals. The number of uncontrollable variables is incalculable.

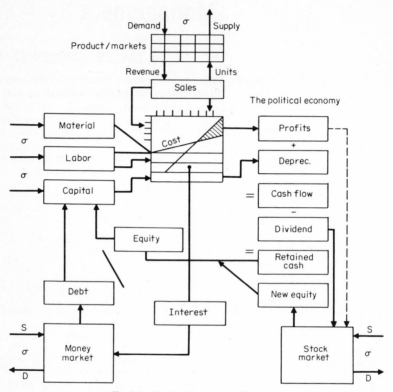

Fig. 2-1   Stochastic aspects of the firm.

Somehow, most businesses are managed fairly successfully without dealing explicitly with very many of these factors.

2. *It is stochastic.* To add complication, few of the relationships within a business are deterministic—or at least, few relationships can be sufficiently specified to permit them to be stated in constants. Frequently the performance outcomes and many determinants are realistically treated as random variables. Statistical methods of correlation, probability, and inference permit the indication of relationships that elude precise descriptions. The natural equilibria that persist in most competitive circumstances tend to provide orderly stochastic distributions and relationships.

3. *It is objective-oriented.* The orientation of business management is toward the achievement of quantifiable objectives. The attempt is to measure all actions and events in terms of their impact on these desiderata. This permits the system to be organized and defined in unambiguous terms, although conflicts between objectives require systems that permit trade-offs within the hierarchy of objectives.

Utility functions are explicit or implied in the definition of objectives. That is, the value of a given plan in terms of profits does not have to be stated explicitly; rather, management can choose between different plans on the basis of a formulation that defines profits as a function of risk in each case.

4. *It is an open system.* The fundamental control aspects of the management process are limited to the controllable variables. However, a significant number of interfaces exist with the larger macroeconomy comprising a large number of variables that are measurable but lie outside the control system. This means that the system must be highly adaptive.

Functions of Management The four principal functions of management are organization, planning, decision making, and controlling. A fifth function, which is usually taken for granted, is knowing and understanding. Figure 2-2 illustrates the general flow of information among these functions. First, we organize the units of operation and the forms of information. We then plan on the basis of these units. Management makes decisions regarding investment in alternative plans, and communicates the de-

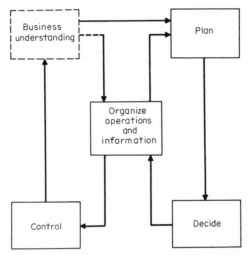

Fig. 2-2   General flow of information among management functions.

cisions back to the operating units. Control information flows back to management from these units. This provides feedback to management.

Control information updates, corrects, and adds to the embodied store of knowledge. In an effective system, improved understanding of the business is fed back to the operating units, and provides a new platform of understanding upon which replanning is based.

Organizing. A prime function of management is to organize the units of production and marketing, and at the same time to organize the information system needed for managing these units. The organization of information, although often neglected, is particularly critical. The design of the information system should at the beginning recognize the management functions it serves (i.e., planning, decision making, controlling, and understanding). Most business firms today are multidimensional: they have a variety of products, and they operate in different markets (including different countries). In order to manage the business effectively, the information units must represent the lowest common denominator of homogeneity with respect to both product and market. Ideally, they should identify discrete and independent product/market units. In larger firms, these units may lie as many as five or six levels below corporate management.

As a result of this complexity, a hierarchy or family tree of these units exists. Furthermore, there are usually multiple concepts of organization that exist simultaneously, e.g., the management organization of responsibility, the legal organization of business units, the accounting organization of information, etc. These complexities are what dictate the system properties, and in general, they are best met by organizing an information system that has the following properties: (1) homogeneity of units; (2) independence of units; (3) matrix structure; and (4) flexible means of organizing and reorganizing units.

Business Understanding. Although the goal of providing improved understanding about performance of the business pervades all management functions, there is a specific need to collect the current inventory of knowledge before each stage of planning or budgeting. This is normally an unthinkable MIS task. Business people, being prac-

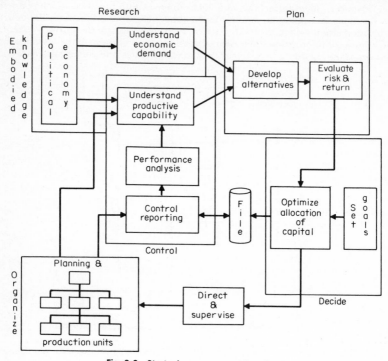

Fig. 2-3 Strategic management functions.

tical problem solvers, do this by gathering together and using their collective memory recall.

Today, we can supplement that process by bringing along flexible tools for the access and presentation of virtually unlimited stores of data and information about the business environment. We can present organized series of historical relationships, models of market behavior (demand, pricing, etc.), models of cost relationships, production possibilities, and practically unlimited financial information. If the vast store of management information is easily accessible, through a good interface system, the management process benefits from more rigorous and precise knowledge without forfeiting all the subjective knowledge that managers possess. Furthermore, both sources of information can be beneficially united if the system design *facilitates human participation.*

The system developed at IU Development Corporation illustrates this in a practical setting. Figure 2-3 shows the wide range of business information that can be brought forward at a plan review meeting. The plans can be subject to extensive screening and analysis prior to review time, using management models. If subjective information is available at the meeting, models can be modified then and there to add a new assumption, and cost functions can be modified to include, say, a new labor rate—if, for example, the manager has new insights into labor contract negotiations. Real-time graphic response while new data are being entered makes this act of changing or adding assumptions a management aid rather than a bookkeeping chore.

Planning. The process of business planning, whether for broad, long-term strategy or short-term, detailed operations, is essentially the process of developing and analyzing alternatives. Given a sound understanding of the external and internal environment of the business, the next difficulty management has is the translation of its understanding of potential threats and opportunities into "scenarios" and timetables of action. Transforming economic scenarios with their elaborate dimensions into business plans with different but equally elaborate dimensions is a process of trial and error in which the planner requires a fairly comprehensive representation of each new scenario as he or she postulates it. The wide use of financial simulation systems in business planning illustrates the way in which computers readily enhance management in this function.

Supplementing the simulator with an interactive graphic output makes this tool even more useful to management. We now have the ability quickly to display proforma business information in the conventional analyses of managers — graphic displays of results in the form of any selected set of inputs or outputs, together with ratios, comparisons, and overlays of different alternatives. The planner can see the impact of changing his or her assumptions, timing, or approach. This tool is to business people what the oscilloscope is to the engineering designer — a means to see what is happening inside the complex system one is planning.

Decision Making. Adapting to changing circumstances is continually demanded. Hence, the availability of a range of options is highly desirable. However, the constant need for choosing among alternatives requires both understanding and judgment. If we expand the range of options, we exponentially expand the problem of understanding. To make judgments among this embarrassment of riches, we now have to integrate all the information we have just developed back into "sensible" forms. Then, the subjective knowledge of executives can be related through their senses to other forms of information regarding their choices.

One illustration of the way in which subjective values can interact with objective choice is a trade-off curve. A representation of all the possible business-mix choices can be boiled down into such a curve that identifies only (1) the risk and return properties; and (2) the "efficient frontier" of mix alternatives. That is, all possible business-mix positions can be screened down to *only those* that give *the highest return for a given level of risk*. Those that give less return for the same amount of risk are obviously less desirable. Figure 2-4 shows a graphic plot of such a trade-off. Using this graphically coupled model, the manager can visualize the region of risk taking that corresponds to his or her value system and see all the business-mix (or investment) budgets that correspond to that level. At the same time, he or she can see what changes imply more return, and what increase in risk exposure goes with the higher-return investments. If the manager wants to consider other criteria, he or she can alter the solution based on other policy considerations or values and determine how sensitive the return (or risk) may be to that choice. Also available are more comprehensive means for simultaneously optimizing a larger number of goals.

Other schemes, such as linear programming, are used to consider simultaneously as many as 50 to 100 goals and constraints. These obviously provide solutions to problems of such complexity that the trade-offs within the process cannot be "sensed." The manager cannot enter the decision process in midstream, and so his or her value system and nonrigorous knowledge are not available to the programming process. This is overcome through extensive visual monitoring of results, and sensitivity analysis of the solution. A series of two- (or three-) dimensional trade-off curves can be graphed to show the effect of an error in any given assumption, or different goals. For example, a trade-off curve can be displayed showing the increased growth of earnings possible for different assumptions, such as increasing borrowings above the level assumed in the initial solution.

Control. Controlling business activities requires a fairly short reporting cycle for data that attempt to identify the rates at which things are happening and the effects brought about by planned efforts and expenditures and by other causes. The analyses

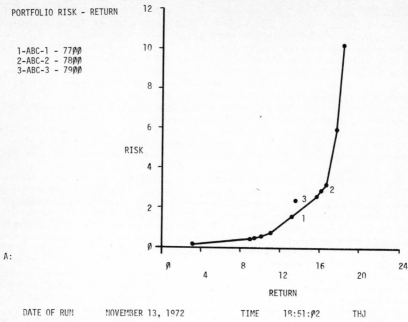

PORTFOLIO RISK - RETURN

1-ABC-1 - 77ØØ
2-ABC-2 - 78ØØ
3-ABC-3 - 79ØØ

RISK

A:

RETURN

Fig. 2-4 An example of a computer graphics presentation of the portfolio analysis of three plans. The convex surface represents the limits of return (return on equity) possible for any given level of risk (expressed as one standard deviation of the return). Plans 1 and 2 are efficient, i.e., provide the maximum return available for the level of risk encountered. Plan 3 is inefficient, i.e., there are investment-mix alternatives available that provide either more return for this level of risk, or less risk with equal return.

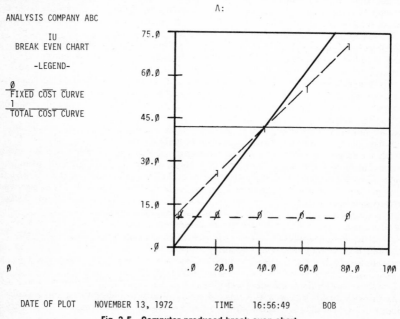

ANALYSIS COMPANY ABC

IU
BREAK EVEN CHART

-LEGEND-

Ø
FIXED COST CURVE
1
TOTAL COST CURVE

A:

DATE OF PLOT   NOVEMBER 13, 1972   TIME   16:56:49   BOB

Fig. 2-5 Computer-produced break-even chart.

which are central to this process are diagnostic in the sense that they attempt to trace the flows of action. The quantity of data required is extensive, and so the manner of data analysis must be efficient.

Simple means have been developed to preset acceptable variance levels and screen all data with the computer, to identify those in which the variance of plan to actual exceeds this level. These items can then be quickly organized and presented graphically in either a prescribed sequence or by direct selection by the analyst who is trying to isolate the performance problem. Actual results are directly superimposed over the original plan or assumption, and differences, ratios, or rates of deviation can be provided. A break-even type of analysis is a typical case (Figure 2-5). Where planned volume is not being realized, the implications to total profit of many alternatives can be estimated and measured by interacting with the computer at the display.

THE STRATEGIC MANAGEMENT SYSTEM

The Strategic Management System attempts to describe and apply the entire "theory of the firm" from product/market demand to capital market theory in a realistic and usable framework.

System Outline   The system consists of:
1. A structured plan input subsystem.
2. A Macroeconomic Model.
3. Microeconomic Models.
    a. Revenue and Capital Functions (Independent).
    b. Production and Cost Functions (Interdependent).
4. Simulation Models.
5. Business-Mix Programming.
6. Goal Optimization Programming.
7. Parametrics.
8. Review and Decision Process (Utility).
9. A Structured Performance Reporting System.
10. Control and Analysis Mechanisms.
11. A Series of Interactive Interfaces.

The entire system is modular, although almost entirely integrated in a single computer system with centralized file handling, data transfer, and compatible programming. Continuous processing is possible throughout the complete microeconomy of the firm by means of a series of related subsystems. This modularity also permits iteration, rerouting, and bypassing of subsystems; that is, the system management procedures permit a heuristic approach to decision analysis throughout. The total system is depicted in Figure 2-6.

The Structure of Planning and Reporting Units and Information   The organization of planning units is classical. The units follow management organization and responsibility (Figure 2-7). The reporting structure is identical. This stems from two principles of structure: (1) responsibility is indivisible, and (2) planning and measuring of results should be parallel.

Within planning units, issues or alternatives are isolated as individual strategic elements, or *strategies*. They are defined as that lowest level of independent events where differential demands and results are definable and measurable. Allocation of costs is not permitted — general expenses remain unabsorbed at a higher level when strategy is being evaluated, and then consolidated when product lines, companies, divisions, or groups are being evaluated. These dimensions derive from the principles of (1) independence among alternatives, (2) scale of decision variables kept as small as possible, and (3) homogeneity of decision variables.

The information structure also is classical. Conventional income, balance-sheet, and cash-flow elements are planned and reported. In addition, market information is developed in the most conventional terms — assumptions regarding market and competitive states, market shares, and market prices (including factor prices) are stated. This structure of information permits a direct interface with all the normal, in-place management methods and systems, especially since the entire management team is educated and familiar with the values of an accounting-based management system.

The only embellishments of these conventional information formats are, again, hardly

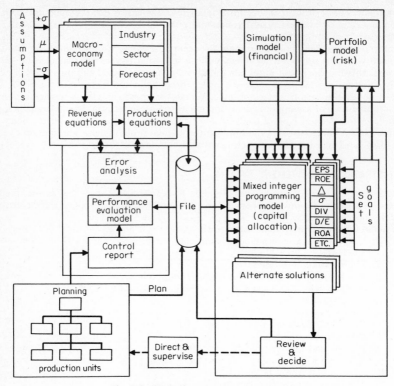

Fig. 2-6   Strategic management system.

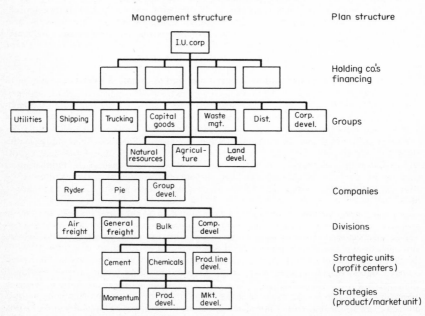

Fig. 2-7   Plan structure paralleling management structure.

new, but not always present in a management information system despite the critical importance of their isolation. They are (1) definition of coefficients of variation, and (2) distinction between controllable and uncontrollable factors. The first embellishment defines the production function, permitting simulation of a broad range of deterministic conditions. The second permits events to be divided into causal subsets that can again permit more logical decision methods as well as better diagnosis of business problems.

Macroeconomic Models None of us can foresee the future, but there is a strong temptation to ascribe prescience to economic models. However, the proper use of macro-

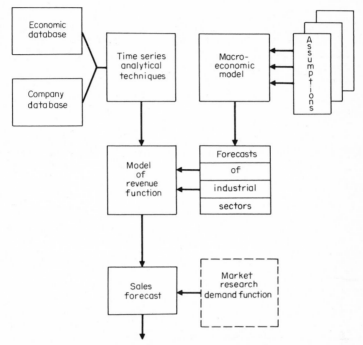

Fig. 2-8   Schematic of a macromodel for strategic decision in the revenue function.

economic models is *not* for forecasting. The major value of large macroeconometric models is that they make it possible to identify the key policy or random variables that can influence business events. We can then build an orderly chain of relationship between these independent variables and the dependent variables within the sphere of business management. The large macromodels available today permit the examination of a broad range of assumptions for policy variables, and the determination of consequences for a fairly large number of industrial and monetary sectors. The manner in which macromodels are used in strategic management systems is illustrated in Figure 2-8.

In general, the macrosystem is used to calibrate submitted plans in a consistent manner, and to provide alternative plan estimates throughout the (more defined) range of *probable* variation. In detail, we proceed through the following steps:

1. Correlation of micro- and macrohistorical series.
2. Formulation of equations for the relationships.
3. Forecast of macromodel under a range of assumptions.
4. Microforecasts by inference.

IU Development Corporation generally works initially between the macromodel and the revenue or sales functions of the company. Subsequently, the production and cost functions are developed using revenue as an independent variable.

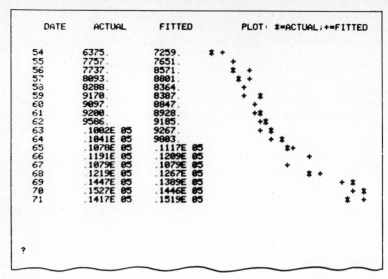

Fig. 2-9   Computer print-out and computer-produced graphic analysis of a correlated series.

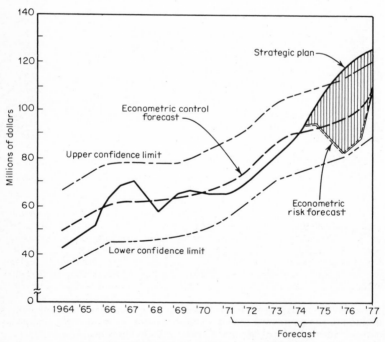

Fig. 2-10   Distribution of probable revenue outcomes.

Revenue Functions, General. Large bases of historical data can be efficiently screened by sequential correlation methods and other statistical techniques. Analysis of correlation matrices for logical causality as well as statistical significance follows a partially subjective process. Further corrections or improvements of relationships are frequently made by the use of lead-lag analysis, the insertion of dummy variables or Boolean expressions for discontinuous events, and the supplementing of equations by the addition of other terms or functions derived from other sources, such as market research or technological forecasts. Graphic analysis of correlated series is helpful in providing clues to improved correlation—i.e., lagged relationships or extraordinary events in one or two periods such as occur where national strikes prevail (Figure 2-9). Revenue functions so developed are filed and later used in a structural manner as a part of forecasting, calibration, and review of plans and results.

Macroforecasts of the United States economy can provide fairly rich sectoral forecasts through bridging equations or input-output models that approach the detail of many historical series. By forecasting these "independent" variables (or first-stage variables) under a variety of optimistic, pessimistic and most-likely policy assumptions, a distribution of revenue outcomes (or the dependent variables) can be established with some probabilistic dimensions (Figure 2-10), at least for a period of time. The wisdom and understanding of the forecaster provide increased assurance that the confidence limits of the equations are warranted.

Production Function. The development of production and cost functions derives almost entirely from company historical data, but usually gains value by the inclusion of analysis of relevant industry data (Figure 2-11). In general, capital output relationships are stable and have equilibrium. Inventory practices change in orderly series. The technologies of processes change slowly (for this purpose) because of the relatively large depreciable asset base and period.

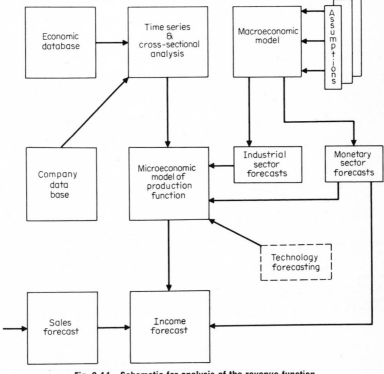

Fig. 2-11 Schematic for analysis of the revenue function.

Capacity utilization varies, but is determinate. After all, the break-even type analysis (Figure 2-5) is widely used, and is generally a useful description of short-term production functions. Labor and capital prices change more abruptly than capital intensity or productivity. Taking a stochastic view, together with an economist's equilibrium view, permits us to deal with these variables in a fashion similar to that of market pricing and other similar disturbances to the revenue functions. The most significant independent factor that affects the production-cost relationships is the volume impact of the revenue variable. Coupling these two functions, revenue, and production (Figure 2-12), implies certain stochastic difficulties—joint probabilities exist, as do conditional

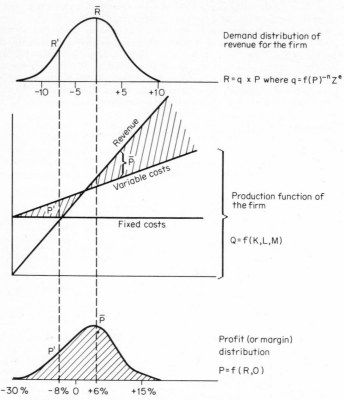

Fig. 2-12   Coupling of revenue and production functions for analysis.

probabilities, and in cases where oligopoly exists, there are significant interactions among presumably "independent variables."

Joint probability and conditional probability are almost always present. They are easily handled today with Bayesian methods. Hence, we can couple our revenue functions and production functions and get equations of good quality for a wide range of economic and business events.

Simulation Models Simulation models conventionally contain the accounting algorithms that describe the case process and accounting measurement convention. (Figure 2-13.) The uses of simulation models in a total system are:

1. To develop the full implications of changes in revenue, production, and finance variables.

2. To permit frequent change in policy assumptions or plan elements.

3. To translate idiomatic business insights into formal statements that can be used in a structured business system.

By implementing interactive processes of simulation, we can rebuild plans to re-

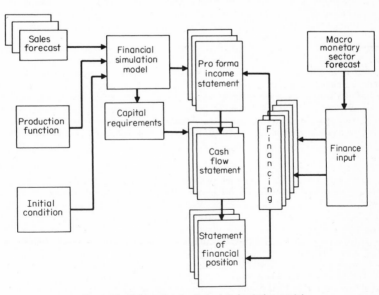

```
                               *
STRATEGY NAME    DEVELOPMENT-SOUTHERN ACQUISITION
                  1973    1974    1975    1976    1977
LN
 1 SALES & REVENUE    5000    6500    8450    9718   11175
 2 COST SALES & OPNS  4750    6110    7858    9135   10337
                     ------  ------  ------  ------  ------
 3 OPERATING PROFIT    250     390     592     583     838
   **OTHER APPLICATIONS**
 6 MGT CST & CMP PROV    9      12      18      15      24
 4 INTEREST            52      16       0       0       0
 5 PROV INCOME TAX     91     173     284     273     402
 7 MINORITY INTEREST    0       0       0       0       0
                     ------  ------  ------  ------  ------
 8 TOTAL OTHER DEDUCT  152     201     302     288     426
                     ------  ------  ------  ------  ------
 9 NET INCOME OPNS      98     189     290     295     412
                     ======  ======  ======  ======  ======
   **APPLICATION OF FUNDS**
15 PP&E GROSS ADD     3121    1966    2302    1840    1764
16 NET INC C ASSETS    326     117     152      99     191
17 NET INC LT INVEST     0       0       0       0       0
19 NET INC OTH ASSETS    0       0       0       0       0
18 NET INC INTANGIBLE  721       0       0       0       0
                     ------  ------  ------  ------  ------
20 TOTAL ASSET ADD    4168    2083    2454    1939    1955
   **LESS INCR**
21 C LIAB EX DEBT      559     100     140      91     176
22 OTH LIAB & CONTRIB    0       0       0       0       0
23 NEGATIVE EXCESS       0       0       0       0       0
                     ------  ------  ------  ------  ------
24 TOTAL NEW INVEST   3609    1983    2314    1848    1779
   **INTERNAL SOURCES FUNDS**
25 NET INCOME           98     189     290     295     412
26 DEPREC & AMORT     1328     807    1164     998    1172
27 MIN INT IN NET INC    0       0       0       0       0
```

Fig. 2-13 Computer print-out of financial results from a simulation model.

Fig. 2-14 Schematic of a financial simulation model.

flect change easily and quickly. We can maintain insight into the nature of the impacts on various goals, and hence more efficiently find solutions to problems of several dimensions. Furthermore, we can methodically translate stochastic distributions of limited dimensions into distributions of much greater richness, by bringing a large number of constants into the decision process in the typical simulation model (Figure 2-14).

The strategic system uses an elaborate simulation model to assist in the development of plan alternatives, and the screening of many of these. The simulating models permit a translation of econometrically derived ranges of possible plan outcome into plans that are calibrated for consistent assumptions of what the "most likely" outcomes will be, and their established degrees of variance. Individual plans can be consistently subjected to various scenarios of risk, and the consolidated impact estimated.

Consolidation of several hundred planning units takes seconds in an efficient simulator. This compares with employee weeks of manual effort or hours of batch processing with conventional accounting consolidation programs. The simulator models also provide a rapid means of consolidating financial statements for the complex organizations and structures that most corporations have to deal with today. When a large number of alternatives are considered, the burden of pro forma consolidation is formidable if it is to consider tax credits, minority interest, amortization of excess, and all the complexities of intercompany elimination. As a result, many analysts have to perform crude approximations of a consolidated view of planning alternatives that mask the true cash flow or reported income effect of decisions.

The major result of the entire system to this point is a liberation of the management decision maker from the deterministic point estimate of the subordinate decision maker. He or she does not have to challenge the subordinate manager's judgment or self-image in order to determine what other alternatives are available or possible, nor "second guess" the outcome of events with respect to which others have greater familiarity and more direct responsibility. At any level of responsibility an analysis of the probabilities of uncertain events is available to help guide judgment and make risk taking more explicitly understood.

Executives' judgments of realistic and unrealistic levels or degrees of undertaking are enhanced, and the initial interaction between the executive level and the operating levels is conducted in a more factual and less emotional milieu. The subjective factors not captured by equations or coefficients can be brought into the system, and a systematic exposition of risk, impact on total corporate goals, etc., can be brought to the operating executive. This interaction improves the system insight, sharpens the executive's insight and value judgments, and bridges the initial difficulty of decentralization, namely the existence of pluralistic viewpoints.

Business Mix (Risk Management) The question of business mix is exactly related to a risk-reward view of strategic management. There may be two or more dimensions to the question, since we recognize that there are more than one type of reward and more than one type of risk. Importantly, this aspect of business, though present at any level of a hierarchy of diversification, constitutes the bridge across the chasm that separates the goals of the two levels of management (strategic and operational). Here we first recognize the different conclusions that can be reached by optimization versus suboptimization of components. This is the critical meaning of *systems management:* the operation of all the subsystems at peak performance does not optimize the total system.

The notion of balance in a business firm is critical, since there is no natural equilibrium state for a firm. A firm's growth path is fundamentally explosive, although there are cyclical deviations from that growth path. On the other hand, once a critical point has been reached in unbalancing a firm's financial flows, the path becomes degenerate. Bankruptcy is a very common fate of entrepreneurs because of the lack of regenerative forces. The concept of optimizing balance between risk and return is the beginning of the explicit treatment of the complex, nontrivial interrelations among business units or fields of investment.

Economists have understood the divergent behavior of different business sectors for many years: the contracyclical aspects of some businesses, the lead-lag relationships among others, and the compensating seasonal patterns of others. In recent years, this same understanding emerged more formally on Wall Street in the form of *portfolio theory.* This basic theory, as well as analogous forms of implementation of the theory, provide the next system element. Especially applicable to conglomerate diversification, it is an extremely useful tool in planning. The system described here maintains a risk-return portfolio programming system as a separate (rather than integrated) subsystem (Figure 2-15). This permits heuristic exploration of the nonlinear dimensions of the business without preconceived utility values or prior knowledge of all the feasible combinations. (Figure 2-16.)

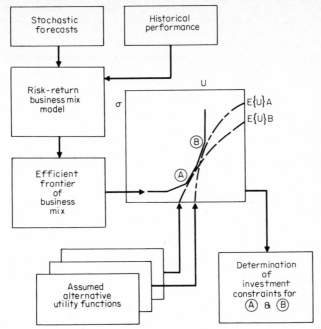

Fig. 2-15   Schematic of business-mix model.

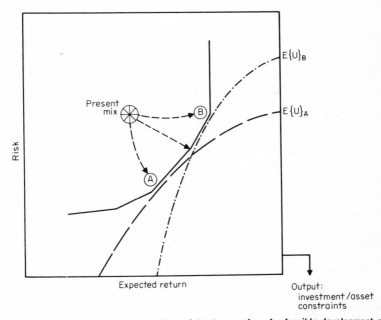

Fig. 2-16   Heuristic examination of nonlinear risk-return surface for feasible development paths.
The models and computer graphics permit exploration of what risk-return goals (A and B) can be pursued from the present position, and develop "menus" of investments that will produce these expected results.   The utility (U) of each can be judged by top management, with an understanding of what changes in investments are required to produce these goals.   See Figure 2-18 for a typical output.

The system defines the efficient frontier of all investments, calculates the risk-return coordinates of any plan variant, and permits exploration of the entire surface. These features permit a knowledgeable business manager to determine where he or she is, examine alternative risk-return goals, and define the multipath means of developing toward these goals with nothing more than judgmental insight into the limits of feasible

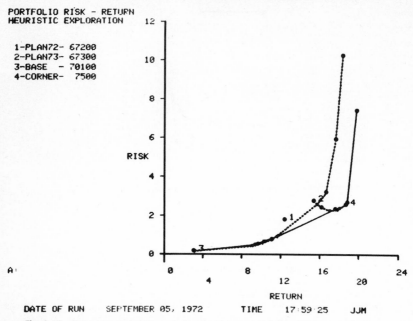

Fig. 2-17 Computer-produced graph showing degrees of risk against expected return.

change in business mix over time, and the utility functions of the chief executive, directors, and stockholders.

This model provides scenarios of the most efficient long-term redirection of investment funds. The risk-return dichotomy is so fundamental to business decision making that it naturally precedes more rigorous multidimensional optimization. But, more importantly, it deals with the stochastic dimensions of the plans. This is done by using alternative sets of forecast values as input to the model, and developing plans for different economic assumptions. Methods are available for giving emphasis to downside risk and upside potential, as well as variance.

The output of this model is a series of "portfolios" of investment (or reinvestment) that provide different degrees of risk and expected return. These can include a series of steps from A (present) to B (goal) that describe the asset or investment weights year by year. (See Figures 2-17 and 2-18.) Using the model independently of the macro-

POINT NUMBER	POINT NAME	BASE	RISK	RETURN	DV/DE
673	PLAN73	3	2.76	15.42	.00
578	IDEAL	3	2.31	16.93	.00

DATE OF RUN   SEPTEMBER 05, 1972   TIME OF RUN   17:02:12

PT NO.	GR 1	GR 2	GR 3	GR 4	GR 5	GR 6	GR 7	GR 8	GR 9	GR10	GR11	GR12
673	16.5	29.5	13.8	11.0	8.3	8.5	.0	.0	.0	4.7	7.8	.0
578	.0	13.7	40.4	.0	8.3	8.6	.0	.0	.0	18.0	11.0	.0

DATE OF RUN   SEPTEMBER 05, 1972   TIME OF RUN   17:02:25

Fig. 2-18 Computer print-out of risk-return analysis.

economy stochastic forecasts provides a shortcut means of considering larger numbers of development issues in a stochastic framework without the econometric work associated with explicit forecasting of distributions. In that case, we use the statistics of the historical distribution in the same fashion as does the security analyst.

Goal Optimization   The central process of management is optimizing the achievement of all the company's goals within the constraints and restricted boundaries of real life. The keystone of the planning process that permits this to be done is the mathematical programming system (Figure 2-19). Most of the time, managers are faced with decision

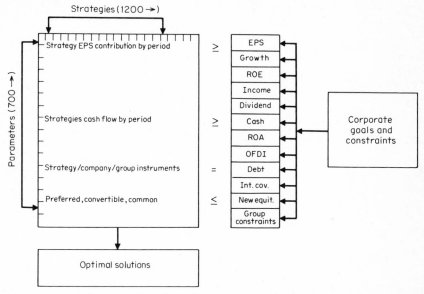

Fig. 2-19   Schematic of multiperiod goal optimization model.

making from an extremely limited menu of perceived alternatives and a one- or two-dimensional view of the consequences of the decisions. The purpose of this system is to enrich the decision process by making it possible to consider the astronomical number of available permutations with full cognizance of the consequences upon a large number of goals.

Optimization of goals is undertaken by feeding a data set of available strategic alternatives (expressed in 30 to 40 parameters per period/unit) to the programming model. These can be plans as submitted, expected values of plans, plans under a given condition of risk, or sets of simulated plan alternatives. The objective function is earnings per share (EPS), with other goals held as constraints (such as the upper and lower limits of growth in individual years) and with a large number of real-world constraints, such as limits on foreign investment, terms of debt covenants, etc. The total matrix is currently about 700 rows and 1,200 columns. The system can be entered at several stages — at the data base level and matrix level, and in a postoptimal stage. This permits several levels of problem modification to be performed, which is desirable because of the essentially iterative nature of the decision process.

The model permits financing to be managed and optimized. Selections from alternative financing instruments are made. These instruments accompany plans when they are tied to the program (e.g., mortgages) or can come from a corporate pool of financing plans.

Parameterization (Development of Alternatives)   The system connection between the stochastic aspects of the system and a deterministic linear programming optimization system is through postoptimal parameterization, or sensitivity analysis (Figure 2-20). These procedures permit a broad range of decision criteria to be applied — expected value maximization, mini-max criteria, minimum income criteria, etc.

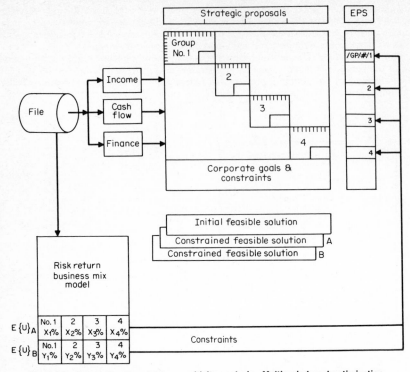

Fig. 2-20 Schematic of model for sensitivity analysis: Multiperiod goal optimization.

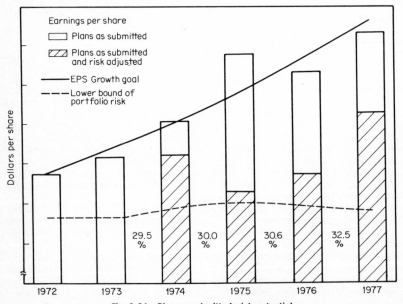

Fig. 2-21 Plan as submitted, risk potential.

The portfolio weights of different business-mix conditions are the input to parameterization. Different portfolios that emphasize different utility functions, other decision criteria, or different development strategies are available from the risk-return
model. These solutions are two- or three-parameter solutions, however, and do not
deal with growth, pattern of earnings, cash flow, capital structure, and many other goals
and constraints. That is, they are naïve solutions. Such preliminary solutions to the
nonlinear, stochastic problem now can be further discriminated by submitting them to

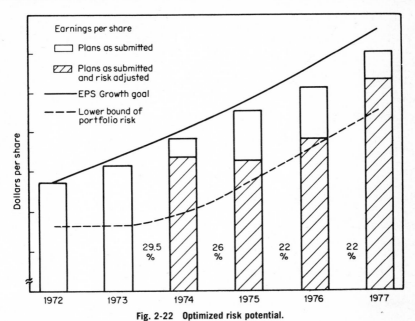

Fig. 2-22 Optimized risk potential.

testing in the complex environment of the optimizer, where several hundred constraints are recognized. Further, the portfolio solutions may not be feasible.

The values of the portfolio solutions are used as parametric variables to the right-hand
side of the optimization model, where group asset and equity constraints are brought
sequentially down to the portfolio values, or until the problem becomes infeasible.
This parameterization can be done using any of the databases available on file—the
plans as submitted, maximum-likelihood estimates, or risk scenarios. The output, as
shown in Figure 2-20, is a series of solutions that offer alternative strategy for the corporation under different decision or utility criteria.

Review of Alternatives   The solutions can be resimulated to smooth out any error resulting from the model approximations or sequential calculation procedures. The
plans can now be presented in highly detailed accounting fashion, in abstract mathematical formats (trade-off curves, frontiers, etc.), or as graphic presentations of typical
management-style information (Figures 2-21 and 2-22). They are arrayed reflecting
the pros and cons of the major decision variable(s), such as risk-return decision trees
(Figure 2-23).

The executive management planning committee considers these alternatives and
trade-offs and recommends one to the chief executive officer. The final review meeting, attended by all major executives, is for the purpose of discussing the trade-offs,
reflecting different viewpoints, and reaching the final decision—for the present. The
plans, as approved, are returned to the operating units and become the basis for subsequent action and reporting.

Control Loop Mechanisms   The next stages of the strategic management process are
more conventional in one sense, but are unconventional in a different sense: conventional, in that the process of reporting variance analysis, fault diagnosis, and plan

change are common control practices of long standing; unconventional in method.

The analysis of causation in this system separates the controllable and uncontrollable aspects of performance and attempts to determine the extent of variance caused by uncontrollable factors. For example, a deviation in sales is related to actual results of external factors contained in the revenue equation. If the changes in the independent variables explain the variance, fine; if they do not, either the equations need revision for replanning, or some change took place in a controllable area. This is the subject

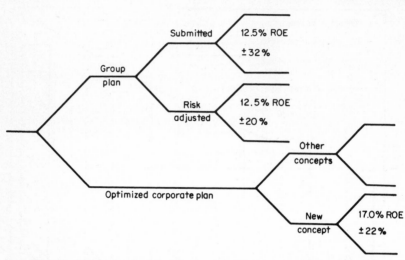

Fig. 2-23 Decision tree for future development alternatives—risk-return potential.

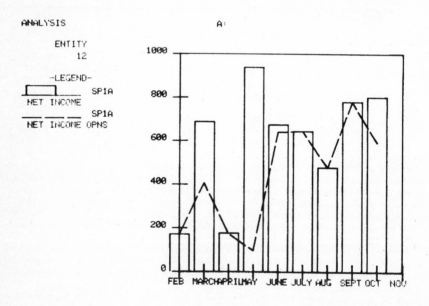

Fig. 2-24 Computer-produced plot for income analysis.

of reviews, and becomes the basis for correcting performance or adding new terms to the planning model. The same is true of the cost factors through feedback and comparison with elements of the production functions. In most cases, the difficulties are isolated much more effectively than through the usual interrogation by successive levels of management in the emotional and threatening climate such meetings tend to have. (Typical comparisons appear as Figure 2-24.)

The replanning is quarterly, and results in either a grass-roots replanning, or a correction of coefficients, terms, etc. In the latter case, it is little more than a mechanical

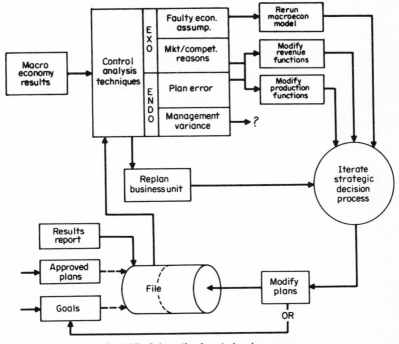

Fig. 2-25 Schematic of control review process.

or automatic recomputation of results. After new plans are established, the cycle is repeated to reassess results vs. goals and determine if the interactions of change dictate any further policy changes (Figure 2-25). If so, policy changes are examined in the form of alternatives and risks, and reviews lead to new decisions that are communicated throughout the system.

CONCLUSION

From the user's viewpoint, the effectiveness of all the management functions depends on proper coordination of these systems and databases through well-structured design. The management system itself provides the means of relating databases, models, and display methods in a way that assists the management process.

Chapter 3

Case Example: Financial Simulation and the Corporate Model System

DONALD K. ABE

Management Consultant; Lecturer, Graduate Business
Program, Saint Mary's College, Moraga, California;
formerly Division Manager and Senior Advisor,
Mathematics, Computers & Systems Department,
Exxon Corporation, Florham Park, New Jersey

The size and complexity of the major oil companies, with their regional and operating organizations and numerous affiliates, have necessitated the development of models for corporate planning. Ideally, we would like to develop a Corporate Model System of an entire corporation. Such a major development must necessarily be an evolutionary process, and in this case study of the "ABC Corporation," a major oil company, we have developed a Financial Corporate Model that can serve as the integrating model for the Corporate Model System.

FINANCIAL CORPORATE MODEL

The Financial Corporate Model, a deterministic simulation model of the corporation, was developed to serve as a long-range corporate planning tool for ABC. In developing such a long-range corporate planning model, we pose a series of questions:
- What should we use as a measure of performance?
- What kinds of information should we generate?
- How should we organize this information?
- What inputs are required?

Focusing on performance measures we can consider, for example, (1) operating ratios, (2) financial ratios, (3) corporate DCF (discounted cash flow), and (4) present value of common stock. Broadly, we need to generate information for (1) operating plans, (2) investment plans, (3) financing plans, (4) financial results, and (5) performance measures. Using the answers to these questions, we can develop a model to generate the desired information. We can then take a further step of developing a Corporate Model System which includes normative techniques to the extent possible.

ABC Corporation—Organization In the Financial Corporate Model, the ABC Corporation is organized into 15 areas (Figure 3-1). We feel that this organization provides a useful level of aggregation. We have attempted to define relatively homogeneous units as areas. Thus, a projection of the ABC Corporation is enhanced by projecting financial results by area, then aggregating the areas. Eight of the areas are geographic. Area 1 is ABC U.S.A.; Area 2, Canada; and so on. Seven of the areas are special. For example, all chemical activities are pulled out of their geographic areas and aggregated in Area 11. The appropriate functional representations, Producing, Refining, Marketing, Logistics, and so on, are included in each of the areas.

10 Functions (J) / 15 Areas (I)	(1) Prod.	(2) Ref.	(3) Mkt.	(4) Log.	(5) NC Ref.	(6) P-S Crude	(7) P-S Prod.	(8) Chem. Feed	(9) Other	(10) Fin. Adj.
(1) ABC U.S.A.										
(2) Canada										
(3) Venezuela										
(4) South America										
(5) Libya										
(6) Europe										
(7) ABC East										
(8) Mid-East										
(11) Chemicals										
(16) ABC Consol.										

Fig. 3-1 ABC Corporation organization.

Input for Financial Corporate Model Within the framework provided by this organization the following data and relationships are used:

Volumes. Volumes represent the basic input. The long-range outlook on volumes is used as the base for our forecast.

Prices. The Gross Operating Revenue Report is analyzed to develop historical prices as a starting point.

Costs. The Costs and Other Charges to Income Report and special studies are used to develop cost relationships.

Capital Coefficients. Two coefficients are used for capital:

1. A coefficient is applied against an increase in volume (next year's volume minus this year's volume) to calculate capital expenditures for expanding capacity.

2. A coefficient is applied against current volumes to calculate capital expenditures for sustaining capacity.

Financial Relationships. These include the equations used for calculating interest income and expense, taxes, minority interest income, etc.

Flow Chart of Financial Corporate Model The model includes volume modules (volumes, prices and costs, capital coefficients) to generate volume-related information such as sales, operating cost, operating income, and capital expenditures; a financial module (financial data bank) to generate financial information; a financing module to analyze financing policy for working capital, dividend, and debt; and a report writer to provide flexibility in generating management reports (Figure 3-2).

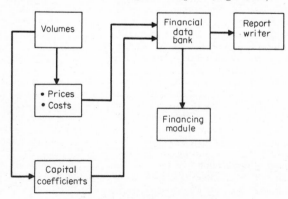

Fig. 3-2 ABC Financial Corporate Model.

   The volume modules are designed to handle 12 areas, 80 products and functions, and 24 time periods. The modules include matrices for volumes, delta volumes, volume growth rates, equations for calculating volumes, prices, costs broken down into cost of goods sold excluding duties and taxes, duties and taxes, operating costs, and capital coefficients for growth and sustaining.

   The financial databank is designed to generate all the financial information needed for fiancial statements, performance measures, and other financial information required by management.

   Financing Module   The financing module is designed to evaluate corporate financial policy regarding (1) working capital, (2) debt, and (3) dividends. Assuming a base case

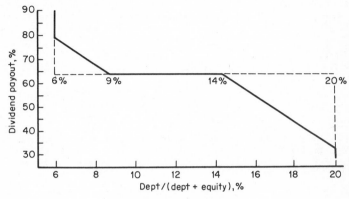

Fig. 3-3   Financing module.

for operating results, we can then use the financing module to simulate various financial policies (Figure 3-3).

   Option 1. Let any one of the three variables float. For example, fix current ratio and dividend payout ratio and let debt be the balancing variable.

   Option 2. Set upper and lower limits to debt. For example, let 6 per cent and 20 per cent (debt, debt + equity) be the upper and lower limits to debt. Debt will float within this range, but at the limits, the debt ratio is fixed and dividend is allowed to float.

   Option 3. Let debt float between debt low and high. Beyond debt low and high, adjust debt and dividends to fit debt ratio to formula, and at the upper and lower limits to debt, allow dividends to float.

   If treasurers would like to develop, for example, an algorithm focusing on coverage or cost of capital as a basis for developing a financial plan, the algorithm can be incorporated independently as another option in the financing module without affecting the other modules in the system.

   Financial Forecast Time Period   In developing the dynamics of the forecast, financial results for 1974 are used as a starting point, and volumes are used as a base for generating a financial forecast (Figure 3-4). Results for 1975 are then analyzed to determine the financial relationships experienced, which are used to generate 1975 results as a benchmark which serves as a basis for developing projected financial relationships.

   Cascading System   To illustrate the flexibility of the model, Figure 3-5 provides a schematic representation of a *cascading system*. Detailed analyses can be conducted which flow into the total ABC model. For example, the ABC Eastern study is a refined study of Area 7 in the ABC model. Even ABC Eastern can be studied in greater detail. The heterogeneity of Area 1, Japan, in the ABC Eastern model led us to study its elements, ABC Sekiyu, ABC Trading, and ABC Refining separately. The results of this study can be fed into Area 1 of ABC Eastern. The results of the ABC Eastern study can then be fed into Area 7 of ABC. This cascading system provides the user with flexibility in selecting the level of aggregation.

   In this cascading system, the results of detailed studies such as business lines or

(1) 1974	(2) 1975	(3) 1976						(15) 1988
Start values	Finan- cial coeff.							
	Capital coeff.							
	Costs							
	Prices							
	Volumes							

Fig. 3-4   Financial forecast time period.

Inputs	Business lines	Area	Region	Exxon
(1) Volumes (2) Prices (3) Costs (4) Capital coeff. (5) Financial rel.	(1) Service stations (2) Consumer (3) LPG (4) Fuel oil (5) Other	(1) ABC Sekiyu (2) ABC Trading (3) ABC Refining	(1) Japan (2) Philippines (3) Hong Kong (4) Viet Nam (5) Thailand (6) Malaya (7) Singapore (8) India . . (11) EEPA . . . (16) AE Consol	(1) ABC U.S.A. (2) Canada (3) Venezuela (4) South America (5) Libya (6) Europe (7) ABC East (8) Mid-East . (11) Chemicals . . (16) ABC Consol

Fig. 3-5   Cascading system: Financial Corporate Model.

special projects can be fed into the system. Significant sectors represented by the model can be continually refined. Steps are also being taken to mechanize the flow of source data from our central data bank into the model.

MANAGEMENT INFORMATION AND PLANNING SYSTEM

The ABC Financial Corporate Model provides not only an organization for information, but also a tool for developing long-range plans. Cases can be run to evaluate investment programs, test sensitivities, and conduct special studies. Used as a management information system, the Financial Corporate Model provides an effective means for conducting a constant and meaningful dialogue between field management and New York Headquarters. Incorporated into the model are crude transfer prices, freight rates, projected volumes, forecast of investments, gross realizations, unit operating costs, financial coefficients such as depreciation rates, interest rates, tax rates, etc., and the integration of agreed-upon bases and assumptions.

Some of the benefits derived from the ABC Financial Corporate Model are as follows:

   1. Serves as a financial planning tool:
- Working capital
- Dividend
- Debt policy

2. Identifies problems and opportunities requiring further study and analysis.

3. Facilitates running alternative cases and sensitivities, and analyzing if-then questions.

4. Provides an evaluation of base load. Also a basis for evaluating corporate objectives.

5. Serves as a management information system—provides an organization for information and a basis for dialogue between headquarters and the field. Documents parameters and assumptions in long-range plans.

6. To the extent that the inputs to the model are built up from detailed standards, information from the model can be used for control purposes.

Corporate Model System   Although the Financial Corporate Model generates a total financial picture of ABC, a number of other models are used to develop inputs for the model. The integration of these models for corporate planning represents the concept of a Corporate Model System.

Linear Programming (LP) Models. Linear programming models are used extensively in corporate planning. LP models are used in refinery and supply planning, and multi-time-period LP models are particularly suitable for the study of timing and sizing of major new facilities such as additional refining capacity. A hierarchy of models can be used for refinery, area, and regional logistics and investment planning.

Simulation Models. Simulation models are also used extensively in the corporate planning process, particularly for facilities planning. To illustrate the kinds of simulation models used, we briefly describe two models, a Crude Supply Simulation Model and a General Marine Terminal Simulation.

Crude Supply Simulation Model. The Crude Supply Simulation Model is a planning tool for aiding in the determination of (1) number of large tankers and (2) the amount of tankage required for the efficient operation of the logistics system. The introduction of large tankers into operation necessitates additional tankage to avoid excessive ullage delays and crude oil runouts, and the delivery of crude oil in large lots results in higher average inventory. The Crude Supply Simulator Model simulates the response of the crude supply system to variations in the tanker fleet and tankage configuration.

Inputs to the model include information about the fleet of tankers, tankage levels at the various refineries, and operating guidelines. Output includes information about ullage delays, crude runouts at refineries, crude oil inventory profiles, and so on. Fleet size and composition, as well as tankage levels required for the efficient operation of the system, may be evaluated by analyzing the results of a number of cases.

The major components of the Crude Supply Simulation Model are refineries, crude oil sources, and a fleet of tankers. Tanker scheduling is centralized. Decisions are made as tankers arrive at geographic locations referred to, in the model, as decision points. The objective of tanker scheduling is to plan the efficient operation of the system by minimizing crude runout, ullage delay, two-porting, and lightening costs. The random elements included in the model are (1) tanker travel-time variations, (2) refinery breakdown dates, (3) storm lengths as well as intervals between storms, (4) tanker breakdown dates, and (5) size and procurement delay of supplemental tankers.

The computer program is designed to simulate the system by generating a representative sequence of events and executing them in chronological order. The execution of an event generally consists of three steps: (1) making any required decisions, (2) updating the system to reflect the impact of the event, and (3) scheduling any future events implied by the current event. If, for instance, a tanker arrives at a refinery, it is necessary to (1) decide whether to unload it or to place it in a waiting line; (2) update inventory levels if unloaded, and update the status of the waiting lines otherwise; (3) schedule tanker arrival at the crude decision point if unloaded, and schedule tanker unloading event if placed in waiting line.

An important feature of this model is its *closed loop* nature, that is, the existence of a "captive" fleet of tankers whose movements have to be monitored and scheduled by the model. The behavior of the model is sensitive to the quality of the tanker scheduling guidelines. The better the tanker allocation within the model, the smaller the tankage requirements estimated by the model. A great deal of experimentation and thought went into the development of tanker allocation procedures that are conducive to the efficient operation of the system.

Another important feature of this model is the fact that it takes into account interactions among refineries. The benefits, to the system as a whole, of adding tankage at a given refinery may far exceed the benefits at the refinery. The use of this model enhances investment decisions by providing a quantitative measure of these interactions.

General Marine Terminal Simulation (GMTS). A number of simulation models have been developed for planning marine terminals. It was observed that these models had a number of logical elements in common resulting in considerable duplication of effort. We estimated that a General Marine Terminal Simulation Model could be developed which would reduce the required programming time for modeling any marine terminal from 6 months to 6 weeks. Experience with GMTS has shown that the reduction to 6 weeks programming time is indeed possible and that GMTS generates reasonable results.

GMTS is used to study the facilities of a single marine terminal including piers, berths, loading lines, and crude tankage. GMTS estimates the incentives for expanding these facilities by determining the duration and consequent cost of ship delays incurred with the present facilities and those delay costs likely with the proposed facilities. Three kinds of delays are explicitly considered:

• Berth delays: Ship A must wait for Ship B to leave a berth before coming in to load or discharge.

• Line delays: Ship A, although berthed, must wait until an appropriate loading or discharge line is available.

• Ullage delays—for crude ships only: Ship A must wait until there is more room in the crude tank(s) before it can discharge.

The simulation models consist of two segments:

1. A ship arrival generator. Crude ships and product ships are generated independently by slightly different mechanisms. Both processes, however, calculate some "good" or "ideal" arrival time and then apply a random factor to represent the fact that a ship may arrive early or late. This list of arrivals can be stored and used in future runs.

2. The main simulator which "operates" the terminal and keeps track of all delays.

Output includes number of delays of each type, duration of delays, and cost of delays, by berth and for the entire terminal. Information on berth occupancy and berth turnaround time is also provided.

SUMMARY

The size and complexity of major oil companies necessitate the use of models to give effect to the many economic factors associated with corporate planning. The use of a Corporate Model System improves the effectiveness of planning through the quantitative and logical discipline imposed by the system and through the close communication which results from utilizing the integrated approach of the system. The use of a Corporate Model System also has the advantage of requiring corporate planners to use consistent data and agreed-upon assumptions and provides the capability for quickly responding to new problems.

Section 4

Functional Applications of Automatic Data Processing

Introduction

IRA M. ADLER   *Principal, John Diebold & Associates, New York, New York*

Data processing's impact on corporate decision making to date has been based on broadening the corporation's fund of information regarding its internal operations and external environment, enabling it to forecast and respond to trends more quickly, and permitting it to automate some lower-level decision-making problems such as production scheduling. The role of the computer in higher-level decision making (e.g., risk analysis), however, is still under debate. We believe that information technology has developed sufficiently to provide some genuine exploratory interaction between manager and computer; some of the principal tools and techniques in use and under development for management decision making in the face of uncertainty are presented in Chapter 1 of this Section.

Such higher-level decision making depends ultimately on the decision maker's concept and comprehension of his or her environment. This comprehension, in turn, depends on the decision maker's own experience and observations, the experiences and observations of peers and subordinates as they are transmitted to the decision maker, and the output of formal data systems using models. The experience of business to date suggests that future, more complex data systems will rely on human interaction to a greater extent than heretofore. Management will continue to draw upon its experience, observations, and intuition, not only because of technical constraints but also because of economic constraints of system design. There is a point at which discretionary decision-making activities cost too much to program. Consequently, the objective and challenge for corporations today is to design computer communications systems which permit an effective cooperation between person and computer.

Another important area is the use of computers and computer-related devices in the product design and development activities of a business. Chapter 2 presents current technology applied to the engineering and design environment in terms of computer-driven graphics displays, automated drafting machines, and data-capture digitizers. The increasing complexity of our culture demands a better ability to represent information in forms convenient for comment and communication. This form of output is actually a picture where the association of data elements, whether graphic or alphanumeric, is easily grasped.

From a broader perspective, the chart and other graphic forms allow visualization of relationships among variables; for example, they can show the growth in sales and relation to profits succinctly and unambiguously. The primary function of a picture output is an expansion of the visualization ability. There is no doubt that the types of technologies represented in Chapter 2 will continue to find increasing utility in other business functions.

The concluding segment of Chapter 2 presents project planning and management by network analysis. A primary virtue of network analysis is that its use encourages a more formal methodology of planning. The value of a thorough, disciplined approach has been demonstrated sufficiently to cause its introduction to other areas of planning; contingency planning, new-product planning, etc. This approach leads to more careful definition of objectives and establishment of well-defined review and approval steps, resulting (if properly utilized) in fewer surprises for management and increased financial control over development efforts. We have occasionally found the technique somewhat difficult to apply, nonetheless, because some managers are unaccustomed to its rigors and may exhibit a great reluctance to any disciplined approach to planning, detailed documentation, definition of project objectives, and a host of other procedures.

A third area covered in this Section entails computerized information storage and retrieval, which is part of the field of information science. This field has emerged from a variety of parent disciplines, including computer science, semantics, and the behavioral sciences. Its focus is the development, processing, and use of essentially textual information. The problems of using textual information have received considerable attention for well over a decade. Nevertheless, after substantial breakthroughs occurred in the initial period, such as computer parsing, the rate of development slowed. The problems of semantics and syntax encountered in natural languages turned out to be a greater barrier than had been anticipated. The present state of the art is still such that automated indexing, abstracting, or classification remain essentially experimental, as do query-answering systems—except for relatively limited-scope or specialized systems (e.g., Aspen System's textual database of trial transcripts for search and retrieval by attorneys). Obstacles to further development have to do with such matters as machine-comprehensible natural language files and the nature of indexing languages, all of which relate to the central semantic problem of the representation of meaning. Chapter 3 provides a current view of computer applications in this field and discusses related topics.

The fourth area presented is the use of computer models in physical distribution. Physical distribution includes transportation, warehousing, shipping and receiving, inventory control, purchasing, materials handling, order processing, market forecasting, protective packaging, customer service, and production scheduling. For too many firms, the emphasis on computers is a reflection of the fallacious assumption that the computer can automatically generate the information necessary to control properly the physical distribution function. As a result, many distribution managers (like other functional managers) have relinquished their responsibility to systems analysts. This approach can all too often result in systems which are not responsive to the real information needs of the manager. The computer, after all, is only a tool which makes possible the development of information systems to control a function. Chapter 4 examines the application of modeling (introduced in Chapter 1) to effective distribution management.

A fifth area concerns the use of computers in personnel management, another function common to all businesses. Traditionally, computers have been used to maintain personnel records and provide input to ancillary functions such as payroll. This has been little more than automation of a clerical activity. In a very real sense, personnel management is an inventory control function in large organizations. A few corporations have successfully implemented computer-based personnel skills inventories as integral components of personnel resource allocation systems, although such systems have formidable updating requirements in order to remain viable. Chapter 5 provides insight into current computer applications in personnel management.

A related area where computers have had significant impact, but in a small number of instances, is in collective bargaining. Labor negotiations supported by computer modeling provide organizations with the ability to focus rapidly on the impact of demands and to formulate counterproposals based on formal analysis. The major drawback is that the labor relations function usually cannot alone cost-justify such a system. It must piggyback onto other functional areas such as production, payroll, and transportation.

A sixth area presented examines the use of computers in marketing and advertising. The cost of marketing has always been a matter of critical importance to most corporations. This contributes to a continuing search by management for new tools and procedures to improve the effectiveness of the marketing dollar. Although initial computer applications in marketing began in the late 1950s, they concentrated primarily on recording and reporting past performance. Current applications and development work tends to concentrate on predictive applications such as more timely sales forecasting and probable competitive marketplace actions, intended to support and optimize the entire sales effort. That these new directions are gaining in importance among data processing and marketing managements is exemplified by an increasing percentage of the computer resource dedicated to the marketing function. In large corporations this allocation reaches 40 per cent of the total computer expenditure.

Computers can and are providing managers with better information to support their decision making in an increasingly complex environment. Computers cannot provide absolute answers to all the marketing manager's problems, but they can enable the manager to choose among many alternatives that can be simulated. In market research, sales strategy alternatives, and advertising media selection, computer models are beginning to provide answers about relationships among various factors affecting individual decision areas. This is the realm of opportunity addressed by Chapter 6.

In summary, the principal contribution to be made by the computer from now on will be to assist functional and corporate executives in managing change rather than reacting to change.

Chapter 1

New Tools for Decision Making

ARNOLD REISMAN, Ph.D., P.E.

Professor of Operations Research, Case Western Reserve
University, Cleveland, Ohio; Vice President, University
Associates, Inc., Cleveland, Ohio

ROBERT REICH

Corporate Planning Officer, The Cleveland Trust Co.,
Cleveland, Ohio; Instructor of Computer and Information
Science, Cleveland State University, Cleveland, Ohio

The complex nature of certain problems encountered in industry, government, and private institutions has produced a demand for procedures to aid management in improving the decision-making process.

These procedures should weigh the relative trade-offs among alternatives and produce a course of action which will benefit the organization as a whole. Benefits should not simply accrue to a unit thereof at the possible expense of other units. The development, during the last quarter of a century, of certain mathematical and/or statistical techniques, along with the computational and data bank capabilities of present-day computers, has further demonstrated the applicability of "new tools for decision making" to management practices. This Chapter discusses some of the decision-aiding techniques used by disciplines and/or professions known by such names as *management science*, *operations management*, and *operations research*.[1]

One may list as follows the steps involved in conducting an operations research study:[2]

1. The formulation of the problem.
2. The construction of a mathematical[3] model to represent the system under consideration.
3. The derivation of a solution from the model.
4. The testing of the model and the solution derived from it.

---

[1] Henceforth in this Chapter the authors refer to *operations research*. The reader should recognize that what is being said is true for all these disciplines.

[2] Russel Ackoff, "The Development of Operations Research as a Science," *Operations Research*, March–April, 1956.

[3] It should be recognized that other models, e.g., computer models, are also used effectively in studying systems.

5. The establishment of controls over the solution.
6. The implementation of the solution.

The most crucial aspects in any application of these methodologies are the identification, definition, and the formulation of the problem. After solving a problem, the implementation of the resulting decision policy is paramount. Thus, the solution procedure is not an end in itself but merely the means to the end.

SYSTEMS, MODELS, AND SOLUTIONS

Since the definition of and the delineating of models plays a significant part in an operations research study, it is important to differentiate between several characteristics of models.

Deterministic vs. Stochastic Models A *deterministic* model does not explicitly allow for chance variation of the system (model) parameters. Events and processes are assumed to occur in a predetermined manner (e.g., the demand rate for a certain product in an inventory control study is assumed known). Conversely, a *stochastic* system ("stochastic" is based on the Greek word meaning to aim, to guess) is one wherein some properties of the situation being modeled do in effect vary according to some probability distribution (e.g., the demand rate for inventory is not certain). Stochastic systems are found in modeling most real-world situations, but are sometimes approxi-

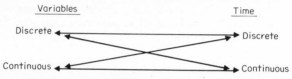

Fig. 1-1 Four types of discrete-continuous relationships.

mated by deterministic models (e.g., the average or expected value of the statistical distribution is used). When the parameters of the probability distribution are known, the process is said to have the property of *risk*, but when these parameters are unknown, the process is said to have the property of *uncertainty*.

Single Period vs. Multiperiod It is important to define explicitly the time period over which the problem is to be modeled. Many situations require only a one-time solution to the problem at hand (e.g., location of a new warehouse). Others require a set of solutions to satisfy many different time points (e.g., determination of production rates over the next 6 months to satisfy incoming demand). In the first case we are concerned only with a single time period and, as a result, the solution is defined for that period only. If the same problem were to be posed 5 years later, it is conceivable that because of changing priorities and/or technology a different solution might result. In the second example, a solution is generated for each time period of interest. If the chosen time period is a month, then the model would generate solutions for the next several months.

Continuous vs. Discrete This category of model description is two-dimensional in the sense that it concerns both the nature and method of change within the model. The components or variables used may change in one of four distinct ways as indicated in Figure 1-1.

Note that in the categories indicated, any independent variable used in the model could substitute for "time." The attributes of the problem will determine which of the above alternatives is most descriptive of the situation at hand.

Constrained vs. Unconstrained All models may be classified as to whether or not they are constrained. When faced with the situation of determining the optimal amount of inventory to have on hand for item X, it might first be postulated that 1,000 units be kept on hand so that virtually no order would face a stockout and hence be backlogged. However, the number of units on hand of item X may be physically constrained in that the warehouse can accommodate only 200 units. Thus the inventory level is constrained by space availability.

Linear vs. Nonlinear A linear functional relationship displays the properties of additivity and homogeneity. When a variable A produces an effect B and a variable C produces an effect D, then if A, C, used together, produce the effect $B + D$, the additivity property is present. If a variable A produces the effect B and if A is multiplied by any real constant C, then the property of homogeneity is present when $C \times A$ produces the effect $C \times B$. For example, let N_A and N_B represent the number of units sold of product A and product B, and let C_A, C_B be the revenue per unit sold of A, B. Total revenue is therefore $C_A \times N_A + C_B \times N_B$, wherein both homogeneity and additivity are present. Thus there is a linear relationship between total revenue and the number of items of A and B produced. Mathematically, a linear functional relationship is defined as that which occurs when $f(aX_1 + bX_2) = af(X_1) + bf(X_2)$.

Optimality, Suboptimality, and Simulation These descriptors are more characteristic of the solution method than of the model. Often in an operations research study a search is made for the *optimal* or best solution. Many mathematical programming formulations have been developed for this single purpose. In solving real-life problems, it is often necessary to make some simplifying assumptions, e.g., linearity, certainty, ability to integrate a certain function, etc. These assumptions should not be made solely for computational convenience. Moreover, tests can often be performed to determine the sensitivity of the solution to the assumptions made.

Because of the many "imponderables and uncertainties" associated with real-world problems, the model's optimal solution is rarely the best possible solution for the real problem. But if the model is well formulated, i.e., if it is an accurate description of the system modeled and all its assumptions can be explicitly defined, then the computed solution should closely approximate the best solution to the real-world problem. In many cases, the marginal value gained from an optimal solution is not worth the additional time and effort involved over a nearly optimal solution.

To illustrate the above, consider the following table.

	$ Cost	*$ Savings*
Good solution	$1,500	$10,000
Optimal solution	$2,000	$10,100

The costs of generating "good" and "optimal" solutions are $1,500 and $2,000 respectively. However, the implementation of the optimal solution, while producing an additional saving of $100, involves an incremental expenditure of $500. Hence, the incremental cost does not justify the incremental benefit. To be sure, real-life problems cannot usually be evaluated with such precision regarding the cost-benefit of extending the study so as to reach "the one best" solution, but the thinking indicated is always applicable. Additionally, it must be recognized that a good solution today is often preferred by management to an optimum solution at some time in the future even if the question of resource and/or cost constraints were not germane, as it often is.

Techniques which do not guarantee optimal solutions do exist. These techniques, known as *heuristics*, produce a good, albeit suboptimal, solution. A large number of problems in the areas of sequencing and searching are solved using heuristic methods. The techniques are based on the fact that an analyst confronted with problems involving a very large number of alternatives cannot feasibly enumerate, test, or consider them all. In the general case where the relevance of the alternatives differs, the analyst may develop these heuristics or rules of thumb to indicate the more desirable alternatives.[4] A general structure for the selection of a decision-making method is shown schematically in Figure 1–2.[5]

OBJECTIVES AND CONSTRAINTS

As discussed earlier, the model may be one wherein constraints are imposed on the available courses of action, or it may exist without such limitations. However, in either case some organizational objective must exist. Management objectives without constraints are rare or nonexistent.

The various objectives or criteria (e.g., profit and/or throughput maximization, etc.) fall into one of two categories, namely monetary and nonmonetary objectives. For

[4] For further discussion of this topic, see Frederick S. Hillier and Gerald J. Lieberman, *Introduction to Operations Research*, Holden-Day, San Francisco, 1968.

[5] For further discussion, see James R. Enshoff and Roger L. Sisson, *Design and Use of Computer Simulation Models*, Macmillan, New York, 1970.

example, one critical factor which affects the monetary criteria, but which is often wrongly omitted from analysis, is the time value of money.

Monetary Objectives and Alternative Investments   A given amount of money if properly invested may earn interest and thus grow in magnitude. Alternatively, there is a cost associated with the use of borrowed money. Moreover, there is a cost of foregone opportunities when such borrowed money is not used at all, but merely allowed to sit idle. All such costs are time dependent; e.g., the longer a unit amount is held, the higher the cost. Thus, in all decisions involving capital over a period of time, the time value of money must be taken into consideration.

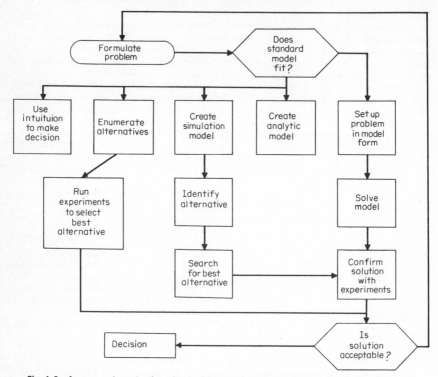

Fig. 1-2   A process for selection of a decision-making method.   (*After Emshoff and Sisson.*)

As a consequence of the concept of the time value of money, it is realized that expenditures that will take place at some future time have different and lower present or current values. Similarly, money in hand at the moment has a potentially higher value at some time hence. Thus, if a single payment P is invested today at some discrete rate of interest per period, i, for N such periods, then the future sum F at the end of the Nth period is $F = P(1 + i)^N$.

Alternately, the present worth of a sum of money F to be disbursed N periods later, if i is the rate of interest, cost of capital, opportunity foregone cost, or the internal rate of return, is given by $P = F(1 + i)^{-N}$.

Furthermore, if instead of a single cash flow, a series of such flows, each described by some F_j, are indicated, then

$$P = \sum_{j=0}^{n} F_j (1 + i)^{-j} = \sum_{j=0}^{n} \frac{F_j}{(1 + i)^j}$$

The computation of P or F in a given situation is simplified by referring to compound interest tables in standard texts.[6]

[6] See, for example, Eugene L. Grant, *Principles of Engineering Economy*, Ronald, New York, 1960.

These concepts can be used to analyze alternative investment opportunities. Specifically they may form the basis of objective functions concerned with optimal strategies. The principal methods available for the evaluation of alternatives may be summarized as follows:[7]

Payback Period Method. This is a simple method which does not recognize the time value of money. It is defined as the length of time required for the sum of net cash returns to equal the initial capital outlay. Projects are selected on the basis of the duration of this period, e.g., the shorter the period, the better the investment is assumed to be. However, because of its simplicity, it does suffer from some major deficiencies, such as the following:

1. It ignores the benefits received after the payback period.

2. It ignores the pattern of returns within the period by not considering the time value of money.

Present-Worth Method. The present-worth method mentioned above can also be used to decide between alternative courses of action. For example, the present worth is calculated for each of the competing alternatives, and the item with the highest value in a profitable situation or the lowest present worth in a cost-minimizing situation is selected. One of the major shortcomings of this method is that it requires the specification of the *rate of discount,*[8] which is not always available.

Discounted Rate of Return Method. This method finds the discount rate which sets the present worth of all revenues exactly equal to the present worth of all disbursements. Fleischer[9] provides an excellent discussion of the concept. In applying it to evaluate alternatives, we must first decide upon the minimum acceptable rate of return, inasmuch as all projects yielding less than this cutoff rate are unacceptable for consideration. All others, i.e., those yielding a rate of return above the given threshold, are ranked in order of preference based on the anticipated return rate thus calculated. The selection is made in the light of budgetary constraints and consideration of the duration of the high-yield investments. Computer algorithms are now available for reducing the computational problem of solving the polynomial involved.[10]

Equivalent Annual Cost (EAC) Method. This method accounts for the time value of money. It may be used to compare competing nonuniform series of cash flows. It accomplishes the above by reducing each of these to an equivalent uniform annual series of payments.

Consider two machines, A and B, which are to be compared over their 5-year service lives. The purchase cost of machine A is $20,000, and its yearly cost of operation is estimated to be $5,000. Similarly, the purchase price of machine B is $25,000 and its annual operation costs are estimated at $3,000. Furthermore, neither machine A nor machine B will have a salvage value at the end of the 5-year period. The deciding organization views 7 per cent as the minimum acceptable rate of return.

To solve the above problem the purchase price must be converted to an equivalent uniform annual series of payments. Mathematical formulations are developed in standard texts on the subject, showing the relationships between the variables involved. For example, if n years is the planning horizon, the annualized equivalent A of an initial disbursement, P, given a discount rate i, may be represented by

$$A = P\left[\frac{i(1+i)^n}{(1+i)^n - 1}\right]$$

As an example, let the discount rate, i, be 0.07 and let n be 5. Standard texts[11] contain tables with the computed value of

$$\left[\frac{i(1+i)^n}{(1+i)^n - 1}\right]$$

[7] The interested reader is referred to Arnold Reisman, *Managerial and Engineering Economics,* Allyn and Bacon, Boston, 1971, for a complete coverage of this and related topics.

[8] The rate of discount is variously the cost of capital, opportunity cost, internal rate of return, etc. *Ibid.*

[9] Gerald Fleischer, "Two Major Issues Associated with the Rate of Return Method for Capital Allocation: The 'Ranking Error' and 'Preliminary Selection,'" *Journal of Industrial Engineering,* April, 1966.

[10] L. Fisher, "An Algorithm for Finding Exact Rates of Return," *Journal of Business,* January, 1966.

[11] See Grant, *op. cit.*

for a given n and i. In the above numerical example this factor is 0.24389. The total annual cost for each machine is the sum of its annual cost of capital recovery (ACCR) and the annual operating cost. The ACCR for machine A is $20,000 × 0.24389 = $4,877.80. Upon addition of annual operating costs of $5,000, the total annual cost for machine A is $9,877.80. The ACCR for machine B is $25,000 × 0.24389 = $6,097.25. Upon addition of its annual operation cost of $3,000, the total annual cost for machine B is $9,097.25. Thus machine B has a lower annual cost by $780.55.

The EAC method is capable of taking into account salvage values, and further extensions are indicated in the reference cited.

The equivalent annual cost method can also be used to evaluate and compare investments which will not yield or require *equal* annual cash flows as was indicated by the above example. In the latter types of evaluations one merely calculates the present worth of the *nonuniform* cash-flow stream and then, using the time value of money, distributes the latter into a series of *uniform* cash flows. The above equation still holds. One merely extends the definition of P to be the present worth of all initial and future cash flows.

The equivalent annual cost method has all the advantages of the present-worth method and yet is more readily acceptable to those managers whose education stopped short of discounted cash-flow analysis.

Continuous Compounding. In certain transactions, cash flows occur on a discrete basis, i.e., at the beginning or end of a time period such as a week, a month, or a year. There exist, however, operations where the cash flows may take place continuously although not necessarily steadily through time. Similarly, interest on money borrowed, on money owed, or on opportunities forgone may be treated either on a continuous or discrete basis. Conceptually, since various alternative investment opportunities are forever present and can be taken advantage of, the continuous basis of treating interest or cost of capital is much more sound. High-speed computers have greatly facilitated the computations associated with continuously distributed interest.

Because of the existence of both continuous and discrete cash flows as well as interest rates, any one of four possible combinations of such treatments (refer to Figure 1-1) may be possible in economic studies. It is therefore important to distinguish between *effective discrete*, coherent interest, i, and *nominal continuous* interest, γ. Discrete and continuous interest are related by the identity

$$i = e^{\gamma} - 1 \quad \text{or} \quad \gamma = \log_e (1 + i) = \ln (1 + i)$$

Tables indicating the values of γ for corresponding values of i can be easily generated by computer or alternately found in the Reisman reference previously cited.

Nonmonetary Objectives In the nonmonetary category there are two classes, namely measurable objectives and nonmeasurable objectives. Criteria such as reliability of equipment, customer service level, job throughput, system turnaround time, to mention but a few, are in the measurable class. Quality of service, the maintainability of a system, flexibility of use, etc., are in the nonmeasurable class. These nonmeasurables, however, can be quantified.

Delphi Technique One of the most successful methods to date for subjectively quantifying these is the Delphi technique.[12] This is a well-established method for eliciting, refining, and integrating the subjective opinions of experts without sacrificing or compromising individuals' suggestions. It has three distinctive characteristics: (1) anonymity, (2) controlled feedback, and (3) statistical group response.

Anonymity. To minimize the impacts of dominant individuals in a panel of experts, separate and individual responses are elicited to previously prepared questions, without divulging the responses of others. This opinion gathering is normally carried out by written questionnaire, but of late, time-sharing computer terminals are being used to relay responses to the experimenter when the experts are not in one location. However, when all panelists are on site, manual processing of data has been found to be more expeditious. The interaction among panel members is through formal communication channels controlled by the experimenter.

[12] See Olaf Helmer, *Convergence of Expert Concensus through Feedback*, The Rand Corporation, 1964, p. 2973; Juri Pill, "The Delphi Method: Substance, Context, A Critique and an Annotated Bibliography," *Socio-Economic Planning Sciences*, 1971; and Reisman, *op. cit.*

Controlled Feedback. This is a device to reduce the variance in parameter estimates. A Delphi exercise will usually consist of several iterations with the results of the previous iteration fed back to the respondents. The feedback is normally in a summarized form, showing the distribution of votes and/or the parameters of those distributions, such as medians and interquartile ranges. Also solicited and fed back after the first round are the various justifications in the form of arguments and counterarguments offered by individual panelists in their attempts to persuade others to their point of view.

Statistical Group Responses. Here the panel of experts will be asked at the end of each round to re-evaluate these dimensions based on the feedback provided. There is no particular attempt to arrive at unanimity among the respondents, and a spread of

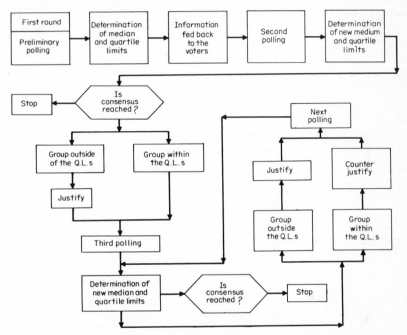

Fig. 1-3   Flow diagram representing the sequence of events in conventional Delphi.

values on the final round is an expected normal outcome. However, the spread will usually be much smaller as compared to the earlier rounds.

A general structure for a Delphi experiment is given in Figure 1-3. The method has been found to be very useful for enriching the database for use in models wherein many of the variables are subjective by nature.

Successful applications include the forecasting of future dates for technological breakthroughs, the study of developing economies, the forecasting of long-range industrial and educational trends, the evaluation of a system of social welfare agencies, and the forecasting of medical and paramedical personnel demands.

Typically, the Delphi experiments would begin with a thorough analysis of the various points of view and institutional functions that must be represented in the panel. The panel design must include all the diverse elements of the organization which can impact the outcome. Next, the results of a preliminary polling of the experts to each question would be fed to an analysis group which would rank the responses, indicate the distribution of these responses, and thus determine for each question the median and quartile limits. If time-sharing computers are utilized they could also perform the task of ranking and determining the distribution medians and quartiles. These parameters would then be returned to the panel of experts, who would undergo a second round of voting. This time, however, the participants are asked to justify their positions. Thus, new median and quartile scores are determined from the last round of voting.

The above process continues with reasons and counterreasons exchanged until consensus is reached. An operational rule is to agree that consensus has been reached when some fixed percentage of the votes lie between some predetermined range of values.[13]

PROBABILITY AND STATISTICAL ANALYSIS[14]

Multiple Alternatives: Criteria and States of Nature The methods discussed up to this point assume a single "state of nature," e.g., forecast of the future. However, many decisions require consideration of several alternative, yet possible, states of nature (forecasts). To demonstrate what is meant here, assume the possibility of only two states of nature.[15] State one, N_1, has a probability of occurrence of .28, and state two, N_2, has a probability of .72. The states will be defined on the basis of several properties, e.g., political, economic, technological, and/or competitive factors. The probabilities of each state of nature may be estimated by the Delphi method. Table 1-1 shows an example of two states of nature.

TABLE 1-1 Summary of Two Possible Future States of Nature and the Estimated Probabilities of Their Occurrence

State of nature N_z	N_1	N_2
Probability of N_z, $z = 1, 2$	Probability $(N_1) = .28$	Probability $(N_2) = .72$
Major assumptions and ground rules political	No hot war in foreseeable future. No substantial disarmament.	Current international conflict ends in 2 years. Limited wars start 5 years from now in Central America and grow in intensity.
Economic	Price levels, interest rates, and spending levels remain steady.	Prices, interest rates, and spending levels reflect political conditions; they remain steady for 2 years, then dip down, and then rise slowly without exceeding original levels at the end of 10 years.
Technological	No major breakthrough in computer design. Steady improvements in reliability, and in maintenance and operating costs.	IBM will market 5th generation computer in 3 years. Maintenance and operating expenses fluctuate for 2 years and then drop below present levels.
Competition	New competitors will enter field. Increased emphasis on this company's public image, i.e., reliable service, modern equipment, "value for your dollar."	Instabilities in the economy and body politic will deter the emergence of any major new competitors. Inflationary trends will be fought by higher productivity.

SOURCE: Reprinted with permission from Arnold Reisman, *Managerial and Engineering Economics*, Allyn and Bacon, Boston.

[13] Pill, *op. cit.*

[14] On the subjects of probability, statistics, and stochastic models, see W. Feller, *An Introduction to Probability Theory and Its Applications*, 3d ed., vol. 1, Wiley, New York, 1963; J. E. Freund, *Mathematical Statistics*, Prentice-Hall, Englewood Cliffs, N.J., 1962; P. L. Meyer, *Introductory Probability and Statistical Applications*, Addison-Wesley, Reading, Mass., 1965; A. M. Mood and F. A. Graybell, *Introduction to the Theory of Statistics*, 2d ed., McGraw-Hill, New York, 1963; and E. Parzan, *Modern Probability Theory and Its Applications*, Wiley, New York, 1960.

[15] The example given here is to show the use of the methodology. A requisite factor is that the states be exhaustive. More than two states become cumbersome for treatment in an overview discussion. If one utilizes the Delphi method, one can easily get a number for the states of nature greater than two, together with probability estimates for them.

Under each state of nature several alternatives are open to the decision maker. Every one of these alternatives may be evaluated on several different criteria—each criterion being as independent of the others as possible. As a result, the overall effectiveness of a given alternative may be measured by an expression called the *criterion function* or the *objective function*. The criterion function, CF, is the sum of the individual effects of each of the criteria K_x, each weighted or proportioned with respect to its relative importance by the weighting coefficients W_x, i.e.,

$$CF = \sum_{x=1}^{a} W_x K_x$$

where W_x = weighting coefficient, measuring relative importances
    K_x = criterion variable, as a system function or parameter

Often the situation arises where the criteria are not all of the same unit of measurement (e.g., cost, throughput capability, staff training needs, hardware configuration, and documentation availability might be some of the criteria used to evaluate or select a computer). To force the various terms of the objective or criterion functions to have the same dimensions, e.g., money or "Brownie points," and to safeguard against certain criteria overpowering others in sheer order of magnitude, it is necessary to calculate a unit conversion factor, F_x, equal to the average value of K for a specific criterion chosen for this purpose, divided by the average[16] of K_x for the criterion in question. The formula for obtaining F_x, in the case where it is desired to convert all terms of the equation to the units of the first criterion, is

$$F_x = \overline{K}_1 / \overline{K}_x$$

Thus,

$$CF = \sum_{x=1}^{a} F_x W_x K_x$$

Now when there exists more than one state of nature, the probability of each state of nature may be included in the criterion function for, say, the yth alternative, given

$$CF_{yz} = \text{criterion for the } y\text{th alternative} = \sum_{z=1}^{a} P(N_z) CF_{yz}$$

where a = the number of states of nature
    $P(N_z)$ = probability of the zth state of nature
    CF_{yz} = criterion for the yth alternative under the zth state of nature

However, in view of the fact that there are multiple states of nature, multiple decision alternatives, and multiple criteria, the introduction of triple subscripts on certain variables is necessary. Thus K_{xyz} represents the xth criterion for the yth decision alternative for the zth state of nature. (Numerical examples of the development and use of these factors are given in the Reisman reference.)

UTILITY

Although the criterion function offers a composite "measure of goodness" for all the criteria relative to each other, it does not explicitly relate achievement on any given criterion to the objectives of the individual, the organization, or the project. This needed measure, for the purposes of this Chapter, is referred to as *utility* and is measured in *utiles*. If one were to select a criterion such as wealth (y) and graph it against utility (u), a resulting typical relationship $u = f(y)$ would be nonlinear and may look like Figure 1-4, wherein the utility function shows an aversion to risk and insensitivity to increments of large amounts of wealth. The way such a curve is drawn will differ from individual to individual. As a matter of fact, it will shift from stage to stage within one individual's lifetime as

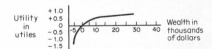

Fig. 1-4 Utility function showing aversion to risk and insensitivity to increments of large amounts of wealth.

[16] Given a range of values of a particular K_x, say, 30,000 to 50,000, the $\overline{K}$ is the arithmetic average of the extremes, namely $(30,000 + 50,000)/2 = 40,000$.

preferences change with time. However, at a particular point in time the utility curve will exist, and the Delphi method may be used to generate it.

Example[17] Consider the situation where $10,000 is available for investment, and three alternative investment decisions A_1, A_2, and A_3 are considered. Three possible conditions of the market (states of nature) N_1, N_2, and N_3 are anticipated (N_1 = continuation of present trends, N_2 = inflation, N_3 = depression). Analysis of each investment decision under each market condition yields the following results.[18]

Alternative 1 (A_1) (Invest $10,000)
   Receive original investment plus $10,000 if N_1 occurs.
   Receive original investment plus $15,000 if N_2 occurs.
   Lose original investment and $5,000 more if N_3 occurs.
Alternative 2 (A_2) (Invest $5,000 and keep $5,000)
   Lose original $5,000 and $5,000 more if N_1 occurs.
   Receive original investment if N_2 occurs.
   Receive original investment plus $5,000 if N_3 occurs.
Alternative 3 (A_3) (Invest $10,000)
   Receive original investment if N_1 occurs.
   Lose original investment if N_2 occurs.
   Receive original investment plus $5,000 if N_3 occurs.

Probability estimates for market conditions are available as follows:
   $P(N_1) = .3$
   $P(N_2) = .2$
   $P(N_3) = .5$

The information so far is summarized in Table 1-2.

TABLE 1-2 Present Worth of Investments at Each of Three Market Conditions

	N_1 $P(N_1) = .3$	N_2 $P(N_2) = .2$	N_3 $P(N_3) = .5$
A_1	$20,000	$25,000	$-5,000
A_2	0	10,000	15,000
A_3	10,000	0	15,000
A_4	10,000	10,000	10,000

Note that the alternative not to invest in any of the three alternatives, but to keep the money, is of course open (i.e., A_4).

A criterion function of expected worth can be computed as follows:
   $EP_1 = .3(\$20,000) + .2(\$25,000) + .5(-\$5,000) = \$8,500$
   $EP_2 = .3(0) + .2(\$10,000) + .5(\$15,000) = \$9,500$
   $EP_3 = .3(\$10,000) + .2(0) + .5(\$15,000) = \$10,500$
   $EP_4 = \$10,000$

Looking at the above, the best alternative is A_3, i.e., the expected worths (EPs) represent utilities in terms of dollars. Suppose, however, that there exists a relationship between the money or wealth and its value to the investor, e.g., it is the investor's life's savings and thus losing any part of it is highly undesirable. It is possible to construct a utility curve defining this relationship between the amount of wealth and its value using methods defined in the Reisman reference. By using the utility function defined in Figure 1-4, Table 1-2 may be converted to Table 1-3.

The expected utility may now be compared to identify the best alternatives.

The best alternative is now A_4, since none of the candidate investments is as good as keeping the initial $10,000. This result, as well as the very poor showing of A_1, emphasizes a significant characteristic of the application of the utility concept, namely that

---

[17] Melvin Lifson, *Applications of Criteria and Measures of Value in Engineering Decision*, Hughes Aircraft Co., TM-818, May, 1965.

[18] The discussion here is to illustrate decision making under uncertainty. The dollar figures could be absolute numbers or the discounted equivalents. The expected values do not differ greatly in magnitude; however, the outcomes are vastly different. The nearness of the expected values is fortuitous because of the numbers used.

attitudes toward risk are automatically incorporated into the value of alternatives by introducing the utility idea.

Decision Trees Another method of evaluating alternative courses of action is that of *decision trees*. This method commences at a trunk decision point and from it spring branches, each portraying a different decision. Each of these branches in turn grows additional branches, and this process continues until all avenues of decision are exhausted. Figure 1-5 is an example from an inventory stockout situation.[19]

TABLE 1-3 Utility of Investments at Each of Three Market Conditions

	N_1 $P(N_1) = .3$	N_2 $P(N_2) = .2$	N_3 $P(N_3) = .5$
A_1	.960	.982	−1.24
A_2	0	.800	.911
A_3	.800	0	.911
A_4	.80	.80	.80

$U_1 = .3(.960) + .2(.982) − .5(1.24) = −.14$
$U_2 = .3(0) + .2(.800) + .5(.911) = +.62$
$U_3 = .3(.800) + .2(0) + .5(.911) = +.70$
$U_4 = .3(0) + .2(.80) + .5(.80) = .80$

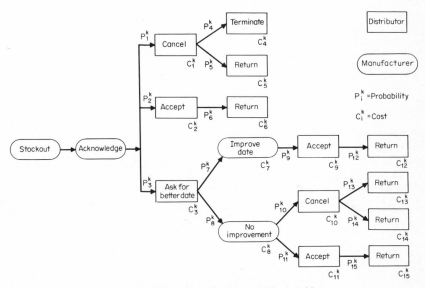

Fig. 1-5 Decision tree for inventory stockout problem.

Suppose an order is met by a stockout condition at the factory warehouse. The manufacturer sends an acknowledgment to the distributor and indicates an expected (belated) delivery date. There are three possible courses of action the distributor can take:

1. Cancel this particular order immediately since the delivery date is far beyond the expectation.

2. Accept the delivery date in the acknowledgement and tolerate the stated delay.

3. Ask for a better delivery date from the manufacturer.

In case one, after the distributor cancels the order with the manufacturer, there are two possible courses of action available to the distributor:

a. Terminate business with the manufacturer for this item only.

b. Return to the manufacturer for the next order of this item.

[19] Arnold Reisman, Burton Dean, Michael Salvador, and Muhitten Oral, *Industrial Inventory Control*, Gordon & Breach, New York, 1971.

In case two, the distributor continues doing business with the manufacturer as usual.

In case three, the distributor requests an expedited delivery from the manufacturer. Then, depending on the production schedule and backlog, the manufacturer is either able to give an improved date or is forced to deny the request. If satisfied with the improved date, the distributor accepts it and continues business as usual. If not, the distributor either cancels the order with the manufacturer or accepts it. If the order is canceled, alternatives *a* and *b* above prevail.

OPTIMIZATION AND MATHEMATICAL PROGRAMMING

As mentioned earlier, an objective or criterion function is often utilized to effect the "best" or "optimum" course of action among several competing alternatives. A major factor influencing the selection of a solution procedure is the determination of whether the objective function has constraints associated with it.

Unconstrained Optimization If the objective function is continuous, has no constraints imposed upon it, and depends only on the value of one variable for its determination, then the simplest case prevails, and classical optimization may be utilized to determine optimum value.

From calculus it is known that for differentiable functions of a single variable, a necessary condition for a particular value of x, say $\bar{x}$, to be a minimum or a maxmum is that $df(x)/dx = 0$ at $x = \bar{x}$. However, the decision as to which of the two alternatives it is requires the evaluation of the second derivative at that point. If $d^2f(x)/dx^2 > 0$ at $x = \bar{x}$, this implies that $\bar{x}$ is a minimum, but if $d^2f(x)/dx^2 < 0$ at $x = \bar{x}$, this implies $\bar{x}$ is a maximum. Note that no reference has been made to whether or not these critical points are local optima or global optima. However, if the function is convex[20] and $df(x)/dx = 0$, then any local optimum is the global optimum, in this case the minimum. Similarly, if $f(x)$ is concave,[21] then $f'(x) = 0$ at $x = \bar{x}$ implies that $\bar{x}$ is the global maximum.

Therefore, to find a maximum or a minimum of a function of several, say N, variables, a necessary condition is that

$$\frac{\partial f(x_1, x_2, \ldots, X_n)}{\partial x_j} = 0 \qquad \text{at } (x_1, x_2, \ldots, x_n) = (\bar{x}_1, \bar{x}_2, \ldots, \bar{x}_n) \qquad \text{for } j = 1, 2, \ldots, N$$

When the objective function is continuous, depends on many variables, and is subject to constraints, a closer examination of other systems attributes is required to effect the choice of an appropriate solution technique—for example, to determine whether the objective function and constraints are all linear. If they are, the problem may lend itself for solution by the technique of linear programming.

Constrained Optimization—Linear Programming Linear programming produces a solution to the problem of allocating scarce resources. A large user of linear programming is the petroleum industry. Crude oil is sent to a refinery to effect the production of a variety of products. Each of these products has associated with it production requirements, profitability contribution, selling price, and market demand. Also, whenever a particular product is produced, other products are generated along with it as an outcome of the production process. The linear program technique solves the problem of crude oil allocation among refineries and the generation of the optimum total production schedule within each refinery.

Another application area of linear programming is the blending problem, of which the diet problem in food processing is one in particular. The objective here is to determine the amounts of certain foods which should be combined to effect certain nutritional requirements at a minimum cost.

In the general case, assume the existence of N independent activities, with activity j having a unit profit of C_j. Also, let there be M different resources available, with resource i having available a total amount of b_i units to be allocated across the N activities. Let A_{ij} be the amount of resource i used by a unit of activity j. If x_{ij} is the number of units of resource i allocated to activity j, then the objective is to find the optimal

[20] A function $f(x)$ is convex if $f(\theta x^1 + (1 - \theta)x^2) \leq \theta f(x^1) + (1 - \theta)f(x)^2$ for any θ, $0 \leq \theta \leq 1$.
[21] If $f(x)$ is convex, then $-f(x)$ is concave.

allocation of the resources to the competing activities to effect the maximization of a function Z equal to

$$\sum_{j=1}^{N} C_j X_j$$

Thus algebraically, maximize

$$Z = C_1 X_1 + C_2 X_2 \cdots + C_N X_N$$

subject to the constraints

$$A_{11} X_1 + A_{12} X_2 \cdots + A_{1N} X_N \leq b_1$$
$$\cdot \qquad \cdot \qquad \qquad \cdot \qquad \cdot$$
$$\cdot \qquad \cdot \qquad \qquad \cdot \qquad \cdot$$
$$\cdot \qquad \cdot \qquad \qquad \cdot \qquad \cdot$$
$$A_{M1} X_1 + A_{M2} X_2 \cdots + A_{MN} X_N \leq b_M$$

where $x_j \geq 0$ for any activity j.

Linear programming has had wide success in solving many diverse problems. In addition to the blending and processing applications mentioned are problems in personnel assignment, scheduling, and inventory planning. The most widely utilized solution method is known as the *Simplex* method. It consists of a number of iterations, where at each such iteration the value of the objective function Z increases.[22] The method converges to an optimum solution in a finite number of iterations. One factor contributing to the wide acceptance of the method at this date is the availability of relatively sophisticated computer (including time-sharing) routines for the solution of linear programming.

Transportation Problem   Although still a linear program, the transportation problem has a structure of its own and as such is treated separately. The problem is formulated as follows:

Suppose that N warehouses are supplied by M factories. The ith $(i = 1, \ldots M)$ factory produces a_i units and the jth $(j = 1, \ldots, N)$ warehouse requires b_j units. If the cost of shipping from factory i to warehouse j (C_{ij}) is directly proportional to the amount shipped (x_{ij}), then what shipping pattern minimizes the transportation costs? Thus, minimize

$$Z = \sum_i \sum_j C_{ij} X_{ij}$$

subject to

$$\sum_i X_{ij} = b_j \qquad i = 1, \ldots, M$$

$$\sum_j X_{ij} = a_i \qquad j = 1, \ldots, N$$

$$X_{ij} \geq 0 \text{ for all } i, j$$

Specialized linear programming computer programs are available to effect the solution to this problem, as, for example, in Dantzig and in Hillier and Lieberman.

Assignment Problem   The assignment problem is a special case of the transportation problem. If in the transportation problem $M = N$ and $a_i = b_j = 1$, for all i and j, then we have the assignment problem. Thus each "source" is assigned a unique destination, and the problem consists of finding how to determine the minimal cost structure. This problem has been found to be very helpful in allocating or assigning personnel to jobs, tasks to machines, etc.

CONCLUDING REMARKS

As mentioned previously, the solution technique adopted must be construed as a means to an end, the end being improved and implementable decision rules. The operations

[22] The special case where Z does not increase but remains constant is called the *degenerate case*. For further elaboration on this point, refer to G. B. Dantzig, *Linear Programming and Exteriors*, Princeton University Press, Princeton, N.J., 1963, and Michel Simmonard, *Linear Programming*, Prentice-Hall, Englewood Cliffs, N.J., 1969.

research project or system study should be structured so as to maximize the probability of success during the implementation phase. To effect this, implementation must be kept in mind during the organization of the project team and when the design of the project is developed, as well as during the entire course of the study. There are four dimensions of project success: (1) technological success, i.e., the project has met technical specifications and objectives; (2) timeliness, i.e., the project was completed on time; (3) budgetary success, i.e., the study stayed within the budget; and (4) political success, i.e., the study results were implemented.[23]

There are certain criteria which must be met in order to effect success along all the above four dimensions. The key fact is simply that unless line management and management at the highest possible levels are intimately involved throughout the course of the study, the probability of success rapidly decreases. Specifically, the manager and the operations research analyst must learn to work together, learn each other's language, problems, methods, etc. This keeps the analysts honest and line managers knowledgeable. Also, top management should receive progress reports for review, evaluation, and feedback on a regular basis. This has the effect of transferring "ownership" of the solution directly where it belongs, to the line management, as well as assuring that the task of one is not led astray and/or sabotaged by people in possession of information and/or data.

Another factor contributing to success is the trade-off between an aggregate approach vs. a detailed approach to the problem. Experience indicates that one should err during the early phases of the study on the side of detail or descriptiveness. However, during the latter phases of the study it is often necessary to aggregate variables, parameters, or even processes to make the methods manageable and therefore implementable.

A third factor for success is initially to document the problem or system either by discourse or verbal documentation, by graphical descriptions (e.g., process charts, flow diagrams, block diagrams, etc.), and/or by symbolic and algebraic relations describing the decision rules used. This aids the operations research analyst in achieving an understanding of the functional relationships between problem subsystems as well as involving the line managers very early in the course of the study.

By using the techniques and methodologies indicated in this Chapter, one may approach problem solving relying upon much more than intuition and subjecting a problem to much critical analysis. Understanding of the basic interrelationships of the processes is gained which effects a much more comprehensive view of the situation at hand.

BIBLIOGRAPHY

Ackoff, R., E. L. Arnoff, and C. W. Churchman, *Introduction to Operations Research*, Wiley, New York, 1956.

———, and M. Sasieni, *Fundamentals of Operations Research*, Wiley, New York, 1968.

Bellman, R., and S. Dreyfus, *Applied Dynamic Programming*, Princeton University Press, Princeton, N.J., 1962.

Dantzig, G. B., *Linear Programming and Exteriors*, Princeton University Press, Princeton, N.J., 1963.

Dreyfus, S., "An Appraisal of Some Shortest Path Algorithms," *Journal of the Operations Research Society of America*, 1969.

Emshoff, James R., and Roger L. Sisson, *Design and Use of Computer Simulation Models*, Macmillan, New York, 1970.

Feller, W., *An Introduction to Probability Theory and Its Applications*, 3d ed., vol. 1, Wiley, New York, 1963.

Fleischer, Gerald, *Capital Allocation Theory: The Study of Investment Decisions*, Appleton-Century-Crofts, New York, 1969.

Freund, J. E., *Mathematical Statistics*, Prentice-Hall, Englewood Cliffs, N.J., 1962.

Grant, Eugene L., *Principles of Engineering Economy*, Ronald, New York, 1960.

Hadley, G., and T. Whitin, *Analysis of Inventory Systems*, Prentice-Hall, Englewood Cliffs, N.J., 1963.

---

[23] A. Reisman and C. A. de Kluyver, "Implementation and Evaluation of Systems Studies," *Proceedings of the International Symposium on Systems Engineering and Analysis*, volume I, Purdue University, October, 1972.

Helmer, Olaf, *Convergence of Expert Concensus through Feedback*, The Rand Corporation, Santa Monica, Calif., 1964, p. 2973.

Hillier, Frederick S., and Gerald J. Lieberman, *Introduction to Operations Research*, Holden-Day, San Francisco, 1968.

Meyer, P. L., *Introductory Probability and Statistical Applications*, Addison-Wesley, Reading, Mass., 1965.

Miller, David W., and Martin R. Starr, *Executive Decisions and Operations Research*, Prentice-Hall, Englewood Cliffs, N.J., 1969.

Mood, A. M., and F. A. Graybell, *Introduction to the Theory of Statistics*, 2d ed., McGraw-Hill, New York, 1963.

Parzan, E., *Modern Probability Theory and Its Applications*, Wiley, New York, 1960.

Pill, Juri, "The Delphi Method: Substance, Context, A Critique and an Annotated Bibliography," *Socio-Economic Planning Sciences*, 1971.

Reisman, Arnold, *Managerial and Engineering Economics*, Allyn and Bacon, Boston, 1971.

Simmonard, Michel, *Linear Programming*, Prentice-Hall, Englewood Cliffs, N.J., 1969.

Wagner, H., *Principles of Operations Research*, Prentice-Hall, Englewood Cliffs, N.J., 1969.

Chapter 2

ADP in Engineering, Design, and Project Management

LEE F. HAYNES

Director, Management Information Services—Corporate,
The B. F. Goodrich Company, Akron, Ohio

This Chapter addresses the engineering and scientific aspects of automatic data processing. Rather than attempting to give an in-depth treatment, the approach is to make the reader cognizant of some of the major facets of the subject. Attention is then directed to available materials which address the subject in detail for those who wish to pursue a particular subject-branch in depth.

Scientific computing, as we know it today, was born in the mid-1940s with the development of the ENIAC computer at the University of Pennsylvania. Shortly thereafter, the ILLIAC computer was developed at the University of Illinois. Thus it may be stated that programmable computing equipment was developed in the university environment, and its first application was in the scientific area.

As indicated in earlier Chapters of this Handbook, computer hardware has evolved through three generations of technology. The first (1954) was the vacuum tube; the second (1958) was the advent of the transistor (solid state) and core memories; the third generation was announced in 1965 with integrated printed circuitry, faster peripherals, and cheaper direct-access storage. The emphasis has been to improve reliability, speeds, and the cost-effectiveness ratio.

Human ingenuity and imagination have thus far only scratched the surface as regards computer use for practical solutions to problems. Technology has progressed more in the years since World War II than in the combined total of the previous 1945 years. The computer has played no small part in these advances. A good example is the United States space program, which could not possibly have progressed to its current state without computer-aided engineering.

In order for large numbers of engineers and scientists to be able to use the computer as a tool, certain aids had to be designed that would allow them to communicate with the computer without becoming "computer experts." High-level languages were developed for this purpose: the American version goes by the acronym FORTRAN (formula translation), and the European version is called ALGOL (algorithmic language). FORTRAN has emerged as the more widely used of the two languages. Both languages have an algebraic notation and are relatively easy for the engineer to learn and use.[1]

[1] See Section 2, Part Four, Chapter 3, "Programming Languages."

Since all computing hardware is designed and maintained by engineers, it is appropriate to take a look at some of the uses engineers have made of their creation. To this end, this Chapter is divided into two sections. The first addresses engineering and design, and the second discusses project management.

ENGINEERING AND DESIGN

Graphics Display   Interactive graphics display terminals have been available to the industrial community since the mid-1960s. These devices must be considered as "top of the line" for computer video terminals. (The "interactive" portion of the name is appropriately derived from the interaction of the human being and the computing hardware.) The type of display discussed here has a screen size approximately that of a 21-inch television receiver. Many of the newer screens are also in the 10- and 12-inch range.

There are various ways of inputting commands to modify or produce graphics displays on the screen: alphanumeric keyboard, function keys, light pen, and tablets. These devices are discussed in greater detail later on in this Section.

The advantages of graphics display are being discovered in many application areas, e.g., architecture, hospital information systems, animated films, financial analysis,

TABLE 2-1   Time Comparisons: Graphics Display and Batch Processing

	Batch	Graphics
Structure design	2 weeks	0.5 days
Printed circuit	2 weeks	1 day
Maintenance drawings	10 hours	1 hour
Tire design	5 weeks	2 days

computer-aided instruction, and others. However, design engineers have been the major users of this technology to date, and if we concentrate on design engineering, we can readily see the significant use categories and benefits.

Some of the advantages of a graphics display system are:

1. The improved design made possible by it will lower start-up and production costs.

2. It allows more "cut and try" iterations in a shorter time span.

3. Repeatability is excellent, and modifications to existing designs are made rapidly.

4. Effective reductions in direct design labor, in orders of magnitude of from five to ten, are routinely achieved.

Use can be placed into three categories, as follows:

1. Computation: e.g., stress analysis and heat flow.

2. Geometry: e.g., printed circuit boards, integrated circuits, tire design, numerical control, and piping.

3. Drafting: e.g., block diagrams, flow charts, and engineering drawings.

Referring to some of the above categories we can apply typical time savings in the design cycle, utilizing graphics as opposed to a batch computing process, as shown in Table 2-1.

The indicated ratios may at first glance seem astonishing; however, the user must remember that *total* design or process cycle will not be reduced by these ratios. Instead, the ratios should be applied only to the portions of the cycle that are directly related.

A typical graphics display has an invisible (to the human eye) but computer-recognizable point grid on the face of the screen, consisting of 1,024 points in both the X and Y coordinates. This obviously produces a matrix in excess of a million points. All these points may be used in the display output; however, a light pen usually has a resolution only to 70 mills, and therefore approximately 170 thousand of these points can be properly detected for input. The light pen is a portable device that senses the presence of light from the screen at a specific X,Y coordinate. The technical explanation is that the light pen receives an input from the screen and in turn relays the coordinate data to the computing circuitry. Hence the light pen is not an input to the screen, but conversely is an output. In order for the foregoing to occur, the supporting software must be expecting an input, and the light must be activated. The design engineer activates the light either by pressing the tip against the screen, or operating a switch on the side of the pen, depending upon the pen manufacturer's design.

The design engineer, graphics console, light pen, keyboard, and supporting software system work in concert for rapid response in displaying and storing selected data at the direction of the user. Software is an important element that must not be overlooked for this type of terminal. Also a good database management system must be employed to store the selected arrays of data to support the visual display. This same data may be "dumped" to a hard-copy device for approvals and retention.

Figure 2-1 illustrates a graphics display console that would be connected to a computer. The screen shows a portion of a tire tread with a *menu* for line, circle, and point.

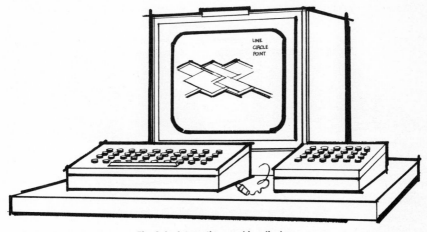

Fig. 2-1   Interactive graphics display.

A menu is a list of options available to the user. The list is generated by the software programs supporting the graphics displays. The options shown in Figure 2-1 are basically asking the engineer what geometric function he or she desires to construct, i.e., line, circle, or point. The light pen lying on the console is used to select one of these geometric functions by, for example, putting the light pen next to "LINE" and activating the pen. The system now knows that a line is to be constructed and will take the next two inputs as the coordinates for the beginning and ending of the line, which then appears on the screen.

The smaller keyboard on the right contains *function keys*. These can be used to complement the menu displayed on the screen or in themselves to set the functions to be performed. Their use depends entirely on the software design of the system, which determines how the user will be allowed to input requests. Numerous functions must be performed, of which a simple example is erase. With respect to the construction of a line previously described, if the engineer had made a mistake, or desired to make a modification, he or she could have depressed an erase function key and then used the light pen to indicate specifically where to erase.

The alphanumeric keyboard located on the left side in Figure 2-1 is used as an input device. Again there is a tremendous amount of flexibility in the method of constructing the supporting software. The alphanumeric keyboard is primarily used to converse with the software system. For example, the user may wish to have a specific section of Tire Tread Drawing No. 187605 displayed on the screen. He or she would input this specific data through the alphanumeric keyboard. The system would then search the library for this drawing number, take the data contained therein, if necessary, convert it to X and Y coordinates, and display Drawing No. 187605 on the screen.

This could be either a completed drawing which the user wishes to modify or a partially complete one which the user wishes to continue working on.

A capsule summary of the process described allows the user to:

1. Maintain a library of partially or completed drawings which can be displayed, and if desirable modified.

2. Construct new designs and enter them into the library.

3. Have the ability to perform desired computation on the design data.

4. Cause this data to be outputted to hard-copy devices applying desired scaling factors.

Computer graphics can be fairly expensive, and a thorough cost-effectiveness study should be performed prior to installation. However, where such justification investigations have been made, these devices have been extremely rewarding.

Automatic Drafting Machines These devices have been essential tools in engineering for many years. The basic concept is to produce good quality output on the devices to be discussed, from various types of inputs. The inputs to automatic drafting machines will probably be derived from complex computation on data in a batch mode.

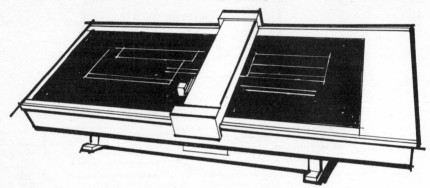

Fig. 2-2 Automatic drafting machine (flat-bed plotter).

The engineer will have supplied the proper parameters and/or data to a program that in turn generates the output to be used as input for automatic drafting. The input will be X and Y coordinates plus device commands, i.e., pen up, pen down, and the like. The output is usually a two-dimensional drawing produced by one or more pens or printed (by dot matrix) on electrostatic plotters.

Many types of devices are included in the automated drafting category. The devices discussed here are activated by a control hardware unit that may be directly connected to a computer or run as a stand-alone or off-line peripheral. The off-line mode will utilize computer-generated data in the form of magnetic tapes, paper tapes, punched cards, etc., as the input media for data and device commands.

Flat-bed plotters of various table sizes, of the type illustrated in Figure 2-2, may be equipped with various output devices, such as:

● One or more pens (ink, felt tip, and ball point) in a program-selectable turret for hard-copy drawing.

● Photo-exposure heads used on light-sensitive material. A turret is again used to select a number of predefined geometric shapes, including various sizes of lines, squares, rectangles, triangles, etc. Selections of these geometric figures, placement on the film, and aperture opening and closing are input data to the plotter. A good example is the precision artwork for printed circuit boards in the electronics industry. The light-sensitive material (film) is then used as a master in the process of setting up the production for the accurate metallic etching of these boards. Accuracy is ±0.002 inches, with repeatability in the ±0.0005-inch range.

● Pattern cutting heads that are used for cutting geometric shapes from pattern material mounted on the drafting table surface. This enables garment manufacturers, for example, to cut, very precisely, many patterns at the same time by using multilayers of material.

The foregoing do not include all the accessories available, but should give the reader an idea of the flexibility of plotters. The pens are the most commonly used devices.

Drum plotters, as illustrated in Figure 2-3, achieve less accuracy than their flat-bed counterparts. A typical use would produce accuracy in the ±0.010-inch range, with repeatability ±0.005 inches. They do operate at a much faster speed (1,200 to 1,600 inches per minute), are less expensive, and in some applications will produce the desired final product. When more accuracy is required, the drum plotter may be used to produce check drawings until the desired result is attained, and then the data are plotted on the slower, more accurate flat-bed.

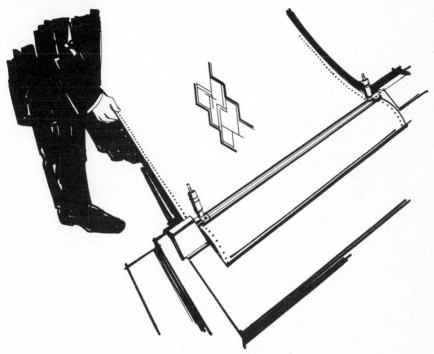

Fig. 2-3   Automatic drafting machine (drum plotter).

Drum plotters are designed to hold a roll of pin-feed paper in excess of 100 feet. Movement along the X axis is accomplished by moving the roll forward and backward. The Y axis is attained by the pen movement across the surface of the paper in a fixed plane.

Electrostatic plotters utilize electrosensitive paper for very high speed output. Speed in this case must encompass the time required for the entire drawing, as opposed to the physical movement of drawing a single line vector with the previously described plotters. A typical example would be to complete an 11- by 10-inch matrix in one second.

The technical concept is to have a writing head composed of several hundred bits or styli. The bits would be equally spaced, 100 to the inch. It can readily be seen that the best resolution would then be 0.010 inches. As the paper moves forward, the entire writing head is conditioned (on or off) from the input, and transferred to the electrosensitive paper for purposes of passing through a toner which will cause the paper to retain the charge and hence the graphic output.

The setting of the matrix or matrices for larger drawings is a function of the supporting software. Character generators are available as optional hardware if alphanumeric data are to be printed. This same function can be performed by additional software. A character, whether hardware or software generated, can be scaled to any reasonable reading size. For example, a 5(X) by 7(Y) character would produce a character 0.05 inch wide and 0.07 inch high. In order to print total characters of this size one would then need to print seven lines of "dots." Some manufacturers may attempt to dazzle a prospective user with "lines per minute" in the 50,000 range. One should remember that for graphical and/or alphanumeric data, they are really referring to a line equal to one-hundredth of an inch in the Y plane.

As can be seen, many types of automatic drafting devices are available. The correlation between speed, accuracy, and cost can generally be stated by placing high speed and less accuracy on the lower end of the cost spectrum, and slower speed but greater accuracy on the other end of the spectrum. An example of this would be an electrostatic plotter on one end and a flat-bed plotter with a photohead attachment on the other end of the spectrum. The electrostatic plotter is characterized by high-speed output over the entire X,Y coordinate area. It does not require the accuracy of the photohead device, but it is also of considerably less cost. The user must decide which of these parameters is the most important for the particular application, and secure the drawing device accordingly.

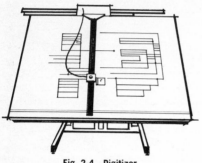

Fig. 2-4 Digitizer.

Digitizers The foregoing has discussed device uses where machine-sensible data are to be transferred to a hard-copy print via various automatic techniques. Let us now consider the situation where there is just the opposite circumstance: hard-copy data are to be converted to machine-sensible form. For this application a *digitizer* is used. The digitizer illustrated in Figure 2-4 is manually operated[2] by moving the cursor over a drawing in pseudotracing fashion and, on operator command, producing X and Y coordinate data. Draftsman-type drawings as well as freehand sketches may be used in developing the input.

In the digitizing process we must determine what resolution is required in the machine-sensible output. For example, we could have an architectural drawing that can properly be represented by 12 points per inch. The criteria would be the turn points and lines needed. However, detailed drawings might require as many as 50 or 100 points per inch. The determination of the proper X and Y coordinates (grid) to be used can readily be made by taking a small square area of the drawing that has the greatest density in lines and turn points, and:

1. Drawing enough equidistant horizontal lines to intersect all turn points and straight lines encountered along the X coordinate direction.

2. Drawing equidistant vertical lines that intersect all turn points and straight lines encountered along the Y coordinate direction.

3. Applying this grid to other sections of the drawing to ensure proper evaluation of the drawing.

4. Taking the maximum number of equidistant lines obtained in steps 1, 2, and 3, and using this in determining what point grid is to be used.

There are other ways to arrive at the proper grid to use, depending upon the expertise of the user.

The desired grid is set up in the digitizer electronics, and the hard copy is placed on the working table and properly aligned with indicators known as *bull's-eyes*. When the cursor is moved to a grid point, a light indicator will notify the operator. The operator must perform two things at each point via keys: (1) indicate that this point is to be input, and (2) indicate the function, i.e., begin, end, turn, etc.

In order to see in detail the motions of the operator, refer to Figure 2-5. We have a line drawn from points A to F, with turns at points B, C, D, and E. The step-by-step process would then be as shown in the listing beneath the drawing. The digitizer will properly determine if a turn is to be in the X or Y direction.

---

[2] There are also automatic digitizers that employ an automatic line follower which performs the same functions as the operator.

While the illustration shows only turns of 90° angles, all angles that fit the grid points may be used. For example, in a grid of 10 points per inch (0.010 grid), given that any two points may be connected, each angle from 0° to 360° may be approximated with a high degree of resolution. Thus, referring to Figure 2-5, if we connect the points as shown in Figure 2-6, we can approximate the angles indicated.

Some applications that are well suited to a digitizing process are:

• Drawings to be put into machine-sensible form for purposes of:

1. Making the drawings appear on an interactive graphics display for modification and then for automatically plotting the new drawing.

2. Transmitting the drawing in the form of digitized data to distant locations, for plotting there in the form of hard copy or of visual display on graphics equipment.

3. Taking engineering drawings from one measuring system to another, e.g., English to metric. Computation would be applied to the input geometry to produce the new dimensional data which would then be placed on the new drawing, in addition to the geometry reproduced by the plotting device.

• Engineering areas that must produce quality drawings but do not have drafting artists. In this case, the engineer can sketch the drawing, possibly on grid paper. The engineer does not have to be concerned with straight lines, etc., but can concentrate instead on the beginning, ending, and turn points in the geometry.

• Any requirement for taking the graphics of a hard-copy drawing into a computing data environment.

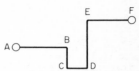

Step	Cursor location	Function
1.	A	Begin
2.	B	Turn
3.	C	Turn
4.	D	Turn
5.	E	Turn
6.	F	End

Fig. 2-5   Digitizer: Motions of operator.

PROJECT MANAGEMENT

While this Chapter is oriented toward engineering uses of ADP, the project management techniques described can readily be applied to all disciplines of management. Project management can best be described as a method by which management can (1) schedule a project and/or related subprojects based on the "best" estimates of time, assuming either fixed or unlimited resources, and apply appropriate cost

Point to point		Approximate angle
A	F	13°
A	E	22°
D	F	47°
C	E	67°

Fig. 2-6 Approximation of angles in digitizer application shown in Figure 2-5.

factors; (2) monitor the "actuals" against the "planned" and generate new project plans upon the occurrence of deviations.

The term *project* can best be described as an undertaking having all the following attributes:

1. A project is *finite* and has a defined end point.

2. A project is *complex*, with requirements for an involved mixture of serial and parallel work efforts.

3. A project is *homogeneous* in that all activities belong within the boundaries of a finite start and end date.

4. A project is generally *nonrepetitive* and viewed as a one-time effort.

The above four parameters of the definition of a project apply regardless of the magnitude.

There are many cases where a totally manual system of project management is highly appropriate and effective. A good manager will go through the "mental gymnastics" of outlining his or her project in the planning process, whether or not this is ever formalized into a manual or automated process. Again, even in a formalized automated process, a high degree of freedom is afforded the manager, based on his or her style of management and influenced by outside or other constraints.

When any formalized project management techniques are to be used, the management and personnel of other resources to be utilized should be involved in the planning process. Also, appropriate reporting and monitoring techniques must be employed to track the project.

There is no rigid set of guidelines as to the detail to be involved in the planning process; procedures will be greatly influenced by the management style of the responsible project manager. The most important requirement is that the project manager should feel "comfortable" with the detailed steps, so that he or she can effectively manage the resources based on established time schedules; and he or she should be able effectively to communicate the project requirements and current status to others.

Many automated techniques are utilized to schedule and monitor the progress of projects. The method employed will most probably be influenced by one or more of the following:

1. Complexity and interaction of many identifiable events.
2. Certain departments of the U.S. Federal Government sponsoring the project (mandatory).
3. Availability of computing software and hardware.
4. ADP departmental budget.

Many project management systems techniques are in use today. The following is a partial unordered list of some of these.[3]

DOD/NASA PERT Cost.
The techniques contained in USAF's and NASA's configuration management.
DOD's Cost Information Reporting System.
Line of Balance.
Multiproject Scheduling.
Resource Leveling.
Resource Scheduling.
Cost Estimating and Validation.
Decision Tree Planning and Risk Analysis.
Life Cycle Analysis.

Two of the most widely used project management systems are project evaluation and review technique (PERT), and critical path method (CPM).

In 1958 the Navy Special Projects Office recognized the need for a project management system that would be effective in a complex and large project. In collaboration with personnel from the management consulting firm of Booz, Allen and Hamilton and Lockheed Missile Systems Division, NSPO developed PERT. This system was first to be used in the Polaris missile program that involved in excess of 2,000 contractors. Its dramatic success in bringing the project to successful completion years ahead of schedule provided impetus to its acceptance as an excellent management tool.

CPM was developed in private industry at approximately this same time to meet a similar management need, by J. E. Kelly, then with Remington Rand, and M. R. Walter, then with E. I. DuPont.

The two systems are quite similar in their functional capabilities, since both rest on the basic concept of utilizing a network for a model of a project. There is naturally a terminology difference among users of the systems, e.g., a PERT *event* is analogous to a CPM *node*. However, over the years the system differences have all but disappeared, and most software systems, in relation to them, available to industry today are of a hybrid nature.

The initial version of PERT took only project time parameters into consideration, since time was the major consideration in the Polaris Missile Program. In 1962 the Department of Defense (DOD) and the National Aeronautics and Space Administration (NASA) published a PERT/cost procedure which was to become mandatory for large defense contracts. Hence today PERT time/cost processors are referred to quite frequently. Most of the major mainframe computer manufacturers have made software packages available to their users which will process PERT and/or CPM type scheduling networks.

The requirements and capabilities of project management systems have evolved to encompass time and then cost. Next came the need for resources. It is imperative to know if one has the proper resources to complete a project. This void, as far as com-

---

[3] List is from IBM PMS IV Manual No. GH20–0855–2.

puter scheduling was concerned, was previously filled by the manager's ability to ensure proper logistics of the resources.[4]

In 1967 IBM developed an additional software system named, appropriately enough, Project Management System (PMS). The initial versions of this system contained time and cost capabilities; with the advent of PMS II in 1969, resource allocation became a reality.

PMS Software   For purposes of illustration, the remainder of this Chapter will address only the PMS software system. The IBM Project Management System consists of the following major modules:

1. Network processor.
2. Cost processor.
3. Resource allocation processor.
4. Report processor.

The *network processor* is the basic feature of PMS, and is utilized for configuring the *time* parameters of the scheduling process. Some of the features of this processor are:

1. A maximum of 255 networks constitutes a project.
2. A network may contain up to 255 subnets.
3. A subnet may contain up to 32,000 activities.
4. Subnets may be interfaced with other subnets in the same network.
5. A variable calendar extends up to 15 years relative to current start time, and takes into consideration flexible holiday and vacation periods.
6. Subnets may have multiple start and end events.
7. A condensation of milestones and activities is provided for purposes of a summary overview.
8. One or three time estimates may be used and broken down into quarters, months, weeks, days, or hours; and additionally these may be expressed in whole or decimal units. The three time estimates are "optimistic," "pessimistic," and "most likely."

An extended version of the network processor is also available. The extended facilities will address the work in progress and deadlines, as well as work planned and work completed. Some of the major features are:

1. Ability to report on in-progress activities in terms of actual start, work done, and duration left or per cent complete.
2. Capability of specifying five types of schedule dates as:
    a. Descriptive only—no computational effect unless entered against an end event.
    b. No later than.
    c. No earlier than.
    d. Imposed—a combination of no earlier than and no later than, and hence a critical activity.
    e. Slack time—a date to initialize secondary late date calculations on predecessor activities.

The *cost processor* is designed to perform the computations usually required for project cost management, accounting, and control functions. The cost and network processors serve to tie the time and cost accomplishments into management objectives. Some salient features are:

1. An accounting calendar must be constructed to reflect the appropriate accounting system; it does *not* have to be the same as the one used in the network processor.
2. A chart of accounts and charge numbers must be established to be consistent with budgets and estimates, so that actuals may be properly recorded.
3. A rate table containing unit rates, overhead and burden rates, and adjustment factors for personnel or materials must be established for proper costing.
4. A company's organization chart may be used to provide the functional responsi-

---

[4] For details on PERT and CPM, the reader should consult the ample literature. Clear statements are to be found in Carl Heyel (ed.), *The Encyclopedia of Management*, 2d ed., Van Nostrand Reinhold, New York, 1973. With regard to available computer software for implementation, consult a computer marketing representative. This is essential because (1) some manufacturers did not develop software for both of these systems, and (2) the implementation will deviate somewhat in functional capabilities.

bilities and associated charges/cost, and again does not need to be consistent with the subdivisions made in the network processor.

The *resource allocation processor* will apply the proper resources for a network in the form of personnel, equipment, and materials. The overall criterion to be used is one of the following:

1. The project is to be finished by a specified time, hence extra resources will be added.

2. The resources are limited but the project is to be completed as soon as possible.

These two situations are known as *fixed time scheduling* and *fixed resource scheduling*, respectively. The method to be employed is at the option of the project manager. Some of the features of this processor are:

1. Up to 25 resources may be specified per activity with the maximum of 32,767 for a computer run.

2. Priorities may be established by activity, resources, subnets, or departments.

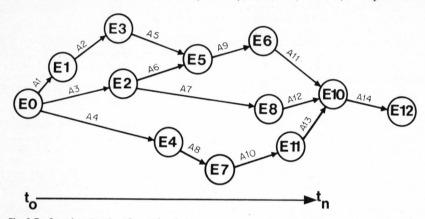

Fig. 2-7   Sample network. The circles designate *events*, i.e., the culminations of specific *activities* which are designated by the numbered arrows. The *critical path* is the path which entails the greatest lapse of time and/or greatest cost. No matter what is done in other activities, if nothing is done to improve this path, it will govern completion. (In PERT networks, probable time estimates are assigned to the activities, indicating "optimistic," "pessimistic," and "most likely.")

3. Resource "splitting" may be used if an activity may be stopped and restarted at a later date from the same point. Certain priorities could cause this to be feasible.

The *report processor* by definition must be used to output the results of the other processors. There are in excess of 30 reports, bar charts, graphs, and listings that may be produced at the user's option.

Network Analysis An example of a network is shown in Figure 2-7. In network analysis, activities are represented as lines, and events are represented as points in time. (In CPM networks, these are sometimes designated as *nodes*.) The duration of activities is expressed in work units which are completely arbitrary and may be chosen to represent days, shifts, months, etc. In the example depicted in Figure 2-7, Activity A4 begins at event E0 and terminates at event E4. Event E0 is considered the predecessor and event E4 the successor for the Activity A4.

All activities are constrained by their predecessors, and interdependencies between activities and subnetworks are expressed in several ways:

1. Any number of activities may originate from or terminate at the same event. Clearly Activity A12 may not begin until Activities A3 and A7 are complete.

2. Subnetworks may be interfaced, i.e., possess one or more events in common. Interfaced subnets may be processed and reported on independently or concurrently.

3. The concept of *slack time* or *float time* may also be introduced; e.g., if Activity A5 has a duration of six working units, and Activity A6 has a duration of five, and since both terminate at event E5, it is clear that Activity A6 might be started one work unit late without interrupting or delaying Activity A9.

As analysis of each activity proceeds through the network, consideration of the duration of each activity and its logical relationship to the rest of the network yields a completion date for the entire project.

For an in-depth understanding of the various options, statistical techniques, etc., of the PMS IV System, the reader is referred to the following IBM publications:

Network Processor	SH20-0899-1
Report Processor	SH20-0901-2
Resource Allocation Processor	SH20-0900-0
Cost Processor	SH20-0898-0

All these publications are *PMS IV Program Description and Operations* manuals for the above four processors.

Chapter 3

Computerized Information Storage and Retrieval

S. E. FURTH

**Retired; formerly Industry Consultant,
Information Systems Marketing,
International Business Machines Corporation,
White Plains, New York**

Management can effectively control its organization only if it is in possession of complete, accurate, and up-to-date information. Today, information is being generated at such a rate that the traditional systems can no longer provide the level of service necessary to alert the people who need to know of new information, or to provide them with prompt access to the documents they need in their work.

Information created within the organization may be in the form of:

- Project reports.
- Technical reports.
- Trip reports.
- Specifications.
- Bids and proposals.
- Drawings and blueprints.
- Patent records.

In addition, a large volume of information comes from outside the organization in the form of:

- Journal articles.
- Patents.
- Government reports.
- Laws.

Access to this literature may be facilitated by the numerous abstracting and index services which publish indexes on paper, microfilm, and magnetic tape.

In many organizations, managements have recognized the need for a formal system for information transfer and have established information centers or staffed their libraries to perform the functions of:

- Indexing and abstracting
- Selective dissemination of information
- Retrospective searching

With the constantly growing volume of information requiring the creation and maintenance of large files, one of the resources which should be provided is access to a

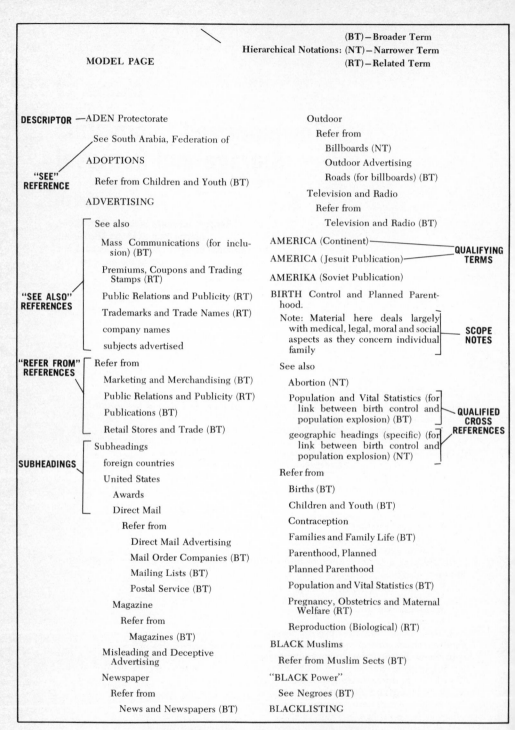

Fig. 3-1 Model page from *New York Times Thesaurus.*

computer. However, the decision to mechanize information retrieval functions should be preceded by a thorough systems analysis, with particular emphasis on the special requirements of the ultimate user. What the users want is to receive documents *relevant to their interest, when* they want them and *where* they want them.

Two approaches can be taken, and there are many options available in both: (1) the user can be provided with references to the documents and it becomes his or her responsibility to obtain the documents themselves; or (2) the full text of relevant documents can be provided by the system—that is, the text may be stored on magnetic tape, or magnetic disks, or on microfilm.

Systems that merely provide document references require only that the contents of the documents be represented by *index terms*, and possibly by an *abstract*. Index terms are assigned by indexers who may select them from the text of the documents, or *key words* may be selected automatically by the computer from document titles, abstracts, or the full text. The selection of index terms may be "uncontrolled" or may be in accordance with an *authority list*. An authority list can be a dictionary which will indicate to the indexer and later to the user of the system the preferred word form and spelling; or it can be a thesaurus which contains cross-references to or from other terms.

Computers are being used to create and maintain such authority lists. Their advantage lies in their ability to arrange and rearrange entries and check cross-references, and to print the lists as well as to store them for on-line use. Computer-prepared subject heading lists, thesauri, or dictionaries can be printed on a line printer in upper and lower case, or can be photocomposed from computer output. Figure 3-1 shows a model page from the *New York Times Thesaurus*, which is used in connection with the New York Times information retrieval procedures.

Thesauri have been compiled and are publicly available for many subject areas. In constructing a thesaurus, reference should be made to the American National Standard Institute's *Guidelines for Thesaurus Structure, Construction, and Use* (Z39.19–1974).

INDEXING AND ABSTRACTING

Manual or automatic methods can be used in preparing indexes to document collections. Manual indexing usually assumes the preparation of a work sheet for each document on which are entered the bibliographic elements such as author's name(s), title, source (journal name; department, book, or the like), and the index terms. Reference should be made to the *Standard Basic Criteria for Indexes*, published in 1968 by the American National Standards Institute (ANSI)(Z39.4–1968).

Where abstracts are to be included, they may be copied from the documents if they are included there and are considered adequate, or they may have to be written. ANSI has also published *Standards for Writing Abstracts* (Z39.14–1971).

Input of the indexing elements and abstracts into the computer can be accomplished by keyboarding the data off-line, that is, by punching cards, creating records on magnetic tape or cards; or the keyboarding can be on-line, that is, the indexer enters the information directly into the computer where it will be stored on direct-access storage devices, such as magnetic disks.

Automatic indexing requires that the information to be indexed be available in a form that can be processed by a computer. The simplest method to prepare an index by automatic means is the so-called *key-word-in-context* (KWIC), developed from document titles. The only steps necessary are:

1. Preparation of a bibliographic record for each title to be indexed, by keypunching a set of cards as illustrated in Figure 3-2.

2. Preparation of a list of *stop words*, i.e., words not to be used as index terms, such as THE, AND, WITH, etc. This list, usually 100 to 200 words long, is stored in the computer.

A program for use of the above consists of three parts: the KWIC index, the bibliography, and the author index. Such programs are available for most types of general-purpose computers.

In line with the above, the input to the KWIC program consists of several types of cards, each identified by a type code; e.g.:

- Author name.
- Title (frequently titles may have to be enriched by adding key words).

- Source.
- Abstract.

Each document is identified by a document number, which can be an existing number or one created for the KWIC index as follows:

- First four letters of the author's last name.
- Author's initials.
- Year of publication.
- Initials of the first three key words of the title.

The KWIC index part of the program using only the title cards will identify each word in the title (that is, each word not on the stop list) as a key word and automatically prepare an index entry for each word, sort all entries into alphabetical sequence, and print them as illustrated in Figure 3-3.

The bibliographic part of the program, using the complete sets of cards representing

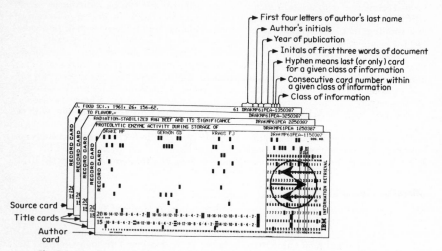

Fig. 3-2 Punched-card record for bibliographical entry shown in Figures 3-3 and 3-4.

the documents to be indexed, sorts the cards into document number sequence as illustrated in Figure 3-4.

It should be noted that because of the structure of document numbers discussed above, all articles by the same author will be shown together. For each author they will be arranged chronologically by year of publication, and within each year by title in alphabetic order. This is particularly useful when it is desired to produce cumulative indexes.

Finally, the author index is prepared by alphabetizing the author cards, as shown in Figure 3-5.

The same computer program with slight modification can be used to produce a more conventional appearing index, usually referred to as a *key-word-out-of-context* (KWOC) index. Using the same set of cards as input, the computer would be instructed to print the key words on the left of the page and on a separate line followed by the title or titles, as illustrated in Figure 3-6.

The KWIC format as shown displays titles in truncated form. However, it is more economical than the KWOC format in volume of paper produced.

The two-column format of the KWIC index reduces the printed index to half the size of the conventional type index, based on the following calculation: Reasonably informative titles should produce five to six index entries from key words selected by the computer. An index to 1,000 documents would, therefore, produce 5,000 to 6,000 lines, which, using the KWIC format, could be photoreduced by approximately 35 per cent, so that two columns could be photoreproduced, side by side, on one $8\frac{1}{2}$- by 11-

inch page. Assuming 50 lines per column, a KWIC index would require 50 pages, while a KWOC index would take up 100 pages.

Citation Indexing Citation indexing is another method of preparing indexes. It has become practical because computers can be employed to arrange and rearrange the entries once they are available in machine-readable form. No selection of key words or assignment of index terms by indexers is required. Citation indexing requires that the references cited by an author in an article, report, patent, etc., be recorded, that is, punched on cards or stored on magnetic tape or disk. After verification and editing of the data, computer programs can prepare the citation index, consisting of two parts, the citation index (Figure 3-7) and the source index (Figure 3-8).

The citation index is arranged by cited author in alphabetic sequence, listing all authors citing him or her in alphabetic sequence. The source index lists all authors in alphabetic sequence and gives complete source information.

To use the citation index, one starts with the name of an author who has published an article or written a report on the subject being searched. The citation index will list under this author's name references to articles citing his or her paper. By referring to the source index one can find complete bibliographic information, including title.

Instead of printing out the indexes, they can be stored on direct-access devices permitting on-line searching. Texts in machine-readable form can be used as input to computer programs which automatically index them, thus eliminating the need for manual indexing. Machine-readable texts of either full documents or abstracts are becoming available in increasing numbers, usually as byproducts of a publishing function.

Computer Processing of Text There are basically two methods of creating machine-readable text:

1. Off-line, that is, by keying the text to an intermediate storage medium, such as punched cards, magnetic cards, or a typescript of the text in an optical character reader (OCR) font. These media serve as input to the computer for later processing, which includes text editing, type composition, and formatting.

2. On-line, where the keyboards, either typewriters or video display devices, are connected directly or through a communications link to a computer. Text editing and modification also can be performed on-line. The text thus created and used to "publish" by any one of a variety of composing devices can then serve as input to the indexing process. It should be noted that the Government and many professional societies and commercial organizations market the machine-readable byproducts of their index and abstract publications on magnetic tape. These can then serve as direct input to computer-prepared and stored information retrieval systems without the need for manual intervention.

Computer processing of text representing documents such as reports, journal articles, patents, memoranda, etc. requires that the elements making up the documents be explicitly identified. A structure of such a record might consist of the following elements:

   00 Document number.
   10 Author.
   20 Title.
   30 Source.
   40 Abstract or full text.

Under the control of the computer program, each word in the elements' title and abstract (or full text) would be indexed automatically, that is, the computer would prepare in alphabetic order a list of all the words in a collection of documents, and store next to each word the specific location of each occurrence as follows:

   Document number.
   Element number.
   Sentence number within each element.
   Position of the word in the sentence.

As was pointed out above in connection with the KWIC method, a stop-words list consisting of words such as THE, AND, WITH, etc., can be used to reduce the numbers of index entries. It is generally estimated that a list of 100 to 200 stop words will reduce the number of word occurrences in a text database by 40 per cent.

Note that the purpose of a computer-prepared index to a full text or text of abstracts database is not to create printed indexes, but to facilitate the computer searching of the files of text, as will be discussed later. The computer-created list of index terms can, of course, be combined with a computer-stored dictionary or thesaurus.

Computer Storage of Indexes If the computer is to be used to search indexes to document files, the index entries must be arranged and stored in such a manner that

From keyword index ... to bibliography ... in one quick step

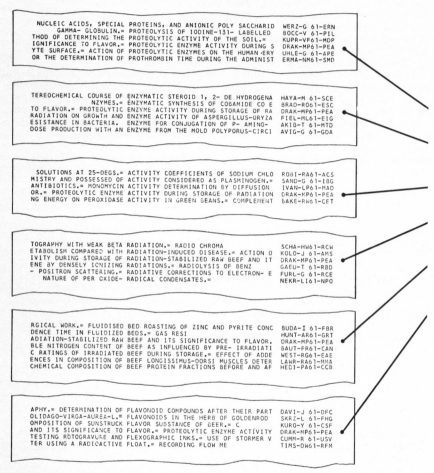

```
    NUCLEIC ACIDS, SPECIAL PROTEINS, AND ANIONIC POLY SACCHARID    WERZ-G 61-ERN
        GAMMA- GLOBULIN.= PROTEOLYSIS OF IODINE-131- LABELLED      BOCC-V 61-PIL
THOD OF DETERMINING THE PROTEOLYTIC ACTIVITY OF THE SOIL.=         KUPR-VF61-MDP
IGNIFICANCE TO FLAVOR.= PROTEOLYTIC ENZYME ACTIVITY DURING S       DRAK-MP61-PEA
YTE SURFACE.= ACTION OF PROTEOLYTIC ENZYMES ON THE HUMAN ERY       UHLE-G 61-APE
OR THE DETERMINATION OF PROTHROMBIN TIME DURING THE ADMINIST       ERMA-NM61-SMD
```

```
TEREOCHEMICAL COURSE OF ENZYMATIC STEROID 1, 2- DE HYDROGENA       HAYA-M 61-SCE
        NZYMES.= ENZYMATIC SYNTHESIS OF COBAMIDE CO E              BRAD-RO61-ESC
TO FLAVOR.= PROTEOLYTIC ENZYME ACTIVITY DURING STORAGE OF RA       DRAK-MP61-PEA
RADIATION ON GROWTH AND ENZYME ACTIVITY OF ASPERGILLUS-ORYZA       FIEL-ML61-EIG
ESISTANCE IN BACTERIA.  ENZYME FOR CONJUGATION OF P- AMINO-        AKIB-T 61-MTD
DOSE PRODUCTION WITH AN ENZYME FROM THE MOLD POLYPORUS-CIRCI       AVIG-G 61-GDA
```

```
   SOLUTIONS AT 25-DEGS.= ACTIVITY COEFFICIENTS OF SODIUM CHLO      ROBI-RA61-ACS
MISTRY AND POSSESSED OF ACTIVITY CONSIDERED AS PLASMINOGEN.=       SAND-G 61-IBG
ANTIBIOTICS.= MONOMYCIN ACTIVITY DETERMINATION BY DIFFUSION        IVAN-LP61-MAD
OR.= PROTEOLYTIC ENZYME ACTIVITY DURING STORAGE OF RADIATION       DRAK-MP61-PEA
NG ENERGY ON PEROXIDASE ACTIVITY IN GREEN BEANS.= COMPLEMENT       BAKE-RW61-CET
```

```
TOGRAPHY WITH WEAK BETA RADIATION.= RADIO CHROMA                   SCHA-HW61-RCW
ETABOLISM COMPARED WITH RADIATION-INDUCED DISEASE.= ACTION O       KOLO-J 61-AMS
IVITY DURING STORAGE OF RADIATION-STABILIZED RAW BEEF AND IT       DRAK-MP61-PEA
ENE BY DENSELY IONIZING RADIATIONS.= RADIOLYSIS OF BENZ            GAEU-T 61-RBD
- POSITRON SCATTERING.= RADIATIVE CORRECTIONS TO ELECTRON- E       FURL-G 61-RCE
    NATURE OF PER OXIDE- RADICAL CONDENSATES.=                     NEKR-LI61-NPO
```

```
RGICAL WORK.= FLUIDISED BED ROASTING OF ZINC AND PYRITE CONC       BUDA-I 61-FBR
DENCE TIME IN FLUIDIZED BEDS.= GAS RESI                            HUNT-AR61-GRT
ADIATION-STABILIZED RAW BEEF AND ITS SIGNIFICANCE TO FLAVOR.       DRAK-MP61-PEA
BLE NITROGEN CONTENT OF BEEF AS INFLUENCED BY PRE- IRRADIATI       BAUT-FR61-CAN
C RATINGS OF IRRADIATED BEEF DURING STORAGE.= EFFECT OF ADDE       WEST-RG61-EAE
ENCES IN COMPOSITION OF BEEF LONGISSIMUS-DORSI MUSCLES DETER       LAWR-RA61-MMA
CHEMICAL COMPOSITION OF BEEF PROTEIN FRACTIONS BEFORE AND AF       HEDI-PA61-CCB
```

```
APHY.= DETERMINATION OF FLAVONOID COMPOUNDS AFTER THEIR PART       DAVI-J 61-DFC
OLIDAGO-VIRGA-AUREA-L.= FLAVONOIDS IN THE HERB OF GOLDENROD        SKRZ-L 61-FHG
OMPOSITION OF SUNSTRUCK FLAVOR SUBSTANCE OF BEER.= C              KURO-Y 61-CSF
AND ITS SIGNIFICANCE TO FLAVOR.= PROTEOLYTIC ENZYME ACTIVITY       DRAK-MP61-PEA
TESTING ROTOGRAVURE AND FLEXOGRAPHIC INKS.= USE OF STORMER V       CUMM-R 61-USV
TER USING A RADIOACTIVE FLOAT.= RECORDING FLOW ME                 TIMS-DW61-RFM
```

Fig. 3-3 Above are six excerpts from the KWIC index proper which contain one document in common. In each case the document is listed under a different key word, but the document always bears the same reference code (DRAK-MP61-PEA). By looking up this code in the bibliography, the user finds the authors' names, full titles, sources, volumes, and page numbers.

access to each entry can be as direct as possible. Index entries, whether manually or automatically created, consist of the index term and the document number, or in full-text systems the occurrence of the term expressed as document element (document number, paragraph number, sentence number, word position).

In creating an index file, the index entries are sorted automatically into alphabetic sequence and stored so that each term appears only once followed by the document numbers or occurrences in the collection where that term appears. Such a file is referred to as an *inverted* file, and is illustrated schematically in Figure 3-9. The inverted file can be stored on magnetic tape or on direct-access devices such as magnetic disks.

Searching the Index by Computer To search the index file, queries must be formulated and fed into the computer. The usual method employed in query formulation uses the logical operators AND, OR, and NOT, as illustrated by Figure 3-10.

A query might read: Find any documents which contain the terms:

A AND (B OR C) NOT D.

The computer will read in the string of document numbers or occurrences following each query term from the inverted file, compare the document number strings, and produce the document numbers which qualify. Document No. 4 will qualify.

In systems which store not only index terms, but the text of abstracts or of the entire documents, words can be asked for in context. Searches can specify phrases by asking

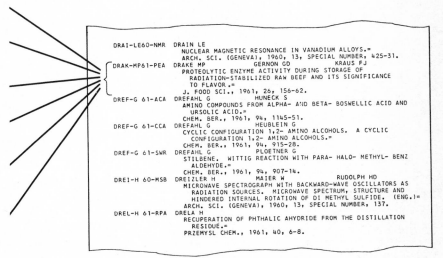

```
DRAI-LE60-NMR    DRAIN LE
                 NUCLEAR MAGNETIC RESONANCE IN VANADIUM ALLOYS.=
                 ARCH. SCI. (GENEVA), 1960, 13, SPECIAL NUMBER, 425-31.
DRAK-MP61-PEA    DRAKE MP            GERNON GD         KRAUS FJ
                 PROTEOLYTIC ENZYME ACTIVITY DURING STORAGE OF
                 RADIATION-STABILIZED RAW BEEF AND ITS SIGNIFICANCE
                 TO FLAVOR.=
                 J. FOOD SCI., 1961, 26, 156-62.
DREF-G 61-ACA    DREFAHL G           HUNECK S
                 AMINO COMPOUNDS FROM ALPHA- AND BETA- BOSWELLIC ACID AND
                 URSOLIC ACID.=
                 CHEM. BER., 1961, 94, 1145-51.
DREF-G 61-CCA    DREFAHL G           HEUBLEIN G
                 CYCLIC CONFIGURATION 1,2- AMINO ALCOHOLS.  A CYCLIC
                 CONFIGURATION 1,2- AMINO ALCOHOLS.=
                 CHEM. BER., 1961, 94, 915-28.
DREF-G 61-SWR    DREFAHL G           PLOETNER G
                 STILBENE.  WITTIG REACTION WITH PARA- HALO- METHYL- BENZ
                 ALDEHYDE.=
                 CHEM. BER., 1961, 94, 907-14.
DREI-H 60-MSB    DREIZLER H          MAIER W           RUDOLPH HD
                 MICROWAVE SPECTROGRAPH WITH BACKWARD-WAVE OSCILLATORS AS
                 RADIATION SOURCES.  MICROWAVE SPECTRUM, STRUCTURE AND
                 HINDERED INTERNAL ROTATION OF DI METHYL SULFIDE.  (ENG.)=
                 ARCH. SCI. (GENEVA), 1960, 13, SPECIAL NUMBER, 137.
DREL-H 61-RPA    DRELA H
                 RECUPERATION OF PHTHALIC AHYDRIDE FROM THE DISTILLATION
                 RESIDUE.=
                 PRZEMYSL CHEM., 1961, 40, 6-8.
```

Fig. 3-3 (cont.)

for words to be adjacent to each other (word position) or queries can state that words must occur in the same sentence or at least in the same paragraph.

Thus, the availability of text should result in higher precision in search results than systems which permit only searches to the document level.

The actual process of querying the index file depends upon the computer configuration available and the medium of storage of the index file. If the index file is stored on magnetic tape, access to each term in a query is sequential because the file is in alphabetic order. This would require that for each query the index tape or tapes would have to be searched from beginning to end, a time-consuming operation even at computer speeds.

The preferred way to query files stored on magnetic tape is to *batch* the queries, that is, accumulate the queries for a day or two and then process all queries against the index file. The batched answers would be sorted out automatically by query and displayed with appropriate identification of the user. Even where the file is stored on direct-access devices, queries may have to be batched unless the available computer facilities provide access by terminal—typewriter or video display sharing the central processing unit with other computer applications.

In batch systems, the user is not able to interact with the computer-based files. The user usually communicates his or her requirements to an information specialist, who in the manner of a reference librarian assists the user in framing the question, then translates it into the language of the computer system and submits the queries for

```
ORAI-LE60-NMR   DRAIN LE
                NUCLEAR MAGNETIC RESONANCE IN VANADIUM ALLOYS.=
                ARCH. SCI. (GENEVA), 1960, 13, SPECIAL NUMBER, 425-31.
DRAK-MP61-PEA   DRAKE MP          GERNON GD          KRAUS FJ
                PROTEOLYTIC ENZYME ACTIVITY DURING STORAGE OF
                RADIATION-STABILIZED RAW BEEF AND ITS SIGNIFICANCE
                TO FLAVOR.=
                J. FOOD SCI., 1961, 26, 156-62.
OREF-G 61-ACA   DREFAHL G          HUNECK S
                AMINO COMPOUNDS FROM ALPHA- AND BETA- BOSWELLIC ACID AND
                URSOLIC ACID.=
                CHEM. BER., 1961, 94, 1145-51.
OREF-G 61-CCA   DREFAHL G          MEUBLEIN D
                CYCLIC CONFIGURATION 1,2- AMINO ALCOHOLS.  A CYCLIC
                CONFIGURATION 1,2- AMINO ALCOHOLS.=
                CHEM. BER., 1961, 94, 915-28.
OREF-G 61-SWR   DREFAHL G          PLOETNER G
                STILBENE.  WITTIG REACTION WITH PARA- HALO- METHYL- BENZ
                ALDEHYDE.=
                CHEM. BER., 1961, 94, 907-14.
OREI-M 60-MSB   DREIZLER H         MAIER W          RUDOLPH HD
                MICROWAVE SPECTROGRAPH WITH BACKWARD-WAVE OSCILLATORS AS
                RADIATION SOURCES.  MICROWAVE SPECTRUM, STRUCTURE AND
                HINDERED INTERNAL ROTATION OF DI METHYL SULFIDE.  (ENG.)=
                ARCH. SCI. (GENEVA), 1960, 13, SPECIAL NUMBER, 137.
OREL-M 61-RPA   ORELA M
                RECUPERATION OF PHTHALIC ANHYDRIDE FROM THE DISTILLATION
                RESIDUE.=
                PRZEMYSL CHEM., 1961, 40, 6-8.
ORES-FK61-IGT   DRESCHER-KADEN FK   GITTMANN J
                INTER GRANULAR TRANSPORT PROCESSES.=
                NATURWISSENSCHAFTEN, 1961, 48, 217-18.
ORES-FK61-ODS   DRESCHER-KADEN FK
                ORIGIN OF THE DARK SPHEROIDS OF ADAMELLO IONALITES.=
                NATURWISSENSCHAFTEN, 1961, 48, 217.
OROZ-NS61-RBU   DROZDOV NS          MATERANSKAIA NP
                RELATIONSHIP BETWEEN THE UNSATURATED CONDITION AND THE AUTO
                OXIDATION RATE IN MIXTURES OF TRI GLYCERIDES DERIVED
                FROM NATURAL FATS.=
                DOKLADY AKAD. NAUK S.S.S.R., 1961, 137, 602-5.
OROZ-VF61-EAC   DROZDOVSKII VF      LAVROVA TV       SOKOLOV SA
                EFFECT OF ANHYDRIDES OF CARBOXYLIC ACIDS ON REGENERATION
                OF RUBBER.=
                KAUCHUK I REZINA, 1961, 20, NO. 3, 11-5.
```

Fig. 3-4   Portion of KWIC bibliography page containing document shown in Figures 3-2 and 3-3.

```
COHEN E        IVAN-T 61-IPU   DANYUSHEVSKII AS
COHEN HL       COHE-HL61-RPU                   DANY-AS61-IPV   DOROGOCHINSKII AZ
COHEN IR       COHE-IR61-NSM   DARRAS R        PAID-J 61-OUC                   KOZO-UI61-CPA
COHEN LA       COHE-LA61-RCA   DAS MR          DAS  -MR60-ESR  DOU NK          BUND-AA61-ECN
COHEN M        BUFF-FS61-SDI   DAS PK          SANY-RK61-BGS   DOUGLASS JE     DOUG-JE61-QDB
               CAPL-D 61-VCO   DAUBEN WG       DAUB-WG61-FST   DOURA T         TAKE-K 61-AOP
               HIRA-K 61-DNI   DAVIDEK J       DAVI-J 61-DFC   DOWNES AM       DOWN-AM61-AAE
COHEN PP       NAZA-M 61-ETE   DAVIDENKOV NN   DAVI-NN61-MLL   DOWNING RG      DOWN-RG61-AAF
COHEN T        ARNE-EM61-LBD   DAVIDSON CS     STOR-JM61-ICF   DOYLE RR        LEVY-EJ61-ICP
COHN HO        COHN-HO61-CNT   DAVIDSON DF     BISH-J 61-HIA   DRACHOVSKA M    DRAC-M 61-CFS
COHN SH        COHN-SH61-ZRW   DAVIDSON ER     DAVI-ER61-CTC   DRAGUT V        CATO-E 61-DIT
COLE T         COLE-T 61-END   DAVIDSON WD     SACK-MA61-EVR   DRAIN LE        ORAI-LE60-NMR
COLEMAN EG     COLE-EG61-SEM   DAVIES M        CLEM-C 60-MRR   DRAKE MP        DRAK-MP61-PEA
COLEMAN LW     COLE-LW61-AHA   DAVIES WD       STEI-M 61-HTA   DRAVNIEKS F     REIT-DC61-ESW
COLEMAN NT     NYE -P 61-IEE   DAVIS DK        PALM-RC61-RSS   DREFAHL G       OREF-G 61-ACA
COLIN Y        LEBO-J 60-DAN   DAVIS GK        HOWE-JR61-BPS                   DREF-G 61-CCA
COLLET A       COLL-A 61-PAQ   DAVIS HT        LAPA-S 61-CMP                   DREF-G 61-SWR
COLLINS RL     COLL-RL61-CCR   DAVIS LE        DAVI-LE61-INH   DREIZLER H      DREI-H 60-MSB
COLLINSON E    COLL-E 61-FRS   DAVYDOV AT      DAVY-AT61-AAE   DRELA M         OREL-M 61-RPA
COLMER AR      MAGE-LA61-OFF   DAY CE          CASS-JW61-ASC   DRESCHER-KADEN FK
COLOMBIE N     COLO-N 61-PCT   DAY EA          YU  -TC61-AOF                   ORES-FK61-IGT
COMBES G       LEDR-J 61-PPS   DE-AGOSTINI C   CAPR-V 61-LAC                   ORES-FK61-ODS
COMSA G        CONS-G 60-FMA   DE-KIMPE C      BRIN-GW61-ALT   DRICKAMER HG    BALC-AS61-EPT
CONDER PC      COND-PC61-VMO   DE-VRIES T      MCNA-HM61-TCE   DRISCOLL JL     BAIL-SC61-VSC
CONDIE RM      COND-RM61-PMS   DEARNALEY DP    DEAR-DP61-STA   DROZDOV NS      OROZ-NS61-RBU
CONIA JM       CONI-JM61-AKU   DERABOV VG      POKO-KT61-CAU   DROZDOVSKII VF  OROZ-VF61-EAC
CONKLIN JH     CONK-JH61-NWI   DEBERDEEEV IK   DEBE-IK61-EVM   DRUCKREY H      DRUC-H 61-PSC
CONRAD D       CONR-D 61-NGA   DECINO TJ       RONZ-AM61-MST   DUBINA TL       DUBI-TL61-ZCA
CONSIDINE JP   BAUM-RP61-OIE   DECOMPS B       DECO-B 60-MRA   DUBININ MM      DUBI-MM61-APS
CONSTANT E     CONS-E 60-HS3   DEDICHEN AJ     HALP-BN61-ILE                   KAOL-O 61-KTD
CONSTANTOPOULOS G              DEEDS F         AMBR-AM61-AST                   ZOZ -NN61-CIM
               CONS-G 61-CHC   DEFORD DD       BOWC-RC61-WME   DUBOIS M        DUBO-M 61-ENI
CONVERSI M     CONV-M 61-NCM   DEGRAW JI       DEGR-JI61-PAC   DUROVIK LI      REIK-VN61-TCP
COOGAN CK      STAL-B 61-PMR   DEHL R          BERR-RS61-NMR   DUBOVITSKII FI  DUBO-FI61-KTD
COOK WA        COOK-WA61-MMM   DEHNICKE K      DEHN-K 61-DCQ   DUBOVITSKY VA   NESM-AN61-SOA
COCKE AM       COOK-AM60-SLR   DEICH AY        DEIC-AY61-VLK   DUBROVSKAYA II  DUBR-II61-PIC
CORBETT NH     CANN-JA61-AEP   DEIMLOVA E      PUDL-P 61-ACG   DUCA A          RIPA-R 61-APC
CORDONE L      CICC-IS60-EMM   DELANEY CFG     CUMM-DO61-OSC                   RIPA-R 61-APC
CORI CF        BROW-DH61-MDS   DELASANTA AC    MILE-TD61-DPH                   RIPA-R 61-SBD
               ILLI-B 61-DSP   DELBARRE F      BUUH-NP61-SBP   DUCASSE Y       LALA-R 61-ALA
CORLATEANU E   HERS-J 61-RX    DELBOVE F       DELB-F 61-DHL   DUCHESNE J      DEPI-J 60-NGR
CORNET N       DEPI-J 60-NGR   DELIA TJ        VING-FA61-CSB                   DUCH-J 61-OFR
CORNILLOT P    CORN-P 61-CGA   DELIMARSKII UK  DELI-UK61-APW                   VAND-A 60-AES
CORPE WA       CORP-WA61-AIC   DELIMARSKY YK   DELI-YK61-CRL   DUCLAUX AM      RAOU-G 60-CPM
CORRAL RA      NAKA-T 61-SJ    DEMCHENKO PA    DEMC-PA61-EMW   DUCROS P        DUCR-P 60-NMR
COSTA-NOVELLA E                DEMETER I       KESZ-L 61-DHE   DUDINSKAYA AA   DUDI-AA61-BCC
               COST-E 60-MTA   DEMIDENKO AA    DEMI-AA61-MTF                   DUDI-AA61-PCN
COUCHMAN JF    GREE-WL61-SHE   DEMIDOV VI      DEMI-VI61-PAM   DUFRESNE ER     DUFR-ER61-RMT
COULL J        HOUG-G 61-SDC   DEMIKHOVSKY IE  DEMI-IE61-SME   DUGAN PR        DUGA-PR61-HSD
COUMES A       COUM-A 60-CTE   DENNEMANN H     BRUN-FH61-CEL   DUGGAL VP       DUGG-VP61-AHS
COUTINHO JMV   VICE-G 61-CTU   DENNEY DB       DENN-DB61-MKT   DUKHIN SS       DERJ-BV61-TFS
COVILL RW      WILL-KW61-LGI   DENNY GB        DENN-CB61-ETN   DUMITRESCU N    DUMI-N 61-DTS
COWAN JC       FRAN-EN61-ALO   DENOEL A        DENO-A 60-CEC   DUNBAR RE       CUNB-RE61-OCM
               TELT-HM61-SOA   DENTICE-DI-ACCADIA              DUNIN AI        GORB-SV61-EFR
```

Fig. 3-5   Portion of KWIC author index page containing reference code for document shown in Figures 3-2, 3-3, and 3-4.   (Note: This document reference code would appear three times in the author index—once for each of the three authors of the document.)

processing. The quality of the search results depends upon the quality of the communication between the user and the person framing the query for the computer.

Computer technology makes it practical to provide the ultimate user with a system allowing him or her to interact with the files, processing one query at the time. This will be discussed in more detail under the next heading.

The result of a search of the index file is a list of document numbers identified by the computer as containing the words or phrases asked for in the query. This is hardly adequate service to the users who would like to be given at least the author and title of each document, preferably also an abstract if not the full text of all relevant items. A complete information retrieval system will have to include these other files, so that

---

MARCH 9, 1971   Subject Index   Page   69

Operators
     71B 00112. OS/360 Job Management Project- Device Independent Display
     Operators Console Support (DIDOCS).
     71B 00112   Page   58

Optical
     USCEE-397. Communication Theory for the Free Space Optical Channel.
     August 1970.
     71B 00024   Page   13

     USCEE-396. Optical Synchronization Phase Locking with Shot Noise
     Processes. August 1970.
     71B 00026   Page   14

     NASA TN-D-6077. Optical Probing of Supersonic Aerodynamic Turbulence
     with Statistical Correlation. Phase I- Feasibility. February 1971.
     71B 00179   Page   92

Optimizing
     71B 00135. PL/I Optimizing Compiler.
     71B 00135   Page   69

Organization
     71E 00193. Generalized Organization of Large Data Bases. A Set
     Theoretic Approach to Relations. June 1970.
     71B 00193   Page   99

Fig. 3-6   Portion of key-word-out-of-context (KWOC) index.

the user can be furnished with as much information about the documents retrieved as possible.

INFORMATION RETRIEVAL SYSTEMS

To meet the information needs of the members of an organization, a system must be set up for acquiring relevant documents and processing them for future retrieval, as well as procedures for alerting users to the availability of the documents.

Documents are created within an organization or may be published by others. The documents may be stored in hard copy or on microfilm or microfiche, or may be available in a form that can be stored in a computer.

We have seen how computers can be used to prepare indexes and how computer-stored indexes can be searched. To provide the user with as much information as possible, it is necessary to put into machine-readable form or to obtain in such form bibliographic data such as author, title, source, publication date, etc., and possibly the text of abstracts or of the document itself. This file, usually referred to as the *document master file*, is maintained in document number order, either on magnetic tape or on direct-access storage devices.

An information retrieval system operating in a batch mode consists then of three basic files:

- Dictionary.
- Inverted file (index terms plus document numbers or occurrences in alphabetic order).
- Master file (bibliographic data, abstract or full text in document number order).

Queries consisting of words in logical combinations are processed against the dictionary to establish that the words exist in the database, and against the inverted file

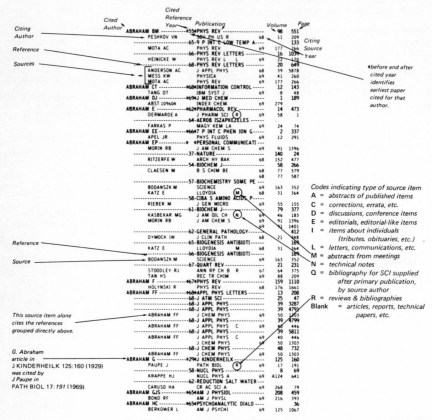

Fig. 3-7 Typical column from citation index.

to produce the document numbers which answer the query. These document numbers are then used to access the master file to display the available information, which may be the author and title only, or in addition an abstract or even the full text of the document.

Interactive retrieval systems, where the user is able to query the files from a terminal at or near his or her desk, permit a step-by-step dialogue with the computer, as follows:

1. The user enters query.

2. The computer responds by indicating to the user the number of documents or word occurrences for each query term and for the entire query.

3. The user may wish to look at the computer-stored dictionary or thesaurus for related terms.

4. The user may ask to see one or more of the documents or document references the query has retrieved.

5. The user may modify the query by adding or deleting terms.

6. The user can narrow the volume of material retrieved by specifying dates or ranges of dates, language of publication, or any of the bibliographic fields in the record or fields that might contain quantities, amounts, or other discrete data.

7. The user may review any or all documents or document references the query has retrieved at his or her terminal, or request that the information be printed out.

In systems where the text of the documents or at least the text of abstracts is stored in the computer, the user may request that the retrieved output be presented in order of

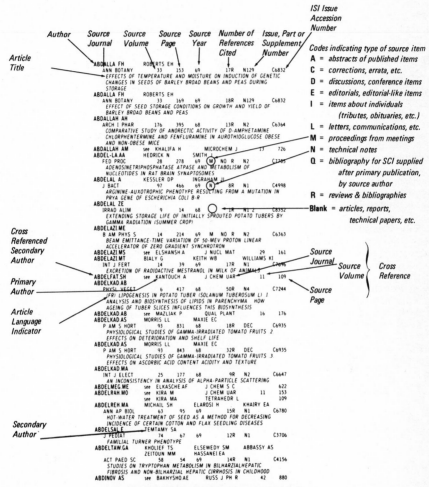

Fig. 3-8 Typical column from source index.

relevance. This ranking capability is based on statistical analysis of text and the resulting occurrence frequency of the words in the query.

If full text of the documents is not available in machine-readable form, the user will decide on the basis of the retrieved information (which may be only author and title or abstracts if available in the system) whether he or she wants the relevant documents.

Where documents are available in microfiche form, it is possible to store them in an image storage device connected to the computer. The video display terminal can be used not only to view the document references and abstracts stored in the computer, but to ask for the transmission of the microfiche images via coaxial cable to the terminal.

These images include not only the text, but also any graphics associated with the document, such as drawings and photographs.

Data Protection Any collection of information must be protected against alteration and abuse. If the information is stored in a computer, the design of the information retrieval system should include procedures to protect against loss, alteration, and unauthorized access to the records. Interactive retrieval systems especially should provide for data protection at various levels. Only certain terminals or persons should be authorized to add, delete, or alter records. For this purpose, authorized personnel can be given a lock word—changed at frequent intervals—and each terminal on which changes to the file can be made should identify itself to the computer.

All persons authorized to search the files from their terminals only must have an identification code and should be given a clearance code. This code can be on several levels, and should match the classification code assigned to a file or to individual documents within a file and even parts of documents. The user "signs on" to the system by identifying himself or herself. A computer file of authorized persons is automatically accessed, and if the computer recognizes the user, it will ask the user to proceed with his or her query.

Next the user must identify the file or files he or she wishes to search. The computer will check the user's clearance level, and if he or she is authorized to search that file or files, it will display the instructions necessary to proceed. Even on the document level, the user may not be allowed to see certain documents or sections of documents in accordance with the classification level assigned to the document.

File Maintenance With new information being generated daily, it is necessary to provide for the updating of records now in the file, deletion of others, and addition of new documents. The usual procedure is to mark records in the computer file to be updated or to be deleted, enter the updated and new documents into a temporary file that can be searched as are all the other files, and periodically merge the temporary files with the "old" file, deleting the records marked, adding the updated and new ones in their respective file locations, and simultaneously updating the index (inverted) files.

Before merging the new records—either those created by the information center or those acquired from external sources on magnetic tape—into the permanent files, the computer can be used to notify persons potentially interested in knowing about the newly acquired material. This can be accomplished by printing and publishing lists,

Index terms

	A	B	C	D	E	F
Document No. (occurrence)	X			X	X	X
Document No. (occurrence)		X		X		X
Document No. (occurrence)	X	X		X	X	X
Document No. (occurrence)	X	X	X		X	
Document No. (occurrence)	X		X		X	X

Fig. 3-9   Inverted file.

Document No.	Index terms			Qualifying documents
	A AND	B OR C	NOT D	
1		X	X	
2	X	X	X	
3		X		
4	X	X		4
5	X		X	

Fig. 3-10   Diagram illustrating file search query.

or by selectively disseminating the information to individuals, teams, or departments in the organization.

Selective Dissemination of Information (SDI) One of the most effective ways to improve the information using habits of members of an organization is to present them periodically with abstracts of documents published internally or of articles and reports appearing in the literature which are most relevant to their interest.

This is accomplished by creating *interest profiles* of individuals or groups. These, like the queries discussed above, are constructed by using index terms in logical combination. A file of these profiles is created which will also include name, location, date of the profile, etc. The creation and maintenance of interest profiles is an important function. It is usually performed by an information specialist or a member of the library staff trained to interview potential subscribers or to translate the user's own description of what he or she is looking for into the query language of the system.

The system should also provide feedback from the users, so that profiles can be continuously monitored. As job assignments change or new projects are undertaken, in-

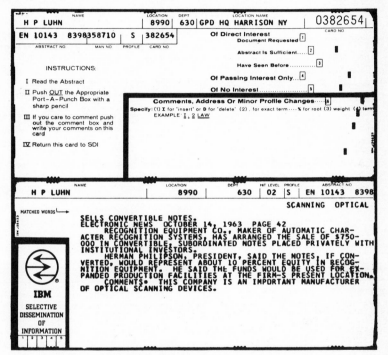

Fig. 3-11   SDI notice on punched cards.

terests will change and the interest profiles must be updated. Individuals, as well as groups, can have more than one interest profile.

Periodically the document records consisting of bibliographic data, index terms, and/ or abstracts are processed by computer against the interest profiles. For every matching record the computer will produce an SDI notice. These notices can be printed on two punched cards attached, side by side, as shown in Figure 3-11, or on continuous form paper, as illustrated in Figure 3-12.

Each batch, individually addressed, is inserted in a window envelope and forwarded to the subscriber, who will review the abstracts and order copies of those documents he or she wishes to read in full. Copies may be furnished to him or her by the information center or library in hard copy or on microfiche.

The user is asked to evaluate each item by indicating that the referenced document is:
1. Of interest, and he or she has ordered a copy.
2. Of interest, but the abstract is sufficient.
3. Of interest, but he or she has seen it before.
4. Of passing interest only.
5. Of no interest.

The user can indicate his or her choice by marking an answer in the position indicated. These cards serve as the feedback to the system, and are used to prepare sta-

```
THE ATTACHED ABSTRACTS WERE SELECTED FOR YOUR REVIEW                411600

AFTER SEARCHING A TOTAL OF 550     IBM DOCUMENTS     11/01/72




                  WE BROOKS JR                    411600
                  D/777  B/10 RYE R
                  VIA ARMONK, NY



IF THE MAILING ADDRESS SHOWN IS INCORRECT, PLEASE INDICATE THE CHANGES
ON THIS CARD AND RETURN IT TO ITIRC.



72A003391                                 IBM DOCS  11/01/72     411600

    IBMC VVIII N2.  AIR QUALITY- A DYNAMIC MODEL.  1972.

  1      IBM COMPUTING REPORT
            AMONG THE MORE NOISOME AND CORROSIVE POLLUTANTS OF THE
    ATMOSPHERE IS SULFUR DIOXIDE, WHICH, IN CONTACT WITH MOISTURE,
    READILY FORMS SULFUROUS ACID.  ACIDIC RAIN, IN FACT, IS NOT UNCOMMON
    IN AREAS WHERE SULFUR CONTAINING FUELS ARE BURNED FOR INDUSTRIAL
    PURPOSES OR TO GENERATE ELECTRICITY.  ONE WAY TO CONTROL SUCH
    POLLUTION WOULD BE TO PREDICT IT SO THAT PREVENTIVE ACTION COULD BE
    TAKEN.  FACTORIES AND INCINERATORS COULD BE SHUT DOWN, FOR EXAMPLE,
    AND THE PRODUCTION OF ELECTRIC POWER COULD BE CURTAILED.
            RESEARCHERS AT IBM'S SCIENTIFIC CENTER IN PALO ALTO,
    CALIFORNIA, RECENTLY DEMONSTRATED THAT IT IS INDEED POSSIBLE TO
    PREDICT SULFUR DIOXIDE CO           ONS IN THE A              THE
          O AN EXPERIMEN                 GRAM T
                  FUR  D
```

Fig. 3-12   SDI notice on continuous form.

```
WE BROOKS, JR.   10/70 ARM  CHQ D/777 B/    MAN NO. 411600            72A21

DOCUMENT ORDER FORM. SEND TO LOCAL IBM LIBRARY. IF NO LIBRARY, RETURN TO
ITIRC. CHECK /M/ COLUMN FOR MICROFICHE, OR /P/ IF PRINTED COPY REQUIRED.

         M     P  ACCESSION NO.              SOURCE CODE NO.

   1   .( )..( )..72A003391              IBMC VVIII N2
   2   .( )..( )..72A003400              IBMD 08-72
   3   .( )..( )..72C001890              TDB 09-72 P1304-1309


WE BROOKS, JR.   10/70 ARM  CHQ D/777 B/    MAN NO. 411600            72A21

PLEASE EVALUATE THE ATTACHED ABSTRACTS AND RETURN THIS CARD TO YOUR LOCAL
IBM LIBRARY (IF NONE, SEND TO ITIRC).

   CHECK

     ( )     GOOD - OVER 75 PERCENT OF THE ABSTRACTS ARE OF INTEREST.

     ( )     FAIR - ABOUT HALF OF THE ABSTRACTS ARE OF INTEREST.

     ( )     UNSATISFACTORY - LESS THAN 25 PER CENT  ARE OF INTEREST.

          ( )  ENTER BELOW - COMMENTS, QUESTIONS, ADDRESS OR PROFILE CHANGES




YOU RECEIVED    3 NOTIFICATIONS FROM   IBM DOCUMENTS          11/01/72

**** IF YOU NEED PROFILE HELP CALL ITIRC 8-254-6640, AREA 914-696-6640 ****
```

Fig. 3-13   Evaluation form.

tistics on the overall performance, as well as the user responses. Periodically these statistics will indicate the degree of user satisfaction and give the system operators the opportunity to take the initiative to contact a user whose profile requires updating.

SDI systems using the continuous form notices do not provide for user evaluation of each abstract. However, as shown in Figure 3-13, provision is made for evaluation of the whole batch.

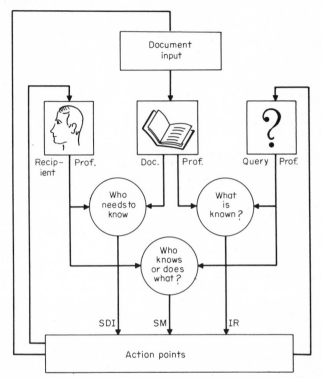

Fig. 3-14   Schematic of business intelligence system.

The computer program to perform SDI is essentially the same as programs used for searching. A program to maintain the interest profile file will also be required. It can be used not only to match interest profiles with document profiles, but also to search for people with desired skills as indicated by their interests.

A BUSINESS INTELLIGENCE SYSTEM

Figure 3-14 indicates how the building blocks discussed in this Chapter can be fitted together into a system that will serve the user groups by answering three questions:

1. Who needs to know?
2. What is known?
3. Who knows or does what?

Once the information about a document, be it an internal report, a journal article, or a patent, is available in machine-readable form, the computer will arrange and rearrange, print, or display the information.

While much of the published literature, especially in scientific and technical fields, is being made available in machine-readable form, usable as input to a computer-based SDI and retrospective search system, management should be alert to the potential offered by technology to capture internally created documents in machine-readable form at the source. It can then use computer technology in the publishing process and thus obtain the input to an SDI or retrieval system as a byproduct.

SELECTIVE BIBLIOGRAPHY

Cuadra, Carlos A. (ed.), and Ann W. Luke (assoc. ed.), *Annual Review of Information Science and Technology,* vol. 9, American Society for Information Science, Washington, D.C. (Contains extensive bibliographies.)

Holm, Bart E., *How to Manage Your Information,* Van Nostrand Reinhold, New York, 1968.

Kochen, Manfred (ed.), *The Growth of Knowledge,* Wiley, New York, 1967.

Chapter 4

Computer Models in Physical Distribution

RONALD H. BALLOU

**Associate Professor of Marketing and Logistics,
Case Western Reserve University, Cleveland, Ohio**

Over the recent two decades, there has been a significant trend toward greater use of quantitative models in the decision-making activities of management. The popularity of the computer along with the great strides that have been made in physical distribution model design and performance have contributed to this trend. Many good models now exist for planning and controlling physical distribution activities ranging from the broad problem of system design to the detailed problem of warehouse layout.

This Chapter focuses on a select number of physical distribution models in the areas of facility location, inventory planning and control, routing and delivery, and warehouse planning. These particular areas are chosen because a number of models exist that require the use of the computer for them to be effective and efficient when applied to real-world problems. The emphasis of the discussion is on a comparison and appraisal of the models rather than a detailed mathematical presentation of how the models work. References are intended to offer further reading on the models mentioned.

CLASSIFICATION OF MODELS

Before treating each planning model on an individual basis, greater perspective will be achieved if all models are classified into a limited number of groups. Planning models are decision-assisting models in that they evaluate alternative courses of action and often seek the best among these. They can be grouped as *algorithmic models*, *simulation models*, or *heuristic models*. Each group has a different computer requirement in terms of the amount of computer time needed to solve the model type, the computer data storage capacity requirements, and the extent of the programming necessary to make the model available on the computer.

Algorithmic Models The distinguishing characteristic of an algorithmic model is, by definition,[1] that it is built on rigorous mathematical procedures to assure that an optimum solution to the modeled problem will be found. Although the guarantee of

[1] *Algorithm:* A prescribed set of well-defined rules, or process, for the solution of a problem in a finite number of steps, e.g., a full statement of an arithmetical procedure for evaluating sin X to a stated precision. (American National Standards Institute.)

an optimum solution is a desirable feature in any decision-assisting model, it is obtained in trade-off with the breadth of the problem that can be attacked within a given computer budget. Many of the operations research models are of this type. Examples are linear programming, calculus-dominated facility location models, some routing models, and inventory control models.

One of the most familiar models of this type is the economic order quantity (EOQ) model for inventory control.[2] The model is not particularly rich in scope, but it does reflect the essence of the problem. Also, the solution to the model provides the optimum quantity to reorder into inventory.

Algorithmic models are the ultimate in model design, though currently many such models lack rich problem definition and computational efficiency when applied to problems of real-world size. Nevertheless, as these problems are overcome, future model development will move from either simulation or heuristic types toward algorithmic model designs.

Simulation Models   Computer simulation models are opposites to algorithmic models. That is, simulations can provide a rich problem description in the form of computer programming statements, but do not seek the best solution as part of the model. Simulation is basically an experimental technique where the associated model is sampled under different input conditions. The user selects the input conditions and interprets the model's output. To the extent that the model replicates in some detail a real-world system or process, sampling the model reveals something of how the real-world system or process would respond to various changes without disturbing the actual system or process. Because developing a simulation model often requires a substantial effort in computer programming, a number of specially designed simulation languages are available to aid in the modeling effort. These include SIMSCRIPT,[3] GPSS,[4] SIMULA,[5] and DYNAMO.[6]

The simulation modeling approach has been successfully applied to a number of areas of interest to the physical distribution manager. Examples of some of these are warehouse location, inventory control, carrier routing, and even total physical distribution system design. These models are elaborated upon later in this Chapter.

Heuristic Programming   The third significant model type is the heuristic model. In many respects it is a hybrid of algorithmic and simulation model types. It can generally achieve the good problem definition of simulation models, yet it includes search rules within the model to guide it toward an optimum solution. Seeking an optimum solution is an important feature of the algorithmic model type. Heuristics in the model contribute greatly to reducing the amount of computational time required to achieve satisfactory solutions to real-world problems. More specifically, heuristics have been defined[7] as:

> . . . a short cut process of reasoning . . . that searches for a *satisfactory* rather than an *optimal* solution. The heuristic, which reduces the time spent in the search for the solution of a problem, comprises a rule or a computational procedure which restricts the number of alternative solutions to a problem, based upon the analogous human trial-and-error process of reaching acceptable solutions to problems for which optimizing algorithms are not available.

Heuristic models are probably the most useful of the model types available to management today. They do not represent the ultimate in model design, but the practical features of broad problem definition with the ability to seek out good solutions has had a lot of practical appeal. The growing list of distribution problems approached by heuristic programming includes locating warehouses, order consolidation for freight savings, local truck delivery scheduling, and airline scheduling.

[2] See Ronald H. Ballou, *Business Logistics Management*, Prentice-Hall, Englewood Cliffs, N.J., 1973, pp. 290–294.

[3] H. Markowitz, B. Hauser, and H. Karr, *SIMSCRIPT: A Simulation Programming Language*, Prentice-Hall, Englewood Cliffs, N.J., 1963.

[4] G. Gordon, "A General Purpose Systems Simulator," *IBM Systems Journal*, September, 1962, pp. 18–33.

[5] A simulation program for the analysis of discrete event system and a library program for the Univac 1108 computing system.

[6] J. Forrester, *Industrial Dynamics*, M.I.T. Press, Cambridge, Mass., 1961.

[7] Charles L. Hinkle and Alfred A. Kuehn, "Heuristic Models: Mapping the Maze for Management," *California Management Review*, Fall, 1967, p. 61.

APPLICATIONS

The above model types provide the basic tools for dealing with physical distribution decision problems. Most physical distribution problems can be identified within the product-information flow network of the firm as shown in Figure 4-1. Figure 4-1 is an abstract representation of the physical distribution system. The nodes in the network represent supply points, warehousing points, and demand points. Locating these is the problem of facility location.

The links connect the nodal points in the network. Which links are to be used is the problem of routing and scheduling the product flows. Within the nodal points there are two additional problems that concern the physical distribution manager. First is the problem of inventory management. Second is the internal design of a warehouse.

There are many additional decision problems that could also be included, such as transport mode selection, order processing system design, and materials handling decisions. Space limitations preclude dealing with these.

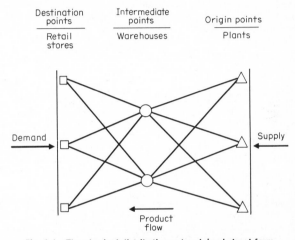

Fig. 4-1   The physical distribution network in abstract form.

Facility Location Selecting the number, location, and size of the nodal points in the physical distribution network is a major problem in system design. In a realistic problem, where a firm may have a hundred warehouses and thousands of customers, finding good nodal point configurations is a significant computational task. Fortunately, a number of good mathematical models have been developed in recent years to deal with the problem. For discussion, these are grouped as (1) classic models and (2) recent improvements.

Classic Models. There are three classic models of note. First is the *modified linear programming* approach of Baumol and Wolfe.[8] This was one of the early models developed to deal with locating multiple facilities (warehouses). Though it tends to be limited to problems where there are few or no warehouse fixed charges as in the case of public warehouses, the method is appealing because it is based on the rigors of linear programming and of mathematical proofs. Because linear programming computer routines are readily available, the task of programming the model for computer use is greatly simplified.

The model can handle location problems of significant size. The author has used this method to solve problems of 4 plants, 120 warehouses, and 325 demand territories, and larger ones are possible. However, large linear programming problems often require substantial amounts of computer time, and this must be a limitation to this approach. The model also requires transportation rates to be linear and cannot guarantee

---

[8] William J. Baumol and Philip Wolfe, "A Warehouse-Location Problem," *Operations Research*, March–April, 1958, pp. 252–263.

an optimum solution, though an improved solution compared with existing company practice is usually obtained.

The second classic model for facility location is a *simulation model* developed by Shycon and Maffei.[9] This model offers a rich problem description as a main advantage. In fact, basic to the model are such features as (1) customer's order sizes, ordering patterns, different types of shipments received, and product mix, (2) detailed transportation costs in the form of vehicle load versus less than vehicle load quantities, and various shipment sizes in differing freight classifications, (3) detailed warehouse operating costs including labor costs, rentals, and taxes for different geographic areas, (4) differing factory source points for each product and factory capacity limitations, and (5) customer demand over the period of 1 year and the location of the demand. Problems of up to 4,000 customers, 40 warehouses, and 15 plants can be handled.

The third classic model is a *heuristic program* developed by Kuehn and Hamburger.[10] The unique feature of this model is that heuristics are incorporated into the model that guide it toward a good solution. For example, one heuristic is to limit the examination of warehouses to those at or near concentrations of demand. This heuristic alone can save a substantial amount of computing time by eliminating those warehouse sites from consideration that have a low probability of being chosen. The problem definition closely resembles that of the Shycon-Maffei simulation, with the exception that a delivery time cost has been added to represent reduced customer service as warehouses are located farther from customers.

What is being described here are three model types that use different mathematical methods for finding the minimum-cost warehouse location patterns. What they do in terms of describing the distribution system is basically the same. That is, each model describes the most important factors that make up the distribution system. These factors include transportation rates, inventory carrying costs, customer service requirements, potential warehouse locations, warehousing costs, warehouse capacity, and product demand. These models permit changing the input data and the potential warehouse location patterns without disturbing the current operating distribution system. They aid in finding the best location patterns and also predict what the anticipated costs will be for operating the distribution system in its new configuration.

Recent Improvements. Several significant improvements have been made that extend the scope of facility location models, improve their computational efficiency, and make them more accessible to the uninitiated user. A few of these are worth noting.

There has been a continuing effort by analysts to express more of the real world in the models, as well as to broaden the models beyond just the problem of warehouse location. An entire systems design model is sought. One such model is Long-Range Environmental Planning Simulator, or LREPS for short.[11] It was developed under the sponsorship of the Johnson & Johnson Company to be a comprehensive model for physical distribution system planning. LREPS represents an extension to the classic models because it overcomes some of their deficiencies by (1) incorporating such additional features as inventory control procedures, order processing and information flows, and multiple transportation mode alternatives, (2) integrating the time dimension of inventory control with the space dimension of geographical location, and (3) incorporating dynamic behavior into the model. LREPS is a simulation model and inherently suffers from substantial computer running time.

Much of the effort since the early model development has been directed toward reducing computational time. Not only are better heuristics being developed, but these efforts are making a relatively new algorithmic model type, called *branch-and-bound*, an attractive way of approaching the facility location problem.[12] The branch-and-bound

[9] Harvey N. Shycon and Richard B. Maffei, "Simulation: Tool for Better Distribution," *Harvard Business Review*, November–December, 1960, pp. 65–75.

[10] Alfred A. Kuehn and Michael J. Hamburger, "A Heuristic Program for Locating Warehouses," *Management Science*, July, 1963, pp. 643–666.

[11] Donald J. Bowersox, "Planning Physical Distribution Operations with Dynamic Simulation," *Journal of Marketing*, January, 1972, pp. 17–25.

[12] See M. A. Efroymson and T. L. Ray, "A Branch-Bound Algorithm for Plant Location," *Operations Research*, May–June, 1966, pp. 361–368; B. M. Khumawala, "An Efficient Branch and Bound Algorithm for the Warehouse Location Problem," *Management Science*, August, 1972, pp. B-718–B-731; and D. G. Elson, "Site Location via Mixed-Integer Programming," *Operational Research Quarterly*, vol. 23, no. 1, pp. 31–43.

technique refers to the way the location problem is solved. The technique realizes an optimum solution by solving a series of linear programming problems, each of which moves closer to the optimum solution until it is reached. Because computational time has hitherto been the chief limitation of this technique, we can expect to see greater use made of it in the future, as faster computer processing procedures are developed.

Major strides are being made to make large-scale location and system design models readily available to a wide variety of firms having different problem descriptions. One model of note is the Distribution System Simulator software package developed by IBM.[13] In addition to being a broad-based physical distribution system simulation, the software package is a collection of submodel types. First the user answers a detailed questionnaire about system design requirements. The questionnaire contains such yes or no questions as: Shipments are to be batched? Never batched? Batch unless order priority is greater than P? Backorders are always accepted? Never accepted? Accepted by item type? In addition, questions are asked as to what should be the form of the program output. In this way the user defines his or her own output format.

Then the questionnaire inputs are processed by the computer. The computer builds a systems model in the form of a computer program by making the appropriate selections from the submodel package as suggested by the input questionnaire. The user receives a "customer made" model to fit his or her particular requirements. The user also receives a data specification list as a guide to what data will be needed and the form in which it will be needed. Such user-oriented models are new and not many exist. However, their potential seems great and we can expect to see many more in the future.

Inventory Planning and Control. Inventories are an economic convenience rather than a necessity in the distribution system. It would be possible to operate the distribution without inventories, but probably not very efficiently or effectively. Inventories serve as buffers to help overcome the uncertainties in and the mismatching of the levels of supply and demand over time. So prevalent are the use of inventories that in the United States roughly 5 per cent of the Gross National Product is represented by these inventories, and approximately one-third of a firm's physical distribution dollar is spent on them. Inventories are important and costly, and nearly every large company utilizes the computer in some way to help to control inventories.

The most interesting and perhaps the most important inventory problem occurs when there are thousands of items located in the many warehouses of a firm's distribution system. It also is the most complex.

Specifically, what is this inventory problem? It is to plan over time for an adequate supply of each product item in a warehouse, so as to minimize the costs of maintaining the stock while providing a desired level of stock availability. A number of computer software programs exist for handling problems of this scope. Examples of these programs are IBM's IMPACT, NCR's REACT, and Honeywell's PROFIT.

These programs both plan for and control inventory levels. First, the computer is used to keep track of the reductions or additions to inventory caused by demand or by replenishment of depleted stock. Second, the computer periodically is called upon to forecast the future demands of each stock item. (Inventory control programs frequently use *exponential smoothing* as the forecasting technique.[14]) The forecast provides the basis for planning the required future stock levels needed to meet anticipated demand. Third, the software program contains decision rules that trigger an order for stock replenishment. Though these decision rules may vary with the particular situation, one such rule is to issue a stock order when the computer records an accumulated deficit with respect to the desired maximum stock level and the actual stock level, for each product in the warehouse. When this deficit equals or exceeds the shipping weight (for example, a truckload weight), the stock order is placed on a plant or a supplier. Figure 4-2 shows a flow chart of the model's operation.

Such inventory models are of great significance in the management of today's physical distribution operations. One survey revealed that it was the most widely used of all

---

[13] Michael M. Conners et al., "The Distribution System Simulator," *Management Science*, April, 1972, pp. B-425–B-453.

[14] For a discussion of exponential smoothing for inventory control, see Robert G. Brown, "Less Risk in Inventory Estimates," reprinted in Norton E. Marks and Robert M. Taylor, *Marketing Logistics: Perspectives and Viewpoints*, Wiley, New York, 1967, pp. 159–170.

physical distribution models and that *all* the firms surveyed had computerized their control over inventories.[15]

Routing and Delivery The physical distribution manager can often improve the efficiency of operations by better utilizing transport equipment and personnel. One way to do this is to route the equipment scientifically over the firm's distribution network. Though scientifically solving routing problems often does not lead to dramatic improvements over the solutions achieved by intuitive methods, the repetitive nature of routing problems means that even small improvements compound into substantial cost savings.

There are two basic problems of interest. First is the separate origin-destination routing problem as shown in Figure 4-3a. For example, it is the type of problem encountered in directing a truck over the interstate highway system, say from New York to Los Angeles. The shortest trip distance, time, or cost is sought. Second is the delivery problem. This is essentially the routing problem where the origin and destination points are the same except that the optimum sequence to visit the points is sought (Figure 4-3b). This is typical of the problem of routing delivery trucks to retail food stores from a central distribution point, routing trucks in a pickup and delivery operation, and even the routing of school buses!

The separate origin-destination routing problem has been approached using a wide variety of quantitative techniques. These include dynamic programming, linear programming, and algorithmic models specially designed to deal with this problem.[16] Selecting the right model for the particular application is the key. The choice generally is a trade-off among complexity of the algorithm, computational time, and richness of the solution. From among the many possibilities, the shortest-route tree method[17] is a good choice.

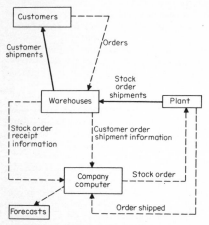

Fig. 4-2 Simplified flow chart of the operation of a typical inventory control model.

The delivery problem is the most complicated version of the routing problem. Not only is the minimum distance or travel time routing sought, but such additional questions are posed as: What is the best sequence to visit the network nodal points? Which nodal points should a single vehicle visit? How many vehicles should be assigned to the delivery problem? Which nodal points should be serviced by which vehicles? What should the capacity of each vehicle be? Methods based on branch-and-bound,[18] graphic,[19] and dynamic programming[20] techniques have been used to approach the problem. However, the complexity of the problem has resulted in heuristic programming receiving a lot of interest as a methodology, mainly because of reasonable computational times and the ease with which realistic constraints can be dealt. Probably

[15] John J. Cardwell, "Marketing and Management Science: A Marriage on the Rocks?" *California Management Review*, Summer, 1968, pp. 3–12.

[16] For a review of these models, see Stuart E. Dreyfus, "An Appraisal of Some Shortest-Path Algorithms," *Operations Research*, vol. 17, pp. 395–412, 1969; Maurice Pollack and Walter Wiebenson, "Solutions of the Shortest-Route Problem: A Review," *Operations Research*, March–April, 1960, pp. 224–30; and Stanley Zionts, "Methods for Selection of an Optimum Route," in *Papers: American Transportation Research Forum*, Oxford, Ind., 1962, pp. 25–36.

[17] The method is described and discussed further in Frederick S. Hillier and Gerald J. Lieberman, *Introduction to Operations Research*, Holden-Day, San Francisco, 1967, pp. 218–222.

[18] John D. C. Little, Katta G. Murty, Dura W. Sweeney, and Caroline Karel, "An Algorithm for the Traveling Salesman Problem," *Operations Research*, December, 1957, pp. 841–845.

[19] L. L. Barachet, "Graphic Solution of the Traveling-Salesman Problem," *Operations Research*, December, 1957, pp. 841–845.

[20] M. Held and R. M. Karp, "A Dynamic Programming Approach to Sequencing Problems," *Journal of the Society for Industrial and Applied Mathematics*, March, 1962, pp. 196–210.

the most popular of such heuristic programs is the "savings" method of Clarke and Wright.[21] Testing the program has shown substantial reductions in computational time compared with other methods and an average error of approximately 3 per cent.

Warehouse Planning Many problems associated with the operation of a nodal point (warehouse) are nicely handled by quantitative methods, but some more than others. Two problems of particular note are stock layout and stock retrieval.

Stock Layout. Stock layout refers to how stock should be arranged within the available storage space of the warehouse. Figure 4-4 shows the product flow through a typical food distribution warehouse where the product moves from the receiving dock to temporary storage in the reserve bays. From there the product is moved to the break bulk or assembly section of the warehouse from which the orders are filled. The question becomes one of deciding where to locate the product in the reserve and assembly bays when thousands of other items are competing for the same space. The stock layout is sought that will minimize the total materials handling cost for moving the product through the warehouse.

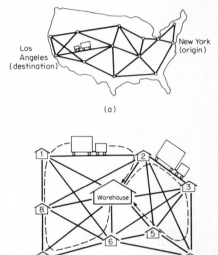

(a)

(b)

Fig. 4-3 Two common types of routing problems. (a) Shortest route through a network. (b) Scheduling deliveries from a distribution center.

Several methods exist for dealing with the layout problem that can be used without the necessity of a computer. These essentially manual methods include layout by popularity,[22] layout by size,[23] and the cube-per-order index.[24] However, more rigorous procedures have been developed that utilize the computer to make the multitude of detailed calculations required to evaluate different layout arrangements.

One such method is based on linear programming.[25] Linear programming as a technique is particularly well suited to this type of allocation problem since it effectively evaluates a greater number of alternative stocking arrangements while meeting such constraints as (1) bay capacity, (2) a minimum volume of each product to be maintained in the assembly bays, and (3) a maximum volume to be stored in the warehouse. Another benefit is that the standard linear programming software programs can be used.

The primary disadvantage of linear programming for the layout problem is computational. When the layout problem involves thousands of product items and many storage bays, the computational time can be excessive. Large-scale problems can be handled by a heuristic model called CRAFT.[26] The CRAFT model works much like linear programming by interchanging product items two at a time within a given storage space unit to see if a reduction in handling cost is possible. Though the model does not guarantee an optimum solution as does linear programming, the CRAFT model solutions are difficult to improve upon.

[21] G. Clarke and J. W. Wright, "Scheduling of Vehicles from a Central Depot to a Number of Delivery Points," *Operations Research*, vol. 11, 1963, pp. 568–581.

[22] Forest L. Neal, "Controlling Warehouse Handling Costs by Means of Stock Location Audits," *Transportation and Distribution Management*, May, 1962, pp. 31–33.

[23] J. L. Heskett, "Cube-per-Order Index: A Key to Warehouse Stock Location," *Transportation and Distribution Management*, April, 1963, p. 28.

[24] Ibid.; and J. L. Heskett, "Putting the Cube-per-Order Index to Work in Warehouse Layout," *Transportation and Distribution Management*, August, 1964, pp. 22–30.

[25] Ronald H. Ballou, "Improving the Physical Layout of Merchandise in Warehouses," *Journal of Marketing*, July, 1967, pp. 60–64.

[26] Elwood S. Buffa, Gordon C. Armour, and Thomas E. Vollman, "Allocating Facilities with CRAFT," *Harvard Business Review*, March–April, 1964, pp. 136–158.

Stock Retrieval. In large warehouses where thousands of product items are stored over a dozen acres, the problem of retrieving the stock on order becomes a significant task. Where the design of the warehouse is to locate stocks on a space-available basis, causing the layout constantly to shift, retrieving the stocks requires some formal plan. An obvious benefit of the random-locator system is that it contributes to better space utilization by better matching the peak space requirements among products.

Some companies use a card coding system whereby products are matched to a location code as identified on a card. The cards are filed by product. Retrieval is made by withdrawing a card according to the product desired. This is a manual system. However, it is easily adapted to a computer. A time-shared computer system is useful here because of its moderate cost, and especially because the input-output device, usually a

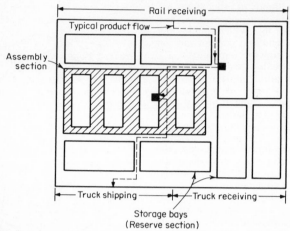

Fig. 4-4 Stock layout and product flow in a food distribution center. (Ronald H. Ballou, "Improving the Physical Layout of Merchandise in Warehouses," *Journal of Marketing*, vol. 31, July, 1967, p. 61.)

teletypewriter, can be located on the warehouse floor to be used by the operating personnel.

IMPLEMENTATION

Obtaining the Models Chief among sources of models are computer companies that offer software packages along with computer equipment and services, software companies specializing in providing computerized versions of the models, consultants who specialize in handling distribution problems, and university professors who are concerned with the physical distribution area.

Perhaps of more concern than simply where to obtain the models is the issue of whether you should use an "off-the-shelf" model, use a customized version of it, or develop a custom-designed model to fit your specific application. This is a philosophical issue and cannot be resolved with hard-and-fast rules. An off-the-shelf model is appealing because it is relatively inexpensive. But too often the design considerations are averaged across a wide variety of problem circumstances so that there may be some problems with matching the model to individual circumstances. Of course, the more custom the model becomes, generally the more expensive it is. Some facility planning models cost as much as $100,000 to develop, whereas off-the-shelf models are in the $30,000 to $40,000 range. However, custom models have a higher potential for manager appeal since they are often more credible to the manager and subordinates, and thus the higher cost may more than be offset by the improved managerial acceptance and model performance. Probably a good decision rule here is to tend toward off-the-shelf models if (1) your problem is fairly well standard with that of many other companies,

(2) the cost of acquiring the model is a concern, and (3) the presence of the model in the organization and its results are likely to be easily accepted by the personnel.

Concerns in Implementation Once a model has been obtained, there are three major tasks that must be performed before the model can become an effective planning or operational tool. These are (1) data collection, (2) personnel coordination, and (3) pretesting the results.

Data Collection. Collecting data for the model is a necessary but often expensive and unexciting task. It can involve many hours of company personnel time that do not show up on the profit and loss statement as an assignable cost. Yet, the performance of any model cannot be better than its data inputs.

Data collection can be facilitated by developing a table that shows the specific data items to be collected, their dimensions, the probable source, date to be acquired, and who has the responsibility for collection. This table is the plan for data collection as well as a control device. It works well where a number of people in different functional areas of the firm must be involved in providing the data.

Personnel Coordination. No model is likely to realize its full potential unless those that must deal with the model and its results accept what it can do. One of the best ways to gain this acceptance or early understanding of what the problems of implementation are likely to be is to set up a coordinating committee of all potentially affected people and *involve them* in the planning stages of the modeling effort. A good bit of the negative organizational energy can then be vented and dealt with before it can undermine the project.

Pretesting the Results. Pretesting is too often overlooked in the haste to put the model to work. Pilot testing the model in an actual but controlled situation can build needed confidence and provide a final opportunity to establish its credibility before making major commitments based on the model results, or making the model operational.

Getting Help Sources of help are readily available. First, look to your own staff people. If you are associated with a large firm, it is likely that such help is available from analysts within the physical distribution function or at least from a centralized operations research group.

Second, a number of consulting groups now specialize in transportation and distribution problems, and may be able to provide a consulting package of both model and expertise.

Third, university professors specializing in the physical distribution, business logistics, or transportation fields can provide such help directly or suggest further sources of help.

SELECTIVE BIBLIOGRAPHY

Ballou, Ronald H., *Business Logistics Management*, Prentice-Hall, Englewood Cliffs, N.J., 1973.

Ford, L. R., and D. R. Fuekerson, *Flows in Networks,* Princeton University Press, Princeton, N.J., 1962.

Heskett, J. L., Nicholas A. Glaskowsky, Jr., and Robert M. Ivic, *Business Logistics: Physical Distribution and Materials Management*, second edition, Ronald, New York, 1973.

Magee, John F., *Physical-Distribution Systems*, McGraw-Hill, New York, 1967.

Starr, Martin K., and David W. Miller, *Inventory Control: Theory and Practice*, Prentice-Hall, Englewood Cliffs, N.J., 1962.

Wagner, Harvey M., *Principles of Operations Research*, Prentice-Hall, Englewood Cliffs, N.J., 1969.

Chapter 5

Computer Applications in Personnel Management

EDWARD A. TOMESKI, Ph.D

Consultant, New York, New York; Associate Professor,
Fordham University, New York, New York

HAROLD LAZARUS, Ph.D.

Dean, School of Business, Hofstra University,
Hempstead, New York

A progressive use of computers, employing integrated information system approaches, can increase the effectiveness of human resource systems. These plans can provide valuable information for decision making and can facilitate human contact and communication by freeing the personnel staff of paperwork burdens.

Various studies have indicated, however, that human resource systems have failed to keep pace with the general advance of computer technology and its other applications, such as the financial ones. A recent survey by the authors, of 87 United States organizations, revealed that little progress has been made in achieving personnel systems which provide information that improves administrative decision making. These organizations were selected from among all the Federal departments, all the state administrations, the 50 largest county and city administrations, and the *Fortune* list of the 500 largest business organizations. Some of the criticisms of the personnel function and related areas include the following.

The personnel function is not management-oriented. It is so absorbed with such fragmented, immediate problems as hiring employees on a crisis basis that it does not have the planning horizon needed at the management level.

The personnel function is not adaptable to change. It is prone to accept conditions as it finds them; consequently the personnel function often appears to be antiquated and unresponsive to organizational needs.

The personnel system is absorbed in relatively unimportant tasks like record keeping. It cannot adequately provide for its central mission of planning for and developing the human resources of the organization.

In general, administrative offices function at low levels of productivity and are measured against inappropriate standards. This suggests poor management and a lack of motivation on the part of employees. Unfortunately, personnel departments have done little to improve managers' leadership techniques and to stimulate employees' needs for achievement.

THE COMPARTMENTAL APPROACH

Most computerization of personnel data has been accomplished on a disjointed basis, in relative isolation from related work and without an overall systems design and plan. Figure 5-1 illustrates how the compartmentalization in such an approach impedes coordination and the achievement of common objectives.

This approach necessitates considerable searching and analysis by the personnel staff. Data are scattered in such files as employee records, recruitment, education and training, payroll, medical, and benefits. Frequently, there is considerable duplication of data, and perhaps more important, there is frequently a disparity among data which should relate or coincide. Furthermore, the files are not always up to date.

Organizations may have hundreds of separate personnel documents designed to collect hundreds or thousands of different items of data. Some data are reported time and time again. As a result, the personnel staff has difficulty in accurately and quickly

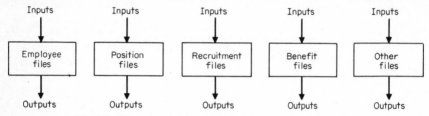

Fig. 5-1   Compartmental approach to personnel computerization.

searching data to find answers. Personnel neglects important activities, including human contact, because of the pressures of handling clerical work.

AN UPDATED APPROACH

An alternative approach is the development of an overall plan for a management information system. A model of such a system is presented in Figure 5-2. When a system is designed within an overall plan, a high degree of coordination and commonality of goals results. Note that there is a single stream of input data through an array of appropriate computer programs. The several databases are linked together for coordinated processing.

Other related areas (such as the budget and financial systems) have clearly defined communication paths to and from the personnel system. Outputs from the system are available to administrators, personnel staff, and authorized employees. Provision is available, via a data terminal, for authorized personnel directly to interrogate and use the system.

It is necessary to incorporate the personnel system within a total organizational system interrelated and interacting with the other systems. This approach entails integrating, by use of the systems approach, the various personnel files. It also aims at maintaining up-to-date records, so that inquiries can be answered with timely and accurate information. Such an approach should result in elimination of much duplication and many inconsistencies in existing files.

If an effective computerized personnel system is to be developed, certain minimum essentials must be met. There must be a personnel database which includes all data needed to make decisions and to fulfill legal and other report requirements. The database includes facts about employees' skills, personal histories, employment records, and benefits. In addition, data about positions, the personnel budget, as well as other relevant facts can be included. Before inclusion in the base, the data must be filtered and edited to assure accuracy, nonredundancy, and consistency. Provision must be made for updating the data so that they reflect a status that is current. Moreover, there is need for assurance that the data are available only to authorized individuals. Figure 5-3 illustrates the movement upward from objective data, used for routine decisions, to subjective information, used for nonroutine decisions.

Since the database usually entails consolidation and integration of formerly scattered and segmented files, it should provide information more pertinent and reliable than that previously used. Provision must be made to give access to those who formerly had access to the unintegrated files.

The same database can be tapped by all interested and authorized individuals to

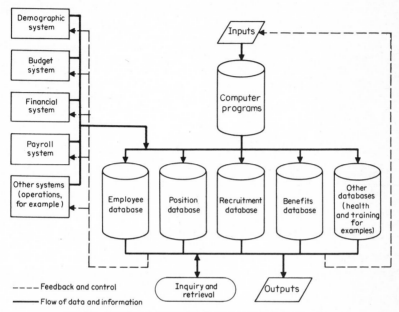

Fig. 5-2   **Model of an integrated computerized personnel system.**

serve their particular requirements. In addition, management can use the database to monitor the personnel effort.

PRIVACY AND PERSONNEL SYSTEMS

The organization using a database for its personnel records may be faced with privacy problems. Some data may be included that are relatively objective and not controversial: name, profession or skills, physical description, etc. Even in this area, sensitive issues arise related to potential bias based on race, color, sex, religion, age, etc. On the other hand, such statistics are required for reports to government agencies and the like.

Other data will be less public, yet hardly private, such as maiden name, former spouse, hobbies, etc. Certain data may contain private material, including results of medical examinations, details of income, alimony, and possibly arrest and conviction records. Finally, there may be records of personal details of which not even the employee may be aware, such as results of psychological tests, reference checks, career potential evaluations, and the like.

Management has a systems obligation to consider carefully who, and under what circumstances, has the right to such data. There must be confidence that:

● Data inserted into the database are correct, or bear some indication as to level of credibility and confidentiality.

● Information, once inside the database, is accessible only to individuals authorized to receive it.

A related question is whether an employee has or does not have the right to inspect his or her complete personnel record in the database. Only by permitting the employee to verify the record is there assurance that the data are indeed accurate and up to date. (There is as yet no legislation requiring such disclosure, but laws now on the books regarding the access by an individual to information about him or her in the files of credit companies are an indication that personnel management will be well advised to keep abreast of developments in this area.)

For the personnel manager, management by exception can be programmed for such ongoing problems as pinpointing those employees for whom salary increases are overdue; determining which recommended pay changes are in excess of or below specified

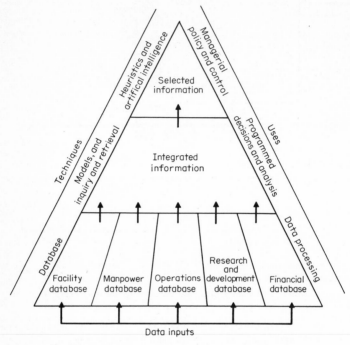

Fig. 5-3   Personnel management information system concept.

criteria; identifying those employees whose pay levels are inconsistent with their performance appraisals; identifying personnel or organizational units that have excessive lost time; and indicating personnel requisitions that have remained unfilled for excessive periods of time.

Management is also in a position to obtain studies that were formerly difficult, if not impossible, to acquire. Employee bargaining groups might want to know quickly the specific costs of extending vacation allowances an additional week for certain employees. It might be desirable to identify all jobs that will be open, in the next several years, because of retirements. A study of recruiting sources, in order to facilitate reduced costs and increased quality and quantity of candidates, could be undertaken.

Eventually, an organization's computerized database might be supplemented by interconnection with external databases. For instance, it would be possible to have computer communications with a cooperative industry-wide data bank, a network of public and private employment offices, and with government facilities like the Department of Labor and the Civil Service Commission.

This type of computer network would provide for such efficient measures as a rapid job–person matching system, consolidated personnel data, and the comprehensive salary surveys. However, such an integrated information network is a substantial undertaking. It requires careful planning for phasing the parts of the system when economically and technically feasible.

SELECTIVE BIBLIOGRAPHY

Dukes, Carlton W., *Computerizing Personnel Resource Data*, American Management Association, New York, 1971.

Martino, R. L., *Personnel Management Systems*, Management Development Institute, Wayne, Pa., 1969.

Morrison, Edward J., *Developing Computer-based Employee Information Systems*, American Management Association, New York, 1969.

Tomeski, Edward A., and Harold Lazarus, *People-oriented Computer Systems*, Van Nostrand Reinhold, New York, 1975.

APPENDIX

ITT's "AIMS" and "REDI" Programs

J. P. O'BRIEN   *Manager, Personnel Administration Center, International Telephone and Telegraph Corporation, World Headquarters, New York, New York*

"AIMS"

At its World Headquarters in New York, ITT's Corporate Personnel Division has put detailed job-related information about all ITT executives, including those of its subsidiaries, into a comprehensive computerized personnel information retrieval system — AIMS, for Automated Information Management System. The information is stored, updated, and processed at the ITT World Headquarters Data Processing Center in New York.

Data are entered and edited via an intelligent terminal and then transmitted for batch processing. Begun in 1969, this skills inventory now covers some 3,200 high-level executives and key managers who provide the leadership for this multinational corporation's 409,000 employees in more than 80 countries.

A three-page Profile Report (see Figure A-1) is available on any executive being considered for promotion or transfer. The print-outs cover (1) personal data, including education and language proficiencies, location preferences, and even nickname and wife's nickname; (2) career history data, including strongest background functions and function interests; and (3) compensation data. The AIMS file is updated weekly, and as a double check there is a complete yearly audit. All personnel transaction information on this executive category flows through the central information center in New York, where the personnel data processing group analyzes it and inputs the appropriate information into the data bank.

"REDI"

ITT's second major personnel system, REDI — Register for Development and Identification — covers some 4,000 middle management personnel in North America. Movement in this group is much greater than in the other, and so no attempt is made to update the file weekly (although termination and hires are inputted immediately). Semiannually, a complete package of profiles is sent to personnel directors at all locations for

ITT'S EMPLOYEE PROFILE PRINTOUTS

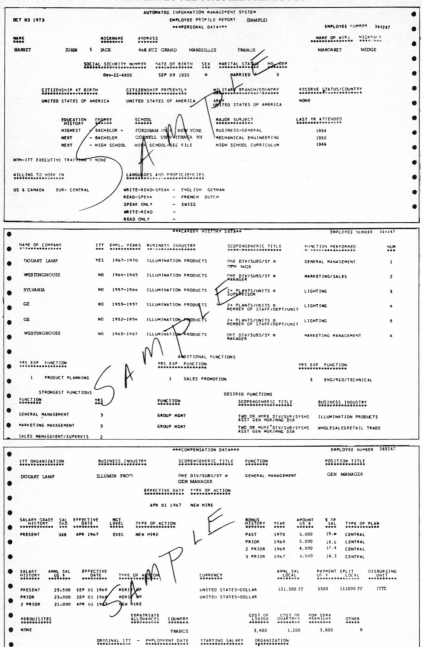

Fig. A-1   ITT's employee profile print-outs.

review and updating. In addition, this system has been made available to ITT groups for their own use; thus these groups can place all their employees into the system.

INFORMATION FOR DECISION MAKING

ITT's comprehensive computer operations and wide-encompassing databases, of course, make possible the assembly, summarization, and interpretation of data for a broad range of human resources decisions, over and above the profile print-out for individual promotion and career-development purposes. Development of information for the profiles has obviously facilitated the production of the other analyses and decision-making reports. Because most requests are for ad hoc reports, both an in-house developed extract/report generator and ASI-ST are used extensively. (ASI-ST, by Applications Software, Inc., is a proprietary general-purpose data management software system that facilitates the retrieval of desired information from computer files and the preparation of standardized reports. The use of a higher-level language enables nonprogrammers to access the computer by simple English statements.) Future plans include a database management system with later conversion to an on-line system.

Chapter **6**

ADP in Marketing and Advertising

EVELYN KONRAD
Evelyn Konrad Associates, New York, New York

The seventies could be called "the decade of realism" in computer use in marketing and advertising.

This sweeping generalization positions this decade in diametric opposition to the "promotional and overglamorized decade" of the sixties. It not only refers to the attitude prevailing among users and sellers of marketing and advertising applications, but also characterizes the types of applications that have found acceptance as compared with those of the sixties that have been discarded.

Broadly, computer applications in marketing, advertising, and media fall into the following categories: (1) data processing, such as tabulations of statistical data; (2) analytical applications, reorganizing raw data input into information for decision making or evaluation; and (3) predictive models. Actually, there is considerable overlap between these three categories, but the classification may help understanding. On the whole, it is a progression from simple computation that may be as applicable to accounting or production data as it is to marketing, advertising, or media data, to finding mathematical relationships between diverse parts of the input for the sake of better understanding, and ultimately, to the most sophisticated attempts to draw a picture of the real world through mathematical relationships and show what may happen in the real world as one or more of the variables change.

EVOLUTION OF COMPUTER USE IN MARKETING

The following capsule summary of the evolution in the use of computers for marketing and advertising processing and decision making is offered to focus attention on the key differences in the state of the art during this decade, in contrast with the decade of the sixties:

1. Marketing professionals in in-house marketing departments, marketing research firms, advertising agencies, and the media have come to accept computers for data processing and for sophisticated analysis of marketing information as routinely as they accept typewriters and duplicating machines as a standard part of office equipment and procedures.

In the early sixties, the workhorse processing capability of the computer was being imbued with magic, and the promoters of hardware and software trumpeted a future when computers rather than people would provide instant total insight, cutting tedious paperwork and clerical costs. Today, data processing in marketing, advertising, and media analysis is viewed not as a magic substitute for human labor, but as a practical tool providing speedier and more precise information based on existing data, without the exaggerated overtones that permeated computer applications a decade ago.

2. The character of model building for the broad spectrum of marketing, advertising, and media decision making is drastically different from the model building of earlier years:

• Modest goals rather than global promises dominate the marketing world. For example, a number of the highly publicized media selection models of the sixties, such as BBDO's linear programming models, Young & Republican's High Assay simulation model, and the COMPASS and COUSINS Group media selection models have been generally abandoned.[1] In their place, advertisers and agencies alike use a variety of so-called intramedia models whose more modest aims can be fulfilled without reliance on the large quantity of doubtful subjective judgments that were required to feed the more ambitious earlier models, which in effect sought to compare apples and oranges without adequate data support.

• The competitive search for "global" models of advertising effectiveness and consumer behavior has been relegated, on the whole, to the academician. In place of these generalized models, with their thus far relatively unproductive and not too reliable output to date, sophisticated marketers today seek highly specific brand-share and brand-switching answers from models based on *single product category* information that lends itself to reliable and valid statistical manipulation.

• Frantic "me-firstism" and "me-tooism" among advertisers and agencies alike have been replaced with a far more wholesome cooperative attitude, as the professionals in marketing have realized that common knowledge can benefit all, and that common effort is better than bankrupting the pioneer, whose time lead with a new application is doomed to be short-lived at best.

• The development of excellent time-sharing facilities has been a great equalizer in the marketing community, making it possible for the pioneering large companies to allocate their major effort to some innovation, but making a wide variety of excellent marketing applications as accessible to the medium-sized firm as they are to the large and powerful one.

3. The communications gap between the computer-oriented operations researchers and marketing professionals has narrowed slightly, but unfortunately not sufficiently to permit free discourse without benefit of translator. This problem does impede, or at least slows, the dissemination of excellent techniques to smaller firms that may lack specialized talent capable of examining and evaluating diverse applications. It also impedes the understanding on the top corporate executive level, where model building must receive financial support.

However, there are some hopeful developments in contrast with the sixties: Most time-sharing applications lend themselves to use by the marketing and media individual, without extensive knowledge of computer programming. This fact has finally made many mature marketing and advertising professionals as comfortable with "the big black box" as grade school children in those elementary schools that are wired to time-sharing systems. Indeed, such early exposure, in our educational system, to new math and to computers gives the hope for the eighties that the new generation will face computers head on without mystique, just as they can take space travel for granted without the overtone of awe that hampers comprehension among the present "over-thirty" generations.

4. In the decade of the seventies, increased computer use in marketing and advertising is also considerably narrowing the gap between the business world and the university world of quantitative analysis and computer models and simulations.

[1] All these models attempted to develop a computerized systems approach to media selection for clients' advertising campaigns. Each of the models quantified certain judgmental characteristics of media in order to weigh the value of a magazine advertisement in comparison with network programming inserts or TV or radio commercial schedules. In contrast with these ambitious early models, the later intramedia models were restricted to alternative choices within specific media without comparing, for example, print to air.

For instance, the marketing personnel at such large, sophisticated firms as General Motors, General Foods, Lever, Colgate, Gillette, P&G, Ford, Bristol-Myers, and Corn Products, to mention just a handful of leaders, are on easy and conversational terms with such leading academic authorities on marketing and media modeling as M.I.T.'s Professor Little, Columbia's Professor Starr, and Harvard's Professor Buzzell, among others.

By the same token, mathematical approaches to marketing problems have left a number of the old stars of academia "out in left field," along with obsolete business executives. Indeed, entire marketing departments in business schools, dominated by consultant professors who had their heyday in the fifties, have become irrelevant to today's marketing world.

5. Some highly sophisticated techniques, originally developed in other disciplines such as economics and finance, are finally seeping through to the marketing leaders. Thus, econometric methods are being applied to certain sales and profit forecasting problems. Dynamic programming, which was conceived for capital budgeting decision making, is creeping into brand-advertising planning.

In brief, the prediction about eventual cross-fertilization which was stressed in an earlier book on computers[2] is starting to come true: Computer sciences are beginning to break down the artificial separation between some of the corporate functions, such as finance and marketing, which must be tightly linked together if a firm's decision making in marketing is to be based on profit responsibility and on profit-oriented goals.

CURRENT APPLICATIONS

Following are some of the computer applications that are in current use among most large and many middle-sized marketers:

The simplest form of sales forecasting, aside from sheer guess, is a regression analysis carried forward on the assumption that the relationships that maintained historically between sales and the particular regressand chosen will persist. Of course, there are some variations on that theme, as additional variables are added to the model and allowed to interact simultaneously, as they do in an econometric model.

Marketers, particularly of consumer products, now frequently subscribe to one or more of the currently popular econometric models, such as the Wharton School model, or the St. Louis monetary model, or the DRI model of Harvard economist Dr. Otto Eckstein. They then take the relevant sector prediction as their base, and relate this sector forecast to their sales according to their own regression coefficient, based on prior internal modeling.

On the other extreme are the multitude of routine tabulations and cross-tabulations of the tonnage of statistics that marketers buy from such syndicated market research services as A. C. Nielsen, Audits & Surveys, W. R. Simmons, MRCA, to cite just a few.

Literally thousands of men and women throughout the country labor in marketing and market research departments of major advertisers, doing analyses and cross-analyses of this research and statistical avalanche that is part of the condition of the marketing and media person today. The use of computer applications to speed up these computations and tabulations has in no way diminished the number of these staff analysts. Rather, it seems to have stimulated the computation of more and more variations and permutations of the basic statistical output. Thus computer applications relate Nielsen Food and Drug data to company sales territories or else to brand-purchase cycles based on consumer panels or to a great variety of marketing or media statistics. These "workhorse" programs are frequently supplied by outside data processing services, and an increasing number of them are offered on a time-sharing basis.

This is not to dismiss the need for these computations simply because they lack the glamour of beating new trails in marketing decision making. They have general application, cutting across industries and company size. In fact, these simple data processing programs are so generally accepted that their user no longer gains much competitive advantage from having them. However, the competitive edge always goes to

[2] Evelyn Konrad et al., *Computer Innovations in Marketing*, American Management Association, New York, 1970.

the marketer who asks the better, more probing questions—a function of proprietary marketing research; and, of course, the rewards also go to the marketer who draws the right inferences from the data.

GUIDELINES FOR ADVANCED APPLICATIONS

As we move into the area of "inferences drawn" or intelligence to be derived from raw figures, we find a handful of new and exciting computer applications that provide useful guidelines for other marketers. An overview of such applications comes, as one would expect, out of the marketing departments of the larger firms. The following comments by Henry R. Kropp, manager of marketing planning systems and analysis, General Foods, sets the tone:

> General Foods uses computers for just about every quantifiable marketing function, starting with data processing and tabulations. In models, we use simulations of marketing processes from advertising spending, budget allocation, competitive pricing to new product introduction, where we do share predictions, as well as profit and sales forecasts. We also use risk analysis, and we use simulation for test marketing.
>
> In forecasting, we use primarily models that look at historical trends in the structural characteristics of the market, understanding what variables affect product competition. That is, we combine competitive interaction, assuming quality parity in advertising with competitors. We are also looking at purchase behavior trends in product categories. This program has been operational for four or five years. Other companies working in this direction include Coca Cola, Lever and Gillette, all marketers who are applying more science to marketing decisions.[3]

At Lever Brothers, William T. Moran, marketing research director, and a Y&R veteran and long-time computer and modeling enthusiast, is at this writing building up the information development and analysis capability within the Lever Marketing Research Department. Lever has developed a substantial inventory of intriguing and apparently effective computer models, some entirely staff-developed, others clearly aided by outside consultants. William Moran explains Lever's philosophy this way: "We work both with staff and with outsiders to develop models. We have programmers on staff, but we don't want their time spent on programming, but rather on analysis of the data and the output."

The firm's basic approach to model building is highly pragmatic, addressing itself to finding useful and understandable answers to urgent and repetitive marketing questions. "We are not looking for theoretic answers to the *totality* of the marketing process," Moran has stated. "Rather, we're looking at those problems that we face daily, and we're studying them in the context of defined product categories. In this way, we can deal with hard fact and easier-to-get research input, rather than having to rely on unproved assumptions."

A typical example is a relatively simple *promotion pay-out* model which Lever developed recently as a usefel and continuing time-sharing application. For example, prior to having this model, the firm used to expose a test panel to sampling, compare the results with a control panel, and interpret the figures in terms of sales results. This approach, which is fairly typical of current marketing research practice, tended to be inconsistent from one time period to another and from one product category to the next.

The promotion pay-out model, on the other hand, works this way: The measured results of each promotion are programmed into the data bank, which also has stored in it (1) the product category consumption rate, and (2) financial information to convert cases of products sold and the time elapsed between launching a promotion and the additional sales volume, into incremental dollar value vs. incremental cost of the promotion, using discounted cash-flow techniques. In other words, the program answers these two basic questions:

1. How much will it cost Lever to get a specific incremental consumption of a particular brand?

2. How long will it take to get there?

A modest program? Yes and no. It could be called modest in the sense that it has cut down the number of variables to the controllable bare essentials, thus making the program relatively inexpensive to use. On the other hand, it is highly sophisticated be-

---

[3] Interview with the author.

cause it relates as aspect of the marketing function, namely promotion, to the basic corporate goal, which is profitability, by studying *incremental consumption* in terms of *incremental costs*. Furthermore, as a reflection of concern with fast-moving competitive pressures, the program takes into account the time effectiveness of the promotion. William Moran has further reported as follows:

> We are now developing empirical response functions to promotions by type and brand. The types of in-store promotions we're studying are (1) dealer allowances, and (2) price-off promotions. Ultimately, we will have a family of curves for each brand in a product category. Right now, we have no effective knowledge about where each brand is on the promotion-budget-to-sales curve. Of course, marketing judgment is pretty good, and we know that most advertising heavy-up tests are not successful because the brand in question is approaching infinite elasticity where its response to promotion is concerned; that is, it has matured.
>
> But if we had response curves for each brand and each part of the country, then we would know rather than having to rely on judgment alone. We're now at the early stage of this study, relating sales to such variables as own advertising weight, competitive advertising weight and sales, and promotions.
>
> Again, our approach to the project has to be on the basis of product category because elasticity to advertising weight differs. Once we have the fully family of curves, then it becomes a question of resource allocation for greater marketing return to investment.

Moran's comments point up two significant developments related to the use of computers in marketing and advertising decision making:

• In the last few years, the concept of brand and product elasticities has been increasingly applied by knowledgeable marketing people. This basic microeconomic concept simply refers to the amount of change in one variable with respect to a finite change in another variable: for instance, what a brand's response in increased market share will be as a result of a unit increase in advertising weight.

• The goals of the marketing function have shifted from overemphasis on sales and market-share objectives to consideration of total corporate profitability. This healthy development is rooted in a changed philosophy, rather than being merely symptomatic of the profit pinch of the early seventies. It is closely related to the concept of *management by objectives* that is increasingly becoming a part of executive-suite thinking.

In discussing more scientific approaches to corporate diversification and mergers, the present author has argued[4] that interdisciplinary approaches, cutting across the artificial functional separation of marketing and finance on the corporate level and applying scientific knowledge from both the social and physical sciences, will be essential to effective corporate planning and decision making in the seventies. This approach is now winning acceptance in profit-conscious corporations.

MARKETING MODELS

The costliest corporate errors in market decisions tend to center around hasty and ineffective new-product development, and excessively long and costly support of moribund product lines. In between these two extremes, going business momentum tends to obscure or at least compensate for lesser errors in judgment. However, as computer-aided marketing decision making relates the probability of success from alternative strategies to the corporate balance sheet and income statement, corporate decision makers will find that the payoff from more innovative strategies in new-product development will minimize the risk involved. Important work in these areas is being done at Wharton, Harvard, M.I.T., and other well-known business schools, centering on the use of marketing models.

An insight into the use of marketing models is furnished by the Hendry Corporation, a firm which has pioneered in this field, whose basic model is used by such companies as Lever Brothers, Coca Cola, General Foods, and others. The *Hendry marketing theory* contends that market structure for diverse product categories is fairly stable, but that marketing environment is changeable. Four innovative marketing models stem from this seemingly modest insight: (1) the *strategy impact* model, which establishes market structure, analyzes the dynamics of the market, and measures the impact of these changes; (2) *advertising weight to share of market and to contribution to profit* model; (3) a *price/promotion pay-off* model; and (4) the *distribution to share of*

---

[4] Evelyn Konrad, "Corporate Planning Shouldn't Be a One-Man Band," *Innovation*, November, 1971.

market and contribution to profit model. All use marginal or incremental analysis to determine the return on the marketing investment. An example of a particular application will clarify the meaning of the term *market structure* and *environment* as used by Hendry.

Let us assume, for example, that a company wishes to make some strategic decision about the effect of a change in advertising weight on a beer brand's share of market, sales, and profitability. As its first step, the company undertakes a consumer research project, using either diary data, personal or telephone interviews, structured questionnaires, or a panel. It is essential to the program that each respondent shows what brands he or she bought on the two immediately preceding occasions. Such information cannot be sifted out of most current syndicated marketing research.

These sample data are entered into the computer, and the model analyzes them in terms of the elasticities of substitution between the firm's brand and the competing brands. The varying brands are then partitioned according to their elasticities of substitution, showing the structure of the beer market. For instance, Brand A may be twice as interchangeable or substitutable for Brand B as it is considered to be a substitute for Brand C and Brand D. On the other hand, Brand C and D may be close substitutes for each other, according to the documented consumer purchase behavior. The computer output therefore shows not only the brand's share of market, but also the competing brands on which it is likeliest to make inroads if the advertising weight is increased.

The model is geared to showing the impact of increased advertising weight not only on brand share but also on the incremental profit of the brand. According to Hendry:

> The elasticities of substitution computed by the model are natural elasticities based on purchase information. The program then defines both the brand share and where the brand's market is. It defines where the marketing strategies will have their impact.
>
> We are now at the "if this, then that" stage, because we have identified (1) the elasticities; (2) the brand or product-type attributes, implicitly as perceived by the consumer in terms of his or her purchase behavior; and (3) the hierarchy implicit in this market structure.
>
> We also program into the model the total competitive environment, that is, price, distribution, and advertising weight of all the brands in the product category. The data are available either from the firm or from the varying syndicated research services the firm buys. It does not require any additional original research. The model then generates a par-share index, a central tendency, and, in the case of a potential new brand, a critical advertising level (namely the minimum advertising budget the brand must have in order to achieve the anticipated market share for a one-time trial).
>
> The model allows variations of (1) price, (2) distribution, (3) promotion, and (4) advertising weight; and by manipulating these, the marketer can determine the likely impact of a change in his strategy both on share and profits.

The above capsule summary, while obviously not a detailed description of the Hendry model, serves to highlight the following elements in the computer model approach:

1. The application of theory from other disciplines, for example that of product elasticities, a basic concept in elementary microeconomics.

2. The link-up of the marketing and financial functions at the critical point where marketing strategies can be measured in terms of their contribution to profit as well as to brand share. This additional and vital information gives management the hard-fact basis for deciding on the sales-versus-profit trade-off that may best suit the corporate short- and long-term objectives.

3. The splitting of a product market into bite-size segments or partitions that lend themselves to tailoring marketing strategies to very specifically defined target markets.

4. The appeal of the Hendry model is at least partially in the fact that it deals, in terms of original research, with definable, attainable, and relatively low-cost consumer probings that are entirely confined within product categories. This feature avoids the disadvantages of the "global attributes" of some of the operations research experimentations fashionable in the sixties.

The Hendry analysts cite the diversity of their applications, encompassing some 200 different product categories over the years, as lending generality to their market structure and market environment theory. However, as the models reach into consumer hard-good areas where the purchase cycle may be far more extended than it is for the package goods and supermarket-product industries where the Hendry track record has been built, there may be need to retool the research design which provides the basic input for the market structure information and for the market partitioning. However, there is little question but that the approaches used in such models are very much geared to the marketing thinking and marketing needs of this decade.

Further Experimentation The modeling and experimentation going on in universities, consulting firms, and using companies do include a number of attempts at more "global" and ambitious approaches. Currently, these tend to be confined to behavioral models that seek to predict consumer action based not so much on their historic purchase behavior within a product category, as on the laws of psychology, sociology, learning theory, and the other disciplines that combine to form a consumer behavioral theory. Two examples of such behavioral models may be mentioned, even though as of this writing neither is commercially available:

Professor John Howard, head of the Columbia University Marketing Department, originally applied his consumer behavior model in 1966 to a General Foods instant breakfast experiment. Then, in 1970, he used it in Argentina, for the largest soap company in the country, in order to determine whether it was culture-free. The model was tried also, on a pilot basis, on a couple of major United States car models. In terms of marketing significance, this program selects out the variables that can be influenced by marketing communications.[5]

Professor Howard's model is currently the only fully articulated buyer behavior model that has been tested. Some others, developed in the academic community but not yet tested, are the Ingo-Collatt & Blackwell system, named for three professors at Ohio State, who developed it at the end of the sixties; and the consumer decision process, developed in 1966 by Franco Nicosea, professor at Berkley. Still another new but untested model is the one recently developed by Professor Allan Andreason of the University of Buffalo.

In the meantime, another group of creative problem solvers, supported by the Advertising Research Foundation, set out in the mid-sixties to develop a model that could take into account the paradoxes of consumer purchasing patterns from the viewpoint of communication theory. This group includes Professor Martin Starr, also of Columbia University; BBDO's M. Lawrence Light, and Lever's marketing research director, William Moran. Their model is "Consumenoid I," which was gearing for a year of experimental test runs in 1973 and 1974.

Advertising Agency Activity BBDO's participation in this model-building effort is far from accidental: While the majority of agencies were racing out of computers (in terms of their own modeling effort) during the recession of the early seventies about as fast as they had been racing in during the prestige-conscious competitive early sixties, BBDO has been one of the few to buck this trend. Indeed, this agency began its Management Science Department in 1969 with two or three people, and four years later had 24 people in this activity, reporting to a senior vice president.

Again, it is interesting to note, and perhaps to be expected in the light of the structural changes in the agency business since the late sixties, that only a handful of agencies are with BBDO in fighting the trend. For example, N. W. Ayer has an advanced methods group. Grey Advertising set up its separate Com-Step Computer subsidiary to sell a media processing system to other agencies and clients. However, this group has been experiencing the problems of other small firms in the highly competitive field of marketing computerized media processing systems, though its problems are doubtless aggravated by the firm's known tie with the Grey agency: It is no secret that agencies are loath to buy from their own competitors.

BBDO, which in the sixties had DEMON, a widely publicized product, has a current model, NEWS. The acronym stands for New Product Early Warning System. This model is being used as a predictive tool, as well as a simulation for test market purposes.

BBDO was also a pioneer of the early sixties in media planning and modeling, with its linear programming approach, developed in partnership with C-E-I-R. This, however, has long since dropped from use. Indeed, linear programming went the way of

---

[5] The Howard model is based on a complex set of variables related to motivations leading to buying decisions. It includes feedbacks over time, as the individual reshapes attitudes based on experience with a brand. A full description is contained in John Howard and James Hulbert, *Advertising and the Public Interest*, Crain Communication, Chicago, 1973.

all flesh even before Y&R phased out its complex simulation model for media selection, the "high assay" model. But then, the entire media planning, buying, and policing practices inside and outside agencies have been dramatically changed since the turn of this decade.

The media allocation problem, at BBDO, is currently handled by a more modest and manageable optimizing program, called MEDIAMAX, which uses integer programming and is written in FORTRAN V. "It is used by our media people in the early planning stage," says BBDO's Edward Brody, but he adds, "It is more generally used in pharmaceuticals than in consumer product media planning."

But at BBDO, as in other agencies, the focus of computer use for media purposes is on far more modest applications than intermedia comparisons and intermedia selection problems. In terms of "tonnage use," the computer is certainly standard operating equipment for media processing, but the key words are *processing* and *analysis*, rather than complex modeling.

In the light of this change of emphasis, it is perhaps not surprising that the service, as often as not, is provided by one of a handful of service companies, rather than being based on programming that is developed within and proprietary to the agencies. The exception, again, is BBDO, where marketing and media are considered to be too intimately linked to full-agency servicing of accounts to allow for outside contribution to their computerized information processing and analysis.

In contrast, Ted Bates's Jackie Da Costa sums up the attitude of the majority:

> The move is more to combining efforts. Agencies are more willing to share costs and pool efforts in some areas. For example, P&G has nine agencies sharing a budget allocation model through Nielsen.
>
> The multi-media selection model is not a dead issue either, if agencies get together and share the expense of reactivating a program like COMPASS or COUSINS. A media allocation model for one agency alone has limited use, because we find that the patterns don't change often enough to make the development and feeding of such a model economically sound.

Activity by Advertisers The delineation of responsibility, as between advertiser and agency, for media planning and modeling is not clearcut or well defined. However, a number of advertisers have plunged deeply into the media planning function that was the undisputed domain of the agencies in the early sixties. Thus Bristol-Myers has its own STAR (Spot Television Analysis and Retrieval) system for spot buying control; General Foods has a selection model. A number of other advertisers have full-blown media departments or media directors, including Gillette, Philip Morris, and Colgate. Not surprisingly, therefore, the focus for media modeling has also shifted away from the agencies in most cases.

Media Applications Aside from the large bulk of sheer processing applications that are implicit and totally accepted within the media function today, the single most popular type of application in the seventies seems to be a "reach and frequency" analysis, which is used as often during the planning stages of an advertising campaign as it is used after the buy to evaluate how close reality came to the stated objectives.

The impetus for postbuy evaluations actually came out of the competitive pressure that media buying services have exercised on agencies since the late sixties. The claim of these services has been that not only are the agencies less efficient in terms of spot TV buying, but they are "still unprofessional in methods used to maintain control over a spot schedule from the initial order to the final step," according to representatives for such services.

As might be expected, this attack, coupled with the increased cost consciousness of advertisers in the early seventies, has plunged into postevaluation even those agencies that had not traditionally performed this function. Young & Rubicam, which was a pioneer in use of computers for media planning, has a complex system for handling spot TV, including reach, frequency, target, demographic levels, and cost measures. BBDO has reach and frequency measures within its MEDIAMAX model. Doyle, Dane, on the other hand, does perform postbuy evaluations, but without benefit of computer programs. Grey Advertising is, quite naturally, a key client of its own Com-Step subsidiary for postbuy evaluations.

The majority of other major and middle-sized agencies are currently relying for this type of analysis on a handful of service companies which are carving out a modest specialized business based on media-related applications. Most of them offer these services on a time-sharing basis today, feeding answers, as required, through a number of terminals within agency media departments. Names of services in this field include Telmar, Interactive Marketing Systems, Donovan Systems, and Marketronics, all located in New York, headquarter city for most agencies.

Both the Nielsen Company, primarily known for its Food and Drug Index, but a strong factor in syndicated television research, and ARB, with its syndicated television and radio research, went into such computerized services in the sixties.

Judging from the price competition that exists between the remaining services, it would not be surprising if the field narrowed to two in this decade. This would not be because the applications they are selling are not in use, since they are, but rather because the economics of a business depending on sale to intermediaries such as agencies tend to be perilous at best.

CONCLUSION

Considering the many emerging techniques and the variety of applications, and the controversy surrounding many of the approaches, the following steps appear to be the logical ones for the marketing, advertising, or media manager to take as regards the application of computers to marketing and advertising:

1. It is essential to start with a thorough understanding of the problem and the way the answers to it are most likely to be used within the organization. In other words, the executive must start with (a) a tentative definition of the problem, although this definition may have to be altered as the investigation proceeds; (b) a tight understanding of the corporate purpose to which the output or information is likely to be applied, such as long-range planning and budget allocation; and (c) insight into the backgrounds of the various other executives who may be able to use these answers, with an idea about the relative importance of this information to them.

2. It is worthwhile to undertake a thorough study of all available applications in a specific problem area prior to taking the plunge. Neither this brief Chapter, nor some of the excellent books totally dedicated to computer use in marketing, pretend to cover the entire field. Such a study should cover at least the following basic questions:

• What types of models or programs address themselves to the particular areas of interest?

• What firms have used them to date, and with what results?

• What are the pros and cons of the specific techniques and approaches used, compared with alternative methods?

• What are the hardware, software, and cost parameters of these approaches?

• What are the financial strength and the fiscal responsibility of the varying outside suppliers of software?

A well-designed investigation of this nature should include a quantified evaluation matrix to help the executive make a selection from among the many sources and approaches available.

Opportunities Where are the untapped opportunities for the computer scientist who would like to develop new answers to marketing problems?

Some of the applications on the outer frontier of investment analysis might provide inspiration for simplified approaches to marketing problems. For example, Professor William F. Sharpe of the University of California, Irvine, has managed to reduce the multitude of variables studied laboriously, expensively, and often ineffectively in Wall Street to two sensible and manageable criteria for the intrinsic value of a security: namely, *risk* and *return*. Of course, there is still a good deal of controversy surrounding the best definition of risk. However, the model represents a valid step in the right direction of sounder investment analysis.

A comparable concept, relating a marketing strategy not only to its own return, but also to its impact on the complexity of consumer budgeting and buying decisions, would obviously represent a breakthrough for marketing.

Perhaps the salient message here is not so much the specific of the example cited, but rather the moral that inspiration for new approaches to modeling solutions for marketing problems may be far more likely to come out of other functional areas than marketing itself, and out of other disciplines. The reason? Not only do good computer models of the marketing world provide us with a new perspective, but we may well need a broadened perspective of marketing in order to create new, simplified, and meaningful marketing models.

Section 5

Managing the ADP Operation

Introduction

THEODORE J. FREISER   *Senior Vice President,*
John Diebold & Associates, New York, New York

Management of data processing in a modern corporation can be said to have two aspects, which might roughly be called the *internal* and the *external* — or, more suggestively, the *housekeeping* and the *functional*. The first, the internal, is actually the less difficult of the two, though it is the more involved with data processing technology and sophistication. It is the area of performance efficiency, software and hardware selection and optimization, project management and control, the management and motivation of data processing people, setting and enforcing standards, assuring data and data center security, setting up and maintaining cost charge-back systems — into this category fall all the details of running the operating and system development resources of a data processing department.

The second responsibility of data processing management, the external or functional one, is to support and enhance the conduct of the company's business on a cost-justified basis, deploying and using the available resources to best serve the company's needs.

The first aspect, the internal, is apt to be the focus of attention of data processing management: It engages more of the data processing manager's technical expertise and presents the kind of problem with which he or she feels at home. Often, this focus extends to an emotional identification with data processing, as a professional and as a social milieu, much stronger than the identification with the industry in which the company operates, or with the company itself.

The external duties of the manager — the duties oriented to the needs of the total enterprise — are actually the more important and the more demanding. The data processing department must be geared to providing service to the user. The gratifications of the technical and managerial people in the department must come from the knowledge that they have helped the company meet its goals, not from technical accomplishments. Satisfaction, that is, comes not from the successful implementation of an on-line order processing system (for example) but from the (perhaps unmeasurable) improvement in customer service and the consequent favorable impact on sales.

It goes without saying that the data processing department must respond to the felt and expressed needs of the functional departments, taking responsibility for bridging the communications gap that so often develops between the user and the data processing professional, and ensuring that needs are well met as they emerge.

Beyond this, however, is the more challenging task: to motivate and guide the functional people to take advantage of opportunities they do not perceive by themselves; to goad them, if necessary, to venture beyond the mechanizing of existing manual procedures into the beneficial approaches to corporate operations opened up by the computer. The potential gains from such applications as financial planning using corporate financial models, product-mix calculations through linear programming, and optimal plant loading through discrete simulation are often among the richest available to a company.

Data processing managers are on the horns of a dilemma: Their operations should be oriented to motivating for change, but their "customers" may not like or want change. As a service organization, the data processing department must be responsive to user requirements, but it must also work to apply its developing technology to support users in areas where there is payoff to the corporation—users may not be responsive to this. A manager who fails in this responsibility becomes an "order taker"—when the user says he or she wants a new or changed system, the data processing manager simply carries out this mandate, reducing the company's usage to the level of the least knowledgeable people in the company. On the other hand, balancing these two roles—that of the responsive service organization and that of innovator and gadfly—is the essence of managing the data processing function.

There are other nontechnical challenges to effective data processing management. The manager must guard against certain types of political conflict unique to data processing—conflict over such issues as centralized vs. decentralized organization, and lines of authority for making data processing decisions. A data processing manager need not fear decentralization of that activity. It may well be in the best interests of the company, and can create a very meaningful and effective role for the corporate data processing manager—guiding and counseling the users, maintaining commonality of hardware and systems, seeing to the development and enforcement of the standards necessary to ensure portability and transferability of systems and to facilitate hardware and software conversions, and monitoring levels of ADP training and ensuring their adequacy.

It is up to the corporate-level data processing manager to see to it that technical decisions by division-level data processing and functional managers are made on the basis of criteria significant to the corporation as a whole—and to see to it that technical groups making studies and recommendations are asking the right questions. (It is easy for such groups to bog down in detailed feature analysis in a hardware evaluation, for example, at the expense of such fundamentals as purchase terms and support commitments.)

On the one hand, data processing managers—who may not be business people by training and experience—sometimes fail to be cost-justification-minded, and may be overly enamored of technology. On the other hand, functional managers have sometimes tended to view data processing as a unique activity not subject to the same oversight and objective management to which such functions as manufacturing and marketing are routinely subjected. Often, data processing is initially permitted to "run away with" management, to be followed by a sense of dissatisfaction, sometimes resulting in management upheavals. Senior management must look at data processing as just another functional organization in the company, its projects monitored and evaluated exactly as if a new plant were being built, a new product being launched, or an advertising budget being set.

For his or her part, the effective data processing manager will not take advantage of any initial lack of control, but will direct the efforts of the organization toward the cost-justified, best interest of the company.

Chapter 1

Effective Corporate Placement of ADP: Organizational Considerations

WILLIAM R. POLLERT, Ph.D.

Manager, Soviet Commercial Development, International
Paper Company, New York, New York

"One of the most difficult, costly, and potentially disruptive problems our company faces today is the integration and repositioning of our ADP activities."

This comment from the executive vice president of a large divisionalized company is indicative of a problem currently facing many corporations. Traditionally, corporate ADP activities have been submerged in one or another functional department. Since ADP was initially used by most companies to process financial and accounting data, it is not surprising that the function often was placed in the finance and accounting department. At the same time the manufacturing, marketing, and R&D departments of many companies have developed their own ADP systems for inventory and production control, scientific calculations, and order entry and processing.

One of the primary reasons why ADP activities have been the organizational "captive" of functional departments has been that until recently management has thought of ADP in terms of a tool to facilitate the performance of a single transactional process. As such, ADP was placed so as to serve one user and only secondarily other potential users within the corporation.

Another factor which contributed to the traditional approach of locating ADP operations within user-departments was that first- and second-generation computers were designed either as scientific machines or as commercial machines. Thus an organization that had a need for both scientific research and commercial-type computing often had to have two or more separate data processing installations. Third-generation computers, on the other hand, have the capacity to perform both scientific and commercial operations. Consequently, it is now feasible for firms to generate both types of information from a single system.

The evolution of the systems approach to management during the sixties has brought with it the concept of comprehensive management information systems (MIS).[1] Unlike the transaction approach, MIS stresses coordinated management decision making.

---

[1] See Section 3, Part One, Chapter 2, "Concepts of Management Information Systems."

At the same time, the availability of third-generation computers with remote terminal capabilities and high-level programming languages has made it economic for a firm to consolidate its ADP activities. As a result, an increasing number of firms are centralizing ADP operations and redefining the role of ADP in terms of the total management information needs.

Problems of "Captive" and Centralized ADP Systems   Perhaps the single greatest weakness of the traditional placement of ADP in the controller's department and/or other user-departments has been that it has hindered rather than facilitated the generation of the type of coordinated decision-making information necessary to deal effectively with the complex business problems of the 1970s. The need for more integrated company-wide data has motivated the management of many firms to consolidate their ADP activities into an independent department that reports at the same organization level as the functional departments it serves. The shortage of experienced ADP personnel and rising system costs also have contributed to the trend toward ADP consolidation. Although the title of these ADP units varies from firm to firm, an appropriate composite title seems to be the Management Services and Information Systems Department.

Despite the apparent advantages in terms of cost and coordination of reorganizing and upgrading the ADP function into a separate department-level unit, several factors may militate against the total centralization of personnel and equipment in one location. For example, problems may arise because:

• The management of departments which currently have their own ADP operations may view ADP reorganization and centralization as a threat to their autonomy, status, and/or power. This in turn may result in costly morale problems, employee turnover, and/or communication breakdown.

• ADP centralization may make it difficult for a firm going through acquisition and merger to achieve system compatability with newly acquired firms. Unless adequate systems planning is done prior to a merger, obtaining ADP compatability between firms may be both costly and frustrating.

• Interdepartmental conflict may arise over billing and budget responsibility for development operation and use.

• The degree of ADP centralization may be inappropriate, given the firm's operating environment. As a result, user information needs may not be adequately met.

Although the above problems are real, many of them can be avoided or at least minimized if adequate organizational planning is done prior to ADP reorganization.

ADEQUATE ORGANIZATIONAL PLANNING

All too often, firms attempt to consolidate their decentralized ADP operations into a centralized "total system" staff unit overnight. This invariably results in costly communication breakdowns and organization disruption. On the other hand, a systematic planned evolution toward the establishment of a central *management service and information systems* unit has resulted in successful ADP consolidation in many companies.

Unfortunately, relatively few firms adequately plan for ADP reorganization or for the effects which such reorganization might have on the total corporate structure. Rather, many firms wait until their existing ADP organization becomes unworkable and then attempt to solve the problem through "instant" reorganization.

The problem of ineffective organizational planning is exemplified by the following statements from two executives of firms that had recently been involved in ADP reorganizations:

> About a year ago in one of our Monday morning executive meetings, our president raised the question of whether our EDP operations, which at that time reported to the controller, adequately met the information needs of our firm. After about an hour and a half of discussion, several areas for improvement were identified. Three weeks later we got a memo saying that all ADP activities would be consolidated under a new MIS department headed by our top systems man. Things have never been the same since. Reports are always late, costs have shot up, and we've lost two assistant controllers and three key ADP people. I think it will take us another year to get back where we were a year ago. . . . The funny thing is that the reorganiza-

tion was a good idea; it's just that we didn't put enough time into thinking the details of the reorganization out.

• • •

We're in our third ADP reorganization in four years. I'd hate to tell you how much these have cost us, both in dollars and cents and in personnel turnover. It seems to me that not enough planning has gone into any of these changes, or we wouldn't have had the problems we've had.

Although it would be impossible to outline all the variables which management might consider when developing an ADP reorganization strategy, the following four factors are essential and should be considered in any restructuring of corporate ADP:

Top-Management Commitment Perhaps the single most critical element in successful ADP organization planning as well as the actual reorganization itself is continuous top-management involvement. The importance of top-management commitment to ADP reorganization is illustrated in a study of 27 large firms with extensive ADP experience. This study found that in firms with effective ADP operations "corporate management had set clear-cut objectives . . . adequate resources had been marshalled to get the job done and the human organizational barriers to progress had been brought down."[2]

The Business Environment In addition to top-management involvement, consideration must be given to the nature of a firm's business environment. Recent studies indicate that firms competing for markets characterized by rapid technological change require a more decentralized ADP system to meet their information needs than firms operating in fairly stable markets where the primary means of competition are service and price. (The impact of corporate environment on ADP placement is discussed in greater detail later in this Chapter.)

Effect on Total Corporate Structure Since all functional departments handle and process information, any major revamping of the information processing structure will inevitably affect other departments and is likely to necessitate further organization changes. For example, ADP consolidation in a corporate staff unit often results in some recentralization of profit responsibilities. Further centralization of ADP has in some cases reduced the sphere of middle-management decision making because the lines of communication between top management and the level of decision implementation have been shortened. Although this may result in less distortion in the implementation of corporate plans, it may at the same time cause a breakdown in communication between top management and middle management and/or a redefinition of the role of middle management. To facilitate such changes, top management should make clear the objectives to be achieved through ADP reorganization, anticipate organization and personnel problems, and encourage participation in ADP planning by management groups potentially affected by ADP consolidation.

Involving a cross-section of corporate management in the development of ADP reorganization plans also is important to help ensure that the information needs of user-groups will be adequately met by the new ADP system. As each user-group's information requirements are evaluated vis-à-vis the potential capabilities of a new ADP department, corporate management will be able to reduce the risk of future communication breakdown.

Personnel Capabilities Finally, management should evaluate the ADP personnel capabilities. Establishment of an independent ADP service department will require that ADP staff be able to interact with and understand the information needs of diverse groups within the corporation. This may require a different type of person from one currently operating a captive ADP unit within a department. A combined strategy of hiring new personnel and staff training may be necessary to develop the right mix of people to manage and run an integrated ADP operation.

To summarize, consolidating and relocating the ADP function in a firm involves more than merely the technical problems attached to reprogramming independent computer systems. It involves people problems as well. As a result, ADP reorganization cannot be left to chance. Rather, for reorganization to be successful, top management along

---

[2] John T. Garrity, *Getting the Most Out of Your Computer*, McKinsey & Company, New York, 1973.

with a cross-section of corporate management must systematically plan for each phase of the reorganization.

FUNCTIONS OF AN ADP SERVICE DEPARTMENT

Consolidating the scattered ADP activities of functional departments into an independent ADP department generally results in broadening the scope of a firm's ADP operations. Existing functions, such as systems and procedures, operations research, and parts of industrial engineering, are often incorporated into a centralized ADP service unit.

In order to bridge the gap between an independent ADP service unit and user-departments, it is useful to conceptualize the functions of the ADP service group in terms of its own *marketing, product development, engineering,* and *production*. Thus, the management information system unit of the ADP department may be thought of as performing a marketing function—since it identifies the information needs of user-groups and develops along with user-groups a cost-benefit *systems project proposal*. Once completed, the proposal can be evaluated by both the user and top management to determine if resources should be allocated to develop the proposed system.

The systems and procedures unit of a consolidated system often performs a function similar to that of product development. This unit links the computer to the firm by translating the information requirements of users into systems, forms, and procedures. The systems and procedures unit also helps to assure product (information) compatability by setting overall standards for corporate ADP.

Once defined, the system requirements are converted into computer language by the computer programming unit. In effect, this is analogous to the applied engineering functions of a firm. Finally, the information "product" is produced ("manufactured") for user-groups by the operations unit.

HOW MUCH ADP CENTRALIZATION?

Current organizational research indicates that there is no one best way to organize a company. This is particularly true when it comes to defining the organizational relationships between an ADP service department and user-departments. At one extreme, management may attempt to consolidate equipment, personnel, and total ADP responsibility in one centralized ADP service unit, i.e., a monolithic-type ADP department. At the other, management may establish a loosely organized ADP "federation" in which standardized general operating policies are set by a central ADP department for quasi-autonomous ADP units located in departments.

The basic dilemma posed by ADP reorganization is the trade-off which inevitably must be made between the benefits of ADP decentralization and the need for an integrated corporate information flow. In general, the greater the degree of ADP decentralization, the greater the chance that the special information needs of functional departments will be met. On the other hand, the more decentralized a firm's ADP, the more difficult the problem of integrating and controlling the flow of decision-making information to top management. How this dilemma is resolved will inevitably affect the flow of management information, corporate planning, coordination, control, and ultimately profitability.

Achieving the proper organizational balance between a firm's ADP unit and user-groups is particularly difficult because of the number and complexity of factors which must be considered. Although the specific mix of factors which are weighed by management when reorganizing the ADP function varies from firm to firm, serious consideration always must be given to the following items: the firm's business environment; the extent to which the firm is vertically or horizontally integrated; and the costs and benefits of reorganization.

The Firm's Business Environment Where product innovation is the major characteristic of the market (unstable type of business environment), flexible, rapid decision making is essential. On the other hand, management decision making tends to be more proceduralized in companies competing for markets in which there is little product innovation and the primary means of competition is price and service (stable type of ' business environment). Thus, firms which are forced to compete through product innovation generally have less rigid bureaucracies, with fewer managerial levels than firms which produce a standard, unchanging product. Further, firms facing constant product innovation generally find that there is a greater difference in the goals, decision-making time frame, and interpersonal relationships among their functional departments (finance, marketing, R&D, and manufacturing) than is found in firms where product innovation is relatively unimportant. As a result, a highly centralized ADP unit may not be able adequately to satisfy the varied information needs of user-departments in firms characterized by rapid product change.

At the same time, however, some ADP coordination is necessary to assure adequate interdepartmental coordination. Under these circumstances, a "federation" type of ADP structure provides the best of two worlds. Departments can continue to operate their own on-line ADP systems. At the same time, these systems are integrated through a corporate ADP department. This is done by having the corporate ADP service unit set overall standards, documentation and operating procedures, and design parameters. The corporate ADP department also has the responsibility for seeing to it that there is an adequate interdepartmental flow of information and that top management receives the type of relevant coordinated information it requires to adjust effectively to changing market conditions.

Although departmental goals, time requirements, and interpersonal orientation as well as information needs differ in firms operating in relatively stable business environments, the difference is usually less than between similar departments in firms operating in unstable business environments. Further, the basic tasks performed by functional departments in firms producing a standard, unchanging product are better defined and more proceduralized than the tasks performed by similar departments in firms faced with constant product innovation. Because of the relative predictability of information requirements and similarity between department orientations, a single central ADP service department with remote terminals may best serve the ADP needs. In addition, a centralized MIS will enable top management better to coordinate and control department activities at the corporate level.

Obviously, between the extremes of a loosely coordinated federation-type ADP system and a single centralized corporate service department, there are numerous organizational variations which may better satisfy a firm's particular information needs. What is important is that in defining the organizational relationships between the corporate ADP service department and user-groups, corporate management consider the organizational constraints and information requirements placed on it by its business environment.

Vertical vs. Horizontal Integration The extent to which a diversified firm is vertically or horizontally integrated is a key consideration in ADP placement. In vertically integrated firms, such as steel companies, one division's output either totally or partially becomes the input of another division. The product divisions of a diversified conglomerate, on the other hand, often produce unrelated products for diverse external markets.

The relatively high sequential interdependence between product divisions in vertically integrated firms requires close management control and coordination to assure the proper flow of products between departments. To accomplish this, corporate management must rely on its MIS to provide detailed financial and nonfinancial information about the operations of all divisions. Under these conditions an independent, centralized corporate ADP service department may be better able to produce the type of total system information needed for effective decision making than a loosely coordinated federation-type ADP organization.

Since the only real interdependence between product divisions in a diversified, profit-decentralized conglomerate is financial, the need for interdivisional coordination is minimal. Corporate management generally controls and manages the firm by *exception*, i.e., management attention is primarily concentrated on divisions not meeting their profit objectives. In this situation, top management's information needs probably could be met adequately by either a centralized or less centralized federation-type ADP system.

If product divisions serve highly diverse and unrelated markets, and the firm is continuing to expand through mergers and acquisitions, a federation-type system in which some or all product divisions have their own ADP units may be most economical.

Each division will then be assured that its information needs will be met adequately. Equally important, the cost of converting the ADP system of acquired firms can be minimized until the parent company is satisfied that the acquisition will work out. As a conglomerate begins to consolidate, management may find cost savings in consolidating some or all divisional ADP units under a single ADP service department.

Multinational Operations   To this point, the question of vertical and horizontal integration has been discussed only in the context of domestic operations. Today, many American companies are rapidly expanding their international operations both horizontally (acquiring unrelated foreign firms) and vertically (where the output of one foreign subsidiary becomes the input of another). These firms, the so-called multinational corporations, are posing many new challenges of ADP control and information flow for management.[3] Because of the geographical distance between the corporate headquarters and foreign subsidiaries, a federation-type ADP organization is generally used.

Depending on the regional concentration of plants and foreign affiliates, some multinational corporations have established centralized, regional ADP units to serve their affiliates either through time sharing or by coordinating the ADP operations of affiliates in that region. Regional information is then fed into the corporate ADP unit in the parent company for integration and use by headquarters. The headquarters ADP department generally has line control over regional and/or affiliate systems, and establishes design, programming, and information standards, and also audits ADP operations. Experience with this type of system generally has been favorable, although problems do occur. According to the vice president of ADP operations in a large multinational corporation:

> We have a regional EDP system in Europe and individual affiliate systems in Latin America and the Far East. Although we have experienced some problems in system design and information transmittal between countries, the system provides the kind of financial, marketing, and operating information we need to compete in world markets.

Other multinational corporations which have subsidiaries scattered throughout the world, and/or are producing highly differentiated products, do not attempt to regionalize their data, but allow each affiliate to operate its own ADP system. Once again, the corporate ADP department sets the general operating framework for the affiliates' units, and affiliate information is periodically updated and maintained on the headquarters system. As with strictly domestic firms, the degree of international interdependence (in this case, between foreign affiliates) will affect both the degree of central control and the type of information transmitted to the parent company.

COST-BENEFIT COMPARISONS

As a result of rapidly rising computer and personnel costs, many managements have become disillusioned with the cost effectiveness of their ADP systems. To reduce these rising costs, many firms are looking to consolidate and reorganize their ADP operations. However, while cost savings often can be obtained through the reorganization and relocation of the ADP function, these changes must be weighed against the future information needs of the firm.

One of the problems frequently associated with the traditional approach of making ADP a "captive" of the user-department has been that it often leads to costly duplication and excess computer capacity. To assess the dollar effect of consolidating and relocating the ADP function, management must evaluate systematically the cost effectiveness of the current and proposed ADP systems.

The calculation of past and current ADP costs is relatively simple. Salaries, programming, design, overhead, and time-sharing costs generally are all available. From these cost figures, fairly reliable cost projections can be made for the continued operation of the existing ADP system. It is considerably more difficult accurately to estimate the cost of reorganizing and operating a new ADP system. Design, programming, and maintenance costs are invariably underestimated, as are organization disruption costs (i.e., personnel turnover, communication breakdowns, information inaccuracies, interdepartmental conflict, etc.) and the costs of retraining and corporate education. Two common rules of thumb are:

---

[3] See also Chapter 9, "ADP Management in the Multinational Company," in this Section.

- The cost of redesigning and reprogramming an existing system is about equal to the cost of the firm's computer.
- The continuing cost of programming after reorganization is approximately equal to the monthly computer rental.

When both sets of cost estimates are developed, comparisons can be made on a discounted present value basis. But costs are only part of the story. Management must weigh the costs of ADP organization alternatives against the real and potential effectiveness of the organizational options being considered.

Unfortunately, most firms do not measure adequately the effectiveness of their ADP operations. Although the majority do have some kind of ADP audit, all too often idle versus productive machine time is the only factor considered. This measurement in and of itself tells little about quality and/or usefulness of the information generated by ADP. At best, this ratio can show scheduling problems, uneven machine loading due to cycles in production, accounting, and reporting, and repair and maintenance problems. Even when supplemented with such ratios as setup time to total time, rerun time to production time, and average turnaround time per job and assembly time to test time, management learns little about the quality and the usefulness of the systems output information.

In addition to measuring machine utilization, management also must assess how well the firm's future information needs will be met by the current and proposed ADP organizations. This requires that management do a systematic information *profile* of the firm and its operating environment as it is now and as it might be in the future. Once this is developed, management can evaluate how the current ADP system and the organizational alternatives being considered conform to the firm's future information needs. Only when this is done is management in a position to decide whether the benefits of following a particular ADP organization strategy warrant the allocation of resources needed to accomplish the reorganization.

CONCLUSION

Traditionally, management has thought of ADP as a tool to facilitate the performance of a single transactional process. As a result, ADP often has been the organizational captive of user-departments and/or under the control of the treasurer's office. Although this approach seems to have worked well in the early- and mid-1960s, rising costs, the introduction of second- and third-generation equipment and software, and the need for coordinated decision-making information to deal with the complex business problems of the 1970s have led many managements to consolidate, reorganize, and relocate the ADP function in the corporate structure. Increasingly, companies are establishing quasi-independent corporate ADP departments reporting at the same level as other functional departments.

Because of the vital role played by ADP in providing all levels of management with timely decision-making information, ADP reorganization cannot be done on a "hit or miss" basis. Top management must become personally involved in developing and implementing the firm's ADP reorganization strategy. In addition, since consolidating and relocating the ADP function in a firm involves people problems as well as program and design problems, a cross-section of middle management should be invited to participate in the planning and implementation process. This will help to minimize potential personnel problems and ensure that user information needs will continue to be met by the new system.

The basic dilemma posed by ADP reorganization is the trade-off which inevitably must be made between the benefits of ADP decentralization and the need for an integrated corporate information flow. Although there is no one best way to organize the ADP function so that this dilemma is completely resolved, a systematic analysis of the firm's operating environment and interdepartmental relationships combined with a cost-benefit comparison of the current system and the proposed organizational alternatives will help management optimize the potential benefits of effective ADP.

SELECTIVE BIBLIOGRAPHY

Congdon, Frank P., Jr., "Advanced Planning for the System Function," *Journal of Systems Management*, August, 1970.

Fredericks, Ward A., "A Case for Centralized EDP," *Business* Automation, January, 1972.

Garrity, John T., *Getting the Most Out of Your Computer*, McKinsey & Company, New York, 1973.

Harvey, Edward, "Technology and the Structure of Organization," *American Sociological Review*, vol. 33, p. 249, April, 1968.

Kantor, Jerome, *Management Guide to Computer System Selection and Use*, Prentice-Hall, Englewood Cliffs, N.J., 1970.

Kelly, Joseph F., *Computerized Management Information Systems*, Macmillan, New York, 1970.

Lawrence, Paul R., and Jay Lorsch, *Organization and Environment*, Harvard Business School, Cambridge, Mass., 1967.

Chapter 2

Selection of ADP Personnel

ELEANOR H. IRVINE, LL.B.

Director, New Concepts, Delhi, New York

Matching people to positions has been a very undisciplined and personalized exercise in employment. Some organizations rely exclusively on their personnel departments to perform this function; in others, management and the personnel department act independently and confuse the total effort; still others depend on personnel departments for records and administrative duties and everyone gets into the employment picture.

The word *select* implies culling, picking the best from a choice. Most individuals consider their capacity to select inate, but seldom function in a way that bears out this assumption. They pick and hire but are ill-equipped to choose the best person for the opening. People responsible for selection fail to recognize their shortcomings because they are rarely held accountable for their choices. Accountability in this area is difficult, laborious, and frequently impossible. Yardsticks are hard to devise for the many variables and the frequency of changing criteria. Many would discover ineptness and serious failure if their records were opened to examination against valid yardsticks.

THE PROBLEM

No longer can an organization afford the luxury of undisciplined selection processes. Results of such latitude are costly, wasteful, and often disastrous to both the employee and the company. Employment of personnel today is a major investment for a firm. The cost of hiring one individual regardless of position is extremely high, and the cost of maintaining the person is even greater. Base salary alone is no longer the primary consideration. Yet more care is taken in spending a company dollar on materials, supplies, and equipment than on the human element.

Mobility of the working population, changing attitudes and career directions, and the impact of automation are typical of the strong influences that have increased turnover rates to unacceptable levels and have brought about costly and tragic human errors, disappointing production rates, overextended budgets, and other equally serious dilemmas in organizations.

Proven tests or a battery of tests which make selection an automatic procedure, or an evaluation of skills, or a prior record of success do not in themselves ensure successful selection. The selection process has become a complex and sophisticated procedure in organizations where human endeavor is valued as highly as any other profit source.

ADP has been a high-priority investment for most companies, and has introduced an entirely new type of professional to its users. ADP has also come under closer scrutiny as it has become integrated into the company as a whole, and as it has become less an unknown experiment and trial. No longer does it enjoy the luxury of "getting personnel at any cost" or "doing its own thing." Personnel is a major expenditure in the ADP budget, and its selection has a serious impact on the organization. Failure to develop an effective selection program has even caused some ADP service companies to become insolvent. Every ADP effort should have as efficient a procedure for selecting its personnel as it has to process its data.

Basic Questions　One of the preliminaries in a sound selection system is the determination of answers to a number of basic questions. Most organizations have well-established policies and attitudes which must be examined and considered before attempting to answer such questions. Some of these standards may appear restrictive, and permission to deviate may seem desirable. Such requests should be honored only when they will not slow down the recruitment effort. Questions vary by organizations, but will generally include the following:

1. What is the long- and short-term view of employment? Is it a one-time need, to put out an immediate fire, or is there a need for someone permanently? If there is a permanent need, is a follower or leader needed? What are the potentials? Will development be possible?

2. What is the time schedule for recruitment? How long a period is available between request and filling the position? Are there latitudes?

3. Is it possible to meet current and continual market demands for the desired person? What is the competitive factor for this type of person? Is it more feasible to buy the service than to hire the individual?

4. Is turnover important? Does the investment in the person require a long term of employment to pay off? What effect would there be on others if employment were of short duration?

5. Are there training considerations? Can the person be productive immediately without special grooming for the position? Are time, personnel, and funds available for training?

6. How much flexibility does the opening require? Are there travel, work schedules, and assignments that narrow the field of possible candidates? Do such requirements slow the recruitment effort? Are they unrealistic?

7. Are there unique features in the position? Do these require special qualifications? If so, are they available or will training be necessary?

8. Does the organization have an "image" to consider? If it is true that "you can tell the company by the people it keeps," what are the desired characteristics here?

9. What are the lines of communication? What exposure will the person have in the position? Is it confined to the immediate working area or does it include other areas within and outside the organization?

10. What is the working climate? What type of individual flourishes in the existing environment? How much variance can be tolerated successfully?

11. What style of recruitment program is applicable? Will applicants be screened originally alone or in groups? How much involvement of company personnel will be needed? How many visits should be planned?

12. What are the goals of the company, department, and position? What kind of person will fit in with each function's present and future plans? Will retraining be required along the way because of changes in direction and in company or personal goals?

Answers to questions such as the preceding chart the course for the first phase of the selection process: recruitment. The objective of this phase is to find suitable personnel in the most efficient manner. This means in the shortest possible time, with the least amount of effort, at the lowest possible cost, and with the highest deportment of all concerned individuals. Too often it becomes a nightmare of extravagance, breakdowns of relationships, and losses of prestige, production, and propriety. The lack of senior-management direction and guidance is chiefly responsible. Recruitment requires management involvement and objectivity to be successful. It can be delegated only after an efficient system has become an integrated part of company life.

RECRUITING

ADP in its infancy was a serious violator of sound recruitment practices. The license to build a department on its own without consideration for the rest of the organization has disappeared in many companies, but few have replaced such license with effective programs. A reliable program should include the following:

Job Description Large organizations have used job descriptions and specification sheets widely. Most firms practice this discipline in some form. It is a useful exercise in thinking out the details of a position and in defining the structure of the job. Job descriptions are helpful to the uninitiated recruiter, and aid in the dialogue between the employer and anyone involved in making referrals on the openings.

Job descriptions are a valuable resource, but their shortcomings make them unreliable to use as sole criteria for openings. Too much inflexibility is inherent in them, and most of their users are prone to attempting fulfillment of specified requirements to the letter. Most job descriptions represent several commonly designated positions, but each opening has its own peculiarities which require identification and clarification. Each recruitment takes place at a peculiar period of time, with a unique group of applicants, and many trade-offs may occur before final selection. The chosen candidate may be a far cry from the one envisioned originally.

Sources It is surprising that many firms are so casual about the expenditure of their recruitment dollar and its return to them. More attention should be given the selection of sources used for referrals, and they should be held much more accountable than at present. The cost of an advertisement, fee, retainer, expenses tells little of the story. How much additional work is required of one's own personnel? Did the source enhance or detract from the company image? What are the future effects from such exposure? What was the return on the money spent? Did the source slow up the recruitment? The answers to questions such as these point out the actual cost of recruitment.

Some ADP organizations with extensive recruitment needs have established records to analyze the effectiveness of their sources. Each recruitment is entered on the page designated for its source. These pages are reviewed periodically with the progress of their respective placements, to ascertain the sources that provide the best service. Pages represent newspapers, trade journals, periodicals, consultants, computer manufacturers, software firms, educational institutions, other activities of the business, agencies, and professional recruiters.

Records are obviously helpful, but alone are insufficient to rely on for all recruitment needs. The evaluation that must be made is illustrated well by analyzing the use of advertisements. The first decision to make is whether to place a blind advertisement or identify the firm. If a blind ad is the choice, many good ADP applicants will ignore it because of the vulnerability of exposing their availability to unknown parties. The ADP community is too close and there is considerable misuse of the blind ad by unethical and misguided people.

If the ad carries the company name, each responder expects and deserves a reply. This practice builds image, reputation, and reliance, but it is costly and time-consuming. Both types of ads attract recruiters, drifters, "shoppers," and incompetents who are nuisances and are difficult for the uninformed to screen out.

An effective ad normally produces three possible candidates for every hundred replies. Company personnel are required to do considerable review of unqualified applicants. The time lag and the cost of speeding up the process may prove prohibitive in themselves. The loss of image which results from repeated advertising deters its use for difficult recruitment. The most important consideration of all is that of goodwill. There is one position and one person to fill it. All other candidates are potential disparagers unless handled with care and expertise, because no one appreciates a turndown. It is soon evident that the cost of the ad was the least of the considerations.

Third-party sources require periodic personal contacts, preferably on their premises when possible. Visits develop interest and keep the visitor informed of a source's situation. Many companies have little personal knowledge of how they are represented by their sources, and fail to recognize the importance of this introduction to a possible candidate.

Sources may vary with different openings. Each choice should result from a careful analysis of factors that are pertinent for the specific opening. Important factors to consider include: what will provide the largest number of qualified applicants; how to get the most effective screening; where the best knowledge of personal credentials exists; who should do the major effort of review, screening, briefing, and interviewing. Time spent in such deliberations is well invested and expedites the recruitment cycle.

Referral System   Completion of the evaluation and selection of sources turns consideration to the handling of referrals. Third-party sources and in-house personnel who will participate in selection require briefing. The emphasis is on promptness. Expeditious handling of each referral indicates interest and concern and encourages similar action in return.

Contrary to popular practice, employers should take the initiative in follow-ups. A source's time is spent best in screening applicants, rather than in tracking down an employer, frequently at an inopportune time. Follow-ups should include a discussion of reasons for the referral, clarification of details of the résumé or supporting documents, and a decision to reject, consider further, or see the applicant. A decision to see the applicant prompts mutual agreement on contact routines. These routines should provide for constant communication among the three parties, identifying substitutes who will function when the prime parties are unavailable.

A selected candidate requires a clear explanation of the opening prior to testing interest in a personal visit to the company. An expression of interest is followed by a thorough briefing to put the candidate in as favorable a position as the employer. The employer has considerable information on the candidate at this point, and the candidate requires similar knowledge of the employer and position. Briefing should include data on the organization, nature of the work, backgrounds of personnel involved in the selection, and evaluations when possible.

A source has a dual responsibility as the objective party in these contacts. Both parties' images must be kept intact, each party must be allowed to make independent decisions, and counseling is given only upon request of the parties. Some of the poorest placements result from a lack of this objectivity, because a source can never be well enough informed to replace either party's judgment.

Phone interviewing is hazardous without skill in its use. It should be avoided unless surrounding circumstances prevent personal contacts. It is easier to be "turned off" than "on" by its use. The applicant should be advised that such a contact will be made to avoid surprise and consequent stress, misunderstandings, and confusion. The employer needs to prepare for such a contact, considering queries which will prompt replies that express attitudes and philosophies rather than salary requirements, skills, and personal needs.

Planning and Preparation on Site   Considerable thought and attention to arrangements precede the visits of candidates. Visits are successful when candidates want the positions or disqualify themselves. Such candidates are ambassadors of goodwill and carriers of favorable publicity. It is the unsuccessful and rejected candidates that cause harm and poor relationships.

Impressions begin with the opening of the first door. First impressions affect the applicant's demeanor and general attitude, and often determine the climate of the entire visit. The first contact point with such vulnerability deserves special concentration. This may be outside the ADP area, and therefore requires the interest and cooperation of other departments. Constant attention by ADP personnel is important in this situation, making sure to advise of candidate visits and gaining cooperation through involving those responsible for reception in the total ADP program. Surveillance of any contact point should be continual, making sure to involve everyone that devotes any time to the area.

Reception   The warmth and friendliness of the reception does much to put a candidate at ease. Deportment of employees and the efficiency of plans for the conduct of the visit attract attention next. This may be a convenient time to convey preliminary information by using a visual presentation rather than the discourse of an employee. Some ADP departments have prepared binders which contain pictures of key ADP personnel that will be met, and describe something of their backgrounds. Other informative detail that belongs in the binders includes a list of applications in process, completed, planned, and under advisement; equipment installed and on order; an organization chart; and employee participation in outside ADP activities. Binders are helpful in prompting questions from the candidates, and ease the first awkward moments of the meeting. They should provide the candidates with a better grasp of the situation and make the visits more meaningful.

Selection of a candidate after one meeting is the exception and not the rule. There are advantages in keeping the first meeting general in nature. Its aim is to furnish the candidate with sufficient information to equalize the knowledge factor of each party, and to place the candidate in a position to appraise the opening accurately. Too seldom is this done or considered important. More care is taken by an ADP sales representative in presenting products than is given the presentation of an ADP effort to a prospective employee.

This is a scheduled visit, and planning goes into its conduct. Every employee of the ADP effort is a host and on display. All should be aware of the visit to show proper recognition, and some should have an opportunity to chat with the candidate. Employees need briefing to function well, and substitutes should be ready to take over for any person not available as arranged.

A tour of the entire ADP facility while in action is essential. Too many visits are arranged off-hours, and the candidate never gets the feel of the organization prior to joining it. One large company hired a keypunch supervisor after night interviewing. The shock of seeing her new responsibility in action was so great that she resigned during the first hour of her new employment. Someone had forgotten to bring out a very important aspect of the position when interviewing her. First-hand information is best observed on the premises.

One way to conclude the general visit is to have an informal preorientation session. This session can be the focal point of the visit. It provides an opportunity to convey any information not covered previously, and a chance to talk informally with the candidate. The meeting concludes with a commitment from the candidate on further interest in seeking the position, taking it under advisement, or disqualifying for personal reasons. Another appointment is arranged when there is interest in pursuing the job further, and it is left up to the candidate to take the initiative in requesting another appointment when interest is questionable. The important point is that the employer does not make the decision to conclude interest or consideration. Skillful handling of the preorientation session will place a candidate in a position to do this well, and will prevent animosity, hurt feelings, and disappointment.

SCREENING

More research and emphasis have been concentrated on this phase of the selection process than on any other. Most selections result from formal criteria that companies set up to use with all applicants. Some ADP installations rely solely on these, but others that place great importance on their personnel have developed their own criteria. A brief review and examination of criteria in use follows:

Tests Selection was not a problem for most installations during the first generation of computers. Many had punched-card personnel who were trained and converted to the computer. Others were promoted from various related departments.

The Federal Government and other large-scale users were an exception. They realized very quickly that new guidelines were needed for qualifications and salaries. The U.S. Air Force installed one of the first commercial computers, and staffing became a personal effort because the U.S. Civil Service had nothing applicable for its recruitment needs.

Other agencies with computers on order found themselves in similar situations and turned to the computer manufacturers for assistance. The manufacturers had developed tests for their own screening needs, and offered these to their users. The *Programmers Aptitude Test* (PAT) developed by IBM was used most frequently. The FBI opened the opportunity to join its computer department to the entire Bureau. Twenty-five employees who scored exceptionally well on the PAT were selected from many applicants who took the test. Five received permanent assignment at the conclusion of the training and proved to be outstanding. The Treasury Department had a tremendous recruitment problem when it installed three large-scale computers. It relied on the PAT with similar results.

PAT consisted of three sections, all math-oriented. The first one covered number sequence; for example, in the sequence 1, 3, 2, 4, 6, what would be the next number? The second section was the largest, and dealt with spatial relationships. The last was composed of accounting problems. Each section had a time limit, the last one being given the most time because of the required care in reading and personal effort.

PAT was such a fast, easy, and reliable way to select that it had general acceptance for trainee staffing of second-generation computers. However, wider application brought out its shortcomings. It screened too well, eliminating some applicants who proved to be successful computer personnel at a time when demands for people were very heavy. Results were lower and questionable for those with experience. Applicants who were given the test several times improved their scores considerably, and misled prospective employers. Familiarity brought an end to its usefulness.

Some software firms developed tests for their own use which simulated computer disciplines, and were highly successful in selecting exceptional personnel. Most of these fell into disuse with the introduction of third-generation hardware. Companies had become more sophisticated in selecting new and unskilled personnel, testing was gaining disfavor nationally because of discriminatory features, and there was general reluctance to invest in the development of new tests to fill the void. The field had more trained and skilled people by the time of the third generation, and a large majority of openings requested skilled personnel. These highly trained individuals would have been turned off immediately if they were to be subjected to testing.

Specialized Training The glamour of the computer world attracted many applicants during the early generations of computers. Employers became enamoured with the impact of their new toy, and set high and unrealistic educational requirements for ADP departments. Systems personnel were required to have masters degrees, programmers needed degrees in math, engineering, physics, or similar disciplines, and doctorates were assured high priority.

These backgrounds were very helpful in scientific and specialized applications, but the thrust of most ADP installations was commercial work, repetitive and routine after the first application was mastered. Continuing challenge was lacking for these highly trained individuals, and turnover and excessive salary demands became serious burdens to their organizations. Too few ivory towers were available for creative thinking, and too many repetitive implementing jobs were daily routines.

Third-generation computers brought stability to the field in the hiring of trainees, but the "numbers game" replaced the "degree game" for the skilled applicant. Computer numbers, number of years, number of applications, number supervised were typical experience specifications. Many colleges had initiated computer courses and programs which prepared their graduates for employment with the computer manufacturers, but their technical orientation made them unrelated to the typical user account. Computer schools found placement of their graduates still limited and confined to the small company which could not compete in the open market, and which seldom had internal resources. Specialized training without hands-on experience never gained the acceptance in the computer field that it has enjoyed in other occupations and professions.

Personal Characteristics The excessive demands for skilled and talented personnel to handle technical requirements of second- and third-generation computers obscured the need for personal-characteristics criteria. This resulted in unusual combinations of people in some organizations. Some of the larger installations attempted to recruit a "company person," but abandoned such efforts when faced with critical requirements for personnel. Even firms that started out with strong images abandoned them with growing pains.

The seventies brought a slight change of emphasis. Project teams and task forces replaced former individualized efforts, and quickly demonstrated the value of team action and support. The integration of ADP into the organization with profit responsibility, deadlines, and other normal demands produced added personal requirements. The ability to cooperate with others, merge personal goals with group goals, adhere to standards, and accept responsibility for schedules were typical attributes which took on new meaning. Managers became aware of their need for additional understanding of behavioral disciplines in selection, and for the more serious consideration of personal attributes.

References Many organizations have abandoned the practice of checking references unless they know the person for whom the applicant worked, or someone who worked with the applicant. This checking may help to ascertain the level of technical proficiency, but it does little else. Too many influences affect a person at work, and they vary with each working environment. A person may perform poorly in several installations and suddenly change into an effective member at a different time and place. The opposite is equally true.

The source of the reference must be considered likewise. References are given based on one's own standards, which may be completely inapplicable for the position under consideration.

Verification of employment dates and knowledge of the commitment of an illegal or immoral act are the most reliable information to obtain from reference checking. Other checking is best left to the experts.

CDP Examination The Certificate in Data Processing Examination has little influence on selection to date. Some firms consider it a desirable asset and feel it expresses extra personal effort and discipline. The chief difficulty is relating the proficiency to specific job requirements.

Phrenology, Handwriting Analysis A few companies have practiced these techniques but have never proven their value.

Related Talents and Skills It has been found that many good programmers are musically inclined, and play chess and bridge well, but these skills have never been considered too seriously as predictive. Some day coefficients may be developed, but to date the records show wide diversities.

Samples of Work and Homework Some concerns have discovered that insight is provided by reviewing an applicant's previous work and by assigning a short problem to resolve at home for presentation on a return visit. Most applicants have unclassified work samples that are available for this purpose. The results may be the work of several persons, but such a review assists the employer in understanding the nature of prior assignments, and gives an opportunity to the applicant to discuss his or her work background with concrete detail.

Assignment of a problem is requesting the applicant to work on his or her own time, and is a good test of serious interest in the opening. It should never be a difficult undertaking, and the applicant should be advised to keep it brief and simple. Content is unimportant to this exercise. The main concern is the approach that is taken to solving the problem and its presentation.

Much can be learned about an applicant in this type of stress situation. Thought processes, conduct, ability to communicate, interest, and many other capacities can be observed quickly.

ADP personnel are exposed to many segments of an organization, and frequently have outside contacts. Presentations are common occurrences. The homework approach makes it possible to obtain a preview of how the applicant would handle himself or herself with such contacts. Proficiency in the use of this technique should increase the number of its adherents.

Workshops Another technique which explores the applicant's approach to solving a problem and working out the necessary details is the workshop. The homework method works well when one person is under serious consideration, but the workshop is used more successfully when several people have been invited to a firm for an extensive program. It has application for college recruitment, when several openings are available, when the firm is in an isolated location, and when there is an urgency and a need to compress the recruitment time.

The opportunity to observe candidates in a work experience is invaluable when sufficient thought has gone into the planning for such a session. It reveals how the work is approached, the level of relating to others, the capacity to communicate, attitudes, needs, priorities, and other necessary indicators. Workshops and formal evaluation sessions will gain popularity when more sensitivity develops in using them correctly.

The Interview The most common and popular technique is the interview. Much weight is given it in determining final selections, frequently on the basis of one interview. Changing attitudes toward the work ethic, loyalties, and discipline place the interview in jeopardy unless it is conducted with professional expertise. Few managers are proficient in its use, and many consider it a perfunctory exercise. Training is required to use it effectively; care must be given its planning; practice is essential to improvement; and attention to its pitfalls must be constant. Pitfalls vary with interviews but some of the frequent ones are:

Loss of Perspective. One is attracted immediately to the person who has common interests and hobbies, likes the same places and people, relates an experience that recalls a similar one from one's past, talks the same language, is referred by a friend. This attraction often distorts the evaluation of a person's ability to do the job and fit in with other staff members.

Inaccurate Diagnosis. Imposing one's own standards on the person needed to do the job is a common failing. This practice may be acceptable when the person works directly and solely with the interviewer, but other considerations become important when this is not the situation. The interviewer must realize that it is the applicant and fellow workers that must enjoy associating with each other. The interviewer must remain alert to the paramount consideration: what the applicant can bring to the job and company. Managers are apt to select for themselves, rather than pay attention to how the applicants fit into the immediate work environments.

Eye and Ear Appeal, Rather than Mind Appeal. The applicant may be a glib talker who knows the right "buzzwords" because of an ability to read well rather than to perform well. The applicant has a winning way and a contagious personality. Beware! It is so easy to be subjective and so difficult to be objective about another person. This is one of the most dangerous and prevalent pitfalls of personal contacts. Even the professional interviewer falls into this trap and must guard against it constantly.

Overemphasis on Skills. Critical time factors, dislike for training, pressures to get someone, and inability to judge personal characteristics lead one to an unsound absorption with a person's skills and complete neglect of personal qualifications. "Can the person do the job, technically?" is the only thought. Left unanswered are the vital issues of whether associates will allow the person to do the job, whether he or she will want to do the job, and how well he or she can do the job.

The Successful Interview   Most ADP personnel have been selected and hired primarily because of an interview, many times after only one interview. Few of these interviews were prepared for in advance, and seldom have the interviewers reviewed thoroughly the applicant's qualifications and histories prior to the meetings. This is uncomplimentary to applicants and foolish for the amateur interviewer.

Sound interviewing results from prior preparation. Briefing personnel that will be involved, scheduling the time allotted to assure thorough coverage of important points, and determination of approach to use for the specific position are significant considerations. The interview is expedited and more meaningful questions can be posed by gaining as much knowledge of the applicant as possible prior to the meeting. It is as important to systematize the interview as the work flow.

Skill and assistance are needed to accurately interpret applicant reactions and answers. A major cause of selection failures is poor interpretation. Multiple interviews and exposing the applicant to several interviewers on a one-to-one basis help to minimize the danger. Team evaluation develops a sounder profile of the person in relation to the opening than the sole decision of a manager or equivalent.

The interview can never be a perfunctory task if employers continue to use it as the primary selection and screening technique. Increased application of some of the other valuable tools, such as the workshop and mock presentation, can provide important data to implement the interview and make it more effective and meaningful, but constant emphasis on improving the use of the interview is desirable and necessary.

HIRING

Screening does not complete the recruitment and selection process. The candidate must accept the offer. Many a good candidate has been lost at this point through inefficiency and lack of understanding.

Final selection should involve a firm offer and a definite acceptance. Instead of this, the system bogs down. Candidates are left dangling for unreasonable lengths of time. Information regarding their status is unavailable when they make inquiries. Neither interest nor concern is expressed, and the seeming lack of enthusiasm about filling the opening prompts equal demeanor on the part of those assisting in the interviewing, and finally from the candidates themselves.

Most of the difficulty is caused by the inability of those responsible for making the offer to get together for a final decision, and no one takes the responsibility to bring the matter to a head. Other common causes for such difficulty are the premature requests for referrals prior to final approval of the opening, the disruptions caused by absences from the firm for vacations, illness, and similar reasons without designated substitutes or someone to act on the situation or to arrange for a delay, sudden changes in requirements or plans which make future needs uncertain, internal changes of personnel involved in the recruitment without naming successors, and revisions in job specifications.

All the effective effort that went into the previous phases is wasted unless the follow-up offer is handled as well. Delays can be arranged and understood when discussed with the candidates. Courtesy alone requires it, and image building, reputation, and need for the cooperation of those who assist the recruitment effort make it imperative. Cost alone should alert one to its necessity. Desired candidates require attention and expressions of serious interest until offers are made them.

Hiring does not end with the acceptance of the offer. The time before reporting for duty and the first days on the job are vulnerable periods. Candidates tend to change their minds during this time, especially if there is a "seller's market" for skilled professional people. They are often uncertain about their choices, and are exposed to many pressures and influences which tend to confuse them. Their enthusiasm for the job needs strengthening, and immediate involvement has merit. This is done by suggesting preparation for the position, seeking their advice and opinions, and remaining in constant communication during the interim period.

This approach also helps the first difficult days on the job. Personal interest and guidance from an older employee, immediate work assignments, orientation sessions, and brief meetings with the manager ease the strain of the new environment. Only when the new employee is acclimated and productive may the selection process be considered over and successful.

THE "TWO-WAY STREET"

Discussion has centered on employer responsibility in selection. Today's selection is very much a two-way street, each party selecting the other. Applicants also have a definite responsibility. Their responsibility is to know themselves well enough to present themselves accurately and to select positions which best suit them. Professional counseling may be necessary because such insight requires not only a basic honesty but objectivity and realism. There is a natural inclination to overestimate one's capabilities and requirements. This is prevalent in the ADP field where no precedents exist and where for a long period demands for personnel were excessive and opportunities practically limitless. Premiums have been paid for aggressive and unprofessional conduct. Such symptoms of rapid growth have nearly disappeared, and with them many of the selfish attitudes and dishonest behaviors. Applicants are beginning to recognize what it means to be a true professional.

Applicants should use care in selecting sources to help them in their job moves and in deciding what position and firms to interview. Too little attention is paid to third-party representation with prospective employers or the exposure with direct sources. The relationship between applicant and third-party source requires good rapport and trust. It should be a team effort with constant communication and follow-through. The applicant who seeks third-party sources merely to pass paperwork and arrange appointments and who feels no need to advise these sources of progress or decision has failed to benefit from the advantages that are possible with a careful selection and a good relationship.

The résumé passer has earned the title of "paper hanger." Many ADP applicants are guilty of this practice. Husbands request wives to go through the advertisements and send résumés to those which sound like ADP openings. Consultants and sales representatives pass résumés among their clients. Friends give résumés to other friends. This has been normal and accepted practice, but often has unsuspected consequences. It has resulted in loss of jobs, prestige, and friendships. It has encouraged unprofessional conduct. It has failed to consider the important details that lead to good matches. What started out to be a favor turns out to be a real disservice to the underemployed and unemployed alike.

The applicant should move generally for reasons of personal growth and opportunities for greater accomplishment, unless specific circumstances make a move for move's sake necessary. Personal affronts on the job, boredom, more rapid success of peers in other companies, failure of one's firm to keep up with the latest technical developments, and similar influences prompt applicant unrest and urgency to make a change. The wise applicant moves when the best change for development and continuity is available. Temporary stopovers and repetitious experiences in a new environment at a better salary do little to advance one's career.

The future will undoubtedly witness changes in the ADP selection process. Practices will change to accommodate a variable marketplace. The purpose of this Chapter has been to place both parties in the selection process on an equal footing to function effectively regardless of time and place.

Chapter **3**

Training and Motivation of ADP Personnel

GERALD M. WEINBERG

President, Ethnotech, Inc., Lincoln, Nebraska

DANIEL P. FREEDMAN

School of Advanced Technology, State University of
New York, Binghamton, New York

In order to achieve perspective on the current state of ADP education, the ADP manager must recognize that ADP is the youngest of the professions. Moreover, formal education is an inherently conservative process and normally lags a decade or so behind the forefront of any field. Therefore, the mere details of any particular training program are of no lasting value to the manager, who must instead understand the dynamics of education in a fast-changing technical field.

The ADP manager needs to understand that the particular training possessed by his or her employees today is but a passing moment in a continuing educational process that began long before their employment and must continue unabated if the ADP function is to remain healthy. The manager needs to know the options open for this continuing education, and how each fits into the entire process of ADP management. In particular, he or she needs to know what to expect and what not to expect from each, what are the costs and what are the pitfalls—to know, in other words, how to obtain true training for employees and not simply the appearance of training which so often passes for the real thing.

PRE-EMPLOYMENT TRAINING

Very few of the early ADP practitioners received any formal training in ADP. They came from diverse educational backgrounds that included principally mathematics, accounting, physics, economics, and engineering, but not excluding any major profession. Today, however, ADP training is evolving toward the pattern normally followed in other professions—formal courses in the subject in public and private institutions followed by on-the-job training to adapt the general education to the specific needs of the employer. The principal institutions providing such pre-employment training are high schools, universities, and a variety of "education-for-profit" companies.

High Schools ADP training has been slow in coming to the high schools, partially because of the equipment expense of maintaining such a program. With the increasing availability of used ADP equipment and time-sharing services, ADP training in the high schools has in recent years experienced a rapid growth. This equipment lag often reflects itself in a training lag, so that rarely is the high school graduate ready to step directly into meaningful ADP employment. Naturally, the lag is less pronounced in those areas where equipment changes have been neither great nor rapid, such as tabulating machines, keypunches, and key verifiers. Nevertheless, few high schools at this writing can provide, for example, a multistation key-to-disk system for keypunch training.

To a great extent, high school ADP training is bipolar. On the one hand, there is training in computer programming, primarily for honor students in mathematics who will be likely to continue their education in the university. On the other, there is training in "lower" skills often for minority or underprivileged students who are expected to terminate their education upon high school graduation. This bipolarity more or less reflects the traditional role of the high school in reinforcing the social stratification of the society at large.

There are little or no data bearing on the question of the value of high school ADP training as a preparation for university studies. In one introductory computer science class in a Canadian university, the instructor noticed that those students who had taken a high school class in FORTRAN programming performed less well on the average than those students who had no previous experience with ADP. While this observation may reflect merely the particular high school course, it is well to be reminded that high school training may not necessarily be an advantage to the student, just as college training may at times prove a handicap in an actual job situation.

Colleges and Universities The colleges and universities have been in the business of ADP education longer than the high schools, but in most of these institutions the faculty are still "first generation" – that is, not the product of university education in ADP themselves. One consequence of this faculty composition is the diversity we find in the placement of ADP education within the academic structure. Though the predominant name for ADP training is *computer science*, we find computer science departments on the graduate and undergraduate levels in such diverse places as physics, management, mathematics, electrical engineering, or as a separate department or school. Moreover, *computer programming* and *systems analysis* courses are even more scattered throughout academia, with courses frequently given by such departments as anthropology, sociology, political science, biology, geology, geography, as well as those mentioned above. Furthermore, most university computing centers offer a variety of credit and noncredit courses in the practicalities of ADP.

To the outsider, the diversity of college and university ADP training may be concealed behind a veil of published formal curricula such as ACM's *Curriculum 68, Computer Science Course Program for Small Colleges,* and *Report of the ACM Curriculum Committee on Computer Education for Management.* These reports tend to provide catalogue copy for courses, but university courses are notorious for their failure to follow catalogue copy. A better indication of course content will generally be the textbook used, though with the publication of "official" curricula, textbooks are beginning to appear which are designed to match the catalogue copy.

In any case, college and university courses, like their textbooks, will tend to lag 3 to 5 years behind industry practice, so that graduates will be more likely to know principles than specific skills that can be put to work immediately on the job. When these principles have been properly chosen and well taught, they will outlive skills training – such as particular programming languages or hardware – and provide a base for postemployment training of university graduates. For instance, one large ADP user routinely permits new employees with an undergraduate major in computer science to skip the first 3 weeks of a 13-week initial training program. On the other hand, some reports indicate that university graduates demand higher salaries for equal work, show less motivation on the job, and generally have a higher turnover rate than nongraduates. The effects seem more pronounced the higher the degree earned, and stronger in computer science graduates than in those not specifically trained in ADP subjects. It should be noted, however, that such reports reflect averages and not individuals, and that the effects may depend on the personnel practices of the reporting organizations.

Education-for-Profit In spite of the dearth of evidence of the value of university education in ADP employment, personnel practices seem to be moving inexorably toward requiring college degrees and even advanced degrees before a candidate will even be considered for programming or systems work. Such practices naturally tend to limit employment opportunities for minority groups which are under-represented in the university population. Under such Supreme Court rulings as *Griggs v. Duke Power Co.*, employment requirements which are discriminatory and not demonstrably related to job performance are not permitted, so college degrees may become less important in the future. For the present, however, many non-degree-holders are turning to a variety of "education-for-profit" schools in an attempt to gain entry to the ADP profession.

Education-for-profit does not have a long tradition in ADP, because of the historical role of manufacturers' training programs which were normally restricted to the employees of hardware customers and prospects. In the past, the normal entry to ADP education was first to get a job and then to be sent to a manufacturer's school. With the "unbundling" of education, manufacturer's schools were opened up to nonemployees, but often at costs so high as to create a niche for the education-for-profit schools.

The resulting proliferation of ADP schools was often accompanied by scandal created by unscrupulous or incompetent operators taking advantage of the desire for "high-paying jobs in the computer field." As usual, the victims of these scandals were primarily those students who could least afford to lose their tuition. Although many schools promised placement services, few could actually obtain jobs for their graduates, who were often convinced that jobs would come easily if they took additional courses. But the students were not the only victims. Legitimate, competent, and conscientious school operators found themselves painted with the same black brush, so that it may be a long time before education-for-profit in ADP can clear its reputation. In 1968 the Association for Computing Machinery (ACM) formed an Accreditation Committee to monitor these schools with the U.S. Office of Education. Eventually these efforts should improve the situation.

Though employers should be cautious about believing the claims of ADP schools about their graduates, the smart manager will realize that graduates even of poor ADP schools might make excellent employees. For one thing, their motivation level is likely to be high, so if their training does not measure up to claims, remedial training can be given. After all, nobody has ever demonstrated the value of university or manufacturer training in ADP, so some caution should be exercised in condemning ADP schools.

POSTEMPLOYMENT TRAINING

From the employer's point of view, the major advantage of pre-employment training—perhaps its only advantage—is its initial price. Expensive as university training might be, for example, it is the employee and not the employer who bears it—initially. Over the long run, however, the more formal education an employee has, the more he or she is likely to demand in salary. Postemployment training, on the other hand, though it entails direct costs for the employer, is more likely to engender employee loyalty and more specifically applicable skills.

Hardware Vendors Because of the strong ideas of T. J. Watson, Sr., on the subject of education, and because the IBM Corporation quickly became the dominant factor in the ADP industry, hardware manufacturers have traditionally found themselves in the training business—if they wanted to compete with IBM. At first such training was free—or rather, the costs were hidden in equipment costs so that the organization which failed to use the manufacturer's schools was paying for a service it was not receiving. While some manufacturer's training remains "free," it is seldom the bargain it appears on the surface. In the first place, a manufacturer normally trains only in the use of its own equipment. Even in "general" courses or "concepts" courses such as are often given to executives, the general concepts will usually turn out to be heavily biased toward the manufacturer's own specific sales features.

In the second place, even when training in specific equipment is desired by the employer, heavy reliance on the manufacturer tends to lock an organization into that manufacturer's equipment, since retraining such narrowly trained employees adds to the burden of conversion. Small organizations, which often have no alternative, may find themselves locked in to a particular manufacturer for generation after generation of hardware.

On the more positive side, the manufacturer brings course development resources to the small organization which it could never afford on its own, and availability of course offerings—both quality and quantity—should be a major factor in hardware decisions for small organizations. In addition, the manufacturer has the incentive of wanting the user to learn to use the equipment effectively, and not simply to collect tuition fees. Yet even this incentive may be tainted by the suspicion that *efficient* use of the equipment is not in the manufacturer's best interests, especially if the equipment is on an extra-shift rental plan. In the long run, however, the manufacturer who fails to inculcate efficient use of its equipment through its training programs will be vulnerable to forays by other manufacturers into its customers' ADP centers.

We cannot leave the subject of manufacturers' training without touching on the quality of texts and manuals provided both for courses and self-study. Such materials suffer the same disadvantages and gain the same advantages as courses, but have the additional handicap of a tradition of inaccuracy and lack of user-orientation. The same may be generally said about some audio-visual courses that are becoming more widespread. While such materials theoretically have the advantage of being the collected work of the best talents available, they are often no more than automated live courses—without the merits of changing quickly with changing technology.

Software Vendors   The inaccuracy of documentation is—with some exceptions—even more pronounced in the training materials of software firms, perhaps because of their more recent entry into the ADP market in general and the educational aspects in particular. Quite often, initial training of user-personnel is a standard feature of a software package—which may be more a result of poor documentation than devotion to education. Without such training and the resulting person-to-person documentation, a sizable proportion of marketed software packages would be unusable.

In general, then, the ADP training provided by software firms has the same advantages and disadvantages as that provided by hardware firms. To the extent that software firms are smaller than hardware firms, they may suffer from less capital investment in their educational packages, though their small size often means that the initial users of a software package have the advantage of being trained by the package's developers. Moreover, to the extent that software is closer to the user than hardware, software companies' training may be closer to user realities. Perhaps this closeness accounts for a trend toward a broadening of the educational scope of some software houses into courses not directly supporting their products, or perhaps such broadening is simply a strategy to broaden the capital base underlying their educational services, or even to obtain a continuing supply of new prospects. Whatever the reason, in the future we may expect software firms to be a growing factor in ADP training services.

Education Vendors   Another growing factor in ADP training is educational or consulting-educational firms specializing in custom courses for industry. These courses may be live or audio-visual packages. If the latter they tend to be more professionally done than such courses obtainable from other sources, since these firms profit only from continuing use of the courses themselves. While such firms might seem to be the same as the education-for-profit schools previously mentioned, an important difference results from dealing with institutions rather than individuals. In order to secure continuing relationships with their clients, custom education companies must provide a continuing high level of training. This feedback does not ensure that every custom course will be of high quality—any more than the generalized courses need be of low quality—and any purchases of such services must provide for continuing evaluation of their quality and applicability to the organization.

Custom courses will tend to give a broader representation of the subject matter, rather than a bias toward one manufacturer or software house. On the other hand, this broad coverage may be a screen for the inability to keep course materials as current as a vendor can. Moreover, since teachers in these firms often come from vendors, the courses may turn out to be just as biased. Even when the instructors seem to carry a grudge against their former employers, they may tend to teach close to the knowledge that former employers gave them, so contracting for an "independent" course will not necessarily give impartial training.

Another potential advantage of custom courses is that their services can be adapted to the specific requirements of the client organization, but though this tailoring is often promised, it is seldom done to any appreciable extent. The economics of education do not permit true custom work, and in the future we can expect to see even more reliance on audio-visual material—not for quality, but for price. The organization that wants customized education will still be better off with in-house training, but for smaller firms, educational packages taken apart and put back together in some new arrangement may prove an economically viable alternative to the full-scale in-house training they cannot afford.

Professional Societies Most of the professional societies with interests in ADP have a chartered concern with the education of their members. To this end, they publish journals, conduct meetings, and sometimes provide seminars and courses directly competitive with the profit-making education vendors. The educational value of the journals for the practicing ADP professional is generally rather small—their role being more to educate the educators from whom the information comes down indirectly. Trade publications tend to be closer to the day-to-day informational needs of the ADP professional, though professional societies do try to make at least some of their publications—such as the ACM *Computing Surveys*—more relevant to the ADP practitioner.

Computer expositions and trade shows, though primarily marketplaces, do provide some educational function. They may be especially useful in providing a broad view of ADP possibilities in the shortest possible time, and many an attendee has returned from a meeting with one new idea or fact that saved his or her organization thousands of dollars. Nevertheless, a regular diet of such meetings should not be substituted for a more solid training fare. It seems unlikely that the average employee can benefit from attendance at more than two national meetings per year.

Local meetings of professional societies can be quite another matter, though these may be unavailable in smaller areas. The major educational benefit of such meetings is probably not in the invited speakers, prestigious as they may be, but in the face-to-face contacts with other ADP personnel from the area.

Similar heterogeneity of classmates is found in the typical seminar or course sponsored by a professional society, and the same broadening of perspective may accrue to the attendee. Heterogeneity has its drawbacks, however, primarily in the retarding effect on the pace with which course material can be covered. These same advantages and disadvantages are found in the out-of-house seminars offered by education vendors, for there is little to distinguish their seminars from those offered by professional societies. The price may be somewhat higher and the presentation may be a little more polished, but the value of each individual seminar or course must be judged on its own merits and not on the type of sponsoring organization.

IN-HOUSE TRAINING

Possibly the major advantage of in-house training programs is the strength of focus that can be obtained because the audience is homogeneous, participants coming as they do from the same organization. It is worth noting, however, that all ADP personnel in a single organization need not be more homogeneous than personnel from similar functional areas in several organizations. Only in sizable organizations are sufficiently large numbers available to ensure homogeneity in training programs. When medium-sized organizations attempt to distribute the costs of a training program over diverse functional areas, the result can easily be poor training-dollar effectiveness.

Yet efficiency is not the ultimate goal of education, and heterogeneity may serve the function of integrating information across divisional lines, thereby restoring some of the organization-wide understanding that is needed even in the most highly structured organization. For example, at the IBM Systems Research Institute, a graduate-level school for ADP personnel within the IBM Corporation, there has always been an explicit policy of constructing each class out of personnel from each major division of the company.

The Training Coordinator The decision to create a training function within an organization is often made on grounds which are oblique to the main function of training. For example, a training program may be established for the prestige which this gives, or one may be discontinued because of lack of manufacturing space. This decision is confused by the general lack of understanding of the role of training in an organization. Too often, training is thought of as giving courses, when in reality, training is a succession of planned experiences intended to bring the skills and knowledge of the ADP employee closer to the future needs of the organization.

The minimum staffing requirement for training is one person who serves as *training coordinator*—though in a small organization, this may be only a part-time function. The training coordinator has overall responsibility for each ADP employee with respect to the maintenance of skills, just as others have responsibility for maintenance of other capital items. Since ADP employees are generally not managed directly by the training coordinator except perhaps at the beginning of their employment, there is always potential conflict between the training coordinator and the employee's current manager.

Conflict between manager and training coordinator regarding the amount and timing of training is no different conceptually from conflict over the amount and timing of any other maintenance. Operating managers, if left to themselves, might run equipment into the ground. Though skills once acquired do not deteriorate if used, they become obsolete quite rapidly in advancing fields such as ADP. Without an actively coordinated training program, the ADP function will steadily become obsolete and nonresponsive to organizational needs.

The training coordinator not only monitors the training needs of the ADP employees but is also responsible for selecting the source of training. It is important that the training coordinator not be in the training department—and especially not at its head. The training department, if there is one, should be regarded simply as one potential source for the purchase of training. If the training coordinator were part of that organization, there would be a conflict-of-interest situation which would easily result in empire building. Though training must always be internally coordinated by the training coordinator, the decision to provide the actual training itself internally should be made just as any other purchase-or-make decision is made. There are many organizations which would never dream of building their own computer, but which never give a second thought to their ability to do their own training. Everybody is an "expert" in education!

Naturally, for teaching employees the particulars of their own organization, internally supplied training is the only way. Much of this training may not differ for ADP employees from what is given to employees in other functions. At the other end of the spectrum, training in specific hardware must originate with the vendor, even if it is passed into the in-house school by training the in-house instructors.

The role of the instructor is obviously critical in ADP training, yet many in-house training programs recruit their instructors from the "rejects" of other ADP functions. Those who do not pass programmer training, for example, are sometimes moved into the position of programming educator. On the other hand, an equally frequent error is to assume that the best programmers make the best programming instructors. Just as some people are not cut out to be programmers, some will never shine as teachers no matter how much time and money is pumped into their development.

The selection of instructors should ideally be from among the successful ADP practitioners, with an eye to the qualities that also make for successful teaching: good verbal skills, ability to listen to and understand questions, a talent for abstracting and organizing technical material, and, above all, a genuine desire to teach. Needless to say, there will be no genuine desire to teach in an organization which regards the educational function as a dumping ground for inadequate employees.

On the other hand, it will not always be desirable or practical to free key technical people for long stints of teaching. For instance, the main developer of a new database application might not be a person who could be spared for the 2 years it might take to train all ADP employees in their use of the system. Probably the best solution to such problems is to have the technically knowledgeable person teach a course *to the teachers*. Even if this person is not an effective communicator, their teaching skills will enable them to draw out of him or her the material they need for building and carrying out the training program.

The Training Function The training program itself, like any other program, must be maintained. Organizations that spend millions for training sometimes neglect the training of the people within the training function itself. One self-defeating technique is to draw people from active ADP work and drain them of their first-hand experience for a few years before returning them to the ADP function. Though this method appears to be a cheap way to obtain qualified instructors, at the end of a stint in the school the employee is obsolete and of little use in his or her previous job. Second, when the employee realizes that he or she is becoming obsolete, morale in the education function begins to suffer. Since the education department has extensive contact with most new ADP employees, it is the last place we want to find a collapse of morale based on a feeling that the organization is "using" people.

Like any other employees, instructors find their motivation raised by more or less regular opportunities to learn. Indeed, the motivation of technically inclined employees is one of the major factors justifying large and protracted expenditures on education. But training is a two-edged sword, for as employees receive higher training, they will desire more responsible job assignments. If such assignments are not forthcoming, motivation will drop and turnover will increase. Therefore, it is not sufficient simply to send employees to school regularly. Great care must be paid to synchronizing educational advancement with job advancement. Though many organizations yield to the financial temptation, education cannot be *substituted* as a motivational factor for such other motivators as salary, benefits, working conditions, responsibility, and appreciation.

Another common structural flaw in in-house training is the lack of contact between instructors and students after courses are completed. For the instructor to learn, he or she must, like anyone else, have feedback about the results of his or her efforts. These results are not scores on final course examinations, but on-the-job performances of the students. Probably the greatest single advantage of in-house training is the feedback that can result to the training program by having instructors in regular contact with their former students and their managers. Probably the greatest single lack in in-house training is the failure of the training coordinator to arrange for such beneficial feedback.

Vendor-Supplied Training Surprisingly, performance feedback from students is more likely to be found when a specialized educational firm contracts to do in-house training. The reason is simple: The outside firm must demonstrate its performance in order to continue receiving contracts and good references. Each new course is a new financial decision for management, while strictly in-house courses go on and on without so much as a once-a-year management review. One of the great benefits of having an outside firm do ADP education from time to time is the alertness it lends to management about the educational function in general.

Though performance evaluation is a strong point of educational specialists, the contracting organization should never accept blindly evaluation criteria set by the educators themselves. No contract for education should be written without specifying, in advance, what operational criteria are to be used for judging the effectiveness of the program. Passing examinations — particularly examinations made by the instructors — is simply not adequate as a performance criteria. In such a field as ADP, where job performance measures abound, there is no excuse for establishing surrogate measures of performance such as are commonly used in classrooms. Moreover, if management would apply to their own educators the cost-effectiveness criteria they are more likely to use when purchasing education from outside, both types of education would benefit.

One severe caution about evaluation is in order: If the student or course evaluation procedure is confounded with the employee selection process, information is lost in two ways. In the first place, the evaluation process becomes self-fulfilling — those students who are selected as good students are marked in advance as good employees. Second, students and teachers alike will soon be working not toward learning but toward good evaluations — and these are not necessarily the same. Moreover, in training programs where there is student choice of course material, "grading" of students for external consumption merely tends to direct the students toward the easier courses, and particularly to things they already know — a serious waste of the training dollar. By all means evaluate the students within the school so as to direct their training and monitor the training process itself, but keep these "grades" within the school and leave to the managers the task of evaluating their employees.

INFORMAL TRAINING

Any survey of formal ADP education and training would pass right over the 90 per cent of ADP education that lies submerged below the surface of formal training programs.

Though the situation may not be desirable, we must face the fact that the vast majority of ADP education and training is obtained on the job and usually without benefit even of a recognized apprentice status. Even at the lowest levels of pay and technical skill, such as input preparation or machine operation, the majority of training comes by imitation or trial and error on the job, while as we move up the scale of skill and compensation to such positions as programmer and systems analyst, the preponderance grows.

Needless to say, such haphazard training can be expensive, not just in the direct costs of education, but also in the far greater indirect costs of inefficient and outright damaging or dangerous operations that may result from poorly trained ADP personnel. How many millions of dollars charged to "reruns" should more accurately be posted to the ledger of "training"? How many tens of millions in undetected inefficiency should be laid on the account of "education"? No doubt the costs of these kinds of "education and training" are an order of magnitude greater than the recognized kind, and the first step toward an intelligent management position on ADP education is to recognize the true costs of education—the costs of obtaining it and the costs of ignoring it.

The second step is to acknowledge the existence of the informal training so that its great mass can be harnessed or at least directed toward beneficial goals. At the very least, the intelligent ADP manager should know how to recognize when education is taking place under some other rubric, in order that he or she not destroy it. All too often we find managers who react negatively and violently to finding their employees "reading manuals" or "going around asking questions" or "running 'unauthorized' tests on the machine." If, for some reason, the manager has an aversion to these activities, he or she should in any case take their continued existence as a symptom that more formal training procedures are not functioning properly.

But no formal training is ever going to inculcate ADP personnel with even a fraction of the knowledge they need to perform their duties. There is a limit to what the human mind can absorb from all-day classes day after day. A more enterprising approach is to encourage training activities initiated by employees on the job, for if nothing else, effective *automatic training* is the best possible investment in education.

Automatic training may take any one of a number of forms. For instance, the entire practice of "egoless programming" can be viewed as a training process of the most automatic kind. The "chief programmer team" provides a master-apprentice situation which can provide the type of training that has classically served in so many other professions. Just the simple provision of an "experimenting budget" of machine time under a special account number can demonstrate to programmers or machine operators that management is behind their efforts to advance in knowledge. Or, for the cost of a few manuals, or copying a few pages, or a taxi fare to a meeting, alert management can purchase what would cost hundreds or thousands of dollars if obtained in more conventional ways. Given the costs of training and of not training, what ADP manager can afford to ignore the possibilities of automatic training?

SUMMARY

There are several sources of pre-employment training for ADP personnel—high school, to introduce the fledgling to a history of the field; the college and university, to teach the theory of it all; and the education-for-profit institutions, to train those who have no prior formal education in ADP. Though each source has characteristic limitations, all train potential ADP personnel. An intelligent ADP manager will evaluate each approach for what it is, rather than for what it claims to be. These pre-employment institutions provide background for later training performance, though the influence is less measurable under the title of *training* than of *motivation*. Any graduate of such facilities must have been sufficiently motivated to study ADP, so it is reasonable to assume that he or she will be receptive to further training opportunities.

Postemployment training, however, is the key source of skills in a data processing installation. Whereas pre-employment training and evaluation is a simulation, postemployment training is a true production test—real criteria must be met. Both in-house and vendor-supplied training programs must be judged as carefully as bought or made hardware or software. Constructive evaluation is needed by training directors, instructors, and education vendors in order to improve courses, but if the evaluation process also serves as an employee selection process, much vital information may be lost.

Formal training, however, is presently but a small part of the learning experience of typical ADP personnel. Informal training through peer group contact, machine experimentation, or reading of the literature and of programs—all contribute the major portion of ADP education. Management can encourage automatic training by providing space, materials, machine time, and other resources—but especially by establishing a general atmosphere that rewards self-education and skill improvement. In such a rapidly changing field as ADP, the most worthwhile training program is the one that motivates and helps people to train themselves.

SELECTIVE BIBLIOGRAPHY

Austing, Richard H., and Gerald I. Engel, "A Computer Science Course Program for Small Colleges," *Communications of the ACM*, March, 1973.

Baker, F. T. "System Quality through Structured Programming," *Proceedings of the Fall Joint Computer Conference*, Fall, 1972.

Beckman, Frank, "The IBM SRI: An Intra-Company Activity," *Proceedings of the Third Annual Computer Personnel Research Conference*, June, 1965.

Curriculum 68, "Recommendations for Academic Programs in Computer Science," *Communications of the ACM*, March, 1968.

Proceedings of the IFIPS Working Conference on Programming Teaching Techniques, Warsaw, Poland, North Holland Press, Amsterdam, 1973.

Report of the ACM Curriculum Committee on Computer Education for Management, "Curriculum Recommendations for Graduate Programs in Information Systems," *Communications of the ACM*, May, 1972.

Weinberg, G. M. "Psychology of Computer Programming," Van Nostrand Reinhold, New York, 1971.

Appendix[1]

Career Paths for ADP Personnel

Most companies do not have a career path for ADP personnel which is an organized plan for advancement. These companies, which in effect have negative career paths, either do not think in terms of advancement, or they do not want such a program because it requires a large commitment to a line activity. In such corporations, a senior programmer, for example, may find that although increased technical competence brings more money, he or she has reached the ceiling and there is no place to go. If such a person wishes to stay in programming, he or she can move on to a company where sophisticated technical capabilities are more important than to the present firm. Or, if this person wishes to move into middle management, he or she can look for the rare company that really has a career-path program. However, many programmers and systems analysts will tolerate low salaries and uninteresting work for a reasonable time if they see opportunities for improving their positions in the future. In this respect they are quite similar to people in other occupations.

Planning a career program can start at any time in the occupational life of a data processing professional, and without regard to experience, education, seniority, or present job classification. The plan can be made by finding his or her present position on a chart, such as the one shown in Figure A-1, whenever it is desirable to encourage working toward promotion within the data processing facility, or to middle-management positions in line functions.

[1] Based on *Turnover among ADP Personnel*, a Diebold Research Program Report.

PROFESSIONAL OPTIONS . . . AND A CHANCE TO ENTER MANAGEMENT RANKS

In some cases, data processing experience will qualify programmers or systems analysts for responsibility in a corporate department with which they have been working for several years, even though they may have had minimum supervisory or management training. The chart in Figure A-1 indicates that career development may proceed along

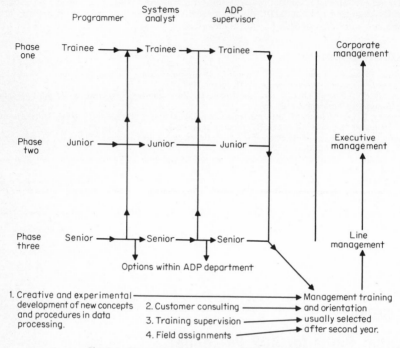

Fig. A-1   Career development in an ADP department.

several lines, with a variety of options for advancement in both data processing and line positions. The direction a person takes will depend on his or her own qualifications and ambitions, as well as on corporate requirements and policies. It is usually enough that a person be given the opportunity to advance. Those who are incapable and who leave because they think they have been bypassed unjustly are usually those the company should be least interested in.

The chart also suggests that management positions must follow a change in training and orientation. The requirement is extremely important and should not be overlooked in a frenzied attempt to keep a man or woman who is anxious to leave. A successful career path requires long-term planning commitment on training by both the firm and the employee.

Chapter 4

Salary Administration in the ADP Function[1]

ROBERT J. GREENE

**Compensation Consultant, A. S. Hansen, Inc.,
Lake Bluff, Illinois**

"One of our employees does systems analysis, writes programs, operates the computer and takes care of customer billing complaints. What should this person be paid? Should the salary range for this job be higher or lower than the ranges for our engineers or our accountants?"

Questions such as this arise frequently, particularly when the salary administrator is not familiar with the duties being performed on the job in question. Too often the questions go unanswered and that employee with the mixed job is paid according to the "best guess" technique. The purpose of this chapter is to look at some of the problems encountered when data processing employees must be hired, retained, and motivated within the constraints of a firm's compensation program. Basic salary administration techniques will not be dwelled upon. Rather, the intent will be to suggest some strategies and types of analysis which are particularly well suited to fitting the data processing function to the organization's salary structure.

ACTIVITIES AND ORGANIZATIONAL STRUCTURE

Within the data processing function there are usually several distinct categories of activities which must be performed. A list of activities common to many firms might be:

1. Management
2. Systems analysis
3. Applications programming
4. Systems programming
5. Computer operation
6. Keypunch
7. Unit record

---

[1] This chapter, updated, follows the treatment by the author in "Salary Administration in the DP Function," *Datamation*®, January, 1973, with permission of *Datamation*®. Copyright 1973 by Technical Publishing Company, Greenwich, Connecticut 06830.

8. Record (input-output) control
9. Facilities and hardware planning

There are many other combinations of, or additions to, the above. For the sake of simplicity let us assume this to be a complete list of activities which must be performed. The first step toward effective operation is to organize these activities properly. To help visualize a common organizational structure within the data processing function, consider the chart in Figure 4-1.

This type of organizational structure establishes the data processing function as an entity reporting to top management. It embraces the centralized approach and bases internal reporting structure on the type of activity performed. Much discussion has

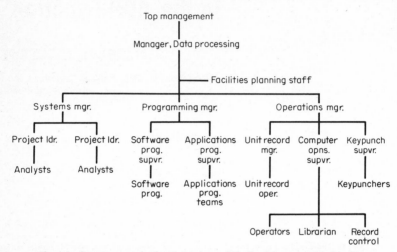

Fig. 4-1   Common organizational structure within the data processing function.

occurred as to which top executive the data processing manager should report to. If there has been a consensus, it is that the executive should not have a strongly vested interest in one aspect of the firm's operation (accounting, marketing, etc.). Data processing applications should work toward the achievement of the overall objectives of the firm, not just toward those of a single department or division. This consideration should be given a great deal of thought by a firm, taking into account the particular applications and the personalities involved.

Definition and Levels of Functions   Once an overall organization has been decided upon, each function should be further defined. Selecting one function, systems analysis, we can look at the various levels within a job family. The level represents the complexity of the tasks performed and the degree of supervision required. Consider the levels and the accompanying descriptions shown in Figure 4-2.[2]

Establishing several job levels within the family has benefits. Most important is that salary ranges can be established for each of the levels. Systems analysts can earn from $8,000 to $25,000, and the adoption of only two levels, such as junior and senior, will result in extremely wide salary ranges. One of the problems of a range which is too wide is that an employee near the top of the range may view the minimum as demeaning and someone near the bottom may view the maximum as not believable (as a "carrot" placed in front of his or her nose by management).

Another advantage of the six delineated levels is that the employee may be shown a clear career path. As he or she attains higher levels of expertise, the employee is awarded promotions which acknowledge technical progress. The new job title is accompanied by a higher salary range and, presumably, a salary increase to further acknowledge accomplishments. During periods of wage controls, the clearly defined

[2] *Position Descriptions for Data Processing Personnel*, published by A. S. Hansen, Inc., Lake Bluff, Ill. 60044.

job levels can act as objective justification for salary adjustments. Governmental inspectors are predictably wary of an increase "due to promotion," but are usually assuaged when the firm can produce standards for job performance and show that they have been well thought out and documented.

Job Descriptions The job description accompanying each of the job levels should be equally well thought out and documented. Many competent authors have described

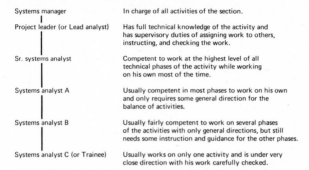

Systems manager	In charge of all activities of the section.
Project leader (or Lead analyst)	Has full technical knowledge of the activity and has supervisory duties of assigning work to others, instructing, and checking the work.
Sr. systems analyst	Competent to work at the highest level of all technical phases of the activity while working on his own most of the time.
Systems analyst A	Usually competent in most phases to work on his own and only requires some general direction for the balance of activities.
Systems analyst B	Usually fairly competent to work on several phases of the activities with only general directions, but still needs some instruction and guidance for the other phases.
Systems analyst C (or Trainee)	Usually works on only one activity and is under very close direction with his work carefully checked.

Fig. 4-2 Levels of positions in the systems analysis function.

the process of writing a good job description, and the subject is outside the scope of this Chapter. One technique for analyzing "mixed" jobs should be described, however. Let us go back to our employee in the opening paragraph of this Chapter. This employee does systems analysis, programs, operates the computer, and handles customer billing complaints. To classify this employee, ask the employee to fill in the grid in Figure 4-3, indicating the level at which he or she operates when performing each of the tasks. Further, have the employee think about the percentage of time spent on each of these tasks and place those percentages next to the check marks. It is unlikely that the employee will be able to do more than approximate the figures, but this information helps analyze the importance of each task.

Level of work	Systems	Programming	Operations	Customer complaints
Manager				
Lead				
Senior			X (1%)	X (9%)
A		X (85%)		
B				
C	X (5%)			

Fig. 4-3 Grid indicating level at which an employee operates in performing specific tasks.

It is clear that if we wish to fit this employee in one of the specific data processing job families and establish the level, we would classify him or her as a Programmer A. Reassigning the other tasks out of his or her jurisdiction is a matter of choice, probably dependent on whether or not these "sidelines" adversely affect the performance of the employee's basic task.

Mixed Jobs Mixed jobs often seem to be convenient, particularly when there are sideline tasks which are essential but would not justify a full-time employee. The old problem of justifying the typing of research reports by a senior engineer is an example. The contention here is that the volume could not keep a typist busy full time and also that it would take the engineer longer to explain it than to do it. But it is wise to consider the negative aspects of this practice. It is doubtful that the engineer would be a proficient typist, and one may certainly question what job satisfaction he or she would derive from the activity. Additionally, it is an underutilization of a scarce talent. This example can be brought back into the context of data processing by considering the typing of systems and programming documentation. Though necessary, documentation is a thorn in the side to a technician who is beset by user-groups demanding new applications and improvements in existing applications. Nowhere in the literature concerning job enrichment via vertical loading is it suggested that additional tasks be loaded on the *bottom* side.

Even if the mixed job consists solely of "rewarding" work, the salary administrator pays a penalty due to its existence. When using salary survey information the administrator can be left without data on the mixed job because no reporting is done on a job with equivalent content. Comparing the Programmer A we previously classified to Programmer A's in other firms may be valid, since only 15 per cent of the employee's time is spent on other functions. But what if the employee in question spent 40 per cent of his or her time on customer complaints? The comparison would then seem to be shaky at best.

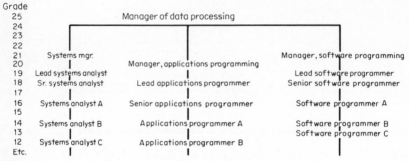

Fig. 4-4   Classification of jobs into grades.

Grades Assuming that the organization structure of the data processing function has been completed along the lines discussed earlier, and that all jobs have been classified into levels, there is a useful technique for determining the appropriate position grades for the jobs within the function. Consider the chart in Figure 4-4.[3]

This is a portion of the chart displayed earlier, but with one concept added: the comparative level of the jobs by position grade. This chart does not imply a systems analyst is universally rated higher than an applications programmer. It merely indicates that in this particular firm the systems manager has been classified two grades above the applications programming manager. It may be that in this evironment the systems function is more complex and that the systems people define their work down to the logic, leaving only the coding operation to the applications programmers.

Once this chart has been completed and the inconsistencies corrected, an additional step can be taken. Other functions within the company can be plotted alongside the data processing group, as shown in Figure 4-5.

This type of comparison can do much to identify inequities in the position grade classification of specific jobs. Any job evaluation plan will erode somewhat over time because of reclassifications, reorganizations, and newly added jobs. Periodic updating and review of a chart such as this can allow inequities to be identified and corrected. The classical technique of *empire building*, that of inserting assistant managers and assistant supervisors and gradually reclassifying jobs upward, is especially vulnerable to this type of cross-functional analysis. We are assuming, of course, that at least one function has remained "pure," so the comparison can be made.

COMPARISON WITH PREVAILING RATES

Once jobs have been defined, the organizational structure solidified, and functional comparisons made, a verification of the firm's pay levels with prevailing market rates is valuable. Since data processing salaries have changed rather dynamically in comparison to the more "settled" functional disciplines, more frequent comparisons are recommended. The comparison process is a difficult one. Salary data which truly reflect market rates are expensive to accumulate, and the mathematical calculations to

---

[3] *1974 Salary Survey Report on Data Processing Positions in the United States* published by A. S. Hansen, Inc., Lake Bluff, Ill.

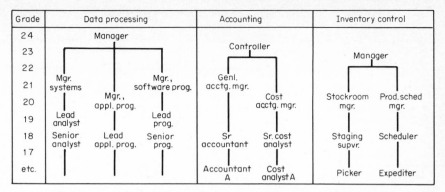

Grade	Data processing			Accounting		Inventory control	
24		Manager					
23				Controller		Manager	
22							
21	Mgr. systems		Mgr., software prog.	Genl. acctg. mgr.			
20		Mgr., appl. prog.			Cost acctg. mgr.	Stockroom mgr.	Prod. sched mgr.
19	Lead analyst		Lead prog.				
18	Senior analyst	Lead appl. prog.	Senior prog.	Sr. accountant	Sr. cost analyst	Staging supvr.	Scheduler
17							
etc.				Accountant A	Cost analyst A	Picker	Expediter

Fig. 4-5 Comparison of data processing positions with those of other functions.

make them meaningful are time consuming. Yet a salary structure which is internally equitable but fails to be comparable to prevailing market rates can cause the firm severe staffing problems.

The one question most often asked about the data processing function relates to the exempt/nonexempt status of the various jobs under the Fair Labor Standards Act. Many firms consider programmers and systems analysts to be managerial people, and therefore exempt. Considering the Standards Act, we find that justification for that position can occur under only two of the six allowed categories: administrative or professional. Professional status has not been officially awarded to the data processing field. Administrative status requires that work performed must be directly related to management policies and that it be performed for a proprietor or in a bona fide executive and administrative capacity. The best advice any consultant can give a client, with respect to exempt/nonexempt classification is that clients should familiarize themselves with the Fair Labor Standards Act in its most recently amended version and then take the matter up with legal counsel retained by their firms. Any general advice regarding the provisions of the act must be suspect, since the true content and level of a job with a specific title will vary significantly between firms.

SUMMARY

Basic salary administration techniques are no less valid for the data processing function than for any other. Some of the techniques mentioned above have been found to be particularly well suited to data processing jobs, but are not limited to data processing alone. The main objective of this Chapter is to point out to the salary administrator that the techniques he or she has been using in other areas of the firm are likely to succeed for the data processing function also.

Chapter 5

Scheduling Operations

KEITH HARVEY

Operations Manager, Computer Communications Group,
Bell Canada, Toronto, Ontario, Canada

ADP operations vary considerably from installation to installation. A number of factors contribute to the difficulty of effectively scheduling the many varied types of processing which a computer center must handle. The measure of a successful computer center is the production of a quality product to a schedule, at the lowest possible cost. Economic and efficient operation is not possible if a number of applications processed in any given month have to be rerun because key materials were not on hand, or because of poor flow of work through the center or unavailability of processing resources required for a given step in the operation.

BASICS OF SCHEDULING

ADP operations are of two major types: those operated by a department of a given organization to provide processing power to other departments, and those which are operated strictly as service bureaus to provide processing power to businesses or academic or institutional establishments which do not have ADP equipment. Some specialized processing needs are handled by service bureaus for companies which do have ADP resources, but do not have installations of the type required, say, for R&D or large-scale "number-crunching" jobs.

ADP centers operated in-house or by independent service bureaus can function either as *open-shop* facilities where users may enter the center and move from device to device to obtain finished results from their source data, or as completely *closed-shop* operations to which the user has no access, but instead submits processing to an input function of some kind. Some ADP operations may be a happy blend of both approaches, allowing certain processes to be performed by the user, but controlling other steps. An open-shop approach is difficult to schedule to keep all users pleased, but does provide some advantages in that the operations staff is kept to a minimum, and documentation for processing runs is generally controlled by the user and does not form part of a central library.

A closed-shop approach is usually desirable in an in-house ADP center, and is mandatory in most service bureau operations. Closed-shop processing must ensure that input to the center follows some specified format, and that processing requirements be well documented and defined. Intermediate steps in the processing are identified, and the materials necessary to complete the operation are specified as to source and quantity, with the retention or disposition of these items also clearly set forth. Samples of the output and input should be included in whatever run procedure is standard at the site, and quality control procedures should be noted so that a quality product can be produced.

Scheduling Challenges   Processing at all ADP centers is generally of the same type and frequency, and only the volume changes. Repetitive operations carried out by all centers include, but are not limited to:

Sales recording.
Inventory reporting.
Shipping document preparation.
Invoicing.
Statement preparation.
Payroll processing.
Accounts payable.
Accounts receivable.
Banking—deposits; check reconciliation.
Systems software testing.
Program testing and development.

Nonrepetitive or infrequent operations such as conversion of manual systems to ADP and special software projects must be scheduled on short notice, and require the operations manager to have a clear map of the current system load and the load expected over the next few weeks.

Two major operations have been excluded from the above list: preventive maintenance and equipment modification. Preventive maintenance is usually scheduled as a block of time daily, weekly, or semimonthly, depending on the configuration. Modifications to the equipment due to a manufacturer's change notice can usually be slotted into weekends or light days, and frequently need software modifications to make them effective or to take advantage of their insertion. This testing must be scheduled along with the hardware work.

Production Coordinator   The function of the production coordinator is vital to effective ADP operation. Depending upon the size of the ADP center, this function may be full time or shared. The production coordinator is the individual who has the resources of the center at his or her command, and attempts to match these resources to the demands of users and of his or her own internal requirements. Internal requirements are usually expressed in terms of loading statistics and performance measurement, on the basis of which the coordinator can plan new equipment or modifications to the existing configuration.

In a small- to medium-sized installation, the production coordinator's function may be served by the operations manager or supervisor. In a medium- to large-sized facility, this function is frequently a full-time job, and an installation with a large-scale system plus smaller specialized ADP equipment will find it desirable to give the coordinator complete scheduling authority and jurisdiction over conflicts for processing resources.

Obviously, the coordinator must have a complete understanding of the capabilities of the system at his or her disposal. The number of available disk drives, tape drives, printers, punches and readers, etc., must be known, as well as their speeds and peculiarities of code sets, etc. Available memory size, processing speeds, channel speeds, and operating system capabilities must be well understood, in addition to the specialized utility programs available which may make job steps simple. The individual assigned the task of coordinating the demands on the center must also be familiar with the capabilities of the operations staff and the level of knowledge each staff member has achieved. Certain complex operations may require a specific level of knowledge in the computer room at the time of their processing, and if this involves shift changes, the coordinator must prepare in advance.

The coordinator must also be familiar with the handling of processing output, e.g., whether it should be burst and bound into covers or left intact. If the output consists of special materials such as microfiche, microfilm, or numeric control tapes, the coordinator must know where to send it, how to package it, and what the successfully produced material looks like.

Scheduling Aids Routine operations of the ADP center assume that no application has been accepted for processing that is too large to handle on the facilities available. Additionally, it is assumed that there is no attempt to schedule more than 24 hours of work into any one day, or that certain housekeeping functions have been sacrificed to add "just one more rush job."

The most useful scheduling aid is a record of all incoming workload, and for want of a better term we shall call this device a *calendar*. The calendar will detail to the co-ordinator the following vital information:

User-department.

Contact.

Due into the ADP center: date/time.

Due out to the user-department: date/time.

Materials to be received: tapes, disk, etc.

Special steps: keypunching, sorting, batch balancing, etc.

Estimated processing time for each step.

Computer resources required: core, tape drives, etc.

Special forms.

Disposition of output.

Ideally, the calendar will be duplicated and form part of the run materials which the operator assigned to the job uses, and will serve as a ready and convenient check along the way. Some method of feedback into the calendar operation will be used to input the actual date/time received, date/time delivered, and the duration of the processing steps, so that the scheduled requirements can be compared with the actual performance over some months or weeks. This will serve to pinpoint those areas where the schedule is unrealistic or the workloads have varied from the original. It will also serve to pinpoint those users who are frequently late with input, but insist on getting the results out on time anyway.

ENVIRONMENTS

There are two basic ADP center environments. In a controlled environment, the ADP manager can specify the limits of the resources of the center which will be pre-empted by any one user. This is usually the case of the in-house facility and exists to serve a manufacturer, distributor, or similar operation. This practice of specifying resource limits also exists in an environment which is devoted to processing a product in volume, e.g., service bureaus providing payroll processing.

The second type of environment is more difficult to schedule. This is the uncontrolled use of resources at any time, experienced by a commercial service bureau or a facility installed at a university for research and development. Similar operations exist in connection with industrial R&D. In the uncontrolled environment, the user dictates his or her consumption of resources at the time the job is submitted. Since the user demand may represent a major percentage of available resources, scheduling such processing is a problem.

The Controlled Environment In the controlled environment, which usually includes small- to medium-scale installations using serial processing of work steps, scheduling can be a simple paper-and-pencil task. Timetables can be drawn up to represent each half-hour segment of the day, and the task assigned to the system for a specific time is entered onto this sheet. When the size of the center increases to the point where multiple machines make it difficult to schedule this way, or in the situation where a serial processor has been upgraded and is now capable of multitask processing, more sophisticated scheduling is called for.

A useful tool for a center such as this is a calendar routine, which can be simple or complex, depending on how much information it is required to carry or generate. Basically what we are after is a machine-generated list of what work is expected at which system component at what time, plus how much of the available resources are demanded. Additionally we must have some method of feeding back to the routine any changes in the schedule, size of job, etc.

We might also carry other information along with the job name and chronological information. We might like to know whom to contact in case of trouble, and what to do with the output. We might like to know how frequently the job is expected, and how soon it will be required after it is presented to the center. Figure 5-1 illustrates the concept. The output from this routine could include a machine-loading report which tells the center manager just how much of the resources are being used at what times of the day or month. Such a report can be invaluable in planning for new equipment.

The Uncontrolled Environment   As indicated earlier, in the uncontrolled environment the user dictates his or her consumption of resources. In the commercial service bureau, or in an operation which is handled like a commercial service bureau, the center manager must have available at all times sufficient resources to handle this demand. Since the demand varies considerably in volume and frequency, the scheduling

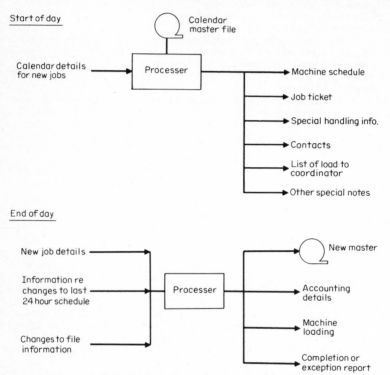

Fig. 5-1 Calendar routine for machine-generated scheduling in a controlled environment.

of the center's workload becomes highly complex. Additionally, the manager must charge for services and the use of resources, since the manager's very existence depends on the proper return on the equipment dollar. Many in-house installations also charge for their services; this is vital if we are to place some self-regulation on the user. In the uncontrolled mode of operation, machine-loading statistics are also vital if we are to monitor usage and plan for growth.

A center operating in the uncontrolled mode usually has a system which is medium- to large-scale in size of processor and peripherals, and will require certain pieces of equipment or certain dedicated resources simply to run itself. The control over the hardware is usually done by a monitor or control system, generally called an *operating system,* and generally furnished by the machine manufacturer. Such an operating system will have a scheduler of some kind built in, but the center manager must fine-tune this to suit his or her requirements. The resources of a center operating such a system are usually measured in terms of memory size to run a job, plus the number of tape drives, disk drives, and printers required to handle the input and output files. Memory size is frequently divided into small units to assist in scheduling, and to avoid waste, and such units are variously called *partitions, pages, chapters,* etc. Tapes and disks may be called *volumes, files,* etc., but the intent is the same: to break the units up into smaller pieces for ease of scheduling.

By experience and by analyzing the data generated by machine-loading reports, the center manager can determine how to charge for services, and also how to establish priority levels to avoid scheduling conflicts or log-jams in the system. The manager may wish to establish five or six levels of priority, with limits for memory and disk/tape, and a decreasing cost for those users who can wait a few hours to have their work processed. These divisions or levels can represent the center's published ground rules for doing business.

An example of such levels and possible costs allocated to them is given in Table 5-1. Assume the central processor has a memory allocation system which uses an actual numbering scheme, and that the system has rows of tape drives and disk storage. The reader will notice that the processing cost reduces as the priority is lowered. This will encourage a user to refrain from demanding a turnaround that is unreasonable for his or her job. The published turnaround times and costs are data which are important to the user when the user must plan his or her own workload and budget for processing.

TABLE 5-1   An Example of Six Levels of Priority, with Associated Costs

Priority level	Price	Turnaround	Resources restrictions
P6	0.75	30 minutes	56K core 100 cps No tapes
P5	0.53	60 minutes	80K core 200 cps 1 tape
P4	0.44	2 hours	None
P3	0.33	8 hours	None
P2	0.25	24 hours	None
P1	0.20	48 hours	None

The published turnaround times may on occasion not be met by the center because of equipment malfunctions or large demands for service at a single priority level. If this is the case, the user will automatically be charged the appropriate priority level representing the actual time his or her job turned around.

From time to time the queue of work submitted may contain so many jobs at equal priority levels that their total exceeds the capacity of the system. At this point, the operator may elect to intervene and control the processing sequence to prevent excessive stacking of the queues. The operator may do this by suspending partially completed jobs, or by raising and lowering assigned priorities to expedite processing that is holding up resources required by other jobs.

BLENDING INTERNAL AND EXTERNAL SCHEDULING

Computer systems operating as previously described do a very efficient job of automatically processing the workload once it is presented to them. Workload can be presented either by communications links or via the computer-room input devices. Control over the presentation of jobs entered via the computer input devices must be external to the built-in scheduler, and can follow the procedure outlined previously in connection with scheduling aids, specifically the table dealing with machine loading and process scheduling (machine-generated timetables).

Machine-generated Timetable for the Center as a Whole   The calendar routine can be enhanced to produce a timetable for the operation of the center as a whole, and a machine-generated timetable can be invaluable in scheduling emergency computer runs. The details for this timetable are taken from all the lines of the calendar, and can produce a *load map* for all the ADP center's equipment.

In a shop where each device has one operator assigned, this timetable will tell the operator what to expect next. In a shop where one operator handles all phases of a given job, the timetable will tell the operator when it is his or her turn on the sorter, collator, or computer.

The calendar will also schedule preventive maintenance and housekeeping functions, such as disk backup and slots of time for software development where the analyst requires hands-on time. Certain sections of the day may be set aside for program testing in batches or for operator hands-on training. These should also be part of the daily timetable and properly indicated.

Some centers may not wish to use a full-blown automatic calendar routine with attendant timetable, preferring to use a hand-generated timetable with a page per day for each machine, divided into 15-minute or 30-minute segments. This is perfectly acceptable, providing the information is kept current and changes to scheduled items are made only by the person acting as coordinator.

Occasionally a center is asked to provide backup time for another site, and a properly kept log or timetable will allow the coordinator to provide a quick yes or no answer to this request. Careful use of the timetable can allow a center to sell off excess time and defray operating costs, since most centers charge for use of their facilities by outsiders.

Priorities in the ADP Center   The best-laid plans of any center can often be disrupted by equipment failure, power failure, or reruns due to a variety of causes. Such is the life of the operations manager that these always seem to occur on the busiest day, when there would just be enough time to handle the load if everything ran smoothly. And in these times of stress, it almost always seems that the users are also demanding their output early because of some special requirement. At this point, the ADP center staff must realize that it cannot please everyone and that certain priorities must be recognized. A quick look at the processing calendar will indicate what the load yet to be processed is, and what was actually in process at the time.

Obviously, certain items are critical to running the business, and certain items are critical to running the ADP operation. Items such as disk backup runs and daily computer accounting must be completed. Any user run which makes sure that the factory or business opens its doors tomorrow must also be completed. If, for example, meat products or perishable goods are awaiting preparation of bills of lading before they can leave the dock, then that must be first on the list. Payroll and other key finance functions must be completed, but runs such as receivables, payables, and mailing campaigns will generally not suffer if kept an additional 12 hours or so.

Developmental Operations   Frequently large-scale software development is undertaken to satisfy future processing demands. Developmental work may also be undertaken to install new operating system software or to convert for newly installed equipment additions. Such large-scale effort will involve every present user of the ADP facility as well as those who simply receive output as part of their daily operation. To launch such an operation demands that a design team or project group be formed. This group will be responsible for blocking out the major steps of a developmental project and have the responsibility of monitoring the process during its lifetime. We must expect that this group will need to conduct extensive surveying of present and future users of the facility and that it will be conducting a great deal of interviewing. This holds true whether the project is to switch to a new operating system, design a new system to automate another section of the plant operation or accounting, or install new features on the existing system.[1]

After the first planning and interviewing phase, an idea of the size of the effort undertaken will be in all project team members' heads. Unfortunately, keeping track of large-scale projects "in team members' heads" is not the most efficient method of project control, since even the best-developed memory can slip when involved in a complex operation such as this. Now is the time to start charting the steps necessary to bring this project to a successful completion. As each team member recruits more input to complete his or her part of the project and actual work begins, an interlocking relationship forms. This *interlocking* is the crux of the problem, since certain key steps must be complete before other operations can begin.

[1] See the detailed discussions in Section 3, Part 4, Chapters 1 and 2: "Organization for Systems Implementation: Timetables and Follow-through" and "Installation and Testing Techniques."

Project Control Inasmuch as each step has some dependency on the step which preceded it and has some effect on those which are planned to follow it, it becomes vital to develop a system of control. Every project has a number of steps or events, and each event does have some forecasted duration. If all the events were processed by one individual, and all the time allotments were added together, the scheduling of the project would be easy: Simply pick a start date, add the number of days necessary to complete all events, and the completion date is the result. But since there is usually a rush for any given project, and more than one person is involved, this serial approach is unworkable. We can, however, put down the things we do know: start date, number of events currently planned and their duration, estimated or desired completion time. As we start listing these items, we begin to see by group discussion which must be delayed until completion of others and which can be conducted in parallel.

To keep all team members informed, we should record and publish this information in a form which is easily understood by all members. This is not too difficult with the normal minutes-of-meeting approach, but as the project marches on in time, it becomes difficult to make changes to the original document as slippages occur or new information is received. A number of application programs are available to ADP users to produce such required documentation automatically, and any of these can be useful in the control of projects. Probably the best-known ones are the following:[2]

PMCS Project Management and Control System.
PMS Project Management System.
PERT Project Evaluation and Review Technique.
CPM Critical Path Method.

The term *interlocking relationships* used earlier is at the heart of the critical path method (CPM) and other management control systems. Simply stated, most events depend upon other events, and should slippage occur in one, another will become critical and should be flagged. These project management control systems do this flagging, and make it quickly obvious to the project leader that something is about to upset the careful planning. While these systems require input in different forms, the information is largely the same in all cases:

Event identification.
Event duration.
Starting point.
Completion point.

The start and completion points are usually termed *nodes,* and the systems mentioned are capable of accounting for many hundreds of events and nodes simultaneously. It is also possible to carry additional information within the system which can assist the project team in meeting its budget target as well as its product target. By pricing employee-hours and material costs into the system, one can produce quickly an estimate of the dollars expended and new dollars required as a result of changes.

We can obtain output from these systems in various forms, the most frequently used probably being the bar chart. By identifying events vertically and forming a calendar horizontally, we produce a grid which can be blocked in to produce a picture of the activities under way. Since most projects contain far too many events for one page, the project report is broken up into sections which are the control for operations within the project. A bar chart is an ideal way to note slippages or early finishes, since this can be done easily with a colored marker on the chart itself. These modifications must of course be re-entered into the system to provide updated reports.

Another form of output is the simple list of events and dates. In this case, the events which are affected when the one we are working on is modified for some reason are identified by number and can be cross-referenced quickly.

Some project leaders prefer to have a chart which displays the interlocking or net effect, and this is very workable for control over the whole operation. Unfortunately, for a large-scale project, the drawing effort to create the chart is quite large, and as the events change in scope and duration, the redrawing becomes a large time consumer.[3]

[2] For a discussion of the network techniques, see Section 4, Chapter 1, "New Tools for Decision Making."

[3] But note the time-saving charting techniques described in Section 3, Part 4, Chapter 1.

If the site is equipped with a plotter facility, then such a chart becomes quite easy to obtain. For large projects at ADP facilities without plotter capability, the project leader may wish to buy this service from an independent service bureau.

Independent of which procedure is used to manage a project, the key is to ensure that all team members understand the system and provide constant input to keep the system up to date.

Chapter 6

The Technology of Database Management

RICHARD F. SCHUBERT

Director of Management Information Services — Technical Advancements, The B. F. Goodrich Company, Akron, Ohio

A database management system (DBMS) is a collection of interrelated software modules that control storage, retrieval, modification, maintenance, integrity, and security of data and data relationships for a company on a hierarchy of secondary memory storage devices such as drum, disk, mass storage, and magnetic tape. A DBMS provides data and information services to all types of application programming languages and generalized software used by nonprogrammer users for data entry and display.

The design and implementation of DBMS is a complicated and difficult task which has been undertaken by hardware vendors, software firms, and users. Of the many systems that have been developed, only a few have survived the test of time and use, and are thereby considered successful. The general reason for failure and abandonment is that the system does not provide one or more of the capabilities required by the user, whether in the design, implementation, or operation of an application. The specific causes of failure which follow outline subject areas that may be considered in the evaluation and selection of a DBMS:

1. Failure of the DBMS to provide a flexible method of describing data and data relationships.

2. Failure to provide adequate language facilities for the manipulation of data and data relationships.

3. DBMS costs in terms of disk and memory utilization, central processor overhead, forced database restructuring caused by DBMS software changes, and user-personnel required to maintain the DBMS.

4. Failure of the DBMS to perform satisfactorily in an operating environment. (This is especially important in an on-line fast-response system).

5. Failure of the user to comprehend how and where to use a DBMS effectively.

The technical aspects of database management contained in this Chapter are based on the concepts and terminology of the April, 1971, report of the CODASYL Data Base Task Group (DBTG).[1] Examples are based on a subset implementation of the DBTG specifications produced by B. F. Goodrich, called *Integrated Database Management*

---

[1] See reference in the Selective Bibliography at the end of this Chapter.

System (IDMS). (IDMS has been used in production since January, 1972, on IBM hardware.)

BACKGROUND

The Conference on Data Systems Language (CODASYL) was organized in 1959 in response to the need for a common business-oriented language (COBOL) designed to be independent of any current or future make or model of computer, which would reduce the cost of program creation, maintenance, transferability, and documentation.

COBOL allowed the user to define data and procedures to fulfill exactly the processing requirements of an application. The original COBOL specification assumed serial processing of data, provided by existing magnetic-tape technology. This, of course, is an acceptable approach in many applications. However, the implementation of more sophisticated business applications combined with the development of disk and drum technology showed the shortcomings of serial methods, and emphasized the need for new methods of data storage and retrieval on direct-access devices.

The onslaught of third-generation hardware and software diverted considerable software resources into development of viable operating systems and language compilers at the expense of database management system development. The primitive access methods provided by many vendors greatly influenced the design, implementation, and performance of many advanced applications. As a result, many applications require additional sort/merge programs, greater data redundancy, and repetitive entry of input data.

Clearly, the increasing information needs of a dynamic company require a database management system to provide: control of data structure, comprehensive language for data description and manipulation, control of data access, adequate execution performance, and system integrity.

Note that the basic needs have not changed; only the hardware technology and application requirements have changed.

The April, 1971, report of CODASYL Data Base Task Group was accepted by the Programming Languages Committee in May, 1971, for inclusion in the COBOL *Journal of Development* language specifications. It marked the culmination of 6 years of effort by many knowledgeable software developers and users to produce a language for the description and manipulation of data stored within a database. The language specifications for describing a database are designed to be independent of any programming language.

However, the language specifications for manipulation of data are designed to be used as an extension of existing programming languages. Like any new language specification, the DBTG report needs refinements which can be created only by implementation and use of the language. As it stands, it offers significant advantages over currently available database management systems, and represents a giant step in the right direction.

DATABASE CONCEPTS

The subject of database management systems, database data description, and data manipulation covers a wide range of topics of varying complexity. However, the basic concepts of a database management system are not difficult to understand.

In its most primitive form, a database is a centralized collection of all data stored for one or more related applications. Current direct-access hardware technology permits data for many applications to share the same storage device. This in turn makes it possible for two or more applications to use a common, single source of data, and thus eliminate the cost and complexity of data redundancy. Once data have been integrated, a need arises for the ability to structure data in a manner which meets the requirements of each application. An application requirement may be to access only a specified portion of data in the database, and thereby remove data required by other applications from view. Furthermore, not all applications are written in the same programming language. This in turn requires that the data and its description be independent of any programming language.

Data independence and the separation of data description from the restrictions and conventions of any programming language allow centralized database maintenance, protection, and control over physical aspects of the database. A database, then, can be viewed as more than an ordinary collection of data for several related applications. The database must be viewed as a generalized, common, integrated collection of company- or installation-owned data which fulfills the data requirements of all applications which access it. In addition, the data within the database must be structured to model the natural data relationships which exist in a company.

The three elements of a database are: (1) physical storage structure, (2) data and control information contained within a database, and (3) logical relationships among data stored within the database.

Physical Storage Structure   The physical storage structure of a database can vary considerably, depending on the design of the direct-access storage device and the manufacturer of the machine. In this discussion, let us assume that an entire integrated database is contained in a single disk unit.

The single unit contains 404 cylinders (or arm positions). Each cylinder contains 19 tracks (or recording surfaces), each of which has capacity for four 3,156-byte blocks of information. Thus, the physical database is subdivided into $404 \times 19 \times 4 = 30,704$ contiguous blocks. Each block of information is called a *page*, and is the unit of physical data transfer between the database and main memory of the system. The pages are numbered in consecutive order, beginning with the first block in the first track of the first cylinder and ending with the last block of the last track of the last cylinder. The page numbers will range from 0 through 30,703. In this manner, every page has a unique number identifier, and occupies a known location within the database.

In DBTG terms, an *area* is a named subdivision of a database. In IDMS, this logical address space is simply defined as a given number of contiguous pages. The area defined for the BFG on-line order processing system (TOPSY) and the area for payables, raw-material inventory, and engineering stores system (PRESTO) are defined as shown in Table 6-1.

TABLE 6-1

	Extent	
Area name	Low page	High page
TOPSY	4,000	12,999
PRESTO	13,000	19,000

Thus the 9,000-page TOPSY area begins at page 4,000 and continues to the page numbered 12,999. A user program which requires access to information stored within the TOPSY area must execute a statement that declares the type of database operations to be executed and whether concurrent access by other independent programs is allowed.

Contents of a Database   The smallest unit of named data in a database is a *data item*. In addition to a name, a data item has other attributes which define its type and length. A data item may be described by:

CUST-NO   PICTURE X(11)

where CUST-NO is the name of the data item and the X(11) picture indicates that the length of the item is 11 bytes and may contain any character in the machine's character set. An occurrence of a CUST-NO data item would have a value such as 71320601011.

A *record* is a named collection of one or more data items. A *record type* is a description consisting of the record name followed by the names and attributes of all data items included within the record. For example, the record type named CUSTOMER contains the data items:

CUST-NO   PICTURE X (11)
CUST-NAME   PICTURE X (32)
CUST-ADDR   PICTURE X (32)

where CUST-NO is the identification number assigned to the customer, followed by the customer's name (CUST-NAME) and address (CUST-ADDR). Any reference to the CUSTOMER record type implies reference to all data items within the record. This description may be considered a model or template for the CUSTOMER record type wherever it appears in the database. An *occurrence* of a CUSTOMER record type exists when a value for each data item exists within the database. Three occurrences of the CUSTOMER record appear in Table 6-2.

TABLE 6-2

Customer record	Cust-no	Cust-name	Cust-addr
Occurrence #1	71320601011	H. Martoyal Inc.	689 Pennington Ave.
Occurrence #2	81182803003	Texoil Inc.	P.O. Box 1608
Occurrence #3	87580701001	Weathering Co.	P.O. Box 310

The distinction between a record type and a record occurrence is important. Note that any number of CUSTOMER record occurrences may appear in the database, and each occurrence will contain a string of characters which are defined by the CUST-NO, CUST-NAME, and CUST-ADDR data item description.

Physical placement of records types within a database is controlled by specification of one or more areas in which record occurrences may be stored. In addition, occurrences of one record type may be stored close to occurrences of another record type to improve execution performance of the system. Any number of record types may be specified within any given area. Unless otherwise restricted, any number of record occurrences may appear for any given record type, subject to the total physical storage space limitation of the specified area. In addition, an occurrence of any record type specified for an area may be stored in any page in the specified area.

In addition to record occurrences, the database also contains system information used to control access to each page, to provide audit trail information, and to inventory available space on each page.

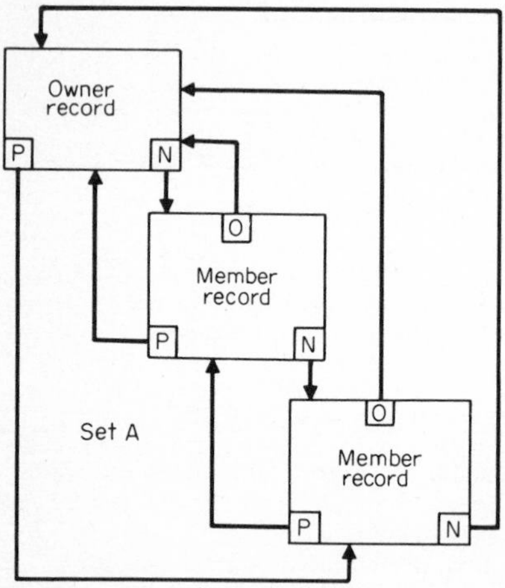

Logical Data Relationships The most common and familiar type of data structure exists within a record type. The CUSTOMER record type is an illustration of intrarecord data structure where the CUST-NO, CUST-NAME, and CUST-ADDR data items have an implied logical relationship to each other by their appearance together within the same record. Intrarecord data relationships are largely determined by the data content of the record and the meaning imparted to it by logical procedures within the application program. Intrarecord data structure is an important and useful capability which is essential in all database applications. The additional provision for a flexible method of establishing relationships between record types is essential to fulfill the complete data structure requirements of an integrated database.

Fig. 6-1 Set occurrence with next (N), prior (P), and owner (0) pointers.

Logical relationships between two or more record types are established by the *set* mechanism. The set establishes a logical relationship between two or more record types and is, in effect, a building block which allows various data structures to be built.

Figure 6-1 is a representation of a set occurrence which includes three record occurrences shown by rectangular boxes. A set must have only one record type which functions as *owner* of the set. In addition, a set must have at least one record type which functions as a *member* of the set. Figure 6-1 shows one owner record occurrence and two record occurrences which participate as members. One of several possible implementations of the set mechanism is to use pointers which are included with the data as part of each record occurrence. The owner of the set contains a pointer marked N (next) which identifies the first member record occurrence.

The first member record occurrence also contains a pointer marked N, which identifies the second member record occurrence in the set. Finally, the last record occurrence contains a pointer marked N, which identifies the owner record. Taken together, all the N pointers form a ring structure which is commonly called a *chain*. Moreover, the N pointers establish a logical chain order in the *next* direction.

The pointers marked P (prior) establish a logical chain order in the *prior* direction. The owner contains a pointer marked P, which identifies the last member record occurrence in the set. The last record contains a pointer marked P, which identifies its logical predecessor, which in turn points to the owner record occurrence. In addition, each member record occurrence may optionally contain a pointer marked O, which identifies the owner record occurrence. The next and prior chains, along with owner pointers, are considered as a model or template for all occurrences of the set named A. Note that a database may contain any number of owner record occurrences, which in turn may have any number of member record occurrences. Each record occurrence in

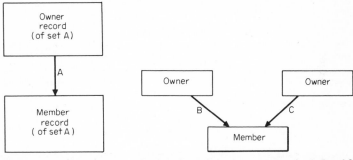

Fig. 6-2 Set represen-   Fig. 6-3 Record type as a member of sets B and C.
tation.

a database is assigned a unique identifier, called a *database key*, by the DBMS when the record is initially stored in the database. In IDMS, the database key represents a logical position in the database which is easily mapped to a physical location within a page.

In Figure 6-1, the owner and member record occurrences each possess a unique database key. Each of the next, prior, and owner pointers are database keys that uniquely identify the record occurrences in the logical order of set A. The owner pointer in each member record occurrence is the database key of the owner record occurrence.

Since the set mechanism can be used to build complicated relationships between record types, an abbreviated, "shorthand" set notation is needed to simplify the graphic representation of data structure within the database. Figure 6-2 shows the owner record type as a rectangle with an arrow pointing to the rectangle representing all occurrences of the member record type.

The arrow is the shorthand equivalent of all next, prior, and owner pointers shown in Figure 6-1. The name of the set (A) appears next to the arrow. The general rules for this representation are: The tail of the arrow touches the record type which is the owner of the set; the point of the arrow touches the record type which participates as a member of the set.

The set mechanism is a basic building block which can be used to construct complicated data structures. There are seven basic rules for the formation of set relationships between record types:

1. Any record type may participate as a member in one or more sets. Figure 6-3 uses the shorthand set representation described in Figure 6-2 to show a record type which is a member of two sets, B and C.

2. Any record type may be the owner of one or more sets. Figure 6-4 uses short-hand set representation to show a record type which is owner of three sets, D, E, and F.

3. Any record type may participate as a member in any number of sets, and also be owner of one or more other sets. Figure 6-5 shows a record which participates as a

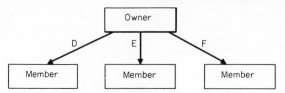

Fig. 6-4   Record type as owner of sets D, E, and F.

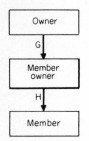

Fig. 6-5 Record type as member of set G and owner of set H.

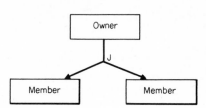

Fig. 6-6 Two record types as members of set J.

member of set G and also is owner of set H. This is the representation of the hierarchial data structure.

4. A set may have only one record type as its owner but may have one or more record types as members. Figure 6-6 shows two record types which participate as members of set J.

5. Any number of set relationships may exist between two record types. Figure 6-7 shows a record type as owner of sets K and L with a single record type as member of each set. This type of structure is used whenever two or more relationships exist for the same data. In a manufacturing application, set K could represent a list of all parts or subassemblies required to produce a given inventory item. Set L could represent a list of where each part or subassembly is used throughout the entire manufacturing operation.

6. A record type may exist without set participation. This means that record occurrences will not participate either as owner or member in any set.

7. Any record type may be defined as an optional member of a set. Participation of a record occurrence in this case is established, or deleted, based on execution of a procedure within a user program. In a retail application, failure to submit payment for a monthly statement would cause the customer's record occurrence to be inserted into the OVERDUE-ACCOUNT set. Subsequent payment would then cause removal of the customer's record from the OVERDUE-ACCOUNT set. The graphic representation of an optional set is shown by a dashed arrow.

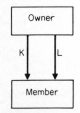

Fig. 6-7   Two record types as owner and member of sets K and L.

The data structure in Figure 6-8 is a portion of the B. F. Goodrich Chemical Company's on-line order entry system, TOPSY. It illustrates how the seven basic rules for set relationships are combined to achieve a data structure required by multiple applications. The alphabetic set names in Figure 6-8 correspond to set names used in Figures 6-3 through 6-7. Record types are identified numerically for discussion purposes.

Starting in the top left of Figure 6-8, note that record types 1 and 5 are owners and

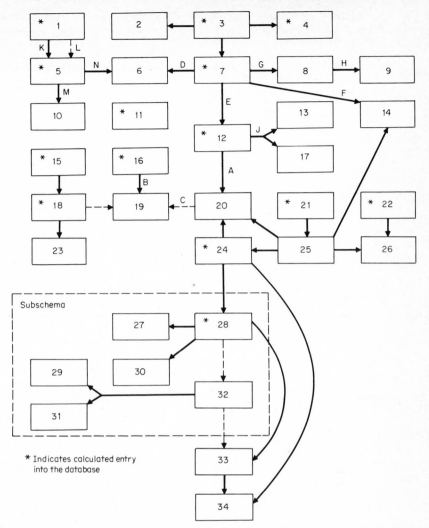

Fig. 6-8 B. F. Goodrich Chemical Company on-line order processing system (TOPSY) network data structure.

members respectively of sets K and L (Rule 5).   Record type 5 also is the owner of set M with record type 10 as member, and set N with record type 6 as member (Rules 2 and 3).   Record type 6 also participates as a member in set D with record type 7 as owner (Rule 1).   Record types 6, 7, 12, and 14 are related by sets D, E, and F (Rule 2). Both record types 13 and 17 are members of set J with record type 12 as owner (Rule 4). Record type 11 shows the absence of structure (Rule 6).   The use of optional set membership (Rule 7) is illustrated by use of dashed-arrow set representations.

A complete description of data items included in each of the 34 record types and the structure provided by the 35 set types in Figure 6-8 is beyond the scope of this discussion.   The design of this part of the database required extensive study and analysis of the actual B. F. Goodrich Chemical Co. data relationships that exist among internal departments, plants, warehouses, sales offices, customers, and products.   Placement of data items and data redundancy within this structure is determined by the logical structure of the database and the manner in which the data will be accessed by all applications involving the database. The objective was to provide an optimum balance between data placement, structural requirements, and execution performance.

The techniques of database design are a complex subject which has not been fully developed by the industry. Database design will remain a black art for a few self-trained people until sufficient insight and experience can be obtained to treat the subject properly.

Schema and Subschema Descriptions A definition of the concepts of a *schema* and *subschema* will complete the description of the elements of a database.

A schema is a complete description of all elements of a database. It includes the names and descriptions of all areas, data items, records, and sets which exist in a database.

A subschema is a logical subset of the schema which names only those areas, data items, records, and sets that are accessed by one or more specific programs. The concept of a subschema is important because it provides a measure of data privacy and programming convenience by "removing from view" all the other areas, data items, records, and sets not included in a given subschema. A measure of data independence is achieved in that certain changes may be made at the subschema level to provide compatibility with existing programming language conventions. However, a subschema must be a consistent and logical subset of the schema from which it is obtained.

In any database there is only one schema, but there may be any number of subschemas. The TOPSY data structure in Figure 6-8 is a large subschema which would not normally be used in its entirety in one processing program. A subschema of more reasonable scope is shown by those record and set types included within the dotted area at the bottom of Figure 6-8. All records and sets outside the dotted area are removed from view of the program which invokes the subschema shown.

DATABASE LANGUAGES

The common approach of data description followed by most programming languages in current use is to include the data description in the same program as the procedures which access the data. The files are frequently designed to optimize processing for only a few programs. Other programs which require access to the same data frequently require extraction of redundant data and sorting to create a file which is then optimized for processing by a few other programs. Moreover, the data files reflect the data formatting characteristics of the language used to create the file. The use of more than one programming language to access the same data normally requires data conversion from one format to another. The cost of handling ever-increasing volumes of data, combined with increasingly complex processing demands, has created the need for a method to create and manipulate a database which is common to all applications but independent of any particular programming language.

The required separation of database description from the programs which access the data has created the need for new languages and extensions to existing programming languages.

DEVICE MEDIA CONTROL LANGUAGE

The Device Media Control Language (DMCL) is used to specify and control the physical properties of a database. The manner in which the DMCL functions are achieved will depend upon hardware and operating system architecture, and implementor preferences. In the IDMS system, the DMCL statements are entered into the system after the Schema DDL and Subschema DDL statements have been entered.

Schema Data Description Language (DDL) The schema DDL is used to name and describe the attributes of all areas, records, and sets included in a database and to specify appropriate control over availability and manipulation of database contents by application programs. The schema DDL entries are grouped into three categories: area entry, record entry, and set entry.

Area Entry. Area clauses within an area entry are primarily used to name the logical address space which will be referenced in clauses used to describe records.

Record Entry. Record clauses within a record are used primarily to specify control over record placement and to describe the contents of a record.

PLACEMENT CONTROL: General placement of a record type is achieved by specification of an area in which all occurrences of the record type will be stored. If the CUSTOMER record type (Table 6-1) is defined for storage within the TOPSY area, then all occurrences of the CUSTOMER record will be placed between the physical page range from 4,000 through 12,999 in the database controlled by DMCL.

Additional storage placement control within an area is achieved by one of several options:

• The DIRECT option allows maximum user control over logical storage location of a record occurrence within an area. In IDMS, the user must supply a "suggested" database key before a record is to be stored. If the suggested database key is available, it will be assigned to the record occurrence. If unavailable, the next available database key will be assigned by the DBMS.

• The CALCULATED (CALC) option stores the record occurrence based on the value of one or more data items within the record. A hashing algorithm uses the item values to produce a logical storage position within the area associated with the record.

• The VIA option specifies that record occurrences will be accessed primarily as members of a named set.

These storage options allow the user to determine the number of entry points (CALC) into the database and to control access performance. Each of these storage placement options also provides one of several ways of selecting record occurrences in the database.

DATA DESCRIPTION: Data description facilities were designed to handle a wide variety of data types and intrarecord structure available in all host languages currently in use. Groups of data items (aggregates) and hierarchical item structures within a record are achieved with an item-level number similar to that used by COBOL and PL/I. The type of data item may be described as bit, character, binary or decimal, fixed or floating, real or complex, and is open-ended to allow additional types. Data aggregates and items may also be repeated. Not all the data item types are compatible with all host languages, and therefore not all may be provided by a given implementation.

A data item may be described as a *result* of a database procedure coded by the data administration staff. The output of the procedure may be an *actual result* data item if it is physically included in the record occurrence in which it is described. A *virtual result* data item is only produced when the data item is accessed by the host program. A data item may also be described as having a *virtual* or *actual source* by naming a data item in an associated owner record type.

DATA VALIDATION: Validation of a data item may be specified as a PICTURE (e.g., all numeric), a RANGE, or a database procedure coded by the data administration staff.

An ENCODING procedure may be specified to perform necessary validation and/or transformation of a data item before it is stored in the database. A DECODE procedure may also be specified to transform a data item into User Working Area before it is accessed by the user program.

Set Entry. Set clauses within a set entry specify the names and characteristics of logical set relationships among record types described in the record entry. It is here that the logical relationships shown in Figures 6-1 through 6-7 are described.

SET ORDER: Many options are provided for ordering member record occurrences within a set. The intraset position a new record occurrence will occupy when stored in the database may be specified as either the *first* record (top of a push-down list) and the last record (bottom of a push-up list), or a position immediately before or after a record occurrence established by the user program. A set may also be ordered by a record type if more than one record type is included in a set (Figure 6-6) as well as by database key.

Each record occurrence may be maintained in ascending or descending order based on the value of one or more data items included within the record. The logical ordering of member record occurrences in a set is independent of the physical placement of the records. Furthermore, the same record occurrences may participate in different sets (Figure 6-8) with different ordering criteria.

SET MEMBERSHIP TYPE: The type of membership may also be different in each set. Set memberships for a record type may be *mandatory* or *optional*, depending on whether the user program is permitted to insert in the set, or remove from the set, an occurrence of this record type. A mandatory set membership means that a record occurrence is a permanent member of the set as long as the record is present in the database. Set membership may also be specified as an *automatic* function performed by the DBMS when a record occurrence is stored in the database, or as a *manual* function to be performed by the user program.

Subschema Data Description Language The subschema DDL is oriented toward the conventions and requirements of the programming language used to create user application programs. This approach allows the schema DDL to function as a common language for database description, and permits separate subschema DDLs to exist for each programming language used to access the database. The subschema DDL provides a measure of data independence in that certain changes can be made to the schema for the database without affecting existing programs.

The subschema DDL may allow certain variations from the schema on which it is based. All subschema DDLs will permit the selection of only those record types, sets, and areas relevant to a particular user application or individual program. Additional capability may be provided to:

- Change characteristics of data items.
- Omit description of data items within a record.
- Alter intrarecord data mapping.
- Rename records, sets, areas, and data items to conform to conventions of a particular programming language.

The IDMS subschema DDL requires only specification of areas, records, and sets to be used by an application. The user may optionally describe only those data items needed by the application program. In IDMS, any number of subschemas may be defined, and may overlap in any manner. The only access a program has to the database is through a subschema, and the same subschema may be used by any number of programs.

DATABASE PROCEDURES

Database procedures are programmed routines written by the data administration staff to provide necessary protection and access control services for all programs which access the database. Database procedures are invoked by the DBMS only when they are needed to perform some specific database service such as:

- Checking PRIVACY key validity to permit: access to PRIVACY LOCKS, schema display, schema modification, retrieval or update of an area, execution of data manipulation language functions, access or modification of specified data items within a record, access or modification of set occurrences, and access to a subschema.
- Performing specific functions which are triggered by data manipulation language functions executed by a user program.
- Computing data-item values as a function of the values of one or more other data items.
- Performing a search algorithm in response to a user program request.
- Performing validation or other manipulation of data items.
- Collecting and reporting database statistics for use by the data administration staff.

Database procedures relate only to the database, and as such are transparent to user programs.

PROTECTION OF DATA

Both schema and subschema data description languages contain provisions to protect both privacy and integrity of the database. The PRIVACY lock/key mechanisms at the area, record, set, and data-item levels protect against unauthorized access of data and other information within the database.

Integrity facilities are separate from privacy mechanisms and are primarily concerned with maintaining the database consistent with the schema description for areas, records, and sets. Rollback/recovery facilities fall in this category, and are primarily concerned with restoring the contents of a database back to some known good condition following a failure of the operating system, user program abort, hardware malfunction, or physical destruction of the storage media.

DATA MANIPULATION LANGUAGE

The DML is designed to provide database access capabilities to an existing programming language. As such, the DML may be viewed as a language extension which conforms to the syntax of the host language.

The schema DDL and DML specifications included in the April, 1971, report of the Data Base Task Group are designed for COBOL and as such may be used as an example for development of subschema DDLs and DMLs for other languages. The DML functions can be grouped into control, retrieval, and modification categories.

Control   Control statements are used to obtain access to an area within the database. The OPEN statement announces the user's intention to begin processing within one or more specified areas of the database. When access is established by the database management system, retrieval or modification statements may be executed. The CLOSE statement announces completion of processing in the specified areas of the database.

Retrieval   Retrieval statements are primarily concerned with locating data in the database and making them available to a program. This is where the greatest language flexibility is needed because of the different data access requirements of all applications which process the data. The DBTG language specifications provide a variety of methods for access of record occurrences within a database:

• Direct access of any record occurrence in the database is possible provided that its system-assigned unique identifier (database key) is known. This type of access is independent of any set relationships associated with the record.

• If specified in the schema DDL, a record type may be stored and retrieved based on the value of one or more data items contained within the record. The DBMS uses the data-item value to "calculate" (CALC) the position within the database to store each record occurrence. To retrieve a record occurrence, the user must furnish the value of the specified data item before execution of the retrieval statement.

Any number of record types in the schema may be defined with a CALC location mode regardless of the set relationships associated with the record. This capability allows as many entry points into the database as needed by the applications associated with the database. The BFG TOPSY subschema illustrated in Figure 6-8 contains 12 CALC entry points, indicated by asterisks.

• Record occurrences may be accessed through their participation in one or more set occurrences. Once a record occurrence has been selected, the sets in which it participates as either owner or member provide an access path for selection of other associated record occurrences.

With this capability, an application program can access related data by stepping along the pathways through the database provided by sets. The upper left of Figure 6-8 shows a record type (5) as a CALC entry point into the database. Once an occurrence of a type 5 record has been selected by the DBMS, associated occurrences of record types 1, 6, and 10 are easily available by DML statements to select the owner occurrences of either sets K or L, the next record occurrence (type 6) of set N, or the next record occurrence (type 10) of set M. If a DML statement to find the next type 6 record occurrence of set N was executed, then an associated type 7 record occurrence could be selected by a statement to find the owner record occurrence of set D.

• Records which participate as a member in a set may be specified as ordered in either ascending or descending sequence, based on one or more data items contained within the record. Selection of a specific record occurrence in an ordered set is accomplished by furnishing the values of the sort-key data items before execution of the retrieval statement. In addition, a nonordered set may be searched automatically to find a record occurrence with data-item values matching values supplied by the program.

• All occurrences of any record type may be accessed by a complete scan of an area, starting with the first page and ending with the last page in the area. This method of access is independent of any other set relationship or location mode.

Modification Modification statements result in a change to the contents of the database. Change includes the addition of new data, modification of existing data by replacement of data-item values, or deletion of data which currently exist in the database. Modification statements are also provided which permit participation of existing record occurrences in specified sets to be established or removed.

SELF-CONTAINED SYSTEMS

A self-contained system provides database access and data display capabilities through the use of a simplified, high-level language, designed to be used by nonprogrammers. The language provides considerably less flexibility than a language such as COBOL, but is easier to learn and use. Such a language would allow a simplified method of describing the format and content of a report for display on a video terminal or a printer. A simplified method of describing the criteria for selection of data to be used in the output report allows users quickly and easily to obtain the desired information in an acceptable format. These languages are nonprocedural in the sense that the user is not required to specify input-output commands or the precise logical sequence of operations required to produce the desired output.

The simplest form of a self-contained system, and the one easiest to implement, is provided by a database inquiry program written in COBOL using DML statements. After the database is designed, it is possible to formulate many "canned" reports which are useful to many users. To operate the system, the user must enter a code to select a specific canned report followed by data values required by the inquiry procedure. The procedure then uses the input to access the database, formats the output report, and transmits the report to a display device. A typical application would allow an accounts payable department employee to enter a code followed by a vendor number and immediately receive a display of information related to unpaid invoices for that vendor.

The need for both self-contained and host (COBOL/DML) languages which provide access to the same database was clearly recognized by the DBTG. The specifications for the data description and data manipulation languages have provided the necessary solid foundation for the development of many different types of self-contained systems —each designed to fulfill specific user needs.

DATABASE ADMINISTRATION

The creation of new languages for data description, combined with the responsibility to design a common database which satisfies the data requirements of many applications, has created the need for a new function of database administration to augment the functions of systems analysis and programming.

Database administration is accomplished by one or more technical experts who are knowledgeable in database design and creation, operation of the database management system, and the use of one or more data manipulation languages. The database administrators must also be capable of working well with systems analysts, programmers, and computer operations personnel. The duties of database administrators are to:

- Work with systems analysts to determine application data requirements.
- Aid programmers in the most effective techniques in the use of DML.
- Specify the content and structure of the database.
- Create subschemas as required by applications.
- Maintain documentation of the database schema and document subschemas for programmer and analyst use.
- Establish appropriate operating recovery and rollback procedures to preserve the integrity of the database in the event of either hardware or software failure.
- Evaluate database loading and program performance characteristics to recommend improvements.
- Supervise the addition of new areas, data items, record types, and set types to the database.
- Initiate database restructuring whenever it is needed to provide additional physical space or changes in data structure.
- Establish appropriate constraints in the use of DML statements for each subschema.

DATA DICTIONARY

The data dictionary is a systems database containing the description and cross-reference of all attributes of data within an installation. It is used to manage all aspects of database usage and access control, and is the common stored data intelligence for compilers, query languages, report generators, and various data administration and systems analysis functions.

Figure 6-9 illustrates the central role of the data dictionary among database and application compilers as well as support and reporting functions.

The schema DDL compiler accepts all schema DDL statements and maintains a stored definition of all attributes of data and relationships.

The subschema compiler accepts subschema DDL statements, validates for logical

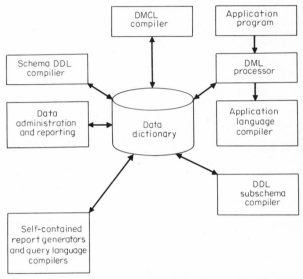

Fig. 6-9   Data dictionary.

consistency, and stores a complete definition of the subschema. Both schema and subschema descriptions are logical views of the database. The physical characteristics of the database are described in the DMCL compiler. Such separation of logical and physical characteristics allows the same subschema to be mapped into differing physical environments for testing and implementation on differing hardware systems.

The DML processor validates all DML statements in an application program, based on the allowable data access and relationships specified in the subschema identified within the application program. The DML processor also uses the data dictionary to create automatically allowable record descriptions and other control statements in an application program. Information about DML usage can also be determined during this operation for later review by the data administration function within an installation. The IDMS implementation of data dictionary is an IDMS network database of 41 record types and 53 set types.

Self-contained language compilers use information contained within the data dictionary to determine the strategy of database access for report generation or response to a query.

Data administration analysis and reporting functions represent the entry point into database technology of the future. Existing technology provides a reporting function which documents and cross-references the attributes of the schema, subschemas, records, sets, data items, application programs, and database usage information. Analysis of the entire database for purposes of tuning, maintenance, and addition of new descriptions is performed by the data administration function within an installation.

Further automation of database analysis functions will lead to greatly improved systems analyst productivity, automation of application programming, reduction of application maintenance, and substantial reductions in the effort and time required to produce new application systems.

CONCLUSIONS

The CODASYL database language specifications represent a significant foundation for development of a common database capability for many programming languages and computer hardware systems, including minicomputers.

The continued stability, memory economy, flexibility, ease of use, and performance of IDMS on IBM hardware since January 1972 have demonstrated the viability of CODASYL specifications. Other successful implementations on Univac, Xerox, DEC, Phillips, and Honeywell hardware attest to the acceptance of CODASYL specifications as the direction for continued future database development.

SELECTIVE BIBLIOGRAPHY

Feature Analysis of Generalized Data Base Management Systems, Association for Computing Machinery, New York, May, 1971.

Lyon, John K., *An Introduction to Data Base Design,* Wiley, New York, 1971.

Report of the CODASYL Data Base Task Group, ACM, New York, April, 1971.

Schubert, R. F., "Basic Concepts in Data Base Management Systems," *Datamation,* July, 1972, pp. 42–47. (Portions of this article were reproduced in the present chapter by permission of *Datamation*).

Chapter 7

Physical Security
of the Computer Center

IRVING M. CRUPAR

Technical Director, Wackenhut Electronic Systems Corp.,
Miami, Florida; formerly Manager of Engineering, Holmes
Protection, Inc., New York, New York

Much has been written on the procedural steps requiring study before installing electronic computers and related data processing equipment. These embrace selection of proper equipment, checking and planning for areas to receive the equipment, utility requirements, orientation and training of personnel, and provisions for expansion of the initial facility. Fully as important as all these is the assurance of uninterrupted operation of the system. By partial or entire loss of equipment, an entire operation of vital importance could be seriously paralyzed, even though the interruption is only temporary.

A computer represents a large capital outlay (or rental commitment), and a continuing heavy operating expense commitment. Thus, when companies consider this form of purchase, they usually make careful studies to determine whether the machinery is really necessary and whether it will accomplish the desired objectives. Equally careful studies should be conducted to assure that after the computer is installed it will be capable of working 365 days a year, 24 hours a day, if necessary, and is secure from any danger such as theft, fire, or vandalism.

Data processing managers often make the mistake of viewing security as they would the security of their homes, without taking into consideration the full business risks involved in loss of vital information over and above the cost of destroyed or damaged physical equipment. They forget that destroyed computer centers have set businesses back years, and have driven others completely out of business. And in this connection, security from intrusion or inside sabotage is perhaps even more important than protection against damage from storm or fire. It is possible for an individual with an inexpensive magnet, given enough time, to erase wholly the information contained on reels of tape.

The obvious areas that must be considered with respect to the degree of security measures to be applied to the computer center are:

1. *How important is the equipment?* This evaluation is of course based both on what the equipment is and what it does. If it controls air traffic safety, it can be vital to

human life; if it controls corporate information, it can be vital to business life; but if its loss would be simply an inconvenience, then perhaps it is not especially important, even though it may be expensive.

2. *Does this equipment need special construction, special access control, and fireproofing and fire-detection devices?* Where new facilities are to be built for the computer center, it is important that all safe-environment factors be considered in the early planning for the structure.

3. *What are the special exposures to the equipment?* Special exposures can exist within the equipment room, in the immediate area around the data processing room, in the floors above and below the computer, and outside the building in which the equipment is located. These exposures must be evaluated and then eliminated or guarded against as needed.

ACCESS TO THE COMPUTER AREA

At the beginning of the computer boom, about 1950, most electronic data processing installations were planned for operation behind glass walls, so that they could be visible to everyone. This was good public and employer relations. Not only was the installation planned so as to be totally visible, but, generally, there were no restrictions regarding access to the computer area. This installation blueprint was satisfactory until some

---

"ELECTRONIC FORTRESS"

A visit to the headquarters of the William J. Burns International Detective Agency, Inc., at Briarcliff Manor, N.Y., provides the visitor a "real life" demonstration of complete physical computer security. The company uses its own computer installation (for its 30,000-employee payroll and general accounting and sales analysis) as a working example of the electronic security package it has been installing and servicing for the past two and a half years.

The computer area is on the first floor in a separate building adjacent to the new headquarters recently erected in this "exurbia" setting. Because the installation is on the first floor of a structure in a fairly secluded area, the Burns controller requested maximum security. Designing it led to the idea of making it a security "demonstration model," representing the ultimate from which a computer user can make customized adaptations for his own needs.

Protection begins with a perimeter defense of the building itself, with burglar-alarm wiring on every door and window. (All windows are bullet-proof.) Any unauthorized attempt to enter the building would trigger a response at the guard position at the Briarcliff Manor location, and in the nearest (White Plains, N.Y.) of the central control stations Burns maintains in 21 cities. At the central stations, signals from warning devices are monitored on a 24-hour basis. In addition to personal response, public police and fire units are notified immediately. As soon as a person enters the building after hours, his motion is detected by ultrasonic detectors. These operate independently of the perimeter warning system, and also signal the local guard force and the control station in White Plains.

To enter the data processing area, one must pass through two maximum-security doors, both operated by a card reader. The first door accesses the data processing area as a whole, but not the main-frame computer room. In this general area, work such as systems design, programming, and keypunching is done. The ID cards for employees here (and, of course, *all* employees receive thorough security checks), operate the door to their area, but not the second door leading to the computer room. Employees with computer-room duties there are issued special ID cards which operate both doors. In addition to these employees, only the data processing manager, the head of administration services, and the controller have "double" cards. Even the highest-level Burns executives, including the president, must borrow a card if they wish to enter.

The computer room itself is completely blanketed by electronic and ultrasonic detection devices, and is additionally kept under 24-hour surveillance by closed-circuit television. (*Note:* No more than one person at a time is allowed in the computer room.) Smoke- and heat-detection devices are in the dropped ceiling space and in the space beneath the raised floor. Access doors for movement of material in and out can be operated only by switches within the computer room itself. And the mover must telephone to get the operator to open the door.

— DIEBOLD *ADP Newsletter*

centers were sabotaged—bombed, burned, maliciously damaged—or subject to theft of information by intruders. It was soon obvious that the computer would have to be adequately protected and hidden from public view. Security measures centered around access to the electronic data processing centers, and the byword was *restriction*.

Restriction varies from organization to organization, but in general includes a preliminary fingerprinting program and complete background investigation of all computer employees. This procedure is then followed by a strictly enforced system of entry, so that only those designated to work in the area are permitted access.

Access-entry systems can be expensive or relatively cheap, according to security needs. For the utmost in simplicity, a doorbell-button arrangement can be used, requiring a person to open the door from the inside after the person requesting entry has been "recognized." More elaborate and expensive is the card reader, an automatic electronic device which will allow entry only if the appropriate card is inserted. This method requires no attention from the inside. In addition, the card reader can be connected to a printer to record specific information, such as the card reader location (if there is more than one), the person desiring entry, and the date and time of the entry.

In 1968, when Burns International Security Services, Inc., installed a computer/data processing system at its Briarcliff Manor corporate headquarters building, it made certain the installation was not visible to anyone. A dual card reader system was installed, and only six people were issued cards providing entry into the main computer area. It is interesting to note that even the president of the company did not receive an access card. (See box, "Electronic Fortress.")

FIREPROOFING AND OTHER CONSTRUCTION AND STORAGE MEASURES

To achieve physical protection against fire, the following specifications will serve as guidelines:

1. The computer area shall be housed in a fire-resistive, noncombustible, or sprinklered building.

2. The computer/data processing system shall be so located as to minimize fire, water, and smoke exposure from adjoining areas and activities.

3. The computer room shall not be located above, below, or adjacent to areas or other structures where hazardous processes are located, unless protective features are provided.

4. The computer/data processing system shall be housed in a room of noncombustible construction. All materials, including walls, floors, partitions, finish, acoustical treatment, raised floors, raised floor supports, suspended ceilings, and other construction involved in the computer room shall have a flame-spread rating of 25 or less (see NFPA *Standard Method of Test of Surface Burning Characteristics of Building Materials*, No. 255, 1966[1]).

5. Floor covering materials, such as asphalt, rubber, or vinyl floor tiles, linoleum, high-pressure elastic laminates, or carpeting may be used to cover any exposed floors.

6. In multistoried buildings, the floor above the computer room shall be made reasonably watertight to avoid water damage to equipment. Openings, including those for beams and pipes, shall be sealed to watertightness.

7. Provisions shall be made for automatic positive drainage of the floor surface to minimize damage to the system and associated wiring due to flooding, sprinkler operation, coolant leakage, and the like.

8. The computer room shall be cut off from other occupancies within the building by noncombustible, fire-resistance-rated walls, floors, and ceiling. The fire-resistant walls or partitions enclosing the computer room shall extend from the structural floor to the structural floor above, or the roof.

9. Decking for raised floors shall be of the following: (*a*) concrete, steel, aluminum, or other noncombustible material, or (*b*) pressure-impregnated fire-retardant treated lumber, or (*c*) wood or similar core material which is encased on the top and bottom with sheet, cast, or extruded metal, with all openings or cut edges covered with metal or plastic clips or grommets so that none of the core is exposed.

10. Openings in raised floors for electric cables or other uses shall be protected to

[1] National Fire Protection Association, 60 Batterymarch Street, Boston, Mass. 02110.

minimize the entrance of debris or other combustibles beneath the floor. This may be accomplished by noncombustible covers, grilles, screens, or by locating equipment directly over the openings.

11. All office furniture in the computer room shall be of metal construction or other materials that do not contribute significantly to the combustible content.

12. Small supervisory office and similar light-hazard occupancies directly related to the electronic equipment operations may be located within the computer room if all furnishings are noncombustible and adequate facilities are provided for containing the necessary combustible material. Supplies of paper or other combustible material shall be strictly limited to the minimum need for safe, efficient operations.

The following shall not be permitted within the computer room:

a. Any activity or occupancy not directly associated with the electronic computer system(s) involved.

b. Supplies of papers or other combustible material in excess of those necessary for efficient operation.

c. Service and repair shops and operations, except that servicing and repairing may be performed directly on machines which are impractical to remove from the computer room.

d. Bulk storage of records.

e. Any other combustible material, equipment, or operation which constitutes a hazard and which can be removed.

When the electronic data processing centers went "behind walls," the draperies and other superfluous decorations tended to disappear. However, a serious fire hazard from paper still exists. The operation of an electronic computer system normally requires considerable quantities of cards, stationery supplies, and other combustible support materials. Paper stock, unused recording media, and other combustibles that must be retained in the computer room should be kept in totally enclosed metal file cases or cabinets.

A most urgent anti-fire precaution is to enforce the rule that smoking is not permitted in the computer center. Also, since fires can occur from electrical wiring, it is extremely important that data processing personnel be warned to be alert to burning odors which may be a symptom of a short circuit in the wiring and a possible smoldering fire. It is essential that fires in the computer center be found at the smoldering stage, before extensive damage has been done to the data processing equipment.

Magnetic tapes should be stored in containers, and these containers should be stored in metal fireproof cabinets. Each tape available in the data processing center with proprietary information should be duplicated and retained at a remote location.

ELECTRONIC DETECTION DEVICES

Many detection devices are now available to prevent intrusion and fire. Intrusion devices which form a system to detect motion are extremely useful measures against theft and vandalism when the computer center is not in operation for 24 hours per day.

Widely used is the ultrasonic motion detection system, which consists of transmitters and receivers located at intervals of 20 feet. Operation is based upon a steady frequency not audible to most people. As long as the receiver receives the frequency emitted by the transmitter, the system is normal. When intrusion occurs, the frequency shifts and the receiver receives a displaced frequency, causing an alarm condition. Such a system gives total coverage throughout the area being protected, and can be installed so as to give zoned protection with certain zones on and other zones off.

Depending on the needs of the situation, other motion detection devices may be employed, some operating on the infrared principle, others utilizing the microwave frequency range, and still others that operate by means of the pulsed infrared photoelectric principle. Any one or more of these systems can be used as a spot-type trap or detector for the protection of an individual door, entranceway, or critical point of a computer center. This protection can be useful even if the computer center is in operation 24 hours a day.

Closed-Circuit Television Surveillance Valuable proprietary information stored on tape may be a temptation to a dishonest employee who plans to make use of it for his or her own purposes. Some precaution must therefore be taken to guard against such an occurrence by surveillance from within. This may be accomplished by installing one or more closed-circuit cameras inside the computer center to scan the highly critical areas for transmission to CCTV monitors located at an appropriate monitoring station or guard console. It is thus possible for a security guard to observe continually the activities in the computer center. At the same time, the employees in the computer center realize that they are under observation, and the temptation to personal use of confidential company information is minimized. An extra precautionary measure that can be implemented in any event is a rule that there should never be less than two employees in the computer center during the normal working hours.

Fire Protection To prevent fire, the computer center should be protected with devices that respond to smoke rather than heat. Today there are ionization detectors that sample the amount of smoke particles in the atmosphere and initiate an alarm when an unsafe smoke density has been sampled. Even though there are less expensive sensing devices available that respond to fire temperature rather than products of combustion, it is more important to be notified of an alarm situation when smoke and products of combustion are produced.

Ionization detectors should also be provided in the air space below the floor and above the suspended ceiling to sound an audible and visual alarm, and to shut down all electrical power passing through the air space.

A portable or fixed carbon dioxide fire-extinguishing system is preferable to an automatic sprinkler system in the computer room or the computer areas. Carbon dioxide fire extinguishers or carbon dioxide hand-hose systems installed in accordance with NFPA Standards for Carbon Dioxide Extinguishing Systems (No. 12-1968 USAS A54.1–1968) can be considered as providing adequate extinguishing protection, provided all the following conditions are met:

1. The equipment is at all times under supervision of an operator or other person familiar with the equipment and trained in the operation of the types of extinguishers or hand-hose systems involved.

2. Adequate controls are readily accessible to shut down power and air conditioning to the equipment.

3. All interior sections are readily accessible to manual application of the extinguishing agents.

4. There is located within the computer room, and not more than 50 feet from the equipment, either a carbon dioxide fire extinguisher or carbon dioxide hand-hose system having a capacity of at least 1 pound of carbon dioxide for each cubic foot of volume of equipment, if the equipment is in open racks; $\frac{1}{2}$ pound for each cubic foot of volume of equipment, if the unit under consideration is enclosed in a cabinet.

A fixed carbon dioxide extinguishing system can be installed, to be activated solely by manual operation, if it is at all times under the supervision of an operator or other person or persons familiar with the equipment. If the extinguishing system is to be activated by automatic means, the detecting means should be of an approved type. Particular attention should be given to the choice of actuation means, to ensure detection under the conditions of air flows usually involved in such systems, and the small heat release under fire conditions. When a suitable fixed carbon dioxide extinguishing installation is planned, it should also be arranged to sound an alarm automatically and shut down the power and air conditioning supplied to the equipment involved.

Halon systems for fire or smoke extinguishing are relatively new and effective for total coverage of hazards involving gaseous and liquid flammable materials and electrical equipment. However, Halon systems will create a toxic environment, symptomized by dizziness and loss of coordination after a minute's exposure at more than 7 per cent concentration. Factory Mutual Engineering Corporation in Norwood, Massachusetts, can provide the names of fire-extinguishing systems that have been tested and approved by it, and will provide recommendations for specific environments.

Protection of Magnetic Recording Media[2] When not in use, magnetic tapes (reel or cassette) and disk packs should be stored in storage cabinets with adequate shielding.

---

[2] Based on National Bureau of Standards Technical Note 735, July, 1972, by Sidney B. Geller.

If they are stored 1 foot from the inner walls of the cabinet, no degradation of recorded signals will be caused by magnetic or electromagnetic devices which are carried into the storage room.   Several manufacturers produce suitable cabinets and shielding materials.

Additional protection is afforded by the normal ferromagnetic metal walls found in many computer installations.   Any metal wall to which a magnet will adhere will provide some shielding against magnetic fields.   Most drum and disk cabinets are made of plastic; however, they could also be made of shielding materials.

A tape vault should be installed as far away as possible from all fixed sources of stray magnetic fields such as large transformers, motors, and generators.

Shielded containers are particularly valuable for transporting tape reels that contain important data.   The tapes in repository should not be subjected to temperature extremes, since these can produce both physical damage and erasure effects.

Since a magnet with a field intensity of 1 tesla (10,000 gauss) can be carried in a briefcase or a ladies' handbag, measures should be taken to prevent the entry of persons possessing such devices.   Magnetic detectors (e.g., magnetometers) may be used at close range to apprehend the would-be saboteur.   Detectors that will warn of concealed magnets without "keepers" are quite inexpensive (less than $1,000).   Detectors for magnets with keepers will cost from $1,000 to $5,000.

It is difficult to retrieve recorded information from a magnetic medium whose timing or clock track signals have been damaged.   This damage can be inflicted with magnetic devices or by interfering with the recording process as it occurs.

Devices such as simple spark gap units plugged into wall outlets or small concealed battery-operated transmitters can cause interference with the magnetic recording process as well as with other computer functions.   Therefore regular searches of the entire facility should be conducted for such devices.   (And, of course, only authorized persons should be permitted to enter the computer area for such inspection.)

Duplicate copies of all important tapes, such as master and program tapes, should be kept in a different, secure location.

CONTINGENCY PLANNING FOR CONTINUING OPERATION

An emergency situation should not totally impede the continued operation of the required electronic data processing.   The planning for continuation or resumption of operation should include:

　　1. A program to protect records in accordance with their importance.

　　2. An analysis of the workload and the effect upon continuity of operations, organized for each computer facility.

　　3. Arrangements for emergency use of other installed computer equipment to cover:

　　　　a. Plans for transportation of personnel, data, and supplies to an emergency computer location.

　　　　b. Agreements and procedures for the emergency use of the computer equipment.

　　4. Programs designed with adequate number of checkpoints and restarts to ensure rapid recovery to normal operations.

All personnel should receive continuing instructions and review in:

　　1. Method required for turning off all electrical power to the computer under both normal and emergency conditions.

　　2. Turning off the air conditioning in the area.

　　3. Alerting the fire department or company fire brigade.

　　4. Evacuation of personnel.

　　5. The location and proper operation and application of all available fire-extinguishing and damage control equipment, including automatic detection and extinguishing equipment.   Computer-room personnel should be fully trained in carbon dioxide usage through actual operation of the equipment on a practice fire.

　　6. The importance of records and their storage requirements.

Emergency Fire Procedure   A written emergency fire plan should be prepared for and posted at each installation, assigning specific responsibilities to designated personnel.

The following major items should serve as a guide, and are suggested as minimum features of this plan:

1. Remove all power to the computer system.
   a. Provide a means, such as a main-line circuit breaker, or equivalent.
   b. Provide a remote control for this purpose near the operator and next to each of the exit doors.
2. Shut down the air conditioning system.
   a. This should be done if the main circuit breaker does not control the air-conditioning system. Emergency means similar to those for the computer system should be provided.
3. Notify proper authority.
   a. Building fire brigades should be notified immediately.
   b. Outside fire-fighting companies should be called immediately to assist.

Damage Control If the electronic equipment or any type of records are wetted down, smoked up, or otherwise affected by the results of a fire or other emergency, immediate action should be taken to clean and dry the electronic equipment. If the water, smoke, or other contaminations are permitted to remain in the equipment longer than is absolutely necessary, the damage may be grossly increased.

Chapter 8

Evaluation of Computer Department Management and Personnel

JOHN A. GUERRIERI, JR., CDP

Consultant, Niles, Illinois

Not much has been written about performance evaluation of data processing personnel. A major reason is that not a great deal of performance evaluation of data processing personnel has been done. It has been, and still is, widely believed that most positions in data processing are not subject to performance evaluation because of the creative and essentially nonrepetitive nature of the work involved. In addition, the rapid and often hectic growth of the industry has made it difficult to keep up with the techniques being used by the people to be evaluated. As long as the components of the work are fluctuating, it is not possible to accumulate the necessary historical base to set the standards common to the usual forms of performance appraisal. That facet of the data processing industry has not settled yet, but refinements in appraisal and evaluation philosophy now permit the evaluation of creative and nonrepetitive jobs without the necessity of predetermined standards.

The *management-by-objectives* technique provides the foundation for achieving performance evaluation in data processing. In very brief terms, management by objectives begins with the establishment of job objectives for a set period of time, objectives that are mutually agreeable to both manager and employee. Those objectives provide the basis upon which performance will be measured. They provide a relatively objective method of determining *how well* an individual performed, because the established goals provide the standard against which actual performance is measured. The *why* of performance, of course, remains a subjective procedure.

DIFFICULTIES OF EVALUATION

Exploring whys, where human beings are involved, is highly complex, often frustrating, and usually not subject to quantification or procedurization. It requires an examination of the psychological factors acting upon an individual and the effect they have upon the execution of his or her responsibilities. The performance of assigned duties requires that some kind of motivational pressure is applied to the individual. The motivation may be as complex as an appeal to the individual's need for self-realization or as simple as money or fear. Whatever the method used, in order for it to be successful it must have a positive effect on the individual's desire to do his or her job. Motivation is a volatile and totally essential aspect of performance. It is the largest single factor in the *why* of performance and, at the same time, it is the most difficult to isolate on an individual basis.

Almost everything that happens in a typical business situation affects the motivation of those involved to some degree. It is the requirement of performance evaluation that the motivation of an individual be given consideration as much as, if not more than, the consideration given to the actual meeting of established objectives. One without the other is not enough to determine the adequacy of the work environment; and the adequacy of the work environment ultimately determines whether or not an individual could have reached his or her predetermined goals.

The determination of why a person performed as he or she did is generally not subject to predefined procedures. It requires an understanding of the principles of human behavior and insight into the application of those principles. The variability found between individuals generally demands a unique approach to each situation, which makes generalizations difficult. Therefore, we shall here concentrate, for the present, primarily on a discussion of performance appraisal.

RIGHTS AND WRONGS IN APPRAISAL SYSTEMS

There are five basic criteria which should be met if a performance appraisal system is to succeed: (1) The system must be objective. (2) It must be acceptable to those concerned. (3) It must appraise the proper factors. (4) It must be workable. (5) The system must be obviously advantageous to those concerned.

Objectivity Experience has shown that subjective appraisals, because they have no clear-cut demonstrable defense, are resented by employees and abused by managers. In such cases employees often come to view the appraisal process as a personality contest rather than a performance review. This inevitably will lead to employees who devote their time and effort to "buttering up the boss," a move calculated to make the boss benevolent at appraisal time. The managers, on the other hand, become reluctant to record instances of above or below average performance in subjective systems, because they leave themselves open to criticism they cannot refute. The solution adopted by many managers using a subjective appraisal system is to rate everyone as average or above average, thus making the unit look good and simultaneously avoiding confrontations with employees. Obviously, such appraisals are useless.

The key to objectivity is to appraise performance using specified goals or accomplishments which can be verified as having been achieved. The establishment of goals for employees allows the manager to identify positively the goals which were achieved and those which were not. It also decreases the potential for criticism of unwarranted bias because of the clear-cut nature of the appraisal. This, of course, assumes that the initial goals were well defined and available to the employee concerned.

Acceptance If the program is not acceptable, the employees will resist implementation and, more than likely, attempt to subvert the system after implementation. The reactions would be analogous to the familiar situation in user-departments in which a new computer system is brought in over the objections of employees. It is wise in the case of a performance appraisal system to go to extra lengths to inform the affected employees and make absolutely sure that they understand and approve of the plans. That may appear to some to be dilution of authority, but since appraisal situations have a significant impact on the future of employees, it is a prudent move to get their consent. Moreover, it is not enough to have an initial push of enthusiasm and support by the upper levels of management that later slips to resigned apathy. There must be continued active support of the program by all levels of management.

Factors A great deal of care must be taken to select the factors that are appropriate measures of performance. The basic reason for problems in this area is fundamental human nature. The employee, anxious to present the best possible picture of his or her performance, will concentrate efforts on those factors used to appraise performance.

This certainly will reflect favorably in the performance appraisal, but it may not be desirable from an organization standpoint. For example, if a manager were to be judged solely on profit, he or she might neglect to make capital investments to improve the current profits. However, the lack of capital investment might seriously hamper company operations in the future. The way to avoid such potential disasters is to take care to select multiple factors as the basis of performance appraisal. The factors may be weighted to allow for special concern in particular areas, but they should be chosen so that the individual reaching to achieve those goals will be contributing to the good of the organization as well as enhancing his or her own performance record.

Workability An appraisal system that is "dug out of mothballs" once a year at traditional appraisal time is destined to be a complete failure. An employee's performance continues on a day-to-day basis. Therefore, if efficiency and effectiveness are expected, that performance must be monitored on a regular basis. Under the once-a-year formal performance appraisal system, situations requiring review or discussion between employer and employee become subject to error because of the sheer passage of time and the natural manipulation of information in the minds of the two individuals. That, however, is not the most serious problem in isolating the performance appraisal system from the mainstream of the work environment. The delay in the appraisal may turn a relatively minor weakness into a major shortcoming that cannot be corrected; or repeated erroneous execution may produce a crisis that could have been avoided by periodic appraisals of performance.

Advantage to Appraisees Finally, the effective performance appraisal system should be an aid to those involved. Personnel generally constitute a significant financial investment for an organization. Therefore, it is desirable to minimize personnel turnover while at the same time promoting maximum productivity among employees. The performance appraisal system can play an important part in achieving these dual objectives. As stated, an effective appraisal is an ideal way of pointing up weaknesses for early correction. By using the appraisal system this way, individuals can be trained to strengthen the weak areas, thus becoming more efficient and productive and usually happier because of their newly acquired ability to handle their responsibilities. This benefits the organization because of the increased output and lower turnover common to people confident and happy in their work. It benefits the employees because they have increased knowledge and grasp of their jobs.

An effective appraisal system can also be useful in identifying individuals who have been placed beyond their capabilities. This is advantageous to the organization because it identifies areas of low productivity and potential turnover, which can then be "shored up." It is advantageous to the individual because it may allow an orderly reassignment to more fitting work before major errors require termination. In any event, an effective appraisal system should be viewed by employees as a learning experience, a chance to identify and correct weaknesses.

There are more poor performance evaluation systems than there are good ones because one or more of the attributes discussed above have been overlooked or given insufficient attention. Even worse, the data processing activity has been noted for the absence of performance evaluation systems of any kind. This is probably due not only to a lack of understanding of how performance of data processing personnel should be evaluated, but also to a reluctance to alienate the specialists who made the computer systems work.

However, this situation has recently been undergoing change. The enormous costs associated with data processing have forced organizations to cast an "eagle eye" on their data processing installations. That, coupled with the growing acceptance of management-by-objectives concepts and techniques, has opened the door to the use of performance evaluation systems for creative personnel such as data processing specialists.

PERFORMANCE EVALUATION OF DATA PROCESSING MANAGEMENT

Management personnel in data processing installations, like any other managers, must be evaluated on two levels. First, they must be evaluated with respect to the total performance of their group, unit, or department. Second, they must be evaluated with respect to their own specific managerial performance—their results in areas such as planning, scheduling, budgeting, cost control, the training and development of their people, and the like. Thus a manager's performance is a combination of multiple individual performances of which only one, his or her own, is under his or her absolute control.

Obviously, it would not be practical to try to combine the individual performance evaluations of all subordinates to determine how well the manager did. Therefore, in most normal situations, roughly the same result is achieved by measuring the unit, group, department, or division as a single entity through the use of common measures of performance such as unit profits, unit return on investment, or similar measures. Almost all common measures of performance for organizational units are based on financial data because of its commonality and recognition across functional boundaries. In the data processing area, however, performance geared to financial goals is frequently misleading and inadequate.

A Service Function Requires Special Treatment   Data processing installations in most companies are not organized for the purpose of making a profit. They exist to provide services to other operations of the organization. Therefore the use of financially based goals will not provide meaningful performance evaluation unless a specialized structure—the cost center—has been established.

Under the cost center concept, the data processing installation is permitted to bill participating departments for the cost of services, thereby offsetting the cost of operation, at least on paper. If the participating departments have the option of contracting with outside sources based on price and/or performance, it becomes feasible to apply financial goals to the data processing installation for evaluation purposes. It is normally expected, in a situation like this, that the best performance is that which achieves complete coverage of costs, competitive with costs of outside sources, because it is not desirable to reap profits at the expense of other functional areas. If such a cost center concept exists, it provides a highly useful measure of all data processing managerial performance, because the charge-backs will usually be broken down to indicate the costs of the various specialty areas such as systems, programming, and operations. However, in most cases the cost center concept is not utilized, and the cost of the data processing installation is usually treated as part of the indirect expenses allocated to revenue-producing departments.

Whether the financial data from the cost center concept are available or not, there are other measures of performance which should be employed. Since the primary nature of data processing is to provide a service, a primary measure of performance for the managers concerned must be the service they do provide to the users of data processing resources. In other words, to a large measure the performance of data processing management must be evaluated by its "customers" in terms of the level of satisfaction expressed by the data processing users. Therefore, a method of interrogating the users regarding the kind of support they received from the various specialty areas of data processing must be included in any effective performance evaluation of data processing management.

Valuable insight into data processing management performance is generally achieved by examining the effort going into the completion of a request for service by a user. Without this kind of examination, it would be easy to draw faulty conclusions, since there is a significant probability that both the users and the data processing specialists do not have an in-depth understanding of one another's requirements and limitations. Thus, an expression of dissatisfaction or only marginal satisfaction on the part of a user may, on the surface, indicate poor data processing performance; however, frequently the changes, oversights, and new requirements originating with the user create problems in data processing which result in service that is less than expected.

Conventional Managerial Skills   As stated, data processing management must also be evaluated with respect to the normal managerial functions of planning, organizing, delegating, controlling, and education and development of subordinates. There are many cases where a data processing manager completely abandoned the managerial functions and became, in effect, another worker. This will tend to increase the short-term output of the unit, but the neglect of managerial responsibilities will later inevitably result in bottlenecks, delays in routine service because of interest in exotic applications, lack of coordination between employees, and any number of other problems.

Measurement of performance of the traditional management functions must, by their nature, be subjective in some aspects. For example, it is difficult to measure precisely and objectively the degree to which the work of subordinates is effectively organized. As to planning, one input in the appraisal process is the tangible evidence of the presence or absence of plans, together with information as to whether actual results were close to the planned results. Similarly, delegation can be judged by examination of the responsibilities given to key subordinates, a matter which can be determined with comparative objectivity.

Control is also a somewhat subjective area as regards performance measurement. It is possible that things may appear to be in control while actually they are not. Of course, it is possible by looking at deadlines to see how schedules are being met. That, however, may be deceiving because deadlines may be reached through a combination of luck and padding.

Education and development of subordinates can be measured by examining increases in the responsibility and scope of assignments successfully handled, as well as by the number of formal training and educational activities engaged in by subordinates.

The above aspects of management must be examined, even if the evaluation must to a large degree be subjective, because they will determine the pattern of long-term growth and development of the data processing organization.

Selected Data Processing Management Evaluation Measures

Quantitative Measures

MANAGERIAL PERFORMANCE (Evaluation of the individual manager)

1. Planning ability indicated by the existence of comprehensive plans for both current and future periods, most often up to 5 years in the future.

2. Organizational ability indicated by the structure of the department in terms of levels of authority, the established *and functioning* lines of authority, and, most especially, the amount of responsibility delegated to subordinates and the absence of overlapping or conflicting authority for execution of those responsibilities.

3. Effective control techniques indicated by documentation on a periodic basis showing the activities performed by subordinates both in terms of types of activities, time expended, and the variance from the expected results.

OPERATIONAL PERFORMANCE (Evaluation of departmental performance as a unit)

1. Actual revenue and expense vs. budget by project and in total.

2. Actual schedule vs. planned schedule by project and in total (generally expressed in employee-days but could be employee-months or employee-years for large projects).

3. Return on investment by project and in total, using actual department costs compared to the dollar benefits estimated by users of the systems or those actually realized and attributable to the projects.

4. Personnel turnover. Should be no more than 20 per cent for large projects, less for smaller ones.

5. Operational efficiency, which must be defined for each project or system in measurable terms. For example, a batch system may require 2-hour turnaround or a real-time system may require 5-second response time.

Qualitative Measures

MANAGERIAL PERFORMANCE:

1. The success in identifying and planning areas for future development.

2. The level of employee morale and the type of staff relationships.

3. The breadth and quality of the training program and its contribution to employee growth and development.

OPERATIONAL PERFORMANCE:

1. Users' acceptance of department activities and systems.

2. The extent to which department activities solve user problems, and contribute to organizational efficiency and growth.

3. The existence and use of standards in all appropriate areas.

PERFORMANCE EVALUATION OF SYSTEMS ANALYSTS

Evaluating the performance of a systems analyst presents a special problem because of the nonroutine nature of the work. It would be very rare to find an analyst who executes the same procedures in the same sequence more than once or twice. The function of the systems analyst is to analyze activities and identify problems and areas where improvements are required, then develop methods and procedures to solve those problems and accomplish the improvements.   Each project an analyst undertakes usually has its own special requirements and pecularities.

The Management-by-Objectives Approach   The management-by-objectives approach is the most effective one for the appraisal of systems analysts.   Briefly, this involves the definition of work objectives by mutual discussion and agreement between the employee and the supervisor.   The mutually developed objectives then become the basis for performance evaluation.

Because of the nature of their assignments, most systems analysts work on a project basis.   Therefore, the application of objective setting and evaluation should be at the project level.   Not only is this a logical and convenient approach to performance evaluation, but it provides an effective method of project control.

A systems analyst should follow a definite sequence of steps in completing a project. The first step is *systems investigation*, the process of gathering all pertinent data related to the assigned project.   The next step is to *analyze the collected data* to determine what actual problems or inefficiencies exist.   Once the problems or inefficiencies have been defined, the analyst must use his or her knowledge, experience, and creativity to *develop alternative methods* to solve the problems or eliminate the inefficiencies.   The alternatives are presented to the appropriate management personnel for *selection of the most desirable*.   Once the selection has been made, the analyst re-enters the picture to prepare the *specifications* to be used by programmers and other personnel in implementing the system.   The analyst again becomes involved in the *testing* stage of the completed system to verify that it accomplishes its objectives. Once again, after the system has been operational for a suitable period, the analyst becomes involved to *audit the system* to make sure the system is performing as designed.

While none of the above steps actually begins and ends in sequence with no overlap, the fact that the steps are defined and common to systems analysis projects makes them more than adequate as units for which objectives may be established and performance evaluated.

Establishing the Objectives   The only appropriate method of setting objectives for the analyst is to reach mutual agreement between manager and analyst on what is to be accomplished and how long it should take for each of the defined steps.   The mutual agreement is necessary for motivational purposes as well as to establish reasonable goals.   The average systems analyst has more loyalty to his or her profession than to an employer.   Therefore, in order to perform up to capacity, the analyst must feel that he or she has had a hand in establishing the criteria for performance evaluation.   Strictly speaking, it is not necessary to enlist the analyst in the establishment of work objectives.   It is entirely within the perogative of management to bypass the analyst in setting work objectives.   However, if the analyst is treated as a run-of-the-mill employee instead of as a professional, having work objectives set unilaterally by superiors, he or she will tend to lose motivation.   The basic advantage in mutual-agreement arrangements is the fact that seasoned analysts are best equipped to estimate what they expect to happen, and how much time they expect to need for the completion of the various stages of assignments.   The participation of both managers and analysts will ensure, first, the contribution of the individuals ultimately responsible for reaching the objectives, and, second, the balance provided by the broader and probably more experienced views of managers.   The latter consideration is obviously even more important in the case of the less-than-seasoned analyst.

Using the Established Objectives   There should be no room for dispute as to the achievement or lack of achievement of objectives.   The clear-cut determination of which of the mutually agreed upon objectives have been met and which have not provides a firm picture of *how* the analyst performed.   That constitutes the appraisal function.   The next step, to determine *why* the analyst performed as he or she did, is the evaluation function.   The evaluation should be done even if the analyst achieved all the objectives, since in such a case evaluation may indicate that the objectives were not challenging enough!   Even if evaluation indicates superior performance on objectives that are challenging, the *why* can be useful in defining the attributes of a superior systems analyst that will assist in future recruiting efforts.

Determining why an analyst performed as he or she did is not always clear-cut.

In a good number of cases, the reasons for a particular performance are rooted in personal considerations. For example, a noncooperative employee who is the only source of vital data may have prolonged the time needed for the data gathering operations. Or unexpected conflicts in information may have extended the time needed.

In determining the why of performance, it is crucial to pinpoint those factors which are controllable or caused by the analyst, and those which are not. Those not under his or her control should be taken into consideration in any indication of poor performance.

From the foregoing it can be seen that it is impossible to offer a simple "how to" formula for performance evaluation of systems analysts. The data processing manager must make his or her own determination of what activities should or should not be included in evaluation, and whether they should be applied organization-wide or individually.

Selected Systems Analyst Evaluation Measures

Quantitative Measures
   1. General performance evidenced by the degree of achievement of objectives established jointly by the analyst and the manager.
   2. Actual schedule vs. planned schedule by project, expressed in employee-days, -months, or -years.
   3. Return on investment by project using departmental costs compared to dollar benefits defined in the systems justification.
   4. Actual project cost vs. project budget.
   5. Operational efficiency of the completed systems using criteria defined at the initiation of the project.

Qualitative Measures
   1. The success with which the systems implemented solve the users' problems.
   2. The extent of users' acceptance of the systems.
   3. The ease of maintenance of the systems.
   4. The development and maintenance of good working relations with both user-personnel and other data processing personnel.
   5. The ease with which the design is translated into computer programs by the programmers.

PERFORMANCE EVALUATION OF PROGRAMMERS

The opinion still exists in many quarters that programmers cannot be expected to conform to standards, or to be subject to performance evaluation, because of the uniqueness of the program assignments and the creativity needed to execute them. This attitude has helped create a good many "programmer frauds"—individuals who are only marginally competent, if that, and survive and prosper by doing as little as possible and moving to a new job just before the truth is discovered. Adding to this situation is the almost complete freedom allowed to programmers in a good many installations. In such a milieu, programmers decide what programming techniques to use, whether or not to prepare a flow chart first, what kinds of documentation to include, and almost every other major aspect of their work. In addition, laxity in supervision and control has resulted from a chronic shortage of experienced programmers in the marketplace, and the consequent fear of losing programming personnel if management reins are tightened.

The foregoing "scenario" of programming is no longer valid. Experience indicates that it is possible to impose standards on programmers and to evaluate their performance. Doing so not only provides a measure of individual programmer competence, but also provides a more efficient and controlled work environment.

Preliminaries to Evaluation   Before evaluation, it is obviously necessary to establish what is required. This involves, first, standards which are to apply to every assignment, generally described as *installation standards*, and second, individual program assignments, or *program objectives*.

Installation Standards.   The object of installation standards is to provide continuity in such areas as documentation, procedures, and certain program techniques. This is important from a management standpoint because it ensures completeness, comprehensibility, and transferability of programs and supporting materials. It is also useful to the programmer because it frees him or her from the decisions of how much and what kind of documentation, run instructions, and program embellishments to include. And finally, it provides both management and the programmer with basic standards against which to compare performance and execution of responsibilities in a generally un-structured work situation.

It is suggested that installation standards be established for all types of program documentation, for sequences of completing various parts of the programming function, for testing procedures, for operating instructions, and for programming techniques which are used for interface of programs or which have general application within the installation. For example, it would be desirable to institute a program documenta-tion manual which specifies in detail what documentation is required and how it should be prepared. Similarly, the format of generally applicable program routines should be specified, so that they may be utilized by any programmer in the installation. In-stallation standards, since they involve repetitive execution, are particularly suited to the application of standard times. This provides the closest thing to traditional performance standards that is possible in the programming environment.

Program Objectives. Establishment of program objectives is a common concept in programming with respect to the expected input and output of the program, and the functions the program itself is to perform. However, the establishment of program objectives with respect to how the program will be executed on the computer is a less common practice. It is important for effective performance evaluation that both kinds of program objectives be established and utilized.

The establishment of program objectives concerning the functions to be performed by a particular program is generally done by a systems analyst during the development of detailed systems specifications. This sequence of events, obviously, sets up ob-jectives that are not subject to input from the programmer selected to write the program, except insofar as discussion between the analyst and programmer exists. They are set and, it is hoped, finalized by the time the programmer begins the task of coding instructions.

The program objectives related to execution on the computer are internal to the data processing installation and, therefore, lend themselves to the technique of establish-ment by mutual discussion between manager and programmer. These kinds of objec-tives would normally be concerned with whether the program should be written for efficient utilization of memory or for speed of execution, and considerations of a similar nature.

Implementing the Evaluation   Once all the objectives have been established, either by external forces or internal arrangement, the process of appraising performance can begin. The primary goal of the appraisal system is to be as free of subjective judgment as possible. The less subjectivity involved, the less complicated and difficult the process should be. The use of objectives makes the initial appraisal a matter of deter-mining whether or not the objectives have been met.

The difficulty remains in determining the *why* of a particular performance. In the case of the systems analyst, a large number of the factors affecting performance are rooted in personnel problems. In the case of the programmer that is usually not the case. The programmer has a technical job which requires a minimum of interaction with other personnel. Therefore, the primary factors affecting programming per-formance are to be found in programmers themselves. In other words, to evaluate the performance of a programmer it is necessary to examine his or her attitudes and motivations, as well as prior training and experience.

Programmers have unique responsibilities which span the breadth between pro-fessional and technician. Significant competing forces tend to exert pressure on the programmer, and these can materially affect his or her performance. For example, a competent, concerned programmer, without proper direction from his or her superior, will have to choose between such opposite considerations as writing programs effi-ciently and writing them quickly; or the desire for "elegant" programs and the need for easily maintained programs. Therefore, it would be wise in establishing objectives to minimize any potential conflicts in philosophy or attitude. Failing that, it becomes imperative to recognize the possibility of such conflicts when examining reasons be-hind a particular performance.

Programmers may initially resist attempts at performance evaluation because they may feel that it poses a threat to their autonomy. However, after programmers are exposed to an evaluation system for a suitable period, such objections generally disappear because of the inherent advantages to the programmers. Of course, there will be definite disadvantages to the "programmer fraud." However, one of the objectives of a performance evaluation system is to uncover those individuals who for one reason or another cannot execute their responsibilities in a competent manner.

Selected Programmer Evaluation Measures

Quantitative Measures
1. Debugged program statements per employee-month. The time allocation includes design, coding, and testing time. The number of debugged program statements produced will vary with the type of program, but business applications in a high-level language should range from 300 to 850 per employee-month.
2. Actual schedule vs. planned schedule by program.
3. Operational efficiency of the program in terms of running time, core usage, number of statements required. The efficiency factors should be defined on a priority basis before programming begins.
4. The number of assemblies or compiles required per program.
5. The extent to which installation, programming, and documentation standards are achieved. These standards must be established by each installation to meet the individual requirements and peculiarities of the installation.

Qualitative Measures
1. The extent to which the program meets the design criteria and users' needs.
2. Ease of maintenance.
3. Ease of operation with emphasis on the quality of communications to the operator, especially in exceptional situations.

PERFORMANCE EVALUATION OF COMPUTER OPERATORS

The primary responsibility of a computer operator is to execute computer programs on assigned equipment. There are three relatively independent activities which take up a significant part of the operator's time: (1) production runs; (2) assemblies and compiles; and (3) special runs, including program tests and one-time runs.

Assemblies and compiles and special runs tend to be variable operations which are usually not subject to standard performance measurement techniques. The run times for these types of operations cannot be defined in advance because each operation is a "one-shot" run. Measurement of performance on these operations must necessarily be limited to consideration of time for job setup; operator error requiring rerun; and efficiency of operator execution.

In the typical installation, the bulk of a computer operator's time is devoted to production runs. For clarification, a production run is defined here as a program or set of programs executed on a regularly defined schedule with no substantial changes to the program or programs. The time for execution of a production run should be determined during the final testing or parallel run stage. Therefore, when the programs go into production status, the run time can be considered the standard against which performance is measured.

Generally, a computer operator's work objectives are established on a daily basis through a schedule prepared by management. The schedule normally is constructed by using standard run times as a basis, with projections for any assemblies and compiles or special programs. The standard run time for a production program should include setup and takedown procedures as well as the actual execution time of the program based on the volume of input. Setup time normally includes obtaining the appropriate files, mounting those files on appropriate devices, mounting the required paper stock, and other actions necessary to prepare the computer system for the run involved and logging in on control sheets where required. The takedown procedure is the reverse of the setup, and results in a computer system ready for the next run sequence.

Performing the Evaluation Since measurements of performance in computer operations are made with discrete values—minutes, seconds, and the like—they constitute the most objective appraisal of performance available. It can be determined accurately whether an operator completed a particular run over or under the standard time, provided of course that appropriate log-in/log-out procedures have been instituted. As long as the operator completes the assigned tasks at or below the times specified in the schedules, there is no further question about the adequacy of his or her performance. It is obvious that in this situation the concern about why a particular performance occurred is limited to failures to meet standard. The reasons can either be outright operator failure, or failures outside the operator's control, such as program malfunctions or equipment failure.

Instances of program malfunction or equipment failure will almost without fail be promptly reported because they absolve the operator of any blame for missed schedules. Operator errors, recognized by the operator before completion and distribution, are not as likely to be noted if there is any way to avoid it. There have been countless cases where time used to correct operator errors is buried in assembly and compile times or in special run times because of the inherent lack of precision in estimates of required time for those jobs. After all, who would question a few extra minutes of time for a compile? It therefore becomes essential for a valid evaluation system to minimize the opportunities for allocation of rerun time to nonrelated runs.

In most cases the use of prenumbered console log sheets requiring specification of program number or name and time in before the program can be activated will eliminate the arbitrary allocation of slack or error time. Such log sheets provide an adequate hard-copy record of the tasks executed by the operator on a particular computer system, and the time devoted to each task. This would be the primary input to the performance evaluation process and would provide, after correlation with standard times and established schedules, a good appraisal of an operator's performance on a daily basis. Such records should be standard practice in installations if valid performance evaluation of computer operators is expected.

PERFORMANCE EVALUATION OF KEY DATA RECORDERS

Among the various data processing positions, the key data recorder (keypunch operator, key-to-tape operator, etc.) presents the fewest problems in measuring performance. It is generally accepted throughout the industry that performance is measured by keystrokes per hour.

Keystrokes per hour, to be precise, is *net* keystrokes per hour, or the difference obtained by subtracting the number of strokes in error from the total strokes per hour. This, however, is not an ideal method of determining the desired figures, so an alternative method is generally used. The alternative is to state the keystroke standard as a rate of keystrokes per hour with a minimum level of accuracy, such as 5,000 keystrokes per hour with 95 per cent accuracy. The keystroke rate then is the total keystrokes per hour, and the accuracy is determined by computing the percentage of *records* keyed accurately.

The exact number of keystrokes per hour to be used as a standard will vary, depending upon the type of data being keyed. Normally, the rate is highest for all numeric data, and decreases as the percentage of alphabetic and special characters increases. It is the responsibility of the manager in charge to establish the rate for his or her people. Historical statistics are useful as a guide, but it would be wise to seek the active involvement of the key data recorders early in the decision process, to ensure their cooperation in the program and pave the way for easier implementation of future adjustments.

As a guideline, the generally acceptable range is 7,000 to 12,000 keystrokes per hour with a minimum of 95 per cent accuracy on a data mix of 80 per cent numeric and 20 per cent alphabetic. In some areas, 7,000 keystrokes per hour is considered above average, but 10,000 keystrokes per hour would be closer to average in most cases.

SELECTED BIBLIOGRAPHY

Brooks, Frederick P., Jr., "The Mythical Man-Month," *Datamation*, December, 1974.

Koontz, Harold, *Appraising Managers as Managers*, McGraw-Hill, New York, 1971.

Lopez, Felix M., Jr., *Evaluating Employee Performance*, Public Personnel Association, Chicago, 1968.

Schefer, Edward A., "Management Control of the Corporate Computer Activity," *Data Management*, September, 1972.

Weinberg, Gerald M., *The Psychology of Computer Programming*, Van Nostrand Reinhold, New York, 1971.

————, "The Psychology of Improved Programming Performance," *Datamation*, November, 1972.

Chapter 9

ADP Management in the Multinational Company

P. J. DIXON

Director, Management Systems, Massey-Ferguson
Limited, Toronto, Ontario, Canada

Managing automatic data processing in a multinational company introduces several new dimensions to a managerial and technological problem which is already difficult enough. The new dimensions which have to be taken into consideration are:

- Cultural diversity.
- Language barriers.
- Variety of approaches to management.
- Varying degrees of decentralization.
- Political considerations.
- Uneven technological levels in different parts of the world.
- Increased complexity of corporate and subsidiary unit organizational considerations.
- Strength of the "not invented here" syndrome—i.e., resistance to suggestions from others regarding new methods, procedures, and equipment.

All these factors are superimposed on the usual problems of managing ADP in a corporation of any size, problems which range from the organizational placement of the function and the methods of project management, to coping effectively with user relations at all levels.

It should be noted that ADP is only a part, although a new and important part, of the overall problem of managing information systems in a corporation, in support of on-going profitable management of the corporation. We are discussing, in fact, systems in support of management—or, in other words, *management systems*—and their introduction, evolution, and ongoing improvement. Computers and related equipment and techniques are, of course, playing an increasing role in this process, and expenditures related to the rental (or other forms of payment) of ADP equipment, software, and telecommunications form the predominant portion of the budgets of most management systems departments.

In order to lay a proper framework for the discussion of the management of systems in a multinational corporation, we shall discuss the nature and special characteristics of a multinational (or global) corporation. We shall then discuss how objectives should be set for the systems function in order to support the management needs of the corporation. Then we shall pick up the appropriate management, technological, organizational, and human questions which have to be tackled. There are no pat answers to what in many cases are apparent and sometimes real contradictions in the demands a multinational company places on the systems function supporting it. But then, often the realization that a problem exists and the identification of the problem lead us more than halfway to a solution.

THE MULTINATIONAL COMPANY

A company which merely has extensive export operations, or even offices abroad, by no means qualifies for the description *multinational*. Let us follow the path from such a company to a true global corporation: First, there is the company which exports and does business abroad. Such a company is just a business with an export division. Then there is the company which manufactures in a number of countries, and even has distribution centers abroad, but the top management and corporate management always come from the parent company nation. We can classify such a company as an international corporation; many oil companies are like that.

Next in line is the company which has manufacturing and distribution facilities well distributed over many parts of the world. These facilities usually take the form of subsidiary companies wholly or partly owned, and usually managed by the nationals of the country in which the subsidiary operates. In such a company, with fully evolved management sourcing concepts, there will be the occasional expatriate in an otherwise nationally staffed subsidiary on a management development assignment, and corporate management will generally include the best of the managerial talent regardless of its national origin. Normally each subsidiary will operate with considerable degree of freedom, and be responsible for its profit and loss statement, and for its balance sheet. However, a number of decisions affecting the balance sheet and profit-loss considerations of the worldwide company as a whole will normally be coordinated by the corporate head office, particularly as far as the development of assets and consistency of financial control and planning methodology are concerned. Such a corporation can truly be considered a multinational company.

Organization   There is no one best organization structure for a multinational company (even in any given industry, such as manufacturing of engineered products). Today the political climate and world economic structure are undergoing a process of change, and the creation of trading blocks, or regions, such as EEC, and the changing relative strengths of individual national economies and currencies require a flexible approach to organization structures and management processes of multinational companies oriented toward the future.

However, after the above considerations have been acknowledged, it is well to return to some fundamentals which any organization structure established must accomplish if the interests of the world community, employees, and shareholders are to be served. Too many systems specialists and executives forget what being in business is about, and what their role in supporting the business is. Why is any company in business? At the risk of being accused of expressing a platitude, let us firmly state as a foundation of this discussion that a company must:

1. produce the right product . . .
2. at the right place . . .
3. at the right time . . .
4. economically . . .
5. sold at the right price . . .
6. year after year . . .
7. while steadily improving net profit . . .
8. while maintaining respectable return on investment . . .
9. with steadily improving debt/equity ratio.

If a multinational business is to survive in today's social and political environment, it must achieve the above basic goals to a degree sufficient to provide adequate return to shareholders, and in addition to be able to help support the reclamation and maintenance of the ecological environment and meet the requirements of social justice as defined by the national governments within whose orbit it functions.

Operational Problems A multinational company operating around the globe continuously faces the challenge of obstacles placed in its path by competitive pressures, regional and national economic action, political pressures, and changing technology. These obstacles can be outlined in terms of the following specific operational problems that a multinational company must solve with ever-improving efficiency:

1. Provisioning materials in a situation of fluctuating markets and increasing product variability.

2. Minimizing inventories while component parts and finished products are changing continuously.

3. Speedily introducing new products in view of shortening life cycles of product lines, to maintain market penetration.

4. Improving reaction to changing technology of engineering and manufacturing processes, and to technology available for worldwide product distribution.

5. Meeting the need for money, management, and investment decisions in politically and financially uncertain environments.

6. Assuring fast reaction to the changes in the character and nature of world markets by each function of the enterprise, and by the corporate management as a whole.

7. Providing data, external and internal to the company, for flexible planning and control to those members of senior management accountable for setting and steering the future course of the company.

Management Processes and Information Flow The following broad interacting processes, taken as a whole, represent the dynamic entity which is the company. Their planning, control, and administration constitute the process of management:

• The market research (including R&D), product definition, and product introduction process.

• The purchasing, provisioning, manufacturing, and wholesale distribution process.

• The sales monitoring, sales forecasting, and factory programming process.

• The financial planning and control process.

Each of the above processes has to be supported by an information system, or information flow, which is the symbolic representation of the process itself. The information system has to provide the data required by management to plan, control, and administer the process.

In defining the interaction between the conduct of a business and the information system, it is useful to state the conceptual framework succinctly, as follows, keeping in mind the special needs of the multinational company:

1. The company consists of ongoing operational and management processes which interact. Each of these has to be planned, controlled, and administered.

2. Each of these processes can be represented by the supporting information flows needed to plan, control, and administer it.

3. The processes, the information flows, and the planning and administrative activities must be recognized to operate over different time spans, and at different management and supervision levels in the company.

4. It is useful to think in terms of strategic, tactical, and operational aspects of the processes—and of related information flows—to represent the differing time spans and the different levels of processes to be planned, controlled, and administered.

MANAGING THE INFORMATION SYSTEMS FUNCTION

A clear awareness of the relationship between ongoing management processes and information systems is particularly necessary for effectively organizing and managing the information systems function *itself* in a multinational company. If it does not exist, or is not reasonably well understood despite language and cultural barriers, it becomes almost impossible to manage the function worldwide in other than a fragmented, uncoordinated manner. The result will inevitably be attendant duplications of effort, communications blocks, and blocks to the effective operation of the management processes themselves.

Once the conceptual foundation has been laid, it is possible to establish an organization, implemented by effective procedures, charged with accomplishing the following specific tasks:

1. Assisting managements at all levels of the company with the formal definition of the process for whose planning, controlling, and administering they are accountable.

2. Assisting with the definition of the information and the format of reports necessary to accomplish the ongoing planning, control, and general administration of the processes.

3. Formalizing the information into disciplined databases and organized information flows.

4. Providing input into the formulation of organization processes and structures which will actively facilitate the organized flow of information, and the formally designed planning, control, and administrative systems essential to effective ongoing management.

Placement, Scope, and Authority   In a multinational company, the corporate division charged with the above responsibilities is variously called Information Systems, Management Information Systems, Management Systems, Management Services Division, or the like.   In most global corporations it is a staff division, with its counterparts in the line organizational entities that make up the operating structure of the company around the world.   In Massey-Ferguson Limited, the corporate division is called Management Information Systems, and the counterpart line operating units are called Management Services.   Its technical scope includes management sciences and operations research, electronic data processing, systems and procedures (in line operating units), and technical aspects of communications.

It should be emphasized that neither at the corporate level nor in the line operating organizations can the management system function, by whatever name it is called, discharge the responsibilities defined for it, unless it is:

1. *Entirely service-oriented.* Its sole justification for existence is to serve the rest of the company by continuously helping all other functions, via improved information systems, more effectively to plan, control, and administer processes for which they are responsible.

2. *Independent of any particular function or department within the company.* It must be able to serve all impartially, and to allocate its resources to projects over the company as a whole, in accordance with established priorities.   The latter will be set by the chief executive.   For management services departments in the operating units of the worldwide corporation, priorities will be set by the managing director or senior executive of the unit.   Since each managing director of an operations unit has profit and loss responsibility, and since different business priorities may have to be considered in different parts of the world to achieve best results, the priorities set for management services departments of individual operations units may vary widely within the overall guidelines set by the chief executive for the corporation as a whole.

3. *Able to identify and bring about interfunctional and interorganizational information flows.* The establishment and control of such information flows is vital to assure optimum coordination among all the functional processes interacting to achieve the goals of the company.

4. *Placed at an appropriate organizational level within the company.* At the corporate level, the function should report either to the president or to a senior corporate executive coordinating all interrelated corporate functions (divisions) on behalf of the president.   Within the line operating units, the function should report to the managing director or to a senior executive coordinating all service functions on behalf of the managing director.

5. *Governed by goal setting and direction by top management.* Without such goal setting and direction, the probability that systems will contribute significantly to profits will be negligible, and the essential direct participation of senior user-management in system definition and project management will be unlikely.

6. Finally, the management services function must be *accepted within the corporation as the vehicle fostering and assisting in the implementation of change.* It has to be a catalyst for bringing about change, since without change there can be no improvement in either profitability or the manner and effectiveness with which a company is managed.   In today's fluid international economic, political, and social environment, the recognition of this need is particularly vital in a multinational cor-

poration. Yet it is precisely when the management systems function attempts to perform this role that it runs into the highest degree of resistance and resentment. The challenge here is to "rock the boat" without either upsetting it or being thrown out of it!

Management and Accountability   Once the role and direction of the management systems are established in terms of supporting continuous improvement in the profitability of the company, it is necessary to ensure that the whole range of activities and procedures be clearly defined by precisely stated cost-effectiveness criteria. This is necessary in order that investment decisions concerning the development of new management systems and the computer facilities needed to support them can be evaluated as would any other capital investment in the company.

The key to successful and cost-effective management systems contribution to the profitability of the company is the way we define *accountability for results* of new and ongoing management systems in relation to definition and control of management systems projects. It is essential to establish that:

1. The *user*-management is accountable to top management for results.

2. The management systems function is accountable to user-management for quality of systems design and technical feasibility.

3. No systems work can be undertaken without an approved proposal; no proposal should be approved unless countersigned by both user-management and management systems senior management.

The relationship between management systems and user-department in connection with project definition, control, and installation, as outlined above, is at the crux of success or failure of modern systems-oriented management. The recognition of this fact must govern the organization and lines of authority established at both the corporate level and the operating levels. In a multinational company, line operating entities may, for example, be national subsidiaries or economic regions. In a large company operating worldwide, such as Massey-Ferguson, profit and loss accountability may be found both at the level of a managing director in charge of a national unit and at the level of executive vice president in charge of an economic region of which the national unit forms a part.

Under such conditions it is essential to establish the accountability for each system to be developed at the appropriate level in the company. The underlying principle must be that managing directors are accountable for systems with which they decide to manage the functions within their control; and that executive vice presidents in charge of economic regions are accountable for systems with which they decide to manage their operations—systems which are entirely within their control, and which cut across—in terms of information flow and functional control—the several national management entities reporting to them.

At the corporate level, the management systems function makes recommendations on those systems whose design and implementation must take into account the requirements of the corporation as a whole. It seeks concurrence on the design and implementation of those systems within each line operating entity, where maintenance of compatibility in system design and implementation would benefit the corporation as a whole. Reduction of design and implementation costs in all organizational units is also a consideration.

Organizationally, it is extremely important to separate the management of system definition, design, and implementation on the one hand, and the management of data centers and telecommunications on the other. The reason is simple. In multinational companies it is not necessary to have a factory to make each product in each location. In fact, from the point of view of investment and sales efficiency, it would usually be most undesirable. Similarly, one can see the potential expenditures if each national operating entity, and, even more, the major functions within such entities, were to operate their own data centers with attendant technical and administrative support. As we shall see later, data center management must be treated in a manner similar to that of factory management, and the factors in decisions as to data center location are similar to those of planning production capacity and factory location. For example, to be specific, the line management of all computer operations and communications at Massey-Ferguson is in the hands of a director, data center operations for the Massey-Ferguson European Region, which includes all operations units with profit-center responsibility in Europe. The communications and computer operating requirements for the whole region are centrally managed, and computer centers supported by a telecommunications network serving several operations units are being created.

However, the conception and implementation of systems are an integral part of the management process at each level of the company. The line executive accountable for the results of his or her operating entity must be accountable for the priorities he or she assigns to system development, and for the effectiveness with which he or she exploits systems as a management tool. For this the line executive must have at his or her command an adequate systems design and development function.

The freedom of action at the national level outlined above is circumscribed by only two constraints:

1. The requirements for compatibility of major systems throughout an economic region, which an executive vice president decides is essential to optimize regional profit and loss and balance sheet results.

2. The requirements for compatibility of major systems throughout the corporation, which the chief executive officer decides, following consultation with corporate staff and senior line executives, is essential to optimize systems contribution to worldwide operating financial results. In this case, long-term implications on the strategic evolution and needs of the company will predominate over the short-term apparent benefits that can often be achieved at local or regional level.

To recapitulate: Systems supporting local (national) sales and distribution networks and accounts control, and other operating-type systems, will often be within the entire discretion of a national managing director.

Systems required to support the supply management within an economic region, whether whole goods or spare parts, will be within the entire discretion of a regional executive vice president.

Systems required for worldwide coordination of financial reporting and planning, supply systems which need to function across economic regions, systems supporting the introduction and management of new product lines, and systems supporting new engineering and manufacturing control processes will very definitely require corporate-level input and coordination.

Steering and Review Committees   The management systems departments within each organizational level should be placed in such a manner that the head of systems is a member of senior management at that level. In addition, the continuous planning and control of systems responsive to the needs of national and regional profit centers requires the establishment of appropriate steering and review committees. These review committees are needed by senior management at each level to:

1. Monitor the direction, progress, and full user-function involvement of each major system, e.g., manufacturing control system or distribution control system.

2. Coordinate system development plans with requirements of existing operating systems, and with data center technical support and computer capacity.

3. Serve as a vehicle for communicating among executives of all functions a better understanding of costs and benefits associated with the use of systems in their respective functions and in the corporation as a whole.

4. Serve as a communications and recommendations vehicle to the executive vice presidents and to the chief executive officer on those major systems where compatibility requirements, dictated by the management needs of supply, distribution, planning, and control, call for the coordination of the system design approach across the boundaries of national and economic-region profit centers.

5. Last but not least, assure that system design and implementation resources are expended *only* on projects which now or in the future will benefit the company profit and loss statement and balance sheet in an identifiable manner.

Such committees should also be set up for specific projects within economic regions, and for the corporation as a whole.

The corporate steering committee will be primarily concerned with overall systems development strategy and monitoring, namely, the major systems which require worldwide compatibility of approach to system design and to the method of system implementation. This will normally comprise systems that support facilities planning and utilization, worldwide asset management, product development and introduction, and overall financial planning and control.

It must be remembered that such committees advise and report, and have no line management function. The accountability for results must remain undiluted in the hands of specific project managers for projects, and in the hands of the management systems directors and the line executives to whom they report, for the effective world-wide utilization of systems by the company as a whole.

Systems evolved within the management framework outlined above have a reasonable chance of being relevant to the key problems of managing the various components of a worldwide corporation now and in the future. What is then needed is *production capacity*, i.e., "information processing factories," to produce the product—information relevant to effective management at all levels of operation.

MULTINATIONAL DATA CENTER MANAGEMENT

Efficient "information processing factories" are required on an international scale to support the management needs of multinational operating units ranging from annual operating levels of ten million dollars or less to hundreds of millions of dollars, and, of course, also to support the management needs of corporate head offices. In addition to developing systems for worldwide management, there is the problem of cost-effective management of the information processing factories themselves. Let us consider some of the problems which have to be solved in this area, and some of the solutions which are evolving, using the European theater of operations for purposes of illustration.

Historically, individual data centers, sometimes several—in individual operating companies and divisions of all types and sizes—grew up like mushrooms all over a given theater of operations, such as Europe. This gave rise to the following management and operating problems:

1. Uncoordinated computer center management resulting in:
    a. Difficulty and added costs in any attempted application transfers.
    b. Duplication of hardware and software specialists, or inadequate technical support of data center operations.
    c. Administrative duplication leading to nonproductive overhead.
2. Inconsistency of documentation standards, resulting in uneven level of service to users.
3. Inconsistency of accounting for and control of data center operations, resulting in poor visibility of costs and of application effectiveness.
4. Lack of central control, resulting in difficult cross-application of data center management techniques.
5. Poor distribution of computer capacity, resulting in imbalance in service to users.
6. Imbalance in the proportion of data center costs relative to total management systems department costs, while suffering from shortage of capacity. (In general, Massey-Ferguson experience shows that some 70 per cent of every management systems dollar is spent on data center operations, as shown in Figure 9-1.)

Consolidation In order to solve these problems so that data center operations can support the improved management of the systems development function, current computer and teleprocessing technology permits the consolidation of the management of data centers throughout Europe organizationally in the first place, and physically in the second place.

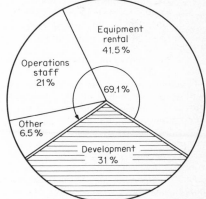

Fig. 9-1 Allocation of the management systems dollar, Massey-Ferguson Limited.

While one has to proceed continuously and test each step, there are indications of rapid potential improvement in telecommunications in the EEC, and of cost-effective mini-computers as semi-independent terminals connected to central high-volume processors are now available. (However, in many parts of the world, e.g., Latin America and

Europe, high-speed telecommunication lines to connect everything together are either unavailable or still very expensive.)

The objectives to be achieved are:

1. Reduce the number of administrative, professional, and technical staff employed in data centers, and increase their quality and effectiveness by reducing the number of fully staffed independently operating data centers.

2. Increase each remaining data center's cost effectiveness.

3. Establish region-wide and corporation-wide standards of effectiveness of staff performance, system, software, documentation, and maintenance.

4. Provide effective control over operation of existing systems, and bring about full visibility of data processing operations costs by operating companies and by user-departments.

5. Provide continuous planning and control of future data center capacity needs of operating companies and of economic regions.

6. Establish a single powerful contact point with vendors, computer leasing companies, and software consultants.

7. Put the company into a position to attract and keep superior staff, operating advanced facilities; these are in particularly short supply outside the United States.

8. Overall, control the cost at which any given desired service level in the data processing operations area is supplied to the operating companies — i.e., design and operate high-throughput, efficient information processing factories.

An action program for achieving these objectives should be centered on people and organization action, rather than on preoccupation with equipment. One should select those whom one considers both first-class professionals and executives as directors of data center operations. These should then proceed to take inventory of existing people resources and develop the organization structure and staff with which to operate, and bring about consolidation. A computer is but a machine tool for management; if you have a first-class director of manufacturing, he or she can get rid of a machine tool that does not work. However, if you have a first-class machine tool, that machine tool cannot get rid of a poor director of manufacturing. The same applies in systems work, and particularly in the data center operations area.

Massey-Ferguson has appointed the directors and implemented the organizational change throughout Europe, each step of the way having been agreed upon with operating unit management. Prior to any physical consolidation of data centers, it was necessary to establish:

1. Forward capacity planning.

2. System software development and maintenance.

3. Operating and documentation standards and their control.

4. Dealings with all computer, peripheral equipment, and software suppliers on a centralized basis.

5. Administration, internal accounting, and methods of charging for data center services.

Detailed planning for major physical consolidation of data centers into a network with teleprocessing is at this writing in the course of execution, and is regularly reviewed by the European Systems Steering Committee. Three computers have already been eliminated, teleprocessing introduced, and capacities and technical skills of major data centers increased to meet planned throughput demands arising out of major current-asset management systems.

The company is well on the way to working out how to remove another complete configuration from the complement in use in continental Europe. The resources released by these moves are available for application to the development of significant new management systems in the Massey-Ferguson operating companies, which otherwise the company might not be able to afford within overall budgetary constraints and profit guidelines established by the president and the general managers.

KEY ADP PROBLEMS IN MULTINATIONAL OPERATIONS

In the course of applying the policies discussed in this Chapter, it is almost certain that one will run into a number of problems, some of which are almost inevitable.

The Language Problem While a multinational company will normally use one language for communication among its management, this lingual facility tends rapidly to disappear once one penetrates deeper into each national organization. Where it is desirable to adapt compatible operating standards, and to adapt successful systems from one area of the company to another, this becomes a very real problem. Technical translations are necessary—and that assumes that the *original* documentation is there in the first place, according to policy, to be translated. Also, imagine, for example, under remote job entry mode of operation, a German-speaking terminal operator trying to solve a problem with a French-speaking central computer shift supervisor. Thus a new dimension of qualification is required of all data processing personnel: fluency of written and spoken communication in one language in common use through the company, in addition to fluency of communication with their own users in their own language.

The Cultural Lag Problem. Most people in senior management positions worldwide, and often in middle management, received their formal education before computers were heard of, and attained their practical experience and managerial growth while the use of computers in business was in its infancy, or before. This lag between availability of modern management technology and the managerial readiness to embrace it varies from country to country. General ability to initiate and implement change—even where clearly desirable from overall company point of view—also varies from country to country. In general, today, where the managing director or regional vice president is not prepared personally to push the introduction of computer-based management systems, progress will be very slow, and the effort required by all concerned will be much greater than otherwise would be necessary. In this management area, lack of positive leadership is very often misunderstood by old, established middle and supervisory management as positive encouragement to resist any change in methods of working—change which is essential to the competitiveness of the company. This general problem can be dealt with only by patience, and by acquiring gradually, through natural turnover, managers who utilize computer-based systems naturally as a tool, the way engineers use a slide rule.

The "Not Invented Here" Problem. This problem is rampant throughout the data processing fraternity. Add to the natural predilection of the analyst/programmer to invent his or her own solutions, regardless of what it costs the company, the language barriers and the national and profit center competitiveness which exists in any multinational company, and it is quickly evident that a major portion of a corporate management systems division's effort must go into overcoming this syndrome.

The Proprietary Problem. Allied to the "not invented here" problem is that of data center consolidation, and the resistance to it. People do not like to lose "their own computer," particularly if the data center is to be in another country. Any slip during consolidation tends immediately to be exploited to show that it cannot, or should not, be done. Unflagging senior executive and corporate management support are called for to steer to completion the consolidation consistent with the economics of modern technology.

The Computer Selection Problem There is enough work to be done, even if all processing worldwide is done on fully compatible mainframes. Hardware selection feasibility studies are a waste of shareholders' money, once the bulk of worldwide data processing is committed to the central processors of one supplier or another. This is a rather harsh assertion. However, the following factors which have to be taken into consideration lie behind it:

1. Development of major new applications is costly in itself. There are sufficient problems in the transfer of major applications from one part of the organization to another, and in adopting corporation-wide information reporting systems, without adding the problems and costs of different and often incompatible hardware and software.

2. At the operator, programmer, systems analyst, and software specialist level, people will often do their work in different languages. That in itself introduces a number of problems. It is desirable to minimize these problems by training one's staff in using compatible system design and programming methodology, supported by common programming languages and compilers, utilizing common operating systems and database management software, and operating compatible hardware.

3. It is important that the full weight of the corporation can be brought to bear on its data processing equipment suppliers, particularly in less industralized areas of the world where the suppliers' support capability may be relatively weak and needs to be assured by the overall importance of the worldwide corporation as a customer.

4. Senior software and hardware specialists are difficult to obtain, and it is important that their services and know-how can be utilized in different parts of the world as problems arise, or as a new stage in development is reached. Further, compatible hardware and software facilitates the transfer of promising systems analysts, programmers, and managers on foregin assignments, to broaden their knowledge of the corporation and improve their language skills.

CONCLUSION

The foregoing discussion presents only some of the major problems which multinational requirements accentuate. The need to compromise between line and staff, balancing corporate recommendations against local line-management accountability, is a problem with a variety of partial solutions (and no absolute one) common to all large companies, and to most functions.

It is to be expected that problems of managing ADP worldwide in the next 10 years or so will be far more managerial than they were in the late sixties and early seventies, calling for executives with professional background, rather than merely sophisticated technicians. This will be so because the key task facing management is to learn how to fit the management systems function into complex multinational companies with their organization processes and structures.

A solution which seems to work is to make the function a true service function, one receiving attention from top management equal to that accorded other important functions. Management systems development is part of the responsibility of general management of operating companies, coordinated from the corporate level. This is the investment multinational companies have to make—like capital investment—in their management future.

The foregoing can be accomplished through maximum centralization of data center operations, made possible by modern technology, consistent with required service levels by operating companies. In this way, multinational companies get the benefits of large "data factories" with first-class management and staff, and retain central control over a major item of capital expenditures, while in no way diluting the line executive's accountability or responsibility for the way he or she manages the operating company.

Actually, the need is to de-emphasize the computer and consider it as merely a sophisticated machine tool available for use in modern management systems. We have on our hands not a new technical problem, but a new managerial and people problem: We have to learn how to fit a major new function into complex multinational structures so that it contributes to, rather than hinders, the process of communication among people, and the process of managing a corporation as a coherent entity.

Section 6

Outside Services for Data Processing

Introduction

THEODORE J. FREISER *Senior Vice President, John Diebold & Associates, New York, New York*

The computer industry can be divided into four broad categories:
- Hardware vendors, who sell (or lease or rent) computer mainframes, peripherals, accessories, supplies, support equipment, specialized furniture, and facilities to users.
- Software and services companies, which assist computer owners to use their machines, selling them software packages, custom application development services (and the use of temporary programmers), facilities management, hardware maintenance, and educational services.
- Consulting services.
- Computer service companies, which supply computation as a service to customers who may or may not also own computers of their own. (Some reasons why computer owners may also buy outside computing services will be cited later.) Such services take two forms: over-the-counter batch processing and remote-access service.

The second, third, and fourth of these categories constitute the services sector of the computer industry, and it is with that sector that this Section is concerned. Services in all the categories have contributions to make to companies of all sizes, with all types of owned ADP resources: They are complementary rather than competitive to internal facilities. Some services, by their natures, will be routinely or continuously used by corporate ADP departments: for example, hardware maintenance, or packaged software in routine use. Other services, such as consulting services and custom programming, are used on an occasional basis, to meet specific needs.

In many cases, management faces the choice of acquiring the service from an outside vendor or using (perhaps developing for the purpose) an internal department or group as provider of the service. In broad terms, an outside service merits consideration to fill any nonrecurring need for which no internal capability exists. But there are a number of other considerations which bear on this decision.

Remote-Access and Time-Sharing Services These are computer service companies which support multiple users simultaneously via terminals on customer premises. These services come in several "flavors":

• Remote job entry (RJE) batch—the customer loads data for batch processing at a terminal; the output may be produced (e.g., printed) at the terminal, or delivered from the computer center.

• Scientific/engineering-oriented time-sharing service—these services make available flexible languages for conversational programming, such as Dartmouth BASIC and Interactive FORTRAN. These are generally used by technically oriented people, who first create and then use (execute) their own programs, working at conversational terminals such as teletypewriters.

• Programmer-oriented time-sharing service—these services make available programmer utilities such as editing programs, language processors, syntax checkers, and environment simulators for test execution. These are used by programmers to create new (batch or interactive) application systems.

• Communications-oriented services—these services are structured to permit each client to access a private database (and/or set of applications) from terminals at multiple locations.

Many companies, including large ones with extensive in-house computer resources, use one or more of these services for selected applications for any of several reasons:

1. Unscheduled work, such as COBOL compiles, disrupts a production-oriented center, while an interactive programming service eliminates turnaround time, greatly increasing programmer productivity.

2. Putting interactive or transaction-oriented applications on an outside service keeps the internal resource in a simple pure batch environment.

3. Similarly, placing communications- and database-oriented applications, such as customer order entry from multiple sales-office locations, on a service avoids the necessity of developing an in-house communications hardware resource and technical expertise—a particularly expensive resource category.

4. The use of proprietary software. This type of software is available from remote-access services as well as in package form, as discussed below.

Proprietary Application Packages These are available to run on the client's computer, and via terminal access from computer service companies.

Wherever a proprietary package exists which fills a need, there is a direct cost saving, compared to developing the application from scratch, because the cost recovery is distributed among a large number of customers. However, the availability of proprietary packages does not eliminate the need for ADP expertise within the user-organization: A closer evaluation is required to assure that the package really is a good fit to the user's need, or can be made so with an acceptable amount of custom revision. The credentials and resources of the vendor must be carefully evaluated, and—even with the best documentation and user manuals—implementing a proprietary package is often a demanding technical task within the user-organization.

Proprietary packages from remote-access services are particularly attractive when a user needs a number of applications with widely fluctuating levels of usage. An excellent example are programs in the financial analysis and economic modeling area: A financial officer may make irregular use of six or seven separate packages of this type to meet specific financial management needs.

Utility Software Packages   Aside from end-use applications, there are several types of general utility software packages available on a proprietary basis:

1. Programming aids — language preprocessors (language short-form processors, macroprocessors, etc.), program documentors, program test facilities, syntax checkers, standards enforcement facilities, and the like.

2. Environment enhancers — spoolers and schedulers, operating system extenders to increase the number of partitions, adapters (e.g., to permit DOS applications to run under OS), etc.

3. Measurement and optimizing facilities — software which accumulates detailed system performance statistics, used in "tuning" for increased system throughput, and high-level-language (e.g., COBOL) optimizers which flag (or automatically correct) program usages which cause unnecessary execution steps.

Consulting Services   There are four main reasons why companies with substantial computer expertise of their own find it useful to call in consultants specializing in ADP:

1. When specialized knowledge in a particular area is temporarily needed: for example, when a user must develop specifications for the RFP of a hardware acquisition. A consultant who prepares such RFPs as often as four or five times a year may often avoid pitfalls and solve problems not readily apparent to the data processing manager who makes one major acquisition every 4 or 5 years.

2. Objectivity. Senior data processing or corporate management often has reason to feel that an internal recommendation involves a vested interest or a bias of some sort. Certain types of "political" problems can also arise which are most effectively resolved by an impartial and objective technical umpire.

3. A technical resource. When there is a nonrecurring need for a technical staff, as during an unusual development project or a big one-time conversion effort, a consultant can provide technical experts on a temporary basis to accomplish or contribute to the effort. One problem this solves for the user is severe fluctuation in the size of the ADP staff.

4. A fresh point of view. Professional people working intently on a problem for an extended period of time often find it extremely useful to call in other qualified minds with a fresh perspective.

Miscellaneous Services   A few significant services are available that do not fall readily into the above categories:

1. Hardware maintenance. Maintenance by a third party is often used by companies with multiple vendor hardware configurations or modified hardware. Some hardware vendors do not readily support second owners of their products, and third-party maintenance houses are finding a market here.

2. Facilities management. Some companies find ADP management a nuisance or distraction, and retain specialists to operate their entire data processing departments: hardware, operations, and system staffs. These companies gain certain economies of scale and learning-curve economies and can sometimes perform this service profitably at less cost to the end user than in-house operation.

3. Communications common carriers. The telephone companies are major suppliers of data communications services. In addition, certain companies specializing in data communications offer economically attractive carrier services to certain types of users — particularly those with high-volume traffic among fixed points.

Chapter 1

Software Houses

L. A. WELKE

**President, International Computer Programs, Inc.,
Carmel, Indiana; Past President, The ADAPSO Software
Industry Association, Montvale, New Jersey**

In the early days of computers, the term *software house* was coined to describe a firm whose primary activity was to produce computer programs for someone other than itself. At the time – roughly in the mid-1950s – this meant custom contract programming. As the computer industry and its markets grew, the term was broadened until it came to cover almost anyone who was doing anything associated with software.

Hence today, software house can include consulting vendors of proprietary program products, contract programmers, education specialists, and even some service bureaus. What is essential for an understanding of the software industry is a recognition that the term is somewhat vague and ill-defined, and that participants (vendors) range from very small companies to divisions of the largest corporations in the United States.

The industry got its start with the realization by Federal Government computer users that while they had difficulty in hiring capable programmers at the prevailing Government salary classifications, they had little trouble getting appropriations to subcontract the work out to a nongovernment source. Indeed, all but one of the first software houses were founded on a Government contract.

Although the Government business volume was good, these early software entrepreneurs lacked credibility in the private sector. Only with the arrival of third-generation computing equipment – notably the IBM 360 Series – and the record of assistance chalked up by independent software firms with respect to this equipment, were the latter able to approach businesses in the United States to get contract programming work. The short supply of good programmers and analysts in the mid-1960s also contributed to the growth of software firms. Contracts were often available to outside programmers because no one was available within a company's ADP staff, or a sudden crisis demanded a new report or system within a time frame that the company's staff could not meet.

This emerging industry was also aided by a completely extraneous factor: the private investor and the new-issue stock craze of 1966–1968. The "man in the street" took a fancy to computer stocks in those years, and eagerly funded hundreds of new companies that were "going into software."

The point of all this is that it was not new technology or even better methodology that led to the creation of the computer software industry. Rather, it was a series of incidents and seemingly unrelated happenings, taking place during a period of business expansion.

RECENT INDUSTRY CHANGES

A high point in software company formation was reached in late 1968, with 2,800 firms counting themselves as software houses. And then the house of cards began to collapse.

In almost all of the 2,800 software firms, technical prowess was greatly overshadowed by weak management, inadequate financing, and immature marketing. Unfortunately, those firms that were not guilty of the foregoing nonetheless were given the poor image of those that were. As a result of the decline of the United States economy during 1969 and 1970, the industry was narrowed down to less than a thousand firms by 1971.

What emerged by the end of 1974 was approximately 800 sources of proprietary software products—many of which also did contract programming. Additionally, there were some 200 firms devoted only to the latter activity. The composite was made up of either divisions or offsprings of more than 100 of the "Fortune 500" companies (through acquisition, sale, or spin-offs), a number of the country's leading service bureaus, 15 of the large CPA firms, about 250 dedicated and "pure" software houses specializing in software products, and 200 firms, more or less, that might be classed as "beginners."

There is little or no pattern to the industry at this writing—but then its very immaturity might well preclude a pattern. The Fortune 500 firms, for instance, took no one set approach to the market, and have not determined a proportioned mix of products or services to be offered. The service bureaus, on the other hand, could usually be counted on to provide software products or services in those areas of expertise that they possessed by virtue of their roles as processors. Hence, certain firms became payroll specialists, others, accounts receivables specialists, and so on. Because service bureaus are more and more specializing in *packaged* services, it is only natural that their software activities take the same course.

In spite of the churning in the software marketplace, the business equations necessary for success are rapidly becoming evident. The leverage to be gained from product as opposed to service has caused most software sources to turn their efforts and resources accordingly. Further, the difficulty in marketing software has dictated the need to specialize in a particular type of software aimed at a specific type of user. This means that those firms specializing in systems software, for example, will not likely be found marketing accounting packages, and vice versa.

SALIENT CHARACTERISTICS

The salient characteristics of software sellers may be noted as follows:

Length of Time in Business As of late 1975, about half the sellers had been in business between 5 and 6 years; all the rest had been in business less than 4 years, with 10 per cent having come into the marketplace within the last year.

Geographic Marketplace All software vendors market nationwide, with rare exceptions.

Marketing Force and Technical Support Only 5 per cent of the software sellers have 12 or more salespeople, and 80 per cent have three or fewer people doing their selling. Brokers, once thought to be a viable route and form for distribution, have fallen by the wayside. And technical support people have a ratio of two-to-one to sales representatives.

Type of Software Sold Sixty per cent of the sellers work with data-based applications; 10 per cent have algorithmic-based applications; 5 per cent deal in database management systems, and the rest deal in systems software and programming aids.

Sales Volume Proprietary software products grossed approximately $20 million in 1969, $45 million in 1970, $110 million in 1971, $220 million in 1972, $355 million in 1973, $525 million in 1974, and $750 million in 1975. Contract programming sold approximately $600 million in 1970, $450 million in 1971, and $400 million in 1972. The noticeable decline in sales volume for contract programming is due on the one hand to fewer sellers being in the marketplace, and on the other to the increasing requirement by the buyer for fixed-fee contracts, with not many software firms being willing to offer them.

POINTERS FOR THE SOFTWARE BUYER

Any firm buying proprietary software will encounter certain potential problem areas which can be minimized if not eliminated with a businesslike approach.

First, it is important to realize that the vast majority of software is licensed for use, rather than sold. The lease/license agreement usually has a term of 3 to 5 years, or is a *lease-in-perpetuity*. The payment terms characteristically require a single payment when the contract is consummated. More and more software firms, however, are offering monthly rental plans of one type or another; these obviously ease the problem of cost justification in the buyer's mind.

Most software products are warranted for the first 6 to 12 months following installation, after which the warranty is followed with an annual maintenance agreement. If the seller does not offer to maintain the product, the buyer has reason for caution. On the other hand, the type of maintenance covered by the agreement must be clearly understood. For example, one must differentiate between the following aspects of maintenance:

- Normal "bug" repair.
- Upgrading of the user's computer configuration.
- Changes in the manufacturer's operating system.
- Modifications in business procedures.
- Changes due to tax or regulatory law.
- Major system enhancements.

Variations in the levels of maintenance offered are dependent on type of product as well as on how long the product has been on the market — and its acceptance in the marketplace. If a software product is new to the market, it will tend to be warranted for a longer period, leased over a longer term, and covered by more aspects of maintenance. All this is due, in most part, to marketing considerations. The converse is true for older, established software.

Again because of the relative newness of the software industry, just about any arrangement is possible with the majority of the 3,000 software products being marketed today. Payment plans can be negotiated; secondary and tertiary marketing agreements can be arranged; support and modification are open to bid. Any and all of these can be potential pitfalls to the buyer.

What is needed by the buyer is a sound, well-planned, structured buying practice. This should be designed as a least-cost approach to the software marketplace, with every opportunity taken for built-in hedging.

Hedging can take many forms. Possibly the most important is devising an acceptance test. This can range from examining other users' experience, through trial use and demonstration, to an elaborate performance of the product against bid specifications. Obviously varying levels of expense are incurred with these methods, and it is necessary to rationalize the cost of acquisition in terms of the total economic impact of that product on the buying firm.

Vendor/Product Selection Most software products have competition in the marketplace — some to a much greater degree than others. For instance, there are more than 80 payroll systems for sale, 30-odd general ledger programs, and two dozen variations of COBOL precompilers, etc. But for any given equipment and language environment, probably no more than a half-dozen programs fit. The buyer must first select those software products that apply. Then, by employing whatever business practices the company normally follows in vendor selection, the buyer can usually narrow the alternative software sources to half the original number.

However, it is important to recognize all the peculiarities of the marketplace mentioned above when evaluating a potential vendor. Size alone is not especially significant; dollar volume can be misleading. Profitability and length of time in business are not as important as the quality and experience of the firm's professional staff — their technical competence and work habits, and their tenacity.

Certainly a most important criterion is the experience of other buyers. No software product or service should ever be contracted for without a thorough analysis of the relationships the software firm has with its clients. To do this, it is necessary to do more than merely ask "binary answer" questions. A questionnaire should be prepared covering the salient points of operation, vendor response to problems, vendor claims, and performance.

Because buying software is so new an activity for most computer users, references on software are easy to get—and the importance of them in the buyer's decision-making process cannot be overestimated.

CURRENT INDUSTRY PROBLEMS

The usual problems that pervade in a young industry are present in the software industry. Additionally, there are several areas that are affected by related and yet separate disciplines. These center around the legal definition of software, the tax treatment of software, and the proper application of accounting principles to the purchase or development of software.

Legally, software products seem to be somewhere between patentable subject matter and something totally intangible and unprotectable. Not only does the industry lack specific legal protection, but the judicial system lacks the knowledge to set proper precedent law at a reasonable cost to the plaintiff.

The question of taxability for software became well focused in 1971 with the proposal by the state of California of a personal property tax on all software, both purchased and developed in-house. At this writing, not only California, but several other states are seeking this new revenue source to offset the difficulty of securing further tax receipts from real estate and other traditional sources. Further complicating the matter is the fact that while almost all states have a sales and/or use tax, some have and some have not extended their definitions to include computer software. Very few states have a clear understanding of what constitutes software and what is or is not included as taxable matter.

Certainly the IRS Ruling 69–21 did not help to clarify the taxability problem, and for that matter, did very little to clarify accounting procedures for software. In consequence, most firms have taken the route of expensing software development and software purchases as well. However, there still are firms that amortize both of these with, again, no discernable pattern. The American Institute of Certified Public Accountants (AICPA), beleaguered by new pressures on its professional status, has not addressed the question, and the software industry suffers as a consequence.

OUTLOOK

All the foregoing notwithstanding, the software industry seems assured of a viable future in the American business scene. United States computer users are spending approximately $8 billion a year on the development of computer software, much of this being obvious duplication and wasted effort. The economy of purchasing specialized and generalized software products and services is ever more evident to user-companies, and the economics of providing them is becoming known to more and more sellers.

What remains to be determined is what the impact of the computer mainframe manufacturers will be on the software firms. IBM should be credited for stimulating the software package industry by unbundling its software. Other manufacturers should take heed: As Martin A. Goetz, president of ADAPSO/SIA remarked as chairman of the Software Industry Panel at the 1973 National Computer Conference, history may prove that IBM's unbundling will result in so much software being developed strictly for IBM computers that a prospective buyer will have to be completely naïve or prejudiced not to buy IBM gear.

Chapter 2

Service Centers

J. L. DREYER

**Executive Vice President, Association of Data Processing
Service Organizations, Inc., Montvale, New Jersey**

Services for payroll preparation, statistical and tabulating, and general bookkeeping—
some extensively equipped with accounting and bookkeeping machines and punched-
card tabulating and sorting equipment—have been available for over 30 years. But it
was not until the early 1960s that the concept of computer data centers began taking
hold, followed in the late 1960s with the newer time-sharing companies[1] which clients
could access directly via terminal equipment on their own premises. In addition, the
age of the computerized "information utility"[2] is now upon us, providing prompt
specialized information on print-out or display terminals of subscribers, upon dialed-in
or keyed-in inquiry.

Data processing computer centers (as distinguished from ticket reservation, hotel
reservation, and other specialized inquiry services) can now bring to small or intermit-
tent users the benefits of large-scale computers. They are also of great advantage to
companies just getting into computer use, because computer processing can be done on
contract, only on those applications where savings will be immediate. Many centers
also provide the programming talent if desired.

Many business managements want the advantages of electronic data processing but
do not wish to become involved in the major investment and personnel problems entailed. It is this gap which the data processing centers, especially those with the
newer time-sharing facilities, fill. In addition, large companies with their own extensive computer systems will often use the service centers for peak loads. And conversely, some companies with large computers of their own will rent out their excess
computer capacity to others, and perhaps perform some data processing services.

One may well ask why a user-company would not rather have its own in-house computer facilities, especially with the advent of minicomputer systems. For the smaller
company the problems associated with an installation may be formidable. First of all,
there is the cost of such equipment—even the simplest system may be in the neighbor-
hood of $10,000 (not including power, supplies, and maintenance). Leasing may run
upward of $500 a month to many thousands of dollars for a small company (again not

---

[1] See Chapter 3, "Time Sharing: An Overview of the Technology and Types of Services," in this
Section.
[2] See Chapter 4, "The Computer Business Utility," in this Section.

accounting for associated costs). Then there is the cost of hiring experienced computer personnel, always in high demand and always scarce.

There are other risks. A company may contract for equipment which is not powerful enough, running into almost immediate obsolescence, or it may find that its installation is not suited to its needs. On the other hand, it may invest in equipment that is unnecessarily powerful, leaving a void of excess computer time. At the same time, most companies do not take full advantage of the computer because they are unaware of the uses to which it can be put in their operations.

A reliable service center makes it possible to avoid these risks, offering highly trained personnel, equipment equal to the job (placing the burden of equipment obsolescence on the center and not the using company), insurance covering loss on destruction of records, service paid for as used, and the opportunity to have electronic data processing without having to provide space for the equipment and associated storage.

For those companies that for a variety of reasons require the physical presence of a computer, a newer element of the business has come into its own in the early 1970s — data *facilities management*. The basic concept of this service is for the service organization to manage the total computer function for the client on an in-house basis for a fee. This includes systems design, program development, personnel selection, and operations.

THE DATA PROCESSING SERVICE-CENTER INDUSTRY

The Association of Data Processing Service Organizations (ADAPSO) estimates that there are some 1,600 data processing organizations in this country and Canada, whose equipment and operations justify the term *service centers*. These figures include centers run as departments or subsidiaries of computer manufacturers, in addition to independent organizations, and count separately each unit in multiple operations. Also included are a few centers with only large-scale punched-card equipment and no electronic computers.

Data centers accept raw data and convert them into input for the computer. The computer correlates and manipulates the data and prepares specified reports and print-outs — financial statements, sales analyses, payroll checks, magazine mailing labels, personalized letters, and the like.

Many data service centers have developed specialties in one or more types of services, as well as industry specialization. For example, some concentrate on payroll and accounting. Some may provide elaborate computerized personnel record keeping and information retrieval — e.g., a company wants to have the names of all employees who speak French, so that it may fill a position in Brussels, and the computer provides the information immediately. Others will offer software services, analyzing a client's data processing and information needs and developing tailormade computer programs. Still others will install transmission terminals in a customer's premises and provide on-line time-shared service to a large-scale computer many miles away, and users can connect with the computer at any time to solve special problems, or to enter queries for specialized types of information in the center's data bank. For real estate people, for example, there is a data bank for instant readings on available property across the country; for merchants, a computerized credit-checking system; for hospitals, GE's Medinet package of data processing services.

Data service centers thus break down broadly into two classes — those specializing in one type of job or customer, as indicated above, and those performing many different data processing jobs. Specialized centers may, for example, serve only brokers or engineers or publishers, or do only payroll or accounts payable, or questionnaires or corporate statistics. Specifically, the range of services includes:

1. *Business services.* Payroll, accounts receivable, order processing, sales analyses, inventory control.

2. *Scientific services.* Engineering, statistics, simulation, numerical-tool tapes, calculation.

3. *Software services.* Custom programming, computer systems design, data conversion, packaged programming, computer systems management.

4. *Information and data-bank services.* Credit ratings, product listings, reserva-

tions, indexing and abstracting, market data, economic analysis, personnel selection, legal searches, and many other types of specialized information.

Batch Processing and On-line Time Sharing   Data service organizations may be further classified according to whether they offer traditional batch processing, the newer on-line time sharing, or both.

Batch Processing.   Batch processing has been described as after-the-fact processing. Data are accumulated, and only at the end of the day, or at some other specified period, are the data fed in proper sequence into the computer, which updates the data previously stored and performs whatever transactions are called for.   Payroll, sales analysis, customer accounting, special mailings, etc. lend themselves to this type of processing.

Time Sharing.   Time sharing is what its name implies—a situation where several clients share time on a single computer.   All medium- and large-scale third-generation electronic computers have time-sharing capabilities, and a data processing center may have a time-sharing computer without necessarily being a time-sharing center.   When applied to the type of service offered by a center, the term means that the clients of the center are *on-line* to the computer, via terminals on the clients' premises connected to the computer by communication lines.

Theoretically, clients have to wait their turn, but because of the time-sharing computer's great speed and the sophistication of its operation, it can perform computations on parts of one user's problems while waiting for another client to key in additional information on a problem, which the computer is working on collaterally.   In effect, the users are getting "simultaneous" service.   To all intents and purposes, the client is the "sole" user and can access the computer at any time.

Clients need not wait for data to have been accumulated, as in the case of batch processing, and they need not wait until the end of a specified period to get the latest updated results.   Data for not-so-vital applications may, however, be saved for non-peak periods, such as night-shift computer operations, and sent all at once.   This is termed *remote batch processing in the time-sharing mode.*

The Industry's Association   The Association of Data Processing Service Organizations, Inc. (ADAPSO), headquartered in Montvale, N.J. was formed in 1961 and represents batch-processing, time-sharing, and software companies in the computer services industry.   It had a roster (in 1975) of 292 member companies, accounting for over 650 data centers in the United States, Canada, and 10 other countries and doing some 45 per cent of the industry's business in the United States.   The association's objectives are defined as follows:

1. To exchange service-center management know-how, to ensure effective and continually improving service to the business community.

2. To develop member appreciation of high performance and ethical standards.

3. To further general acceptance of the service-center concept.

4. To provide mutual assistance in times of individual member-company emergencies.

5. To provide a forum for the discussion of operational and policy problems.

ADAPSO has established a Committee on Ethics and Professionalism and a Committee on Customer Relations.   Customers and the member service companies benefit in terms of effective standards of service evaluation and a greater degree of uniformity in operations.   Four major points in relation to customers are under continuing observation by the committees: (1) clear expression of terms of agreement, and adherence to them; (2) recognition that computer terminology can be confusing to the layperson, and acceptance of responsibility to educate and inform; (3) proper security for clients' documents, records, and programs; and (4) quality performance.

FACTORS IN UTILIZATION

The cost of service-center use will of course vary, depending upon the type and volume of services.   In typical situations, billings may range from as little as $300 a month to as much as $30,000 or more.   In a recent year, IBM's former subsidiary, SBC (Service Bureau Corporation), reported that with centers in 70-odd cities, it was doing work for more than 12,000 scientific and commercial accounts whose billings ranged from as little as $15 a month to as much as $20,000. About half of its regular customers were companies with fewer than 100 employees. Statistical Tabulating Corporation reported that with a dozen data centers across the country, its customers ranged from giant corporations with millions of dollars of computing equipment of their own to "small shops with barely an accounting machine."

It must be remembered that for its fee (depending upon the type of contract entered into) the service center may advise the customer on how a computer may best be used in the customer's operations, set up realistic work goals, and develop special programming. In billing operations, for example, the monthly fee will fluctuate in accordance with the total number of invoice lines. But the expense is offset by the number of employee-hours the client would find necessary if the operations were performed in-house by a manual system. It often takes only one customer employee to prepare all the raw data for the service center—the rest of the job is up to the center.

Most on-line time-sharing users find it profitable to rent their terminal equipment. By doing so, they can hold the cost of a minimal time-sharing service to under $250 a month. The teletypewriter communications unit typically rents for about $100 per month. The telephone company's Dataset runs about $35 a month. A separate telephone line might mean an additional $7 per month. Thus the total for the terminal would come to about $140. To this must be added the minimum charge for use of the computer, which may range from $80 to $100 a month, depending upon the service center, which usually allows 4 hours of computing time for this service charge.

Of course, most users end up spending much more than minimum charges. Normally, customers of a data service center soon find more profitable uses for the computer system than they had considered possible at the start.

Skill Requirements Where completely off-premises services are used, as in batch processing, the customer needs no computer-trained personnel, unless, of course, the company is buying computer time at a center for operation by its own personnel, or is using the center as a supplement to an in-house computer for peak work.

Experience of on-line time-sharing computer centers shows that for typical business operations, an employee can be trained in perhaps 2 days, because it is only a matter of learning how to run the terminal, rather than learning any "computer talk." For sophisticated, problem-solving uses, a time-sharing center beginner[3] can sit down at a terminal and start using it as a tool to solve problems after only three sessions lasting 3 hours each, using a computer language called SUPER BASIC. Centers have reported that clients learn enough BASIC or FORTRAN after attending a 1-day class to enable them to begin writing their own programs.[4]

Of course, the simplicity of operation in an on-line time-sharing business application (as distinguished from use in solving individual problems) is possible only with a well-planned computer program, which the time-sharing center prepares as part of its service. After that, it is simply a matter of putting in new data and entering inquiries —which is why a clerk with no electronic data processing experience can work with so little training.

Liaison Service organizations stress the fact that a computer is not infallible, and that it cannot automatically correct or even catch all sloppy clerical work. The customer company must thus share the responsibility for incorrect results if it is not careful to provide valid input. A person should be designated in the user-company to act as liaison between the company and the center. This person should be responsible for seeing that information is correct and that all editing has been done properly.

ECONOMICS OF USE: SERVICE CENTERS VS. IN-HOUSE COMPUTERS

Use of on-line time sharing for a broad range of data processing (i.e., more than simple inquiry or specialized services) instead of traditional service-center batch processing requires careful economic justification. A powerful, complete time-sharing service can be used to do what a general-purpose computer would do on the premises. However, counting line charges, it can also be expensive. This brings us to the question of cutoff.

[3] Note that here the word *beginner* is applied in terms of computer-language knowledge. The user will, as rule, be a seasoned scientist or engineer or business specialist.

[4] For a discussion of computer languages, see Section 2, Part Four, Chapter 3, "Programming Languages."

Who can actually afford complete on-line time sharing? Who can afford traditional data-center service? Where does the small company fit into the scheme of things?

Not many years ago it was assumed that the computer was exclusively the tool of the largest corporations. Only they, it was felt, could afford to buy or rent these costly machines and hire the skilled personnel necessary to operate them, to say nothing of the administrative and operating expenses involved. Soon, however, manufacturers began to offer small computers (recently, minicomputers), bringing electronic data processing within the reach of medium-sized and small companies. (These low-cost computers, of course, did not have the versatility, speed, and sophistication of the large-scale equipment whose high cost could be justified by sufficient volume to keep them busy.) With packaged programs — a basic set of computer instructions that apply, with little change, to a number of related or similar businesses — these developments have made electronic data processing increasingly feasible for small users.

Complete on-line time-shared service, providing all the outputs obtainable from an on-premises general-purpose computer, is a development still in the future.[5] Under this concept, even a fairly large-scale business would have only a console and certain types of display and print-out terminals on the premises. The time-shared computer at the service center would give the customer all the capabilities and economic advantages of a large-scale computer, without the trouble and expense of developing its own programming and computer operating staffs. The only specialized staffing would be a key liaison executive and one or more systems analysts to aid in the center's development of the required software to suit the company's particular information needs. Code input signals would assure complete privacy of proprietary information stored in the computer. The subscriber would use special *password codes*, so that even within its own organization, only authorized personnel could access the computer for certain types of information.

Such an evolution would sharply raise the cutoff point in terms of size and type of operation at which it would be advantageous for any company to have a computer of its own. The decision would depend on trade-offs between equipment and software costs, speeds, line charges, and the like, taking into account also the less tangible factor of the desirability of complete in-house control over company information. In this connection, an economic factor is that as one goes up the scale in computer systems, doubling the cost of operation normally produces perhaps four times the output, in the equipment rental range about $10,000 per month. Thus a center with many customers can effect large-scale economies with the high pooled volume. The need to stay competitive will then tend to turn the attention of small and medium-sized businesses to the on-line multiple-access centers. Even some of the larger corporations may scrap their in-house computers in favor of a center. Many large companies, of course, are already feeding out overload and peak-period work, and many are using a service organization for specialized jobs or jobs too large or too small for economical performance on their own facilities.

The Small Business   In the light of the various data processing systems available, what criteria does the small-business management use to decide whether to purchase (or rent) equipment, or to use a data center for batch processing, or to make use of an on-line time-sharing service?

A major consideration for the low-volume user is the cost of converting existing files to punched cards and magnetic tapes, in addition to the cost of the computer itself. However, as indicated earlier, manufacturers have been bringing out lower-cost equipment and packaged programs, and newer peripheral equipment has simplified the problem of data input.

For the small business, the most economical setup will still be the traditional type of data service center (i.e., not on-line time sharing) for the bulk of its total data processing on the center's computer, doing other work with conventional (but now some of it quite sophisticated) accounting machines. Under such circumstances, the low-volume user buys computer service as needed and pays only for what is used. The input of data to the center is usually simple and relatively inexpensive.

[5] See the discussion of the "phantom computer" in the chapter on data processing service centers in Carl Heyel, *Computers, Office Machines, and the New Information Technology,* prepared for Business Equipment Manufacturers Association, Macmillan, New York, 1969.

Applications No matter what the size of the using company, it is important to know what to ask for in a conventional data center or time-sharing operation. The service representative knows the capabilities and limitations of the equipment, and is familiar enough with most types of businesses to help the customer save time and money. He or she may recommend a packaged program, or if the company's needs are more specialized, he or she can help it develop completely new software for its particular needs.

An actual checklist of what to ask for in each type of business would be of little value, for needs vary too widely. One small company may need services equal to those required by a medium-sized one. However, it is important to know some of the options available to the prospective client.

For example, almost any business, large or small, can benefit from more efficient accounts receivable and accounts payable operations. These are in fact the two most popular data-center services. Reduction of losses on accounts that will not pay up is possible with an aged accounts receivable procedure, providing clients with monthly comparisons as a guide so that they may look at their receivables from one month to the next and make necessary judgments as to follow-up.

Sales analysis is also well suited for computerization and handling by a data service center. Statistical analyses of market surveys have long been a staple service of punched-card data centers. Computerized centers now have added speed and versatility capabilities for such work.

With the enlarged capabilities of modern time-sharing computers (not necessarily connected to the client on-line), the service center can now be of greater value in (1) general office procedures such as payroll, order writing, and billing; (2) sales costing and sales analysis; (3) inventory control from raw materials to parts and finished product; and (4) production control and scheduling.

In connection with payroll, for example, a service organization can prepare the payroll on the computer, and at the same time assemble information on labor distribution for management analysis and perhaps for special Government reports where progress payments are involved. A service center can set up a vendor file that will keep track of items received, defective stock returned, and items removed for processing. The program can be made to include safety points to indicate when reorders are necessary, and the papers for replenishment can be prepared automatically.

Where control is critical — for example, in certain types of raw-materials control — updating and reporting can be arranged for as frequently as necessary: several times a week, daily, or on spot request. As far as equipment and communications capability are concerned, such information could actually be made available immediately (on-line, real time), giving the status of any item as of any time a query is keyed in. Under present circumstances this would be costly and is usually unnecessary. However, material-control services are in operation where a raw-material count is updated twice a day, with print-outs issued showing where the critical levels are and what is to be ordered, and alerting the purchasing agent responsible for the particular raw material involved.

Production control systems can be developed to keep close track of parts and components, and to provide analyses of scrap and rework. Controls can be provided to make sure the product is not coming out with components whose specifications have been modified, and reports can be prepared on direct-production time, overhead allocations, material costs and efficiency of use, and the like to aid in margin-of-profit analysis and pricing decisions.

SERVICE-CENTER SELECTION

The Yellow Pages in cities of significant size will provide a listing for data service-center organizations. And ADAPSO issues an annual directory of service centers. A specialized organization, if available for the application in question, will often provide better service and be more economical than a general-purpose center, since it will probably have proprietary software packages suited to the particular client need.

An initial free consultation is generally offered, explaining the service firm's experience with businesses similar to that of the prospective client. At that time, an estimate of cost can be obtained. However, the decision should not be made on the basis of cost alone. The pertinence of claims should be weighed against the class of service needed. Considered should be service factors such as speed of response, format of reports, number of relevant packaged programs available, and record of meeting cost and time estimates. Ask for references to clients with problems similar to yours. Find out about protection of data and files, and procedures for safeguarding programs and equipment to ensure continuity of processing.

After selecting an outside data service organization, get a written contract to avoid future misunderstandings. Be sure the following points are covered.

Cost of Services You may be billed by the complete job, by unit price, by machine time, or by monthly contract. Be sure to understand the terms, including which services cost extra.

Description of Services It is important to be aware of the format and contents of the reports and the method of preparing data and transporting them to the service organization.

Schedules How and when will reports come back to you? Do you need monthly or daily statements? Be sure to make a provision if either party fails to meet the schedule.

Ownership of Software Input and Storage This can be a sore spot if the program is designed jointly by the customer and the service organization. It must be agreed who owns the software. It is important that you establish that you own cards, tapes, disks, or other storage media, and the information they contain. This will prove valuable should you decide to terminate the agreement with the service organization.

Insurance Coverage Be sure to make provisions to protect data from fire or other disasters while on service-center premises, and determine whose insurance will cover all losses and data reconstruction costs.

Term of Agreement One-year, or even five-year, contracts may be expected for the sale or leasing of packaged programs. Overly long contracts may be unwise because of industry growth. It is always smart to include a cancellation clause in the event that either party should want to terminate the contract.

Liaison When you have signed a contract with a service center, it is wise to name someone in your company as a liaison; this way, whatever problems develop can be handled by that employee. The service center should do the same. A clearly defined line of responsibility makes for smoother work flow.

Use of Standard Formats When discussing a program with the service center, you will usually have a choice between standard formats already in use at the center or a specialized format suited to fit your particular needs. For economy, time, and accuracy, you are better off taking the standard programs, if you can. The programs represent tried and true formulas which the center knows how to operate with facility.

Specialized Formats These require specialized software, which requires specialized prices. It is important to agree in writing with the center that you are the owner of all programs designed for you, and that you will receive a credit or a refund if the center should use the software for other customers. Also be sure of what you are paying for—just what is included as part of the service and what are the special extras.

Procedural Steps Set up procedural steps for control totals. In sales processing, for example, this may mean running tapes from adding machines, but that is better than handing in a pile of invoices to your center and expecting it to punch cards and come up with an accurate report. A tape on every batch gives the center a balancing figure.

Chapter 3

Time Sharing: An Overview of the Technology and Types of Services[1]

ALDEN HEINTZ

Vice President, Corporate Development, Tymshare, Inc., Cupertino, California

This Chapter deals primarily with general-purpose time sharing, or, more specifically, with time-sharing services offered by commercial firms to a number of user-organizations. This is as opposed to special-purpose systems such as airline reservation systems, which involve the application of time-sharing technology to a single specific application. However, the technological and functional descriptions developed apply in general to special-purpose as well as general-purpose systems.

TIME SHARING DEFINED

Time sharing is a term used to describe a method of computer access and use which is both conceptually and technologically different from other computing environments, such as local batch or remote batch processing. Time sharing differs conceptually by presenting a unique philosophy of how to access and use a computer. It differs technologically as a result of the enhancements required for implementation of its unique computing philosophy.

A definition of time sharing, while potentially controversial, can best be developed by describing the functional characteristics which typify such systems. The literal interpretation of time sharing is, quite simply, the sharing of computer resources by multiple concurrent jobs. However, most local and remote batch-processing systems perform such sharing to some degree, and one must go beyond this definition to identify time-sharing systems uniquely.

A second characteristic of time sharing is that its users are physically removed from the computer and from each other. The geographic separation may involve only a few miles or several thousand miles, and may even be intercontinental. This characteristic alone, however, is insufficient, since remote access is available in remote batch-processing systems.

[1] The author wishes to acknowledge the assistance of Ronald A. Bamberg, Manager of Business Planning and Analysis, Tymshare, Inc.

The most definitive and the unique characteristic of time sharing is the manner in which the person–machine interface is effected. Time sharing provides a direct interaction between the user and the computer, with the computer reacting to user inputs in a near-instantaneous time frame. This rapid interaction can exist when there are 10, 20, or even 100 concurrent users. As a result of the person–machine dialogue, each user has the distinct impression that he or she alone is using the computer. In short, there exists a symbiotic relationship between a user and a distant computer.

If the three general characteristics given above are combined, one might define time sharing as follows: *Time sharing is a computing mode or environment whereby multiple simultaneous users share the resources of the computer from remote locations, each user having a direct interaction or dialogue with the machine.*

ADVANTAGES OF TIME SHARING

One of the long-standing problems in computer use has been that the interaction between person and machine has been more nearly at the machine level. That is, the user has been forced to communicate with the computer in terms which are not fully natural to people. Time sharing effectively moves the person–machine interface closer to the user, and in so doing, makes the computer available to a broader spectrum of people.

A second advantage is convenience of computer access. An individual can access and use the computer anywhere a standard telephone is available, whether at his or her own desk or even at home. The user also has access to the computer on an *as-needed* rather than *as-available* basis. In fact, the two become synonomous. There are no human intermediaries between the user and the computer, and the time-sharing computer can handle many simultaneous users.

A fourth advantage is that the user pays for only the amount of system resources used, rather than paying a fixed rental fee. There is little, if any, initial outlay, and no long-term financial commitment. This is extremely important for smaller organizations.

Finally, any technological advancements or system enhancements developed by a time-sharing service bureau are immediately available to the user. That is, the costs of research and development for the service are borne by the time-sharing firm and are spread across all its customers.

TECHNOLOGICAL REQUIREMENTS

The computer system itself requires hardware and software enhancements for time sharing, and special telecommunications capabilities are needed to satisfy the remote-access criterion.

Computer System Requirements While there are specific hardware/software requirements in time sharing, it is perhaps more meaningful to evaluate functions which are necessary in the hardware/"system software" subsystem. *System* software is used in this discussion as opposed to *user* software, which is covered later. Certain major computer system functions will now be discussed.

Memory Management. An extremely important system function involves the allocation of main memory to user jobs or, more specifically, the use of multiprogramming. This simply means that multiple concurrent jobs may reside in main memory as long as sufficient space exists. The central processing unit may operate on any job in main memory, and can move from job to job as the need exists. Limited multiprogramming capabilities also exist on most batch and remote batch systems, but typically they work on the principle that any given job remains in memory until it is completed. Only then can another job be moved into memory for processing. If sufficient space is freed by the completed job, then multiple new jobs can be brought into memory. This improves the overall efficiency of the system since a job can be moved into memory at the same time the central processor is operating on another job.

The normal approach to multiprogramming is not sufficient for time sharing, however, because of the need to provide very quick response to all jobs, not just those in main memory. Generally, it is not possible for all current jobs to reside in memory at once. Hence, time sharing requires an expansion of the multiprogramming concept, essentially one which ensures that every job has a periodic and frequent opportunity to use the central processor if the need exists.

Since every job must be in memory periodically for execution by the central processor, and since it is usually not possible for all jobs to be in memory at the same time, there must be a method for moving jobs in and out of memory. This is called *swapping*. Current jobs not in memory are stored on a device which provides extremely fast access, typically a magnetic drum. This device allows swapping to take place at the same time the central processor operates on a job in main memory.

When the central processor begins execution of a job, it continues to operate on that job for a maximum length of time referred to as a *time slice*, or *quantum*. The job has control of the processor until that maximum time elapses, until the job is completed, or until the job requests a function not requiring the central processor, such as input or output. As soon as one of these events occur, several things happen:

1. The central processor immediately begins operating on another job in main memory if there is a job that requires processing.

2. The previous job is swapped to the high-speed storage device.

3. A job on the storage device is swapped into memory to occupy the space vacated by the previous job.

Only through such a scheme can time sharing provide near-instantaneous response, and one should realize that the maximum length of time any job can hold the processor must be very short if there are other jobs which require the central processor.

Memory Protection. When a job is swapped from memory to the high-speed storage device, it may or may not require further processing. If it does, then the system must swap not only the program, but the current values of all data items. In addition, there must be an indication of the job status when swapped and the point at which execution is to be restarted. When the job is returned to memory, the central processor must be able to begin execution at the exact point where previous processing terminated.

In most time-sharing systems, it is not necessary for a job to occupy the same portion of memory every time it is swapped in. That is, the job is relocatable. This means that the system must have an indirect addressing scheme so that the most effective use of memory can be made.

Job Priority. Since at any point in time there may be several jobs in memory ready for the central processor, and several other jobs on the storage device ready to be swapped into memory, the system must have a means for establishing priorities. For example, of several jobs in memory ready for processing, the central processor may be assigned to the one which has had the longest wait. Of the jobs on the storage device, the system may consider only those which are ready for the processor as candidates for swapping.

A number of priority algorithms have been used in time sharing. However, many time-sharing services have combined features of several algorithms to arrive at one unique to their system. The selection of algorithms for processor assignment and swapping and of the maximum time slice is largely dependent on the expected mix of job requirements. For example, memory management for a special-purpose system is much simpler than for a general-purpose system, since job characteristics of the former are known in advance of system design.

Files and File Protection. It must be possible for the time-sharing user to save data and program files temporarily or permanently, and to gain access to them quickly and without human intervention. Magnetic disks are most often used for this purpose. Since there may be hundreds of potential users of a time-sharing system, there must be a means for segregating the files belonging to each user. This could be done by allocating some portion of the disk for each user, then writing each new file in that allotted space. However, this prohibits effective utilization of the disk, since some users would use only a fraction of their allocation while others would exceed their allotted space.

A more efficient approach involves the maintenance of a *directory* or *dictionary* for each user, containing the disk address of each file. In this way, any available space on the disk can be used by any user, even if the space is not contiguous with the user's other files. When a user wishes to access one of the files, the system need only locate the file address from the user's dictionary. Of course, the system must always maintain a *map* of the disk in order to allocate space when a new file is to be written.

The users of a time-sharing service generally represent different organizations; thus, it is imperative that the system protect files from access by unauthorized users. The highest-level restriction usually imposed is that only the *owner* of a file can access it unless it is specifically declared as *public*. Most systems provide more detailed levels of control, with the user having the ability to specify that data may only be appended to the file, or that a program may be run by other users but not copied.

The ultimate degree of file security is the ability to cipher or scramble a file. Essentially, this means that the file is broken into meaningless bits and pieces and scattered throughout the disk. Prior to the file being scrambled, the user supplies a password which serves as the key to file reconstruction and use. When the file is to be used, the password is given, and only then can the data be reconstructed and made available. Even if another user gains access to the file, it is of no use unless the associated password is known.

Access Security.[2] It is absolutely necessary that a time-sharing system be able effectively to control who can gain access to it. Not only must a user have confidence that he or she alone can get access to his or her files, but the user must also be sure that no one else can use computer resources for which he or she will be charged. Such matters make obvious the need for access control.

Most time-sharing services require two distinct but related pieces of information before a user can be connected to the computer. The first is some kind of *user identification* which is required for accounting purposes. The second is a *password* associated with the user identification. Only when these two items are entered in combination can one successfully "log on" to a time-sharing system. Knowledge of one without the other is of absolutely no value. For accounting purposes, the user identification is unique and usually cannot be changed by users themselves. However, on many services, users may change their passwords as often as they choose.

System Reliability. While we have said that a time-sharing system is available at all times, this statement should be tempered somewhat, since a service may not operate 24 hours a day, 7 days a week. However, planned operations may cover the greatest percentage of time anyone might want to use the system. Hence, the computer should be available at any time during the stated hours of operation.

While the internal reliability of computers has improved dramatically over the years, there will inevitably be times when the machine is inoperable. This can have a drastic impact on the time-sharing service, since the work of hundreds of organizations may be affected. For this reason, time-sharing firms make a concerted effort to ensure maximum reliability. For example, there may be a backup power supply in the event of a power outage. There may be redundant central processors, one or more of which may be able to take over the load of one that fails. Spare peripheral devices may be available if another one becomes unusable.

Most time-sharing services periodically copy the entire contents of their disk units to other disks or magnetic tapes. In this way, even if disk contents are completely destroyed, recent files can be recovered.

Telecommunication Requirements   Since the distance between the time-sharing user and the computer may be quite extensive, and since person–machine dialogue must occur on a near-instantaneous basis, the telecommunications system must be widespread and capable of transmitting data reliably at high speeds.

Because of general availability, widespread coverage, and relatively low cost, the standard telephone system has most often been used as the telecommunications medium in time sharing. Attempts are being made to develop specialized data transmission networks, but it appears that the telephone system will continue to be of greatest use in time-sharing telecommunications through the decade of the 1970s.

Figure 3-1 illustrates a general structure for time-sharing telecommunications, although the configuration used by a specific time-sharing service may be more complex or less complex. In any case, the components shown in this schematic are those typically required for the completion of telecommunications functions.

User Terminals. To send data to and receive and display data from the computer, the time-sharing user must have some kind of terminal. A multitude of low-cost data terminals are available, the differences occurring in how certain functional requirements are handled.

First, the terminal must have some method of transmitting data to the computer. Most terminals have a keyboard which closely resembles a standard typewriter keyboard. There are certain special-function keys which are required for data transmis-

---

[2] See also Section 8, Chapter 4, "The Computer and Privacy."

sion, and there may be a special 10-key "scratch pad" for the entry of numeric data. Terminals often provide for optional additional methods for input, such as paper tape, magnetic-tape cassettes, or punched cards.

Second, the terminal must have some way for displaying data transmitted from the computer. There are three common mechanisms for accomplishing this function:

1. Impact printing, where a mechanical action causes an image to be printed on paper. This is similar to the action of a standard typewriter.

2. Thermal printing, where heat is generated on heat-sensitive paper to create an image.

3. Graphic display, where a cathode-ray tube or similar device produces a televisionlike image on a screen.

In addition to displaying data received from the computer, the terminal output mechanism also displays data entered through the terminal input mechanism. The terminal may have an optional output device such as a paper-tape punch, a magnetic-tape cassette writer, or a card punch.

A third terminal characteristic involves the speed at which data can be transmitted

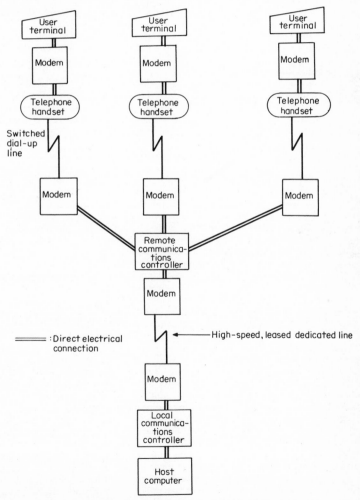

Fig. 3-1   General structure for time-sharing telecommunications.

or received. Most time-sharing terminals operate at speeds ranging from 10 to 30 characters per second, with a greater tendency toward the higher speeds. Some terminals can operate at 60 or 120 characters per second, but these are not yet commonplace for technical and economic reasons.

A fourth, but less significant, terminal characteristic is related to the data coding structure used. While several codes are in use, there is an increasing tendency toward the use of standardized codes. The most widely used code is the American Standard Code for Information Interchange (ASCII).

The development of time-sharing terminals has, in large part, been controlled on economic grounds. Because time sharing is intended for widespread use, it is necessary that terminal costs remain quite low. Cost is largely a function of speed, size, type of output mechanism, and optional input-output devices. There will be a growing tendency toward higher-speed terminals as it becomes possible to provide these at lower cost. Time sharing is also likely to feel an even greater impact from so-called intelligent terminals, devices which allow stand-alone use in addition to use in a time-sharing environment.

Modems. At several places on the telecommunications schematic (Figure 3-1), there are components labeled as *modems*, a name given to modulation-demodulation devices. These are required to interface digital devices, such as terminals, communiation controllers, and computers, with the telephone system, which carries analog signals. When the modem receives a digital input, it produces an analog output; when an analog signal is received, it is converted to a digital output. The fact that the telephone system is analog is one of the overriding reasons for attempts to develop fully digital communications systems.

Different types of modems are required in the time-sharing telecommunications system, depending on the speed at which it must receive and send signals. The modem connected to the user terminal must also be able to perform an acoustical-to-electronic (or electronic-to-acoustical) conversion, since the telephone handset is basically an acoustical device. Hence, the name *acoustical coupler* is often applied to the modem which connects to the terminal.

It should be remembered that some type of modulation-demodulation device is required at every point where a digital device must interface with the telephone system.

Communication Controller. Communication controller is a name used here for a device which may alternately be called a *communications processor, concentrator,* or *multiplexer.* The name used, in large part, depends on the complexity of the functions performed by the device. The most basic function required of the controller is that of *multiplexing.* This is a two-fold function consisting of (1) accepting messages from multiple sources and constructing a single output stream, and (2) receiving a single input stream and constructing multiple output messages.

At any point in time, the remote communication controller may have current dialogues with many user terminals. On the one hand, it is receiving messages from those terminals and must construct a single message stream directed to the computer, such stream containing messages or inputs from multiple terminals. On the other hand, it is receiving a single message stream from the computer and must construct individual messages to be directed to the appropriate user terminals. This implies that the controller must be able to determine the source and destination of each user message, even when it is interspersed with messages from other users.

The role of the local communication controller is similar in that it must (1) accept message streams from multiple remote controllers and construct a single stream for use by the computer, and (2) accept a message stream from the computer and construct individual messages for individual remote controllers. The problems of message identification are essentially the same as for the remote controller.

Increasingly, communication controllers are used for functions beyond simple multiplexing. One of the more important of these may involve the implementation of an error-detection and retransmission system. Since there may be noise on a telephone line which impairs the transmission accuracy, it is helpful to have a means for ensuring data validity. This tendency toward error increases as the distance of transmission increases. In some time-sharing systems, the remote and local communication processors interact in such a way as to detect transmission errors and retransmit any data altered as a result of faulty transmission. This virtually ensures that invalid transmission cannot take place between these devices.

Increased sophistication in communication controllers has tended to make them an ever more important part of the time-sharing telecommunications system. Multiplexing alone is an important and necessary function, but more and more the communication controllers take on responsibilities formerly held by the host computer, allowing the latter to concentrate on functions for which it is more directly suited.

Communication Lines. The point has been made that the standard telephone system most often satisfies the telecommunications requirements of time sharing. No doubt it will continue to play an integral role in such systems even as specialized data networks are developed. It is important for time sharing that a user has access to the computer wherever there is a standard telephone.

In general, time sharing makes use of two types of telephone lines when connecting the user terminal to the host computer. The link between the terminal and the remote communication controller is made through a switched line on a dial-up basis. The line may be strictly local, a "Foreign Exchange" line, or an incoming WATS line, depending on the location of the controller relative to the terminal. A high-speed, dedicated line provides the link between the remote and the local controller. Typically, these lines are specially conditioned for data transmission, and operate at speeds ranging from 2,400 baud to 9,600 baud. The baud rate represents the number of bits per second which can be carried along a line.

Another line characteristic important in a time-sharing environment is the manner in which two-way transmission is handled, particularly in the link between the terminal and the remote controller. Some systems use half-duplex lines, meaning that data may be transmitted in either direction, but in only one direction at any point in time. Full-duplex lines allow transmission in both directions simultaneously. This implies that the user terminal may be sending and receiving data at precisely the same time. When full-duplex lines are used, depression of a terminal key does not result in a character being printed or displayed on impact. Rather, the communication controller "echoes" the character back to the terminal for display, and simultaneously sends it to the host computer for processing. However, this echo occurs so rapidly that typically the user is not aware that such a scheme is in force.

The use of full-duplex lines affords several distinct advantages in a time-sharing environment. First, the user may enter data from the terminal at the same time data from the computer are being printed or displayed. If input is taking place simultaneously with output, the echo of input characters back to the terminal is deferred until all available output has been displayed. The input data are then displayed. Second, since an input signal is echoed from the remote controller, the user can observe the character received by the controller. If an error in transmission occurs between the terminal and the remote communication controller, it is known immediately and can be corrected.

Communication Security and Reliability. The value of a time-sharing service to a user can hardly be greater than the accuracy with which data are transmitted and received. Incorrect data produce spurious results which may be of great cost to the user, and, for this reason, time-sharing firms have exerted great efforts to ensure optimum reliability in data transmission. As mentioned, some time-sharing systems have implemented error detection and retransmission to ensure data validity between the remote and local communication controllers.

Another aspect of reliability involves the availability of the telecommunication facility. When a user cannot access the time-sharing system as a result of communications problems, the consequences are as great as when the host computer is inoperable. This situation would rarely occur with the local, switched line, but might with the long-distance dedicated line. To alleviate problems of this kind, some time-sharing services have developed a capability for alternate communications routing. It would be possible to accomplish this by having a redundant dedicated line between the remote and local communication controllers. However, the distance between the two devices may be quite great, and the cost of the redundant line might be excessive. In this case, a line between two remote controllers (the distance between which is less than the distance between the remote and local controllers) could allow data from one to "pass through" the other, thus, sharing a single line to the local controller.

Security in data transmission is an obvious necessity, just as is security in system and file access. Data intended for one user must reach that user alone. Users would simply not use a time-sharing service if they felt that certain of their data were being received by other users.

USER SOFTWARE

The time-sharing system discussed thus far is, essentially, a vehicle through which a product can be delivered to a customer. Nothing has been said about that deliverable product or, more specifically, about how the user directs the time-sharing computer to do something.

The user of a time-sharing system, like the user of any computer system, can establish a workable relationship only through a *language* or protocol understood by the computer. This interaction is accomplished through *user* software as opposed to the *system* software required in conjunction with hardware.

User software in time sharing can be classified in three categories: languages, general-purpose application programs, and special-purpose application programs. With computer languages, the user specifies the operations the machine is to perform, limited only by the user's own imagination and skill and the functional capabilities of the language. Application programs are prewritten instructions (in a language) to which the user need only supply input data.

Languages[3] While the structure and content of time-sharing languages are much the same as in local and remote batch processing, they are usually implemented in a way which takes advantage of the time-sharing environment. Most time-sharing services offer several languages, the most popular of which are BASIC and FORTRAN. The former was designed specifically for time-sharing use, is easy to learn and use, and is popular as a "first" language for time-sharing users. Many versions of the language are available, with features beyond the scope of the originally implemented version. One typically finds different versions of BASIC from company to company, as there has been little attempt at standardization.

FORTRAN has been and is a popular time-sharing language, partly as a result of its historical acceptance in the computer industry. The language has been standardized to some degree, even though time-sharing companies have often enhanced it to take advantage of the time-sharing environment. There is little reason to doubt that FORTRAN will continue to receive widespread usage among time-sharing users.

Other languages sometimes found on time-sharing systems include COBOL, ALGOL, PL/I, APL, and SNOBOL. Some time-sharing firms have developed new languages, and certain general-purpose application programs *might* be construed as languages. However, there is no evidence that any of these have approached the general acceptance or use of FORTRAN or BASIC.

Because of the interactive environment of time sharing, and since many time-sharing users are not computer professionals, time-sharing languages are frequently implemented quite differently from their local or remote batch counterparts. Broad new vistas of computer assistance in program development are opened as a result of the person–machine interactive dialogue. One technique which has received considerable attention is that of *incremental compilation*. In this mode, each program statement is checked syntactically as it is entered. If the statement has no syntax errors (i.e., errors in statement form or unrecognized key words), it is accepted by the computer; if such errors exist, the machine immediately informs the user of the errors and allows the user to re-enter the statement. This ensures that when a program has been completely entered, it will be syntactically correct, since only correct statements will have been accepted by the computer.

Another capability opened by time sharing is *stop-and-go* execution. This means, simply, that the user may interrupt execution at various places in the program. Upon such interruption, the user may inquire as to the current value of variables or array elements, change certain values, or even change program statements. Execution may then be restarted at the beginning of the program or at the point where execution was interrupted.

One can reasonably expect further advancements in computer-assisted program de-

[3] See also Section 2, Part Four, Chapter 3, "Programming Languages."

velopment. More and more, time-sharing systems will improve their ability to analyze user programming heuristically. If certain errors are made relatively often, the computer will make the user aware of that fact and offer suggestions as to how the problem might be overcome. This concept will be expanded to include an analysis of program logic prior to execution, rather than waiting for the errors to occur during execution.

While such programming aids can be invaluable during program development, they tend to lessen the efficiency of execution. As a result, time-sharing firms are likely to provide two modes in which a given language can be used: one in which, during program development, full advantage will be taken of the interactive mode; and another in which a special run-time mode will enable optimum efficiency in execution once the program is debugged.

There is little doubt that program development can be accomplished more quickly and easily in time sharing than in other environments. The interactive dialogue permits the development of user aids which simply cannot be duplicated by local or remote batch-processing systems.

General-Purpose Application Programs The point was made that the functional characteristics of time sharing permit computer usage by a broad audience, many of whom have little if any computer experience. The development of prewritten programs which satisfy a common need or solve a common problem has been, perhaps, of equal importance in expanding computer use. A user need only supply inputs which define his or her particular situation, allowing the user to utilize the computer without writing a single program of his or her own. Most time-sharing firms have extensive libraries of such programs available to any user.

One group of such application programs are general purpose; that is, their use is essentially independent of the functional area of application. These might more accurately be called *utility programs*. One might include in this category programs designed for sorting, merging, and updating data files; programs for information retrieval and inquiry, report generators, and generalized modeling systems; programs for general statistical analysis; and so on. These programs are of value not only to the unsophisticated user, but to programming professionals as well, since the functions performed typically require a significant programming effort.

Special-Purpose Application Programs The second category of time-sharing application programs is those intended to solve specific, well-defined problems. Numerous such programs exist for use in management, finance, accounting, statistics, operations research, manufacturing, engineering, mathematics, electronics, and basic science. One problem with such programs is that they may not totally meet the needs of a given user with a specific problem. That is, the user may be required to restate the problem in terms necessary for the program. Nonetheless, these special-purpose programs can often obviate the need for extensive user programming and can be of great value to the time-sharing user.

THE TIME-SHARING USER

Frequent mention has been made of the "user" in this discussion without having attempted to describe that user. Descriptions of the time-sharing user may be made on the basis of:

1. Level of computer knowledge or experience.
2. Job function.
3. Size or complexity of the organization which employs him or her.
4. Industry to which his or her company belongs.

User Knowledge or Experience Time sharing has effectively dispelled the mystery and fear surrounding computers by moving the person–machine interface closer to the user level. It has provided an environment whereby inexperienced individuals can take full advantage of the power and capability of the machine. The number of people having at least nominal programming skills has increased dramatically as a result of the ease of use and common availability of time sharing. Countless others have improved their job effectiveness through the use of time-sharing application programs. The required technical skill level of the computer user has been reduced significantly without decreasing the machine capability, and without insulting the intelligence of the more sophisticated user.

User Job Function In its earlier days, time sharing was intended primarily for the scientific user—the engineer, mathematician, statistician, or scientist—to make the computer readily available to a group which was already familiar with it and its language. However, it soon became apparent that time sharing could be extended beyond the originally intended user-group, making the computer available for business as well as scientific analysis and application. Today, time sharing is effectively used throughout organizations, from top management to production lines, and most time-sharing firms state that a majority of their usage comes from traditionally business areas.

Company Size While it was observed that time sharing allows smaller organizations to use a computer without any significant financial commitments, it should not be assumed that the use of time sharing is restricted to organizations which cannot afford their own computer. Indeed, the greatest number of time-sharing users are found in companies which *do* have their own machines, some of which have immense computing capabilities. This is because the features of time-sharing services are desirable regardless of the extent to which local or remote batch processing are available internally.

This is not to say that time sharing can or should replace internal computer systems; local or remote batch processing is far better than time sharing in certain application areas. Time sharing is *complementary* to other computing modes, rather than only *supplementary*. As this awareness is achieved, it will be possible for diverse computing environments to coexist successfully, allowing use of the mode best suited for a given application.

Industry Just as time sharing knows no functional bounds, so does it transcend industries. It is used in practically every imaginable setting, encompassing both public and private organizations.

SELECTION OF A TIME-SHARING SERVICE

There are a great many time-sharing firms in business today, so that the question of how to go about selecting a particular service is pertinent. At the outset, one must be aware that there *are* differences in time-sharing services, some qualitative and some quantitative. In general, one can infer that as capability and quality increase, so does cost.

Many time-sharing users obtain service from several vendors, primarily because there are strong points and weak points in any time-sharing firm. If a user has diverse needs, he or she may find that one system cannot effectively satisfy all of them. However, there are overriding reasons in favor of using a single time-sharing service. The importance of any given selection criterion varies from situation to situation, and a potential time-sharing customer must determine what factors should receive highest priority. Much of this decision-making process relies on the intended applications and the level of user sophistication and experience.

Pricing Structure Most time-sharing firms base the cost of their service on three pricing elements:

1. Connect time: The length of time the user is connected to the computer regardless of what he or she is doing.
2. Processing units: A measure of the computer resources utilized.
3. Disk storage: The amount of disk space occupied by the user's program and data files.

It is sometimes dangerous to evaluate potential costs simply on the basis of stated prices, since one is really concerned with how much can be accomplished in one *unit*. This is particularly true with processing units because different computers produce varying amounts of "work" in a unit. In addition, one should be aware of what computer resources are included in calculating the number of processing units. Often, the term *cpu seconds* is used instead of processing units, the inference being that one processing unit is exactly equivalent to one second of central processor time. Increasingly, however, time-sharing firms include system resources in addition to the central processor in defining a processing unit. The number of disk accesses, main memory used, and the total number of characters swapped are typical candidates for inclusion in the algorithm for processing units.

Connect time is a straightforward component and is usually balanced in some way against the price for processing units. One should evaluate the cost of connect time relative to the types of applications for which the system is to be used. If an application requires a significant amount of computer connection but relatively insignificant processing, one would prefer a low connect charge, even if the cost of processing were high.

On some systems there is a separate charge for terminal input and output, and on others this charge may be included in the processing unit. There may be several pricing options which balance the input-output charge against the connect time charge, and the selection of an option should depend on the relationship between connect time and terminal input-output requirements.

There are several considerations in evaluating the cost for disk storage. The first of these concerns the method by which storage is measured and includes the following possibilities:

1. Storage is measured once each day, usually at night. The user is charged on the basis of the highest of these daily measurements.

2. Storage is measured once per day, but the user is charged on the basis of average daily measurements.

3. Storage is measured periodically throughout the day, perhaps on a near-continuous basis. The user is then charged either by a monthly peak, by an average of daily peaks, or by the integral (area under) the storage-utilization curve.

When storage is measured once per day, it is usually done at night; hence, a user may create temporary files of any size during the day and not be charged for them, provided they are deleted before the storage measurement is taken.

A second storage consideration concerns the *block* size used. This is the minimum number of characters which can be stored. The disk is essentially divided into many of these blocks whose size may range from a few hundred characters to several thousand. A given file might require a large number of blocks, and if any portion of a block is used, the user is charged as if the entire block were used. When the block size is large, there can be a considerable amount of unused storage for which the user is charged.

Of course, the user must have a terminal to use the time-sharing system; this represents an expense above and beyond computer costs. The choice of a terminal, with regard to speed, size, display mechanism, and optional input-output devices, depends on the types of applications to be developed. The time-sharing firm can assist in determining the terminals best suited for the user's applications. The terminal can then be purchased or leased from the time-sharing firm, a terminal marketing organization, or directly from the manufacturer.

Telecommunications The potential time-sharing customer should ensure that he or she has access to a service without placing long-distance calls. This should be possible except in certain lightly populated areas, and even then there should be some services which provide coverage by Foreign Exchange or in-WATS lines. If the customer has multiple offices which will use the service, he or she should determine the ability of the time-sharing firm to provide access without long-distance calls.

The potential user should determine whether desired terminal speeds can be handled, and whether there is any surcharge for higher-speed transmission. The ability of the system to detect and retransmit errors should be ascertained, particularly when data must be transmitted for a significant distance. If full-duplex transmission is desired, one should determine if a system provides for it.

Customer Support The ability to use the computer effectively often depends on the extent to which the time-sharing firm provides training and ongoing support. This need may have an inverse relationship to the skill level and experience of the user, but even the most skilled user typically requires some assistance.

On-going customer support should include both on-site visits and telephone assistance, and should be provided at no additional cost to the customer. The user should understand that the time-sharing firm does not provide extensive free programming, but only assists in the solution of problems. Some time-sharing firms can provide contract programming and/or systems analysis for a fee.

Documentation Closely related to customer support are the availability and quality of system and software documentation. High-quality documentation can alleviate the need for a certain amount of personal support. One should determine what initial documentation is provided at no cost, and the time-sharing firm's policy regarding additional documentation and its cost.

Software Software is of extreme importance in evaluating a time-sharing service, since that represents the ultimate product to be delivered to the user. The evaluation of software is typically difficult, since so many of the considerations are qualitative in nature. One must first determine that the service provides the languages with which the users are familiar or which the customer wishes to use. For each language, one should determine the maximum number of statements, the maximum memory size available for programs and data, special editing and debugging features, and any special or nonstandard syntactical features. These items can then be weighed relative to user skill level, application types, and, of course, the costs of program creation and execution.

Available application programs should be viewed quite closely, particularly when the customer does not anticipate a significant amount of internal programming. Even when users will be writing many programs, one should look for a text editor, data management utilities, report generators, and any special-purpose software suited to the customer's needs.

Auxiliary Services In some cases, the time-sharing user may have a need for high-speed peripherals such as printers, card reading/punching equipment, or magnetic tape units. A potential customer requiring such devices should determine if they are available, their location, how materials are transferred between the customer and the service firm, the cost of such services, and the normal transaction timing.

Benchmarks If several firms are being considered, certain common programs may be used to obtain direct cost comparisons from the alternative vendors. Extreme care should be taken to use benchmarks which are realistic in the sense that they approximate the types of applications to be used on an ongoing basis.

Cost differences should also be considered in light of the qualitative differences of the competing firms. In addition, one should consider the personnel time requirements for use of a system, since those costs may exceed or approach direct computer costs. This may be an extremely important factor where there is to be considerable programming.

Financial Stability Many firms have entered the time-sharing industry only to fail after a period of time. Therefore, there should be confidence that the firm is financially able to remain in business. Changing time-sharing services can be a trying and costly experience.

SELECTIVE BIBLIOGRAPHY

Datapro Research Staff, *All About Remote Computing Services,* Datapro Research Corporation, Delran, N.J., 1975.
Martin, James F., *Telecommunications and the Computer,* Prentice-Hall, Englewood Cliffs, N.J., 1969.
Remote Computing Directory, Quantum Science Corporation, Palo Alto, Calif., 1974.

Chapter 4

The Computer Business Utility

LEON WEISBURGH
President, Anstat, Inc., New York, New York

Not long ago, the computer served as a tool only to individual companies. With the advance of computer technology and communications, time sharing now offers mobility to computer users, allowing them to tap into specialized knowledge wherever it exists. By eliminating the necessity of locating the computer near its source of data, the *computer utility* becomes a reality in servicing the needs of the business community.

Initially the utility was restricted by slow communication equipment to scientific calculations or financial analysis, where the data from the user was relatively small and the processing requirements relatively large. With the development of faster and more flexible terminals, larger core memories, and faster disk drives, the utility can now service commercial applications where there is a huge amount of data to be transmitted, with relatively simple processing.

From the low teletype speed of 10 characters per second, terminals now reach the speed of conventional line printers. The terminals can be placed near the input machines; they can also be located in remote areas such as warehouses, branch offices, etc. To handle the input, CRT (cathode-ray tube) units display both the data that are keyed in and the response from the computer, allowing the operator to verify accuracy immediately. Tape cassettes provide inexpensive storage of data at the terminal for subsequent processing. Larger core memories allow more complex operating systems which, in turn, keep track of a greater and more varied mix of programs to be handled by the system at one time. Faster disk drives permit rapid interchange of segments, or pages, of a program between core and disk with little loss in computer efficiency.

With equipment now able to handle work from many companies simultaneously, and with the data being fed into the computer from, and being printed back at, the user's offices, the computer utility now offers significant cost advantages over the in-house installation. As larger and more powerful computers are operated, the cost per transaction decreases, providing, of course, that the computer is used to its capacity.

Of even greater significance than the reduction in processing cost is the availability of a reservoir of specialized knowledge. The utility gains from its exposure to the executives of many different businesses and the constant improvement of its programs through these contacts. The prime function of a computer should be the extraction of the specific information which management needs from the vast amount of data available, and the presentation of that information in a meaningful way. As the computer has moved beyond record-keeping applications into support of management information systems (MIS), the effort of designing the necessary computer programs has become more costly than the hardware itself. A large number of smaller companies, moreover, lack the expertise to formulate the requirements for a management information system, much less actually design and write the programs. Once a utility has created a series of programs that could be offered to one firm, it is practical to reuse those same programs with minor modifications for other firms.

There is, of course, a continuing conflict between the desire to operate the computer program as a package and the need to address the specific problems of clients requiring major changes in the design of the program. Some utilities refuse to alter their programs in any but very minor ways, and thereby offer their services at lower prices. Other computer service companies have designed the main element of their programs as a package with many branches from the main routines allowing for custom design. Once the goal of supplying management information is firmly fixed, the need for specialized treatment of individual companies becomes critical.

COMPUTER UTILITY VS. IN-HOUSE INSTALLATION

While the developments of time sharing, larger core memories, and terminals have made the computer utility more practical, the cost of the *in-house* installation has rapidly decreased for the smaller businesses. Computers renting for as low as $500 to $2,000 per month do many of the chores previously performed by bookkeeping machines. These lower-priced systems have opened a vast market for computer systems. The hardware vendors have also incorporated prepackaged application programs so that a small business with little outside expense can take advantage of the higher speed of computer systems.

With the development of low-cost computers and prepackaged application programs, why use a computer utility? First of all, many firms would prefer not to assume the responsibility for installing and managing a computer system. They would far prefer to devote their efforts to managing their businesses as long as their data processing can be handled satisfactorily. Furthermore, since the computer utilities are developing along specific lines of business, the utility offers specializations that would seldom be available to a small firm installing its own computer system.

A second problem of an in-house installation is the user's dependence upon one key individual to manage the installation. In fact, many of the low-cost systems are being sold as operable without any experienced computer supervision. As long as the computer operates perfectly, and there are no changes to the package application programs, a minimum of supervision is required. However, as soon as parity errors occur on disk, or tapes get mislabeled, or any number of miscellaneous and often extraneous complications arise, a supervisor, intimately knowledgeable with the data processing system, becomes a necessity. If such an individual is not available (and turnover is notoriously high in ADP), the entire data processing system may stop.

Another significant consideration is machine failure. Most computer service organizations maintain spare equipment, either a dual computer system or at least extra disk and tape drives, so that if a peripheral unit requires service the system can still operate.

Reliability of people is as important as the equipment. In the utility there are many highly skilled individuals who not only supply backup to each other if one should be away, but also supply specialized knowledge for solving individual business problems.

The efficiency of application programs supplied by hardware vendors or offered as "shelf" items by software suppliers for in-house use is another important factor. The vendor of such programs cannot afford to design a system for each user. Vendors must develop programs which have generalized use. Thus, many of the idiosyncracies of individual users have to be ignored. If, on the other hand, the user attempts to modify these generalized packages, he or she then takes on the huge risk that programming bugs may not be noticed for a period of time—and when they are noticed, there may not be immediate capability within the organization to solve the problems that arise.

An even more important consideration is that the computer should be more than just a record-keeping machine—it should be a tool for management. The system should be designed to give management the type of information it needs to improve its performance. The information which is needed can be determined only by detailed discussions with the key executives of the company, by studying how the managers are running their individual departments, and then incorporating their views into the system design. Such flexibility usually is not permitted within the package program.

Advantages of Being On-line As part of a time-shared system, the main files of a company are on-line and are, therefore, available for immediate inquiry. This proves extremely important, for example, to a distributor who must tell a customer whether it can deliver an item from stock within a specific time. An inquiry to the on-line inventory file immediately provides information on the quantity on hand, the open purchase orders, and assigned inventory for other customers. Similarly, the customer files, being on-line, provide the credit manager with instant information as to the accounts receivable balance, the amount of shipments over a period of time, and how the customer is paying its bills. Many systems even provide the back orders on-line to the user so that when an item is received into inventory, the shipping department can get an immediate print-out of all customers who have open orders for that product.

A further benefit to the user of having the key files on-line lies in the rapid response at the input station. Normally, errors that pass through the input departments are not caught until the editing run, or even later when the input data are merged with the inventory or customer files. An unmatched situation must then be referred to the input department, where it has to be checked against the original media. Often a full day or more elapses before the data are corrected. When the files are on-line to the input department, however, as soon as the data are entered into the terminal, the computer verifies that the correct products and customers exist. Those systems using CRT terminals display the descriptions of the customers and the products on the television-like screen for a further check by the input operator.

Finally, having the key files on-line allows updating of these files as soon as information is entered into the system. Inventory, for example, can instantly reflect the latest shipments, and send back a notice as soon as the remaining balance on hand falls below a prespecified level. Customer orders can be rejected when the credit limit has been exceeded by the previous order that the user has authorized.

HOW TO CHOOSE A COMPUTER UTILITY

While the computer utility industry is in its infancy, one should beware of the firm that offers a "supermarket" of products. To accomplish its purpose of providing detailed management information to its clients, rather than merely bookkeeping services, the utility should delve deeply into the practices of each of the industries it serves, and of its clients within those industries. Such studies require considerable effort from the ablest and most creative personnel the utility can muster. Spreading these talents over a wide range of industries will only diffuse the results in any one area. As the utilities mature, there will be a consolidation of skills from various companies into a few broad-based, national organizations.

The most important representative of the computer utility is the systems engineer who will handle the assignments. The systems engineer is responsible for analyzing the user's requirements at both the management and accounting levels; later, he or she oversees the conversion of the user's system to the utility. In interviewing someone for this position, it is necessary to view the individual as an applicant for a critical position in the user's company. What experience has he or she had in solving similar problems? How will the applicant's personality fit into the client's organization as he or she works shoulder to shoulder with the executives and office staff?

Once the systems engineer has finished his or her assignments, the internal control department becomes the client's contact with the utility. This department takes responsibility for the daily auditing of the input and output data, and reviews all the periodic reports before they are released to the user. With time sharing, it is no longer necessary for the computer to be located near the source of data. The computer can process the information 4,000 miles away as easily as it can next door. With its continuous contact with the client's staff, however, it is extremely important that some representative of the internal control department be located nearby. As problems arise they can be solved immediately, either over the telephone or with personal visits.

Most utilities provide backup equipment to their systems, but the user also depends upon the reliability of the terminal in his or her office, where there is seldom spare equipment. It is important, therefore, to check the reliability of the terminals with other users. Many utilities will deliver spare equipment if the user should be experiencing terminal difficulties, or at least provide backup terminals at their computer centers for use by their clients. However, it is far better to select terminals that are well constructed than to have to revert to backup procedures.

AN ORDER PROCESSING SYSTEM

In designing a data processing system, a prospective user starts with a rigorous examination of its own requirements. What files require constant reference and how often do these files require updating? In particular, what are the needs of the executives who will receive the reports?

In this examination, management-by-exception reporting should be a critical goal. It is no longer necessary to bury a manager with reams of paper. Instead, the computer should select, from the masses of data it has stored, the specific information each manager needs. In this Chapter, effort is made to stress the less obvious, but nevertheless critical, areas in which the computer can serve the user.

In this discussion businesses are separated into three functions: distribution, manufacturing, and importing. This provides a simple way of grouping related business problems and practices. In the business world, however, such divisions are rarely so definite. A distributor often imports part of its product line, while a manufacturer can distribute most of its products from a large finished-goods inventory and import various products. In this Chapter, reports listed for one type of business often may serve the other classifications equally well.

Distribution Client service is a key ingredient to the successful distributor; one's products often bear few distinguishing characteristics from those of competitors. By keeping a large variety of products in inventory, by maintaining a high percentage of in-stock products, by the rapidity with which the customer's order is filled and the merchandise is delivered, the distributor attracts and retains customers. Thus the success of the distributor depends upon the way inventory is maintained and handled.

With many distributors, a staff of order takers receives the customers' orders over the telephone. On a manual system, during the peak hours, the order taker seldom has time to do more than write down the customers' requirements. Only as the volume of calls subsides will the order taker inquire at the warehouse whether the items are in stock. This system then requires a return telephone call to notify the customer of those items that are not in inventory, at which point the customer may request a substitute item, resulting in another inquiry to the warehouse. Such a system is inefficient to the distributor and provides poor service to the customer. With a data processing system in which the inventory file is immediately accessible to the salesperson while the customer is on the telephone, the order taker can inquire into the computer file and determine the availability of inventory at that point. Furthermore, the inventory file can also specify the quantity of open purchase orders and the item cost. Thus, the customer receives an immediate and complete response.

Since the purpose of the distributor is to maintain an adequate inventory to service the customers, the greatest expense and largest investment lie in the maintenance of that inventory. Studies by management consultants point out that proper inventory management can reduce the inventory investment by as much as 30 per cent. A distributor carrying an inventory valued at $2 million could possibly reduce this investment by as much as $600,000 through an inventory management system. The cost of carrying inventory, including the cost of money, warehouse space, labor involved in moving the inventory within the warehouse, and obsolescence, has also been estimated at approximately 30 per cent. If the distributor with $2 million in inventory could reduce this investment by $600,000 it could, therefore, achieve a saving of up to $180,-000 per year. Such savings alone more than pay for many data processing systems.

The computer services the distributor in many ways in the control of this inventory investment. Each time the product is shipped, the computer immediately matches the remaining balance on hand against a reorder point level, and notifies the distributor whenever this reorder point is reached. Thus, the distributor knows when to replenish the inventory without waiting for a periodic review of all items that would occur on a manual basis. Similarly, the computer warns the distributor when it is necessary to expedite delivery of a product that has fallen below the safety stock position and when the critical moment arises that the product is out of stock. For those distributors that handle a substantial volume of drop shipments, the computer prepares a *hit analysis* (the frequency a nonstocked product is ordered) to determine which items should be kept in inventory instead of being purchased individually from the manufacturer.

Periodic analyses can also aid in inventory management. Most distributors have a fast turnover of a relatively small percentage of the total inventory and a much lower turnover of the remaining items. By spotting certain changes in the sales trend, the computer can warn management when to adjust the prescribed inventory levels for the new activity. Analyzing changes in the gross profit pinpoints that product which is nearing the end of its life cycle, or where a competitive product is entering the marketplace.

Many distributors order in carload lots from the manufacturer to take advantage of special discounts. When a product falls below a reorder level, the computer can examine all the other products for that vendor and prepare a list of those products that are within a specified percentage of their reorder point, thereby allowing the purchasing agent to place a carload order.

Finally, a whole series of programs are available to the distributor for adjusting the EOQ (economic order quantity) to reflect the serviceability versus size of investment desired by the distributor. Once a computer has stored historical data on the movement of a product, it can begin to vary the inventory levels to reflect recent sales activity and allow for seasonal and cyclical trends. The computer can then estimate the serviceability of the inventory level (the frequency with which the product will be in stock when the customer requests it), and graph the serviceability versus the investment of inventory required at each level. The distributor may find that a $10 million inventory is required to offer 99 per cent serviceability

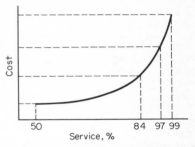

Fig. 4-1   Cost-service relationship.

to a client; a $5 million investment will provide 97 per cent serviceability; a $3 million investment, 95 per cent serviceability, and so forth. (See Figure 4-1.) Once the distributor determines what investment it is willing to make to obtain the desired serviceability, the computer will then adjust the reorder point and EOQ for each product. The inventory projection reports offer a high degree of accuracy for staple products, and more than satisfactory accuracy for seasonal items.

For distributors that maintain warehouses, whether public or private, the computer can keep track of the inventory in each warehouse and in total for a company. This facilitates shipping merchandise to the customer from the nearest inventory location. Where in-plant inventories are kept at their customers' location, the computer signals when to replenish that inventory. To control the movement of high-priced merchandise, the computer may also produce daily reports to reconcile sales with manifests for each product released from the warehouse.

Next to control of inventory, the pricing of products is the most complex function of the distributor. In the simplest form, the price may vary depending upon the type of customer or the quantities ordered.

Sometimes, however, a customer will receive varying prices or discounts depending upon the type of product ordered. A building contractor, for example, may receive one level of discount for quantities of wire ordered from an electrical distributor and an entirely different discount for lighting fixtures. Sometimes the prices a customer receives depend upon the relationship with the distributor and might go back for decades. Other distributors use the latest price negotiated by their salespeople as a standard price for that customer from that point. With some purchasing agents, it is even necessary to overbill the products and then grant equivalent advertising allowances. While many distributors prepare a price schedule that appears to resemble some of the categories discussed above, there is always a list of special prices that fall outside these categories. A computer system that does not encompass all the price variances causes the clerical department to check each order for these special prices. Thus, to be effective, the files must allow for a complete and flexible pricing matrix.

As a result of the huge variety of prices that can exist for the same product, a gross profit analysis can be very valuable to the distributor. The computer will check the gross profit for every product on each order and reject those orders in which the gross profit falls below certain parameters. These parameters can vary for every product or for every product category. Later in the reporting, the computer will analyze the profit margin by customer and by salesperson.

The distributor operates under what is sometimes called a *one-pass system*. Under the one-pass system, the order is received and a picking slip for the warehouse is immediately produced. This warehouse slip can be printed in bin location sequence to facilitate the picking of the merchandise and may also be extended with all the prices to be used as the invoice. For many distributors, however, this form will serve the picking function alone, and the invoice will be prepared after the picking slip returns to the accounting office.

Manufacturing While a distributor maintains a wide variety of products to provide immediate service to the customer, the manufacturer more often maintains a much smaller product list without the need to provide immediate shipment to fill a customer order. Instead, many manufacturers create their production orders once they have received the customer orders, while others with seasonal business begin with samples and then release large production orders once they are able to spot the sales trend of the product line. For a typical manufacturer, the customer's order is filled over a period of time and often by partial shipments.

The distinction between a distributor and a manufacturer, however, is rarely so simple. Even manufacturers that produce their products to order often maintain a parts inventory for immediate shipment to their customers. Many manufacturers, moreover, have set up divisions which take over the distributive function for the customers.

The manufacturer operates under what often is called the *two-pass system*. Orders are entered and stored in the computer and then released partially or totally as the merchandise is available for shipment. Keeping track of the large volume of unfilled orders becomes a requirement of the computer system. Because of the importance of tracking these unfilled orders, the computer produces a variety of reports. To answer customer inquiries, one report maintains every open order for that customer, listing the customer's purchase order number, the date of the order, its volume, and the number of partial shipments already made against that order. The open-order position also is analyzed by shipment date, with the computer signaling those orders that are past due, those scheduled for immediate shipment, and those which will not be completed as scheduled. It is far better to notify the customer that an order will be late than to await an angry inquiry from the purchasing agent. The unfilled orders can also be keyed to the products ordered, so that when the product is received into stock, the shipping department can receive an immediate print-out of all customers who have open orders for that product. (See Figure 4-2.)

For many manufacturers, the most important analysis plots the open customer orders against an inventory projection for each product. This report begins with an overall *availability to sell* for each product. (Availability to sell represents the balance on hand in inventory, plus the quantity released for production, minus the open customer orders.) Then the production orders are projected over the future in timed intervals (generally 1 or 2 weeks per interval) and the open customer orders are plotted within the same time intervals. Thus it is possible to see that while there may be sufficient availability to sell the product based upon production orders released, the actual filling of the customer orders could be delayed because of the time lag in the replenishment of the inventory. Once the computer has signaled these discrepancies, it is possible to revise the production schedules, to switch the customer into substitute products, or to delay the filling of the customer order until the expected receipt of the production.

Similar to the distributor, the manufacturer gains many advantages by having the computer analyze the inventory position. The products of the manufacturer, moreover, become more involved as the products become multilevel. The textile manufacturer,

EXCEPTIONS - INVENTORY STATUS FOR PERIOD ENDING 3/31/75

ITEM NUMBER	ITEM DESCRIPTION	CLS	VENDOR	U/M	STD COST	SAFETY STOCK	RFORD POINT	QTY ON ORDER	LAST ORD DATE	LEAD TIME	CURR ISSUES	LAST ISSUE	BALANCE ON HAND	DAYS SERVICE	EXC
113101341	GASKET	100	118470	BOX	1,500	1000	2000	0	5/04/70	2	0	6/70	1861	120+	IN
113101352F	CYL HEAD	100	134200	DZ	15,000	30	100	0	1/20/71	5	15	3/71	0	0	SO
113101483A	GASKET	100	118470	BOX	.090	3000	6000	1500	3/20/71	2	0	2/71	5700	46	RP
114261051GX.362	MUFFLER DUAL	300	310765	DZ	50,000	125	350	120	3/27/71	1	240	3/71	297	43	RP*
115251053I.X	MUFFLER DUAL	300	310765	DZ	52,500	470	875	0	1/16/71	2	300	3/71	421	22	BS*
211251157	TAIL PIPE	301	310765	DZ	21,500	125	380	120	3/25/71	3	330	3/71	362	36	RP
211257157G	TAIL PIPE	301	310765	DZ	30,500	300	600	240	3/19/71	3	420	3/71	563	41	RP
211282748XX-JERI	HORN RACING	905	541983	DZ	182,500	50	110	0	1/29/71	4	50	3/71	124	48	*

EXCEPTION CODES

RP = BELOW REORDER POINT
BS = BELOW SAFETY ALLOWANCE
SO = STOCKOUT
IN = INACTIVE ITEM
* = SIGNIFICANT ITEM

Fig. 4-2 Exceptions: Inventory status for period ending 3/31.

INVENTORY PROJECTION ANALYSIS REPORT   REPORT DATE 10/31/75

ITEM NUMBER	ITEM DESCRIPTION	CATEGORY	--TOTAL--	--1--	--2--	--3--	--4--	--5--	--6--	CODE
							PROJECTED PERIODS			
18002	ICKY BEAR W/STCKY PW	+ BOH	4762	4762	3286	486	4514	1902	1313-	****
		+ ON ORDER	11340	1240		6600			3500	
		= TOT AVAIL	16102	6002	3286	7086	4514	1902	2187	
		- CUST ORD	16035	2716	2800	2572	2612	3215	2120	
		= NET AVAIL	67	3286	486	4514	1902	1313-	67	
18029	JR TWEED MONKEY	+ BOH	1472	1472	607	585	643	824	712	
		+ ON ORDER	6000		1200	1200	1200	1200	1200	
		= TOT AVAIL	7472	1472	1807	1785	1843	2024	1912	
		- CUST ORD	6568	865	1222	1142	1019	1312	1008	
		= NET AVAIL	904	607	585	643	824	712	904	

CODE: **** INDICATES THAT INVENTORY HAS
DEVELOPED A NEGATIVE QUANTITY
FOR THIS ITEM DURING THE
PROJECTED PERIOD.

XXXX

Fig. 4-3 Inventory projection analysis report.

PURCHASE ORDER REGISTER FOR PERIOD ENDING 08/31/75

ITEM DESCRIPTION AND NO.																
	------ORDER INFORMATION------						CONFIRM-ATION	------ON WATER INFORMATION------				RECEIPTS INFO		BALANCE INFO	
VENDOR NO	VENDOR NAME	DATE	PO NO	QTY	UNIT PRICE	EXT PRICE	DATE	DATE	QTY	BOAT NAME	UNSH-IPPED	DATE	QTY RCVD	BAL DUE	$ BAL OPEN

001 5-40X13/4F   MACH SCREW 1 PL

61576	ROTHSCHILD BRO	03/15/71	12135	100M	1.215	122	04/22/71	06/07/71	100M	CONSTITUTN	0			100M	122
		04/19/71	21976	1200M	1.200	1440	06/07/71	06/29/71	1100M	TITANIC	100M			1200M	1440
		08/11/71	35071	800M	1.210	968	08/29/71							800M	968
69275	ARROWSMITH CO	05/19/71	24390	850M	1.200	1020	06/19/71	06/30/71	400M	QUEEN MARY				850M	1020
								07/04/71	500M	MAYFLOWER	50M-			300M	360
		07/12/71	44103	300M	1.200	360	08/01/71								
71365	HARRISON INC	07/19/71	46538	975M	1.090	1063	07/26/71					08/15	975M	0	0
		08/26/71	58301	1450M	1.100	1595								1450M	1595

127 1204   INT LK WASHERS

1309	HNG KNG WSHRS	09/16/71	7162	30000M	.015	450	12/25/70	07/01/71	1000M	AFRICAN QN				30000M	450
								07/08/71	1000M	QN OF ORNT					
		12/24/70	10372	10000M	.016	160	03/16/71	07/15/71	9500M	HAPPINESS	500M			10000M	160
		08/12/71	41972	20000M	.020	400	08/15/71	08/15/71	6000M	SHANGRI-LA	4000M			20000M	400
27563	ATHENS PRODS	12/15/70	9917	90	.020	90	02/16/71					08/16	4500M	0	0

****
****
**

NEW STANDARD COSTS
001 5-40X13/4F   1.245
127 1204   .027

XXXX

Fig. 4-4 Purchase order register for period ending 8/31.

for instance, must maintain its inventory not only by style, but also by color spread within style. The latter is displayed on the order, but summarized by style only on the invoice. Similarly, the garment manufacturer will maintain its inventory by style with a size spread within that category. The subdivisions keep the same characteristics as the main record, as far as selling price, cost, and replenishment time are concerned, but require their own inventory statistics for customer inquiries and reordering. To reduce computer costs, some utilities implement these subdivisions as multiple records attached to the primary style record.

A manufacturer, moreover, must maintain its inventory beyond the finished-goods level down to its raw materials. The computer, therefore, must be programmed to explode the sales statistics by the bill of materials and summarize requirements by each raw-material item. The bill-of-materials explosion, in reverse, provides the material cost for a direct-cost system of finished goods.

Importing   Although lacking productive facilities, the importer falls more closely in the pattern of the manufacturer than that of the distributor. With the importer there is also a time lag between receipt of the order and shipment of the merchandise. Thus, the importer must also track the unfilled customer order.

The importer depends on the docking of ships for replenishment of inventory. A shipment from overseas generally covers a wide number of products, and may constitute the only receipt of those products for the entire season. While waiting for the shipment, the importer needs to record order position not only when the purchase orders were issued, but also when the merchandise was placed on board the ship. Once the goods are in transit, the importer can gauge when the items will be received. By keeping track of the in-transit position, the importer can answer customer inquiries and take orders with specified delivery dates. The inventory report, projected on a time scale, becomes critical to the importer. Once the merchandise has been received, the computer is called upon to expedite delivery to the customer, by first producing reports analyzing the unfilled customer orders by product, and then printing out the invoices.

Despite the complexities of tracking the purchase order through its various stages, the computer can reduce the clerical chores. The system will match the purchase order with the acknowledgment of the order by the exporter, followed by the notice of shipment of merchandise and finally by receipt of the goods. Since many importers issue blanket purchase orders to cover a release of merchandise over a period of time, the computer can maintain a record of the unfilled portion of each purchase order and the in-transit position.

ACCOUNTS RECEIVABLE AND SALES ANALYSIS

When companies first moved from bookkeeping machines to tabulating equipment and then to computers, the types of information supplied to the credit manager were generally insufficient for this manager to perform his or her job properly. The credit manager had been accustomed to an account ledger card which provided a visual history of the account's activity. The typical computer print-out, however, reflected only the current status. As its capacity increased, the computer became capable of generating more meaningful information than the manual system. Unfortunately, most credit reports have not kept up with the advance of technology.

On the bookkeeping machine ledger, every invoice and cash posting appeared, including all the items that had been keyed off. Picking through all these postings to determine the open items was a time-consuming, error-prone effort. On the equivalent computer ledger, only the active items appeared individually, listed in date sequence. The historical data were summarized at the bottom of the form in a manner which aided the manager in analyzing the sales and payment trends of the customer.

The computer ledger still retained one shortcoming over the manual ledger—it was updated infrequently, in most instances only once a month. This drawback has now been overcome with the on-line system. All credit files are accessible to the credit manager through use of the terminal. These files, of course, are updated with every shipment to the customer. For a manufacturer, in addition, the files are updated as soon as an order has been approved for shipment. By establishing credit limits based either on a fixed dollar amount or on the aging of the unpaid invoices, and by rejecting orders from a customer who has exceeded his or her credit limit, the computer can relieve the credit manager from the chores of checking every order. The credit manager can then devote more time to delinquent accounts. (See Figure 4-5.)

On the aged trial balance, the computer has now advanced beyond merely segregating the unpaid invoices by month, and now helps analyze the paying habits of the customer by tracking the number of times he or she has fallen into each past-due category. To aid the cash-flow projections, those invoices with future dating are separated from those invoices already due for payment and summarized by due date. For many companies, the computer is even instructed to compute service charges on past-due balances.

Analysis of sales trends is valuable as long as the reports pinpoint those areas that require management activity. Most salespeople are partial to certain products and to particular customers within their territories. Developing new territories, opening up difficult accounts, and selling the more profitable products require considerably greater effort. The computer should, therefore, pinpoint those products the salesperson is not moving and those customers and territories not called upon. One meaningful report lists customers according to the volume of sales for the year. The largest customer is printed first, followed by the second, third, and so forth. For many companies with 3,000 to 5,000 customers, the top page of the report accounts for over 50 per cent of the sales volume, while the rear two-thirds of the report often accounts for less than 5 per cent of the sales volume. Management's attention should be constantly directed to its largest customers, and periodically to its smallest customers to determine the worth of handling these customers at all. If this report further analyzes the percentage of credit returns to sales, it calls attention to those customers who are taking advantage of their favored position at possibly too high a cost.

```
4/22/ –          15:11
CUSTOMER # 225372

BALANCE                 645.18
CREDIT LIMIT            11,000
UNSHIPPED BAL.        4,672.97
MONTH TO DTE SLS        252.68
YEAR TO DTE SLS.      1,678.23
DATE LAST PURCHASED     4/22/–
AMOUNT LAST PAID      1,012.45
DATE LAST PAID          3/15/–

JOHN L. ADAMS INC.
109 FERRY ST.
METROPOLIS, ILL.
```

Fig. 4-5 Customer-credit inquiry.

For companies with seasonal business, a sales report that compares bookings to date by customer in addition to shipments to date will spot trends occurring early in the season when it is still possible to take management action. The gross profit analyses, on a comparative basis, also pinpoint the products which are nearing the end of their life cycle as well as those customers who are negotiating too intensively. Examining these calculations by salesperson may also identify the weaker salespeople.

Sales reports can be prepared in a multiplicity of ways to study sales trends. Reports reflecting sales in any combination of territory, salesperson, customer, trade class, product category, and product will produce reams of paper that most managers will scarcely study. In designing any sales report, it is far more important to determine which data the manager requires and have the computer extract that specific information from its vast data banks. Only the figures which fall outside of defined boundaries should appear on these reports. A sales manager may, for instance, want to know which customers have increased their business by 25 per cent, or decreased their orders by 15 per cent. If the computer is used to select relevant data, it becomes an important adjunct to management.

CONCLUSION

The advent of time sharing has unleashed the energies available to establish the computer utility industry. Heretofore, the industry was limited to those applications that could be serviced on a periodic basis, and where the user was willing to send out data and depend upon the service company to process them according to its own schedule. Now the user can transmit data directly to the utility's computer, can interrogate the computer files whenever necessary, and can schedule the printing of many reports — all from the user's own office.

With its limiting factors now overcome, the advantages of the utility becomes significant. Of prime importance is the knowledge the utility builds up as it services many different businesses. This knowledge exists in the library of computer programs available to a prospective user; it also exists in the experience of the systems engineers who are responsible for designing the user's system. For those utilities whose basic programs allow for substantial flexibility in meeting the needs of its individual users, the resulting range of problems already solved simplifies the installation and reduces the initial programming costs. As the utility uses larger, more powerful computers, the processing costs also decrease relative to the in-house installation.

For normal, commercial businesses, the utilities have already attacked the main areas requiring data processing. Because the utility can spread its development cost over its many clients, it can afford more sophisticated programming which takes the computer out of the mundane bookeeping requirements into the more useful management information systems. Reporting changes in inventory, sales, and credit activities can pinpoint the areas needing immediate management attention. The greatest savings to the user should be found in those areas where the computer can effectively screen the data and report only the exceptions.

Because of the huge amount of knowledge to be absorbed, the utility must initially restrict itself to specific lines of business. As these utility companies mature, there are economies to be gained by sharing the communication network and the research on new technologies, so that eventually the smaller utilities will merge into large national organizations. By that time, the computer utility will have established itself as a necessary and valuable adjunct to the business community.

With the growing complexity of business, governmental, and institutional operations, managements must depend increasingly on automation. Heretofore, the computer has been limited largely by the talents of its masters. Now time sharing has made it possible for the computer to disseminate the knowledge of specialists wherever called upon. We have seen the computer progress from a high-speed adding mechanism to directing men to the moon. The Bob Cratchits have long ago been removed from their counting tables.

Chapter **5**

Interactive Teleprocessing Network Services

GEORGE J. FEENEY

Vice President and General Manager, Information
Services Business Division, General Electric Company,
Rockville, Maryland

One of the most fundamental changes in the data processing industry in the 1970s has been the development and widespread acceptance of broad-scope, extensively deployed, interactive teleprocessing network services. The most important characteristic of such interactive networks is the shared use of central computer power through an integrated communication system which provides instant access to data, programs, and computer resources to multiple, geographically dispersed locations.

Although interactive networks are a relatively recent phenomenon, the services they provide represent the culmination of the first two phases of a three-phase evolution within the industry, paced by a series of technological innovations in the intersecting and gradually merging disciplines of computing and communications.

THREE MAJOR PHASES

Time-Sharing Service First offered commercially in 1965, time-sharing service provided the user with direct, continuous access to computer power through dozens of local terminals simultaneously connected to a central system. The principle was simple: to provide medium- and large-scale computer capacity directly to individuals without third-party intervention. For problem-solving applications, this, in effect, reversed the traditional arrangements. Instead of having the user juggle a number of projects in parallel so that the computer could work on one job from start to finish, time sharing made the central computer handle many jobs in parallel. A design engineer, for example, could work on one task from start to finish with sustained attention through the creative process of deciding what option to try next on the basis of results so far. The effect was a significant increase in user productivity along with a substantial reduction in task completion time. In planning, production management, statistical analysis, programming, and many other major fields as well as engineering, this amplification of user productivity produced a decisive increase in the usefulness and relevance of computers.[1]

[1] See Chapter 3, "Time Sharing: An Overview of the Technology and Types of Services," in this Section.

Information Networking Service   First offered commercially in 1969, this service was a logical outgrowth of the original time-sharing applications, meeting an increasingly vital business need.   In a large, complex, geographically dispersed industrial society, some of the most important computational tasks involve real-time inputs that must be collected from many different locations, and produce real-time outputs that must be distributed to many different locations.   Conventional batch-processing systems did not accommodate these requirements.   For example, the day-to-day interactions between the production schedules of a manufacturer's material sources and the delivery requirements of its customers were totally outside the scope of conventional computer systems and services.   These interactions had to be augmented by secondary message-passing systems that were expensive, cumbersome, error-ridden, and slow.

By the late 1960s, it was apparent that interactive computing represented a solution to many of these information logistics problems.   The relevance of networks to business applications is largely the result of three major extensions to the technological base provided by time sharing.   First, data communication systems were developed and deployed which made it possible to access shared corporate files and programs from a large number of business locations.   Second, on-line data manipulation and storage capabilities were extended consistent with the large volumes of information involved in business applications.   And third, continual improvements in computer availability, reliability, and data security made the services increasingly suitable for time-critical and highly sensitive aspects of a business operation.

Networking, as it is organized today, encompasses both time-sharing and information logistics, but it has begun to move into a third—and perhaps ultimate—phase: total service networks.

The Total Service Concept   The "total" concept is just emerging.   To understand this new phase, it is helpful to examine the parallel development of electric utility services since the turn of the century.   In 1905, approximately 50,000 small, privately owned generating stations produced roughly 50 per cent of the total United States power supply—largely for their own internal needs.   Today only about 6 per cent of the nation's total electric power is produced for internal consumption; the bulk of the country's power needs are met by some 200 large utilities.

Innovative work by scientists such as Steinmetz and Stanley in the technologies of power generation, transmission, and distribution made the electric utility approach possible.   Highly concentrated power-generation facilities resulted in major economies of scale.   High-voltage transmission technology made it practical to transmit power over long distances.   Local distribution facilities deliver the power efficiently to end users.

The information industry is on the verge of similar change in the middle 1970s.   Despite the presence of some 70,000 widely scattered and mainly privately operated general-purpose computers, there is an emerging trend toward centralization both among in-house data processing organizations and service firms.   This trend is largely due to three unifying forces:

First, there are economic pressures of potential savings through the inherent efficiency of fewer large-scale machines and the standardization of procedures and software.

Second, improvements in communications, computers, and terminal technology have greatly reduced the technical and economic obstacles to remote computing, especially in the area of remote high-speed printing.

And third, there are strong business incentives for large national firms to centralize their computing.   More and more multilocation companies are discovering that they cannot manage vital national and international operations such as order service, inventory control, field sales, factory scheduling, and financial planning with a scattered collection of "cottage" computers.

There is another related trend accompanying the move toward centralization.   Even though the value of computing continues to grow, the glamour surrounding computers themselves has largely faded.   Many companies are looking for relief from the unending cycle of system upgrade, overcapacity, undercapacity, and then yet another system upgrade.   Even larger firms, which could afford to provide their own centralized computer networks, are questioning why they must operate their own systems to enjoy the benefits of efficient computing, any more than operate their own generators to obtain the full benefits from electricity.

Centralization within individual firms will contribute substantially toward the efficient utilization of computers. However, as data communication becomes less expensive and more manageable, as dynamically accessed mass files become bigger, cheaper, and more reliable, as the need for physical security and environmental control grows, as business requirements for reliability and availability at levels attainable only through system clusters and interconnected spinning reserve capacity multiply, it will become increasingly clear that optimum system size often exceeds the resources of even the largest industries and organizations.

Pooling of common requirements through third-party service organizations—networks that are evolving into true total service systems—will be the consequence of these mushrooming needs and expectations. With respect to the needs of any individual company or corporate location, the capacity of the total service networks will be virtually unlimited. Computer power will be available 24 hours a day, 365 days a year to satisfy all data processing needs and will be provided, like electric power, on a variable-cost basis that is a function of usage.

In addition to reduced and variable cost, joint users of these ultralarge system complexes will enjoy greater operational autonomy than they have in the past through individualized operating systems. Greater privacy and data security will be provided through built-in cryptographic techniques in terminals, transmission, and storage, and through access verification procedures. Because the total service concept incorporates worldwide access, the workday peaks and valleys of interactive network users can be balanced across many time zones with a resulting system utilization efficiency that is a substantial factor in overall networking economy.

To summarize: In developmental terms, the first networking phase—time sharing—is a fully mature activity that has settled into an undramatic but steady and consistent growth pattern. The second phase—information logistics—is at the crest of its development. In the past 5 years we have seen its birth and rapid expansion to a major worldwide service offering. Today thousands of successful user experiences attest to its dependability and productivity. Though still in a rapid growth period, the technology is approaching maturity and future innovations in information logistics will be primarily in the applications area.

The third phase—total service networks—is at the beginning of its growth cycle and is still in its formative stages. It is not clear what form these service networks will ultimately take. The next 2 or 3 years will be decisive in determining their eventual shape and direction.

ADVANTAGES OF INTERACTIVE NETWORKS

While the development of information network services has been largely technology-driven, their phenomenal growth and acceptance have been due to their usefulness in a broad range of computing tasks and business problems. Networking offers a number of significant advantages both to the users and to the network operators. Through a series of specific examples, let us examine five key benefits of network services: (1) teleprocessing, (2) data sharing, (3) load sharing, (4) program sharing, and (5) facility sharing.

Teleprocessing Geographically distributed organizations are highly dependent upon the timely exchange of information among their components. Interactive networks are well suited to such tasks.

Example. XYZ Industrial Corporation is a large multinational firm which operates on a decentralized basis and employs a very small headquarters organization to do staff work. Some time ago, management realized that to preserve its operating philosophy, it would have to improve the information flow between divisions and headquarters. The information would have to be faster and more accurate, and in much greater volume.

Specifically, the target was to shorten the financial closing cycle significantly, establish a company-wide database, limit increases in central staff, and develop tools for forecasting and financial analysis. To meet these requirements, XYZ developed a financial consolidation and reporting system for use on an international teleprocessing service network, covering its domestic and international locations. As a result, the company reduced the enormous amount of manual data preparation formerly required. Today, when XYZ acquires a new subsidiary, management can quickly consolidate the pertinent financial information, almost as a matter of routine. The analyzed results of the consolidated data are immediately available, on-line, not only to the central staff, but to key personnel around the world.

Example. Over twenty affiliated companies of a major oil company throughout Europe forward their profitability plans to the parent international division's regional service company in London. There the data are entered via local telephone access into a worldwide teleprocessing network for consolidation and processing. Other affiliates forward their reports to the New York office for similar entry and processing. Working at a remote terminal in New York, the international division then accesses the file, processes the data, and reports them back in various required forms.

All data that affect the profit plan are consolidated into a total report which compares current profit figures with projections previously made by affiliates. A key advantage is that the data received in New York do not have to be reprocessed, as required under the previous computer and manual systems. The following advantages are reported: quick access to the database; quick changes to the database as required; reliable, consistent, and uniform reports; elimination of a large amount of preparatory work for reports; and quick turnaround service.

Example. An industrial firm's foam products, which are manufactured to order, expand in volume 100-fold during production, presenting the following problem: Because raw material at each of the firm's eight factories literally "comes in a test tube and leaves in a boxcar," finished-goods inventories necessarily must be minimized. Yet the competitive nature of the business demands immediate response to customer delivery requirements.

The solution was a network-based on-line order entry system that now instantly checks stock on hand, moves the order into production if it is not in stock, determines a delivery date based on the production schedule, informs the salesperson of that date, initiates a credit check, and, if a credit problem is uncovered, notifies the sales and accounting office even as the flagged order goes on through the cycle so that work can begin pending credit approval.

This system involves close cooperation between the network and the firm's in-house IBM 360/40 computer. Each night new order summaries are transmitted to the in-house computer by a direct computer-to-computer link. Invoices are then prepared and a number of sales databases are updated. The sales are automatically credited to the proper office, the proper item account, the right salesperson, and the appropriate customer account. This information is then transmitted back to the network to expedite the next credit check.

Data Sharing   Because networking provides a means of maintaining, structuring, and analyzing large sets of data, it has become a highly useful tool for financial and market analysts, management consultants, and business and economic planners in academic, government, banking, publishing, manufacturing, and other corporate and noncorporate entities. Coupling data management capabilities with broad geographic accessibility, an interactive network presents unique opportunities for data sharing.

Example. The Management Analysis and Projection System (MAP) is an economic analysis and forecasting system offered by General Electric that combines advanced statistical techniques with an economic database. The latter includes over 2,000 historical time series, and short- and long-range projections of these, and a wide variety of additional general economic and selected industry indices. MAP was designed by corporate economists and mathematicians who had a responsibility for formulating and implementing strategies within their own business, and it is addressed to senior managers and planners with similar responsibilities.

More than a data bank, MAP is a comprehensive multiprogram service package that includes a subscription publication (MAPCAST), a seminar and workshop series, and consulting-services offered in conjunction with private firms specializing in management systems. But the heart of the MAP program is an on-line databank and manipulative software system. Sociological, political, demographic, and government data (e.g., SEC, FTC, and other Federal agency and commission reports) going back almost three decades are part of a portfolio that includes such obvious macroeconomic indicators as gross national product and balance of payments. Additionally, a good deal of more detailed information on the current business environment is made available by region and by specific industry segment.

MAP's software allows subscriber data files to interact with MAP databases for plotting, model building, and forecasting specifically tailored to meet pragmatic and discrete individual business needs. Though used extensively by large companies, MAP has particular appeal to executives in small- and medium-sized firms that cannot afford their own staff economists.

Example. One of the country's largest property and casualty insurers has 29 regional offices, 100 territories, and an independent agency system of roughly 7,000 agents throughout the United States and Canada. Since each regional office is a nearly autonomous profit center, the company had never found a satisfactory method of operational control and planning.

With the help of a commercial network's technical services staff, an on-line planning model was designed which, in effect, provides an independent management system for each regional office. The system, which operates on a database generated monthly on an in-house computer and then transferred to the network, has enabled the company to make the power of shared computer time available to decision makers at all levels of management for the first time in the insurance industry.

Load Sharing Since the fundamental requirement of interactive computer systems is highly responsive service, such systems must be designed to accommodate peak customer demands. These peak usage periods typically occur during midmorning and midafternoon on business days, with little or no demand during nonprime shift and weekend time. The result is that interactive systems typically are significantly underutilized. Computer networks, which can serve multiple time zones from a centralized facility, extend the number of hours of equipment utilization and distribute the peak demand periods from the different time zones throughout the day.

The savings that accrue to the network from better equipment utilization more than offset the increased communication costs of transmitting computer power over long distances. Customers benefit by receiving more responsive and predictable system performance.

Surprisingly, network expansion to Europe and the Far East is economically sound because it extends to as many as 18 the number of time zones, collectively equalizing demands on the system over a 24-hour period—an efficiency that more than sustains the otherwise prohibitive costs of international data transmission.

Example. One of the world's largest chemical producers reaches from its home plant in England to network computers based in Cleveland, Ohio, to get time-critical computer backup for its own system.

The firm's in-house system processes 10,000 tightly scheduled jobs a month. In dealing with urgent and highly unpredictable equipment maintenance and malfunction problems, production would be crippled by waiting in the queue to get access to the in-house computer. So the company sends the fraction of its processing load consisting of handling malfunction data 4,000 miles across the Atlantic under a "quiz and answer" management information system network application. The 6-hour time differential allows this essentially local application to be processed in a highly cost-effective manner by a computer located in the United States.

Example. In Japan, a major international department store and mail-order chain is developing a network application that will process catalogue orders. The orders will be entered via CRT devices at the store's Japan locations. The network will edit each order for validity, sort the orders, and establish a sequenced error-free transaction file. Using a direct computer-to-computer link, this order file will then be transferred to the firm's headquarters each night for additional processing on its in-house system. A United States–based international network was selected for this application since (again, because of the time differential) it was able to supply the desired service at a competitive price.

Program Sharing Information networks provide a useful vehicle for distributing specialized application services on virtually a worldwide basis. This benefits not only the users, often lacking the resources to duplicate highly sophisticated packages themselves, but also the application creators for whom a network is an effective marketing channel.

Example. Established computer service networks provide vehicles for software authors and users requiring programs that reflect the knowledge and expertise of specialized businesses and disciplines. A typical service program is SITE, a computerized system developed by CACI, Inc., a management consulting firm specializing in quantitative analysis and computer techniques.

According to CACI, the SITE system provides the user with detailed demographic profiles for any area within the United States. These areas may be of any shape or size. SITE has been applied to a wide variety of tasks, including trade area analysis, site selection, market analysis, sales forecasting, merchandising, advertising, and market research. The service user simply specifies requests by providing answers to a series of questions posed on the terminal. SITE then generates profiles for the requested areas. With such program-sharing capability, software authors can use the reach and power of the information processing network to create their own mininetwork for software distribution.

Facility Sharing Facility sharing is largely synonomous with the final phase of network evolution: total service networks. We have already discussed the manner in which pooled central-site operations can provide substantial advantages in the areas of scale economy, improved service reliability, and unprecedented provision for data integrity and security.

Advantages of this sort are obvious, but there is another important though less tangible byproduct of the total service concept: Because computer services relieve users of administrative and operating burdens for data processing activities, they allow management to concentrate on the higher-priority business of the organization. Total service networks eliminate the recurrent upgrade problem with a flexible-capacity approach that lets the user obtain as much or as little computer power as needed at a particular time at a cost determined by the resources actually used.

Example. A large operating division of the General Electric Company — the Switchgear Equipment Division in Philadelphia — has transferred its entire data processing load to a commercial network. Since early 1973, all Switchgear's data processing has been performed by network computers which are several hundred miles from its headquarters in Philadelphia. All input and output are processed through a series of high-speed terminals located in what was formerly a local computer center. As an indication of the magnitude of this operation, the daily printing load is approximately 800,000 lines, with twice that volume at month-end closing.

Unit pricing and administrative project controls enable Switchgear to judge the cost effectiveness of every application — even of every report. These management factors, in combination with the scale economies of total service computing, are producing significant cost reductions. To date, Switchgear's data processing costs have dropped more than 10 per cent. Further, management reports significantly higher reliability and faster response than from the local remote batch operation.

NETWORK TECHNOLOGY

Current network technology is discussed here in the form of a detailed examination of one system: the General Electric network. This is presently the largest general-purpose information network in the world, and its technical aspects provide insight into advanced utilization of on-line systems.

The GE network is a modified "star structure," radiating from very large computer "supercenters" near Cleveland, Ohio, and Washington, D.C. Logically, the network can be represented as a mosaic of concentric circles as shown in Figure 5-1. The two outside rings of the mosaic represent communications equipment which interconnects users with their data files and computer power on a worldwide basis. These outer rings are operationally invisible to the users, and essentially act as conduits to the two inner rings, where the actual processing and file manipulation are performed.

Fig. 5-1 Schematic of the General Electric "star structure" network.

The Network Mosaic Let us now look in greater detail at the individual rings comprising the mosaic. The two outside rings represent the communications system. The outermost ring consists of a series of programmed communication concentrators which are deployed in 13 cities in the United States, 7 cities in Europe, 2 cities in Australia, and in Tokyo, Japan. Through regional subnetworks, the communications concentrators in these 23 cities are connected to local dial-up points in over 500 cities throughout North America, Europe, Japan, and Australia. These computers converse directly with user terminals and are responsible for translations between the terminals' individual character sets and capabilities and the standardized communications format within the network.

Low-speed keyboard terminals which operate at 10, 15, 30, and 120 characters per second are handled by Honeywell 416 and GE Diginet 1600 concentrators, each of which may converse with up to 96 separate terminals simultaneously. Another version of the Diginet 1600 handles high-speed remote batch communications at speeds of from 2,000 baud (approximately 200 characters per second) through 9,600 baud. In addition to interfacing with a wide range of remote batch terminals, these high-speed concentrators can "interprocess" directly with users' in-house computers.

The second ring, which is located at the supercenters, consists of a series of central communications computers. These machines manage the overall communications traffic of the network, talking to the remote communications concentrators via pairs of land telephone lines plus satellite and undersea cable channels and to the central systems by means of direct memory channels. The central and remote concentrators utilize a store-and-forward message discipline for transmitting data back and forth. This, together with the duplicate communication paths, assures continuous error-free communication over tens of thousands of line miles between the 23 remote locations and the supercenters. The individual central concentrators at the two supercenters are themselves completely interconnected by means of special switching computers. This interconnection permits a user dialing in from any network location to be linked to the particular system containing the user's files.

All but the outer ring of equipment is located at the supercenters. Such centralization not only facilitates worldwide access to common shared files, but also makes possible economies of scale and levels of security and reliability not obtainable on a decentralized basis.

This high degree of centralization has enabled GE to provide a service of extremely high reliability. A million dollars worth of power supplies with batteries intervening between utility power and computer equipment and with automatic diesel backup power have been installed at the supercenters to protect against blackouts, brownouts, and destructive power-line transients.

The two inner rings of the mosaic comprise the central processors where the users' computing and file manipulation are actually performed. The outer processing ring consists of a series of systems which provide interactive, or "foreground," computing. These machines supply reliable, responsive service for time-critical problem solving and teleprocessing applications. The foreground systems at each supercenter are actually interconnected to form system "clusters." This pooled resource approach allows dynamic load balancing for optimum performance, and automatic backup and load redistribution in the event of system failures.

Extended versions of FORTRAN IV, BASIC, and ALGOL are provided for program development as well as a comprehensive EDITOR for data file manipulation, in addition to data management languages and complete file protection and data-sharing capabilities. Foreground allows a customer to place a terminal user under complete program control so that clerical personnel can use the system effectively without extensive training. Application packages are available in such areas as business management, financial management, manufacturing, engineering, accounting, project control, and statistical analysis. Foreground provides convenient access to the background processors which are described below. Foreground processing is performed on Honeywell 6000 computers utilizing proprietary software developed by General Electric.

The inner processing ring consists of a series of Honeywell 6000 and IBM 370 processors which are used to provide large-scale remote batch-processing service. Background processing provides maximum economy through deferred execution for those jobs where there is no requirement for direct interaction or immediate turnaround.

Background service, using Honeywell's Generalized Comprehensive Operating System (GCOS III), and IBM's OS/VS2 Operating System, provides full ANSI versions of FORTRAN IV and COBOL. The large-core storage on the background systems makes it well suited for processing very large jobs. In addition to extensive storage and data management facilities, background offers magnetic-tape processing to accommodate sequential files of virtually any size. Foreground processors are connected to background processors by means of high-speed channels. Users may change from one mode to another by issuing a simple command; in addition, they can transfer files back and forth when necessary.

The foreground/background configuration employed in the GE network combines the reliability and interactive responsiveness of specialized time-sharing technology with the efficiency and scope of full-scale batch data processing without the performance compromises and additional overhead generally characteristic of most systems which try to combine interactive and batch processing on a single computer. The approach is readily generalized to include additional types of background systems in the future.

In total, the network consists of nearly 100 computer mainframes, over 3,000 access ports, 150,000 miles of dedicated communications lines, and a variety of transoceanic satellite and cable circuits. The network is on the air 24 hours a day, 365 days a year, and provides local dial-up service to over 500 cities in the United States, Canada, Western Europe, Japan, and Australia.

The network structure incorporates a high degree of circuit redundancy and compartmentalization to limit the impact of failures within the system. Dual components and diversified routings are used throughout the communications system in order to assure continued operation in spite of singular outages. In addition, the widely separated supercenters assure that the network will continue normal operation in the unlikely event of a major failure.

This particular structure was chosen for the GE network because it is capable of indefinite growth and expansion. Rigid software and hardware interfaces are provided between each ring in the mosaic. This permits each ring to be modified and evolved as needed in order to offer new products and services to customers and to take advantage of the improved reliability or economies of scale presented by new technology.

Alternative Network Organizations The GE network represents a centralized network, one in which processing and data storage equipment are concentrated in a single installation, and communications facilities radiate out to the user locations. Many of the centralized networks originally made heavy use of IN-WATS telephone service to obtain broad geographic coverage. This approach is gradually being replaced by communications concentrator systems similar to GE's, to achieve the advantages of economies of scale, backup, and load balancing already described.

The principal alternative approach is the distributed network. Examples of this organization are CDC's CYBERNET and the Federally-developed ARPA network. Distributed computer networks are typically a series of regional computer systems which are interconnected by high-speed communication lines. Each regional center generally serves its own local community of users. Although network-wide file sharing is usually possible, it is often less convenient than in centralized networks. One of the primary advantages of distributed networks is that they are easy to establish: relatively autonomous regional systems can form a network without serious disruption to their current processing missions. This makes the approach particularly attractive to organizations such as universities which, although the predominant processing load is local, desire a modest amount of program and data sharing with remote locations.

OTHER MAJOR NETWORK SERVICES[2]

Computer Sciences Corporation Computer Sciences Corporation, headquartered in El Segundo, California, solicits the large-scale user with its INFONET communications network, which offers both batch and interactive capabilities. It provides a full-

[2] Competitor information was provided to and not researched or developed by the author. In each case, the statement provided here has been authorized by the subject vendor, as of the time of writing. While changes in detail are to be expected over time, it is felt that the composite picture here given provides a "flavor" of the services available.

service remote computing network linking approximately 100 cities in the United States, as well as major cities in Europe, including both a centralized network for national service and three regional computer centers in Los Angeles, Chicago, and Washington. Batch and interactive processing are conducted on the same computer. The national service is provided out of Los Angeles.

INFONET features an applications library of some 1,000 programs, with languages including COBOL, FORTRAN, BASIC, and assembly. All these programs can access common data files, and programmers with divergent language skills can work together on the same system.

Bulk jobs can be conducted at any one of nine priority levels, with costs depending on the rapidity with which the customer wants the job completed. The national service is available 22 hours a day, with precise operating schedules for each regional INFONET center determined by local requirements.

CSC customers furnish the necessary compatible remote input-output devices (terminals) and data sets. Standard telephone communications services tie into the INFONET system, and CSC assumes full responsibility should fault isolation of communications occur from user terminal to one of the computer systems.

Within the operating system, a subsystem concept permits divergent systems to function in the same environment. In addition, programmable computers are utilized as remote concentrators, and serve to alleviate the central computers of much of the communications workload, including error detection and correction.

The concentrators serve to accept various transmission codes and speeds, which are available up to 4,800 baud; by separating communications from data processing functions they serve, in effect, as a secondary backup system. CSC provides a variety of user training courses, and maintains a "hot line" at each computer center to ensure quick response. The service can accommodate over 300 users simultaneously.

Com-Share, Incorporated   Com-Share's Commander II remote computing system offers integrated interactive, batch, and remote job entry services. Based on the Xerox Sigma 9 Series computers, the service features a program development system, COBOL, BASIC, and FORTRAN languages, and easy-to-use management, information retrieval, and reporting application packages. The company's international DATAGRID network provides local-call telephone access to Commander II service from 60 cities in the United States and Canada.

Computer systems are located at computer centers in Ann Arbor, Michigan, and Toronto, Canada. Commander II is available from 7:00 A.M. to 11:00 P.M. weekdays, and 10:00 A.M. to 6:00 P.M. Saturdays and Sundays. Data may be transmitted at 110, 300, 1,200, 2,000, and 4,800 baud and from a wide variety of compatible terminals. Commander II and DATAGRID are also available in the United Kingdom, Continental Europe, and Japan. Service offices in the United States, Canada, United Kingdom, Belgium, Holland, France, and Japan provide local consulting and technical support assistance for client problem solving and applications development.

Control Data Corporation   Control Data Corporation, Minneapolis, Minnesota, has been offering remote-access computer services since the announcement of its CYBERNET Service data communications network in 1969. The company now offers interactive time sharing in the United States, Canada, Brazil, Europe, South Africa, and Australia. Major CDC CYBER 70 or 6000 Series installations are located in seven metropolitan areas in the United States (New York, Boston, Washington, Minneapolis, Houston, Palo Alto, and Los Angeles) and in Paris, Stockholm, The Hague, Frankfurt, Johannesburg, Sydney, and Melbourne. A full complement of applications software is installed in all centers, including such disciplines as structural analysis, electrical engineering, database management, graphics, operations research, and general commercial packages.

A number of Control Data subsidiaries also provide various data offerings, as follows:

The Service Bureau Company. Control Data acquired SBC in 1973 as part of the settlement of the IBM-CDC lawsuit. SBC offers its business-oriented CALL/370 time-sharing service to customers throughout the United States and Canada, and via satellite to Europe. SBC's major processing center is in Cleveland, where multiple IBM 370 computer systems are linked by toll-free access lines to most major metropolitan areas in the United States. In Europe, SBC's services are marketed under the name "CALL/CDC."

ACTION Data Services. A St. Louis–based subsidiary, ACTION Data Services, provides real-time processing on a dedicated network for the consumer finance industry.

Greenwich Data Systems. Headquartered in Greenwich, Connecticut, Greenwich Data Systems specializes in commercial data processing, real-time systems analysis, and data processing services. Three major organizational groups correspond to the airlines, brokerage, and consumer finance industries.

Systems Resources, Inc. A Dallas-based subsidiary, SRI provides computer services to the utility and health insurance industries, ranging from complete facilities management to consulting, systems analysis and design, programming, and computer operations.

ADP Network Services, Inc. This international telecommunications network (formerly The Cyphernetics Corporation), Ann Arbor, Michigan, provides computer-based information management services in principal cities throughout the United States and Western Europe. In operation since 1969, the system includes conversational time sharing, remote job entry, and deferred processing, all available 24 hours a day. The company also offers facilities management services for large customers.

Communications computers in principal cities perform sophisticated error detection and retransmission to provide error-free data transmission between network cities and the firm's Technical Center, as well as support line-print and card-reading service in each major city. An international staff assists clients on problems involving data management, information retrieval, management sciences, financial services, and business analysis, reporting, and forecasting. Expertise in interactive computer graphics and computer-based text processing and photocomposition service is also offered. Programming languages available include extended versions of BASIC, FORTRAN IV, COBOL, and assembly language, as well as an easy-to-use command language.

McDonnell Douglas Automation Company McDonnell Douglas Automation Company (McAuto) of Saint Louis, Missouri, performs data processing nationwide through a telecommunications network that links the customer with data centers in St. Louis; Peoria, Illinois; and Long Beach and Huntington Beach, California. Services include remote batch, interactive time sharing, conversational/batch, and on-line processing of large databases. Eighty-seven computing systems are installed, including two IBM Model 195s, each with 4 million bytes of main core; six IBM 370/168s with a combined total of 24 million bytes of main core; two Xerox Sigma 9s, each with 192K words of core; and three CDC 6000 Series computers.

The network supports most low-speed and high-speed terminals through dial-up and leased lines at line speeds of 9,600 bps. Large walk-in facilities with remote batch terminals are also maintained in 11 cities to accommodate the user without a terminal of its own.

National CSS, Inc. With headquarters in Norwalk, Connecticut, and computer centers in Stamford, Connecticut, and Sunnyvale, California, National CSS, Inc., offers batch and interactive services in the United States, Canada, and Europe. To service this market, NCSS developed the Virtual Control Program/Conversational Software System (VP/CSS). The nature of the VP/CSS software has been a primary strength of National CSS. It is now stated to be the most powerful operating system available for IBM 370 hardware.

Featured are interactive compilers, proprietary syntax checker, and symbolic debuggers. Interactive processing as of this writing is available from 7:30 A.M. to 12:00 A.M. weekdays and from 7:30 A.M. to 6:00 P.M. Saturdays, while remote batch processing can be conducted from 6:00 P.M. to 7:30 A.M. weekdays and on Saturdays as needed. The NCSS computer network consists of a System 370 Model 168, a System 370 Model 145, and three System 360 Model 67 processors capable of performing large-scale general-purpose computing. Transmission speeds are 110, 134.5, 150, 300, 600, 1,200, 2,000, and 4,800 baud.

Tymshare, Inc. Based in Cupertino, California, Tymshare's international telecommunications network, Tymnet, serves some forty-five cities in the United States, and is also operational in Canada and Europe. Primarily for conversational time sharing and remote job entry processing, the system employs satellite and analog communications circuits. Utilization of the system, in operation since 1969, has gradually shifted from scientific to business orientation.

The service, available 7 days a week, 24 hours per day, is structured on a centralized approach, with major computer centers in Cupertino, Houston, Valley Forge, and Paris. Typical applications include order processing for companies with geographically dispersed operations, information retrieval, and engineering and scientific computations.

Over forty major computers are interconnected to Tymnet as of this writing, and provide a wide range of computer languages, applications programs, and databases. Interface is via a local telephone call in all major United States cities and in Europe. Languages include Batch FORTRAN, FORTRAN IV, COBOL, SUPER BASIC, EDITOR, and EXECUTIVE, as well as others. Tymnet is compatible with a wide variety of terminals and can accommodate many hundreds of users simultaneously.

Special-Capabilities Services   In addition to the foregoing, numerous services offer special capabilities for smaller users, regional users, or users with specialized application requirements. Thus Keydata Corporation, in Watertown, Massachusetts, provides interactive processing for invoicing, inventory control, accounts receivable, record keeping, work-order accounting, and the like. On-Line Systems, Inc., in Pittsburgh, has moved increasingly into the business field from origins that were primarily scientific. It has capabilities in interactive information retrieval, facilities management, professional programming services, management information systems, and financial modeling. Boeing Computer Services, Inc., in Dover, New Jersey, has dual batch and interactive capability.

Internationally, the French firm SEMA has developed an offering through its service bureau, SIA. Canadian universities are linked through a national system, Canunet, and in Japan, Nippon Telephone and Telegraph offers a dual-capacity service (batch and interactive) over its switched telephone system. More are bound to follow.

Section 7

Special Industry Applications of Automatic Data Processing

Introduction

PHILIP A. RICCO   *Principal, The Diebold Group, Inc., New York, New York*

Certain major segments of industry have specialized needs, with little resemblance to those of other industries. The airline industry is one example: A seat reservation system for an important national or international line involves management of a very large, complex, and perishable inventory (seat space on future flights), with simultaneous re-entrant access from many points (reservation offices and telephone reservation centers). Retailing, with its special point-of-sale data capture problems, and manufacturing are other examples.

Organizations in fields with extensive specialized needs face a fundamental decision with respect to data processing: to expend very large sums of money and extensive time on the in-house development of special systems, accepting the high risk levels of such development projects, or tailoring a vendor's available application package to the company's need. The latter course, while less risky and costly, foregoes any possible competitive advantage of a unique in-house development and foregoes the flexibility to meet unique needs.

Regardless of the ultimate decision to buy or develop, the data processing manager in such an industry must put more emphasis on evaluating available application packages, as an aspect of evaluating competitive vendor offerings, than a manager in an industry with less stringent requirements. With today's level of maturity in hardware offerings, the manager can be sure of being well served *at the hardware level* by any of several vendors, but the quality of the application packages in these demanding categories can vary significantly — both in general quality and in suitability to a particular user's operations. It is also important to note that certain hardware vendors have chosen to place heavy competitive emphasis in specific special markets. This is certainly true in retailing, banking, and airline reservations, and is true in a different sense for users with extensive applications in the on-line scientific-engineering area or with plans for supporting extensive in-house time sharing.

An example of the problem faced by industries with highly specialized needs is retailing. Until recently, retailing had a low priority with most vendors — in the United States context, with all vendors except the one mainframe supplier which historically has marketed cash registers and other special equipment to the retailing industry. Only quite recently, with the emergence of low-cost point-of-sale equipment with facilities for automatic data capture, has the potential of retailing caught the interest of the computer industry at large.

One other recent change in the environment followed the introduction of small-business computers, widely proffered as "programmerless" systems, with application packages available from the hardware vendors and from a variety of OEMs, system houses, and software vendors, for a large number of specific applications. These packages should be carefully evaluated by small companies contemplating hardware purchases, as well as by larger companies preparing distributed data processing systems. The quality of packages in such areas as order entry, inventory management, and production scheduling can be the most important evaluation criterion in comparing small-business computers for use at small-scale remote sites.

Chapter 1

The "Less-Cash, Less-Check" Society

WILLIAM M. ADAMS

Metropolitan Marketing Manager, Recognition Equipment Incorporated, Indianapolis, Indiana; formerly Associate Director, Operations/Automation Division, The American Bankers Association, Washington, D.C.

The concept of a "checkless society" has been with the banking industry since data processing technicians first recognized that a check could ultimately be replaced with data from any electronic source. The lure of technology picked up momentum during the early sixties as the volume of checks to be processed continued to grow. Some visionaries foresaw a collapse of the check processing system similar to the one that had taken place in the securities industry. Early disciples advocated isolating several cities in order more quickly to develop electronic payment facilities. The thing that had begun as a concept soon began to take the shape of a system in the minds of its proponents. The checkless society, much needed and desired, would, it was felt, soon become a reality. Many articles were prepared, talks were given, and with each communication, the system became more sharply defined.

As its supporters envisioned it, the mechanism of the checkless society would, in effect, be a national financial utility. Banks would be linked with their business customers and other banks through their computers and communications lines. A consumer carrying a single bank identification card could avail himself or herself of any financial service at any terminal in the system. The customer's financial database would be at the heart of the system, and funds could be added to or subtracted from it from Touch-Tone phones, teller terminals, and point-of-sale devices located anywhere in the country. Retailers would no longer extend credit (the system would take care of that), but would concentrate their efforts on moving merchandise without fear of bad-debt losses and fraudulent checks.

A part of the rationale for the development of the checkless society was, as mentioned earlier, the collapse of the check processing system. During the late sixties, the check came under a great deal of scrutiny. Concern was expressed regarding the continued use of the check as a primary source of payment in the United States. It was out of this concern that the American Bankers Association established its Monetary and Payments System Planning Committee, which came to be known as the MAPS

Committee. This committee was composed of policy-level bankers who undertook a 2-year extensive study to determine if, among other things, the industry's check payment system could survive the decade of the 1970s. This study was undertaken in 1968, and the committee's summary and conclusions were publicly presented in the spring of 1970.

The MAPS Committee found cause for concern. Check volume is increasing at an annual rate of 7 per cent. By 1980, the industry will be processing 44 billion checks a year—double the 1970 volume of 22 billion. The check processing system remains highly labor-intensive (60 per cent) even with almost total conversion to MICR (magnetic ink character recognition). Considering growth in volume, rising costs, and the available labor supply, the system is likely to be extremely expensive by 1980.

Nevertheless, the MAPS Committee found the system to be operationally sound and capable of handling the volume of checks anticipated by 1980. It recommended evolutionary rather than revolutionary change. The committee's major recommendations were for development of local and regional facilities for clearing and processing electronic payments and for development of the charge card to its full potential.

Market studies undertaken at the time revealed satisfaction with our present payments system. Bankers are very happy with the check as the primary payment method, and see no real reason for change. The same feeling exists on the part of business people and consumers. The committee concluded that change will not be desirable until the benefits of the change are more clearly perceived by all parties.

The MAPS Committee's works and recommendations had a settling effect on the industry and effected change in perspective. With the removal of the fear of system collapse, the urgency and desirability of the checkless society soon faded from center stage. The report gave the industry overall direction and enough time for competitive innovation and consumer acceptance to shape the payments system of the future. The emerging payments system will offer the consumer a wider choice for making payments, and less checks and less cash will be used because of the attractiveness of the alternatives. However, instead of the *checkless* society, tomorrow's version will, speaking in more practical terms, be a *less-check, less-cash* society.

This new payments system is being developed in pieces in different parts of the country. Bank customers will be able to have their pay deposited, and to have regular, fixed-amount bills paid automatically because of developments in California. Monthly utility and retail statements can be signed and returned by the customer without checks, because of developments in Atlanta. Purchases can be made in retail stores with bank cards that cause balances to be shifted automatically from customer accounts to merchant accounts because of developments in Columbus and Long Island. Customers can withdraw funds and make deposits at merchant locations because of a grocer savings and loan innovation in Lincoln, Nebraska. Cash can be borrowed or withdrawn from checking or savings accounts at 24-hour, peopleless, teller stations located in shopping centers, airports, or branch bank exteriors because of developments in the cash dispenser and automated teller area.

Tomorrow's payments system will of course evolve from the one we have today. This evolvement will come from a number of forces, factors, and developments that are not predictable with any measurable degree of certainty. A great deal will depend on whether or not the consumer finds the new developments to be more attractive in terms of convenience, cost, and safety.

THE PRESENT PAYMENTS SYSTEM

Before going further, let us first consider the present payments system. To the average consumer, a payments system is mostly just cash, checks, and charge accounts. To the Federal Reserve System, whose duty it is to provide an efficient payments system for the public, it is primarily a system created to clear checks and settle accounts with member banks.

The check clearing or check collection system, as it is often referred to, is somewhat complex, primarily because of the volume of checks handled by the system, the relationship of the banks involved, and the distances between them. Checks deposited by individuals and corporations with a given bank are presented for collection or payment of funds back to the banks upon which the checks are drawn. This would be a simple procedure if only two banks were involved, as they could simply exchange checks and settle for the difference in some manner. Essentially this is the way a city clearinghouse is run. Banks in the city get together and exchange bagsful of checks and settle for the difference, usually with funds deposited in their local Federal Reserve branch.

When two banks from different cities are involved, the same procedure could be utilized if the banks were willing to pay the cost of transporting the checks. This is not necessary, however, since it is one of the functions of the Federal Reserve System. Checks to be collected in distant cities can be presented to a Federal Reserve branch, and the latter will, in turn, forward them to another Federal Reserve branch, located in or near the city where the bank on which the checks were drawn resides. Many

Entities Involved With the Check Collection System

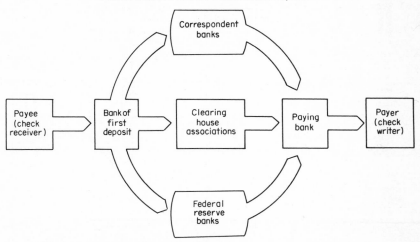

Fig. 1-1   Entities involved with the check collection system. (*From "The Check Collection System: A Quantitative Description," Bank Administration Institute, Park Ridge, Ill.*)

banks do not belong to the Federal Reserve System, however, and those banks send or receive their checks through a member bank by establishing what is known as a correspondent relationship. In actual practice, the system is more complex than described, because banks with a large correspondent business oftentimes can speed up the collection process by sending checks directly to similar banks in other cities. (See Figures 1-1 and 1-2.)

A check given to a Federal Reserve branch that is drawn on a bank in another city theoretically could not result in collected funds for the depositing bank until enough time has passed for the check to be sent and the funds received. Because of the volume of checks, there is no practical way to keep track of the actual date collected funds are available at the depositing bank for each individual check. What the Federal Reserve does is to establish zones around each office, and grant deferred credit for deposited checks based on the zone in which the drawing bank is located. For checks drawn on banks within the immediate area, the Federal Reserve gives immediate, same-day credit. Checks drawn on banks within the next zone are eligible for credit the following day, and in the next zone, credit 2 days hence.

Until 1972, the Federal Reserve had been granting deferred credit on a scheduling basis, which was better than the actual physical collection and settlement capabilities of the system. In this manner the Federal Reserve in effect created money, often referred to as *float*, by allowing a bank to utilize funds before they were actually collected. However, during 1972, the Federal Reserve began making significant changes to the system in order that the majority of checks drawn in the United States could be cleared in a single day.

Individual banks also create a form of float by allowing consumers immediate credit for checks deposited even though they themselves may not receive credit for those checks for several days. Most banks use a system of deferred credit similar to that of the Federal Reserve for their corporate accounts, but it, too, results in additional float. Studies have shown that many checking account customers, both individual and corporate, have learned to use float and mail delay to their advantage.

An electronic funds transfer system, such as the one envisioned by checkless-society proponents, would virtually eliminate float. Funds would be moved immediately. The elimination of float apparently will be somewhat painful to banks, corporations, and individuals, and has been one of the stumbling blocks for the rapid implementation

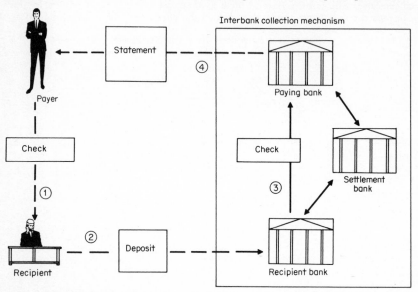

Fig. 1-2 Check collection system. *(From "The Check Collection System: A Quantitative Description," Bank Administration Institute, Park Ridge, Ill.)*

of electronic funds transfer systems. This is one of the reasons that the Federal Reserve System has chosen to eliminate float gradually, to provide a more orderly evolution into electronic funds transfers.

THE PAYMENTS SYSTEM IN DEVELOPMENT

The payments system of the future is already taking shape in the form of three developments presently occurring. The first is the development of automated clearing facilities for interbank exchange of prearranged depositing and bill-paying services. The second is the development of point-of-sale terminal systems for linking customers with their checking and credit-card accounts when making purchases at a retail store. The third is the development of unattended, automatic banking services equipment, providing the customer with 24-hour cash withdrawal, cash advance loans, intra-account funds transfers, and deposit services.

It appears likely that these three developments will continue to emerge separately, and will be accepted because of different forces at work. However, at some point in time they will probably become more interrelated in the customer's eyes. The sophisticated customer will learn to utilize the components of the system and to avoid using cash or checks whenever he or she so chooses.

Automated Clearing Facilities   In the early seventies, local and regional clearinghouses established payments system study groups, often referred to as SCOPE committees (Special Committee On Paperless Entries). At least 24 cities across the country had established a payments system study or SCOPE group by the end of 1972.

The original SCOPE Committee was the one formed in California in 1968. California's system design and organizational activities led to the establishment of automated clearinghouses in San Francisco and Los Angeles on October 16, 1972. These facilities have the capability of processing previously arranged electronic payments and deposits. Entry of either of these two types of transactions can be made by a participating bank from magnetic tape or punched cards. For example, the participat-

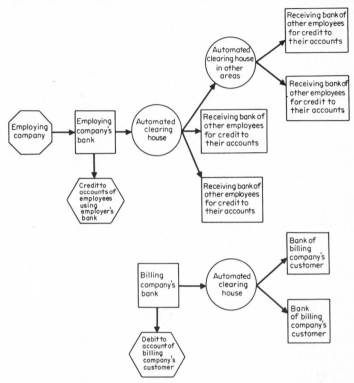

Fig. 1-3   Automated payments to employees. Top: Mechanism to credit employees with payroll amounts from employer. Bottom: Mechanism to debit employee's account and credit accounts of those to whom he or she authorized payment of fixed-frequency, fixed-amount bills. (*From "Banking," October, 1971.*)

ing bank accepts a reel of magnetic tape from an employer, representing the company's payroll. (Participating employees do not then receive a check.) The bank retains all the deposits for the participating employees who bank with it, and duplicates the remainder of the tape for submission to the automated clearinghouse in San Francisco or Los Angeles. The automated clearinghouse accumulates and merges tapes from all participating banks. At the end of the merge, the participating banks get a reel of tape representing employee deposits submitted by other participating banks. In this fashion an employer can deposit payroll earnings to employee checking accounts in any bank across the state of California. (See Figure 1-3.)

The Atlanta banking community implemented an automated clearinghouse in mid-1973. Initially the automated clearinghouse accepted preauthorized payments with a system it developed, known as Bill-Check. The project team developed the system while working with all the major utilities in the Atlanta area.

The idea behind Bill-Check is to have the firm continue sending its bills to customers, with one slight difference. At the time that the consumer wants to pay the bill, he or she merely signs it and returns it to the firm. The customer does not remit a check.

The firm processes the bill as it does any other accounts receivable item. As the accounts receivable files are updated, a tape is prepared showing the amounts of the bills that have been paid by the Bill-Check plan along with consumers' checking account numbers. The tape is submitted to the bank as the firm's deposit. The bank retains payments made by its own customers, and submits the rest of the tape to the automated clearinghouse in Atlanta. Ultimately the payment will appear on the consumer's statement as a paid item. In market research studies done by the group, 63 per cent of the consumers polled stated that they would like to use such a service if it were made available. For the consumer, the Bill-Check eliminates the need to write a check, yet gives the consumer complete control over the timing of the payment.

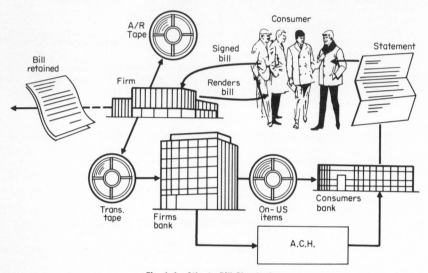

Fig. 1-4   Atlanta Bill-Check plan.

Each of the Atlanta banks will market the Bill-Check service to its own individual bill-rendering customers. In addition, it is planned to market individually a direct-deposit payroll service soon after the implementation of the automated Bill-Check program. (See Figure 1-4.)

The automated clearinghouse seems certain to be an integral part of the payment system of the future because of three significant events that occurred in 1974. First, the U.S. Treasury announced its plans to use the system for the payment of Government employees and Social Security recipients. This began on a trial basis with Air Force employees in California and Georgia, and with Social Security recipients in Florida and Georgia. The second event was the formation of the National Automated Clearing House Association (NACHA) in early 1974. Eighteen regional clearinghouse groups, each having made a commitment to establish an automated clearinghouse, became members of NACHA. The third event was the publication of industry standards for interregional exchange of paperless entries by the Automated Clearing House Task Force set up by the American Bankers Association in 1973.

Point-of-Sale Systems Among the point-of-sale system developments that took place in the early seventies was the Instant Transaction system tested by the Hempstead Bank of Long Island. Twenty-nine hundred customers of the bank's Syosset, New York, branch were offered an Instant Transaction or IT card to use in place of cash in local Syosset stores. Cooperating merchants utilized a special terminal connected on-line to the bank's computer. As the customer concluded a transaction, he or she gave the merchant the IT card, and this was inserted along with a sales slip into the special terminal. The customer authorized the transfer of funds from checking account to the merchant's account by keying his or her own secret, personal identification code into a special box connected to the terminal. During the test, the average Syosset customer used the card four times a month, with the greatest volume generated at supermarkets, long-time cash bastions.

In the Columbus, Ohio, suburb of Upper Arlington, a somewhat similar test was conducted jointly by City National Bank, BankAmericard, and IBM. Special bank cards were issued to selected Upper Arlington residents, and they were encouraged to use the card in place of cash at stores in the area's two major shopping centers.

Both tests were judged successful in terms of customer and merchant acceptance. The customers enjoyed the convenience of cashless and checkless shopping, particularly in places where credit had not before been available. The credit or funds transfer through the terminal added little time to the transaction, and system downtime was not a serious problem. As in the previously described test, customers were selected from more affluent neighborhoods, and tended to be better educated. The tests pointed toward a need for two types of payment for purchases: checking accounts withdrawals and deferred charges. The merchants appreciated the guaranteed payment feature of these electronic purchases.

During 1972, the two major bank-card organizations announced their plans to implement nationwide computer-based authorization systems that will ultimately be capable of supporting on-line terminals and electronically transferring funds. The two organizations' plans appear to be a logical evolution of their services, inasmuch as bank cards have had growing national acceptance. Not as apparent is retailer acceptance of multiple terminals for credit functions only.

The large national retailers have been building on-line point-of-sale systems on their own. These systems utilize a terminal capable of capturing inventory reorder information while also recording credit sales against the retailer's own customer base. Often the same terminal performs other cash register functions. To these national retailers with profitable credit operations and substantial system investment, additional terminals at the point-of-sale station have little appeal.

However, these same retailers desire the advantages of a check verification system, according to an extensive point-of-sale study undertaken in 1972 by a payments project sponsored by Atlanta's major commercial banks. In what was planned to be a historical first, these otherwise major competitors jointly sponsored a project to design a cooperative point-of-sale system for the Atlanta area. Knowing that bad-check losses are substantial, project members proposed that their system's terminals first be installed for check verification at the point of sale. At the time of purchase, the consumer would present his or her check and bank card to the merchant. The card would be inserted in the terminal and the check amount keyed by the merchant. The bank's computer would then verify that the customer had funds available and would guarantee the check to be good.

The Atlanta system, as proposed, would connect individual bank computers with merchant terminals through a cooperatively owned computer switch. Ultimately the system would allow consumers to utilize their plastic card for purchases against their checking accounts, for charges against their bank-card account, or for check verification. The terminals would be either bank-owned, merchant-owned, or shared, depending upon the relationship and volume. National retailers with their own point-of-sale systems could transmit accumulated bank-card transactions to the central switch at the end of their business day.

The Atlanta point-of-sale project may, however, serve only as a model, since the Atlanta banks tabled the project indefinitely in 1974. This action came as a result of inquiries made by the Justice Department and a denial by the Federal Reserve to operate the switching center for the banks experimentally.

It is not clear, at this writing, how many point-of-sale systems will be developed across the country, or how significant banking's involvement will be. Action by members of the thrift industry indicates their strong desire to be involved in this development from the very beginning. Early in 1973, a segment of the thrift industry announced plans for its own card-oriented electronic funds transfer system known as MINTS (Mutual Institutions National Transfer System). In 1974, First Federal Savings and Loan, in Lincoln, Nebraska, rocked the financial world with the installation of teller terminals in two Hinky-Dinky supermarket locations. Surviving several lawsuits, the Hinky-Dinky System is apparently legal, and has since been expanded to include multiple associations and additional merchant locations. Basically, the system allows consumers to make deposits and withdrawals at the courtesy booth within the supermarket.

Outside the financial area and in place is a nonbank network connecting oil company point-of-sale terminals with a central computer in Atlanta. Total point-of-sale system packages are available from several sources. It seems likely that consumers will be making purchases with electronically transferred funds at retail outlets within a few short years, but they will probably be carrying a number of cards in their billfolds in order to accomplish this.

Cash Dispensers and Automated Tellers　Probably the most glamorous recent banking innovation may prove to be the "money machine." Dispensing packets of dollars at the insertion of a card at any time, night or day, these electromechanical machines primarily offer convenience to the customer. Money machines are in reality either cash dispensers or automated tellers. The cash dispenser's only function is to dispense cash and charge the withdrawal to the customer's checking account. The automated teller can, in addition, make savings account withdrawals, accept deposits, and grant loans.

Initially these money machines were off-line, stand-alone devices located in bank lobbies or at bank exteriors. Whether or not these devices can be placed elsewhere without constituting a bank "branch" has not been legally tested at the time of this writing. Commercial banks apply for branch permits in states where branching is legal, and house them separately.

One of the first banks to install this type of equipment in a separate, stand-alone, automated branch was the Huntington Bank of Columbus, Ohio. This tellerless branch was known as the Handy Bank. At one of these, a customer can complete most normal demand deposit and savings account transactions with the automated tellers installed. The Handy Bank branch, located in a convenient shopping center, is open 24 hours a day and, while completely peopleless, is not altogether paperless.

Federally chartered savings and loans were given permission in 1972 by the Federal Home Loan Bank Board to install three automated tellers or cash dispensers at locations of their choosing. This may ultimately lead to the machines' being installed inside shopping malls or even in nonbank stores.

More recently, equipment manufacturers have begun to deliver on-line versions of these machines that will eventually broaden their use because of the broader access to authorization files. Off-line versions contain only a limited negative authorization file, and information regarding credit limits has to be stored within the magnetic stripe on the back of the card.

On-line systems will make it possible for banks to share terminals, or, more importantly from a competitive standpoint, to allow interbank exchange. A group of banks in West Virginia has already begun this through a program called "Mr. Cash." Participating banks issue "Mr. Cash" cards that can actuate on-line cash dispensers at their own banks and at any of the other banks in the system.

THE FEDERAL RESERVE SYSTEM'S ROLE FOR THE FUTURE

The evolution of the payments system will be influenced along the way by the actions of the Federal Reserve System. With a public announcement in June, 1971, the Fed signified its intention to make the check processing system more efficient, as a first step toward ultimately providing facilities for the electronic transfer of funds. With this first step, the Federal Reserve began implementation of regional check processing centers at selected cities which will soon give them a national network for same-day check clearing. As mentioned previously, the goal of same-day clearing is the elimination of the float which exists in the present system. Although the Federal Reserve is primarily interested in removing float to make the system more equitable and efficient, its removal is a necessary precedent to implementation of some of the proposed electronic alternatives.

The Federal Reserve System has also installed an extensive communication network known as the Federal Reserve Wire, which it envisions as the linkup between regional and local networks serving automated clearinghouses and point-of-sale systems. From its commitment in terms of personnel and resources, it is clear that the Federal Reserve will be a strong influence in reshaping the nation's payments system. By funding study projects and the equipment necessary to operate automated clearing facilities, it is making it economically more attractive for the commercial banking industry to move in this direction.

THE CONSUMER'S ROLE

Market studies undertaken in the late sixties indicated that the consumer was not ready and perceived no need for the checkless society. Most of these studies, however, were done by sampling consumer attitude on proposed or conceived alternatives to the check, because actual experience was nonexistent at the time. The generally negative results of these studies, as much as anything else, caused the banking industry to proceed with caution in trying new developments.

In the early seventies, competition for checking account funds led banks in several areas of the country to do away with check charges and to offer free checking accounts. Just how many checks this added to the system is unknown, but to the consumer receiving free checks, it lessened the attractiveness of electronic alternatives. Banks in cities where free checking is common continue to remain profitable. The capacity of the check processing system also seems quite capable of handling at least double its 1970 volume. These two facts by themselves are enough to assure us that the check will be around for a considerable number of years.

On the other hand, the inconvenience of checking accounts when compared to the convenience of newer alternatives will hasten acceptance of the new developments. Checks are sometimes difficult or inconvenient to cash and fraud losses are high — merchants who support the system suffer bad-debt losses and customers must obtain check-cashing cards and must frequently wait in lines to have checks cashed or to deposit funds. The sophisticated customer who has obtained cash quickly from a cash dispenser will remember this the next time he or she waits in line to cash a check for a similar amount. Consumer attitude and consumer demand will grow more positive with familiarity. The implementation of the electronic alternatives described earlier should accelerate at a rapid pace in the last half of the seventies.

Other developments outside the financial sector will have an influence on consumer acceptance. An example of these is the payments procedure set up for the Bay Area Rapid Transit System in San Francisco. Riders on that system purchase special magnetic-stripe cards for fixed amounts, such as $20. The rider inserts the card in an entry device when boarding the train and again when exiting. The fare for the ride is calculated and subtracted from the remaining balance stored in the magnetic stripe. The device also accepts cash or a second card when the remaining balance is insufficient.

COMPETITION AND THE CHANGING BANKING STRUCTURE

Changes to the payments system emanate primarily from the commercial banking sector. However, other financial sectors will increasingly play a more important role in the development of the system of the future. As mentioned earlier, savings and loans have already gained authority to install card-actuated cash dispensers and automated tellers. The mutual savings banks are installing their own national transfer system, and in several states provide various forms of checking accounts. As the seventies unfold, it appears likely that savings and loan institutions will also in some manner be granted checking account powers. Considering the fact that these types of institutions have no investment in equipment capable of reading the magnetic characters on checks, they will probably bypass them in favor of electronic alternatives. Because of the competitive nature of these types of institutions, their entry into the field will tend further to spur developments by the commercial banking industry.

In Massachusetts, mutual savings banks are allowed to issue a form of a check called a *negotiable order of withdrawal* (the NOW) on savings accounts that bear interest. Although illegal in most other states, the practice is gaining in popularity, and could be approved by regulatory bodies in states where they are now prohibited. If NOW should become common practice, it would probably hasten the development of electronic alternatives. The Federal Reserve and the FDIC and other regulatory agencies have long felt that interest paid on checking accounts was undesirable. However, they are more likely to be receptive if the practice is limited to special savings accounts where previously arranged electronic deposits and payments (which can be processed less expensively) are the only types of transactions accepted other than at lobby teller stations.

THE SYSTEM OF THE FUTURE

In the last half of the seventies, sophisticated consumers will have learned the ways of a less-cash and less-check life-style. They will have electronic accounts at their banks or savings and loans that draw somewhat less interest than their regular savings accounts. Their paychecks will be deposited automatically into these accounts twice a month, and at regular intervals during the month, automatic withdrawals will be made for savings accounts transfers, mortgage payments or rents, insurance premiums, annually leveled utility bills, and fixed amounts to their bank-card accounts.

These same customers will have limited-use checking accounts. They will use these for the payment of bills accumulated through purchases at retail stores, which will still be administering their own credit programs. In most cities, customers will avoid the writing of checks by sending all bills rendered back to their banks. Banks in turn will pay the bills and subtract the total payments from customers' checking account balances. This will be a natural refinement of the Bill-Check program that was in use in 1974. The retailers will abandon their practice of having the signed statements returned directly.

Our customers of the future will use their bank cards for all purchases made at other retail establishments and for the withdrawal of cash at convenient downtown and shopping center locations. Since customers have regular amounts withdrawn from their automatic savings accounts, their bills will be paid at the last possible moment. This will leave them with either positive or negative balances in their bank-card accounts. Any positive balances will be transferred to the checking accounts, and any negative balances will automatically create loans, and customers will be so notified.

Because banks will use combined statements showing available balances in all account relationships, statements will begin to serve better the customers' financial planning requirements. Customers will receive periodically profit and loss type statements showing expenditures by classification. These will facilitate income tax preparation at the end of the year, and, where desired, allow banks to advise customers properly through financial budget programs. This will be done entirely at the customer's own option, inasmuch as public concern over the creation of personal financial data bases will limit this practice.

All this may sound like a variation of the checkless society originally rejected. In truth, some of the elements are still there, but then again so are checks and cash. Most importantly, all the options will still exist, and the choice will be left to the wishes of the consumer.

Chapter 2

ADP in Retailing: Point-of-Sale Automation

IRVING I. SOLOMON

President, Aris Associates, Plainview, New York; formerly
Vice President, Information Systems Division, National
Retail Merchants Association, New York, New York

Manufacturers of data processing equipment early saw a potential market in retailing operations. They saw quite clearly that the retail business was made up of many transactions on a daily basis, and recognized an important sales opportunity in helping the retailer handle those transactions. A number of manufacturers—notably IBM, NCR, and, to a lesser degree, Honeywell and Burroughs—had long maintained close contact with retail organizations. They not only saw a future market, but also had a pressing need to retain their existing markets in retailing.

FIRST PHASE

The initial applications in most retail establishments were, in fact, not specifically retail applications. Rather, computers were sold for payroll, general ledger, and similar uses. In some cases, inventory control systems at the warehouse and wholesale levels were also installed. But only rarely was there an attempt to install systems that dealt specifically with true retailing problems: inventory management, store-level merchandise planning and control, and the like. In other words, during the early stages, the computer was kept away from the store per se.

As long as the manufacturers were selling general business and accounting systems, neither the manufacturers' technical staffs nor the customers' ADP management needed to have any significant retail orientation. Thus ADP in retailing was dealing with the same problems as were, for example, companies engaged in manufacturing. As a consequence, there was little difference between applications in department stores, food chains, discounters, variety stores, specialty chains, etc., despite the widely differing nature of their operations. Moreover, these nonretail applications constituted only a very small portion of the total administrative workload of most retail companies, and the market for these applications soon became relatively saturated.

By 1963–1964, however, the computer manufacturers became convinced that the real market for their products in this area lay in actively dealing with the heart of the retail business—that is to say, in the control of merchandise and sales in the store. This marketing phase coincided with the development of the third-generation computers. Unless the computer manufacturers could persuade retailers to expand their applications, the latter were likely to retain their second-generation equipment, or worse yet (from the vendors' point of view), replace two or three second-generation rental machines with a single, less expensive third-generation computer.

The situation at this point was that although the manufacturers were stepping up their sales pressure, their sales representatives as a group did not clearly understand the real nature of the many different kinds of businesses that are lumped together under the term *retail*. (Indeed, the charge was made that some computer manufacturers were training their people at the expense of the retailers.) As a result, their sales to retailers increased substantially, although the gain to the latter was, unfortunately, less clear.

At the same time it must be admitted that in most retail organizations, ADP management itself was not fully cognizant of the problems of the retail business. In many cases, the retailer's ADP staff was largely composed of computer professionals taken from other industries or, frequently, from the equipment manufacturers. In all too many situations, the tendency was to impose applications on the retail buying and selling organizations without adequate changes in the manual procedures that were needed to provide the system input data, or in the necessary re-education in regard to them.

A related problem was that most ADP systems tended to force retail organizations toward increasingly centralized merchandise control. At this very time, however, many retailers had come to believe that only by decentralizing profit responsibility to store managers and department heads could they gain the flexibility to be fully responsive to the demands of the marketplace. Consequently, the increasing use of computers ran directly counter to the decentralization policies many retailers were trying to implement.

Using the computer for automatic merchandise ordering and control normally worked satisfactorily where the merchandise was stable in nature—characterized by relatively steady and predictable sales demand, depth of stock greater than was normal for most items, infrequent assortment changes, and reasonably constant vendor delivery schedules. Unfortunately, such merchandise probably constitutes less than 30 per cent of the collection in the variety stores and even less in department stores. One might also observe that such merchandise is typically the easiest to control by non-automated methods.

The data processing people had a language all their own, and so did the retailers. Communication consequently was poor, and there was insufficient effort on the part of ADP personnel to understand fully the needs of the using departments. Thus the systems that were developed were oriented heavily toward hardware. Programmers and analysts were primarily concerned with how efficiently their programs ran, and with what programming techniques. There was insufficient control over the data processing function. Management of the store had little alternative other than to accept whatever the data processing department said it should have. As a result, a new expense center, the computer, was established in retail organizations, from which the store managements had little or no tangible benefits.

SECOND PHASE

Company managements were now saying, "We must have ADP, at any cost! Convert! Mechanize! We'll be lost in the shuffle if we don't." So automation projects were initiated that had little or no cost justification. Major programs such as credit authorization were undertaken on the sole basis that the store just down the street had installed such a system. In some cases, advertising departments were dictating how credit operations should be run on the computer in order to accommodate their direct mail programs. Accounts payable systems were being developed without considering the store buyers' needs. Some of these systems actually hindered the buyer rather than helped. What was happening essentially was that decisions regarding data processing were being made by the wrong people and for the wrong reasons. Systems were implemented that produced a multitude of reports. When a report that was produced by the computer did not meet the exact needs of the user, the ADP department simply designed an additional report, and then ran both. A retail operations computer became primarily a printing press. At one large chain, merchandising reports produced for the buyers became so voluminous, and were printed on such large paper, that they became known affectionately as the "horse blanket." The size of this report on a weekly basis was measurable not in number of pages, but by weight of paper.

As the using departments became more and more disenchanted with the results of the computer, they became less meticulous about the input information they were submitting to the keypunch department. GIGO systems ("garbage in, garbage out") appeared in many department stores. The systems output became less accurate, and the information that was produced was largely not usable. For example, in one company the merchandise identification stubs that should have been forwarded to ADP for each garment sold were discarded; merchandise reports represented only 60 to 70 per cent of the goods that had actually been sold, and were thus worthless to the buyers. Non-ADP personnel in the store challenged the rising cost of ADP in the light of such poor results. Finally one store president questioned whether "we are not now in the computer business instead of the merchandising business."

THIRD PHASE

In some companies, communications broke down totally. User-departments, deciding that their efforts could be directed more profitably elsewhere, failed to cooperate with data processing. ADP became isolated. In one store, the results of the separation between ADP and the user-departments had such catastrophic effects that the overall profits were completely eliminated. One large store, in converting its accounts receivable system, failed to include the proper controls necessary for managing the delinquency of customers' accounts. As problems that would normally be associated with any data processing conversion occurred, the dunning of delinquent accounts was stopped. The ADP Department and the Credit Department had not spent sufficient time together to understand fully the system as a whole. Had they done so, this problem would never have occurred. When start-up problems began to lessen as the system entered its third and fourth months of conversion, the dunning that had been neglected was resumed—but with the dunning procedures out of sequence. The net effect was a bad-debt write-off approaching $2 million.

In sum, at the close of Phase 3, systems in many stores were producing inaccurate figures, reports were late, and the cost of ADP operations was escalating. Top managements of retail companies became increasingly dissatisfied with their ADP systems. As increased competition in a period of business decline led to severely reduced profit margins for many retailers, ADP expenses loomed steadily larger. Many of the fastest growing, most dynamic, and most profitable retail companies made relatively little use of computers.

PRESENT STATUS

In the past few years, many retailers have worked their way out of the type of unfortunate situations described above. As of 1975, it appeared that ADP in retailing had entered a period of stabilization and integration.

Stabilization The stabilization of the ADP function in retailing is being aided by four developments. First, top management is becoming directly involved in the ADP program. Store presidents have begun to do more than merely attend a vendor's "executive computer concept" seminar or symposium. Intensive seminars have been set up within the store, run by the store's strengthened internal ADP department. The seminars have involved all levels of store management.

Second, management teams have been established within the store to oversee the priorities and plans, and to establish controls for the ADP department. Management has begun to get involved at the critical stages of systems development.

Third, the technical versus retailing gap is being reduced. Personnel from outside the systems area have been transferred from the retail side, and have become systems analysts. Systems personnel have been promoted to management positions outside of the ADP department. For example, at one medium-sized department store, the vice president and treasurer is a former ADP manager. In addition, systems personnel are going through the store's orientation program for other store personnel, and are being exposed to each facet of the store's operations. The isolation of the ADP systems department is tending to disappear.

The fourth major development is the growing sophistication of ADP people in retailing. Through the activities of the National Retail Merchants Association in the United States and the International Association of Department Stores, as well as of associations in other phases of retailing, a large number of systems and management personnel have been brought together to learn what other stores are doing, and to exchange useful ideas to improve operations.

Integration   Another major change has been the integration of ADP applications within the store. There has been a great focus on the basic requirements of retailing and how they can best be served through automation. The early systems developed for retailing—each on an isolated basis—have become refined and restructured, so that one system naturally flows into another. The output from one system is the input to the next. The flow of the systems work in many stores is comparable to the flow of information through the stores and the flow of transactions that take place. The overall impact is to merge the detailed component systems into a few major systems.

Finally, this integration of the various systems into an overall framework increases the utilization of all resources, human as well as machine. This phase of consolidation and integration is well under way, but it is by no means completed. Only a relatively small number of retailers can say that their ADP activity is fully under control and making optimum contribution to profitability.

But even before consolidation and integration are fully implemented, a new phase of automation is taking place, the most important development in retail ADP today—the installation of point-of-sale (POS) terminals.

POINT-OF-SALE SYSTEMS

The first attempt to capture all the sales transaction data at one register and also to perform credit authorization was the UNITOTE (General Instrument Corp.) system developed in the sixties. UNITOTE was an electromechanical POS system with a specially designed keyboard register to capture transaction code, employee number, account number, price, and quantity of each item. The register automatically printed the subtotal but required manual entry of tax. The data were placed onto paper tape or magnetic tape, which was then fed to a computer. The unit also performed credit authorization via a negative credit file.

The UNITOTE system represented a method for control recording of all POS data off-line. A succeeding trend was toward a combined cash register, recording device, and credit authorization terminal. The next move was to an on-line POS terminal, exemplified by General Electric's short-lived Tradar System in 1969, which used simple terminals connected to a central computer. Tradar included provisions for sensing machine-readable merchandise tags and forwarding the data directly to the central computer.

Typical System   Today's typical POS system configuration consists of self-contained terminals that can perform all sales recording independently of a central computer. However, the computer or minicomputers tied together are used for credit authorization and merchandise control. Following are the basic components of such a POS system:

Data Entry. At present, most POS data are entered manually at a terminal keyboard. Recording of merchandise data is accomplished automatically by optical, magnetic, or punched-hole readers sensing machine-readable merchandise tickets. Credit purchases are recorded automatically from machine-readable cards. Manual keyboard entry is still needed to define the type of transaction, make price changes, and enter discounts or merchandise adjustments.

Calculations. Each terminal is a self-contained calculator, and performs all the item-price and tax calculations.

Output. Types of output for the salesperson include: (1) visual display of transaction recording, (2) hard-copy sales receipt, (3) manager readout, and (4) presentation of credit information. The output to the computer system is by cassette, magnetic tape, or directly by data transmission.

Credit Checking. On-line verification of customers' accounts stops customers with bad accounts or those who have exceeded a given dollar limit. The machine-readable credit card using embossing or an optical-readable font is part of the current technology.

Merchandise Inventory Control. The heart of the integrated POS system is its merchandise inventory control software, which makes possible an accurate accounting of each item and implements specific purchase policies and economic reorder points. The central computer program processes the data input from the POS terminals and presents the resulting information to management. Without the implementation of inventory control, an integrated POS system is not justified economically.

Implementation. The total effect of implementing POS in all areas is:

1. Reduction of buyers' workload through valid data reporting.

2. Better merchandise reporting and hence improved inventory mix.

3. More accurate identification of merchandise ticketing, and therefore more reliable data read by the sophisticated POS registers.

4. Dramatic reduction in the cost of the receiving, order checking, and accounts payable operations.

5. Lower inventory carrying charges and greater sales because of the ability to maximize inventory turnover, minimize stockouts, maximize customer service, and minimize stock on hand.

Impetus As of now, the consideration by retailers of new electronic POS equipment is most commonly in conjunction with the installation of registers in new stores. Traditionally, retailers plan the opening of new stores with considerable foresight. Stores cannot put off the decision about POS until the scheduled date for opening new units is close at hand. This pressure is a source of concern because the retailer frequently feels that there is not enough time to evaluate the alternative equipment available. However, even when complete information is available, the final decision is at best a trade-off among alternatives.

It seems likely that the offerings from various manufacturers will become less divergent as time goes on, and that the selection of one manufacturer or another will not cause the retailer any serious problem. Certainly, those problems which arise from having selected an "incorrect" vendor are less serious than the problems that will arise because no vendor was selected at all. Moreover, as of mid-1975 there were no more mechanical registers available in the market, and thus all choices had to be of electronic POS.

The second most important impetus to installing POS equipment is the need for more information, for both merchandising and credit. Third is the requirement for accurate capture of increased amounts of data. The fourth requirement is for speedier check-out in order to solve the problem of customers queueing up at the registers, thus avoiding the loss of good credit customers who become annoyed at the length of time it takes to check credit. The last-named three items together — the need for more information, the need for accuracy, and the need for speed — point up the problems to be solved at the point of sale.

The automatic reading of merchandise information and customer credit cards provides a great amount of data accurately and quickly. Further, the POS register is programmed to guide the salesperson through cash register procedures quickly and accurately. Studies indicate that these features enable a clerk to accomplish a check-out between 10 and 20 per cent faster than with the traditional register, at the same time identifying himself or herself. Thus, if all the data capturing requirements were to remain the same and the sales volume and customer volume were to be constant, the average retailer would be able to operate his or her store with approximately 15 per cent fewer registers. Naturally this figure varies with the type of operation, transaction mix, and the physical location of registers.

Evaluation of POS Proposals After all POS systems have been evaluated technically, the decision often rests heavily on seven factors, most of which have very little to do with the technical capabilities of the machines. These are (in approximate order of importance):

1. *Vendor's financial stability.* The retailer must be concerned with the stability of the vendor in terms of long-range commitment to the POS market and ability to supply additional units of equipment in the future.

2. *Maintenance.* Retailers should expect the same level of maintenance and service that has been available for traditional cash register equipment and electronic

computers. POS maintenance should include the POS device, ticketing equipment, and computers and controllers. Questions of special maintenance importance are:

a. Who manufactures the equipment? Generally the user is more comfortable if the equipment is manufactured locally or at least in the United States.

b. Who services the equipment? Critical questions here include:

    (1) How many maintenance personnel are available?

    (2) Where are they located, and what is the guaranteed elapsed time between placing of a service call and arrival of a maintenance person at the customer's site? The retailer who has branches or "twigs" in extremely remote locations is particularly concerned about the vendor's ability to provide quality service on a timely basis.

    (3) What hours do the maintenance people work and what are their premium rates for second- and third-shift maintenance?

c. What are the cost arrangements for maintenance: Is it included in the equipment price or is it contracted for separately?

d. Frequently equipment is tailored to meet the customer's specifications. While this is certainly of advantage functionally, it can pose problems if the maintenance staff is not trained on the custom hardware. Generally it is preferable to obtain standard units or units with minimal modifications involving maintenance problems.

3. *Special requirements.* Almost every retailer has one operation that is of special concern. One store may be extremely concerned about credit checking and authorization, another may be especially interested in the register's ability to handle employees' discounts accurately. A third may be primarily interested in the security of handling returns or voids, or other operations open to theft or fraud.

4. *Availability.* A very practical consideration is the ability of the vendor to supply equipment in time for a new store opening. Indeed, this consideration may overshadow all others.

5. *Software.* A vast amount of data will be captured at the point of sale. Frequently stores do not have the time or personnel to develop the necessary programs to process all these data through computers. As a result, they may look to outside sources to provide this assistance. If the equipment manufacturer can also provide the software for sales audit control, inventory control, accounts receivable, accounts payable, etc., the store may consider that obtaining all these from a single vendor is an attractive option.

6. *Backup.* Investigation should be made into the backup procedures available in case one or more units in the system become inoperative. Generally when a POS device is connected to some other unit, it has the ability to function independently of that unit in an energency. The question then becomes, what capabilities are lost when, for example, the central controller goes down and the register units are left to operate on a stand-alone basis? Generally two functions are lost: the credit-checking capability (since the unit does not have access to the credit file attached to the controller), and the ability to produce machine-processable output in the form of magnetic tape. This is because the unit, not designed to operate as a stand-alone, frequently uses the computer to control the recording device. When this unit is unavailable, there is no recording medium at the terminal, and the only output is the register journal tape. In order to recapture transaction information, it is necessary to keypunch this journal tape and process the resulting punched cards. As of 1975–1976, cassette backup promises to be almost standard for stand-alone.

One solution to this problem is to provide optical font on the register print mechanism so that the journal tape can be optically scanned. There should be assurance that the quality of the printing is sufficiently high to achieve good optical scanning results. It is important to include an indication on the journal tape of information not recorded on the output magentic tape. In addition, some system for immediate supervisor notification should be developed so that when the controller is inoperative corrective action can be taken as soon as possible.

7. *Flexibility.* Many POS manufacturers have designed their equipment to adapt to either optical or magnetic input. One important criterion for selecting a manufacturer should be the ability to accommodate changing technology at minimum cost. Flexibility also extends to the total modularity of equipment. A unit installed today which re-

quires manual keying of merchandise information should be adaptable to a wand reader or other hand-held device, as the technology of OCR becomes cost-feasible. The retailer should determine at the outset what the cost of making such adjustments to the equipment configuration will be, and include it in the purchase contract.

Unfortunately, no single manufacturer satisfies all the criteria, and compromises will be called for. The decision is not easy or clean-cut. Not to be overlooked are units and components available from OEM (original equipment manufacturers) which will tie in to one or more of the currently available systems. For example, it is possible to get a wand reader from one manufacturer which will plug into the POS register of a second manufacturer, which in turn will log information out of the cassette available from yet a third manufacturer. In addition, it may be possible to utilize multiple vendors to supply the controllers, minicomputers, tapes, disks, and other files in order to achieve an optimum combination of units for a particular operation. As of 1975–1976, it appears that this will be a complete POS with all equipment serviced by one vendor. Indeed, in the future some manufacturers will undoubtedly become so well known for their particular components (wand readers, printers, controllers, etc.) that they will find their major market is in OEM equipment rather than in selling the total system.

Conversion Conversion to the more sophisticated POS environment involves the training of personnel and the modification of current data processing procedures to accommodate new data sources. Even more difficult, however, are some of the functional problems created. For example, if merchandise marking and identification techniques are to be changed, what will be done in the interim when there may be two types of merchandise tags or a variety of customer identification cards, etc.? Another problem is how to operate in an environment where not all units have the new registers, or where one selling unit has a combination of new and old registers. Some manufacturers have attempted to solve this problem by providing marking techniques which combine the old technology and the new. Transitional problems face the industry today and for the next 3 to 5 years.

A similar problem exists in connection with reading credit cards. In this instance the technology is critical, since it may involve reissuing all outstanding credit cards, which is economically onerous if not unfeasible. An alternative might be to add the appropriate encoding to the existing cards by some simple means such as affixing an OCR strip as customers request changes of address, etc., in their accounts.

Hardware can yield only a partial solution to these problems. The full solution lies in the analysis and design of a total system wherein careful consideration is given to the requirements of the implementation and transition periods. In many cases this may mean operating dual systems for a time. If so, adequate attention should be paid to the cost of such an operation to ensure that the time period for this dual operation is reduced to a minimum.

Standards Optical Character Reading, OCR-A, Size 1, is a standard that has been available for a number of years, sponsored by the American National Standards Institute and published as a document available to anyone who wishes to use this technology. As of October, 1974, the retail industry has agreed on a standard, Optical Character Reading, Type A Font, for identifying merchandise, credit cards, and even the salesperson. This standard has been published and made available to the manufacturers of equipment, who have agreed to supply equipment with this capability for the next 2 to 5 years. Additionally, the manufacturers of merchandise are now conforming to this standard for tickets, tags, and labels.

Another standard, Universal Product Code (UPC), originally announced on April 3, 1973, has been established during 1974 and 1975 for the marking of merchandise by the supermarket food industry and its suppliers. This code consists of a group of black and white bars identifying the items of merchandise on the supermarket shelves.

There are a number of differences in concept between the two standards. In the supermarket industry, marking is based on the fact that the major items on the shelves are staples regularly recurring and available to the customer. The purpose of the UPC code is to allow for high-speed check-out through a laser beam at a conveyor belt, and a minicomputer look-up for the identification of price. A 10- to 15-digit code is printed on the labels.

The supermarkets and their food suppliers are working under a different concept from that of the department stores. The supermarkets can have their merchandise — 6,000 to 8,000 items — marked at point of manufacture, since most of the items either have labels affixed to cans or glass containers, or have label information directly printed on the container, as for example on a cereal box. However, all the merchandise in the department store area must be marked not only with price, but also with other significant information — e.g., style, class, season — far in excess of the 10 digits assigned to the UPC code.

The original 10-digit code assigned by the supermarket industry was not expandable at the time of discussion between both industries. It was only machine-readable via laser beam scanner on a conveyor belt, whereas the department store industry was looking for a merchandise ticket/tag/label that could be entered manually into a keyboard of a register, or read by a wand, at a much lower cost. The department store is not a check-out operation, since it uses registers located within each individual department in the store. It is perhaps logical to expect that compatibility in marking merchandise under both concepts can be attained in the future. However, at present both industries are attacking their own marking problems independently. In this connection, it must be understood that normally the consumer going through a supermarket will buy from 10 to 30 items, going up and down the aisles, while a department store customer averages about 2.7 items per purchase.

System Choice   POS devices range from models that merely duplicate cash registers (except that the mechanical and electromechanical equipment has been replaced by electronics) to terminals that will only operate when connected to a central computer. Equipment manufacturers range from giant companies such as NCR (which has a computer background and has been marketing equipment to the retail industry since its founding) to small electronics companies composed of no more than half a dozen technical people. There is substantial turnover in the latter category.

The potential purchaser of point-of-sale equipment is confronted with the huge task of deciding which vendor to use and which features are really needed. Without question, it is a buyer's market, but what may be the right device for one store may fall far short of meeting the requirements of a competitor down the street. Retailers must look ahead to what their future requirements will be. Even well-thought-out systems that meet today's needs could be totally inadequate in the future. POS may be the largest single decision that the retailer's ADP department will be involved in, and can have a major impact not only on the future of ADP for the store, but on the future of the store as well, in terms of maintaining its competitive status in the market.

PROGNOSIS AND PRESCRIPTION

There have been three great electromechanical developments in retailing history. The first was the cash register; the second, the computer; and the third is the point-of-sale terminal. The last is ushering in a new age in merchandise control. It should do much ultimately to reduce the cost of inventory, cut down on stockouts, improve turnover, increase sales by a faster and more accurate response to customer demand, and economize in many support operations. The key to success lies in the system area. The level of effort in retail systems development must be increased if we are to see these expectations fulfilled.

Packaged Programs: Application-Oriented vs. Non-Application-Oriented   Systems standardization is part of the answer. Utility packages (operating systems, file management systems, terminal polling, etc.) are available from equipment manufacturers and software houses, and will be utilized. But total retail application packages developed by manufacturers or software firms will have little impact on most retailers. Although there will be a market for such packages in the smaller stores, it is more economical for the medium- and large-sized retailer to do its own application development. Most stores will utilize outside expertise from time to time; however, the majority of their systems development and programming will probably best be done with their own in-house capabilities. Only in this way can stores assure themselves that the systems they are developing will truly meet their needs.

Minicomputers   One hardware area that will effect dramatic changes is the minicomputer designed for the retail industry. In one type of installation, the unit located in the branch stores that controls point-of-sale terminals is, in fact, a minicomputer.

With the new technology of large-scale integrated circuits continuing to bring down the price of computing power, minicomputers now provide more power than did many of their larger predecessors, at a fraction of the price.

In typical installations, the minicomputers will be connected via communications lines to a central computer that will still be required to store the large files of data, and to handle the larger data processing requirements. These systems will enable store personnel ranging from salesclerks to store manager to president to use the computer with the same ease with which they are using typewriters and adding machines and calculators today.

SELECTIVE BIBLIOGRAPHY

Lev, Joseph, *EDP Systems in Retail: Why They Fail*, Cresap, McCormick & Paget, New York, November, 1972.
Shaffer, Richard P., *Point of Sale Report, 1972–1973*, Gambit Strategies, Inc., New York.
Solomon, Irving I., *Management Uses of the Computer*, Harper & Row, New York, 1971.

Chapter 3

ADP in Banking

JOHN D. BEDNAR

Manager, Industry Marketing Development—Financial,
Burroughs Corporation, Detroit, Michigan

Banks and other financial institutions were among the first commercial users of automatic data processing equipment. Over the years, much equipment has been developed specifically for use by banks, beginning before the turn of the century with the first adding machines.

Through a process of evolution, these adding machines gradually acquired greater capabilities and became the accounting machines that served as the mainstay of a bank's depositor accounting system. They stored information on a hard-copy record — a ledger card — which was a convenient and efficient way of keeping the records for a relatively small number of customer accounts such as loan, demand deposit, and savings. Many of these machines in versions that make use of the latest technology are still in use today, typically in smaller institutions. These units performed their function well, but the volume of items handled made their limitations apparent. Although faster than manual methods, they were too slow for processing the rapidly increasing volumes of paperwork, notably checks and related documents.

The popularization of checking accounts by the banking industry accounts for a considerable portion of the increase in the number of transactions handled by a typical commercial bank. Until the post-World War II period, checking accounts were almost exclusively used by business and professional people. Personal checking accounts were unusual.

Because they were relatively few in number and characterized by high levels of activity per account, commercial checking accounts were almost ideally suited to the ledger-card approach provided by accounting machines. The promotion of personal checking accounts changed this picture by introducing large numbers of new accounts, each with relatively low activity. This type of operation was well suited to automation, and banks were among the first business establishments to recognize the potential of the computer and to adapt it to their needs.

At first, mechanical tabulating equipment oriented to punched cards was used extensively. These machines were already available and were relatively easy to use in punching a record for each check, deposit slip, and other bank documents. The machines had the advantage of greatly speeding up document handling at comparatively lower cost.

With the advent of paper-tape and magnetic-tape equipment, banks were provided with an additional capability, that of being able to store records in some chosen sequence for later rapid entry into a computing machine. To the bank customer the new systems meant the availability of lower-cost checking accounts, while to the bank they meant a more practical way of handling the large volume of new accounts.

The rapidly growing numbers of documents made further new approaches to paper handling necessary. Several methods were tried, including checks that were written directly on punched cards, and others that were coded with ultraviolet-sensitive material for machine reading.

After much effort, the banking industry, through the American Banking Association (ABA), standardized on magnetic-ink character recognition (MICR), using a stylized font called E13B for numeric and special characters. These characters are printed in standard format across the bottom of such documents as checks and deposit tickets that are used to introduce data into the data processing system. MICR printing has the advantage of being both human- and machine-readable. The ink used in printing the MICR coding on documents is so formulated as to be able to accept a magnetic charge. This allows the data to be read directly by equipment designed to recognize the magnetically encoded characters.

CONVERSION TO COMPUTERS

The number of banks that could afford to convert to computer-based systems was dramatically increased with the development of the second-generation computers in the early 1960s. Based on the transistor instead of the vacuum tube, these lower-cost systems were practical in smaller configurations to the point that ledger-card-oriented systems could be developed for use in the smallest banks. Both the customer and the bank benefited by the lower unit cost of handling financial transactions, resulting in still higher volumes of checks to be handled and services to be automated, such as trust accounting, and the initial on-line operation with remotely located terminals.

Developments in programming techniques also helped in reducing the cost of the computer installation. The introduction and acceptance of such commercially oriented languages as COBOL (Common Business Oriented Language) and RPG (Report Program Generator) helped to reduce the level of expertise needed by the programmers, and enabled them to concentrate more on finding solutions to problems and less on the basic methods of making the machines operate.

A basic breakthrough in data storage was the development of random-access disk files for both program and data storage, and disk drives with removable packs. These allowed an almost unlimited file size and made practical the processing of data without prior sorting.

The third generation of computers in the sixties and seventies was marked by a shift in emphasis to the operating system. These systems allowed the computer manufacturers to introduce to the banks a series of program packages specifically designed to solve the problems encountered by the typical financial institution. Complete item processing systems, for example, could be installed within a few days. Advances in random-access storage technology also made the processing of data practical at the time that the transaction was taking place. For the banking community, a system that updates customer records immediately has the advantage of reducing float and virtually eliminating the practice of check-kiting within the bank.

Today, advances in technology are so rapid that significantly faster processing speeds and larger, less expensive memories are making practical the use of more complex automatic operating systems within the computer, permitting less and less involvement by the human operator, and the capability for a greater variety of machine functions.

DATA PROCESSING IN THE BANKS TODAY

Data processing systems as used for accounting purposes in commercial banks in the United States today can be divided into three basic approaches:
1. Batch-mode accounting systems.
2. On-line systems.
3. Item processing systems.

Batch Mode Batch-mode accounting systems today are essentially a much improved version of the processing that was most typically used in systems during the previous 20 years. In batch accounting, the items (monetary transactions, nonmonetary transactions such as name/address changes, etc.) are prepared and accumulated for a consolidated entry into the accounting system process. There are usually many steps or processes in a predetermined sequence to edit, balance, update, and report on these transactions as they affect the master file of accounts.

Typical of these accounting systems in the commercial bank are those that handle such functions as demand deposits (checking accounts), credit cards, installment loans, saving accounts, real estate loans, trusts, and commercial loans. All these services usually require a daily accounting of transactions.

An example is the demand-deposit function. During the course of a business day, checks drawn on customer accounts and funds deposited to customer accounts are received in the bank. New accounts are opened by customers, accounts are closed, and customers change some aspect of their account, such as the address, and all these changes require corresponding changes in the bank's records. All the transactions are collected by the bank's various operating areas and forwarded to the data processing system for conversion to machine-readable media after the close of business.

The computer programs, in a predetermined sequence, are executed on the computer system to edit the transactions, balance monetary items to controls established by the various operating departments, and apply these transactions to the customer account record. Reports are produced on high-speed printers. These reports are used to answer customer inquiries as well as to inform the bank's management of unusual situations, such as overdrawn accounts, that need attention.

In the batch-processing mode, magnetic-tape or magnetic-disk storage devices are typically used to store the customer account data. These storage devices provide large amounts of data in a short time to the computer processor. Typically, the account data and the transaction data are arranged in account-number sequence, so that all transactions for a given customer account may be processed before the transactions of the next customer are handled. This sequential mode of operation also offers high efficiency (from the point of view of work accomplished in a unit of time), and therefore substantial economies. However, it also requires additional sorting processes to arrange the work into its sequential account-number order.

On-Line Systems Although batch-mode accounting is used by most commercial banks today, the on-line approach is gaining in popularity. On-line systems have been made possible primarily by the availability of lower-priced, larger-capacity disk file memories on today's third- and fourth-generation computer systems, by the multiprogramming capabilities offered, and by the advanced data communication capabilities, including economical, sophisticated terminals.

On-line systems generally can be divided into two categories: (1) on-line inquiry, and (2) on-line, real-time update.

On-Line Inquiry. In on-line inquiry systems, the processing of customer transactions is accomplished in the same manner as in the batch-mode accounting systems. The customer records are, however, available for inquiry through terminals connected to the computer system via telephone lines or other communications media. Examples of these terminals include on-line teller terminals, visual displays, audio-response units using the familiar telephone headsets, and typewriters. These devices are sometimes special-purpose units designed for the specific functions to be accomplished at the operating station. Use of on-line inquiry terminals allows much more rapid and complete retrieval of customer account data than do the printed output journals produced in batch mode. It reduces the number of clerical personnel required to service a large base of customer accounts, provides more rapid service, and provides more timely information to customers as well as to bank management.

On-Line, Real-Time Update. The on-line, real-time update system usually includes on-line inquiry, and goes on to replace many of the functions of the batch-mode accounting systems. Customer transactions, instead of being collected for consolidated entry into the accounting systems after the close of business, are used to update the customer accounts throughout the business day, as they occur. Although this eliminates the processing of transactions after the close of business, it still usually requires a process similar to that used in batch systems to report on the total customer transactions that have occurred, and on situations requiring management attention that come to light only after the day's business has been processed.

On-line, real-time offers some very significant advantages. First, the bank's computer is used to process customer transactions throughout the whole business day instead of being restricted to a period of concentrated usage after the close of one business day and before the opening of the next — typical of batch-mode systems. Second, customer accounts are kept current on an up-to-the-minute basis, as opposed to the delayed basis inherent in batch processing. This provides improved audit and control over errors and fraud. It also provides greatly improved customer service. Third, since much of the clerical function of maintaining accounts and opening new accounts becomes part of the on-line process, devices such as visual displays can be used to eliminate several intermediate preparation steps. Fourth, bank management has instant access to accurate up-to-the-minute information to assist in decision making processes. Bank offices can monitor the cash flow at any time, and more effectively assist their customers or review their accounts.

Central Information Files. Many banks today are using a combination of batch processing, on-line inquiry, and on-line, real-time update systems to produce a central information file. Very simply, this is a system where all the accounts of a given customer are either contained in a single record on the disk file subsystem, or are linked to a common customer record which contains name, address, and other pertinent data. Central information file systems were initially used by a few of the larger banks in the middle and late 1960s.

In the 1970s, many more banks have internally prepared for or are already using central information files. The advantages of a CIF are many. Much redundant clerical work (name, address, etc., maintenance of different types of accounts) is eliminated. In addition, the bank has a consolidated picture of all the accounts and other information regarding a single customer. It can access this total customer file information instantly, using such devices as visual displays. The central information file systems also allow the bank much more easily to analyze its mix of accounts, its account concentration by geographic area, its success in attracting new customers and new accounts from existing customers, and customer profitability on all accounts. CIF systems also allow much more efficient and higher-quality customer servicing by responding more quickly and accurately to inquiries.

Item Processing Item processing involves the handling of the millions of items flowing into and out of banks, and forms a large share of the work performed on bank computer systems. (Responsible industry observers estimate that the 10 years ending in 1980 will see the check rate increase from 22 to 42 billion a year.) Most transactions today are encoded in magnetic ink, using the E13B font mentioned earlier. Documents are read by high-speed computer-peripheral reader-sorters. Generally the bank number, account number, and other information are already encoded on the document when it is issued to the customer. The dollar amount is later encoded on the document by the bank when it is returned by the customer, e.g., when he or she makes a deposit or cashes a check.

Documents flow into a bank from many sources. The Federal Reserve System, serving as a clearing and interchange function for banks in the United States, will send a bank the checks drawn on accounts in that bank. Additionally, local banks in a given area have exchange agreements and locally controlled clearing centers. Documents also come into a bank through the teller windows as business is transacted.

All these documents are processed through the bank's computer system. Those items which affect the bank's own accounts are retained for processing against these accounts. Those items deposited or cashed by customers, but drawn on other banks, flow out of the bank either directly to the proper bank, to the Federal Reserve System, or to a local clearing center. Credit-card documents are handled in much the same manner.

Recent Advances Recent advances in microcircuitry have led to the development of compact and relatively inexpensive but powerful document processing systems for use in bank branches or in individual smaller banks. A full complement of electronic logic enables these systems to encode, read, verify, prove, and capture completely "clean" data with a single handling of each document. "On us" items — which typically constitute the bulk of a bank's item processing workload — go directly back to the customer, thus eliminating most of the multiple handlings required in the conventional clearance cycle.

Meanwhile, each document's electronic image, recorded on tape or disk, is immediately available to the bank's own computer, or for electronic transmission to a correspondent bank or data center, for account processing and management reporting. Errors, unnecessary float, and redundant labor are eliminated, with attendant reductions in real cost.

The advent of low-cost, "do it once" electronic item processing systems, concurrent with the development of small-scale data processors, portends a profound shift in future bank automation in favor of dispersed processing points and databases linked in networks to central information management systems.

RELATED DEVELOPMENTS

Financial Information Systems Banks are increasingly using the computer as a tool to manage their business professionally. The outgrowth of this is a new type of system: the financial information system. With the aid of the computer, the modern bank can establish cost or responsibility centers within its organization, perform complex budgeting and cost-accounting functions, and generally monitor each of the parts of its business and make necessary changes required by its management goals.

The Thrift Industry Electronic data processing plays a big role in the fast-growing thrift industry. In the past decade, savings and loan associations, mutual savings banks, and credit unions which make up this segment of the financial community have experienced tremendous growth. To meet this growth, many institutions have turned to computerization.

The early sixties saw thrift institutions begin to employ on-line processing. Prior to this time, some of the larger institutions used tabulating equipment and computers for back-office or batch processing of account transactions similar to the previously described functions in commercial banks. The majority of institutions used some form of accounting machines or sometimes simply pen and ink systems.

When on-line capabilities became economically feasible, some of the larger thrift institutions installed computer systems and terminal devices capable of implementing this new technology. These types of systems were also installed by service-center operations for the purpose of providing on-line processing services to several customer institutions. With terminal devices installed at teller windows—and connected to a central computer either locally or remotely located—the customer found that the speed and accuracy of handling his or her transactions and inquiries had been greatly enhanced.

Initially these systems accommodated limited types of accounts—usually only savings accounts. As personnel became more familiar with the computer as a new accounting and management tool, and as a new technology provided faster, more flexible computers and teller terminals, on-line services were expanded to include mortgage and other forms of loan payments.

By the late sixties, third-generation computer systems began to replace many of the initial on-line computers. Many of these new systems allowed faster processing speeds, multiprogramming capabilities, and the capability to support more extensive data communication networks.

Perhaps of even greater value to those thrift institutions using on-line processing was a new approach to the design of the teller terminal itself. Whereas the original terminals installed in the early and middle sixties were nonprogrammable and had to rely upon the computer for virtually all error checking, sequence control, data editing, and formatting, the new approach to terminal design was to make the terminal "intelligent." In other words, the terminal could be programmed to an individual institution's requirements, and the flexibility of the overall system was greatly enhanced. Now the terminal could interact with the computer by performing some of the processing, reducing a great deal of the work formerly required of the central computer system.

This meant that more terminals and greater account activity could be handled by the same computer system. Tens of thousands of these terminals have been installed in thrift institutions, and today every major teller terminal manufacturer is taking this approach in the design of its units. Many thrift institutions have begun to install other new devices in their on-line networks: display devices, remote teller units, cash dispensers, remote high-speed printers, and specialized window terminals.

Electronic Funds Transfer Because of on-line capabilities, thrift institutions and commercial banks are in a good position to take advantage of electronic funds transfer systems which are now in various stages of discussion, study, and implementation. Changing legislation is enabling some of these institutions to offer additional services which have not been possible in the past.[1]

Financial institutions are looking very closely at the cash/credit-card concept. By taking advantage of their existing on-line computer networks, institutions will be able to offer their customers a wide range of additional services through the use of an industry-wide plastic identification card. The industry's experience in on-line data processing and remote terminals should allow financial institutions to continue their use of computerization to meet the needs of the seventies.

Expanded Services The expansion of on-line facilities will lead to an increase in customer services offered by banks, such as 24-hour banking through remote teller terminals that require no human intervention for most transactions. Deposits can be made by simply placing the deposited items into a container after the amount has been keyed into the terminal by the customer. Withdrawals require only that the customer enter the amount of money desired through a keyboard. Currency enclosed in clips can be dispensed to the customer through the machine.

Many such terminals are in operation, and the future will undoubtedly see a dramatic increase in their use. The advantages to the customer are obvious. To the bank, it will mean decreased labor costs and more efficient use of the computer, by spreading work out over the full 24-hour day.

The use of the automated facilities requires some positive means of customer identification, such as an identification card. This card can be used by the customer at other facilities allied with the bank's system. The customer could, for example, draw on his or her funds on deposit at the bank to pay for an item at a retail store. Revolutionary methods such as the use of hand prints or voice prints are being investigated to replace or supplement secret code numbers and the like.

The variety of bank services is bound to increase. It is conceivable that one day customers will depend on the banks to handle all their financial dealings. These could include everything from paying utility and charge-account bills to calculating income tax and setting aside funds for a more carefully planned investment program—performing the functions of a business manager for the customer. This could be practical because of the central information file concept that makes all the customer records readily available, and the increased use of automated equipment that will make more time for customer contact available to bank personnel.

Until recently, banks have been forced to adapt their methods of doing business to meet the requirements of the computer. The future will no doubt see new approaches that will result in changing the computer system to the needs of the banking industry, resulting in happier customers and higher profits for the financial community.

[1] See Chapter 1, "The 'Less-Cash, Less-Check' Society," in this Section.

Chapter 4

ADP in Manufacturing
1. The Process Industries

JOHN W. HOAG

Director, Strategic & Business Planning, Honeywell Inc.,
Process Control Division, Phoenix, Arizona

The basic functions performed by data processing systems in administrative operations are pretty much the same wherever they may be installed. In the manufacturing process control area, however, processes vary from industry to industry, and the job of the computer will vary from process to process. The available computer array is far wider and, in some cases, more complex than in the data processing world.

WHAT IS PROCESS CONTROL?

Generally speaking, process control is the ability to control multiple variables such as temperature, pressure, flow, and level to obtain the desired results from a process. Consider a mixing tank into which two products of different temperatures are flowing. We want to maintain the temperature in the tank at a certain value. We insert a temperature sensor such as a thermocouple into the tank. This sensor sends to a control instrument a small electrical signal proportional to the actual temperature. The controller compares the actual temperature with the desired or set-point temperature and sends out a control signal to one or both valves controlling product flow into the tank.

This can be further complicated by adding level control to the tank. Now we have the problem of controlling the temperature as we have just described, and controlling the level by regulating the flow of product leaving the tank.

While these simple examples show how one or two loops are controlled, most processes today are much more complex. We have to control many loops and, since some of these loops may be interdependent, we have to control on a multivariable basis. Prior to the emergence of digital computers, this was extremely difficult to do, and even now it is often difficult to develop the relationships of the interdependent or interacting variables. Once these relationships are developed, however, computers can do an outstanding control job.

SPECIAL COMPUTER REQUIREMENTS FOR A PROCESS CONTROL SYSTEM

Before we go into the evolution of digital computers in manufacturing, let us examine the special computer requirements for a process control system.

Environment Ability to stand up under adverse environment is one of the key requirements. Data processing computers in offices, banks, and department stores usually operate in a clean, air-conditioned environment. The process control computer, on the other hand, must be able to operate in the environment of the processing area. It must be able to tolerate temperatures ranging from 40°F up to around 130°F, and relative humidities up to 95 per cent. The atmosphere may contain oily vapor, metal dust, or gases such as hydrogen sulfide or chlorine. In some cases, vibration and shock are encountered. And under these conditions, the computer must be able accurately to read millivolt-level signals from thermocouples and other sensing elements on the process despite a high electrical noise environment.

Real Time The process control computer must also be capable of working in real time; that is, it must be able to respond in microseconds to changes that take place in the process.

Multiprogramming It must operate in a multiprogramming environment, which means that it not only picks up and reads live instantaneous inputs from the process, but also makes decisions and sends out control signals to valves and other final control elements.

Instead of printing out for an operator some action that should take place, the process control computer frequently brings in the data, analyzes it, runs it through a mathematical calculation, and takes any needed corrective action, all in a matter of fractions of seconds.

Continuous Operation As contrasted with data processing systems, the process control computer must operate in tandem with the process. If the process runs 24 hours a day, 7 days a week, the computer is expected to keep the same hours. Many users have requested, and some computer manufacturers have responded to, a guaranteed uptime availability of 99.5 per cent. Very few process control computers operate on only one or two shifts, 5 days a week.

Software The process control computer must have extensive software capability. For example, the computer may be performing a calculation when an interrupt comes in saying that there is a critical alarm in the process. The software must jump to the routine that has been put into the computer to handle this particular alarm. After handling the alarm, the computer jumps back to its calculation. While still doing the calculation, it may have to scan inputs for a control operation. So it again stops its operation, does its input scanning, performs control calculations, sends out some control signals, and goes back to the calculation. Then comes the time to print out a log for the operator, so it must jump out and do that. And it does all these things at super speed.

It is thus obvious that the process control computer is entirely driven by external events, and it is evident that highly sophisticated software is needed. To give some idea of the speed and need for multiprogramming, several thousand instructions might be executed during a calculation between the striking of the keys on a logging typewriter.

EVOLUTION OF PROCESS CONTROL

Growth of the Instrumentation Industry The instrumentation industry emerged during the industrial revolution, with some companies being formed in the mid-1800s. These companies developed sensors and measurement and control devices. While primitive by today's standards, these devices were valuable in controlling single loops in the early days of technological growth.

Control systems in those days, and even through the 1940s, had little regard for optimizing processes or making them more efficient. While some work was done in that area, instrumentation and control were more often used for reasons of safety and accuracy, and because experience told processors that by controlling certain flows in certain ways, they came up with better products. Processes were not as completely understood as they are today. The technology to analyze a process was not available, and competition and operating costs did not demand optimum control as do today's conditions.

In the early days, measurement and control instrumentation was scattered throughout a plant. For example, each processing unit would have its own control panel. This was wasteful of personnel and, since many processing units were interdependent, made it very difficult to obtain smooth, efficient overall plant operation. During the late 1940s industry started to pull all control instrumentation together into central control rooms. In addition to permitting more efficient use of operating personnel, this centralization enabled the operators to keep the process under much closer control.

As both processes and instrumentation continued to grow more complicated, the user's engineers and those of the instrumentation companies worked closely together to develop new measurement and control techniques and new hardware to meet the increasing demands of new processes.

Early control systems were mostly pneumatic, and used compressed air to operate valves and other final control elements. They were explosion-proof, inexpensive, and understood by the instrument engineers, and they did an adequate job. Then, in the 1940s, the age of electronics began to emerge, and the instrumentation industry began a trend toward electric and electronic control. While this type of control is more expensive than the pneumatic variety, it is faster and highly reliable, and has made the newer, more complex control loops easier to handle.

Also in the 1940s, more sophisticated control techniques began to emerge. *Feedforward* control is a typical example. This type of control predicts changes in a processing unit and takes corrective, or rather preventive, action before they actually occur in the unit. Thus in our mixing tank example, if we knew that a certain temperature change was going to occur in one of the product feed lines, we could open or close a valve in this line to compensate for the change before any temperature change was sensed in the tank.

Early Process Computing While there was nothing like today's digital process control computer in the late 1930s and early 1940s, process control systems began to do some modest computing. Instrument engineers started to tie a number of control elements together to perform computations, and began to take into account multivariable control.

The first known use of an analog computer in process control in an on-line mode was in the power industry in the mid-1950s. The computer was connected into the control system on the Southern Services power system to optimize the generation and dispatch of electric power. It is only natural that this first application would be in the power industry, where there are a great many companies with common technical problems. There are no proprietary processes in the industry, and there always has been a great deal of cooperative effort by many elements of the industry to develop better controls. Efforts to achieve a better understanding of the electric power dispatch process had been going on for 20 years prior to the installation of this first on-line analog computer.

Shortly after the start-up of this computer, a digital computer was installed in an oil refinery at Port Arthur, Texas, for control and data acquisition. This is generally accepted as the first digital process computer.

The Data Logger During the 1950s, several companies began to develop and offer data logging systems. These systems could scan a large number of inputs, linearize any nonlinear signals, provide high and low alarms, and print out log sheets at periodic intervals. They were well accepted by industry because they made it possible to get a lot of data into one control room in a relatively simple format.

These early data loggers had little or no computational capability. They were hardwired devices and rarely had any kind of memory. However, they did make a contribution to the soon-to-be-developed digital process control computer. The instrumentation industry learned from them how to take low-level analog signals, accurately convert them to digital form, and present them in print-out form. The result is today's accurate, reliable, analog-to-digital and digital-to-analog converters.

Pitfalls As is often the case in a pioneering effort, the early users of digital process control computers encountered many pitfalls and disappointments in applications. Manufacturers entered the field with enthusiasm, but many did not survive. Some manufacturers made claims that could not even be met today, 20 years later. Some users wrote specifications that could not be achieved today, while others wrote no specifications at all but expected the computer to do everything. As a result, many computer manufacturers and many users lost large amounts of money because the computer system had been oversold, misunderstood, misapplied, or just plain would not work. Unfortunately, these early setbacks gave process control computers a bad name and held back the growth of the market in the early 1960s.

Let us take a look at two representative examples of the early pitfalls:

The "Big Bite." In the early days, most of the computer manufacturers felt they could provide systems that could do more than was actually possible at that time. Many of them offered to undertake the total task of understanding the user's process, and developing hardware and software to control it. Some even guaranteed savings from the use of their computer systems.

The problems, however, turned out to be manifold: The early computers were not yet highly reliable. Many processes were not thoroughly understood, even by process engineers (to say nothing of the computer manufacturers), in terms of the sequential and detailed steps required for computerization. Moreover, the software personnel needed to do analysis and programming were often not available. To complicate the situation further, neither the computer manufacturer nor the user knew how to write definitive specifications that would enable both of them to understand what had been committed for in the computer system. Ill feeling and law suits often followed.

The "Paper Maker." Many early systems performed, in a slightly more sophisticated manner, the same functions as did the data loggers discussed earlier. The computer system would be sold to the user on the basis that it would first perform data acquisitions only, and that then, from an analysis of all these data, would evolve a great control system. The problem here was that the computers usually generated more paper than anyone could possibly analyze and make use of. It became apparent that this, too, was the wrong approach to the ultimate goal of computer control.

The Team Approach It soon became evident that no computer manufacturer could ever hope to understand fully all the ramifications of the user's processes. Similarly, it was seen that the user's process and instrument engineers had to be intimately involved in the application of a process control computer. This *team approach* led to some highly successful results. In addition to the user, who understood the process, and computer manufacturer, who understood the computer system and software, the team included, in some cases, a consultant, who understood all three quite well. The team approach offers an additional user benefit: By working with the computer people in developing systems, users acquire quite a knowledge about both the hardware and the software. Consequently, if they want to change or expand their systems at a later date, they can usually do the software portion themselves.

Software While there were some hardware problems in the early days, software was usually the major problem. Early computer systems had very little in the form of standard, usable software. Most machines had to be coded in machine language or in FORTRAN, with very little in the way of advanced executive control or any extensive multiprogramming capability. While hardware costs were dropping rapidly, software costs were not.

The computer industry tackled this problem, and in the 1960s, several improved software systems were developed. Among the significant packages at that time were Real-Time Multiprogramming Operating Systems (RTMOS) and Basic Control Engineering Programming Systems (BICEPS) developed by General Electric.

RTMOS was a sophisticated multiprogramming system, a monitor that allowed foreground and background work to be done. This meant that the computer system could continue to control the process with all its event-driven devices and rapidly needed outputs, and at the same time compile and execute an engineering program in the background.

RTMOS and BICEPS made it possible for the process engineer simply to fill in program "blanks" with process data. To perform data acquisition or control, the engineer did not have to be a programmer. The software was written so that he could enter data into the system in engineering units and other familiar process terms. The software would then translate the data into machine language and link it into the appropriate parts of the control software within the computer.

Other major computer companies developed systems similar to RTMOS and BICEPS. All these standard packages tended to reduce the software and programming costs of a typical process control system.

Advent of the Minicomputer One of the reasons for developing large computer systems with foreground/background capability was the cost of the computer and the software, which was usually too high to justify the use of the system merely to control the process.

The emergence of the relatively inexpensive minicomputer caused some changes in this thinking. While large, comprehensive, foreground/background systems are still available today, the dedicated minicomputer systems installed on process control applications far outnumber the large systems.

A dedicated computer system is one which repeatedly performs a specific group of tasks within a process. And this is all it does. This type of computer process control system falls within the $40,000 to $100,000 price range, depending on the number of inputs, outputs, and tasks to be done. In this price range, it is usually fairly easy to justify a computer system, especially if it is applied to a part of a process where payout will occur. Moreover, users of dedicated minicomputer process control systems are finding that a system applied successfully to a part of a process in one of their plants can usually be applied equally successfully in other plants throughout their companies. These systems are relatively simple, since the tasks performed by the computer are limited to a specific part of the overall process.

Minicomputers as Preprocessors As more is learned about a process in a plant, additional minicomputer systems will be applied. It is quite likely that a typical industrial plant will have 10, 12, or 20 minicomputer systems controlling different parts of the process. But how can we be sure that they are all doing the right thing as far as overall plant operation is concerned?

The logical next step is to tie these minicomputers into one large machine which would be considered the supervising computer system—a data processing system for which the minicomputers throughout the plant can become the eyes and ears, feeding it real data on a real-time basis. No need to wait for cards to be punched and loaded into the computer.

The minicomputers are "intelligent" eyes and ears. They can format, consolidate, average, and otherwise edit data going to the supervising computer.

Also, they can accept instructions from the large machine. These may be in the form of production schedules, changes in operating conditions, changes in grade of product, control settings for optimal control, or other parameters that are being generated or worked upon in the supervising computer.

While the minicomputers may be regarded as preprocessors for the supervising computer, they also have the ability to stand alone and keep doing their job according to the last set of instructions they received from the large machine. This means that the process will continue to function even though the supervising computer is down for maintenance or otherwise occupied.

THE FUTURE

The trend we have just described will probably continue throughout industry. Technology will soon bring forth the computer that sells for one or two thousand dollars. The control will be implemented on one or two single integrated chips and will probably be a throw-away-and-replace device if it should ever fail. Such devices are currently being used by the military and are called *dedicated task devices*.

To make this possible in process control, however, the process industries must find ways to break down what must be done into small, repeatable common tasks. Once this has been accomplished, the computing devices can be manufactured in quantity. Until this can be done, no appreciable savings can be realized.

Hierarchical Control Systems Ever since the beginning of process control by computer, leaders in the industry have talked about and planned for the day of the hierarchical control system, a multilevel control system with dedicated task controllers at the lowest level. In a complex process, there could be dozens of these small, dedicated task controllers.

At the next higher level would be a supervising computer that would manage and control groups of these dedicated task controllers. This supervising computer could eventually be tied into the top level of the hierarchy—the data processing system.

To reach this goal, work must be done and costs reduced in the process interface equipment that enables field-mounted sensors such as thermocouples (which generate analog signals) to communicate with the dedicated digital task controllers. In the not-too-distant future, one may hope to see digital transducers which would eliminate the analog-to-digital conversion problem.

Reduction in Installation Costs Installation cost is an area where we see significant improvement. On some past computer control systems, the combined costs of the wire and its installation actually exceeded the cost of the computer system. Today, a major breakthrough is in "data highway" concepts. For years, the computer industry has been seeking a good method of remote multiplexing. Instead of requiring 200 pairs of

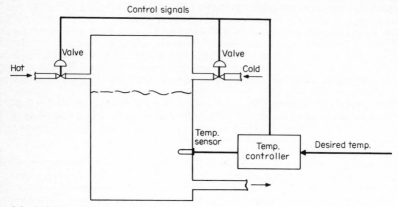

Fig. 4-1 A simple process control system. A temperature sensor in the tank sends to the control device a signal proportional to the temperature of the fluid in the mixing tank. The controller compares this with the desired temperature and repositions valves in hot and cold incoming product lines to maintain tank contents at desired (set-point) temperature.

wires to carry signals from 200 temperature sensors to the computer, now a multiplexer near the process can convert these 200 signals to digital form and transmit the data to the computer over a single pair of wires. For example, Honeywell's HS4450 for in-plant locations up to 2,500 feet from the process computer, or HS7024 Telecontrol Stations for remote operation over telephone lines or microwave.

For a recap of the concepts discussed thus far, see Figures 4-1 through 4-5.

Improvement Over Inferential Control Today most control systems use *inferential* control. That is, through formulas or experience, process engineers know that if they

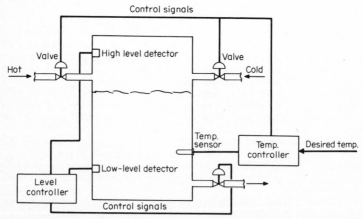

Fig. 4-2 A slightly more complex control system. Both temperature and level of tank contents are controlled. Temperature is controlled as described in Figure 4-1. Level is controlled by relating the flow of product leaving the tank.

maintain certain temperatures, pressures, and flows at specific values, they will most likely get a good product yield. However, they cannot be sure that they are getting the optimum yield of a top-quality product.

The answer is some means of continuously analyzing the output of the product and automatically controlling the process to obtain the desired product characteristics. In recent years most analyzers of this sort have been designed for laboratory work.

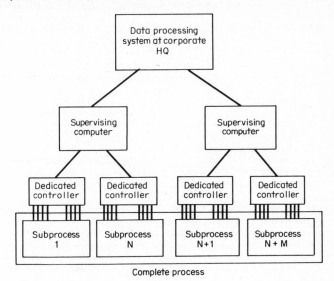

Complete process

Fig. 4-3 The hierarchical control system of the future. Many small dedicated task controllers will be monitored and managed by one or more supervising computers which will, in turn, be tied into the data processing system.

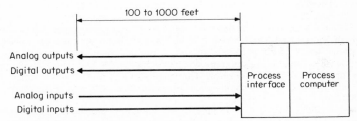

Fig. 4-4 A hard-wired process computer control system. A pair of wires to connect each field-mounted sensor and final control element to the computer is required. On some installations, cost of wire plus installation can be very high.

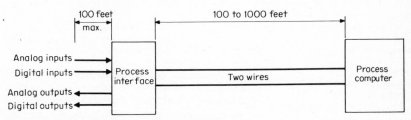

Fig. 4-5 A remote multiplexer. The process interface can be moved close to the process and connected to the computer with a single pair of wires. This greatly reduces wire and installation costs.

They have not provided on-line, real-time analysis, and have not held up well under the rigors of continuous operation on the process. However, today there are rugged, high-speed analyzers that can provide continuous on-line, real-time product analysis.

What does this mean to industry? Let us assume that some gaseous/chemical product is being produced in a continuous process, and that we want to determine the quality of this product. In the past, a sample of the product would be either piped or carried over to the laboratory where it would be run through a gas chromatograph, and the results interpreted by laboratory personnel. If they found the product was "off spec," they would notify the operating people. The latter, in turn, would juggle process temperatures, pressures, and flows to try to get the product back "on spec." Of course, they would not know whether or not they had been successful until after another sample had been taken and run through the laboratory analysis procedure. And, while all this was going on, the process was turning out a lot of off-spec product, which might have to be reprocessed.

Today's on-line, real-time gas chromatograph could continuously sample the product leaving the process and send corrective signals back to the computer system immediately when any variation from product specifications occurred. The end results would be a higher yield of a more uniform product, fewer reruns, and reduced utility costs.

The hardware to achieve this end-point control is available right now. To make the best use of these valuable tools, an extensive knowledge of the process is needed. We must be able to develop the mathematical interrelationships between the product and the process variables such as temperatures, pressures, flows, feedstock quality, catalyst wear, and others.

Cooperation: The Key to Success In some companies, there are conflicting opinions as to whether the data processing people or the process control people should control all the computers in the particular company. In others, there is a sincere cooperative effort between the data processing and process control people. The latter approach is obviously by far the more practical and profitable. In the not too distant future, it appears that data processing and process control equipment will be tied together physically, electrically, and also in terms of personnel.

As indicated earlier, in complex process control people are needed who know the process intimately and understand the chemical and other reactions involved. Only they can best handle the analysis and study required to develop increasingly better process control systems. However, in the area of programming, process control systems also call for an entirely different skill than that required in data processing. Data processing is a batch operation. In process control, the computer depends on external devices to tell it what to do, and, when it is told, it must do these things instantaneously.

Experience has shown that in most process control applications it is easier to teach a process engineer how to be a programmer than it is to teach a data processing programmer the intricacies of process control. Conversely, if a process control engineer were asked to implement inventory control on a large data processing system, he or she would most likely have quite a struggle.

The process control systems of the future will need data processing equipment backing them up to give better guidance and direction and to provide the more complex production control, inventory, and optimization calculations to make the entire plant run more efficiently. If it is to do these things, the data processing system will need fast, accurate, edited data from the process control system. The real-time data will also enable the data processing system to provide management with reports that are more accurate, more quickly prepared, and, consequently, more meaningful.

In short, to ensure successful future growth, there is a very real need for cooperative effort between the data processing people and the process control people. One is reminded of the old argument about the relative importance of the Army, Navy, and Air Force. Without any one of the three, the other two are in bad shape.

What is needed is an ever-increasing exchange of information and a better understanding of each other's needs and problems. This can be achieved only by closer working relationships between the data processing and process control people.

Chapter 5

ADP in Manufacturing
2. General Manufacturing: Serial and Job Shop

R. L. DAUBENMIRE

**Director, Information Systems Center, International Business
Machines Corporation, Sterling Forest, Suffern, New York**

Today, the computer is appearing everywhere in industrial operations as the key to better productivity. It is being used with equal success for planning, execution, and control of manufacturing operations – and its applications range from stand-alone plant floor functions to vast, nationwide integrated systems affecting the resources of entire companies. Whatever their size, manufacturing control systems are proving that the most profitable process is also the best controlled process.

The term *manufacturing control* is a broad one, taking in two major areas. One covers the broad-scaled planning and support functions carried out in integrated systems. The other is computer-aided manufacturing, which covers the execution of actual plant floor manufacturing operations, including direct control of production equipment. Computer-aided manufacturing systems are used to ensure that production is following plans and to give management more direct control over operations.

Plant floor production applications generally include some of the following functions:

- Real-time communications with and collection of data from machine sensors and manual entry devices.
- Analysis of retained data.
- Comparison of critical data against plant production schedules.
- Provision of direct production machine control or guidance to operators through messages, lights, and displays.
- Production of periodic exception reports as output.
- End-of-shift summary reports.
- Response to local and remote inquiries.

Computer-aided manufacturing systems are specified by manufacturing, quality control, and industrial engineers, and they are used by supervisors and line management, and by operators, inspectors, and expediters performing make-move-test operations. However, the systems do not stand alone. They must interface and feed back to other company systems in such functional areas as production planning, engineering, plant management, and administration, to update plans and schedules with current operating data. These relationships are further extended in integrated systems, to the point where computers offer new approaches to the solution of critical operating problems, rather than merely speeding up existing procedures.

INTEGRATED PLANNING AND SUPPORT SYSTEMS

Computer manufacturers have led in the development of integrated systems for their own internal production planning needs. This was the case with the Common Manufacturing Information System (CMIS) developed by the IBM System Products Division. This division produces many of IBM's computing systems in the U.S.A., and uses many computer installations in various stages of production in its North American plants. CMIS was developed to support the logistics system needed to make this production more efficient and more responsive to changes in planning and scheduling.

For the System Products Division manufacturing complex, control information is vital because, generally, each computer part is made in only one plant, and a high degree of interdependency exists among plants. Since the 1950s, IBM had steadily increased the size and number of its production facilities. As each was established, it was considered to be essentially an autonomous manufacturing entity, and each plant tended to develop information systems tailored to its own specific requirements — with independent records, files, and programs. The manufacturing planning and control systems thus developed were of high quality, but they were not always compatible with those in other plants. In addition, lacking a common system, division-wide material requirements generation — operations planning — depended on batch processing and manual methods. It could take as long as 3 months to implement a major schedule change. CMIS, as described later herein, now supports a wide variety of operating functions, including multiplant materials requirements planning and materials logistics, which, together, form the basis for a manufacturing information system.

As indicated, CMIS was designed for IBM's internal use in its own manufacturing operations. Development effort for it began in 1967. In the marketing of its computer systems, IBM had already, in the early 1960s, developed an effective bill of material processor for customer use, followed in 1966 by the broader concept of Production Information and Control System (PICS). These led to the first widespread use of computers in manufacturing applications.

The PICS concept evolved into Communications Oriented Production Information and Control System (COPICS), introduced in 1972. COPICS is essentially a set of "application road maps" — databased, interactive — that describe an approach to advanced manufacturing applications. It defines the levels and nature of integration that can be achieved within a single manufacturing system, and comprises 12 conceptual application modules corresponding to various company-wide planning, execution, and control functions.

It is emphasized that COPICS is not a set of application programs or a proprietary software "package." It is described in some detail here, as is CMIS, as a conceptual approach to an integrated manufacturing system, dealing with problems common to most manufacturing companies, proceeding from a forecast of customer requirements, through development of the master production schedule, to the production and shipment of the product. For individual applications, specific equipment and software must be selected and developed to fit the conceptual framework.

CMIS, an operational system, performs many of the functions subsumed in the COPICS application modules. Four COPICS modules, however, extend beyond the current range of CMIS applications. They are Cost Planning and Control, Plant Maintenance, Customer Order Servicing, and Plant Monitoring and Control. These functions were not designed into CMIS, since the latter was conceived primarily as a logistics and planning system.

The design of CMIS, COPICS, and other integrated systems and approaches increasingly reflects the combination of the two basic approaches to manufacturing control. The *top-down* approach calls for integration of all manufacturing applications in the total plant information system. The *bottom-up* approach emphasizes the individual, stand-alone, sensor-based application as the basic building block of a successful computer-aided manufacturing program.

COMMON MANUFACTURING INFORMATION SYSTEM (CMIS)

The combination of bottom-up implementation and top-down planning is exemplified in CMIS. Created to solve the problem of getting the right information to the right place at the right time, the system coordinates the growing interdependence among the various functional areas of manufacturing. With the availability of data processing systems of all sizes with improved cost-performance ratios, and of high-bandwidth communications facilities, this interdependence no longer means that a system must be physically consolidated in one location. Thus CMIS elements are distributed among local plant installations operating on-line, linked by telephone lines. At a plant, CMIS replaces much previous data processing activity with new programs that use an integrated database. It also substantially adds to local capabilities for retrieval of information.

Planning, Implementation, and Control   There are striking similarities in the ways that IBM and the automobile manufacturers plan their future production activities. Both begin with a forecast of future orders. In IBM's case, this forecast—the product schedule—is the result of negotiations among various functional areas of the company, including manufacturing, planning, forecasting, and marketing. There are, however, a great number of feature options open to customers for computer systems—ranging from memory size and configuration of system hardware down to the color of the cabinets. In effect, IBM, like the car makers, "finishes to order."

Once drawn up, the product schedule is "exploded"—broken down to provide a list of all the parts and subassemblies that should be on hand when the order is released for final assembly of a machine. The product schedule also provides a basis for assignment of delivery dates for customer orders. These orders go through the order processing system that translates sales features into manufacturing bills of materials. They then go to the plants where each order is matched with one that has been preplanned for assembly to meet the schedule. The particular features ordered determine the parts and subassemblies required for final assembly. Inventories of these parts and subassemblies are maintained at plants on the basis of statistical forecasts of their order patterns.

The role of CMIS in the process includes the explosion of the product schedule into a manufacturing plan that controls the release of purchasing and manufacturing orders, stocking of the resulting parts and assemblies, their issuance to the plant floor for inclusion in larger subassemblies, and the stocking of the latter. This process is repeated and escalated until CMIS finally supports the issue of parts for the final assembly of complete machines.

The great variety of functions that CMIS performs at all management levels reflects the fact that it is not enough for a system to be technically and economically sound. It also must be designed for the people who use it. This will generally place emphasis on systems design features that help managers in planning, implementation, and control.

Planning.   Planning involves choosing between alternatives for such activities as setting resource levels, determining production schedules, and stating inventory policy. This function, which is undertaken by middle and top management, largely governs day-to-day operating decisions.

Implementation.   Implementation begins once the master schedule has been established with the generation of purchase and shop orders. Features that can be designed into the system through appropriate programming to make the schedule's implementation more effective include:

● Testing the effect of any large order on production capacity to confirm order delivery date.

● Implementing engineering changes promptly, resulting in lower parts obsolescence and fewer production shortages.

● Confirming availability of tools and materials before releasing an order to the shop floor.

● Controlling tool issue and recall of tools to reduce production delays and ensure maximum tool usage and reduce scrap caused by worn tools.

● Dispatching work and controlling reporting procedures to ensure that operators work on assigned jobs in proper sequence.

• Providing purchase-order procedures to speed order release, with rush orders being automatically expedited.

The previously mentioned features provide the rapid implementation of changes that manufacturing systems require, particularly if they are geographically distributed. The computer networks that implement them can operate either on-line or off-line, depending on data processing requirements. This is the case with CMIS, whose information is stored in local data banks. Very little data are held at the CMIS center, at which computers are used chiefly for communications switching. Because CMIS is an on-line system connecting all plants, processing of routines and production of reports can be accomplished at individual plants as though all CMIS computers were under the same roof.

Control. Control involves the monitoring and measurement of actual conditions against standards to make certain that all is going according to plan. The responsible manager can be alerted automatically when a deviation from plan, is reported, such as nondelivery of materials, production facility downtime, excessive scrap, or imminent exhaustion of the work backlog.

More thorough control can be obtained by linking the computer directly to the production process. For example, a sensor-based system can, when connected to such facilities as machine tools or stamping presses, monitor the actual production rate, operating conditions, etc. Computers can also be attached directly to automated production facilities, such as heat-treatment plants or foundry processes. These techniques result in significant increases in productivity and product quality.

COMMUNICATION-ORIENTED PRODUCTION INFORMATION AND CONTROL SYSTEM (COPICS)

Unrelated and incompatible systems can be eliminated through the creation of a comprehensive systems framework that prevents duplication of effort and compartmentalization of information, and is also flexible enough to address unique local plant needs. The resulting integrated system should:

• Allow a common base for effective management evaluation.
• Improve central coordination of the activities of interconnected plants.
• Simplify transfer of responsibility for manufacturing specific products from one plant to another.
• Ease promotion and transfer of employees between plants using similar systems.
• Allow easier start-up of new plants using the same systems as older plants.
• Avoid duplicate creation of common data.

Such a system framework is outlined in the IBM COPICS concepts.

The Application Modules COPICS defines 12 integrated applications, or systems modules. Each of the 12 modules can be implemented separately so long as interfaces between applications areas are carefully defined. These interfaces are essentially fixed-format segments of information exchanged between applications. System development and improvement can thus take place in small, manageable increments without disrupting existing applications.

The COPICS emphasis throughout is on the use of display and shop floor terminals, and other communications equipment, to help communicate management policy and to monitor and control actual operations. The system concepts are thus oriented to production and related manufacturing applications, and only indirectly toward other major areas such as finance, marketing, and personnel. Not every company will want to implement all sections of COPICS. The suitability of a particular module will depend on the type of manufacture, product line, management priorities, etc. However, each company will be able to develop a system tailored to its own needs through implementation of some or all of the 12 following application modules (see Figure 5-1):

Engineering and Production Data Control creates and maintains basic engineering records such as bills of material, manufacturing routings, and manufacturing facilities data, to constitute a common database for all departments.

Customer Order Servicing links the sales information system to manufacturing to improve handling of customers' orders and inquiries. Orders are controlled from receipt of quotation requests and/or the entry of orders through terminals to shipments of finished products. The system's guidance of the clerk through all phases of order entry increases accuracy. The system also audits data and indicates errors.

Forecasting supports the development of the master production schedule, which specifies production for future periods, and the projection of management performance standards and inventory requirements. The difference between production forecast and actual demand is called the *forecast error*. Anticipation of this error will aid plants more easily to absorb normal fluctuations in business volume.

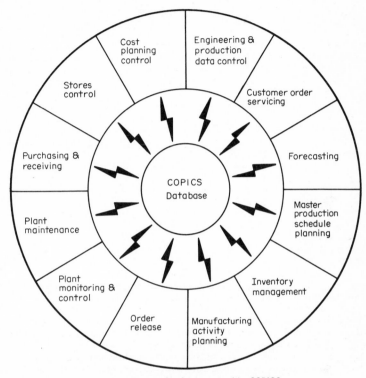

Fig. 5-1   **The applications covered by COPICS.**

Master Production Schedule Planning allows quick assessment of the impact of alternative production plans on plant capacity. The result is a reaslistic master production schedule, a statement of future requirements specified by date and quantity, which reflects management inventory policy as well as customer demand. It provides input for the Inventory Management application to use in determining short-term production requirements for lower-level subassemblies, components, and raw materials. It is also used to estimate long-term demand on company resources such as production capacity, engineering, and cash.

Inventory Management determines the optimum quantities and timing of each item to be ordered—both manufactured and purchased—to meet the requirements of the master production schedule.

Manufacturing Activity Planning is designed to ease the problem that exists in most manufacturing companies, where shop orders spend much more time (often 10 times as much) queued up at work centers than being processed. Detailed capacity requirements are planned, and the dates of planned order releases are adjusted to be consistent with plant capacity. Objectives include the achievement of reasonably level loads, and the minimizing of work-in-process inventory manufacturing load, and idle machine time.

Order Release is concerned with the connection between the planning and execution phases of the system. It changes, on the appropriate dates, the status of orders from "planned" to "released." This change initiates the placing of either a purchase order or a manufacturing order. Physical availability of materials required for shop orders is verified at order release time. Requisitions for production components, tools, and manufacturing drawings needed are generated, and a requisition action file is maintained in priority sequence to ensure that important shop orders are serviced first.

Plant Monitoring and Control implements the production plan and serves to reduce the number of delays and waiting time by more effective monitoring and feedback of production and shop floor status data. These data may be obtained either through terminals located on the shop floor or through direct connection of the computer to the machine tools. With these data readily available, the system minimizes delay by means of communications links to production support departments such as maintenance and materials handling. In addition, it can broadcast the effect of a delay to other affected departments, so that they can have the option of shifting their attention to other orders.

The first objective is to ensure that the production schedule is being met. The second is to improve coordination between production and supporting activities, such as inspection, material handling, and tool cribs. A third objective is the improvement of the efficiency and utilization of production, testing, and material handling equipment through direct machine monitoring and control.

Plant Maintenance is concerned with maintenance personnel planning, work order dispatching, and costing, as well as preventive maintenance scheduling. The chief objective is to reduce production costs by extending the life of production equipment.

Purchasing and Receiving maintains current purchase quotations, creates purchase orders, and follows the progress of orders from the time of requisition, through acknowledgment, follow-up, receipt, quality control, and deposit in stores. Like maintenance, this area has not until now received as much management attention as production planning and control. Yet, timely delivery of correct materials is obviously vital. As important are savings on purchased materials and services, which can account for 30 to 60 per cent of many manufacturers' costs of sales. A small reduction in purchase costs can have a large effect on profits, particularly in cost-competitive situations. Thus, in a situation where materials and services account for half the cost of sales, and profits are only 9 per cent, a 2 per cent reduction in purchase prices would raise profits to 10 per cent, giving an increase in profit of 11.1 per cent.

Stores Control keeps track of materials location and determines where to store new material, and where and when to retrieve it. Objectives are to increase the utilization of storage space and its economy, and to reduce picking time and picking errors. Automated warehousing techniques are also addressed. Stores Control and Inventory Management together create a complete inventory control capability.

Cost Planning and Control is basically concerned with the difference between what it *should* cost a company to make and sell each of its products, and what it *does*. Information created within the system for production purposes is available for budgeting and accounting applications. Every company activity provides information for specific functions of Cost Planning and Control.

Response to Exceptions The COPICS framework also incorporates a variety of features for prompt response to exception situations. These "control aids" include:

A set of standards for such functions as production labor, sales quotas, budgets, etc., used both to measure performance and to provide incentives. Control is the weakest part of many business systems today owing to the lack of effective standards.

Action files, which are consulted by the computer to determine what the appropriate response should be to a particular exception situation, and what message should be directed to whom for appropriate action, and in what sequence. The production plan is continually being affected by changes and interruptions. Two approaches—real-time and net-change processing—are used to reduce delay in determining the impact on the plan.

Real-time data processing permits on-line entry of data into the plant communications system for immediate updating of affected records. For instance, if an employee reports the completion of an operation, the data (employee number, shop order number, and quantity completed) go directly from the plant floor terminal to computer memory. There the data can update the following records:

- Shop order record, reflecting job status and accumulated labor and material cost to date.
- Work queue at the completing work center to remove the completed work from that center's backlog.
- Queue list of the next work center to indicate the job's imminent arrival.
- Material handling action file to move material to the next work center.
- Employee's payroll record.

Net-change processing makes possible rapid determination of the effect of new on-line data on the production plan. Replanning thus need not be on a weekly or monthly cycle, as in most previous manufacturing control systems. Instead, it can be done daily, or even continuously. Together with real-time processing, this approach reduces the two major causes of delay in information and control systems—collecting data and communicating the answer. In addition, data acquisition costs are reduced, and so are inventory and workload fluctuations caused by communication delays.

Figure 5-2 gives a schematic overview of COPICS.

COMPUTER-AIDED MANUFACTURING

Many companies that do not yet feel ready to undertake full integration of their activities have nevertheless been actively implementing systems for computer-aided manufacturing—the execution and control of actual production activities. The sophistication of these systems varies greatly. Some are made up of extensive networks of remote terminals and other communication devices linked to teleprocessing front-end data processing systems, while others still consist chiefly of oral communications and a stack of paper. However, whatever their form, they are all designed to provide for the following six major direct manufacturing requirements:

- Conformance to the floor logistics plan—shop order documentation and control; material requests, handling, and control; expediting and status reporting; manufacturing activity reporting.
- Manufacturing resource management and measurement of internal resources consumed—attendance reporting; job assignment; machine assignment; tool control and recall; maintenance scheduling, monitoring, and reporting.
- The optimum level of operations assistance, monitoring, and control.
- Conformance to quality control plans and standards through reject criteria and analysis for testing, inspecting, and sampling; and results comparison and reporting.
- The means for manufacturing execution—designing, evaluating, selecting, and building tools, testers, and process equipment, and for developing procedures.
- Conformance to environmental standards and facility monitoring and control—water purity, air purity, power consumption, access security.

System Data Hierarchy   As can be seen from the preceding lists, computer-aided manufacturing involves a great deal more than control of individual tools and testers. The complex, multilevel structure that exists even in the least automated system relies on the assembly of information in common databases, and exchange of this information among the databases.

Databases within a computer-aided manufacturing system are typically organized in a hierarchical sequence. The first is logically the technical or *planning* base, which describes the product to be manufactured. Developed by the Production Engineering Department, the base also accepts data from and feeds back to Product Planning and Control and to the Marketing, Engineering, and Administrative Departments. It contains basic records (such as bills of material, routings, parts list, capacity requirements) and technical data, including a parts program file, test process and quality procedures, tool records, and manufacturing standards.

Production Engineering uses product descriptions and design specifications and secondary information, such as customer order configuration and quality rules, to generate an in-process database. This database contains both operations data (work-in-process, order status, work-center status, inventory) and manufacturing data (numerical control parts program, assembly instructions, statistics, move sequences, and main-

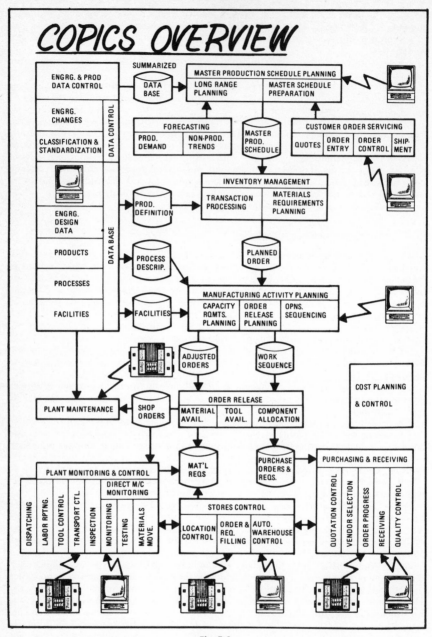

Fig. 5-2

tenance records). Raw data received from the plant floor are analyzed to develop trend statistics, initiate corrective action within the system, and ultimately, to feed back information to other systems.

The in-process manufacturing database communicates with one or more specific operations application databases. Communications among all the databases in the system are generally through a central facility that supports all plant floor applications. Its nature will vary according to the degree of automation in the plant system. In a completely manual plant, this facility may exist only indirectly through the several departments responsible for parts chasing, information dissemination, quality report gathering, production and process status acquisition, etc. At the other extreme, this central facility will be implicit in the design of a computer-based network controlling all production application operations, and this facility may itself be part of a nationwide, distributed system.

The acceptance of distributed systems is relatively recent. Potent arguments were previously raised against them, based on database redundancy and functional duplications. These arguments, however, are steadily losing their power as the cost of storage continues to decrease and the computer increasingly becomes an indispensable working tool. Thus, a break-even point is being reached at which integrated decentralization becomes ever more advantageous. Incentives include greater reliability, faster response, and simplified but more thorough management control.

Successful implementation of distributed systems requires a clear definition not only of the work to be done by each of the systems, but also of the information exchange procedure to be used among systems. If this is done properly, redundancy between the computer-aided manufacturing system files and other plant system files will be quite low. The manufacturing files, being transient in nature, contain information which is redundant only until it is transformed into a suitable form for manufacturing support.

Database Design and Characteristics The need for a clear definition of the work to be done by each system is matched by a need for assignment of database responsibility to specific systems. The task is one that requires special care, for structuring of computer-aided manufacturing databases can follow a virtually unlimited variety of formats. Attainment of standard interfaces for process equipment is far behind the relatively high level achieved for business-oriented data processing applications, such as payroll and accounting.

The relatively uncertain nature of database organization helps explain the creation of a new manufacturing personnel title, that of Computer-Aided Manufacturing Engineer, which is borne by members of that new professional subgroup in an increasing number of plants. However, despite this uncertainty, certain key data categories and types are generally included. Among them are the following:

- Serial number of personalized item or part of shop-order number for product tracking and technical data.
- Machine ID and operation number for maintenance/performance/station assignment and fixed procedures and process tracking.
- Station ID for job queue status, intermediate work-in-process (WIP) status, quality reporting, scrap reporting, labor claiming, etc.
- Process variables and parameters for process analysis and control.

In addition, there are at least six basic factors that should be considered when planning the distribution of database responsibility among the various systems:

- Data traffic patterns.
- Access time requirements.
- Subsystem interdependence.
- User responsibilities.
- Data volumes.
- Data redundancies.

The design of the resulting databases should emphasize availability of data that are used often or needed quickly. For applications that draw chiefly on stored information, only currently needed data should be stored at the process system. The larger-volume libraries should be stored by the computer-aided manufacturing system subhost (if the system stands alone, and is not part of an integrated manufacturing system). The reverse will often be true for data collection-oriented applications that chiefly contribute process information. The volume will frequently be the greatest at the process system level. Sometimes shared databases are most practical, with two levels of system accessing the same I/O device.

PLANT FLOOR SYSTEMS AND APPLICATIONS

Thinking big, but starting small is the computer-aided manufacturing approach followed by a growing number of industrial firms. Their future plans call for integration of all their manufacturing and related operations into a single control system. Currently, however, they are installing sensor-based plant floor computers on a unit basis for individual applications. From this base, they are gradually assembling the equipment, database, and experience needed to bring these applications together into a cohesive computer-aided manufacturing system. The latter can then itself be integrated with other large functional systems, such as production planning and engineering.

Advances in the development of economical sensor-based systems have made it increasingly easy to justify the start-up of plant floor computer applications. Computers such as the IBM System/7 can offer improved control of operations regardless of whether a production process is manual or highly mechanized. What is important is that *people* remain in charge and benefit from the system's capabilities.

Computers dedicated to specific applications are generally sensor-based systems with sufficient CPU and memory capabilities to support local processing needs on a stand-alone, quick-response basis. They are used to monitor and guide production through sensors and manual input terminals, and to communicate information to plant management. Developing problems can be highlighted at an early stage through exception reporting techniques. Computer control can extend directly to production equipment. Thus, in the case of transfer lines, where high-production parts are machined, the computer is a flexible and powerful alternative to the relay panels often used to control machine cycles and to initiate protective action in case of malfunctions.

Examples of plant floor computers include IBM 1800s and System/7s. These systems can be interconnected in a plant-wide computer-aided manufacturing system and communicate with it on a broad-bandwidth basis. This will bring added economy by eliminating the need to add functions and peripherals, such as disk files for buffering, to the low-end systems. These functions will instead be centrally located in the plant-wide system, with higher-bandwidth communications being traded off for reduced buffering.

Linkage to a central system also permits the use of remote line controllers to control applications. These devices can execute only fixed programs, and are totally dependent on the system for program loads, data processing support, and terminal support. They cannot support large processing tasks, and are dedicated to machine interfacing and control.

The Computer-Aided Manufacturing Network   A multilevel hierarchy of plant floor systems can be created within a computer-aided manufacturing network. Sensor-based systems can, for instance, be used as line controller concentrators or dedicated to large process-control jobs. The advantage of concentrating the line controllers through a sensor-based system is that the controllers are buffered to some extent from heavy dependence on the central computer, and better support response can be achieved.

The computer dedicated to the computer-aided manufacturing system will have sufficient data processing and communication capability to accept information from other plant systems, translate this information into a form suitable for manufacturing use, and communicate it to the process computers and terminals. It will also monitor information originating at the process level, analyze it and create necessary management reports, and collaborate in initiating corrective action within the computer-aided manufacturing or other systems. In addition, it will support the processing needs of the Product Engineering Department.

Development Approaches   Development of an integrated computer-aided manufacturing system can proceed in either of two directions. In the top-down approach, a computer already being used for production planning and scheduling can provide additional control through connection to sensor-based plant floor systems as they are installed. The bottom-up approach proceeds one application at a time.

The following six areas of plant floor applications can provide the basis for the bottom-up approach:

• *Plant communications:* operator guidance through such equipment as display terminals and terminal printers, for customized assembly information and live status reporting and collection through terminals of various types of operator-, expediter-, inspector- and supervisor-originated data. The IBM 2790 data collection system is representative of equipment used for this purpose.

• *Electronic testing:* complete appliances and units, extending downward through subassemblies, power supplies, harnesses, cables, boards, semiconductors down to chips and wafers, and also testing systems themselves.

• *Mechanical testing:* engine testing, motor-generator set testing, precision parts measurement, brakes, carburetors, and turbines.

• *Facility monitoring:* such as for air and water purity, controlled access, power demand, and alarm systems.

• *Machine control:* for numerical control (NC), digital numerical control (DNC), induction molding machines, forming machines, furnace time-temperature controls, and conveyor synchronization.

• *Machine monitoring:* for transfer lines, stamping presses, and maintenance, and yield and productivity monitoring for all special-purpose machinery.

Transfer Line A typical production application for small, sensor-based computers, drawn from the preceding list, is the monitoring and/or control of a transfer line. A typical transfer line consists of many machine stations, mechanically connected work-piece transfer mechanisms, and closely interlocked electrical controls. These lines may be inoperative for extended periods because of their difficult environment, and for other causes such as control problems, tool replacement, and mechanical breakdowns.

Computer control can reduce transfer line downtime by connecting the limit switches and other line sensing devices to sensor inputs on the computer. The computer then continuously compares sensor status with a programmed table of conditions. If conditions are proper, the computer activates solenoid valves and other control devices on the line to accomplish the next step in the operating cycle. This cycle is interrupted if improper conditions are detected. A logical determination of the fault is made by the diagnostic program, and a recovery program clears the line for maintenance and restart.

Besides taking protective action, the computer can automatically type out a complete report, enabling the operator to call for suitable maintenance assistance and giving the operator the correct restart procedures. The computer can also keep a count of the number of operations performed by each tool, reporting when a replacement level has been reached. Cutters, for instance, can thus be changed at the optimum point on a planned basis, conserving materials and tools and minimizing unscheduled downtime. Finally, the computer can generate production reports to management either on demand or at scheduled intervals. These help management plan material flow, minimize inventory of tools, and reduce overall machine maintenance time.

Application Growth The use of stand-alone plant floor computers makes it possible to begin with monitoring of a single production area and later to broaden the application without scrapping the initial investment in equipment systems design and programming. Application growth can take several forms, such as more sensor inputs to accommodate additional machine tools, more data entry terminals, and more data processing or storage capability. The sensor-based computers can be interconnected with a larger computer already being used for planning and scheduling. The two computers can then accomplish tasks that neither could effectively perform alone. However, this expansion of applications and interlinkage to create a production system is an evolutionary process. It is one that requires management involvement.

Management's role is to take a systems look at the various production operations with the objective of improving productivity and profits—to identify as the first plant floor application the one that will provide immediate benefits, and that will later serve as a satellite in a total manufacturing information and control system.

Chapter 6

Reservation Systems

EUGENE J. JONES

Management Consultant, Data Processing Systems, Huntington, New York; formerly Vice President, Systems & Programming, Avis Rent-A-Car System, Inc., Garden City, New York

The travel industry, airlines, hotels, motels, car rental companies, and even such facilities as ferry boats and campsites all use extensive reservation and customer service computer systems. All these systems have the common objective of ensuring maximum utilization of available space. An airline seat, a rented car, or a hotel room if not used on a flight or day when it could be used is revenue irretrievably lost. An associated objective, of course, is improved customer service in the highly competitive travel market.

All these on-line systems basically have a common design: a single data processing center connected via communication lines with terminals installed at reservation and service locations spread over a wide geographic area. In many cases, the systems interconnect locations thousands of miles or more apart, and some of these systems are truly global in scope.

While most of the travel industry systems are still known as reservation systems, and virtually all started with reservations as their single major function, it is no longer totally accurate to designate them as such, since their capabilities have expanded far beyond this single service. In addition to handling reservations, these systems now perform such functions as pricing and printing airline tickets, renting cars, performing credit checks, and pre-preparing hotel guest registrations.

HISTORY

Traditionally, reservations were tracked by having the originating locations send a telex or telegraph message to the service location, or center, where the counts were manually adjusted. Because of the time lag in transmitting and posting, at some point before all the space was actually recorded as sold, a "stop sell" message would have to be generated to all locations, cutting off acceptance of further bookings. The hope was, of course, that there would not be more reservations still in the pipeline than space remaining available.

In the mid-1950s, the first generation of computers were used to record the counts automatically, advising reservation management when the danger availability level was reached. As the technology improved, a limited number of terminals located in principal cities were added to these systems, allowing the first recording of reservations at the point of sale. Reservations made at outlying locations still had to be sent as messages for delayed posting in the computer.

In order to confirm the fact that a customer had a reservation, in addition to adjusting the inventory count, the customer name would be transmitted to the location where the service was promised. Here the reservation would be filed for reference on the needed date. However, as the volumes increased dramatically during the early 1950s, in the airlines in particular, this method of handling reservations became less and less satisfactory both in terms of utilization of space and customer service.

SABRE   Using the experience gained from military systems such as SAGE (Semi Automatic Ground Environment), the early warning defense system installed for the Air Force, computer technology had advanced during the 1950s in terms of hardware and programming to such a degree that an effort comparable in scope to that of the pioneering SABRE system was committed to in 1958 by American Airlines and IBM. This system, operational in 1963, is generally regarded as the "granddaddy" of the current-generation reservation systems. SABRE actually offered many of the application features found in today's systems, even though it operated entirely with second-generation computer mainframes and peripheral storage tied to hard-copy-only (printing) terminals. The two major features of the SABRE concept were that it extended the same immediate level of access to inventory to all reservation locations and for the first time in the same system recorded all the customer data. With the availability of the flight inventory at all reservation points, sales could now be made down to the last seat available at any of these locations. And with the customer information in the same system, the passenger could be dealt with by name at any location regardless of where he or she made the reservation. This significantly increased the customer's confidence that the reservation would be honored.

With SABRE, a uniform and high degree of computer editing was for the first time used for all reservations. This processing ensured, for example, that a connecting flight was, in fact, scheduled to leave after the incoming flight.

Based upon their experience in developing SABRE, and the similar PANAMAC (Pan American Airlines) and Deltamatic (Delta Airlines) systems installed slightly later, IBM constructed the PARS—Passenger Airline Reservation System—for use with its third-generation 360 computers. The PARS package provides at least the basic foundation of the systems operational in over 20 airlines, several reservation service organizations, and in the Avis Rent A Car "Wizard of Avis" System. In terms of number of systems installed, the other manufacturer providing a substantial number of major reservation systems is currently Univac.

SYSTEM ARCHITECTURE

The cross-section of the structure of all the large reservation systems, regardless of manufacturer, is quite similar. First, they are dedicated real-time systems. The expression *real-time* connotes the system's ability to respond—provide an answer—in a time frame appropriate for it to be used. In reservation systems, this means a response measured in seconds. This term also refers to the ability to enter any transaction into the system at any time. This is as opposed to the batch-processing discipline of having to adhere to pre-established application input schedule. *On-line* refers to the fact that the terminals have constant availability to the computer via communication lines. Reservation systems, because of their fast response-time requirements, are normally dedicated solely to this function together with those related customer service functions added in recent years, and are not shared with other applications.

Processing   Processing in reservation systems is performed at a single computer center with a duplex computer configuration, one system on-line and the other maintained for backup. The principal medium for peripheral file storage is disk and drum, because of the need for rapid retrieval of information. Key data on these devices are duplicated in two separate on-line storage locations to ensure their integrity and availability. Each night a copy is made of the exact state of all data files. All critical transactions, anything that changes a file during the processing day, is written out (logged) to magnetic tape for use in restoring the system to a current state (restart) should the files be destroyed or damaged at any point in a day. This is done by rapidly re-executing the file-change transactions in the sequence in which they occurred, against the previous night's file capture. Spare disk and drum capacity is also available for insertion into the on-line system should a mechanical failure occur in any of these units.

System throughput is maintained by a control program resident in main memory. This program controls all the input-output file functions and application program execution. The sophistication of the control program can best be appreciated by the 2-second response times commonly found in reservation centers.

Terminals Regardless of whether they involve a CRT (cathode-ray tube) or hard-copy terminal, the agent sets used are of two types, either *stand-alone* or *cluster*. A stand-alone terminal has sufficient memory or buffer capacity built in to allow message composition (storage) directly within the unit. In the clustered version, terminals, from two to eight normally, do their buffering in some remote device which either is cable-connected or uses some portion of the communications network.

When the message is complete and ready for transmission at the terminal level, the operator indicates "send" or "end transaction." Each terminal in the system has a unique address. The common method of communicating with the terminals is through *polling:* the communication control software, either as part of the central site computer control program or in some systems remoted to communication concentrators, asks in a prescribed sequence, by address, if a terminal unit is in the send state (that is, has data ready to transmit). If it is, the control program accepts the data and passes them on to the task management portion of the control program. Here the transaction code is interpreted and the appropriate sequence of application processing is commenced. When the transaction processing is complete, either in terms of a satisfactory response as to application execution or an error message produced by an edit check, control is returned to the output portion of the communication control program. The communication handler determines that the addressed terminal is ready to receive a message and transmits it.

All reservation systems tend to have the same field configuration of agent sets or terminals. Reservation input is normally handled through reservation *hub* centers. Each of these centers services a geographic area through use of IN-WATS or tie-line telephone service. These reservation center concentrations of personnel and equipment can range from as few as 30 terminals to as many as 600 or more in the largest of the airline centers.

In airlines, in terms of percentage of total terminal population, the terminals installed in such centers have historically far outnumbered the other terminals in the system. In the hotel and car rental applications, while centers are used for booking reservations, the number of points serviced and their wide geographic distribution have resulted in more remote terminals than those housed in the purely reservation locations. As the auxiliary or additional customer service applications have grown in number and importance in the airline systems, however, there has also been a considerable expansion in the number of remote resident terminals.

Reservation Service When a customer places a call to the number published for a company's reservation service, he or she is normally connected with a reservation center where automatic call-distributing equipment places the call with the next available sales agent. Since a printed record is not normally required, each reservation sales agent position is usually equipped with a CRT (cathode-ray tube) terminal instead of the slower hard-copy-type terminal.

The major expense of a reservation center is a direct result of the number of inbound telephone lines and the number of agent personnel needed. A *reservation standard of service* is used to establish the communication lines and the personnel staffing required at any reservation center. This objective is defined in terms of the percentage of all calls to be answered within a specified time period. The time period is called *answering time,* and is the time from first ring until an agent answers the call ready to give service.

A typical objective would be to serve 90 per cent of all calls in 20 seconds. Since a telephone line and sales agent can serve only one customer at a time, the reservation *holding time* becomes a major factor in meeting this objective. Holding time is the elapsed time from the moment the agent picks up the call until the disconnect. It therefore becomes critical not only to respond to each agent input in seconds, but to handle all aspects of the reservation in as few computer responses as practical to reduce this agent holding time. This leads to the reservation application and how it is typically done in three major users of reservation systems—airlines, hotels, and car rentals.

RESERVATION AVAILABILITY

The starting point in any new reservation transaction is the selection of the desired service and the determination of its availability.

The exact starting point is actually determined by the customer. There are two types of customers, the potential customer and the "action" customer. The action customer is normally the experienced traveler who knows exactly the service he or she requires, whether it be a room in a particular hotel, space on a specific flight number, or a car rental at a specified location. The potential customer either does not know the service available or is comparison shopping for the best service. Thus the opening customer request can vary from, "Do you have any flights to St. Louis that leave New York around 12 noon on the fifteenth?" to "I want one first-class ticket on your flight number 122 leaving JFK Airport at 12:55 on September 15." Regardless of the type of customer initiation, the starting transaction and first computer action in all three applications is the availability request and/or availability file search.

Availability Control An airline controls its availability on a *flight leg* basis. For example, if a flight number 122 is scheduled to serve cities A, B, C, and D, this gives legs AB, BC, and CD. Each leg for each date of service has a fixed departure and arrival time and airport. For the quick determination of the availability of space, each leg of airline service is represented in the system by a simple yes/no indicator for each date for as much as 1 year in advance.

Passengers, however, book reservations in terms of segments. In this example, a passenger could require segment AC or AD as easily as any individual leg of the flight. Therefore, while the availability is maintained by leg, the reservation computer search must combine legs into segments to be certain the total service is available. Unavailability of any leg in the segment, of course, means that the entire segment is unavailable.

Hotel systems confirm space for specific types of rooms within individual hotel properties. Each hotel is represented in the system, and for each there is division in terms of rooms of differing type or capacity—single, double, suite, etc. Some hotels, particularly resorts, also segregate rooms by such distinctions as ocean view. In the hotel application, for each hotel room type for each day for the next year, availability is again represented by a yes/no indicator. The fundamental difference in the hotel availability search is that it must span the duration of the intended stay from date of guest arrival to date of departure. A day of unavailability in the requested room type during the reservation period denotes that the service is unavailable.

In car rental, availability is usually controlled on a city basis, or on the basis of a car control area within a large city, even though the actual reservation request is made for a specific rental station. This level of control is feasible because of the ability to transfer cars from one location to another to meet demand, a flexibility not afforded an airline or hotel whose capacity is fixed. Cars are normally reserved by class. A rental car class contains cars of similar quality, but of different makes and models. Availability is determined by checking the city or car control area for the class of car for the date of planned rental. If a customer has a unique reservation requirement—for example, a convertible—this is handled via a specific computer-generated request to the rental station involved and confirmed to the customer only after a confirmation from the local management that it will be able to provide exactly what is required.

In the case where an airline or hotel availability request is in terms of an approximate departure time for a flight or general geographic area for a hotel, the computer must first determine those flight segments or hotels most nearly fitting the requirement. In the airline situation, the agent inputs the approximate departure time, date, and city pair (origin and destination) desired. The computer then searches out and displays back to the agent a number of available flights which most nearly suit the request, scheduled to depart both before and after the requested time. (In the case where an availability request is for a specific flight and that flight is not available, most airline reservation systems respond to the agent with the alternative flights, if any, with available seats which most nearly match the request.)

Request/Response The general request for a hotel reservation is input in terms of geography, check-in and check-out dates, and, at times, price range. The geographic description coded in the inquiry for hotel space can range from a city or section of a city to such conditions as proximity to an airport or even in some systems in terms of a city's shopping versus business section. The response is similar to that of the airline, some number of properties fitting the parameters and having availability space. (If a specified hotel property is requested and is not available, alternative available properties will also be displayed as in the airline application.)

One level of computer-selected alternative common in all three applications is the class. Reservation computer systems do an upward and downward search if the specific flight, hotel room, or rental car class shows no availability, to determine the closest class that *is* available. In airlines, the selection is between first class and tourist. In hotels, class can be made up of the configuration of the room (twin beds as opposed to a double bed), capacity of the space (double versus single) etc. In Europe, it can also be the rating of the accommodations in terms of luxury, first, standard, and economy. For car rentals, in the United States, the class has been representative of the degree of luxury provided, from subcompact to luxury. As the distinctions widen in the type of cars produced, however, considerations such as passenger and luggage capacity figure more and more importantly in the class selection, adding a new level of sophistication to selection of alternatives.

Since the costs of operating a reservation center are dictated by the length of time an agent must spend with each customer, every reservation system aims to respond both quickly and with sufficient information for the normal customer concerns. In an airline situation, this would be such items as the exact time of departure and arrival and the number of stops the flight makes, and whether there is meal or snack service. For the hotel, the exact hotel address and the room price are included in the usual availability response. For car rentals, the specific vehicle makes and models in the available class and the exact rental rates or plans available at the rental station are part of every availability response.

Once availability is determined and the customer selects or confirms his or her desire for a particular flight, hotel room, or car rental station, the variously called *ticket, sell,* or *book* transaction occurs with its resulting inventory action.

RESERVATION INVENTORY CONTROL

All inventory systems, including reservation systems, basically work on the formula that opening stock balance, plus units due in, minus units on order, equals units available. The travel industry is no exception. Nevertheless, the area in which the three example applications probably differ more than any other is in their approach to calculating inventory levels. And this area more than any other can represent the largest cost saving or revenue increase.

Of the three, the airline has perhaps the most stable *on-hand* situation. The exact equipment—airplane—to be used on a specified flight is known in advance, and thus the capacity in terms of both first-class and tourist seats is known. Therefore, as each reservation is booked, the number in the reserved party is subtracted from the starting balance for each leg of the flight covered by the reserved segment, leaving an exact number of seats available. When the number of seats available for any leg reaches zero (or in some cases a predetermined minus number to allow for a forecastable number of no-show passengers) the availability indicator for the leg is turned from on or yes, to off or no.

One of the many added capabilities of an on-line airline reservation system is that it can *wait-list* passengers. That is, even though the flight is booked, a first-in, first-out list of potential passengers—the wait list—can be stored by the computer. If a confirmed passenger cancels his or her space, the computer automatically searches out the next eligible wait-listed customer and advises the proper reservation center to make contact to confirm the reservation.

One of the most complex inventory actions in the airline system occurs on a large scale twice a year. At these times, spring and fall, there is a general schedule change.

Because the system contains not only inventory counts, but a PNR (passenger name record) for each customer, if a flight is canceled, or its equipment changes drastically in capacity, the computer system will automatically notify the correct reservation center in order that the customer can be contacted to make alternate reservations. This, however, occurs only after the computer has attempted to protect the passenger by reserving the closest alternative flight available in the new schedule.

Hotel system inventory control is, in large, still under the control of each individual hotel's management. In the majority of the on-line hotel reservation systems, each property specifies a given number of rooms by type to be counted as initially available. As space is confirmed, this number is decremented. At zero, reservations are stopped and an advisory message is sent to the local hotel management. The decision is then made locally as to whether more rooms should be released to the systems control.

One of the complicating factors in controlling a hotel inventory, and one of the reasons for not fully allowing remote computer control, is that the use of the inventory item occurs across a period of time. An airplane flight works on a fixed date and time schedule. Once a flight has departed from a city, there is no longer a single thing that can be done to improve its occupancy, and its load is precisely known. A hotel can check in or check out customers at any time of the day. Of even more concern, however, in determining availability of rooms at some fixed point in the future is the fact that just as some number of customers with reservations will not arrive (no-shows), some number of registered guests will not depart on the date planned. This has led to the practice of maintaining the precise room control at the local level, parceling out blocks of space to the computer.

Flights have fixed times and capacity. Hotels have established capacities, but a nonspecific time. Since rental cars are totally mobile, another factor is added to the difficulty of establishing the availability of service for a specific rental location for a point in time in the future. While the ability to move cars can present an advantage in meeting demand, it presents a considerable challenge in inventory planning. On the plus side is this ability to move cars to meet demand. On the negative side is the consideration that a car can also be moved away from a location before the customer arrives.

For car rental inventory control, three factors must be considered. The first, and the only "known" in the car rental situation, is the number of cars physically present at a specific station (renting location) at the current point in time. (And this is available only if each car movement is entered into the system as it occurs.)

Also known, but subject to the same no-show possibility found in all service systems, are the number, date, and time of customers with reservations. The third and unique number which must be developed is a count of cars due in at any period in the future. That is, when a customer rents a car, he or she is asked the planned return location, date, and time. If this is recorded in the system, a forecast of when and where this car will next become available is possible.

In order to develop the future car inventory number from any point in time, first the remainder of the current day and each day in the future are divided into time periods, and within each period the count of reservation customers and due-ins (for each class) are summarized. Using the number of cars currently on hand, the inventory position for the first time period is calculated by adding the due-ins and subtracting the reservations. For example, if at the current moment there are 40 cars on hand, and in the remainder of the current time period 20 are due in and there are 25 reservations, there should still be 35 cars available for rent at the start of the next time period ($40 + 20 - 25 = 35$). The same equation is then executed for the next time period, now using the forecasted 35 as the probable opening on-hand count. This exercise can then be rolled forward as far as desired in the future to determine probable availability of cars. Since both reservations and due-ins, however, are subject to a customer not following his or her original plan, a history of fluctuation must be developed and used to prepare these numbers to increase their meaning in inventory planning.

To determine when cars are no longer available, the number of reservations is measured against the possible supply. When the per cent of reservations reaches a predetermined limit, a warning message is automatically generated to the local car control management. Management there reviews the local conditions and the availability status of other near rental locations to determine the true ability to meet the demand. If the reservation demand for cars in the area, not only at an individual station, has reached a critical level, the local management informs the system to suspend confirming reservations for that area.

The fact that, to date, the system of this type does not automatically suspend reservations for a prescribed local area is due to the impact of the immediate local conditions. In dry, sunny weather, it may be practical to move cars; in a snowstorm, impractical. Or there simply may not be sufficient local labor at a given time to "nonrevenue" or move the cars from one location to another. The car rental inventory control system described above is at the present writing used only in the Wizard of Avis System.

CUSTOMER INFORMATION

From a customer viewpoint, the ability of the reservation computer system to remember the customer by name and retain on-line all the particulars about his or her travel plans, and to make this information available at any terminal in the system if the customer needs to confirm or change plans, is perhaps the most visible addition to the state of the art with the full computer reservation system. A number of the reservation systems now will even permanently retain on-line for a customer all static personal data such as credit-card number, billing address, class of service preference, etc. With this information available, all the customer need provide at reservation time is his or her unique identification code to have the computer automatically marry this permanent data to the specifics of this reservation.

The amount of customer data desired at reservation time varies from application to application, and even within the systems offering like service, such as car rentals, depending upon the sophistication of the individual systems. In particular in car rentals, considerable customer data are requested at reservation time, since this customer information is needed on a car rental contract. If the information is captured at reservation time, it can be entered onto the rental contract before the customer arrives, reducing wait time at the counter.

In a single airline passenger name record, multiple reservations can be stored if the reservation is for more than one individual. The same is true of a hotel guest name record. In car rentals, normally only the name of the driver is required, the count of the number in the party not being important.

The second portion of the customer record is the service detail reserved for the customer. For an airline, this would be each flight segment detail, including date, flight number, class, origin, and destination, and departure and arrival times. In the hotel record, information would be the specific property name, guest arrival date and time, departure date, type of room, and rate quoted. For car rental, it would include the station, class of car (or car make and model on a confirmed request reservation), check-out (rental) date and time, check-in (return) station date and time, and rate quoted.

Another custom feature of keeping the customer information on-line for each reservation is the ability to indicate unique requirements. These can range from an unusual food preference, the need to supply fresh flowers to a VIP's room, or the requirement for some special automobile feature such as a ski rack.

DEPARTURE, RENTING, AND HOTEL ARRIVAL PROCESSING

A number of airlines have now implemented fare quote and ticketing. This allows the ticket in a high percentage of itineraries to be printed directly out of the central computer. Depending upon the lead time and customer preference, the ticket can be printed directly after the reservation is made and sent to the customer, or printed shortly before his or her arrival at the boarding point for the first flight in the plan.

The one limiting factor in producing tickets on-line is the extreme complexity of fare plans available in the airline business. The price charged for on-the-surface identical passenger itineraries can be subject to a variety of considerations. There are promotional fares which demand that to be eligible, a customer leave on a certain day of the week—and even at a certain time—and stay a minimum but less than maximum number of days. Even the number of hours requested between connecting flights can affect a fare. And in international travel it is the location of the furthest point of journey which determines the charges for a multisegment trip.

Another service now being offered by some airlines is seat selection at time of reservation.

At an increasing number of locations, when the airline customer arrives for departure, receipt of the boarding pass is the transaction which confirms in the central computer his or her use of the reservation. This same transaction also increments the actual on-board count for any passenger who did not have a reservation. With this total input, the actual flight load count is automatically calculated as soon as the plane departs, and is available for use at its next "down leg" boarding point.

In the car rental application, in the case where the system has all the needed customer data, the rental agreement is now normally pre-prepared before the time indicated for arrival in the reservation. But the rental or check-out of a car is only half the transaction. The charge for the rental must still be computed when the rental is completed. This action is analogous to the airline fare calculated, but is in one way more involved than ticket preparation. The normal car rental return (check-in) requires a minimum of four additions, four subtractions, and one multiplication. In some car rental systems, the check-in is now also done on-line, ensuring the accuracy of the charge.

In the vast majority of the current hotel systems, the customer information is sent for each reservation at the time of its confirmation. These data are then filed or posted manually for date of arrival. When the hotel has an in-house minisystem, the data are keyed into the system. If the reservation included all the customer billing data, a guest registration can be pre-prepared before the customer arrival in the same manner as the airline ticket or car rental contract.

FUTURE TRENDS

The airlines have developed interline message disciplines to the extent that all airlines now interchange reservation requests between systems. In some cases, airlines actually maintain availability status in their systems for connecting flights of other airlines. These are automatically opened and closed by the other airline's system as the status changes. In some instances, airlines, as part of their reservation, will also book a hotel or rent a car for the customer, feeding this information directly to that company's system. It is probable that the future will see an even greater degree of communication between systems representing all travel interests.

For years, travel agencies and major corporations have envisioned a single terminal which would allow them to book space as required, with all the various suppliers of travel service. Early efforts in this direction encountered serious legal and cost obstacles, however, and were not successful. As the interchange of reservation capability becomes more common, the possibility of a single terminal reserving hotel, rental car, and airline space becomes realizable.

One of the functions becoming ever more important in customer processing occurs at time of airline ticketing, or of preparing the car rental contract, or when a customer checks into (or certainly before he or she checks out of) a hotel — the credit check. This credit check is certainly important in airlines and hotels, but it is vital in car rentals. If a stolen credit card is used in the airline or hotel situation, the actual out-of-pocket loss will normally be confined to the food and liquor consumed. Only if the fraudulent customer used space in a fully booked hotel or on a fully booked flight, where potential revenue is lost through having denied a legitimate customer this service, is there a considerable loss.

In a hotel situation, with the potential for material loss due to the availability of in-house shops, etc., a duration of stay is usually involved which makes possible credit check at other than that initial moment of contract, thus reducing the exposure. A car rental company, however, is trusting an inventory item worth many thousands of dollars to the renter based on his or her credit identification. (In the Wizard of Avis System, a credit check is now performed as part of each rental, and airlines will soon add the feature to their ticketing capability.)

One experiment has been conducted on the use of a vending machine to produce airline tickets. The airlines have agreed to a common format for encoding a magnetic strip which can be placed on the back of credit cards. This machine-readable strip can be scanned by a unit such as a vending machine. The customer inputs his or her flight requirements via some key device, and the fact of the reservation is confirmed, or availability requested and confirmed, a credit check on the customer is made, a passenger name record is created, and a ticket is issued by the vending machine—all in seconds, through on-line conversation with the control reservation computer.

This same concept certainly can be applied in varying degree by hotel and car rental companies. (In car rentals, one problem is that there is always the need to inspect the customer's driver's license visually to be certain it is still valid, and to observe the customer to be certain he or she is in a condition to drive.)

Some hotels now have operational in-house minicomputer systems, recording all guest charges and automatically preparing the guest's bill at check-out time. These in-house systems are capable of communicating directly with the central reservation computer, to allow establishing more accurately the number of rooms available for reservation. These in-hotel systems will no doubt also use a central system for credit-check purposes.

As systems ability and use in airline fare quote and ticketing grows, so does the probability that the airline ticket data will be fed directly into the airline's accounting system. The facility to bypass the assembling and data recording of the information from a ticket represents a savings in terms of both personnel and cash flow. With the ability of airlines, hotels, and car rental companies to store all the required data on-line and on a credit card, it is even possible that at some future point the customer possessing such identification can actually be handled without the physical issuance of a ticket! The more data that are captured on-line in machine-processable form, the better will transportation companies become in terms of having detailed information for market analysis, trend analysis, and future space forecast requirements.

However, it is the ever-increasing power and flexibility provided by the minicomputer which will bring the computer sharply into every facet of the processing of the customer in the travel industry. While many applications must have the central-site processing capability—the reservation itself, maintenance of the fare, and rate plans, credit check, etc.—there are functions which can be processed and given interim storage at the local level ranging from being the intelligent base for vending operations to seat selection and the hotel front desk.

CONCLUSION

The 1960s were the travel industry era of reservation inventory systems. With the efforts visible in the 1970s, it is clear that this period will be the decade of the *full customer service computer system*. By the end of this decade it is probable that the customer will interact with some type computer system at virtually every point in his or her travels.

Section **8**

The Computer and Society

Introduction

JOHN W. OPLINGER *Marketing Manager, The Diebold Group, Inc., New York, New York*

The computer is a powerful tool, with enormous potential to enhance and enrich the quality of human life. Like any powerful tool or strong medicine, it can cause harm if abused. But used with intelligence and restraint, it will improve the quality and lower the cost of many of our goods and services, and will make available new goods and services scarcely imagined today. And it will do so with little or none of the adverse effects so widely feared today.

In parts of the world, such as the West, where further advances in the standard of living are tightly related to increases in productivity, the computer is already making a major social contribution, largely unnoticed by the public. It is helping factories, utilities, and railroads operate far more efficiently, by improving work routing and production scheduling, inventory and resource management, pinpointing mechanical problems, responding to customer inquiries and needs, and eliminating much routine drudgery. In manufacturing particularly, it is enriching life by enabling factories to produce a wide spectrum of options and variations on the basic product (e.g., automobiles) at little or no loss in production efficiency.

The computer permits more efficient generation and use of electric power, thus conserving fuels, and improves police dispatching, thus making police departments more effective guardians of the peace. In the form of computer-aided instruction it helps students get a better education. It improves airline and hotel booking procedures, makes new telephone features available, creates new credit and funds transfer conveniences for the shopper, and aids doctors in electrocardiogram analyses.

As we shall see, the computer increases rather than decreases the levels of employment. A whole new industry has been created: $20 billion a year in the United States alone, or far more than that if all the related new businesses are included. And beyond the computer industry itself, a wide spectrum of new careers — satisfying and rewarding new skills and professions — has developed. Moreover, a fascinating variety of direct computer-based services to the individual citizen or consumer is waiting in the wings — many of them technically feasible now, waiting only for better understanding and acceptance by the public to make them economically feasible, too.

There could, for example, be new, far more convenient modes of shopping, conserving not only time but valuable energy resources. Closed-circuit television or two-way CATV could enable the shopper to view merchandise while he or she selects purchases by operating an in-home computer terminal. Instant calculations would display unit prices and accumulated costs at the terminal. Supermarkets would give way to automated, computer-controlled warehouses, and the significant cost savings would be passed on to the consumer. For those few items — meat and fresh produce — which the buyer would reasonably wish to examine physically before purchasing, small counters would remain available for this limited shopping. The related electronic funds transfer to simplify such modes of shopping is already being implemented.

Books and reference information can be stored in computer memories and accessed via home display terminals. This would eliminate waiting for borrowed books to be returned and would enable efficient search by the individual for all kinds of information on the basis of key words or subject indexes. Computer recreations are a fascinating possibility, as are computer aids for tax preparation, household budget management, activity scheduling, and homework preparation.

But the negative image of the computer persists. What are the anxieties felt by so many people, and why are they so widespread? The perceived menace is that of the "mechanical brain" or "electronic brain" or "blinking monster" which will put us all in numbered categories, and — deaf to our protests — keep us so pigeonholed the rest of our lives. What is feared, then, is a controlling force, impersonal and depersonalizing, insensitive, making decisions by crude criteria, and substituting its mechanical processes for the human nexus in our affairs.

There are, in our view, three reasons for the growth of these anxieties:

First, there has been a certain amount of mishandling of the computer, sometimes verging on abuse, on the part of companies which deal with the public. Especially in the early years, systems were implemented grossly lacking in error checking and prevention facilities, so that consumers' money accounts were frequently in error. This was compounded by the failure of at least some of these companies to correct the errors promptly, even when presented with incontrovertible documentary proof of the error. And even more seriously compounded again when the error *and* the failure to correct it were explained to the consumer as "computer error." This very widely used term is a particularly unfortunate one, since it is grossly misleading or false at worst, and too vague to be meaningful at best. Very few of these so-called computer errors are actually machine failures. Such failures usually cause the machine to stop processing, or to produce total gibberish readily discernible. Almost all "computer errors" are either programming errors or data entry errors — both categories of human and not a machine error, in the same sense that a typo in a letter is a human rather than a typewriter error.

Consumers have been frightened, not because people made mistakes (people always have), but because the people who formerly would have

corrected the errors are now shrugging them off as "computer errors." And
—worst of all—these "computer errors" are often rectified with inexcusable
slowness.   True, it may not be economically feasible to correct an erroneous
record as an isolated transaction (particularly in a batch environment), but
one wonders why these errors often persist through three, four, or five
processings of the master file.

It is true that the programming process exposes us to the possibility of a
new kind of error, which was not a risk under manual procedures.   The
programmer must foresee all possible future combinations of circumstance,
input, operator error, and data entry error, and provide for each, either in
procedure logic or error routines.   Otherwise, the system will act in unforeseen ways, and someone may be abused.   But commercial computing is a
quarter of a century old.   We know now how to live with these possibilities,
and how to cushion the innocent citizen or consumer from adverse effect, if
we have the will to do so.   There is no more reason for a citizen to be "im-
personally" treated by a company using a computer than by a company using
a typewriter.

The second reason that many ordinary citizens are uneasy about computers
is the image presented in all the media—sometimes with the complicity
and almost always without the protests of the computer industry or community.   We have seen—many times!—press releases from computer manufacturers, extolling new computer applications, which describe the processor
as the "brain" or "nerve center" of the system.   "Giant brain," "electronic
brain," and "mechanical brain" are common terms for the computer in
fiction, feature articles, and news stories.   On television, computers are often
depicted doing things any programming tyro knows to be absurd.   (Interestingly, many of these marvels are accomplished by running a card sort,
which television directors apparently regard as the most photogenic computer procedure.)

The simple facts of the nature of the computer have never been communicated adequately to the public: It is a programmed mechanism, with much
more in common with such programmed devices as the loom, the printing
press, the machine tool, or the two-barreled carburetor, than with any brain,
even that of a fly.   Despite an unfortunate piece of jargon applied to terminals,
the computer has no intelligence.   (The voice answer-back and voice recognition systems now in various stages of development are sure to cause
further confusion along these lines—despite the fact that the computer is
in no way processing natural language with these systems; it is simply
making programmed responses.)

The third reason for fear of the computer is the fear of technological unemployment.   It is certainly true that some individual skills have been or are
being displaced by the computer—just as, in the past, the locomotive fireman,
the telephone operator, the street sweeper, and the flight engineer have been
reduced in number or eliminated.   But the computer industry, which en-
riches any society that it enters, creates jobs as well as eliminating them—
creates more rewarding and interesting jobs than those it eliminates.

It is a valid question whether the computer, which is marketed as a cost
reduction system, can in the long run create as many jobs as it eliminates.
In the short run it has created more jobs than it superseded because it has
grown so rapidly as an industry.   In the long run, it will create jobs in a
different way, by enriching—economically and culturally—the society, bringing new forms of enterprise into being, marketing new services and new
products only possible in a computerized society.   Many such products are
already being introduced, or are clearly on the horizon: highly optioned

automobiles, new specialty machine tools, vending machines, building utility controls, computerized ignition and fuel injection systems for vehicle engines, novel telephone and communication services, specialized business and professional information services, medical diagnostic instruments, and many more.

The so-called hardware ratio employed by many companies to indicate relative spending for computer support personnel and hardware indicates that most companies are spending significantly more money to hire and train people in the new computer employment categories than they are on the machines themselves. If the society takes the necessary measures to accommodate the computer, it can benefit greatly while suffering minor dislocations at worst.

The first, and most important, measure is a significant increase in education. The computer modifies the statistical distribution of work in the society, eliminating unskilled jobs and adding new highly skilled ones. The distribution of education must be altered to correspond. The second measure is the control of abuses — fraud, abuses by credit extenders, the development of dossiers, and the abuse of privacy. The third measure is the responsibility of the computer industry itself: education of the media and the public as to the real nature of the computer, and its potential value to the society.

Only when, on the one hand, systems and their operators are responsive to the legitimate concerns of the society, and, on the other, the citizens understand that there is nothing intrinsically harmful in a numeric identifier or an MICR font, will we start fully exploiting the computer as a tool for improving the environment.

Chapter 1

Computer-Aided Education

LEONARD C. SILVERN

**President, Education and Training Consultants Company,
Los Angeles, California**

The issue of systematizing the method of instruction has been alive since the 1800s, when educational psychology began its evolution from roots in philosophy. It grew into a problem with international proportions in the twentieth century as mass education became a public function, and as more time was devoted to formal education and training. School population growth is usually accompanied by expansion of the faculty, and this brings with it a wide variety of instructional methods to communicate precisely the same subject matter. The search for a better method for a particular subject has become a national quest in the United States as new forms of education develop: preschool, vocational-technical secondary school, junior college, community college. These new forms are rapidly assuming a permanent role in the burgeoning educational system.

HUMAN INSTRUCTION

Handing down the knowledge accumulated by one generation to the next has been a function performed traditionally by the teacher—the process of *human instruction*. The model for human instruction in Figure 1-1 describes two-way communication between the instructor and the learner.

This model is a generalization. It can represent the college professor–student, kindergarten teacher–student, military instructor–recruit trainee, or the supervisor–employee relationship. It can even represent the mother–child relationship in a learning situation. Each arrow, or signal path, carries information, and in Figure 1-1 there is two-way communication or interaction: information flows between the functions represented by the rectangles. However, it is widely agreed that to obtain good

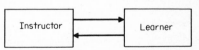

Fig. 1-1 Model of instructor-learner interaction.

communication, the instructor must prepare his or her material in a form which will afford maximum or optimal learning. This process is the preparation of the lesson plan —a systematic step-by-step sequence of events in the lesson. (See Figure 1-2.) Thus, instruction consists of lesson plan preparation and the implementation of the plan in the form of a presentation to the learners. The lesson plan, regardless of the subject matter, should be based on real-life societal requirements which can be determined by conducting a *human activity analysis* or a *job analysis* (the terms are synonymous). This relationship appears in Figure 1-3.

Also, the job analysis–human activity analysis, known as JA-HAA, is the basis for developing a text which has long been the basic tool for the learner in addition to

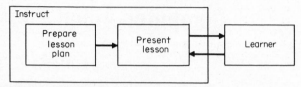

Fig. 1-2 Model describing preparation and presentation as subsystems of human instruction.

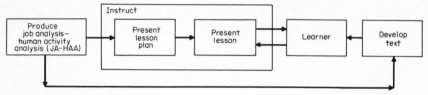

Fig. 1-3 Model describing the JA-HAAA as the source of information for instruction and texts.

human instruction. It should be understood, at the outset, that Figure 1-3 and subsequent models represent ideal situations, since not every teacher, in every education or training program, relies on the JA-HAA. Many texts are based on the personal experiences and biases of the author and may not accurately reflect the needs of real life.

Most instructors use aids of one kind or another, the most common being the chalkboard. A large number now rely on slides, filmstrips, 8-mm and 16-mm films and filmloops, charts, models, and similar visual and audiovisual aids. When the aid is employed as the basis of communication, it is said to be *mediated*—it is between the instructor and learner, and the instructor teaches through it. (See Figure 1-4.) In contrast to mediation is the library function which influences the learner directly without instructor mediation. Both the aid and the library are based primarily upon the JA-HAA.

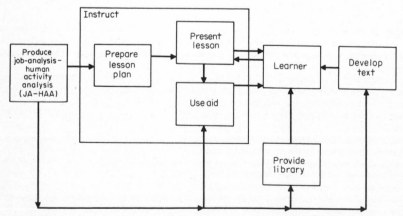

Fig. 1-4 Model describing human instruction which also utilizes a visual or audiovisual aid and the library function.

Having set the stage through flow-chart models of the instructor-learner relationship, attention may now be turned to computers in the learning environment.

COMPUTER AID

The term *computer-assisted teacher* (*CAT*) was created by the present author[1] to identify the use of a computer by an instructor in demonstrating a subject — it is in the same category as the aid. CAT is shown schematically in Figure 1-5, and the model reveals with clarity that an instructor can indeed rely on a computer while he or she is instructing any subject matter which requires or permits digital or analog computation.

This application is *not* administrative — it is instructional, but it is *instructor-centered*. For example, assume that the instruction is in engineering mechanics, and deals with

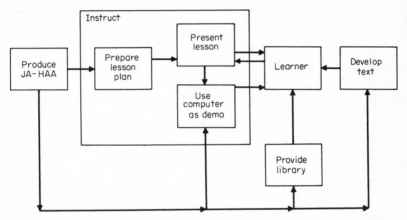

Fig. 1-5 Model describing the computer as an aid — the computer-assisted teacher (CAT).

the design of a cantilever beam. The instructor is teaching beam design and uses the computer to solve the problem on-line, by the direct numerical-integration method. In Figure 1-5, both the library and text functions are in the engineering mechanics domain, not in computing.

A different example for which Figure 1-5 is applicable requires the instructor to teach how to write a computer program in BASIC language; the course is Introduction to Computer Programming. The instructor will utilize the digital computer to demonstrate how to write and debug a BASIC program. In this illustration, the library could be a library of computer programs stored in the machine, the text could be a manual on BASIC. Functionally, there is no difference between a chalkboard, a slide rule, or a computer when it is used solely by the instructor to ensure optimal communication. A comparison of Figures 1-4 and 1-5 will certify to this statement. This represents mediation.

In Figure 1-6 is seen the model for *computer-assisted student* (*CAS*) where, in addition to previously explained instruction, the learner engages in laboratorylike problem-solving activity with a digital or analog computer. Laboratory activity in the computing field has been called *hands-on*, but it differs not at all in principle from student activity at a lathe in a machine shop course. Again, using the cantilever beam design case, the learner designs beams using a computer — or writes and debugs programs in BASIC, using a computer. However, this differs from pure *instructor-centered* communication and, because it is planned around the learner and to suit the learner's particular needs, it falls midway between instructor-centered and *learner-centered* instruction. It is not pure learner-centered, because the human instructor can quickly mediate himself or herself between the problem and the learner when the latter is in

---

[1] Leonard C. Silvern, *Systems Engineering of Education VI: Principles of Computer-Assisted Instruction Systems*, Education and Training Consultants Co., Los Angeles, 1970.

trouble. Since the instructor realizes this when designing the lesson, he or she hesitates to make the instruction completely independent of the instructor.

The software necessary to process either the learner's data or program, or both, is entered into the computer as an external function, but it is based on the real-life situation represented by the JA-HAA. The model in Figure 1-6 may be altered in this manner: delete the entire function of INSTRUCT. What remains is the computer laboratory component of the instruction—without any human instruction. In this

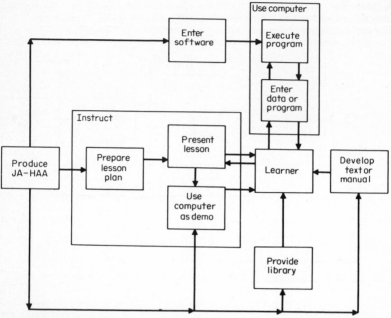

Fig. 1-6 Model describing learner experience with a computer in a laboratory setting, along with human instruction—computer-assisted student (CAS).

model, the learner interacts with the computer, relying exclusively on the manual supplied with the system, any texts provided for the subject matter, and library support which might be stored in the system, such as the editor language to modify listings, etc. If the manual is, in fact, a carefully written laboratory manual, then the learner will not have too much difficulty in obtaining solutions and data. However, the environment still represents computer-assisted student, since the learner merely utilizes the computer—the computer does not instruct the learner.

In all these models, the objective is learning through the process of teaching, and the administrative aspects of instruction are ignored. At least, the administration does not involve the computer system. In Figure 1-7, the recording of grades, scores, attendance, and similar information is accomplished and entered into the computer. Tabulations of various types, including statistical treatments, may be obtained by the instructor or members of the institutional management. This is *computer-assisted management (CAM)*. The administration selects the software which will produce the results, but the major user of the system is the human instructor.

Figure 1-7 does *not* deal with payroll processing, inventories of supplies, processing of purchase orders, or other business office tasks. Since there is very little difference between the computer tasks in a private business and those in the business office of a school or university, it is understood that such events occur and, in fact, can occur in the same computer system.

Now, in Figure 1-8, a model describing *computer-managed instruction (CMI)* appears. The difference between CAM and CMI is not subtle. With CMI, the software

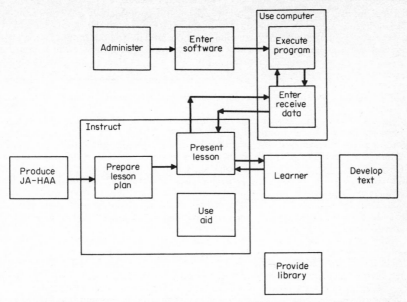

Fig. 1-7 Model describing computer-assisted management (CAM), used for reporting and statistics.

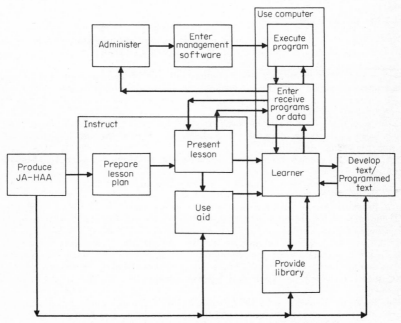

Fig. 1-8 Model describing computer-managed instruction (CMI).

in the computer system receives inputs concerning individual learner progress, and it then outputs the next lesson for the learner. Of course, all decisions made by the computer at computing speeds have been determined during the programming stage. Parameters have been identified and tolerances established. When the data are received and processed, the computer simply follows the prescriptions previously programmed. However, the effect is an illusion that the individual learner is being treated on an exclusive basis.

In a CMI system, the computer does not instruct. It simply tells the learner what the next lesson or part of a lesson is and where he or she may obtain the information. In some instances, the learner may read a regular text or chapter of a text. In other situations, he or she may examine a short, 4-minute filmloop. The learner might take 25 minutes of programmed instruction or be asked to work with a microscope under control of a laboratory manual. Each time, a test of some kind is administered and the scores are entered into the computer system. These scores are quantitative measurements of learner progress and form the basis for computer decision making. CMI does not exclude human instruction; it is just another means of instructing the learner, rather than the sole method. CMI affords both the instructor, who is responsible for the individual learner, and the administration immediate knowledge of learner progress without being actively involved in the instructional process.

While not specified in Figure 1-8, information entered by a counselor can be input, and, along with learner requests for certain courses, could produce custom-tailored schedules in a structured school environment. In an ungraded school environment, each learner receives a custom-tailored schedule on an almost daily basis. In all the foregoing, the computer performs housekeeping chores, but does not instruct.

The trend in progressing from the model in Figure 1-1 to the model in Figure 1-8 is to *reduce the mediation* by a human instructor gradually but not completely eliminate it.

MACHINE INSTRUCTION

Instruction completely by a nonhuman—which was not one-way communication, but had the characteristics of human instruction—entered the scene with the introduction of programmed instruction and teaching machine technology.[2] The programmed instruction movement in the late 1950s emphasized individual instruction, and this was a *learner-centered* concept. The criteria which distinguish this technology are:

1. Instruction is provided without the presence or mediation of a human instructor.

2. Learner learns at his or her own rate.

3. Learner receives immediate knowledge of progress through feedback which controls his or her behavior.

4. There is a participative, overt interaction or two-way communication between learner and program.

5. Sequence of the lesson is carefully controlled and consistent.

6. Reinforcement is used to strengthen learning.

7. Program shapes and controls learner behavior.

Historically, this movement erupted at a time when the Federal Government was preparing to furnish very large sums to local school districts, state educational agencies, and both state-operated and privately controlled universities. Consequently there was a sudden rush to market unproven products and programs, and this left a very bad taste in the mouths of the consumers. There were wild gyrations in the marketplace as companies entered and quickly folded, leaving behind a trail of unhappy and frustrated customers.

The peak year of activity was 1962, with a dip in 1963 and a slow, gradual rise since that time. Today, nearly every major publisher introduces several new programmed texts each year, but this effort is fairly small and is not believed by the publisher to be a major source of income. The dream in the 1960s that publishers would concentrate on programmed materials to the virtual exclusion of standard texts has vanished in a rude awakening. Only a handful of small firms remain throughout the United States

[2] Leonard C. Silvern, *Fundamentals of Teaching Machine and Programmed Learning Systems,* Education and Training Consultants Co., Los Angeles, 1964.

concentrating on the custom writing of programmed materials. Instead, *in-house* capability has evolved within those organizations interested in producing programmed materials for internal use.

Typically, military technical schools, banks, insurance companies, and public utilities have managed to keep internal programming efforts alive and growing. One should not disparage programmed instruction as an efficient method of instruction simply because the marketing techniques were inferior. Actually, programmed instruction introduced to education and training the concept of *tryout* or field testing which had been reserved mainly for the production of commercial testing instruments. Curriculum materials had rarely been tried out and revised before release. Beginning in the early 1960s the tryout concept grew and prospered. However, tryout always results in high development costs and, for this reason, has not been accepted by publishers who work on very narrow profit margins.

About the same time, and evolving from an independent source, systems engineering concepts were introduced to education and training.[3] Models based on *anasynthesis* (analysis, synthesis, modeling, and simulation) incorporated the notion of tryout and revision for product quality control. In the early days of programmed instruction, two basic formats were introduced: *recall design,* typified by the multiple-choice response, and *written-completion,* in which the learner was expected to construct a response without any assistance. Today, written completions in text form constitute most of the programs produced in the United States.

COMPUTER-ASSISTED INSTRUCTION

On the basis of pure logic, the use of a computer system to instruct should be categorized as machine instruction. Why does it deserve a separate category? Only because

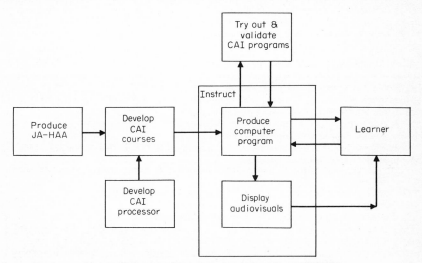

Fig. 1-9 Model describing computer-assisted instruction (CAI).

it is believed that *computer-assisted instruction* (*CAI*) holds such great promise that it should be examined as an independent movement rather than be subsumed under machine instruction.

In systematizing instruction, particularly where courses are to be offered to large numbers of learners, two elements are present in all good models: (1) the JA-HAA is the source of all course content; and (2) courses are tried out and validated *before* release. The model in Figure 1-9 incorporates these elements but, more importantly,

[3] Leonard C. Silvern, *Systems Engineering of Education I: The Evolution of Systems Thinking in Education,* Education and Training Consultants Co., Los Angeles, 1965, 1971, 1975, and *Systems Engineering Applied to Training,* Gulf Publishing Co., Houston, 1972.

represents a *learner-centered* environment where the human instructor has been eliminated and a computer system substituted. This avoids *mediation,* since the only human in the system is the learner. Of course, this is the case in an education or training program where management has elected to rely exclusively on CAI. In practice, CAI is selected for certain subject areas, and other instructional methods, including human instruction, are utilized for other areas. The criteria for selection would involve such parameters as number of learners, social characteristics of group instruction, nature of subject matter, form of learner response to stimuli, criterion test design, length of instructional exposure, etc.

In human instruction, the lesson plan is normally developed by the instructor, but in CAI, it is the *instructional programmer* who has the responsibility for this function. Instructional programmer is a newly emerging occupation, and is differentiated from the established occupation of *computer programmer.* In real life, depending on the size of the development project, the instructional programmer may be a team of persons, one senior individual who works with a staff of specialized technical personnel, or one individual performing all the tasks subsumed by the title. The tasks are:

1. Perform job and human activity analyses for existing activities (JA-HAA).
2. Perform job and human activity syntheses for newly emerging activities (JS-HAS).
3. Establish behavioral objectives to be achieved at the terminal point.
4. Create examinations to measure behavioral objectives, such as pretest, unit tests during the course, and post-test.
5. Develop course outlines to the teaching-point level.
6. Write steps in the instructional program.
7. Evaluate, debug, and validate the lesson.

It is quickly seen that a computer programmer would be out of his or her element when engaging in these tasks. They require the full-time services of an educator or training specialist. The key task is the function of organizing and sequentializing subject matter—and this is still an art for many areas.

TASKS IN COMPUTER-ASSISTED INSTRUCTION

Training the Instructional Programmer   From experience in training programmers and managing CAI installations, it is concluded that the following are the *ideal* prerequisites for entry into a training program:

1. Bachelor's degree in any field; degrees in psychology or education are undesirable unless programming is to be in psychology or education courses.
2. Five years of active classroom, shop, or laboratory teaching experience at level and in subject area to be programmed.
3. Two years of active management experience.

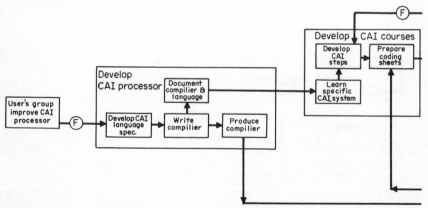

Fig. 1-10   Model describing relationships in and between the user's group role, developing the CAI

4. Two years of writing material of an instructional nature.

Mental and personality characteristics are:

1. Excellent memory for details.
2. Excellent memory for and acceptance of a whole.
3. Nominally without fear of or antagonism toward hardware.
4. Nominally without fear of or antagonism toward abstractions.
5. Nominally able to create a learner-centered sketch or drawing.
6. Excellent tenacity and without punitive-level emotion in debugging.
7. Nominally undisturbed by and responsive to feedback.

The Computer-Assisted Instruction Systems course created by the present writer has two components: (1) Forty hours of programmed instruction which is sent by mail to the participant and which is worked through prior to the first class meeting. Individuals who have a strong background in writing programmed instruction, from the JA-HAA through tryout and validation to course implementation, are expected to work through this material rapidly. (2) Ninety-three hours of classroom and computer laboratory. A graduate of the combined 133 hours should be able to select an existing CAI system, manage installation, and operate a CAI facility which is essentially the development of CAI courses. It is understood that the hardware would be supervised by a computer facility specialist.

Creating CAI Programs Refer to Figure 1-10. It is assumed that the decision to use CAI has already been made. Unless an existing CAI processor is to be acquired or accessed, it will be necessary to develop one and insert it into a time-sharing computer system. Most educational organizations are willing to accept a commercially available CAI language such as LYRIC, PLANIT, ASET, or COURSEWRITER II or III. A very large organization may wish to develop its own CAI language or make major modifications of an existing language, provided it has a computer facility staff able to do this. The first step is to develop language specifications which can be quite extensive and extremely technical. The education specialist must have experience in instructional programming to make realistic and practical recommendations.

The processor may be a compiler, precompiler, interpreter, or other software package. Writing the compiler is the function of developing software which will take an instructional program written in natural language on coding sheets and transform this into a learner's program *without* the instructional programmer knowing anything about

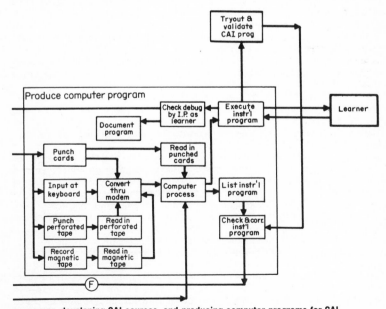

processor, developing CAI courses, and producing computer programs for CAI.

computing or what is happening in the computer. In producing the compiler, the compiler program is run iteratively in the computer under various practical conditions to be certain it is reliable and effective.

Documentation is the process of collecting, organizing, storing, citing, and dispensing documents or information recorded in these documents. The documentation function in developing the CAI processor is the responsibility of the *computer* programming staff—*not* the instructional programming staff. One end product of the documentation effort is a manual prepared by the compiler-processor software group. It is the basis for the instructional programmers learning the specific CAI system which has been selected or created for his or her use. This group may also offer a formal training program going beyond the manual and providing experience in a laboratory setting.

As may be seen in Figure 1-10, with a CAI processor and a computing system, it is possible to begin developing CAI courses. The instructional programmer must learn at least two things: (1) operation codes (*opcodes*) of the specific language, and (2) strategies allowed when using opcodes. These opcodes constitute the step-by-step ground rules for writing CAI programs and *must be learned*. When the CAI step is produced, it is converted into opcodes on the coding sheet, as in Figure 1-11, and is translated into machine-input and stored in the computer system.

To produce the computer program, one has a choice of four methods of input: punched cards, manual keyboard input, perforated tape at terminal input, magnetic cassette at terminal input. It is also possible to input cards at the computer facility, but this tends to degrade a time-sharing system designed for remote input-output for both the learner *and for the instructional programmer*. The model in Figure 1-10 is predicated on the remoteness design concept and incorporates a modem allowing transmission to and from the computer via telephone, microwave, or coaxial lines.

When a program is processed, the instructional programmer or his or her editing assistant will call for a listing as in Figure 1-12. Errors due to typing or transmission are checked and corrected, using an editing language which is usually available in all time-sharing systems. Errors due to strategy, incorrect opcodes, or labeling are fed back and entered on the coding sheet, thereby closing the feedback loop and controlling the quality of output. This loop deals *only* with the original or unexecuted program in the form of a listing—it does not deal with the version translated by the compiler into FORTRAN, some lower-order machine language, or binary code. To produce a learner's version of the program, shown in Figure 1-13, the program must be executed or compiled, and stored. Then, it may be called up by the instructional programmer acting the role of learner and checked and debugged. Changes are documented, and steps are redeveloped when necessary. Coding sheets are corrected and the process is iterated until the instructional programmer is satisfied that the learner's version is ready for tryout on actual learners who represent a sample of the target population.

In working with a large CAI hardware/software system which has been created by a commercial producer, a formal organization known as a *user's group* attempts to advise the producer on changes recommended by the various group members. These recommendations invariably involve software rather than hardware and can result in a modification or expansion of the basic language specifications.

Learner-Computer Program Interaction   It has been pointed out that there is no human to mediate the instruction—the learner interacts with the program through a console, and the transaction appears as in Figure 1-13. A stimulus is printed out by the computer, and then it halts and expects the learner to respond. Some stimuli have blanks inserted in the question following the practice in the programmed instruction text. However, the illustration in Figure 1-13 consists of open-ended questions, which are preferable.

The computer signals the learner that a response is requested by returning the teleprinter carriage to the left margin, printing a ?, a space character, then halting. In many systems, the machine will wait 10 minutes for a response before signing the learner off, but this time can be controlled by the computer program and the time set by the instructional programmer. The learner then types his or her answer in one character, one word, or a group of words or symbols constituting a sentence. Each system has a line length limit, which is usually between 30 and 135 characters, in-

LYRIC Coding Sheet

COURSE NAME _MEASURES OF CENTRAL TENDENCY_ COURSE CODE _3.13 81_

INSTRUCTIONAL PROGRAMMER _ROWLAND F ROBERTS_ DATE _23 JUL 69_ TEAM _____ PAGE _8_ OF _64_

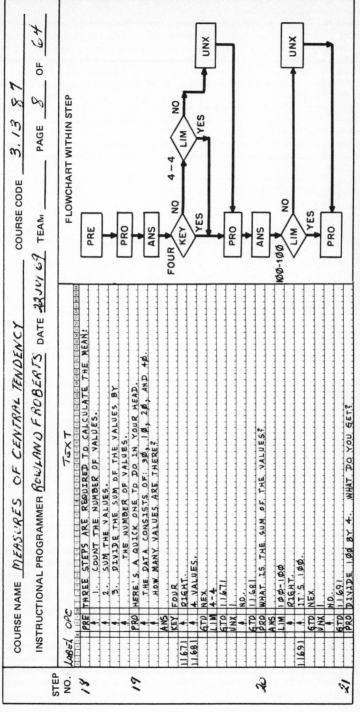

FLOWCHART WITHIN STEP

STEP NO.	Label	OPC	TEXT
18		PRE	THREE STEPS ARE REQUIRED TO CALCULATE THE MEAN:
			1. COUNT THE NUMBER OF VALUES.
			2. SUM THE VALUES.
			3. DIVIDE THE SUM OF THE VALUES BY
			THE NUMBER OF VALUES.
19		PRO	HERE'S A QUICK ONE TO DO IN YOUR HEAD.
			THE DATA CONSISTS OF: 30, 10, 20, AND 40.
			HOW MANY VALUES ARE THERE?
		ANS	
		KEY	FOUR
	11671		RIGHT.
	11681		4 VALUES.
		GTD	NEX.
		LIM	4-4
		GTD	11671
			UNX. 1
			N.D.
		GTD	11681
20		PRO	WHAT IS THE SUM OF THE VALUES?
		ANS	
		LIM	100-100
	11691		RIGHT.
			IT'S 100.
		GTD	NEX
		UNX	
			N.D.
		GTD	11691
21		PRO	DIVIDE 100 BY 4. WHAT DO YOU GET?

Fig. 1-11 Typical coding sheet showing strategy in flow-chart form and opcodes.

cluding spaces. CRT consoles have shorter line lengths, while teleprinters run between 72 and 135 characters.

When the learner has completed typing the response, he or she hits the RETURN or ENTER key and the computer processes the input, analyzes the response, follows the program in Figure 1-12, and provides feedback as seen in Figure 1-13. In the model of Figure 1-9, slides or filmstrip are rear-screen-projected on the console under computer control. The program can control a display, search forward or backward, and provide new information as well as remedial instruction when the learner's response is inappropriate. In addition, the program can display audio by storing it on magnetic tape, either Philips-Norelco cassette or computer storage, and play a selected track, searching forward or backward, just as for displaying visuals.

Getting Started in CAI Getting started in CAT (Figure 1-5), CAS (Figure 1-6), CAM (Figure 1-7), and CMI (Figure 1-8) presents few problems, since all the hardware and much of the software have been available commercially for many years. If a par-

```
335 10780 PRO  WHAT DOES THE CIRCLED F MEAN?
338       ANS
340       KEY  FEED
342       '    CORRECT
345       GTO  NEX
349       UNX  1
352       '    IT REPRESENTS A FEEDBACK SIGNAL GOING TO IDENTIFY.
355 10790 PRO  THE COMBINATION MAY BE GOOD BUT NOT THE LARGEST WHOLE.
358       '    THEN, WHAT MUST BE DONE?
360       ANS
363       KEY  IDEN
366       '    YEP....RE-IDENTIFY
369       GTO  NEX
372       UNX  1
375       '    NO, YOU RETURN AND RE-IDENTIFY
378 10800 PRO  WHAT DO YOU DO IF THIS IS LARGEST WHOLE?
380       ANS
383       KEY  LIMIT
386       '    EXCELLENT
389       GTO  NEX
392 10810 PRO  BUT IF ANOTHER ELEMENT IS SUDDENLY DISCOVERED ---
395 10811 '    WHAT WILL YOU DO?
398       ANS
400       KEY  IDEN
403       '    TRUE
406       GTO  NEX
409       UNX  1
412       '    A NEW ELEMENT IS PERCEIVED.  NOW,
415       GTO  10811
418       UNX  1
420       '    YOU MUST RE-IDENTIFY.
423       PRE  WELL, YOU SHOULD BE READY TO GO THROUGH A PROBLEM
426       '    WITHOUT ASSISTANCE.  LET'S GO........
429       PRE       (NEXT SLIDE --> 33)
432       PRE  STUDY THESE ELEMENTS WITH GREAT CARE.
435 10820 PRO  HOW MANY INDEPENDENT ELEMENTS DO YOU PERCEIVE?
438       ANS
440       LIM  6-6
443 10821 '    EXACTLY.  YOU PERCEIVE SIX.
446       GTO  NEX
449       KEY  SIX
452       GTO  10821
455       UNX  1
458       '    WRONG.  ONE AT THE VERY TOP.  COUNT 'EM AGAIN.
460       GTO  ANS
463       UNX  1
466       '    SIX
469 10830 PRO  USING SHAPE AS A CRITERION, YOU SHOULD LOCATE ELEMENTS
472       '    WITH CONTOURS WHICH MIGHT INTERFACE WITH EACH OTHER.
475       '    SO YOUR FIRST STEP IS WHAT?
478       ANS
480       KEY  IDEN
483       '    YES, IDENTIFY.
486       GTO  NEX
489       UNX  1
492       '    THE FIRST STEP IS ALWAYS WHAT?
495       GTO  ANS
498       UNX  1
500       '    ALWAYS START BY IDENTIFYING ELEMENTS.
```

Fig. 1-12 Listing of instructional program. The numbers beginning 335 are line numbers used solely for editing. The numbers beginning 10780 are labels for addressing. The opcodes and text field complete the listing.

```
WHAT DOES THE CIRCLED F MEAN?

? FEEDBACK
CORRECT

THE COMBINATION MAY BE GOOD BUT NOT THE LARGEST WHOLE.
THEN, WHAT MUST BE DONE?

? IDENT
YEP....RE-IDENTIFY

WHAT DO YOU DO IF THIS IS LARGEST WHOLE?

? LIMIT
EXCELLENT

BUT IF ANOTHER ELEMENT IS SUDDENLY DISCOVERED ---
WHAT WILL YOU DO?

? IDENTIFY
TRUE

WELL, YOU SHOULD BE READY TO GO THROUGH A PROBLEM
WITHOUT ASSISTANCE.  LET'S GO........

          (NEXT SLIDE --> 33)

STUDY THESE ELEMENTS WITH GREAT CARE.

HOW MANY INDEPENDENT ELEMENTS DO YOU PERCEIVE?

? SIX
EXACTLY.  YOU PERCEIVE SIX.

USING SHAPE AS A CRITERION, YOU SHOULD LOCATE ELEMENTS
WITH CONTOURS WHICH MIGHT INTERFACE WITH EACH OTHER.
SO YOUR FIRST STEP IS WHAT?

? IDENT
YES, IDENTIFY.
```

Fig. 1-13 Learner's version of the instructional program listed in Figure 1-12.

ticular software package is needed but not available, it can be written and embedded in an existing executive package with very little difficulty — and at a reasonable cost. However, the same solutions do not apply to CAI. It has been demonstrated that a high-order CAI language must be available, and the instructional programmer need not know such languages as FORTRAN, PL/I, or COBOL to program effectively and quickly.

There are seven alternative methods of getting started, some of which are better than the others:

1. Contract with a computer manufacturer to lease a CAI language for your time-sharing computer system.

2. Contract with a software firm to lease a CAI language for your time-sharing computer system.

3. Contract with a commercial time-sharing firm to subscribe to and use a CAI language on its computer.

4. Affiliate with a university time-sharing system to subscribe to and use a CAI language for writing your courses on its computer.

5. Affiliate with a university time-sharing system to enroll in and take its course on its computer.

6. Contract with a commercial time-sharing firm to subscribe to and use one of its non-CAI languages; write your course in this non-CAI language on its computer.

7. Lease or buy a computer; obtain a software package which includes a suitable non-CAI language; write a course in this language on your time-sharing computer.

Of course, it is assumed that one of these alternatives is selected when (1) there is inadequate in-house capability to develop a CAI processor (Figure 1-10), and (2) funds are available to support the decision. These alternatives do not exhaust all possibilities.

The basic difficulty for a training director involves persuading his or her management, or the computer facility supervisor, that training is important and deserves storage space in the system. Storage is the obstacle since everyone is fighting for a share! In an educational enterprise, such as a university or secondary school, competition may not be so keen, but there is usually less money available unless a research grant has been obtained.

Economics of CAI Systems   Computing is expensive when compared with other forms of data handling if one considers initial investment or outlay. The cost of computing to produce an outcome drops dramatically when the cost of labor increases, as has been occurring in the United States. However, generally speaking, public school teachers and university professors constitute relatively cheap labor, and this fact, along with the high cost of computers, continues to place the computer out of reach for most teaching applications.

In addition to the economics issue, there is a philosophical issue dealing with the alleged "dehumanization" of the learner when he or she is subjected to machine instruction. It is almost impossible to counter this attitude with facts. Dehumanization may not, per se, be an important factor, but the *feeling* that it is definitely works against ready acceptance of computers in the educational environment.

For the realist, there is only one measure of utility: the cost per learner per hour of one method of instruction in comparison with another, such as CAI. Clearly, one must be absolutely certain that the learning effectiveness in both methods is identical — otherwise instead of one variable (cost/learner/hour) there would be two variables (learning effectiveness; cost/learner/hour) and this would complicate the comparison process. Today, the cost per learner per hour in the public schools is about $0.40, in the university about $1.10, in the university professional school about $2.00, in the typical military school about $2.50, and in the typical employee training program about $4.00. Whenever the learner is in a pay or remuneration status during instruction, his or her hourly wage or salary must be added to the basic cost; costs for military trainees and private-sector employees are therefore higher than the case where the learner is not paid to learn.

Assume that a CAI language, similar to the one shown in Figure 1-12, is available, a well-maintained time-sharing system can be accessed, and a group of trained instructional programmers is ready. The *development* costs, devoid of profit, to produce a JA-HAA, develop a COTP, write CAI steps, try out steps on a sample of the target population, debug and deliver CAI software which will take an average learner *one hour* on-line should be about $1,200; the computer time and equipment are furnished to the developer without cost. In human instruction, *development* costs either are hidden in the overhead or disguised — it is assumed that human instructors are prepared and ready to teach at a moment's notice!

A college course of 45 hours (two-semester system) which earns 3 units or credits would cost about $48,735 to produce using CRT consoles for both instructional programmer and learners. This is an in-house estimate, without profit or company overhead. When CAI experts speak of the cost per learner per hour of $0.25, one wonders if this includes the *development* costs just enumerated. If development is paid for by someone else, notably the Federal Government, then the question has been answered, but many are not able to scrounge the U.S. Office of Education or the National Science Foundation. Based on the author's experience, the cost per learner per hour *with* development costs is about $4.83 and *without* development costs is about $2.98. Both figures are far removed from the talking cost of $0.25!

THE FUTURE OF COMPUTERS IN EDUCATION

The educational use of a computing system is tied inexorably to the growth of computers in business, industry, and government noneducation activities. Breakthroughs in the exotic educational areas so often touted in the Sunday Supplements and in business/marketing trade papers must wait for evolutionary advances in other, more profitable fields. Despite the statistics of the public education system, and the college and university system, it is difficult for even a large company to remain in the education market for a sustained period of time. Large numbers of students and teachers, even when counted in millions, do not automatically mean an expenditure for new-fangled hardware/software systems. Most of the budget in an educational enterprise goes for faculty and support-personnel *salaries*, and the salary line item will continue to be the single largest item in a budget. Therefore, computers may be expected to enter the educational bastion gradually.

So far as elegant, interactive, conversational software goes, the present state of the art allows very flexible programming. Memory has been expanding rapidly, coupled with a decrease in cost per bit, and response time has been decreased—both of these technological improvements are in the field of computing from which the education and training field profits.

Trends in Computer-Assisted Teacher Systems (CAT) In addition to growing interest in individualizing instruction, the use of computers as an instructional aid is growing, and this is aside from applications in research or noninstructional domains. The 19 campuses of the California State University and Colleges service 263,000 students and 15,000 staff. The state is covered from the Oregon border to Mexico and from the Pacific Ocean to the neighboring states of Arizona and Nevada. All campuses are tied together into two regional data centers: San Jose (CDC 3300) and Los Angeles (CDC 3300). The University of California is a separate and distinct system from the above. However, the University of California, Los Angeles (UCLA), IBM 360/91 is now tied into the California University system for large-scale, complex or highly specialized problems which cannot be handled on the smaller machines.[4]

There are about 2,600 institutions of higher learning in the United States (offering associate, bachelor, master, doctorate, and professional degrees), and of these, it is estimated about 70 per cent have one or more computers at their campuses. However, of the 910,000 secondary (high) school teachers in public day schools, certainly less than 1,000 (0.1 per cent) have regular access to a computer *for demonstration* in a class. Large public and parochial districts have computers, but these are reserved for business and other noninstructional applications. While very few would question the need to expand the use of computing equipment in an instructional setting, a mix of mental inertia and reluctance on the part of taxpayers will continue to restrict and constrain expansion in the secondary schools.

Trends in Use of Computer-Assisted Student Systems (CAS) In addition to previously described methods of using the computer, the individual learner can write computer programs, solve problems using a library program, and use a library program for localizing software and hardware malfunctions and thus maintain the computer electronics and electromechanical hardware. Writing programs is usually instructed in a department of mathematics or computer science, although engineering and business administration courses are offered which also accomplish this. Computer science and information science are approximate equivalents, depending on the institution. Learners acquire skill in writing and debugging in such languages as COBOL, ALGOL, BASIC, SUPERBASIC, FORTRAN, PL/I, APL, SNOBOL, RPG, or a specialized assembly language. Since it is essential that a program be converted into machine-acceptable language, cards or tape are produced and the program is executed. The laboratory or hands-on philosophy requires the learner to go through all the manual steps and the hardware operating procedures to obtain a print-out of his or her program. While the objective is not to learn how to press buttons or detect system malfunctions, students do acquire this kind of experience on the way.

When a computer is used primarily for problem solving, the learner inputs data rather than a program, and there is no great need to have the learner physically interact with a hardware system. However, when problem solving is on-line and is like an MIS activity, the CRT–learner relationship is important. Access to a system is more significant than manipulation in this category.

When maintenance training is the object, a physical system is mandatory. Trying to simulate computer malfunctions on paper is an interesting but ineffective academic exercise—there must be a real-life system into which malfunctions may be inserted, and then isolated and corrected.

While secondary schools and universities are gradually expanding computer usage, various user-groups and computer manufacturers are introducing higher-order languages which make it possible for more nonmathematically oriented students to write and debug programs. These learners are asked to learn only the language for programming, and each language is taking on the outward characteristics of the English

[4] "California's State University Computer Network," *The Office*, May, 1972.

language—or whatever spoken language is in local use. For example, programming of machine tools, direct numerical control, would be included in this category.

In the future, more learners are expected to learn programming for their particular field of specialization in the university, and a small but growing number of secondary school students will be exposed to programming, probably using a mini. Problem solving receives greater attention in the colleges, so one would expect an increase in activity there, but almost no activity in this area is anticipated for the secondary school; the reason for a lack of activity is primarily economic.

Papert and Solomon contend that everyone regardless of age or level of academic performance should be introduced to programming, so that they can receive education in mathematics, physics, and all formal subjects including linguistics and music by means of a computer.[5] These authors believe that inertia and prejudice and not economics or lack of good educational ideas stand in the way of implementing these computer-based experiences for learners. The present author in a review of this position reacted negatively.[6] Papert and Solomon talk of instruction costing about $0.84 per learner per hour in contrast with the $0.40 average alluded to earlier. The quotation, "If every child were to be given access to a computer, computers would be cheap enough for every child to be given access to a computer," simply reveals a lack of sensitivity to the issues of cost, programming development, teacher employment, system maintenance, and the basic fact that teachers as a rule detest machines.

Maintenance training occurs in military schools, private trade schools, and at company schools for employees often conducted by computer manufacturers. Without question, computer usage in these environments will expand in step with computer applications growth outside.

Trends in Computer-Assisted Management (CAM)   The use of computer systems to accept data on student progress and tabulate them for statistical purposes is growing rapidly in educational enterprises of all kinds. Probably within the next 20 years, *every* higher education institution will be relying on computers to turn out reports and grade cards and tabulate various kinds of attendance records. There will always be a large number of public school districts too poor to lease or buy a computer or even purchase tabulation services in the community. While CAM furnishes data for management decision making, it does little to assist management, as is done in a CMI system.

Trends in Computer-Managed Instruction (CMI)   The trend in education is toward individualizing instruction, but the principle is given more lip service than actual support. One expects to go forward by returning, in fact, to the one-room schoolhouse where each learner was of a different age and grade—and all of them progressed with a single teacher. Because subject matter was comparatively simple, as was life in those days, the incredible feat of a young schoolmarm maintaining a learning environment which was essentially *ungraded* was a daily accomplishment.

Today, such success is impossible on a large scale. However, by using a computer coupled with various self-instruction techniques, it is possible to direct and control a learner to the next learning event, and this makes for individualized instruction in an ungraded environment. There is a very gradual trend in this direction, and it is expected to continue without picking up much speed for another half a dozen years, when it probably will expand more rapidly.

Trends in Computer-Assisted Instruction (CAI)   The future of CAI is predicated on cost and the computer state of the art, and it is closely tied to the national economy. The substantial investment by RCA in CAI was washed away when that firm closed down its computer divisions. The exploratory activities at General Electric dealing with CAI disappeared, along with the entire computer production facility, when it went out of the business, leaving only a commercial time-sharing function to continue. IBM entered the CAI field as a pioneer in 1958, and has continuously developed hardware and specialized software up to the present. However, there has been a measurable diminution of CAI activity in the IBM marketplace, although IBM is still at work developing COURSEWRITER language capability.

---

[5] Seymour Papert and Cynthia Solomon, "Twenty Things to Do with a Computer," *Educational Technology*, April, 1972.

[6] Leonard C. Silvern, "Review of the Papert-Solomon Paper in *ET*," *Computing Review*, Journal of the Association for Computing Machinery, New York, 1972.

In 1970, *Datamation* pointed out that Mitre Corporation's TICCET CAI System was being developed "at a time when most firms are retrenching their CAI efforts in disillusionment after overoptimistic predictions of past years, and illusory profits.[7] The cost/learner/hour was estimated at $0.23 (presumably the course development costs were not included). Two years later, it was reported that Mitre management thought the cost/learner/hour would be about $0.35, and this was exclusive of development costs. The initial field trial of TICCIT[8] began in junior colleges in 1974 for a 2-year tryout period. With TICCIT, freshman English and mathematics will be taught for 2 years. Hammond[9] concludes, "The impending demonstration will not bring about the use of the computer in the American classroom overnight, nor . . . [is it] likely to convince the many critics who believe that the answer to educational reform does not lie in new technology. . . . [However, it] seems likely to have a substantial impact on education in this country."

It is not enough that a computer be superior to a good human instructor—it must be less expensive and more reliable; it must be consistent and faceless. The day when a learner can converse in spoken language with a machine, a la *Star Trek*, is bound to come, but it may take a few more years for it to arrive on a cost-effective basis!

[7] "Twenty-Three Cent CAI System Aimed by Mitre," *Datamation*, August, 1970.

[8] TICCET became TICCIT when Time-Shared Interactive Computer-Controlled Educational Television was renamed Time-Shared Interactive Computer-Controlled Information Television.

[9] *Science*, June, 1972.

Chapter 2

The Impact of ADP
on Public Administration

EDWARD W. KELLEY

Vice President, Griffenhagen-Kroeger, Inc.,
San Francisco, California

A discussion of the impact of computer technology in the administration of public affairs must, in order to maintain perspective, recognize that it was largely due to the administrative requirements of government that computer technology came into being.

ADP IN THE FEDERAL GOVERNMENT

In anticipation of the requirements for processing data collected in the 1880 census, the United States Government secured the services of Dr. Herman Hollerith, a distinguished statistician, to devise an improved methodology for tabulating census statistics. After several years of research Dr. Hollerith developed a processing system based on the use of punched cards and electronic circuitry. Data were tabulated on electromagnetic counters activated by pins inserted through punched holes in the cards. The system had little impact on the 1880 census, which despite use of the system required over 7 years to tabulate, but it was also used for the 1890 census, and reduced the overall processing time to $2\frac{1}{2}$ years. From that time until World War II, improvements in electromechanical data processing techniques were steadily developed and implemented.

In 1945 the University of Pennsylvania completed and placed into operation the first electronic digital computer. Called the ENIAC, this computer was built for the U.S. Army to execute ballistic missile trajectory calculations. Though limited in comparison with today's computers, the ENIAC was able to execute in 30 seconds a calculation which, as a manual process, would have taken a person many hours to complete. From that relatively rudimentary application, the growth in the use of computers by the Federal Government reached the point where, in 1965, there were estimated to be 2,188 digital computers installed in 35 agencies; by 1971 almost 6,000 computers were in use in Federal agencies.

The primary user of computers in the Federal Government is the Department of Defense, which has over 50 per cent of all computers in the Federal Government. Applications for this large block of computers are in the fields of both research and management systems. Highly complex computer-based simulation models are used by the

DOD in areas of missile technology and combat theory. In addition, computers are used as integral elements of guidance and navigational systems aboard naval vessels and aircraft, as well as in calculating courses of interception and in the reduction of data resulting from target identification by radar. More mundane, but no less important, computer applications within the DOD are involved with the function of material and supply distribution. Were it not for the application of ADP to this vast management area, insurmountable problems of operation and control would accrue.

The next largest users of computers within the Federal Government are the Atomic Energy Commission and the National Aeronautics and Space Administration. Both of these agencies rely heavily on ADP in fields of research and applied technology. In addition to playing a basic role in space exploration and extraterrestial research, computers are also being used to process vital data, obtained by satellite, regarding natural resource utilization and pollution of the earth's environment. In a related area, ground-based computers are used by the U.S. Geologic Survey to monitor and anticipate seismic and volcanic activity.

Virtually all departments and agencies within the Federal Government rely on ADP technology for the processing of management and operational data. Throughout the Federal Government computers are used in general accounting, payroll, and operational data reduction applications, as in private industry. In the Treasury Department, for example, millions of checks and bonds are issued each year through the use of computers. The Internal Revenue Service uses computers to process and audit income tax returns, and has experienced improved accuracy and completeness of reported income data as a result of publicity of the use of ADP technology. ADP has been similarly adapted to the needs of practically every other activity within the Federal jurisdiction.

Clearly, the United States Government has been at the forefront of data processing automation, both as a major user of ADP technology and as a stimulus to research and development activities, with major impact in both the public and the private sectors. While the effect of many ADP applications at the Federal level has been to increase operational efficiency through reduced processing time and personnel requirements, the impact of ADP in such agencies as NASA, the AEC, and the DOD may never be fully appreciated by the layperson. There is no question, however, that human beings would never have walked on Earth's moon or photographed the surface of Mars in the absence of ADP technology.

ADP IN STATE AND LOCAL JURISDICTIONS

In state and local government, as in the Federal Government and in private industry, early ADP applications were developed to accommodate record systems having a high volume of routine transactions. At all levels of government such systems have included general revenue and expenditure accounting, employee payroll and related applications, and the processing of payments to vendors, pensioners, and public aid recipients.

In addition, many early ADP applications were addressed to various systems which were unique to specific levels of government. Thus, among state governments, in addition to ADP systems developed to process state income tax payments and refunds, such systems were addressed to the massive task of maintaining records associated with vehicle registrations and vehicle ownership titles. At the level of city and county government, one of the first ADP application areas involved the maintenance of property ownership records and associated property tax assessments. More recently the maintenance of voter registration records, as well as the processing of local and general election vote counts, have been adapted to ADP technology by cities and counties.

Even as private industry has developed computer-based systems for the process control of automobile assembly lines and crude-oil production facilities, certain processes which are the responsibility of governments have been benefited by computer control techniques. Thus, the traffic signal networks of many urban areas are controlled and monitored by computer, as are many sewage treatment plants. Mass rapid transit systems now in operation or under development rely heavily on computer technology to control the actual movement of vehicles. In California, the massive distribution system which transports water from the northern part of the state to arid farms and communities in the southern half is controlled by computers. The development of such process control systems is becoming increasingly widespread among specialized public agencies, and will continue to expand.

But despite all the foregoing, it must nevertheless be stated that the application of ADP in state and local public administrations (which collectively overshadow by far the apparatus of the Federal Government) has fallen short of the needs of government and the potentials of the technology. The evolution in sophistication of computer technology over the past decade has rendered obsolete the computer hardware that was considered revolutionary 10 years ago. However, the information management techniques utilized by public administrators are not as sophisticated as would be possible with the available technology.

Admittedly, the resource capacity to process data, within most public agencies, has been fully utilized in keeping abreast of the detail of daily operations. However, the advent of ADP has for the most part resulted in the automation of manual processes, allowing only for the derivation of the same limited information at higher processing speeds. This characteristic of conversion from manual to automated processes may have been justified 10 or 15 years ago, when only unit record equipment was in general use. Yet, subsequent conversions and reconversions involving increasingly sophisticated computer hardware have resulted in data processing systems whose physical output is remarkably similar in format and utility to the manual systems of 15 years ago. For example, the computer-based payroll system now processed by the average city or county was designed for obsolete and long-since-replaced hardware, and has rarely been improved, in spite of the subsequent installation of third- and fourth-generation computer equipment.

More important than the shortcoming cited above is that which is reflected in the fact that most applications of ADP developed for public administrators have been addressed to internal "housekeeping" problems, and neither enable governments to improve the quality of their current services nor enable them to respond more effectively to new and emerging problems for whose solution society increasingly relies on public administrators.

CONTEMPORARY PROBLEMS IN PUBLIC ADMINISTRATION

Evolution in Scope of Public Services The present role of governments has far exceeded that of the day when they were called upon only to mint coinage, build roads, and deliver mail. The increasing complexity and sophistication of our society have led to the assumption by governments, at all levels, of the responsibility for providing an ever-broadening scope of services. Many of these services are protective in nature, and are addressed to problems of crime, public health, the environment, and socio-economics. Others are regulatory in nature and are embodied in land-use plans, building codes, and business licenses. Still others are designed to enrich the general quality of life, and include the provision of education, libraries, parks, and a forum for aesthetic culture.

The continuing increase in scope of services provided by public agencies has, during the past 200 years, been attended by a proliferation in the number of jurisdictions which provide services. In the 50 states of the United States there are over 3,000 counties and 18,000 incorporated cities and towns. Within California alone, in addition to its 58 counties and 407 cities, there are in excess of 4,000 special districts which provide single and multiple public services.

Interdependence of Public Agencies No one jurisdiction mentioned above can be considered independently of any other jurisdiction; they are all interactive and interdependent, in varying degrees. However, units of government have traditionally organized themselves into structures that isolate services and obscure the interdependent nature of such services. In part, such isolation has been necessary in order to focus specialized disciplines on the solution of public problems, yet the problems are neither as specialized as the disciplines which are marshaled for their relief, nor as well-delineated as the organizations through which those disciplines are provided.

The problems for whose solution government agencies have assumed responsibility have come to transcend departmental lines, geographic jurisdictional boundaries, and hierarchical levels of government, and will need to be addressed and resolved through the cooperative and coordinated efforts of all these entities. John Gardner, of the Urban

Coalition, has said, "The plain fact is that most cities are not organized to cope with their problems. Their haphazard growth has brought such rampant administrative disorder that good government is scarcely possible."[1]

Major Issues The following constitutes a listing of what are considered to be some of the major issues confronting state and local jurisdictions:

● Government costs: the need to find new tax sources and to reduce current tax burdens.

● Program evaluation and measurement: the need for better measures of efficiency and effectiveness, and the need to eliminate obsolete procedures.

● Service equity: the need to provide more services, with greater equity in distribution.

● Law and order: the need to reduce crime and create better public–police relations.

● Environmental concerns: the need to preserve, protect, and restore the environment.

● Housing: the need to provide better housing at a reasonable cost.

● Health care: the need to provide better health care to all, with better control of health costs.

● Transportation: the need to provide new and better means of public transportation.

● Labor relations and equal opportunity in government employment: the need to be aware of the issues, and to reduce friction.

● Intergovernmental cooperation and merger: the need to reduce costly duplication.

● Education: the need to provide adequate services and to utilize existing resources more effectively.

All the issues on this list have been with us in the past. However, it was only during the late 1960s and the early 1970s that they reached critical proportions. The environment in which governmental managers at all levels now operate has changed drastically within the last 10 years. Thomas W. Fletcher, former City Manager of San Diego and now head of the National Training and Development Institute, stated recently, "Ten years ago if we had been asked were our cities manageable, we would have answered an unqualified *yes*. Today, I am sure that most of us in city management would be concerned as to whether or not we have the capacity to manage the types of problems we are now facing."[2]

Much has been written about the causes of the problems, and their detailed consideration is beyond the scope of this Chapter. Many people trace the origins of the problem to World War II and the years immediately following. The central theme of this approach is that scientific knowledge and technology have grown at such a pace that they have shaken the very foundation of our public and private institutions. Whatever the basic causes, it is clear that in the 1970s, governmental jurisdictions have placed increasing emphasis upon problem identification and problem solving. There will continue to be greater acceptance of and dependence upon new technologies, more sophisticated decision processes, and increasing concern about impact and cost effectiveness. This will inevitably mean a greater reliance upon and more development and use of ADP systems by all levels of government.

THE "PROGRAM" CONCEPT IN PUBLIC ADMINISTRATION

In recent years increasing interest among public agencies has been directed to the concept and application of the Planning Programming and Budgeting System (PPBS), and a number of jurisdictions have implemented such systems, with varying degrees of success. An even more recent development has been that of Program Management Systems (PMS). Both systems concepts are based upon the element of *program* as a governmental activity.

---

[1] John W. Gardner, *No Easy Victories*, Harper & Row, New York, 1968, p. 23.
[2] Thomas W. Fletcher, "What Is the Future of Our Cities and the City Managers?" *Public Administration Review*, January–February, 1971.

In current budgeting and fiscal management terminology, a *program* is a grouping of activities that contribute to the achievement of a common objective or a set of related objectives. Such programs are the central core and very essence of the program budget. The program structure is a hierarchical arrangement of programs that graphically illustrate the relationship of activities to goals and objectives. Since the costs and measurement criteria are related to the activities, the program structure is the basis of fiscal management and control. Thus, in this context, traffic patrol would be a *service* while traffic safety would be a *program*, contributed to by such services as traffic patrol; street design, maintenance, and construction; and public education.

The advent of the concept of *program* among public administrators reflects their emerging recognition that the traditional structures through which public services have been delivered in the past have become inadequate to serve public needs now and in the future. While individual services may remain the same in their basic outward appearance, it will be the orientation of service administrators which will change. No longer can the chief of police direct the patrolling of streets without regard for the activities of the public works director, who is responsible for constructing and maintaining those streets. Both activities share a common goal: traffic safety. That goal will not be achieved efficiently in the absence of coordination between these agencies.

Because past applications of available technology by public administrators has, as noted earlier, generally not been sophisticated, significant efforts have not widely been directed toward effecting needed coordination and exchange of information, either among components of an individual public agency or between agencies. Even where it may have been recognized that such integration was desirable *and possible*, there has been a reluctance to divert data processing personnel and equipment resources from accommodating ongoing operations to accomplishing needed research and development efforts. The cost of such efforts is great.

Current Efforts in Coordinating Information With the current evolution in orientation of public officials from a perception of departmental or jurisdictional service to one of interdepartmental or interjurisdictional programs, the status of information integration is changing from that of luxury to that of necessity. Administrators are coming to realize that the computer for which they are already paying can achieve that integration, and large amounts of money are now being made available to satisfy that demand.

One of the more significant developments in the United States contributing to the emergence of integrated municipal information systems has been the creation of the Urban Information Systems Inter-Agency Committee (USAC). USAC grew out of the recognition, at the Federal level, that local governments need better tools with which to manage the increasingly complex scope of programs for which they are responsible. Many of these programs are funded by various Federal agencies and, therefore, have reporting requirements which are common to all participating local jurisdictions.

USAC is comprised of representatives of a number of Federal departments, including those of Housing and Urban Development; Labor; Justice; Health, Education and Welfare; and Transportation. It is the purpose of USAC to coordinate and channel available resources of its member agencies toward the development of prototype municipal information systems. Through contractual arrangements, these resources are made available to selected municipalities to be used for systems development, while USAC monitors the progress of that development. It is a requirement that the resulting system be transferable for implementation by other local governmental jurisdictions. Several such developmental projects are now under way throughout the United States.

Another, earlier impetus for the development of integrated information systems at the local level has come from the Law Enforcement Administration Agency (LEAA), a component of the Federal Department of Justice. Through LEAA, funds have been available, by grant, to local jurisdictions for the purpose of developing information systems in support of criminal justice administration. The Federal Department of Transportation has also provided funds, primarily to state governments, in support of the development of information systems oriented toward traffic safety.

While the initial projects funded through USAC are aimed at the development of information systems for individual city governments, it is anticipated that other levels of local government will subsequently be encompassed by the program. Many of the other information systems whose development was sponsored directly by the Federal Government have been designed as multilevel, interjurisdictional systems. Most notable among these are criminal justice information systems which provide for the exchange and integration of crime information among cities, counties, states, and the Federal Government.

Needs for Information Exchange Just as the activities of departments within a jurisdiction are interrelated, so also are the activities between jurisdictions. Very few of the services provided by a city or county are directed toward problems which are defined by jurisdictional boundaries. When a manufacturing plant in one city emits its industrial waste products into an adjacent river, that effluent will shortly become of concern to the cities and counties immediately downstream from the plant. When a person commits a felony and flees the scene of the crime, his or her travel plans are of interest not only to the law enforcement agency of the jurisdiction where the crime occurred, but also to those of neighboring jurisdictions. Thus problems of crime and public safety, poverty, education, fire protection, health, and recreation, among others, are not simply problems which occur in every local jurisdiction; they are problems which, wherever they occur, affect multiple jurisdictions. This interrelationship has been accentuated by urbanization and the development of sprawling metropolitan areas.

In recent years, steps have been taken to create organizational structures which would provide a forum in which to exchange and discuss ideas of common interest to neighboring public jurisdictions. Such councils of governments generally do not have powers of legislation, and any tangible result of deliberation in such a forum must be implemented separately by each individual member jurisdiction. While effective progress is often slow through this structure, the mere focusing of attention on the fact of interdependence has been a constructive result.

Information as a Tool Program management, in the context of PPBS and PMS concepts, consists of three activities: planning, control, and evaluation. These activities are both cyclical and ongoing, and they share among them a common foundation: information. Without adequate information about current services and the community, positive and justifiable service goals cannot be developed for future operations. Without adequate information reflective of the degree to which goals have been achieved, evaluation of effectiveness in service provision is impossible. Without adequate information, control of day-to-day operations can be based on only intuition and reaction.

No aspect of effective program management can be conducted in an information vacuum. Historically, public administrators at all levels have characteristically managed affairs in an information vacuum. In effect, the quantitative achievements of the past year, for any given public service, became the goals of the coming year, adding, say, 10 per cent for population increase and economic inflation. Little else was possible in the way of planning, and effective evaluation was virtually impossible. Control was effected simply through, for example, assuring that "all the garbage trucks are running."

This lack of perspective in service and program management was not due to insufficient available data. Governmental entities, particularly at the local level, gather immense volumes of data regarding a broad spectrum of phenomena and activities. These data have generally become lost, however, through a lack of preparedness and an inability to contend with such volumes on the part of public officials responsible for their collection. Prior to the development of rudimentary ADP applications, and continuing in public agencies to which ADP has not been introduced, massive banks of file cabinets became repositories of the diverse data that flow into public agencies. It has been a major activity simply to maintain such files; efforts of inquiry to such files can only be haphazard and ineffective. In the end, these data files are shredded in order to accord space to the data of the ensuing fiscal year.

Even with the advent of ADP technology and its applications, this information vacuum has persisted. The processing of data by computer has generally resulted in the production of voluminous and detailed daily, weekly, monthly, quarterly, and annual reports to which few public administrators refer, and which still fewer comprehend, with justification. Thus, public administrators have had an abundance of available *data* and a dearth of useful *information* with which to manage programs and services.

IMPLICATIONS FOR THE FUTURE

What can we expect to experience, in the management of public affairs, as a result of the full utilization of available and emerging ADP technology?

New Management Processes First, public administrators will come to rely upon different kinds of information, and different modes of management, than have been made available to them in the past. Instead of detailed reports reflecting year-to-date revenues and expenditures, managers of government programs will increasingly demand, and get, information which reflects the community setting in which these programs are operating. Certainly payrolls and purchase orders will continue to be processed, for the internal affairs of public agencies cannot go unattended. The emerging perspective of public administrators toward the *community*, in contrast with the *government* of the community, however, will lead to the increased utilization of available information processing resources in maintaining that perspective.

In addition, management by exception and management by objectives will become more available to, and accepted by, public administrators. ADP technology can provide the capability, lacking in manual systems of processing data, to *monitor* any public service environment and, with predetermined activity limits, to alert administrators when a given activity has become suboptimal in the community and, therefore, in need of management attention. Because of the increasing volume and diversity of data generated in the course of activities administered by cities, counties, and states, the manual identification of such suboptimal situations can at best be accomplished only on a sporadic or random-sample basis. Managers cannot personally review every property tax account for delinquency, or evaluate every incidence of diphtheria to determine that the localized health problem exists. While administrators have not utilized exception reporting with confidence in the past, more widespread experience with the technique, utilizing ADP technology, should instill such confidence in the future.

The use of simulation models, utilizing computers, can also be expected to become more widespread among public administrators. Rather than basing management decisions regarding public services solely on past experience with the community setting, a process which is slow and only reactive, public administrators will be able economically to simulate the community setting by computer, and artificially and experimentally to alter conditions in order to project what would occur if a given set of circumstances were changed. With this tool, public administrators will be able to anticipate changes in the community, to prepare proactive programs in advance of such changes, and to avoid many of the crises which occur daily, and unnecessarily, in today's urban setting.

Increased Sharing of Information A second impact on public administration resulting from the application of ADP technology will be the increased utilization of shared information among public jurisdictions, as well as among organizational components within jurisdictions. With the increased recognition among public administrators of the interactive relationships which exist between individual services of an agency, more processing systems will be developed which correlate service data and generate information reflective of the programs of which individual services are components. A result will be the maintenance of a more cohesive body of information upon which service managers can base their decisions. Planning, control, and evaluation will become significantly more refined as management activities.

Similarly, data generated within multiple neighboring jurisdictions and reflective of community activities which are of common interest will increasingly be shared among such jurisdictions.

The role which ADP technology will play in this increased interdepartmental and interjurisdictional cooperation will be its facility (1) to reduce diverse and voluminous data to manageable yet significant information on a timely basis; and (2), through teleprocessing, to allow immediate-response access to information of common interest by physically dispersed administrative personnel.

Sharing of ADP Resources Third, neighboring public jurisdictions will increasingly come to share both ADP software and computer hardware. In the United States, most cities or counties within a given state operate within organizational and record-keeping frameworks which are established by the state. This is particularly true within the larger, more populous states. This characteristic of many local governments, supplemented by the fact that all cities or all counties within a given state generally provide approximately the same scope of service programs, results in a setting in which the basic information processing requirements of comparable jurisdictions are nearly, if not exactly, alike. Thus, the payroll or accounting system software used by one city should be able to satisfy the basic requirements of other cities.

Traditionally, the parochial interests of individual governmental agencies have resulted in the development of a unique manual or automated processing system for each application area within every jurisdictional agency. This continual and widespread reinvention of the wheel has been costly and inefficient. Developmental efforts of USAC and other agencies, cited earlier, are leading to the creation of ADP application systems which can be installed by many jurisdictions; the increased professionalism of public administrators will lead to the acceptance of such generalized systems, at the expense of forsaking local report format designs in favor of more prudent and productive utilization of available resources in service to the community.

Jointly operated computer installations have been developed in the recent past, with mixed success, among both large and small city and county public agencies. One of the more successful of such installations has served public agencies in San Gabriel Valley, California, for several years. The advantages of such intergovernmental ADP service centers are as appropriate to multiple jurisdictions within a geographic region as they are to multiple departments within a single jurisdiction's organization.

The emergence in recent years of economical multi- and real-time processing capabilities of computer technology has brought ADP within the practical reach of almost any governmental jurisdiction, regardless of size, through the cooperative development of computing centers for joint use. The increasing demand for better information among public administrators at all levels of government, coupled with the application characteristics which are unique to public agencies and common among them, should result in the more widespread establishment of such centers.

Impact on Public Services Abraham Lincoln stated that "the proper function of government is to do those things for the people which they cannot do as well or as cheaply for themselves." One may argue that in practice these objectives of government have been far exceeded, but the basic premise remains true. For this reason, if the application of ADP technology cannot be demonstrated to have a beneficial impact on the quality of public *services*, any impact which it may have on public *administration* will be of dubious value.

The effects of increased utilization of ADP technology in government will enable public administrators to improve the quality of services through an improved basis upon which to make decisions. Additionally, operational economies will free already limited public funds for direct application to the needs of the community.

Chapter 3

The Computer in the Living Room

HUBERT J. SCHLAFLY

Chairman and Vice President, Transcommunications
Corporation, Greenwich, Connecticut

The computer in the living room, available to every member of the family for natural and productive use, may well be a reality within a relatively few years — certainly before the end of the 1980s, and possibly within the next 10 years. The time for this to happen is right because:

1. Our society has continuing need for new conveniences, economies, and opportunities.

2. The public, after more than two generations of conditioning by television, supersonic travel, and walks on the moon, can accept and absorb even the most startling new developments as a matter of course.

3. Advances in the applicable fields of technology have combined small size, long life, low power consumption, and high performance with tolerable cost.

4. A new broadband communications network, permitting full spectrum transmission over a shielded and low-loss cable and capable of serving all the homes in a local community, has been developing over the past 20 years. It now serves some 30 million people and is rapidly expanding toward a fully "wired nation."

5. The general regulatory climate has been healthy and progressive in spite of endless delays required for studies and evaluations, and in spite of opposition by protectivists and alarmists and the slowness of industry in developing specific hardware and standards.

THE TECHNOLOGICAL BASE: CATV

The missing link has been a reliable, low-cost, high-speed transmission medium which would permit bidirectional mass-entry operation. Almost by accident, and certainly for completely different objectives, the basic transmission means has been developing on an impressive scale in the United States, Canada, and, to a lesser extent, in certain other countries. This new transmission facility is CATV — Community Antenna Television, now called *cable television* — rapidly becoming known by the sophisticated term *broadband communications*.

CATV was originally, and still is predominately, simply a convenient means for distributing broadcast television signals from a point of more advantageous antenna reception of "off-the-air" signals to the point of utilization, the subscribers' television receivers. Almost from the first, the 6-megahertz bandwidth of even a single standard television channel made the use of coaxial cable desirable. Although some early systems used balanced pairs—that is, a two-wire, ungrounded conductor system—and many British systems continue to use that transmission mode, the industry fortunately selected as a "backbone" a transmission means having broad bandwidth, good shielding, and low loss. Widespread use has stimulated improved cable designs, lower costs, and good installation techniques.

The CATV service originally developed in communities that had poor television reception, when signal reception depended on rooftop antennas. It also flourished in locations where the broadcast allocation plan of the FCC provided an inadequate choice of programs. The concept, implemented as a high-risk entrepreneurial venture, caught on, and system operation became viable through the development of a favorable cash flow. The public demonstrated a willingness to pay a modest monthly fee for better signal quality and a greater selection of programs.

The business expanded to larger communities with more broadcast stations, and finally to densely populated areas such as New York City and Los Angeles. Even in these communities the basic service attracted subscribers by offering better signals, equal access to UHF stations (these were converted to unoccupied VHF channels at the cable system headend, and thus acquired "equal status" with their better established rivals), reception of more distant signals, and freedom from the problem of a local antenna.

Cable does not have the spectrum limitation of a single-channel broadcaster. Removal of that limitation brought a new dimension to television. System operators found that they could attract additional subscribers and create community and regulatory support by generating new programming of a specialized and local-interest nature. Now channel space could be "squandered" on programming that was not directed at mass audience ratings. *Local origination* supplemented the broadcast stations' program offerings. The Sloan Foundation report on cable TV characterizes its subject as "the television of abundance."[1]

New Opportunities The new local-origination capability prompted thinking about services of greater scope than the distribution of television programs. If the spectral capacity of the cable could accommodate additional television channels, why could not other types of communication signals be carried on the new community network? Even in 1960, and possibly before, national magazine writers and feature writers for the newspapers were speculating on the day when a viewer would "talk back" to the television set. Proposals for participation television and record keeping for billing of pay-TV contemplated two-way transmission at an early date.

The possibilities opened up by such two-way transmission are exciting. More details of the technology of interactive home terminal services are discussed later in this Chapter. It does not take a great vision to foresee innovations in consumer marketing. A retailer might display wares—by television or through any other medium—and the consumer, in his or her home, might now place an order by entering the item number into the terminal keyboard. The local processor computer would identify the customer and the item indicated, process instructions for delivery, and enter the transaction onto that individual's monthly billing statement. In addition, consumer preference polling, community attitude surveys, progressive selection of information or computer-assisted education, medical aid, real-time audience participation, and many other applications come to mind.

The CATV industry, as of the end of 1974 comprising nearly 3,200 operating cable systems serving about 14 per cent of the nation's television homes, is a mammoth test-bed for new and improved hardware, techniques, and imaginative services. The natural growth of demand for basic services, accelerated by recognition of the full broadband potential, will fulfill predictions of the "wired nation." Forecasters have suggested that perhaps 21 million homes will be wired by the end of the seventies, and perhaps 60 million homes by the end of the eighties.

---

[1] "On the Cable: The Television of Abundance," *Report of the Sloan Commission on Cable Communications*, McGraw-Hill, New York, 1971.

TRANSMISSION

Cable Networks   As channel capacity requirements increased because of expanded broadcast carriage and local origination sources, tube-type amplifiers evolved into low-voltage, cable-powered solid-state devices which today can accommodate 250 MHz or more of usable spectrum.

The most common cable networks are king-size party lines, generally of a tree structure. Main *trunks* have bridging amplifiers for signal insertion onto *feeder* "limbs" which are taped to direct a portion of the signals to *drop* cables that serve individual viewer locations. Direct routing by multiple radials from the headend and from subsplitter locations minimizes total transmission paths, avoids massive cable bundles and splicings, and eliminates multiple central-station switching operations. Channel-shared time-shared signals of a broadband cable network are available to all drop locations, using frequency multiplex selection. Other multiplex techniques are being studied. Selection of an individual terminal or group of terminals for reception or transmission of signals on a specific channel, by means of head-end command to those terminals selected, is a cable technique now under study and test. It is called *terminal switching*, as contrasted with central-station switching normally used by telephone networks.

Two-Way Transmission   It can readily be seen that a broadband transmission network can be made into a bidirectional facility. The cable and the passive devices are insensitive to direction as long as the transmissions are within their useful frequency range. Signals at different frequencies on the same cable can be sorted out by filters for amplification appropriate for the desired direction of transmission.

There are a number of proposals for establishing a two-way broadband network. All of them seem workable. More prominent among these are the following:

1. *Single cable with crossover* filter below TV Channel 2 (54 MHz) and an "upstream" amplifier in the 5- to 30-MHz range.

2. *Single cable "round-robin"* where the cable loops back to its origination point for collection or reinsertion. All transmissions are in the same direction around the loop.

3. *Dual cable,* using one cable for one direction, the second cable for the opposite direction.

4. *Second cable bidirectional,* using one cable for normal CATV subscriber service, one-way transmission, and second cable with a mid-band (110 to 170 MHz) crossover. Lower frequencies in one direction, higher frequencies in the opposite direction.

5. *Hybrids*—combinations of the above.

The single cable, subchannel return may be the least expensive bidirectional method. Many existing systems can be retrofitted with crossover filters and upstream amplifiers at existing downstream amplifier locations. One of the early experimental installations, Los Gatos, California, certainly indicated that this approach is feasible, that upstream video and data channels can be transmitted simultaneously and that the data error rate on a fully loaded cable system was surprisingly low. At the same time these tests, conducted for over a year, highlighted the following cautions:

1. Design, installation, and maintenance precautions are necessary to minimize interaction, which affects amplifier balance and band-pass characteristics.

2. Additional equipment necessary on the subscriber's line increases the possibility of downtime, with consequences of a reduced level of service to the basic customer.

3. The subchannel upstream band may have insufficient capacity for expanded use requirements.

The round-robin method merits further study, but may be impractical in many situations because of the geometric configuration of the community and the increase (by a factor or two) of the number of amplifiers in cascade on a single trunk. The dual cable is attractive for new construction because installation of a second cable, simultaneous to the first cable, requires comparatively little additional cost in terms of labor and construction equipment.

As a hedge on futures, farsighted cable system operators are installing a dual "shadow" cable now and sealing exposed ends but holding back on purchase or installation of electronics for the second cable until they are more certain of equipment performance and need. Thus for a relatively small initial cost, they have a second cable and have preserved their option for later decision on the details of electronic implementation. The second cable can be equipped to operate one-way, in the opposite direction to the first cable, using readily available equipment, established techniques, and a minimum of complication. Since such an upstream system need not have the full capacity of a modern downstream (30 or more channels) plant, it offers a means of salvage of earlier equipment that has been replaced by wideband amplifiers.

It is likely, however, that many operators may elect to make the second cable bi-directional, such as is suggested in item 4 above. Equipment for this type of system is at this writing being field-tested but is not as yet in ready supply or common use. Advantages and disadvantages of a bidirectional second cable are being studied.

It is not yet contemplated that the second cable will require a second drop line to the terminal of every cable subscriber. Return transmissions from a subscriber can be accommodated upstream in the 5- to 30-MHz band, back through passive portions of the feeder line to the first amplifier and there transferred (with or without frequency conversion) over to the second cable for the journey back to the head end.

Outlets to commercial terminals, stores, banks, reservation offices, police stations, schools, libraries, and the like, where the spectrum demand and traffic may require more channels and greater flexibility, will include a dedicated drop from the second "limited-access" cable. Such a cable with bidi.ectional electronics could, for example, permit two computers to "talk" to each other, regardless of their location on the network, at high speed (possibly 250 Kb) with a low error rate (possibly as low as 10^{-8}) on a time-shared channel-shared basis with terminal switching, under the control of a local processing unit at the head end of the cable system.

SUBSCRIBER RESPONSE SERVICES

It is obvious by now that broadband networks are being planned in which the cable outlet in the home may deliver signal to many terminations other than the television receiver or the FM radio. The interactive home terminal using high-speed data transmission will enable many Subscriber Response Services (SRS). Indeed, it will bring about the era of the "Computer in the Living Room."

Terminals There are numerous versions of terminal configuration and capacity. It is far too early to try to describe a specific terminal or a specific method. In fact, the cable operators hope that there will be many competing designs, both in function and in price range, so that a variety of alternatives may be available to match developing market needs and economics. Generally, however, certain system specifications do seem to be emerging, such as:

1. *Low cost.* If necessary, many extra dollars could be spent on head-end equipment to keep a few cents of cost out of the home terminal. The multiplying factor of the mass consumer market for the home terminal may impose requirements for investment capital that will equal or greatly exceed the plant investment in the cable system itself. The industry is contemplating the need for billions of dollars invested in terminal hardware.

2. *High speed.* Each terminal must be capable of almost real-time entry and response. Delays of over 2 or 3 seconds at any terminal may be too great. Considering that many systems are expected to have 10,000 or more terminals, data speeds as high as 1 Mb may be necessary. The speed limit will probably be determined by cost and reliability of components before it is determined by bandwidth limitations.

3. *Keyboard.* This is desirable to permit human insertion of reply messages. The keyboard might be as simple as a yes/no choice; multiple choice (several keys); a decade keyboard plus some elementary function selections; or it might be as elaborate as a complete typewriter or commercial data terminal input device. At this point of development, the decade keyboard—already popularized by the Touch-Tone telephone and the electronic calculator, seems to offer flexibility and low cost without excessive shock of unfamiliarity to the general public and still compatible with present habits and skills.

4. *Verification.* Verification of orders or transactions seems to be a must. This can be provided by various types of "soft" displays. LED (light-emitting diode)

displays, alphanumeric graphics generators, using the television screen as a readout, and other electronic devices are being considered. A hard-copy verification permits convenience of record storage and referral. A hard-copy printer that will accommodate graphic displays for handwriting, line drawings, business forms, and the like, as well as alphanumerics, has great attraction. Such a printer for the home has been designed for production in a manner that is consistent with the low-cost criterion.

5. *Flexibility.* Flexibility of use of the terminal is considered a protection. Those entrepreneurs who are courageous enough to invest in system and terminal hardware are concerned by the very real spectre of obsolescence. Until there has been considerable exploration into the field of viable services, and until reasonable time has been provided for evaluating entrepreneurial ventures, commercial uses, and social applications, there will be great reluctance to standardize. Early terminals therefore must have sufficient capacity and flexibility to accommodate add-on devices. This requirement may not be as disconcerting as it would first seem. The fundamental requirements are individual or group addressing, recognition of commands, and a reply capability. These seem to be the basic ingredients for flexibility. Any auxiliary terminal devices may or may not within themselves include elaborate circuits and mechanisms, but it is always essential that they be able to interface with a relatively simple primary terminal.

Head-End Controls The processing control at the head end of the broadband cable network does not need to have in itself all the capacity and programs that might be necessary to deliver or utilize the information from the home terminals. It is anticipated that such a head-end controller will interface with and provide store-and-forward functions for specialized processors which are owned and operated by others, possibly at locations quite remote from any particular cable system performing the "grass roots" transmission and data collection function. It is obvious therefore to think in terms of long-haul microwave data carriers or equivalent facilities, including two-way services on domestic communications satellites, as well as on the local cable network.

CURRENT STATUS

In the past decade, a great deal of thought has been given to the potential of interactive home terminals. "Participation television" was publicly demonstrated in 1960, and it is possible that certain farsighted pioneers could claim dates earlier than that. Certain forms of pay television employed a return signal capability in order to determine who was looking at what, for billing purposes. Satellite networking in conjunction with privately owned and operated earth station terminals has come into use more rapidly than anticipated. The first such earth station was placed in operation September 30, 1975, and at this writing almost 30 of these are operational, with the number expected to approach 100 within a year.

Continuing Studies Government agencies—particularly the Federal Communications Commission and the President's Study of Telecommunications Planning, established in the Johnson administration and continued as the Office of Telecommunications Planning (OTP) under President Ford—have developed a substantial body of information on broadband communications potential. These agencies were sufficiently impressed with the possibilities to take special measures to avoid hasty action which might have discouraged or prohibited development of this new communications medium. In fact, the FCC, after conducting perhaps the most extensive hearings and studies in the history of that agency, released its cable television *Report and Order* on February 3, 1972, which *requires* nonbroadcast services on cable systems, including provisions for leased channels, guaranteed access, and two-way service.

Provisions in these rules created an Industry Advisory Committee on Technical Standards for Cable (C-TAC). One of the nine working panels of this committee is specifically addressing the question of two-way. A study of home terminal services for two-way broadband communication by the U.S. Department of Commerce, Office of Telecommunications,[2] predicts $19 billion of national gross revenues by the end of the 1980s. Other important studies of interactive services are being funded by the

---

[2] *Potential Market Demand for Two-Way Information Services to the Home, 1970–1990*, Report No. IFF-R-71-26, U.S. Department of Commerce Office of Telecommunications, 1970.

National Science Foundation and by other Government agencies, such as HEW, Justice, Transportation, and others. Technical and marketing studies have been made and are under way by foundations, by "think tanks" such as Mitre and RAND, by consulting groups and professional and trade organizations, and by major electronics manufacturers. The National Cable Television Association, which represents a good portion of the cable systems operating in the United States, created a Standards Committee and an Engineering Advisory Committee whose subpanels include "Future Services."

The real pioneers who are hastening the day of the interactive home terminal are some of the cable operators and a few engineering and manufacturing groups, who have backed up their beliefs with considerable investment of time, facilities, and money. Hardware and systems tested in Los Gatos, California; Overland Park, Kansas; Reston, Virginia; Irving, Texas; Orlando, Florida; El Segundo, California; and elsewhere have attracted less publicity. Not all of these experimental installations will be successful. Some will demonstrate that their methods are not practical or competitive, but they, too, will contribute valuable information and guidance. All are stepping stones to a mammoth new industry.

Competitive Counterforces   Obstacles to the establishment of the era of the "Computer in the Living Room" are not technical. Nothing has to be invented—proven concepts have to be implemented. Opposition to the growth of a new broadband communications network can be expected from industries that have had a monopoly on the electronic communications links into the home—the broadcasting industry, particularly the networks, and the telephone companies. Broadcasters see the emerging new opportunities for use of the television set and the greater variety of available programming as "fractionating" their audience. The telephone companies see a new wire into the home, using newer communication methods, as a threat to their long-held monopoly. It is natural that they would prefer to exploit the new services at some future date after an orderly amortization of current capital investment. The new medium will have to make its way in the face of such counterforces, by demonstrating the public benefit that will accrue from its offerings.

Regulation   CATV and its expanded concepts have been and continue to be examined and regulated at all levels of government. Federal, local, and now, increasingly, state bodies see areas of broadband communications which relate to their authority and jurisdiction, and which present new revenue-producing opportunities.

Effective regulation cells for investigation, understanding, evaluation, reporting, protection of the public interest, and performance monitoring. If these activities are not adequately funded and are not performed intelligently, efficiently, and fairly, regulation becomes an obstacle. But by the same token, regulation, properly administered, can provide assistance and protection to the industry as well as to the public. The FCC rules promulgated in February 1972, to regulate the cable television industry, although slow in coming and arguable in certain details, do provide protection against abuses and do define an area of operation that will allow the industry to grow and to prove its worth.

Problems of Growth   Let us assume that the growth of broadband cable and interactive home terminals is such that it will evolve into the predicted "wired nation." The industry is then faced with the following normal problems of growth:

1. *Equipment.* The manufacturers are reluctant to design equipment when there are no standards. However, new hardware will probably be installed first in systems owned and operated by the larger cable corporations. In this case, the performance specifications will be approved (and sometimes generated) by the cable operator's engineering staff. For some time at least the cable operators will have control of the system, including the terminals. They are in a position to set their own standards on their own system—just as is the telephone company. This means that the manufacturer, although serving a mass market, does not have to make mass sales. The manufacturer has to satisfy one, or comparatively few, prime customer(s).

When we talk about the computer in the living room, we are definitely talking about a mass consumer market—a potential of 70 million or more homes affluent enough to afford television sets. And we are talking about a need for a potential family of devices, varied in nature and purpose, having as a common ingredient their linkage to communications facility for command, input, and readout. The market for the hardware, therefore, is large and varied. Manufacturers willing to invest moderately in advance study and product development will have a good chance to benefit from that demand.

2. *Standards.* Standards that are set too soon may well be detrimental to innovation and opportunity; set too late, they may limit broad expansion and use, prevent interchangeability, and increase costs. Therefore some will call standards an obstacle, and others will just as vigorously claim that lack of standards is an obstacle. Standards will develop—some as an outgrowth of use in the marketplace, some by careful advance industry planning. The C-TAC Committee of the FCC, previously mentioned, and the Electronics Industry Association's Cable Television Systems Committee (CSTC) and others are aggressively studying the issues.

3. *Financing.* The industry must be prepared to deploy tremendous amounts of capital for plant and equipment—in the order of magnitude of billions of dollars. Sources of capital appear to be willing to provide this financing, but they will be looking for well-organized, stable operators with good performance records to minimize their risk. They will keep a close eye on regulatory and tax requirements. Excessive demands for free services or excessive limitations on services, unusually heavy tax burdens, or ceilings on reasonable expansion could dry up sources of private capital. The thought of leaving the development of this facility dependent on Federal subsidy or municipal ownership is not attractive. The public might easily end up with something as costly, inefficient, and poorly managed as transportation is today.

THE SHAPE OF THE FUTURE

To try to predict, at a time when the whole field is in its early prototype stage, which services will be most popular, most useful, or most profitable is a crystal-ball undertaking of sobering magnitude. Two-way, mass-entry, substantially real-time data communication between individually selective addresses and a nation full of computer processing capability, provides a flexibility of use that challenges the imagination. In spite of all the research, logical deductions, and educated guesses of trained market analysts, some unpredictable fad-type use could conceivably capture a top-rating position.

The challenge and the opportunity lie in the variety of applications both for home use and businesses that the computer network and two-way mass terminal combination will accommodate. Add to these the display and instruction potential of color television and its associated sound channels, and one begins to experience the excitement of anticipation as regards the services and conveniences that can be offered.

There is much work still to be done. Not only must the existing networks be adapted to the two-way transmission mode which itself must be expanded into the "wired nation," but specific data services will require careful planning and production of related software and hardware. Each service will require study, specialized attention, and hard work to achieve implementation. But the concept is understandable and glamorous, and it is to be expected that strong pressure for development of services will come from the public as well as from entrepreneurs, once the media begin to talk and write about working examples instead of prophecy.

A Hypothetical System   By way of example, let us assume a bidirectional broadband cable system that has sufficient outside plant in place to serve 10,000 outlets within a community. Each outlet has a data terminal, capable of recognizing a binary address unique to that terminal. Once the terminal address has been recognized, the equipment is programmed to accept commands, instructions, and messages, in the form of digital code, at speeds of 250 kb to 1 Mb per second. The terminal includes a television tuner capable of selecting any of the downstream television channels on the cable, delivery of the selected channel to a standard television receiver, and reporting the selection back to the system computer. Certain channels may be designated for selection only when authorized by remote command, permitting programs for which special charges might be made (premium television), or special viewer qualifications required (i.e., doctor, enrolled student, etc.). The terminal has a keyboard with the numbers 0 through 9, a few symbols that can be assigned arbitrary meanings, and a few function buttons such as "send," "cancel," "purchase," and "TV." It has an indicator light to attract attention, or acknowledge a response.

Auxiliary devices, for starters, will include some form of hard-copy graphic print-out and the television receiver. At a later date, video storage devices such as individual "frame grabbers" and home video recorders or other appliances may be added, with appropriate control functions supplied by the keyboard or by remote command. The terminal will also accept and store and forward, upon routine interrogation, automatic binary inputs from meter readers and medical, fire, intrusion, and other sensors.

Although the keyboard provides only decade and functional buttons, alpha characters can be transmitted by a simplified double-button code. On the other hand, a full typewriter keyboard could be considered on auxiliary device, and the terminal should accommodate such input codes.

After the address recognition and command or message signals have been received, a brief time will be allowed for transmission of an appropriately identified return message.

It has been calculated that a 1-Mb data rate could permit interrogation and reply from 10,000 homes in 1 second—almost a real-time relationship. In actual practice, such a terminal contract cycle might be stretched to 2, 3, or more seconds for routine or "dormant" terminals, and speeded up to once or several times a second for those terminals that indicate they wish to transact active business. Thus *every home* is, in effect, in constant communication with a computer which is programmed to inform, monitor, and serve.

The above generalizations require some concentrated thought before the full impact and scope of opportunity can be appreciated. The U.S. Department of Commerce Report, referenced earlier, has broken down this potential into 30 specific areas of service that are indicated to have greater or less revenue-producing potential. Many other reviews and reports itemize specific services ranging from premium television programming to medical sensor monitoring. This writer prefers to provide a generic analysis of the potential (limited by his own understanding and background) in order to permit the reader greater freedom to generate his or her own ideas for specific uses. At this time all of us may see only the tip of the iceberg.

Seven Generic Uses   A broadband, high-speed interactive data terminal in the home and certain business locations suggests the following operational potentials:

1. Address selection and identification (in terms of prestored demographics or instructions) of individual or groups of subscribers.

2. The enabling (or restriction) of reception or transmission of specific television, data, or other communication channels to or from the selected addresses.

   a. Central processor record of the source, responsible entity, type, duration, time, frequency of such activation or use—for billing, authorized analysis, support, identification, or other purposes.

3. Reinsertion of terminal transmissions into the network (or interconnection with other networks) immediately or on a store/forward basis for general or selective delivery to other addresses.

4. Terminal access on demand, or by preauthorization, to computer processing, readout, and reply of external or terminal-supplied data.

5. Terminal access to information storage, and delivery to the terminal auxiliary devices for hard-copy or soft-copy capture, display, and/or record.

   a. Delivery of communications generated by others, to such auxiliary devices at selected addresses.

   b. Verification or confirmation of terminal-generated transactions.

6. Continuous and real-time monitoring of automatic sensors for computer analysis or recognition of need and:

   a. Immediate notification, if necessary, of assistance requirement to appropriate human agencies, with accurate identification of the name, location, and nature of the difficulty.

   b. Emergency alert notification to the terminal location.

   c. Processing of such data for statistical readout.

7. Terminal-generated instructions or orders for processing and/or delivery to external agents or agencies for terminal-requested services or goods, including buy/sell, credit, and other financial transactions.

It is not generally contemplated, nor does this writer believe, that the broadband network and the home terminal should be cluttered by the undisciplined exchange of human sensory interactive communication on a central-station-switched, "anybody-to-anybody" basis, as is presently provided by telephone message networks that include possible future extention to Picturephone® networks.

Costs and benefits It is recognized that the cost of plant for the two-way broadband transmission network for the "wired nation," and the data terminals and auxiliary devices for the home, with the associated local processing and control equipment, will require many *billions* of dollars of capital investment by the system operators. Despite this huge investment, which must be amortized by charges to the user, this writer is prepared to say that widespread use of the services will *reduce* the cost of living of the individual. This saving will be realized not only in terms of dollars that the user would have paid for equivalent services and conveniences, but also in terms of tax reduction or deferment of tax increases.

The above statement is, in this writer's view, based on a reasonable premise. The efficiency and convenience of the interactive home terminal represent, for the supplier of goods and services, a possible reduction of overhead and economies in terms of support expenses and personnel time and a reduction of error and spoilage that substantially exceeds the cost of the system hardware and operationsl services rendered.

As an example of tax benefit, a meaningful percentage of the ill and the aged receiving community- or government-supported care might be able to live at home, with better attention and opportunity to participate in community life than they would receive at an institution. Such a social benefit may well be realized, not only in terms of human dignity, but tangibly as a saving in tax dollars. The opportunity for citizens, rich or poor, to avail themselves of services and access to information and assistance that previously had been available only to the wealthy, to big business, or to government, offers a chance for self-help and development that has never before been realized in any society.

Timetable How soon? That is a good question. The answer will be "never" if special interests and unimaginative regulation prevail. But given the opportunity of a democratic, free-enterprise society, the era of the interactive home data terminal, or the "Computer in the Living Room" as the editors of this volume have chosen to classify this revolution, should be showing good signs of life by 1980, have substantial support by the end of this decade, and be generally accepted by the end of the 1980s.

In spite of national and worldwide economic problems which have already delayed timetables, an increasing number of system operators and equipment manufacturers are risking financial involvement. Already, some businesspeople are becoming sufficiently aware of this communications medium to see that it may provide new opportunity or more efficient methods for their own special business interests. They are beginning to insert a financial toe into the water.

After a period of time to take the rough edges off some of the hardware and operating techniques, certain small community systems will be established and offer limited services. If these services live up to their potential, with the news media spreading the story, the demand will explode suddenly and dramatically. Those who have done their homework and are technically, financially, and operationally qualified, will prosper. More importantly, society will have made another quantum move in its access to knowledge and in its quest for an expanded life potential.

Chapter 4

The Computer and Privacy

LANCE J. HOFFMAN

College of Engineering, Department of Electrical Engineering
and Computer Sciences, University of California at Berkeley,
California

HOWARD H. CAMPAIGNE

Department of Mathematics, Slippery Rock State College,
Slippery Rock, Pennsylvania

Along with the increasing use of computers in industry and government, a slow but steadily increasing public concern has developed over potential threats to privacy posed by the advent of the computer. Fears of Orwell's "1984" and "Big Brother" have developed, as well illustrated by the *Newsweek* issue of July 27, 1970. Its cover features a computer system wearing an Uncle Sam hat and equipped with (as peripheral devices) a tapped telephone, videotape camera, sound recording tapes, microphone, and other listening or snooping devices. All these are focused on one poor couple illustrated in a spotlight. This magazine sitting on every drugstore and supermarket rack in the country focused the attention of millions of Americans on privacy, data banks, and the computer—and its latent power for good or evil.

The worry that some members of the public have expressed about huge memory banks which contain personal dossiers is well founded, from the technological point of view. The technology for storing enormous amounts of data in computer systems is here. Several firms are now marketing as standard products bulk memories that could store a one-page dossier on each of the 200 million citizens of the United States in a small area—about 225 square feet. In one system already delivered by Precision Instruments, Inc., all these dossiers could be available on-line, with an access time of approximately 6 seconds.

A later system, that of Ampex in Sunnyvale, California, has a $1\frac{1}{2}$-trillion-bit memory that uses videotape recording techniques; it allows on-line accessing of the equivalent of up to 32,000 reels of tape or 350 IBM 3330 disks. This amount of memory is equivalent to cover 30 double-spaced pages per person for everybody in the United States. Average access time is under 10 seconds.

IBM has delivered a special order system, the IBM Mass Photodigital Storage System, which consists of trays of film chips. Each small $3\frac{1}{2}$- by 7-mm ($1\frac{3}{8}$- by $2\frac{3}{4}$-in.) chip contains 4.72 million bits of memory (read-only after once written). In each cell is contained 151.04×10^6 bits, and in an entire system one could have either 3.36×10^{11} or 1.0×10^{12} bits.

The average access time here is 10 seconds. One could write as little as one file per frame (there are 32 frames on a chip). There are 206,640 bits per frame, and the bit size is 8.5×8.0 microns.

The Grumman MASSTAPE system can store 16 billion bytes in 16 square feet. Up to eight of these units may be combined to provide a trillion-bit (128-billion-byte) system at a cost of about 0.0001 cent per bit (= $1 million).

As we have seen, the technology in memories is here. How extensive, then, are the dossiers currently kept in computer data banks? What data are kept in them and who has access to these data?

A RECORDS-ORIENTED SOCIETY

If we take a look at the panorama of data banks which exist today, we find that the United States has become a records-oriented society. Records are kept on our education, employment, credit, and health, and in government files such as taxation and law enforcement. During the past two decades, as most government agencies and large private organizations have been computerizing their large-scale files, the American public has become concerned that because of the computer's enormous capacities, far more personal data might be assembled about individuals than it had been feasible to collect before, and that at the same time there might be a decrease in an individual's ability to see and challenge records on himself or herself.

The files of the Social Security Administration take 700,000 reels of magnetic tape. The Federal Bureau of Investigation keeps 201 million fingerprints, and 56 million records in a name-check file. Its National Crime Information Center processes 76,000 inquiries a day into its 3.3 million active records. R. L. Polk and Company have 135 million names on their mailing list, which they vend in 1,500 different packages. Their records reside on 50,000 reels of tape. The Geneological Society of the Church of the Latter Day Saints has its subsidiary, Management Systems Corporation, keep 35 million records. There are 13,700 commercial banks each with extensive records; the banks are required by law to report any "unusual transactions." The Bank of America, for example, does 31 million transactions each year through its BankAmericard, and keeps 14 million accounts of 100 different types. The National Driver Registration Service processes 15 million inquiries a year, from which there are 121,000 reports of suspension or revocation of licenses. Mutual Insurance Company of Omaha keeps health records on 8.5 million people. From these they write 9,000 checks each weekday. There are 26,000 hospitals and health services. One of them, Kaiser-Permanente, processes 1 million laboratory tests each year, and a third of a million prescriptions. There are 3,700 municipalities, each with a police force and its blotter. One of them, Kansas City, has 224,000 records in its file of warrants, pick-up orders, and suspicious persons. Its Automatic Law Enforcement Response Team (ALERT) computer system processes 2 million inquiries a year, resulting in 21,700 identifications. *Databanks in a Free Society* has still more examples. (See Selective Bibliography at the end of this Chapter.)

However, the fact is that computerized data banks which contain sensitive information on people are not nearly as advanced as one might think after reading some of the literature warning of potential misuse of these systems. The vision of a general-purpose total management information system providing key executives the information they need on a cathode-ray tube at the touch of a button—the image so popular in much of the glossy literature of the sixties—is still just that: a vision. In practice, it is nowhere to be found in 1976.

More important, the most sensitive information—information which is text (character strings) rather than numerical values and which is therefore more likely to be subjective—is usually not going into computer systems. With the technology that has been available to date, it has simply been too expensive to store large amounts of text in most computer systems. For a combination of technological and organizational reasons, central data bank developments are far from being as advanced as many public commentaries have assumed. Organizations have so far failed to achieve the "total" consolidation of their information about individuals which raised civil liberties alarms when such goals were announced in the 1960s by various government agencies or private organizations.

Further, in computerizing their records on individuals, organizations have generally carried over the same policies on data collection and sharing that law and administrative traditions in each field had set in the precomputer era. Where new law or practices have evolved to protect individual liberties over the past decade, organizations with computerized systems have followed such new policies as fully as those that still use manual files and procedures. Even the most highly computerized organizations continue to rely heavily on manual record keeping and retain in their paper files the most sensitive personal information they possess.

We should not infer, however, that organizational and technical limitations will hold down the amount of information in computer data banks forever. Precisely because of the technological advances in memories mentioned earlier, it is becoming economically feasible to store more and more data in relatively fast on-line memories. As the cost of these memories is driven down, more and more textual and subjective information is likely to be stored in computer systems.

Some areas where data banks with sensitive information on people already exist are law enforcement (e.g., the FBI's National Crime Information Center Computerized Criminal History file), retail credit bureaus (e.g., TRW-Credit Data Corporation's completely computerized credit history data bank), and state welfare system data banks.

These and other computer systems all reflect the age-old problem of resolving the conflict between privacy on the one hand and data acquisition for use in better, rational decision making on the other hand. One has to make trade-offs. If society desires better medical systems, speedy and accurate airlines reservation systems, fewer police officers shot when they stop cars, or faster distribution of welfare checks (just to give a few examples), it will have to give some "private" data to the computer systems which provide these advantages, and thus increase the risk of unauthorized disclosure in order to gain the benefits. Note that sometimes the risk is decreased in computer systems as opposed to manual systems. Data are often better protected in computer systems than in manual file folders that may be presided over by flattery-prone or even bribery-susceptible clerks working for low wages in large offices.

PRIORITIES FOR PUBLIC ACTION

As reported by the National Academy of Sciencies Project on Computer Databanks[1] in late 1972:

> The real issue of databanks and civil liberty facing the nation today is not that revolutionary new capacities for data surveillance have come into being as a result of computerization. The real issue is that computers arrived to augment the power of organizations just when the United States entered a period of fundamental debate over social policies and organizational practices and when the traditional authority of government institutions and private organizations has become the object of wide-spread dissent. Important segments of the population have challenged the goals of major organizations that use personal records to control the rights, benefits, and opportunities of Americans. There is also debate over the criteria that are used to make such judgments (religious, racial, political, cultural, sexual, educational, etc.) and over the procedures by which the decisions are reached, especially those that involve secret proceedings and prevent individuals from having access to their own records. Computers are making the record keeping of many organizations more efficient precisely at the moment when trust in many large organizations is low and when major segments of the American populations are calling for changes in values that underlie various social programs, for new definitions of personal rights, and for organizational authorities to make their decision-making procedures more open to public scrutiny and to the review of specific individuals involved.

The report identified six areas of priority for public action:

1. Development of laws to give the individual a right of access and challenge to almost every file in which records about him or her are kept by government agencies.

2. Development of explicit laws or rules which balance confidentiality and data sharing in many sensitive private record systems which today do not have such rules. These include bank records and travel and charge-card records.

3. Limiting the collection of personal information and its use in such areas as arrest-only records in licensing and employment decisions; and selling of name and

[1] A. F. Westin and M. A. Baker, *Databanks in a Free Society*, Quadrangle Press, New York, 1972.

address lists collected by government agencies to mailing list sellers (unless the individual consents).

4. Increased work by the computer industry to make technological safeguards "available and workable products."

5. Reconsideration by Congress and the executive branch of the "current permissive policies toward use of the social security number." The report contends that a minimum level of trust must be maintained between American citizens and their government. "Under these conditions, adopting the social security number as a national identifier or letting its use spread unchecked cannot help but contribute to public distrust of government."

6. Experimentation with special information-trust agencies. For example, the handling of national summary criminal histories (rap sheets) might be taken away from the FBI and given to an independent national agency under control of a board which would have public representatives as well as law enforcement officials on it.

In its closing paragraphs, the report sums up the data banks and civil liberties problem as follows:

> If our empirical findings showed anything, they indicate that man is still in charge of the machines. What is collected, for what purposes, with whom information is shared, and what opportunities individuals have to see and contest records are all matters of policy choice, not technological determinism. Man cannot escape his social or moral responsibilities by murmuring feebly that "the Machine made me do it."[2]

SAFEGUARDS FOR SECURITY

To turn now to security measures in computer systems, one must first realize that most safeguards for privacy are not delivered as standard, off-the-shelf items when computer systems are bought or rented today; they do not come with the hardware or with the software. Usually little or no mention of privacy problems is made when the computer system is contracted for. If security safeguards are supplied, they are generally furnished as special optional items, tailored to each individual installation with commensurate cost to that installation. Since concern about the problems of personal privacy in computer systems is just now beginning to surface, manufacturers are just now starting seriously to address these problems. But today there is not one standard system — that is, one that can be bought "off the shelf" with no optional hardware or software — which contains adequate privacy safeguards for personal data.

Probably the most important controls of all are administrative, not technical. Administrative controls determine what gets collected in the first place, and to a large extent to whom it is disseminated once it is collected. Even then, one should realize that no system will ever work exactly as designed; we live in the age of the Xerox machine, and in the age of the information "buddy system." This buddy system functions in any information system, and there will probably always be a few unauthorized leaks. Interestingly enough, computer systems are very possibly more secure than manual systems, since with the advent of the computer, people must be instructed in how to use the automated system. No longer is it the case that anyone who can read can open the file cabinet and scan a neighbor's folder.

---

[2] See also "Records, Computers, and the Rights of Citizens," *Report of the Secretary's Advisory Committee on Automated Personal Data Systems*, U.S. Department of Health, Education, and Welfare, July, 1973. The Committee recommends the enactment of a Federal Code of Fair Information Practice for all automated personal data systems. The proposed code would rest on the following five principles: (1) There must be no personal data record-keeping system whose very existence is secret. (2) There must be a way for an individual to find out what information about him or her is in the record, and how it is used. (3) There must be a way for an individual to prevent information about him or her that was obtained for one purpose from being used or made available for other purposes without his or her consent. (4) There must be a way for an individual to correct or amend a record of identifiable information about him or her. (5) Any organization creating, maintaining, using, or disseminating records of identifiable personal data must assure the reliability of the data for their intended use, and must take precautions to prevent misuse of the data. (For related discussion, see Chapter 5, "The Computer and Society," in this Section. The recently enacted Public Law 93-579 regulates most personal information systems operated or funded by the U.S. Government. Its provisions are specific and it is "must" reading for those concerned with privacy and security in computer systems.

Another important nontechnological control method is physical security.[3] This can be very important and is often overlooked. One may be using all the passwords and other technological safeguards, but without physical security at the computer center and at the files, one's efforts will be for naught. There is now a substantial literature on physical security, one of the best short works being an IBM booklet on the subject, "The Considerations of Physical Security in the Computer Environment."

Technical Methods for Security Assuming that physical and administrative safeguards have been taken, one can now turn to technical methods for security in computer systems.

Authentication and Identification. Current software identification techniques are generally based on something the user knows, something the user has, or something the user is. Comparisons are made between the proper "something" and what the computer expects, and a decision to permit or deny access is made accordingly.

In the category of "something the user knows," there are several techniques. Simple passwords offer protection against what might be called *casual* infiltration. They are used to protect files, records, data fields within records, or groups of these items. Once the computer verifies that a proper password can be associated with a given user, that user can obtain all the information authorized to that password.

While the simple password scheme is easy to use and inexpensive to implement, it requires the authorized user to remember the password, and it can be compromised by wiretapping, electromagnetic pickup, or (more simply) an interloper discovering the password written down somewhere, such as on an office calendar, a scrap of paper tossed in the wastebasket, or on discarded console output. There is also an inverse relationship between the length of time a password is in use and the degree of security it maintains. For this reason, passwords should be changed periodically to thwart unauthorized users. Passwords should not be printed (echoed) at consoles; overprinting them there is not always effective. Passwords should also undergo some minimal encryption before being stored in computer systems.

There are a number of variations on password schemes. One of these which eliminates some of the disadvantages named above is the following. The user remembers a password as before. When signing on, he or she is requested by the computer to type certain characters of the computer's choosing. In this way the possibility of compromise by ribbon reading or wastebasket searching is greatly reduced. However, all the other disadvantages of the passwords remain.

One-time passwords can also be used. These protect against stolen password utilization because once a password is used it is no longer valid.

Further along the spectrum, many disadvantages of passwords are not present if the computer system requires successful execution of an algorithm for the authentication process. This is often called a *handshaking* procedure. Questions asked by the computer can be personal information ordinarily unknown to anybody but the authorized user (such as brand of hair tonic used). Alternatively, the user can be asked to apply a secret transformation to a pseudorandom number generated by the computer. The transformation is never transmitted in the clear over communication lines or typed on a console.

Electronic combination locks are also available (from, for example, Datalock[4]) where a Touch-Tone-like keyboard is used. The user must press the right combination in order physically to enter the area of the computer terminal.

In the category of "something the user has," the user's photograph and signature can be attached to a medium something like a credit card. This prevents illegal users from easily passing a guard and getting to computers or remote consoles. These credit-card-like devices come complete with threat-monitoring printer units. For example, one access control system is a locking and identification unit which is like an ordinary door lock and key, except that the key is a binary coded printed circuit. A central printer can record the date, time, key identification number, and door number of each entry.

There are also some devices that allow access to a user based on "something the user is." In this category there is the Identimat,[5] which identifies individuals by measuring

---

[3] See Section 5, Chapter 7, "Physical Security of the Computer Center."

[4] Datalock, Sacramento, Calif.

[5] Identimation Corp., Northvale, N.J.

hand geometry. This system claims 99.5 per cent accuracy, but the cost per station is relatively high.

Another authentication method is the dial-up and call-back method. When data are desired by a user who is connected to the computer via telephone line A, a message is sent to the user asking him or her to provide the password of that data to the computer operator by voice over a different telephone line B. Alternatively, the operator calls the user back over phone line B to make sure the user is authorized and at the right place.

In addition to the authentication methods which are used to control access to files, or to the computer system itself, other methods are necessary to handle shared databases and files which contain information needing different degrees of protection.

Compartmentalization Methods. Various technical methods for compartmentalizing computer memories are in use. By *compartmentalizing* is meant those methods used to subdivide the memory into parts with different access privileges. We use the inelegant word *compartmentalizing* because words in more common use (e.g. *partitioning* or *segmenting*) are too closely linked to specific hardware. There are two types of compartmentalizing techniques: those which are necessary for the proper operation of the computer system (especially a time-sharing system) and those which are used to enhance information security in a shared system.

1. Hardware compartmentalization. In any multiprogramming, multiprocessing, or time-sharing system, each user must be prevented from disturbing the program or data of other users. Furthermore, a user should not be allowed to interfere with operations by improper or untimely input or output or halt commands. This latter restriction is generally obtained by denying to the user certain instructions which may be executed only by privileged programs, such as the operating system. The former capability generally is provided by memory protection schemes such as relocation and bounds registers, segmentation, paging, and memory keys.

The techniques mentioned in the preceding paragraph protect contiguous portions of (real or virtual) computer memory from alteration by an errant or unauthorized program. These hardware countermeasures do not, however, provide protection of a user file in auxiliary storage from unauthorized access. To this end, software schemes have augmented the hardware methods.

2. Software compartmentalization. Only a few installations are using the more sophisticated of the methods described below. Computer users are pleased (even astonished) when their programs work, and most—if they use any security protection at all—use simple passwords to guard their files. In many cases this level of protection is all that is justifiable. More detailed descriptions of some of the methods mentioned below appear elsewhere.[6,7]

A system involving concentric *rings* for protection, developed at M.I.T., has recently been announced by Honeywell. It provides flexible but controllable access by a number of different users to shared data and procedures. On the negative side, as implemented, it requires hardware segmentation; and if a file has many different data fields with many different levels of access, the swap times necessary to access each datum in its own segment may cause prohibitive overhead. It also imposes a hierarchy on all information in the database, and this is not desirable in every instance.

Software compartmentalization below the file level is not in general commercial use. This is probably due in varying degrees to the obscurity of the methods, the lack of reliable information on overhead costs, and (until recently) manufacturer and user indifference toward data security.

Privacy Transformations. Privacy transformations are reversible encodings used to conceal information. They are useful for protecting against interception on communication lines, neutralizing of electromagnetic radiation from terminals or computers, or wrongful access to data in removable files. This last threat is probably the most significant.

Simple privacy transformations are one of the most effective methods of preventing disclosure of data. Even if an infiltrator somehow obtains the data, he or she must still

[6] L. J. Hoffman, *Modern Methods for Computer Security and Privacy*, Prentice-Hall, Englewood Cliffs, N.J., 1977.

[7] James Martin, *Security, Accuracy, and Privacy in Computer Systems*, Prentice-Hall, Englewood Cliffs, N.J., 1973.

decrypt them; often this person does not have the time or resources to do this, and even if he or she does, a mass of uninteresting data must be decrypted just to find what is wanted. It would usually be much simpler to bribe a legitimate user. Figure 4-1 is an example of a very simple (and fairly insecure) privacy transformation.

Privacy transformations can be effected by either hardware or software. Scrambling devices which use group theory, pseudorandom number techniques, and other methods are now available commercially from, for example, Ground Data in Ft. Lauderdale, Florida, and Technical Communications Corp. in Lexington, Massachusetts. These boast hardware at the terminal and software or hardware at the computer. More detailed information on privacy transformations can be found in David Kahn's excellent work, *The Codebreakers*,[8] and in Hoffman's anthology.[9] A recently proposed Federal standard is described in Reference 6.

Threat Monitoring. Software, when used in conjunction with administrative rules and compartmentalization methods which protect the operating system from un-

Cleartext:	P	L	A	N	E	S		A	T	T	A	C	K		A	T		0	5	0	0
Cleartext in numbers:	16	12	1	15	5	19	0	1	20	20	1	3	11	0	1	20	0	27	32	27	27
Key (π)	3	1	4	1	6	3	1	4	1	6	3	1	4	1	6	3	1	4	1	6	3
Ciphertext in numbers:	19	13	5	16	11	22	1	5	21	26	4	4	15	1	7	23	1	31	33	33	30
Ciphertext:	S	M	E	P	K	V	A	E	U	Z	D	D	O	A	G	W	A	4	6	6	3

Fig. 4-1 Privacy transformation, using π as the key and addition as the method.

authorized changes, can detect attempted or actual security violations, and either provide an immediate response (e.g., job cancellation or tracing procedures) or provide an ex post facto analysis. It can also record all attempts or all rejected attempts to obtain certain sensitive information, unusual activity of a given file, attempts to write into protected files, or excessively long periods of use. Indeed, the last is perhaps the only known method to attempt to cope with the fact that, given enough work and some a priori information, it is possible to obtain a specific "dossier" from a "statistical" data bank—the "statistical inference problem."[10]

The use of such software is called *threat monitoring*. The log kept is called an *audit log* or an *audit trail*. The monitoring or auditing provides a method for recording the identification of each request and the name of each requestor. The audit trail can be examined periodically by appropriate authority to determine if unauthorized access has occurred, and then suitable steps can be taken.

Threat monitoring has a beneficial side effect: It often will help improve the efficiency of the system by recording widespread use of particular facilities. These facilities can then be altered to eliminate bottlenecks. Also, if some security restriction is unduly interfering with operations, threat monitoring should help pinpoint the offending restriction.

Costs of Countermeasures   There is almost no information available on the cost or overhead of security techniques for computer systems. Fixed costs of security controls are very dependent on the vicissitudes of the particular installation. These include the capital cost, the one-time outlay to get into operation, and the expenses of buying, building, or programming a system. These also include administrative costs such as costs of guarding doors, having telephones elsewhere, and perhaps even having some people devoting their time to penetrating the system.

Many of the costs of security are variable, even at a given installation. These costs depend on the frequency with which records are used, since this determines how often some safeguards are invoked.

---

[8] Macmillan, New York, 1968.

[9] L. J. Hoffman, *Privacy and Security in Computer Systems*, Mellville (Wiley), Los Angeles, 1973.

[10] L. J. Hoffman and W. F. Miller, "Getting a Personal Dossier from a Statistical Data Bank," *Datamation*, March, 1970.

In addition to these fixed and variable costs, there are other costs even harder to quantify: the development cost; the expense of experimenting and rejecting approaches before finding an acceptable one; the social cost of being secretive; the social cost of not being secretive; the cost of doing some functions manually because adequate security controls are not available in the computer system; and others. It is impossible to evaluate or even enumerate these latter costs.

Administrative Rules. Administrative rules do not come free; they take effort on the part of the administrators. Also, restrictions of access to tapes, documents, or other items must be enforced by employees who have other tasks to perform as well.

Such precautions as logs and artificial data for demonstrations cost money to generate and maintain, as well as requiring constant alertness. Accounting for sensitive punched cards, tapes, printed forms, carbon paper, and ribbons is not very expensive, but is not free either, for someone must be responsible that pains continue to be taken that this chore be done and done thoroughly.

Physical Security.[11] The most elementary precaution is to control physical access to the system and its files. This means either arranging partitions and doors so as to limit the approaches and arranging for locks and keys, or else having personnel in the area night and day. The latter is very expensive if the workload would otherwise not demand it.

The costs of elaborate physical security measures vary widely, depending on the particular installation. Newspaper accounts have stated that the William J. Burns International Detective Agency data processing center in Briarcliff Manor, New York, has been "soaked" with ultrasonic traps and other measures at a cost of about $12,000. A *Wall Street Journal* account states that Data Processing Security, Inc., of Hinsdale, Illinois, "will put a team of consultants to work running through a 172-point (security) checklist and preparing a survey report for $3,000 to $5,000."

One can use double-door *buffer* systems with electric locks, magnet sensors, and closed-circuit television to control access to computer centers. In contrast, locks and keys can also be obtained for under $100.

Partitioning for security may mean somewhat inefficient use of space, another cost. Identification badges cost very little, but they do require someone to supervise, monitor, and maintain them, a half-time job for even a small installation. Very small installations can rely on personal identification.

Authentication Methods. Hardware in terminals which identifies the terminal or the user to the system is still an optional extra in most cases.

The ordinary password is an inexpensive method, well tested and perfected by much use. It can be implemented on existing systems without special hardware. The use of one-time passwords is not nearly so well known. It is more secure, and involves little incremental software cost over the simple password, but it is much harder on the user, who must know either by memory or by algorithm the current password.

A handshaking algorithm is a much more elaborate procedure than any other involving the user. It takes more of the user's time, more communication line time, and more programming effort. It is, of course, more effective, and is worth what it costs to those who need it. Since the complexity of the handshaking algorithm is adjustable to the requirements of any given system, the procedures can meet a large variety of needs, and offer much promise for the future. But for the same reasons, they can be arbitrarily expensive.

The use of simultaneous software keys from different terminals, which has been suggested as a very secure procedure, throws a quite demanding requirement on the coordination of the people involved. The cost of equipment and of software to do this is relatively low. But the necessity for the people involved to be at certain places at certain times will limit this procedure to very unusual situations.

The dial-up and call-back method is relatively cheap for the protection it provides.

Compartmentalization Methods. Hardware compartmentalization of memory is necessary for the proper operation of any multiprogramming system; therefore that facility is free, so to speak.

The use of individual field authorizations is not widespread, and costs are not completely known. The incremental costs of methods which allow individual field au-

---

[11] For further details, see Section 5, Chapter 7, "Physical Security of the Computer Center."

thorizations are unknown, although they are clearly at least as expensive as those methods which do not allow them. Even if they cannot be made cheaper than the other methods, they still offer much promise because of their flexibility and comprehensiveness.

Privacy Transformations. Methods of encrypting are such that a good deal of security, measured by the amount of work required to break a cipher, can be had with only a very modest increase in expense.[12]

Products for encrypting transmission over vulnerable communication lines are currently available. Ground Data Corp. of Ft. Lauderdale, for example, was in 1972 selling such a system with immediate delivery for $975; rental of the same unit was $34 per month. Relatively inexpensive chips for implementing the Federal encryption standard will soon be available also.

Privacy transformations lose much of their utility if an entire file must be decrypted and re-encrypted using a different transformation many times. This can happen if an installation has a large encrypted file and changes encrytion frequently in order to maintain a high level of security. The computer time required by this can be quite considerable. Frequent passing of a large (possibly multivolume) file, the only effect of which is to change the encipherment, is nearly always prohibitively expensive. For this reason, many experts feel that cryptography will not generally be used for encrypting entire data sets, but will be used for transmissions over communication lines, where encryption and decryption are done only once. Frequent re-encryption of an entire file can be avoided by instead providing adequate physical security of the place where the file is kept and complete security of the transmission channels, where applicable. Here, as usual, resources saved on one safeguard (privacy transformations) can be used to strengthen another safeguard (physical security) and thus achieve better results.

Threat Monitoring. The costs of threat monitoring are not known accurately now, but they are principally the cost of deciding what information should be kept in logs, the operating cost of examining those logs, and the maintenance of the software. Sufficient magnetic tapes or other storage on which to record the audit trails will be required, and additional system overhead will be caused by the recording of accesses and refused admission.

SUMMARY

In summation, security of private or sensitive information in computer systems involves legal, administrative, physical, and technological controls. Often one can arrive at a desired level of security by trading off safeguards in one area (such as technological) to increase them in another (such as physical). In the final analysis, this decision must be made by each installation based on its own needs.

SELECTIVE BIBLIOGRAPHY

Hoffman, L. J., *Modern Methods for Computer Security and Privacy,* Prentice-Hall, Englewood
——, and W. F. Miller, "Getting a Personal Dossier from a Statistical Data Bank," *Datamation,* March, 1970.
Kahn, David, *The Codebreakers,* Macmillan, New York, 1968.
The Considerations of Physical Security in the Computer Environment, G520–2700–0, IBM, White Plains, N.Y., 1972.
Westin, A. F., and M. A. Baker, *Databanks in a Free Society,* Quadrangle Press, New York, 1972.
"Records, Computers, and the Rights of Citizens," *Report of the Secretary's Advisory Committee on Automated Personal Data Systems, U.S. Department of Health, Education, and Welfare, July,* 1973.
Westin, A. F., and M. A. Baker, *Databanks in a Free Society,* Quadrangle Press, New York, 1972.

[12] T. D. Friedman and L. J. Hoffman, "Execution Time Requirements for Programmed Encipherment Methods," *Communications of the ACM,* August, 1974.

Chapter 5

The Computer and Society

BRUCE GILCHRIST

Director of Computing Activities, Columbia University, New
York, New York

To consider the role of computers in society, we must consider the ways in which over-all society is changing, since there are many sources of change in society besides the computer. In addition to its own part in bringing about changes, the computer has been instrumental in furthering the changes brought about by other forces, and in helping society to adapt to change. Gone are the days when we realistically could debate whether or not society would be better off without computers. For better or worse computers are as essential to the operation of industry and government as, say, the availability of electric power is to the operation of New York City.

Recognizing current reality does not necessarily commit us to abandoning all attempts to improve the current situation. Nor does it say that we must adopt a "whatever will be, will be" attitude toward the future. Rather, it tells us to look at the future in a broader context of the development of a society in which the computer is already firmly embedded. The development of new computer technology and applications will of course play a significant part in the evolution of society, but the rate of development and the public's reaction to computers will be highly dependent on the way in which society as a whole develops.

SOURCES OF CHANGE

Daniel Bell, in the introductory article of the 1967 report of the work of the Commission on the Year 2000,[1] suggests that there are four sources of change in society. These are (1) changes in technology; (2) the diffusion of existing goods and privileges in society; (3) changes in the structure of society; and (4) the relationship of the United States to the rest of the world. (The last of these Bell felt will perhaps be the most important.)

In general, the import of Bell's four sources of change is clear from the mere listing of them. However, it will be helpful to consider how the computer is involved in each of them, since the computer is in many ways more than just another in a long string of technological advances.

Changes in Technology The development of the computer from a relatively slow and cumbersome device in 1950 to the high-speed, versatile, and universally applied tool

[1] "Toward the Year 2000: Work in Progress," *Daedalus*, Summer, 1967.

of the 1970s is an example of a rapid change in technology which has brought a profound change in society. But other technological changes may be equally or even more important. For example, advances in biomedical engineering, with the possibilities of genetic modification and the control of disease, may result in a substantial increase in life expectancy. Bell suggests that the prolongation of life by the control of aging could accentuate a tendency, already visible, in which the chief concern of a person (particularly in middle age) is not death from disease but staying young, thus strengthening the hedonistic elements in our culture.

The nature of technology itself is changing, and this in itself may be one of the more important kinds of changes in the next quarter century. Technology, as Bell points out, is not simply a "machine," but a systematic, disciplined approach to objectives, using a calculus of precision and measurement and a concept of system that are quite at variance with traditional and customary religious, aesthetic, and intuitive modes. Instead of a machine technology, we shall have, increasingly, an "intellectual technology" in which such techniques as modeling and simulation, aided by computers, become the new tools of decision making.

Diffusion of Goods and Privileges The second source of change, the diffusion of existing goods and privileges in society, has long been important in the United States where equality was one of the principles upon which the republic was founded. An organization or system designed to serve a privileged *minority* has to change not only its methods but often its very character when it has to service the *majority*. Higher education is a prime example. As the percentage of youth entering higher education has grown, we have seen enormous growth in the state universities, the establishment of numerous community colleges, and at the same time, major financial problems for the private colleges and universities. Another example is banking, where the traditional ways have had to change as checking accounts became the rule rather than the exception for the average worker. Similarly, as the courts have ruled that virtually all defendants, irrespective of means, are entitled to legal counsel and reasonably speedy trials, there has been major growth in legal aid services and a recognition by some that court procedures need streamlining. These may in the long term affect the basic way law is administered. The provision of medical services is another area which is changing as the majority is demanding the sort of care previously enjoyed by only the wealthy. Even if a national health service on the European style is not adopted, there is little doubt in most people's minds that there will be extensive changes in the health care delivery system in the coming years.

Changes in the Structure of Society Bell cites two major contributors to the structural changes in our society. The first is the continuing centralization of the political and economic systems. More and more decisions are being made at a national level with implementation left to the local level. This is true of governmental organizations as well as private companies. There are many reasons for this move, among them being the ease of transportation and communication which tends to break down geographical barriers and the economies of scale which foster the growth of single organizations serving a large constituency or marketplace. The second is the steady movement of the economy from a goods to a service orientation. This increases the importance of information and intellectual developments as compared to product invention, and changes the values assigned by society to the individuals and organizations involved. This topic will be covered more fully in our later discussion of post-industrial society.

Relationship to the Rest of the World The fourth source of change, the relationship of the United States to the rest of the world, has become important not only because of the nuclear age, but possibly more because of the realization by the less developed and poorer nations that they are entitled to more of the world's material benefits. Moreover, these nations have found that by uniting they can exert pressure, political and moral, on the wealthier nations.

The United States, like other industrialized nations, has relied in the past, and continues to rely heavily, on overseas markets and overseas sources of raw materials. As these are affected by national movements around the world, there will be major impacts on industries and on the standard of living in the United States. The rapid increase in worldwide oil and commodity prices in 1973 brought this aspect home to the American family in a most vivid way, namely in soaring energy and food prices.

THE COMPUTER'S INVOLVEMENT IN CHANGE

The computer is intimately involved in each of these four major sources of change. In the first, technology, the role of the computer is obvious. In addition to the computational aids in traditional areas of science and engineering, modern developments in weather prediction and, ultimately, climate control, and our space-age achievements would be impossible without large high-speed computers. And in decision making, the techniques of simulation and operations research require computers if real-life situations are to be modeled.

In the area of diffusion of goods and privileges, computers may well be a vital tool of change. For example, despite the failure to live up to early expectations, computer-aided instructions may still be a key to successful mass education at reasonable cost. Similarly, banks can provide service to large numbers of customers only through the use of computers. Likewise the credit-card companies need computers to process charges, bills, and payments at economical rates. In the administration of our courts, computers are finding increasing application for the streamlining of operations, and lawyers are beginning to use computer-based retrieval systems to search statute and case law. In health care we also find numerous applications of computers, ranging from the keeping of hospital and health insurance records to the control of the many aspects of multiphasic screening.

In both types of structural change previously mentioned—centralization and a service-oriented economy—the computer is playing a key role. In the early days of computers, multiplant organizations tended to have a computer at each major location for payroll, accounting, inventory control, and the like. The subsequent development of large efficient computers and associated data communications encouraged the replacement of many on-site computers by terminals connected to a single central computer site, or by large central computers connected to local satellite computers. Similarly, computers have allowed large Government agencies such as the Social Security Administration and the Internal Revenue Service to centralize their systems and exercise the control inherent in centralized systems. For example, its highly centralized and standardized computer system enabled the IRS to process the great majority of 1974 tax rebates in only 6 weeks, despite the necessity to examine some 70 million returns.

Finally, in the area of international relations the computer is important because of its use as a planning tool. Most of the developing countries have strong central government planning activities to ensure that their scarce resources are appropriately allocated. The computer is an almost essential requirement for such work because of the need to accumulate and analyze large quantities of statistical information upon which to base planning decision and also because of the need to simulate the effects of alternative plans.

The Need to Consider the Whole Picture The fact that the computer is important in each cause of change must not lead us to the simplistic view that if we can only control the development of computers and the way they are used, we shall be able to control change. On the other hand, we cannot ignore the role computers play and only address the other components of the causes of change. As is so frequently the case, causes and effects are intimately and inextricably tied together, and to ignore any one may result in the drawing of wrong conclusions. All this could lead to the conclusion that the subject of computers and society in the future is just too complicated to study. But this is too pessimistic a view, and much can be learned without studying the whole problem.

The important thing to remember in any partial study is that there are other factors which, because they are being ignored, may invalidate the results. For example, 20 years ago studies of transportation envisioned the almost never ending, unquestioning demand for cars and new highways. As a consequence, no thought was given to the possible pollution problems, energy crises, and the public's concern for ecology. Each of these three ignored factors have now become highly significant and possibly dominant in the future development of automobile transportation. Similarly, not many years ago many computer experts felt that only technological breakthroughs were necessary to achieve large databanks, whereas now there are a growing number of proposals to limit such banks, not for technological reasons but for social ones.

Public Reaction to Computers   Turning to the question of the current public reaction to computers, we should first note that the last few years have seen a vast increase in interest on the part of the general public in the problems produced by modern technology.   The work of Rachel Carson and others has made the public highly aware of the adverse consequences of insecticides, and Ralph Nader has made well known the price the public is paying in terms of death and injury for the convenience of the automobile.   Similarly, conservation groups have pointed out many of the serious negative consequences of construction of atomic power plants.   In each of these areas it had hitherto been assumed that either there were no adverse consequences or that they were negligible in relation to the benefits.   The public awareness and concern have been translated into action on both the political and legal fronts, and a number of major projects have been abandoned or significantly modified as a result.

Public concern has not been limited to the physical environment but has extended into such areas as privacy.   For example, Congress and the press made loud outcries when it was found that the United States Army was collecting data on individuals the Army thought were connected with disturbances on college campuses.   The resulting congressional hearings under Senator Sam Ervin developed considerable criticism of the Army and resulted in the discontinuance of the practice.   Similarly, a proposal to create a Government-wide data bank in the mid-sixties ran into very strong congressional opposition led by Representative Cornelius Gallagher, and was abandoned.

The continuing concern over the invasion of privacy by Government units led eventually to the passage of the 1974 Privacy Act.[2] This act sets firm privacy standards for Federal agencies, and prescribes penalties for officials who disregard its provisions.

Government action, of course, whether it be by the executive or legislative branch, reflects public opinion.   Unfortunately, few surveys have been made of public attitudes toward computers.   However, some indication may be drawn from a 1971 survey by AFIPS and Time Inc.[3] and from a smaller and earlier survey in the Greater Boston area.[4]

The AFIPS/Time Survey.   In the widely publicized AFIPS/Time study 1,001 telephone interviews were conducted with a statistically drawn sample of the adult population of the United States.   Although the sample included people from a wide range of incomes, occupations, ages, and locations, 49 per cent said that they had once had a job requiring contact directly or indirectly with a computer, and 30 per cent said that they still had such jobs.   When asked whether they presently had a job requiring working directly with a computer, 7 per cent responded affirmatively.   Despite the possible ambiguities in the questions these responses clearly indicate that the American public is being exposed to the computer in a major way.

Looking at the detailed responses we find that:

• Eighty-nine per cent agreed that in the future computers will help provide many kinds of information services to us in our homes.

• Sixty-five per cent agreed that computers are helping to raise the standard of living for American people.

• Eighty-seven per cent agreed that we can do many things that would be impossible without computers.

• Fifty-three per cent agreed that safeguards are used by the Government to make sure that personal information stored in computers is accurate.

However,

• Thirty-four per cent reported "problems" because of a computer.   Two-thirds of the problems related to financial transactions.

• Fifty-five per cent agreed that people are becoming too dependent on computers.

• Fifty-four per cent agreed that computers are dehumanizing people and turning them into numbers.

• Fifty-three per cent agreed that computerized information files may be used to destroy individual freedom.

[2] Public Law 93–579, December 31, 1974.

[3] Bruce Gilchrist and Clark Schiller, *A National Survey of the Public's Attitudes toward Computers*, AFIPS Press, Nontvale, N.J., 1971.   (A survey conducted by *Time* and AFIPS, reported upon at the Fall Joint Computer Conference, 1971.)

[4] Taviss, Irene, "A Survey of Popular Attitudes toward Technology," *Technology and Culture*, vol. 13, no. 4, October, 1972.

• Thirty-eight per cent agreed that computers represent a real threat to people's privacy.
and

• Eighty-four per cent agreed that the Government should be concerned about regulating the use of computers.

Greater Boston Survey. The Greater Boston study was based on only 200 interviews but found the same kind of concern as well as confusion about the role of computers. Over 90 per cent of the Boston sample agreed that "machines have made life easier," but over 75 per cent also felt that "people have become too dependent on machines." A large number agreed that computers would increase the efficiency of government, but over half were opposed to the development of data banks because of the threat to privacy.

A Canadian Survey. The findings of the two American surveys are similar to those of a Canadian survey[5] conducted at about the same time. This supports the general conclusion that the average citizen recognizes both the benefits and the potential problems of computers. Whether these opinions are based on facts or on newspaper headlines or gossip is really irrelevant, since it is what the voter perceives that is converted into political action.

Government Reaction to Public Concern Congressional reaction in two areas of concern—surveillance and databanks—has already been noted, but there are a growing number of other examples. Two interesting ones that reflect the conflict between Government economy and privacy are the 1974 Privacy Act and the Social Services Amendments of 1974.[6] The first protects individual privacy with respect to Government records and as a result will increase the costs of Government record-keeping systems; the second sets up a Parent Locator Service to help reduce welfare payments to dependent children but at the same time allows many Government records to be used for purposes other than was intended when they were collected and will possibly result in the invasion of personal privacy.

The 1974 Privacy Act. The 1974 Privacy Act was the culmination of some ten years of effort by many people and groups to eliminate the growing number of instances of misuse of computerized Government files. Along the way there were several congressional hearings in both the House of Representatives and the Senate. Of particular significance was an exchange in 1971 between Elliot Richardson and Senator Sam Ervin which led to the appointment by Richardson, who was then Secretary of Health, Education and Welfare, of a broad-based Advisory Committee on Automated Personal Data Systems. The 1973 report of this Committee[7] clearly enunciated the following five principles:

• There must be no personal data record-keeping systems whose very existence is secret.

• There must be a way for an individual to find out what information about him is in a record and how it is used.

• There must be a way for an individual to prevent information about him that was obtained for one purpose from being used or made available for other purposes without his consent.

• There must be a way for an individual to correct or amend a record of identifiable information about him.

• Any organization creating, maintaining, using, or disseminating records of identifiable personal data must assure the reliability of the data for their intended use and must take precautions to prevent misuse of the data.

Specific Committee recommendations included:

• Federal legislation guaranteeing individuals the right to find out what information is being maintained about them in computerized systems, and to obtain a copy of it on demand.

• That the legislation also allow a person to contest the accuracy, pertinence, and timeliness of any information in a computer-accessible record about him.

• That record-keeping organizations be required to inform individuals, on re-

---

[5] *Survey of Public Attitudes towards the Computer*, Information Canada, Ottawa, 1973.

[6] Public Law 93–647, January 4, 1975.

[7] *Report of the Secretary's Advisory Committee on Personal Data Systems*, U.S. Department of Health, Education, and Welfare, July, 1973. (Publication No. (OS) 73–94.)

quest, of all uses made of information that is being kept about them in computerized files.

In connection with the Social Security number, the committee further recommended:

● Congressional action giving each individual the right to refuse to disclose his Social Security number to any person or organization that is not authorized by a Federal statute to collect and use the number.

● That organizations with authority to use the number be prohibited from disclosing the number to organizations that lack such authority.

The HEW Committee's report was discussed widely and was quickly followed by bipartisan legislative proposals. Eventually, in the final days of 1974, a bill was agreed to by Congress and signed by President Ford. The 1974 Privacy Act excludes from its provisions essentially all law enforcement agencies and the entire private sector, but otherwise it follows quite closely the recommendations of the HEW Committee. Of special interest is the provision of civil and criminal penalties for officers or employees of a Government agency who violate provisions of the act.

The Privacy Act was to become effective in September, 1975, but as early as May, 1975, there were growing complaints of the cost of implementing its provisions. In particular, the Government agencies covered by the act will have to publish annually in the Federal Register a detailed description of all existing record systems and to respond promptly to requests from individuals for information about their own records. Doubtless the Federal Register will have plenty of information to print and if there are many individual requests for records the agencies will have a significant increase in workload. If the increased costs are too high, there will certainly be an ongoing debate as to the economic value of privacy legislation. Hopefully this aspect will receive attention from the Privacy Commission which was established by the Privacy Act to monitor progress and to explore future directions.

The Social Services Amendments of 1974. For many years there has been a growing concern about the rising costs of welfare, and especially the costs of supporting children of runaway parents. It has been estimated that there are 1.3 million fathers in the United States who have deserted their children, leaving their support to welfare agencies. Such support payments cost the Federal Government nearly $1.5 billion each year, passed on to the states to match their own welfare contributions.[8] In order to help cut back on the need for such payments the Social Services Amendments of 1974 included the establishment of a Parent Locator Service within the Department of Health, Education and Welfare. Moreover, the act penalizes states which do not use the service by withholding 5 per cent of their matching Federal funds.

The act requires that, upon the request from an authorized person for the most recent address and place of employment of any absent parent, the Secretary of Health, Education and Welfare, notwithstanding any other provision of law, must provide the information if it is contained in HEW files or can be obtained "from any other department, agency or instrumentality, or the United States or of any state."

The definition of "authorized person" is very broad and includes state authorities, courts, and "the resident parent, legal guardian, attorney or agent of a child *without regard to the existence of a court order against an absent parent who has a duty to support and maintain such child*" (emphasis added). The Secretary of Health, Education and Welfare is already reported to have made arrangements with the Internal Revenue Service and the Social Security Administration to have their files searched for evidence of the whereabouts of missing parents.[9]

The operation of the Parent Locator Service clearly violates a number of privacy principles. For example, it allows data collected for one purpose, namely Social Security and income tax, to be used for another without the agreement of the individuals concerned. Furthermore, the relatively large number of persons authorized to request information may give rise to harassment of innocent individuals. President Ford recognized some of these privacy faults in the act but signed it nevertheless because he felt that the benefits outweighed the disadvantages. He promised to submit corrective legislation, and we must wait and see whether any of the potentially money-saving aspects of the Parent Locator Services will be weakened in favor of increasing personal

[8] *Computerworld*, April 23, 1975, p. 1.
[9] Ibid.

privacy. The fundamental question which will undoubtedly arise is: Does the welfare cheater have the same privacy rights as the innocent citizen even if such rights protect the cheater from detection?

In practice the Congress will have to come to a pragmatic balance between the benefits of privacy and its cost. It will indeed be interesting to see how much the public will be willing to pay in higher taxes or less-than-expected services in order to preserve or protect privacy. The cynic will suggest that the public will be willing to pay very little, and will support this surmise by citing the fact that the opposition to the Alaskan pipeline decreased markedly when the gasoline shortage developed in 1973.

POST-INDUSTRIAL SOCIETY

In his book on the "post-industrial" society, Bell develops some of his ideas mentioned earlier in this Chapter, and describes the kind of society he believes is rapidly developing in the United States.[10] The concept of post-industrial society is a large generalization, and Bell suggests that its meaning can be more easily understood if one specifies five dimensions, or components, of the term:

1. Economic sector: the change from a goods-producing to a service economy.
2. Occupational distribution: the pre-eminence of the professional and technical class.
3. Axial principle: the centrality of theoretical knowledge as the source of innovation and of policy formulation for the society.
4. Future orientation: the control of technology and technology assessment.
5. Decision making: the creation of a new intellectual technology.

Such changes do not come about overnight, but there are definite signs in the United States of movement in each of the five components.

A somewhat similar view of the future prompted a Japanese group in 1972 to propose a plan for Japan to develop into an *information* society.[11] Whether it be named *post-industrial* or *information*, the society of the future will certainly be highly knowledge- and information-oriented.

The ability to collect and assimilate data is already a prime requisite in many industries for a company to compete successfully; new devices are increasingly being developed from a strong base of theoretical knowledge rather than by self-educated inventors; the number of professional employees is a growing percentage of the work force; and economic growth as a national goal per se is being challenged.

If goods were the main product of the industrial age, then services play the same role in post-industrial society. The definite move in this direction is shown in Table 5-1, in which employment is divided between the goods-producing industries (agriculture, mining, construction, and manufacturing) and the service-producing industries (wholesale, retail, transportation, finance, government, and special services).

TABLE 5-1   Percentage of United States Work Force Employed in Goods-Producing and Service-Producing Industries

	1900	1920	1940	1960	1973
Goods-producing	69	60	51	43	34
Service-producing	31	40	49	57	66

SOURCE: U.S. Department of Labor reports.

The portion of the gross national product that is accounted for by services has also risen, but much more slowly. Services now represent about 42 per cent of the GNP. The slow change in the services component of GNP is due to the service industries' being highly labor-intensive, in contrast with the goods-producing industries which have seen large increases in output per employee-hour.

The standard of living has been rising steadily and will continue to do so as the

[10] Daniel Bell, *The Coming of Post-Industrial Society*, Basic Books, New York, 1973.
[11] *The Plan for Information Society: A National Goal toward Year 2000*, Japan Computer Usage Development Institute, May, 1972.

United States moves into the post-industrial society. However, there will not be universal affluence in which goods are available for next-to-nothing.

One of the chapters in *The Coming of Post-Industrial Society* is entitled "Who Will Rule? Politicians and Technocrats in the Post-Industrial Society." This is a vital question from many points of view, and in particular, the way it is answered will determine to a major extent the degree to which computers are used in the future. The attributes outlined above of post-industrial society all suggest that the professional manager and technocrat will lead the new society. This elite bureaucracy has grown over the past few decades, and indicators such as academic enrollment suggest that the trend will continue. But as usual there is another side to the picture.

A populist movement is developing, and, as was pointed out earlier, has had a number of successes in fights to limit technological "progress." Best known is probably the defeat in Congress, after a great deal of public pressure, of the supersonic transport (SST) program. In addition, there are numerous examples of the construction of nuclear power stations being stopped or delayed by public pressures, despite the efforts of the technological bureaucracy to push ahead with them.

Which side wins or where the compromise will be fixed between technocracy and pure democracy will clearly affect the way the country develops, and which value system will be appropriate for judging the suitability of a particular computer system or application. It is easy to say that social values will replace economic growth as a national goal, but it is difficult to define such values. Furthermore, the current generation of Americans has become used to economic growth, the ready availability of goods, and the ability to satisfy personal desires. Whether or not this or the next generation will give up some of these for social goals is a moot point. For example, will we voluntarily give up the convenience of driving our personal automobiles in order to reduce pollution? Or will we give up personal privacy to obtain better health care or easier credit?

Knowledge in the Post-Industrial Society   A key attribute of post-industrial society and one that has great significance to the data processing field is that of the centrality of knowledge. Civilization has always depended on knowledge, and on the ability of humans to pass on knowledge to others and especially to the next generation. However, today we are more dependent on knowledge than ever before, and this dependence is increasing daily. The development of knowledge and its transmission between people and/or organizations account for a significant share of the gross national product of the United States.

Using a very broad definition of knowledge, Machlup[12] estimated that in 1958 just under 30 per cent of the gross national product was devoted to the production and distribution of knowledge. Without getting involved in the question of defining knowledge and debating whether or not Machlup's 30 per cent figure is exaggerated, we can note a few relevant statistics.[13]

From 1930 to 1972, the percentage of the gross national product accounted for by education rose from 3.1 to 7.8, and enrollments doubled. From 1955 to 1973, the annual expenditures for basic research in the United States increased from $600 million to over $4.5 billion. In 1955, 44 per cent of workers had white collar jobs, whereas in 1972 the percentage was close to 50, of a much larger total work force. By 1972, over 94 per cent of households had telephones, and over half a billion phone calls were being made daily. From nothing in 1950, cable television by 1972 was being used by approximately 10 per cent of United States households. The number of possible statistics is endless, but the ones given clearly show the growth of the knowledge-producing and -transmitting parts of the economy.

The Computer in Post-Industrial Society   In a knowledge-based society, the computer will clearly play a major role. However, it will be an integrated role, and the key decisions as to whether or not particular parts of the system will be computerized will be based on the overall goals of society. For example, if it is generally accepted that a universal credit system is desirable, computerized data banks of financial information and a computer-controlled communications system will inevitably be involved. To be sure, various controls will be built in to protect rights which society feels are important,

---

[12] Fritz Machlup, *Production and Distribution of Knowledge in the United States*, Princeton University Press, Princeton, N.J. 1962.

[13] U.S. Bureau of the Census, *Statistical Abstract of the United States*, 94th ed., 1973.

but here again the decision will tend to be based more on overall goals than on matters specific to the computer.

The maintaining of criminal records is another example. If society decides that records should be kept and made available to certain organizations and/or people, then computers will inevitably be involved. On the other hand, if society decides that it would be better served if such records were not retained, then computerization will not proceed. Most likely what will happen is that it will be realized that careful computerization of a record-keeping system can allow for very effective control mechanisms, and society will opt for the first alternative.[14]

A third example, and one which has a number of very interesting implications, is the possible combination of computers and cable television (CATV) which could allow for on-line polling of the population. It is already technologically feasible to equip every CATV receiver with simple yes/no buttons which could be pressed in response to questions.[15] The responses could then be fed into a computer and rapid analyses of the results could be obtained. Using this sort of scheme, politicians could get virtually instantaneous readings of their constituents' opinions following either a presentation of the "facts" or a political speech.

The value-judgment question is, would representatives under such circumstances be able to exercise independent judgment, or would they always have to cast their votes in accordance with the latest poll on the matter in question? The argument might be raised that we already have public opinion polls, so why should more accurate and frequent ones change the situation? The point is that there is a lot of difference between occasional polls of questionable accuracy based on a limited sample, and frequent ones of *all* constituents willing to spend a few minutes at their CATV set. It will simply be much more difficult for a politician to reject the findings of the latter, although he or she may still believe that they are not appropriate to the situation. In the extreme, we shall have the contrast between an electronic town meeting of whole cities, states, or even the nation, and the representative form of government which has served us for 200 years. It is interesting to ponder whether one approach would be more democratic or practicable than the other.

CONCLUSION

Detailed projections have been deliberately avoided in this Chapter. Rather, the stage has been set for readers to make their own projections in the light of the way they see society developing.[16] As we each write our own scenarios of the future, we shall not only begin to see what the influence and consequences of computers will be, but also, perhaps more importantly, we shall learn what we should be doing now to ensure that the future is better than the present, at least on *our* scale of values.

SELECTIVE BIBLIOGRAPHY

Bell, Daniel, *The Coming of Post-Industrial Society*, Basic Books, New York, 1973.

Forecast 1968–2000 of Computer Developments and Applications, Parsons and Williams, Copenhagen, 1968.

Matchlup, Fritz, *Production and Distribution of Knowledge in the United States*, Princeton University Press, Princeton, N.J., 1962.

Nanus, Burt, Michael Wooton, and Harold Borko, "The Social Implications of the Use of Computers across National Boundaries," *Proceedings of the 1973 National Computer Conference*, AFIPS Press, Montvale, N.J., 1973.

A National Survey of the Public's Attitudes toward Computers, AFIPS Press, Montvale, N.J., 1971. (A survey conducted by *Time* and AFIPS, reported upon at the Fall Joint Computer Conference, 1971.)

The Plan for Information Society: A National Goal toward Year 2000, Japan Computer Usage Development Institute, 1972.

[14] See Chapter 4, "The Computer and Privacy," in this Section.

[15] See Chapter 3, "The Computer in the Living Room," in this Section.

[16] For contrasting scenarios of "closed" and "open" information-rich societies, see Murray Turoff, "Opposing Views," *Proceedings of the 1973 National Computer Conference*, AFIPS Press, Montvale, N.J., 1973.

"Records, Computers, and the Rights of Citizens," *Report of the Secretary's Advisory Committee on Automated Personal Data Systems*, U.S. Department of Health, Education, and Welfare, 1973.

Survey of Public Attitudes towards the Computer, Information Canada, Ottawa, 1973.

Taviss, Irene, "A Survey of Popular Attitudes toward Technology," *Technology and Culture*, vol. 13, no. 4, October, 1972.

"Toward the Year 2000: Work in Progress," *Daedalus*, Summer, 1967.

Turoff, Murray, "Opposing Views," *Proceedings of the 1973 National Computer Conference*, AFIPS Press, Montvale, N.J., 1973.

Wessel, Milton R., *Freedom's Edge*, Addison-Wesley, New York, 1974.

Index